POLITICS IN CANADA

CULTURE, INSTITUTIONS, BEHAVIOUR AND PUBLIC POLICY

THIRD EDITION

ROBERT J. JACKSON
DOREEN JACKSON

PRENTICE HALL CANADA INC., SCARBOROUGH, ONTARIO

Canadian Cataloguing in Publication Data

Jackson, Robert J., 1936-
  Politics in Canada

3rd ed.
Includes index.
ISBN 0-13-064007-7

1. Canada-Politics and government.   I. Jackson,
Doreen, 1939- . II. Title

JL65 1994.J32 1994   320.971 C93-095112-3

Prentice-Hall, Inc., Englewood Cliffs, New Jersey
Prentice-Hall International (UK) Limited, London
Prentice-Hall of Australia, Pty. Limited, Sydney
Prentice-Hall Hispanoamericana, S.A., Mexico City
Prentice-Hall of India Private Limited, New Delhi
Prentice-Hall of Japan, Inc., Tokyo
Simon & Schuster Asia Private Limited, Singapore
Editora Prentice-Hall do Brasil, Ltda., Rio de Janeiro

ISBN 0-13-064007-7

Acquisitions Editor: Michael Bickerstaff
Developmental Editor: Linda Gorman
Copy Editor: Ruth Chernia
Production Editor: Norman Bernard
Permissions/Photo Research: Angelika Baur
Cover Design: Alex Li
Cover Image: First Light/Ron Watts
Page Layout: Jerry Langton

1 2 3 4 5   RRD   98 97 96 95 94

Printed and bound in the United States

TABLE OF CONTENTS

PREFACE

The third edition of *Politics in Canada* has been thoroughly revised to keep students abreast of the momentous political changes that have taken place in the last few years. Since the 1990 edition, there have been new census data revising our portrait of Canadians as a people, a General Election which ushered in a realignment of the party system, a new, fractious Parliament, new party leaders, a new government with new ideas about how to structure Cabinet and the bureaucracy and new approaches to solving grave constitutional problems. Canada is facing separatist disruption and fiscal chaos emanating from a mushrooming deficit and federal debt. These problems and the unique composition of the House of Commons will focus attention on the federal government as never before. Contemporary Canadian politics is a serious, exciting, creative and demanding venture, and we have tried to capture that mood in this book.

Politics in Canada stresses the importance of *politics* in the study of Canadian government. It is a general treatment of Canadian federal politics, useful for both introductory and advanced courses. The book purposely avoids the rigidity imposed by the adoption of a single approach or framework for the study of politics, but goes beyond mere description of governmental institutions and processes. It attempts to provide a coherent understanding of Canadian politics, eschewing the simplicities of myths, but reckoning with the resistance to order exerted by the incoherent events in the day-to-day world.

This volume's orientation is comprehensive, drawing upon a wide variety of concepts and theories about Canadian politics. Each chapter is organized around one or two central concepts, which are discussed in general terms before being applied to the Canadian context.

Politics in Canada retains its original structure, but each section has been thoroughly revised and rewritten to make it as clear, concise and up-to-date as possible. There are five parts. The first is introductory; the remainder correspond to the four elements incorporated in the title: culture, institutions, behaviour and public policy.

Part I, the Introduction, consists of two chapters. Chapter 1 establishes Canada's place in the world, discusses elements of its physical and international environment, introduces some key concepts in the study of politics — power, state, nation, nationalism and democracy — and offers a rationale for the organization of the book. Chapter 2 provides necessary historical, economic and contextual background through an examination of the origins and development of the Canadian people and the Canadian state. It traces the growth and changing nature of the population from the aboriginals who originally inhabited the land to the multicultural society of today. Similarly it traces the development of the Canadian state, both in terms of the physical boundaries of the country and the expansion of the role of government in Canadian society.

The two chapters comprising Part II provide a more intimate portrait of Canadian society. Chapter 3 examines Canada's political culture in terms of the ethnic and regional cleavages which define politics in Canada. It focuses on the different background and aspirations of French Canadians, English-speaking Canadians and Native Peoples, stressing the importance to the Canadian political community of overarching commonly shared values which help preserve the unity of the country. This edition provides a new examination of current issues such as immigration and language policy. Chapter 4 asks how Canadians acquire the political ideas that underly their political behaviour. Families and schools play a role here, as do institutions such as the media and even government. Also significant are two cleavages that cut horizontally across Canadian society: gender and class. They too help to define how Canadians think and behave politically. The extent to which each of these factors contributes to the political orientations and behaviour of Canadians is described and assessed.

Part III concerns political institutions. It argues that political institutions reflect both the structure and the values of society. It presents five chapters dealing in turn with the constitution, federalism, the inner circle (Cabinet and central agencies), Parliament and bureaucracy. This section has been considerably expanded in the third edition, with new material on the growing role of the courts and rights in the political process, and especially on the constitutional developments leading up to and following the failed Meech Lake and Charlottetown accords. Chapter 6 takes an up-to-date look at the challenges to federalism in Canada today, financial arrangements, nationalism, separatism and regionalism. Chapter 7 considers the new Executive, the inner circle comprising the new Prime Minister, Jean Chrétien, his ministry, Cabinet and the central coordinating agencies that will form the nexus of political power in Canada for at least the next five years. Chapter 8 focuses on Parliament, and includes completely revised discussions of the committee system and the issue of Senate reform. Chapter 9 details the changes in government organization and the public service that were brought about by the short-lived Kim Campbell government, and then slightly revised under Jean Chrétien and the Liberals.

Part IV demonstrates how both culture and institutions structure individual and collective behaviour in the political process. Its three chapters respectively discuss political parties, elections and electoral behaviour and interest groups. This edition focuses on the results and massive implications of the 1993 General Election. The party system has undergone a major realignment; new regional parties have taken the place of the traditional opposition parties and are having a significant impact on the traditional functioning of Parliament. Chapter 12 deals with the new rules governing interest groups and lobbying. It also considers the growth of movements that share many of the same functions of interest groups, and examines the women's movement in particular.

Lastly, in Part V, culture, institutions and behaviour are linked together as determinants and components of Canadian public policy and the policy-making process. Chapter 13 deals with domestic public policy, including approaches to the study of public policy, policy instruments and a discussion of current economic problems and policy constraints. Chapter 14 deals with Canadian foreign and defence policy, including Canadian-American relations, free trade, NAFTA, national security policies, peace-keeping and disarmament issues.

Politics in Canada offers a new perspective on politics. It focuses on issues that are vital to the country and to students of politics today, issues such as the role of Native Peoples in Canadian society; the role of women; nationalism and the threat of Québec separatism; the negative image of politics and politicians in society; how Parliament can be reformed; and the crushing economic implications of the national debt. The analysis presents the most recent research and an expanded selection of important readings for each topic. A number of key features provide highlights:

1. **Focus on the political:** This book emphasizes the importance of *politics* to an understanding of how the federal governmental process works; it is not limited to institutional or socio-economic determinism.
2. **Focus on the four key concepts:** Instead of adopting only one approach, the text takes an objective and detached perspective on the relations among

culture, institutions, behaviour and public policy. It provides a well-rounded view of the entire political process.

3. **Focus on the newest social science research:** Including books, journal articles, findings of the latest census, government publications and official government inquiries which highlight aspects of Canadian society at the turn of the century.

4. **Focus on the contemporary:** The book discusses the historical development and background of Canadian politics, but it concentrates on the present, offering the latest information and perspectives on such vital topics as the Constitution, Cabinet, federalism, Quebec nationalism, interest groups, conflict of interest, and the most recent elections and party leaders.

5. **Focus on comparison:** This book gives credit where it is due for substantial achievement, but also finds many political reforms desirable. The authors are optimistic but concerned about the fundamental ability of the Canadian political process to meet its major challenges — its ability to transcend regional and cultural cleavages and assure the survival of Canada. Politics is an honourable and worthy profession which has been tarnished by misunderstandings and the greed and corruption of a few.

6. **Focus on style:** The text is simply, clearly and concisely written with little academic jargon.

7. **Focus on the global:** This book examines Canada's role in the world, examining the interrelationship of domestic, foreign and defence policies. In particular, Canada's increasing economic integration with the United States and Mexico is considered.

The authors are extremely appreciative of the many students, professors and interested readers who have taken time to comment on aspects of *Politics in Canada* and given support and encouragement to bring out this third edition. Many friends and scholars have contributed, directly and indirectly, to the discussion of ideas and issues it contains. The very long list must include Michael Atkinson, David Bellamy, Scott Bennett, Alan Cairns, Barbara Caroll, Terry Caroll, Brian Crowley, Piotr Dutkiewicz, Jean-Pierre Gaboury, Brian Galligan, Janice Gross-Stein, Jack Grove, Ken Hart, Kal Holsti, Bill Hull, Carl Jacobsen, Christian Jaekl, Ken Kernaghan, Peyton Lyon, Roman March, Bill Matheson, Ken McRae, Greg Mahler, Henry Mayo, John Meisel, Kim Nossal, Randy Olling, K. Z. Paltiel, George Roseme, Donald Rowat, David Siegel, Richard Simeon, Michael Stein, Elliott Tepper, Hugh Thorburn, Martin Westmacott and Patrick Weller. Over a decade, several reviewers of the various editions have diligently ferretted out errors of omission and commission in the preliminary manuscripts. We gratefully acknowledge the insight and detailed knowledge that Nicolas Baxter-Moore, Donald Blake, Fred Englemann, Susan McCorquodale, Mary Beth Montcalm, David E. Smith, Robert Williams and Nelson Wiseman brought to our manuscript. We thank them for their thoughtful suggestions and corrections.

We are grateful to our friends at Prentice Hall, including Cliff Newman, Herb Hilderley, Michael Bickerstaff and Norman Bernard for their enthusiasm and helpfulness in bringing this new edition to fruition. Ruth Chernia edited the manuscript quickly, carefully and professionally. At Carleton University, Marion Armstrong and Gail Mordecai provided organization and support in a myriad of ways that enabled time and energy to be focussed on this project.

Finally, we wish to express our gratitude to two very special people — Velma, a wonderful mother and friend whose enthusiasm for politics is indefatigable, and to Nicole, our extraordinary daughter whose love of government and politics has taken her abroad to a new world of challenges.

Robert J. Jackson
Doreen Jackson

ABBREVIATIONS USED

AEI–*American Enterprise Institute*
APSR–*American Political Science Review*
BJPS–*British Journal of Political Science*
CIIA–Canadian Institute of International Affairs
CJEPS–*Canadian Journal of Economics and Political Science*
CJPS–*Canadian Journal of Political Science* (replaced the CJEPS as of March 1968)
CPA–*Canadian Public Administration*
DEA–Department of External Affairs
IIR–Institute of Intergovernmental Affairs
IRPP–Institute for Research on Public Policy
PAR–*Public Administration Review*

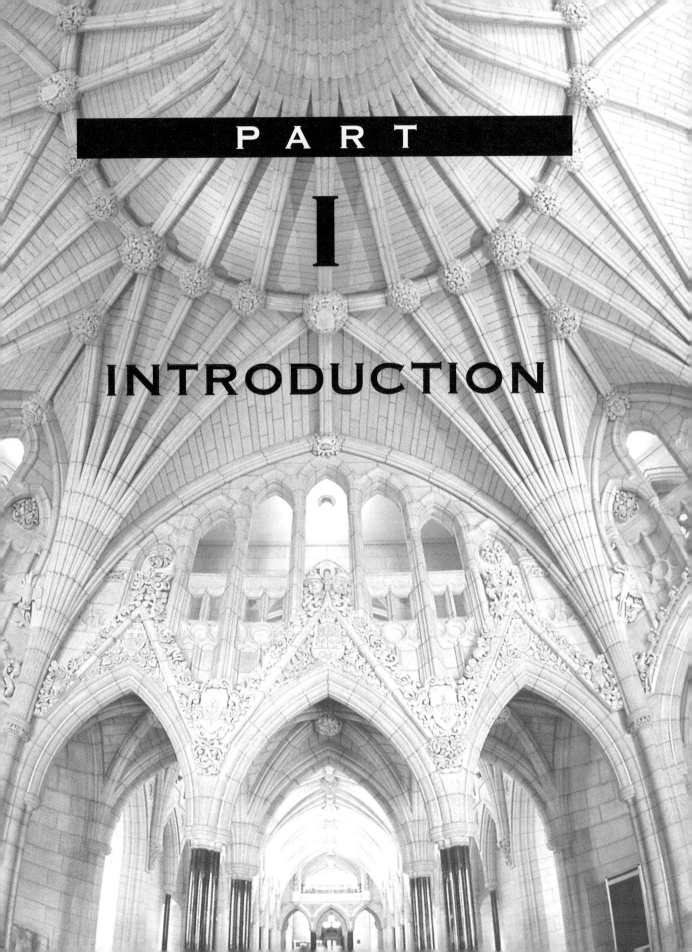

PART

I

INTRODUCTION

CHAPTER 1

GOVERNING CANADA

A COMPARATIVE PERSPECTIVE

The election of October 25, 1993 marked the end of an era in Canadian politics. The massive defeat of the Progressive Conservative government that had ruled for almost a decade was unprecedented. A strong, new Liberal majority government reflected widespread but cautious optimism that the gloomy state of economic, social and foreign affairs in the country would be improved.

Understanding Canada as we approach the twenty-first century will not be easy for politicians, professors or students. Rapid social and economic developments are changing the political culture, behaviour and public policy of the country. To comprehend modern Canada, students must confront themselves: Who are they? Who could they be? Who do they want to be? Their questions must be directed to the future. As a whole, Canadians will have to reassess who they are as a people, what values they wish to uphold and what languages they want to speak. They must decide how they should organize themselves and what institutions are worthy of their loyalty. These questions can be answered realistically only by maintaining a comparative perspective — how does Canada compare to the rest of the world? In short, the time for political maturity has come.

The earliest political science texts on Canada were concerned with the country's march to independence and autonomy. More recent volumes have concentrated on understanding Canada in the context of new academic developments in political science — concepts, frameworks and theories that came mostly from the United States. Today, the challenge is to understand how Canadians will confront the next century. The questions concern not whether the next century belongs to Canada but whether there will indeed *be* a Canada in the twenty-first century.

There have been many turning points in Canadian history. But possibly none were more important than 1867, 1931, 1982 and 1992. These dates mark Canada's march to political maturity. In 1867, the new state was born. In 1931, it received independence from Britain. It took another half century, until 1982, before Canadians had the courage and confidence to patriate the Constitution and break the last link with the mother country. Finally, in 1992 a massive constitutional reform proposal, the Charlottetown accord, which had been fashioned and sold to Canadians by the leaders of Parliament and all ten provinces and territories, was defeated when the people stood defiantly against it in a referendum.

These four historical events, and others like them, had a profound effect on the evolution of Canada's culture, institutions and public policy. The 1992 referendum marked the end of the politics of the twentieth century. It indicated a shift to a new politics, one that is more open, less elitist and, perhaps, more threatening to the status quo and the institutions of Canada.

Today, cleavages of the past continue to divide French and English, aboriginal and settler, westerner and easterner, men and women. But these cleavages have been given new direction and emotion in parties and movements and in novel approaches to old problems. What will their legacy to Canadians be in the next century? In this and subsequent chapters we shall marshall evidence about what is old and what is new in Canadian politics. We shall, for example, assess arguments about individual versus collective rights; examine movements and parties; and consider issues such as whether Québec will integrate more into Canada or become independent.

The 1993 election has given some indication of who the main political players will be and what directions Canadians will take as the new century approaches. But more information is required. We need to examine contemporary politics in view of the experience of the past as well as the dimmer light of the future.

Today, as the last vestiges of a colonial past are being erased, Canada ranks proudly among the world's states. A brief profile of the country — its political base, people and socio-economic status — reads impressively when examined in a comparative perspective.

Since Confederation, Canada has enjoyed a stable, liberal-democratic government; it is one of the very few countries in the world never to have experienced a civil war or a military coup. This stability has been achieved despite the many factors that complicate political decision-making in this country. Its size alone is a great barrier to progress. Canada has several thousand square kilometres more area to administer than all of Europe combined. A Canadian driving from St. John's, Newfoundland to Victoria, British Columbia covers the same distance as a Spaniard driving from Madrid and traversing at least ten countries almost to Mongolia. Québec, homeland of the French-Canadian nation, is almost equal in size to the entire European Community.

This enormous land mass housed 29 million people in 1993 — about .006 of the world's population. Yet Canada has a population problem — not in the traditional sense of over-populated countries afflicted by high birth rates, but in a demographic sense. Four-fifths of the territory has never been settled permanently. This results in great regional imbalances in population, from congested urban centres to uninhabited wastelands. Certain areas are being depopulated, while there is an undesirable rate of growth in others. Large tracts of land are being devoured by greedy cities. Today, in this country that was settled originally by farmers, most of the population lives in urban areas that occupy only one percent of the land. Only one-eighth of the territory is suitable for agriculture; settlement has therefore been confined to a long thin line along the southern border, linked by the world's longest national highway.

To these problematic demographic and geographic factors must be added the unique ethnic composition of the population. Besides the original Native groups and the two founding French and English nations, at least 100 other ethnic groups make their homes here. The French-Canadian nation is centred in Québec but is in no sense limited to that province. Large pockets of French-speaking Canadians live in Manitoba, New Brunswick and Ontario. Of the Native people, more than half reside in the Prairies and British Columbia. The many other ethnic groups scattered across the country add a multicultural dimension that has been the source of much division but also much pride for Canadians.

Canada is a land of extremes, in terms not only of territory and population but also of landscape and climate. Fertile rain forests, arctic barrens, mountains and plains — the variety is as large as the country itself. Most Canadians endure harsh winters, but even here there is great diversity. For example, the area near Kitimat holds the record for the highest average snowfall at 1071 cm a year, but there is almost no snow at all in Victoria. At Eureka on Ellesmere Island it snows all year round, yet at the other extreme towns like Midale in Saskatchewan hold record summer temperatures of 37°C.

Even with these disparities, Canada is one of the elite rich among the world's states. Canadians enjoy clean, abundant water, great resource wealth, a plentiful food supply, modern industries, safe cities and good health-care and educational facilities. These attributes add up to one of the highest material standards of living in the world.

The facts bear out this conclusion. In 1993, the United Nations placed Canada second in the world in terms of a combination of purchasing power, life expectancy, literacy and educational attainment — called the Human Development Index.[1] Only Japan bested Canada on that statistical index. (See Table 1.1.) More specifically, Canada beat out its traditional competitors, the Nordic countries, as well as the United States, Britain and Germany.

Trade accounts for a very significant proportion of Canada's wealth. As one of the world's top trading nations, Canada is among the very few countries in the world with a greater volume of exports than imports. A high percentage of these exports consists of natural resources: fish, lumber and energy.

TABLE 1.1   1993 HUMAN DEVELOPMENT INDEX

	Country	Human Development Index
1.	Japan	0.983
2.	Canada	0.982
3.	Norway	0.978
4.	Switzerland	0.978
5.	Sweden	0.977
6.	USA	0.976
7.	Australia	0.972
8.	France	0.971
9.	Netherlands	0.970
10.	United Kingdom	0.964
11.	Iceland	0.960
12.	Germany	0.957

The Human Development Index includes: life expectancy at birth; adult literacy rates; mean years; educational attainment; real purchasing power.

Source: United Nations, *Human Development Report 1993* (New York: Oxford University Press, 1993).

Yet even within the economy problems exist. Approximately three-quarters of all Canadian merchandise exports go the United States, a convenience that costs dearly in terms of de-

---

[1]   United Nations, *Human Development Report 1993* (New York: Oxford University Press, 1993).

pendence on American markets. Both lumber and fish stocks are dwindling, and will not be as lucrative in the years ahead; many other resources are not renewable. Native supplies of oil, gas, coal and electricity, many as yet untapped, have allowed Canadians to become energy gluttons: consumers of more energy *per capita* than any other state. Better planning and management of these resources and development of a broader industrial base are fundamental political challenges.

In 1992, Canada placed first in the UN's Human Development Index. This cartoon indicates that Canadians may be more comfortable with their more recent, 1993, second-place ranking.
Reproduced with permission, Alan King, *The Ottawa Citizen*.

ISSUES IN CANADIAN POLITICS

A political scientist once commented that "asking a person to say what government is about is like asking for a description of an inkblot. Its form is ambiguous, signifying different things to different people."[2] However, it is clearly the task of government to create some uniform conditions and standards for all citizens within the diversity of Canada. Sharing the wealth and resources of the country and assuring certain minimal national standards in areas such as health, communications and education are primary functions of governing in Canada. Unfortunately, there is no consensus about the degree to which it is desirable for governments to be directly involved in the lives of its citizens by directing the economy or providing social services, let alone agreement about how these things should be accomplished.

---

2   Richard Rose, *What is Governing? Purpose and Policy in Washington* (Englewood Cliffs, N.J.: Prentice-Hall, 1978), p. 2.

Since 1867, the Canadian government has developed into an institution respected throughout the globe as well as within its own borders. Its significance derives from its size, resources, economic power and moral suasion in many parts of the world. Among other world links, Canada is a member of the Commonwealth and the North Atlantic Treaty Organization (NATO), contributes to United Nations peace-keeping forces in various parts of the world and has taken a leading position in developing a dialogue between countries of the North and South in order to ameliorate the conditions of the world's poor.

Internally, the government is paramount in making laws and regulations for its citizens. The battle to control the offices and activities of this mammoth institution should be understood by every inquiring and intelligent citizen. The constant evolution of governmental structures and priorities necessitates an unceasing re-evaluation of the policies and direction of government and even of the institution itself. In many areas, there is room for reform and improvement. It has been suggested, for example, that one test of a good government is how well it provides for the most vulnerable of its citizens: the young, the aged, the sick and the handicapped. The Canadian government does subsidize a great range of social services whose primary intent is sharing the resources of the country more equally. However, despite these efforts, between three and five million Canadians, depending on definitions and statistics, live below the poverty line. The high GDP disguises the fact that the country's wealth is very unevenly distributed among Canadians.

Within Canada, the political struggle is focused on institutions, behaviour and policies. The result is an agenda for the resolution of conflict over the very basics of life. Before the turn of the century, many fundamental questions need to be addressed. Will the country achieve economic stability or go bankrupt? Will the distribution of wealth, education and power remain heavily influenced by membership in privileged groups, or will the government continue to attempt their redistribution among individuals and regions? Will women receive their rightful place in Canadian society? Will Canadians of Indian, Métis and Inuit origin and new immigrants be successfully harmonized into Canadian society? Will Canada prosper under a North American Free Trade Agreement with the United States and Mexico? Will Canada adopt new foreign and defence policies now that the Soviet Union has disintegrated and the influence of communism has waned?

In the broader context of Canada in the world, there are many more unknowns in the years ahead. A report commissioned by the Canadian government predicts that, as basic resources become scarce in the world, pressures upon Canada to provide them will increase.[3] For instance, in times of famine, Canada may well find itself in the unenviable position of having to decide who eats and who does not. The government will have to conserve resources and ensure that the exploitation of natural wealth will be dictated not by short-term gains or political expediency but by longer-range national and global interests. It will become increasingly important for Canada to turn outward, pursuing foreign trade and playing a role in the resolution of global issues. Ad hoc decision-making will have to give way to greater government investment in research and development and in planning for the future.

The supreme test of any polity is whether it has the capacity to establish acceptable and enduring solutions from multiple conflicting demands. The crucial challenge to the present Canadian political system concerns its ability to manage the policy conflicts discussed above and others equally critical.

---

[3] G.O. Barnes, P.H. Freeman and C.A. Ulinski, *Global 2000: Implications for Canada* (Toronto: Pergamon Press, 1981).

This book is based on the premise that Canadians need to agree on one major issue — how these choices will be made. In a country as diverse as Canada, realists cannot expect agreement on fundamental philosophies about people and their community. What can be expected is a fair, open process of democracy, responsive to the public will, and consensus about how this process ought to work.

POLITICS AND GOVERNMENT

Politics is as old as human history. It is a fascinating form of behaviour, concerning disputes and decisions about human ideals and interests. Defined by the non-specialist as manipulation or the struggle for advantage, it is omnipresent: in relations between husband and wife, parent and child, employer and employee — in short, in all societal relations. However, political scientists do not study all social relations; they are concerned primarily with organized dispute and its collective resolution.

Two definitions of politics contend in the literature. The most widespread of them, put forth by David Easton, one of the foremost experts of systems analysis, is general and abstract. He defined politics as "the authoritative allocation of values."[4] By values, Easton did not mean moral ideas, but rather the benefits and opportunities that people value or desire. The second, a more restricted definition, was conceived by Harold Lasswell, who pointed out that politics always concerns "who gets what, when and how" in society.[5] In the present volume, we delimit the subject by proferring a definition of politics that combines the insights of both Easton and Lasswell: **Politics** embraces all activity that impinges upon the making of binding decisions about who gets what, when and how. It is an activity through which contending interests and differences may be reconciled for the supposed advantage of society.

Since valued possessions such as wealth and status are invariably scarce and unevenly distributed, disagreement can be expected to arise among people as they attempt to satisfy their seemingly endless wants. It is such general dispute that gives rise to the organized conflict pervading society, whether in the election of the president of the National Action Committee on the Status of Women (NAC), in the struggle within the United Church over policy toward human sexuality or in the election of the Canadian Prime Minister.

To reduce this endless conflict over power, mechanisms have evolved to enforce decisions for all members of society. We refer to these mechanisms as government. Politics and governing are both about organized dispute over power, but are often artificially demarcated: politics is concerned with influencing the governors, while governing consists of the actions of public officials in making decisions. Much of the dynamic character of politics comes from the pervasive conflict between the rulers and the ruled.

Government is thus the organization of people for the resolution of dispute and conflict. Even the simplest societies have some means of settling disputes. In modern societies, government not only provides law and order but also regulates many aspects of private and public affairs. It is one of the most complex and important of institutions.

While anthropologists and sociologists study the rules that regulate all forms of behaviour, political scientists concentrate on describing and analyzing the institutions and behaviour of the political governance of states. Insofar as social processes influence or are influenced by politics or governance, they are also part of the study of political science.

---

4   David Easton, *A Framework for Political Analysis* (Englewood Cliffs, N.J.: Prentice-Hall, 1965), pp. 50–6.

5   Harold Lasswell, *Politics: Who Gets What, When and How* (New York: McGraw-Hill, 1936).

The concept of *power* is central to the study of politics. The word comes from the Latin verb *potere* which means "to be able." Thus, in the broadest meaning of the word, power is being able to achieve what one wants. Power has been part of the vocabulary of politics since the time of Machiavelli, yet it remains the most perplexing issue within the discipline of political science. Even the fundamental question of whether it can be possessed like gold or is simply the result of social relationships remains unanswered.[6] But where would our understanding of politics be without the notion that some individuals hold power over others? Substitution of words such as "influence," "coercion," "compulsion," "control" and "persuasion" for "power" only compounds the difficulties. The essential problem stems from the difficulty of ascertaining whether power is absolute or relative. A person's ability to influence other individuals to act in a certain way often relies more upon bargaining than on the application of naked force. Thus **power** must be understood to include the ability to influence (convince) and/or to coerce (force) others to accept certain objectives or behave in a particular manner.

APPROACHES WITHIN POLITICAL SCIENCE

Each generation brings to the study of politics its own interests, values and methodologies. It usually carries over ideas from other disciplines such as history, law, philosophy, sociology, economics or anthropology. In this sense, the study of politics includes multiple approaches and is in reality a multi-disciplinary subject. The inconsistencies caused by this diversity in the tools for obtaining political understanding are reduced by the accepted principle that scientists should be self-consciously analytical and comparative and should avoid basing generalizations on casual observation.

Theories provide explanations of *why* politics takes place the way it does. The concept of theory derives from the Greek word *theoria* which means contemplation. Casual observation or opinion about facts is not theory. To use **theory** in political science (or in physics) means to make sense of the facts of a situation by explaining how they are interconnected. It means distinguishing the significant from the irrelevant by elucidating the most convincing explanation about the facts. Whether political research is based on experiments, statistics or configurative case studies, it is disciplined by the desire to be explicit in the rules employed to describe and analyze politics. Students must be aware, however, that some authors may use analysis as the proverbial drunk uses a streetlight — more for support than illumination.

Some scholars believe that the only way to study politics is to employ a general theory of the polity in an effort to obtain scientific, law-like, generalizations about politics.[7] Such general theories purport to identify all the critical structures and processes of society, to explain all the inter-relationships and then to predict a wide variety of outcomes.[8] Few Canadians have adhered to this view of the discipline. Beginning with William Ashley,

---

[6] For a discussion of the complex methodological issues see R.A. Dahl, "Power," *International Encyclopedia of the Social Sciences* (New York: Macmillan, 1968), vol. 12, pp. 405–15; R.A. Dahl, *Modern Political Analysis*, 2nd ed. (Englewood Cliffs, N.J.: Prentice-Hall, 1970), pp. 14–34; and H.D. Lasswell and A. Kaplan, *Power and Society: A Framework for Political Inquiry* (New Haven: Yale University Press, 1950).

[7] An introduction to the basic concepts and theories is found in Robert J. Jackson and Doreen Jackson, *Contemporary Government and Politics; Democracy and Authoritarianism* (Scarborough: Prentice Hall, 1993).

[8] For an intelligent overview criticism see Joseph LaPalombara, *Politics Within Nations* (Englewood Cliffs, N.J.: Prentice-Hall, 1975), chs. 1, 2.

who gave the first political science lecture in the country over 100 years ago, the discipline has been pluralistic; there has been no commitment to one theory or approach. Early writers such as George Bourinot, Stephen Leacock, Harold Innis, R.A. MacKay, Alexander Brady, H.M. Clokie and J.A. Corry commanded academic and public esteem, but they did not slavishly accept a single theory.[9]

In terms of influence in Canada, MacGregor Dawson's 1946 institutional analysis probably came closest to imposing a single approach on the discipline. Dawson and some of his students adhered to a strict **legal/formal** description of Canadian government and politics.[10] Critics of this style of analysis founded their arguments on the position that Dawson and much of his generation eschewed the study of culture, behaviour and public policy while concentrating exclusively on formal institutions.

Other general theories of politics have been applied to Canada; the best-known among them is **systems analysis**. It has been used as an introduction to many textbooks since about 1965.[11] While it was rarely employed in a methodical fashion, it usually served as a short-hand introduction to the study of politics. The essence of this general theory is that the politics of a country can be depicted by the interaction between the societal environment and an abstract political system that processes its demands and supports into outputs, producing an overall stability or homeostasis.[12]

A related general theory is **functionalism**. In essence, functionalism specifies the activities of a viable political system and explains how they help to maintain stability. If the polity does not perform these functions, it ceases to exist.[13] Though it has influenced writing about politics, functionalism has never found a place as a theory to explain the Canadian polity. Somewhat more in vogue is **structural functionalism**. In this approach researchers attempt to determine which "structures" perform which "functions" — as in these statements: "interest aggregation" is expressed by political parties, or "rule-making" is performed by Parliament.

The **political economy** approach has always had many advocates in Canada and has gained popularity among Canadian researchers in the 1990s. Political economy studies are concerned with the relationships between economics and government and in particular with the study of **public policy** — or, what governments do. Since different ideologies and political beliefs conflict over what this relationship should be, two opposing views are reflected in contemporary studies of political economy — a relatively new **public choice** school, sometimes referred to as "liberal political economy" because it tends to follow the logic of classical economics; and **neo-Marxism** based on Karl Marx's ideas about the structural relations among society, economy and politics.

All these schools of thought, except the Marxists (and some élite theorists) at least partially accept **pluralism** — the idea that power is widely dispersed and many groups

---

[9]   Robert J. Jackson, "The Classics in Canadian Political Science," *Research Tools in Canadian Studies*, vol. X, no. 4 (1988) pp. 7–18.

[10]   R. MacGregor Dawson's celebrated *Government of Canada* (Toronto: University of Toronto Press) was first published in 1947.

[11]   For one version see Richard Van Loon and Michael Whittington, *The Canadian Political System*, 4th ed. (Toronto: McGraw-Hill Ryerson, 1987).

[12]   Easton, *A Framework for Political Analysis*, passim.

[13]   See Gabriel Almond and G. Bingham Powell, *Comparative Politics: A Developmental Approach* (Boston: Little, Brown, 1966).

compete for it — in their fundamental conception of the polity and government. As a compromise, a new **state-centered** approach views the state as being able to act without responding to the demands of society. The state is visualized as being at least partially autonomous from the public's interests as expressed in the pluralist model.[14]

The essential problem with systems analysis, as well as other general theories such as functionalism, public choice and traditional Marxism,[15] is that often they are at such a high level of abstraction that they are remote from empirical research. They describe the polity in such general terms that they neither generate testable propositions nor aid our understanding of concrete political phenomena or problems. Moreover, such general theories have also failed in their fundamental task of identifying all the critical structures and processes of the political system and explaining the relationships among them.

In Canada, no single general theory of politics has ever been totally accepted. The various theories have been used as heuristic devices to help authors and students collect and analyze fragments of political reality. In Chapter 13 we outline in detail the contemporary determinist, pluralist, public choice and neo-Marxist theories of public policy, but let it be clear that by the middle of the 1990s no single theory or approach is taken as uniquely valid; few, if any scholars accept the notion that one approach can exhaust all that is to be known about Canadian politics.

Even if no single theory or approach is, or should be, pre-eminent in the study of Canadian politics, students ought to be aware of the underlying principles governing many of the basic arguments in the field. Gabriel Almond and Stephen Genco point out that two analogies summarize the core of the debate on the status of theory in political science. According to these authors, the discipline is divided over whether the analogy underlying the profession should liken it to the shifting formlessness of clouds or to the precise causation involved in a machine such as a watch. They conclude that "the current quandary in political science can, to a large extent, be explained by the fact that, by themselves, clock-model assumptions are inappropriate for dealing with the substance of political phenomena."[16] What this argument suggests, then, is that there is no adequate theory about politics that must not perforce include transient and fleeting phenomena. Politics is not totally predictable; its study has not uncovered a world of cause and effect. Almond and Genco's article contends that political reality has distinctive properties that make it unamenable to the forms of explanation used in the natural sciences. Thus, the science of politics should not be seen as a set of methods with a predetermined theory, but as a "commitment to explore and attempt to understand a given segment of empirical reality." Such an argument calls for an eclectic approach to Canadian politics and to comparative government.

Entirely eschewing approaches or theories in the discipline is not much help either. What political scientists call "hyperfactualism" or "barefooted empiricism" may simply lead to the

---

[14] See Eric Nordlinger, *On the Autonomy of the Democratic State* (Cambridge Mass.: Harvard University Press, 1981). For use of these theories see William Coleman and Grace Skogstad, eds., *Policy Communities and Public Policy in Canada* (Mississauga: Copp Clark Pitman, 1991).

[15] For neo-Marxism see Barrington Moore, Jr., *Social Origins of Dictatorship and Democracy: Lord and Peasant in the Making of the Modern World* (Boston: Beacon Press, 1966) and Ralph Miliband, *The State in Capitalist Society* (London: Weidenfield and Nicholson, 1969); for an application to the Canadian context, see Leo V. Panitch, ed., *The Canadian State* (Toronto: University of Toronto Press, 1977).

[16] Gabriel A. Almond and Stephen J. Genco, "Clouds, Clocks and the Study of Politics," *World Politics*, vol. 29, no. 4 (July 1977), p. 505.

collection of facts without purpose. Collecting parts of reality without any reference to hunches and ideas from theories is as misleading as the wholesale adoption of a single theory of the polity. We need guides to the facts to be examined.

In this volume, we adopt a variety of analytic and institutional approaches — what Joseph LaPalombara has called "partial" theories.[17] Our information and conclusions are based on the best available research, but not on the basis that knowledge is obtained uniquely by scientific methods. To adopt a purely scientific approach would be tantamount to declaring that the only knowledge we can have about torture must come from conducting experiments in this field.

If no general theory underlies the framework of this book, what segments of politics have been selected for examination? The choice of the analytical dimensions to be studied is always difficult, but the subject must somehow be delimited. In this volume we analyze Canadian culture, institutions, behaviour and public policy. These four dimensions all impinge on the competing ideas, interests, issues and people that make up the polity. They direct us toward those aspects of the political process that can be observed, compared and evaluated; they are the primary segments of a society concerned with politics and power.

The formal institutions of government are the most visible elements of the political process. Such structures as constitutions, parliaments, bureaucracies and executives are well known to students of Canadian politics and government. And formal institutions do explain much about politics. Too often they are treated as epiphenomena — that is, as being caused by self-interested individuals and groups. Institutions are important in their own right as units of analysis — they shape the interests, resources and conduct of political leaders who in turn shape the institutions.[18] The way institutions are structured affects political actors, bureaucrats and citizens — as well as who gets what, when and how.

Whereas traditional Canadian political science focuses on studies of institutions, contemporary political culture and socialization studies tend to emphasize the study of values and beliefs. The assumption of the latter studies is that political outcomes are determined by amalgamations of individual preferences. Certainly, the values of members of society influence social and political decisions. However, institutions also affect social outcomes. Institutions, therefore, can be thought of as "congealed tastes" or conventions about values that are condensed into institutions that make rules for society.[19]

It is extremely difficult to assess the relative significance of institutions and values for the development of government policy. Probably both are necessary. If institutions are constant or stable, we ought to be able to predict outcomes from tastes. If tastes are constant, we ought to be able to predict outcomes from institutions. In turbulent times, institutions, and often values, are in constant evolution. "One fundamental and unsolved problem of social science is to penetrate the illusion and to learn to take both values and institutions into account."[20]

---

[17] Joseph LaPalombara, "Macro-theories and Micro-applications in Comparative Politics: A Widening Chasm," *Comparative Politics*, vol. 1, no. 1 (October 1968), pp. 52–78.

[18] See Robert J. Jackson, "Australian and Canadian Comparative Research," in Malcolm Alexander and Brian Galligan, eds., *Comparative Political Studies* (Sydney: Pitman, 1992).

[19] William H. Riker, "Implications from the Disequilibrium of Majority Rule for the Study of Institutions," *APSR*, vol. 74, no. 2 (June, 1980) pp. 432–46. Alan Cairns has also made use of this distinction in his introductory essay to *Constitution, Government and Society*, edited by Douglas E. Williams (Toronto: McClelland & Stewart, 1988).

[20] Riker, ibid., p. 432.

The distinction between individual behaviour and institutions is also blurred. If, in calling institutions "structures," we are referring to a process of change so slow as to be negligible for the purposes of investigation,[21] then institutions are stable configurations that change only over long periods and so are merely the organized collective behaviour of individuals. The collectivity may be more than the sum of its parts, but there is no doubt that its parts are individuals behaving in some routine manner. The study of behaviour and institutions is therefore intertwined at the logical as well as the empirical level of analysis. As Karl R. Popper so aptly put it, "institutions are like fortresses. They must be well designed *and* properly manned."[22]

Public policy is a more recent jargon-concept in political science. As government has grown, the vast array of government programs and policies have become more difficult for the average Canadian to comprehend. In response to this complexity, the study of public policy has flourished in the discipline of political science. Usually, policy is defined by its ability to set the parameters of future decisions by developing a long-term perspective in an issue area. Policy-making is the activity of arriving at these perspectives. Policies result from the interaction of culture, institutions and behaviour. They feed back into the politics of a country, helping to determine political culture, to structure institutions and to limit political behaviour.[23]

Thus, culture, institutions, behaviour and public policy all interact to form the Canadian variety of politics. There are two basic approaches to the study of these and other factors in Canadian politics. In the **synchronic** approach, specific political factors in Canada are compared with those of other states. In the **diachronic** approach, political factors are examined in one or more countries over historical time. Both approaches are important. Dynamic (over a period of time) and static views of the four dimensions are also useful in formulating generalizations about the Canadian polity.[24]

In this volume we search for significant regularities, similarities and differences in Canadian culture, institutions, behaviour and policies. The approach used is eclectic, seeking evidence through both dynamic and comparative avenues. Too many volumes on Canada have been parochial and cynical about Canada and its future. Too many texts attempt to compress the facts into immutable pigeon-holes that provide an improper, negative understanding of the country. Canada's system of government is best understood and appreciated when it is compared, even briefly, with those of other countries. The democratic equilibrium is fostered by a comprehensive interplay of culture, institutions, behaviour and policy. Understanding this phenomenon requires sensitivity to the political and administrative environment within which government has to operate, as well as an appreciation of both the cohesive and the disruptive forces of our history and society.

---

[21] See Karl W. Deutsch, "The Crisis of the State," *Government and Opposition*, vol. 16, no. 3 (Summer, 1981), pp. 331–43.

[22] Karl R. Popper, *The Poverty of Historicism* (London: Routledge, 1961), p. 157. For neo-institutional approaches in general see Jeffrey Pfeffer, *Organizations and Organization Theory* (Marshfield, Mass.: Pitman, 1982).

[23] For an introduction to this literature see Peter Aucoin, "Public-Policy Theory and Analysis" in G. Bruce Doern and Peter Aucoin, eds., *Public Policy in Canada* (Toronto: Macmillan, 1979), pp. 1–26; Anthony King, "Ideas, Institutions and the Policies of Governments: A Comparative Analysis," *BJPS*, vol. 3, no. 4 (October 1973), p. 423; and Stephen Brooks, *Public Policy in Canada* (Toronto: McClelland & Stewart, 1989).

[24] See Jackson and Jackson, *Contemporary Government and Politics*, chs 4. and 5.

STATES AND NATIONS

A useful starting point in placing Canada within a comparative context is to consider it as a "state." As one of the 181 states currently recognized by the United Nations, Canada may be compared synchronically with a multitude of other more-or-less similar political entities. Furthermore, a consideration of the origins and development of the Canadian state provides a basis for diachronic comparison and an historical setting for contemporary Canadian politics.

Since the rise of absolutism in the sixteenth and seventeenth centuries, when sovereigns in certain parts of Europe began the process of integrating feudal fiefdoms, petty principalities and conquered territories into unified kingdoms, the state has emerged as the dominant form of political organization. Of course, other types of political systems have existed and continue to exist. Empires have come and gone. Considerable decision-making power may be wielded at sub-national levels of government, especially in federal systems; and the number of international actors, such as the United Nations and the European Community, has grown. States, too, are born and disappear over time. For example, the Baltic states of Estonia, Latvia and Lithuania, which were recognized as independent countries after the First World War, were forced into the Soviet Union after the Second World War and then recently became independent again. The Soviet Union itself has fragmented into multiple republics of which Russia is the largest. The general tendency has been for the number of states to grow almost yearly. Of the 181 members of the United Nations, well over half have become independent since 1945.

While everyone can share sunshine, politics is a zero-sum game in which some win and some lose in the struggle for advantage.

Reproduced with permission (Bas.-Tachydromos, Greece/Rothco).

THE STATE

The **state** is usually defined as a form of political organization in which governmental institutions are capable of maintaining order and implementing rules or laws (through coercion if necessary) over a given population and within a given territory.[25] The usual point of departure for such formulations is German sociologist Max Weber's definition of the state as a human community that "successfully upholds a claim to the monopoly of the legitimate use of physical force in the enforcement of its order...within a given territorial area." Thus, the state as an organization is defined in terms of its relation to power.[26] A state is normally admitted to the United Nations, for example, when it has satisfied the members of this international body that, like themselves, it wields state power and is capable of maintaining order within its territorial boundaries — that is, when it is considered to be **sovereign**. It should be noted, however, that some states recognized as sovereign are not members of the UN — for example, Switzerland and the Vatican.

While many practical problems circumscribe the concept of **sovereignty**, a state usually is recognizable by its internal and external powers: its ability to tax its citizens and its ability to conduct external relations. Or, as Joseph LaPalombara puts it: "As applied to *internal* matters, national sovereignty means that supreme and final authority rests in the national government as opposed to all other private and governmental organizations that may compose the nation-state itself."[27] External sovereignty, on the other hand, represents the recognition by the international community of the right of a people or government to run their own affairs, free from interference by other states or governments.

A state is also characterized by the degree of subjective feeling its citizens have about it. While some states do exist without widespread public identification with their institutions, this is not usually the case, especially in developed democracies such as Canada. Normally people strongly identify with their state. When citizens accept that a government ought, or has the right, to make decisions for them, political scientists refer to the system as **legitimate**.[28]

Legitimacy in this sense is closely linked to the concept of **authority**, which we may define as the government's power to make binding decisions and issue obligatory commands. According to Weber, authority may be said to stem from three main sources. **Traditional authority**, which arises from custom and history, is most frequently gained through inheritance and thus has been enjoyed by royal dynasties throughout the ages. **Charismatic authority** is derived from popular admiration of the personal "heroic" qualities of the individual in whom it is vested — whether prophet, warlord or orator. Lastly, **rational-legal** or **bureaucratic authority**, the most common form in western societies, is vested not in individuals *per se* but in the offices they hold and the mechanisms that placed them there.[29] Thus, the authority of the Canadian Prime Minister (though charismatic to some) is derived primarily from the fact that he or she is a leader of a government placed in power by the routine and legitimate process of popular election. As soon as one leader ceases to be Prime Minister, the authority currently vested in that person will pass to the new incumbent of the

---

[25] Max Weber, *The Theory of Social and Economic Organization*, edited and translated by A.M. Henderson and Talcott Parsons (New York: Oxford University Press, 1947), p. 154.

[26] The reader must be wary of all single definitions of the state; as early as 1931 one scholar found 145 different usages of the term "state." See Sabine Cassese, "The Rise and Decline of the Nation or State," *International Political Science Review*, vol. 7, no. 2 (1986), p. 120. For an illuminating essay on the "the state" see Gabriel A. Almond "The Return to the State," *APSR*, vol. 82, no. 3 (Sept. 1988), pp. 853–75 and the symposiums pp. 875–901.

[27] LaPalombara, *Politics Within Nations*, p. 36.

[28] Jean Blondel, *Comparing Political Systems* (New York: Praeger, 1974), p. 49.

[29] Weber, *The Theory of Social and Economic Organization*, ch. 3.

office. In Canada and many other modern societies, therefore, legitimacy and authority tend to be vested not in individuals but in the political institutions and offices of the state.

The concept of legitimacy may be applied not only to regimes and governments but also to their individual acts. Thus, a legitimate government may do some things that are perceived to be illegitimate. Legitimacy in this sense should not be confused with **legality** — while the former denotes the degree of subjective authority vested in the government by public opinion, the latter relates to the constitutional or legal propriety of undertaking certain activities. Some events may therefore be legal (that is, within the letter of the law) without being considered legitimate. The Canadian government's use of the *War Measures Act* to suppress civil liberties during the 1970 Québec crisis was legal, but many Canadians did not think it was legitimate; they did not believe that the federal government ought to have exercised such powers. Or, to cite a more recent example, a majority of the Supreme Court of Canada concluded in 1981 that, while Prime Minister Trudeau's attempt to patriate the Constitution unilaterally was strictly legal, it was not legitimate because it flouted the convention that provincial assent should be obtained. Conversely, certain events can be viewed as legitimate without being legal. Some Canadians, for example, supported the action of the RCMP in burning a barn to prevent a "subversive" meeting, but the action was not legal; in fact, it was a criminal offence.

The ability of a state and its political institutions to govern a given population and territory rests on the twin foundations of sovereignty and legitimacy. In the resolution of conflict, a government requires the consent necessary to allocate values and resources authoritatively. All states attempt to maintain political order and viability, to resolve societal conflicts without tearing the country apart, to defend the territory against external enemies and to maintain essential services such as the food and water supply, transportation, health facilities and educational institutions. The manner in which these and other policy-making activities are performed, while a balance is maintained between power on the one hand and legitimacy and support on the other, is at the core of the study of politics and government.

THE NATION

The identification of citizens with their state, and therefore its legitimacy, may be enhanced by the perception that the state and its institutions serve to represent the interests of the population as a whole — in other words, the interests of the *nation*.

In popular usage, and as the title of the United Nations Organization suggests, "nation" is often taken to refer to all people living within a certain territory and under a single government. In this sense, however, the meaning of nation becomes indistinguishable from that of the citizenry of a state. Alternatively, a nation is sometimes identified with respect to certain objective criteria, such as the possession of a common language, racial or physical characteristics, ancestry or cultural heritage. But this usage fails to explain why all peoples who share such characteristics, for example, Argentineans and Chileans, continue to think of themselves as constituting separate nations.

The key to understanding the concept of nation is that, "like any other form of social identity," national identity (and its associated concept, ethnic identity) is "essentially subjective, a sense of social belonging and ultimate loyalty."[30] While objective criteria such as lan-

---

[30] George De Vos and Lola Romanucci-Ross, *Ethnic Identity: Cultural Continuities and Change* (Palo Alto, Cal.: Mayfield Publishing Co., 1975), p. 3; and Anthony D. Smith, *National Identity* (London: Penguin, 1991).

guage or race may play a part in reinforcing these identities, the essence of a *nation* is that it is a collectivity of people united by a shared sense of loyalty and a common feeling of belonging together. Thus, immigrants to Canada from Eastern Europe or Lebanon may feel themselves to be just as Canadian, as much a part of the Canadian nation, as those who were born in Canada. On the other hand, while some French Canadians are first and foremost "Canadien," others, who share the same language and cultural heritage, consider themselves "Québécois."

National identity is therefore a sense of belonging to a particular community, often (but not necessarily) reinforced by a common language, culture, customs, heritage or the shared experience of living under the same government. At the same time, national identity consists of a sense of distinctiveness from other peoples who may or may not share certain of these characteristics. This dual subjective aspect of the nation is clearly expressed in one satirical definition of a nation as "a society united by a common error as to its origins and a common aversion to its neighbours."[31]

Not all collectivities that consider themselves culturally or linguistically distinct necessarily constitute separate nations. When individuals and minorities do share cultures distinct from those of other groups, social scientists label them "ethnic groups" or "ethnic minorities." **Ethnicity**, like national identity, is primarily a subjective phenomenon, although it is usually reinforced by the presence of objective traits such as a language or dialect, customs and cultural heritage and, often, distinct racial or physical characteristics. In many societies, such as the United States or much of Canada, ethnic groups may live side by side and consider themselves, though culturally distinct, to constitute one nation. In others, however, certain ethnic groups may think of themselves as nations in their own right. In the latter case, as in Québec, they may mobilize and pursue political action in order to gain independence. The boundary between ethnic group and nation is therefore rather tenuous, but it is possible to relate the two if, as in this volume, we define a **nation** as a politically conscious and mobilized ethnic group (usually with a clear sense of territory) that possesses, or aspires to, self-government or independent statehood.

The concepts of "nation" and "ethnicity" are important to the study of politics because, despite the widespread lip-service paid to the principles of national self-determination, only rarely do territorial and ethnic boundaries coincide. For example, the co-existence of several languages is generally taken as one indication of ethnic pluralism. At the same time, in only about half of the world's states do more than 75 percent of the population speak the same language. Few states in the world consist, as do Japan and South Korea, basically of one ethnic group. The term **nation-state** is used to represent this conceptual marriage between the cultural principle *nation* and the territorial and governmental principles inherent in the idea of the *state*. Some states, such as Canada and the United Kingdom, contain aspiring nations within them. Other nations are governed by more than one state — for example, Koreans in North and South Korea or Palestinians in a number of middle eastern states. The politicization of demands for the re-unification of nations, as in Korea or Ireland, or for the division of multinational states into more ethnically homogeneous self-governing communities, as in Cyprus, results in highly emotional and frequently violent conflict and causes serious problems of accommodation for political authorities. Attempting to account for these strains and find solutions for them is a major concern for politicians and political scientists alike.

---

[31] Julian Huxley and Alfred Court Haddon, *We Europeans: A Survey of "Racial" Problems* (London: Jonathan Cape, 1935), p. 16.

NATIONALISM AND REGIONALISM

A generation ago, "nation-building" was a dominant theme in political science, especially among those studying the political development of new states in the so-called Third World, many of which faced the task of integrating fragmented societies into cohesive political units. The prevailing view was that the ongoing processes of economic development, urbanization and industrialization would reduce territorial and cultural tensions, just as they had already apparently enhanced the integration of western advanced industrial societies.[32] In the last decade, however, many advanced states have been subjected to pressures of a nationalist or regional nature, which had previously been dismissed as threats only to "new" nations.

Nationalism has manifested itself in many forms over the centuries since the state emerged as the major form of socio-political organization. It has been used as a justification for economic expansionism, protectionism and imperialism; as an ideology espousing the supremacy of a particular nation or people (as in German National Socialism); as a quest for emancipation from colonial rule; or as an integrative process in multi-racial or tribal societies of the Third World after independence.[33] In most cases, these forms of nationalism were devoted to integrating the members of an existing or future state. But, as it is found in a number of western societies today, nationalism is a potentially divisive force. In several cases, territorially concentrated ethnic minorities, previously subjects of a larger state, have been roused to search for increased self-determination and even total independence. The breakdown of Yugoslavia into multiple republics and then the violent fragmentation of one of them, Bosnia, is one of the most visible of these circumstances.

Ethnic minorities have not been totally assimilated or acculturated by the forces of modernization in most advanced industrial societies. Indeed, since the Second World War, they have become increasingly visible and vocal. However, not all examples of organized ethnic interest should be labelled as nationalism. Many ethnic demands, such as those of Italian or Ukrainian minorities in Canada, involve no challenge to the integrity of the existing state and quite easily may be accommodated within its confines. Examples are demands for minority-language education or ethnically oriented television programs. Nationalism should rather be viewed as that part of the continuum of ethnic activity in which demands move from those that may be accommodated within the existing state structure to those for political (and usually economic and cultural) autonomy, or even for total separation from the larger state.[34] Thus, in this volume **nationalism** is defined in its contemporary sense as the collective action of a politically conscious ethnic group (or nation) in pursuit of increased territorial autonomy or sovereignty.

Examples of contemporary nationalist movements (often labelled "ethno-nationalist" or "neo-nationalist") may be found in many advanced industrial societies: the Scots and Welsh

---

[32] A critique of these forecasts is found in Arend Lijphart, "Political Theories and the Explanation of Ethnic Conflict in the Western World: Falsified Predictions and Plausible Postdictions," in M.J. Esman, ed., *Ethnic Conflict in the Western World* (Ithaca, N.Y.: Cornell University Press, 1977), pp. 46–64. For a discusion of the fundamental issues in this field, see Robert J. Jackson and Michael Stein, *Issues in Comparative Politics* (New York: St. Martins Press, 1971).

[33] On the types of nationalism see Anthony D. Smith, *Nationalism in the Twentieth Century* (Oxford: Martin Robertson, 1979). On Québec see Robert J. Jackson and Abina Dann, "Quebec Foreign Policy? Canada and Ethno-Regionalism," in Werner J. Feld and Werner Link, eds., *The New Nationalism* (New York: Pergamon, 1979), pp. 89–105.

[34] See James Lightbody, "A Note on the Theory of Nationalism as a Function of Ethnic Demands," *CJPS*, vol. 2, no. 3 (September 1969), pp. 327–37.

in the United Kingdom, Basques and Catalans in Spain, Bretons and Corsicans in France, Flemings and Walloons in Belgium and, of course, the Québécois in Canada.[35] In such cases, the ethnic minorities have apparently reduced any previous commitment they may have had to the larger state and have acted collectively to develop political parties, nationalist and cultural organizations and, sometimes, even terrorist groups, in order to pursue fundamental changes in the territorial boundaries and sovereignty of the state.

In the above-named countries and elsewhere, territorial tensions have also been manifested by movements espousing regionalist demands and protests, even where a separate ethnic or national identity has been absent. In contrast to nationalist demands, which seek to alter existing political structures, **regionalist** territorial tensions are "those brought about by certain groups that...demand a change in the political, economic and cultural relations between regions and central powers *within* the existing state."[36] Regionalist discontent is most often articulated in economic terms, especially by representatives of poorer, peripheral regions within a country. They demand a share of the affluence enjoyed by the rest of their society. However, such discontent can also find expression in political terms, particularly as in the case of *nouveau-riche* regions objecting to the central government's power to impose constraints that prevent them from "cashing in" on their new-found prosperity.

In the short term, because regionalism does not directly challenge territorial sovereignty, it appears to present less of a threat to the existing state structure than does nationalism. In the long term, however, persistent neglect of regionalist demands by central authorities may result in a serious loss of legitimacy for the state in certain parts of the country. Moreover, it may also reinforce or provide the basis for the development of a distinct ethnic or national identity that seeks separation from the state. At the very least, regionalist protests add to the flow of demands that must be considered by policy-makers. Because most political parties have regional concentrations of support, regionalism has become an important dimension of political life in many countries, especially Canada.

THE DEVELOPMENT OF THE MODERN STATE

Territorial strains manifested in nationalism and regionalism are one aspect of what some writers have referred to as a "crisis" of the contemporary state.[37] The modern state originally emerged in western Europe before the industrial revolution as a strategic and economic unit. As John Herz has aptly put it, the territorial state provided a "hard shell" toward the external environment. Strategically, the hard shell of the state "rendered it to some extent secure from foreign penetration, and thus made it an ultimate unit of protection for those within its boundaries."[38] At the same time, the state became the major locus of economic activity

---

[35] For case studies of a number of ethnic and nationalist movements, see, among others, Esman, ed., Ethnic Conflict; Charles Foster, ed., *Nations Without a State: Ethnic Minorities in Western Europe* (New York: Praeger, 1980); Jeffrey Ross et al., eds., *The Mobilization of Collective Identity* (Lanham, Maryland: University Press of America, 1980).

[36] Riccardo Petrella, "Nationalist and Regionalist Movements in Western Europe," in Foster, ed., *Nations Without A State*, p. 10 (emphasis added).

[37] For example, Deutsch, "The Crisis of the State"; John H. Herz, *The Nation-State and the Crisis of World Politics* (New York: David McKay Co., 1976), esp. ch. 3; Gordon Smith, "The Crisis of the West European State," in D.M. Cameron, ed., *Regionalism and Supranationalism: Challenges and Alternatives to the Nation-State in Canada and Europe* (Montréal: IRPP, 1981), pp. 21–36.

[38] Herz, *The Nation-State and the Crisis of World Politics*, p. 101.

and the guarantor of economic autonomy. In many countries, the state institutions themselves played an active role in promoting economic development, providing transportation networks and other forms of industrial infrastructure, if not actually developing certain industries under state ownership. Less directly, almost all states provided a hard shell for their domestic markets through the imposition of tariffs, quotas and other protective measures and through the management of external trade relations.

With the emergence of the concept of national self-determination, the hard, hollow shell of the territorial state was given substance. The modern state emerged in Europe in the sixteenth and seventeenth centuries and was carried by colonists to the Americas, Australasia and Africa where new states were formed for self-defence or in emulation of Europe. The idea that the state should govern on behalf of all the people, instead of a privileged minority, was first realized by the French Revolution of 1789. With the spread of the principles and institutions of popular sovereignty, often in the form of liberal democracy, the strategic and economic unit also became the primary focus of cultural and political loyalties.

Today, the hard shell of the state has been rendered somewhat less resistant by changes in the world economy, technology and communications and by the development of new instruments of warfare. As strategic units, most western states are no longer able to defend their citizens against realistic external threats. They are forced to rely instead on the protective cloak offered by the United States and NATO. The economic autonomy of states has been challenged by the increasing inter-dependence of national economies, the growing importance of international finance capital and multi-national corporations, dependence on energy supplies and raw materials imported from more assertive Third World countries and the need for economic markets greater than those encompassed by traditional state boundaries. In some cases, these factors have led to the development of new economic and political institutions on a transnational level, perhaps best exemplified by the growth of the European Community. More generally, and especially in Canada, the result has been dependence on foreign capital investment, especially from the United States. Overall, it has become increasingly difficult for states to control the internal dynamics of their own economies.

It is in this context that one author refers to the economic and strategic "inadequacy" of the contemporary state.[39] The state is no longer able to maintain its hard shell toward the outside world. The implied danger for the state and its authorities is that, if this inadequacy is widely perceived by the general public, the legitimacy and loyalty owed to the state will be undermined. Herein may also be found one factor behind the nationalist demands of ethnic minorities; many of the original economic and strategic advantages of remaining within the larger state no longer exist.[40]

Until the twentieth century, the role of the state was by and large restricted to the maintenance of law and order, the administration of justice, the defence of the realm and the conduct of diplomacy. In order to maintain or enhance their legitimacy or popular support, states have assumed many new tasks. In particular, state authorities have increasingly taken on service functions — such as education, health care, housing, pensions and unemployment insurance — to provide for the welfare of their citizens. This growth of the "welfare state" has been accompanied by a more interventionist role for the state in the econ-

---

[39] Smith, "The Crisis of the West European State."

[40] On this and other potential lines of explanation for nationalist movements in western industrial societies, see Nick Baxter-Moore, "The Causes of Nationalist Movements in Developed Democracies," in D.C. Rowat, ed., *The Referendum and Separation Elsewhere: Implications for Québec* (Ottawa: Carleton University, 1978), pp. 49–76.

omy. Many governments have intervened directly with budgetary policies or through state ownership of particular industries, for example, air and rail transport, telecommunications, energy development and public utilities. Others have played less overt economic roles, for example, through regulation of the private sector (environmental regulations and health and safety standards) or with tariff policies designed to protect domestic industries or markets.

> *"The measure of a nation's greatness does not lie in the conquest, or its Gross National Product, or the size of its gold reserves or the height of its skyscrapers. The real measure of a nation is the quality of its national life, what it does for the least fortunate of its citizens and the opportunities it provides for its youth to live useful and meaningful lives."*
>
> **The Ottawa Citizen, October 16, 1993**

The influence of the state in the daily lives of its citizens is therefore immense. As the scope of government activity has enlarged, the machinery of government has grown more complex and decision making has become more centralized and bureaucratized. The increased number of state functions, and the personnel to carry them out, must be paid for. The average share of the national income consumed by the public sector in western societies has risen from 5 to 10 percent in the late nineteenth century to between 35 and 50 percent today. In countries with large and well-developed welfare state programs, such as Sweden or the Netherlands, total government expenditures actually exceed half the national income. Consequently a large proportion of each wage-earners' income disappears into the hands of the government, either directly in the form of income tax and pension contributions or indirectly through sales tax and customs duties.

This growth of the state in the twentieth century underlines another dimension of the perceived crisis of the contemporary state. Some political scientists and politicians allege that in addition to being strategically and economically inadequate, as outlined above, the institutions of government are *overloaded*.[41] The "overload" thesis consists of two complementary aspects: first, that the state has taken on more functions than it can perform and/or afford; second, that the policy-making process has become too complex and cumbersome to respond effectively to the expectations of the citizens. Particularly in liberal democracies, the state faces a loss of public support and legitimacy if it cannot cope with the demands of its citizens. Thus, the resurgence of nationalism and regionalism may be attributable in part to a reaction against the centralization of economic and political decision making. More generally, in a number of western societies there has also been a backlash against "big government" and high levels of government expenditure and taxation.

Though under fire, the state remains the pre-eminent political actor in both the domestic and the international arenas. International organizations, such as the European Community, NATO and, particularly, the United Nations, remain the creatures of the states that comprise them. Debates regarding nationalism, regionalism and political decentralization are carried to the state capital. Indeed, nationalist movements perpetuate the logic of the nation-state

---

[41] See, for example, Michel J. Crozier, Samuel P. Huntington and Joji Watanuki, *The Crisis of Democracy* (New York: New York University Press, 1975); Richard Rose and B. Guy Peters, *Can Government Go Bankrupt?* (New York: Basic Books, 1978); Richard Rose, ed., *Challenge to Governance: Studies in Overload Polities* (Beverly Hills, Cal.: Sage Publications, 1980).

by demanding secession from the larger state in order to form another, smaller one. Although the state, by and large, may not be quite as sovereign as it once was — even questions of sovereignty or foreign ownership of the economy have become national political issues — its institutions, policy-making processes, functions and powers remain at the heart of the study of politics. Thus, an examination of the origins and development of the Canadian state is an essential precursor to the more detailed analysis of politics in Canada. Before turning to this examination in Chapter 2, we shall first discuss the type of state that Canada has adopted.

THE BASIC PREMISES OF DEMOCRACY IN CANADA

States vary greatly in their governmental forms, politics and policies. Canada is a democracy, and its governmental form is that of a constitutional monarchy with a federal basis. The principles and structures inherent in this description will be fleshed out in detail throughout this volume. Though these concepts may appear fuzzy and debate over their meaning is to be expected, they are extremely important in the daily lives of Canadians.

The type of political system enjoyed by a state is usually encapsulated in the kind and limits of power exercised within it. Aesop's fable of the frogs and their search for the right leadership in their pond comes readily to mind. It seems that the frogs longed for a king, so they appealed to the god Zeus to send them one. He sent them King Log. When the log lolled about without exercising any authority the frogs demanded another king. Zeus sent King Stork, who immediately gobbled them up.

Aesop's fable illustrates the principle that in political systems there is a continuum between total freedom and the government's use of persuasion or coercion. In the real world, an element of power — and so coercion — is always present or implied. The poet Yeats expressed the idea that violence is always available to the state when he wrote in "The Great Day":

> *Hurrah for revolution and more cannon-shot!*
> *A beggar upon horseback lashes a beggar on foot.*
> *Hurrah for revolution and cannon come again!*
> *The beggars have changed places, but the lash goes on.*[42]

States differ remarkably in their openness and types of participation. Certain features of each polity are unique, yet the essentials of political systems are similar because all perform the same basic functions. A question, then, at the heart of the study of comparative politics, has been whether political systems tend to fall into distinguishable categories or classes.

The search for understanding on this subject usually begins with Aristotle's analysis of the Greek city-states in the fourth century before Christ. This Greek philosopher, the godfather of comparative politics, set out the fundamental rules for scientific investigation and developed the first significant classification of types of political systems.

Aristotle's classical division of polities was based on his knowledge of the 158 Greek city-states. While he lived in Athens, with its principle of equal access of citizens to government positions, he studied the constitutions and governments of other city-states to determine the causes of political instability and change. He employed two criteria to classify these states: the number of people who participated in governing; and whether they ruled in their own or in the general interest. A six-fold classification resulted. Aristotle found that only two

---

[42]   Quoted in Michael Curtis, Comparative Government and Politics (New York: Harper & Row, 1968), p. 43.

categories —*aristocracy* and *polity* — were reasonably stable, and concluded that stability depended on active participation, or at least some degree of representation, of all citizens. (See Table 1.2.)

TABLE 1.2   THE ARISTOTELIAN CLASSIFICATION

Number of Rulers	Rule in the General Interest	Self-Interested Rule
One	Monarchy	Tyranny
Few	Aristocracy	Oligarchy
Many	Polity	Democracy or Ochlocracy

This classification of rule by the one, the few or the many (with its resultant spectrum from tyrannical rule to democracy) has become part of western thought. While considerably simplifying reality, the classification helped introduce some order into the immense variety of political ideas and systems. It has gradually become clear, however, that there is no right or wrong classification, and that comparison requires agreement on at least principles and definitions.

In the contemporary world the governors are never in total control, so a classification that forces either/or distinctions can only be a starting point. The next step is to examine political systems on a spectrum. The most standard continua are those between democratic and authoritarian governments, and traditional and modern societies. In both cases, the difficulty lies in determining the degree to which a state is democratic or modern. This task of measuring the degree of forms of government is very difficult. In this volume, we use the following basic definitions: a **democratic** system conciliates competing political interests; an **autocratic** system imposes one dominating interest on all others.[43] Thus, in these terms the form of government is determined by its method of reconciling political diversity and conflict. In autocratic regimes, representative institutions are absent or are facades.

Democracy is an ambiguous concept. It is used as a *source* of authority for government, as well as for the *purposes* served by government, and for the *procedures* for constituting government.[44]

Originally, the word democracy came from two Greek roots — *demos*, meaning the people, and *kratos*, meaning authority. As we have seen, in ancient Greek culture democracy meant government by the many. In some Greek city-states all citizens participated in making and implementing laws. Save for rare exceptions (an example occurs in some Swiss communes), such systems no longer exist. Instead, most democracies, Canada among them, consist of a system of elected representatives who make laws for the country. In other words, democracy is a set of procedures for constituting governments.

For Aristotle, "democracy" was characterized by the "poor" ruling in their own favour. When we characterize Canada as a democracy we tend to place it in the "rule in the

---

[43] Classification of the world's states is discussed in Robert J. Jackson and Doreen Jackson, *Contemporary Government and Politics*, chs. 4 and 5. In many classifications a third basic form is added. See Bernard Crick, *Basic Forms of Government: A Sketch and A Model* (London: Macmillan, 1973) for a discussion of "totalitarianism" following a reasonably similar definition.

[44] Samuel P. Huntington, *The Third Wave: Democratization in the Twentieth Century* (Norman: University of Oklahoma Press, 1991).

general interest" category under which, to some extent, the people govern themselves. Unfortunately, today practically all states describe themselves as "democratic" in some fashion. Even the former East Germany referred to itself as the German Democratic Republic. The British writer Bernard Crick played lightly but brilliantly with this problem of the meaning of words and their usage in the real world. For him, "democracy" is perhaps the most promiscuous word in the world of public affairs: "She is everybody's mistress and yet somehow retains her magic even when her lover sees that her favours are being, in his light, illicitly shared by many another. Indeed, even amid our pain at being denied her exclusive fidelity, we are proud of her adaptability to all sorts of circumstances."[45]

Yet, if a democracy is defined as a state in which opposition parties have a reasonable chance of winning office, not all members of the UN would be called democratic. Only about a third of the states have established over time that they can change their governments without recourse to revolution, coups d'état or other violent forms of change, and Canada is one of them. The fact is that democracy in the sense just cited is not very widespread in the developing world.

The pure model of democracy envisages popular assemblies as in the Athenian sense. Readers may like to recall that, at that time, elections to high office were carried out by lottery because the Athenians believed that if choices between individuals were made then the richer, or better connected, candidates would win. In the modern day few observers expect democracy to be rule by the people as a whole. The closest to this goal is representative democracy, in which the people choose those who are to make and administer the laws. In principle, all citizens should have equal access to and influence on government policy-making through participation in fair and competitive elections. In this book, we define **representative democracy** as a political system in which the governors who make decisions with the force of law obtain their authority directly or indirectly as a result of free elections in which the bulk of the population may participate.

Thus, democracy in Canada is not equivalent to rule by the people as a whole. Our form of government is, properly speaking, a representative democracy, in which those elected to high office are invested with the legitimacy of power to make decisions having the force of law. The system provides a method of electing and monitoring these representatives. It also allows regular and institutionalized opportunities for changing those responsible for governing the political system.[46] Moreover, the elected representatives do not mirror the views of the people or the various regions they represent. If they did so, formulating coherent policy might well be impossible.

Representative democracy requires complex structures, but its basic attributes may be fairly easily outlined. Its essential characteristic is reconciling the need for political order with a degree of influence for competing political interests. Associated with this basic feature are the values of liberty and equality. The primary premise is that representative democracy is the best means or technique of governing a complex society. It is a political means and not necessarily an end in itself. However, representative democracy is generally thought to be accompanied by other political values that are embedded in the notion of reconciling diverse interests through the majority principle: freedom of press and opinion, contested elections,

---

[45] Bernard Crick, *In Defence of Politics* (London: Penguin, 1964), p. 56.

[46] See Seymour Martin Lipset, "Some Social Requisites of Democracy: Economic Development and Political Legitimacy," *APSR*, vol. 53, no. 1 (March 1959), pp. 69–105.

competing political parties, civil rights, rule of law, limited terms of office and constitutional limits on the power of the elected. The assumption is that political weight and authority can shift from one group to another, and that any group or party seeking power will have to enlist the cooperation of other groups. No single élite or oligarchy will remain in control over time and over all issues. In other words, *pluralism* is assumed.

The values of democracy are often debated. Some authors consider democracy to be essentially equivalent to certain fundamental values such as the protection of individual liberty or equality or other goals. In this volume we shall describe, analyze and assess the Canadian political system as a *means* or *technique* of government. It is the procedures of democracy that will be in question, not the substance of the policies produced. For example, it is possible to have a democratic political system with either a capitalist or a socialist economy.

Since public policies are not scientifically determinable, we are best advised to put our faith in free and fair elections with the concomitant necessary values.[47] Placing such high hopes in the "system" of democracy is best defended by Winston Churchill's well-used maxim that it is the "least worst" system of government. If it were possible to determine scientifically the best government policies, then the obvious connection of intelligent citizens should be to agree with Plato and set up an élite of philosopher kings to rule. However, this contention is difficult to uphold. The ruler of Bahrain, the smallest and least prosperous of the independent Gulf states, personally makes the rules or laws for his citizens. Citizens merely appear on Friday morning, make a verbal appeal, hand in a written petition and wait for the judgement to come down from on high. While there may be some merit — such as efficiency — in such a process, it is certainly not procedurally democratic. There is no institutionalized way for the citizens to change their ruler. The outstanding worth of democracy is that it allows citizen participation in the orderly succession of rulers. Governments elected by the people will more likely produce government *for* the people. As Aristotle put it, an expert cook knows best how to bake a cake, but the person who eats it is a better judge of how it tastes.

Countries are "more" or "less" democratic. While the level of democracy that a country possesses changes over time, cross-national (diachronic) comparisons indicate that Canada always appears high on a list of states on this criterion. Yet within the sub-set of developed democracies, Canada has been placed first on an index of democratization by two authors, but ninth and eleventh out of twelve respectively, by two others.[48] Therefore, although Canada is usually complimented when placed in global comparison, our ability to be "as democratic" as some other developed countries has been challenged by a few serious scholars.

In adopting a democratic system, Canada did not shed its ties to the monarchy, as occurred in the United States where a republic was established. The number of monarchies in the world has steadily decreased. Even members of the Commonwealth, such as India, have opted to become republics. Canada, on the other hand, like the United Kingdom, continues as a constitutional monarchy — monarchical because Queen Elizabeth II sits on

---

[47] Henry B. Mayo, *An Introduction to Democratic Theory* (New York: Oxford, 1960).

[48] Compare Lipset, "Some Social Requisites of Democracy"; Phillips Cutright, "National Political Development: Its Measurement and Social Correlates," in N.W. Polsby, R.A. Dentler, P.A. Smith, eds., *Political and Social Life* (Boston: Houghton Mifflin, 1963), pp. 569–82; Deane E. Neubauer, "Some Conditions of Democracy," *APSR*, vol. 61, no. 4 (December 1967), pp. 1002–9; and Robert A. Dahl, *Polyarchy: Participation and Opposition* (New Haven: Yale University Press, 1971).

the throne of Britain and presides as the Queen of Canada. The symbols that historically indicated this attachment — "God Save the Queen" as our national anthem and the Union Jack as our flag — have disappeared, but our monarchical origins have had a lasting impact on the system of central government and administration. Symbols such as those on the Great Seal, badges of the Royal Canadian Mounted Police and the reverse side of coins and some bills, illustrate the monarchical ties that remain.

Canada is further, a **constitutional democracy**, because the Constitution shapes and limits political power. The documents and behaviour that comprise the Constitution limit the powers of the government by specifying the form of involvement of elected representatives and the division of authority among the partners in the federation. The Constitution also defines the power of those chosen to govern us. The choice of a parliamentary system rather than a presidential one followed logically from the adoption of a monarchical form. In the presidential system of the United States, the chief executive and symbolic head is the elected president. In the parliamentary system, the monarch retains the latter honour and the chief political executive officer is relegated to a lower status for purposes of protocol. In other words, in the presidential system the president is both the nominal and political head of state, whereas parliamentary systems usually have a nominal head of state whose functions are chiefly ceremonial and whose influence is marginal.

Throughout this volume (particularly in Chapters 5 and 6), we shall describe and analyze these constitutional mechanisms. The basic form rests on British parliamentary traditions, but the Constitution also divides power by a federal principle. The essential difference between a unitary and a federal form of government is simply that a **unitary system**, such as that found in France, has a central government that possesses total authoritative power, whereas a **federal system** divides such power among jurisdictions and over geographical areas.

OVERVIEW

In twelve decades of independent existence Canadians have shown the vision required to master the huge desolate spaces of the northern hemisphere, to exploit the riches of the land and to solve the puzzles of a bilingual and multicultural society. The Fathers of Confederation created a structure of government that has met the tests of viability and flexibility under stress. In the decades ahead the tests may be more difficult, but they will nonetheless relate to past Canadian crises and to the way politics is played in Canada.

To describe, analyze and explain contemporary politics in Canada requires an understanding of the origin, territorial expansion and development of the Canadian state. In the next chapter, a brief developmental history will introduce this subject and illustrate the major importance of the growth of the state.

The four parts of the volume that follow examine those dimensions of politics in Canada that the authors regard as the most significant: political culture, institutions, behaviour and public policy. All four have an impact on the Canadian people, directing daily life and shaping the future.

Part II (Chapters 3 and 4) describes the Canadian political culture, how it is acquired through such means as gender, class, education and the media and how it is transferred from generation to generation. Part III (Chapters 5, 6, 7, 8, 9) outlines and dissects the institutions, such as the Constitution, federalism, the executive and the legislature, that give structure to the culture and to political options. Part IV (Chapters 10, 11, 12) assesses the activities of individuals within these formal institutions and other organizations in the political process. The last section, Part V (Chapters 13 and 14), evaluates the impact of Canadian culture, institutions and behaviour on public policy-making. Woven throughout the discussion is the importance of the development of the Canadian state, and its social divisions over the allocation of the resources of the territory— in brief, politics.

SELECTED BIBLIOGRAPHY

Almond, Gabriel A., and G. Bingham Powell, Jr., *Comparative Politics* (Boston: Little, Brown, 1978).

Ball, Alan R., *Modern Politics and Government*, 3rd ed. (London: Macmillan, 1983).

Banting, Keith, ed., *State and Society: Canada in Comparative Perspective*, vol. 31, Royal Commission on the Economic Union and Development Prospects for Canada (Toronto: University of Toronto Press, 1985).

Bertsch, Gary K., et al., *Comparing Political Systems*, 3rd ed. (New York: Macmillan, 1986).

Best, Paul J., et al., *Politics in Three Worlds* (New York: Wiley, 1986).

Bill, James A., and Robert L. Hardgrave, Jr., *Comparative Politics: The Quest for Theory* (Columbus, Oh.: Charles E. Merrill, 1973).

Blair, R.S. and J.T. McLeod, eds., *The Canadian Political Tradition* (Scarborough: Nelson, 1993).

Coleman, William and Grace Skogstad, *Policy Communities and Public Policy in Canada* (Mississauga: Copp Clark Pitman, 1991)

Crick, Bernard, *In Defence of Politics,* 2nd ed. (Harmondsworth, Eng.: Penguin Books, 1972).

Dahl, Robert, *Democracy and Its Critics* (New Haven: Yale University Press, 1989).

Di Palma, Giuseppe, *To Craft Democracies* (Berkeley: University of California Press, 1990).

Dogan, Mattei, and Dominique Pelassy, *How to Compare Nations* (Chatham, N.J.: Chatham House, 1984).

Gamble, John K. Jr., et al., *Introduction to Political Science* (Englewood Cliffs, N.J.: Prentice-Hall, 1987).

Hague, Ron, and Martin Harrop, *Comparative Government* (London: Macmillan, 1982).

Holt, Robert T., and John E. Turner, eds., *The Methodology of Comparative Research* (New York: Free Press, 1970).

Huntington, Samuel P. *The Third Wave: Democratization in the Late Twentieth Century* (Norman: University of Oklahoma Press, 1991).

Jackson, Robert J., and Michael B. Stein, *Issues in Comparative Politics* (New York: St. Martin's Press, 1971).

Jackson, Robert J. and Doreen Jackson, *Contemporary Government and Politics: Democracy and Authoritarianism* (Scarborough: Prentice Hall, 1993).

Kavanagh, Dennis, *Political Science and Political Behaviour* (London: Allen and Unwin, 1983).

LaPalombara, Joseph, *Politics Within Nations* (Englewood Cliffs, N.J.: Prentice-Hall, 1974).

Laver, Michael, *Invitation to Politics* (Oxford, Eng.: Martin Robertson, 1983).

Lewis, Paul G., et al., eds., *The Practice of Comparative Politics*, 2nd ed. (London: Longman, 1978).

MacPherson, C.B., *The Real World of Democracy* (Toronto: CBC Publications, 1965).

Macridis, Roy C., *Modern Political Regimes* (Boston: Little, Brown, 1986).

Mayer, Lawrence C., *Comparative Political Inquiry* (Homewood, Ill.: Dorsey, 1972).

Mayo, Henry B., *An Introduction to Democratic Theory* (New York: Oxford University Press, 1960).

Nordlinger, Eric, *On the Autonomy of the State* (Cambridge, Mass.: Harvard, 1981).

Ponton, Geoffrey, and Peter Gill, *Introduction to Politics* (London: Martin Robertson, 1982).

Przeworski, Adam, and Henry Teune, *The Logic of Comparatiave Social Inquiry* (New York: Wiley, 1970).

Ranney, Austin, *Governing*, 4th ed. (Englewood Cliffs, N.J.: Prentice-Hall, 1987).

Redekop, John H., ed., *Approaches to the Study of Canadian Politics*, 2nd ed. (Scarborough, Ont.: Prentice-Hall Canada, 1983).

Roberts, Geoffrey K., *An Introduction to Comparative Politics* (London: Edward Arnold, 1986).

Roskin, Michael G., *Countries and Concepts*, 2nd ed. (Englewood Cliffs, N.J.: Prentice-Hall, 1986).

Roth, David F., et al., *Comparative Politics* (New York: Harper and Row, 1989).

Sartori, Giovanni, *The Theory of Democracy Revisited*, 2 vols. (Chatham, NJ: Chatham House, 1987).

Shively, W. Phillips, *Power and Choice* (New York: Random House, 1987).

Wesson, Robert, *Modern Government*, 2nd ed. (Englewood Cliffs, N.J.: Prentice-Hall, 1985).

Wilson, Jeremy, *Analyzing Politics* (Scarborough, Ont.: Prentice-Hall Canada, 1988).

Also see the periodicals *Canadian Journal of Political Science*, *American Political Science Review* and other national and regional quarterlies.

THE CANADIAN NATION AND STATE

YESTERDAY AND TODAY

How and why have present cultural attitudes, institutions and modes of governing developed in Canada? What has made Canadians who they are? How and when were the territorial boundaries for today's state and nation determined? Answers to these vital questions indicate to what a large extent contemporary politics is circumscribed by the broad constraints of the past. Without some understanding of Canada's economic, social and political history, it is impossible to grasp how Canadians forged a positive and dynamic system of government when the country was vulnerable to dangers on all sides. In this chapter, therefore, a historical framework will be developed as a context for an appreciation of contemporary politics.

> *"Not to know what happened before one was born is always to remain a child."*
>
> **Cicero, as cited in *Harper's Magazine* (November 1993), p. 10.**

In chronological terms, Canada is one of the world's oldest states. With the passage of the *British North America Act* (*BNA*) in 1867, Canada became the 45th of the present members of the United Nations to receive independence. It is now one of a very few states that can claim continuous existence as an independent entity for over a century. Yet Canada is considerably "younger" than the majority of current West European countries.

Canada also postdates most of the countries of South and Central America, which gained their independence from the Spanish Empire largely between 1810 and 1840 and many of which are still considered to be part of the developing, as opposed to the developed, world. Unlike many of these Latin American examples, however, Canada has established a highly stable political system based upon the western European norm of parliamentary democracy, and has become very much a part of the "developed world" of advanced industrial societies, as evidenced by its membership in the Organization for Economic Cooperation and Development (OECD), the North Atlantic Treaty Organization (NATO) and, especially, the "Group of Seven" economic summits attended by the leaders of selected major western economies.

Other aspects of contemporary political life in Canada are similar to problems faced by newer states. Until 1982, concerns were voiced over political and constitutional dependence on the United Kingdom. Economic dependence on the United States is an ongoing issue, as is the enormous debt that the state has accumulated. And internal linguistic, nationalist and regional conflicts suggest a lack of political integration typical of many countries in the developing world.

Thus, Canada may justifiably be labelled one of the "first new nations,"[1] inasmuch as it shares with many developing countries the past experience of European colonization and colonial rule before gaining independence as a sovereign state. Furthermore, in spite of its high level of economic development, Canada continues to face many of the problems of state building and national integration suffered by newer, less affluent states in the Third World. Canada is therefore something of a paradox. A stable parliamentary democracy, with over a century of self-government and a highly industrialized economy, it still faces some of the difficulties of much younger states. How Canadians have attempted to cope with these problems constitutes much of the subject-matter of this book and comprises the source of many key issues in Canadian politics.

In this chapter, we link the past and the present, the history of yesterday with the politics of today. Taking a historical perspective, we outline Canada's early colonial settlement and examine the expansion and development of the nation and the state from 1867 to the present. The many obstacles to nation-building in Canada are considered. We conclude with a discussion of how the role of the state has grown and affects the everyday lives of Canadians.

PRE-CONFEDERATION HISTORY

The development of Canada as a modern state began with the act of Confederation that united three British North American colonies: New Brunswick, Nova Scotia and Canada (East and West), in 1867. But that act of union, and the federal nature of the new political entity founded thereby, must itself be placed within an historical context.

EARLY SETTLEMENT

Archaeologists have discovered traces of human life in Canada dating back as far as 30 000 years, but relatively little is known about this early pre-history. We do know that the native Indian and Inuit populations are descended from Asiatic nomads, who probably crossed on foot from Siberia into Alaska and northern Canada during the last Ice Age. Slowly, they spread over the continent, creating diverse languages, lifestyles and social and political structures. Most tribes were nomadic, but by 1500 AD Indian population patterns in Canada were fairly well defined. About 45 different tribes had identifiable territory.[2]

---

1   For use of the term "new nation" applied to former colonies that are now mature and affluent states, see Seymour M. Lipset, The First New Nation: The United States in Comparative Perspective (New York; Basic Books, 1963).

2   The first comprehensive study of Canadian Indians, Diamond Jenness, *The Indians of Canada* (Toronto: University of Toronto Press, 1932, 1977) identifies seven main groups, each associated with a particular "cultural area" or "physiographic region": Algonkian tribes of the Eastern Woodlands, the Iroquois in the St. Lawrence Valley and lower Great Lakes; the Plains tribes in the western plains; the tribes of the Pacific coast; the tribes of the Cordillera or Mountain Barrier, and the Inuit, a distinct people who migrated from Asia much later than the southern Indians.

Around 1000 AD, the Vikings became the first Europeans to discover and briefly settle on the Canadian east coast, which they called "Vinland". However, not for another five centuries did permanent European settlements tentatively begin and eventually thrive. John Cabot first arrived on the Atlantic shores in 1497, five years after Columbus' historic "discovery," and within seven years St. John's, Newfoundland, was established as an English fishing port. The French, Portuguese and Spanish also began to use east coast harbours as bases for the exploitation of the rich North Atlantic fisheries.

Thirty years later, in 1534, Jacques Cartier explored the coastal area, describing it contemptuously as "the land God gave to Cain." The following year, however, he discovered the Indian settlements of Hochelaga (Montréal) and Stadacona (Québec) in the St. Lawrence valley and established a French interest in this more promising region. Yet it was not until 1605 that the first French colony was established at Port Royal in Acadia. Three years later, Samuel de Champlain, the first governor of New France, founded Québec City. In the next century and a half, approximately 10 000 French immigrants arrived to settle along the shores of the St. Lawrence.

Early English settlement in North America was restricted primarily to what is now New England and the eastern seaboard of the United States, although the area around Hudson Bay was also claimed by London-based commercial interests. In the early eighteenth century, successive wars in Europe between England and France began to spill over into North America. In 1710, a combined force of British troops and American colonial militia captured Port Royal; the *Treaty of Utrecht* (1713) subsequently recognized British possession of Hudson Bay, Newfoundland and the new colony of Nova Scotia. The French retained the rest of eastern mainland Canada, Isle St. Jean (now Prince Edward Island) and Isle Royale (Cape Breton), which was defended by the newly constructed fortress of Louisbourg.

In 1754, war broke out again in North America. In rapid succession the British expelled the French-speaking Acadians from Nova Scotia, shipping them off to other British North American colonies, and captured both Louisbourg and the Lake Ontario stronghold of Fort Frontenac (present-day Kingston). In 1759, the forces of Wolfe and Montcalm met on the Plains of Abraham outside Québec City and the capital of New France fell into British hands. A year later, the remnants of the French army surrendered at Montréal, ending military resistance to the British conquest. The French colony was formally ceded to Britain in 1763 as part of the *Treaty of Paris*, which ended the Seven Years War in Europe. The British now controlled all of North America north and east of the Mississippi, except for the tiny islands of St. Pierre and Miquelon, which remain part of France to this day. But British domination was not to endure.

FROM COLONY TO CONFEDERATION

For over 250 years, between the establishment of the first permanent European settlements on the North American mainland and the time of Confederation, parts of what is now Canada were governed as colonies, primarily through laws made on the other side of the Atlantic Ocean. From the founding of the first French colony at Port Royal in 1605 until the British conquest of Québec in 1759, much of the future Dominion (together with the Ohio and Mississippi River valleys) was in French hands. Although many settlers established themselves in the St. Lawrence valley and on the coasts of Nova Scotia and Cape Breton, the primary function of these colonies was to provide raw materials (especially fish and fur) to the economy of mainland France.

In serving this purpose, the colonies of New France and Acadia (now Nova Scotia) were no different from most others. A **colony**, in general terms, is an area of land geographically remote from the metropolis (the centre of the colonial power) and incorporated into the colonial empire either by right of first possession or by conquest. Its laws are usually made in the metropolis and are administered by either a civilian governor or the military authorities. Colonies serve three major functions for a colonial power. First and most importantly, they are exploited for their natural resources, which are exported to serve the interests of the metropolitan economy. Second, they may be used for settlement, especially for surplus population (for example, during the great potato famine in Ireland in the 1840s) or, occasionally, as a means of getting rid of undesirable elements (for example, the penal settlements of Australia). Third, their possession acts as a symbol of the international importance of the colonial state, and they are therefore frequent subjects of international dispute and war between rival powers.

For the British in the mid-eighteenth century, the French colonies of North America offered substantial natural resources. They also posed a threat to both the British colonies on the eastern seaboard of what is now the United States and the rich fur-bearing interior then owned by the Hudson's Bay Company. As an extension of repeated wars between Britain and France in Europe, Britain gradually acquired, through treaty concessions and by conquest, the French colonies in North America. Along with access to the natural resources of the region, the British acquired the problem of how to deal with the French-speaking population that had settled there — a problem that grew in complexity as the number of British merchants and English-speaking immigrants to the colonies increased.

A further generalization to be made about colonies is that their inhabitants tend to develop their own interests separate from those of the imperial economy and may eventually rebel against the imposition of laws made in the colonial metropolis. Since World War Two, many new states have been created as a result of armed uprisings, usually by indigenous populations against their European colonial masters. But over 200 years ago, the first challenge to British supremacy came from descendants of British settlers in North America who had become disaffected with the policies of George III and his administrators in the American colonies. Following the success of the American Revolution and the establishment of the world's first post-colonial state, the major threat to Britain's remaining North American colonies was the danger of invasion from or absorption by the United States. As well, resistance to colonial rule emerged inside the future Canada, as demands developed within the colonies for some degree of self-determination and responsible government.

Thus, the origin of the Canadian state, from colony to Confederation, must be traced with reference to at least three major sets of historical relations: the trilateral relationship among the British North American colonies, the United States and the United Kingdom; the relations among the colonies themselves; and the conflict, particularly within the colony of the United Canadas, between the English- and French-speaking populations.

THE AMERICAN REVOLUTION

In 1776, the southern colonies of British North America revolted against the British crown in order to found the United States of America. Forty thousand Empire Loyalists, American colonists loyal to the crown, sought refuge in the remaining British colonies, particularly in the Maritimes (where their influx resulted in the creation of the colony of New Brunswick in 1784) and in what was then western Québec (now Ontario).

The boundaries between the newly sovereign United States and the British colonies were gradually settled over the next century. The *Treaty of Paris* had established an approximate southern border for the new British acquisition of Québec between the Atlantic Ocean and the western tip of Lake of the Woods (now the Ontario-Manitoba border). Large parts of this border were subsequently adjusted by *Jay's Treaty* in 1794 and the *Webster-Ashburton Treaty* of 1842. The *Rush-Bagot Treaty* of 1817 clarified the boundary through the Great Lakes. In 1818, the *Treaty of London* fixed the westward border along the forty-ninth parallel to the Rockies and paved the way for western settlement. The final step, to the Pacific Ocean around the southern tip of Vancouver Island, was determined by the *Oregon Treaty* of 1846. This formalized the bulk of the borders well before Confederation, but two remaining treaties settled smaller land disputes: in 1872 the San Juan Islands were ceded to the United States, and the boundary between Alaska and British Columbia was finally agreed upon in 1903. British dominion over the Arctic Islands had been passed to Canada in 1880.

These boundary agreements were often preceded by disputes, but were always achieved without violence. The single major hostile outbreak between the United States and Canada was occasioned less by overt dispute over territory than by America's desire to demonstrate the complete nature of the break from Britain. Although some American leaders may have hoped that the colonists to the north would throw off British rule in order to join the United States, the War of 1812–14 was mostly an affirmation of American sovereignty against what was seen as continued British interference. First, the U.S. resented the seizure of neutral American ships on the suspicion that they were trading with the French, with whom Britain was once again at war. Second, British traders were accused of arming and inciting a potential Indian rebellion in the American midwest. Despite incursions by each side into the territory of the other, the *Treaty of Ghent* of 1814 left the pre-war boundaries intact. If the war achieved anything on the Canadian side, it was to lay the basis for a future Canadian nationalism that would come to fruition with Confederation, as well as for the periodic upsurges of anti-Americanism that still manifest themselves within Canadian political culture.

FOUNDING NATIONS: ABORIGINALS, FRENCH AND ENGLISH

The relations of the British Crown with the aboriginal population in British North America were, in the early colonial years, straightforward and accommodating. Before 1867, Indians were seen as valuable allies who helped extend the fur trade to the Pacific, and in doing so helped define the boundary between Canada and the United States.[3] Later they were allies in the struggle against threats of American incursion. The royal *Proclamation of 1763* recognized native land rights and described a rough "Proclamation Line" dividing hunting grounds from land that could be settled by Europeans. The Crown retained title to the land mass of Canada, but recognized the right of aboriginal peoples to use and occupy the land. The *Proclamation* did not, however, state the exact eastern or western extent of the reserved lands. It was a vague document that belied the harsh treatment aboriginals would later receive.

As settlements grew and pushed farther westward the Crown undertook separate treaty negotiations with tribes that occupied different sections of land, striking bargains concerning land use. In 1830, Indian settlement on reserves commenced under government trustee-

---

3   Randall White, Voice of Region (Toronto: Dundurn Press, 1990) p. 16 and ch. 2.

ship, and efforts began to integrate aboriginal peoples into non-aboriginal society. Meanwhile, contact with Europeans was disrupting and radically changing traditional Indian and Inuit ways of life, exposing them to European technology, religion and disease. Before Europeans arrived there were about one million aboriginal people in what is now Canada. By Confederation, only about 140 000 were left.

Among the Europeans, the cessation of hostilities with the United States allowed the British colonial administrators in Canada to return to the long-term problem of relations between the two European founding nations[4] of British North America. The history of French–English relations leading up to Confederation illustrates the agonizing indecision of the British government about how to deal with the conquered French population, the original European settlers.

The intention of the British government in 1763 was to promote immigration by English-speaking Protestant settlers and to assimilate the French-speaking Roman Catholic population as rapidly as possible. However, in the first few years, only about 200 English families, mostly merchants, settled in the new colony. For this reason, neither of the first two British Governors was prepared to establish the representative assembly in the new colony as promised in the Royal Proclamation of 1763. They both considered that such a body would have represented only the 600 English settlers and not the 90 000 French who, as Roman Catholics, were excluded from the franchise under British law at that time.

With the failure of the assimilation strategy and the growing realization that French Canadian loyalty might prove vital as the southern colonies became increasingly restive, Governor Carleton persuaded the British government to revise its policy toward Québec. The *Québec Act* of 1774 withdrew the provision for an assembly, placing full authority in the hands of the governor and an appointed advisory council consisting of both English and French speakers. The French culture was to be preserved. Neither language was specifically guaranteed, but Roman Catholics were allowed freedom of worship and the right to hold civil office. The Catholic Church was given official sanction, and both French civil law and the seigneurial landholding system were retained to protect the property rights of individuals.

The decision to respect the cultural heritage of French Canada was clear, and the French population warmly approved of the *Act*. Many English Canadians, on the other hand, resented it. The break in the tradition of representative government in the British colonies arising from the special circumstances of a French-speaking majority was anathema to many English-speaking colonists, who felt unjustly deprived of their right to a representative assembly and British civil law — rights to which they had grown accustomed. The English merchants were slightly mollified by the expansion of the colony's boundaries to encompass the rich fur-trading area between the Ohio and Mississippi Rivers — but most of that gain was lost under the *Treaty of Versailles*, which, in 1783 finally settled the American War of Independence.

Partly in response to demands from the Empire Loyalists who had settled in what is now Ontario, the British next attempted to satisfy both ethnic communities with the *Constitutional Act* of 1791. This Act maintained the commitment to the French culture established by the *Québec Act*, but within a new political context. The old colony of Québec was divided in two: Upper Canada, west of the Ottawa River, which was predominantly English-speaking, and

---

[4] These are the people present from early settlement to 1867. It should be noted that the western provinces were later settled largely by immigrants who were not of French, English or Aboriginal extraction. In this larger sense, Canada has many founding nations, including Ukranians, Germans and a host of other ethnic groups all of whom are usually included under the English-speaking umbrella.

Lower Canada, which was predominantly French. The right of representative government was now granted to each group and, whereas French civil law and seigneurial landholding were retained in Lower Canada, English common law and freehold land tenure were established in Upper Canada. Thus, English Canadians outside Montréal were placated and the French Canadians were largely protected from absorption and conflict.

This promising new arrangement deteriorated over the next few years as the representative assemblies grew increasingly frustrated by their lack of control over the executive. The appointed members of the Governors' legislative councils often abused their privileged positions in order to enhance their personal wealth and power and paid scant attention to the elected members of the assemblies. Political and social agitation began against Upper Canada's "Family Compact" and Lower Canada's "Château Clique." Finally, open rebellion under the leadership of William Lyon Mackenzie in Upper Canada and Louis-Joseph Papineau in Lower Canada forced Britain to re-evaluate its policies.

In 1838 Lord Durham was dispatched to report on the situation and recommend a course of action. In Lower Canada he found all the problems of the other British colonies, plus an ethnic war. Britain's approach, he decided, had been wrong; the colony of Canada should have remained united so that the French population gradually would have been assimilated. Consequently, his recommendations included a reversion to the pre-1791 union and the granting of responsible government, which he believed would, given the first condition, function effectively.[5]

The British government did not see fit to accept Durham's philosophy wholeheartedly; instead, it took a middle course. The *Union Act* of 1840 re-established the two Canadas as one political unit (although each was to retain its own version of the law), with English as the sole official language of record. Although Durham had recommended representation by population, the two former colonies were each granted 42 members in the assembly. Canada West (formerly Upper Canada) with its lesser numbers, gladly accepted this equality of representation. Not surprisingly, however, a decade later, after rapid immigration had elevated its population to majority status, Canada West declared the allocation grossly unfair. Durham's other major recommendation, that the government be made responsible to the elected assembly, was not implemented in 1840, though it became effective in practice some eight years later. Also at this date, the English-only language policy was deemed unworkable and the two languages were declared officially equal.

Perhaps because of the half-hearted adoption of Durham's recommendations, or because of the separation of the two Canadas 50 years earlier, relations between the two founding nations did not unfold according to Durham's desires and predictions. Repeated attempts to find a workable solution to the ethnic problem showed the leadership's great determination to satisfy both cultures. From about 1849, Cabinets in the colony included representatives from both ethnic groups. Rather than a single prime minister at the head of government, there were two party leaders, one from each group, as well as separate attorneys-general to mirror the dual legal system. Some legislation applied to one or both; sometimes dual legislation was enacted. For a number of years, even the capital of the colony alternated between Toronto and Québec City until Queen Victoria settled the problem by deciding on the (then) backwoods logging town of Bytown (Ottawa).[6]

---

5   Gerald M. Craig, ed., *Lord Durham's Report* (Toronto: McClelland & Stewart, 1963).

6   David B. Knight, *Choosing Canada's Capital: Jealousy and Friction in the Nineteenth Century* (Toronto: McClelland & Stewart, 1977).

The theory of cooperation was excellent, but the practice impossible. Soon, Montréal merchants in Canada East were openly supporting union with the United States, while George Brown's Reformers in Canada West demanded "Rep by Pop" (representation by population) and, eventually, a federal solution to the colony's governmental problems. Ethnic and religious antagonisms were exacerbated under these circumstances until it became almost impossible for any government to retain the confidence of the assembly. By about 1857 the government had reached a virtual impasse, which representatives of both groups sought a way to break. It was in this common search for a solution to political deadlock that both French and English leaders came to embrace the goal of British North American unity.

CONFEDERATION

A handful of representatives from the colony of Canada took their vision to Britain for approval as early as 1858, but the concept of a "British North America united from sea to sea" had not yet penetrated British government circles and the Canadians were sent home. Nevertheless, they kept sight of their goal and in 1864 they gatecrashed a meeting of Maritime representatives in Charlottetown in order to sell their idea there. Over the next three years, they laboriously patched together a successful proposal for an *Act of Union* involving three of the five colonies — Canada, New Brunswick and Nova Scotia — and paved the way for the later accession of other colonies and territories.

It should be noted that Confederation was not directly approved by the people. There was no referendum or election to determine public sentiment, nor was the omission deemed significant at the time. Confederation grew out of the gentlemanly agreement of a few men united by a noble ideal regarding the type of political system most appropriate to achieving their common goals. In the final analysis, it was a series of external circumstances that eventually allowed the Fathers of Confederation to marry their ideals with practical necessity and proceed on the path to statehood. Had these men not clung tenaciously to their dream and acted when they did, it is questionable whether the Canadian state ever would have existed. The Canadian colonies almost certainly would have been annexed or absorbed by the United States by the turn of the century. As one historian has observed, "perhaps the most striking thing about Canada is that it is not part of the United States."[7]

In many ways, the fulfilment of the Canadian dream at that particular time was a response to events in the United States; such decisions have since become commonplace in Canadian history. In the mid-1860s, Anglo-American relations were at a new low and the Canadian colonies were isolated and vulnerable to attack. The American Civil War was drawing to a close and the army of the northern states would soon be available for an attack on Canada. Westward migration in the United States had become a threat to the political vacuum west of the colony of Canada. Furthermore, Britain had neither the resources nor the desire to protect these colonies from American aggression.

In 1864, therefore, after having discouraged for several years the efforts by those few Canadians (notably Macdonald, Cartier, Galt, Tupper, Tilley, Brown and McGee) who wished to have the issue of a federal union of British North America taken seriously, the British government suddenly deemed it propitious to encourage Canadian unity and independence. It was recognized that if British North America were united it would be not only be more economically viable and easier to defend, but also, as a self-governing dominion,

---

[7]   J.B. Brebner, *Canada: A Modern History* (Ann Arbor: University of Michigan Press, 1960), p. ix.

more responsible for the cost of its own defence. The colonies of New Brunswick and Canada, which shared long boundaries with the United States, supported a union, but Nova Scotia, with no American land border, was less easily persuaded.

The 1864 Charlottetown Conference, instigated by Nova Scotia Premier Dr. Charles Tupper, was originally called to discuss the prospects for Maritime union. The Canadians invited themselves and had the agenda changed to deal with their proposals for a larger entity. The Québec and Maritime leaders were adamant that the new arrangements should be federal in order to prevent Canada West from dominating the future Dominion by virtue of its size. John A. Macdonald was willing to accept federalism as a second choice rather than delay or thwart the project on this point. Thus, Charlottetown concluded with a basic agreement that the new larger union would be a federal, not a unitary, arrangement and that another meeting be held to discuss proposals in more detail.[8]

The Québec Conference that followed in October 1864 was very brief. Within three weeks the leaders had produced the 72 resolutions that were to provide the basis for Confederation. They concluded that "the sanction of the Imperial and Local Parliaments shall be sought for the Union of the Provinces on the principles adopted by the Conference."[9]

The future provinces acted on this item in very different ways. Prince Edward Island and Newfoundland rejected any association with the Conference or its proposals. The legislature of Canada debated at length and finally adopted the 72 resolutions by a three-to-one majority (with most of the "nays" coming from Canada East). Canada was the only colony to approve the project formally. The government of New Brunswick called a general election on the question and was soundly defeated. Premier Tupper, afraid of similar unpopularity in Nova Scotia, avoided an assembly vote on the resolutions by introducing a motion to approve a Maritime Union. Nevertheless, the Canadian group persevered and took the results of the Québec Conference to London where, this time, they received a more sympathetic audience.

Although the colonies were by then internally self-governing, Britain retained direct influence over their policies through its colonial governors. Britain refused to consider Nova Scotia's stated preference for a Maritime Union, and the governors of the Maritime colonies were instructed to sway their respective political executives in favour of the wider confederation. By 1866, the legislatures of both Nova Scotia and New Brunswick (the latter now under threat of invasion from the United States by the Fenians[10]) had reconsidered their earlier dismissal of the Québec Resolutions and sought a renewal of consultations toward a union with the Canadas.

In December 1866, delegates from the three participating colonies incorporated the essence of the Québec Resolutions into an Act of Confederation at the Westminster Palace Conference in London. The *British North America Act* was given Royal Assent on March 29, 1867 and came into effect three months later on July 1, 1867, without any of the colonies having had a further opportunity to discuss or approve the birth of their future state.

---

8   See Chapter 6, Figure 1 for further explanation of federal government, unitary government and confederation.

9   Quoted in R. MacGregor Dawson, *The Government of Canada*, 5th ed., revised by Norman Ward (Toronto: University of Toronto Press, 1970), p. 32.

10 The Fenian Brotherhood, an organization of Irish-Americans, sought to pursue the cause of Irish independence by provoking war between Britain and the United States.

The *British North America Act* brought into formal existence the Dominion of Canada. In the light of the continuing tensions between English and French Canada, it is somewhat ironic that it was the combined leadership of the United Canadas that provided the direct impetus for Confederation. The French Canadian leaders at that time supported the federal union, although there was some disquiet within the newly created province of Québec on the part of those who feared that the addition of the largely English-speaking Maritimes would further exaggerate the minority status of French Canadians within Canada. However, it was Nova Scotia, not French Canada, that welcomed Dominion Day in 1867 by draping the streets in black!

The union of 1867 provided immediate solutions for three major problems facing the former colonies and the British government. The reorganization of the internal government of the United Provinces of Canada (by the creation of the separate provinces of Ontario and Québec) provided relief from the political impasse there. The threat of American invasion was allayed once Nova Scotia and, particularly, New Brunswick joined Canada and arrangements had been made to connect the provinces by rail. Lastly, the provisions made in the act of Confederation to bring other territories into the union enabled the political vacuum west of Ontario to be filled and laid the basis for a "Dominion from sea to sea."

These tentative steps toward the development of a Canadian state were merely the beginning of a long and sometimes arduous process of territorial consolidation, national integration and state building that even today is not complete.

THE LAND AND THE PEOPLE

The concept of a country or state embodies four interrelated ideas: a clearly defined area of territory, a set of state (or political) institutions that govern the territory and maintain both internal and external sovereignty, a given population that is subject to the state and a sense of community or common identity ("nationhood") among that population. The Dominion of Canada founded by the act of Confederation in 1867 was considerably smaller, in both area and population, than it is today. Consequently, before we examine the problems encountered by the new Dominion in developing a sense of "nationhood" and attaining sovereign status, we need to outline the territorial and population expansion of Canada.

TERRITORIAL EXPANSION

The territorial outline of the state formulated at Confederation was gradually expanded and filled in over the succeeding years. In 1670, England's King Charles II had granted all the lands that drained into Hudson Bay to a company of that name. Proceedings were initiated in 1867 to bring this territory under Canadian control, and eventually the Company sold it to the Canadian government for $300 000. In 1870, both Rupert's Land and the Northwestern Territory were formally annexed to the Dominion. (See Figure 2.1.) In the same year, the Red River Colony (under the new name of Manitoba) became the first additional province in the union, although it was much smaller then than today. Lured by the promise of permanent railway communications with eastern Canada, British Columbia was admitted by Imperial Order-in-Council in 1871. Two years later, the previously uninterested Prince Edward Island also decided to join.

The next major jurisdictional change occurred in 1905, when Alberta and Saskatchewan were carved out of a large portion of the Northwest Territories and granted provincial status. Seven years later, Manitoba, Ontario and Québec were allowed to annex more land from the Territories to assume more or less their current forms. The tenth and final province,

FIGURE 2.1 CANADA'S HISTORICAL BOUNDARIES

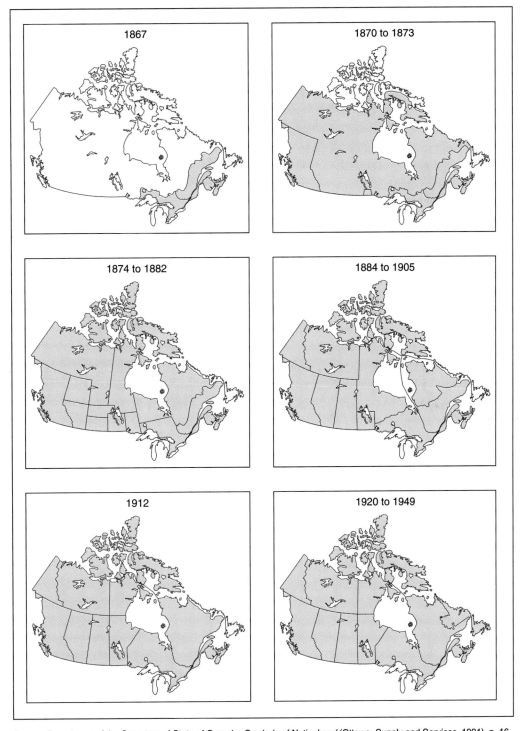

Source: Department of the Secretary of State of Canada, *Symbols of Nationhood* (Ottawa: Supply and Services, 1991), p. 16. Reproduced by authority of the Minister responsible for Statistics Canada 1993.

Newfoundland, entered the federation in 1949, over 80 years after the original invitation and even then only after two referendums to decide its future.[11]

The rest of the land within the boundaries of the Canadian state, the Yukon Territory (created out of the Northwest Territories in 1898) and the Northwest Territories currently remains under federal jurisdiction, however changes are underway. In May 1990 an agreement on the largest land claim in Canadian history gave about 18 000 Inuit ownership of an area about half the size of Alberta.[12] Shortly after, in October 1992, a political accord made provisions to divide the Northwest Territories and create a new territory, Nunavut (which means "our land" in Inukitut), to be set up by the end of the century. (See Figure 2.2) It is anticipated that by the year 2008 the Nunavut government will be given full powers along the lines of the Northwest Territories legislature in Yellowknife. Inuit constitute about 80 percent of the territory's population, so they will have virtual self-government when this arrangement is complete.

Canada's external boundaries have therefore changed very little since shortly after Confederation. Except for the tardy addition of Newfoundland, all of Canada's current ter-

FIGURE 2.2 MAP OF NUNAVUT

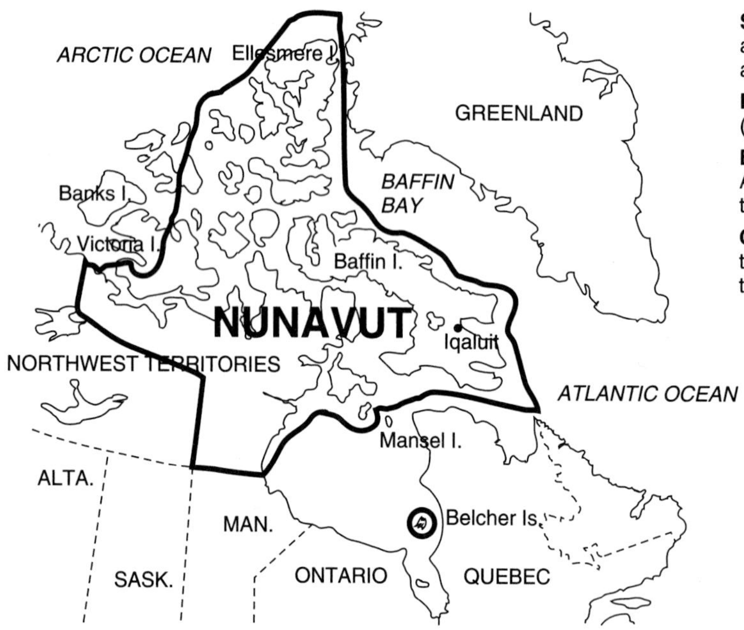

Size: 2.2 million sq. km, about one-fifth of Canada's area

Population: About 22 000 (17 500 Inuit)

Boundaries: Entire Eastern Arctic from the treeline 60° to the North Pole

Government: Democratic territorial system similar to N.W.T.

Nunavut — the new territory carved from the Northwest Territories, creating the northern territories: Yukon, Northwest Territories and Nunavut. The area is twice the size of British Columbia, but its entire population would not fill half of Toronto's 50,000-seat SkyDome.

11 See Henry B. Mayo, "Newfoundland's Entry into the Dominion," *CJEPS*, vol. XV, no. 4 (November 1949), pp. 505–22; Richard Theoret, "The Uses of the Referendum in Canada," in D.C. Rowat, ed., *The Referendum and Separation Elsewhere: Implications for Quebec* (Ottawa: Carleton University, 1978), especially pp. 26–9.

12 The Inuit relinquished title to about 80 percent of their ancestral land claim, which encompassed two million square kilometers.

ritory was formally part of the Dominion by 1873. Thus, the territorial development of the Canadian state has been primarily a process of internal adjustment: creating or admitting new provinces and territories or extending the boundaries of existing ones. But, as a number of contemporary political issues would suggest, this process is not necessarily complete. There is, for example, a lingering boundary dispute between Québec and Newfoundland over the status of Labrador. Québec has never accepted the 1927 decision of the Judicial Committee of the (British) Privy Council that gave more than 260 000 square kilometres of Labrador to Newfoundland. As well, maritime boundaries have taken on new importance in recent years, with ownership of potentially huge reserves of offshore oil and natural gas at stake.

In addition, Canada has been and continues to be subject to the regionalist and nationalist territorial strains often observed in states with multi-ethnic populations. In particular, recurring secessionist aspirations of dissatisfied groups in Québec, and to a much lesser degree in western Canada, impose a certain degree of doubt on the long-term integrity of Canada's external boundaries. After a century of growth, it is possible, but currently unlikely, that the number of provinces and the amount of territory encompassed by the Canadian federation may one day decline.

POPULATION GROWTH

At the time of Confederation, the population of the member provinces totalled approximately 3.5 million people. The number of Canadians has steadily increased to 29 million in 1993. As the size of the population has grown, so too has its ethnic diversity. Today, Canada is regarded as a multi-ethnic or multicultural society, a view given formal recognition by the *Constitutution* in 1982.

This was not always the case. In 1763, when the French Empire in North America was officially ceded to Britain by the *Treaty of Paris*, the total European population of what is now Canada was fewer than 100 000. The vast majority were French Canadian descendants of immigrants from the Old France to the New. By 1812, partly "as a result of one of the highest birth rates in recorded history,"[13] the French Canadian population of Lower Canada had reached about 330 000; but the number of English-speakers had also increased rapidly, swelled by immigration from Britain and by the large influx of Loyalist settlers from the United States into Upper Canada and the Maritimes. After further immigration from Britain, the United States and Ireland, the English-speaking population reached parity with the French and then surpassed it. In 1867, the new province of Ontario was the most populous of the four founding provinces of Confederation, and the predominantly French-speaking majority in Québec constituted only about one-third of the total population of Canada. New aboriginal populations were gradually absorbed, including Pacific Coast Indians, tribes of the Yukon and Mackenzie basins and the Inuit. By the start of the twentieth century, however, the French and the Indians had become minorities.

Even when referring to the time of Confederation, however, it may be a misleading oversimplification to see Canada's population purely in terms of the two founding European nations or, as John Porter labelled them, "the charter groups" of the society.[14] For one thing, the English-speaking segment was by no means homogeneous, consisting as it did of

---

[13] Ramsay Cook et al., *Canada: A Modern Study* (Toronto: Clarke, Irwin and Co., 1963), p. 21.

[14] John Porter, *The Vertical Mosaic: An Analysis of Social Class and Power in Canada* (Toronto: University of Toronto Press, 1965), p. 60 ff.

immigrants from England, Scotland and Ireland and their descendants, the descendants of the Empire Loyalists, and many subsequent settlers from the United States who had migrated north in search of farmland or employment offered by the economic expansion of Canada West. Even among those who had migrated directly from the British Isles there were profound differences.

For instance, many of the Scots and Irish settlers were Catholic, not Protestant, a distinction that proved a source of conflict in Ontario and the Maritimes. Religious division was reflected in the creation of denominational schools and "a whole network of colleges, newspapers, hospitals and charitable and welfare institutions" that served to separate Catholics of both language groups from Protestants in everyday life.[15] Furthermore, many of the Scots and Irish immigrants originally spoke Gaelic rather than English, and although their descendants have long been assimilated into the English Canadian linguistic majority, small enclaves preserving the Gaelic language and culture have survived, especially in Newfoundland and Cape Breton.

Second, as the census of 1871 illustrates, although members of the two charter groups constituted over 90 percent of Canada's population at that time, representatives of other ethnic groups were already becoming established or had been previously established in the new Dominion. In addition to the Native peoples, both Indian and Inuit (about 0.7 percent of the total population), there were nearly 30 000 Dutch (0.9 percent), over 200 000 Germans (5.8 percent), and a smattering of other ethnic minorities, including some American Blacks (chiefly in Nova Scotia and southwestern Ontario) who had arrived around the same time as the Loyalists.

Since Confederation, the population of Canada has grown rapidly through a combination of natural increase (the excess of births over deaths in any given period), a generally high rate of immigration and, to a lesser degree, the incorporation of new territory (for instance, approximately 360 000 people were added to Canada's population by the accession of Newfoundland in 1949).

IMMIGRATION AND ETHNICITY

Canada is a settler society. The early colonists were all immigrants: the French settled Québec, the British colonized the Maritimes and what is now Ontario, the Loyalists followed. Each group multiplied; the population of Canada in 1867 consisted largely of their descendants. Although much of Canada's population growth may be ascribed to natural increase, after Confederation the new Dominion sought more immigrants to settle the vast western spaces uninhabited by Europeans.

Well over 12 million immigrants have entered Canada since Confederation. In 1991, over 16 percent of Canada's population were immigrants, nearly half of whom had lived here more than 20 years. (See Figure 2.3.) As new immigrants and their descendants helped swell Canada's population after Confederation, the ethnic composition of the Canadian population began to change. Although English-speaking immigrants from the British Isles and the United States continued to form the largest groups, other Europeans arrived in increasing numbers. Significant concentrations of Germans, Dutch and Scandinavians were present by 1900; they were joined in the early decades of the twentieth century by Eastern Europeans, chiefly from Poland and Ukraine. After 1945, large numbers of new Canadians came from countries devastated by the Second World War, especially Germany, Italy, the

---

[15] Kenneth D. McRae, "Consociationalism and the Canadian Political System," in McRae, ed., *Consociational Democracy: Political Accommodation in Segmented Societies* (Toronto: McClelland & Stewart, 1974), p. 243.

FIGURE 2.3   IMMIGRANTS AS A PERCENTAGE OF TOTAL POPULATION, CANADA, 1901–1991

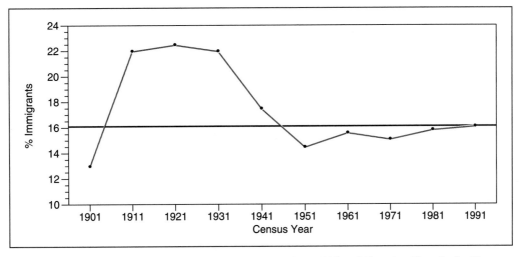

Source: 1991 *Census Highlights: The Daily* (Statistics Canada, December 8, 1992), p. 3. Reproduced by authority of the Minister responsible for Statistics Canada 1993.

Netherlands and Eastern Europe. In 1991, Europeans are still the largest group of immigrants in Canada (54%) but declining proportionately to, for example, Asian immigrants who have increased to 25%. (See Figure 2.4.)

After 1962, when the regulations were changed to eliminate explicit discrimination on the basis of race or nationality, the preponderance of English-speaking and European immigrants began to decline. Previously, the only significant groups of non-white immigrants were from China and Japan. By the late 1970s, over one-quarter of new immigrants came from Asian countries (Hong Kong, India and the Philippines among them), and there were also significant increases in the numbers entering from Africa, South and Central America and the West Indies. Immigration is discussed in more detail in Chapter 3.

As a consequence of changes in immigration patterns over the last century, Canada today is a truly multicultural society. In 1871, 61 percent of the population was of British origin, 31 percent French. In the 1991 census, 28 percent of Canadians who claimed a single ethnic heritage said they were of British origin, 23 percent, French.[16] Apart from these two large groups, the census also categorized over one hundred smaller ethnic groups, the most significant of which were Germans (3.4 percent), Italians (2.8 percent) and Chinese (2.2 percent). Native peoples formed the sixth largest group (1.7 percent). Interestingly, 2.8 percent claimed their single ethnic origin simply as Canadian.

Citizenship Oath:

I swear (or affirm) that I will be faithful and bear true allegiance to Her Majesty Queen Elizabeth the Second, Queen of Canada, Her Heirs and Successors, and that I will faithfully observe the laws of Canada and fulfil my duties as a Canadian citizen.

Citizenship Act (6)

---

[16] The 1981 census was the first to allow respondents to identify more than one ethnic background. In 1991, 14 percent reported some combination of British and/or French and other origins, and 4 percent said they had British and French ethnic backgrounds.

FIGURE 2.4   IMMIGRANT POPULATION BY PLACE OF BIRTH AND PERIOD OF IMMIGRATION, CANADA 1991

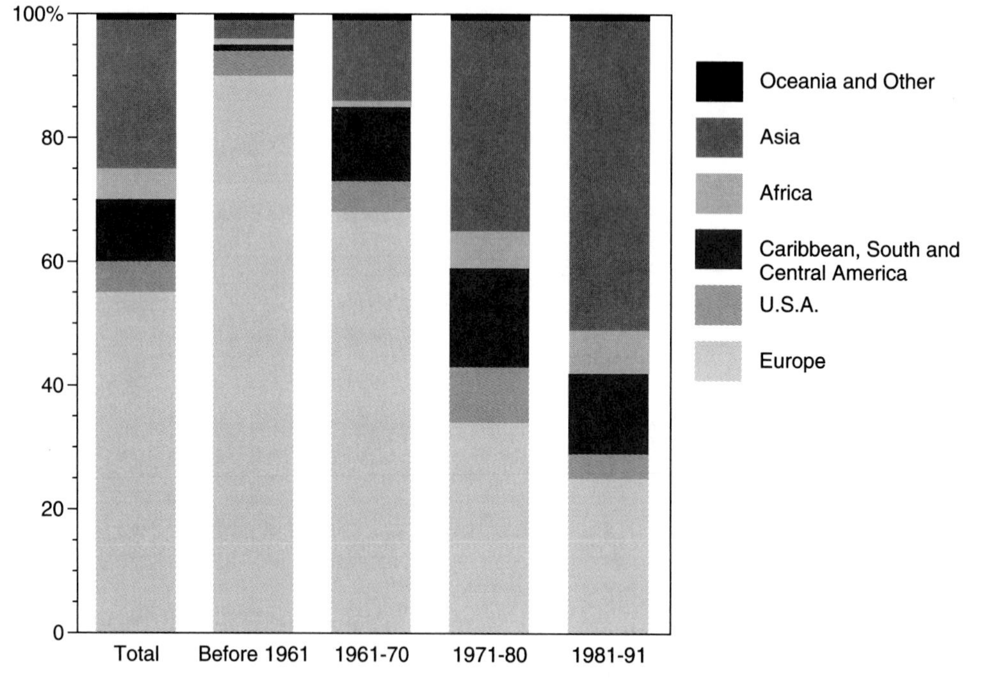

Source: *1991 Census Highlights: The Daily* (Statistics Canada, December 8, 1992), p. 6. Reproduced by authority of the Minister responsible for Statistics Canada 1993.

Furthermore, despite the bicultural image projected by conflict between the two major language groups, Canada is a "nation of many tongues." Although the 1991 census showed that about 85 percent of Canadians had English or French as the language first learned in the home, the remaining 15 percent cited over seventy other languages, each one claimed as a first language by at least a thousand and, in some cases, by up to half a million people. The integration of this multicultural and multilingual population into Canadian society and the creation of a sense of national identity and political community among them have posed additional challenges for the development of the Canadian state.

CANADIANS TODAY: DEMOGRAPHIC TRENDS

From Confederation to 1991 Canada's population grew from 3.5 million to 27.3 million. It continues to grow at slightly more than one percent per year; about two-thirds is caused by natural increase and one-third by immigration.

As we have noted, the population is extremely concentrated and highly urban. It is concentrated in three ways: 90 percent live in a 320-kilometre strip along the Canada–United States border; about 60 percent live in central Canada in Ontario and Québec; and over three-quarters of Canadians live in metropolitan areas. Thirty-two percent live in the country's three largest cities: Toronto, Montréal and Vancouver. (See Figure 2.5.)

FIGURE 2.5   POPULATION DISTRIBUTION IN CANADA 1951 AND 1991

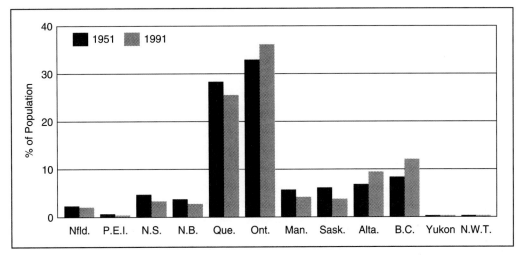

Source: *1991 Census Highlights: The Daily*, Statistics Canada (April 28, 1992), p. 5. Reproduced by authority of the Minister responsible for Statistics Canada, 1993.

Four basic variables affect demography: fertility, mortality, migration and immigration. As in other developed countries, Canadian fertility rates began to decline in 1961 after the baby boom of the late 1940s and 1950s. The highest fertility rates correlate with women who marry young, remain married the longest, live in rural areas, are not well-educated and who work in the home. Given current social patterns, these variables indicate that low fertility rates will continue in the near future.

Mortality rates are also changing. The average life expectancy at Confederation was about 45; in 1992 it was closer to 77. Women live six to seven years longer than men. The lowest life expectancy correlates with unskilled and blue-collar workers, the unmarried, and Native Indians.

Immigration has played a vital role in Canada's development. Canada has one of the largest proportions of foreign-born residents of any country in the world — double that of the United States. Migration, too, has played an important role in Canada's demography. Canada has a very mobile population, enabling swift population changes in response to challenging economic circumstances, although most of the migration is generated by a small minority of the population.

In overall composition, Canada's population is now "middle aged" and aging rapidly. In 1881, the median age was 20; by 2001 it will be over 30. This trend is due mainly to declining fertility and the stabilization of a low birth rate.

To acquire a more complete picture of the Canadian population these demographic facts must be combined with social stratification data. This is discussed in detail in Chapter 4, but here we should note that social class can be characterized by such variables as economic circumstances, education and occupation. Canadians as a whole have experienced an absolute increase in real wealth in this century and, as we saw in Chapter 1, they are also very well-off compared to citizens of other countries. This rosy picture masks a plethora of problems. There are significant inequalities of opportunity and distribution of wealth in Canada that the political system has failed to address adequately.

THE DEVELOPMENT OF THE CANADIAN NATION

In the mid-1960s, political scientists evinced a growing concern with the problems of developing countries that in turn led them to focus on the relations between "nation-building" and "state-building." Particular emphasis was placed on identifying patterns in the historical evolution of established states that might serve as models for comparison with contemporary processes of political development. The majority of historical analyses concentrated on the experience of western European countries, although some also investigated the process of state formation in older "new nations" such as Canada and the United States.[17]

Most authors agreed that two factors — successful national integration and a clearly defined and legitimate role for the state — are prerequisites for the emergence of stable political systems. In ideal terms, the development of a sense of national identity among the inhabitants of a territorial state — otherwise known as **nation-building** — serves to increase the sense of loyalty and legitimacy accruing to that state. The state thus replaces region, church or ethnic group as the primary focus of citizen allegiance, thus reducing the number and intensity of potential sources of conflict within the population.

The establishment of the second factor — called **state-building** — similarly involves integration and consolidation. Again in ideal terms, the imposition of the supreme authority of state institutions and laws throughout the land serves to integrate the various parts of its territory into a single cohesive unit and to guarantee its domestic sovereignty — that is, its authority over and above the rival claims of other internal sources of political influence. In addition, the state requires external sovereignty, which frees it to manage its own domestic and international affairs, independent of constraints imposed by any other country.

We have already referred to the regional, religious and ethnic conflicts, and the problems of geographic diversity and external influence that hampered the processes of forming a sense of national integration and building a sovereign state in Canada. The remainder of this chapter will examine the impact of these factors on the progress Canada has made since Confederation toward the "ideal-typical" model of an integrated and sovereign modern state.

PROBLEMS OF NATION-BUILDING IN CANADA

The concept of national identity is rather like a coin in that it bears two sides. The "heads" of the national identity coin consists of a sense of belonging together in a single political community, while the "tails" represents a sense of distinctiveness from all other peoples. In different countries and different periods, one side or the other will appear to predominate. It sometimes seems that in the case of Canada there is a distinct bias in favour of "tails."

On one side of the coin, the emergence of a separate Canadian identity has largely involved a process of differentiation from the United Kingdom and the United States. The need

---

[17] For example, Gabriel Almond and G. Bingham Powell, *Comparative Politics: A Developmental Approach* (Boston: Little, Brown and Co., 1966); Karl Deutsch and William J. Foltz, eds., *Nation Building* (New York: Atheston Press, 1966); Samuel Eisenstadt and Stein Rokkan, eds., *Building States and Nations*, two volumes (Beverly Hills, Cal. and London: Sage Publications, 1973). For studies of older "new nations," see Kenneth D. McRae, "Empire, Language, and Nation: The Canadian Case," in Eisenstadt and Rokkan, eds., *Building States and Nations*, vol. II, pp. 144–76; Lipset, *The First New Nation*.

for Canadians to cut the colonial ties that bound them to the United Kingdom in the nineteenth and early twentieth centuries has more recently been transformed into the problem of establishing a Canadian identity and culture distinct from that of the United States.[18]

The other side of the coin, the development of a sense of belonging together has been hindered by several obstacles: the historic relationship of conflict between English-speaking and French-speaking Canadians; defining a satisfactory relationship with aboriginal peoples; the problems attendant on integrating minority ethnic groups into the community; and the pervasive effects of regionalism, exacerbated by the federal nature of the political system, the uneven distribution of economic activity and the peculiar configuration of settlement in Canada. Many aspects of each of these problems will be examined in greater detail in other parts of the book (notably, Chapters 3, 4 and 6), but an overview linking the various obstacles to nation-building in Canada will be provided here.

A DISTINCT CANADIAN IDENTITY?

The American Revolution and the entry of the Empire Loyalists into the northern colonies marked the initial differentiation of Canada from the United States, based on loyalty to the British Crown and Empire. The identification with Britain was further strengthened by the successful defence of Canada in the War of 1812 and by massive immigration from Britain in the next few decades. As McRae argues, "the literature of the period suggests that they [the newcomers] did not see migration as involving a change of allegiance. They remained simply British subjects who lived in the colonies."[19]

Canadian Confederation was "largely a response to the American presence; as a defence strategy, as imitation, and as a general alternative."[20] Faced with a potentially expansionist United States, the Fathers of Confederation were motivated by "the fear of slow death by absorption and a quick one by annexation [that] hung over Canadian constitutional debates."[21] The British, for their part, were increasingly unwilling to devote resources to the defence of their North American colonies and were happy to give self-government to a new Dominion whose inhabitants remained loyal to the Crown and the Empire. Indeed, for many Canadians of British stock, there appeared to be little conflict in values between the new Canadian nationality created at Confederation and continued loyalty to the British Empire — a dual allegiance that remained widespread, although dwindling, among English Canadians up to the First World War.[22]

Since 1920, this duality has gradually declined in favour of a more exclusive identification with Canada. Growing national consciousness has been bolstered by the adoption of specifically Canadian national symbols, such as the Maple Leaf flag to replace the Red Ensign, the substitution of "O Canada" for "God Save the Queen" as Canada's national anthem and, most recently, the patriation of the "made-in-Canada" Constitution. A degree of imperial and

---

[18] See J.B. Brebner, *North Atlantic Triangle: The Interplay of Canada, the United States and Great Britain* (Toronto: McClelland & Stewart, 1966).

[19] McRae, "Empire, Language, and Nation: The Canadian Case," p. 149.

[20] John H. Redekop "Continentalism: The Key to Canadian Politics," in Redekop, ed., *Approaches to Canadian Politics*, 2nd edition (Scarborough, Ont.: Prentice-Hall Canada 1983), p. 35.

[21] Janet Morchain, *Sharing a Continent* (Toronto: McGraw-Hill Ryerson, 1973), p. 108.

[22] Carl Berger, *The State of Power: Studies in the Ideas of Canadian Imperialism, 1867–1914* (Toronto: University of Toronto Press, 1970).

monarchical sentiment lives on, partly because of reinforcement by continued immigration from the United Kingdom and by the activities of organizations like the Imperial Order of the Daughters of the Empire and the Monarchist League, and partly because remnants of the Tory and Empire Loyalist traditions remain a component of Canadian political culture. A movement pressuring to depose the Queen as Head of State and to make Canada a republic has never taken hold here as it has in Australia. But these elements aside, the separation of the Canadian national identity from British influence is complete. In the eyes of many Canadians, a far more pressing concern is the need to emphasize Canada's distinctness from the United States.

The relationship with the United States is hardly a new factor in the development of the Canadian state. But the major source of anxiety has changed over time. Although Canadians no longer fear direct military annexation by the Americans, concern is now directed toward economic and cultural penetration of Canada by its much larger neighbour. Economic relations, including Canada's trade dependence on the United States, American ownership of Canadian industry and natural resources and the impact of economic interdependence promoted by the 1989 free trade deal are among the major foreign policy issues examined in detail in Chapter 14. But, just as important for many Canadians, and more pertinent to the present discussion, is the issue of cultural independence from the United States (see Chapter 4).

It is, of course, difficult to separate the economic from the cultural dimensions of Canada–US relations, since the concern for cultural independence seems to mirror economic realities. Since World War Two, the United States has been responsible for over 70 percent of foreign investment and simultaneously has been viewed as a major cultural threat. Concern over assimilation into America, or continental North American culture, is real. The proximity of most Canadians to the border with the United States, the existence of a shared language, the relative size of the two populations and the penetration of Canadian society by American mass media and other culture-bearers are all viewed as potential threats to the emergence or maintenance of a distinct Canadian identity. Some observers suggest that a determination to resist total cultural assimilation remains a fundamental component of the Canadian national identity. As one writer has put it, despite a tendency to embrace many aspects of popular American or continental culture,

> being 'non-American' and, at times quite pointlessly, anti-American, is part and parcel of the Canadian forms of patriotism and nationalism. Such negation is perhaps a somewhat weak basis for a national sentiment to focus itself on, nevertheless it is integral.[23]

INTERNAL IMPEDIMENTS TO NATION-BUILDING

There are several *internal* impediments to nation-building in Canada, all of which have been present to different degrees since 1867. These are discussed fully in the next two chapters, but the most important of them must be noted here.

First, a harsh conflict between English and French Canadians has surfaced on numerous occasions since Confederation. The execution of Louis Riel, the conscription crises of 1917 and 1944, the October Crisis of 1970, the exclusion of Québec from the constitutional set-

---

[23] George Heiman, "The 19th Century Legacy: Nationalism or Patriotism?" in Peter Russell, ed., *Nationalism in Canada* (Toronto: McGraw-Hill, 1966), pp. 337–38.

tlement of 1982 and the failure to resolve the constitutional dilemma with the Meech Lake or Charlottetown Accords are among the low points in relations between the two charter groups. (For details, see Chapters 5 and 6.) No satisfactory long-term *modus vivendi* has ever been apparent between the founding nations. Today, the Parti Québécois and the Bloc Québécois in Québec officially espouse separation from the Canadian state and the foundation of an independent, sovereign state of Québec.

Nation-state building requires political co-operation.

Rodewalt illustration, originally appeared in *Policy Options*.

Next is the question of the integration of non-charter, ethnic groups into Canadian society. To a degree, government policies and popular support for multiculturalism have allowed each ethnic minority to preserve its own cultural identity and heritage, while becoming part of Canada's social tapestry. A few minority groups, such as the Sons of Freedom sect of the Doukhobors, have refused to acknowledge the sovereignty of the Canadian state. However, the general pattern among immigrants has been one of willingness to concur with the norms of their host society. In turn, the host society usually has been willing to accept them. However, examples of both institutionalized (governmental) discrimination and public racism, even racial violence, have surfaced at various periods of Canadian history.[24]

Perhaps the most disruptive impact of minority ethnic groups on nation-building in Canada has occurred with respect to the French-English relationship. The fact that, until recently, the majority of new immigrants, even in Montréal, have tended to learn English rather than French as their first official language has exaggerated the minority status of French-speaking Canadians in Canada and exacerbated relations between the two charter groups.

Canada's Native peoples, for a long time, were deliberately excluded from the nation-building process. The expansion of the Canadian colonies and state in the nineteenth century brought Native and European groups into direct competition for possession of land. Following the conquest of Québec, the British authorities made repeated attempts to accommodate the interests of the French-speaking population but they demonstrated little regard for the rights and customs of Canada's aboriginal peoples. Successive colonial and, later, Dominion administrations deprived the Indians of their land (by fair means or foul) as part of the process of opening up western Canada for settlement and railway construction, herding them onto reserves and subjecting them to the draconian, paternalistic measures of the nineteenth century *Indian Acts*. (See Chapter 3.)

Although some of the more discriminatory provisions of the legislation pertaining to Native people have since been relaxed — for example, after 1960 Indians on reserves were at last allowed to vote in federal elections — status Indians still occupy a dependent, quasi-colonial position vis-à-vis the federal government.[25] Non-status Indians and Métis who attempt integration into mainstream society usually find themselves among the poorer and under-privileged sections of the Canadian population, often being subject to discrimination and racial stereotyping.[26]

Because of their geographical isolation the Inuit were largely by-passed in the process of nation-building and modernization until about four decades ago. Like status Indians, the Inuit, until 1950, were explicitly excluded from the federal franchise. Even then, many Inuit living in the high Arctic could not actually exercise their right to vote until 1963, following the creation of a new parliamentary riding covering the entire Northwest Territories.[27]

During the past four decades, the Inuit have been forced into co-existing with an advanced industrial society within the Canadian state. Their traditional lifestyle has been

---

[24] Alan B. Anderson and James S. Frideres, *Ethnicity in Canada: Theoretical Perspectives* (Toronto: Butterworths, 1981), pp. 200–2 and ch. 9 passim; D. Hill, *Human Rights in Canada: A Focus on Racism* (Ottawa: Canadian Labour Congress, 1977); Evelyn Kallen, *Ehnicity and Human Rights in Canada* (Toronto: Gage, 1982), chs. 1 and 6; B. Singh Bolaria and Peter S. Li, *Racial Oppression in Canada*, 2nd ed. (Toronto: Garamond Press, 1988); Neil Nevitte and Allan Kornberg, eds., *Minorities and the Canadian State* (New York: Mosaic Press, 1985).

[25] See, for example, Mel Watkins, ed., *Dene Nation: The Colony Within* (Toronto: University of Toronto Press, 1977).

[26] For a critical view of the situation of the Indian population from a human rights perspective, see James Wilson, *Canada's Indians*, MRG Report No. 21 (London: Minority Rights Group, 1982), especially Parts Three and Four.

[27] From 1953 to 1962, there was a constituency of "Mackenzie River," which excluded the territorial districts of Keewatin and Franklin. From 1963 to 1979, the "Northwest Territories" riding covered all three districts. Since the 1979 General Election, the N.W.T. has been represented by two MPs, one for "Western Arctic" and one for "Nunatsiaq." In addition, the N.W.T. and Yukon were finally given representation in the Senate, one Senator each, in 1975.

encroached upon by attempts to develop Arctic energy and other mineral resources and by the construction of the Distant Early Warning (DEW) line of radar stations and other military installations. Many Inuit, like the Indians, are resentful of the disruption of their customary mode of life by modernization and economic development.[28]

For Native organizations like the Inuit Tapirisat of Canada or the Dene Nation, minority status and the lack of institutionalized channels have made it difficult to compete within the established mechanisms of federal–provincial negotiation. It is perhaps not surprising that some Native groups feel themselves to be non-participants in the Canadian state, and actively oppose further modernization and development.

Fourth in this examination of the impediments to nation-building in Canada comes regionalism. Regionalism is not a new phenomenon in Canada. Even in pre-Confederation days there was little contact between the colonies of British North America. The events leading up to the establishment of the Dominion suggest profound regional differences in attitudes toward the founding of the Canadian state. Today, well into the second century of Confederation, many of those differences and local interests continue to exist.

The persistence of regionalism within the Canadian state can be ascribed to several factors such as the sheer size of the country, the very different historical backgrounds of the provinces and their populations and the uneven development of economic activity across Canada. The regions have separate economic interests to advance and protect. Thus, there are several economic bases for regional conflict: oil producing *versus* oil consuming regions, agricultural *versus* industrial areas, resource-rich *versus* poorer provinces, among others.

Another factor that promotes regionalism in Canada is the country's peculiar pattern of settlement, with 90 percent of the population clustered within a strip 320 km wide extending along the American border. One result is that, unlike in many other western societies, there is no single centre of population concentration to serve as a cultural and economic core. Nor is there a dominant city in Canada. Rather, Canada has a "polycephalic" city network,[29] with several regional centres (Halifax, Montréal, Toronto, Winnipeg, Calgary, Vancouver, etc.) as the political, economic, social and cultural foci for the populations clustered around them. Instead of possessing a single metropolis dominating and easing the integration of the peripheries of the state (such as Paris and London), Canada consists of a series of core–periphery (or city–hinterland) relationships that divide the country into more-or-less self-contained regions and communication networks. (See Figure 2.6.)

Even within central Canada (that is, Ontario and Québec), which is sometimes portrayed as the centre in relation to the peripheries of east and west, no dominant city emerges. Ottawa is the political capital of Canada, but little else; Toronto is the economic and cultural centre of Ontario, as well as a provincial capital; Montréal is the economic core of Québec and the cultural centre for French Canadians; Québec City is increasingly viewed as the political capital by Québec nationalists. Clearly, none of these can claim to dominate central Canada, let alone the whole country.

---

[28] On the constitutional status of the Territories, see Chapter 5, page 232.

[29] On the impact of "polycephalic" city networks on nation-building, see Hans Daalder, "On Building Consociational Nations: The Cases of the Netherlands and Switzerland," in McRae, ed., *Consociational Democracy*, pp. 107–24; or Stein Rokkan, "Cities, States and Nations: A Dimensional Model for the Study of Contrasts in Development," in Eisenstadt and Rokkan, eds., *Building States and Nations*, vol. 1, pp. 73–97.

FIGURE 2.6   CORE-PERIPHERY RELATIONS: TWO SIMPLIFIED MODELS

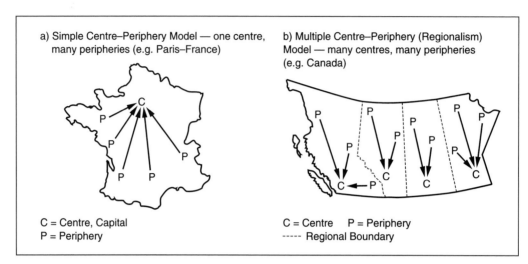

a) Simple Centre–Periphery Model — one centre, many peripheries (e.g. Paris–France)

b) Multiple Centre–Periphery (Regionalism) Model — many centres, many peripheries (e.g. Canada)

C = Centre, Capital
P = Periphery

C = Centre   P = Periphery
----- Regional Boundary

Another factor contributing to regionalism is the federal system of government adopted at Confederation, a system that compounds the effect of this core–periphery network. Regional interests are primarily articulated by provincial governments in competition with each other or with the federal government. It is this factor that is chiefly responsible for the frequent equation of "regions" with "provinces" in Canada. But the representation of regional interests by provincial governments tends to exaggerate differences between regions and to understate intra-regional variations. Richard Simeon, for one, has argued that the provincial governments have a "vested interest in maintaining and strengthening the salience of the regional dimension"; each one therefore, "is motivated to accentuate the degree of internal unity, and to exaggerate the extent of difference with Ottawa."[30] Thus, while Canada's federal system was intended to reflect and take into account the diversity among the original provinces, it has served to perpetuate, institutionalize and, perhaps, exacerbate regional differences and conflicts among the members of the now much larger Canadian federation.

A final factor contributing to the persistence of regional particularism in Canada is the absence of nationally oriented mass media that, according to many theorists, often serve as an integrative force. Where the media focus is upon local news about political and social issues, there is little opportunity for the consumer to acquire knowledge about other parts of the country or to learn what people elsewhere think about his or her own region. Despite their best efforts, little nationally integrative force has emerged among the Canadian mass media (see Chapter 4). As one discussion suggests, "the present national [media] system has been only moderately successful at best in fostering interregional communication."[31]

---

[30] Richard Simeon, "Regionalism and Canadian Political Institutions," in J.P. Meekison, ed., *Canadian Federalism: Myth or Reality*, 3rd ed. (Toronto: Methuen, 1977), pp. 301–2.

[31] Frederick J. Fletcher and Daphne F. Gottlieb, "The Mass Media and the Political Process," in M.S. Whittington and G. Williams, eds., *Canadian Politics in the 1980s* (Toronto: Methuen, 1981), p. 149.

We conclude that a number of factors combine to ensure the persistence of regionally based attitudes and interests in Canada: the sheer size of the country, historical patterns of ethnic settlement, variations in economic activity and wealth, uneven population distribution and the polycephalic city network, the institutionalization of regional differences by the federal system and the vested interests of provincial governments and the lack of information and awareness of the regions of Canada about one another and about national affairs. The results are that Canadians often do not share a strong sense of belonging together, and regional or provincial interests frequently take precedence over those of the state. These factors must be counter-balanced by nation-building.

NATION-BUILDING AND CONTEMPORARY POLITICS

Canadians today have, on the whole, accepted that their country is a country of differences. This willingness to accept diversity may well be one of the distinguishing marks of the Canadian national identity — a contrast to the pressures toward conformity that characterize many other national cultures. However, potential dangers lie in store for the Canadian state when these latent cleavages become politicized.

Some of the most bitter recent debates among Canadian politicians, including the long-drawn-out wrangling over the constitution, reflect the persistence of divisions among regions and between the two founding nations. Concern about anglophone oppression, real or reconstructed, fuel the nationalist aspirations of the Parti Québécois in its quest to lead Québec out of Confederation. Though based on a sense of physical and political marginality rather than ethnic discontent, similar resentment against "the Centre" or "the East" underlies potential separatist threats in the West.[32] Further, a combination of regional economic disparities, perceived historical grievances and (in some cases) a sense of physical remoteness often exacerbates tensions among the provinces and between the provinces and the federal government.

Relations between the various levels of government and tensions with Native populations also reflect the impact of what might be called "the unfinished nation-building process" on contemporary politics. The relative isolation of most indigenous groups, whether on reserves or in the far north, is gradually being broken down by the expansion of state activity and by the ongoing process of economic development. Native people have increasingly been drawn into the mainstream of economic and political life. As they have become more politicized, they have introduced new political issues with which governments are inadequately prepared to cope. Consequently, pressures for and conflict over self-government and the settlement of Native land claims are likely to continue over the coming decades.

In a country as large and diverse as Canada, it may be unrealistic to expect the process of nation-building to eradicate all differences or integrate all disparities. As Chapter 3 will argue, certain overarching values and attitudes shared by all Canadians have developed that counterbalance the potentially disintegrative effects of regionalism and ethnic differences. But the historic rivalries remain. Chapter 6 will discuss in detail the continued impact of these divisions upon the contemporary politics of Canadian federalism. Perhaps, when all is said and done, one of the fascinations of Canadian politics is the fact that Canada has survived for as long as it has, despite the persistence of strains and conflicts left unresolved in the nation-building process.

---

[32] See various articles in Larry Pratt and Garth Stevenson, eds., *Western Separatism: The Myths, Realities and Dangers* (Edmonton: Hurtig, 1981).

THE DEVELOPMENT OF THE CANADIAN STATE

By 1873, Canada's borders were established virtually as they are today, with the exception of the Alaska–British Columbia boundary, settled in 1903, and the addition of Newfoundland in 1949. But, while the boundaries of the Canadian Dominion were defined early in its history, the acquisition of sovereignty over the territory enclosed by them was a somewhat slower process.

The major task was the establishment of external sovereignty. This process was naturally linked to Canada's gradual acquisition of independence from Britain. The quest for external sovereignty in fact began even before Confederation, as the elected assemblies of the British North American colonies strove for some measure of responsible self-government within the context of Britain's colonial administration. Progress was slow. Between 1758 (in the case of Nova Scotia) and 1791 (Lower Canada), each of the colonies was granted what might be called a popularly elected assembly. The early years of these assemblies saw them dominated by the respective Governors and their appointed Executive and Legislative Councils.

By the time Lord Durham recommended the political union of Upper and Lower Canada under "responsible government" in his *Report* of 1838, the power of the Governors was under strenuous attack. Although the first of Lord Durham's recommendations, the *Act of Union*, was implemented by the British government, the second, responsible government, initially was ignored. But the first Governor of the new united colony of Canada, Lord Sydenham, combined his gubernatorial duties with those of Prime Minister and leader of his own party of adherents, appealing directly to the population to provide his followers a majority in assembly elections. This practice was followed by other colonial Governors, but eventually proved to be counter-productive since the "appeal to the electorate worked in the end to confirm that power resided, in part at least, in the people, and not solely in the crown."[33]

In 1846, a change in the British government produced an administration more sympathetic to responsible government in the colonies, and newly appointed Governors of Canada and Nova Scotia were instructed in 1847 to select their Councils from the leaders of the majority factions or parties in their respective assemblies. Within a year, non-confidence motions passed in the popular assemblies resulted in changes of ministries in united Canada, Nova Scotia and New Brunswick.

In this fashion, the principle of **responsible government**, whereby the Governor retained his advisors only as long as they were collectively able to retain majority support in the assembly, became established in British North America. The next stage in the development of representative and responsible self-government occurred over the next decade with the effective separation of the political executive ("Cabinet") from the formal executive (the Governor). Governors increasingly absented themselves from the deliberations of their political advisors, while acting on their recommendations.

Thus, even before Confederation, the Canadian colonies had achieved a moderate degree of self-government through the development of responsible government and parliamentary democracy. But their assemblies and governments were not sovereign; there were constraints

---

[33] Thomas A. Hockin, *Government in Canada* (Toronto: McGraw-Hill Ryerson, 1976), p. 6.

upon their autonomy and on the supremacy of their parliamentary institutions. When the British North American colonies were each granted assemblies in the eighteenth century, they were given the power to legislate on local matters, subject to two conditions: first, that they did not attempt to enact laws having effect outside their territorial boundaries and second, that their laws did not contravene the established law of England.

Obstacles to the outright independence of governmental institutions continued, even after the creation of the new Dominion in 1867. First, legislative competence within Canada was divided between two different levels of government: federal and provincial. This in itself did not directly affect the external sovereignty of the Canadian state, but it did have an indirect impact: neither the federal division of powers nor any other provisions of the *BNA Act* could be amended by any Canadian legislature, only by the British Parliament. Moreover, the creation of separate fields of legislative competence had important and restrictive consequences for internal state-building.

As well, certain matters were withheld from all levels of government in Canada. In particular, legislation having extra-territorial effect (such as laws pertaining to copyright or merchant shipping) was reserved exclusively for the United Kingdom Parliament. Similarly, the Canadian government was not regarded as an independent actor in the world of international relations. Canada was effectively an appendage of the United Kingdom when it came to the conduct of diplomatic affairs, which remained the exclusive preserve of the British government.

Third, even within the legal competence of Canadian federal or provincial legislatures, parliamentary supremacy could be overridden by the powers of reservation given to the governor general and the lieutenant-governors (as representatives of the Crown in Canada) and by the powers of disallowance retained by the British government.

These factors and others (for example, the retention until 1949 of the Judicial Committee of the Privy Council in the United Kingdom as the highest court of appeal, a device that permitted substantial outside meddling in Canada's internal affairs) combined to maintain Canada in quasi-colonial relationship with Britain long after Confederation.

EXTERNAL SOVEREIGNTY AND ITS CONSTRAINTS

In the present century, however, two major periods of constitutional change, some fifty years apart, have served to secure Canada's *de facto* and *de jure* independence from the United Kingdom.

The first series of events revolved around the Imperial Conferences of 1926 and 1930, culminating in the 1931 *Statute of Westminster*. At the Imperial Conference of 1930, the disallowance and reservation powers of the British government and the governor general were declared constitutionally obsolete. They had, in any case, long ceased to be of much practical relevance. The **Statute of Westminster** paved the way for the Dominions to emerge as independent foreign-policy actors by stating that a Dominion Parliament had full power to make laws having extraterritorial operation.[34] A further provision of the Statute laid down that the United Kingdom Parliament no longer had the right to legislate for any Dominion except at the request of the Dominion concerned — for example, by way of a petition to amend the *BNA Act*.

---

[34] It should be remarked that, a few years earlier, Canada had already negotiated and signed its first treaty with the United States, the *Halibut Treaty* of 1923, after the King gave specific permission to do so.

These changes highlight the role of the *Statute of Westminster* as the watershed between the effective ending of colonial status for the Dominions and their emergence as more-or-less independent states. According to the historian A.R.M. Lower,

> *the* Statute of Westminster *came as close as was practicable without revolutionary scissors to legislating the independence of the 'Dominions'. There is good ground for holding December 11, 1931 as Canada's Independence Day, for on that day she became a sovereign state.*[35]

However, Lower slightly exaggerated the significance of *Statute of Westminster*. There is no doubt that it was important for all the Dominions, but in the case of Canada reminders of the colonial heritage lingered, despite Canada's emergence as an international actor in its own right.

Some more colonial remnants were removed in 1949. The Supreme Court replaced the British Judicial Committee of the Privy Council as Canada's highest court of appeal. In addition, the *British North America Act* (No. 2) of 1949 permitted the Parliament of Canada to amend certain portions of the Act without recourse to Westminster. However, in order to achieve Constitutional reforms, it was still necessary for the Canadian government to go cap-in-hand to Westminster to ask for amending legislation from the United Kingdom Parliament. While Westminster was traditionally willing to accede to any such requests from Canada, the necessity remained a limitation to Canada's self-determination.

Thus, one of the dominant political issues of the 1970s was Prime Minister Pierre Trudeau's crusade to patriate the Canadian Constitution — a quest that finally came to fruition with the passage of the *Canada Act* by the British Parliament in 1982. This Act gave effect to Canada's request for Britain to consent to the *Constitution Act, 1982*. At last, Canada, like other sovereign states, had its own Constitution and was able to determine its internal political structure without reference to external authorities. In formal terms at least, it was the year 1982, over half a century after the *Statute of Westminster* and 115 years from Confederation, that marked the final stage in Canada's evolution from colony to sovereign state.

The final, formal severance of ties with the United Kingdom did not mean, however, that Canadian governments could do just as they please. In the modern era, increasing interdependence among states and their economies has severely constrained the capacity of governments to act independently of all external pressures. This is especially the case for countries that have a high degree of economic integration with a larger, more powerful neighbour.

While Canada is a genuinely sovereign state in international law, the nature of its relationship with the United States imposes limits upon government policy-making. Canada's defence policy is conducted within the context of the NATO alliance, in which the United States is the largest single actor — a position it uses to attempt to sway the policies of its partners. Canadian fiscal and budgetary policies are heavily influenced by American interest rates and by capital flows between the two countries. Energy and industrial policies have to take into account American ownership of Canadian branch-plants and American investment in Canadian resources. The success of Canadian environmental policy is partly dependent upon the extent to which American governments can be persuaded to impose their own controls on the emission of industrial pollutants. Acid rain and the level of toxic waste in the

---

[35] Arthur R.M. Lower, *Colony to Nation: A History of Canada,* 4th ed. revised (Don Mills, Ont.: Longmans Canada, 1964), p. 489.

Great Lakes are but two examples of such cross-border issues. A few large international corporations have acquired more economic power than most provincial governments. Thus, contemporary issues of external sovereignty now revolve, not around Canadian–British, but around Canadian–American relations (to be further examined in Chapters 4 and 14).

INTERNAL STATE-BUILDING IN THE NINETEENTH CENTURY

In contrast to the long, drawn-out process of Canada's acquisition of external sovereignty, the initial stages of internal state-building were quite rapid. After the political unification of the original provinces in 1867 and the subsequent expansion of Canada's territory, it was imperative to integrate this vast area into a governable political entity. The three major components in this late-nineteenth century integration process were the imposition of law and order over the entire territory, the development of means of transportation and communication and attempts to create a viable national economy.

One of the key characteristics of the modern state is the government's ability to ensure that its laws are obeyed and, where necessary, to utilize its monopoly of the legitimate use of physical force in order to maintain its authority. Since the birth of the Dominion, Canadian governments have not been averse to using large-scale coercion when deemed necessary. On at least four occasions — the Riel Rebellions of 1870–71 and 1885, the Winnipeg General Strike of 1919 and the 1970 October Crisis — large numbers of police and troops were mobilized to crush perceived or actual uprisings against the Canadian state.

One year after Confederation the federal government created the Dominion Police to enforce laws in central and eastern Canada. The major symbol of central authority in the west of Canada in the late nineteenth century was the red coat of the Mountie. Four years after the annexation of lands from the Hudson's Bay Company in 1869, the North-West Mounted Police force (later combined with the Dominion Police to become the Royal Canadian Mounted Police or RCMP) was created to impose a uniform code of law on the territories. The Mounties were responsible for keeping the peace in all federally administered lands from the American border to the Arctic and between Hudson Bay and the Rocky Mountains. The RCMP still maintains a federal presence throughout Canada. In addition to its tasks of enforcing federal laws everywhere, acting as the sole police force in the two remaining territories and, until recently, providing Canada's internal security, the force is under contract to perform police functions in every province except Ontario and Québec and in a vast number of municipalities.

The second medium of internal state-building in the new Dominion was the improvement of transportation and communications among its provinces and regions. An efficient system of transportation was necessary for security purposes, for economic reasons and for the movement of people, mail and other sources of information. In the second half of the nineteenth century, the most efficient form of transport for all such purposes was the railway. Thus, one of the conditions under which New Brunswick and Nova Scotia were willing to join Confederation was that a railway be built linking Halifax and the Saint John valley to the St. Lawrence. The construction of this "Intercolonial Railway" was enshrined in the original *BNA Act* as one of the duties of the Dominion government.[36]

---

[36] *British North America Act,* section 145 — repealed in 1893 after the government had fulfilled its duty.

Transportation became even more of a challenge as the Dominion spread from sea to sea. The building of a transcontinental railway consequently became one of the most important political issues and objectives of Canada's first 20 years. Through a mixture of government intervention and private enterprise, Canada's railway system slowly took shape, highlighted by the completion of the transcontinental Canadian Pacific Railway when the famous "last spike" was driven in 1885.[37]

Railway construction was also very much a part of the third aspect of nineteenth century state-building. The so-called "National Policy," first publicized by John A. Macdonald in the general election campaign of 1878, became the basis for Canada's economic development for the next 50 years. The **National Policy** consisted of three interrelated objectives: the development of a comprehensive railway system; the opening up of western Canada through the encouragement of immigration, settlement and agriculture on the prairies and national economic development through protection of Canadian industries by means of an external tariff.

In order to realize the dream of a Dominion stretching *ad mare usque ad mare*, and also to forestall the danger of United States expansion into western Canada, it was deemed necessary for Canadians to populate the vast open plains between Manitoba (at that time little more than the area around Winnipeg) and British Columbia. The government therefore opened the door to immigrants, largely from Central and Eastern Europe, who were willing to settle and farm on the prairies, and gave them land grants and financial aid to help them become established. The railways were of great importance to such settlement, particularly for the transportation of wheat and other prairie products to consumer markets in the east and to the coasts for export abroad.

At the same time, the Macdonald government attempted to develop other sectors of the Canadian economy. In particular, the high rate of emigration from Canada in the 1870s brought home the realization that Canada required secondary or manufacturing industries to provide jobs for its non-agricultural labour force. But such emerging industries required protection from more advanced foreign competition. Interprovincial tariffs had already been removed to aid the free flow of raw materials and goods within Canada. Now, as the third plank of the National Policy, the government imposed an external tariff designed to reduce the flow of imports (especially certain manufactured products) into the country.[38] Creation of the tariff did aid indigenous economic development in certain industries. As well, in combination with the new railways, it increased the volume of east-west trade within Canada at the expense of north-south trade with the United States. These measures taken together therefore represented a major step toward the emergence of Canada as a national economic entity.

The National Policy was an explicit attempt by Canadian governments of the late nineteenth century to enhance the economic and political integration of the Dominion. To a certain extent, it was as important for its symbolic contribution to nationalism and independence as for its con-

---

[37] See Pierre Berton's detailed history of the transcontinental railway in *The National Dream: The Great Railway 1871–1881* and *The Last Spike: The Great Railway 1871–1885* (Toronto: McClelland & Stewart, 1970 and 1971).

[38] Ironically, while this move was intended to increase Canada's economic independence, it may have had the opposite effect in the long run. British and American companies, faced with a tariff on goods sold to Canada from outside, started to set up branch plants inside the country. This policy helped to create the pattern of foreign ownership of Canadian industry which has become a major political and economic issue in the present day. Michael Bliss, "Canadianizing American Business: the Roots of the Branch Plant," in Ian Lumsden, ed., *Close the 49th Parallel* (Toronto: University of Toronto Press, 1970), pp. 26–42.

tribution to Canada's economic development;[39] in fact, its economic impact has recently come under critical re-evaluation by historians and political scientists.[40] But the National Policy is also noteworthy in that it represented the first major incursion of the state into economic life in Canada, an influence of increasing importance to Canadians in the twentieth century.

THE GROWTH OF THE STATE IN THE TWENTIETH CENTURY

One important trait of the modern state has been the inexorable growth of its role in the lives of its citizens. Whether this phenomenon is referred to as the growth of the state, the expanding sphere of government or the enlargement of the public sector, it has been common to all countries, particularly the industrial societies of the western world. The author of a study of increasing government expenditure in sixteen western democracies introduces his subject with this observation:

> *Government, it seems safe to say, is one thing that has been growing rapidly in the West. Wherever governments were once small they have become big and wherever they were big they have become bigger. Nothing is so rare as a shrinking government.*[41]

In the second half of the nineteenth century, when the Canadian state began to take shape, the role of government was everywhere considerably more limited than today. The main functions of central state institutions were providing for external defence and for the maintenance of internal law and order, conducting foreign policy and trade relations, managing the currency and the national debt and overseeing a few services such as the postal system and harbour and navigation facilities. Additional tasks were performed by local or municipal authorities: building and maintaining roads, ensuring a water supply and employing local law enforcement officers. Municipalities might also provide for some elementary education and minimal health care and social services, although these were more often the preserve of private, charitable or religious organizations. In brief, in the nineteenth century, there were no major welfare state programs.

In many contemporary societies, including Canada, the state now offers free primary and secondary education to all students and subsidizes university and college education; provides massive medical care, unemployment and old age pension programs; and has become involved in a wide variety of other social welfare policies ranging from family allowances to low-cost public housing. In addition, it has become increasingly important in the economic sphere: as an owner and entrepreneur in resource development, transportation and other nationalized industries; as a regulator of both the public and the private sector; and as a manager of the national economy, through economic and regional planning, intervention in the capital and credit markets, budgetary policy and its own spending decisions. Consequently, in many western societies, total government expenditure per annum is fast approaching, and

---

39 Craig Brown, "The Nationalism of the National Policy," in Russell, ed., *Nationalism in Canada*, pp. 155–63.

40 For an overview of some of the critiques of the National Policy, see Michael Bliss, " 'Rich by Nature, Poor by Policy': The State and Economic Life in Canada," in R.K. Carty and W.P. Ward, eds., *Entering the Eighties: Canada in Crisis* (Toronto: Oxford University Press, 1980), especially pp. 78–81, and Wallace Clement and Glen Williams, eds., *The New Canadian Political Economy* (Kingston, Ont. and Montréal: McGill-Queen's University Press, 1989).

41 Warren G. Nutter, *Growth of Government in the West* (Washington, D.C.: American Enterprise Institute for Public Policy Research, 1978), p. 1.

in some cases (for example, Sweden and the Netherlands) has exceeded 50 percent of the total national income.

This last point raises the question of how the growth of the state can be measured in real terms. As the state has expanded its activities, so government expenditure has grown. Of course, even if a government continues to perform exactly the same functions over time, expenditure in money terms will increase as the cost of goods, labour and services purchased by the government also grows. Therefore, when an attempt is made to measure the growth of government (and the growth of the state) in real terms, it is usually expressed as a proportion of the country's gross national product (GNP), its gross domestic product (GDP) or some other indicator of national income, expenditure or product.[42]

As well, the growth of the role of the state can be measured in terms of the increase in governmental activities: the number of new programs adopted by the government, the number of new laws and regulations and the statutes establishing new public corporations or nationalized industries. A third way of expressing the growth of the state is in terms of the actual size of government, that is, either the number of governmental organizations or the percentage of the labour force employed by the state. Lastly, these government activities and employees must be paid for; the state must have revenues in order to meet its expenditures (despite the tendency toward budgetary deficits displayed by many governments in recent years). Thus, a final indicator of the growing role of the state is the size of government revenues, especially those accruing from the taxation of individual and corporate citizens. Once more, this is usually expressed as a percentage of the GDP or other national income statistics.

THE EXTENT OF THE STATE IN CANADA

In this chapter we have been using the terms "government" (in the singular) and "state" more or less interchangeably. Doing so is quite reasonable when discussing the "state" in abstract terms, or when referring to centralized unitary countries like Britain, France or Sweden in which most state activities are performed by a single level of government and the majority of public expenditure is centrally funded and controlled. In the Canadian context, however, things are somewhat different. As in other federal systems, the functions of the state in Canada are shared among two major levels of government, federal and provincial, and a third tier, local or municipal government. Thus, a definition of the extent of the Canadian state and the measurement of its growth should take into account activities, expenditures, organizations and employment at all three government levels.

The Canadian state, then, consists of multiple layers of government, rather than a single hierarchical structure. In order to get a complete picture of the growing role of the state or the size of the public sector in contemporary society, we must include not only the regular government departments in each tier (in other words, the "civil service" component), but also the numerous federal and provincial regulatory boards and commissions, Crown corporations and other public enterprises, as well as the so-called "parapublic" service, in particular the health care and educational sectors.[43] Indeed, as suggested earlier, the very

---

[42] See, for example, Richard G. Lipsey, Douglas D. Purvis and Peter O. Steiner, *Economics*, 6th ed. (New York: Harper and Row, 1988) ch. 26.

[43] The problem, even for government policy-makers, of specifying the boundaries of the state (or the "public sector") is well-illustrated by the discussion in Dan Butler and Bruce D. Macnaughton. "Public Sector Growth in Canada: Issues, Explanations and Implications," in Whittington and Williams, eds., *Canadian Politics in the 1980s*, especially pp. 87–9.

proliferation of these non-civil-service bodies may be used as one indic[...] sion of state influence.

In Chapter 13, we will attempt to measure the growth and current ex[...] expan- tivities in terms of the various indicators suggested above. Before leaving th[...]te ac- ever, it will be useful to outline briefly the ongoing process of state-building h[...]ow- the twentieth century that has given birth to the present "interventionist state[...] in

Internal state-building in Canada since the National Policy has been more than in many states because of the federal nature of the political system. Rather tha[...]x ple one-to-one relationship between unitary state and society, Canadian state-buildin[...] consisted of a trilateral relationship among society, federal institutions and the set of pro[...] cial governments. Competition between the particularistic objectives of province-buildin[...] and the centralizing bias of federal state-building has served to aggravate existing reg[...]al conflicts and the broader context of federal-provincial relations. Despite these complexit[...]s, political institutions have assumed an increasingly activist role in Canadian society a[...] the economy.

The initial thrust of state intervention in Canada was primarily economic. As the example of the National Policy indicates, the role of the state was originally conceived as one of in- direct intervention (through taxes, land grants and so on) to provide the infrastructure and other conditions conducive to private sector economic development. In the twentieth century, however, the state has intervened more directly in the economy, especially through public ownership of Crown corporations. The federal government takeover of Canadian National Railways in 1917 was followed in the 1930s by the establishment of the Canadian

Reproduced with permission, Dennis Pritchard.

...casting Commission (now the CBC), the Bank of Canada and Trans-Canada Railway Air Canada); more modern examples include Atomic Energy of Canada (1952), Telesat Canada (1969) and Petro-Canada (1976). Moves by Brian Mulroney's government (1984–93) to reduce the role of the federal government have considerably this original pattern and are discussed in Chapter 13.

But while Canadian state institutions have a long history of intervention in the economic sector, the development of social policies leading to the current welfare state system occurred relatively late. This tardiness has been attributed to the delayed nature of Canada's industrial revolution; to the weakness and late emergence of the working class as an organized political force; to the strength of the business community in restricting the role of the state to promotion and protection of its own interests; and to the peculiarly Canadian form of conservatism, which reconciles strong state leadership of the economy with private responsibility (through family or community) for individual social welfare. With the last point in mind, it is perhaps not surprising that many innovations in social policy have been initated by provincial governments in the prairies, where frontier isolation created a somewhat more collectivist culture.

Although some programs had been introduced earlier (for example, Worker's Compensation in almost every province by 1920 or the federal government's Old Age Pension legislation of 1927), it was not really until the period between 1930 and 1945 that the Canadian welfare state began to take shape.[44] The combined impact of the depression and the Second World War created a climate more conducive to social intervention by both federal and provincial governments. A number of factors have been cited as contributing to this change: the growing militancy of western farmers and industrial workers in the depression; the threat posed to government parties by the electoral successes of the CCF in the early 1940s; the inability of municipalities and private welfare agencies to cope with the demand for relief during the depression; the emergence of a more collectivist national spirit induced by the shared tribulations of economic disaster and world war; and reduced opposition from a business community which saw that its interests might be served, rather than hampered, by welfare legislation. At first, the federal government provided a series of temporary relief measures to alleviate poverty in the depression, but more permanent legislation followed, especially in the fields of unemployment insurance (1940) and family allowances (1944).

Since the Second World War, both federal and provincial governments have introduced many programs into the welfare state system, including health care plans and hospital insurance, the Canada and Québec Pension Plans, housing policies, grants for higher education and guaranteed income supplements, among others. As a percentage of national income, total government spending at all levels on welfare state policies (health, education and social welfare) approximately tripled from the end of the Second World War until the 1990s. But from a state-building perspective, it may be argued that it was in the decade preceding 1945 that the major shift in perception of the role of the state occurred, allowing Canada to join the ranks of other "welfare societies." At that time Canadians began to view poverty less as a sign of individual weakness, and more as a social problem whose alleviation could be beneficial to the rest of society and that therefore could be regarded as a responsibility of the Canadian state.

---

44 Alvin Finkle, "Origins of the Welfare State in Canada," in L.V. Panitch, ed., *The Canadian State: Political Economy and Political Power* (Toronto: University of Toronto Press, 1977), pp. 344–70.

Once governmental responsibility for social welfare functions was accepted, as it had already been for economic development, the last major step in the state-building process was accomplished. Since that time, the role of the state (or "government," or "public sector") in Canadian society, with minor reversals, has continued to expand. Whether the size of the state is measured by the proportion of national income spent by governments, the number of laws and regulations or the number of public servants, twentieth century Canada differs greatly from the nineteenth century laissez-faire state.

POLITICS IN AN INTERVENTIONIST STATE

Questions about the growth and the absolute size of the Canadian state are topics of controversy and political debate. As the sphere of government activity expanded, more aspects of everyday life became political and more individuals and organizations were directly affected by public policies and the political process. In return, popular expectations of what governments can do have been raised, increasing demands on the political system. Today, some observers suggest that the Canadian political system is overloaded, and that its institutions (collectively or individually) are unable to cope with the pressures being placed upon them.

Other critics argue that the growth of the state stifles individual initiative and redirects resources away from the private sector, thereby endangering Canada's prospects for economic growth. They demand a reduction in public expenditure and deregulation of the economy so that private enterprise can prosper, unfettered by government controls.

Finally, even where the actual size of the state or the overall rate of growth of the public sector is not directly at issue, a persistent source of federal-provincial conflict concerns the relative distribution of state funds among the levels of government in Canada. Thus, provincial critics of federal government spending or involvement in certain fields are often not so much condemning government action per se as claiming federal interference in provincial jurisdiction. Once again, the politics of the present is haunted by the unresolved conflicts of Canada's past.

OVERVIEW

Politics is more than the product of historical, social and economic forces. But these forces do influence political life, and the historical development of the Canadian state and its people continues to have a profound impact on Canadian politics.

Many of the major issues and conflicts emerging from the processes of nation-building and state-building in Canada have been only partially resolved. Consequently, some of the most contentious subjects of debate in the political arena today have their origins in the strains and antipathies created by the evolution of the state. Furthermore, these same strains often hamper the reconciliation of other, apparently unrelated disputes among actors in the Canadian political system.

Even the settlement of Canada's sovereign status vis-à-vis the United Kingdom served to exacerbate tensions. The proclamation of Canada's new Constitution on April 17, 1982 was accompanied by political controversy and acrimony in parts of the country. Some 20 000 Québécois joined René Lévesque in a Montréal demonstration to protest the exclusion of Québec from the constitutional accord between the federal government and the nine other provinces. Meanwhile, Native Indian organizations, whose demands for the entrenchment of Native rights in the Constitution had not been fulfilled, also boycotted the ceremonies in Ottawa and declared that any Indians celebrating the event were committing treason against their nation.

Although the major question of external sovereignty has been resolved, relations with the United States are still at issue. Fears of assimilation into a US-dominated North American culture and the impact of American economic influence in Canada remain important topics of political debate.

With regard to internal nation-building, conflicts among regions or provinces and between the two founding nations continue to intrude on the political agenda. The threat of separation by Québec cannot be ignored. Jurisdictional disputes, especially over ownership and control of natural resources, exacerbate federal-provincial relations. Attempts to reduce regional economic disparities are frequently declaimed as unfair by the "have" provinces and inadequate by the "have-nots." The politicization of Native movements adds another new dimension to contemporary ethnic politics in Canada. Despite all these differences, however, the country stays together, united by the almost indefinable sense of "being Canadian."

Lastly, the growth of the Canadian state from the nineteenth century National Policy to the present day has also provided a subject for political debate. Today, conservatives argue that governments are too interventionist, while socialists condemn them for not being active enough. Meanwhile, provincial governments criticize the expansion of federal spending and budgetary deficits, simultaneously protesting cutbacks in federal contributions to provincially managed programs such as health care and higher education.

Many of the major issues in contemporary Canadian politics have their source in the origins, expansion and development of the state over the past 300 years. Furthermore, the attitudes, myths and grievances that evolved from the nation- and state-building experience profoundly affect the approach of contending sides to other, less directly related questions. Those attitudes and myths will be examined in more detail in the next two chapters; other issues raised above will receive further attention elsewhere in the book. The purpose of this chapter has been to draw together various strands of Canadian historical evolution in order to provide a base from which to commence the exploration of politics in Canada in the 1990s.

SELECTED BIBLIOGRAPHY

Asch, Michael, *Home and Native Land* (Toronto: Methuen, 1984).

Baldwin, Douglas and Emily Odynak, *Canada's Political Heritage: Conflict or Compromise?* (Regina: Weigh Educational Divisions, 1985).

Banting, K., ed., *State and Society: Canada in Comparative Perspective,* vol. 31, Royal Commission on the Economic Union and Development Prospects for Canada (Toronto: University of Toronto Press, 1986).

Bellan, R.C. and W.H. Pope, eds., *The Canadian Economy: Problems and Options* (Toronto: McGraw-Hill Ryerson, 1981).

Bennett, Paul, Cornelius Jaenen, Jacques Manet and Richard Jones, *Emerging Identities: Selected Problems and Interpretations in Canadian History* (Scarborough, Ont.: Prentice-Hall Canada, 1986).

Berger, Thomas, *Northern Frontier, Northern Homeland: The Report of the Mackenzie Valley Pipeline Inquiry*

(Ottawa: Supply and Services Canada, 1977, republished by Douglas and McIntyre, Vancouver, 1988).

Bothwell, Robert, Ian Drummond and John English, *Canada Since 1945: Power, Politics and Provincialism* (Toronto: University of Toronto Press, 1981).

Brebner, J.B., *North Atlantic Triangle: The Interplay of Canada, the United States and Great Britain* (Toronto: McClelland & Stewart, 1966).

Bumsted, J.M., *The Peoples of Canada*, 2 vols. (London: Oxford University Press, 1993).

Carty, R. Kenneth and W. Peter Ward, eds., *Entering the Eighties: Canada in Crisis* (Toronto: Oxford University Press, 1980).

Clement, Wallace and Glen Williams, *The New Canadian Political Economy* (Kingston, Ont., and Montreal: McGill-Queen's University Press, 1989).

Dacks, Gurston, *A Choice of Futures: Politics in the Canadian North* (Toronto: Methuen, 1981).

Doern, G. Bruce, ed., *The Politics of Economic Policy* (Toronto: University of Toronto Press, 1985).

Easterbrook, W.T., and Melvyn H. Watkins, eds., *Approaches to Canadian Economic History: A Selection of Essays* (Toronto: McClelland & Stewart, 1967).

Glenday, Daniel, Hubert Guindon and Allan Turowetz, eds., *Modernization and the Canadian State* (Toronto: Macmillan of Canada, 1978).

Granatstein, J. L., Irving Abella, David J. Bercuson, R. Craig Brown and H. Blair Neatby, *Twentieth Century Canada: A Reader* (Toronto: McGraw-Hill Ryerson, 1986).

Granatstein, J.L. and Paul Stevens, *A Reader's Guide to Canadian History: Confederation to the Present* (Toronto: University of Toronto Press, 1982).

Harp, John and John Hofley, *Structured Inequality in Canada* (Scarborough: Prentice-Hall Canada, 1980).

Laxer, Gordon, *Open for Business: The Roots of Foreign Ownership in Canada* (Toronto: Oxford University Press, 1989).

Maslove, A.M. and S. Winer, eds., *Knocking at the Back Door* (Halifax: IRPP, 1987).

McDaniel, Susan A.M. *Canada's Aging Population* (Toronto: Butterworths, 1986).

Pal, Leslie A., *State, Class and Bureaucracy* (Kingston, Ont. and Montréal: McGill-Queen's University Press, 1988).

Pammett, Jon and Brian Tomlin, eds., *The Integration Question: Political Economy and Public Policy in Canada and North America* (Toronto: Addison-Wesley, 1984).

Panitch, L.V., ed., *The Canadian State: Political Economy and Political Power* (Toronto: University of Toronto Press, 1977).

Ponting, Rick, ed., *Arduous Journey, Canadian Indians and Decolonization* (Toronto: McClelland and Stewart, 1986).

Savoie, Donald J., *Regional Economic Development: Canada's Search for Solutions* (Toronto: University of Toronto Press, 1986).

Statistics Canada, *Population Projections for Canada, Provinces and Territories 1989–2011* (Ottawa, March 1990).

Trebilcock, M.J. *et al.*, eds., *Federalism and the Canadian Economic Union* (Toronto: University of Toronto Press, 1983).

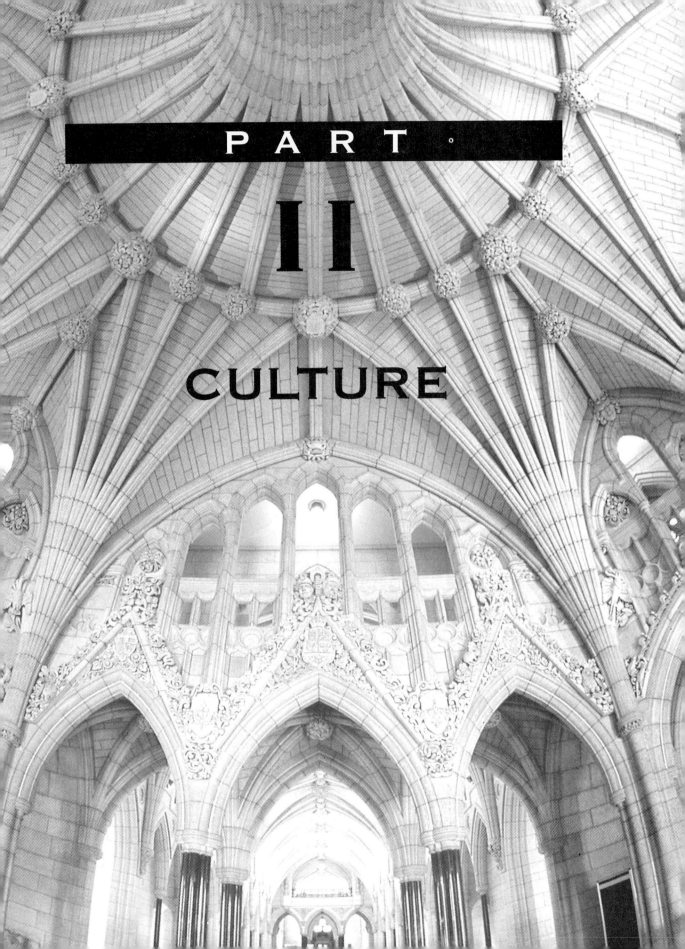

PART ·

II

CULTURE

POLITICAL CULTURE:
THE FABRIC OF CANADIAN SOCIETY

Certain myths about Canada and Canadians are common in foreign countries. Some are based on reality; some not. These include conceptions of Canadians as a solid, stolid, northern, reliable, prosperous, tough, not sexy people blessed by good government and policies and one of the world's greatest police forces.[1] At home, Canadians often characterize themselves as modest, hard-working, tolerant peacekeepers who distrust personal achievement among their peers. Potential Canadian heroes are regularly cut down to size. The story is told of a Nova Scotia fisherman who observed some lobsters, several of which appeared to be trying to climb out of a pail. "These are definitely Canadian lobsters," he concluded. "One is trying to crawl out so the rest are trying to pull it down."

This chapter looks beyond such impressionistic generalizations in the search to learn in a systematic way who Canadians are and what motivates them to act politically. It examines the attitudes and values that Canadians hold about themselves, their country and their system of government, all of which in turn affect their political behaviour.

Citizens of all countries develop perceptions and expectations of what their political system can and should do for them and what obligations they have in turn. This interaction provides the value structure within which political decisions are made. It delineates the accepted parameters of government and individual political activity and enables organizations and institutions to function coherently.

The political culture of Canada is like a colourful tapestry. When examined closely, a tapestry can be separated into different strands or elements. Only when these basic units are interwoven and viewed together as a whole is the unique design of the tapestry visible. This chapter aspires to understand three important strands of political culture in Canada in order to achieve a more meaningful view of the whole. But first, the concept of political culture must be clarified.

WHAT IS POLITICAL CULTURE?

Political culture is a relatively new concept in political science, and certainly one of the most controversial. The term was first coined in the United States in the 1950s and

---

[1] See for example "The Maiden Aunt Among Nations," *International Herald Tribune*, Paris, November 1,

only later applied in Canada.[2] It has been defined in a multitude of ways.[3]

We use the term **political culture** in this book to refer to the broad patterns of individual values and attitudes toward political objects. These may be concrete objects such as government institutions or national symbols such as the flag, but they may also be intangibles like power. In the latter case, it is important to understand how Canadians perceive the distribution of power between themselves and government, and what institutions or positions they view as the greatest sources of political power. Students of political culture therefore attempt to determine the degree of the individual citizen's knowledge and awareness of the political system, as well as the attitudes held about politics and political objects and the perceptions of the personal role in societal affairs.

Political culture, though but a small part of the general culture of a society, serves many purposes: it draws individuals together; supports thought, judgement and action; constitutes the character and personality of a community; differentiates it from other communities; and encourages its members to seek common objectives. What citizens know and feel about their political system will affect the number and kinds of demands they make on the system and also their responses to laws and political leadership. Political culture renders the government's decision-making processes acceptable by demarcating the boundaries within which it can legitimately act.

Political leaders often appeal to the appropriate values and standards of citizens in creating and justifying policies. For example, one of the most effective electoral slogans in recent decades in Canada was Pierre Trudeau's appeal for "a just society." This was an appeal to fundamental values in the electorate and an attempt to link the Liberal Party platform to those values.

Understanding the relationship between political culture and the political system assists in identifying and appreciating how political change can be effected. The extent to which values and beliefs are shared greatly affects the degree of national cohesion and stability in a country. Deep cleavages within a state over such issues as language or economic well-being obstruct the sharing of values and beliefs and contribute to political instability. Knowledge about the political attitudes of individual citizens helps to predict their political actions both inside the system through such means as voting and outside the electoral process through demonstrations, strikes and, even, violence.

The study of political culture is a multidisciplinary endeavour to which political science, sociology and psychology all contribute. Citizens' beliefs and values that formerly were ignored by political scientists are now scrutinized to determine their effect on voting behaviour and other forms of political participation or non-participation.

Political culture studies in Canada have been influenced, among others, by the empirical work of Gabriel Almond and Sidney Verba, American pioneers in the field. These

---

[2]   The concept was first introduced by Gabriel Almond in "Comparative Political Systems," *Journal of Politics*, vol 18, no. 3 (August 1956), pp. 391–409; reprinted in Gabriel Almond, *Political Development* (Boston: Little, Brown, 1970). For a concise history of the term "political culture" and its application to the Canadian situation see David Bell and Lorne Tepperman, *The Roots of Disunity* (Toronto: McClelland & Stewart. 1979), ch. 1.

[3]   See Sidney Verba, "Comparative Political Culture," in Lucian W. Pye and Sidney Verba, eds., *Political Culture and Political Development* (Princeton: Princeton University Press, 1965), p. 513; and Gabriel A. Almond and G. Bingham Powell, *Comparative Politics: A Developmental Approach* (Boston: Little, Brown, 1966), p. 50.

political scientists conducted the first statistically based cross-national study of political beliefs, symbols and values in an attempt to measure and compare national political attitudes.[4]

In the course of their study, Almond and Verba encountered serious difficulties with survey research, not all of which have been resolved. For example, large-scale opinion surveys and interviews are extremely expensive to administer and difficult to interpret. The answers elicited are not always truthful or thoughtful and can be affected by temporary events or personalities, and so may not reflect deeply held beliefs on which people will act. As well, an empirical approach to comparing states is limited because it lacks an historical or contextual dimension and therefore fails to recognize the constantly changing nature of political culture. Despite such limitations on this type of study, however, Almond and Verba effectively demonstrated that national cultures vary considerably with regard to beliefs about government and politics, and that these beliefs affect essential aspects of political behaviour.

As we shall see, social scientists have studied Canadian political culture in quite different ways. Some have employed empirical methodology, using surveys and questionnaires to learn about mass attitudes and behaviour. Others have carried out more qualitative research on the historical development of political ideas. Although they cannot be compared directly, and each has shortcomings, both methods contribute to an understanding of the Canadian political system.

THE THREE STRANDS OF CANADIAN POLITICAL CULTURE

We now return to our analogy of Canadian political culture as a tapestry composed of separate but interwoven parts. We can identify three major strands, each of which is valid and important but if taken in isolation gives only one part of the picture. For the sake of simplicity, in this chapter, the subject of political culture is divided into three sections that correspond to the three strands.

The first section examines Canadian political culture in terms of the values and attitudes common to *all* citizens of the state, searching out the roots of the Canadian heritage. It attempts to determine whether there is a common ideology behind Canadian political thought and, if so, what its origins may be. This broad level of interpretation also considers what characteristics distinguish Canadians from citizens of other countries. These pan-Canadian attitudes and values reveal one strand of Canadian political culture.

The second section examines the most important subcultures created by *ethnic* and *linguistic* cleavages in the country. The literature dealing with this strand of political culture focuses on three distinct groups: 1) the French Canadian community, whose cultural and linguistic differences were reinforced by historical, geographical and economic circumstances; 2) the broad range of members of ethnic and visible minorities who constitute the "English-speaking" sector, as it is generally called because of the official bilingual status of the country; and 3) the aboriginals who constitute yet another subculture of the Canadian community.

---

4   Gabriel A. Almond and Sidney Verba, *The Civic Culture* (Boston: Little, Brown, 1965). For comments on the above study see Gabriel A. Almond and Sidney Verba, eds., *The Civic Culture Revisited* (Boston: Little, Brown, 1980).

The third section examines *regionalism* in Canada. Regional boundaries may vary from one academic study to another, but they often coincide with political boundaries. According to such regional interpretations, the values and beliefs Canadians hold about their political system are conditioned by the distinct geographic and economic characteristics of the region in which they live. People of different origins and interests settled in areas which offered greatly varied resources and potential for industrial development. Canada's federal system of government has helped to reinforce and perpetuate these regions and the attitudes related to them. Individuals within the different regions often maintain unique attitudes toward national problems. How distinctive are the regions, and what evidence exists that there are several geographically based political cultures in Canada?

Because political values and beliefs are far from uniform across the state, some scholars argue that there is no such thing as a Canadian political culture, but rather several cultures based on ethnic or regional divisions. This chapter argues that a multitude of regional and ethnic political subcultures exist, but that they are tied together by the overarching values of a national culture. Subcultures can, and do, affect the dominant culture of the political community, sometimes acting as a disruptive force when group ties are stronger than loyalty to the whole. But they are only one part or strand of the country's cultural fabric.

We will examine the three strands of Canadian political culture under three headings: nation-state political culture, ethno-linguistic political cultures and regional political cultures.

NATION-STATE POLITICAL CULTURE

Nation-state political culture encompasses the values and attitudes that pertain to the entire Canadian political system. These values and attitudes include traditions of personal freedom and civil liberties, respect for the law and co-existence of heterogeneous communities that underlie the political system. These are the heart of Canada's political culture. There are deep historical roots to this political thought that forms the parameters of mainstream political culture in Canada.

HISTORICAL ROOTS: IDEOLOGY AND POLITICAL CULTURE

A few classic arguments about what traditional attitudes, if any, form the base of Canada's political system underlie all discussions of political culture. Before we look at these arguments in detail, it is important to clarify a confusion that sometimes arises between the terms "political culture" and "ideology." Both refer to political attitudes, values and beliefs, but ideologies are more coherent and explicit.[5] As used in this book, ideology is narrower in scope than political culture. **Ideology** refers to an explicit doctrinal structure, providing a particular diagnosis of the ills of society, plus an accompanying "action program" for implementing the prescribed solutions. Political culture, on the other hand, refers to vaguer, more implicit orientations whether or not they embrace any explicit, formal ideology.

Within Canadian society, for example, we can identify certain ideologies — socialism, conservatism and liberalism among them. Liberalism and conservatism originated in Europe in the nineteenth century as philosophers and thinkers struggled to create logical and con-

---

[5]   See Bell and Tepperman, *The Roots of Disunity*, ch. 1, for a brief examination of the concept of ideology as used by Karl Marx and Karl Mannheim.

sistent patterns of thought about how to restructure the medieval social and political order that new technological developments were rendering obsolete. **Liberalism** became the ideology of the rising commercial class that chafed under the confines of the old social order, while **conservatism** justified the positions of the aristocracy and church. Both ideologies spawned political parties. Liberal thought became dominant in the western world in the latter part of the nineteenth century, and for that reason some view the nineteenth century as the century of liberalism. **Socialism** developed slightly later, but, again, in response to fundamental changes in society: the technological advances of the industrial revolution had brought the growth of a large urban working class that existed in wretched conditions. Socialists sought to ameliorate the lot of these workers. By the beginning of the twentieth century, the ideological and party battlefield was a three-way contest as the socialist ideology produced Socialist, Labour and Communist parties in Europe.

There are several competing interpretations about the origin of political thought in Canada. Louis Hartz's book *The Liberal Tradition in America* is a source of many ideas concerning the traditional attitudes which underlie Canadian political culture.[6] This volume was published before the popularization of the concept of political culture and consequently the word "ideology" is used in this and subsequent writing on the topic in a way that differs from the usage in the present text — not as an action-oriented system of ideas, but as a relatively vague set of attitudes that form the foundation of political culture. Had the systematic discussion of political culture begun a decade later, Hartz and other authors might have substituted "political culture" for "ideology." As it is, much of the literature that followed Hartz, and that is discussed here, uses the latter term in the loose sense of a set of general principles.

The thesis put forward by Hartz, and later expanded by Kenneth McRae,[7] is that North America, like other societies founded by European settlement, is a "fragment society." According to Hartz, the New World societies based their political cultures on single European ideologies brought as "cultural baggage" during colonization. Immigrants to the new land did not represent all elements of the society that they had left. Institutions and myths set up and passed on by the founding peoples perpetuated those beliefs and values. McRae argues that, because it has two founding nations, Canada is a classic instance of a "two-fragment" society.

The settlers in New France represented one fragment, the feudal strain from France. As a result, a kind of "feudal catholicism" dominated rival ideologies there, and excluded others through expulsion or assimilation. The second fragment, English Canada, was very similar to its liberal American counterpart. English-speaking immigrants were predominantly liberal. In pre-revolutionary United States, the liberalism of the philosopher John Locke became the prevailing ideology. The beliefs, of which Locke was the primary spokesman, were based on the importance of the individual, free enterprise and the right of the individual to pursue personal interests without government interference. Loyalists who flooded into Canada at the time of the American revolution brought these liberal values with them — along with strong anti-American, pro-British sentiments.

---

6   Louis Hartz, *The Liberal Tradition in America* (New York: Harcourt Brace & World, 1953).

7   Louis Hartz, ed., *The Founding of New Societies* (New York: Harcourt Brace & World, 1964). See McRae's analysis in "The Structure of Canadian History" in Chapter 7. See also Kenneth D. McRae, "Louis Hartz's Concept of the Fragment Society and Its Applications to Canada," *Canadian Studies/Etudes Canadiennes*, vol. 5 (1978), pp. 17–30. For a strong argument that the Hartz framework is too abstract, see Walter C. Sodurlund, Ralph C. Nelson and Ronald H. Wagenberg, "A Critique of the Hartz Theory of Political Development as Applied to Canada," *Comparative Politics*, vol. 12, no. 1 (October 1979), pp. 63–85.

The differences that developed between English Canada and the United States were subtle and minor, according to Hartz and McRae. In both cases, the liberal ideology "congealed" before socialism developed in Europe; therefore, socialism did not take hold in North America. Liberal thought, with its belief in maximizing individual freedom and satisfaction of private desires, is widely diffused and dominant in the political culture of English North Americans. However, Hartz, McRae and others argue, Canadian thought is more conservative and collectivist than that of the United States.[8] For instance, Canadians feel strongly that the state is responsible for its citizens and is obligated to provide for their collective well-being. Americans, on the other hand, believe in non-interference by the government and the primacy of individual liberties.

George Grant, writing on this matter, lamented the widespread diffusion of liberal thought in Canada. He warned that the triumph of liberalism over conservatism and socialism in Canadian society represents the defeat of Canadian nationalism because it brings total conformity with the ideological structure of the United States.[9] Others have argued that Canadian anglophones have never been able to accept liberal ideology totally, because it was the natural culture of the Americans. They see the tension between adhering to the British connection and the fostering of antipathy toward the American culture, which was ideologically very similar to Canada's own, as the origin of a serious identity crisis for Canadians.[10]

Hartz's "fragment" theory of political culture considers the culture of founding groups as a kind of "genetic code," one that does not determine, but rather imposes boundaries on, later cultural developments. This approach offers the advantage of historical depth, since political thought is viewed as a phenomenon that develops over time, rather than being static. A drawback is that it fails to explain how fragment cultures survive, how they are transmitted to new immigrants and new generations. Why, for example, did new immigrant groups not establish new competing cultures? This question is considered in the next chapter.

Part of the Hartz and McRae thesis has been challenged by Gad Horowitz, who maintains that the respective heritages of Canada and the United States indeed are very different because Canadian liberalism did not "congeal" before British and European immigrants arrived in Canada in the late nineteenth and early twentieth centuries, bringing with them newer ideas from the old societies.[11] The fact that a socialist movement grew illustrates that, unlike the United States, Canada has had an enduring, though small, socialist "fragment." Thus, political thought in Canada was not totally buried beneath an unqualified liberalism. Even among the English-speaking group, Horowitz maintains, there is no single dominant ideology.

In a more recent study, Roger Gibbins and Neil Neville find that American respondents "displayed far greater attitudinal coherence, and stronger ideological linkages among sets of attitudes," than did English-Canadian respondents. French Québec respondents diverged even more from the Americans in that they demonstrated the "virtual absence of an ideological right." The authors conclude that there is evidence that the political culture of the United

---

[8] Gad Horowitz, "Conservatism, Liberalism and Socialism in Canada: An Interpretation," *CJEPS*, vol. 32, no. 2 (May 1966), pp. 143–71. See also Horowitz, "Notes on 'Conservatism, Liberalism and Socialism in Canada'," *CJEPS*, vol. XI, no. 2 (June 1978), pp. 383–99.

[9] George Grant, *Lament for a Nation: The Defeat of Canadian Nationalism* (Toronto: McClelland & Stewart, 1965) and also Grant, *Technology and Empire* (Toronto: Macmillan, 1970).

[10] Bell and Tepperman, *The Roots of Disunity*, ch. 3.

[11] Horowitz, "Conservatism, Liberalism and Socialism in Canada."

States "is more ideologically structured than that found in English Canada, and even more so than that found in francophone Québec."[12]

Other authors, such as Seymour Martin Lipset, conversely stress the conservative inheritance of the Canadian political culture.[13] Using census data and a comparative framework comprising the United States, Britain, Australia and Canada, he concluded that Canadian values are generally conservative, closer to those of Europeans than Americans. He bases this conclusion on evidence that Canadians are more elitist than their American neighbours. For example, he found deferential attitudes in Canada, evidenced by a widespread respect for political leaders, the law and public authority. He noted that compliance forces such as the RCMP and the military are generally viewed with respect, not as symbols of oppression as they are in many countries. Finally, Lipset found that, compared to the United States, Canada has a much lower per capita crime rate, and less political corruption — both of which facts, he believed, might be traced to elitist values.[14]

These and other Canadian–American differences, Lipset posited, are the result of very different "formative events" in the history of the two countries. Canada became independent through evolution, the United States through revolution. Canada had a relatively civilized westward expansion, not a "wild west." The religious traditions too, differed: Canada was settled predominantly by Anglicans and Roman Catholics rather than by Calvinists and fundamentalists.

Colin Campbell and William Christian have added to the debate by rejecting the view that the Canadian ideological system congealed in the way suggested by either McRae or Horowitz.[15] They maintain that the Loyalists introduced strains of Tory thought into English Canada. The Loyalist presence shifted the patterns of settlement in subsequent years so that more liberally inclined immigrants went to the United States, while more conservative individuals chose to remain under the British Crown. Close ties with Britain reinforced this Tory strain. Of course, French Canada was even further removed from the liberalism of John Locke. "Many of the immigrants to New France had left France at a time when liberal ideas were virtually nonexistent, and hence they brought with them to the new land an attitude to the state and to the society which was more tory/feudal than liberal."[16] As for Canadian socialism, Campbell and Christian contend that it was indigenous, a natural product of the post-First-World-War depression.

In yet another approach to the topic, Gordon Stewart traces the roots of Canada's political culture to the historical circumstances of Canada's colonial political system. Stewart builds on the work of Hartz and McRae by assessing the "workings of politics" during the colonial period. He concludes that the impact of the 1790–1850 formative period was so

---

[12] Roger Gibbins and Neil Neville, "Canadian Political Ideology: A Comparative Analysis," *CJPS*, vol. 18, no. 3 (Sept. 1985), pp. 577–98.

[13] Seymour Martin Lipset, "Revolution and Counterrevolution: Canada and the United States," in O. Kruhlak et al., eds., *The Canadian Political Process: A Reader* (Toronto: Holt, Rinehart and Winston, 1970), pp. 13–38. This article was first published in 1965. See also by the same author, *The First New Nation: The United States in Comparative Perspective* (New York: Basic Books, 1963).

[14] Lipset, "Revolution and Counterrevolution," p. 19.

[15] William Christian and Colin Campbell, *Political Parties and Ideologies in Canada: Liberals, Conservatives, Socialists, Nationalists*, 2nd ed. (Toronto: McGraw-Hill Ryerson, 1983). Also see Gibbins and Neville, "Canadian Political Ideology."

[16] Christian and Campbell, *Political Parties and Ideologies in Canada*, pp. 227–28.

powerful that "it created a distinctive and enduring pattern of Canadian politics."[17] Stewart argues persuasively that characteristics of the Canadian political culture such as patronage, influence, active government and intense localism were imported and firmly established during the colonial period and "went from strength to strength" after Confederation in 1867.

All of these interpretations suggest that Canadian political culture, unlike its American counterpart, was open to both conservative and socialist thought. Canadian political culture has a European flavour, placing a high value on tradition, order, historical continuity and group rather than individual interests. But, liberalism is, as David Bell and Lorne Tepperman aptly phrase it, "the ideology of the dominant class; it has the full force of the state, Church, media and educational system behind it: it has been trained into all of us."[18] It is our contention that liberal values, based on belief in a capitalist society, a market economy and the right to private property, dominate in Canada, although not to the exclusion of other perspectives.

OVERARCHING VALUES AND SYMBOLS

The political values of a country form the broad base of its political system. Though generally taken for granted and not articulated, they set the parameters of acceptable behaviour and underlie citizens' attitudes toward specific political objects, providing guidelines to define what is right or wrong, what is or is not valuable or acceptable. In Canada these include certain democratic rights and, as we have seen, liberal values with strains of socialist and conservative thought. These values are reflected in political symbols such as national emblems or institutions, and are often enshrined in the country's constitution.

In April 1982, the *Canadian Charter of Rights and Freedoms* was proclaimed. It became the first comprehensive statement of the fundamental values of Canadians to be entrenched in the Constitution. The preamble sets out the premise that "Canada is founded upon principles that recognize the supremacy of God and the Rule of Law." The Charter then proceeds to guarantee the fundamental rights of Canada's "free and democratic society." The implicit values of Canadians, as formalized in the *Charter*, are rooted in the western political tradition and the Judeo-Christian religious tradition.

Democracy, as we discussed in Chapter 1, is such an ambiguous concept that it has become a cliché to claim it as a basic value. It is espoused by all types of political systems. In Canada, democratic rights are outlined in the *Charter of Rights and Freedoms*. Embedded in the process of representative democracy are a great many values. One is the individual right to *fundamental freedoms*. These include 1) freedom of conscience and religion; 2) freedom of belief and expression, including freedom of the press and freedom of association; 3) freedom of peaceful assembly; and 4) freedom of association. Another democratic right is *equality* before and under the law, without discrimination. (These and other constitutionally approved values will be detailed in Chapter 5.) In the political sphere, equality presumes associated values such as *universal suffrage* and elections contested by competing political parties that give voters alternatives from which to choose. Another associated value is acceptance of the

---

[17]   Gordon T. Stewart, *The Origins of Canadian Politics: A Comparative Approach* (Vancouver: University of British Columbia Press, 1986) p. 92.

[18]   Bell and Tepperman, *The Roots of Disunity*, p. 232. For a discussion of dominant ideologies and counter-ideologies, see M. Patricia Marchak, *Ideological Perspectives on Canada*, 2nd ed. (Toronto: McGraw-Hill Ryerson, 1981).

rule of law, with civil rights for all citizens. Still another implicit value of representative democracy is *majority rule*. In Canada, governments are based on an ability to retain a majority of votes in the House of Commons, and Members of Parliament are elected in a system that gives credence to the majority principle but that, in fact, allows Members to be elected by a plurality.

It is deemed necessary to protect *minority rights* in Canada, so a few specific collective rights are also protected in the *Constitution*. These include French and English minority language rights in the federal and Québec legislatures and courts and Roman Catholic and Protestant minority education rights. Basic collective rights are generally considered inviolable, beyond even the right of the majority to change.

Comparing Canada to the United States can help to identify Canadian values. Lipset, for example, finds Canadians are more 1) aware of class, 2) elitist, 3) law abiding, 4) statist, 5) collectivity-oriented, and 6) particularistic than Americans.[19] He traces many of these differences to British values that remained strong in Canada long after they were abruptly curtailed in the United States by the American Revolution.

Canadians, Lipset maintains, tend to be more class-conscious than Americans, who see their social structure as more fluid. Canadian society is characterized more by elitism, hierarchy and deference. The educated elite is smaller, creating a more rigid conception of social hierarchy that can be viewed as a part of the feudal and monarchical traditions inherited from Britain and reinforced by the Roman Catholic and Anglican churches. Canadians also show more respect for authority than do Americans — for the law, police, RCMP — those whose duty it is to provide "peace order and good government."

Lipset notes that in politics Canadians prefer to divide their economy relatively evenly between the public and private sectors, whereas Americans promote a much stronger private sector. In Canada, the state is expected to interfere more in the economy, acting as a distributive force to share the benefits of being Canadian. Government expenditure in Canada accounts for more of the GDP than in the United States. Compared to the United States, Canada has a relatively comprehensive public health insurance system, many federal and provincial Crown corporations and a more comprehensive social security system. Canadians are much more willing than Americans to pay higher taxes in order to have such benefits. The belief that governments should interfere in the economy when necessary makes Canada a more "caring" society.

Canada also demonstrates more "particularistic" characteristics. This is especially true with respect to the integration of immigrants. Beyond Lipset's reasoning, it can be said that Canada encourages ethnic minorities to preserve their culture, so that Canada can be seen more as a "fruitcake" than the "melting pot" of the United States. Multiculturalism is a reflection of the ideal of tolerance that, though not always lived up to, is highly valued by Canadians. Compromise, too, is highly valued. This is evident in the workings of the federal system of government itself that seeks to accommodate diverse regional interests. It can also be seen in the international reputation Canada has earned as a peace-keeper under the United Nations' auspices.

These facets of the Canadian identity can be rounded out by a picture of Canadians as inhabitants of a huge, diverse country with a harsh northern climate, a federal system of government and a parliamentary system adopted from Britain with some modifications

---

[19] Seymour Martin Lipset, *Continental Divide* (New York: Routledge, 1990), p. 8.

inspired by the United States. Canada has evolved from aboriginal peoples and two European nations to a country that includes people of widely diverse heritage. The values of that heritage are expressed in official policies of bilingualism and multiculturalism.

The political values of a country are symbolized by such objects as flags, anthems, leaders, national holidays and historical heroes. These symbols help enforce respect for and emotional attachment to political institutions and can be a focal point for national unity. The name Canada itself symbolizes the aboriginal heritage of the country. "Kanata," the Huron-Iroquois word for "village" or "settlement" became "Canada" and by 1547 was used on maps to designate everything north of the St. Lawrence River. The first use of "Canada" as an official name was in 1791 when the Province of Québec was divided into the colonies of Upper and Lower Canada. In 1841 the two Canadas were reunited as the Province of Canada. At Confederation the new country assumed the official title the Dominion of Canada.[20]

Canada's passage from colony to nation is clearly reflected in the country's changing national symbols. In the early stages, they manifested a dual allegiance to Britain and Canada, but were gradually transformed to reflect national pride and unity without reference to Britain.

The evolution of the Canadian flag is perhaps the best illustration. At Confederation in 1867, Canada was granted permission to fly the red ensign, the flag of the British Merchant Navy. Attempts to replace it with a uniquely Canadian flag began as early as 1925 but did not succeed until four decades later. The transition was difficult. There were bitter debates both in and outside of Parliament concerning not only the specific choice of a replacement but also the basic question of whether Canada should jettison the flag that represented its historical attachment to Britain. In the end, of course, a flag was selected that features a red maple leaf, a distinctively Canadian symbol that had been adopted quite separately by both English and French Canadians well before Confederation, and that has deep historical roots in heraldic arms, regimental colours and literary publications.[21] The present flag was flown for the first time on February 15, 1965, and today many Canadians would not leave the country without a tiny facsimile on their lapels.

A similar evolution occurred in the acquisition of a Canadian coat of arms. Following World War I, representation was made to the Crown for a coat of arms that was uniquely Canadian. For years a controversy simmered over whether Canada should be symbolized by living green leaves or dead red ones. (Sir Robert Borden, then Prime Minister, thought green far more appropriate.) The dispute was not settled until 1957 when it was agreed that three red leaves would adorn the base of the shield, and a lion would proudly display a fourth.

Another progression to a specifically Canadian symbol occurred in the choice of the national anthem. The English version of "The Maple Leaf Forever" was quite unacceptable to French Canadians for the good reason that it referred to the French defeat at Québec. At the time of Confederation, therefore, "God Save the Queen" became the unofficial anthem. Finally, on July 1, 1980, "O Canada," based on music written by Calixa Lavallée a century earlier, was proclaimed Canada's national anthem. There have been many English versions, and disagreement over the wording often has been intense. Rather than inspiring loyalty and devotion, phrases that include "native land," "sons command," "true North," and "God" tend to give rise to resentment among immigrants, women, westerners, easterners and

---

[20] Department of the Secretary of State, *Symbols of Nationhood* (Ottawa: Supply and Services, 1991), p. 5.

[21] Strome Galloway, "Why the Maple Leaf is Our National Emblem," *Canadian Geographic* (June 1982). Red and white are the official colours of Canada, appointed by George V in 1921.

atheists. And of course, there are also royalists who still prefer "God Save the Queen." The French version of "O Canada," whose lyrics resemble the English only in that they refer to the same country, also contains some questionable wording.

It is important that a symbol of unity cause as little friction as possible, and Canadian efforts to compromise and please were evident at the formal adoption ceremony for the new anthem. There had been hot debate over whether the choir should sing first in English or in French. What was later called a "typically Canadian" solution was found: the choir was divided in two and sang both versions simultaneously.

Other minor conflicts and reminders of the British heritage have emerged from time to time with regard to other symbols. One concerns the country's official name, the Dominion of Canada. For most of our history, the first of July, Canada's national holiday, was known as Dominion Day. Although the word "Dominion" had been chosen explicitly by the Fathers of Confederation to mean sovereignty from sea to sea, many Canadians came to feel that it smacked of colonial dependence. With some trepidation because of the controversy the topic engendered, in November 1982, the Canadian Parliament finally changed the title of the holiday to Canada Day — in spite of the country's official name as reaffirmed by the *Constitution Act, 1982.*

In many countries, the constitution provides a concrete focus for pride and unity. This has only recently been the case in Canada. As with the other symbols we have discussed, the process of wrenching away from British ties and establishing a unique, Canadian symbol was not easy. The *British North America Act,* Canada's written constitution, was passed by the British Parliament. It was increasingly embarrassing to Canadians in the twentieth century as a national symbol both because it could not be amended without British approval and because it contained no formal guarantee of rights. The remedy finally came in the spring of 1982 when the revised *Constitution* was patriated. Like the American Constitution, the new document has begun to provide a common focus of pride for Canadians.

Two other predominant political symbols deserving of mention here, although they are discussed extensively in Chapter 5, are the monarch and her representative, the Governor General. Canada is a constitutional monarchy, and the role of Her Majesty Queen Elizabeth II as Sovereign of Canada and head of state is ceremonial. As Sovereign, she personifies the nation and is a symbol of allegiance, unity and authority. Federal and provincial legislators, cabinet ministers, public servants, military and police personnel and new citizens all swear allegiance to the Queen (not the flag or *Constitution*). Laws are promulgated and elections are called in the Queen's name. She is custodian of the democratic powers vested in the Crown. Historian W.L. Morton pointed out that allegiance to a monarch alleviates pressures for uniformity: "Anyone...can be a subject of the Queen and a citizen of Canada without in any way ceasing to be himself."[22] The monarchy, in this sense, is well adapted to the bilingual, multicultural, regional character of Canada.

Yet, the relevance of the English monarchy as an appropriate symbol for French Canadians has often been questioned. An overtly hostile reception for the Queen during a Royal visit to Québec in 1964, for example, prompted officials of the Québec government to take increasing pains to disassociate themselves and their constituents from the monarchy. It is evident that the ability of this institution to serve as a unifying symbol for Canada's two founding cultural groups is limited.

---

[22] Quoted in *Symbols of Nationhood*, ibid., p. 7.

The role of Governor General has evolved considerably from its British origins. The Queen's representative to Canada was originally selected by Britain. However, since 1936, the Governor General has been appointed only after consultation with the Canadian Cabinet, which means, in effect, that the Prime Minister makes the choice. The appointment of the first Canadian, Vincent Massey, came in 1952. This final transition to a Canadian Governor General nominated in Canada has increased the potential of the position as a unifying symbol for Canadians.

Finally, we must allude briefly to historical heroes as symbols of national pride and unity. Gradual evolution to nationhood, as opposed to dramatic revolution, does not produce charismatic hero material. And independence on the installment plan has no glamour as a national event. To compound the difficulties, French and English Canadians each tend to cultivate their own heroes, based on different interpretations of history. In fact, Canadian heroes often gained reputations in their own communities by resisting or defeating their counterparts. The dearth of common national heroes and events around which to rally has undoubtedly encouraged substitutions from south of the border, a problem discussed more fully in the following chapter. F.R. Scott aptly described this situation in a satirical poem entitled "National Identity":[23]

The Canadian Centenary Council
Meeting in La Reine Elizabeth
To seek those symbols
Which will explain ourselves to ourselves
Evoke unlimited responses
And prove that something called Canada
Really exists in the hearts of all
Handed out to every delegate
At the start of the proceedings
A portfolio of documents
On the cover of which appeared
In gold letters
   not
A Mare Usque Ad Mare
   not
E Pluribus Unum
   not
Dieu et Mon Droit
   but
Courtesy of Coca-Cola Limited.

POLITICAL ATTITUDES

Overarching values set the general parameters of political behaviour in Canada. Specific attitudes toward political objects are more differentiated than basic values and more fleeting, but they may be more immediate determinants of political behaviour. Three types of attitudes can be distinguished: cognitive, affective and evaluative.[24] **Cognitive** attitudes reflect

---

[23] From *The Collected Poems of F.R. Scott*, John Newlove, ed. 1981. Used by permission of the Canadian Publishers, McClelland & Stewart Ltd., Toronto.

[24] Almond and Verba identified and elaborated on these three types of political orientations in their study, *The Civic Culture*.

the degree of knowledge, accurate or otherwise, that citizens have about political objects. **Affective** attitudes reflect the degree of citizens' attachment to or rejection of the political objects that surround them: how do Canadians feel about their country, their government or the political symbols we have discussed? **Evaluative** attitudes reflect the moral judgements made by individuals about the "goodness" or "badness" of political objects. The three types of attitudes are interrelated and often difficult to distinguish in practice.

Attitudes toward specific political issues of the day, as opposed to more permanent political objects, are ephemeral. Issues change and so do people, but institutions and symbols remain. These transient attitudes are sometimes defined as public opinion, and although they can be important in determining short-term behaviour they are less helpful in understanding the overall political culture of a country.

With respect to cognitive attitudes, Canadians appear to have the basic information necessary to allow them to operate effectively at both provincial and federal levels of government. They also demonstrate a high degree of affect for both their country and their province of residence.[25]

FIGURE 3.1   NATIONAL INSTITUTIONS 1990: LEVELS OF PUBLIC RESPECT AND CONFIDENCE

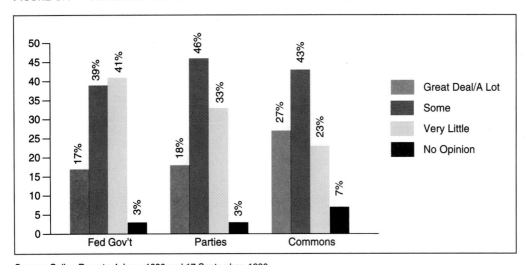

Source: *Gallup Reports*, 4 June, 1990 and 17 September, 1990.

Despite these positive attitudes, however, there are disquieting findings about the nature of affective evaluative attitudes toward objects in the Canadian political system.[26] (See Figure 3.1.) In the 1970s, a study by Clarke et al. found that Canadians lacked faith or trust that politicians and the political system would respond positively to their interests.[27] Public cynicism continued to grow in the 1980s, fuelled by government scandals and mismanagement. A 1992 survey concluded that "Canadian political discontent is at its highest since polling began."

---

[25] Harold D. Clarke, Jane Jenson, Lawrence LeDuc and Jon H. Pammett, *Political Choice in Canada* (Toronto: McGraw-Hill Ryerson, 1979). For a recent study of the sources of political knowledge, both factual and conceptual, see Ronald D. Lambert, James E. Curtis, Barry J. Kay and Steven D. Brown, "The Social Sources of Political Knowledge," *CJPS*, vol. 21, no. 2 (June 1988) which is discussed in Chapter 4.

[26] Clarke, et al., *Political Choice*, ch. 3.

[27] Ibid.

FIGURE 3.2 NATIONAL INSTITUTIONS 1979–92: LEVELS OF RESPECT AND CONFIDENCE

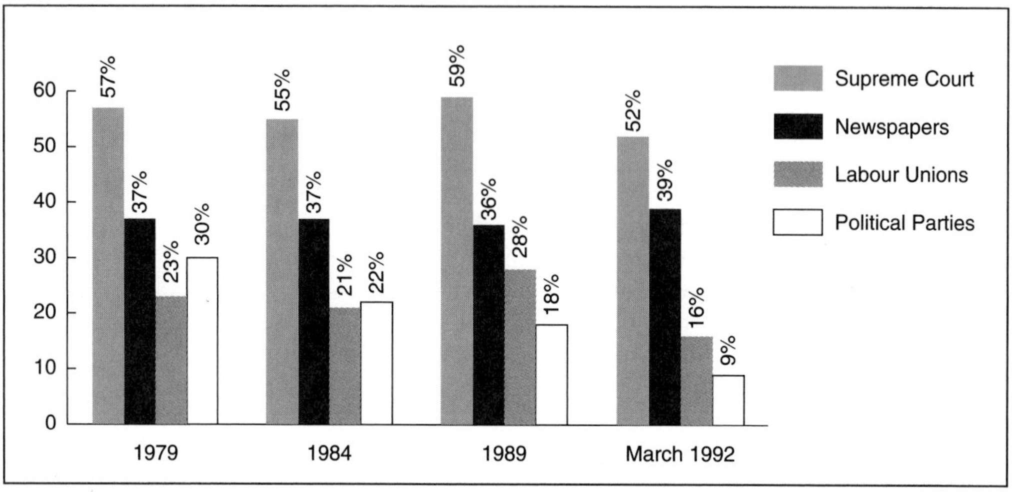

Respondents were asked to rate how much respect and confidence they had for the institution listed. Scores are for those who answered "A Great Deal" or "A Lot," as opposed to "Some" or "No Opinion."

Source: *Gallup Report*, 16 March 1992.

Questioned about honesty and ethical standards of MPs in 1989, for example, Canadians ranked MPs 11th of 12 professions, below labour unions and building contractors. [28]

Declining respect and confidence in government institutions and politicians was evident in the fall of 1992 when the Mulroney government called a national referendum on a set of constitutional proposals. The proposals were widely rejected despite massive financial and political support from all provincial governments and the major political parties. As Figure 3.1 shows, none of the major institutions, Parliament, political parties or the federal government commanded high respect at that time. Respect for political parties dropped from 30 percent in 1979 to only 9 percent in March 1992 (see Figure 3.2).

In 1991, André Blais and Elizabeth Gidengil also found political discontent to be at a historically high level in Canada.[29] They discovered that 49 percent of Canadians did not trust the federal government, and that 52 percent even believed that "quite a few of the people running the government are a little bit crooked." Two government commissions in the early 1990s also confirmed a high degree of discontent and considerable lack of confidence in politicians and institutions. The Citizen's Forum on Canada's Future (the Spicer Commission) and the Royal Commission on Electoral Reform and Party Financing both witnessed an outpouring of criticism that Canada lacked responsible leadership, that current leaders were not trustworthy, that Canada lacked strong leaders, and so on.[30]

---

[28] Peter Dobell and Byron Berry, "Anger at the System: Political Discontent in Canada," *Parliamentary Government*, no. 39 (1992), p. 5.

[29] Andre Blais and Elizabeth Gidengil, "Representative Democracy: the Views of Canadians (1991), Royal Commission on Electoral Reform and Party Financing," *Reforming Electoral Democracy*, vol. 1 (Ottawa: Supply and Services, 1992), p. 225.

[30] Citizen's Forum on Canada's Future, *Report to the People and Government of Canada* (Ottawa, Supply and Services , 1991) and Royal Commission on Electoral Reform and Party Financing, *Reforming Electoral Democracy*, vol. 1 (Ottawa: Supply and Services, 1992).

Such attitudes can fluctuate over a relatively short period and are not uniform across the population; however, they have been persistent in recent years. Some negative emotion was undoubtedly due to the economic recession and unpopularity of policies such as the free trade deal with the United States and the Goods and Service Tax. Cynical attitudes do not, of course, preclude diffuse support for the government in Canada or hamper political participation at either level of government. Neither do they indicate a rejection of government authority. Individual Canadians are quite willing to comply with basic political laws, and major political groups rarely offer unconditional resistance. Acts of Parliament are automatically considered legitimate and are carried out voluntarily by citizens without the need for coercive security forces.[31] Crimes against the state are rare, even when laws are unpopular.[32]

Reproduced with permission, *The Globe and Mail*.

BEHAVIOUR: PARTICIPATION AND EFFICACY

Values and attitudes are often difficult to ascertain. Impressionistic studies and survey research are helpful, but as we have noted both have limitations in the answers they can provide. Another approach is to deduce from people's behaviour the attitudes and values that make

---

[31] A good deal of research has been done on support for the Canadian political community and the national political regime. See especially Allan Kornberg and Harold D. Clarke, eds., *Political Support in Canada: The Crisis Years* (Durham, N.C.: Duke University Press, 1983).

[32] The empirical data suggest that Canada experiences an incidence of violence comparable to that of most industrialized democracies. Robert J. Jackson, Michael J. Kelly and Thomas H. Mitchell, "Collective Conflict, Violence, and the Media in Canada," Ontario Royal Commission on Violence in the Communications Industry, Report. Volume 5: *Learning from the Media* (Toronto: Queen's Printer, 1977).

them act in a certain way. One of the best deductive methods is to examine the extent to which people *participate* in the political world about them and to generalize from this behaviour. The individual's self-perception as a political object is an important factor here, because self-esteem can affect the degree and intensity of participation.

Relative to most democratic countries, Canadians participate very readily in electoral politics; about 75 percent vote regularly in federal and provincial elections. French Canadians are less active politically at the national level than English Canadians, but more active at the provincial level. Corresponding to this relatively high level of electoral participation, feelings of political efficacy with regard to voting are very high: Canadians feel that their individual vote is important. Their reasons for feeling they should vote are mixed. Some are committed to the principles of democracy and a feeling of civic duty; others feel it important to render judgement on a government or certain politicians, perhaps seeking to punish parties or politicians by voting them out of office.

Apart from the act of voting, however, overall feelings of political efficacy are low. As a result, Canadians are said to have a "quasi-participant" political culture.[33] Canadians are not confident that they can understand and affect the political process. In general, they express feelings of distrust, cynicism and powerlessness in the face of government domination by powerful interests. But Canadians are not alone in harbouring these sentiments. Comparative analysis of responses to similar questions raised in surveys undertaken in Canada and the United States indicates that, on most items, Canadians have as high a sense of efficacy as Americans and similar levels of trust in government.

Active participation in politics beyond casting a ballot is low in Canada.[34] Only 4 or 5 percent of the electorate participate regularly in political parties or hold elected office at either the federal or provincial level. Unless the level of interest is artificially high because of colourful personalities or issues, Canadians retain only a vague spectator interest in politics and rarely show strong ideological commitment. Political protest, even peaceful demonstration, is engaged in by a very small percentage of Canadians. Moreover, political participation aside from voting is very uneven across different groups in Canadian society. The higher an individual's social status, the more likely he or she is to participate politically. The most active participants tend to be wealthy, well-educated, male, middle-aged Protestant members of the English "charter group." Women participate less than men, and that pattern does not appear to be changing quickly.[35] Lower socio-economic and less well-educated groups participate only infrequently. Participation in parties and elections is discussed further in Chapters 10 and 11.

Although there is a drastic drop in political participation when voting is excluded, it must be noted that only 25 to 30 percent of Canadians confine their participation exclusively to casting a ballot. About 60 percent of the public participate in at least one political activity in addition to voting. Although Canadians are less active in political life than would befit the

---

[33] See Robert Presthus, *Elite Accommodation in Canadian Politics* (Toronto: Macmillan, 1973). Rick Van Loon uses the term "spectator-participant" in "Political Participation in Canada," *CJPS*, vol. III, no. 3 (September 1970), p. 397.

[34] For a survey of participation in Canada see William Mischler and Harold D. Clarke "Political Participation in Canada," in Michael S. Whittington and Glen Williams, eds., *Canadian Politics in the 1990s,* 3rd ed. (Toronto: Nelson, 1990), pp. 158–81.

[35] Barry J. Kay, Ronald D. Lambert, Steven D. Brown and James E. Curtis, "Gender and Political Activity in Canada, 1965–1984," *CJPS*, vol. XX, no. 4 (Spring 1987), pp. 851–64.

democratic ideal, they are considerably closer to that goal than citizens of the majority of the world's states.[36] Unfortunately, the least influential in society — the poor, the young and the old, for example — participate the least in the political process, and exhibit the least political efficacy.

ETHNO-LINGUISTIC CLEAVAGES AND POLITICAL CULTURE

Under the veneer of national political culture in Canada, as in all societies, there are many political subcultures that do not share all of the values and attitudes discussed above. Among the most significant of these subcultures are ethnic groups. **Ethnicity** is primarily a subjective phenomenon, although it is often reinforced by different customs, language, dialect and cultural heritage, and sometimes distinct racial or physical characteristics. **Ethnic origin** refers to the ethnic or cultural group(s) to which an individual's ancestors belonged; it pertains to the ancestral roots or origins of the population and not to place of birth, citizenship or nationality.

Ethnic group members maintain their distinctiveness through such means as preserving their mother tongue, attending an ethnic-oriented house of worship or maintaining certain customs. Ethnically, of course, there is no such thing as a Canadian race. If an original decision had been made to engulf minorities in a unitary rather than a federal system of government, cultural diversity might not have been sustained, and perhaps ethnic groups would not have the political significance they do today. In Canada, cultural pluralism has also been encouraged by the size of the country, its sparse population and, particularly, the federal system of government.

There are three major ethno-linguistic cleavages in Canada that profoundly affect the country's political culture. The first, between the two founding European nations, French and English, is based on the conception of Canada as a bicultural, bilingual state. The second important division is within the large non-francophone majority, and is based on the conception of Canada as a multicultural country. The third concerns the country's original inhabitants, the aboriginals, who today are struggling for recognition and self-government. We shall consider each in turn.

HISTORICAL ROOTS OF THE FRENCH-ENGLISH CLEAVAGE

We have discussed Hartz's and McRae's concept of New France as a fragment founded by bearers of a feudal tradition who had left France before the liberal revolution. From 1663, when it came under royal control, the political development of the colony was dominated by French-style absolutism, modified somewhat by circumstances in the New World. When the British conquest ended French rule, most merchants and officials returned to France, and the forces for modernization and change departed with them. Isolated from the turmoil of the French Revolution, the culture of New France was enveloped and preserved by a few remaining institutions: the Catholic church, the French language and civil law and the feudal landholding system.

---

[36] Mishler, "Political Participation and Democracy," p. 178.

So tightly sealed was French Canadian society in Québec that most of the francophone population there today are descendants of the original 10 000 French colonists who arrived before 1760.[37] From this inheritance of political thought, historical events produced a political subculture very different from its English Canadian counterpart. The most visible differences are language, a civil law code unique to Québec and traditions, myths and heroes based on early Québec history. Less tangible is the fear of assimilation that permeates politics because of the francophone minority status.

In direct contrast to the encapsulated and preserved feudal fragment in New France, Canadian anglophone society was open to outside influences. An extremely high percentage of the early inhabitants of the northern British colonies were Loyalists who fled the American Revolution; indeed, their numbers — 30 000 to 60 000 — submerged the fewer than 15 000 English colonists already in Canada. The Loyalists brought with them attitudes still prevalent in English Canadian society: some aspects of the liberal American tradition, but also anti-American sentiments and a corresponding loyalty to the British Crown. Some authors have termed this bond with Britain a colonial mentality, "an artificial loyalty to the Crown that grew ever more strained as new Canadians without British origins poured into the population."[38] Arguably the net effect was to delay the development of a unified and coherent nation.

As noted in Chapter 2, one fundamental difference between the French and English in Canada lies in each group's understanding of the term "nation." To French Canadians the word "nation" means "people" or "society." To English Canadians it means "nation-state," the combined people of a country. Léon Dion's description of this difference is tripartite: francophones see Canada as two distinct societies or nations, one French-speaking and the other English-speaking; these two societies are qualitatively equal in every way; and the Canadian Constitution should accordingly give special status to francophones within federal political institutions and also to the province of Québec.[39] Thus, while it is thought that many anglophone Canadians view Canada as one nation, with an enclave of French Canadians in Québec, francophones begin with the dualistic conception of a political system composed of "Québec" and "the rest of the country." This conception of Québec as a separate "nation" can be traced in the history of the province.

In 1867 the Fathers of Confederation created what has been called a "political nation," giving Canada every power a political nation needed to thrive. George Etiènne Cartier negotiated for Québec and gave his strong support to this vision. He saw it as the responsibility of the provinces to preserve what he called "cultural nations" — cultures imported from England, Ireland, Scotland and pre-revolutionary France. After Cartier's death, however, his Québec critics claimed that Confederation was really a "compact" between French and English nations. This myth flourished, nourishing the notion of "two founding nations" that provided French Canadians with a collective claim to equality rather than simple minority status within Canada. The word "compact" also implies a right to secede from the bargain.

Whether Canada is one nation or two is obviously a matter of definition. Constitutional expert Eugene Forsey expressed the situation this way: "In the ethnic, cultural, sociological

---

37   Jacques Henripin and Yves Peron, "The Democratic Transition in the Province of Quebec," in D.V. Glass and Roger Revelle, eds., *Population and Social Change* (London: Edward Arnold, 1972), pp. 213–31.

38   Bell and Tepperman, *The Roots of Disunity*, p. 63.

39   Léon Dion, *Québec: The Unfinished Revolution* (Montréal: McGill-Queen's University Press, 1976), p. 180.

sense, Canada is 'two nations'... In the political, legal, constitutional sense, Canada is one nation."[40]

It is generally accepted today that the Confederation arrangement was an implicit bargain between French and English to create one strong political unit, a country that would protect the rights and assist the advancement of two culturally diverse peoples. English- and French-language communities were to be protected. But it did not work that way in practice. From the outset, English was a legal language in the Québec legislature and courts. In the other provinces, however, the practice until the 1940s was for English-speaking Canadians, wherever they were in the majority, to deprive French-speaking Canadian minorities of public school facilities in their native langage, and to refuse them the use of their language in government institutions.

Several historical crises marked the breakdown of good will between English and French in Canada and stimulated the growth of frustration and eventually separatist movements. Although they are given relatively cursory recognition by Canadians outside Québec, French Canadians dwell upon these events and find in them the emotional justification for the need to defend themselves as a distinct, cultural minority in Canada. They include the Manitoba schools question (1885–96), conscription issues during both World Wars (1917, 1942) and the rejection of the Meech Lake constitutional accord (1987). These events and the growth of nationalism in Québec are discussed fully in Chapters 5 and 6.

FRENCH CANADIANS: A CULTURAL NATION

Today, just under 24 percent of Canadians claim French as their mother tongue (Figure 3.3, 1991 census). They are concentrated mainly in Québec (81 percent) with other significant group-

FIGURE 3.3 PERCENTAGE DISTRIBUTION BY MOTHER TONGUE OF THE POPULATION, CANADA 1991

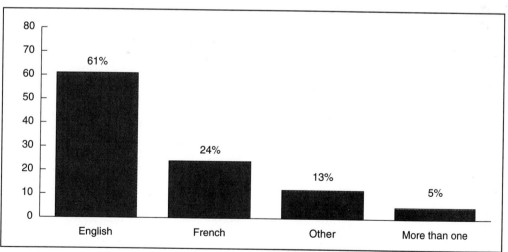

Source: *1991 Census Highlights: The Daily* (Ottawa: Statistics Canada, September 15, 1992). Reproduced by authority of the Minister responsible for Statistics Canada 1993.

---

[40] Eugene Forsey, "Canada, One Nation or Two?" *Le Canada, expérience ratée...ou réussie?* (Québec: Congrés des affaires canadiennes, 1962), pp. 55–7.

ings residing in Ontario and New Brunswick. Over the years, the French Canadian culture has developed and thrived, but not without political controversy with the rest of Canada.

Until the 1960s, the Roman Catholic Church was fairly successful in directing and fostering attitudes of withdrawal and non-participation among French Canadians in Québec. They were concerned mainly with *la survivance*, cultural preservation, that necessitated resistance to change and withdrawal from external influences that would alter the composition of francophone society. French Canadians were content, even within their provincial government, to resist change rather than control it. They neither participated as a group in the political affairs of the country nor even exploited to any degree the control that they, the majority, could have wielded within the provincial jurisdiction.

The situation began to change in the early 1960s, when the election of the Jean Lesage government on a *"maîtres chez nous"* platform revealed a change in the character and aspirations of French Canadian society — the beginning of the "Quiet Revolution." The influence of the Catholic church declined dramatically. Québec francophones had come to believe that if they were to maintain their identity, they had to take control of their own destiny. The cultural spectrum of Québec politics expanded from defensive, conservative nationalism to ideologies of liberalism, socialism and more radical thought.

The Quiet Revolution soon became a challenge to Canadian federalism (*see* Chapter 6). The Royal Commission on Bilingualism and Biculturalism confirmed that the state of affairs established in 1867, and never before seriously questioned, was being rejected by Québécois. The strategy of *la survivance* had been replaced by *l'épanouissement* — in this case, a desire to develop French Canadian culture to its full extent and participate actively in fulfilling their aspirations.[41] Thus, the relationships between francophones and anglophones and between the federal and Québec governments have changed over time. Until the Quiet Revolution, the needs and aspirations of both communities and governments were relatively congruent; since then they have often diverged or conflicted.

During the 1960s, the federal Liberal government responded to the Quiet Revolution by declaring Canadian federal instituions to be officially bilingual. It increased the number of bilingual civil servants in the government and improved government services in both languages. In 1973, for example, many public service positions were designated bilingual, a process that continues to this day.

The rise in Québec national consciousness directed and channelled economic, social and political change in that province. The provincial government became the focus of political modernization, assuming a much greater role in the economy and society than ever before. Traditional socioeconomic patterns gradually shifted as the anglophone business elite left the province in great numbers in the 1970s and francophones began to occupy an ever larger proportion of the economic middle class in Québec. A prolific and dynamic francophone business elite eventually moved beyond Québec into other Canadian and international markets. By the mid-1980s "francophone firms represented ten of the fifty largest financial institutions in Canada and five of the twenty-five largest insurance companies."[42] Francophones today control a greater portion of the province's economic base and hold more senior management positions than ever before.[43]

---

[41] For a more detailed discussion of the Quiet Revolution see Kenneth McRoberts, *Quebec: Social Change and Political Crises*, 3rd ed. (Toronto: McClelland & Stewart, 1988).

[42] McRoberts, *Quebec*, p. 428.

[43] A report on the use of French released by the Québec government and quoted in the *Globe and Mail*, June 19, 1991, pp. 1 and 2, noted that francophones held 58 percent of senior management positions in 1988 compared to 34.6 percent in 1969.

At the same time, however, language issues have become increasingly politicized. By the mid 1980s the province's economy was in decline, and language policy was seen as a contributing factor because restrictive policies had driven large numbers of English out of Montréal.[44] Because of the importance of language in French–English relations, we turn next to an examination of language policy and then to an evaluation of nationalist attitudes in Québec.

LANGUAGE POLICY: A SOURCE OF DIVISION

Canada's Confederation arrangement was essentially a bargain between the French and English in British North America to create one strong political unit — a country that would protect the rights and assist the advancement of two culturally diverse peoples. On this basis, linguistic duality was embedded in the *British North America Act* of 1867.[45] This duality has had both positive and negative repercussions for Canadians. For decades language has been at the root of most social and political tensions between French- and English-speaking Canadians. At the same time, however, the establishment of two official languages has provided one of Canada's most distinctive traits and, for many, has enriched the experience of being Canadian.[46]

The legal basis for language regulation in Canada is divided across three spheres — the *Constitution*, federal law and provincial law.

Constitutional law establishes the framework of language use and development. As early as 1867, the *BNA Act* specified that Parliament and the Québec National Assembly were to function in French and English. Much later, in 1982, the *Charter of Rights and Freedoms* enshrined English and French as the two official languages of Canada and the province of New Brunswick for matters pertaining to Parliament, the New Brunswick legislature and courts in both jurisdictions.

Minority language rights are enshrined in section 23 of the *Charter*. It stipulates that citizens of Canada whose first language is that of the French or English minority of the province in which they reside (mother tongue clause), or who have received their instruction in one of these languages in Canada, have the right to have their children educated in that language wherever numbers warrant. The clause does not apply to non-Canadian immigrants who move to Québec. These rights are entrenched. In other words, to amend the minority-language guarantees in the *Constitution*, all provinces and the federal government would have to agree. As well, governments cannot use the "notwithstanding clause" to exempt the application of the *Charter* guarantees.[47] In early 1993, Parliament and the New Brunswick legislature passed a constitutional amendment guaranteeing equal status for New Brunswick's French- and English-language communities.[48]

---

[44] See Alain G. Gagnon and Mary Beth Montcalm, *Québec Beyond the Quiet Revolution* (Toronto: Nelson, 1990), chs. 1 and 8.

[45] A good discussion of the foundations of the English/French relationship is found in Roberto Perin "Answering the Québec Question: Two Centuries of Equivocation," pp. 14–30 in Daniel Drache and Roberto Perin, *Negotiating with a Sovereign Québec* (Toronto, James Lorimer, 1992); or Gagnon and Montcalm, op. cit., ch. 6. Also see William D. Coleman, "From Bill 22 to Bill 101: the Politics of Language under the Parti Québécois" *CJPS* (Sept. 1981), pp. 459–85.

[46] See Marcel Côté's introduction to *Survival: Offical Language Rights in Canada* (Toronto: CD Howe Institute, 1992), p. 8. This book, No 10 in The Canada Round: A Series on the Economics of Constitutional Renewal, edited by John McCallum, presents a debate between English and French points of view.

[47] See Chapter 5 for a discussion of this clause.

[48] See Chapter 5.

In the federal domain (after the publication of the Report of the Royal Commission on Bilingualism and Biculturalism) the federal Liberal government responded to the Quiet Revolution in Québec by declaring Canadian federal institutions to be officially bilingual. This was accomplished in the *Official Languages Act* of 1969. This *Act* was amended and updated in 1988, extending the reach and primacy of the earlier version and bringing it into conformity with the *Charter of Rights and Freedoms*. The *Official Languages Act* has two parts: it regulates bilingualism in federal institutions and in federally regulated institutions like banks and airlines; and it provides a framework for promoting the official languages. For example, it gives Canadians the right to be served by federal institutions in the language of their choice where "significant demand" exists; provides federal employees with the right to work in the language of their choice; and attempts to provide an equitable distribution of English- and French-Canadians in the public service.

Provincial language legislation has often been controversial. In 1870, the *Manitoba Act* created that province on a bilingual basis, but from 1890 to a Supreme Court judgement in 1979 that law was ignored. Several provinces have language legislation, and all provinces except Newfoundland and British Columbia have legislation on minority language rights. Ontario, for example, has a *French Language Services Act*, Bill 8, which outlines what services must be provided to francophone minorities in the province.

Sometimes provincial legislation goes further than federal law, and sometimes provincial leglislation and federal law conflict. The *Charter of Rights and Freedoms* in 1982 expanded the basis for legal challenges about language rights on constitutional grounds. Since it came into effect, many cases have been brought to the Supreme Court to challenge provincial governments and force them to accommodate language minorities in their laws and schools.

In March 1990, the Supreme Court gave its first ruling based on Section 23 of the *Charter of Rights and Freedoms*. The court supported the rights of francophone parents in Edmonton to manage and control their own publicly financed French-language schools. It called Section 23 of the *Charter* "a linchpin in this nation's commitment to the values of bilingualism and biculturalism," saying it was designed "to correct, on a national scale," the progressive erosion of minority official language groups. But it temporized its remarks. It concluded that rights of members of minorities to an education in their own language were subject to practical financial constraints.[49] A later Supreme Court ruling in March, 1993 rebuked Manitoba for not complying with the *Constitution* and ordered the province to give exclusive control over French-language education to the province's francophones "without delay."

ATTITUDES IN QUÉBEC CONCERNING LANGUAGE

Language permeates politics in Québec. The fear that French language and culture is in decline in Canada, or may soon be, is widespread. Some facts back up this argument. In 1992, Québec's fertility rate was 1.5 children for every woman, compared to 1.7 for all of Canada. A rate of 2.1 is needed to maintain the current population level nationally and provincially. It is not surprising, therefore, that Québec nationalists claim the province must attract, hold, and integrate immigrants into the French culture and language.

Motivated by such demographic concerns, in the 1960s Québec authorities began to assert and protect the province's distinctive character. A spiral of restrictive language laws began with an attempt to force immigrants to have their children educated in French. In 1968,

---

[49] *Globe and Mail*, March 16, 1990.

the Catholic school board of St-Léonard in suburban Montréal attempted to force children of allophones (those whose mother-tongue is neither English nor French) to attend French language schools, denying English education to its largely Italian population. The next year, the provincial Union Nationale government introduced Bill 63 that confirmed the right of parents in Québec to educate their children in the language of their choice.

Nationalists resented Bill 63, and to mollify them, in 1974 (following the Québec Gendron Report that advocated strong measures to support French in the province), the government of Premier Robert Bourassa passed Bill 22. It declared French to be the official language of Québec. French was given primacy in the work force but linguistic dualism was preserved in several areas. The bill required children of immigrants to be enrolled in French schools, except for children who could demonstrate a sufficient knowledge of English.

In 1977, under the new Parti Québécois government of René Lévesque, Bill 101 was introduced as the *Charter of the French Language in Québec*. It was much stronger in its promotion of French than Bill 22 had been, and circumscribed the use of English. For example, it restricted access to English schools. Regardless of where a child came from — even from another province within Canada — he or she had to be educated in French unless one of the parents had been educated in an English school *in* Québec. It also took measures to make French the language of commerce and business. Any company with more than fifty employees was instructed to conduct all internal business in French. Furthermore, English, or even bilingual, commercial signs were to be illegal by 1981. And towns, rivers and mountains that bore English names were to be renamed in French.

In the mid 1980s, due to considerable court challenges, francophone attitudes toward enforcement of Bill 101 began to soften. Bill 57, passed in 1984, incorporated into Bill 101 guarantees for the survival of English institutions, modifying certain requirements for bilingualism and rules for internal and inter-institutional communications. These special arrangements were meant to encourage businesses to stay in Montréal.[50] On December 22, 1987, the Québec Court of Appeal ruled that the ban on languages other than French on commercial signs violated freedom of expression as protected by the Canadian *Charter of Rights and Freedoms*, and also that of Québec. The next year, in December 1988, the Supreme Court ruled on Section 58 of Bill 101, finding it violated both the Canadian and Québec guarantees of freedom of expression. The sign law was ruled invalid.[51] Nationalists were enraged and feared a massive unravelling of the Québec language charter.

Almost immediately, Premier Robert Bourassa invoked the notwithstanding clause of the *Canadian Charter of Rights and Freedoms* that allows the federal Parliament or any provincial legislature to pass legislation infringing on individual rights. (Such legislation has an automatic "sunset clause" that causes the legislation to lapse after five years unless it is re-passed in the legislature concerned.) Using the notwithstanding clause, the National Assembly passed Bill 178, a controversial sign law that expanded on Bill 101. Bill 178 banned languages other than French on *outdoor* signs, but allowed languages other than French on *indoor* signs,

---

[50] Gagnon and Montcalm, p. 187.

[51] The Supreme Court presented two judgements: one was a challenge to Section 58 of Bill 101 by five businesses that questioned the rule that commercial sign laws in Québec had to be in French only. The second was the case of Allan Singer dealing with the legality of English-only signs. In the first case, the Supreme Court declared that the sign law was a violation of freedom of expression and stated that a ban on other languages was not needed to defend the French language. In the second case, the court ruled that the province was entitled to pass a law requiring the predominant display of the French language.

providing that French was predominant. Use of the notwithstanding clause made this action constitutionally valid and the Supreme Court could not intervene. Predictably, language wars within the province of Québec esclated with ridiculous debates over the size, colour and placement of letters on signs. Self-appointed language "police" reported offenders.[52]

Before December 1993, when the five-year limit on the invocation of the notwithstanding clause concerning Bill 178 was to expire, a new and less controversial law was put in place. (See Table 3.1.) In June 1993, the National Assembly passed Bill 86 replacing all of Bill 178 and parts of Bill 101. It changed the sign law so that French was required to appear along with any other languages. Bill 86 was therefore in keeping with the spirit of the earlier Supreme Court ruling and did not require the notwithstanding clause to be used again. This legislation, passed only a few weeks before Premier Bourassa retired, helped to defuse the volatile language issue in Québec, at least in the short run.

TABLE 3.1   LANGUAGE POLICY IN QUEBEC 1968–1993

1968	Catholic school board of St. Leonard attempts to coerce children of allophones to attend French language schools.
1969	Québec's Union Nationale government responds: **Bill 63** allows parents in Québec to educate children in language of choice.
1970	Union Nationale defeated by Robert Bourassa's Liberal Party.
1974	**Bill 22** replaces Bill 63. French is given primacy in the work force, but linguistic dualism is preserved in several areas. Children of immigrants have to be enrolled in French schools, except children who demonstrate sufficient knowledge of English.
1977	**Bill 101**, Charter of the French Language declares French the official language of Québec. It promotes French much more than Bill 22, and restricts use of English. It further restricts access to English schools and takes measures to make French the language of commerce and business in Québec.
1982	*Charter of Rights and Freedoms* passed with the *Canada Act, 1982*.
1984	**Bill 57** is incorporated into the Charter of the French Language, providing guarantees for the survival of English institutions and modifying certain language requirements for businesses.
1985	Supreme Court rejects Québec's 1982 argument over Bill101, and declares that sections of it are incompatable with the *Canadian Charter of Rights and Freedoms*.
1987	PQ Court of Appeal rules that banning languages other than French on commercial signs violates freedom of expression as provided by the Québec and Canadian Charters of Rights.
1988	Supreme Court invalidates section 58 of Bill 101 requiring French-only commercial signs in Québec.
1988	Premier Bourassa invokes the notwithstanding clause from Section 33 of the *Canadian Charter of Rights and Freedoms* in order to pass Bill 178.
1988	**Bill 178** passed in the National Assembly — continues ban on languages other than French on outdoor signs and allows English and other languages on indoor signs if French is predominant.
1993	Bill 178 was up for renewal (the five-year limit expired on the use of the notwithstanding clause to override the Supreme court judgement on the language of signs) but, in June, the National Assembly passed **Bill 86** that replaced parts of Bill 101 and all of 178. Since Bill 86 was in line with the *Charter* and Supreme Court decisions, it did not require a notwithstanding clause.

[52] In April, 1993, the United Nations Human Rights Commission found that Bill 178 contravened the International Covenant on Civil and Political Rights, which Canada has signed. It stated that any limitation on an individual's right to freely express ideas, including advertising, violates the principle of freedom of expression, and argued that francophone rights are not threatened by the ability of others to advertise in a language other than French. *Globe and Mail,* February 6, 1993.

ARGUMENTS FOR AND AGAINST BILINGUALISM

Language policy in Canada thus has become highly politicized. It has been used as a "social engineering" tool by governments at both federal and provincial levels. Any government interference with language is highly sensitive and subject to distortion based on motivations from fear to racism and this has often been the case in Canada. Institutional bilingualism has become a magnet for intolerance, often based on misinformation and misunderstanding.[53]

Bilingualism in Canada does not mean that all Canadians must speak both French and English. Rather, it means that Canadians can communicate with their federal government and federally regulated institutions in the official language of their choice, and that they have the right to have their children educated in that language wherever numbers warrant. The policy is based on the belief that a highly bilingual government could be expected to increase sensitivity, tolerance and respect between the two language communities.

By these criteria, official bilingualism has had mixed results. On one hand, immersion programs in the schools are producing more bilingual Canadians. In the 1981 census, only about 5 percent of English-speaking Canadians outside Québec claimed they were bilingual, but this represented a 78 percent increase in a decade. The 1991 census indicated that bilingualism had again progressed generally across the country (See Figure 3.4) and had risen in all provinces and territories except Alberta where it remained unchanged. Over 16 percent of Canadians said they were bilingual.[54]

FIGURE 3.4   PROPORTION OF THE POPULATION ABLE TO CONDUCT A CONVERSATION IN BOTH ENGLISH AND FRENCH, CANADA, 1951, 1961, 1971, 1981 AND 1991

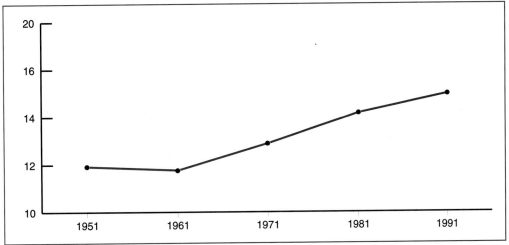

The increase from 1981-91 would have been greater except for a surge of immigrants (1986–91) who could not speak both official languages.

Source: *1986 Census Highlights: The Daily* (Ottawa: Statistics Canada, April 20, 1988) and *1991 Census Highlights: The Daily* (Ottawa: Statistics Canada, January 12, 1993), p. 11. Reproduced by authority of the Minister responsible for Statistics Canada 1993.

---

[53] See, for example, Kenneth McRoberts, "Making Canada Bilingual: Illusions and Delusions of Federal Language Policy," in David Shugarman and Reg Whitaker, eds., *Federalism and Political Community* (Peterborough: Broadview Press, 1989).

[54] Canada's Official Language Commissioner, D'Iberville Fortier, lamented the absurdity that "hundreds of thousands of parents across Canada enroll their children in French-immersion programs, while our French-language minority communities are seriously on the wane... Who will say 'bonjour' to all those budding bilinguals?" Quoted in *The Globe and Mail*, Monday, January 6, 1986.

On the other hand, the assimilation of francophones outside Québec has continued. Although more than 6.3 million Canadians spoke French at home in 1991, up from six million in 1986, the increase has not kept pace with overall population growth.

In English-speaking Canada, particularly since Québec's decision to make French pre-eminent, demands have arisen to end official bilingulism. Unilingualism, however, is often merely a superficial response to separatists who do not speak for all French Canadians, not even a majority of those who live in Québec. Often, too, it is based in frustration at seeing certain jobs labelled "bilingual." In fact, however, very few government jobs require the holder to be bilingual. Across the four western provinces, where the complaints are often strongest, only 3 percent of government jobs are designated bilingual (See Figure 3.5). Francophones represent just over 2 percent of the population there so the match is appropriate. In fact, the only place where bilingual employment and the composition of citizens are not closely related is in Québec outside of the National Capital region. There, a huge disparity exists between bilingual positions and linguistic origins — in favour of anglophones. The anglophone population in Québec City is 2.2 percent, but the designated bilingual positions are 41.8 percent of the total.[55]

FIGURE 3.5   FEDERAL GOVERNMENT BILINGUAL POSITIONS BY REGION, 1991

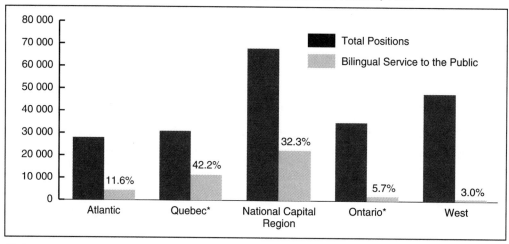

*Excluding the National Capital Region

Source: Official Languages Information System. Treasury Board, September 1991. Published by the Commission of Official Languages, *Annual Report 1991* (Ottawa: Minister of Supply and Services, 1992), p. 50. Reproduced by authority of the Minister responsible for Statistics Canada, 1993.

In these difficult economic times, it is not surprising that claims arise that official bilingualism is a punitive and expensive failure that deprives anglophones of jobs and impoverishes Canadians as a whole. Such claims are highly exaggerated. In fact, the federal government spends only about one-third of one percent of the total federal budget to provide federal services in both official languages. The cost to the federal government of providing services in both official languages represents $13 a year for each Canadian, or 3.5 cents a day. This is hardly an outrageous amount to pay in order to treat fellow Canadians with dignity and respect.[56] The

---

[55] See Robert J. Jackson and Doreen Jackson, *Stand Up for Canada* (Scarborough: Prentice-Hall Canada, 1992), ch. 2.

[56] Office of the Commissioner of Official Languages, *Official Languages Some Basic Facts* (Ottawa: Supply and Services, 1992), p. 16.

often exaggerated claims about the impact of official language policies on job opportunities for unilingual anglophones create genuine concern that must be addressed and dispelled by governments. As D'Iberville Fortier, former commissioner of official languages stated:

> It is clear that support for bilingualism in Canada has gained ground since the first Official Languages Act was adopted in 1969. It is no less clear that dissident groups have become better organized and more vocal, yet only a few political leaders appear prepared to meet the challenge.[57]

Ironically, while bilingualism is on the rise, it is now accepted that Québec is a pre-eminently francophone province: official bilingualism there is no longer considered a goal. Rather, Québec aspires to be recognized as a "distinct society" with unique rights to enable it to protect its distinctiveness if it deems it necessary to do so.[58] This policy is based on the fact that francophones exist in an English-speaking continent and are fearful of being assimilated. Neither federalists nor nationalists in Québec, however, necessarily want official bilingualism ended. Following a call by former Alberta premier Donald Getty to do so, Bernard Landry, vice-president of the Parti Québécois said

> whenever you start questioning the principle of linguistic duality, there is no more Canada... If you tamper with that, you're touching the core of the country.[59]

IS THE FRENCH LANGUAGE IN DANGER IN QUEBEC?

Many French Canadians in Québec fear the prospect of becoming a minority in their own province. As we have noted, Québec's overall birth rate is declining. This makes the selection and entry of immigrants of particular concern to policy-makers in that province. Immigrants, even in Québec, demonstrate a marked preference to learn English as their new language. In the face of this cultural threat (real or perceived), since 1968 the Québec government has had a separate Department of Immigration to deal with recruitment and settlement of immigrants and has launched a series of programs and regulations to encourage immigrants in Québec to integrate into the francophone community.

Certain myths that are propagated in Québec in order to keep the francophone population vigilant against assimilation should be dispelled. Separatists encourage the myth that French-Canadians have no voice in Ottawa, that Ottawa does not represent Québec's interests. This ignores the fact that from 1968 to 1993, Canada had a Prime Minister from Québec for all but about a year and a half. Québec has always been well represented in federal cabinets. Senior government posts rotate between French- and English-speakers. Although francophones still hold slightly less than their statistical share of jobs in the civil service, they are certainly not discriminated against in Ottawa.

The 1991 census reveals what is happening to the francophone population in Canada.

1. The proportion of francophones in Québec changed little over the century. In 1900, 83 percent of the population spoke French; in 1991, 83 percent still spoke French. French in Québec is thriving despite the low birthrate in the province.

---

[57] D'Iberville Fortier, "Language Tensions: People Should be Informed," *Globe and Mail*, Feb. 14, 1990.

[58] This was Québec's demand during the constitutional bargaining over the Meech Lake and Charlottetown accords and is discussed in detail in Chapter 5.

[59] *The Globe and Mail*, Jan. 13, 1992.

2. The English-speaking community in Québec dropped from 24 percent at Confederation to 16 percent in 1970, and to 10 percent in 1991.

3. The English are learning more French in Québec and so are immigrants to that province. Québec's requirements for immigrant children to go to French schools has increased the assimilation rate of these children into French.

4. In most other provinces, however, the proportion of francophones continued to decline largely because of a high rate of assimilation — down from 24.7 percent in 1981 to 23.3 percent in 1991. About one-third of francophones outside Québec speak English at home; less than 1 percent of anglophones speak French at home.

These demographic trends show that, despite federal initiatives, Canada's francophone population is increasingly concentrated in Québec. The francophone presence outside of Québec is projected to continue its steady decline, as illustrated in Figure 3.6. The percentage of Canadians with French as their first language began to drop in 1951. At that time the French language group accounted for 29 percent of the total population, compared to about 25 percent in 1986. Policies such as the *Official Languages Act,* expansion of French radio and television and various efforts by the provinces to expand education for francophones have not halted the decline of French-speaking communities outside Québec. At the present rate, by the year 2000 close to 95 percent of Canada's francophone population will live in Québec.

FIGURE 3.6   PERCENTAGE OF THE POPULATION WITH FRENCH AS MOTHER TONGUE, CANADA, 1951–91

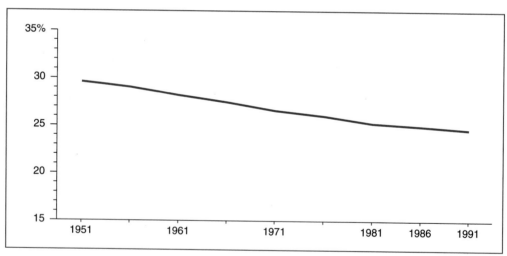

For 1986 and 1991, multiple responses were distributed among the language indicated using a method which makes the data approximately comparable to those of previous censuses.

Source: *1991 Census Highlights: The Daily* (Ottawa: Statistics Canada, September 15, 1992), p. 7. Reproduced by authority of the Minister responsible for Statistics Canada 1993.

As well, Québec's low birthrate indicates that its demographic weight within Canada could decline below its present 24 percent by the year 2000. Canadians, therefore, must expect Québec francophones to continue their struggle to preserve the pre-eminence of the French language and culture within their province using whatever tools are available to them. As Léon Dion has argued persuasively, national identities are constructed not only of current sociological realities but also of myths about the past and visions of the future.[60]

NATIONALIST ATTITUDES OF FRENCH CANADIANS

What attitudes do francophones hold about their province, country and federal and provincial governments? Attitudinal surveys of French Canadians have, for practical reasons, generally been confined to citizens of Québec. In this unique province, where political and ethnic boundaries more or less coincide, Canadians often hold political attitudes that are distinct from those of other regions or provinces.[61]

Public opinion polls in the province of Québec show considerable ambiguity concerning French-Canadian desires for federalism, sovereignty and independence. *L'actualité* polls in 1992, for example, showed beyond a doubt that confusion and indecision reign on all questions about the future of the province. A CROP poll conducted in April 1992, found that 16% of Québec residents were hard-core Québec nationalists, 22% were moderate Québec nationalists, 26% were hard-core Canadian nationalists, 18% were moderate Canadian nationalists and 18% were very undecided. A cartoon summarizing the results of the polling showed a young boy saying essentially, "It's like having to choose between chocolate and ice cream for life... it's very hard when you like them both!"[62]

Surveys that measure the relative attachment of French Québécois to Canada and Québec indicate an attachment to Québec that is somewhat or much stronger than attachment to Canada. Maurice Pinard examined the system of dual loyalties in Québec in terms of attachment to, perceived importance of, and interest in the two levels of government. He concluded that "in ethnically segmented societies, precisely because of this segmentation, people tend to develop a system of dual loyalties."[63] In a 1970 survey of Québec, Pinard concluded that Québec francophones feel the provincial government looks after their interests better than the federal government, and that they are correspondingly more loyal to the former. His surveys show that, in any conflict between the two governments, 40 percent of the francophone population favour the Québec government, compared to 15 percent who support the federal government. Therefore, "if there is a system of dual loyalties, loyalty to Québec nevertheless seems often much stronger than loyalty to Ottawa."[64]

The intensity and forms of loyalty among French Canadians appear to have changed in recent years. Between surveys done in 1970 and 1977, the group's self-identification increased

---

60 Léon Dion, *A la recherche du Québec* (Presses de l'université Laval, 1987). Even in France there is concern about the steady infiltration of the English language since the 1960s. Recently, concern about the growing adoption of the English language, particularly through French-owned multinational corporations led to action. In June 1993, they added the following sentence to their Constitution: "The Language of the Republic is French." *New York Times*, July 10, 1993.

61 Research on Québec attitudes is replete with controversy. The results seem to shift because of particular events and the manner and type of questions asked in the surveys. The more questions are posed in terms of outright separation of Québec from Canada the fewer positive responses are found. The more the question implies a "renewed" Canada, a "reformed" constitution or the like, the more positive the responses are. In other words, responses rely totally on the type of questions posed.

62 "Mon père m'a dit que c'est un peu comme s'il fallait choisir entre le chocolat et la crème glacé pour la vie ... c'est très difficile quand on aime les deux!" *L'Actualité*, July, 1992, p. 20.

63 See Maurice Pinard, "Ethnic Segmentation, Loyalties, Incentives and Constitutional Options in Quebec," p. 4. Paper presented at twinned workshop organized by the Canadian Political Science Association and the Israel Political Science Association at Sde Boker, Israel, December 11–16, 1978.

64 Ibid., p. 12.

substantially from "French Canadian," in which identification was with all French in Canada, to "Québécois," limited to the francophone population in the province of Québec. These results correspond to a rise in support for greater autonomy for Québec. (Escalating support for separatism in Québec is discussed in Chapter 6.)

In a 1992 study, however, Pinard concluded that in spite of the growth of support for sovereignty association in recent years, Québécois prefer federalism.

> *From 1977 to 1991, many studies have measured both support for sovereignty-association and support for some form of renewed federalism, and they have in all instances found greater support for the latter.*[65]

Outright independence has always been less popular than sovereignty-association. If and when the Parti Québécois returns to power again, however, it could easily raise very volatile emotions about language. As Pinard noted:

> *One should certainly not underestimate the propensity of entrenched ethnic parties to exacerbate ethnic divisions and keep them at the top of the political agenda.*[66]

And, as columnist Jeffrey Simpson pointed out, French-speaking Québécois display a schizophrenic attitude to English. Individually they learn English, but collectively they seek to restrict it. "Superbly bilingual Cabinets, whose members have greatly benefited from their bilingual capacity, reject all suggestions that Québec should be a bilingual province."[67]

A majority of Québec francophones have long demonstrated strong preference for remaining in Canada. But polls indicate that they only want to stay if their culture and language can be protected. This implies special powers for Québec, a privilege that raises objections and hostility in other provinces.

ENGLISH-SPEAKING CANADIANS: A CULTURAL FRUITCAKE

When Acadian author Antonine Maillet was awarded the prestigious Prix Goncourt for French literature in 1979, she was asked how she regarded herself — as Acadian, French, French Canadian, French Acadian, Canadian or some other. She replied that she considered herself to be *all* of them in different proportions. Like Antonine Maillet, Canadians have "layered" cultures. Belonging to an ethnic group does not detract from being a Canadian. When non-English- or French-speaking immigrants choose Canada, they learn to speak either English or French and the cultural layering begins.[68]

According to the 1991 Census, people with British or French ethnic backgrounds constitute the largest ethnic groups in Canada. English, Irish, Scottish or Welsh ethnic background, as well as multiple combinations of these, were reported by 28 percent of the population;[69]

---

[65] Maurice Pinard "The Dramatic Reemergence of the Quebec Independence Movement," *Journal of International Affairs* (vol. 45, winter 1992), pp. 471–97.

[66] Ibid.

[67] *Globe and Mail,* Feb. 23, 1991.

[68] See also Antonine Maillet, "Canada: What's That?" *Queen's Quarterly,* vol. 99, no. 3 (fall 1992), pp. 642–50.

[69] This was a drop from 34 percent in 1986. Statistics Canada speculated that this group contributed to the substantial increase in respondents who gave their ethnic ancestry simply as "Canadian" (4 percent including multiple responses).

23 percent reported uniquely French heritage. Other ethnic groups form a large and grow-ing part of Canada's population. (See Figure 3.7 and Table 3.2.)

FIGURE 3.7 ETHNIC ORIGINS, CANADA, 1991

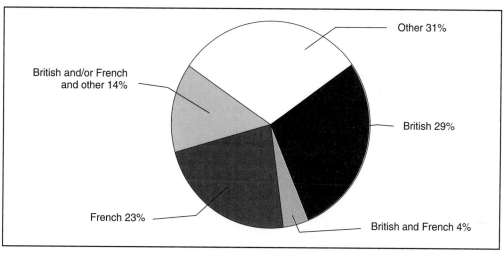

British-only origins include single responses of English, Irish, Scottish, Welsh, or other British as well as multiple British-only re-sponses. French-only origins include the responses of French, Acadian, Québécois and the multiple French-only responses.

Source: *1991 Census Highlights: The Daily* (Ottawa: Statistics Canada, February 23, 1993), p. 4. Reproduced by authority of the Minister responsible for Statistics Canada 1993.

As we noted in Chapter 2, there are over 100 ethnic groups in Canada and they are very unevenly mixed throughout the population. Many are first generation Canadians. According to the 1991 census, about 16 percent of the Canadian population is foreign-born, and more than half of them live in five large cities: Toronto, Montréal, Vancouver, Edmonton and Winnipeg. Toronto's population, for example, is more than 38 percent foreign-born. World history shows that many states can successfully accommodate vast ethnic differences, but they do so in different ways. The United States is often viewed as a "melting pot," because it was built through shared experiences and commitment to similar political ideals and values. Canada, on the other hand, is more of a "fruitcake." The Canadian approach has been to encourage different cultures to exist side by side in harmony and tolerance — not to "boil them down" in one melting pot. As the flow of immigrants to Canada increases and the eth-nic composition of the country changes, the challenge will be to maintain a balance between national unity and respect for diversity that has been such an important part of the Canadian political culture.[70]

Since Confederation, immigrants have come to Canada in four large waves, the first three of which were related to depressed economic and/or post-war conditions in Europe. The first was between 1896 and 1914, and was composed mostly of British labourers, eastern European peasants, and American farmers. The second wave was in the mid-1920s, when more hands were needed, particularly in the West, to clear marginal land and increase settlements. The majority of newcomers in the second wave were central and eastern Europeans. Many were refugees and most were very poor. Immigration ceased almost

---

[70] See Robert J. Jackson and Doreen Jackson, *Stand Up For Canada* (Scarborough: Prentice-Hall, 1992), ch. 1.

completely during the depression in the 1930s. The third wave did not begin until after the Second World War; it lasted until 1960. Predominantly European in origin, it included significantly more well-educated professionals than the earlier waves. A fourth large wave began about 1990 as refugees and immigrants, predominantly from Third World countries, flooded into Canada.

TABLE 3.2   TOP 10 SINGLE RESPONSE ETHNIC ORIGINS, CANADA, 1991

	Canada	Number	%
	Total population	26,994,045	100.0
	Single responses	19,199,795	71.1
1.	French	6,146,605	22.8
2.	British	5,611,050	20.8
3.	German	911,580	3.4
4.	Canadian	765,095	2.8
5.	Italian	750,055	2,8
6.	Chinese	588,645	2.2
7.	Aboriginal	470,615	1.7
8.	Ukrainian	406,645	1.5
9.	Dutch (Netherlands)	358,185	1.3
10.	East Indian	324,840	1.2
	Multiple Responses	7,794,250	28.9

Source: *1991 Census Highlights: The Daily* (Ottawa: Statistics Canada, February 23, 1993), p. 10. Reproduced by authority of the Minister responsible for Statistics Canada 1993.

Over the years, the reception and accommodation of newcomers to Canada has changed considerably.[71] Though the tendency was always toward assimilation, three quite different conceptions of assimilation succeeded one another. They approximated the first three major waves of immigration.[72] These changes can be attributed to various factors, perhaps the most important being prevailing economic conditions, the number of new arrivals and the origin of the newcomers.

The first conception of assimilation held that immigrants should renounce their former culture and adopt the patterns of behaviour and values established by Anglo-Canadians. This view was based on the belief that the English Canadian nation should be patterned exclu-

---

[71] Howard Brotz, "Multiculturalism in Canada: A Muddle," *Canadian Public Policy*, vol. VI, no. 1, 1980, pp. 41–6. See also Lance W. Roberts and Rodney A. Clifton, "Exploring the Ideology of Canadian Multiculturalism," in *Canadian Public Policy*, vol. VIII, no. 1 (Winter 1982), pp. 88–94 and Allan Smith, "The Ascendancy of the Ethnic Idea in North America," *CJPS*, vol. XIV, no. 2 (June 1981), pp. 227–57.

[72] See Howard Palmer, "Reluctant Hosts: Anglo-Canadian Views of Multiculturalism in the Twentieth Century," in *Multiculturalism as State Policy: Conference Report, Second Conference on Multiculturalism* (Ottawa: Minister of Supply and Services, 1976), pp. 81–119.

sively on the British model. Consequently, non-British and non-French groups in Canada were relegated to the bottom of the social, economic and political ladder.

After World War I, as Canadians began to loosen their ties to Britain, a new conception of assimilation replaced anglo-conformity. This "melting pot" approach held that conformity was necessary, but regarded assimilation as a relatively slow process in which immigrant groups would intermarry and blend with the established population in order to create a distinctive new society. The new view acknowledged that the British way was not always innately superior and that other cultures might have something to offer Canadian society. Often, however, Anglo-Saxon biases persisted. For example, one western historian advised readers in 1924 that "there is enough Anglo-Saxon blood in Alberta to dilute the foreign blood and complete the process of assimilation to the mutual advantage of both elements."[73] During the depression years of the 1930s, when competition for jobs was severe, there was considerable discrimination and overt prejudice toward ethnic groups, and the melting pot approach to assimilation was more talked about than practised.

During the high immigration period of the later 1940s and the 1950s, (a period of economic recovery marked by a rising tide of Canadian nationalism), a third conception, **cultural pluralism** or, more commonly, **multiculturalism**, gained popularity. It postulated that within the context of Canadian citizenship and economic and political integration, ethnic customs and cultures should be valued, preserved and shared.

There are many reasons for the growth of more liberal views toward ethnic groups at this time. Economic prosperity eased cultural conflicts, and the new wave of immigrants (many of whom were educated or professional Europeans) helped break down the rigid correlation between class and ethnicity. Britain was declining as a world power and therefore provided a less attractive model; at the same time, rising Canadian nationalism required a new self-image to distinguish Canada from the American melting pot. Perhaps the most immediate reasons for the advance of pluralist ideas at this time were the dramatic changes brought about by the Quiet Revolution in Québec. Many ethnic groups found the dualist image conveyed by the recommendations of the Royal Commission on Bilingualism and Biculturalism offensive and sought official assurance that their own aspirations and interests would not be overlooked. In fact, in response to their pressures, the Royal Commission produced a fourth volume dealing with the role of "other ethnic groups" in Canada.[74]

In the early 1970s, the federal government and the provincial governments of Ontario, Manitoba, Saskatchewan and Alberta formally adopted a policy of multiculturalism. In 1971, the federal government defined Canada as being multicultural within a bilingual English-French framework, and established the cabinet position of Minister of State for Multiculturalism. Services on which ethnic groups could draw were steadily increased throughout the 1970s. A comprehensive *Multiculturalism Act* was passed in 1988, and a separate Department, Multiculturalism and Citizenship Canada, was established in 1991, later to be merged into the portfolio, Canadian Heritage, as part of Kim Campbell's 1993 reorganization of the public service.

The current policy of the federal government is to promote the retention of characteristic cultural features of ethnic groups that want to maintain their identity, and to encourage the sharing of these features with all Canadians. The basic assumption of this policy is that confidence in one's own cultural foundations helps to break down prejudice and discrimination be-

---

[73] John Blue, *Alberta Past and Present*, vol. I (Chicago: Pioneer Historical Publishing Co., 1924), p. 218.

[74] *Report of the Royal Commission on Bilingualism and Biculturalism*, Book 4 (Ottawa: Queen's Printer, 1970).

tween ethnic groups. To this end, Ottawa spends millions of dollars to fund projects such as ethnic group histories and language schools designed to further the objectives of multiculturalism.

This high multicultural component creates a tension between duality and plurality in Canadian society. A commitment to multiculturalism makes it difficult to discriminate between "ethnic" and "official" languages in geographical areas where other-ethnic groups are concentrated and outnumber French-speaking or English-speaking minority populations. In Toronto and western Canada, in particular, where high other-ethnic populations exist under an English-language umbrella, there is pressure to make French no more important than other minority languages.

Since the Second World War, only Israel and Australia have accepted numbers of immigrants in proportion to their populations on a scale comparable to Canada. To date, Canadian society has proven remarkably resilient in accommodating such large numbers of newcomers with relatively little social stress. However, infrastructures such as language, culture and citizenship training to help immigrants adapt and integrate successfully should be implemented to meet the needs of these new Canadians. A rapid influx of immigrants into urban areas results in competition for housing, jobs and social facilities and can create a high degree of social tension, particularly in times of economic stress. As well, the pattern of immigrant sources has changed dramatically over the last decade so that a growing majority are now refugees from Third World countries, and their needs may be greater than for immigrants in the past.

The nature of immigration in Canada has changed. Canada used to seek immigrants to populate a new country. In the early 1990s, as a new, fourth wave of immigration was initiated, immigration policy became a more humanitarian gesture. As many as 100 million people from poor and war-torn countries around the world currently want to relocate in richer, more peaceful areas, including Canada. Some are refugees, others simply seek better living conditions. In 1992, perhaps the pinnacle of the fourth wave, Canada accepted a record 250 000 immigrants and refugees, representing about 0.92 percent of the population.[75]

Eighty-five percent of these immigrants entered Canada as either refugees or relatives or fiancé(e)s of people already living in Canada. Only 15 percent (down from 32 percent in 1971) were selected through the point system that had been set up in 1967 to restrict the entry of individuals who might not adapt quickly to Canadian society. Business immigrants, including investors and entrepreneurs therefore represented a very small percentage of total immigrants. To help redress the balance and increase the proportion of business immigrants, in early 1993, Parliament approved a new immigration law that included measures to give the government more control over who becomes a Canadian.

Reproduced with permission, Nease.

---

[75] Immigration rarely exceeded 200 000 until 1990.

In promoting a fourth wave of immigration, the Conservative government argued it was important for humanitarian reasons and also for Canada. Its studies showed that immigration generates benefits for Canadian residents in the form of higher income for everyone.[76] The number of firms expand in response to the larger market and new jobs are created. For this reason, the government argued, immigration does not increase unemployment in the long run. As well, with the country's low birth rate of 1.7 children per family and an aging population (by 2013 one in every four Canadians will be 65 or older), proponents of the high immigration policy argue that Canada needs to accept significantly more immigrants than it did up to 1991 in order to curb a population decline.

Such a population decline in itself is no reason to accept massive immigration. It is not difficult to find small states with low population that prosper economically and states with high populations that do not. However, as one of the world's most prosperous countries, Canada has a moral obligation to reach out to those in need. Immigration is one way to do this. At the same time, informed Canadians should be aware of how immigration is changing the country and ensure that immigrants receive the time and attention necessary to adapt to their new circumstances.

IMMIGRATION AND CULTURAL TOLERANCE

Contemporary immigration trends indicate that Canadians must anticipate a greater racial mix in the population than ever before.[77] A recent study by Professor John T. Samuel concludes that the current 2.5 million Canadians who are members of a visible minority will rise to 5.7 million by 2001 — an increase from 9.6 to 17.7 percent of the total population. In large metropolitan areas the percentage will be higher: Toronto 56 percent; Vancouver 39 percent; Edmonton and Calgary 25 percent, for example.[78] As a group, the report concludes, these visible minorities will be relatively affluent, controlling about 20 percent of the country's GDP. This will represent a significant change in Canada's societal composition, and the potential for increased racial tension is high.

Unfortunately, cultural tolerance is a self-congratulatory ideal that Canadians have not always lived up to. Incidents of racial bigotry in Canadian history include the shameful internment of Japanese Canadians during World War II and the often shabby treatment of Native peoples. Racist ideologies are condemned, but still persist. Some sociologists even maintain that "...racism is a virulent ideology held by Canadians. There is a belief that certain groups (non-whites) are inferior to whites and this justifies invidious distinctions and behaviours directed toward them."[79]

Immigration policies are a good measure of cultural tolerance. As we have seen, Canada's immigration regulations were traditionally based on the principle that all immigrants should be assimilated into the dominant French and English ethnic groups, with the result that less

---

[76] Judith Maxwell (Chair, Economic Council of Canada), "The Value of Immigration," *Ottawa Citizen*, March 8, 1991.

[77] See Seymour Vincent Wilson, "The Tapestry Vision of Canadian Multiculturalism," Presidential Address, CPSA, June 1993; and O.P. Dwivedi et al., eds., *Canada 2000: Race Relations and Public Policy* (Guelph: Department of Political Studies, 1989), particularly the articles by Elliot L. Tepper "Demographic Change and Pluralism," pp. 20–52, and James W. St. G. Walker, "Race Policy in Canada: A Retrospective," pp. 1–19.

[78] T. John Samuel, "Social Dimensions of Immigration Policy in Canada," paper presented at the International Conference on Race Relations: Policy Practices and Research in 1990. Toronto: York University, June 27–30, 1990; and Pamela M. White and T. John Samuel, "Immigration and Ethnic Diversity in Urban Canada, *International Journal of Canadian Studies* vol. 3 (Spring 1991), pp. 70–85.

[79] Alan B. Anderson and James S. Frideres, *Ethnicity in Canada* (Toronto: Butterworths, 1981), p. 229. See also Jean Leonard Elliot and Augie Fleras, *Unequal Relations: An Introduction to Race and Ethnic Dynamics in Canada* (Scarborough: Prentice-Hall Canada, 1992).

easily assimilable groups were restricted. In the early days of the country, when white immigrants were actively sought by the Canadian government, immigration policies were restrictive toward non-white groups. For instance, the federal government took the position after 1900 that non-whites, specifically Asians, would not fit into Canadian society and would be a disruptive element. And, during World War II, Jewish refugees from Europe had extremely limited access to a safe haven in Canada.[80]

Since 1952, consistent attempts to broaden admission policies have been tempered by the notion of "ethnic balance" — that is, that no new immigrant group should disturb the existing ethno-racial balance of Canada. In practice, this concept has tended to ensure that ethnic groups that are not already well-represented remain that way. A point system introduced in 1967 was designed to restrict entry of individuals who might not adapt quickly to Canadian society; these obviously tended to be poorly educated non-whites from developing countries.

The discrimination evident in the history of Canada's immigration policy can also be traced in the social, economic and political development of the country. John Porter's *The Vertical Mosaic* revealed the existence of a pecking order for various ethnic groups that allowed them unequal chances to move between classes and succeed in Canadian society.[81] The ethnic pecking order that existed in immigration policy was identical to the "vertical mosaic" of ethnic stratification. The British were on top in establishment positions; Chinese and blacks, on the bottom rung, held the most menial occupations. Before World War II, members of ethnic groups other than British or French were poorly represented even in middle-echelon jobs in politics, education or the civil service and almost none had penetrated elite positions.[82]

A survey of attitudes in 1974 concluded that the vertical mosaic described by John Porter in the 1960s still existed but was significantly diminished.[83] An ethnic pecking order was still part of the mental baggage of Anglo-Canadians inasmuch as northern European groups were more highly regarded than southern Europeans or non-whites. The same survey showed a correlation between the attitude toward a group and how that group feels it is being treated. However, a great deal of evidence suggested that these attitudes were in the process of breaking down. The 1974 survey further revealed that, despite the fact that knowledge about the federal multicultural policy was very limited (only 19 percent of Canadians indicated they had heard about it), Canadians demonstrated a mild acceptance of a policy of multiculturalism.

By 1978, the new multicultural policies were finally reflected in a more liberal *Immigration Act* that declared that immigration policy was to be founded on principles of non-discrimination, family reunion, humanitarian concern for refugees and promotion of national goals. Provincial and federal governments began to consult to provide an annual forecast of how many immigrants can be absorbed. This forecast is a global limit, rather than a quota system for specific countries or areas. The humanitarian move to consider refugees in particular is an attempt to make the multi-ethnic ideal of the cultural mosaic more than merely a platitude. As noted in Chapter 2, by 1991 almost 75 of percent immigrants came from Asia, Africa, Latin America and the Caribbean.

---

[80]   Irving Abella and Harold Troper, *None is Too Many: Canada and the Jews of Europe 1933–1948* (Toronto: Lester & Orpen Dennys, 1982).

[81]   See Porter, *The Vertical Mosaic,* and Clement, *Canadian Corporate Elite.*

[82]   *Report of the Royal Commission on Biculturalism,* ch. 2. Also see Dennis Olsen, *The State Elite* (Toronto: McClelland & Stewart, 1980).

[83]   A good summary of this survey was published in the Report of the Second Conference on Multiculturalism: J.W. Berry, R. Kalen and D.M. Taylor, "Summary—Multiculturalism and Ethnic Attitudes in Canada," in *Multiculturalism as a State Policy,* pp. 149–68.

Except in Québec, minority groups are most valued where they are most concentrated. The 1991 census results showed Ontario to be by far the largest centre for nearly all ethnic groups, followed by British Columbia, Alberta and Manitoba. Almost one-quarter of Ontario's population was comprised of immigrants. Newfoundland, at the other extreme, counted fewer than two percent of its population as immigrants.

Low acceptance of minority groups by Québec respondents reflects the tendency of some French Canadians to regard other cultures and languages as a potential threat. Any acceptance of other ethnic claims, it is argued, undermines the concept of dualism for the country and reduces the French claim to that of the largest of the minority cultures. This problem was studied by the Task Force on Canadian Unity set up in the wake of the November 1976 election victory of the Parti Québécois in Québec. To ensure that ethnic pluralism remained subordinate to dualism, it recommended that "the provincial governments should assume primary responsibility for the support of multiculturalism in Canada."[84] So far, there has been no significant move in that direction.

Besides fearing that their place as a founding nation will be undermined, French-speaking Canadians make two other criticisms about multiculturalism as a government policy. First, they argue that it will perpetuate the vertical stratification of Canadian society and decrease social and economic mobility. However, stratification by ethnicity is losing its rigidity and today there are numerous examples of ethnic diversity of personnel in middle level and establishment positions. Second, multiculturalism is said to fragment Canadian society. There is, however, no evidence that this is the case. As Antonine Maillet illustrated, one can have many cultural identities and still be Canadian.

In 1981, evidence of both overt and covert racism in Canadian society resulted in the federal government announcement of a national program to combat racism, and the establishment of a Race Relations Unit within the Multiculturalism Directorate. Shortly after, a Special Committee on the Participation of Visible Minorities in Canadian Society was set up to seek positive ideas for ameliorating relations within Canada between visible minorities and other Canadians. Their report, published in 1984, presented evidence of discriminatory mechanisms in Canadian government and society.[85]

Four years later, in 1988, the government issued an apology to Japanese Canadians and provided financial redress for those whose civil liberties had been abrogated five decades earlier. It was an official acknowlegement of the responsibility of the Canadian government and society for the infringement of civil liberties based on race. Immediately, other groups, such as the Chinese who were subjected to a head tax from 1885 to 1923, began demanding compensation for the institutionalized discrimination they had endured. In 1993 the federal government informed Chinese, Italian and Ukrainian Canadians that it would *not* provide financial redress for the wrongs done to them.

ETHNICITY AND POLITICAL CULTURE

The existence of significant subcultures within a country can be disruptive to the dominant political culture if group ties are stronger than loyalty to the country. Does ethnic diversity in

---

[84] The Task Force on Canadian Unity, *A Future Together: Observations and Recommendations* (Ottawa: Ministry of Supply and Services, 1979), pp. 55–6. A study of attitudes toward minority groups is found in J.W. Berry, R. Kalen and D.M. Taylor, *Multiculturalism and Ethnic Attitudes in Canada* (Ottawa: Minister of Supply and Services, 1977).

[85] Report of the Special Committee on the Participation of Visible Minorities in Canadian Society, *Equality Now!* (Ottawa: Queen's Printer, 1984).

Canada fragment the overall political culture and make the country less cohesive? Certainly, Canada has experienced several ethnic crises in which group loyalties conflicted strongly with larger community loyalty, though these were confined to the two founding groups. In these extreme situations, doubts were raised about the efficacy of the federal system of government to meet the needs of an ethnically diverse country and even about whether the country should stay united. However, it would be pessimistic to regard such crises as the norm.

Optimistic conclusions about the multi-ethnic nature of Canadian society can be drawn from research by David Elkins that reinforces the suggestion of the Bilingualism and Biculturalism Commission that multiculturalism is a strengthening feature of Canadian unity. Elkins concluded that ignorance of one's own and other nations is associated with parochial, localist sentiments, while knowledge about and appreciation of other nations is an enriching experience that encourages individuals to feel warmer toward their own country.[86] A partial explanation, he suggested, lies in the fact that most immigrants to Canada are from countries with strong central governments. For example, the largest single group of immigrants comes from Britain, which has a unitary system of government. It is logical that these newcomers would support the familiar idea that the central government should be the strongest and most important voice in the country. Elkins found that native-born Canadians are more provincially oriented than immigrants, and that the longer immigrants are in the country, the more provincial they become.

Another counter-intuitive finding about immigrants to Canada is that they are on average slightly more efficacious in their political attitudes than native-born Canadians. Elkins speculates that individuals who act positively to improve their personal environment by emigrating may demonstrate self-reliant, efficacious behaviour that might explain their high score on political efficacy.[87]

As well as having warmer feelings toward the whole country than do native-born Canadians who remain in one region, immigrants and internal migrants adopt norms and patterns of behaviour characteristic of the province in which they settle. This assimilation to provincial values and attitudes appears to be a function of both length of residence and type of background. Relatively recent or first generation immigrant minorities tend to be concerned primarily with problems of adjustment to their new circumstances, whereas well-established minorities are less concerned with the persistence of their ethnicity than with increasing their collective economic and political strength.[88] When language, religious affiliation and adherence to custom are used as criteria, ethnic identity is not static, but changes steadily from one generation to the next as individuals adapt to Canadian circumstances. The 1981 census, for example, showed that 10 percent of those with a first language other than English or French are able to speak not one but *both* official languages — 2 percent higher than those whose first language is English.

---

[86] David Elkins, "The Sense of Place," in David J. Elkins and Richard Simeon, eds., *Small Worlds* (Toronto: Methuen, 1980), pp. 1–30.

[87] Ibid., and David Elkins, "The Horizontal Mosaic: Immigrants and Migrants in the Provincial Political Cultures," in Elkins and Simeon, eds., *Small Worlds*, pp. 106–30.

[88] Wsevolod Isajiw, "Immigration and Multiculturalism — Old and New Approaches." Paper presented at the Conference on Multiculturalism and Third World Immigrants in Canada, University of Alberta, Edmonton, September 3–5, 1975, p. 2. Results of a more recent study in Toronto indicate that, regardless of country of origin, immigrants are able to draw on their past political experiences and adapt quickly to their new political context. See Jerome H. Black, "The Practice of Politics in Two Settings: Political Transferability Among Recent Immigrants to Canada," *CJPS*, vol. XX, no 4 (Dec. 1987), pp. 732–53.

The Canadian commitment to cultural diversity in the forms of bilingualism and multiculturalism serves to unite Canadians by helping to combat two threats: American cultural domination and threats of separation by any province or region. Bilingualism and multiculturalism are uniquely Canadian responses adopted to deal with uniquely Canadian circumstances. To date, research supports the positive effect of the cultural mosaic and indicates that multiculturalism is not to be feared, but encouraged. Some, however, question whether enough effort is being made to do so. One author questions bluntly whether Canadians genuinely aspire to cultural diversity. What, he asks, does multiculturalism amount to other than folk-dancing on the weekends? The "rhetoric of the Canadian mosaic may be no more than sugar coating on the bitter pill of assimilation."[89]

There is no doubt that ethnic cultures are eroding: studies of language, religion and customs as indicators of ethnic strength all support this view. Many factors hasten language assimilation. Even where a given first language is used in the home, the first language is not often used outside a very small community of friends and family, so that linguistic assimilation becomes inevitable over time. Provincial legislation restricts the use of languages other than English and French in schools. Migration from rural to urban areas also erodes former bastions of ethnic culture. Intermarriage, too, weakens ethnic ties, although it is not a major factor in Canada, where in-group marriages are characteristic of most ethnic groups.

> *"There cannot be one cultural policy for Canadians of British and French origin, another for the original peoples and yet a third for all others. For although there are two official languages, there is no official culture, nor does any ethnic group take precedence over any other... A policy of multiculturalism within a bilingual framework commends itself to the government as the most suitable means of assuring the cultural freedom of Canadians."*
>
> **Pierre Trudeau, in Parliament, Oct. 8, 1971**

Given this dilemma, it is often argued that multiculturalism is a form of assimilation. In fact, the term "multicultural" is misleading: multi-ethnic describes the Canadian reality more accurately. Whether or not one views multiculturalism as a viable policy depends on how it is defined. Jean Burnet addressed the issue by saying, "multiculturalism within a bilingual framework can work, if it is interpreted as is intended — that is, as encouraging those members of ethnic groups who want to do so to maintain a proud sense of the contribution of their own group to Canadian society."[90] In this way, the policy becomes something very Canadian: a voluntary, marginal differentiation among peoples who are equal participants in society. Cultures cannot be preserved in their entirety; immigrants do adapt to the language and customs of the majority. But in doing so they add a richness, variety and depth to the cultural tapestry. The formal adoption of bilingual and multicultural policies enshrines ethnic tolerance among the other important values of Canadian government but it does not necessarily mean that they are realized in society.

---

[89] D. Forbes, "Conflicting National Identities Among Canadian Youth," in Pammett and Whittington, eds., *Foundations of Political Culture*, pp. 288–315.

[90] Jean Burnet, "The Policy of Multiculturalism within a Bilingual Framework: An Interpretation," in A. Wolfgang, *The Education of Immigrant Students: Issues and Answers* (Toronto: Ontario Institute for Studies in Education, 1975). See Stephen Brooks, Public Policy in Canada: An Introduction (Toronto: McClelland & Stewart), ch. 9, for a good summary and comments on federal policy on language and ethnicity.

NATIVE PEOPLES: INDIANS, METIS AND INUIT

A third ethno-linguistic division lies between Canada's native peoples — the aboriginals who consist of status and non-status Indians, including Métis and Inuit — and other Canadians (See Table 3.3). Today's aboriginal issues are rooted deep in the past. While 19th century British authorities made many efforts to accommodate the French minority, they demonstrated little such concern for the rights of the "First Nations."

TABLE 3.3   CANADIAN ABORIGINAL ORIGINS 1991

Canada	Aboriginal % of total population	N.A. Indian % of all aboriginals	Metis % of all aboriginals	Inuit % of all aboriginal	Other multiple aboriginal origins*
	3.7	74	17	4	4
Region	**Aboriginal % of total population of Canada**	**Aboriginal % of total population of the region**	**% of all North American Indians in Canada**	**% of all Métis in Canada**	**% of all Inuit in Canada***
Atlantic	5	2	5	2	16
Québec	14	2	15	10	19
Ontario	24	2	29	12	7
Prairies	36	8	30	64	7
B.C.	17	5	19	10	3
Northern Territories	4	49	2	2	49

Note: North American Indian, Métis and Inuit figures include single origins and multiple non-aboriginal origins, 1991, but not other multiple aboriginal origins.

The total aboriginal origins include all single and multiple aboriginal origins claimed in the 1991 census.

Source: Compiled from Statistics Canada data, *Catalogue 94327, Aboriginal Data, Age and Sex 1991* (Ottawa: Minister of Supply and Services) pp. 2 and 3.

These numbers are approximate. 76 Indian settlements were incompletely enumerated, and some individuals provided unusable responses to the question. The 1991 census did not ask about Indian status, but most registered Indians are North American Indians.

* These figures do not add up to 100 percent because of rounding.

At Confederation the federal Parliament was assigned legislative jurisdiction over Indians and the land reserved for them.[91] Shortly thereafter, Parliament passed legislation that represented a clear policy of assimilation of aboriginal peoples. Essentially, Indians on reserves were to be protected temporarily until they learned European methods of farming. They would then be qualified to relinquish their Indian status. Reserve privileges were considered as a kind of probationary period of Canadian citizenship.

The term "Indian" was legally defined in the first *Indian Act* in 1876. Since then, anyone whose name appears on the band list of any Indian community in Canada or on a central registry list is considered to be Indian. The concept of "status Indian" was adopted in order to determine who had rights to Indian land. Status Indians are either treaty Indians who are

---

[91] *BNA Act* 91:24. For background see J.R. Miler, *Skyscrapers Hide the Heavens: A History of Indian-White Relations in Canada* (Toronto: University of Toronto Press, 1989).

registered members of a band that "took treaty" with the Crown, surrendering land rights for specific benefits, or registered Indians who did not. Since they are registered, both types of status Indians received benefits and privileges from the federal government. Non-status Indians were all others of Indian ancestry and cultural affiliation who, actively or passively, had given up their status rights but not their Indian identity. Métis, for example, are descendants of unions between whites and Indians who retain their Indian identity but do not enjoy special status under federal policy.[92]

The Inuit in Canada, scattered throughout the Arctic in eight distinct communities, have never been subject to the *Indian Act* and were largely ignored by government until 1939 when they officially became a federal responsibility. Since that time they have been classified as "Indians" for the purposes of the *Constitution*.

The *Indian Act* of 1876 was amended frequently in subsequent years, but always with the aim of suppressing Indian traditions and extending government control over status Indians on reserves. The current Act, passed in 1951, remains an essentially nineteenth century statute that reflects early biases and intent.

Court decisions over the years have been unable to define aboriginal rights adequately. Until the *Constitution Act 1982*, Parliament had the power to pass laws extinguishing any or all such rights. However, Native groups never agreed that Parliament had such sweeping powers. The *Constitution Act 1982* clears up the situation to a degree. It recognizes aboriginal and treaty rights and provides a new basis for court challenges. In 1985, Parliament provided a procedure to restore Indian status to those who had lost it. In 1991, the total aboriginal population was estimated at 1 002 675, of whom 741 979 were Indians and 170 454 were Métis. There were just over 40 000 Inuit. (See Table 3.3.)

Native peoples still occupy a dependent, semi-colonial position in regard to the federal and provincial governments. Proposals to end Indian status and repeal the *Indian Act* have been called for by natives who want greater recognition of their traditional rights, settlement of land claims and power to manage their own lands and affairs. Grand Chief of the Assembly of First Nations, Georges Erasmus, put the case this way: "we want to have a relationship with this country that is nation to nation" as expressed in the "two-row wampum" analogy of the Mohawks.

> The two-row wampum is an agreement whereby two nations co-exist and travel the River of Life
> in peace and friendship.... Legally, it means that each of the two nations retains its own
> respective laws and jurisdiction. Neither of the two nations can apply or impose its laws over the
> other.[93]

The *Indian Act* was intended to protect native people within Canadian society and to provide a broad range of social programs. All Indians receive the same benefits as other Canadians, such as family allowances and pensions, and status Indians also have a right to a wide variety of other benefits in the field of education, health care and housing. In fact, however, these people have been left dependent on government.

As a whole, unlike many other minorities, Canada's native peoples are economically deprived. Many are plagued by alcoholism and depression as they strive to cope with the loss of their traditional lifestyle because of the encroachments of modern society and envi-

---

92 See *Canada, Aboriginal Peoples, Self-Government, and Constitutional Reform* (Ottawa: Supply and Servies, 1991).

93 As recorded in documents sent to Québec Premier Robert Bourassa, August 20, 1990.

ronmental disasters. Métis and non-status Indians usually find themselves among the under-privileged sections of Canadian society and are subject to similar racial stereotyping and prejudice. The Inuit, because of their location in the Northwest Territories, northern Québec and Labrador, largely have been by-passed in the economic and political modernization of Canada.

Past treatment of native peoples is a point of shame for Canadians. The condition of status Indians who live on reserves is indicative of the problem. In modern times, this population has grown substantially, largely because of reductions in infant mortality rates and high rates of fertility. Their rate of population growth is well over twice that of the rest of Canadians. Approximately 40% of the Indian population is between the ages of 15 and 35, compared to 35 percent of the total Canadian population.

During the post–Second-World-War period, Indian migration to the cities increased dramatically due to poor conditions on the reserves. There, the migrants suffered from the same type of conditions as they had hoped to escape — high unemployment and economic deprivation.

Despite (some would say because of) government assistance, Indians live in abysmal social conditions. Examples of these conditions in the 1980s and 1990s can be summarized as follows:

- High school completion rates are low: 20% compared to about 70% for non-natives.
- Only 22% of the adult Indian population has training beyond high school compared to 40% of the rest of the Canadian population.
- Participation in the labour force is low: 50% compared to 65% for non-natives.
- Unemployment is about twice as high as the national average.
- Employment pay is about 2/3 the national average.
- Life expectancy, infant mortality, suicide and violent death are all worse for natives than non-natives.
- Native children are four times as likely to die by the age of 14 as non-natives.
- The rate of death by fire on reserves is six times that of the Canadian population.
- Environmental hazards threaten traditional ways of life: industrial and resource development have polluted waterways and disrupted fish and game stocks on which many depend for food and livelihood.
- Reserves endure low housing standard, with overcrowding and insufficient access to indoor plumbing, running water and electricity as the norm. One government task force concluded that fewer than 50% of Indian houses were fully serviced with sewers and water compared to a national rate of 90%.[94]

Further evidence that Indians in Canada constitute an extremely deprived group is found in studies commissioned by the Department of Indian Affairs and Northern Development on the future of aboriginal life in Canada. These studies of demographic trends, social conditions and the economic future for Canada's native peoples for the years 1981 to 2001 indicate that while improvements are being made, the gap between them

---

[94] For figures see Eric Nielsen, *New Management Initiatives* (Ottawa: Government of Canada, 1985). A 1992 study by Health and Welfare Canada found that Natives are more than three times as likely to die a violent death before age 65 as non-natives and about twice as likely to die of any cause before 65. *The Globe and Mail,* Dec. 30, 1992.

and their fellow Canadians will remain fairly constant unless there are major policy innovations.[95]

REDRESSING HISTORICAL GRIEVENCES

While they are divided on many other issues, Native peoples are united in a quest for settlement of their land claims and recognition of their "inherent right of self-government." Their demands on Canadian society are made through several groups, the most important of which include The Assembly of First Nations, the Native Council of Canada, The Inuit Tapirisat of Canada, and the Métis National Council.

As we noted in Chapter 2, land claims are an urgent problem. In some areas no treaties have been signed: in others they are blatantly unfair or not respected. Despite the federal government's authroity over Native peoples, provincial governments are in control of public lands, so negotiations are complicated. Only in the North, where the federal government is in charge of the land, have claims moved relatively quickly. As of 1993, all of Canada's North above the 60th parallel is covered by final agreements or agreements in principle about land claims. Further south, the reserves are generally inadequate for economic development and the resource needs of the aboriginal communities. In order to become economically self-sufficient, these peoples must be assured of a secure and expanded land base. The alternative is for them to remain dependent on governments, and for increasing numbers of aboriginal groups to seek court settlements over disputes in such matters as logging and mining on Crown lands licenced by provincial governments.

About half the over 600 status Indian bands of Canada have not ceded their traditional territories by treaty with the Canadian government. The Indians of most of British Columbia, Québec and the territories have not entered into such treaties, and claim outstanding aboriginal rights over, and title to, their traditional lands. They have asserted historic rights to roughly half the country. In British Columbia, for example, native groups claim most of the land mass of the province, 85 percent in Québec.

The current land claims process is notoriously complicated and slow: only six claims across the country are in negotiation at any one time. All other groups must wait until those negotiations are completed, and each case takes about 20 years to settle. At this rate injustices will continue, and claims will still be heard well into the next century.

Apart from a few settlements in Alberta and Manitoba, Métis and non-status Indians do not have reserves at all. In fact the exact size of the Métis population is not even known. According to Martin Dunn, a very rough and conservative estimate is that there are three Métis and non-status Indians for every registered Indian.[96] They are thinly scattered across the country and do not benefit from the special provisions for reserves and services under the *Indian Act*.

Several other issues about aboriginal rights are on the political agenda. One complication of territorial claims is that Québec's Indians do not want to remain part of that province if it decides to separate from Canada. The Assembly's Report on the Charlottetown Constitutional proposal stated: "If Quebec has the right to separate from Canada, First

---

[95] Department of Indian Affairs and Northern Development, *Highlights of Aboriginal Conditions 1981–2001: Demographic Trends, Social Conditions, Economic Conditions* (Ottawa: DIAND, 1989).

[96] Martin Dunn, *Access to Survival: A Perspective on Aboriginal Self-Government for the Constituency of the Native Council of Canada* (Queen's Institute for Intergovernmental Relations, Kingston, 1986).

Nations have the right to make their own decisions. And if that means separation from Quebec, so be it." This is a serious issue. The Cree claim more than a million square kilometers of sparsely populated land, a tract bigger than Ontario and nearly twice the size of France. The claim includes the land on which the James Bay power installations, which generate nearly half of Québec's current electricity are located, as well as the vast untapped hydro potential of other northern rivers.

Another broad, contentious issue concerning native peoples concerns their demand for the right to "self-government." Although attempts to achieve constitutional recognition failed with the Charlottetown accord (see Chapter 5), progress toward self-government arrangements within the existing constitutional framework are proceeding. However, according to some Native leaders, such rights should not be defined in documents such as the *Constitution* because they are "inherent rights." As well, there is no agreement among the Natives themselves about what self-government means. For some it is to be a level of government much like a municipality. For others the "first nations" would constitute a third order of government.

Public opinion polls indicate strong support for native self-government, although it appears that neither the Canadian public nor Native groups themselves have a clear idea of what exactly is meant by the term nor what it will cost. Canadians are ashamed of how aboriginals have been treated. However the concept of self-government is vague. For years, Native peoples have argued that no Canadian government is in a position to grant a right that predates it and that has no source in any imperial, colonial or Dominion authority. They consider that their right to govern themselves is a pre-existing, continuing, natural right given to them by the Great Creator. It cannot be given or taken away by any government. They reason that they have never themselves given up their right to self-government, and it has never been extinguished by any legislation (because such power could not exist), as it is not the gift of any Canadian government.

These are some of the issues currently being addressed by the Royal Commission on Aboriginal Peoples that was set up in April 1992. The recommendations of the Commission and experience with the Nunavut government as a prototype for other self-government settlements will help to shape attitudes toward native issues in the years ahead. Native self-government is discussed further in Chapter 6.

THE REGIONAL DIMENSION OF POLITICAL CULTURE

There is widespread acceptance in the theoretical literature of comparative politics of the thesis that strong regional interests are incompatible with mature statehood, that state-building involves a gradual reduction of conflict between regional and national interests. While this contention is not without its critics, it remains one of the primary hypotheses about the growth and development of states and their legitimacy.[97] In this section we address the question: How strong is regionalism in Canada and is it increasing or decreasing?

Impressive factual data exist about distinct regional forms of social behaviour in Canada. Such regionally-based behaviour may be caused by differences in political culture between

---

[97] See Almond and Powell, *Comparative Politics*; Raymond Breton, "Regionalism in Canada," in David Cameron, ed., *Regionalism and Supranationalism* (Montréal: IRPP, 1981).

regions or may be the cause of regional differences in values and attitudes. On a practical level, educational and professional standards, as well as licensing requirements, for example, differ from province to province and are often not easily transferable.[98] The provinces also restrict mobility of individuals through numerous other variations in standards, laws and services such as driver's licences, pension plans and medical insurance. Regional behaviour is strong in the economic sphere, too, especially in the area of natural resources where the conflicts over revenue-sharing between federal and provincial often arise.[99]

Not surprisingly, therefore, some researchers have argued that Canada has not merely one or even two "political cultures," but several that are regionally based. In view of the distinctions we made earlier, these are not "cultures" per se, but rather important subcultures within the overarching Canadian political culture. The establishment of a federal form of government gave a structural guarantee that some form of regionalism would flourish in Canada; indeed, it was chosen partly because it would allow regional diversity.

Numerous factors promote and sustain this constitutionalized regionalism.[100] People of varying historical, cultural and linguistic backgrounds settled in different parts of the country. Geographical and economic disparities among the regions fostered distinct viewpoints, loyalties and attitudes toward national political problems. As one author put it, Canada became "a country displaying a complex of political cultures which are regionally based...the extent of the diversity of Canada's political cultures and its scope...are quite astonishing."[101] The institutions and policies of the various provincial governments reflect differences in the values and attitudes of their citizens.

The term **regionalism** is particularly obtuse. It implies a socio-psychological dimension in that the population displays an emotional identification with or attachment to a given territory. There is also a political dimension in that specific interests — cultural, economic and political — can be defined and articulated for a particular area. There is thus general agreement that regions are more than purely scientific artifacts, but many different opinions surface about exactly what they are, how many there are or what their boundaries might be.

Some researchers hold that the boundaries of each of the ten provinces demarcate regions with separate political cultures.[102] Others maintain there are three, four or five regions. In the following pages, we have adopted a popular conception of Canadian regional boundaries wherein six regions are identified: the Atlantic provinces (Newfoundland, Nova Scotia, New Brunswick and Prince Edward Island); Québec; Ontario; the Prairies (Manitoba, Saskatchewan and Alberta); British Columbia; and the North (comprising the Yukon and Northwest Territories). However, the reader should be aware that basing regions on

---

[98] Garth Stevenson, *Unfulfilled Union* (Toronto: Macmillan, 1979), p. 125.

[99] See Garth Stevenson, "Federalism and the Political Economy of the Canadian State," in Leo Panitch, ed., *The Canadian State* (Toronto: University of Toronto Press, 1977) and Kenneth Campbell, "Regional Disparity and Interregional Exchange Imbalance," in Daniel Glenday, Herbert Guindon and Allan Turowetz, eds., *Modernization and the Canadian State* (Toronto: Macmillan, 1978).

[100] For an economic explanation see D. Glenday et al., eds., *Modernization and the Canadian State* (Toronto: Macmillan, 1978).

[101] John Meisel, *Working Papers on Canadian Politics* (Montréal: McGill-Queen's University Press, 1972), p. 25. For a collection of important articles on regional identities in Canada see Eli Mandel and David Taras, *A Passion For Identity* (Toronto: Methuen, 1987).

[102] John Wilson, "The Canadian Political Cultures: Towards a Redefinition of the Nature of the Canadian Political System," *CJPS*, vol. 7, no. 3 (Sept. 1974), pp. 438–83.

provincial boundaries (or groups of provinces) is largely a convenience, and that significant variations in cultural patterns may well occur within these borders — for example, between northern and southern Ontario.

SIX REGIONAL PROFILES

Four main categories of regional differences lead researchers to expect cultural diversity: physical factors (such as climate, terrain and land quality); demographic factors (including ethnic and religious composition and urbanization); economic development (including natural resources and type of economy); and services that affect the quality of life (such as transportation, health and welfare). The following brief profiles of six regions illustrate some of these important differences.

As Figure 3.8 shows, the *Atlantic provinces* possess 9 percent of the population of Canada. The inhabitants are largely of British and Irish ancestry, with pockets of Acadian French, centred in New Brunswick. The majority are Protestant, but Roman Catholics constitute the largest single denomination. Their formal educational level is relatively low, they are relatively poor (refer to Figure 3.8), and they usually have the highest unemployment levels in Canada. Most reside in rural areas and small towns. Economically, the major contribution comes through the fisheries, of which more than half Canada's total are located here. The region is seriously deficient in secondary industries and contributes less than the other regions to the national wealth in proportion to the population. Federal transfer payments make up 30 to 50 percent of provincial revenues. Both internal and external communications are relatively inadequate. Low immigration and a tendency toward outward migration have often meant a net loss of inhabitants for the region as a percentage of the country's total population.

TABLE 3.4   PERCENTAGE DISTRIBUTION OF CANADIAN POPULATION BY PROVINCE AND REGION

Province	%	Region	%
Newfoundland	2.1	Atlantic Provinces	8.6
Prince Edward Island	0.5	Quebec	25.3
Nova Scotia	3.3	Ontario	36.9
New Brunswick	2.7	Prairie Provinces	16.9
Quebec	25.3	British Columbia	12.0
Ontario	36.9	Northland	0.3
Manitoba	4.0		100.0
Saskatchewan	3.6		
Alberta	9.3		
British Columbia	12.0		
Yukon Territory	0.1		
Northwest Territories	0.2		
	100.0		

Source: 1991 Census data. *The Daily* (Ottawa: Statistics Canada, April 28, 1992), p. 5. Reproduced by authority of the Minister responsible for Statistics Canada 1993.

FIGURE 3.8   POPULATION AND FAMILY INCOME IN CANADA BY PROVINCE, 1991 CENSUS

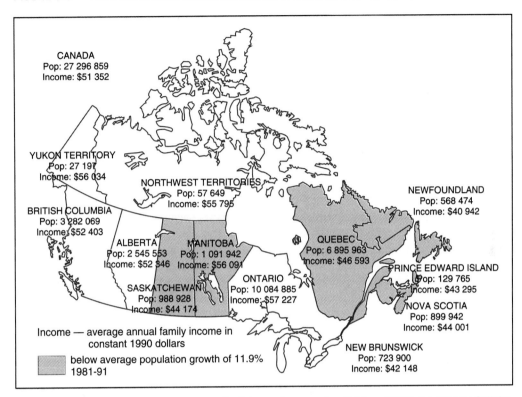

Source: Population figures are from the 1991 census. Family income figures are from *Catalogue 93-331, Select Income Statistics*, Table 6, p. 160. Ottawa: Statistics Canada, 1993. Reproduced by authority of the Minister responsible for Statistics Canada 1993.

Québec houses just over one quarter of the Canadian population. It is the bastion of French language and culture and is largely Roman Catholic in composition. Eighty-three percent of Québec residents were French-speaking at the time of the 1991 census. The province's population growth of 7.1 percent from 1981 to 1991 is below the country's average. Economically, Québec and neighbouring Ontario are the most industrialized regions, with major contributions to agriculture, mining, forestries, electric power, manufacturing and construction. Québec has a rapidly growing urban population that is located in a few major cities; 80 percent of its population was classified as urban in 1986.

Ontario contains 37 percent of the Canadian population. Although still predominantly of British stock, Ontarians include large groups of French, Italian and German, in that order, and many other ethnic groups in lesser numbers. In 1991, 48.6 percent of the Canadian population with non-official first languages resided in Ontario and immigrants represented almost 25 percent of the provincial population. Roman Catholic and Protestant denominations dominate, but many other religious groups are also represented. As noted above, Ontario, along with Québec, forms the industrial heartland of Canada. Economic readjustments required in the early 1990s left the Ontario government with a ballooning deficit and a severe decline in its customary economic position. However, urban, well-educated Ontario residents continued to be well-serviced medically, and to own more televisions, telephones and automobiles *per capita* than most of their fellow Canadians. Ontario residents increased by just over 16 percent between 1981 and 1991, well above the national average of 11.9 percent.

The three *Prairie Provinces* ethnically are extremely diverse and still reflect the influence of the European peasants who flocked to settle the prairie farmlands in the late nineteenth and early twentieth centuries. The first European settlers in the region were Scottish crofters in the Red River valley in Manitoba. Today, the largest single group in the prairie region is still of British origin, but there are exceptionally large numbers of German and Ukrainian descent, a large percentage of Native Indians, as well as many citizens of Polish, Dutch and Scandinavian origin. No single religion dominates. Economically dependent on natural resources for their above-average wealth, the prairie provinces make outstanding contributions in agriculture, particularly wheat, mining and oil and gas production. Development of the Alberta oil fields has dramatically increased the prosperity and prestige of that province in recent years.

Since the Second World War, the agrarian nature of the prairie region has been changing and an increasing percentage of the population is urban, although Saskatchewan is still one of the least urbanized Canadian provinces. Alberta, the richest and most urban of the prairie provinces, and the most attractive for immigrants because of the oil and gas industries, accounts for much of the significant increase in net migration in the prairie region during the past two decades. It sustained the most rapid population growth of all the provinces and territories between 1971 and 1991 (39.1 percent) but most of that gain was prior to 1982. Manitoba and Saskatchewan grew least.

British Columbia is cut off from the rest of the country by the Rocky Mountain chain. Immigrants in the early years were primarily British but today the ethnic composition is diverse because of high immigration and internal migration. In 1991, British Columbia had 12 percent of the total Canadian population. Almost 25 percent of the province's population were foreign-born. Religious affiliation is also diverse; however, the United and Anglican churches make up the majority. Economically prosperous, British Columbia makes major contributions through fisheries and forestry and, to some extent, through its manufacturing and construction industries. Despite reliance on primary resource industries, the region is relatively urban, with a number of heavily populated centres.

Canada's largest region, the vast *Northland* of the Northwest Territories and the Yukon Territory, comprises 39 percent of the country's total land mass. However, the thinly scattered population, which includes the Dene (Indian) nation, several Inuit peoples and Métis and a small white population constitutes only .3 percent of the Canadian population, in spite of rapid growth in percentage terms since 1971. Only about 34 percent of Yukon's population is of non-British, non-French ethnic origins. However, about 51 percent of the population of the Northwest Territories report single aboriginal origins: the largest group are Inuit (32%), about 15 percent are status and non-status Indians, the remaining 4 percent, Métis.

The economy of the Yukon Territory has grown rapidly over the past decade largely because of demand for certain minerals, but the economy of the Northwest Territories remains precarious. Communications in the entire region are tenuous. For Canada's Native peoples, as we have seen, living conditions are difficult.

In November 1982, the federal government agreed to reshape the political boundaries of the Northwest Territories, so that eventually the inhabitants will not have to rely on a single regional government in Yellowknife. In Chapter 2 we noted that a new territory, Nunavut, will begin acquiring self-government in 1999. Nunavut is the first major self-government agreement that gives Native peoples powers equivalent to those of a province. It will be reflective of Native values and cultures. Currently, NWT is the only political division in Canada where the Native people constitute a majority. When the Inuit leave

Yellowknife's legislature to form their own territorial government there will be a major change in the ethnic make-up of NWT. For the first time, non-Natives will represent a slight majority of the NWT's population.

The differences in historical development, ethnic and demographic make-up and economic structure within Canada are evident in these brief profiles of the six regions. However, since provincial governments provide the only institutional focus through which regions can mobilize, it is questionable whether particular groups of provinces can ever be as effective as individual provinces in political terms. Indeed, it is not even clear that they want to be. A former premier of Prince Edward Island, Alex Campbell, once said publicly that "we in Atlantic Canada have not yet made the decision to develop as a region. We are four separate competitive, jealous and parochial provinces."[103]

REGIONAL ALIENATION: DISTANCE AND DIVISION

In the mid 1990s, Canada continues to face particularly strong demands from alienated regions, especially the western provinces. Western discontent reflects the region's unique history and population mix. A dominant perception of Canada's national needs has been built around the concept of two founding peoples because of the long historical relationships between French and English Canadians. This is not, however, the western vision of Canada. According to western political scientists the western vision is largely ahistorical; since the population is ethnically varied and relatively new to the West, the people do not state their interests in terms of the early history of central and eastern Canada.

In the prairie region, particularly Alberta and Saskatchewan, there is a commonly held belief that their region is exploited by Easterners. This feeling is based on the perceived economic and political domination of the rest of the country, especially by the tiny Golden Horseshoe area of southern Ontario and Montréal. Former Alberta Premier Harry Strom's imagery illustrates it well: "We have always had a sense of economic exploitation. This notion has marked all political parties in the West. The cartoon that has captured these sentiments is one of a large cow standing on a map of Canada munching grass in Alberta and Saskatchewan, with milk pouring from a bulging udder into the large bucket in Ontario."[104] The main thrust of western discontent, however, hinges on a feeling of marginalization and alienation from the centres of economic and political power rather than on a simple desire for separation from it, and may "reflect frustration at the lack of national integration as much as it does resistance to integration."[105]

The underlying problem of regional alienation is easily stated, but not easily resolved. The population of two provinces, Ontario and Québec, considerably exceeds 50 percent of the entire country. Because of this fact, the outer regions generally perceive that the federal parliamentary system only represents central Canada and, therefore, to an extent, is merely a regional government for citizens in that part of the country. Many solutions to alienation have been proposed over the years by westerners: switch political parties,

[103] Quoted in Roger Gibbins, *Regionalism: Territorial Politics in Canada and the United States* (Toronto: Butterworths, 1982), p. 178.

[104] Quoted in David Elton and Roger Gibbins, "Western Alienation and Political Culture," in R. Schultz et al., eds., *The Canadian Political Process*, 3rd ed. (Toronto: Holt, Rinehart and Winston, 1979), p. 85.

[105] Gibbins, *Regionalism*, p. 181. See also J.F. Conway, *The West: The History of a Region in Confederation* (Toronto: James Lorimer, 1983).

abolish parties, electoral reform, Senate reform, abolish party discipline and so on. The landscape is littered with reform initiatives. Westerners have agreed only on a goal — a more effective voice at the centre — but not how to achieve it.

It is important to note, however, that these regional economic disparities and the manner they are dealt with are distinguishing features of Canadian politics. Since Confederation, the belief that the rich provinces and regions should help the poorer ones has been a fundamental part of the Canadian political culture. Sharing through redistribution is built into the political system and is viewed by Canadians as the "just" way to cope with differences in wealth.[106]

Disputes over formulas and provincial jostling for a fair share of the economic pie take place within this basic redistribution framework. One study commissioned by the Task Force on Canadian Unity in 1978 concluded that attachment to either region or province does not threaten national integration.[107] It has even been suggested that regional discontent may be more a fabrication of elites than a strong feeling of the mass public.[108] It is often to the benefit of the political elite to exacerbate differences between provinces or regions and the federal government. Provincial premiers can play on regional sentiments to gain support in striking tough financial bargains with the federal government. The impact of western alienation on federalism is discussed in Chapter 6.

REGIONAL POLITICAL CULTURES

Richard Simeon and David Elkins are among those who have argued that Canada embraces several regional political cultures.[109] Basing their argument on survey data, they compared the provinces, examining differences among their populations regarding patterns of political orientations and explanations of these differences. They concluded that "there are indeed differences between the provinces which may be called cultural, which are rooted in the matrix of historical and sociological factors unique to each province."[110]

It is interesting to speculate on the possible sources of the cultural variations among the provinces. Some of the factors outlined in the regional profiles are undoubtedly significant. Levels of industrialization and economic development are extremely low in the Maritime provinces, high in Ontario and British Columbia. Emigration from the Maritime area is high, immigration low. The extreme weakness of the economy and the consistent historical inability of Maritime governments to solve the problem likely engenders lack of political trust and feelings of inability to change their situation. The provinces that scored highest in the efficacy/political trust scale have the opposite of these characteristics. As well, the peculiar pattern of settlement along the American border and the poly-

---

[106] See, for example, Herschel Hardin's concept of "The Canadian Redistribution Culture," in H. Hardin, *A Nation Unaware: The Canadian Economic Culture* (Vancouver: J.J. Douglas Ltd., 1974), especially ch. 13.

[107] Relevant findings from the Atlantic Provinces Study conducted for the Task Force on Canadian Unity can be found in Gibbins, *Regionalism*, pp. 179–80.

[108] See, for example, Richard Simeon and Donald E. Blake in "Regional Preferences: Citizens' Views of Public Policy," in David J. Elkins and Richard Simeon, *Small Worlds*, pp. 77–105.

[109] Richard Simeon and David J. Elkins, "Regional Political Cultures in Canada," *CJPS*, vol. 7, no. 3 (September 1974), pp. 397–437. The revised version of this article is "Provincial Political Cultures in Canada," in *Small Worlds*, pp. 31–76.

[110] Ibid., p. 68.

cephalic city network discussed in Chapter 2 help perpetuate regionally based interests and attitudes.

The six regions profiled above might well exhibit differences of which their residents are unaware. But if there is little or no regional consciousness, it can be argued that residents cannot be politicized into action over regional interests or problems. If there is no regional consciousness, "regionalism" cannot be treated as an explanatory variable for analytical purposes, but must be limited to the role of "container" for other variables. Researchers would have to let Canadians themselves describe the regions in which they live and articulate their feelings about these regions in order to demarcate lines of regional consciousness.

This "self-assigned" concept of regions causes theoretical problems of the highest order. The term is used in so many ways by Canadians that it may have little causal effect on behaviour. Clarke et al. in the 1974 election study, concluded that the diversity of responses about what the regions are "makes it unlikely that regional consciousness will provide a major explanatory variable in the definition of Canadian party politics and in the explanation of Canadian electoral behaviour." However, they also stated that enough regional feeling was discovered to indicate that the "potential exists for both politicization of regional cleavages and for region to be an explanatory variable in itself."[111]

Thus, although it has become widely accepted among Canadian political scientists that regionalism is an important facet of Canadian life, the salient spatial boundaries of the regions have not been determined. Nor has the theoretical explanation of their persistence been satisfactorily developed. Some argue that it is premature to conclude that Canadian politics is largely regional, because there has been no thorough study of class structure in Canada, or of the socio-economic issues dividing right and left branches of public opinion. After analyzing a national sample survey, one study, for example, concluded that Canadian politics is regional only if political views are narrowly defined as attitudes towards electoral politics and governmental institutions.[112] Other researchers have shown that regional variations in opinions are neither strong nor consistent on topics that have no readily apparent territorial connotations, and that Canadians have been, over the past 30 years, becoming more alike in their responses to important public policy issues, regardless of region.[113]

Regional cleavages, like ethnic divisions, are not necessarily detrimental; they can be normal and healthy, and non-threatening to national cohesiveness. One study showed that although regional loyalty is often high in Canada, it is not at the expense of national loyalty. In fact, feelings toward province and nation were strongly correlated: positive feelings toward the province were usually accompanied by positive feelings for the country. In addition, the more knowledgeable Canadians were about their country, and the more sensitive they were to regionalism, the more they favoured the federal government over their provincial governments. Canadian nationalists tended to be not only well-informed about Canada but also cosmopolitan people who felt warmly about other countries.[114]

In conclusion, then, the divisive effect of regional differences should not be exaggerated. Not enough is known about whether territorial identities are compatible with strong national identification. But it is clear that strong regional identities alone do not prove that

---

[111] Clarke et al., *Political Choice in Canada*, p. 64.

[112] M. Ornstein et al., "Region, Class and Political Culture in Canada," p. 267.

[113] R. Gibbins, *Regionalism*, p. 184 and Simeon and Blake, "Regional Preferences," p. 100.

[114] David Elkins, "The Sense of Place," in *Small Worlds*, pp. 23 and 25.

national identification is weak or threatened. Western regional demands are not inherently nationalistic; they usually do not call for the development of a new state as is often the case in the province of Québec. Western regional leaders restrict their demands to changes in the economic and political arrangements between the region and the central government.

There is enough evidence to indicate that, in the case of ethnic identities, multiple loyalties alone need not be feared; in fact, they make Canada richer as a country. However, when strong regional loyalties are linked to general perceptions of injustice, regionalism may become a potent political force. The federal government must be sensitive enough to relieve tensions on these occasions. Canadians should not be forced by governments to choose whether they prefer to be Acadians, French Canadians or Canadians first. David Elkins expressed the matter this way: "Multiple loyalties can have...a civilizing result, since they encourage us to reject absolute choices and teach us to give assent and express dissent in graduated and qualified terms."[115]

OVERVIEW

Canadians have a rich variety of perceptions and knowledge about their country, their provinces and their regions. The very nature of the country, with its geographical, historical, economic and demographic differences, dictates that this will be so. Surely it is this very diversity that is at the heart of the distinctive Canadian political culture.

Canadians did not create an ideologically based nation. Ideological diversity resulted naturally from a combination of such factors as strong American influence, a high rate of population turnover and strong regional, economic and ethnic differences. Canadians also suffered a prolonged condition of colonial mentality that delayed the development of national symbols and pride. When the Constitution was brought home from Britain in 1982, Canada finally matured politically. Perhaps social and cultural maturity will follow.

It is difficult to measure something as elusive as a sense of political community. However, while we recognize that regional and ethnic variations do exist, we can also say that the models of governing that Canada inherited from Britain and the United States have fostered certain types of values, attitudes and behaviour toward the political system and government-related activities. The collective heritage of beliefs, opinions and preferences shared by Canadians is greater than the rhetoric of provincial autonomy and regional cleavages would lead one to believe. The federal structure and the party system, with their apparent inability to bridge regional and linguistic cleavages, exaggerate differences that exist among Canadians. In fact, it is often in the interests of the provincial or federal political elites to frame issues so that their own interests and ambitions are accommodated. In a successful federal system, citizens should feel positively about both federal and provincial levels of government. We know that Canadians do. Those who feel strongly about their province also generally feel strongly about their country. The two are not mutually exclusive; rather, they are strongly correlated.

The most basic values and attitudes demonstrated by Canadians are democratic attitudes toward political participation and governmental authority. Canadians participate very readily in electoral politics but otherwise participate only passively — only 4 or 5 percent participate on a continuous basis. Concomitantly, authority patterns exhibit a strong element

---

[115] Ibid., p. 26.

of deference toward political elites, but there is a declining trust in government. Despite geographical differences, Canadians in all regions are becoming increasingly similar in their expectations and preferences with respect to most areas of public policy. They want equity in government services and programs.

Three major political developments during the 1980s and 1990s could dramatically affect the direction of the Canadian political culture in the coming decades; the *Charter of Rights and Freedoms*, which shifts Canada toward a more individualist focus and away from the country's communitarian, collectivist roots; the Free Trade Agreement with the United States could have a "homogenizing" effect on Canadian culture by opening the borders further between the two countries; and the North American Free Trade Agreement with the United States and Mexico will have further repercussions along these lines.

The Earl of Balfour wrote in 1927 in his introduction of Bagehot's book on the British constitution that "our whole political machinery presupposes a people so fundamentally at one that they can safely afford to bicker: and so sure of their own moderation that they are not dangerously disturbed by the never-ending din of political conflict."[116] It is not clear exactly what the British people were "fundamentally at one" about, nor is it clear today for Canadians, but the cohesion in the Canadian political culture has been strong enough to permit division and conflict without the eruption of widespread and continual violence. Politicians and government officials can rely on deep-seated attitudes to maintain the authority of government in Canada.

There is a distinctive Canadian political culture. Within the country, provincial political cultures are strong, and provide an assimilative framework for immigrants and internal migrants. However, this should not be seen as subversive of the whole. The provinces also have many features in common. There is unity in diversity, just as the strength and beauty of a tapestry is determined by the very different strands of which it is composed.

---

[116] Introduction by the Earl of Balfour to Walter Bagehot, *The English Constitution* (London: World's Classics Edition, 1955), p. xxiv.

SELECTED BIBLIOGRAPHY

POLITICAL CULTURE – GENERAL

Almond, Gabriel and Sidney Verba, *The Civic Culture* (Boston: Little, Brown, 1965).

———, eds., The Civic Culture Revisited (Boston: Little, Brown, 1980).

Bashevkin, Sylvia B., ed., *Canadian Political Behaviour: Introductory Readings* (Toronto: Methuen, 1985).

Brooks, Stephen, ed., *Political Thought in Canada* (Toronto: Irwin, 1984).

Christian, William and Colin Campbell, *Political Parties and Ideologies in Canada: Liberals, Conservatives, Socialists, Nationalists*, 2nd ed. (Toronto: McGraw-Hill Ryerson, 1983).

Clift, Dominique, *The Secret Kingdom: Interpretations of the Canadian Character* (Toronto: McClelland & Stewart, 1989).

Courtney, John C., Peter MacKinnon and David E. Smith, eds., *Drawing Boundaries: Legislatures, Courts and Electoral Values* (Saskatoon: Fifth House Publishers, 1992).

Forbes, H.D., ed., *Canadian Political Thought* (Toronto: Oxford University Press, 1985).

George M.V. and J. Perreault, *Population Projections for Canada, Provinces and Territories, 1984–2006* (Ottawa; Statistics Canada, 1985).

Grant, George, *Lament for a Nation: The Defeat of Canadian Nationalism* (Toronto: McClelland & Stewart, 1965).

Hartz, Louis, ed., *The Founding of New Societies* (New York: Harcourt Brace & Jovanovich, 1964).

Kaplan, William, ed., *Belonging: The Meaning and Future of Canadian Citizenship* (Montréal: McGill-Queen's University Press, 1993).

Mandel, Eli, and David Taras, *A Passion for Identity: An Introduction to Canadian Studies* (Toronto: Methuen, 1987).

Marchak, M. Patricia, *Ideological Perspectives on Canada*, 2nd ed. (Toronto: McGraw-Hill Ryerson, 1981).

McDaniel, Susan, *Canada's Aging Population* (Toronto: Butterworths, 1987).

Nevitte, N. and A. Kornberg, *Minorities and the Canadian State* (Oakville, Ont.: Mosaic Press, 1985).

Porter, John, *The Vertical Mosaic: Analysis of Social Class and Power in Canada* (Toronto: University of Toronto Press, 1965).

Qualter, T.H., *Conflicting Political Ideas in Liberal Democracies* (Toronto: Methuen, 1986).

Resnick, Philip, *Parliament vs People: An Essay on Democracy and Canadian Political Culture* (Vancouver: New Star Books, 1984).

Schmeiser, D.A., *Civil Liberties in Canada* (London: Oxford University Press, 1964).

Smiley, Donald V., *The Canadian Political Nationality* (Toronto: Methuen, 1967).

Underhill, Frank H., *In Search of Canadian Liberalism* (Toronto: Macmillan, 1960).

Stewart, Gordon T., *The Origins of Canadian Politics* (Vancouver: University of British Columbia Press, 1986).

POLITICAL PARTICIPATION

Milbraith, Lester W. and M.L. Goel, *Political Participation: How and Why Do People Get Involved in Politics?* 2nd ed. (Chicago: Rand McNally, 1977).

Mishler, William, *Political Participation in Canada: Prospects for Democratic Citizenship* (Toronto: Macmillan of Canada, 1979).

ETHNIC RELATIONS/MULTICULTURALISM

Beach, Charles M. and Alan G. Green eds., *Policy Forum on the Role of Immigration in Canada's Future* (Kingston; Queen's University Press, 1988).

Berry, John W., Rudolf Kalin and Donald M. Taylor, *Multiculturalism and Ethnic Attitudes in Canada* (Ottawa: Minister of Supply and Services, 1977).

Bibby, Reginald W., *Mosaic Madness: The Poverty and Potential of Life in Canada* (Toronto: Stoddart, 1990).

Bienvenue, Rita M. and Jay E. Goldstein, eds., *Ethnicity and Race Relations in Canada*, 2nd ed. (Toronto: Butterworths, 1985).

Breton, Raymond, Jeffrey Reitz and Victor Valentine, *Cultural Boundaries and the Cohesion of Canada* (Montréal: IRPP, 1980).

Brym, Robert J. and Bonnie J. Fox, *From Culture to Power: The Sociology of English Canada* (Toronto: Oxford University Press, 1989).

Cairns, A. and C. Williams, eds., *The Politics of Gender, Ethnicity, and Language in Canada*, vol. 34, Royal Commission on the Economic Union and Development Prospects for Canada (Toronto: University of Toronto Press, 1986).

Driedger, Leo, ed., *Ethnic Canada: Identities and Inequalities* (Toronto: Copp Clark Pitman, 1987).

Dwivedi, O.P. et al., *Canada 2000: Race Relations and Public Policy* (Guelph: Department of Political Studies, 1989).

Elkins, David and Richard Simeon, eds., *Small Worlds: Provinces and Parties in Canadian Political Life* (Toronto: Methuen, 1980).

Elliot, Jean Leonard, ed., *Two Nations, Many Cultures* (Scarborough: Prentice-Hall Canada, 1979).

——— and Augie Fleras, *Multiculturalism in Canada: The Challenge of Diversity* (Scarborough: Nelson Canada, 1991).

——— *Unequal Relations: An Introduction to Race and Ethnic Dynamics in Canada* (Scarborough: Prentice Hall Canada, 1992).

Granatstein, J.L. and Kenneth McNaught, *English Canada Speaks Out* (Toronto: Doubleday, 1991).

Horowitz, Gad, *Ethnic Groups in Conflict* (Berkeley: University of California Press, 1985).

Kallen, Evelyn, *Ethnicity and Human Rights in Canada* (Toronto: Gage, 1982).

Magee, Joan, *Loyalist Mosaic: A Multi-Ethnic Heritage* (Toronto: Dundurn Press, 1984).

Miller, J.R., *Skyscrapers Hide the Heavens: A History of Indian-White Relations in Canada* (Toronto: University of Toronto Press, 1989).

Taylor, Charles, *Multiculturalism and 'The Politics of Recognition'* (Princeton: Princeton University Press, 1991).

Ujimoto, V. and G. Hiranayashi, eds., *Visible Minorities and Multiculturalism* (Toronto: Butterworths, 1983).

REGIONALISM

Bercuson, David J. and Barry Cooper, *Deconfederation* (Toronto: Key Porter, 1992)

Brym, Robert J., *Regionalism in Canada* (Toronto: Irwin, 1986).

Friesen, Gerald, *The Canadian Prairies: A History* (Toronto: University of Toronto Press, 1984).

Gibbins, Roger, *Regionalism: Territorial Politics in Canada and the United States* (Toronto: Butterworths, 1983).

FRENCH CANADA

Behiels, M.D., ed., *Quebec Since 1945: Selected Readings* (Toronto: Copp Clark Pitman, 1987).

Bourhis, R.Y., ed., *Conflict and Language Planning in Quebec* (Clevedon: Multilingual Maters Ltd., 1984).

Caldwell, G. and E. Waddell, eds., *The English of Quebec: From Majority to Minority Status* (Québec: Institut Québécois de recherche sur la culture, 1982).

Coleman, W.D. *The Independence Movement in Quebec 1945–1980* (Toronto: University of Toronto Press, 1984).

Doern, Russell, *The Battle Over Bilingualism in the Manitoba Language Question 1935–85* (Winnipeg: Cambridge Publishers, 1985).

Gagnon, Alain G., ed., *Quebec: State and Society* (Toronto: Methuen, 1984).

——— and Mary Beth Montcalm, *Quebec Beyond the Quiet Revolution* (Scarborough: Nelson, 1990).

Guindon, Hubert, *Quebec Society: Tradition, Modernity, Nationhood* (Toronto: University of Toronto Press, 1988).

Joy, Richard J., *Canada's Official Languages* (Toronto: University of Toronto Press, 1992).

MacLennan, Hugh, *Two Solitudes* (Toronto: Collins, 1945).

McRoberts, Kenneth, *Quebec: Social Change and Political Crisis*, 3rd ed. (Toronto: McClelland & Stewart, 1988).

Monière, Denis, *Ideologies in Quebec: The Historical Development* (Toronto: University of Toronto Press, 1981).

Richards, John, François Vaillancourt and William G. Watson, *Survival: Official Language Rights in Canada* (Toronto: C.D. Howe Institute, 1992).

Scowen, Reed, *A Different Vision: The English in Quebec in the 1990s* (Toronto: Maxwell Macmillan, 1992).

Young, Brian and John A. Dickinson, *A Short History of Quebec: A Socio-Economic Perspective* (Toronto, Copp Clark Pitman, 1988).

NATIVE PEOPLES

Asch, Michael, *Home and Native Land* (Toronto: Methuen, 1984).

Berger, Thomas, *A Long and Terrible Shadow: White Values, Native Rights in the Americas* (Vancouver: Douglas and McIntyre, 1991).

Cassidy, Frank, ed., *Aboriginal Self-Government* (Halifax: Institute for Research on Public Policy, 1991).

Comeau, Pauline and Aldo Santin, *The First Canadians* (Toronto: James Lorimer, 1990).

Elliott, J.L. and Augie Fleras, *The 'Nations Within' Aboriginal State Relations in Canada, the United States and New Zealand* (Toronto: Oxford University Press, 1992).

Frideres, James, *Native People in Canada: Contemporary Conflicts* (Scarborough, Ont.: Prentice-Hall Canada, 1983).

MacLaine, Craig and Michael Baxendale, *This Land is Our Land* (Toronto: Optimum, 1990).

Purich, Donald, *The Métis* (Toronto: Lorimer, 1988).

Tennant, Paul, *Aboriginal Peoples and Politics* (Vancouver: University of British Columbia Press, 1990).

York, Geoffrey, *The Dispossessed: Life and Death in Native Canada* (Toronto: Lester & Orpen Dennys 1989).

Wright, Ronald, *Stolen Continents* (Boston: Houghton Mifflin, 1992).

TRANSMITTING POLITICAL IDEAS

EDUCATION, GENDER, CLASS, MEDIA, GOVERNMENT

We have seen that there is an overarching political culture that draws the diverse Canadian population together and provides a degree of national unity. Since 1867, ethnic, linguistic and regional differences within the population have become layered and intertwined, like the strands of a tapestry, to create a prosperous and enviable country. At the same time, however, the differences represented by these cultural strands have created tensions in the body politic. They contribute to cleavages that permeate society, providing the foundation for political orientations and ideas in Canada.

Not all Canadians have equal chances to succeed in life. They have different personal characteristics, abilities and health, and are born into different social and economic circumstances. Factors such as gender, education and socio-economic class help to shape an individual's general political culture and ideas and orientation to politics. For example, a woman from a poor family with little education has experiences and develops self-expectations that are very different from those of a man raised in a wealthy, well-educated, professional family. These two individuals experience unique treatment by parents, peers, teachers and employers. What is expected of them, and the kinds of opportunities that will be open to them in life, differ greatly.

The chance circumstances into which one is born, then, help to shape an individual's general political culture. Gender assignment and socio-economic class, in particular, provide and also deny opportunities and experiences. On these bases individuals may be inclined to take particular stands on issues, orient themselves on such abstract constructs as a left-right continuum, and decide how and even whether they wish to participate in the political process.

In this chapter, we examine some of the major ways that Canadians acquire their political ideas and orientations. We begin by looking briefly at the general process of socialization by which values and attitudes are learned, then at how it occurs in families, peer groups and the educational system in Canada. We then examine the role of two cleavage structures — gender and socio-economic class — that also condition political orientations.

In the last sections, we focus on the controversial roles played by the media and government in transmitting ideas and contributing to political orientations in Canada.

ACQUIRING POLITICAL ORIENTATIONS

Acquiring general political culture and more sophisticated political ideas and orientations is a life-long process by which political culture is learned and transmitted at both the individual and community levels. It is known as **political socialization**. In Canada, children experience casual, informal learning of values and attitudes from family and peers, and more direct learning in schools. As they mature, other more explicit agents of political socialization and such factors as socio-economic class become influential. While political socialization is a continuous, life-long process, some stages may be more important than others.

Development of the political self begins early in childhood.[1] By five or six years of age children in western societies acquire emotional attachments, which are nearly always positive, to the political community to which they belong. Authority figures are seen as benevolent "helpers"; symbols of the political community such as the Queen and the flag generally are regarded positively. Concurrently, children identify with a gender grouping, social and economic class and an ethnic or racial group, though again with little or no factual information. Laws are regarded as absolute and unchanging; authority is seen as people such as police officers or teachers, rather than in abstract terms such as law or responsible government. Political attitudes and beliefs learned at this time are less likely to change than those learned later, which involve more information. This is important for the political culture and the political system inasmuch as it allows a high degree of continuity and intergenerational agreement about basic values to be taken for granted by the government, making it relatively easy to predict citizens' reactions and expectations on many topics.

Between the ages of seven and thirteen, children increasingly understand and relate to more abstract political symbols. As they develop the capacity to see political leaders more critically, and their factual knowledge increases, they gain a better understanding of their political system and its leaders. Ages eleven to thirteen may be the most significant in terms of the ability to reason and grasp abstractions. This stage is followed by a gradual and steady increase in political participation and involvement in the remaining adolescent years.[2] Of course, political learning continues during adulthood, but it is less likely that changes in basic political culture will occur. Adults may alter their ideas and orientations toward specific government policies and develop evaluations of political parties and leaders, but they are less likely to change broad cultural attitudes and beliefs about ideological goals or conceptions of the legitimate means of selecting political rulers.[3]

Though basic political attitudes are formed early and tend to persist, they are retained to different degrees by individuals as a result of discontinuities in their political socialization. If, for example, socialization is inconsistent, or a long time elapses between socialization and the assumption of a political role, then attitudes may be weakly held. The more diverse agents

---

[1] One of the best studies of childhood socialization is R.D. Hess and J.V. Torney, *The Development of Poltical Attitudes in Children* (Chicago: Aldine, 1967).

[2] The early development of political orientation is discussed more fully in Richard E. Dawson, Kenneth Prewitt and Karen S. Dawson, *Political Socialization*, 2nd ed. (Boston: Little, Brown, 1977), ch. 4.

[3] Ibid., ch. 5.

of political socialization to which an individual is exposed, the greater the likelihood that contradictory messages will be received and changes or discontinuities in attitudes occur. Experiences at one stage of life can contradict others later.

Complex societies provide more discontinuities or contradictory messages than simple ones where the family is the major, perhaps even the sole, agent of socialization. As well, a socially and geographically mobile individual experiences relatively more discontinuities in political learning. The strong regional and ethnic subcultures in Canada ensure that the minority of Canadians who move between provinces or regions will be exposed to very different influences. A final condition causing discontinuity in political learning is the amount of change in the structure and process of government. In Canada, institutions have changed very little since Confederation, but in newer, politically unstable countries, discontinuities are enormous as children who have been socialized to certain loyalties are engulfed by a larger state or narrowed to a smaller one.

Political learning occurs in a variety of ways. Some forms of socialization are indirect in that they are not overtly political. Others are much more direct in that they transmit or develop specifically political orientations. Those that socialize individuals *implicitly* into political values and orientations are known as **primary agents** of socialization, while those such as schools and the media that are less personal, closer to the governing process and involved to varying degrees in the process of direct, *explicit* political learning, are known as **secondary agents**.

FAMILIES AND PEER GROUPS

As the basic unit of our society, the family is a primary socializing agent. Families are rarely specifically political in teaching their young. The political learning they offer is likely to be sporadic and incomplete and does not adequately prepare an individual for participation in the political world.[4] However, families are generally important in determining the *extent* and *direction* of political learning.[5] Attitudes and beliefs learned in childhood, such as love of country, tend to be the most intensely held and lasting. Families influence children in three main ways. They provide examples or role models and sometimes even direct teaching about politics. Children from families that are actively concerned with partisan party politics are likely to be politically active when they grow up.[6] Families are also important in instilling social attitudes and personality traits that eventually will be significant in influencing how children react to the political world. Finally, families provide social and economic surroundings, determine the social class of children, their educational values, first language and, often, even direct which other socialization agents will affect the child.

The family, therefore, helps to perpetuate traditional values, attitudes and behaviour patterns. This influence, which is essentially conservative, is not easily manipulated by

---

4   Proponents of the view that learning experiences are cumulative and harmonious include R. Hess and J.V. Torney, *Development of Political Attitudes in Children*, pp. 20–2. This view was modified by K. Keniston, *The Young Radicals: Notes on Committed Youth* (New York: Harcourt Brace and World, 1968), ch. 2.

5   See M. Kent Jennings and Richard Niemi, "The Transmission of Political Values from Parent to Child," *APSR*, vol. 62, no. 1 (March 1968), pp. 169–84. Also see Russel J. Dalton, "Reassessing Parental Socialization: Indicator Unreliability Versus Generational Transfer," *APSR*, vol. 74, no. 2 (June 1980), pp. 421–31.

6   Kenneth Prewitt, "Political Socialization and Leadership Selection," *The Annals of the American Academy of Political and Social Science*, no. 361 (September 1965), pp. 105–8.

political leaders. Families, thus, generally are considered to be beneficial in countries trying to maintain the status quo, but as a hindrance to those trying to alter the political culture or to instigate radical changes in society. In the latter case, the family unit can come under attack, as it did in China during the cultural revolution, and as it did in the early years of the former Soviet Union when it was maligned as a "bourgeois institution."[7]

Peer groups constitute another primary agent of socialization. Friends, associates, sports teams, clubs and groups of all sorts comprise this amorphous group that acquires increasing significance as the child's dependence on the family wanes. The peer group is especially important at about age 13 or 14, and continues to be influential throughout adulthood. Political socialization by peers resembles that by the family. It is haphazard because it is not usually the primary aim of the relationship. Individual relationships are highly personal and emotionally involved. Peer group socialization can alter or reinforce the earlier political learning that has taken place in the family, or, in cases where family socialization was weak, provide fundamental political learning.

Peer groups often assume relatively greater importance in complex urban settings that are normally more impersonal and less family oriented than simpler societies that maintain large, extended families. Peers use subtle persuasion, or blatant methods such as ostracism and ridicule, to pressure individuals to conform to group norms and attitudes. Peer group and family socialization can be given much credit for the persistence of minority groups in Canada. The Doukhobors are an extreme example of a minority group that has attempted to limit close personal relationships to group members so that traditional values will be reinforced.

EDUCATION

Education, together with occupation and income, is a principal determinant of social status. It "conveys important political advantages, increasing political interest and awareness, expanding opportunities and developing the political skills necessary for effective participation."[8] Post-secondary education has become a virtual necessity for holding high public office.

As a formal agent of political socialization, the educational system in Canada ideally would reinforce common bonds of national unity while at the same time celebrating the ethnic, linguistic and regional differences that exist. Unfortunately, however, the system is poorly equipped to build a strong Canadian identity. The fact that responsibility for education in Canada is largely in the hands of the provinces and extends downward to the municipal level makes it difficult to establish uniform standards and provide equitable funding across the country. The constitutional division of powers also makes it impossible to ensure that nation-wide interests are put ahead of parochial, provincial interests in terms of curriculum or subject content — or indeed, even considered at all.

The 1991 census showed that Canadians have more education than ever before and are staying in school longer. (See Figure 4.1.) The number of Canadians with more than a high-school education reached a historic high in 1991. Forty-three percent of all who were 15 years and over had a university degree or some other post-secondary education. More

---

[7]   The changing Soviet attitude toward the family is outlined in K. Millett, *Sexual Politics* (London: Rupert-Hart Davis, 1971), pp. 217–19.

[8]   W. Mishler, "Political Participation and Democracy," in M.S. Whittington and Glen Williams, eds., *Canadian Politics in the 1980s*, 2nd ed. (Toronto: Methuen, 1984), p. 183.

than one in 10 had a university degree. Women accounted for much of the increase in university graduates from 1971 to 1991.[9]

FIGURE 4.1   EDUCATIONAL ATTAINMENT FOR PERSONS 15 YEARS AND OVER, CANADA 1961–91

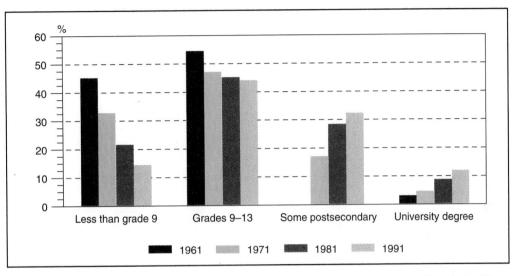

Source: *1991 Census Highlights: The Daily* (Ottawa: Statistics Canada, May 11, 1993), p. 3. Reproduced by authority of the Minister responsible for Statistics Canada 1993.

Canada's expenditures on education, as a percentage of gross domestic product (GDP), are among the highest of the industrialized countries. In 1990–91, the total cost to taxpayers was about $50.6 billion. About 28 percent of the total is spent on post-secondary education. Yet despite this impressive expenditure there remains deep concern about the quality of education in Canada.[10] The harshest criticisms are levelled at elementary and secondary schools. Dissatisfaction centers on academic performance,[11] high numbers of student dropouts, inadequate career counselling, minority and gender inequalities, school violence and lack of national goals for education. Even the number of school days in a standard school year is questioned as being inadequate — there are 180–185 days in Canada, compared to 243 in Japan or 226–240 in Germany, for example. Consequently, pressures have increased to centralize the existing provincial systems, adding national testing and a core curriculum.[12] At the same time, however, provincial ministries and school boards are under pressure to decentralize to give parents and employers more control over local issues. The fact that Canada is ethnically and regionally diverse, with an inclusive rather than an elite school system, impedes efforts to centralize education in any way.

---

[9]   *1991 Census Highlights: The Daily* (Ottawa: Statistics Canada, May 11, 1993) p. 3.

[10]   A Gallup poll in 1992, for example, found that 58 percent of those polled expressed dissatisfaction with the educational system. *The Globe and Mail,* Dec. 28, 1992.

[11]   Two studies by the Economic Council of Canada document the poor showing of Canadian students *A Lot to Learn* (Ottawa: Supply and Services, 1992) and *Education and Training in Canada* (Ottawa: Supply and Services, 1992).

[12]   See, for example, the federal government publication *Learning Well...Living Well* (Ottawa: Supply and Services, 1991) that argues for an increased role for the federal government in education.

Education is the primary means by which people achieve upward mobility and escape from poverty. A university education does not guarantee financial success, but it certainly improves the odds (See Figure 4.2). In 1990, the average family income for university-graduate-headed families was approximately double that of a family whose head had less than eight years of education.

FIGURE 4.2   POVERTY RATES BY EDUCATION, 1990

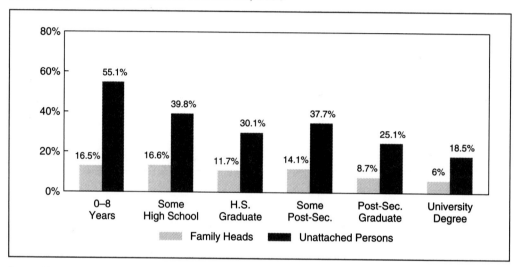

Source: National Council of Welfare, *Poverty Profile 1980–1990* (Ottawa: Supply and Services, 1992) p. 37.

Canada's education system is failing to prepare a high percentage of the population to earn an adequate living. In 1990, the reading skills of 16 percent of Canada's adults were too limited to deal with much of the printed material found in everyday life. Twenty-two percent of the adult population could read only simple materials and could not cope with more complex reading contexts.[13] For the functionally illiterate and those with less than a high school diploma there are few opportunities to enter the work force.

As well as directing students toward particular roles and class positions in society, educational institutions are secondary agents of political socialization. As in other modern societies, classrooms in Canada are the focus of deliberate attempts to shape the social and political outlooks of young citizens. Schools prepare young people for the political world by teaching them relevant facts, values, predispositions and skills. Schools are also the main community facility in which numbers of immigrant children learn one or both official languages and acquire basic citizenship training. Recent research indicates that education is significantly associated with both factual and conceptual knowledge, especially the latter. Furthermore, it indicates that "education establishes a receptivity to acquire further knowledge long after formal education has terminated."[14]

---

[13]   Statistics Canada, *Adult Literacy in Canada: Results of National Study* (Ottawa: Minister of Industry, Science and Technology, 1991) p. 19.

[14]   See Ronald D. Lambert, James E. Curtis, Barry J. Kay and Steven D. Brown, "The Sources of Political Knowledge," *CJPS*, vol. 21, no. 2 (June 1988), p. 373.

It's a good thing this school provides a lot of individual instruction. At least I'm falling behind at my own pace.

Reproduced with permission. Warren, *The Globe and Mail.*

One might think it would be easy to ensure that Canadian students learn the history and literature of their country, understand its culture and environment, and learn to speak, read and write in two or more languages. That has not proven to be the case.[15] There are several reasons why this is difficult in Canada. The fact that education is largely a provincial jurisdiction allows great diversity across the country in curriculum content, standards and administration. The varied historical developments, cultural traditions and geographic, social and economic conditions within the provinces and territories are reflected in twelve unique educational systems. Provincial and regional political cultures are nurtured and perpetuated by this structural fragmentation. The impact of these problems is examined in the next two sections.

LEGAL AND FINANCIAL STRUCTURES

During Canada's early colonial years, education was dominated by the church. Not until the mid-1800s was a public system of education developed in each colony, supplemented in

---

[15] A survey conducted in 1991, for example, revealed that fewer than 6 people in 10 polled could even name the first Prime Minister or the date of Confederation. The survey was part of the Heritage Project developed by Canadian billionaire Charles Bronfman to spotlight the nation's cultural heritage. Reported in *The Ottawa Citizen*, April 1, 1991.

Québec by schools and colleges operated by Roman Catholic orders. In 1867, the Fathers of Confederation awarded education to the provincial sphere of jurisdiction, but also tried to protect English and French minority schools. Section 93 of the *British North America Act* placed education "exclusively" under the control of each province, recognizing the differences that existed at the time of Confederation. The *Constitution*, however, retained the rights and privileges of Protestant and Roman Catholic minorities in relation to education, and the federal government maintained direct control over the education of persons beyond the jurisdiction of the provinces such as Native peoples.

Today, elementary and secondary schools consume about two-thirds of all educational spending in Canada. The federal government contributes a very small amount for primary and secondary education within the provincial jurisdiction (about 5 percent of the total expenditure on these services).[16] Free and compulsory primary and secondary education is provided by the state to all Canadian children. However, the length of actual attendance in school is closely related to factors such as the class, wealth and occupation of the family. Significant inequalities in opportunities for education exist among children of different class backgrounds for reasons such as family interest, financial need or variation in quality of schools in different municipalities.

Post-secondary education in Canada also began under religious auspices. At Confederation the few degree-granting institutions in Canada were largely supported and controlled by religious groups for the primary purpose of training clergy. Shortly thereafter, however, English language institutions began to offer practical and scientific studies under secular control while the French language sector continued to emphasize classical studies under clerical control. Demands for university education escalated after the Second World War, coming to a head in the 1960s when baby-boom children graduated from high school in record numbers. Provincial governments increasingly became involved in planning university development.

During the 1950s, in an attempt to build a world-class educational system, the federal government inaugurated a system of grants to be distributed to the provinces according to their population size. The provinces in turn distributed the funds to the universities based on full-time enrollment figures. In this manner the universities, which had operated as private institutions, became heavily dependent on public support. Religious sponsorship and control diminished.

Since the late 1970s, when Ottawa removed spending conditions from such transfer payments, the provinces have contributed a decreasing proportion of post-secondary education costs. The fact that the provinces retain the constitutional responsibility for education, while the federal government bears approximately half of the financial responsibility for post-secondary education, has obviously hindered the development of a cohesive, national educational system. As well, the current system of university finance penalizes provinces for attracting students from outside their borders. Federal financial transfers to the provinces for post-secondary education are based on population, not the number of students. And provinces fund their own universities directly rather than paying the cost of a student's education wherever he or she may study in Canada. Since students pay only a fraction of the cost of their education, a system with a disproportionate number of out-of-province students is a drain on that province.

---

[16] *Support To Education by the Government of Canada* (Ottawa: Minister of Supply and Services, 1983), p. 7. The federal government also sponsors programs in vocational and technical training.

TABLE 4.1 FEDERAL FINANCIAL SUPPORT FOR EDUCATION, 1990

Federal Support	$ Billion
Post-Secondary Education	5.8
University Research	0.8
Student Aid & Scholarships	0.7
Direct Federal Responsibilities	1.0
Official Languages in Education	0.3
Other Programs	0.4
Canadian Jobs Strategy	0.5
Adult Training	1.5
Total	11.0

Source: Government of Canada, *Learning Well...Living Well* (Ottawa: Supply and Services, 1991).

Today, Canada spends more on education as a percentage of the GDP than most countries in the world — over 7 percent in recent years. (See Table 4.1 for a breakdown of federal spending on education.) In 1992, of the top 30 industrialized countries, no other country spent more. And only the United States rated higher than Canada in terms of mean years of schooling (12.3 years compared to 12.1).[17] Higher education in Canada is much less exclusive than in some countries such as Britain, but not as accessible as in others such as the United States. In 1991, there were 69 public, degree-granting universities across Canada, as well as 203 specialized colleges and institutes.[18]

CURRICULUM AND SUBJECT CONTENT

The educational curriculum is a potentially major instrument of political socialization. Political instruction can range from general civic education to indoctrination. The former model imparts how a good citizen participates in the political life of his or her country; the latter, undesirable model (known pejoratively as brainwashing) goes well beyond this to teach political values in a restrictive and highly structured manner as directed by the state. Political socialization in Canadian schools is of the former type. Subject material is stressed or ignored to reinforce desirable values and beliefs, and texts can be selected to reinforce biases. However, political instruction is diffused and ad hoc.

Across Canada generally, some attempts are made in the educational system to have children understand and relate emotionally to their country from an early age. In Ontario, for example, the Ministry of Education dictates that national symbols are to be brought to the children's attention daily and the proper reverence for them instilled. "O Canada" is part of the daily opening or closing exercises, and schools must fly the Canadian flag when the school-board directs.

[17] According to the *1993 United Nations Human Development Report* Canada spent 7.2 percent of GDP on education and, in the G7, Germany spent 6.2 percent, France 5.7, Japan 5.0, Italy 4.8 and the UK 4.7. Mean years of schooling are from the same source. Federal contributions to post-secondary students are outlined in *Federal Sources of Financial Aid* (Ottawa: Minister of Supply and Services, 1983).

[18] Statistics Canada, *Education in Canada, A Statistical Review for 1990–91* (Ottawa: Ministry of Industry, Science and Technology, 1992) p. 30.

Democracy is considered to be an important value in all Canadian schools.[19] Consequently, an important aim of the Canadian educational system is to strengthen the cooperative social conscience that underlies a common concept of democracy. However, there is no agreement on how that goal is to be achieved. Doubts have even been expressed as to whether schoolchildren can learn freedom and equality from schools that enforce constraint, hierarchy and inequality. According to one theory, the undemocratic nature of schools provides a "hidden curriculum" that undermines the values the schools profess to teach. In other words, the basic attitudes toward authority learned by children at school may have an impact on the attitudes they develop toward political authority; and, because schools are not democratic, children do not learn democratic values in schools.[20]

In accordance with the hidden curriculum notion, the 1960s saw a general democratization within Canadian schools and universities. Compulsory courses were minimized or eliminated and "interest" courses were widely expanded at the expense of core courses such as mathematics, English and history. The move had no visible impact on democratic values, but it did lower educational standards sufficiently to raise an outcry from universities about the growing illiteracy of their students. The 1980s and 1990s have witnessed a tentative reversal of this policy, with a general re-imposition of basic core subject requirements for graduation.

Other countries have tried to solve the dilemma of teaching democratic values within authoritarian institutions in equally unsatisfactory ways. According to Richard Merelman,

American schools adapt to demands that they transmit the democratic values of popular sovereignty and political equality by deemphasizing the academic competence of their teaching staffs, by setting their grading standards at levels which insure that the majority of students perform acceptably, if perhaps poorly, by glossing over the difference between facts and values in politics. In short, American schools adapt by reducing the quality of education.[21]

This type of adaptation to teach democratic values, Merelman claims, causes many of the most promising students to become disillusioned and alienated and actually limits the transmission of democratic values in schools.

The social sciences provide a good example. An important aim of many of the subjects taught in schools is to impart an awareness of a common heritage and build national pride. The general assumption is that learning the history, geography, literature and language of one's country is important in creating citizens with positive attitudes and beliefs about their state. In Ontario, Canadian history is generally introduced in the elementary grades. Civics

---

[19]   Researchers have been unable to demonstrate that schooling contributes directly to the development of democratic values in children. Analysis of formal education as a socializing agent is plagued by the problem of measurement. Studies have generally been unable to exclude non-educational variables (such as socioeconomic environment) or other school-based influences (such as peers or teachers) in order to isolate the impact of strictly educational variables on the acquisition of values, attitudes and political orientations. For a discussion of the relation between education and values in Canada see Peter C. Emberly and Waller R. Newell, *Bankrupt Education: The Demise of Liberal Education in Canada* (Toronto: University of Toronto Press, 1994).

[20]   See Richard M. Merelman, "Democratic Politics and the Culture of American Education," *APSR*, vol. 74, no. 2 (June 1980).

[21]   Ibid., pp. 319–32. For a somewhat comparable view of the state of Canadian universities see David J. Bercuson, Robert Bothwell and J.L. Granatstein, *The Great Brain Robbery: The Decline of Canada's Universities* (Toronto: McClelland & Stewart, 1984).

or Canadian government courses are sometimes introduced at the secondary level but they are not compulsory. Course offerings are, for the most part, at the individual discretion of each school, with final approval from the Ministry, with the result that a "Canadian Politics" course may be optional in one school and not offered at all in another.

The goal of fostering national pride and awareness of a common heritage is therefore not easily accomplished within single provinces or across the country. Because the curriculum and subject material is not standardized, students in different parts of a province and across the country may learn quite different material and from quite different points of view. This was very evident in a study conducted by Marcel Trudel and Geneviève Jain for the Royal Commission on Bilingualism and Biculturalism. Surveying 10 000 Grade 12 students and comparing 14 representative Canadian history textbooks, they found that English and French texts were very different from each other in organization, themes and objectives.[22] These significant differences corresponded to the wide attitudinal and political cleavages between the French and English. Canadian history courses in the French-language Roman Catholic schools in Québec were preoccupied with survival of their own society, while the English schools across the country neglected the interests and development of French Canada. The textbooks expounded different myths and different historical memories. The English books stressed economic interpretations, whereas the French texts stressed the importance of religion and the survival of the French ethnic group.

The Royal Commission study found that key figures and common experiences in Canadian history were depicted quite differently as well. For example, the French saw Lord Durham as a great assimilator; the English considered him a great decolonizer. To the French, Riel was a defender of minority rights, but to the English he was a traitor and murderer. Similarly, the early period of French colonization to 1663 was covered at great length in French texts, but only very briefly in English texts. The periods of the British regime and Confederation were handled so differently that the authors concluded that the two groups did not even seem to be talking about the same country. Books used by francophones attempted to give the students a moral education, while anglophone books attempted to convey a political and social education. Elementary school children in French-language Roman Catholic schools developed strong identification with their own ancestors. At the secondary school level, the interpretations tended to become bitter, resentful and vindictive, with frequent references to resistance.[23]

In the light of the Royal Commission findings, many school textbooks were revised to eliminate blatant biases, as well as other glaring stereotypes, such as the portrayal of Canada's Native peoples as "savages," "heathens" and "fiends."[24] In spite of these changes, differences remain. The Québec nationalist interpretation has become standard in textbooks used in Québec, and is the accepted filter with which to analyze political issues. Students continue to learn the nature and glory of the established order through a combination of facts and myths. Many people in Canada's two founding nations have never shared a common national mythology.

---

[22] Marcel Trudel and Geneviève Jain, *Canadian History Textbooks: A Comparative Study*, Studies of the Royal Commission on Bilingualism and Biculturalism, no. 5 (Ottawa: Queen's Printer, 1970), ch. 4.

[23] Ibid.

[24] Garnet McDiarmid and David Pratt, *Teaching Prejudice* (Toronto: Ontario Institute for Studies in Education, 1968). Also David Pratt, "The Social Role of School Textbooks in Canada," in Robert M. Pilke and Elia Zureik, eds., *Socialization and Values in Canadian Society*, vol. 2 (Toronto: Macmillan, 1978), pp. 100–26.

Conflicting interpretations of Canadian history are not unique to the English- and French-speaking communities. There are regional variations as well. Contrasting theses have been developed by leading historians from western and central Canada. Donald Creighton, for example, saw Canada as an extension of Ontario. The "Laurentian thesis" that he expounded holds that Canada developed around the extension of the trade routes.[25] Creighton argued that the crucial drive behind Confederation was the commercial development of the St. Lawrence, and that the annexation of the West was an extension of this drive. W.L. Morton, on the other hand, gave a western interpretation when he stated that Creighton's thesis does not take account of regional experience and history, but distorts local history and confirms "the feeling that union with Canada had been carried out against local sentiment and local interest."[26]

Morton contended that the study of Canadian history has been limited to the history of the economic and commercial development of Upper and Lower Canada, with little regard for the vigour of regional sentiment. For Morton, the prairie provinces, unlike British Columbia or the Maritimes, had no option but to join Canada, as the colony of a colony, and have never existed outside that subordinate position. According to Barry Cooper, the result of this emphasis on commercial development and economic exploitation of the West by the "loyalist heartland" has led to a split between political allegiance and local identity. "That split appeared and still appears, as a sense of sectional or regional injustice."[27] Often, political movements or minor political parties such as Social Credit or the United Farmers of Alberta have served to channel such regional grievances against Ottawa and provide a western sense of identity.

The cleavages within Canadian political culture are revealed not only in historical interpretations but also in the works of novelists and poets. These works become instruments of political socialization; they mirror and reinforce attitudes about such issues as national unity and regional identity, as the following examples illustrate. Literary critic Northrop Frye wrote that the literature of one's own country can provide the cultivated reader with "an understanding of that country which nothing else can give him."[28] He found in Canadian literature signs of a closely-knit, beleaguered society held together by unquestionable morals and authority — what he termed a "garrison mentality." Margaret Atwood expanded this theme, basing her conclusions on a survey of both English and French Canadian literature. The aim of garrison life is survival, and survival, she claimed, is "the central theme for Canada."[29] Literary critic Dennis Duffy further concluded that the strong garrison will of central Canada was reinforced by political strength. The Canadian identity, he argued has been restricted to the Loyalist heartland and does not extend to the Maritimes or the West.[30] Such

25 Donald G. Creighton, *The Commercial Empire of the St. Lawrence, 1760–1850* (Boston: Houghton Mifflin, 1958).

26 W.L. Morton, "Canadian History and Historians," in A.B. McKillop, ed., *Contexts of Canada's Past: Selected Essays of W. L. Morton* (Toronto: Macmillan, 1980), pp. 33–4. See also David Jay Bercuson and Philip A. Buckner, eds., *Eastern and Western Perspectives: Papers from the joint Atlantic Canada/Western Canada Canada Studies Conference* (Toronto: University of Toronto Press, 1981).

27 Barry Cooper, "Western Political Consciousness," in Stephen Brooks, ed., *Political Thought in Canada* (Toronto: Irwin Publishing, 1984), p. 228. See also Howard and Tamara Palmer, "The Alberta Experience," *Journal of Canadian Studies*, vol. 17, no. 3 (Fall 1982), p. 23.

28 Northrop Frye, *The Bush Garden: Essays on Canadian Imagination* (Toronto: Anansi, 1971), p. 183.

29 Margaret Atwood, *Survival: A Thematic Guide to Canadian Literature* (Toronto: Anansi, 1972), p. 32.

30 Dennis Duffy, *Gardens, Covenants, Exiles: Loyalism in the Literature of Upper Canada/Ontario* (Toronto: University of Toronto Press, 1982), pp. 131–32.

literary analyses correspond to the emphasis by historians on the importance of central Canada and may, as Cooper speculates, help to explain western political consciousness. If national unity is a symbol expressing "Canadian" identity, and that identity is limited to the Loyalist heartland, then Westerners distrust national unity "because it appears as the manifestation of the garrison will."[31]

The tradition of a "political novel" that celebrates Canadian unity is weak in Canada. Hugh MacLennan's *Two Solitudes* is one of only a very few works of fiction to explore the French-English dynamic in Canada. MacLennan drew his inspiration from Rainer Maria Rilke's words "Love consists in this, that two solitudes protect and touch and greet each other." As an English Canadian he struggled to understand the different historical and cultural realities of the French and English in Canada, and suggested in his novel that hope *did* exist for understanding and tolerance between the two large linguistic groups. He maintained that, as long as the fate of a person or nation is still in doubt, the person or nation is alive and real. It is only of the dead that no questions are asked.[32] The issue MacLennan wrote about is still relevant today.

Literature and theatre in Québec is flourishing, but it exists in isolation from English-speaking Canada. It is often highly political and supportive of Québec nationalism. For example, in 1993, Marcel Dubé's 1965 play *Les beaux dimanches* was revived. This popular, classic text of Québec nationalism treats the audience to long speeches about the historical humiliation of the Québec people and diatribes on federalism sugar-coated in an appealing story of sexual infidelity and moral aimlessness. Dubé's highly political message is that independence can lead the Québécois out of their misery.

Today, as the Canadian ethnic tapestry has become increasingly complex, one could perhaps more accurately speak of Canada's three, ten or even more solitudes. Ethnic and regional interpretations of Canadian history are encouraged and often subsidized by the state. They tend to exhibit subtle differences that contribute to or reflect political divisiveness at the expense of national unity. Education of the country's registered Indian and Inuit population presents a unique situation. It is the responsibility of the federal government, and is administered by the Department of Indian Affairs. The traditional, tacit goal of the Canadian school system, which has been to provide Native children with the knowledge and skills of mainstream Canadian culture and encourage them to identify with common values, has shifted in recent years to celebrate ethnic pride. Some would even argue that Native students have learned neither Canadian nor ethnic pride, but instead have become alienated and disillusioned and that this has contributed to high drop-out rates at school and social and economic problems. As in other facets of educational socialization, the task is to establish an appropriate balance — to celebrate the ethnic differences and contributions that aboriginals make, while at the same time ensuring that they are not isolated and that they learn to share and help develop the values of a strong and united Canada.

Language teaching in Canada is also fragmented and inadequate to meet the demands of a bilingual, multicultural society. Apart from the two official languages, teaching of foreign languages in the regular school program has declined dramatically in the past decade. Non-official languages are often confined to special heritage language programs designed to meet the needs of ethnic communities. These programs help

---

[31] Cooper, "Western Political Consciousness," p. 235.

[32] Hugh MacLennan, *Two Solitudes* (Toronto: Collins, 1945).

ethnic groups retain their language and culture but are not designed to encourage other Canadians to share or appreciate the achievements or contributions of these groups to Canadian society. Admission and degree requirements for second languages in universities are almost non-existent.

Political socialization in Canada's educational institutions is fragmented not only by the ethnic and regional divisions within the country but also by pressures from the United States. Textbook markets are so much larger and more lucrative south of the border that it is financially advantageous to adopt American texts rather than use Canadian-written and -published material. Factors of major concern are the limited availability of Canadian books in the school system and the small amount of Canadian content in textbooks, both of which contribute to a stunted knowledge of Canada and Canadians. A study by Statistics Canada determined that 45 percent of school texts used across Canada were Canadian.[33] As would be expected, French texts have much higher Canadian content than do those in English. Considerable efforts have been made to rectify this situation in English Canada. In Ontario, a primary or secondary school book now must have Canadian authors and be manufactured in Canada to be approved as a text, and every province has a "Canada First Policy" that means that if a Canadian text is available, it must be given priority.

Similarly, at the university level, rising nationalist feeling in the 1960s and 1970s unleashed widespread concern for the high percentage of both foreign texts and professors and their possible influence on higher education in Canada.[34] In 1975, a Report of the Committee on Canadian Content conducted for the Canadian Political Science Association revealed concern by political scientists across the country that introductory courses in their field (with the exception of Canadian government courses) relied too heavily on American texts and were therefore overloaded with American examples.[35] The study emphasized the vulnerability of Canadian education to influences from the United States as yet another factor contributing to the fragility of the political socialization process.

The Canadian educational system, fragmented from within by regional and ethnic interests and pressured from without by American cultural influences, strives in an ad hoc and diffused way to impart to students an awareness of a common heritage and instill national pride. Lack of centralized control makes this difficult, if not impossible. In the 1990s in particular, Canadians have often acted as little more than an irascible collection of self-interested groups, provinces, ethnic affiliations and special interests. It has become more politically correct to respond to minority demands than to argue for national standards. Diversity is supported to such a degree that it often undermines pride in Canada. Yet diversity is only one small part, important though it may be, of the Canadian identity. The educational system must share responsibility for this weakness that undermines Canadian unity.

---

[33] Quoted in *The Globe and Mail*, October 20, 1976. Statistics Canada, *The English Elementary and High School Report on Canadian Education and Publishing in Canada* (Toronto: Pepper Wood Inc., 1982), p. 92.

[34] The Nationalist arguments are expounded at length in Robin Matthews and James Steele, eds., *The Struggle for Canadian Universities* (Toronto: New Press, 1969). See also Alan Cairns, "Political Science in Canada and the Americanization Issue," *CJPS*, vol. 8, no. 2 (June 1975), pp. 191–234.

[35] R. Drummond, P. Clarke and R. Manzer, "Report of the Committee on Canadian Content," meetings of the *CPSA*, June 1975.

HORIZONTAL CLEAVAGES AND POLITICAL ORIENTATIONS

In the last chapter we discussed several cleavages that separate groups of Canadians from each other. Ethnicity, language and provincial and regional boundaries constitute **vertical cleavages** in that they divide Canadians into separate groups that co-exist side by side within the state. There are also several **horizontal cleavages** that cut relatively evenly across all of Canadian society, creating different "layers" of political culture. Some of the most important of these stratifications are based on class and gender.[36] Each strata or grouping of Canadians makes unique demands on governments and society. Some act as organized units in society to achieve their ends; others have little or no cohesiveness. Some groupings have considerable power and influence; others have very little.

These cleavages are influential in forming the political ideas and orientations of group members. In the next sections, we examine gender and class in Canada, two horizontal stratifications that affect how individuals think and behave politically.

GENDER STRATIFICATION

According to a recent United Nations study, no country treats its women as well as its men. When the UN figured gender inequity into its 1993 human development index, Canada dropped from second place to eleventh among the world's states. As in most countries, many women in Canada have fewer job opportunities and lower earnings than men.[37] Political scientists debate the underlying causes of gender inequality but there is no doubt about its impact.

Gender theory explanations about the causes of gender inequality have gained credibility as a subdiscipline in some parts of all of the social sciences.[38] The question is not new. In the nineteenth century, John Stuart Mill argued that the subjugation of women was a selfish, egotistical conspiracy by men who wanted to keep women as a free source of domestic labour.[39] It was, he said, in men's interest to preserve a male-dominated society, so they claimed that the subjugation of women was natural, even divinely ordained. Karl Marx and Frederick Engels held that the subjugation of women is based on economic reasons. It serves the interests of the capitalist class because the female homeworker is unpaid, and this keeps the working class without resources. The traditional family is seen as part of the scheme to ensure the subordination of women, keeping them dependent on their wage-earning husbands.[40]

---

[36] Some academics believe that the importance of class in society has declined in recent years. Individuals born after 1945 have distinctive "post-materialist" orientations. That is, they are more concerned with issues that have to do with quality of life — such as the environment — than were older generations. See Neil Nevitte, Herman Bakvis and Roger Gibbins, "The Ideological Contours of 'New Politics' in Canada: Policy, Mobilization and Partisan Support," *CJPS* (Sept. 1989), pp. 475–503.

[37] United Nations, *Human Development Report, 1993* (New York: Oxford University Press, 1993).

[38] See, for example, Michèle Barrett and Anne Phillips, *Destabilizing Theory: Contemporary Feminist Debates* (Stanford: Stanford University Press, 1992) and Sandra Lipsitz Bem, *The Lenses of Gender* (New Haven: Yale University Press, 1993).

[39] John Stuart Mill, *On the Subjection of Women* (London: Dent, 1970). First published in 1869.

[40] *Women and Communism: Writings of Marx, Engels, Lenin and Stalin* (Westport, Conn.: Greenwood Press, 1973).

TABLE 4.2   IMPORTANT DATES IN ATTAINMENT OF LEGAL AND POLITICAL EQUALITY FOR WOMEN IN CANADA

1916	Manitoba, then Saskatchewan and Alberta give vote to women in provincial elections
1917	British Columbia and Ontario give vote to women
1917	Women serving in Armed Forces and women with male relatives in uniform are allowed to vote in federal elections
1918	Nova Scotia gives vote to women
1918	Women given franchise in federal elections
1919	New Brunswick approves women's suffrage
1919	Women gained the right to stand in federal elections
1921	Agnes Macphail first woman elected to Parliament
1922	PEI approves women's suffrage
1925	Newfoundland approves women's suffrage
1928	Supreme Court rules women are not "persons" and cannot be appointed to Senate
1929	British Privy Council overturns Supreme Court decision
1931	Cairine Wilson first woman appointed to the Senate
1940	Québec gives vote to women (the last province to do so)
1947	Married women restricted from holding federal publicservice jobs
1955	Restrictions on married women in federal public service jobs removed
1957	Ellen Fairclough sworn in as first federal cabinet minister
1967	Royal Commission on Status of Women established
1971	Canada Labour Code amended to allow women seventeen weeks of maternity leave
1973	Supreme Court upholds section of Indian Act depriving aboriginal women of their rights.
1973	Supreme Court denies Irene Murdoch right to share in family property
1977	Canadian Human Rights Act passed, forbidding discrimination on basis of sex.
1981	Canada ratifies UN Convention on the elimination of all forms of discrimination against women
1982	Bertha Wilson became first woman appointed to the Supreme Court of Canada
1983	Affirmative action progams mandatory in the federal public service
1984	Twenty-eight women elected to Parliament, six appointed to cabinet
1984	Jeanne Sauvé became Canada's first female Governor General
1985	Section 15 of *Charter of Rights and Freedoms* comes into effect. Employment Equity legislation passed.
1989	*Indian Act* amended to remove discrimination against aboriginal women
1989	Audrey McLaughlin became first woman to lead a significant political party, the NDP
1991	Rita Johnston served briefly as BC premier, becoming Canada's first female premier.
1993	Catherine Callbeck, PEI, first woman *elected* premier.
1993	Kim Campbell served briefly as Canada's first woman Prime Minister.
October, 25 1993 election — the largest number ever, 53 women, elected to Parliament.	

The belief that women inherit physical attributes that determine their personality traits (generally emotional, intuitive, nurturing and passive) was accepted even by early feminists who won political rights for women. Current, second-wave feminists argue that gender role differences are not inherent, but learned. Some scientific research supports the view that inherent differences are considerably less significant than once believed.[41]

Early feminists such as Agnes MacPhail, Canada's first woman elected to Parliament, believed that womens' inequality was based on their lack of political and legal rights. Over time those battles were won; women received the right to vote in 1918, and gained legal equality rights in the *Charter of Rights and Freedoms* in 1982. However, women still did not participate fully in public life. Gender roles still were learned in childhood through family, school and other social contacts and carried through to the workplace and other adult social settings. Society's attitudes toward traditional gender roles and stereotypes were targeted by a new wave of feminists, and new issues were brought into the country's political agenda.

Gender is a powerful factor in socialization. Children tend to identify with role models of the same gender as themselves. Social learning patterns have tended to discourage females from participating fully in public life. Role models shape the aspirations of children and help to provide continuity in society. By the same token, however, they can make attitudinal change slow and stressful. In Canada, the role of women has changed dramatically. In 1901 only 13 percent of Canadian women worked outside the home. By 1990, nearly 60 percent of Canadian women did so.[42] Most of that change has taken place since the 1950s. Women entered the work force for economic reasons and in response to the new feminist argument that women cannot be dependent and equal at the same time.

As women increasingly rejected their traditional roles as full-time wives and mothers in favour of jobs and professions outside the home, specific attempts were made to change the role socialization of boys and girls. Books that contained traditional stereotypes of adventurous, mischevious boys and docile little girls were replaced with more suitable material; toys became less gender specific; girls were encouraged to study mathematics and science and aspire to a career other than teacher, nurse or secretary; boys were encouraged to be more sensitive and share household chores. Changes were not restricted to childhood socialization; gender biases were detected and removed from everyday speech. The issue of gender became highly politicized.

In some respects, however, women's role in the workplace has been slow to change. Significant differences still exist between the economic and social conditions of men and women in Canadian society. In 1991, nearly 51 percent of Canadians were female. Yet this figure bears little relation to their representation in the economic or political elite of the country. As Figure 4.3 shows, women earn considerably less than men who have equivalent educational qualifications, and they are less well represented in political and occupational hierarchies. In 1990, the average female worker earned about 60 percent of what the average male earned. This was largely because about 60 percent were employed in low-paid

---

[41] E.E. Maccoby and C.N. Jacklin, *The Psychology of Sex Differences* (Palo Alto, Calif.: Stanford University Press, 1974).

[42] Canadian Advisory Council on the Status of Women, *Women and Labour Market Poverty* (Ottawa, 1990), pp. 114–15.

[43] Ibid. According to the 1991 census, men spent 17 percent of their time at work compared to 10 percent for women; but women spent 19 percent of their time on unpaid housework compared to 11 percent for men. Statistics Canada, *The Daily* (Ottawa: April 23, 1993), p. 5.

FIGURE 4.3   AVERAGE INCOME, ALL WORKERS BY SEX AND AGE, 1990

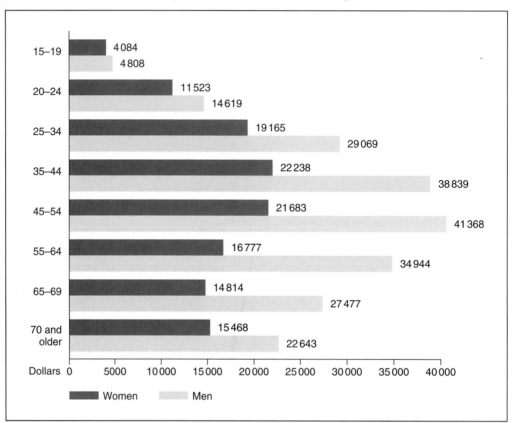

Source: *1991 Census*, Catalogue No. 93-331, (Ottawa: Statistics Canada) Table 2, pp. 20–32. Reproduced by the authority of the Minister responsible for Statistics Canada.

"traditional" clerical and service occupations with few opportunities for advancement.[43] The federal government often is expected to set an example in employment equity. In 1990, women constituted 44 percent of the federal government work force, but only 15 percent of managerial positions.[44]

With their increased participation in the work force women have brought new issues to the government policy agenda: affirmative action, legal equality rights, equal access to opportunities in the public sphere with men, pay equity, abortion rights and child care. (See Table 4.2.) Issues such as sexual assault have also moved more visibly into the public sphere and confronted and reversed the established view of wives as the property and responsibility of their husbands. Women have argued that the "personal is political" and moved many topics that were previously private into the political sphere. A plethora of reforms have taken place. In 1988, for example, the federal government passed an *Employment Equality Act* that called for affirmative action within departments, Crown corporations and federally regulated businesses.[45] But

[44] Public Service Commission, Annual Report, 1990.

[45] For a good overview see Sandra Burt, "Rethinking Canadian Politics: The Impact of Gender" in Michael S. Whittington and Glen Williams, *Canadian Politics in the 1990s*, pp. 208–20.

much more needs to be done to enable women to have equal opportunities. Women are disproportionately represented among the poorest in Canadian society. Single mothers represent the fastest-growing segment of the Canadian population in recent years. From 1976 to 1991, this group grew to 444 000, increasing 66 percent. They were among the most economically disadvantaged in the country.[46]

TOWARD LEGAL AND POLITICAL EQUALITY

More will be said about the role of women in Canadian government and society in Chapters 7, 12 and 13. However, we should note here that despite their changing role in society, and the fact that no *formal* barrier to the full and equal participation of women in politics exists, women are still less active than men in politics. They vote and join activities like political campaigns as frequently as men, but they participate significantly less in more active or demanding jobs. There have been many firsts for women in recent years — Bertha Wilson was the first woman to serve on the Supreme Court (1982); Jeanne Sauvé was the first female Governor General (1984); Audrey McLaughlin was the first woman to lead a federal political party (1989); and, in 1993, Kim Campbell became the first female Prime Minister.

However, these women are still the exception. Women with professional occupations or college education participate in politics as much or more than men do. However, women without college education or middle- to low-status occupations are considerably less active politically than men. Since more women than men now attend university, it can be expected that women's participation in politics will reflect that change. As socialization patterns change and cease to mark politics as a predominantly male occupation, more women can be expected to enter political life. Currently, however, relatively wealthy, well-educated, middle-class men are highly influential in politics and determine the policy agenda at both the federal and provincial levels. We will discuss the issue of women in political parties in Chapter 11 and women's movements in Chapter 12.

CLASS STRATIFICATION

Socio-economic class provides another horizontal cleavage in society that helps define political ideas and orientations.

Defining class is controversial and problematical. **Class** refers to a rank or order in society by such characteristics as education, occupation and income. These characteristics provide "objective" indicators that sometimes are different from "subjective" or self-assigned rankings. Depending on which types of indicators are used different class lines can be detected in the Canadian population.

Class was an important component of Karl Marx's thought. He divided capitalist societies according to economic criteria into the **bourgeoisie** (the economic elite), a small **petite bourgeoisie** (small business people, farmers, self-employed professionals), a **new middle class** (civil servants, teachers, salaried professionals) and the **proletariat** (workers). Marx expected the proletariat eventually to revolt against exploitation by the bourgeoisie and create a new and egalitarian, classless society. History has not unfolded this way. In Canada, as elsewhere, the "new middle class" has grown, the elite "bourgeoisie" has become increasingly more powerful and internationally based, and, as a group, the "proletariat" is too weak, fragmented and dependent on state subsidies to be able to revolt.

---

[46] Statistics Canada, *Perspectives* (Ottawa: Supply and Services, 1993).

In the mid-1990s, class divisions based on wealth and income remain apparent in Canada. At the top of the economic scale, a tiny elite, or *upper class* of about two to three percent of the population holds the top positions in business, industry, professions and the bureaucracy. The extensive holdings of a very few individuals and families in real estate, natural resources, communications and various commercial enterprises, including large corporations, set them apart from other Canadians.[47]

Strictly economic interpretations of the highest classes are complicated by ethnicity, language and other social factors. Historically, Canada's economic elite was dominated by individuals of British origin. In the early 1900s, Canadians of Anglo-Saxon background constituted more than 90 percent of industrial leaders; French Canadians only about 7 percent.[48] John Porter's classic study, *The Vertical Mosaic*, showed that this was still true in the early 1960s. Furthermore, this exclusive group tended to be composed of socially and educationally interconnected individuals from at least middle-income families.[49] Another study in the late 1960s and early 1970s revealed that French Canadians had increased their representation in this group to over 8 percent, and other ethnic groups, especially Jews, composed over 5 percent of the economic elite.[50] This indicates that Canadians of Anglo-Saxon heritage still dominate the economic elite but that the situation is changing with the evolving of the ethnic population of Canadian society.

The vast majority of Canadians today are part of the huge *middle class* — over 80 percent of the population — that is sandwiched between this tiny economic elite and about 16 percent of the population who are economically deprived. The shape of the economic hierarchy, therefore, is not pyramidal but is shaped more like a bulging onion. Income, occupation and lifestyle subdivide the members of the middle stratum into upper-middle and lower-middle class. The upper-middle tier is generally well-educated and financially secure. It does not function as a single unit but has a variety of economic interests and political demands. This group can be further subdivided in various ways, such as between those who are self-employed and those who work for someone else.

The lower-middle class, or working class, is generally considered to consist of those who do manual as opposed to intellectual work. As a group, this class is less educated and generally earns less money than others in the middle class. Despite the fact that some of them are unionized, changes in the Canadian economy in the 1980s and 1990s dramatically increased unemployment in this group. The proportion of blue collar jobs in the work force increased only marginally, while unskilled and labourer's jobs in fishing, mining, agriculture and other primary resources declined sharply. These job losses, combined with inflation and increased taxation, made individuals in this stratum particularly vulnerable to dropping into the lowest grouping of economically deprived Canadians.[51]

---

[47] In 1990, the *Financial Post* listed Canada's wealthiest families. They included the Irving Family, Ken Thompson, the Reichman brothers, the Bronfman family, Ted Rogers and Robert Campeau *Financial Post Moneywise*, May 1989. As well, Canadian corporations employ a select handful of corporate executives who earn over $6 000 000 a year. This stratum also includes senior executives of branches of foreign-owned firms.

[48] T.W. Acheson, "Changing Social Origins of the Canadian Industrial Elite: 1880–1910," *Business History Review*, vol. 47, no. 2 (1973), pp. 189–217.

[49] John Porter, *The Vertical Mosaic* (Toronto: University Toronto Press, 1965).

[50] Wallace Clement, *The Canadian Corporate Elite* (Toronto: McClelland & Stewart, 1975).

[51] Economic Council of Canada, Legacies: Twenty-Sixth Annual Review (Ottawa: Supply and Services, 1989) p. 35.

Within the large, middle economic tier, Canadians of Anglo-Saxon origin appear to have no particular advantage over other groups. Jews, Asians, Dutch and Italians, for example, do equally well or better in terms of average income, percentage of white collar jobs and percentage with some university education. One ethnic group ranks consistently low in socioeconomic stratification characteristics, however — Native people, many of whom live in extreme poverty.[52]

The *poor* in Canada are considered to be those who exist below the **poverty line**, a theoretical line set by Statistics Canada. Depending on the precise definition of the poverty line, about 4 to 5 million Canadians are poor. They rely on state benefits such as unemployment insurance and welfare to exist.

A 1992 report on poverty by the National Council of Welfare showed that 4.2 million people — or over 15 percent of the population — were living on or below the poverty line.[53] It included those who spent more than 70 percent of their income on food, shelter and clothing. In dollar terms, Statistics Canada defined this line according to family type and location, for example, as an annual income below $26 049 for a family of four in a city of 100 000 to 5 000 000.[54]

FIGURE 4.4   POVERTY RATES FOR PERSONS BY AGE AND SEX, 1990

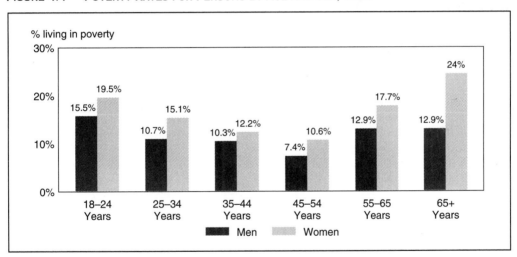

Source: National Council of Welfare, *Poverty Profile 1980–1990* (Ottawa: Supply and Services, 1992), p. 31.

[52]   John Kralt, *Ethnic Origins of Canadians* (Ottawa: Information Canada, 1977). Statistics Canada Catalogue No. 99-709.

[53]   National Council of Welfare, *Poverty Profile 1980–90* (Ottawa: Minister of Supply and Services, 1992).

[54]   In Canada, anyone who falls below the poverty line — Statistics Canda's so-called Low Income Cut-off (LICO) — is defined as poor. However, LICO is a relative measure, closely tied to the average income and average consumption patterns of the average Canadian. As such, some claim it tells more about how well off the typical Canadian is than it does about the condition of the truly poor. Furthermore the line itself is disputed. Christopher Sarlo, for example, in *Poverty in Canada* noted that half of the households headed by someone 65 years of age or older were considered poor, but almost half of them owned a home, 90 percent mortgage free. Canadian figures measure *relative* poverty, unlike the U.S. poverty line that is stated in *absolute* terms. U.S. figures are based on estimate of the cost of a minimum adequate diet, multiplied by three. The official U.S. poverty line is significantly lower than almost every poverty measure in Canada.

Those economically worst-off in Canadian society are most likely to be one-parent families, more than 60 percent of which are headed by females; the young, of whom more than a million are children under 16 years of age (an astounding 18 percent of all Canadian children); the single elderly, who are mostly widows; and Native people. (See Figure 4-4 for distribution of poverty rates by age and sex.)

This brief examination of social stratification in Canada indicates that horizontal cleavages are such that Canadians do not have equal chances to prosper. The educational system and social programs currently in place are not adequate to break the cycle of poverty for the least fortunate in society. The odds of leading a secure, healthy life decline as one moves down the social scale. Poverty means fewer educational opportunities, higher mortality rates, more physical and mental illness, poorer, more hazardous working conditions, higher crime rates (poverty is the greatest predictor of delinquency), and higher suicide and divorce rates.[55]

The inequalities of opportunity and distribution of wealth in Canada also have significant implications for politics. Some writers have concluded that the economic elite is also a dominant political force, that the state and economic elite are linked together and share a "confraternity of power."[56] There is no doubt that the elite exercises considerable influence in the direction of economic development of the country. On the other hand, the economic elite is far from a ruling class. One study, for example, showed that about three-quarters of the state elite was of middle-class origins.[57] This indicates that political power in Canada is diffused downward to at least the middle class. As well, the political decision-making process is extremely complex and virtually precludes control by one small group. Governments must maintain popular support, and this puts considerable power in the hands of the majority of the people through voting, membership in political parties, running for election, and so on.

Unfortunately, as we have noted, members of the lowest socio-economic stratum express low feelings of personal political power and efficacy, and participate least in the political system. They are preoccupied with survival. A wide range of federal, provincial and municipal welfare programs exist to help those who live in poverty, however these have come under attack in the recession years of the early 1990s as governments at all levels attempt to balance their budgets. Pressure on government institutions to expand and make these services more efficient, however, will increase in the twenty-first century as societal problems, such as an aging population, are demographically compounded.[58]

---

[55] See for example James J. Teevan, ed., *Introduction to Sociology: A Canadian Focus*, 2nd ed. (Scarborough, Ont.: Prentice-Hall Canada, 1986), p. 78.

[56] The ideological elite is described in John Porter, *Vertical Mosaic*, p. 460, and later elaborated on by Wallace Clement in *Canadian Corporate Elite* (Toronto: McClelland and Stewart, 1975)

[57] Dennis Olsen, "The State Elites," in Leo Panitch, ed., *The Canadian State* (Toronto: University of Toronto Press, 1977).

[58] Some argue that welfare policies simply legitimize existing social inequities by preventing the poor from becoming a potent political force. See for example Leo Panitch, "The Role and Nature of the Canadian State," in Panitch, *The Canadian State*, p. 8. Also see Allan Moscovitch and Jim Albert, eds., *The 'Benevolent' State: The Growth of Welfare in Canada* (Toronto: Garamond Press, 1987).

THE MEDIA AND POLITICAL ORIENTATIONS

The mass communications media constitute an increasingly important socializing agent both within and across state borders, breaking down the barriers of distance.[59] The media have the potential to reach vast audiences and manipulate subject content to either reinforce or challenge the norms of society. Political leaders recognize the value of controlling communications in order to standardize messages, set community goals and educate and unify a mass population. Efficient and effective internal communication among citizens is a basic requirement of national unity.

Communications media reflect the values and tastes of the society they serve. But they do much more. They act as gatekeepers for the citizenry by selecting which facts, beliefs and perspectives will be covered and how they will be presented. In doing so, they help to shape the values of society and influence the political process. At best, the media offer citizens a broad range of information and informed commentary and provide a voice for governments and opposition parties alike. At worst, they offer a distorted selection of facts and unbalanced, biased viewpoints.

The media's most significant political role is in setting the agenda for public discussion and debate; that is, in helping determine which issues and individuals people think and talk about. Newspaper headlines, in particular, influence what the public perceives to be the most important problems facing the country.[60] The media focus public debate, help legitimize issues and actors and confer or withhold status on individuals. They build and destroy the public images of political figures by awarding labels such as "brilliant," "slick" or "poor debater," which become indelible, and also by selective reporting and commentary. Investigative journalism, in particular, exposes corrosive issues, focusing public attention across the country and inviting strong reactions.

Nation-wide television networks, and the CBC in particular, as well as one English-language newspaper, *The Globe and Mail*, contribute greatly to developing the national political agenda in Canada. Two other newspapers, *The Toronto Star* and *Le Devoir* help set the agenda for national and public affairs, though they are regionally based. The only network other than the CBC to provide national television service from coast to coast is the English-language CTV, which also has a French subsidiary, TVA.

The media face many restraints on their attempts to set the agenda for public debate. The obstacles include editorial policy, technological limitations, and financial constraints — including the need to attract the large middle class and therefore obtain substantial advertising money.

Prime ministers, cabinet ministers and leaders of opposition parties have become adept, particularly in the past two decades, at dealing with the media and getting their ideas across to the public. John Diefenbaker was the first prime minister to employ a press secretary, but was unable to employ him effectively.[61] Several decades later, under Brian Mulroney, media relations had advanced to a highly sophisticated level. As David Taras noted:

---

[59] See John Meisel, "Communications in the Space Age," *International Political Science Review*, vol. 7, no. 3 (July 1986).

[60] See Frederick J. Fletcher, *The Newspaper and Public Affairs*, vol. 7, Research Publications, Royal Commission on Newspapers (Ottawa: Minister of Supply and Services, 1981), p. 17.

[61] David Taras, *The Newsmakers: The Media's Influence on Canadian Politics* (Toronto, Nelson, 1990), p. 137.

> *What distinguishes Mulroney's media relations system is the degree to which it is planned and centralized. While there was a good deal of coordination under Trudeau, Mulroney seems to give higher priority to the communications committee of the cabinet, whose job is to plan media strategy on a regular basis.*[62]

The modern prime minister has a director of communications, a press secretary, speech writers and other staff who help formulate media strategy and deal with journalists. Their job is to package and control what the public hears from government.

Cabinet documents now contain communications strategies that describe, often in considerable detail, how policies are to be sold. The Prime Minister's Office constantly monitors media coverage, wages image-building campaigns, and attempts to orchestrate issues, events and situations so that the most favourable public relations juice is squeezed out.[63]

It is standard practice today for the prime minister's press office to centralize government information and organize and stage events to ensure that the prime minister appears in carefully controlled settings that convey a dignified image. There are other ways that the press or public relations office uses the media to get its message reported and hinder coverage that might be detrimental.[64] It can release information late on a Friday afternoon, or close to the time that journalists have to file their stories, so that there is no opportunity to do anything but accept unquestioningly what is given. Access to the prime minister can be restricted to reporters who provide favourable coverage, while those who are critical are "frozen out." Stories may be "leaked" not just as a favour to the journalist, but to give extra media exposure to an impending policy announcement or to test public opinion about an issue.

Press and communications offices specialize in setting specific conditions for interviews that will produce favourable coverage, ensuring, for example, that the text of an interview is not edited. The "scrums" that take place regularly in Parliament allow party leaders to convey a few, well-prepared, short, newsworthy sentences that will be just right for a television news clip. Another trick is to distract the public from a negative story by timing a "good news" event to be released at the same time, or by making the announcement outside of Ottawa where local reporters or coverage might not be as informed or as critical. Efforts are made to make announcements that are newsworthy, simple and credible.

The relationship between politicians and the media is complex. It is particularly intense during elections where every aspect of the campaign involves the media, as shown in Chapter 11. We turn now to an examination of the broadcast media, particularly television, and the print media, particularly newspapers. In each case, we assess how they affect national unity and what Canadians think about politics. We focus throughout on three main problems: American influence, regional divisions and ethnic divisions. First, however, we consider briefly the history of communications networks in Canada.

DEVELOPMENT OF THE MEDIA IN CANADA

In many ways, Canada represents a triumph of communications. The pattern of the lines of communication is, as Walter Young commented, an "armature on which the figure of

---

[62] Ibid., p. 146.

[63] Ibid., p. 125.

[64] Ibid., pp. 125–47.

Canada as a political community has been shaped."[65] Rivers, lakes, canals and railways were not only avenues of commerce and transportation but also vital means of communication. Communities developed along these lines, and communications links between them were gradually strengthened by technological advances. The network of communications moved steadily outward, from centre to periphery, conquering enormous distances and facilitating political, social and economic movement. The central Canadian elite that directed the development of the media also formulated national goals and aspired to preserve establishment values. That interlocking group, which John Porter described as the ideological elite at the top of the mass media, the educational system and the churches, ensured that its central, national perspective dominated the development of the communications system.[66]

To build a strong national identity it is important that citizens of any political unit exchange ideas and information within that unit more than with other people outside it. In this respect, it is unfortunate that Canada shares the North American continent with the most powerful country in the world, a country that not only is English-speaking, but that extends along the most densely populated border of almost every Canadian province. North-south communications between the proximate English groups in Canada and the United States flow naturally, while internal communications between French and English regions as well as the widely separated provinces of English Canada are artificial and must be protected and nourished. The development of modern communications systems since the early 1840s has facilitated the natural north-south communication links between English-speaking Canadians and Americans and increased the threat of cultural domination from the south.

The history of media development in Canada is to a great extent the record of a struggle by the Canadian government to counter the influences of foreign penetration and bind the country together through better internal communications. Americans outnumber Canadians by ten to one, and nearly all Canadians live within easy reach of American mass media and other cultural influences. That any form of distinct Canadian identity or culture exists at all is contrary to the expectations of most theories of national integration. As one author noted, it is surprising that two centuries of contiguous territory, common language and culture (for English-speaking Canadians at least), inter-migration, trade, travel and communication have not produced formal political integration.[67]

While north-south communications have been easy to establish, east-west communications links have always been a challenge for Canadians. All the principal cities of the United States were linked by telegraph by 1846, but the first Canadian line between Toronto and Montréal was not complete until 1847. The most important centres in the Canadas and the Maritime colonies were linked by 1861, but by then north-south channels of information were already established.

The 1850s were a great growth period for newspapers because of the high interest in war reports, particularly from Crimea. However, from the beginning Canadian newspapers found it easier and cheaper to fill their pages with news from the United States than to hire their own reporters. And the competition from established American newspapers was

---

65 Walter D. Young, "The Voices of Democracy: Politics and Communication in Canada," *CJPS*, vol. 14, no. 4 (Dec. 1981), p. 685.

66 See Porter, *Vertical Mosaic* and Clement, *Canadian Corporate Elite*.

67 Kenneth D. McRae, "Empire, Language and Nation: The Canadian Case," in S.N. Eisenstadt and S. Rokkan, eds., *Building States and Nations*, vol. II (Beverly Hills, Cal.: Sage, 1973), p. 151.

always intense. In the Maritimes in 1865, Canadian newspapers were "a rarity where the foreign and certainly not superior sheets of New York have established a regular circulation."[68] Rather than reading news from the provinces, Canadians of the time devoured the shocking and gory events, mainly murders, lynchings and riots, that filled American papers.[69]

Canadian radio services, and later television, were also established as a direct response to American infiltration of the Canadian market. From radio and television channels, through cable and pay television and, finally, to satellite transmission, the issue has been how best to protect Canadian cultural sovereignty from massive U.S. media penetration. In November 1981, for example, Secretary of State for Communications Francis Fox warned that Canada would be "an occupied land, culturally" unless action were taken against the spread of American television channels, and urged his government to adopt a national cultural policy similar to its National Energy Program.[70] However, steps to achieve such a policy have been slow and uncertain, particularly in the face of the new technological advances.

Several federal commissions from the Aird Report in 1929 to the Davey Report on the mass media in 1970, which were set up to study and direct the course of broadcasting in Canada, have all agreed that national goals and values should be pursued and preserved through the media. The values they referred to were predominantly those of the anglophile elite of central Canada.[71] In late 1982, the controversial Applebaum-Hébert Report added a new dimension to discussions of cultural policy in Canada.[72] It was followed in 1986 by the comprehensive report of a federal Task Force on Broadcasting Policy that recommended an industrial and cultural strategy of broadcasting over the next 15 years.[73] These reports set the agenda for discussions of federal cultural policy to the present day.

Little scientific evidence concerning the impact of the mass media on national cohesion is available. However, it is generally accepted that the extent to which the media provide common images and a cross-regional flow of information, as well as the way in which they present regional and ethno-linguistic conflict, have a significant bearing on national unity. In Canada, with its federal structure, there is danger in a communications system that is either too strongly centralized or too fragmented. Regional and ethnic cultures may be strong enough so that centrally controlled media that are not sufficiently attuned to such differences might, as one media specialist suggests, "produce alienation and hostility rather than assimilation to a national culture."[74] Certainly, the domination of the Ontario heartland in

---

68 *Montreal Gazette*, November 15, 1865; reprinted from a British periodical, *Saturday Review*.

69 R. Brunskill, *A Newspaper Content Analysis of Canadian Integration 1845–1895*, Carleton University Ph.D. Dissertation, 1976, ch. 1, p. 55.

70 See *The Toronto Star*, Sunday edition, November 29, 1981. For a useful account of government policy in the cultural industry field see Stephen Brooks, *Public Policy in Canada; An Introduction* (Toronto: McClelland and Stewart, 1989), ch. 10.

71 Young, "Voices of Democracy," p. 687.

72 Among the Applebaum-Hébert's many wide-ranging recommendations, the report proposed that the CBC continue as a broadcasting outlet but that its own productions be limited to news, and that all commercials should be eliminated. It strongly supported a federal system of "arm's-length" funding for all major cultural agencies including the CBC, to avoid political interference in independent agencies.

73 It made several proposals for strengthening Canadian broadcasting, including a recommendation to gradually phase out foreign programming on the CBC so that 95 percent of CBC content would be Canadian.

74 Fletcher, *The Newspaper and Public Affairs*, p. 25.

areas other than communications has been an important facet of regional alienation. Although the Canadian communications system aims to foster Canadian identity and support regional diversity, central Canadian domination of the national media remains a problem.

BROADCAST MEDIA: TELEVISION AND RADIO

Television is a powerful medium. There is at least one television set in 97 percent of Canadian households; 84 percent of adults, 87 percent of teens and 90 percent of children watch it every day.[75] Canadians spent an average of 23.3 hours a week watching televison in 1991.[76] (See Table 4.3 for a percentage distribution of television viewing time.) Television is primarily an entertainment medium in which impressions and images are more influential than issues. However it is also the primary source of information for most Canadians, and the chief means of communication between political leaders and the general public. As television has gained ever larger audiences, the relationship between politicians and Canadian citizens increasingly has been filtered by televison journalists and by the restrictions of the medium itself. As television has placed demands on political leaders, they in turn have learned ways to maximize their exposure and get the message they want to the public.

TABLE 4.3   PERCENTAGE DISTRIBUTION OF TELEVISION VIEWING TIME — 1991

Type of Program	Canadian Programs	Foreign Programs	Total
News and Public Affairs	17.2	5.6	22.7
Documentary	0.8	0.8	1.6
Instruction			
Academic	0.8	0.4	1.2
Social/Recreational	1.6	0.4	1.9
Religion	0.2	0.1	0.3
Sports	5.0	2.4	7.3
Variety and Games	4.5	5.0	9.5
Music and Dance	0.6	0.5	1.1
Comedy	1.4	15.6	17.0
Drama	4.5	24.7	29.2
Other/Unknown	*	8.2	8.2
Total	36.5	63.5	100.0

* Too small to be expressed

Source: *1991 Census Highlights: The Daily* (Ottawa: Statistics Canada, April 26, 1993), p. 3. Reproduced by authority of the Minister responsible for Statistics Canada 1993.

---

[75] Lambert et al., "The Sources of Political Knowledge," p. 103.

[76] Statistics Canada, *The Daily* (April 26, 1993), p. 2.

Consider some of the ways politicians, and the prime minister in particular, are constrained by television. It is perhaps not absolutely essential for a political leader to project well on television, but those who do certainly reap enormous benefits. As David Taras notes:

> Television by nature coarsens and distorts reality. Virtually all mannerisms are exaggerated: imperfect chins look more imperfect, a hand seems to shake more than it actually does, sudden movements give someone a frenetic look.[77]

Physical attributes and speaking style that formerly would not have been important in a leader's relationship with the public now threaten to damage an individual's chances for political success. Citizens who meet well-known political leaders in person often are surprised at how different the real-life impression is from the television image. Much personal charm is often lost in the electronic translation, as are intelligence and persuasive arguments. Politicians can learn techniques to become more "mediagenic." Speech must be lively rather than slow and deliberate, but not too fast or staccato. One must have the ability to express a complex idea in 10 or 15 seconds; there is no time for deep or thoughtful arguments.

Given the amount of television exposure and the strong north-south attraction in communications in North America, how real is the danger of assimilation into the dominant American cultural milieu? Selected facts and figures from the current scene give some indication of the degree of American penetration into Canadian popular culture.[78] Over 80 percent of Canadians have access to American television channels. Both of Canada's national networks, the CTV and CBC English networks, show a preponderance of American programs — and surveys show that Canadians overwhelmingly prefer them to Canadian alternatives.[79] Former CBC President A.W. Johnson expressed his concern about the U.S. influence this way:

> The plain truth is that most of our kids know more about the Alamo than they know about Batoche or Chrysler's Farm. They know more about Davey Crockett than they do about Louis Riel.[80]

Over the years, the federal government has attempted to increase the quantity and quality of Canadian programming. In 1932, Prime Minister R.B. Bennett created the publicly owned non-profit radio network that evolved into the CBC and now broadcasts nationally in English and French. In the 1950s, the CBC also took on a national television service. The CBC was created to be a unifying force in Canada and its primary concern has been Canadian content.

The Board of Broadcast Governors and the Canadian Radio-television Commission (which now covers telecommunications) were established to regulate both the CBC and all private broadcasting in Canada. The stated goal of the CRTC is to safeguard, enrich and strengthen the cultural, political, social and economic fabric of Canada by broadly regulat-

---

[77] Taris, *The Newsmakers*, p. 122.

[78] See S.M. Crean, *Who's Afraid of Canadian Culture?* (Don Mills, Ont.: General Publishing, 1976); Janet Morchain, *Sharing a Continent* (Toronto: McGraw-Hill Ryerson, 1973).

[79] Manzer, *Canada: A Socio-Political Report*, p. 110.

[80] A.W. Johnson, *Broadcast Priorities for the 1980s*, CBC Corporate Statement to the CRTC, 1978, p. 3. According to a 1987 federal government publication, just 24 percent of prime-time television watched by English-language viewers is Canadian in origin, the rest is virtually all from the United States. *Vital Links* (Ottawa: Supply and Services, 1987), pp. 59–67.

ing the content and standards of Canadian programming.[81] It sets and enforces a complicated Canadian content guidelines for all licenced broadcasters in Canada.[82] It determines the percentage of Canadian content in programming and the time frame within which it must appear for both television and radio. The nationalistic recommendations of the CRTC are often highly controversial and not politically acceptable. For example, its proposals for tougher Canadian content rules often have been rejected by the Cabinet on the grounds that stiff regulation of programming and scheduling might mean loss of audience and advertising revenue, or, more recently, that an interventionist approach is obsolete given satellite television and video cassettes.

The extent to which the CBC, under the watchful eye of the CRTC, has been successful in its mission as a public service is controversial. It does ensure that some of the major people involved in broadcasting in Canada are Canadians. However, the subjects, values and ideas conveyed are often "Americanized" in order to increase their appeal to a broader North American audience and, therefore, make them more profitable. Canadians have shown a predilection for domestic news and public affairs programs, but like other media programming these rely heavily on American sources. For example, U.S. foreign reports tend to displace not only Canadian foreign reports, but also Canadian domestic news.[83]

Since the media sets the agenda for public discussion and debate, it is reasonable that a society that depends on another one for its view of the world will absorb some of the latter's norms. The inevitable effect of this American influence is to encourage attitudinal integration with the United States. Clearly this fact has a bearing on the fragility of the Canadian national identity.

The question of American cultural penetration through the mass media presents a serious dilemma for Canadians. If Canadians believe in a free press and free information flow, then they should leave the borders open to all communications without restriction. Yet this philosophy hinders the development of a distinctive Canadian culture and identity. One author described the Canadian solution to the dilemma this way: in Canada, we "follow a classical liberal ideology and let the media directors, advertisers and people choose the media and the media content they wish." This "reinforces U.S. influence and presumably weakens Canadians identity as such."[84]

Financing is another major problem for the CBC. It generally has been underfunded since 1953 and this has hampered effective planning in the face of severe competition from a rapidly expanding private television broadcasting system. Contrary to early expectations, the CBC remains dependent on advertising revenue for about $300 million a year in revenue, more

---

[81] The CRTC, for example, allows the prime minister special access to the broadcast media. Of course, the prime minister can ask for time on CBC television and radio at any time, but through an instruction from Cabinet, the CRTC can invoke section 18(2) of the Broadcasting Act and gain access to all stations. Such an invocation constitutes a directive to all licencees to broadcast any program deemed to be "of urgent importance to Canadians generally."

[82] See Stephen Brooks, *Public Policy in Canada* (Toronto: McClelland & Stewart, 1988), pp. 312–13.

[83] Conrad Winn, "Mass Communication," in Conrad Winn and John McMenemy, *Political Parties in Canada* (Toronto: McGraw-Hill Ryerson, 1976), p. 143.

[84] Frederick Elkin, "Communications Media and Identity Formation in Canada," in B.D. Singer, ed., *Communications in Canadian Society* (Toronto: Copp Clark, 1975), p. 232. See also Steven Globerman, *Cultural Regulation in Canada* (Montréal: IRPP, 1983).

than a third of its budget.[85] This has resulted in CBC schedules that continue to include a substantial amount of foreign content.[86]

The economic dilemma of all Canadian broadcasters is that profitability rests largely on their use of imported programs. The United States exports expensively made programs for which costs are amortized in the domestic market, which is ten times the size of Canada's. Therefore, they can be purchased for a fraction of their cost by Canadian networks. Private broadcasters try to provide programming with the highest possible appeal at the lowest cost and, therefore, want to import American shows. This pits them against the CRTC whose role is to enforce minimum Canadian-content levels.

The CBC has to cope with these same economic problems, and also the difficult task of carrying out two conflicting mandates. It is required to promote a singe national identity and culture, but at the same time cater to regional, ethnic and other minority interests. Establishing an appropriate balance has proven difficult. As a vocal medium, broadcasting is particularly suited to appeal to awareness of languages and cultures. It does a great deal to develop regional identities but is less successful at reinforcing national values and promoting national unity.

The media in Canada also fail in the quest to provide national unity because they cannot bridge the country's ethnic cleavage. Rather than providing a powerful unifying link for the whole country, television broadcasting in the early years achieved the contrary. In Québec, where the full range of programming was local, the identity that was reinforced was not Canada's but Québec's. Television helped shape and preserve the distinctiveness that promoted Québec nationalism in the 1960s. Montréal sociologist Maurice Pinard commented:

> The Québec nation was born with television...I mean by that the Quebec nation, as opposed to the French-Canadian people, which is something else altogether.[87]

Today, despite the growing availability of English-language television stations, 87.5 percent of francophone viewers watch French-language stations.[88]

Even entertainment shows separate the two communities. In the 1960s and 1970s, French-Canadian entertainers such as Pauline Julien and Robert Charlebois were at the forefront of the independence movement. Their role was so prominent that Parti Québécois leader Jacques Parizeau quipped that the Quiet Revolution was brought about by "three or four ministers, 20 civil servants and 50 chansonniers."[89] Today, in the mid-1990s, many Québec artists have moved away from their separatist crusade and are building careers in the American market, in English. English television programs often feature Americans but only rarely francophone Canadians. A wonderful example of unique television programming in Québec was the TV series "Les Filles de Caleb," a 20-part series on Radio-Canada. It was based on Arlette Cousture's novel about the true experiences of her grandmother. The series was the most popular in Québec history; an estimated 3.5 million people — half of Québec's entire population — regularly watched the shows. The English-language version was not at all popular in the rest of the country. Director Jean Beaudin commented:

---

[85] *The Globe and Mail*, April 15, 1992.

[86] Paul Audley, *Canada's Cultural Industries* (Toronto: James Lorimer and Co., 1983), p. 255.

[87] Quoted by Daniel Drolet in "TV shapes Quebec's distinctiveness," *The Ottawa Citizen*, Feb. 3, 1991.

[88] Rhéal Séguin, "Use of French rising in Québec," *The Globe and Mail*, June 19, 1991.

[89] Peter Maser, "The Muting of the Strident Indépendantists among the artistic community," *The Ottawa Citizen*, June 20, 1992.

Québeckers like Québec television and Québec movies. When you are a Québecker, you can watch American television, but you don't connect.[90]

Different agendas in the French and English media are often evident in political biases. For example, while English CTV is judged to be neutral and the CBC to be establishment-oriented in political leanings, Radio-Canada is more partisan to the left and to the Parti Québécois. A good example is the four-part series broadcast on Radio-Canada in 1992 titled "The History of Nationalism in Québec." It was, as Montréal journalist William Johnson commented, really "the nationalist mythology of Québec history." French-speaking Québeckers were presented as oppressed victims persecuted by *les Anglais* for more than 200 years. All the social and economic problems of French Canada were depicted as the fault of *les Anglais*. It was nationalist mythology presented on television as fact.

Apart from the relative inability of the national media to provide an integrated service between the two official language communities, there are other communication issues that have generated considerable friction between federal authorities and ethno-cultural groups other than French and English. Native audiences, for example, have grievances. East-west radio and television networks were understandably the government's first priority. CBC's Northern Television Service (NTS) began live satellite transmission in 1973, and their stations receive programming by satellite, mainly from CBC networks in southern Canada. In 1982, the Inuit Broadcasting Corporation (IBC) began on a modest scale to air television programs across the Northwest Territories and northern Québec. This has assured more community control of northern broadcasting, but decisions about policy and funding are still made in the South. By 1993, all communities of 500 or more had, or were in the process of getting, radio and television services. As with education in the North, efforts are being made to fund and develop programs that are relevant to northern communities and to Native people in particular. Again, the problem is one of majority versus minority rights — how to balance the need to foster national unity while at the same time celebrating differences.

Technological changes will make regulatory control of Canadian content much more difficult in the years ahead. In early 1993, the establishment of DirecTv Canada signaled the first serous threat to Canadian broadcasting from private satellite television operators. The company plans to launch its first high-power direct-broadcast satellite in December, 1993 and begin offering services in April 1994.[91] The new service will offer Canadian TV viewers 150 channels of entertainment and information in the first direct broadcast satellite service backed by a major U.S. company. The CRTC will have no jurisdiction over what the satellite carries, but it will, in effect, contribute to the Canadian broadcasting system. In future, Canadians will be able to order the information and entertainment they want, when they want it. They will be able to put together their own newscasts, choosing areas that interest them. Eventually networks, if they exist at all, will be transformed and broadcast executives will lose their power to decide what transmissions individuals receive.[92]

---

[90] Ibid.

[91] Cable companies adopted the term "deathstar" to describe the satellite service that will challenge their existence.

[92] See Richard Collins, *Culture, Communication and National Identity: The Case of Canadian Television* (Toronto: University of Toronto Press, 1990).

In the decades ahead, debates over the merits of public-versus-private sector broadcasting will also increase. Nationalists will fight for a stronger mandate for the CBC to promote cultural identity. Internationalists, however, will argue in favour of dropping restrictions against foreign programming and even for killing the CBC. The argument for abandoning restrictions is that there is no direct link between television and political sovereignty, and there is little evidence about how TV actually affects beliefs and attitudes. Richard Collins, for example, calls the CBC's national unity mandate narrow-minded and ineffectual. Controversially, he maintains that political institutions, not a strong national culture, hold the country together, arguing that there is no direct link between television programming and political sovereignty. Canada can even be seen as an example of how a country can survive as a political entity *despite* the fact that its citizens consume huge amounts of foreign TV programming.[93] In the end, technological advances rather than the CRTC will probably determine what Canadians watch on TV.

PRINT MEDIA: NEWSPAPERS

The print media, unlike the broadcast media, do not require a special licence to operate. They regulate themselves through press councils and are free of direct regulation by government. Newspapers were established to inform and persuade rather than entertain. They have a more restricted but more attentive public than television does. Only about half of all Canadians read newspapers, but they tend to be the best educated. Data show that "the most politically attentive individuals regard newspapers as the single most important source of political information."[94] There is strong evidence supporting the effectiveness of the print media in contributing to political knowledge. Reading newspapers and magazines appears to be more 'instructive' on both factual and conceptual knowledge than is viewing television. This is particularly significant in view of the fact that television is growing as the preferred source of political information among Canadians, and that fewer young people are reading newspapers.[95]

The Globe and Mail is read by nearly three-quarters of the country's top decision-makers, and more than 90 percent of media executives read it regularly for ideas and trends. Until satellite transmission made the scheme practical in the 1970s, distance prevented simultaneous publication from British Columbia to the Atlantic provinces. Since *The Globe* became available on a nation-wide, day-of-issue basis early in the 1980s, it has gained considerable strength as a national newspaper, although its share of the market outside of Ontario is still relatively small. It is Toronto-based and, although it does carry regional, national and international material, it is still strongly biased toward central Canada coverage and basically reviews the periphery and the whole from a central perspective. *The Toronto Star*, Canada's largest independent daily, can be considered national only by virtue of a few widely syndicated articles. *Le Devoir* is comparable to *The Globe and Mail* for the francophone community. The Canadian Press (CP) (a cooperative news agency owned and operated by Canadian dailies that provides information to more than 100 media outlets), Southam News (the largest Canadian newspaper chain) and a few national magazines must also be included as part of the national scene.[96]

---

93 Ibid.

94 Lambert et al., "The Sources of Political Knowledge," pp. 373–74.

95 Ibid., p. 103.

96 Fletcher, *The Newspaper and Public Affairs*, passim.

Because of factors such as distance, time and the federal political structure, these national networks of communication are supplemented by a wide range of regional daily newspapers that primarily are community oriented and limited to the regions concerned. Their influence on the country as a whole and on federal decision-makers is small. They depend on centre-oriented agencies such as the Canadian Press for national and international news, reinforcing the influence of the central establishment on content and values. The steadily improving quality of CP and increased regional coverage by *The Globe and Mail* and Southam News in recent years appears to have contributed to a better cross-regional flow of information, as has the development of major newspaper chains at the expense of independent dailies.

Given the importance of newspapers in setting the national agenda, ownership is an important issue. In 1992, three major chains, Thomson, Southam and Black, dominated the newspaper market in Canada, controlling over 64 percent of all dailies (Thomson 37 percent, Southam 16 percent, Black 11 percent). Ninety dailies out of 108 belonged to chains. Many independent newspapers, such as the *Toronto Telegram*, the *Winnipeg Tribune* and the *Ottawa Journal* have been forced to close. This domination poses serious questions about both lack of competition and conflict of interest. The Thomson newspapers, for example, are part of an international conglomerate that includes insurance, television, oil, real estate and import companies, among other holdings. It is questionable whether the running of a newspaper is compatible with such interests. The Kent Royal Commission on Newspapers recommended in 1981 that the government limit further concentration of media ownership, but no action was taken.[97] Kent's stated aim was:

> *To preserve the daily newspaper industry; that is, to save newspapers from further absorption into conglomerate business empires within which they are...valued by their proprietors chiefly for the large cash flow that they can contribute to further empire-building.*[98]

His concern about an increase in conglomerate ownership of the dailies was justified, as Southam took over several community newspapers in the Vancouver area where it already owned both dailies. Kent's concern was about profit maximization rather than bad intent by the owners. A media property is worth more to a proprietor if it spends less on staff and research. Nearly a decade later, in 1990, he commented,

> *For much of history everywhere, and still today in many countries, it is...government that suppresses or at least limits the freedom of the press. Even in a society as liberal as ours, it's not easy to recast our thinking to recognize that now the more effective enemy is within.*

He went on to say...

> *In an economy as dominated as ours by large corporations with diverse wide-reaching interests and large degrees of monopoly power, the problem for journalists is to obtain*

---

[97] The Kent Commission was set up after the *Ottawa Journal*, owned by Thomson Newspapers, and the *Winnipeg Tribune*, owned by Southam Inc., shut down on the same day in August, 1980. Government legislation to freeze the size of the two largest chains and restrict the size of developing chains to 20 percent of national circulation, among other changes, died at the end of the parliamentary session in late 1983. In order to ensure editorial quality and diversity, the government, during the same period, directed the CRTC, which grants licences to broadcasters, to restrict cross-ownership between broadcasters and owners of daily newspapers. In December 1983, Southam Inc. and Thomson Newspapers Ltd. were acquitted in the Ontario Supreme Court of criminal charges for conspiracy and merger in the closing of the *Ottawa Journal* and the *Winnipeg Tribune* and undue lessening of newspaper competition in Vancouver.

[98] From a comment by Tom Kent on concentration of newspaper ownership. *The Ottawa Citizen*, June 6, 1990.

the resources required to inform the public, accurately and fairly, intelligently and interestingly.[99]

Although it would appear to be in the national interest to maintain diversity of news sources, as the Kent Commission claimed, researchers have been unable to prove that chain ownership affects newspaper quality, news or editorial coverage, although it obviously does affect their credibility.[100] However, the issue points out the need for vigilance and for high quality, professional journalism. As Kent maintained, journalists always endure conflicting pressures, and when matters become too complex only the most diligent cope by becoming more sophisticated — others abandon the topic. As the possibilities for manipulation of the press by industry increase, the need for sophisticated, investigative journalism is even greater.

Chain ownership does not necessarily guarantee national coverage. Southam News, for example, ensures that articles on the federal government are available, but regional papers need not publish them. Despite centralized coverage, therefore, it is often lamented that Canada still has no "national" agenda. A common agenda is temporarily created by events such as general elections but then fragments when regional conflict arises. Regional differences in the selection of stories and the amount of local coverage for specific events do not tend to be based on explicit differences of interpretation.[101]

Studies conducted since the mid-1960s found consistent regional differences in news selection to be based largely on geographical proximity to given events as well as on cultural preferences. For example, a study of 29 daily newspapers for the Bilingualism and Biculturalism Report showed great regional differences in amount of coverage and subjects stressed; this difference was more pronounced between French and English newspapers, which tended to be preoccupied with the affairs of their own language-group.[102] Similarly, the amount of news coverage of Québec-related issues, such as language policy a year after the election of the Parti Québécois, corresponded to the results of public opinion surveys: there was most coverage and most concern for these issues in Québec, somewhat less in Ontario and the Atlantic region and least in the West. Press content, Fred Fletcher speculates, probably both reflects and reinforces regional differences.[103] Media emphasis and public concern about issues generally correspond, so that regional differences in public opinion also correspond to differences in newspaper emphasis.

The argument over media ownership will continue, with specialists such as Noam Chomsky fighting for vigilance. Chomsky argues that the media are mere tools of the corporate and political elite. He maintains they use the media to "manufacture consent" among the small, educated, relatively articulate elite whose approval matters, and to divert the other

---

[99] Ibid.

[100] Royal Commission on Newspapers (Ottawa: Minister of Supply and Services, 1981). See especially Fletcher, *The Newspapers and Public Affairs*, ch. 3.

[101] See, for example, Walter C. Soderlund et al., "Regional and Linguistic Agenda-Setting in Canada: A Study of Newspaper Coverage of Issues Affecting Political Integration in 1976," *CJPS*, vol. 13 no. 2 (June 1980), p. 356.

[102] See, for example, Donald Gordon, *National News in Canadian Newspapers*, Report to the Royal Commission on Bilingualism and Biculturalism, 1966.

[103] Fletcher, *The Newspaper and Public Affairs*, p. 26. The Studies were by W.C. Soderlund et al., "Regional and Linguistic Agenda-Setting." The public opinion poll study was by F. Fletcher and R. Drummond, *Canadian Attitude Trends 1960–1978* (Montréal: IRPP, 1979).

80 percent whose main function is "to follow orders and not think."[104] In the movie *Manufacturing Consent*, Chomsky argues 1) concentration of media ownership in the United States is "clubby" if not cabalistic, 2) errors and omissions made by the media are too "systematic" to be coincidental (his best example is the media ignoring the genocides in Cambodia and East Timor), and 3) the media seem to allow free expression, but in reality marginalize those who dissent.[105] Others argue that this is an extremist and unproven opinion, and that journalism is too confused and chaotic to lend itself to manipulation on such a grand scale — that Chomsky misinterprets "ignorance, haste and deadline pressure for conspiracy."[106]

NEWS AND EDITORIALS

News presentation and editorial comment have a considerable impact on the political agenda in Canada. We have seen that economics constitutes a powerful factor in American influence on all Canadian media. Its effects are particularly evident in news reporting. The relative cost of "made in Canada" news gathering is prohibitive, so that Canadian news, in all the media, relies heavily on U.S. agencies and wire services. This is particularly true in international news, where American news chains sponsor teams abroad, and where national daily newspapers such as the *Washington Post* and the *New York Times* have considerable prestige and influence on the American political scene. No Canadian newspaper has nearly the equivalent influence in Canadian foreign policy discussions. At least part of the reason is that most news from outside North America is taken from American sources.

Canadian news is therefore distorted in the amount of coverage accorded to U.S. domestic news, and the selection and perspectives of foreign news is also heavily influenced. Topics of interest to Americans automatically become of interest to Canadians, and American viewpoints and justifications are well-aired in Canada. It has also been argued that another possible effect of the pre-eminence of U.S. sources in Canadian news is that it could undermine NDP support in Canada in subtle ways by supporting right-wing bias.[107] As we have noted, however, one must bear in mind that studies have been unable to prove that the media have a direct affect on citizen behaviour.

The primary barrier to the development of a "national" political agenda in Canada is that the two founding communities live in separate media worlds which reinforce the linguistic and cultural differences in Canadian society. In Québec, as in the rest of Canada, newspapers are the major source of news for top decision makers. The newspapers serving anglophone and francophone communities focus on different headlines and stories, and often view events from quite different perspectives.[108] There is also a degree of stereotyping of French Canadians in the English press and of insularity in the French press, although coverage of issues outside Québec by francophone newspapers has improved since the mid-1970s.[109]

---

[104] Quoted from the movie *Manufacturing Consent: Noam Chomsky and the Media* by film critic Rick Groen in "The scholar from another planet," *The Globe and Mail*, October 2, 1992.

[105] Ibid.

[106] This was argued by Karl Meyers of the *New York Times*, quoted in ibid.

[107] Winn, "Mass Communication," p. 148.

[108] Elkin, "Communications Media and Identity Formation in Canada," p. 235. See also Arthur Siegel, *Politics and the Media in Canada* (Toronto: McGraw-Hill Ryerson, 1983), ch. 10.

[109] André H. Caron and David C. Payne, "Media and Canadian Politics; General and Referendum Applications," paper presented at the Duke University Conference on Political Support in Canada: The Crisis Years (Durham, North Carolina, 1980).

Paul Gilligan, Citizen

'Having decreed that only violence will successfully attract their attention, the media then denounces violence.'

Concentration by the media on divisive news stories and issues builds emotional barriers between Canadians. A 1976 study of editorials on Québec language issues showed the Ontario and Québec press to be generally integrative, stressing compromise, in contrast to editorial writers in the West and the Atlantic region, who tended to condemn Québec nationalist aspirations.[110] Public opinion data showed that public attitudes closely parallelled this same regional division.[111] As might be expected where local cultures thrive, inter-regional conflicts that occasionally surface in editorials often can be described as parochial, hysterical and combative. These generally concern regionally based issues such as western alienation or language rights and, as Fletcher points out, although they are unlikely to create new tensions, they often reinforce existing ones.[112]

Canadian newspapers reflect community norms and generally support the status quo, tending to reinforce the prevailing institutional and cultural patterns of authority and orientation. Most newspapers are anti-union. Rarely do they challenge dominant community interests or endorse political parties other than the Liberals or Conservatives. The Southam group, for example, traditionally has made political contributions to the federal party in power and also to the official opposition party. It does not give money to the NDP. According to Southam's president, the reason is: "Because we believe in the Canadian two party system."[113]

This "middle of the road" tendency has been explained by two factors. First, the media are appealing to mass audiences so they tend to reinforce community values rather than challenge them. Second, as the Special Senate Committee on the Mass Media suggested, many newspapers may be unwilling to challenge the existing power structure in their community because of "lassitude, sloppiness, smugness and too chummy a relationship."[114] Underlying both of these situations is the fact that, with the exception of the CBC (and some minor stations), the print and electronic media are all privately owned and are run primarily to make profits, not to inform the public or challenge the status quo. They must compete for advertising revenue, which necessitates maximizing their audience or readership by such methods as packaging their news as entertainment and conforming with existing values.[115] Of course, they must also keep their commercial sponsors happy, which allows advertisers to wield indirect influence on the content and direction of news and programming. Editors or station managers would certainly hesitate, and probably decline to run, a story that was adverse to the interests of a generous sponsor.

There has been a trend toward judgemental journalism in recent years, with an increase in commentary that focuses on or accentuates certain issues. Both this and the predominantly negative tone of political coverage may have negative consequences for the political system by encouraging lack of respect for politicians, civil servants, government agencies and

---

[110] Soderlund et al., "Regional and Linguistic Agenda Setting," p. 320.

[111] Fletcher and Drummond, *Canadian Attitude Trends*, pp. 22–35.

[112] Fletcher, *The Newspaper and Public Affairs*, p. 29.

[113] Quoted in Audley, *Canada's Cultural Industries*, p. 29. Canada, of course, does not have a "two party system" as the United States does. For further discussion on the party system in Canada, see Chapter 10, especially the section on "The Origin and Development of the Canadian Party System."

[114] The Special Senate Committee on the Mass Media, *The Uncertain Mirror*, vol. 1 of the Report (Ottawa: Information Canada, 1970), p. 87.

[115] For a study of the structure of radio, television and cable television markets and its impact on the pricing of advertising and profitability, see Stuart McFadyen, Colin Hoskins and David Gillen, *Canadian Broadcasting: Market Structure and Economic Performance* (Montréal: IRPP, 1980).

Parliament.[116] The question here is how to ensure that the media behaves thoughtfully and ethically. There is no doubt that journalists occasionally assume a role that is beyond their abilities and destructive to others. At such times they become what former U.S. vice-president Sipro Agnew termed "the nattering nabobs of negativism."

Media concentration on fault-finding and crisis might also be a factor in alienating citizens from the political process. In 1992, a two-hour television program, "The Betrayal of Democracy" (PBS) examined the role of television and the press in the breakdown of the democratic process and the alienation of the body politic from decision-making. It said that the decay of democracy in America is rooted in the "power relationships surrounding the government itself. Political power has gravitated from the many to the few."[117] The thesis of the special was that government intentionally excludes citizens from the process of decision-making. "It reduces democracy to a charade in which power is exercised for the benefit of assorted coroporate elites...and the elected officials who rely on them for the funds to remain in office." Television has a major role in this charade. It reduces the amount of air time television allots to political figures to about five seconds per appearance, reducing political discourse to meaningless slogans and simple-minded catch phrases. Public cynicism, the documentary maintained

> ...is very largely the product of 40 years of commercial television and its relentless trivializing of everything in the human experience, conditioning people so that they are now convinced of the indifference of elected officials, and worse, convinced that they have no access to power.[118]

These comments apply in Canada as well as the United States. Canadian newspapers and public affairs programs are considerably less influential than their counterparts in other countries because policy-makers tend to lack respect for the expertise of columnists and commentators. Too often, Canadian journalists treat public affairs as theatre and gossip, stressing personalities rather than social issues, style rather than substance. This orientation is not, however, entirely the fault of the journalists. As one study noted,

> ...the vast majority of viewers/listeners/readers want all things on their information menu to be black or white, true or false, good or bad — preferably seasoned with a pinch of sensationalism and intimate personal detail of the famous, and served on a platter of conventional belief.[119]

Communications in Canada are at a vital juncture. The current revolution in information technology is fraught with social and political implications. Distances are becoming meaningless, and the sheer volume of information available to individuals is overwhelming. In the decades ahead who will select and supply the information that Canadians will receive? Will the government find ways to control the flow of information without outlawing private direct broadcast satellite receivers, thereby depriving Canadians of the lower costs and vastly improved communications they offer? Will the free flow of information increase American cultural domination? What will the overall effect be on Canadian political culture?

---

[116] Allan Kornberg and Judith D. Wolfe, "Parliament, Media and the Polls," in Harold D. Clarke, et al., eds., *Parliament, Policy and Representation* (Toronto: Methuen, 1980) pp. 35–58; and James P. Winter and Alan Frizzell, "The Treatment of State-Owned vs. Private Corporations in English Canadian Dailies," *Canadian Journal of Communications*, vol. 6 (Winter 1979–80), pp. 1–11.

[117] Quoted by John Haslett Cuff in "Media and democracy's decay," *The Globe and Mail*, April 15, 1992.

[118] Ibid.

[119] Michael J. Trebilcock et al., *The Choice of Governing Instrument* (Ottawa: Minister of Supply and Services, 1982), pp. 16–17.

GOVERNMENT INFORMATION AND POLITICAL ORIENTATIONS

The federal government plays a major role in shaping and reinforcing the political culture of Canada. It constantly taps citizen's reactions and attempts to inform, educate or propagandize in order to increase public support and loyalty. We have noted that public information about government affairs stems mainly from the mass media. There are many ways to inform citizens and influence their attitudes. Governments time their political announcements and broadcasts for peak exposure, advertise their parties and policy positions, televise parliamentary debates and record statements in *Hansard*. They advertise in the various media; public servants answer questions and distribute information; MPs deliver speeches and attempt to maintain personal contact within their constituencies; schools often use government booklets on a variety of subjects. As well, government ceremonies are held with traditional pomp and dignity, instilling feelings of respect and a sense of historical continuity.

For a variety of reasons government communications have increased dramatically in recent years. One is the perceived need to refurbish the image of Parliament and federal institutions; another is an attempt to promote national unity and combat the centrifugal forces of regionalism. Such concerns among political leaders have been prevalent since the late 1960s when protest movements and vocal separatists underlined the growing cynicism and hostility of Canadians toward their federal government and its work. Why was the federal government not reaping credit for its programs? Was the problem a breakdown of communications between the government and its citizens? Should the federal government be doing more to create a national consciousness? Where is the line to be drawn between information and propaganda?

EARLY GOVERNMENT INFORMATION SERVICES

To address the problems of government information, the Federal Government set up a Task Force on Information. Its 1969 report revealed that a majority of the respondents in a national survey could not recall having seen *any* federal advertisements, and tended to be ill-informed about the responsibilities of their provincial and federal governments. On the other hand, the minority who remembered having been exposed to government advertising was relatively knowledgeable. The report noted, however, that exposure of the informed group to the advertising did not appear to have favourably influenced their attitudes toward the federal government. Those who used government services held the most positive attitudes toward government officials, finding them helpful and friendly.[120]

The same study found that the public obtained far more government information from the public service than from MPs. However, this communication was one-way, in that information in the opposite direction from the public to the government passed not through public servants but mainly through MPs or MLAs.

This Task Force report ushered in a controversial era in government information programs. Modern Canadian governments have always advertised to inform the public about such topics as new unemployment regulations. Each government department has a budget for this purpose. However, in response to the report a new agency, Information Canada, was set up in 1970 to provide a direct information service by selling and distributing

---

[120] *To Know and To Be Known*, Report of the Task Force on Information (Ottawa: Queen's Printer, 1969).

government pamphlets and other information across the country. It included a small "federalism" section, the aim of which was "a defence in depth of Confederation." This section was to set up information centres run jointly by the federal and provincial governments and generally provide easier access to government departments.

The agency was immediately viewed with suspicion as a partisan government party propaganda device by both the media and the opposition parties. It was inadequately defended by the government and was disbanded in 1976. The problem of negative public attitudes to government remained, and a year after the demise of Information Canada other efforts were instigated to improve access to federal programs and help the government departments advertise their services. The government, in a word, went into the marketing business — to sell itself.

THE ISSUE OF GOVERNMENT ADVERTISING

The greatest danger for government information services is that they can be viewed, justifiably or not, as a vehicle for publicizing programs, policies and views of the governing party — as a partisan political instrument.[121] This was the case when the Liberals established the Canadian Unity Information Office (CUIO) in 1977, a year after the election of the Parti Québécois in Québec. This office was intended to organize major advertising campaigns and handle media contracts and payments. Initially, it coordinated publicity about the federal government's position on the 1980 Québec referendum; subsequently, it directed advertising supporting the government's views in the bargaining with the provinces that led to the patriation of the Constitution. The CUIO conveyed the federal government's message through both print and broadcast media, making certain that the federal viewpoint reached citizens in all provinces. While the Conservatives were in opposition, they consistently accused the Liberals of using the CUIO to build an image for their own political ends. One of the first Conservative acts on assuming power in September 1984 was to disband the CUIO. The Secretary of State retained responsibility for promoting national unity, and the Minister of Supply and Services was given responsibility for government advertising.

There remain two important controversies about government advertising. One is the use of advocacy advertising techniques; the other is the large financial cost to the taxpayer. In essence, advocacy advertising means selling ideas rather than products or services. Such advertisements attempt to build the legitimacy of their sponsor by sustaining or changing public attitudes concerning long term fundamental values that underlie social and political institutions.[122] Liberal government spokesmen in the days of the CUIO viewed advocacy advertising as a means of building national unity and ensuring that Canadians were informed without the intermediary interpretation of the press. Their advertisements therefore did not contain much information but were designed to underline what the federal government saw as basic national values and to promote understanding of national goals. For instance, ads extolling the virtues of Canada's multicultural society carried logos like "Growing Together" and "We have a lot to offer each other."

This type of service becomes controversial when advertisements extol clearly partisan policies. One of the best examples was government advertising over patriating the

---

[121] See Bob Phillips, "Opening Up," *Policy Options*, vol. 4 no. 2 (March/April, 1983), pp. 34–5.

[122] See Duncan McDowall, "And Now a Word from Our Sponsor: Ottawa Turns to Advocacy Advertising," *The Canadian Business Review*, vol. 9, no. 3 (Autumn, 1982), p. 30.

Constitution. In October 1980 contracts were awarded (without competition) to three agencies that had filled contracts for the Liberal Party in the previous election campaign. The advertisements they generated were designed to convince Canadians that the Constitution should be rewritten and patriated despite the differing opinions of provincial premiers and political parties. This aggressive approach, the government declared, was necessary for informing the public on a matter of national interest. Many who opposed the government viewpoint felt that the powerful political sales effort weakened Parliament and democracy in Canada by undermining traditional relations between MPs, the electorate and the government. One widely criticized television commercial featured Canada geese as the backdrop for a constitutional message. A federal member complained at the time, "I'll never be able to look at Canada geese or a beaver in quite the same way again. I'll see them as Liberals in disguise."[123] There is little doubt, however, that the advertisement contributed to setting a national agenda and ensuring that the federal message was heard in all provinces. Given the regionalization of the press, which often allows provincial premiers and opponents of the federal government to monopolize news coverage, federal government advertising may well be necessary for informed debate and for redressing any distortions in the information received by the public.

The scenario was repeated in 1992 by the Mulroney Conservative government. Canada's 125th birthday celebrations coincided with the government's efforts to "sell" to the public the Charlottetown accord. Making Canadians feel good about themselves and their country was expensive, and "just happened" to try to make them feel good about the Conservative party as well. The Department of the Secretary of State is responsible for promoting national celebrations such as Canada Day or special occasions such as Canada's 125th birthday. However, as political commentator Hugh Winsor noted:

> It is also clear that this relatively minor department is merely a convenient umbrella for the cabinet's propaganda thrust, and the shots are being called in the Federal Provincial Relations Office (FPRO) and Mr. Murray's committee.[124]

"Warm tummy, feel good" advertising filled the media when the government spent $21 million on a year-long 1992 federal advertising campaign, awarding the most lucrative advertising contracts in Canadian history (without competitive bids) to companies with close political ties to the Mulroney government.[125] The ads were to reflect the government's twin themes of unity and prosperity. One controversial ad was a song about pride in one's country sung by a young Mila Mulroney look-alike over a montage of familiar wheat fields, Rockies, fishing harbours and totem poles. The syrupy lyrics had been composed for the Conservative party and, arguably, created a partisan "add-on" for the Tories.[126] The primary goal was to make viewers more receptive to government advertising when Ottawa tried to sell them a Constitutional package later in the year.

When the referendum on the Charlottetown accord was called for October 28, 1992, it was packaged and "sold" by the government with taxpayer's money. Its expenses were limited only by the depth of the taxpayer's pockets.

---

[123] Quoted in Frances Phillips, "And Critics Have a Go at Ottawa," *The Financial Post*, May 13, 1982.

[124] See Hugh Winsor, "Bidding to Quicken Patriotic Heartbeat," *The Globe and Mail*, May 28, 1992.

[125] Mark Kennedy and Chris Cobb, "Ad contracts given without bids," *The Ottawa Citizen*, Feb. 6, 1993.

[126] See Hugh Winsor, "The high cost of feeling better," *The Globe and Mail*, May 26, 1992.

The "Yes" support consisted of the leadership of all three major federal parties and almost all of their provincial counterparts, as well as 191 local or community-based non-partisan organizations, "prominent" Canadians recruited as voluntary "National chairs," and the leadership of the Native, labour, corporate, media, and cultural élite."[127]

The "Yes" side had state-of-the-art technology and luxurious campaign offices. Polling contracts were handed out freely (largely to Conservative agencies); a bureaucrat from FPRO remarked confidentially, "there is no budget here. The sky is the limit."[128] The "No" side, in contrast, had a tiny one-room office, no government funding, and no logistical support. With their superior structure, organization and financing the "Yes" side dismissed their opponents as malcontents and "enemies of Canada." Instead of an informative campaign that countered the objections of their opponents, the government waged a campaign based on emotion, throwing their resources completely behind one side of the referendum question. As Brooke Jeffrey points out, "None of the political parties was above using the referendum as a vehicle to enhance its organizational and public relations efforts in preparation for the next election."[129]

The federal government's rising tendency to use advocacy advertising on controversial issues has stimulated occasional ad wars between the federal and provincial governments. The most notable occurred when the Parti Québécois spent $600 000 on an ad campaign to counter Prime Minister Trudeau's constitutional proposals. The eye-catching advertisements, entitled "Minute: Ottawa!" showed a "federal" hand crushing the provincial flag. Such ad wars exacerbate federal/provincial differences, the very thing the federal government says it aspires to eliminate. At the same time, however, the parochialism and anti-federal bias of much of the press demonstrate the need for the national or federal viewpoint to be expressed across the country.

The second major criticism of government advertising concerns its cost. The federal government does not release a comprehensive figure for all advertising expenditures, but industry experts estimated the total for 1982–83 to be $70 million. This figure did not include advertising for such Crown corporations as Air Canada, CN, Petro-Canada or for agencies that are not required to advertise through the Department of Supply and Services.[130] Such huge outlays made the government the largest single advertiser in Canada by the early 1980s, up from 17th position just over a decade earlier. Advertising expenditures have inflated and in 1992 the government spent over $100 million on television advertising.[131]

Advocacy advertising clearly needs close regulation. Even when money is spent to advertise less controversial topics, it is sometimes debatable whether the sum could not be put to better use. For example, to show the federal government's concern about high unemployment in the 1980s, the Department of Employment and Immigration spent $46 million on billboards depicting men and women working. The only print was "Helping

---

[127] Brooke Jeffrey, *Strange Bedfellows, Trying Times* (Toronto: Key Porter, 1993), p. 115.

[128] Quoted in Jeffrey, *Strange Bedfellows*, pp. 117–8. Elections Canada revealed that the "Yes" forces spent more than 13 times the "No" forces spent. See Chapter 11.

[129] Ibid., p. 118. This book discusses the reasons the "Yes" forces lost in spite of their massive resources.

[130] Ibid. Finance Minister Wilson was in the ironic position in May, 1989 of having to defend a $2.7 million government television advertising campaign designed to convince the public of the need to cut the deficit. *The Globe and Mail*, May 5, 1989.

[131] Hugh Winsor, *The Globe and Mail*, May 26, 1992.

Canada Work" and, in smaller type underneath, "Employment and Immigration Canada." It may not be unduly sceptical to suggest that the money might have been better spent on creating jobs.

The question of government advertising promises to play a conspicuous role in the years ahead. The federal advertising budget is high compared to private sector advertising, but given the size of the country, two major languages and the cultural divisions within it, as well as the high number of social programs in which the government is involved, much of it is justifiable. The federal government has a responsibility to inform Canadians about its policies and programs and yet refrain from using its resources to disseminate partisan propaganda. The ethnic and regional divisions in Canada's political culture can be alleviated to a degree by ensuring that all citizens are exposed to views that represent the country's interests, not just those of a particular region, province or ethnic group. It is the responsibility of the opposition parties to ensure that the government does not abuse this right, and to date they have shown a marked ability to detect and publicize infractions.

OVERVIEW

Many factors condition the political ideas and orientations of Canadians. Informal socializing agents such as the family and peer groups, and more formal institutions such as the educational system, the media and even government itself shape to varying degrees the factual knowledge and attitudes Canadians have about politics and politicians. Other factors such as gender and socioeconomic class define the environment in which a person lives, determining life chances and also shaping politial attitudes and values.

Political socialization in Canada is a haphazard affair. Early socialization through families and peer groups is casual and informal with minimal interference by the state. The three important secondary agents of socialization that we have examined — educational institutions, the mass media and the federal government — are all closer to the political process and are the object of deliberate attempts by the federal government to influence the values and beliefs of Canadians. But even then, state direction is severely limited. Education, for example, is not within the federal jurisdiction, and mass media, including broadcasting, television and the press, all act independently, to varying degrees.

We have discussed many powerful obstacles to building a strong Canadian political culture. American influences are pervasive. French and English language media in Canada, through their selection and treatment of news, reinforce the linguistic and cultural differences between the two official language groups. Educational institutions display significant regional and French-English differences with respect to both structure and curriculum. Both the media and education reflect and reinforce the regional, linguistic and ethnic cleavages in the political culture. Such obstacles are to be expected given the constraints of a democratic federal political system and a society that is bilingual and multicultural.

In liberal democratic societies basic freedoms must be respected. The state cannot assume direct control of the agents of socialization. Would Canadians want totally centralized government socialization in order to instill a stronger national culture? Would too much centralization have the opposite effect and simply deepen regional and ethnic cleavages? Such weak centralization as exists is already at the root of regional discontent. The federal government has moved in the last two decades to combat strong divisive forces in the Canadian political culture. It continues to build on the goals of strengthening communications, facilitating access to government and improving the circular flow of information between government institutions and the public. Its methods, though often controversial, are geared to bring government closer to the people.

The Canadian political culture, initiated and reinforced as it is by the socialization process described in this chapter, contains at least the minimal level of national identity required to legitimize the Constitution and the democratic political process. Canadians expect to live in a liberal society free of government control and indoctrination. They have learned to value the assumptions and processes of parliamentary democracy and to expect the political system to manage the tensions caused by linguistic and regional cleavages — and to do so democratically.

In the next part of the book, and the next two chapters in particular, we shall examine how the institutions of the Canadian political system are based upon, and reflect, the essential characteristics of Canadian political culture.

SELECTED BIBLIOGRAPHY

GENERAL SOCIALIZATION

Dawson, Richard E., Kenneth Prewitt and Karen S. Dawson, *Political Socialization*, 2nd ed. (Boston: Little, Brown, 1977).

International Political Science Review, Issue Title: *Political Socialization* (vol. 8, no. 3), July 1987.

Johnstone, John C., *Young People's Images of Canadian Society* (Ottawa: Queen's Printer, 1969).

Zureik, Elia and Robert M. Pike, eds., *Socialization and Values in Canadian Society, Volume I: Political Socialization* (Toronto: McClelland & Stewart, 1975).

WOMEN/GENDER

Barrett, Michèle and Anne Phillips, *Destabilizing Theory: Contemporary Feminist Debates* (Stanford: Stanford University Press, 1992).

Bégin, Monique et al., *Some of Us: Women in Canada in Power and Politics* (Mississauga: Random House, 1991).

Bem, Sandra Lipsitz, *The Lenses of Gender* (New Haven: Yale University Press, 1993).

Brodie, M. Janine, *Women and Politics in Canada* (Toronto: McGraw-Hill Ryerson, 1985).

Brym, Robert J. and Bonnie J. Fox, *From Culture to Power: The Sociology of English Canada* (Toronto: Oxford University Press, 1989).

Burt, Sandra et al., eds., *Changing Patterns: Women in Canada* (Toronto: McClelland & Stewart, 1988).

Campbell, Robert and Leslie Pal, *The Real Worlds of Canadian Politics*, 2nd ed. (Peterborough: Broadview Press, 1991)

Canadian Advisory Council on the Status of Women, *Women and Labour Market Poverty* (Ottawa: Supply and Services, 1990).

Hirsch, Marianne and Evelyn Fox Keller, *Conflicts in Feminism* (N.Y. Routledge, 1990).

Kealy, Linda and Joan Sangster, eds., *Beyond the Vote: Canadian Women and Politics* (Toronto: University of Toronto Press, 1989).

...el and Glen Williams, eds., *Canadian Politics in the 1990s*, 3rd ed. (Scarborough: Nelson,

Clement, Wallace, *The Challenge of Class Analysis* (Ottawa: Carleton University Press, 1988).

————, *Class, Power and Property: Essays on Canadian Society* (Toronto: Methuen, 1983).

Curtis, James, Edward Grabb, Neil Guppy and Sid Gilbert, *Social Inequality in Canada: Patterns, Problems, Policies* (Scarborough, Ont.: Prentice-Hall Canada, 1988).

Fleming, James, *Circles of Power: The Most Influential People in Canada* (Toronto: Doubleday, 1991).

Forcese, Dennis, *The Canadian Class Structure* (Toronto: McGraw-Hill Ryerson, 1975).

Newman, Peter C.,*The Canadian Establishment Vol. 2: The Acquisitors* (Toronto: McClelland & Stewart, 1990).

Olsen, Denis, *The State Elite* (Toronto: McClelland & Stewart, 1980).

Sarlo, Christopher, *Poverty in Canada* (Vancouver: Fraser Institute, 1992).

Veltmeyer, Henry, *Canadian Class Structure* (Toronto: Garamond Press, 1986).

EDUCATION

Canada, *Learning Well...Living Well* (Ottawa: Supply and Services, 1991).

Economic Council of Canada, *Education and Training in Canada* (Ottawa: Supply and Services, 1992).

————, *A Lot to Learn* (Ottwa: Supply and Services, 1992).

Emberly, Peter C. and Waller R. Newell, *Bankrupt Education: The Demise of Liberal Education in Canada* (Toronto: University of Toronto Press, 1994).

Murphy, R., *Sociological Theories of Education* (Toronto: McGraw-Hill Ryerson, 1979).

Pammet, Jon and Jean-Luc Pépin, eds., *Political Education in Canada* (Halifax: IRPP, 1988).

Royal Commission on Bilingualism and Biculturalism, *Report* (Ottawa: Queen's Printer): Book I, *General Introduction and the Official Languages*, 1967; Book II, *Education*, 1968: Book III, *The Work World*, 2 vols., 1969; Book IV, *The Cultural Contributions of the Other Ethnic Groups*, 1970; Books V and VI, *Federal Capital, and Voluntary Associations*, 1970.

Sigel, Roberta S. and Marilyn A. Hoskin, *The Political Involvement of Adolescents* (Rutgers, N.J.: Rutgers University Press, 1981).

Wardhangh, R., *Language and Nationhood: The Canadian Experience* (Vancouver: New Star, 1983).

MEDIA

Audley, Paul, *Canada's Cultural Industries: Broadcasting, Publishing, Records and Film* (Toronto: Lorimer, 1983).

Babe, Robert E., *Telecommunications in Canada: Technology, Industry and Government* (Toronto: University of Toronto Press, 1990).

Bird, Roger, ed., *Documents of Canadian Broadcasting* (Ottawa: Carleton University Press, 1988).

Black, Edwin R., *Politics and the News: The Political Functions of the Mass Media* (Toronto: Butterworths, 1982).

Chomsky, Noam and Edward Herman, *Manufacturing Consent* (New York: Pantheon, 1988).

Collins, Richard, *Culture, Communications and National Identity* (Toronto: University of Toronto Press, 1990).

Comber, Mary Anne and Robert S. Mayne, *The Newsmongers: How the Media Distort the Political News* (Toronto: McClelland & Stewart, 1986).

Commissioner of Official Languages, *Annual Report* (Ottawa: Supply and Services, 1988), and annually from 1971.

Communications Canada, *Canadian Voices, Canadian Choices: A New Broadcasting Policy for Canada* (Ottawa: Supply and Services, 1988).

Desbarats, Peter, *Guide to Canadian News Media* (Toronto: Harcourt Brace Jovanovich, 1990).

Doran, C.F. and J.H. Sigler, eds., *Canada and the United States* (Scarborough, Ont.: Prentice-Hall Canada, 1985).

Eaman, Ross A., *The Media Society: Basic Issues and Controversies* (Toronto: Butterworths, 1987).

Ericson, R.V., P.M. Baranek and J.B.L. Chan, *Negotiating Control: A Study of News Sources* (Toronto: University of Toronto Press, 1989).

Hayes, David, *Power and Influence: The Globe and Mail and the News Revolution* (Toronto: Key Porter, 1992).

Holmes, Helen and David Taras, eds., *In the Public Interest: Mass Media and Democracy in Canada* (Toronto: Holt, Rinehart and Winston, 1992).

Kent, Tom, et al., Royal Commission on Newspapers, 9 vols. (Ottawa: Supply and Services, 1981).

Lorimer, Rowland and Jean McNulty, *Mass Communications in Canada* (Toronto: McClelland and Stewart, 1987).

Lorimer, R. and D. Wilson. eds., *Communication Canada* (Toronto: Kagan and Woo, 1988).

McLuhan, M., *Understanding Media* (New York: McGraw-Hill, 1964).

Raboy, Marac, *Missed Opportunities: The Story of Canada's Broadcasting Policy* (Toronto: McClelland & Stewart, 1989)

Siegel, Arthur, *Politics and the Media in Canada* (Toronto: McGraw-Hill Ryerson, 1983).

Soderlund, Walter C. et al., *Mass Media and Elections in Canada* (Toronto: Holt, Rinehart and Winston, 1984).

Staines, David, ed., *The Forty-Ninth and Other Parallels: Contemporary Canadian Perspectives* (Amherst, Mass.: The University of Massachusetts Press, 1986).

Taras, David, *The Newsmakers: The Media's Influence on Canadian Politics* (Scarborough; Nelson, 1990).

Task Force on Broadcasting, *Report* (Ottawa: Supply and Services, 1986).

Torrance, Judy M., *Public Violence in Canada* (Montreal: McGill-Queen's University Press, 1986).

Trueman, Peter, *Smoke and Mirrors: The Inside Story of Television News in Canada* (Toronto: McClelland & Stewart, 1980).

Vipond, Mary, *The Mass Media in Canada* (Toronto: Lorimer, 1989).

West, Edwin G., *Subsidizing the Performing Arts* (Toronto: Ontario Economic Council, 1985).

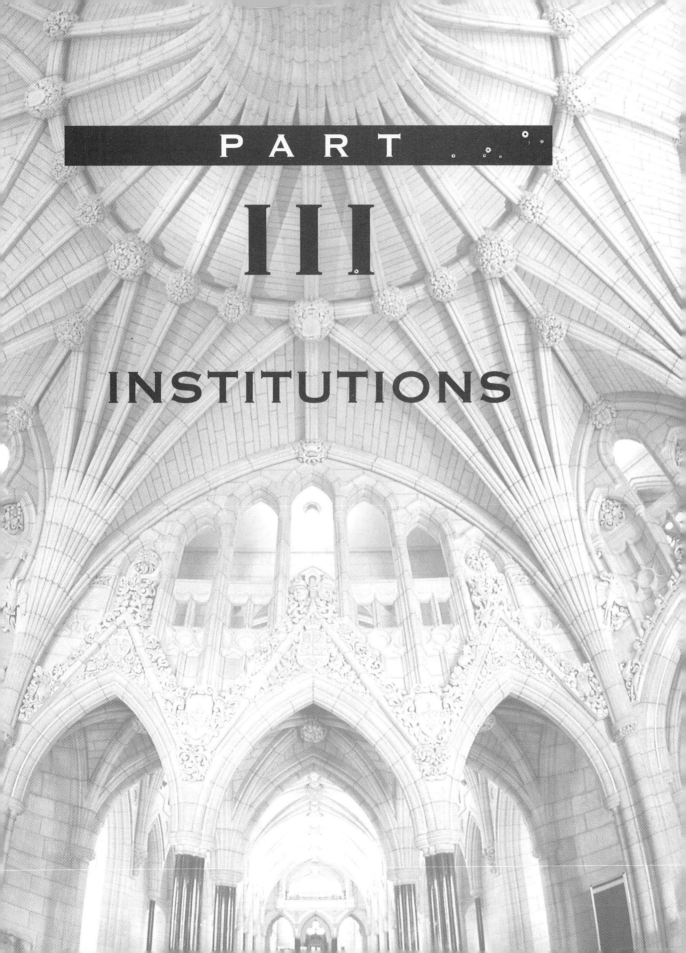

PART

III

INSTITUTIONS

CONSTITUTIONAL FOUNDATIONS

LAW, COURTS, THE CROWN AND CONSTITUTIONAL DEVELOPMENT FROM 1867 TO TODAY

T he establishment of stability and order is a persistent goal of all societies. One way to achieve this end is to create a set of laws and principles that embody the aspirations of the society and, at the same time, provide guidelines for political activity. Although it may take an infinite variety of forms, such a set of rules and procedures is commonly referred to as a constitution. Some societies choose to depend on a constitution in the form of a single written document that is both a statement of principles and a detailed explication of the relative authority and jurisdiction of the various actors in the political process. In other societies, values and political traditions are so firmly rooted in the political culture that no attempt to codify them is considered necessary. The true test of the significance of a constitution, be it written or unwritten, is the nature of its relationship to the society that produced it. Some constitutions are nothing but a set of lofty platitudes that are rarely observed, while others play an integral role in political affairs.

In this chapter we explore the meaning of the term "constitution," and trace the evolution of the Canadian *Constitution* since 1867. Of particular interest will be the provisions for the formal executive, the role of the courts and the problems and difficulties inherent in constitutional amendment and change.

While matters of fundamental law and legal procedure can be complicated for those unfamiliar with the principles of jurisprudence, this chapter will attempt to approach the subject in a non-technical manner, yet remain sensitive to the political implications of constitutional institutions. As we shall determine, the various efforts to patriate the *Constitution* and develop an amendment procedure acceptable to all the provinces created enormous controversy in the past half-century. Though the British Parliament passed the 1982 *Canada Act* that brought the *Constitution* home, the situation is far from resolved and arguments over the nature of the Canadian *Constitution* remain a lively political pastime. The defeat of the Meech Lake and Charlottetown agreements has not ended constitutional wrangling.

LAW, COURTS AND THE CONSTITUTION

All societies, primitive or modern, require some regularized patterns of interaction. Rules imposing obligations and assuring structures for the solution of conflict must be adopted. In primitive societies, these rules are developed through custom and usage; in modern societies they are regularized and formalized. These fundamental rules delineate the authority structures of society and grant leaders the power to act in authoritative ways.

Early societies tended to be dominated by individuals who sought to establish traditions and informal rules to govern their people. In more recent times, there has been a tendency for basic rules to be formalized into what is commonly referred to as a "constitution." The origin of the concept constitution can be traced to Greek and Roman times. Further significant constitutional development flourished during the eighteenth and nineteenth centuries, and since then it has become practically universal for political power to be organized by some form of constitution.[1]

In every political system, there is a need to have guidelines for government action — a supreme law or constitution of the state that defines and limits political power. Thus, the fundamental aspect of a **constitution** is that it states the governing principles of a society. In modern times the word constitution is used both empirically and normatively: to depict the organization of government, and to advise restraints on its action.

Though constitutions are products of historical development, they also tend to reflect current conditions. In absorbing contemporary elements, constitutions are able to help shape the future through their incorporation of norms about political life. As well, constitutional authorities in most countries insist on the need to incorporate **individual rights** into the supreme law as well as to set the parameters for government action. Therefore, the vast majority of contemporary written constitutions contain a discussion of natural rights and the goals of universal liberty, peace and prosperity. Even the most repressive regimes are likely to make reference to these objectives in their constitutions.[2] The French *Declaration of the Rights of Man and Citizens* and the American *Constitution* with its *Bill of Rights* include quite similar statements supporting the principle of the natural rights of *individuals*.

Many constitutions also acknowledge **group rights**. Group claims, privileges and rights are often worked into the Constitution. In Canada, such "rights" were accorded to the ethno-religious-linguistic francophone group of Québec and some historical communities in the eastern seaboard by the *British North America Act* of 1867. Both "individual" and "group" rights are found in today's *Charter of Rights and Freedoms*. Of course, the fact that such rights are incorporated into a constitution is no guarantee of their actualization. In situations of real or perceived emergency, such claims may carry little weight in even the most liberal of societies.

Above all else, the existence of a constitution embodies the *rule of law*. In addition to setting out a commitment to certain general goals, a constitution is intended to provide a guarantee of impartiality and fairness. The authority of the state is to be exercised rationally and without malice, with all citizens being protected from the abuse of power. The **rule of law** means that the citizen, no matter what the transgression, cannot be denied the due process

---

[1]   For details see Robert J. Jackson and Doreen Jackson, *Contemporary Government and Politics: Democracy and Authoritarianism* (Scarborough: Prentice-Hall, 1993), chs. 10 and 11.

[2]   For a discussion of the history of constitutionalism, see Charles M. McIlwain. *Constitutionalism: Ancient and Modern*, 2nd ed. (Ithaca, N.Y.: Cornell University Press, 1947).

of law. It therefore regularizes the relationship between citizens and their government. No individual or institution is above the law, no one is exempted from it and all are equal before it. No government or administrative official has any power beyond that awarded by law. Whether or not it is formally included, the rule of law is a fundamental principle without which any constitution, written or unwritten, would be meaningless.

The courts are the guardians of the rule of law, and as such should be beyond partisan influence. The principle of the independence of the judiciary is firmly established, with a history of nearly 300 years. It can be traced to the English *Act of Settlement* of 1700 that resulted from the English Revolution of 1688, and provided that judges could be removed only if both Houses of Parliament formally asked the Crown for their removal. Following these traditions, Canadian judges remain free to deliver decisions against the interests of influential individuals, institutions or governments without fear of recrimination.

In Canada today, judges of the highest courts (the Supreme Court of Canada and the Federal Court) and also the most important provincial courts (the Superior Court of Québec, the highest court of the other provinces, as well as the provincial courts of appeal) are removable only by an address to the Governor General by both Houses of Parliament. No higher court judge has ever been removed in this fashion. As a further precaution against undue influence on judges, the Canadian *Constitution* provides that almost all courts are established by the provincial legislatures but that all judges from county courts up (except courts of probate in Nova Scotia and New Brunswick) are appointed by the federal government. This tradition of the independence of the judiciary is particularly important in constitutional development because courts interpret the written constitution and therefore define the limits of federal and provincial power as well as apply the *Charter of Rights and Freedoms*.

Aside from the *Constitution*, the two main sources of law in Canada are **statutory** enactments — legislation passed by the Parliament of Canada and the provincial legislatures — and case law developed by the courts, also known as **common law** or unenacted law. While Canada's *Constitution* grants legislative authority to the eleven legislatures, the legislative competence of each is specifically limited to certain classes of matters.

Common law is based upon the rule of precedent, ***stare decisis***. That is, the judiciary is bound by previous decisions in deciding current cases. This has resulted in the development of a body of case law that provides guidelines for judges in rendering decisions. As new problems are brought before the courts, judges refer to previous decisions that are deemed relevant, and apply the deciding arguments when making their own judgements. If there is no appropriate precedent, judges rely on common sense and reason. Existing principles are thereby broadened and the body of case law is expanded. Judicial interpretation is, thus, an important source of our law.

The relationship between these two major sources of law is defined by the doctrine of **parliamentary supremacy**, a basic premise of parliamentary democracy, which is that all 11 legislatures have the authority, in theory, to repeal or modify any principle set out in common law that applies to their jurisdiction. This power is not absolute, however. The Supreme Court's ability to declare an Act *ultra vires* (beyond a legislature's jurisdiction) on the basis of Canada's federal division of power is an important qualification. The *entrenchment* of individual and group rights in Canada's *Charter of Rights and Freedoms* also limits the extent of parliamentary supremacy by placing that body of rights beyond the reach of any legislature.

As well as stating fundamental principles, written constitutions describe the organization of government. Some are remarkably complicated documents outlining the entire government structure and the relative powers and limitations of the various institutions in the political process. There seems to be a general belief that the greater the detail in explicating these relationships, the less the likelihood for the abuse of power. At a minimum, most written constitutions outline the powers and duties of the executive, the legislature, the judiciary and sometimes other institutions such as the bureaucracy or the military. However, in modern, complex societies it is not easy to assign one specific function to any one of these bodies since they all perform multifunctional tasks. The courts, for example, adjudicate the law, but, as we have seen, in their accumulated judgements they also legislate.

However restrictive the legal restraints are on the exercise of power, nearly all constitutions contain provisions for enhanced executive power in emergency situations. War, civil unrest or natural disaster may require a government to act in a way that, under normal conditions, would be illegal. The real test of a constitution is whether, after such a crisis, there is a speedy return to compliance with constitutional strictures. The case of the late Indian Prime Minister Indira Gandhi's invocation of certain emergency provisions of her country's constitution and the subsequent return to normal procedures after the perceived crisis was a vindication of India's constitutional democracy. The use of the *War Measures Act* to suppress civil rights in Québec in 1970 by the Liberal government of Prime Minister Trudeau was another worrisome example of how constitutions allow governments to handle crises.

We need not search far to find examples in other countries where constitutional restraints on the exercise of power have been easily subverted by exaggerated crises. Once a group obtains a power base in society, either inside the institutional structure or outside of it, the potential always exists to manipulate the provisions of the constitution or even suspend it entirely. As we have said, a written constitution is no guarantee that fundamental principles will be upheld. Unless a constitution is congruent with the prevailing political culture, it stands little chance of having a lasting effect.

One form of government in which a written constitution is almost a necessity is *federalism*. The establishment of federalism usually requires some sort of "federal bargain,"[3] in which the constituent elements of the union agree to give up a degree of autonomy in exchange for certain benefits which they perceive as arising from being part of a more powerful political entity. It is difficult to imagine a federal system that is not based on some sort of written document enshrining powers and guarantees to the various levels of governments. This is not to say that a federal constitution cannot be altered by judicial interpretation or by amendment. What is important to remember is that federal states are, for the most part, initiated through the adoption of written constitutions, and that their provisions and limitations help shape the nature of federalism in the given states.

We mentioned earlier that some countries possess what are referred to as **unwritten constitutions**. This is not a contradiction in terms; rather, the existence of such a constitution indicates that certain fundamental principles may be so firmly entrenched in the political process of the state that no formal document outlining them is considered necessary. The United Kingdom is perhaps the best-known example of a country with an unwritten constitution.[4] In this case such documents as the *Magna Carta* of 1215, the *Habeus Corpus Act* of 1679 and the *Reform Bill* of 1832 exist, but they do not make up "the" constitution. Despite these and other documents and legal precedents, the real core of Britain's unwritten constitution is the set of values and norms embedded in the political culture: the right

---

[3] See the detailed discussion in Chapter 6.

[4] See R.M. Punnett, *British Government and Politics*, 4th ed. (London: Heinemann, 1980), pp. 163–93.

of freedom of speech and assembly and the right of the opposition to participate in the political process, among others. The existence of an unwritten constitution provides certain advantages for a state. It makes it possible for instance to adapt more readily to change without the constraints required by a formal constitutional amendment process.

THE ORIGIN AND EVOLUTION OF THE CANADIAN CONSTITUTION

This section examines how the Canadian *Constitution* evolved from the period before the 1867 *British North America Act* (now the *Constitution Act, 1867*) to the passing of the 1982 *Canada Act*.[5] While many Canadians assume that until 1982 the *BNA Act* was the entire Canadian *Constitution*, this assertion should be qualified. The Canadian *Constitution* has always been something of a hybrid of the written and unwritten types.

In reading the *BNA Act*, it is wise to follow the French adage, "read between the lines; it's less fatiguing on the eyes." Important elements of Canada's unwritten *Constitution* evolved in Britain for many centuries before Confederation.[6] Common law precedents and the parliamentary form of government are examples. As British colonists emigrated to Canada they brought with them basic constitutional principles such as the rule of law and the right of parliamentary opposition. The *BNA Act*, with its provision that Canada was to have a form of government "similar in principle to that of the United Kingdom," intended not only that certain institutional arrangements with respect to the formal executive were to be reproduced in Canada, but also that the British parliamentary system, with all its embedded values, was to be transplanted. Important elements of the Canadian *Constitution* were therefore already implicitly in place when the Fathers of Confederation met at Charlottetown in 1864.

As Professor Ronald I. Cheffins phrased it, "a literal reading of the *Act* itself is not only of little value in understanding the realities of political life, but is in fact dangerously misleading."[7] Even vital procedural matters bearing on the governing of the country go unmentioned in the *BNA Act*; for example, the executive roles of the Prime Minister and Cabinet are not mentioned specifically. Constitutional rules that are accepted practice or tradition without being enshrined in the written constitution are called **conventions**. Canada would not be able to govern itself without conventions such as the concept of **responsible government** that requires the government to resign when it is defeated in Parliament over a major issue. Moreover, many issues that preoccupy governments today were not covered in the 1867 document. Over time all levels of government have found ways to expand their responsibilities without increasing their constitutional authority.

Given these elements of the unwritten Canadian *Constitution*, what is the significance of the *British North America Act*? Simply put, the *Act* sets out the basic terms of federalism and sketches the machinery of government based on the British model.[8] The *Act* was the

---

5   Two copies of the original *BNA Act* to which Queen Victoria gave Royal Assent on March 29, 1867 can be seen in London, England: one in the Victoria Tower of Westminster Palace and the other in the Public Records Office. Reproductions are in the National Archives of Canada.

6   See W.P.M. Kennedy, *The Constitution of Canada, 1534–1937* (London: Oxford University Press, 1938) and E. Russell Hopkins, *Confederation at the Crossroads: The Canadian Constitution* (Toronto: McClelland & Stewart, 1968).

7   Ronald I. Cheffins, *The Constitutional Process in Canada* (Toronto: McGraw-Hill, 1969), p. 9.

8   W.H. McConnell, *Commentary on the British North America Act* (Toronto: Macmillan, 1977).

product of lengthy, complex negotiations between the political leaders over the terms of union. The leaders had differing expectations of what federalism would mean for their regions. They all made efforts to obtain concessions and guarantees that would protect matters of vital local concern. For example, French Canadians sought protection for their culture and language as the price for joining the union, while Nova Scotians were concerned about economic concessions and subsidies. Agreement on the organization and structure of the Senate proved particularly difficult to achieve.

The *BNA Act* is a relatively simple, straightforward document. It lacks the stirring rhetoric of the American *Constitution*, and whatever commitment it has to the fundamental rights of individuals is merely implied. In some respects the statute is as significant for what it does not say as for what it does say. The *BNA Act* was a document designed to enable the provinces to join in a political union. It was not intended to establish a truly independent state. It provided that the formal authority of Canada was to continue to be vested in the British monarch and that the *Act* itself could be amended only by the British parliament.

The established provinces continued to adhere to their colonial constitutions, and the provinces added after Confederation later received their constitutions from the Ottawa government. The heritage from the United Kingdom in English-speaking provinces included the common law tradition. However, since Confederation did not change existing law, Québec continued to have a system of civil law based on French traditions such as the *Code Napoléon*. According to the *BNA Act*, criminal law was to be a federal responsibility and similar throughout the land. However, general principles such as liberty and the rule of law were considered to be protected by common law and hence were not included in the *BNA Act*.

The *Act* is reasonably detailed with respect to the machinery of formal executive power and on matters concerning the division of authority between the federal and provincial governments. Over time the *Act* has become less clear-cut on the latter matters as jurisdictional issues have become more complicated.[9] The intent of the authors of the document was the creation of a strong central government. The federal government was given responsibility for the important topics of trade and commerce, defence and foreign affairs. Jurisdiction over education, welfare and other matters perceived to be of lesser and only local interest in 1867 was left to the provinces. As we shall see in the next chapter, the responsibilities of the provinces became relatively more important over time and, when legal disputes did ensue between the two levels of government, the British Law Lords often sided with the provinces. At times, therefore, the *BNA Act* has been a very restrictive document and has created an impasse in federal/provincial relations.

We have said that the *BNA Act* did *not* contain a procedure for amendment except by the passage of a bill in the British Parliament. Over time, the role of the British Parliament in amending the *BNA Act* was restricted. In 1931 the *Statute of Westminster* established the principle that the British Parliament could not legislate for Canada except at the request of the Canadian government. In 1949, Louis St. Laurent's government secured an amendment to the *BNA Act* that widened the scope of the Canadian Parliament's authority to undertake amendments: it was empowered to amend the Canadian *Constitution* on its own except when it affected provincial interests, the five-year term of Parliament and the language and educational rights of minorities. Despite these changes, the *BNA Act* remained an Act of the British Parliament, serving to raise the ire of Canadian nationalists. It was not until

---

[9]   See Garth Stevenson, *Unfulfilled Union: Canadian Federalism and National Unity*, rev. ed. (Toronto: Macmillan, 1982).

1982 that the *Canada Act* was passed, ending forever this link between Canada and the United Kingdom. In total, there were 18 amendments to the *BNA Act*.[10]

Although the *BNA Act* was the centrepiece of Canada's written *Constitution*, there were other relevant documents. Besides the various amendments to the *BNA Act*, and the *Statute of Westminster*, the Canadian *Constitution* before 1982 could be said to include the Royal Proclamation of 1763, the *Colonial Laws Validity Act* of 1865, the various Acts admitting new provinces to the federal union, letters patent concerning the office of the Governor General and a whole range of common law precedents and Orders-in-Council.

Whether a constitution originates as a single written document or as a cluster of laws and agreements, there is no doubt that major changes to it occur through judicial interpretation. There is always a need for a court or an arbitration process to resolve disputes over jurisdictional authority in every federal system. For most of Canadian history the court of final appeal was the Judicial Committee of the Privy Council (JCPC) of the United Kingdom. For the most part, as we noted, it tended to define federal authority as narrowly and provincial authority as widely as possible. The emergency powers of the federal government, expressed in the clause "Peace, Order and good Government," granted extensive residual power to the federal government, but were interpreted by the JCPC in a way that virtually nullified the apparent centralizing intentions of the drafters of the *BNA Act*.[11] The rulings of the JCPC on the law of Canadian federalism were the source of considerable controversy. It was widely felt that the Law Lords were too far removed from the political realities of Canada to render appropriate decisions.[12]

The reign of the JCPC as the court of last appeal ended in 1949 with the establishment of the Supreme Court of Canada as the arbiter of constitutional review. Consisting of nine federally appointed judges, the Supreme Court is the highest court for civil, criminal and constitutional cases. (The Federal Court of Canada, a separate body, oversees matters of law, equity and admiralty.) Until 1982, the Supreme Court was somewhat hampered by the nature of the parliamentary system and the absence of an entrenched bill of rights.[13] It was concerned mainly with jurisdictional disputes, and did not take the activist role for which the American Supreme Court is widely known. In recent years, the provinces have displayed notable reticence to take jurisdictional matters to the Supreme Court because of an alleged pro-centralist bias. Disputes between the federal and provincial governments increasingly tend to be resolved outside the judicial process through the mechanism of federal/provincial conferences. The development of a new style of federalism has meant that the terms of federalism can be adjusted by methods other than judicial interpretation.[14]

---

[10] See Paul Gerin-Lajoie, *Constitutional Amendment in Canada* (Toronto: University of Toronto Press, 1950) and Alan C. Cairns, "Recent Federalist Constitutional Proposals: A Review Essay," *Canadian Public Policy*, vol. 5, no. 3 (Summer 1979), pp. 348–65.

[11] See Peter J.T. O'Hearn, *Peace, Order and Good Government* (Toronto: Macmillan, 1964).

[12] See Alan C. Cairns, "The Judicial Committee and Its Critics," *CJPS*, vol. 4, no. 3 (September 1971), pp. 301–45.

[13] For a review of the Supreme Court's recent interpretations on federalism, see Paul C. Weiler, "The Supreme Court and the Law of Canadian Federalism," *University of Toronto Law Journal*, vol. 23, no. 3 (Summer 1973), pp. 307–67; James Lorimer, ed., *The Supreme Court Decisions on the Canadian Constitution* (Toronto: James Lorimer and Company, 1981); Peter Russell, et al., *The Court and the Constitution* (Kingston, Ont.: IIR, 1982); and Garth Stevenson, *Unfulfilled Union*, 3rd ed. (Toronto: Gage, 1989).

[14] See Richard Simeon, *Federal-Provincial Diplomacy: The Making of Recent Policy in Canada* (Toronto: University of Toronto Press, 1972).

This is not to argue that the Supreme Court is irrelevant. On the contrary, there have recently been important decisions by the Court on matters such as offshore oil and mineral rights and resource taxation, not to mention its rulings on the federal government's plan of unilateral patriation of the *Constitution*. Of late, the court is also taking a renewed interest in cases involving civil rights and liberties. After over 40 years, the Supreme Court of Canada is beginning to assert itself by its interpretation of the *Charter of Rights and Freedoms*. A discussion of this topic is found in the section below on the evolution of the *Charter*.

The second important determinant of power between federal and provincial governments rests on the financial strength of the two jurisdictions. In a federal state, revenue sources must be divided reasonably between the two levels of government. If not, the federal reality will quickly wither. A key question always concerns how to distribute these funds to the provinces and the federal government while at the same time maintaining federal control of the national economy.

The *BNA Act* conferred on the federal government the ability to *raise* money by any system of taxation, while at the same time it gave most areas of growing expenditure responsibility to the jurisdiction of the provinces. From the beginning, provincial authorities were restricted to collecting revenue through direct taxes or the sale of natural resources. (Direct taxes must be paid by the individual or firm assessed, but indirect taxes may be passed along to other persons or institutions.) Thus, it appeared from strict interpretation of the 1867 *Act* that the provinces could not levy a sales tax (indirect) on commodities that would be passed along to consumers. However, by the ingenious device of making vendors tax collectors for the provincial governments, the rules of the *BNA Act* were evaded and the

Reproduced with permission, Raeside, *Victoria Times.*

provinces were able to employ both types of taxation. Today, even such ploys as this are insufficient to alleviate provincial budgetary needs.

The *British North America Act* was an attempt to graft a federal system of government onto a British heritage of representative and responsible cabinet government. Its authors had to take into account two dissimilar linguistic groups, a federal system and complex financing regulations. The result was a division of jurisdiction between the two levels of government, federal and provincial. While the Crown, government and Parliament are the central governmental institutions, they are therefore not totally sovereign in Canada as they are in the United Kingdom.

There are, then, three fundamental cornerstones of the Canadian system of government, all of which are embedded in the *Constitution*. They are the executive and responsible government, the rule of law and federalism. In the following sections, we examine the formal executive, which is bound by principles of responsible government; the court system, which is the guardian of the rule of law; and, finally, the basic federal bargain, which is a key element in Canada's political system.

THE FORMAL EXECUTIVE: CROWN, MONARCHY AND GOVERNOR GENERAL

The *Constitution Act, 1867* (formerly the *BNA Act*) sets out in general terms the powers and prerogatives of formal authority in Canada. Section 9 declares that the "Executive Government and Authority of and over Canada…is vested in the Queen." This principle is fleshed out in the Letters Patent and must be understood in the light of the traditional royal prerogative.[15] While there is no question that the powers of the formal executive are largely ceremonial, it would be incorrect to dismiss them as trivial and meaningless. There have been situations in which the formal executive has proven a very important element in the political process itself.

Following British tradition, the supreme authority of the Canadian state resides with the Sovereign. Government functions are carried out in the name of the *Crown*. In Britain the Crown has been defined as "the sum total of governmental powers synonymous with the Executive."[16] In Canada, the term **Crown** refers to the composite symbol of the institutions of the state. The Crown may be involved in court proceedings[17] and it assumes a variety of duties and responsibilities. Government property is held in the name of the Crown.

The Crown retains some rights from the feudal period, but most of its present authority comes from statute law. The few "prerogative powers" can be traced to the period of authoritarian rule in Great Britain when the Crown possessed wide discretionary authority. With the rise of Parliament and the gradual movement toward popular sovereignty, the authority of the Crown eroded to a very few reserve powers. Although Parliament and the political executive still govern in the name of the Crown, there is little question that the monarch is severely limited. Even the ability of the monarch to stay on the throne is no longer a right. In the cases of both James II and Edward VIII in Britain

---

15   See Andrew Heard, *Canadian Constitutional Conventions* (Toronto: Oxford University Press, 1991).

16   E.C.S. Wade and A.W. Bradley, *Constitutional Law*, 8th ed. (London: Longman, 1970), pp. 171 ff., 678 ff.

17   Since the passage of the *Crown Liability Act* of 1952, the Crown can be sued like any other litigant.

it was clear that they could not retain their crowns unless the ministers and Parliament were prepared to accept them.

The reigning monarch is the personal embodiment of the Crown. The contemporary functions of the monarch are largely ceremonial and non-partisan. The monarch reigns, but does not govern. As British constitutionalist Walter Bagehot put it, the monarch's functions are mainly of the "dignified," not of the "efficient," type.[18] By this Bagehot meant that the monarch does not actually govern the country, but rather carries out a myriad of ceremonial responsibilities that generate mass support for government, while the ministers carry out the "efficient" procedures that operate the machinery of government.

Since the monarch was not based permanently in Canada, a representative known as the Governor General was appointed by the British government. As Canada evolved out of colonialism towards autonomy, this executive link was modified. The Imperial Conference of 1926 sought to make the Governor General a representative of the Crown, not of the British government. In 1947, new Letters Patent completed the process by allowing the Governor General the power to exercise the powers of the sovereign. However, the monarchical link was never ended. The Queen continues to be Canada's monarch: she makes royal tours to Canada and acts as the symbolic head of the Commonwealth of which Canada is a member.

As the Queen's representative, the Governor General is appointed by Her Majesty on the recommendation of the Canadian prime minister and the cabinet. In 1952, the office was further Canadianized by the appointment of Vincent Massey, the first Canadian to hold the position. (See Table 5.1.) It has since become customary to alternate the position between English- and French-speaking Canadians. The appointment of Edward Schreyer in 1978 added a new dimension to this trend, since he was an English-speaking Canadian from neither charter group. The next appointee, in 1984, Jeanne Sauvé, a French Canadian, became the first woman to hold this high office. Governors General have often been selected from outside the partisan political sphere, mainly from the diplomatic or military establishment. The appointments of former Manitoba Premier Edward Schreyer, former Liberal MP Jeanne Sauvé, and former Conservative minister Ramon Hnatyshyn (appointed in 1990) have marked a departure from this pattern.

The Governor General, in performing the Queen's "dignified" roles in Canada, provides little practical input into the political process. The tenure of office is usually five years, but the officially recognized term is six years, which has on occasion been extended to seven. In the event of death, incapacity, removal or absence of the Governor General, the chief justice of the supreme court, Canada's leading judge, acts as the Administrator and may carry out all duties of the office.

The functions of the Governor General as head of state provide the official monarchical structure of Canadian government on an everyday basis. First, many purely ceremonial functions such as conferring Order of Canada awards or reviewing troops may be carried out by the appointee. In order to fill these roles, the Governor General presides over the official residence, Rideau Hall, a staff of about 100, a budget of several million dollars annually and another residence in Québec City. Second, the Governor General acts as a representative for the state. In studying loyalty in political regimes, theorists have found that individuals are socialized into acceptance of authority through their attachment to authority figures such as the Governor General.

---

[18] Walter Bagehot, *The English Constitution* (London: World's Classics, 1928).

TABLE 5.1   CANADIAN-BORN GOVERNORS GENERAL (1952–1993)

Vincent Massey	1952
Georges Vanier	1959
Roland Michener	1967
Jules Léger	1974
Edward Schreyer	1979
Jeanne Sauvé	1984
Ramon Hnatyshyn	1990

The Governor General is bound to act on practically every piece of advice given by his or her ministers. Nevertheless, certain functions are the Governor General's alone. The most important of these stem from the prerogative powers left to the monarch — powers that have not been by-passed by constitutional or statute law. The Letters Patent provide the Governor General with all the powers of the Queen "in respect of summoning, proroguing or dissolving the Parliament of Canada." Clearly the most significant power is the duty to appoint a Prime Minister. In order to exercise this significant prerogative power, the Governor General must have a reasonably free hand to make decisions based on the circumstances and precedents.[19]

On two occasions in the 1890s the Governor General had to help find someone to be Prime Minister because the Conservative Party had no clear successor to the outgoing leader.[20] In cases where there is a leader of a party who can command a clear majority of the seats in the House of Commons, the Governor General has nothing to do but select the obvious candidate.[21] Today, if there were no obvious leader after a Prime Minister died in office, for example, the Cabinet and/or caucus would undoubtedly name an interim leader pending a leadership convention, and the Governor General would name this person Prime Minister.

A major issue remains. If there were no majority for any leader in the House of Commons, the Governor General might be forced to use his or her discretion in selecting the Prime Minister. In 27 of the 35 elections since Confederation, one of the two major parties obtained an absolute majority of the seats in the House, so the Governor General was not required to exercise personal discretion. However, after an election in which the results are confused or which produces no majority in the House, the Governor General could be forced to exercise the prerogative in an independent manner. Such discretionary power would always be subject to controversy and in every case but one (discussed below) the Governor General has chosen as Prime Minister the leader of the party that

---

[19] For a thorough study of the precedents see Andrew Head, *Canadian Constitutional Precedents* (Toronto: Oxford University Press, 1991).

[20] J. T. Saywell, "The Crown and the Politicians," *Canadian Historical Review* (December 1956), pp. 309–37. John A. Macdonald (in 1891) and John Thompson (in 1894) both died in office without an obvious successor.

[21] Since the 1890s, when Sir John Abbott and Sir Mackenzie Bowell held the prime ministership from the Senate, all Prime Ministers have held seats in the House of Commons.

received the largest number of seats in the House of Commons — even if he or she did not obtain a majority of the seats.

For purposes of discussion, the dissolution of Parliament is too often separated from the appointment of the Prime Minister. But the two are logically related. It is generally agreed that only a Prime Minister can ask for and obtain a dissolution of parliament, although a Governor General once refused such a request. This incident was the famous Byng-King case in 1926.

Normally, a Prime Minister who is defeated in the House, or feels he or she may be, can ask to have Parliament dissolved rather than submit his or her resignation.[22] Liberal Prime Minister Mackenzie King, who headed a minority government at the time, did so in 1926. The Governor General, Lord Byng, declined King's request for dissolution and an election. Instead, he called on Arthur Meighen to form a new administration. The Governor General was cognisant of two special factors: the House was in the process of discussing a censure motion against the minority Liberal government, and the Conservatives held the largest number of seats in the House. It was theoretically possible that the Progressive Party, which held the balance of power in the House, could have supported a Tory minority government.

As it turned out, however, the Progressives would not give their continued support to the new Conservative government and within three days the government fell. Meighen, in turn, had to ask the Governor General for a dissolution of Parliament.[23] In the election that ensued, the Liberals charged that the Governor General had favoured the Conservatives and that the British were again interfering in Canada. The electoral victory of the Liberals demonstrated that, although the Governor General may possess some constitutional powers about the dissolution of Parliament, the people are the final arbiters of whether or not the action is appropriate.

The precedent is now fairly firm that Governors General should follow the advice of their Prime Ministers on the dissolution of Parliament. In December 1979, Conservative Prime Minister Joe Clark, who headed a minority government, was defeated on the budget. Although theoretically the Liberals could have been asked to try to form a government, the Governor General consulted Mr. Clark and dissolved Parliament without discussing the matter with any of the opposition parties.

Can a Governor General dismiss a government? It has always been assumed that this would prove impossible when one party controls a majority in the House. However, the Australian "Canberra case" of November, 1975 has upset the certainty of this contention. While the Australian constitutional structure differs from that of Canada in many respects (especially in the fact that the upper house is an elected body), it has generally been assumed that the Governors General of both countries were unable to dissolve Parliament. In the "Canberra case" the Australian Senate had continually held up supply bills from the lower House, until a financial crisis threatened the country. The Senate was controlled by the Liberal and Country parties, while the lower House was controlled by the Prime Minister, Gough Whitlam, and his Labor party. The Governor General wanted to dissolve both Houses. Whitlam refused, and the Governor General dismissed him. The Governor

---

[22]   The results of the 1925 election were Conservatives 116, Liberals 99, Progressives 24 and others 6 seats.

[23]   See Eugene A. Forsey, *The Royal Power of Dissolution of Parliament in the British Commonwealth* (Toronto: Oxford University Press, 1943).

General asked the leader of the opposition to form a government on the condition that he would immediately request a dissolution. In the bitter election campaign that followed, the Liberal-Country coalition was elected. In other words, the Governor General's recommendation was electorally upheld. The effect of this precedent on Canada is difficult to determine, since nothing equivalent has occurred during this century. In view of the changing nature of the Commonwealth and the weakening bonds between the members, constitutional precedents are likely to prove inconsequential. It is thus fairly safe to say that no Governor General will act in Canada following the manner chosen in Australia, but the matter is not entirely settled.

Perhaps more important than formal constitutional power is the Governor General's opportunity to advise ministers. The Governor General meets regularly with the prime minister to discuss general points, personnel or appointments, and on such occasions prime ministers have been known to solicit advice on policy matters as well. In other words, the Governor General has a degree of access that is denied to most individuals. Sir Wilfrid Laurier confided: "The Canadian Governor General long ago ceased to determine policy, but he is by no means, or need not be, the mere figurehead of the public image. He has the privilege of advising his advisers, and if he is a man of sense and experience, his advice is often taken."[24]

THE STRUCTURE AND ROLE OF THE COURTS

The Canadian judiciary has the task of ruling in disputes about the law.[25] Whether the law is *civil* (regulating disputes between two or more private parties) or *criminal* (regulating crimes such as theft or murder), the judges deliberate in courts. The basic, unitary structure of the judiciary or court system in Canada is that of a pyramid with a very wide base and a narrow tip with the Supreme Court of Canada at the apex. Immediately below the Supreme Court of Canada in the judicial pyramid are the provincial superior or supreme courts.

Each province has a superior or supreme court of general jurisdiction that is charged with administering all laws in force in Canada, whether enacted by Parliament, provincial legislatures or municipalities. They are usually divided into trial and appeal divisions. Some may also have county or district courts of both civil and criminal jurisdiction. Article 96 of the *Constitution* stipulates that appointment to these superior district and county courts is made by the Governor General, in practice by the federal cabinet. In other words, while each province determines how many judges it will need in these federal courts, Ottawa determines who will be appointed and how they will be paid. All provinces have courts staffed by judges appointed by the province to deal with lesser criminal and other matters. These provincial courts include magistrates' courts, family courts and juvenile courts. The appeal divisions of the provincial supreme or superior courts hear appeals from the lower courts and from certain provincial administrative tribunals.

---

24 O.D. Skelton, *Life and Letters of Sir Wilfrid Laurier*, vol. II, David L. Farr ed. (Ottawa: Carleton University, 1965) p. 86n. Originally published Toronto, 1921.

25 Peter Russell, *The Judiciary in Canada* (Toronto: McGraw-Hill Ryerson, 1987), p. 5.

The Supreme Court of Canada was established in 1875 by the *Dominion Act* as a general court of appeal for Canada. It was not the final court of appeal, however; that function was performed in Britain by the Judicial Committee of the Privy Council (JCPC) until 1949. Today nine judges serve on the Supreme Court, three of whom must come from Québec. All are appointed by the governor-in-council[26] and do not have to retire until age 75. In 1990, the Prime Minister appointed Antonio Lamer to succeed Brian Dickson as Chief Justice of the Court (See Table 5.2). Since 1949, only three of the judges have been women. All but one of the judges in 1993 were appointed by Prime Minister Mulroney, and half of them had had some connection with the Conservative Party.

TABLE 5.2   SUPREME COURT JUDGES, DECEMBER 1993

Judge	Year Appointed	Province of Birth	Appointing Prime Minister
Chief Justice Antonio Lamer	1980	Québec	Trudeau
Mr. Justice Gerard LaForest	1985	New Brunswick	Mulroney
Madam Justice Claire l'Heureux-Dubé	1987	Québec	Mulroney
Mr. Justice John Sopinka	1988	Ontario	Mulroney
Madam Justice Beverley McLachlin	1989	Alberta	Mulroney
Mr. Justice Charles Gonthier	1989	Québec	Mulroney
Mr. Justice Peter Cory	1989	Ontario	Mulroney
Mr. Justice Frank Iacobucci	1991	Ontario	Mulroney
Mr. Justice John Major	1992	Alberta	Mulroney

As the highest court in the land (See Figure 5.1), the Supreme Court's decisions are binding on all the courts below. It primarily deals with cases that have already been appealed at least once in the lower courts. In these situations, the Supreme Court of Canada is appealed to in order to render "an authoritative settlement of a question of law of importance to the whole nation."[27] On rather rare but important occasions, Canada's highest court also deals with questions referred to it directly by the federal government.

Canada's Supreme Court does not accept to hear all appeals. In fact, the significance of its work lies in the fact that it can be highly selective, concentrating its efforts on questions that are of fundamental importance to Canadian society, and then shaping the direction of the law by applying general rules to the specific circumstances at hand. One should remember as well that, as a general court of appeal, the Supreme Court of Canada has a right to the final say in all areas of law for the country. This combination of selectivity and breadth gives the Supreme Court an extremely powerful role. Since the adoption of the *Charter of Rights*, the Supreme Court also greatly increased its competence to adjudicate in cases involving civil liberties. It has become the final arbiter "not only of the division of power

---

[26] "Governor-in-council" is the formal or legal name under which Cabinet makes decisions. For a full explanation see the section entitled "What is the Canadian Executive?" in Chapter 7.

[27] Peter H. Russell, "The Jurisdiction of the Supreme Court of Canada: Present Policies and a Programme for Reform," *Osgoode Hall Law Journal* (1969), p. 29.

FIGURE 5.1   THE CANADIAN JUDICIAL SYSTEM

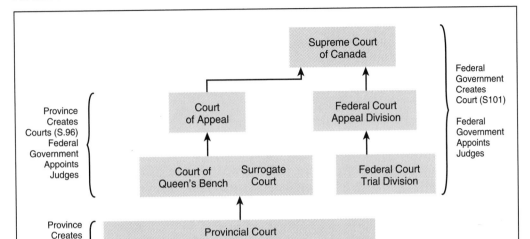

between governments but also of the line between the powers of both levels of government and the rights and freedoms of citizens."[28] In 1991, the Court heard 126 appeals — the most important of which involved either seven or nine judges.

Also below the Supreme Court of Canada but separate from the provincial court structure is the Federal Court of Canada, which was established by Parliament in 1971. The Federal Court, which has both a trial and an appeal division, settles claims by or against the federal government on matters relating to maritime law, copyright, patent and trade-mark law and federal taxation statutes. It also has a supervisory jurisdiction related to decisions of tribunals and inferior bodies established by federal law. There are a few other specialized federal courts such as the Tax Court of Canada whose decisions are also subject to review by the Federal Court. Decisions of the Federal Court of Appeal can be appealed to the Supreme Court of Canada when the matter in controversy exceeds a set amount of money. Otherwise, an appeal to the Supreme Court of Canada requires either the volition of the Supreme Court itself or the agreement of the Federal Court of Appeal. If the dispute is inter-provincial, or federal/provincial in nature, the route of appeal to the Supreme Court is automatically open.

Compared to other countries that operate under a federal rather than a unitary system of government, Canada's judicial system is one of the most integrated in the world. A purely federal judicial power is not even mentioned in the Canadian *Constitution*. Instead, the constitution provides for an integrated system with federally appointed judges to provincial superior and intermediate courts. Canada is the only federation to have this element of judicial integration.[29] As well, Parliament established the Supreme Court of Canada as a

---

28 Peter H. Russell, *The Judiciary in Canada: The Third Branch of Government* (Toronto: McGraw-Hill Ryerson, 1987), p. 335.

29 Ibid., pp. 419–50.

"General Court of Appeal" rather than one that is limited to federal law and constitutional law. Another integrating feature of the judicial system is that Parliament has exclusive jurisdiction in the area of criminal law, while the provincial legislatures have powers to establish courts of criminal jurisdiction. This means that provincially established courts administer federal law.

However, constitutional expert Peter Russell notes that there has been a tendency, particularly in recent years, to "move away from the integrated model to a more bifurcated system of dual courts."[30] Evidence for this is found in the proliferation of both provincial and federal courts that are established and staffed by their own respective levels of government. Increasingly, the federal government is relying on judges appointed and paid by the provinces to administer federal laws and the federal government is showing some tendency to establish federal trial courts for cases involving federal laws. This combination of events illustrates a move in the direction of federalizing Canada's judicial structure. The merits of such a move are highly debatable, in particular because the unitary system has emphasized that the law is impersonal and applies to Canadians equally regardless of region.

The structure of the judicial system in Canada has evolved slowly since Confederation. Over time the unitary nature of the system has become slightly more federal, with the proliferation of both provincial and federal courts that are established and staffed by their own respective level of government. But what of the role of the judicial system; has it changed as well?

The answer is a definite yes. The essential judicial function of the courts is that of **adjudication** — the responsibility to provide authoritative settlements in disputes about legal rights and duties. Canadian judges have always exercised legislative powers by making decisions on the common law, interpreting statutes and "umpiring" the federal division of powers in the country's written constitution. However, this essential role of the judicial system has adapted and expanded as the social and political environment of the country changed.

The Fathers of Confederation did not establish the Supreme Court in the *Constitution*, but left Parliament to propose and establish it through legislation. In the early years of its history, the Supreme Court of Canada was a subordinate, secondary institution. Until 1949, Canadians only had access to the British Judicial Committee of the Privy Council, the Supreme Court of the British Empire. Not until appeal to that body was abolished did the Supreme Court of Canada assume the leadership of the Canadian judicial system. The next major evolutionary change came in 1974 when the Supreme Court of Canada's jurisdiction was changed, allowing it basically to control its own agenda. Finally, the patriation of the *Constitution* with its *Charter of Rights and Freedoms* heralded a new and expanded role for all courts in Canada, especially the Supreme Court.

In a 1981 hallmark decision, the Supreme Court judges ruled in the *Patriation Reference* case that the Trudeau government could legally patriate and amend the *Constitution* unilaterally, but warned that to do so would violate an established "constitutional convention." This ruling on a question of "constitutional convention" was unique in that it reached beyond the law into the realm of politics.[31] It amounted to a legal green light combined with a political red light. Under the circumstances, Mr. Trudeau chose to return to the constitu-

---

[30] Ibid., p. 51.

[31] Peter H. Russell, "The Supreme Court in the Eighties — Wrestling with the Charter," in *Politics: Canada*, 6th ed., Paul W. Fox and Graham White, eds. (Toronto: McGraw-Hill Ryerson, 1987), p. 151.

tional bargaining table with the provincial premiers and seek an acceptable compromise before proceeding with patriation.

The *Constitution Act, 1982* greatly increased the political importance of the Supreme Court of Canada, mainly because of the *Charter of Rights and Freedoms*. Under the *Charter* the Supreme Court of Canada can "overrule legislation and executive acts of government not only on the grounds that they violate the federal division of powers, but also on the grounds that they violate the fundamental rights and freedoms of citizens."[32] The consequences of this new development are discussed more fully in the section on the Charter, but here it is important to note that the Canadian judiciary has gradually become more powerful since its inception.

The mandate of judges has remained constant — to respect the laws governing the disputes that they arbitrate and to contribute to the development of those laws. In doing so, they must act, and must also be seen to act, totally impartially and independently. Increasingly, however, judges are perceived less as fulfilling an essentially technical and non-political role and more as promoting change in public policy. As Canadians become more conscious of judicial power they will undoubtedly want to scrutinize more closely the impartiality claims of judges.[33] The appointment procedure in particular will become the object of public debate. Since the Supreme Court was not established by the *Constitution*, but by federal legislation, there is also no mention in the *Constitution* either of its composition or the method by which judges are appointed. The only mention of the Supreme Court in the *Constitution Act* concerns the amending formula — that requires the agreement of Parliament and all of the provincial legislatures for any change in the composition of the Supreme Court, and the agreement of Parliament and two-thirds of the provinces representing 50 percent of the population for any other constitutional change of the court. Current reform proposals for the Court, therefore, centre on establishing it in the *Constitution* so that it will not have to depend on federal legislation for its existence and so that its composition or method of appointment cannot be changed more easily.

THE FEDERAL CONSTITUTIONAL BARGAIN

We have seen that federalism is a key element in the Canadian system of constitutional monarchy. The federal dimension was necessitated by the exigencies of the Confederation period and subsequently developed through two forces: judicial interpretation of the constitutional documents and the evolution of financial relations between the federal and provincial governments.

Today, federalism is central to the way Canadians think about their politics. The winning entry in a 1967 contest for Canadian jokes was a Canadian version of the ancient elephant joke: Of three students, the American wrote his essay on "The President and Elephants," the French student discussed "Sex and the Elephant," while the Canadian's topic was "Elephants: A Federal or Provincial Responsibility?" In fact, the details of federalism are so significant that the entire *Constitution* is printed in the Appendix of this book.

---

[32] Ibid., p. 152.

[33] For an excellent summary see Andrew D. Heard, "The Charter in the Supreme Court of Canada: The Importance of Which Judges Hear an Appeal," *CJPS*, vol. XXIV, no. 2 (June 1991), pp. 289–307.

The need for a "federal bargain" that would apportion powers between the central and the regional governments was obvious in the nineteenth century. There had been a tradition of local government in the colonies, and the lack of adequate transportation routes and communication among the provinces meant that no matter what type of system was adopted some independence had to be granted to the local entities. Moreover, Sir Georges Etienne Cartier and other French Canadian leaders demanded an element of isolation from central government authority as part of the bargain to be struck with those Fathers of Confederation who favoured a more centralized system of government. John A. Macdonald, for example, would actually have preferred a unitary to a federal form of government.[34] The federal principle was therefore accepted as a necessary compromise for the unity of the political system and as a protection for provinces and language groups. Since then, for better or worse, the federal dimension has pervaded the history and development of Canada.

Provincial constitutions follow the federal pattern. In each of the provinces, the Queen is represented by a Lieutenant-Governor appointed by the governor-in-council on the advice of the prime minister. The Lieutenant-Governor acts on the advice and with the assistance of his or her ministry or Executive Council, which is responsible to the legislature and resigns office under circumstances similar to those for the federal government. Provincial legislatures are elected for a maximum of five years and, unlike Parliament, which has two houses, today they are all unicameral.

The two vast northern territories remain under the constitutional authority of the federal government. Several federal statutes — *Yukon Act, Northwest Territories Act, Government Organization Act* and the *Federal Interpretation Act* — provide their legal structures and the *Charter* also provides a degree of independent legitimacy in sections 3 and 30 by referring to the legislative assemblies of the two territories. In real political terms, the two territories have fully elected assemblies, responsible executives, called Councils, and a form of delegated responsibility for most of the matters under provincial jurisdiction. The Commissioners, who are appointed by the Minister of Indian and Northern Affairs, act as quasi–Lieutenant-Governors under the authority of the minister.

As well as being under the laws of the federal and provincial governments, Canadians are regulated by local governments. Whether designated as city, town, village or township, these authorities are created by the provinces and territories to provide such services as transportation, public health, garbage disposal, recreation, fire-fighting and police work. Local school boards are usually empowered to administer education at the primary and secondary levels.

THE FEDERAL/PROVINCIAL DIVISION OF POWERS

The constitutional status of the provinces appeared insignificant in early Canadian history. The *Constitution* provided such disproportionate power to the national government that some experts have even referred to the period as one of "quasi-federalism," that is, one whose appearance is federal (i.e., with divided jurisdictions), but whose reality is unitary because no significant power rests in the sub-units. This assertion is based on certain constitutional facts. First, the central government could disallow provincial legislation even when the

---

[34] P.B. Waite, The Life and Times of Confederation, 1864–1867 (Toronto: University of Toronto Press, 1962). See Chapter 6, Figure 6.1 for further explanation of the terms federal government, unitary government and confederation.

subject matter of the legislation was assigned to the provinces by the *BNA Act* (now the *Constitution Act, 1867*). This rarely used power could be employed in extreme circumstances. For instance, during the depression years of the 1930s, it was used to stop several acts of William Aberhart's Social Credit government in Alberta. In *disallowing* Aberhart's proposal to print money, the federal government argued that such an action would destroy the banking system.[35] Although the power was employed 112 times after Confederation, it has not been used since 1943. As well, it should be remembered that although the federal government could negate provincial laws, it could not legislate in provincial fields.

The second and third major powers were those of *veto* and *reservation*. The Lieutenant-Governors may at one time have had the ability to employ the royal prerogative of vetoing legislation. Since they did not exercise this power, however, it atrophied as a weapon. On the other hand, the constitutional ability of Lieutenant-Governors to reserve provincial legislation for federal approval has been employed quite often: some 70 bills have been reserved since 1867.[36] The most recent case occurred in 1961, when the Lieutenant-Governor of Saskatchewan, Frank Bastedo, without first consulting the federal government, reserved provincial legislation that he believed was of doubtful validity. (The Department of Justice quickly decided that the Bill was within provincial jurisdiction and assent was given.) It seems unlikely that such extreme power will be wielded again in Canada, except perhaps in a circumstance as grave as the secession of a province from the federal union. Moreover, while the federal government may have the legal authority to block any provincial legislation initiating secession, a "technical" solution of this type would not be satisfactory. A provincial movement toward secession, if it were clearly supported by a popular mandate, could not be prevented by legal devices alone.

The Fathers of Confederation regarded the American Civil War as an example of what could happen if a central government did not have strong powers and referred to this when they wrote the residual clause of the *BNA Act*. This clause might have allowed the federal government to interfere in any matter except those specifically assigned to the provinces. In section 91, it states: "It shall be lawful for the Queen, by and with the Advice and Consent of the Senate and the House of Commons, to make Laws for the Peace, Order, and good Government of Canada, in relation to all matters not coming within the Classes of Subjects by this Act assigned exclusively to the Legislatures of the Provinces..." In addition to granting this sweeping authority, section 91 specified 29 items as belonging exclusively to the federal government, among them trade, commerce, banking, credit, currency, taxation, navigation, citizenship and defence. Section 92, on the other hand, delineates 16 specific areas of provincial jurisdiction, including direct taxation, hospitals, prisons, property and civil rights. These latter subjects, though of only limited and local concern in 1867, were later to become much more important than the Fathers could have foreseen in their era of more-or-less *laissez-faire* government.

While the *BNA Act* was a centralist document, it is important to note that the meaning of many key words has changed over time. Leaving aside for the moment the matter of how judicial interpretation has changed the document, it is clear that certain terms were not defined precisely enough in the beginning and others took on new meanings over time.

---

[35] For a discussion of the power of disallowance, see J.R. Mallory, *Social Credit and the Federal Power in Canada* (Toronto: University of Toronto Press, 1954), especially chs. 2 and 9.

[36] R. MacGregor Dawson, *The Government of Canada*, 5th ed. revised by Norman Ward (Toronto: University of Toronto Press, 1970), pp. 213–17.

Certain matters, of course, could not have been foreseen by the Fathers of Confederation. These omissions created a void that both federal and provincial authorities have sought to fill to their own advantage. For example, section 109 gave control over natural resources to the provinces — but did this control include off-shore resources and the taxation of resources? Section 93 gave power over education to the provinces, but today it is a matter for debate whether education, as a provincial responsibility, encompasses cultural matters, broadcasting, occupational training and research.

The conflict over division of powers is well-illustrated by the case of natural resources. The *BNA Act* clearly assigned "ownership" of resources to the provinces, but gave the federal government a major voice in the sale of resources through its control of inter-provincial and international trade. Thus, the provinces own the oil because it is under the ground, the oil wells are in the hands of private or public companies and the Parliament of Canada exercises some control over oil through taxation and jurisdictional powers. Moreover, through use of the "declaratory" power (*BNA Act* s. 92.10(a)), the federal government can assume jurisdiction over any "work" that is for the benefit of Canada as a whole. For example, in the 1920s Parliament declared that every grain elevator was under federal control but it did not assume ownership. Federal control over uranium exploration is a more recent example. The provinces have always contested the declaratory power, but the courts have continually backed the federal authorities.

Recent breakthroughs in technology permitting exploitation of off-shore resources have also resulted in hot disputes. In 1967, the Supreme Court ruled in an advisory opinion that Ottawa, not British Columbia, owned the resources off the west coast. In 1977, the federal government proposed temporary arrangements with three Maritime Provinces that would have given Ottawa 25 percent and the provinces 75 percent of their off-shore resources. Newfoundland never accepted this bargain, and Nova Scotia quickly backed out after a provincial election. In 1979, the Conservative government of Joe Clark offered to give complete control of off-shore resources to the provinces; however, the return of the Liberals in 1980 left the situation in limbo. Disputants on both sides of the east coast question finally applied to the courts for settlement: Newfoundland to the provincial Court of Appeal, Ottawa to the Supreme Court of Canada. After a long-running battle, the courts awarded ownership of off-shore resources along the east coast to the federal government.

It is clear that the *Constitution* has been inadequate in clearly demarcating all jurisdictions. As Garth Stevenson has pointed out, there are now very few areas of policy that are handled exclusively by one level of government. "The only exclusively federal areas appear to be military defence, veterans' affairs, the post office and monetary policy. The only exclusively provincial areas appear to be municipal institutions, elementary and secondary education and some areas of law related to property and other non-criminal matters."[37] In all other areas, there is either tacit or explicit agreement by the two major levels of government to engage in activities in the same fields. Sometimes this is harmonious, as for example when the federal government allows the provinces to regulate inter-provincial highway transportation. In other areas, such as external trade, manpower training, communications, language and culture, the two levels are in constant conflict.

---

[37] Garth Stevenson, "Federalism and Intergovernmental Relations," in M.S. Whittington and G. Williams, eds., *Canadian Politics in the 1980's*, 2nd ed. (Toronto: Methuen, 1984), p. 378.

Another aspect of the division of powers that continues to cause controversy is the delegation of joint responsibilities. Section 95 of the *Constitution* declared joint jurisdiction between the Parliament of Canada and the provincial legislatures in the areas of agriculture and immigration. Moreover, de facto concurrent powers have arisen in some fields because of the federal government's control of spending power. While the federal government may have little or no jurisdiction over a particular matter such as education, consumer protection or the environment, this does not prohibit Ottawa from spending money in these areas. The provinces have had great difficulty in saying no to such largesse. Although not mentioned in the *Constitution*, scientific research, recreational activities, tourism and protection of the environment all are handled as if they are areas of concurrent jurisdiction.

Conflicts over jurisdictional boundaries are to be expected in federal systems. Canada certainly has been no exception to this rule. Successive court decisions by the Judicial Committee of the Privy Council of the United Kingdom and, later, the Supreme Court of Canada have cleared up some, but by no means all questions about jurisdiction in various policy fields. The precise lines of authority remain blurred in many areas. Dissent has risen mainly over the fact that matters that have grown in significance over the years, such as property and civil rights, are within the provincial sphere, while the "Peace, Order and good Government" clause conveys competing authority to the federal government in the same fields in the case of an emergency. With changes in the nature of social and economic policy, this federal power has increasingly conflicted with the specific powers accorded the provinces.

In such disputes, court decisions have varied from restrictive interpretations that left the federal government with very little authority except in the gravest emergencies (e.g., *Local Prohibition*, 1896; *Hodge v. The Queen*, 1883; *Board of Commerce*, 1992; and *Toronto Electric Commissioners vs. Snider*, 1925) to granting the federal government such wide scope that the specific powers that appeared to fall exclusively in the provincial field were undermined (e.g., *Canada Temperance Act*, 1878; and *Russell v. the Queen*, 1882). Even such major events as the Great Depression were not considered significant enough to offset clearly and permanently the arguments that, first, social legislation was under provincial jurisdiction because of the property and civil rights clause and, second, Canada's federal Parliament was restricted to those fields in its specific jurisdiction (*Snider*, 1925). Thus, even in the face of this supreme test of government authority, the federal government could do no more than supply funds to the provinces for fighting the effects of the depression. It could not act itself. Prime Minister R.B. Bennett's legislation for social insurance, marketing schemes and minimum wages was another piece of legislation struck down by the JCPC in 1937, an action that seriously undermined the federal government's ability to provide any relief in the crisis.[38]

This constitutional position was short-lived. During the Second World War, a surge of nationalism made it possible to circumvent restrictive interpretations of the *BNA Act*. The federal government assumed almost unlimited powers, and the JCPC, apparently sensing the national mood, seemed to shift its position. The result was the 1946 *Canadian Temperance Federation* judgement that declared that laws going beyond local interests could be the concern of the federal authorities. This decision revised the concept of federalism dictated by earlier cases.

An amendment to the Supreme Court Act in 1949 gave the power of final arbitration over jurisdictional authority to the Supreme Court. The JCPC's authority was terminated. Since then

---

[38] See Mallory, *Social Credit and Federal Power in Canada*, p. 51.

the federal government has been able to refer either its own legislation or that of a province to the Supreme Court, while a provincial government can refer either its own or federal legislation to the superior court of that province, from which the case may proceed to the Supreme Court on appeal. Since the federal government appoints not only federal judges but also all judges to provincial superior and county courts, it can exercise great power in this field.

The belief that a wholly Canadian court would be somewhat more inclined to take into account Canadian reality and adopt a broader interpretation of federal powers seems to have been borne out by history. Largely since the ascendancy of the Supreme Court of Canada, the federal government has obtained authority over radio, telecommunications and nuclear energy. A classic example of the centralist orientation of the Court is indicated by the 1952 *Johannesson* case, in which the Court upset earlier judgements by proclaiming that since aeronautics was of "national importance" it belonged to the federal authority. James Mallory concluded from this case that the Supreme Court "has begun to develop a more generous interpretation of the federal power than has existed, except in wartime."[39]

In the 1975 *Anti-Inflation* case the Supreme Court interpreted the federal division of powers in Canada in a similar way. It ruled that the federal government could impose pay restraints on Canadians if a national emergency existed. The Judicial Committee of the British Privy Council had limited the use of the federal government's authority to emergencies such as war, pestilence and famine, but the Canadian Court now added economic factors to the list. It thus broadened greatly the interpretation of the "Peace, Order and good Government" clause. The Court did not approve the federal government's contention that controlling inflation concerned all of Canada, only ruling that Parliament could enact legislation in the field of economic regulation during an emergency.

As mentioned earlier, since the Second World War, the terms of federalism have increasingly been adjusted through the mechanism of federal/provincial conferences rather than exclusively through the judicial process. A feeling has arisen among the provinces that if matters of federal/provincial jurisdiction reached the courts for a resolution, they would probably lose. This contentious subject is fully discussed in Chapter 6.

RHETORIC OVER CONSTITUTIONAL AMENDMENT

In political science terminology, a *rigid* constitution is one that is difficult to amend, whereas a *flexible* constitution can be more easily adapted to changing circumstances. Though arguments may be articulated both for and against the use of either type of amending formula, it is clear that all constitutions must provide *some* means to adapt themselves to new circumstances (See Table 5.3).

Changing the Canadian "federal bargain" struck in 1867 has been extremely difficult.[40] The 1931 *Statute of Westminster* declared that the Parliament of the United Kingdom could no longer legislate for Canada except at the latter's request. At the time of its passage, the British government attempted to persuade Canada to accept a specific amending formula and cut the last tie with the United Kingdom. Unfortunately, Canadian politicians could not

---

[39] J.R. Mallory, *The Structure of Canadian Government* (Toronto: Macmillan, 1971), p. 354.

[40] See R.D. Olling and M.W. Westmacott, eds., *The Confederation Debate: The Constitution in Crisis* (Toronto: Kendall-Hunt, 1980) and, by the same authors, *Perspectives on Canadian Federalism* (Scarborough, Ont: Prentice-Hall Canada, 1988); and David Milne, *The Canadian Constitution: From Patriation to Meech Lake* (Toronto: James Lorimer, 1982).

agree on how the mechanism should work. The British Parliament therefore remained responsible for constitutional amendment in Canada. On several occasions after this date, the *Constitution* was amended in the United Kingdom after a request from Canada. Provincial compliance was obtained, for example, in the 1940 amendment that gave the federal Parliament jurisdiction over unemployment insurance; the 1951 amendment that gave Parliament shared power over old-age pensions; and the 1960 amendment dealing with the retirement of judges. On the other hand, no provincial agreement had to be found (nor was it!) when representation in the Senate was amended in 1915 or when representation in the House of Commons was altered in 1946, 1952 and 1974.

TABLE 5.3   CONSTITUTION-SPEAK: SOME JARGON YOU NEED TO KNOW

Amending formula: The rules for changing the Constitution. The debate over the amending process is essentially over whose voices are needed to make a change in the law — the provinces, the regions or the people themselves.

Asymmetry: Different provinces would have different powers. Essentially, Québec wants powers that not all other provinces want. Should Canada accommodate differences between the provinces, or would it violate the idea of equality?

Bi-Polar Federation: A Canadian federation of two units — Québec and the Rest.

Concurrency: Refers to powers that could be exercised by both Ottawa and the provinces.

Confederation of Regions: A loose confederation of four or five regions.

Common Market: Five to ten constituent units would exist with a minimal federal government.

Concurrency with provincial paramouncy: Concurrency, but the provinces have the final say if federal and provincial governments disagree

Executive federalism: Essentially means decision-making by the Prime Minister, the 10 premiers and their governments — pejoratively called bargaining behind closed doors.

Residual Power: The federal government has the ultimate power to deal with matters of national concern to safeguard "peace, order and good government."

Seven and 50: Not a cocktail mix. Stands for seven provinces with more than 50 percent of the national population — the requirement for most constitutional changes. Other important changes require unanimous consent.

Suspensive veto: If the House of Commons votes against a proposed constitutional amendment the resolution dies. If it passes in the Commons but the Senate votes against it, the amendment does not die. It is merely delayed for six months. Then the Commons votes on it again, and, if it passes, it proceeds without Senate approval.

Triple-E Senate: Stands for equal, elected and effective — an elected Senate that has an equal number of seats for each province and that would be just as effective as the House of Commons.

In view of the practices adopted on these occasions, it is clear that a constitutional convention or protocol had developed with regard to the amendment of the *BNA Act*. The British Parliament accepted each of the 18 amendments that emanated from a Joint Address of both Houses of the Canadian Parliament. On those amendments that affected the federal balance, the provinces were always consulted and agreed to the proposals. On the other hand, no substantial amendment was ever made at the request of any province or group of provinces, since only communications that arrived by way of the federal Parliament were accepted as legitimate by the British Parliament.

Many aspects of the *Constitution* could be changed without the passage of British legislation. From the beginning, the provinces were allowed to amend their own constitutions in all spheres except those concerning the powers of the Lieutenant-Governor. With the passage of the *BNA Act* (No. 2) in 1949, the federal Parliament was empowered to amend the *Constitution*, except with regard to provincial powers, rights and privileges; the rights of minorities with respect to schools and language protection; the extension of the life of Parliament beyond five years; and the necessity to call at least one session of Parliament per year. These were extensive exceptions, however, as they prevented Ottawa from amending anything that touched on the nature and division of federal/provincial responsibilities, the fundamental cornerstone of the Canadian political system. Moreover, some institutions like the Senate and the Supreme Court may be considered to be either purely in the federal sphere or to belong to both Ottawa and the provinces. The Senate has a regional basis to its representation and the Supreme Court is the final arbiter of federal/provincial disputes.

From 1931 until 1981, strenuous efforts were made to cut the remaining ties to Britain. The question in Canada had never been *whether* we should have our own constitution, but *what* it should be. Bringing the *Constitution* home (or patriation) involved two seemingly insoluble conundrums: how much provincial participation should there be before an agreement to patriate the *Constitution* and what type of amendment process should ensue. Only when Canadian leaders came to an agreement over these two matters would they be able to amend the *Constitution* without recourse to Britain.

Changing a constitution is an amazingly complex process. The late Senator Eugene Forsey put it forcefully:

> *...let us never forget that, because a constitution is what it is, pervading and shaping every human being in the community, changing it by formal amendment is an immensely serious business. It is not like getting a new hair-do, or growing a beard, or buying new furniture or new clothes, or putting in a new bathroom. It is more like marriage — In the words of the Anglican Prayer Book — 'not by any to be enterprised, nor taken in hand unadvisedly, lightly or wantonly...but reverently, discretely, advisedly, soberly, and in the fear of God.' What we are dealing with in constitutional change is not paper or things. It is human lives.*[41]

Though efforts to find an acceptable constitutional agreement started in the 1930s, only in the 1960s did coherent discussions take place between the federal government and all of the provinces. Two of the resulting proposals almost succeeded: the Fulton-Favreau formula of 1964 and the Victoria Charter of 1971. The former was significant in Canadian constitutional development because it was the first mechanism that ever received the unanimous support of all ten provincial premiers. Nevertheless, it was bitterly criticized in Québec, and therefore the Liberal government of Premier Jean Lesage did not ask the Assembly to concur with it.

The Fulton-Favreau formula proposed drawing up a set of amending mechanisms that would have changed depending on the issue at stake. Parliament would have been able to amend the *Constitution* subject to approval of the provinces. The rules for this approval would vary issue-by-issue. Matters such as the powers of the provinces, the use of French and English and the number of Senators, for example, would be amended only if all the provinces agreed with Parliament. Changes in education, on the other hand, could be made with the consent of all the provinces except Newfoundland. Still other portions of the

---

[41] *Senate Debates*, May 4, 1976, p. 2080.

Constitution would only be changed if Parliament could obtain the agreement of two-thirds of the provinces, representing at least 50 percent of the population of Canada. The reality behind this latter proposal was that either Ontario or Québec would have had to concur with all changes in this domain. Further, those aspects of the *Constitution* directly related to the functions of the federal government could be changed by Parliament acting alone. For a time it appeared that the Fulton-Favreau formula might gain acceptance and thus form the basis of patriation of the *BNA Act*. However, opposition in Québec prevented the adoption of the arrangement.

In the summer of 1971, another federal/provincial conference came to a tentative agreement on an amending formula.[42] Unlike the Fulton-Favreau formula, the Victoria Charter would not have required the unanimous consent of the provinces for any amendment. Rather changes would have required the agreement of Parliament and a majority of the provinces including all provinces with over 25 percent of Canada's population, at least two Atlantic provinces and two western provinces having 50 percent of the population of the West. As with the Fulton-Favreau formula, it seemed for a time that the Victoria Charter might gain acceptance, but it too failed to receive the support of Québec.

The essential stumbling block to finding an amendment formula was always Québec's desire to be treated as a province unlike the others (*"pas comme les autres"*). To many Québécois, the idea that federalism refers to a process involving ten equal provinces and the federal government working as one state is unacceptable. They argue that Canada is a union of two "founding peoples," not ten equal provinces. This premise is based on the view that the Canadian *Constitution* is basically a "compact" between two cultural groups or between English and French provinces.[43]

By extension, some Québécois argue that it is the Québec state that is best able to protect their interests. From this standpoint they develop one of two possible strategies. Some accept the federal system, but want a *special status* for Québec, in which cultural fields such as education and communications are left totally to Québec, and in which the federal government does not intervene in such matters as language policy. In practice, all premiers of Québec since Maurice Duplessis have taken this stand as their minimum position. Premiers Lesage, Johnson and Bourassa all argued that Canada consists of "two nations."[44]

The second strategy advocated by some Québécois is separation from Canada. The rise to power of the Parti Québécois in November 1976 made this strategy a possibility. The Parti Québécois argued that it was not possible for Québec francophones to protect their language and culture within the federal system, and that separate status was essential. The history and detailed development of this option are discussed in the next chapter; however, a word on the right of constituent provinces to secede from their state may be useful here. As a general rule, such a right does not exist in any of the established federal states — Canada, the United States, Australia, the Federal Republic of Germany or Switzerland. On one occasion, in 1935, the state of Western Australia did attempt to secede from Australia and actually passed a referendum to this effect, 136 653 votes to 70 706. The Parliament of the United Kingdom, however, would not allow the case to go forward as British legislation and the proposal died.

[42] See Simeon, *Federal-Provincial Diplomacy*.

[43] See Ramsay Cook, *Provincial Autonomy, Minority Rights and the Compact Theory, 1867–1921*, Study no. 4, Royal Commission on Bilingualism and Biculturalism (Ottawa: Queen's Printer, 1969).

[44] See Edward McWhinney, *Quebec and the Constitution 1960–1978* (Toronto: University of Toronto Press, 1979) and *Canada and the Constitution, 1979–1982* (Toronto: University of Toronto Press, 1982).

PATRIATION OF CANADA'S CONSTITUTION

The long and at times bitter debate over patriation ended in 1982 with the passage of the *Canada Act* by the British Parliament. While patriation of the Canadian *Constitution* was primarily symbolic in that it did not represent any changes in federal/provincial jurisdictions or the structure of central government, the inclusion of an entrenched *Charter of Rights and Freedoms* and an amending formula has had substantial importance.

The catalyst responsible for what became the final round of the constitutional negotiations leading to patriation was the Québec referendum on sovereignty-association. In May 1980, Premier René Lévesque's Parti Québécois *indépendantiste* government sought authority to negotiate sovereign political status for Québec with continued economic association with Canada.[45] During the provincial referendum campaign, opponents of this proposal — including the federal Liberal party — pledged that Canada would begin a process of "renewal" and constitutional change to address the concerns of Québec citizens if they rejected the referendum. Québec voters ultimately did reject Lévesque's plan by a convincing margin, 60 to 40 percent. Patriation of the *Constitution* was thereby given new momentum, with Prime Minister Trudeau and the Liberal party exhorting Canadians to renew federalism in order to reciprocate Québec's gesture of confidence in Canadian federalism.

The concept of renewed federalism, while vague, allowed Trudeau to renew his efforts for patriation. The federal government and the provinces conducted a series of meetings culminating in September, 1980 in Ottawa. However, government leaders made no progress on the agenda items, which included patriation, an amending formula, a *Charter of Rights and Freedoms*, the principle of equalization, reform of the Senate and the Supreme Court and redistribution of powers between the two levels of government. Faced with an intransigent group of provincial premiers, Prime Minister Trudeau decided that the federal government would proceed unilaterally.

Trudeau's unilateral patriation package proposed an entrenched *Charter of Rights* as well as equalization and amendment formulas. Of the ten provincial governments, however, only New Brunswick and Ontario supported the federal government's course of action, agreeing with Trudeau that unanimous provincial agreement had proven impossible. The federal government justified its action on the premise that, as the representative of all Canadians, it legitimately spoke for the interests of all Canadians. A special Joint Committee of the Senate and the House of Commons was formed to review the government's resolution. After prolonged debate and more than 70 substantial changes, the government's resolution was adopted. The federal Conservative party opposed the government's unilateral action. The NDP, however, supported the package after it won amendments guaranteeing provincial ownership of natural resources.

THE ROLE OF BRITAIN

The federal government's decision to act unilaterally moved the site of the political battle from the Canadian to the British Parliament — a situation that strained relations between

---

[45] See Québec's White Paper on sovereignty-association, *Québec-Canada: A New Deal* (Québec: Gouvernement du Québec, 1979).

the two countries. British MPs became the targets of intensive lobbying efforts. In London, Prime Minister Trudeau and several of his cabinet ministers attempted to ensure quick passage of the request, suggesting that failure would have serious international repercussions. Dissenting groups and provinces also sent representatives to argue their case.

The 1949 amendment to the *BNA Act* had made it clear that the federal Parliament could amend only those provisions that were already under federal jurisdiction. The procedure for other constitutional changes required a Joint Address from the House and Senate to the British Parliament. While Britain had always acted automatically on receiving such an Address, Britain's role in this particular crisis was uncertain. Canada had seldom made requests affecting the division of powers without first obtaining provincial consent, and British parliamentarians were faced with a dilemma, since either accepting or rejecting the Canadian federal government's unilateral request for patriation would leave many Canadians unhappy. Prime Minister Trudeau's remark that British MPs should "hold their noses" and pass the request made their task no easier.

The British House of Commons Select Committee on Foreign Affairs issued a report that questioned Trudeau's assertion that Westminster had no choice but to pass any request from the Canadian Parliament, arguing instead that some measure of provincial consent was required for any constitutional changes affecting provincial powers. Though it did not define the extent of provincial support needed, the committee recommended that it should be the same as that required in the amending formula proposed in the patriation package. The Trudeau government naturally attacked the Committee's conclusions, charging that Britain was interfering in Canadian internal affairs.

THE SUPREME COURT'S DECISION

British politicians hoped to escape the dilemma by telling their Canadian counterparts that, given strong provincial opposition, Westminster would be reluctant to pass the request without a ruling by Canada's Supreme Court on the legality of unilateral patriation. By this time, six of the provinces had brought the question before the Court. However, the Supreme Court's ruling, delivered September 28, 1981, offered both sides a measure of support. By a vote of 7 to 2, the judges ruled that the federal government could "legally" and "unilaterally" submit the constitutional resolution to the British Parliament. However, by a 6 to 3 vote, the Court ruled that a constitutional convention requiring provincial consent also existed, and that the process embarked upon by Ottawa "offended the federal principle." The Court left vague the extent of provincial consent required by this convention: the consent of more than the two supporters (Ontario and New Brunswick) was needed, but unanimity was not essential. The Court further noted that conventions are not enforceable by law. Federal Justice Minister Jean Chrétien agreed, arguing that it is not up to the courts but rather to politicians to decide what political conventions should be.[46]

The patriation package was thus tossed back into the political arena. As a result, another First Ministers' Conference was held in November. The federal government was adamant that a patriation package should include a charter of rights, and an amending formula similar to that offered at the Victoria Conference in 1971. It proposed that constitutional change should require the consent of Parliament and a majority of legislatures in Canada's

---

[46] *The Globe and Mail*, December 29, 1981.

four major regions: two in Atlantic Canada, Québec, Ontario and two in the West. The two largest provinces' veto power would thereby be guaranteed. This formula was opposed by almost all the provinces.

Earlier in 1981 those premiers who were opposed to the federal plans had argued for a patriation package of their own. They had proposed that constitutional change should require the consent of Parliament and seven provinces, representing 50 percent of the population.[47] This proposal would have allowed a province to "opt out" of any amendment that took away existing provincial rights or powers, and would further have entitled any such province to fiscal compensation.

The "Gang of Eight," as the opposing provincial premiers were dubbed, was also against many clauses in the proposed charter of rights. The eight premiers feared that it would give new powers to federally appointed judges and reduce provincial authority. Their other concerns included the prospect of expensive and time-consuming redrafting of provincial legislation to comply with the new charter, the hint of importation of American jurisprudence in the language of the legal rights section and the direct recourse to the courts that the charter would grant to individuals.

The most general provincial opposition to the entrenched charter of rights was based on the contention that it would be difficult to amend it in order to adapt it to changing circumstances or particular regional problems. While most provincial premiers did favour the inclusion of clauses about basic democratic and fundamental rights, they opposed the more controversial mobility, legal and equality rights ideas, which they feared would conflict with provincial legislation. Newfoundland, New Brunswick and the Northwest and Yukon Territories were particularly concerned that provincial legislation allowing preferential local hiring policies for their disadvantaged jobless would be challenged. Québec had similar reservations concerning its language requirements and job programs.

FEDERAL/PROVINCIAL CONSTITUTIONAL AGREEMENT

The November 1981 federal/provincial conference, unlike most of those of the previous 54 years, ended in agreement between the federal government and nine out of ten of the provinces (Québec was the exception). Several compromises were made to obtain this high degree of consensus. The major compromise was over the inclusion of a *notwithstanding* clause that allowed Parliament or a provincial legislature to override most *Charter* provisions by declaring that they were doing so when passing legislation. A "sunset clause" requiring renewal of this exemption every five years was included. In the absence of renewal, the *Charter*'s provisions would take precedence.

Those who favoured inclusion of the notwithstanding clause argued that it provided an important check, maintaining the pre-eminence of the legislatures in the event of an "awkward" court ruling. The idea is of long duration in Canada. It is found in the *Canadian Bill of Rights* passed by the federal Parliament in 1960, as well as in the provincial *Bills of Rights* passed by Alberta, Québec, Saskatchewan and Ontario. The federal government used it only once, during the October Crisis in Québec, in 1970.

Critics of the notwithstanding provision argue that it circumvents the very purpose of an entrenched charter, which is to give the courts the authority to protect fundamental

---

[47] Acceptance by Québec of this plan was the basis for later federal efforts to discredit arguments that traditionally Québec had a constitutional veto.

individual freedoms in the event that legislatures and governments fail to do so. According to one constitutional expert, "if legislatures are given the power to cancel…judicial authority they are most likely to use it when there is a failure of restraint."[48]

There were other compromises concerning the *Charter*. The case of Native people provides a pertinent example. Recognition of their treaty rights was originally excluded from the *Charter* at the insistence of those provinces that were concerned that Native land claims might impede provincial control over natural resources. It was only after intense lobbying by Native groups that recognition of these rights for Indian, Inuit and Métis peoples was later restored. In Section 25 Native people were guaranteed that the *Charter* could not be construed "so as to abrogate from any aboriginal, treaty or other rights or freedoms that pertain to the aboriginal peoples of Canada." For greater assurance, Section 35 specified that "treaty rights" were defined as "rights that now exist by way of land claim agreements or may be so acquired."

Another important lobbying effort ensured the restoration of the rights of an overlooked majority group — women. Section 28 of the *Charter* — which simply stated, "notwithstanding anything in this *Charter*, the rights and freedoms referred to in it are guaranteed equally to male and female persons" — was excluded by one of the early agreements. In response to this the Ad Hoc Committee of Canadian Women on the *Constitution* was formed and in just three weeks had successfully lobbied all 10 provincial premiers to reverse their stand on the issue. Equality of men and women was thus placed outside the reach of the notwithstanding clause.

A further major compromise leading to the success of the November 1981 conference concerned the amending formula. Instead of the federal Liberal proposition, the formula preferred by the provincial "Gang of Eight" was adopted. It called for jurisdictional amendments to be made by a joint resolution of both the Senate and the House of Commons, as well as by a resolution of the legislative assemblies of at least two-thirds of the provinces, representing at least 50 percent of the population of Canada.[49] In addition, it granted dissenting provinces the right to opt out of all amendments that affected their status and powers.

While federal/provincial agreement on a patriation package removed much of the hesitancy of British politicians to grant the federal government's request for patriation, Native Indian groups continued to press their opposition in the British courts, arguing that the British Crown was still responsible for them. The British courts rejected this claim, however, finding that while no government should derogate the Indian rights guaranteed in treaties signed with the British and Canadian governments, responsibility for Native groups had long since passed from the Crown in Britain to the Crown in Canada.

The British Parliament was finally presented with the Canada Bill in mid-February of 1982. The Bill was speedily passed at every stage by large majorities.[50] On March 29, the Queen gave Royal Assent to the *Canada Act*, 115 years to the day after the *BNA Act* had received Royal Assent. In Ottawa, on April 17, 1982, the Queen proclaimed the *Constitution Act, 1982*, completing the patriation process (see Table 5.4).

---

[48] Noel Lyon, *The Globe and Mail*, November 17, 1981.

[49] The latest general census would be referred to for such information. The Senate does not possess an absolute veto on constitutional change. After 180 days an amendment may be concluded without its agreement.

[50] All the major British parties supported the bill.

TABLE 5.4   CANADA'S CONSTITUTIONAL HIGHLIGHTS

1867   *British North America Act* (now the *Constitution Act, 1867*)

1931   *Statute of Westminster:* Britain can no longer legislate for Canada except at the request of the Canadian government.

1949   An amendment to the *BNA Act* widens the scope of the Canadian parliament's authority to undertake further amendments.

1949   Supreme Court of Canada becomes final court of appeal.

1961   Diefenbaker *Bill of Rights*

1964   Fulton-Favreau formula rejected by Québec

1971   Victoria Charter rejected by Québec

1980   Québec referendum on sovereignty-association defeated

1981   Supreme Court rules Trudeau's constitutional resolution is valid but violates political convention.

1981   First Ministers make three significant changes to resolution: package rejected by Québec

1981   Constitutional Resolution passed by Parliament.

1982   *Canada Act* passed by British House of Commons and patriated. A *Charter of Rights and Freedoms* and an amendment formula become part of the Canadian *Constitution*. Québec does not sign.

1987   The Meech Lake accord fails.

1991   The Spicer Royal Commission reports

1992   The Dobbie-Beaudoin Joint House and Senate Committee report followed by Constitutional Conferences

1992   The Charlottetown accord is approved by federal and provincial leaders.

1992   The Charlottetown accord is massively rejected in a referendum.

THE NEW CANADIAN CONSTITUTION

As part of the final patriation package, there were several changes to the *Constitution*, none of which affects the main structure of government or significantly alters the division of powers between Parliament and the provincial legislatures. These changes are listed below and in the next section on the *Charter*.[51]

Change I: There are now five legal formulas for amending the *Constitution Act*. The first formula concerns amendments that require unanimous consent (Section 41). These deal with amendments to the office of the Queen, the Governor General, the Lieutenant-Governors, the right of a province to at least as many seats in the House of Commons as it has in the Senate, the use of the English and French languages (except amendments applying only to a single province), the composition of the Supreme Court of Canada and amendments to the amending formulas themselves. Amendments in these areas must be passed by the Senate and the House of Commons (or by the Commons alone, if the Senate has not approved the proposal within 180 days after the Commons has done so) and by the legisla-

---

[51] These amendments are concisely summarized by Eugene A. Forsey in *How Canadians Govern Themselves* (Ottawa: Minister of Supply and Services, 1982), pp. 12–18; and more fully by Peter Meekison, "The Amending Formula," in Olling and Westmacott, eds., *Perspectives on Canadian Federalism*, pp. 61–76.

ture of every province. This means that every province has a veto over these types of amendments.

The second formula concerns amendments under the general procedure (Section 38). They include amendments that

1. take away any rights, powers or privileges of provincial governments or legislatures,
2. deal with the proportionate representation of the provinces in the House of Commons,
3. deal with the powers of the Senate and the method of selecting senators and their residence qualifications,
4. concern the constitutional position of the Supreme Court of Canada (not including its composition, which is covered under formula 1 above),
5. concern the extension of existing provinces into the territories, and
6. concern the Charter of Rights and Freedoms.

Amendments in these areas must be passed by the Senate and the House of Commons (or by the Commons alone if the Senate delays more than 180 days), and by the legislatures of two-thirds of the provinces with at least half the total population of all the provinces (excluding the territories). This means that any four less populous provinces or Ontario and Québec together could veto any amendments in this category, and that either Ontario or Québec would have to be one of the seven provinces needed to pass any amendment.

The third formula deals with matters that apply to one or several but not all provinces (Section 43). Amendments in these cases must be passed by the Senate and the House of Commons (or the Commons alone, if the Senate delays more than 180 days), and by the legislature or legislatures of the particular province or provinces concerned. This would include changes in provincial boundaries or changes relating to the use of the English or French language in any province, or provinces.

The fourth formula concerns changes in the executive government of Canada or changes in the Senate and House of Commons that are not covered by the first two formulas. Such amendments can be made by an ordinary act of the Parliament of Canada. (Section 44)

The fifth formula concerns amendments that can be made by individual provincial legislatures alone (Section 45). In the original *BNA Act, 1867* (Section 92), with the exception of the office of the Lieutenant-Governor, provinces could amend their own constitutions. Section 92 (1) was repealed and this amendment clause moved to Section 45, which places the provinces in a position equivalent to that of the federal government.

Change II: The first three amending formulas "entrench" specific parts of the written *Constitution*. This means that neither Parliament alone nor any provincial legislature has the power to touch them. All changes must be made according to the particular formula that applies. Procedural requirements are also set out (Section 39) that establish maximum and minimum times within which constitutional amendments must be passed.

The amending process under the first three formulas can be initiated in the Senate, or the House of Commons, or a provincial legislature. Under the fourth formula it can, of course, be initiated in either House as any ordinary act of parliament, and in the fifth formula the provincial legislature concerned initiates the process.

Change III: The provinces obtained wider powers over their natural resources than they had had before. Each province now controls the export within Canada of the primary production from its mines, oil wells, gas wells, forests and electric power plants, provided it does not discriminate against other parts of the country in prices or supplies. The federal government can legislate on these matters, however, and, in case of conflict, the federal law will prevail. The provinces can levy indirect taxes on their mines, oil wells, gas wells, forests and electric power plants and primary production from these sources. Such taxes must be the same whether or not the products are exported to other parts of the country.

Change IV: Provisions were included concerning Native peoples. First, the *Charter* "shall not be construed so as to abrogate or derogate from any aboriginal, treaty or other rights or freedoms that pertain to the aboriginal peoples of Canada" (Section 25). Second, the existing aboriginal and treaty rights of the Native peoples of Canada are recognized and affirmed (this includes Indian, Inuit and Métis peoples).

Change V: In Section 36 (1) on equalization and regional disparities the *Constitution Act* declares that the national government and Parliament and the provincial governments and legislatures "are committed to promoting equal opportunities for the well-being of Canadians, further economic developments to reduce disparities in opportunities, and providing essential public services of reasonable quality to all Canadians." In Section 36 (2), the national government and Parliament "are committed to the principle of making equalization payments to ensure that provincial governments have sufficient revenues to provide reasonably comparable levels of public services and reasonably comparable levels of taxation."

Change VI: Official English and French versions of the whole written *Constitution* are equally authoritative.

Change VII: The new *Constitution Act* includes a *Charter of Rights and Freedoms*. (This important addition is discussed in considerable detail below.)

Change VIII: The *Charter* shall be interpreted "in a manner consistent with the preservation and enhancement of the multicultural heritage of Canada" (Section 27).

The constitutional amendment system that is now in place is quite rigid, so that the chances of further change to the *Constitution* by amendment are minimal. Despite constant efforts and even a national referendum, there have been only two minor amendments to the *Constitution* since 1982. Section 35 (1) now provides for consultation with the aboriginal peoples of Canada before any amendment is made with respect to their rights. And, in 1993 the New Brunswick legislature and the federal Parliament used Section 43 to make New Brunswick a bilingual province. The right to amend the *Constitution* is finally in Canadian hands, but those hands are fairly firmly tied.

THE CHARTER OF RIGHTS AND FREEDOMS

The desirability of an entrenched *Charter of Rights and Freedoms* has been a subject of debate since Confederation and no doubt will remain so despite its adoption in 1982. The constitutional entrenchment of rights can be said to have two primary functions, one symbolic, the other substantive. Symbolically, such a charter is a statement of the ideals valued by a society. While they are not always observed in practice, protection of these principles is a test by which the polity should be judged. A more tangible impact of a charter of rights lies in its restraint of the actions of a government vis-à-vis its citizens, preventing authorities from violating the rights of individuals and groups as defined in the charter. It is this restraint that makes the entrenchment of rights contentious, especially in a parliamentary system such as Canada's where it constitutes a reduction in legislative authority.

Why did Canada need a written and entrenched *Charter of Rights*? Critics have posed this question in light of the fact that Canada existed as a relatively free society for more than one hundred years without such a document. In Britain, civil liberties were, and are, protected by traditions, customs and political culture. Civil liberties are, if you wish, ingrained in the values and beliefs of politicians and the people. Canada relied, too, on the traditional rights provided by British common law and, after 1960, on a statute, the *Canadian Bill of Rights*, which listed the fundamental freedoms that existed in Canada but which was never entrenched in the *Constitution*. Despite these safeguards many Canadians believed that there was a need for a charter of rights and freedoms that would restrict the actions of governments. Why?

Despite the rule of law and British traditions, Canada's record of ensuring the protection of its citizens' rights is not without blemish. The most celebrated example was the Québec Padlock law of 1937, legislation enacted by the Québec government banning the propagation of "Communism and Bolshevism." The law would have allowed Premier Duplessis to padlock any premises allegedly used for such purposes and to move arbitrarily against other groups opposed to his regime. In 1938, the Alberta legislature enacted the Press Bill that allowed the government to force newspapers to reveal the sources of unfavourable comment. In 1953, Québec restrained the freedom of religion of Jehovah Witnesses by restricting their right to hand out pamphlets without permission. Although these pieces of legislation were subsequently overturned by the courts, the rationale cited by the judges in their decisions strengthened the argument for entrenchment of basic rights in the *Constitution*. The courts based their rulings not on the fact that the legislation represented a violation of fundamental rights (although this view was expressed by some of the presiding judges), but rather on the contention that provincial governments did not have the right to restrict civil liberties because of the constitutional division of powers. In all these cases the courts declared the actions *ultra vires* — i.e., not within provincial jurisdiction. Under the new 1982 constitutional provisions, it is the recognition of rights within the *Charter* that will be the basis for such court decisions.

Another notable example of a violation of basic rights in Canada's history was the internment of Japanese Canadians during World War II. Under the *War Measures Act* thousands of people were uprooted from their communities and placed in camps for the duration of the war — for "security" reasons. Decades later, in 1970, Prime Minister Trudeau again invoked the *War Measures Act*, this time in response to FLQ terrorist activities in Québec. This action, which suspended civil liberties and allowed the arbitrary detention of hundreds of suspects, is the most recent major example of government violation of basic human rights in Canada. Both cases raised concern that such violations of basic democratic rights could not be prevented without written constitutional guarantees — hence a charter was necessary.

The *Charter* in its final form was the result of a long process of extensive discussion and amendment of the Liberal government's initial constitutional proposal, tabled before the House of Commons in 1980. It is a significant improvement on the *Canadian Bill of Rights* because it applies to the federal and provincial governments equally and because, unlike ordinary legislation, it is entrenched in the *Constitution*, and therefore can be altered *only* through the constitutional amendment process.[52]

The *Charter* consists of a short preamble — "Whereas Canada is founded upon principles that recognize the supremacy of God and the rule of law..." — followed by 34 sections. It is the first section that actually defines the limits of Canadians' rights and freedoms,

---

[52] Only two attacks on federal legislation based on the earlier *Canadian Bill of Rights* were ever successful.

stipulating that they are "subject only to such reasonable limits prescribed by law as can be demonstrably justified in a free and democratic society."

The *Charter* protects fundamental freedoms, including those of conscience and religion, of thought, belief, opinion and expression, and of peaceful assembly and association. The basic democratic rights named in the document include the right of every citizen to vote; a five-year limit on the terms of federal and provincial legislatures, except in time of real or apprehended war, invasion or insurrection; and the requirement for legislatures to meet at least once every 12 months.

The *Charter* also protects mobility rights, i.e., the right of Canadian citizens to enter, remain in and leave Canada, and to move to and work in any province. These rights are limited, however, by recognition of provincial residency requirements as a qualification for the receipt of social services. Affirmative action programs, whose purpose is to ameliorate the conditions of a socially or economically disadvantaged people, are also allowed if the rate of employment in that province falls below the national employment rate.[53]

Legal rights such as the traditional right to life, liberty and security are listed, along with new legal rights provisions. For example, unreasonable search or seizure and arbitrary detention or imprisonment are prohibited. A detained individual is guaranteed the right to be informed promptly of the reasons for detention, to have counsel without delay and to be instructed of that right, as well as to have the validity of the detention determined and to be released if detention is not justified. Individuals charged with an offence have the right to be informed without delay of the specific offence and to be tried within a reasonable time. They have a right against self-incrimination and are to be considered innocent until proven guilty by an impartial and public hearing. Individuals are not to be deprived of bail without just cause, are permitted trial by jury where the maximum punishment for the offence is imprisonment for five years or more, except in the case of a military offence tried before a military tribunal. And they are not to be punished for an action that was not illegal at the time of commission. If acquitted, an individual may not be tried for the same offence again or, if found guilty and punished, may not be tried or punished again. Finally, if the punishment for the offence has changed between the commission of the crime and the time of the sentencing, the individual will be subject to the lesser punishment.

Individuals are also protected against cruel and unusual treatment or punishment. Witnesses who testify in any proceedings have the right not to have any incriminating evidence they might give used against them in any other proceedings, except in prosecution for perjury. Evidence obtained in a manner that infringes upon an individual's rights and freedoms shall be excluded, but only if its admission would "bring the administration of justice into disrepute."

The *Charter* further provides equality rights guaranteeing that every individual is equal before and under the law without discrimination, particularly without discrimination based on race, national or ethnic origin, colour, religion, sex, age or mental or physical disability. However, affirmative action programs aimed at improving the conditions of groups discriminated against are allowed.

The importance of linguistic rights is acknowledged in the *Charter*. English and French are recognized as Canada's official languages and have equal status in all institutions of Parliament and the federal government. Both languages are also recognized in the province

---

[53] Section 6 (4).

of New Brunswick. Thus, in Parliament and New Brunswick's legislature, both languages may be used in debates and other proceedings. Parliamentary statutes and records, as well as proceedings of the courts, are published in both languages. Individuals have the right to communicate with any head or central office of Parliament or government of Canada in either official language, and the same right is extended to other offices where there is significant demand.

Under the *Charter*, all citizens of Canada who received their primary education in Canada in either French or English have the right to have their children educated in the same language if it is the minority language of the province in which they reside. This right, however, is applicable only "where numbers warrant," i.e., where the number of children warrants the provision of public funds for minority language instruction. Minority language education rights are also guaranteed to the children of Canadian citizens whose first language learned and understood is that of the English or French linguistic minority of the province in which they reside, whether or not the parents were able to receive their primary education in that language. This latter guarantee is not applicable to Québec until it is approved by the Québec National Assembly — and to date it has not been.

The *Charter* includes a variety of other specific rights. The rights of the Native peoples are not to be diminished by the *Charter*'s provisions; for example, the provision that guarantees language education rights in French and English may not be interpreted to deprive the Indian people of James Bay of their right to educate their children in Cree. More broadly, the *Charter* may not be used to deprive anyone of existing rights and freedoms, and its interpretation must recognize Canada's multicultural heritage. The *Charter*'s provisions are to be applied equally to males and females. Significantly, in recognition of Canada's federal nature the *Charter* states that neither level of government gains power as a result of its provisions.

Despite this impressive list of rights, however, they are not all inviolable. Readers will recall that the new *Constitution* was only patriated through a series of political compromises. The leaders agreed to allow restrictions on citizens' rights in two general ways. First, the *Charter* begins with an overarching exception when it claims that the rights and freedoms are guaranteed "subject only to such reasonable limits presented by law as can be demonstrably justified in a free and democratic society." This means that the courts are allowed to decide that a piece of federal or provincial legislation that restricts freedoms is still valid according to their definition of "reasonable limits." The Supreme Court, for example, has allowed the Ontario legislature to impose film censorship as long as its criteria are prescribed by law.[54] Second, Section 33 also allows the province or Parliament to enact laws overriding *Charter* provisions. They can pass legislation *notwithstanding* the *Charter* on fundamental freedoms, legal and equality rights by means of a "notwithstanding" clause. Such a bill becomes inoperative after five years and must be re-passed if it is to remain valid.

CHARTER CASES AND THE CONSTITUTION

Charter cases involve extremely difficult questions on issues ranging from Sunday closing of stores to missile-testing to abortion. In 1987, on the fifth anniversary of the *Charter*, Supreme Court Judge Gerard LaForest commented that he found working with the *Charter* almost overwhelming at times because of the abstract principles and lack of familiar paths:

---

[54] *Ontario Film and Video Appreciation Society v. Ontario Board of Censors*, (1984) 45 O.R. (2d)80.

What is liberty? What should the limits be to it? We all know what we think ourselves. But when it comes to defining liberty, each and every state restriction exists in a proper context. There is no way to escape these problems....When you are dealing with the Charter, you really don't know what path to choose. This is all new. We are still groping — and I think it's healthy to grope.[55]

The early court cases were very important for the development of *"Charter* politics." The first *Charter* decision of the Supreme Court was *Law Society of Upper Canada v. Skapinker*, in May, 1984. It involved the claim that Ontario legislation making Canadian citizenship a condition for practicing law violated Section 6, the mobility rights section, of the *Charter*. The court declared that the Ontario law was not designed to impede movement across provincial borders and therefore did not thwart the mobility guarantee in the *Constitution*.

The next four *Charter* cases to be decided — the *Protestant School Boards, Southam, Singh*, and *Big M Drug Mart* — all were upheld by the Supreme Court. These decisions went beyond a traditional legalistic approach. The interpretations were based on broad historical and philosophical considerations. In *Southam*, for example, Chief Justice Dickson "traced the right to security from unreasonable searches back to the common law concept of trespass and its application by English judges in the 1700s to make an Englishman's home his castle. He then followed the evolution of this private property interest into a wider concern with personal privacy as a fundamental value of a liberal society."[56]

Many of the Court's other early *Charter* decisions were more restrained. In *Operation Dismantle*, for example, a coalition of unions and peace groups tried to use the *Charter* to overturn the decision of the Canadian government to allow testing of American cruise missiles in Canada. They claimed that the agreement increased the likelihood that the country would be involved in a nuclear war, and that this threatened to deprive Canadians of their right to life, liberty and security of the person under Section 7 of the *Charter*.

The Federal Court of Appeal concluded that executive actions and cabinet decisions could be reviewed by the courts; however, it upheld the government's authority to make decisions on matters of defence and national security. Four of the five judges declared that the coalition had failed to prove that the decision to test the missiles was a break with principles of fundamental justice. The decision of the Supreme Court was that this issue was not a proper question to bring before the courts because "even with the best available evidence, judges could do no more than speculate about the consequences of cruise missile testing."[57] The Court was indicating that *Charter* claims should be rejected when they involve "complex determinations about future behaviour which cannot be satisfactorily assessed through the judicial process."[58] According to one of the most persuasive arguments of the Court, the *Charter*'s guarantees are not, and cannot be, absolute. "We must all die, and many are, at one time or another in their lives, imprisoned or made insecure."[59]

---

[55] Quoted in Kirk Makin, "Charter's mandate gives judges role of wary surgeons," *The Globe and Mail*, April 14, 1987.

[56] Peter H. Russell, *The Judiciary in Canada*, p. 360. For a detailed study of *Charter* cases and the *Constitution* see Michael Mandel, *The Charter of Rights and the Legalization of Politics in Canada* (Toronto: Wall and Thompson, 1989) and Rainer Knopff and F.L. Morton, *Charter Politics* (Scarborough: Nelson, 1992).

[57] Russell, *The Judiciary in Canada*, p. 360.

[58] Ibid.

[59] *Operation Dismantle v. The Queen* [1985], Supreme Court Records 651.

The first cracks in judicial unanimity appeared in the Supreme Court of Canada's decision with the eighth *Charter* issue — the *Therens* case — in which the judges split seven to two on whether breathalyzer evidence was admissible in court. Since this event, there have been enough dissenting opinions in other cases that some experts say that it is tentatively possible to assess the judges, or groups of judges, in terms of "liberal," "activist" or "conservative" tendencies. In 1987, Peter Russell named one judge as having quite liberal or activist leanings, two more as likely to join this stand, five with relatively conservative tendencies and one as unpredictable.[60] Since that time, however, many of these judges have changed, so the pattern of interaction has already altered. As ideological differences between the judges become more apparent, we can expect the choice of Supreme Court justices to become more politicized, as is the case in the United States. Governments will want to choose judges of their persuasion in order to ensure that their legislative programs survive future court challenges. Obviously, the process of appointing judges will become more controversial.

Some of the best known public policy issues involve *Charter* decisions by the Supreme Court on fundamental freedoms. The Supreme Court threw out the *Lord's Day Act* as an infringement on the religion of people who did not accept the Christian sabbath.[61] On the other hand, the same Court upheld an Ontario Act preventing Sunday shopping as long as it was based on a secular rather than religious foundation.[62] Other court cases concerning fundamental freedoms included those on language legislation, pornography, freedom of the press, street prostitution and the right to die.

The *Charter's* equality provisions took effect in 1985.[63] Although it has become a fast growing area of *Charter* litigation, it is still too early to determine to what degree the Supreme Court will use these provisions to expand rights for women, the disabled and others. Drawing a line between acceptable and unacceptable forms of discrimination is, according to one Supreme Court Justice, one of the most difficult tasks under the *Charter*: "We are talking about inserting equality into life which is not equal."[64] There are several problems. The court could require citizens to show that an instance of alleged discrimination is unfair, or it could require governments to justify differing forms of treatment. Prohibitive costs and poor public financing for test cases may make litigants reluctant to challenge governments in court for alleged discrimination. Another issue is deciding how to prove discrimination. Mr. Justice Lamer asked: "What the courts will want is up in the air. Will we need statistical evidence? How will we get at the records we need?"[65] Furthermore, can the courts determine what constitutes equality without Parliament having an opportunity to respond legislatively? In 1988, for example, the Federal Court decided that a section of the *Unemployment Insurance Act* discriminated sexually against natural fathers because it denied them paternity leave benefits. Eventually, the federal government agreed and extended the benefits to fathers. Clearly this type of ruling affects the balance of power between Parliament and the courts.

---

[60] Ibid., p. 362

[61] *R. v. Big M Drug Mart Ltd.*, (1985) 1 S.C.R. 295

[62] *R. v. Edwards Books and Art Ltd.* (1986) 2 S.C.R. 713

[63] The Courts were immediately flooded with serious, but also quite imaginative cases such as one in British Columbia where a chicken-lover argued against pet discrimination, saying a local bylaw was unfair because it prohibited fowl within city boundaries. The bylaw was upheld.

[64] Mr. Justice Lamer quoted in *The Globe and Mail*, April 14, 1987.

[65] Ibid.

The controversy that began with the introduction of the *Charter of Rights and Freedoms* continues. Supporters of both pro- and anti- sides can point to disappointing judgements and unfulfilled expectations. However, a definitive verdict on the value of the *Charter* will not be clear until much more time has passed.

R.I. Cheffins and P.A. Johnson say the importance of the *Charter* for Canada's constitutional future is that it is "centralizing, legalizing and Americanizing."[66] By centralizing they mean that it provides a common national standard for the protection of civil liberties and engenders national debates that transcend federal/provincial or regional differences. Peter Russell summed up the legalizing and politicizing effect of the *Charter* this way — it tends "to judicialize politics and to politicize the judiciary."[67]

Clearly, today the nine justices of the Supreme Court of Canada play a very powerful political role. They can overturn legislation that, according to their judgement, conflicts with rights guaranteed in the *Charter*, and they can have the final say on social policy matters such as union rights and abortion that used to be in the exclusive domain of politicians. This power has been particularly evident in cases concerning legal rights. In January, 1988, for example, the Supreme Court declared that the federal abortion law did not conform to the Canadian *Charter of Rights and Freedoms* and struck it down, leaving Canada with no legislation in this field of social policy. In the famous *Morgentaler* case a majority of the Supreme Court judges ruled that the law violated the security of the person of the woman and constituted a "profound interference with a woman's body."[68] Despite parliamentary efforts to regain control of abortion policy, the Supreme Court's judgement remains in place with little likelihood of successful legislation. In 1991, the Supreme Court reaffirmed the position that an unborn child (a fetus) is not a person.

Critics of the *Charter* insist that it will inhibit rather than foster progressive social change. They claim that by framing the agenda for debate the courts can limit the progression of social reform. The rights protected under the *Charter* are, they claim, a reflection of middle-class preoccupations; no basic entitlement is included for a decent level of education, housing, nutrition or health care. However, Section 36 of the *Charter* does enshrine the commitment of both federal and provincial governments to provide "essential public services of reasonable quality to all Canadians." And, although it does not protect present social and economic arrangements, the *Charter* identifies and protects the political and legal rights essential to those who promote social change.

Critics also contend that the *Charter* confers too much power on lawyers and judges, enabling judges who are not elected to strike down measures enacted by the majority. One supporter, Robert Sharpe, answers these criticisms by pointing out that we cannot equate democracy with "the raw will of the majority.... A true democracy," he states, "is surely one in which the exercise of power by the many is conditional on the respect for the rights of the few."[69] It is unfortunate, but true, that the majority at times overlooks minority rights. What the *Charter* does is assign the courts the responsibility to ensure that the claims of

---

[66] R.I. Cheffins and P.A. Johnson, *The Revised Canadian Constitution: Politics as Law* (Toronto: McGraw-Hill Ryerson, 1986), pp. 148–49. This point is also discussed by Peter Hogg in *Constitutional Law of Canada*, 2nd ed. (Toronto: Carswell, 1985), pp. 651–52.

[67] Peter H. Russell, "The Political Purposes of the Canadian Charter of Rights and Freedoms," *The Canadian Bar Review*, 61, 1983, p. 51.

[68] *R. v. Morgentaler*, (1988) 1 S.C.R. 30.

[69] Quoted in *The Toronto Star*, April 11, 1987.

minorities and those without influence must be listened to. Ultimately, of course, elected officials have the final say, because the *Charter* provides that equality rights are subject to the legislative override provision (the notwithstanding clause) that can be used if legislatures disagree fundamentally with the courts.

Another controversial aspect of *Charter* cases will be more familiar to Americans than Canadians. Section 24(2) of the *Charter* declares that a court shall exclude from the proceedings evidence that was obtained in a manner that infringed upon or denied any guaranteed right or freedom. Canadian judges are proving willing to dismiss illegally obtained evidence because it might "bring the administration of justice into disrepute," but these new exclusions are making law enforcement more difficult. Until 1982, illegally obtained evidence was accepted in the courts; today it is not.

One further area of apprehension concerning the *Charter* lies in the realm of political culture. Some scholars see the *Charter* as promoting a shift of values toward those of the United States. They maintain that the traditional, collectivist values that emphasize tradition, order and historical continuity (as discussed in Chapter 3) are becoming more closely aligned with American values that stress individual interests above those of the collectivity. This is a reflection of the emphasis the *Charter* puts on individual versus group interests. As Cheffins and Johnson put it, the *Charter* "will bring an essentially counter-revolutionary, non-rationalist communitarian society into direct collision with individual-focussed legal rights based upon *Charter* arguments." Doing so, they maintain, will accelerate the Americanization of Canada.[70]

However, the *Charter* also has a clearly positive side. Judges have taken the stand that citizens should be allowed to ask courts to declare laws unconstitutional when there is a potential infringement of their rights; they do not have to wait until their rights are actually violated. In response to this, many laws that threatened to deprive individuals of basic rights have been struck down. Supreme Court Judge Lamer commented that because of this, governments have been more careful since 1982 in drafting laws:

> We are all very conscious that these laws were passed by elected representatives…I don't think there is going to be much of this law knocking-down once those laws that are on the books have been cleaned up. And the legislatures are cleaning them up. Whole teams are going through the books.[71]

This was evident in 1986 when a parliamentary subcommittee presented 85 recommendations for making federal law conform to the *Charter*. Part of that list, including mandatory retirement for public servants and discrimination against homosexuals in the federal jurisdiction, was quickly acted upon and outlawed.

A comprehensive study of the *Charter* cases from 1982 to 1985 by F.L. Morton showed that the success rate for *Charter* challenges increased from 27 percent in 1982 to 35 percent in 1985. The most successful cases dealt with minority language rights (92 percent of 25 cases); the least successful dealt with aboriginal rights (all 19 failed). The most litigated legal right was the right to "life, liberty and security of the person."[72] In the first 100 *Charter* cases

---

[70] *The Revised Canadian Constitution*, p. 152. For other criticisms of the *Charter* and the way it was implemented see the excellent collection of essays in William R. McKercher, ed., *The U.S. Bill of Rights and the Charter of Rights and Freedoms* (Toronto: Ontario Economic Council, 1983).

[71] Quoted in *The Globe and Mail*, April 14, 1987.

[72] F.L. Morton, "Charting the Charter 1982–85: A Statistical Analysis," summarized by David Vienneau in "Courts and the Charter of Rights and Freedoms," in Robert J. Jackson, D. Jackson and N. Baxter-Moore, eds., *Contemporary Canadian Politics* (Scarborough, Ont.: Prentice-Hall Canada, 1987), pp. 59–60.

decided by the Supreme Court, the judges struck down provisions in 19 laws. In the late 1980s and the 1990s to date the Supreme Court has been more cautious and more reticent to strike down laws. It also has had more split decisions. In 1991, the Supreme Court handled 126 appeals, approximately one-third involving significant *Charter* issues.[73]

We conclude that Canadian judicial tradition will continue to influence the conduct of judges when they assess *Charter* implications. While the opportunity for a more active, interventionist and, some might argue, more creative, role for the judiciary now exists, this will not bring about sudden change. There will be a gradual but constant evolution in the power of the Supreme Court. It will take considerable time for precedent-setting cases to be brought before the courts and for judges to determine the nature of their new role. In the meantime, the *Charter* has become an important Canadian symbol and a significant part of the policy process, a balance to legislative power.

QUÉBEC AND THE 1982 CONSTITUTIONAL PATRIATION

Despite the facts that Prime Minister Trudeau was French Canadian, one-third of his Cabinet was from Québec and 74 of 75 MPs from Québec were Liberals (almost all of whom supported patriation), Québec's political leaders and government opposed the 1982 constitutional reform. The dissent of René Lévesque, as the lone premier opposing the agreement, caused grave concern in the rest of Canada. Québec's opposition prompted some to question whether the Supreme Court's call for "a substantial measure of provincial consent" had been achieved, given Québec's position as representative of French Canadians.

Lévesque opposed several elements of the patriation agreement. He argued first that Québec's cultural security was threatened by the restriction of its exclusive rights in linguistic matters. As we noted in Chapter 3, the *Charter*'s guarantee of access to English-speaking schools conflicted with Québec's Bill 101, which restricted admission to English schools in that province. Lévesque felt that the *Charter* tampered with his province's exclusive right to legislate on education and was therefore a threat to French dominance in Québec. He also objected that the measure of bilingualism imposed on Québec was not also imposed on Ontario although the latter has the largest minority French-speaking population of any province outside Québec.

Lévesque criticized the *Constitution*'s failure to recognize "in any tangible way" the character and needs of Québec as a distinct national society. The document treated Québec as merely another province of Canada, like all the others, he alleged. Finally, he disliked the amending formula's removal of what Québec considered its traditional veto over constitutional changes. While the *Constitution* gave Québec and the other provices financial compensation in the important areas of education and culture, Lévesque charged correctly that the amending formula does not guarantee financial compensation for provinces that choose to opt out of other programs by constitutional amendments.

The Québec government's extreme displeasure with the new federal *Constitution* was demonstrated by its strategy to circumvent it. Bill 62 was introduced and passed in the Québec Assembly. It attempted to ensure that Quebeckers' fundamental freedoms, and legal and

---

[73] *The Globe and Mail*, April 6, 1992.

equality rights would be subject only to the provincial charter of human rights, not to its new federal counterpart. According to the provisions of Bill 62, which came into force in June 1982, a new clause was to be appended to each Québec law, stating that it would operate "notwithstanding" the provision of the *Charter*. However, the notwithstanding clause does not apply to language-of-education articles in the *Constitution*. To by-pass this obstacle, Québec relied on Section 1 of the *Constitution* that states that the federal *Charter of Rights and Freedoms* guarantees the liberties it sets out "subject only to such reasonable limits prescribed by law as can be demonstrably justified in a free and democratic society." The Québec government hoped to prove in court that Bill 101's provisions could be justified on these grounds. However, in 1985 the Supreme Court rejected the Québec government's argument that the threat to the survival of the French language in North America justified Bill 101's restrictions on English school enrollment. The Court ruled that the section of Bill 101 limiting eligibility to attend English language schools to children one of whose parents had received primary education in English in Québec was "incompatible" with the constitutional guarantees set out in the Canadian *Charter of Rights and Freedoms*. In a further case in late 1988, the Supreme Court again had to rule on the constitutionality of certain clauses of Bill 101. This time it ruled that the law prohibiting business signs in languages other than French was against the *Charter*'s provisions on freedom of expression and speech. The Québec government chose to invoke the "notwithstanding" clause of the *Constitution* that allows Parliament or provincial legislatures to escape from this section of the *Charter*. It then introduced Bill 178 that required French to be used on outside signs but allowed the use of English on signs inside shops provided that French was "prominently" displayed. Once more, Québec's language law sparked intense criticism.[74] The details of these language policies were discussed in Chapter 3.

THE FAILED 1987 CONSTITUTIONAL ACCORD (MEECH LAKE AND LANGEVIN)

As indicated above, Québec was the only province that did not sign the 1982 *Constitution* Act. René Lévesque's government could not agree on the formula reached by the Prime Minister and nine other first ministers for patriating the *Constitution* and for entrenching the *Charter of Rights and Freedoms*.

The new federal Conservative government, which was elected in 1984, conducted months of bargaining to design amendments that would secure Québec's political assent to the Act. In April, 1987, Prime Minister Brian Mulroney and the ten premiers reached unanimous agreement on a constitutional text that culminated in a draft of the Meech Lake accord. The final text for the proposed constitution amendment was agreed to after an all-night bargaining session in June in the Langevin Block on Parliament Hill and is known as the Langevin amendment to the Meech Lake accord (we refer to the entire package simply as the Meech Lake accord).

---

[74] In 1993, Bill 178 was replaced by a less restrictive Bill 86 that did not require a notwithstanding clause. For opposing arguments about Québec's use of the notwithstanding clause in the *Charter of Rights* to defend its language bill, see Reg Whitaker, "The Overriding Right," and P.K. Kuruvilla, "Why Quebec was Wrong," in *Policy Options*, vol. 10, no. 4 (May 1989), pp. 3–6 and 7–8.

Québec Premier Robert Bourassa had five conditions going into the bargaining session of April 1987 at Meech Lake: a formal voice for Québec in Supreme Court appointments, a say on immigration policy, limits to federal spending powers in areas of provincial jurisdiction, a veto on constitutional amendments affecting the province and recognition of Québec as a "distinct" society. While it was generally agreed that Québec should be granted "renewed federalism," the nine other premiers also made demands concerning the Senate, federal spending power and the constitutional amending formula. Virtually all were accommodated, and therein lay the crux of the criticism of the accord — that to achieve an agreement the Prime Minister gave away powers that were necessary to maintain a strong federal government. There were seven main areas of change in the Meech Lake constitutional accord: distinct society, the Supreme Court, spending powers, veto power, immigration, the Senate and the amending formula.

Agreement on the Meech Lake accord was billed as an "historic breakthrough." However, when the euphoria subsided, serious flaws in the accord made it the subject of national dissension and concern. But none of the federal political parties was willing to risk the political consequences of voting against the accord in the House of Commons; however, the Liberals submitted eight amendments and the NDP, two. While none of these changes was accepted, John Turner and Ed Broadbent demanded party discipline in voting in favour of the resolution. Parliament passed the Meech Lake accord with little dissent. But, as the Meech Lake amendments called for a major constitutional revision, it required the approval of Parliament and *all ten* provincial legislatures.

In other quarters the "historic breakthrough" was called a "suicide pact." They argued that in the rush to accommodate Québec, the rights of other groups had been trampled and that these injustices would now be entrenched in the *Constitution*.

The Meech Lake accord, though hotly discussed in 1987, was not a significant issue in the 1988 General Election. It was overshadowed by the issue of free trade. All three major political parties agreed that the benefit of winning Premier Bourassa's support for a revised *Constitution* was greater than the problems inherent in the ambiguities of the accord. No party wanted to risk the wrath of Québec voters by endangering the agreement, although the Liberal party did present a series of amendments that it promised to implement as soon as the accord became law.

The essential criticism of the accord was that, in the pressure to win over Québec, important federal powers that would weaken Parliament and the federal government were given away. To give the provinces this kind of control of national institutions would represent a change in the established notion of federalism. Provincial influence is extremely important in the federal system, but it has always been subject to a unique system of checks and balances. The Meech Lake accord would have changed the established lines of demarcation. Regionalists argued, however, that the Meech Lake accord was a positive affirmation of cooperative federalism and that it would solve many problems in federal/provincial relations. Individuals and groups launched numerous challenges against the government, arguing that the federal Government was handing over so much power to the provinces that Canada would be transformed from a federation into a confederacy. Said one of them: "We are seeking a declaration that the federal Government does not have the constitutional power to destroy Canadian federalism."[75]

---

[75] *The Globe and Mail*, Sept. 26, 1988.

In the final analysis, the Meech Lake accord was defeated because it required unanimity from the provinces, and two provinces (Manitoba and Newfoundland) failed to pass the necessary resolution before the ratification deadline of June 23, 1990. When the proposals did not obtain unanimity, the whole package died and constitutional matters became even more complicated. Canada did not expire with the Meech Lake accord, as the Prime Minister had threatened. Life went on. However, the Québec independence issue — dormant since the 1980 referendum — was given a new burst of respectability. Predictably, Premier Bourassa announced he would not attend any future federal-provincial conferences, and the Québec National Assembly passed Bill 150, which required a referendum on "sovereignty" to be put to the people by October 26, 1992.

For over two years Canadians debated the pros and cons of the Meech Lake accord. But it was the wrong debate. The question should not have been "Meech Lake or no Meech Lake?" but "What is the best constitutional arrangement for Canada?"

A NEW CONSTITUTIONAL APPROACH

Following the death of the Meech Lake accord, there was an appropriate period of political mourning followed by numerous government-sponsored conferences, symposiums, federal-provincial meetings and even a Royal Commission. Having insisted that it was Meech or death, Prime Minister Mulroney needed time to resuscitate the corpse. Unfortunately, the federal government ignored the report of the Charest parliamentary committee that had provided detailed proposals to amend the Meech Lake accord but left its substance intact. That sober report had received all-party agreement in the House of Commons, but was left shelved and forgotten. Instead, another new strategy was devised that created new constitutional packages even larger and more indigestible than the Meech Lake accord.

In a June 1990 confidential briefing to *The Globe and Mail*, Prime Minister Mulroney made some candid remarks that revealed what his new constitutional strategy would be. He indicated that he would delay and temporize until all the political forces could come to some agreement.

> *Anything that happens…is going to be killed with kindness in the future. You will not be able to get me to ever cut off debate on a constitutional resolution. They can go on for as long as they want — years. I want to hear everybody, I want them recorded. I want them filmed. I want documents. I want…and if I've missed anybody I'm going to reopen it…*
>
> *And then when it's done, then we are going to take it and we're going to pass it. Which means that other people are going to have to do the work and they'll be — the country will be better off, the process will be better off, the politicians will have a lot less say in it, which is what should happen and it'll be better for Canada because it will be close to the people.*[76]

Following this strategy, the Prime Minister responded to the wave of populism in the country by raising more democratic procedures — some new, some old. In order to quell the populist element, the Prime Minister and his new constitutional minister Joe Clark initiated new consultations with the people and the premiers, minus the Premier of Québec who boycotted all meetings. The earlier harder-line strategy based on a set of perceived principles about how a decentralized federation should operate changed to an absolute brokerage model of negotiation.

---

[76] *The Globe and Mail*, private transcript, June 20, 1990.

THE SPICER COMMISSION

The first concrete step in "killing with kindness" was the Spicer Commission. Headed by the former official language commissioner Keith Spicer, its mandate was to consult the public about grievances and wishes for new constitutional proposals and clarify the very idea of Canada. And, of course, it was meant to keep the public occupied while the government prepared a new proposal to replace the Meech Lake accord.

The Commission provided a forum for concerned Canadians to express themselves. But by the time the report was completed on June 27, 1991, the commissioners were almost as divided and quarrelsome as the people they had interviewed. The Commission's mandate had been to listen and to educate. But, since the critics they listened to were self-selected rather than chosen by a proper sampling technique, there was no way of knowing how representative their disgruntled views were of Canadians as a whole. The report did, however, help to clarify some perceived problems. And since one must be clear about a diagnosis before offering a prescription, that was helpful. But just what was the cause of the illness and what political prescription would remedy it?

Unfortunately, the Spicer report was unable to sustain a logical connection between the complaint and its cure. It provided no clearly defined idea of what Canada is or could be, and no coherent suggestions for how to actualize Canadian aspirations. For example, the report upheld a vision of a united Canada that respects diversity. But then it recommended taking government funding away from multicultural groups; an action that would have increased charges of favoritism.

The report found that Canadians were worried and unhappy about the country's economic direction. Consequently, it recommended that the government clarify why traditional values needed to be usurped by market forces. The report addressed some of the country's major fault lines. It said that many Canadians were upset with bilingualism as a national policy. It recommended an independent review of the official language policy and how it is applied. But since the Commissioner of Official Languages already issues a report that is discussed in Parliament and examined in minute detail every year, this proposal was not particularly helpful. Native Canadians, too, received respectful recognition by the comissioners, with a recommendation in favour of Native self-government and recognition in the *Constitution*.

After great expense and enormous publicity, the Spicer Commission report fizzled like a defective firecracker. The public had had its say, and the report was shelved.

THE LAST, THE ALMOST LAST AND THE NEXT PROPOSALS

The stage was set for a new government initiative. The Prime Minister introduced his new constitutional package known as *Shaping Canada's Future Together* on September 24, 1991. Unlike during the Meech Lake accord disussions, this time the proposals were *not* supposed to be engraved in stone; comments and proposed changes were encouraged.[77] For a while, there was little reaction as Canadians of all political persuasions were nervous about being depicted as naysayers or, worse yet, against Canada. Much commentary centred on the good intentions of the government rather than on the contents of the package itself.

In presenting its new proposal, the government promised to mend its ways and listen to the people, and even offered a definition of "distinct society," a term that had been kept

---

[77] *Shaping Canada's Future Together* (Ottawa: Supply and Services, 1991).

ambiguous the first time round. However, apart from that one definition, practically everything else cried out for precision and explanation. *Shaping Canada's Future Together* included hundreds of concrete amendments hidden in the garb of 27 global suggestions. Not only were the proposals themselves vague, but the result of the relations among them was completely unknown, possibly even unknowable.

Once again, the proposals were too decentralizing and too multi-layered to allow effective and efficient government. Again they created the possibility of a checkerboard Canada. A few examples make this clear. The residual clause — peace, order and good government — that has been used in the past to give necessary powers to the federal government, was to be weakened by giving "non-national matters" to the provincial authorities. This indicated that the environment, for example, might be construed as a provincial matter so that federal regulations would not apply. As well, the "declaratory power" that was used to allow the federal government to take control of grain elevators and keep its transportation moving during the Depression was to be eliminated. The West had supported the decision to use such power during that period, but later worried that Ottawa might use the same power to control oil wells during the energy crisis of the 1970s.

Besides giving up these precise powers, the federal government proposed to withdraw from several specific jurisdictions. Some withdrawals were reasonable, such as in job training, but proposals to "streamline" other powers were more controversial. Another major area of concern arose over the reform proposals that would have created a complicated Rubik's cube of federal institutions. The Senate, as proposed, was too powerful as a policy and law-making body compared to the House of Commons — giving it the right, for example, to ratify major order-in-council positions, a right that is denied to the House.

The document also committed the government to give MPs "more free votes and to reduce the application of votes of confidence." This was mere rhetoric. The government had made this same recommendation in the mid-1980s but never acted on it. The government already can "free" its backbenchers at any time, on any vote, but it does not do so because cohesive political parties are, and should remain, an integral part of Canada's form of government. At any rate, the motivations and behaviour of future MPs cannot be significantly moulded by the *Constitution*. (See Chapter 8.)

The *pièce de résistance* in the proposal was a new layer of appointed government — the Council of the Federation — to be added on top of the House of Commons, an elected, powerful Senate and First Ministers' conferences. This undemocratic body, consisting of 13 representatives — one appointed by Ottawa, one by each of the provinces and territories — would have had a major influence on shared-cost programs, would have ratified the federal government's new economic powers and would have set up guidelines for raising and spending taxes. Of course, such a powerful council would be in constant conflict with the elected Parliament of Canada over these important tasks.

Instead of streamlining government, and making it more efficient and less expensive, *Shaping Canada's Future Together* proposed to create a cumbersome monster of institutions with the potential to generate more problems than it could solve.

DOBBIE-BEAUDOIN AND THE FIVE CONSTITUTIONAL CONFERENCES

The federal constitutional suggestions in *Shaping Canada's Future Together* were examined at length by a joint House and Senate Committee on a Renewed Canada (known as Dobbie-Beaudoin), in order to produce yet another set of proposals. As the government's 27 proposals were mildly criticized by the committee and savagely attacked in Québec, the Dobbie-

Reproduced with permission, Dennis Pritchard.

Beaudoin committee itself became the object of debate and derision for its poor organization.

In keeping with its promise to allow public input, the joint House and Senate committee held five constitutional conferences across the country. However, there was no deeply hidden consensus about political arrangements in Canada waiting to be plumbed by public meetings, merely a confused and discordant babel of social, economic and language interests. In fact, in the conferences, efforts were made to add even more controversial proposals to the constitutional deliberations, such as ensuring that half of all Senators would be women, entrenching agriculture protection for western farmers and guaranteeing price protection for Prince Edward Island potatoes.

No one was surprised that the conferences did not produce a consensus. The few participants who attended the conferences emerged with glowing reports about how much they had learned about other Canadians and about the system of government and its problems. They felt renewed in their commitment to the country and projected the image of having attended veritable love-ins. But, since it was impossible to provide such an intensive learning situation for every Canadian, it was, from an overall perspective, a waste of time and money.

After these extensive hearings, the joint committee presented a revised set of proposals on February 28, 1992. Québec remained aloof. Neither the government's *Shaping Canada's Future Together* nor the Dobbie-Beaudoin proposals were formally offered to Québec and the other provinces, but they were turned down in principle by members of Québec's political elite as insufficient to provide the type of framework required to keep Canada together.

As for the Official Opposition, the federal Liberals had issued their own nine-point agenda on constitutional reform in April 1991, but by July 1992 their leader, Jean Chrétien, was sufficiently disillusioned to suggest that a moratorium on constitutional reform should be considered.

THE CONSTITUTIONAL DEBATE CONTINUES

Despite all these reports and public consultations the federal government still had no acceptable proposals. And instead of collapsing with exhaustion from all the kindness, public cynicism and criticism of the whole process was growing. Since Québec in effect vetoed *Shaping Canada's Future Together* and the Dobbie-Beaudoin committee report, the federal government was forced back to the drawing board yet again.

The Prime Minister put the next phase of constitutional meetings in the hands of Joe Clark. Under Clark's guidance the federal government called several meetings with nine provinces, two territorial governments and four aboriginal groups. The aboriginal groups themselves then enlisted economic, women's and nationalist umbrella groups to advise them. Québec did not attend. The first of these meetings to draft new constitutional proposals to offer to Québec took place on March 12, 1992. Four months later, on July 7, 1992 an agreement was reached by these leaders in what they termed the "Pearson agreement."

The Meech Lake failure had not killed Canada, but it had ended Conservative Party unity. When the accord died on June 23, 1990 Mulroney's hand-picked, former separatist leader, Lucien Bouchard, left the Cabinet and formed the Bloc Québécois, with a band of dissident Québec nationalists who already held seats in the House of Commons. The Québec government, meanwhile, continued to be bound by Bill 150 that called for a provincial referendum on sovereignty by October 27, 1992. The National Assembly set up the Commission on the Political and Constitutional Future of Québec (known as Campeau-Bélanger) — hearings that led to provincial consultations and, eventually, two parliamentary committees: one to examine the costs of sovereignty and the other to examine any offers on renewed federalism that might come from Canada.

Québec's most divisive input into the constitutional debate came on January 28, 1991 from the Liberal Party's Allaire report, *A Quebec Free to Choose*, a document that proposed drastic decentralization of the country. Québec would "exercise exclusive discretionary and total authority in most fields of activity." According to the report, 22 domains should be in the exclusive power of Québec, including communications, energy, industry and commerce, regional development and income security. Ottawa was assigned only currency, customs and tariffs, debt management and transfer payments. Decisions of Québec courts on these jurisdictions and other questions would no longer be appealable to the Supreme Court of Canada.

The strong decentralizing thrust of the Allaire report was totally unacceptable to most Canadians because it would have greatly weakened the country. However, it was intended to keep pressure on the federal government and set a strong negotiation position for Québec, and that it accomplished.

The Allaire proposals cried out for asymmetry with different status for different provinces or regions within the country depending on their special needs. Canada already has some asymmetry in such areas as agriculture, immigration and the environment. But this does not mean that further asymmetry would be acceptable to the country.

THE PEARSON BUILDING PROPOSALS

By the spring of 1992 it was time for Mr. Mulroney to begin a countdown. Both the federal government and the provinces were under pressure from Québec's looming referendum. On July 7, 1992, the federal government (led by Mr. Clark), the nine provinces, two territorial governments and native leaders came to a tentative agreement on, to a large extent, what the major provincial players bargained for. In total the proposals would have given more power to the provinces and weakened federal authority. Québec representatives, of course, had neither attended the meetings nor agreed to the proposals it produced.

Characterized by those present at that decisive meeting in the Lester B. Pearson building as a "constitutional breakthrough," the proposals would have amended the *Constitution* in multiple respects. The thrust of the deal can be described simply. Québec would have gotten everything mentioned in the Meech Lake accord, including a veto over future constitutional amendments and recognition as a 'distinct society,' in return for satisfying Alberta's desire for a triple-E Senate. Aboriginals, too, would have their wishes granted, with a form of self-government. News commentary tended to concentrate on whether the agreement would "fly" with all the provinces and "sell" in Québec. An "agreement at any price" was necessary to save Canada. The "do or die" atmosphere was shades of Meech all over again.

THE FAILED 1992 CHARLOTTETOWN ACCORD

The Pearson Building agreement drew Bourassa out of his bunker in Québec City. After two years of boycotting constitutional discussions, he returned to the bargaining table on August 4, 1992 along with the Prime Minister, the other premiers and the leaders of the territories and the aboriginal communities. The result was a complex and highly controversial constitutional deal known as the Charlottetown accord, agreed to on August 28, 1992. It consisted of an agreement on principles — not a legal text — about what changes should be made to the *Constitution*, further political accords to be negotiated, and an agreement to put the tentative principles to the Canadian people in a country-wide referendum. The contents can be summarized under the following six headings.

MEECH PLUS OR MINUS: THE RESPONSE TO QUÉBEC

The Meech Lake proposals essentially had consisted of five parts — distinct society, a veto, immigration powers, restrictions on federal spending, and appointments to the Supreme Court — each of which responded to an earlier demand by the government of Québec. The same demands were addressed by the Charlottetown accord, but it went much further. It also included proposals to add a definition for distinct society to the *Constitution* in a new clause that would ensure that "Quebec constitutes within Canada a distinct society, which includes a French-speaking majority, a unique culture and a civil law tradition." As well, the proposals affirmed the role of the legislature and Government of Québec "to preserve and promote the distinct society of Quebec."

In other areas, such as immigration, the Charlottetown proposals slightly softened the Meech Lake accord. Under Meech, Québec was to obtain a fixed share of immigrants to Canada. Under Charlottetown, Ottawa would only have been committed to negotiate agreements with the provinces, a policy that was already the practice. And, if the federal government spent money in a new Canada-wide shared-cost program in a field of exclusive provincial jurisdiction, as in Meech, a province would have been able to claim compensation if it had a program that was "compatible with the national objectives." On Supreme Court appointments, there was no change from Meech. The current practice of appointing three Supreme Court judges from Québec would have been constitutionalized, only now Ottawa would have been required to select all judges from lists supplied by the provinces.

The main difference between the Meech Lake accord and the Charlottetown proposals was over the constitutional veto. Charlottetown would have given all provinces a veto over future constitutional changes to the country's major political institutions. On the surface this looked as though it met Québec's earlier demands, but in fact it fell far short. The veto would have applied only "after" the Charlottetown changes were made part of the *Constitution*, in particular those concerning reform of the federal institutions. As in Meech, Québec wanted the veto to ensure that it could prevent a Senate reform of which it did not approve. Québec also wanted a veto over the creation of new provinces, but the Charlottetown accord would have allowed the federal Parliament to create new provinces through a simple bilateral agreement with Ottawa. Moreover, since the proposed changes to the amending formula would have increased the number of matters that required unanimity, every province — not just Québec — would have had an even greater capacity to veto further constitutional proposals. If this change were accepted, it would have been almost impossible to correct any deficiencies in the *Constitution* at a later time.

Clearly, most of the "offers" that were made to Québec in Meech Lake were included in Charlottetown, but some were damped down. The deal, therefore, was bound to find opposition both inside and outside Québec.

THE CANADA CLAUSE

The Charlottetown deal called for a major innovation in the way Canada is governed. A "Canada Clause" was to be included in the *Constitution* to express fundamental Canadian values. That clause was extremely important as it would have been justiciable — that is, the courts would have been able to use the Canada Clause to guide *all* future interpretations of the *entire Constitution*. As an interpretative provision it would have been binding on the courts in every constitutional case.

Eight "fundamental values" were expressed in the Canada Clause. They included values related to democracy, aboriginal rights, the distinct society of Québec, linguistic duality, racial and ethnic equality, individual and collective human rights, the equality of female and male persons and the equality of the provinces.

On careful scrutiny, the Canada Clause proved to be replete with errors of consistency and fairness. It proposed a hierarchy of fundamental Canadian values. While "Canadians and their governments" would have been committed to the development of language minority communities, only "Canadians" were committed to racial and ethnic equality, individual and collective human rights, the equality of female and male persons and the equality of the provinces. The implication was clear. Governments would have been committed to take action — and presumably to spend money — to defend some groups but not others.

Moreover, some Canadian groups were left out of the Canada Clause altogether. Whereas the *Charter of Rights and Freedoms* stipulates equality for people who are physically or mentally handicapped, and asserts that individuals should not be discriminated against by age, the proposed Canada Clause overlooked these values altogether. Thus, the clause provided a hierarchy in which some groups would be protected by government, other groups would be protected only by Canadians, and still other groups such as the handicapped, seniors, and children would not be mentioned at all.

DIVISION OF POWERS

The new proposals called for the decentralization of some current federal authority. Job training and culture were to be given to the provinces congruent with their present authority in the field of education. The Charlottetown accord was nuanced on these two topics, however. In job training, the federal government's power would have been narrowed to exclusive jurisdiction for unemployment insurance and involvement in the establishment of national objectives for labour market development. As well, the federal government would have been excluded from a meaningful role in retraining workers for the new global economy. Culture, too, would have been divided artificially between two levels of government. The provinces would have had exclusive jurisdiction over culture "within the provinces," and the federal government would have retained powers over existing national cultural institutions, including the grants and contributions delivered by those institutions. If these proposals had been constitutionalized, the designation of "culture" as an area of exclusive provincial jurisdiction would have led to endless constitutional wrangling in the Supreme Court. As well, the Charlottetown accord called for the federal government to withdraw from several areas including forestry, mining, housing, recreation, tourism and municipal and urban affairs.

At best, in all of these decentralizing proposals, policies on which Canadians have grown to depend might remain intact. At worst, some important policies, such as subsidized housing for the needy, might have been discontinued. This rather wide spectrum of possibility proved that the federal government still did not have a handle on viable constitutional change.

NATIVE SELF-GOVERNMENT

The demands of Native peoples were not addressed by the Meech Lake proposal and, in the final analysis, this omission contributed to its demise. Native MPP Elijah Harper was the key figure in the Manitoba legislature's rejection of that accord. His dramatic action made him a folk hero and stimulated increased pressure for native self-government in the next round of constitutional negotiations. As the post-Meech negotiations began, new Native positions were staked out. In one early demand, the leader of the Assembly of First Nations, Ovide Mercredi, asked for all 54 aboriginal languages to have equal status with English and French and for all aboriginal groups to have equal political status with the provinces. In May, 1992, Joe Clark announced that all provinces except Québec had accepted the "third level of government" principle for Native peoples. Clark admitted, however, that the details of how such a third level would relate to existing federal and provincial jurisdictions would have to be negotiated politically rather than entrenched in the *Constitution*.

The Charlottetown proposal went some way toward satisfying aboriginal demands. The Canada Clause said that aboriginals "have the right to promote their languages, cultures and traditions and to ensure the integrity of their societies, and that their governments constitute one of three orders of government in Canada." The proposals also included an expanded definition of aboriginal people, a political accord for the Métis and treaty rights to be affirmed in the *Constitution*. During the first five years of the agreement native groups would not have been able to employ these clauses in cases before the courts.

Even among staunch supporters of the aboriginal cause, there was considerable controversy over these undefined rights. Newfoundland Premier Clyde Wells expressed concern about whether the same or different laws would apply to Native and non-Native

Newfoundlanders. The most direct attack on the concept of aboriginal rights, however, came from a Québec government report entitled "An Analysis of the Impact of the Constitutional Recognition of the Inherent Right to Self-Government." It described the proposal as "unquestionably the most profound change to the political structure of Canada since 1867."[78]

The report declared that a self-government clause would "threaten Québec's territorial integrity and weaken provincial powers," and without Québec's approval would probably be unconstitutional "because creating a new order of government requires the unanimous consent of all the partners to Confederation." Further, it argued that such an agreement would violate the *Charter*, which calls for all Canadians to be treated equally under the law. It judged that approval of aboriginal self-government would be exorbitantly expensive, and that territorial disputes and land claims would have a much stronger legal basis. As the report put it: "There is reason to believe that the aboriginal peoples will not be satisfied with the lands they now occcupy; they will seek to acquire new land." Brian Craik, Director of Federal Relations for the Grand Council of Crees of Québec, replied that Québec has nothing to fear, that in time the Crees would claim vast areas of northern Québec and the Mohawks huge parts of southern Québec, but only as a "starting point for a workable solution for all parties involved."[79]

Elsewhere, the main complaint was that too many small governments might emerge if native self-government were placed in the *Constitution*. Worries were also expressed that band and tribal councils would want to negotiate their own laws to govern schools, justice systems, child-welfare agencies, and other community organizations. Critics asked if self-government could mean up to 600 tiny governments. If so, would this constitute a new form of segregation? Would the Criminal Code apply to Native peoples? Would educational standards or environmental regulations apply?

Advocates said there was no cause for worry on either theoretical or practical grounds. The Charlottetown deal stated that a law passed by a government of aboriginal peoples "may not be inconsistent with those laws which are essential to the preservation of peace, order and good government in Canada." But this did not eliminate the fear, because the text also specified that "this agreement would not extend the legislative authority of Parliament or the legislatures of the provinces." The practical aspects of native self-government were clearer. The process would have been extremely drawn out and only about 30 aboriginal governments could have been created in the next half-dozen years. The proposals also circumscribed the power of aboriginal groups to act precipitously by calling for an orderly transition negotiated "in good faith." Moreover, some provinces may still have been able to opt out of the agreement, and there was no guarantee how much federal or provincial funding would have been available to pay for self-government.

Even among those who favour self-government for Native peoples, there was a concern that the participants in the negotiations did not fully understand the implications of change for such issues as jurisdictions, lands, resources, human rights and economic and financial considerations. The Charlottetown accord was replete with such ambiguities and contradictions. Should constitutional amendments of such magnitude be left to the courts to rule on after five years elapse? One wondered if the self-government clause was a "blank

---

[78]   *The Globe and Mail*, July 23, 1992.

[79]   Ibid.

cheque," and why it was necessary to make such massive changes in such a short time. As Ed Roberts, a Newfoundland minister, put it when he described the first aboriginal package as an "incredible mess":

> "We are doing things and we know not what we do. I don't say that with any joy or any happiness, but believe me we have not thought them through."[80]

SOCIAL AND ECONOMIC UNION

If the Charlottetown agreement had been passed the country would have enjoyed a "social and economic union." The agreement set out objectives for the social union on such topics as providing "a health care system which is comprehensive, universal, portable, publicly administered and accessible," "high quality primary and secondary education to all individuals resident in Canada" and "reasonable access to post-secondary education." Laudable as these goals are, they are reminiscent of the constitution of the former USSR — they are merely slogans and platitudes. Even the Canadian first ministers realized this when they concluded in the agreement that citizens could not rely on these statements in the courts. They were — as they agreed — "not justiciable." Honest politicians would also have pointed out that a non-enforceable social charter is no substitute for real legislative capacity to set national standards.

The Charlottetown agreement also committed governments to free trade within Canada. Among other clauses it called for "the free movement of persons, goods, services and capital," "full employment" and a "reasonable standard of living." These clauses (which were to be placed in the *Constitution*) could not have been taken before the courts. Canadians were asked to trust the rhetoric of political leaders. Even Michael Wilson, the government's trade minister, attacked the Pearson proposals as providing too many exceptions — enough to outweigh any good done by the provision of an economic union. The final Charlottetown agreement was even worse than Wilson imagined. It did not *commit* the eleven governments to anything at all; nor did it allow the courts to make decisions on the basis of the economic union clause.

PROPOSED INSTITUTIONAL CHANGES

The Charlottetown proposals called for a drastic overhaul of the federal institutions. The changes can be summarized briefly as follows:

House of Commons   If the Charlottetown proposal had been accepted, the membership of the House of Commons would have been increased to 337. Ontario and Québec would have obtained 18 additional seats, BC four, and Alberta two. As well, Québec would have been guaranteed no fewer than 25 percent of the seats in the House of Commons. The issue of female and aboriginal representation would have been left for future consideration.

Senate

1. The Senate was to be elected either by the population of a province or territory or by a legislative assembly.

---

[80] *Ottawa Citizen*, July 29, 1992.

2. The Senate was initially to total 62 Senators. It was to be composed of six Senators from each province and one Senator from each territory.
3. The Senate would not be able to force the resignation of a government.
4. The Senate would have had some authority over legislation:
    i) It would have been able to delay revenue and expenditure bills for 30 days by a suspensive veto. After that period, the House of Commons would have been able to act on its own. But fundamental policy changes to the tax system (such as the Goods and Services Tax and the National Energy Program) were to be excluded from this section and handled as ordinary legislation.
    ii) It would have had veto power over all legislation on natural resources.
    iii) It would have been able, by a majority vote, to trigger a joint sitting with the House of Commons on all ordinary legislation. The joint sitting would have ultimate authority over this referred legislation.
    iv) On matters that materially affect the French language or culture a double majority of anglophone and francophone Senators would have been required.
5. The Senate would have had to ratify the appointment of the Governor of the Bank of Canada and other key federal appointments.

INSTITUTIONAL COMPLEXITY

Critics listed 10 ways that these proposed institutional arrangements were inadequate.

1. It increasingly would be regarded as unfair to give Québec 25% of the seats in the House of Commons in perpetuity. In 1992, Québec had 25.3% of the population. Demographers predicted it would drop below 25% by the end of the decade and down to 23.5% by the year 2011. By contrast, Ontario, British Columbia and Alberta are all predicted to grow substantially.
2. Equal provincial representation in the Senate would be a source of constant irritation. Ontario, with a population of 10 million, would have been awarded six Senators, the same number as Prince Edward Island, which is the size of Nepean, a suburb of Ottawa. The distortion was too great.
3. National standards should be maintained in federal institutions. With these new proposals Canada would have had Senatorial elections in some places and nominations in others. It would not have been seen as an improvement to allow the Québec National Assembly rather than the federal Prime Ministers to appoint Senators.
4. Since there were to be simultaneous elections for the House and Senate, appointed Senators from Québec or elsewhere made no sense. After a General Election that swept one party into power in Ottawa, the Québec National Assembly could have appointed Senators who did not reflect that change. The electoral results would count everywhere but Québec — or wherever Senators were appointed.
5. There would have been too many ways for the Senate to tie up the government and prevent it from acting. Fifty percent of the Senate (representing at minimum only 13.2% of the Canadian population) would have been able to

block all taxation on natural resources and force all ordinary legislation to a joint sitting with the House of Commons.

6. The Senate's power to send all ordinary legislation, including such major issues as the Goods and Services Tax, to a joint sitting with the House was controversial. Government business might have been disrupted and responsible government diminished.

7. The double majority of anglophone and francophone Senators required to pass language and cultural legislation might have proven troublesome. A double majority meant that as few as three Parti Québécois Senators (likely there would be only be six francophones) would be able to block all the remaining Senators from action. And, a majority of English Senators could have blocked something Québec wanted in this field.

8. The Senate was to have a controlling veto over higher government appointments. The House of Commons, the major democratic institution, would only have been able to scrutinize appointments. Why? So that a tiny proportion of the public representing the smallest five provinces could prevent appointments that the government, majority of the members of the House of Commons and most of the people wanted?

9. If the Senate delayed the legislation of a minority government, the situation would have been destabilizing for responsible government. When there was a divided House, the joint sitting would not have been controlled by MPs. The combination of House and Senate could have blocked legislation and forced the formation of a new government, a new cabinet coalition or a general election. As well, politicians often block one bill in order to prevent a totally different one from getting through. Senators would have been able to block appointments, taxation on resources and language and culture bills, and force ordinary legislation to a joint sitting until they got compromises on other matters of which they disapproved.

10. The costs of Parliament would have been much too high given the size of the Canadian population. Taxpayers would have picked up extensive new bills. A House of Commons with 337 seats would have made it more than three-quarters the size of the United States House of Representatives (435) with one-tenth the population. As well, Members cost more than Senators and elected Senators would cost more than appointed Senators. The costs of paying for the new Parliament would have been too great.

The proposed Rubik's cube of institutions would have worked effectively *only* when the following *two conditions* prevailed. First, Canada would need a majority, not a minority, government. Since the Second World War, almost half of the governments have been in a minority situation. Second, there would have to be a federalist government in Québec. Without these two conditions in place, the constitutional arrangements would further weaken government and fracture the federal system. If there were a separatist government in Québec, the federal government would be handicapped in dealing with it.

THE CHARLOTTETOWN SENATE: A DANGEROUS ATTRACTION

Prime Minister Mulroney was cornered by the proponents of a triple-E Senate. His 1984 and 1988 electoral successes and the composition of his cabinet and caucus were based on a

Québec-Alberta alliance. If he opted for what Québec wanted — namely Meech Lake plus — he would lose support in the West, particularly in Alberta, unless he also bought off westerners with a form of triple-E. For that reason, he accepted the Charlottetown proposals for the Senate — a combination of deals.

The Prime Minister was wise to prevent the adoption of a full triple-E Senate as was advocated particularly by Don Getty, Gary Filmon and Clyde Wells (then premiers of Alberta, Manitoba and Newfoundland, respectively). Triple-E is not the answer to regional discontent. In fact, it could prove to be a serious threat to equal rights, responsible government and legislative efficiency in Canada. However, according to the critics of the Charlottetown deal the Prime Minister was wrong to accept even the equality provisions of the triple-E concept as he did in the Charlottetown accord. They argued that the most democratic form of representation is one person, one vote — "rep by pop." Ideally, all citizens should have the same amount of political weight, no matter who they are, where they live or how they vote. Distorting this basic democratic principle to provide extra representation for less populous regions is no more worthy a goal than to provide extra representation for special groups such as the rich. Regional aspirations should be met, but establishing a basically unjust system of representation is not the way to do it.

Supporters of triple-E point to the examples of Australia and the United States to illustrate what a good idea it is. They use rose-coloured glasses that filter out some very harsh realities. Take the United States comparison. The Canadian and American political systems are very different, and no single feature transferred from one to the other will work the same way in its new surroundings. In particular, the American system has a strong President whose powers can be used to overcome the divisions caused by a deadlock between the House and Senate.

This is simply not the case in Canada. We do not have a President to promote unity for the country and effectiveness for government. Deadlock and delay would paralyze government in this country if Senate powers were equal to those of the House. How could a do-nothing government solve regional alienation?

Even assuming the best, which would be that a U.S.-style Senate could work as well in Canada as it does in the United States, there still would be no justification for adopting it. There is no reliable evidence that the United States' political system delivers peace, order or good government any better than the Canadian system.

Triple-E supporters argue that Australia may be an even better model than the United States for Canada to follow, because it has a relatively similar system of government. This is true. But even here one should be extremely cautious. The reality is that triple-E down under has done little to ameliorate regional tensions and has sometimes made matters worse. The problem with simple comparison is that one must look beyond the similar formal-legal structure of Australian government to the politics within it. For example, Australian politics is organized by parties, and party discipline in the upper chamber ensures that Senators only rarely vote against measures supported by their own party in the lower chamber. In effect, this means that Australian Senators are *not* more effective advocates for the regions they represent than the members of the lower house.

The Australian Senate can also become a house of obstruction. During the mid-1970s, an intractable deadlock between the Senate and the House of Representatives over the budget precipitated dissolution of both houses and a constitutional crisis. The political process has since returned to "normal," but the possibility of another such crisis remains and is worrisome to Australian experts. Under the Charlottetown proposals, such deadlocks would have developed regularly between the House and Senate.

Canada and Australia both have responsible government in which the majority party dominates. Citizens know who to credit or blame for different policies and outcomes, and ideally can support the incumbent party or choose among other competing visions or platforms at election time. In Australia, responsible government is preserved at the expense of regional representation. If the proposed new Canadian Senate had blocked legislation, what would have happened to the idea of responsible government?

How would the government have been held responsible to the people when the proposals it initiated were ultimately turned down by the Senate? Clearly, the two concepts of responsible government and regional representation are in irremediable conflict. If we decide regional representation should dominate, then we have to jettison responsible government, separate the executive and legislative branches, and adopt the American congressional system and possibly elect a President.

The main problem with the existing Senate is that it lacks legitimacy because it is based on political appointments. The Charlottetown agreement pretended to remedy this. In fact, it would have made it worse. The Senate would have consisted of a hodge-podge of elected and appointed members because the rules could be different for each province. Québec, for example, would have appointed its six Senators by a vote in the National Assembly. Ordinary citizens would not even have had to be consulted. Such a Senate would have no more legitimacy than the current upper house.

THE 1992 CONSTITUTIONAL REFERENDUM

On August 28, 1992, the Prime Minister, the 10 premiers and leaders of the major aboriginal communities agreed on the constitutional text discussed above. More significantly, they agreed to put the Charlottetown package of proposals to the people in a referendum on October 26, 1992. All three federal party leaders also agreed to the Charlottetown accord and to the referendum. The opponents of the accord appeared weak and disunited. Jacques Parizeau, leader of the Parti Québécois and Lucien Bouchard, leader of the Bloc Québécois in Québec were opposed. Preston Manning was the most outspoken leader outside of Québec although he was joined by Liberals such as Sharon Carstairs in Manitoba and Gordon Smith in British Columbia. But the real leader of the "no" side proved once again to be former prime minister Pierre Elliot Trudeau who attacked the constitutional deal with fervour and logic.

As the third national referendum in Canadian history (for the constitutional campaign, politics and earlier referenda see Chapter 11) it proved a divisive, corrosive event. In the final analysis, six provinces decisively voted against the deal and only Newfoundland, Prince Edward Island and New Brunswick voted strongly for it. Ontario very narrowly supported the deal while Yukon voted against and the Northwest Territories voted for the deal. At the national level 72 percent of the Canadian electorate cast their votes and defeated the proposal 54.4 percent to 44.6 percent. The Charlottetown proposal was dead.

The unexpected defeat led federal and provincial politicians to one inexorable conclusion — it was time for a moritorium on constitutional discussions. With a federal election due before the end of 1993 and a Québec provincial election in 1994 the leaders turned to "politics as usual." Only one amendment came out of all this constitutional wrangling from 1984 to 1993. In February 1993, Parliament passed an amendment approved by the New Brunswick legislature to the effect that "The English linguistic community and the French linguistic community in New Brunswick have equality of status and equal rights and priv-

ileges, including the right to distinct cultural institutions as are necessary for the preservation and promotion of those communties." Since this amendment only affected one province
it did not need the agreement of the others. Even this small change, however, took two parliamentary efforts to have it passed. As New Democrat Lorne Nystrom ruefully put it, "It had
to be that way. It had to be screwed up in the end."[81]

In the next chapter we examine in greater detail federalism and its challenges in
Canada.

OVERVIEW

It is clear that the Canadian *Constitution* is not a single document that provides clear direction to the political process. As in most democratic countries, it is both a product of the political system and a significant factor in shaping it. The Canadian *Constitution* can be said to
include both written and unwritten dimensions. Among the unwritten elements are the
British parliamentary heritage and the democratic norms and values inculcated in the
Canadian political culture. The written dimensions of the Canadian *Constitution* include the
well-known *British North America Act* of 1867 (now the *Constitution Act, 1867*) and the *Canada
Act* of 1982, as well as a number of other acts and documents. The *Constitution Act* has been
altered or expanded numerous times since 1867 by formal amendments and by legal
interpretations by the Judicial Committee of the Privy Council and the Supreme Court of
Canada.

Since the patriation of the *Constitution Act, 1982* with its new amending formula and *Charter
of Rights and Freedoms*, the role of the courts in the political process has increased considerably. The new *Charter* is even more comprehensive than the *Bill of Rights* in the United States,
and it has strengthened the position of the judicial branch of government in Canada. The
Charter ensures that legislators who enact laws must be prepared to justify any inequality
of burdens those laws may impose. By doing so, it allows an avenue for minorities and other
previously unempowered groups to participate more effectively in the law-making process.
This new feature in the *Constitution* will greatly increase litigation, but should also enhance
the democratic quality of government and provide arbitration by a forum that is less
vulnerable to the influence of powerful majorities than is the political arena. Court decisions
have already begun to subtly alter the makeup of the country by reducing situations where
laws vary from province to province.

The 1992 Charlottetown accord was designed to accommodate provincial interest in
Confederation. Its defeat has prevented Canada from becoming even more decentralized.
But challenges to the viability of the state continue unabated. Have we patriated the
Constitution only to find ourselves mired in constitutional deadlock? The amendment pro-
cedures may well prove too rigid to resolve deficiencies that are already glaringly evident
in the country. The constitutional dilemma of how to solve regional aspirations as well as
Québec's precise demands while retaining a powerful federal government is probably the
most vital political challenge facing Canadians in the mid-1990s.

As Niccolo Machiavelli warned, there is nothing more difficult to arrange, more
doubtful of success, and more dangerous to carry through than initiating changes in a state's
constitution.

---

[81] *The Globe and Mail*, Dec. 12, 1992.

SELECTED BIBLIOGRAPHY

Asch, M., *Home and Native Land: Aboriginal Rights and the Canadian Constitution* (Toronto: Methuen, 1984).

Banting, Keith G. and Richard Simeon, eds., *And No One Cheered: Federalism, Democracy and the Constitution Act* (Toronto: Methuen, 1983).

————, eds., *Redesigning the State: The Politics of Constitutional Change in Industrial Nations* (Toronto: University of Toronto Press, 1985).

Beck, Stanley M. and Ivan Bernier, eds., *Canada and the New Constitution: The Unfinished Agenda,* 2 vols. (Montreal: IRPP, 1983).

Beckton, C.F. and A.W. MacKay, eds., *Recurring Issues in Canadian Federalism,* vol. 57, Royal Commission on the Economic Union and Development Prospects for Canada (Toronto: University of Toronto Press, 1985).

————, eds., *The Courts and the Charter,* vol. 58, Royal Commission on the Economic Union (Toronto: University of Toronto Press, 1985).

Behiels, Michael, ed., *The Meech Lake Primer: Conflicting Views of the 1987 Constitutional Accord* (Ottawa: University of Ottawa Press, 1989).

Bercuson, David J. and Barry Cooper, *Deconfederation: Canada Without Quebec* (Toronto: Key Porter, 1991).

Berger, T., *Fragile Freedoms: Human Rights and Dissent in Canada* (Agincourt, Ont.: The Book Society, 1983).

Bernier, I. and A. Lajoie, *Law, Society and the Economy,* vol. 46, Royal Commission on the Economic Union (Toronto: University of Toronto Press, 1985).

————, eds., *The Supreme Court of Canada as an Instrument of Political Change,* vol. 47, Royal Commission on the Economic Union (Toronto: University of Toronto Press, 1985).

Bilodeau, R., ed., *Human Rights and Affirmative Action* (Montréal: Canadian Human Rights Foundation, 1985).

Borovoy, Alan, *When Freedoms Collide: The Case For Our Civil Liberties* (Toronto: Lester & Orpen Dennys, 1988).

Boyer, J.P., *Equality for All — Report of the Parliamentary Committee on Equality Rights* (Ottawa: Supply and Services, 1984).

Cairns, A.C., *Constitution, Government and Society in Canada* (Toronto: McClelland & Stewart, 1988).

————, *Disruptions: Constitutional Struggles* (Toronto: McClelland & Stewart, 1991).

———— and C. Williams, *Constitutionalism, Citizenship, and Society in Canada,* vol. 33, Royal Commission on the Economic Union (Toronto: University of Toronto Press, 1985).

Cheffins, Ronald I. and Ronald N. Tucker, *The Constitutional Process in Canada,* 2nd ed. (Toronto: McGraw-Hill Ryerson, 1976).

Cheffins, Ronald I. and Patricia A. Johnson, *The Revised Canadian Constitution: Politics as Law* (Toronto: McGraw-Hill Ryerson, 1986).

Davenport, P. and R.H. Leach, eds., *Reshaping Confederation: The 1982 Reform of the Canadian Constitution* (Durham, N.C.: Duke University Press, 1984).

Gall, Gerald L., *The Canadian Legal System,* 3rd ed. (Toronto: Carswell, 1990).

Gibbins, Roger, ed., *Meech Lake and Canada: Perspective from the West* (Edmonton: Academic Printing and Publishing, 1988).

Greene, Ian, *The Charter of Rights* (Toronto: Lorimer, 1989).

Heard, Andrew, *Canadian Constitutional Conventions* (Toronto: Oxford University Press, 1991).

Hogg, Peter, *Constitutional Law of Canada,* 2nd ed. (Toronto: Carswell, 1985).

——————, *Meech Lake Constitutional Accord Annotated* (Toronto: Carswell, 1988).

Jackson, Robert and Doreen Jackson, *Stand Up for Canada: Leadership and the Canadian Political Crisis* (Scarborough, Ont.: Prentice-Hall, 1992).

Knopff, Rainer and F.L. Morton, *Charter Politics* (Scarborough: Nelson, 1992).

Langford, J. Stuart, *The Law of Your Land: A Practical Guide to the New Constitution* (Toronto: CBC Publications, 1982).

Mandel, Michael, *The Charter of Rights and the Legalization of Politics in Canada* (Toronto: Wall and Thompson, 1989).

McDonald, D.C., *Legal Rights and the Canadian Charter of Rights and Freedoms: A Manual of Issues and Sources* (Toronto: Carswell, 1982).

McKerchen, William R., ed., *The U.S. Bill of Rights and the Canadian Charter of Rights and Freedoms* (Toronto: Ontario Economic Council, 1983).

MacKinnon, Frank, *The Crown in Canada* (Calgary: Glenbow-Alberta Institute: McClelland & Stewart West, 1976).

McWhinney, Edward, *Canadians and the Constitution 1979–1982: Patriation and the Charter of Rights* (Toronto: University of Toronto Press, 1982).

Millar, Perry S. and Carl Baar, *Judicial Administration in Canada* (Montréal: McGill-Queen's Press, 1981).

Milne, David, *The New Canadian Constitution* (Toronto: Lorimer, 1982).

Monahan, Patrick J., *Meech Lake: The Inside Story* (Toronto: University of Toronto Press, 1991).

Olling, R.D. and M.W. Westmacott, eds., *The Confederation Debate: The Constitution in Crisis* (Toronto: Kendall-Hunt, 1980).

——————, eds., *Perspectives on Canadian Federalism* (Scarborough, Ont.: Prentice-Hall Canada, 1988).

Romanow, Roy, John Whyte and Howard Leeson, *Canada Notwithstanding: The Making of the Constitution 1976–1982* (Toronto: Methuen, 1984).

Russell, Peter H., *Constitutional Odyssey* (Toronto: University of Toronto Press, 1991).

——————, *Leading Constitutional Decisions: Cases on the British North America Act*, rev. ed. (Toronto: McClelland & Stewart, 1973).

——————, *The Judiciary in Canada: The Third Branch of Government* (Toronto: McGraw Hill Ryerson, 1987).

——————, R. Decary, W.R. Lederman, N. Lyon and D. Soberman, *The Court and the Constitution 1976–1982* (Kingston, Ont.: Institute for Inter-governmental Relations, 1982).

Schwartz, B., *First Principles: Constitutional Reform with Respect to the Aboriginal Peoples of Canada, 1982–1984*, (Kingston, Ont.: Institute for Inter-governmental Relations, 1985).

Sheppard, R. and M. Valpy, *The National Deal: The Fight for a Canadian Constitution* (Toronto: Macmillan, 1984).

Smiley, Donald, *The Canadian Charter of Rights and Freedoms* (Toronto: Ontario Economic Council, 1981).

Snell, James G. and Frederick Vaughan, *The Supreme Court of Canada: History of the Institution* (Toronto: University of Toronto Press, 1985).

Strayer, B.L., *The Canadian Constitution and The Courts*, 2nd ed. (Toronto: Butterworths, 1983).

Tarnopolsky, W.S. and G.A. Beaudoin, eds., *The Canadian Charter of Rights and Freedoms: Commentary* (Toronto: Carswell, 1982).

Tetley, W., *Reshaping Confederation: the 1982 Reform of the Canadian Constitution* (Chapel Hill, N.C.: Duke University, 1986).

Watts, Ronald L. and Douglas M. Brown, eds., *Options for a New Canada* (Toronto: University of Toronto Press, 1991).

Weaver, R. Kent, ed., *The Collapse of Canada?* (Washington: The Brookings Institution 1992).

Williams, Douglas E., ed., *Constitution, Government and Society in Canada*: Essays by Alan C. Cairns (Toronto: McClelland & Stewart, 1988).

Fred Sherwin/*The Globe and Mail*

FEDERALISM AND ITS CHALLENGES

FINANCES, NATIONALISM, AND REGIONALISM

Although to some students federalism has the reputation of being a dry subject, this assessment is certainly not accurate for Canada. Federalism is an active force that helps shape the issues and priorities of contemporary politics. In a general sense, Canadian politics can be said to be the politics of federalism.

The threat of Québec separation, the sense of grievance in several western provinces, the controversies over language and educational rights for minorities, the disputes over resource control and many similar troublesome matters — all of these political issues are manifestations of conflicts over the authority and jurisdiction of the federal system in Canada. Developments in federalism reach into everyone's lives. The vast array of social services and programs available to Canadian citizens today is the outgrowth of federal/provincial interaction. While certain programs may be supported by only one level of government, the majority require the financial cooperation of both Ottawa and the provinces. The procedures that lead to the interaction of the federal and provincial governments in these activities reveal much about Canadian politics. On the other hand, the federal system complicates the handling of many issues — for example, economic planning, control of inflation and modern concerns such as job creation, pollution, safety, women's rights and the overall impact of large cities.

In Chapter 5, we outlined the constitutional provisions that formally define the relationship between the federal and provincial governments. However, the conduct of politics within Canada's federal structure is also affected by the dynamic social and economic realities in which it operates. Therefore, more is required to comprehend Canadian federalism than a discussion of the legal division of powers and jurisdictional niceties. We need to understand the complex financial relations among governments as well as the political challenges, such as separation and regionalism, that threaten to tear the country apart.

In this chapter, we explore the meaning of federalism and its implications for Canadians. One conclusion is obvious. Rather than being a fixed, immutable institutional structure, Canadian federalism has changed dramatically over the years. It is not a simple, static division of powers, but a process whereby the two levels of government adapt and change in order to reduce tensions within the political environment. Further, the chapter explains why federalism was initiated and how it has been adapted to Canadian realities.

Although the Canadian federal structure has proven remarkably resilient, during the past three decades powerful pressures have emerged that threaten to overwhelm the system. The ultimate outcome of what is often referred to as the "crisis of Canadian federalism" is by no means certain. Whether these forces will result in a truncated Canada or serve to strengthen the federal system will depend on an array of factors, including leadership and political circumstances. The concluding portions of the chapter survey the contemporary regional challenges to federalism, including Québec nationalism and regional alienation, and outline possible scenarios for the future.

WHAT IS FEDERALISM?

In his influential book on the subject, William Riker contends that the twentieth century is an "age of federalism" and lists numerous federal countries, including the United States, Australia, Germany and Canada.[1] Federalism, he argues, has replaced empire as a means of governing diverse peoples living on large land masses.[2] This statement is partially correct. Seventeen of the world's states are federal, including many of the large ones. However, it is also apparent that in 1993 there are more than 10 times as many unitary as federal states, and that, even within the systems labelled "federal," the term means quite different things to different people. There is little similarity in the federal aspects of countries such as the United States of America, Australia and Canada compared with Argentina, Brazil, Mexico, Nigeria, the Federated States of Micronesia and the United Arab Emirates. Moreover, some historically federal countries have imploded — the U.S.S.R. has been dismantled, Czechoslovakia has divided and the component parts of the former Yugoslavia are at war. We shall have to be precise in the use of the term federalism.

Simply put, federalism refers to a division of jurisdiction and authority between at least two levels of government. It is usually characterized by the existence of one central government and two or more regional governments operating simultaneously over the same territory and people. Therefore, **federalism** can be defined as "a political organization in which the activities of government are divided between regional governments and a central government in such a way that each kind of government has some kind of activities on which it makes final decisions."[3]

This definition implies that each level of government has more-or-less complete authority over some specific spheres of activity, while on a few other matters there may be a degree of concurrent jurisdiction. There is certainly no single, ideal way in which this authority is divided. What is important is that each level has a degree of autonomy. In the federal form, the various levels of government obtain their respective powers from the country's constitution, not from each other. Citizens owe some loyalty to more than one level of government, and both levels may act directly on the citizens.

---

[1] William H. Riker, *Federalism: Origin, Operation, Significance* (Boston: Little, Brown, 1964), p. 1.

[2] Ibid., pp. 3–5.

[3] William H. Riker, "Federalism," in Fred I. Greenstein and Nelson W. Polsby, eds., *Handbook of Political Science Vol. 5: Government Institutions and Processes* (Reading, Mass.: Addison-Wesley, 1975), p. 101.

The history of the concept of federalism has been traced back to the fusion of ancient Israelite tribes. In North America, its first occurrence has been ascribed to the Five Nations of the Iroquois Indians. Its modern meaning, however, is best dated to the eighteenth century. During that period, the United States Constitution provided a system of government that has been emulated ever since. The dual essence of the theory of American federalism was the idea of distribution of government power on an area basis, and the philosophy that unity and diversity can co-exist.

CONCEPTS OF FEDERALISM

Since the beginning of political science, one problem has dominated debate about the meaning of federalism. It concerns those systems that have a federal constitutional structure, but political and social forms that reduce the significance of the bargain between the central and regional governments. An example is Mexico, where the near one-party system links the political forces together in such a way as to produce a state very similar to those that are unitary. However, some unitary states are highly decentralized. In summary, therefore, federal states may be *centralized* or *decentralized* — and so may unitary systems.

William Riker offers a useful continuum by which to measure various federalisms.[4] This continuum ranges from centralized federalism, in which the central government dominates or encroaches on the sub-units, to what is referred to as peripheralized or decentralized federalism, in which the sub-unit governments dominate (See Figure 6.1). For a variety of reasons, most federal states today are of the centralized variety. The requirements of national security, the welfare state and, in general, the growing complexity of society are all factors conducive to a centralization of power at the national level. There are, however, states in which the various regional sub-units retain significant powers. Furthermore, there are countries in which it is possible to discern pendulum swings along the continuum over a period of decades. Although centralized federalism is the more common form today, there is nothing intrinsically superior or inferior about the arrangement.

FIGURE 6.1   CONTINUUM OF THE DEGREE OF CENTRALIZATION OF AUTHORITY

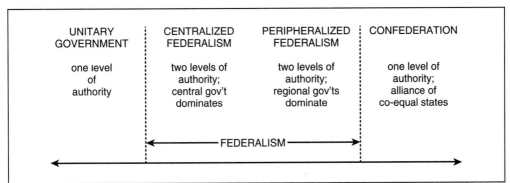

Source: Adapted from concepts proposed by William H. Riker in *Federalism: Origin, Operation, Significance* (Boston: Little, Brown, 1964).

---

4   Riker, *Federalism: Origin, Operation, Significance*, pp. 5–10. See also K.C. Wheare, *Federal Government*, 4th ed. (New York: Oxford University Press, 1963), pp. 31–2.

While considering the continuum of federalism, it is important to note its polar ends: the *unitary* and *confederation* forms of government. As its name implies, **unitary** government is characterized by one level of political authority. In this form the central government grants and amends the powers of local or provincial authorities. The archetype of this form may well be France, where virtually all significant final decisions about political life are made at the national level, in Paris. On the other hand, except in Canada and Switzerland, **confederation** government refers to a loose alliance of sovereign states that band together for very narrow reasons. The United States in the period of the *Articles of Confederation,* 1781–87, is a good example of this form. Even earlier, from 1643 to 1648, the New England Confederation was founded solely for reasons of defence and external relations. Admittedly, there may be a fine line between certain peripheralized federalisms and confederal states. Perhaps the only way to differentiate between the two types is to ascertain whether the various "regional" units are completely, as opposed to partially, sovereign. Despite its imprecision, Riker's continuum is useful for exploring the federal phenomenon.

Many authors dislike the apparent formalism in these legal, political and territorial definitions of federalism. Economists[5] and some political scientists speak of a "federal society," defined as a society in which economic, religious, racial or historical diversities are territorially grouped. W.S. Livingston, for example, believes that certain societies are intrinsically federal because they are pluralist, and that federalism is simply the institutional outcome of the forces that exist in these societies.[6] The inherent difficulty with such definitions is that they concern more than federal unions and could just as well apply to any state composed of more than one ethnic group. Other authors believe that non-territorial federalism can exist. They cite examples such as Estonia in 1925 or Cyprus in 1960. In these instances, legal jurisdiction over cultural and educational affairs was accorded to groups wherever they lived, and was not based on a geographic division of the state.[7] These kinds of examples lead researchers away from rigid, formalistic definitions of federalism; however, at the same time, the concepts become so loose that any form of delegation of power can be included, with the result that the definitions become so general that federalism can mean practically anything to anybody.

EVALUATIONS OF FEDERALISM

Why is federalism adopted? What are its advantages? On these questions there is much disagreement among scholars. Some argue that federalism is synonymous with liberty, that it is a protection for minority rights. Others believe it is chosen essentially to achieve unification without the loss of separate identities by the units. On the other hand, Graham Maddox has argued that many of the so-called altruistic objectives often attributed to federalism are inaccurate and perhaps even misleading.[8] Britain, perhaps one of the world's most liberal

---

[5]   See, for example, Wallace Oaks, *Fiscal Federalism* (New York: Harcourt Brace Jovanovich, 1977).

[6]   See W.S. Livingston, "A Note on the Nature of Federalism," in J. Peter Meekison, ed., *Canadian Federalism: Myth or Reality,* 2nd ed. (Toronto: Methuen, 1971), p. 24.

[7]   See Karl Aun, "Cultural Autonomy of Ethnic Minorities in Estonia: A Model for Multicultural Society?" paper presented at the Third Conference of Baltic States in Scandinavia, Stockholm, 1975; Carl J. Friedrich, "Corporate Federalism and Linguistic Politics," paper delivered at the International Political Science Association, Montréal, 1973; and Kenneth D. McRae, "The Principle of Territoriality and the Principle of Personality in Multilingual States," *International Journal of the Sociology of Language,* vol. 4 (1975), pp. 33–54.

[8]   For a critique of some of the justifications often cited in the adoption of federalism, see Graham Maddox, "Federalism: Or Government Frustrated," *Australian Quarterly,* vol. 45, no. 3 (September 1973), pp. 92–100.

democracies, is a unitary state, while a number of non-democratic countries have, on paper at least, adopted the federal form. Maddox also questions the popular argument that federal governments are "closer to the people."[9] William Riker, too, dismisses the notion of lofty motives, and suggests that federalism is ultimately the result of a rational political bargain.[10] Franz Neumann concludes simply that federalism may be good, bad or indifferent, depending on other circumstances.[11]

We have stated that the federal form is adopted characteristically because the leaders of the constituent units believe that they have something to gain that they could not achieve if they were to remain completely separate and autonomous. The two most often-cited motivations underlying federal unions are the desire for military security and the desire for economic or political expansion.[12] A large geographic unit with a degree of coordination of resources provides a more effective defensive unit than a collection of smaller, independent states. And, of course, such a unified entity stands a good chance of being able to expand economically and politically. The possibility for self-aggrandizement, rather than lofty idealism, seems to be a more accurate assessment of the motivations for federalism.

While the various sub-units may perceive gains from a federal union, they must also take certain drawbacks into consideration: in order to realize their objectives, the sub-units will be obliged to give up some privileges and powers to the central government. Before doing this, they may seek certain guarantees and safeguards so that they may maintain at least a modicum of separate authority. These guarantees are usually in the form of a written constitution clearly dividing political authority and jurisdiction and spelling out certain limitations and restrictions.[13]

A constitution is therefore often referred to as the "umpire" of federalism, serving to protect as well as limit. Whether the constitution is a single written document or an unwritten collection of statutes and understandings, what is important is that the "federal principle" be enshrined in a way that recognizes the diversity of the country and at the same time provides a check on arbitrary rule by the central government. The component units are usually given equal or disproportionately strong representation at the centre. This is often achieved by having two legislative chambers — one based on population, the other based on a recognition of regionalism.[14] The importance of federal constitutions is demonstrated by the controversy over how they may be amended or altered. Much of the evolution of federalism depends on how a given constitution is interpreted, in particular by the judiciary.

To establish a federal union at all, to make the necessary promises and concessions, requires considerable persuasive powers. Once the union is achieved, it will inevitably evolve on the basis of many, perhaps unforeseen, factors. But to establish the union itself is an extraordinarily complex and difficult task. Individuals who accomplish the

---

[9] Ibid., pp. 93–4.

[10] Riker, *Federalism: Origin, Operation, Significance*, p. 12.

[11] Franz Neumann, *The Democratic and the Authoritarian State: Essays in Political and Legal Theory* (Glencoe: Free Press, 1957).

[12] Riker, *Federalism: Origin, Operation, Significance*, pp. 12–16.

[13] Wheare, *Federal Government*, pp. 15–34.

[14] Ibid., pp. 10–14. For a discussion of the relevant examples with different facts, see Ivo D. Duchacek, *Comparative Federalism: The Territorial Dimension of Politics* (New York: Holt, Rinehart and Winston, 1970), ch. 8, and Daniel J. Elazar, "Federalism," in David L. Sills, ed., *International Encyclopedia of the Social Sciences*, Vol. 5 (New York: Macmillan, 1968), pp. 353–67.

task usually end up enthroned in history as near-mythical figures, like the Canadian "Fathers of Confederation."

Many apparently stable federal constitutional systems have endured stresses and strains and, on occasion, even failure. Ronald Watts has found four common conditions of failure: regional divergences of political demands, weak communications, a diminution of the original impetus for union and external influences.[15] All these conditions are present in Canada to some degree; in fact, they are present to some extent in all federations — both those that have failed and those that have succeeded. Examples of peaceful secessions include very loose confederations such as Malaysia (Singapore was virtually expelled) and the tenuous arrangements of Syria-Egypt and Senegal-Mali. Two former communist countries — the U.S.S.R. and Czechoslovakia fell apart when the glue of communism was removed. The other cases involved violence — such as Yugoslavia's violent division into several fragmented states, or the termination of colonial regimes that did not have contiguous territories with the parent countries, such as Algeria's break from France. The lesson is clear — rancour and civil war have been the usual means by which federal states have divided.

Thus far, we have described federalism in terms of constitutions that divide the authority of the central and sub-unit governments and balance regional interests. Nonetheless, readers must be careful not to take too legalistic an approach and overlook the fact that federalism is fundamentally based on a sociological reality.[16] Were it not for societal diversity, federalism would not be as prevalent in the world as it is today. While federal states may be formed for essentially narrow, pragmatic reasons, this political arrangement is ultimately a recognition that the various sub-units are different and that there is something about them that should be preserved and protected. Keeping this in mind, let us now turn to a consideration of how federalism came to be adopted in Canada and how it has evolved over the years.

THE ORIGIN AND EVOLUTION OF CANADIAN FEDERALISM

THE ORIGIN OF FEDERALISM

Throughout the first half of the nineteenth century, Britain's Canadian colonies moved toward a type of political union. The creation of a united Upper and Lower Canada (the present Ontario and Québec) in 1841 was the first step. As the population of Upper Canada grew in relation to that of Lower Canada, there was a corresponding demand by the former for more political influence. Meanwhile, Lower Canada steadfastly insisted on non-interference with the French, Catholic way of life. As a political deadlock developed, tension mounted and the experiment of joining the two Canadas failed. It was obvious that a more broadly based union was necessary.

As noted in Chapter 2, the motivations for the establishment of a federal union in Canada in the 1860s were mixed. Both military security and economic expansion were

---

[15] R.L. Watts, "Survival or Disintegration," in Richard Simeon, ed., *Must Canada Fail?* (Montréal: McGill-Queen's University Press, 1977), pp. 42–60.

[16] See Michael Stein, "Federal Political Systems and Federal Societies," in Meekison, ed., *Canadian Federalism: Myth or Reality*, 2nd ed., pp. 30–42.

central themes of the speeches and political programs of the contemporary leaders. The persuasiveness and political acumen of the Fathers of Confederation on these topics was impressive. Foremost among this handful of politicians was Sir John A. Macdonald, who played the leading role in establishing the federal union in 1867 by placating the objections of the smaller Maritime provinces and holding forth the prospect of a glorious national destiny.[17] By the 1860s, Macdonald, among others, was keenly aware of the need for greater military security. The victory of the northern states in the American Civil War had sent a shiver up the spines of Canadian leaders. British interests in Canada had made no secret of their support for the American Confederacy and, after Appomattox, there was some expectation that Canada might be annexed as part of the spoils of war. Raids by fanatical Fenians across the border into Canada further served to add a note of urgency to plans for some type of national unification. The British, for their part, were tired of the burden of defending their colonies in North America and were not averse to the prospect of turning over to Canadians the responsibility for their own defence.

At the same time, Macdonald recognized the great potential of the unsettled western territories for the development of a transcontinental nation. The possibility of economic development and expansion was therefore another significant motivating factor in establishing federalism. A political union would not only improve internal trade between the Maritime provinces and Upper and Lower Canada, but it would also help in the drive to settle the prairies and the far west before the Americans moved into the vacuum.

Each of the British colonies in North America saw certain specific advantages for itself in the enterprise. The leaders from Upper Canada, a growing and prosperous area, looked forward to further economic expansion and development. Those from Lower Canada, while uneasy about their English Canadian neighbours, were willing to consider a federal union if their language and culture could be protected by law. The sparsely populated Maritime colonies of Nova Scotia and New Brunswick were perhaps the most reluctant, but at the same time were attracted by economic advantages, namely the building of a transcontinental railway and various subsidies from the future federal government. The Charlottetown and Québec conferences, discussed in Chapter 2, culminated a long process of negotiation resulting in the Dominion of Canada.

THE EVOLUTION OF FEDERALISM

While the *BNA Act* authorized the establishment of a type of government in Canada "similar in principle to that of the United Kingdom," the resulting form of government necessarily differed, in that jurisdiction and authority were divided between the central government and the provinces. We have seen that the architects of the federal system sought to establish a strong central government, mindful as they were of the threat posed by the movement for states' rights in the American union, which led to the bloody Civil War of 1861–65. Even a cursory reading of the *BNA Act*, revealing the sweeping jurisdiction given the central government, confirms the impression that it

---

[17] See Donald Creighton, *John A. Macdonald: The Young Politician* (Toronto: Macmillan Canada, 1952), *John A. Macdonald: The Old Chieftain* (Toronto: Macmillan, 1955) and *The Road to Confederation: The Emergence of Canada 1863–1867* (Toronto: Macmillan Canada, 1964); and Peter Waite, *The Life and Times of Confederation, 1864–1867* (Toronto: University of Toronto Press, 1967).

was meant to be predominant. Reversing the American example, it was the federal government in Canada that was to be the beneficiary of the residual "Peace, Order, and good Government" clause. The limited jurisdiction of the provinces was meant to underscore their subordinate position in the federation. While reference is often made to the "Confederation Agreement" and the "Fathers of Confederation," it is clear that the authors did not intend Canada to be a confederation in a genuine political sense, but rather a centralized federation.

In a summary article, Howard Cody has traced the evolution of federal/provincial interaction in Canada since 1867.[18] While his argument lacks a rigorous definition of "interaction," the précis does provide a short history of federal/provincial relations. Cody identifies four eras, and suggests that there have been several pendulum swings between centralization and decentralization. (See Figure 6.2.) While Canada clearly began as a centralized federation, during the latter part of the nineteenth century the relative power of the provinces grew, due to a series of judgements by the Judicial Committee of the Privy Council. We have noted that in jurisdictional disputes referred to the JCPC there was a consistent pattern of interpretation favouring provincial rights.[19] Led by such forceful provincial leaders as Sir Oliver Mowat and Honoré Mercier, the original dominance of the central government was eroded to the point that the *BNA Act* was being interpreted by the JCPC as an international treaty rather than as the founding document of a country, which led to decisions that went against the central government.[20] This period of decentralized or peripheralized federalism, lasting into the early twentieth century, has been roundly condemned by Garth Stevenson:

> *This peculiar situation, which even the Australians had the foresight largely to avoid, had the effect that for almost a century the most influential concepts of Canadian federalism were largely defined by outsiders, men who had no practical knowledge of Canada, or of federalism, and who were not even required to live in the society that to a large degree was shaped by their opinions.*[21]

According to Cody's historical summary, the pendulum began to swing back toward a centralization of authority with the introduction of what became known in the system of funding provinces as "conditional grants." Under the *BNA Act*, the provinces assumed jurisdiction over such matters as education and social welfare, which originally required very little expenditure. As the demand for social services grew in the twentieth century, the provinces found themselves starved for funds. The provisions of the *Act* made it virtually impossible for them to raise the revenues needed to meet public needs. To help them escape from this impasse, the central government in Ottawa offered the provinces grants on the con-

---

18 Howard Cody, "The Evolution of Federal-Provincial Relations in Canada: Some Reflections," *American Review of Canadian Studies*, vol. 7, no. 1 (Spring 1977), pp. 55–83.

19 See Alain C. Cairns, "The Judicial Committee and its Critics," *CJPS*, vol. 4, no. 3 (September 1971), pp. 301–45; V.C. MacDonald, "The Privy Council and the Canadian Constitution," *Canadian Bar Review* (December 1951), pp. 1021–37; and Martha Fletcher, "Judicial Review and the Division of Powers in Canada," in Meekison, *Canadian Federalism*, pp. 100–23.

20 See Donald Swainson, ed., *Oliver Mowat's Ontario* (Toronto: Macmillan Canada, 1972), especially Bruce W. Hodgins, "Disagreement at the Commencement: Divergent Ontario Views of Federalism, 1867–1871," pp. 52–68, and Christopher Armstrong, "The Mowat Heritage in Federal-Provincial Relations," pp. 93–118.

21 Garth Stevenson, *Unfulfilled Union*, revised ed. (Toronto: Gage, 1982), p. 43.

dition that the money be spent in a specified manner. The provinces, for their part, resented this intrusion but had no choice. The Depression further deepened the dependency of the provinces on the federal government.[22] In addition, the necessity for placing Canada on a war footing in 1914 and again in 1939 naturally tended to centralize power in Ottawa. Except perhaps in Québec, where there was considerable opposition to the two World Wars, and especially to the policy of conscription, the national government became a focus of patriotism and loyalty for most Canadians, endowing it with enormous prestige and symbolic influence.

FIGURE 6.2   THE EVOLUTION OF CANADIAN FEDERALISM FROM 1867 TO 1993, INDICATING SWINGS OF CENTRALIZATION AND PERIPHERALIZATION

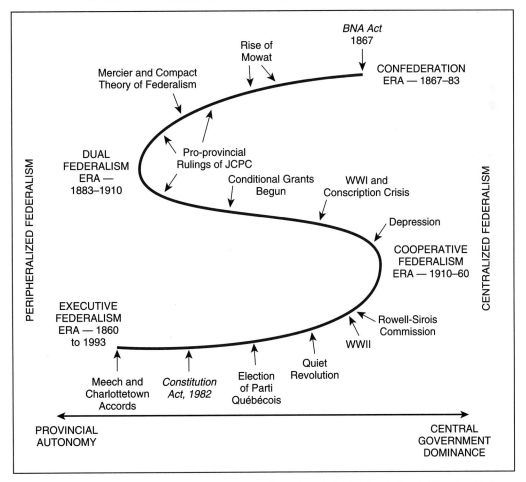

Source: Based on original from Howard Cody, "The Evolution of Federal-Provincial Relations in Canada," *American Review of Canadian Studies*, vol. 7, no.1 (1977), pp. 55–83.

The factors contributing to centralization of power continued for some time into the postwar era, but there were signs that the provinces would seek to regain their lost ground. The dominance of Ottawa can be said to have continued until the late 1950s, when the

---

22 Cody, "The Evolution of Federal-Provincial Relations in Canada," pp. 66–67.

most recent pendulum shift occurred. New ideas about decentralization began to circulate as early as 1937, with the recommendations of the Royal Commission on Dominion-Provincial Relations, perhaps better known as the Rowell-Sirois Commission.[23] This Commission was charged with investigating the reasons for the near-bankruptcy of the provinces and recommending ways in which to revitalize the federation. While its suggestions could not be implemented until after the Second World War, the Rowell-Sirois Commission came out strongly against the conditional grants procedure. In addition, it recommended that Ottawa take over such expensive responsibilities as unemployment insurance and pensions, and generally seek to equalize the financial resources of the provinces.

As the provinces began to obtain relief from their heavy financial burdens through new fiscal mechanisms, important changes were also occurring in postwar society. Beginning in the 1960s and increasing in momentum through the decade, Québec underwent a "Quiet Revolution" in which traditional French Catholic values and occupational patterns were transformed. A new, confident French Canadian elite, epitomized perhaps by the government of Jean Lesage, led the assault on Ottawa's "paternalism."[24] Ottawa countered with an expansion of what were referred to as "shared cost programs" or "conditional grants," which nonetheless tended to be regarded as distorting provincial spending priorities and therefore still engendered antagonism. In the spirit of Mowat and Mercier, Québec politicians insisted on the right to exercise their independence by "opting out" of certain programs so that they could go their own way. Ottawa had no coherent or effective response with which to meet this challenge. Québec's agitation in the 1960s for "special status" only served to give the other provinces ideas.

The longstanding sense of grievance in the western provinces against Ottawa also began to erupt during this period. Made confident by their enormous resource revenues, the provinces of Alberta and British Columbia, in particular, sought greater political clout within the federation to match their recent wealth. While they were not sympathetic to the cultural and linguistic aspirations of the Québécois, the western provinces shared with them a degree of antipathy toward the perceived paternalism of the federal government in Ottawa as well as a perceived favouritism toward central Canada.

FEDERAL/PROVINCIAL MECHANISMS FOR CONFLICT RESOLUTION

The constant interplay of federal/provincial relations has brought into being numerous institutions for coordinating policies and resolving disputes. As we pointed out in the previous chapter, most fields of public policy are managed by both levels of government and many are jointly financed. Both facts necessitate much federal/provincial interaction.

In the early days of Confederation, there was not much need for formal federal/provincial consultations, and what meetings did occur were of an ad hoc nature, convened to discuss specific problems. However, increased financial power expanded the fields of influence

---

[23] See D.V. Smiley, ed., *The Rowell-Sirois Report: An Abridgement of Book I of the Royal Commission Report on Dominion-Provincial Relations*, The Carleton Library No. 5 (Toronto: McClelland & Stewart, 1963).

[24] See Claude Morin, *Quebec versus Ottawa: The Struggle for Self-Government, 1960–72* (Toronto: University of Toronto Press, 1976), pp. 12–28.

and concern of both levels of government. Commitment to economic policies aimed at full employment, economic growth and trade liberalization, as well as to a wide range of social policies, resulted in a dramatic increase in intergovernmental relations. Effective intergovernmental consultation has thus become a basic requirement for the maintenance of Canadian federalism. This development is perhaps best indicated by the establishment, in the federal government and provincial governments, of departments or offices whose sole purpose is dealing with federal/provincial issues.

Intergovernmental relations immediately after the Second World War were characterized by constant, reasonably harmonious exchanges of ideas, financial decisions and policies. This period has been labelled one of **cooperative federalism**, albeit with a decided federal predominance. Economic times were good as a result of the postwar boom, and federal/provincial relations were primarily concerned with social programs that did not necessarily involve regional conflict.[25] As a rule, bureaucrats from both levels of government dominated intergovernmental relations, resolving problems before they reached the political agenda.

The 1960s and 1970s, however, were characterized by less cooperation and more confrontation between the two levels of government. Economic downturns and the ascendancy of provincialism — concern for the jurisdictional integrity of the provinces — changed the conduct of federal/provincial relations. The term coined to describe this new relationship is **executive federalism.**

The clearest sign of the change from cooperative to executive federalism was the movement of intergovernmental talks from among public servants behind closed doors to among politicians, often in the full glare of publicity. The most public institution in intergovernmental relations today is the First Ministers' Conference, during which the leaders of the eleven governments meet to hammer out deals, in recent years under the scrutiny of television cameras.

Some of the most important of these meetings lately have been named Constitutional Conferences. In recent years, the necessity for these First Ministers' Conferences has even found a place in the *Constitution* itself. For example, two substantive meetings of the leaders were required by the 1982 constitutional amendment to deal explicitly with the rights of Canada's aboriginal peoples. And, if the Meech Lake accord had been ratified (see Chapter 5) two annual meetings would have been forced upon the First Ministers thereafter.

Such "constitutionalizing" of these meetings could prove excessive. Compulsory meetings on the *Constitution* would draw the premiers away from dealing with their own provinces and politicize jurisdictional issues on an annual basis. Garth Stevenson is even more critical: "the conferences on the economy serve no useful purpose, provide premiers with a platform for irresponsible and partisan criticism of the federal government's policies, and negate the principle that each government is responsible for its own field of jurisdiction."[26]

While Ottawa may have thought that it could placate opposition through such conferences, some have argued that the meetings only provide an instrument for the expression of provincial discontent and resistance.[27] Certainly, the conferences have increasingly

---

25 Timothy B. Woolstencroft, *Organizing Intergovernmental Relations*, Institute Discussion Paper No. 12 (Kingston, Ont. IIR, 1982), p. 12.

26 Stevenson, *Unfulfilled Union*, p. 264.

27 Don Stevenson, "The Role of Intergovernmental Conferences in the Decision-Making Process," in Richard Simeon, ed., *Confrontation and Collaboration — Intergovernmental Relations in Canada Today* (Toronto: The Institute of Public Administration of Canada, 1979), p. 94, and Gordon Robertson, "The Role of Interministerial Conferences in the Decision-Making Process," in Simeon, *Confrontation and Collaboration*, pp. 28–88.

become political forums in which each Premier appeals not to the other heads of government, but directly to his own electorate. Richard Simeon has argued that intergovernmental bargaining has become more like the diplomatic relations between states than the usual
politics within a single state.[28] Responsible only to the people who elected them, provincial
leaders today are well organized and prepared to take on the federal government through
counter-proposals and independent programs. Moreover, a dangerous new practice has
developed: the 10 provincial premiers have tended to meet in advance of First Ministers'
Conferences and approach the final bargaining table as a unified group opposed to the federal government. Ottawa is no longer able to overwhelm its partners in the federation.[29]

There is little question that the era of executive federalism has been one of decentralization characterized by intergovernmental conflict. D.V. Smiley, for example, argues that
the result of the rise of intergovernmental specialists has made federal/provincial conflicts
more intractable, perhaps to the point of being irreconcilable.[30] Representatives of each
level of government, jealous of their position, promote their own narrow interests, thereby impeding compromise.

Yet this argument confuses the process of intergovernmental relations with the causes
of conflict. Intergovernmental specialists have also facilitated cooperation and compromise
between governments. As Simeon points out, intergovernmental interactions promote consultation between governments and thus contribute to the effectiveness and harmony of intergovernmental cooperation.[31] The appearance of intergovernmental specialists is more a
consequence of the need for consultation than a source of conflict. As well, the concern for
jurisdictional integrity has not displaced the ability of government officials to resolve conflicts as, for instance, in the oil pricing agreements of 1973–74, the Alberta/Ottawa energy
agreement of 1979, the Constitutional accord of 1982, the Meech Lake agreement of 1987,
and the Charlottetown accord of 1992. Intergovernmental interaction provides a means of
communications between governments, encouraging an awareness of the views of their respective Cabinets and bureaucracies — a necessary precondition to achieving compromise.[32]

Thus, while relations between the federal and provincial governments are often characterized by disagreement, the mechanisms of conflict resolution are important for the
functioning of federalism. The ability of the Canadian federation to cope with the fundamental
divergences of interest that animate federal/provincial conflict is based largely on the continued effectiveness of these mechanisms.

As the preceding discussion of the evolution of Canadian federalism has demonstrated,
an understanding of federalism requires an awareness not only of the formal divisions of responsibility and powers, but also of the economic and social context in which the political
contest takes place. While relations between the levels of government are defined by the
Constitution, they are subject to the pressures of the day, and are far from static.

---

[28] Richard Simeon, Federal-Provincial Diplomacy: The Making of Recent Policy in Canada (Toronto:
      University of Toronto Press, 1972); and Donald V. Smiley, Canada in Question: Federalism in the Eighties
      3rd. ed. (Toronto: McGraw-Hill Ryerson, 1980).

[29] See Donald V. Smiley, "Federal-Provincial Conflict in Canada," in Meekison, ed., *Canadian Federalism:
      Myth or Reality*, 3rd ed. (Toronto: Methuen, 1977), pp. 2–18.

[30] D.V. Smiley, "An Outsider's Observations of Federal-Provincial Relations Among Consenting Adults," in
      Simeon, ed., *Confrontation and Collaboration*, pp. 109–11.

[31] Simeon, *Federal-Provincial Diplomacy*, passim.

[32] Woolstencroft, *Organizing Intergovernmental Relations*, p. 80.

The constitutional details described in Chapter 5 and this general review of the evolution of federalism reveal the basic patterns of political interaction. Figure 6.2 portrays the pendulum swings that we have been describing, and illustrates some developments in federal/provincial interaction. While specific dates are given, in reality, changes of this nature take place very gradually, and we have simply used some specific event or individual as marking a turning point when, in fact, the transformation may have been building for some time.

Despite the imprecision with respect to time in Figure 6.2, it is important that federalism be perceived as something other than a static phenomenon. Of utmost concern today is the fact that the pendulum has been moving toward decentralization with such intensity that it has threatened to overwhelm the Canadian federal system. While change is to be expected as the normal course of events in any federation, such pressures threaten federalism in Canada. In the following sections, we shall examine what may be referred to as the dual crises of Canadian federalism: federal/provincial fiscal relations and the Québec nationalist and western regional challenges to federalism.

FINANCING FEDERALISM

Since Confederation, money and ways of obtaining and spending it have been a crucial aspect of federal/provincial interaction in Canada, the source of considerable difficulty for the federation. While some conflicts within the federal union revolve around highly symbolic issues, others are overtly mundane — one of them is the central issue of money.

Four general economic problems have been identified as being at the root of federal/provincial financial arguments; all four are interwoven with political sensitivities and historical exigencies.[33] In this section we examine these problems, tracing the conflict they have engendered from 1867 to the current era.

The first and most obvious problem of federal/provincial financial relations is that there has always been a fundamental incongruence between jurisdictional responsibilities and sources of revenue at the two levels of government. At the birth of the union the central government acquired the most significant revenue sources while agreeing to pay some limited subsidies and annual grants to support the obligations of the provinces. The intention was to create a highly centralized federal system. The *Constitution* entitled the federal government to raise money "by any mode or system of taxation" (BNA 91.3), while the provinces were limited to direct taxation (BNA 92.2). As provincial expenditure grew rapidly, the provinces found it necessary to acquire more revenues. This became a constant source of tension and political conflict.

The second problem can be traced to the fact that the provinces differed widely in their fiscal capacities. In the early years, a relatively prosperous province like Ontario or even Québec was fortunate in having a strong tax base in the form of a concentration of corporate activities and personal fortunes and, therefore, had the ability to raise adequate funds to provide social services. Poorer and relatively depressed provinces like those in the Maritimes were plagued with the problem of being unable to obtain sufficient tax revenue: increasing the rate of provincial taxation would only lower individual incomes and undermine economic growth. While in every federation some regions are better off than others, in Canada the discrepancies have been extraordinarily sharp. Over time, the ability to obtain high tax revenues has shifted from province to province — for example, from Ontario to Alberta during the period of high energy prices. But the problem of lower revenues persists for the poorer provinces.

---

[33] J.C. Strick, *Canadian Public Finance*, 2nd ed. (Toronto: Holt Rinehart and Winston, 1978), pp. 100–1

The third problem has resulted from the joint occupancy of tax fields. As mentioned above, the *Constitution Act, 1867* gave the provinces control only over direct taxation, while the federal government was granted a blanket authorization to tax in any manner. "Direct taxation" refers to individual income tax, corporate income tax and succession duties, among others. The federal government could levy indirect taxation through customs and excise duties, but could also institute its own direct taxation in competition with the provinces. Moreover, the provinces eventually managed to obtain the right to collect indirect taxes as well. Thereafter, both the provinces and the federal government began to levy taxes on the same sources. The competition for revenue sources became one of the most contentious aspects of federal/provincial fiscal relations.

The fourth problem relates to the implementation of fiscal policy. In an age of modern economics, with its long-term budgetary manipulation of the economy, the possibility exists that, without close cooperation between federal and provincial taxation and spending policies, the overall economy will not be effectively controlled. If, for example, the federal government were seeking to cut taxes to stimulate the economy, while at the same time the provinces were deciding to increase taxation, the impact of the federal initiative would be negated. Without a degree of cooperation there is a significant danger that federal and provincial policies could work at cross-purposes. Today a degree of coordination and consultation between the federal government and the provinces exists, but certainly not all difficulties of this type have been resolved.

Bearing in mind these four problems, we next survey the historical evolution of federal/provincial financial relations in Canada.

A BRIEF HISTORY OF FISCAL FEDERALISM

In 1867, the federal government took over existing provincial debts and agreed to pay per capita subsidies and annual grants to the provinces to support their activities.[34] However, the provinces did not acquire enough revenue from direct taxation because of rapidly escalating obligations. The federal subsidies promised in 1867 were helpful, but never sufficed to meet the growing need. Federal subsidies continued to decline as a proportion of provincial revenue — from 58 percent in 1874 to 8 percent in 1929. As well, as time went on, economic disparities between the provinces widened.

The First World War period was characterized by strong economic regulation by Ottawa. Increased military expenditures required the imposition of additional taxes to cover the federal debt, which exceeded two billion dollars at the end of the war. Not surprisingly, the federal government soon took up direct taxation in the form of personal and corporate income taxes to meet its own obligations.[35]

The early twentieth century saw an important development in federal/provincial fiscal relations: the use of **conditional grants** — sometimes called grants-in-aid or shared cost grants. The federal government was willing to provide funds to the provinces for specific pro-

---

[34] Almost from the beginning, however, the provinces were hard pressed for revenue sources. As early as the 1870s, one province began enacting personal and corporate income taxes as well as estate taxes. British Columbia introduced a personal income tax in 1876; Prince Edward Island followed suit in 1894. By 1896 all provinces were levying estate or succession taxes. See A. Milton Moore, J. Harvey Perry and Donald I. Beach, *The Financing of Canadian Federation: The First Hundred Years* (Toronto: Canadian Tax Foundation, April 1966), pp. 3–4.

[35] Strick, *Canadian Public Finance*, p. 102.

grams *on condition* that the money was spent in accordance with federal standards. These grants closed the provincial budgetary gap somewhat but did little to redress the fundamental problem of unequal fiscal capacity. The money was typically offered on a "take-it-or-leave-it" basis and, while tempting for most provinces, it could be disruptive of budgetary planning and priorities. Perhaps more significantly, the provinces grew increasingly annoyed at the paternalistic way in which the grants were set up and administered.

Before 1930, then, the provinces were already straining under various new obligations. The Great Depression had a devastating impact on their fragile finances. Their tax base was eroded, yet the demand for services, especially in the welfare field, increased dramatically. Federal conditional grants were stepped up but were not sufficient and led to a certain amount of heavy-handed federal intervention. The 1930s became known as the "decade of the tax jungle." Uncoordinated joint occupancy of tax fields, duplication of administrative bureaucracy and high regressive taxation (sales taxes) all served to exacerbate the effects of the Depression. While other countries were able to launch coordinated assaults on economic stagnation, Canada was caught in a serious bind. The Depression revealed that the division of federal/provincial fiscal jurisdictions was inadequate for the twentieth century; some major restructuring would be necessary if the country were to survive as a coherent federal system.

The Royal Commission on Dominion-Provincial Relations (the Rowell-Sirois Commission) was established in 1937 to study the issue. Experts were given a sweeping mandate to examine the problems of the federal system and to offer recommendations that would bring about a degree of congruence between obligations and revenue sources. The Commission presented its recommendations in 1940. It suggested that the federal government assume responsibility for personal and corporate income tax collection, the accumulated debt of the provinces and the support of the unemployed through a social security program.[36] In addition, the Commission recommended a system of national adjustment grants to subsidize the poorer provinces so that the level of social services could be standardized across the country. The latter proposal ran into immediate opposition, especially from some of the wealthier provinces, which did not wish to support their poorer compatriots. The outbreak of the Second World War diverted everyone's attention from the issue. Finally, as R.M. Burns concluded: "Patriotism accomplished what financial reasoning could not."[37]

The wartime period of relative economic prosperity eased the burden of the provinces. Citing the emergency, the federal government usurped the income tax and succession duty fields for itself. In return, the provinces were given compensatory payments. Thus began a complicated series of *tax-rental* and *tax-sharing* agreements.[38] The federal government took over, in effect, virtually all provincial sources of revenue from direct taxation in exchange for a payment of "rent." It is clear from this why the federal government in the war years and in the postwar decade was in a position of considerable dominance over the provinces.

By the end of the Second World War, the federal government was spending approximately three-quarters of the money spent by all governments in Canada. It had built up an impressive bureaucratic infrastructure and was intent on implementing its vision of Canada's future. As the war emergency disappeared, the federal government began to assume

---

[36] Moore, Perry and Beach, *The Financing of Canadian Federation*, pp. 11–13.

[37] R.M. Burns, "Recent Developments in Federal-Provincial Fiscal Relations in Canada," *National Tax Journal*, vol. 15, no. 3 (September 1962), p. 228.

[38] See Stevenson, *Unfulfilled Union*, pp. 136–41, and Strick, *Canadian Public Finance*, pp. 106–12.

"... MY NAME IS BOB, AND I'M AN ASYMMETRICAL FEDERALIST ..."

Reproduced with permission, Gable, *The Globe and Mail*.

responsibility for the problems of postwar reconstruction. At this time, a distinct change in attitude concerning the role of government in society arose. The concept of the balanced budget was replaced by Keynesian economic theory: the federal government committed itself to maintaining a high and stable level of economic growth and employment throughout the country. To do so, the federal government had to adjust federal tax rates and levels of expenditure. It was able to obtain provincial agreement for an extension of the tax rental arrangement until at least 1952.[39] The pre-eminence of the federal government began to erode during the later 1950s, as the various tax rental agreements between it and the provinces began to engender opposition. Québec, for its part, began to resent both this arrangement and the conditional grants scheme.

As the 1960s approached, there was an accentuation of the lack of correlation between revenue sources and expenditure responsibilities. The welfare state was entering the "big money" era. The provinces began to feel the financial pinch for education and health care again. The federal government was virtually left out of these important jurisdictional areas. Increased provincial responsibilities were matched by the increasing competence and aggressiveness of provincial bureaucrats, perhaps seen most clearly in Québec. The federal government seemed to be losing its grip on the economy as the country experienced a recession and slow economic growth. Sensing weakness, the provinces began to claim more responsibility for their own economies and questioned the feasibility of a national economic policy.

The most obvious indication of provincial self-assertion was in the area of tax-sharing. Tax-sharing was a continuation of the tax-rental program; however, instead of per capita

---

[39]   Strick, *Canadian Public Finance*, p. 107.

grants, the provinces were to get a fixed percentage of three standard taxes: personal income taxes, corporate tax and federal succession duties. Tax-sharing protected provincial autonomy to some extent and was supplemented by an unconditional grant. Despite this apparent liberalization of federal policy, Ontario and Québec objected to the arrangement, and the federal government introduced a tax abatement system for the two provinces. This meant that the federal government moved out of the tax field to a considerable degree so that the provinces could levy their own taxes. This agreement only encouraged agitation by all the provinces for a better deal.

During the 1960s, the abatement system was gradually extended to all provinces. The federal government thus partially withdrew from the personal and corporate income tax field. Although the federal government continued to collect the tax (and return part of it to the provinces) as long as the provincial tax base remained the same as the federal tax base, the provinces had more room for increasing their taxes. In other words, the provincial portion could vary considerably. In 1966, the tax arrangements were opened up for periodic review, with the provinces asking for even more tax room and more federal money. At that time Ottawa was not in a mood to compromise and the arrangement was extended virtually unchanged.

By 1972, however, the abatement system was practically at an end. The federal government introduced a guarantee program to prevent provincial loss of revenues resulting from a rationalization of their tax base with that of the federal government.

Today, Ottawa still collects income taxes for all the provinces except Québec (at rates set by the provinces); Québec takes in its own personal and corporate income taxes. With the exception of Ontario, Québec and Alberta, all provinces have tax collection arrangements with the federal government for corporate income taxes.

BASIC CONCEPTS OF FISCAL FEDERALISM

Before outlining the most recent federal/provincial agreements, we shall examine in greater detail two of the most important elements of the financial relationship: conditional and unconditional grants and equalization programs. The two are, of course, related, and under various formulas have been a major part of overall federal/provincial policy for decades.

CONDITIONAL AND UNCONDITIONAL GRANTS

As mentioned earlier, conditional grants were one of the means by which the financial gap of the 1930s was bridged. Such transfers between central and regional governments often occur in federations because of the need to provide equal standards in services across the country. In Canada, they are essential because of the imbalance of resources across the land. The first conditional grants in Canada were paid out for agricultural instruction in 1912.[40] Larger-scale grants were offered in 1927 to help the provinces finance old-age pensions. After the Second World War, increased expenditures on health and welfare necessitated another major expansion.

The federal government was able to act in these fields because of its spending power. **Spending power** refers to the federal government's blanket authority to spend money for any purpose in any field even if it has no legal jurisdiction over the area. In most cases, Ottawa offered to pay half the costs of a certain program, with the provinces paying the rest. These so-called "50-cent dollar" programs were an attractive proposition for some provinces, but they had the effect of enticing provincial legislatures to spend their resources on programs chosen by

---

40 Cody, "The Evolution of Federal-Provincial Relations in Canada," p. 66.

the federal government. On certain occasions, provincial leaders might have wished to spend their money on other programs, but there was no way to shift resources unless Ottawa agreed. Budgetary priorities were inevitably affected. Québec was particularly dissatisfied, because it was left with reduced powers in what it felt to be important matters of provincial concern.

As a result of such criticisms, in 1964 the federal government began to allow any province that did not want to be involved in a joint-cost venture to receive an equivalent sum of money either as a federal tax withdrawal or in another form. Only Québec took up this offer, thereby highlighting its claim to special status within Confederation. Québec's special status was also confirmed by the development of its own hospital and old age pension schemes.

As the provinces grew in financial health, it was inevitable that they would seek a revision of these fiscal arrangements. In 1977, led by a militant Québec, and to some extent Alberta and Ontario, they won the struggle to end the restrictive conditional grants system. Ottawa increasingly offered **unconditional grants**, which the provinces could spend in any way they wished, as they were not designated for any specific policy field. This shift can be considered an indication of the current decentralization of the federal system. Figure 6.3 highlights the correlation between conditional and unconditional grants, and constitutional centralization and decentralization.

It has already been pointed out that a continuing problem of federal/provincial financial relations has been the different fiscal capacities of the various provinces. In 1867, the financial gap between the colonies was already wide; it has been growing ever since. A primary objective of post–Second World War fiscal policy has been to narrow this gap and to provide a degree of economic stabilization. The instrument for accomplishing this is the provision of equalization payments to the provinces. **Equalization payments** are unconditional transfer payments to the provinces from the federal government calculated on the ability of each province to raise revenue. (See Figures 6.4 and 6.5.) They enable less affluent provinces to provide an average level of public services without the need to resort to excessively high levels of taxation. Until 1957, such grants were tied to the tax rental scheme. Since then they have been calculated by bringing provinces up to a national average based on a number of provincial revenue sources.

FIGURE 6.3   DEGREE OF CENTRALIZATION AS AFFECTED BY THE FEDERAL/PROVINCIAL FINANCIAL TRANSFERS AND THE DISTRIBUTION OF POWER

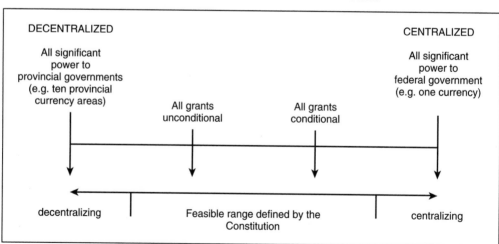

Adapted from Thomas J. Courchene, "The New Fiscal Arrangements and the Economics of Federalism," in *Options*, Proceedings of the Conference on the Future of the Canadian Federation (Toronto: University of Toronto Press, 1977), p. 315.

FIGURE 6.4 FEDERAL TRANSFERS TO THE PROVINCES, 1984 TO 1992 (BILLIONS OF DOLLARS)

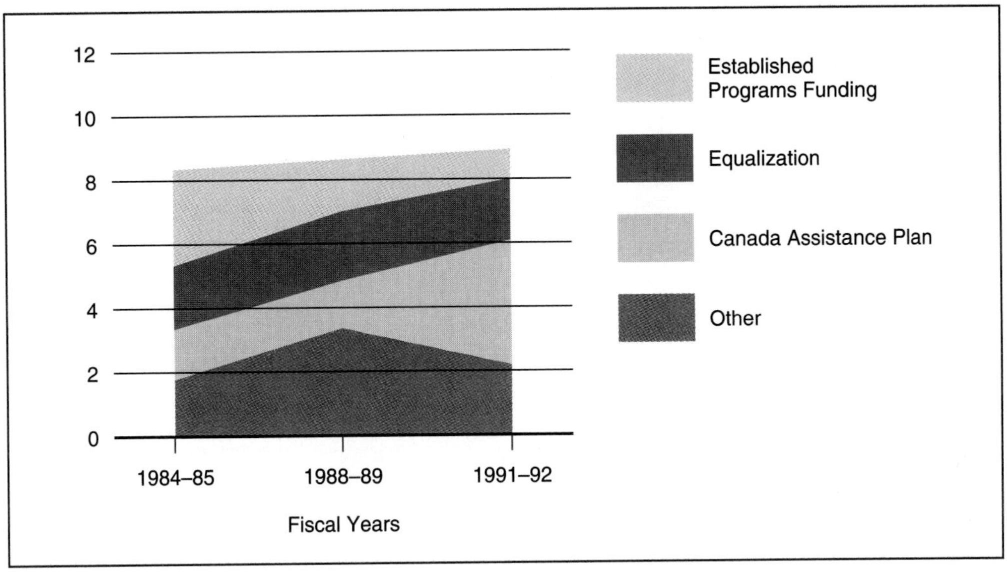

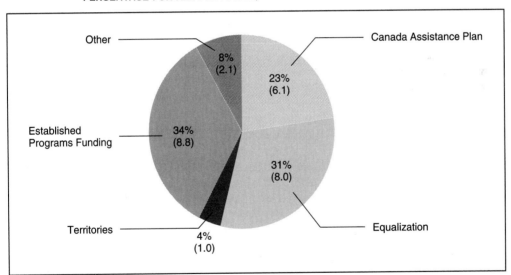

Source: Derived from figures in *The Economic and Fiscal Statement* (Ottawa: Department of Finance, 1992).

FIGURE 6.5 COMPOSITION OF FEDERAL TRANSFERS, 1991–92 (BILLIONS OF DOLLARS AND PERCENTAGE FOR ALL PROVINCES)

Source: Derived from figures in *The Economic and Fiscal Statement* (Ottawa: Department of Finance, 1992).

How successful have the equalization efforts been? In terms of allowing for an increase in per capita provincial expenditures, they can be considered successful. They have brought the "have-not" provinces up to the level of the "have" provinces. However, they have not erased interprovincial and interregional disparities. The ultimate objective of equalization policy, of course, is to strengthen federalism by meeting the needs of the weaker elements in the union and thereby establishing a national standard for social services. While its intentions are undoubtedly noble, the federal government has not been able to convey much sense of urgency to this endeavour. For their part, the so-called "have" provinces object loudly to any increase in their financial commitment.

Apart from the equalization program, federal transfers to all but the two poorest provinces are paid mostly by federal taxpayers in the province concerned.[41] Thus, the equalization program is critical for attainment of **horizontal equity**, the reduction of disparities between provinces in the treatment of persons in similar economic circumstances, as well as **vertical equity**, the reduction of inequalities in real income among individuals. It should come as no surprise, then, that the concept of equalization was enshrined in the *Constitution Act, 1982*.

CONTEMPORARY FISCAL ARRANGEMENTS

The entire federal/provincial fiscal arrangement was changed in 1977. The new system replaced the programs under which the federal government aided the provinces to fund medical care, hospitals and post-secondary education on a shared-cost basis. The 1977 *Federal/Provincial Fiscal Arrangements Act* offered the provinces a more-or-less unconditional block grant to be earmarked for health and education: hospital insurance, health insurance and post-secondary education.[42] For the years 1977 to 1982 the *Act* provided for two types of funding — a tax transfer of personal and corporate income tax points and a cash transfer of about 50 percent for provincial expenditures on health care and post-secondary education. While the federal government interpreted the *Act* as giving more autonomy to the provinces, it also placed the burden of two of the most expensive areas of social services squarely in the lap of the provincial governments. From the provinces' point of view the federal government got them into these expensive fields and, since costs were rising rapidly, it was attempting to disengage itself from the responsibilities.[43] In spite of the move to block funding in the Established Program Financing (EPF) the federal government was able to determine how some of the funds were used. In 1984, the *Canada Health Act* was passed declaring that the health transfer would be reduced for any province that allowed doctors to extra bill or employ user fees.

Changes were also made in the equalization programs. The number of revenue sources in the formula was increased, but a limit was placed on the use of provincial revenues from non-renewable resources in the calculation. If the old formula had not been amended, many more provinces would have become "have-not" provinces, thus qualifying for equalization payments. However, even with this restriction, Ontario, the only province that has never received equalization payments, would have become eligible for equalization transfers. To prevent Ontario from qualifying, legislation known as the "Ontario rider" was introduced by the federal government. It disallowed the payment of equalization grants to any province in which personal per capita income had been above the national average in both the current and two previous years. Although this legislation was not passed until 1981, regulations were enacted to prevent Ontario from receiving equalization grants in the years 1977 to 1980. The resultant savings to the federal government were substantial.

---

[41] D.O. Sewell and D.W. Slater, "The Case for Equalization," *Policy Options*, vol. 3, no. 3 (May/June, 1982), p. 17.

[42] David B. Perry, "The Federal-Provincial Fiscal Arrangement Introduced in 1977," *Canadian Tax Journal*, vol. XXV. no. 4 (July/August, 1977), pp. 429–40.

[43] Marsha Chandler and William Chandler, *Public Policy and Provincial Politics* (Toronto: McGraw-Hill Ryerson, 1979), p. 165.

The next round of negotiations over the renewal of fiscal arrangements came in 1982. Although Ottawa has exclusive jurisdiction over fiscal arrangements, an informal consensus clearly existed that decisions would be made in consultation with the provincial governments. The atmosphere of the negotiations was strained. The federal government sought to correct what it perceived as two fundamental problems.[44] First, a growing fiscal imbalance between the federal and provincial governments had to be arrested. While the federal government's deficit was increasing, there was an overall surplus in provincial revenues. Second, the federal government was concerned with maintaining a proper "political balance." Ottawa argued that its contributions to provincial government services were not sufficiently visible — it did not get political credit for what it did — and that this both hindered proper government accountability for taxes and expenditures and deprived the federal government of recognition for its assistance. The federal government thus sought to cut back the level of transfers to the provinces in order to reduce the growth of its own deficit and to ensure the integrity of national programs, including the national health system and post-secondary education.

The provinces, on the other hand, generally favoured maintenance of the status quo. The federal deficit, they argued, was due not to federal transfers to the provinces, but rather to federal policies of indexation, tax expenditures, the subsidization of oil and gas prices and interest rate policies. The provinces also noted that the overall provincial revenue surplus was the result of the resource wealth of a few provinces and did not reflect the general provincial fiscal capacity. Thus, provincial leaders rejected the concept of "fiscal imbalance." The Report of the Parliamentary Task Force on Federal-Provincial Fiscal Arrangements agreed, stating that "the mere existence of deficits at one level of government does not indicate the existence of such a structural imbalance nor does it mean that such deficits have to be rectified at the expense of another level of government."[45] The "have-not" provinces especially were concerned with the future of the equalization program. The wealthier provinces, for their part, sought to protect the money they received from established programs.

Nonetheless, Ottawa was determined to reduce federal transfers. After four months of inconclusive bargaining, the federal government enacted a new set of fiscal arrangements that continue today in their basic form. In 1982, the EPF formula was amended so that the provincial entitlement was determined for a base year and escalation indicators were applied for economic and population growth. From this aggregate number the federal government subtracted the amount of revenue generated by the tax points given to the provinces and then paid out the remainder as a cash grant. In the succeeding years, the federal government reduced the escalation factor and thus limited the total EPF entitlement of the provinces. This device has had the effect of transfering an increasing share of the burden of these programs to the provinces. As Allan M. Maslove summarized the situation:

> *Given that the tax points transfer continues to generate more revenue from year to year, the residual cash transfer is diminishing and is projected to approach zero in the not too distant future."*[46]

---

[44] Allan J. MacEachen, Deputy Prime Minister and Minister of Finance, "Federal-Provincial Fiscal Arrangements in the Eighties: A Submission to the Parliamentary Task Force on the Federal-Provincial Fiscal Arrangements" (Ottawa: Supply and Services, April 23, 1981), pp. 8–11.

[45] *Fiscal Federalism in Canada*, Report of the Parliamentary Task Force on Federal-Provincial Fiscal Arrangements (Ottawa: Supply and Services, August 1981), p. 33.

[46] Allan M. Maslove, "Reconstructing Federal Fiscalism," in Frances Abele, *How Ottawa Spends, 1992–83* (Ottawa: Carleton University Press, 1992), pp. 57–77.

Changes were also made in the calculation of equalization payments. The federal government had proposed Ontario as the standard for determining eligibility for equalization payments, thereby ensuring that province's continued exclusion from receiving such grants. However, the poorer provinces (and Ontario) objected to having their level of receipts contingent upon Ontario's economic performance, especially in light of that province's stagnation in recent years. Ottawa therefore dropped the "Ontario standard," replacing it with a formula based on the average revenue of five provinces. In total, the federal equalization payments account for about one-quarter of all federal transfers to the provinces and about the same proportion of the revenue of the poorest provincial governments.

For the 1988–93 period, transfers from the federal to the provincial and territorial governments remain mostly in the EPF, the equalization program and the Canada Assistance Program. Total transfers for all programs for 1991–92 was $36.8 billion — divided into 26.1 billion in cash and 10.7 billion in tax points. Under the EPF, financial assistance continues to be provided to the provinces for health care services and post-secondary education. For 1991–92 these transfers, provided on an equal per capita basis, were projected at $8.8 billion in cash transfers. The equalization program, which distributes funds to the provinces in order to enable them to provide reasonably comparable level of services, is projected at $8.0 billion cash while the Canada Assistance Program, which finances welfare and other provincial social services is forecast at $6.1 billion cash.[47] (See Figure 6.5.) The only restriction on federal funding for the CAP is that the provincial social assistance programs must be based on "need." Programs may vary widely across the country.

NATIONALIST AND REGIONAL CHALLENGES TO FEDERALISM

In the last three decades, there has been a proliferation of books, articles and editorials expressing alarm at the possible break-up of Canada. In this period, the smugly confident view that Canada was breaking down old barriers and divisions and progressing toward a highly unified federal state was replaced by profound anxiety and pessimism. The immediate cause of this crisis of Canadian federalism was the election of the separatist Parti Québécois to power in Québec in 1976. However, while the rise to power of René Lévesque was certainly disturbing to the federalist cause, it represented only one element of a much larger and more complex problem.

In the discussion of the concept in Chapter 1, **nationalism** was defined as the collective action of a politically conscious ethnic group (or "nation") in pursuit of increased territorial autonomy or sovereignty.[48] In a federal system, especially in one as decentralized as Canada, an option for nationalist movements in their quest for self-determination is to gain control of provincial government power. Ethnic nationalist groups in Canada, especially in Québec, have pursued varying degrees of autonomy, up to and including independent statehood. Often, they utilized the mechanisms of federalism to challenge the federal status quo. However, since federalism institutionalizes territorial divisions through its political

---

[47] Government of Canada, *Economic Fiscal Statement*, 1992.

[48] Nationalism is a multi-faceted phenomenon. For a recent discussion of theories and literature pertaining to Québec see Hudson Meadwell, "The Politics of Nationalism in Québec," *World Politics*, vol. 45, no. 2 (Jan. 1993) pp. 203–41.

structures, provincial power may also be employed to express *regional* conflicts that lack an ethnic dimension. Throughout Canadian history the power of provincial governments has been used to press both ethnic nationalist and regionalist demands on Ottawa. The discussions that follow trace the development of these territorially based conflicts, first with regard to French Canadian nationalism in Québec and, second, to the expression of regional discontent.

THE FRENCH/ENGLISH DIMENSION

Between about 1840 and 1845 the French, for the first time, became a minority in Canada. As we noted in Chapter 3, the Roman Catholic Church was a powerful influence in determining the initial strategy for minority survival. After the conquest, in 1760, the Church successfully encouraged its flock to remain socially separate from the English in the province, maintaining an essentially agrarian society. French Canadians generally remained aloof from political affairs, and even after Confederation the English minority within Québec dominated urban and political economic life. It was not until much later, in the late 1950s and the 1960s, that fundamental change became apparent in the aspirations of Québec francophones. A "Quiet Revolution" eventually blossomed into an outright challenge to Canadian federalism and the very existence of the Canadian state.

French/English relations in the years leading up to this challenge have sometimes been stormy. However, the discord has not been constant; rather, periods of unrest have been interspersed with more-or-less prolonged periods of quiet. Several crises trace the breakdown of goodwill between the two communities and the growth of the separatist movement. It will be helpful to recall these events before examining the growth of modern nationalism within Québec. The history is not a particularly proud one for English Canadians.

As we have seen, the ethnic conflicts that periodically erupted had their roots in the linguistic and educational rights of the provinces. Manitoba, with its large French-speaking community, was created in 1870 on the same basis as Québec, with Roman Catholic schools and bilingual education. In the other provinces, the languages to be used locally were left as a matter of solely provincial concern.

By 1885, French-speaking Métis in the West were being swamped by English-speaking settlers. To protest land losses they rallied around the Métis leader Louis Riel, who returned from exile in the United States to lead a rebellion against the government. Eastern Canada viewed his action as treason and sent troops to quell the disturbance. Riel was defeated, tried and executed. French Canadians grieved for Riel as a patriot who died in the struggle to preserve the "Frenchness" of his people. English Canadians saw him as a traitor or a madman. The ethnic groups were thus polarized, and the stage was set for the limitation of French language rights in Manitoba.

Only five years after the Riel rebellion, the government of Manitoba established a completely non-sectarian educational system in which Roman Catholic schools no longer received provincial aid and French could no longer be used in the secondary schools.

Two British Privy Council decisions upheld the validity of the Manitoba law, but affirmed the power of the federal government to restore school privileges. The situation posed a unique problem for French Canadians inasmuch as it divided them over whether to support their ethnic group or their church. To have the legislation removed they had to support a federal disallowance of provincial legislation, and French Québec was against the principle of federal veto power. The faltering federal Conservative government introduced remedial legislation in 1896, but under pressure it had to be withdrawn. A bizarre election ensued in which Manitoba francophones supported the Roman Catholic Church and the federal Conservative Party in demanding federal disallowance of the Manitoba law. Québec francophones, on the other hand, supported the Liberal Party, which demanded provincial autonomy and opposed the federal use of the disallowance power. Ironically, the Liberals were also supported by anti-French, anti-Catholic forces. The Liberals won in 1896, and Québec francophones thus stopped the legislation that would have protected French Canadian interests in Manitoba. Despite the ironical twist, the Manitoba Schools Question is widely viewed as the most significant example of the loss of French and Catholic rights outside of Québec.

The Confederation arrangement allowed all provinces to legislate in the field of education but gave constitutional protection to both English and French languages in the federal Parliament and the legislature of Québec. (BNA 133). In the other provinces, however, the practice until the 1940s was for English-speaking Canadians, wherever they were in the majority, to deprive French-speaking minorities of public school facilities in their native language, and to refuse them the use of their language in government institutions. Even within the federal government, where the *BNA Act* had stated the right of both groups to use their own language in debates, records, journals and courts, most government employees were unilingual English-speakers.

In 1935, French Canadian nationalist and historian Abbé Lionel Groulx published the following summary of French language and school rights (or lack of rights) outside Québec:

1864 NOVA SCOTIA: French-speaking Catholic Acadians are forbidden to have French schools.

1871 NEW BRUNSWICK: Catholic schools are closed and teaching of French (and in French) is forbidden in public schools.

1877 PRINCE EDWARD ISLAND: Catholic and French schools are outlawed.

1890 MANITOBA: Separate (Catholic) schools are outlawed and teaching of French (and in French) is forbidden at the secondary level.

1892 NORTHWEST TERRITORIES (including what is now Alberta and Saskatchewan): Teaching in French is outlawed in public schools and Catholic schools are prohibited.

1905 ALBERTA AND SASKATCHEWAN: The regulations of 1892 (Northwest Territories) are confirmed.

1915 ONTARIO: By regulation (regulation No. 17), French is outlawed in Ontario schools.

1916 MANITOBA: Teaching of French is forbidden at all levels.

1930 SASKATCHEWAN: Teaching of French is prohibited even outside school hours.[49]

Abbé Groulx argued that each of these rulings deprived French Canadians of their basic human rights. This succession of ethnic crises formed the history of the loss of French rights outside of Québec. The result was virtual abandonment by the Québécois of French Canadians outside their province, and the gradual assertion of Québec nationalism.

---

[49] André Bernard,*What Does Quebec Want?* (Toronto: James Lorimer, 1978) p. 27, taken from Abbé Lionel Groulx, *L'enseignement Français au Canada* (Montréal: Granger Frères, 1935).

The language division appeared in another guise in the conscription crises of both the First and Second World Wars. French Canadians were strongly opposed to conscription. André Bernard maintains that one of the main reasons behind this opposition was the fact that the recruiting officers and the military hierarchy were English-speaking.[50]

The 1917 federal election on the conscription issue divided the country along linguistic lines: every riding in which French was the majority language voted against the government and conscription. Fortunately, the war ended before conscription could be enacted, and the issue died. The legacy of bitterness remained, however, and its residue in federal politics and parties has not yet been fully erased. In the federal election campaign that followed the conscription bill, the pro-conscription Conservatives and English Liberals united to run Union candidates. They won the election, but captured only three seats in Québec. In the first postwar election in 1921, the Liberals formed the government, this time winning all the Québec seats. Provincially as well as federally, the Conservatives were severely defeated and, except for the Diefenbaker sweep in 1958, the party did not regain the confidence of French Canadians until the Mulroney victories of 1984 and 1988. This ended with the party's ignominious defeat in 1993.

In 1942, during the Second World War, there was a second conscription crisis. The federal government called a plebiscite, an expression of opinion by the voters that was not legally binding. The campaign was bitter.[51] French-speaking Québec voted against conscription by a huge majority of 85 percent, while English-speaking Canada was overwhelmingly in favour. Liberal Prime Minister Mackenzie King postponed the imposition of conscription in order to allay the fears of French Canadians. The delay minimized the crisis because the war ended before the conscripts were sent into battle. However, the apparent impotence of the French in face of an English majority decision on a topic of life or death remained as a humiliating residue and helped to fuel Québec nationalism.

NATIONALISM IN QUÉBEC

Québec nationalism has been present in some form since the British conquered Québec in 1760. In the first century, it took the form of resistance to assimilation by the English: what mattered was *la survivance*. As a conquered people, the French did not become integrated with their victors, but formed an isolated and basically rural society, for the most part living in small parish units where economic activity centred on the family farm. The French elite, especially the clergy, maintained control over the masses through the Church, the educational system and the continuation of the French language. It can thus be said that in general the English dominated politics and commerce, while the French elites controlled the cultural institutions.

After Confederation, two strains of nationalism developed in *La Belle Province*.[52] The first, depicted by the historian Abbé Lionel Groulx, was based on early French Canadian

---

[50] Ibid.

[51] See Richard Thoret, "The Uses of the Referendum in Canada," in D.C. Rowat, ed., *The Referendum and Separation Elsewhere: Implications for Quebec* (Ottawa: Carleton University, 1978), pp. 19–34.

[52] See Léon Dion, *Quebec: The Unfinished Revolution* (Montréal: McGill-Queen's University Press, 1976); Herbert Guindon, "The Modernization of Quebec and the Legitimacy of the Canadian State," in D. Glenday, et al., *Modernization and the Canadian State* (Toronto: Macmillan Canada, 1978), pp. 212–46; Denis Monière, *Le développement des idéologies au Québec: des origines à nos jours* (Montréal: Editions Québec/Amérique, 1977); Marcel Rioux, *Quebec in Question* (Toronto: James, Lewis and Samuel, 1971).

history. It called for a rural vision of Catholic, anti-materialist values and, on occasion, re-sulted in proposals for an inward-looking, corporatist and authoritarian solution to the Québec situation. The second, led by Henri Bourassa, politician and editor of *Le Devoir*, called for a pan-Canadian vision and an equal partnership between English and French Canada. For Bourassa, the Canadian dilemma was to be resolved by building a state that was both bicultural and bilingual.

The inward-looking strain of nationalism characterized the Union Nationale governments of Maurice Duplessis, 1936–39 and 1944–60 (Duplessis died in 1959). The predominantly rural Union Nationale based its philosophy on an old-style nationalism and its action on pa-tronage and intimidation. It was very successful until the 1949 Asbestos Strike. This strike of 5 000 workers lasted four months and consisted of an alliance between the American-owned asbestos company and the Duplessis government against the workers who were sup-ported by members of Québec's developing intelligentsia. Québec was never the same again.

The 1950s were characterized by widespread reaction to both clerical influence and Duplessis manipulation. Industrialization and urbanization helped erode the basis of Union Nationale support, and values in the province changed rapidly from rural to urban, from re-ligious to secular.

The new outward-looking strain of nationalism was typified by the Québec Liberal Party, which Jean Lesage led to victory in 1960 after 16 years in opposition. In the subse-quent "Quiet Revolution," Lesage's Liberals reversed the guiding philosophy of previous gov-ernments in Québec. Instead of preservation of the *patrimoine* (the language, religion and culture of a traditional rural Québec) they defined their job as defending *la nation* in terms of the economy and social structure of the province. Drastically increasing the role of gov-ernment in society, the new government secularized the school system, nationalized hydro-electricity and reformed the civil service. Technological and economic changes had already altered the educational and social structure of the province; now a new administrative élite was set up to manage the state machinery of education, welfare and health care.[53]

Led by this new middle class, French Canadian nationalism gave away to Québec na-tionalism. Nationalists were struck by the fact that use of the French language was on the decline in Canada and that Québec's share of the Canadian population was dropping. The *épanouissement* or flowering of Québec-based nationalism was encapsulated in the 1960 political phrase *maîtres chez nous* (masters in our own house). From now on a state-centred nationalism replaced the traditional nationalism.

Québec's new challenges to Canada came in many guises — judicial, social and political. Objections ranged from precise attacks on centralizing mechanisms such as the power of disallowance to general claims that the *BNA Act* did not define a true federal system. On the latter subject, Marcel Faribault stated: "Our present Constitution is at variance with a genuine conception of federalism, which alone can keep Canada united."[54] And journalist Claude Ryan, later leader of the Liberal Party of Québec, argued that "it is the document [the *BNA Act*] as a whole, the general ideas underlining the text, that must be revised."[55]

---

[53] See Kenneth McRoberts, *Quebec: Social Change and Political Crisis*, 3rd ed. (Toronto: McClelland & Stewart, 1988) for a discussion of this period and the impact of economic development on Québec nationalism.

[54] *Le Devoir*, June 30, 1967.

[55] Ibid.

Claims were also made that the division of powers between the federal and provincial governments discriminated against Québec. Marcel Chaput summarized the situation in *Why I Am a Separatist*: "The Federal government has exclusive legislative authority in the main fields of administration...."[56] The grievance was expressed in more detail by André Allemagne in *Le colonialisme au Québec*:

> By virtue of the BNA Act, which serves as Canada's constitution, the Ottawa government retains powers of which the Québec government is deprived within its own territory. These powers are enormous. They give the federal state supremacy in economic matters and allow it considerable scope for intervention in socio-cultural affairs.[57]

Some Québec francophones saw the federal union as lacking the free consent of the contracting parties — in other words, as blocking self-determination. The following is a sample of representative opinions: "No referendum enabled the people to express their will in 1867" (Raymond Barbeau).[58] "This system (confederation)...was not established by the express will of the people affected, but imposed by statute by an imperialist mother country" (*Le rassemblement pour l'indépendance nationale*).[59] "Once Confederation had been voted by the House and approved by London, in complete disregard of popular opinion, Québec, which 30 years earlier, under the influence of the Patriots, had dreamed of becoming a republic, was de facto turned...into a minority...." (Pierre Vallières).[60] "The Canadian state is a purely political and artificial entity formed originally by armed forces and maintained by a submission of the French-Canadian to the Federal Government" (Marcel Chaput).[61]

These viewpoints were underpinned by real economic injustices. In their volume on Québec, Kenneth McRoberts and Dale Posgate show that in the early 1970s the province's economy was characterized by a predominance of non-French capital and ownership in large corporations. According to their data, only 26 of 165 enterprises with an annual production worth $10 million were owned by French Canadians. The export-oriented, resource-based corporations tended to be under American and multinational control. Modern light industry (such as electronics) tended to be owned by Anglo-Canadians. As McRoberts and Posgate demonstrate, French Canadians predominated in the ownership of labour intensive, lower productivity industries such as textiles, leather products and food processing. Finally, the financial institutions were predominantly controlled by Anglo-Canadians.[62]

At the individual level as well, Québec residents fared worse than many other Canadians during the period in question. In *What Does Quebec Want?* André Bernard found that since 1926 the gap between per capita incomes in Québéc and Canada was around an average of 15 percentage points lower for the former. The rate of unemployment in the province was regularly over 25% above the Canadian average, and Québec rates for standard taxes were 10% to 15% above the Canadian average.[63]

---

[56] Cited in Gilles Lalande, *In Defence of Federalism* (Toronto: McClelland & Stewart, 1978), p. 63.

[57] Cited in ibid., p. 63.

[58] Raymond Barbeau, *J'ai choisi l'indépendance*, cited in ibid., p. 67.

[59] Le rassemblement pour l'indépendance nationale, *L'action nationale*, February 1961, cited in ibid., p. 63.

[60] Pierre Vallières, *White Niggers of America*, cited in ibid., p. 71.

[61] Marcel Chaput, *Why I am a Separatist*, cited in ibid., p. 76.

[62] Kenneth McRoberts and Dale Posgate, *Quebec: Social Change and Political Crisis*, 2nd ed. (Toronto: McClelland & Stewart, 1980), p. 42 and *passim*.

[63] Bernard, *What Does Quebec Want?* p. 48.

The 1956 Report of the Québec Royal Commission of Inquiry on Constitutional Problems (The Tremblay Report) summed up Québec's cultural situation: "Because of the religion, culture and history of the majority of its population, the Province of Québec is not a province like the others…. The 1867 *Constitution* made the Province of Québec, which was already historically its national focus, the French-Canadian centre *par excellence*, and the accredited guardian of French-Canadian civilization."[64]

Québec increased its political pressure on the federal government throughout the 1960s. *Maîtres chez nous* became a serious option for some French Canadians, who adopted separatism for Québec as their goal, maintaining that only with their own government could they preserve their culture and fulfill the aspirations of their community. Their slogan *"Vive le Québec libre"* drew international credence when used in 1967 in an important speech by visiting French President Charles de Gaulle. Nationalists focused on the use of English in the private sector, banks and the federal public service as well as on the economic domination of Anglophones.

As Québec nationalism grew in the 1960s and 1970s, Québécois intellectuals became increasingly divided. Pierre Elliott Trudeau and his friends Jean Marchand and Gérard Pelletier moved into federal politics, where they offered a policy of a bicultural and bilingual federal state, but with no special status for Québec. As Prime Minister of Canada, Trudeau became the major spokesman for Henri Bourassa-style nationalism. According to him, the Parti Québécois (PQ) simply replaced traditional Québec clericalism with the "clericalism of nationalism."[65]

The Front de la libération du Québec (FLQ), represented the most extreme separatists. It initiated terrorist activities that culminated in the October Crisis of 1970, with the kidnapping of a British diplomat and the murder of the Québec Minister of Labour, Pierre Laporte. The *War Measures Act* was invoked by the federal government to deal with what Prime Minister Trudeau considered an acute emergency; in legal terms, it was an "apprehended insurrection." This was the first and only time that the statute has been invoked in peace-time and the basic freedoms of Canadians, mostly French-speaking, were infringed. Hundreds of Québécois were arrested. When the crisis atmosphere faded, it left uncertainty among many Canadians that the crisis had been of sufficient proportion to necessitate such large-scale repression.[66] Prime Minister Trudeau labelled critics of the *War Measures Act* "bleeding hearts."

Meanwhile, the Québec separatist challenge had grown in the political arena. In the 1966 provincial election, the Ralliement nationale (RN) and Le Ralliement pour l'indépendence nationale (RIN) had gained 10 percent of the vote. Former provincial Cabinet minister René Lévesque left the Liberal Party in 1968 and formed the Parti Québécois. This new party brought together the left-wing RIN, the right-wing RN and other nationalists under a new umbrella organization.

---

[64] See David Kwavnick, ed., *The Tremblay Report, The Report of the Royal Commission of Inquiry on Constitutional Problems*, The Carleton Library, No. 64 (Toronto: McClelland & Stewart, 1973), p. 45.

[65] For Trudeau's position see Pierre Elliott Trudeau, *Federalism and the French Canadians* (Toronto: Macmillan Canada, 1968), pp. 207–9. For an overview of the challenge and response see Robert J. Jackson and Abbie Dann, "Quebec Foreign Policy? Canada and Ethno-Regionalism," in Werner Link and Werner J. Feld, eds., *The New Nationalism* (New York: Pergamon, 1979), pp. 89–106; and Robert J. Jackson, "Federal Government Strategy and Response to the Victory of the Parti Québécois" in *La Vie Politique au Canada, Etudes Canadiennes/Canadian Studies*, Numéro Spécial, 1979, pp. 103–19.

[66] See Denis Smith, *Bleeding Hearts…Bleeding Country: Canada and the Quebec Crisis* (Edmonton: Hurtig, 1971).

Reproduced with permission, Gable, *The Globe and Mail.*

Such nationalist organizations with aspirations for provincial independence were not new in Québec history. The first, the Parti Patriote of the first half of the 19th century, was elected to office with a large majority under its very popular leader Louis-Joseph Papineau. In an attempt to win parliamentary control over government expenditures and other concessions, the party instigated an armed rebellion in 1836–37. It was quelled by the troops of the British governor. The second, the Parti Nationale led by Honoré Mercier, was elected in 1886. It was defeated in 1892 because of financial problems, corruption and lack of support for constitutional change. Then, in 1936, the Union Nationale, led by Maurice Duplessis, came into office as the third successful nationalist party. It played the nationalist game within the context of Canadian rules. Gradually, however, the more progressive element split off because the party promoted insular nationalism, not wholesale independence.

In the 1970 election, the Parti Québécois received only 24 percent of the popular vote, and Liberal leader Robert Bourassa formed the government. The October Crisis intervened between this election and that of 1973. Playing on the fear of separatism and on his success with the James Bay Hydro development project, Bourassa won another landslide victory despite an increase in PQ votes to 30 percent.

In reaction to these defeats the Parti Québécois softened its stand from outright political independence to sovereignty-association — political independence with economic association. But the purpose of sovereignty-association was to reassure those who were apprehensive about the economic consequences of separatism. The party continued to promote its vision of a Québec in which no tax would be paid to the federal government and citizens would be subject to no federal law. In the 1976 election, Lévesque ran on an *étapiste* (gradualist) strategy and a platform of "good government." He offered a referendum on sovereignty-association. This approach worked.[67] Forty-one percent of Québec voters cast their ballots for the Parti Québécois on November 15, 1976, and the PQ became the fourth nationalist party to gain control of the government in Québec.

While the new government proved to be moderate in fiscal and monetary policies, it frightened the business community, especially by nationalizing the Asbestos Corporation. The election also escalated French/English tensions. Bill 101, the Charter of the French language, was introduced in the Québec legislature in April 1977, declaring the province unilingual. (See Chapter 3.) The non-francophone reaction was swift — over 100 000 anglophones left Montréal within the next four years.

The May 1980 referendum on sovereignty-association proved a setback for Lévesque. The vote forced Québec residents to choose between "oui" — to negotiate sovereignty-association — and "non" — not to negotiate. It did not ask them to vote on independence. Even this mild resolution was defeated by almost six out of ten votes. The *"non"* forces, buttressed by Prime Minister Trudeau's promise of "renewed federalism," captured a satisfactory majority in Québec.

The threat of independence did not die with this vote, however. According to PQ strategists, Québec had all the ingredients necessary to form an independent state: both people and resources. If Québec had been independent in the 1970s, it would have had a population in the top one-third and a greater geographical territory than 90 percent of UN member states. Lévesque knew that his support came overwhelmingly from voters under age 35 and he thought that he could afford to wait. In the 1981 election, the Parti Québécois promised *not* to call a sovereignty referendum before another election. It received 47 percent of the vote and 80 of 122 seats in the National Assembly. The Liberals under Claude Ryan, former editor of *Le Devoir*, were crushed.

After the 1981 election defeat, the provincial Liberals replaced Ryan with former premier Robert Bourassa. Lévesque, on the other hand, stayed on as leader of the Parti Québécois. He attacked the federal government for selling out Québec, and refused to sign the 1982 amendment package that patriated the *Constitution*. Within his own party he tried to soften the separatist policy. But the December, 1981 convention passed a resolution to delete the word "association" from the PQ policy of sovereignty-association. Lévesque would not accept the decision; he insisted on a vote of the entire membership of the party and won — the party policy remained sovereignty-association. After the Conservatives won control of Ottawa in the 1984 election Lévesque ended his provincial boycott of federal/provincial meetings. He began a campaign to delete the very idea of sovereignty-association from the party manifesto, and, in January 1985, the party convention endorsed his position and officially became a moderate, nationalist party.

Before the next provincial election, however, the party developed major splits (half the cabinet had resigned in 1984) and Lévesque died. Pierre Marc Johnson became leader of the party and led it into the 1985 election with a moderate, nationalist platform. The party found, however, that it had abandoned its ideological roots only to be badly defeated in the elec-

---

[67] For a summary see William Coleman, *The Independence Movement in Quebec 1945–1980* (Toronto: University of Toronto Press, 1984); John Saywell, *The Rise of the Parti Québécois* (Toronto: University of Toronto Press, 1977); and Vera Murray, *Le Parti Québécois* (Montréal: Editions Hurtubise HMH, Lté., 1976). For the official position, see Government of Québec, *Québec-Canada: A New Deal* (Québec: Editeur Officiel, 1979). On PQ voting behaviour see Maurice Pinard and Richard Hamilton, "The Parti Québécois Comes to Power,"*CJPS*, vol. XI (1978), pp. 739–76.

tion. Bourassa's Liberals won 56 percent of the vote and 98 seats while the PQ was left with 38 percent of the vote and only 24 seats.

In 1988, the PQ replaced Johnson with Jacques Parizeau, an arch-nationalist who rejected the party's moderate stance and revived the *indépendantiste* spirit. In 1990, following the advice of Parizeau, it declared

> ...we must break the iron collar of a federal system that serves us badly, that will always subordinate our national interests to those of another majority. The acquisition of sovereignty is a normal development, taken by all peoples in the world. If others have become sovereign why not us?[68]

However, the province-wide decline in nationalist feelings persisted.[69]

Premier Bourassa continued to espouse policies of federalism with nationalism. In 1985, he successfully demanded that his five conditions be included in the Meech Lake constitutional accord (see Chapter 5), and in 1988 he employed the "notwithstanding" clause of the new *Constitution* to prevent the use of English signs for business purposes in the province (see Chapter 3). With these successes he easily won the 1989 provincial election, although the strong showing of a new English-rights party dampened the victory. The Equality Party took four seats in the predominantly English ridings of Montréal.

Today, Québec leaders are divided about the future. Four leadership groups have emerged: the Indépendantistes, who favour outright statehood for Québec; the Sovereignists, who favour an increase in the *degree* of independence for Québec, but who do not necessarily wish to define sovereignty as meaning an absolute break from Canada; the Devolution Sovereignists, who favour an extreme decentralization of Canada in which very few powers would be left to the central government; and the federalists, who favour the continued existence of Québec within Canada but most of whom wish a readjustment of federal/provincial powers.

By 1989, the nationalist challenge in Québec was subdued by the improved state of the economy, a new entrepreneurial spirit and Bourassa's successful dealings with Ottawa. The fourth nationalist cycle was in decline. The desire for Québec autonomy was not dead, however, only waiting for another cycle of grievances with the federal system of government to surface. The fifth cycle began in 1990.

When the Meech Lake accord failed in May 1990, several Québec members of the Liberal and Conservative federal caucuses left their groups to form an *indépendantist* party in the House of Commons, the Bloc Québécois. The Bloc was led by Lucien Bouchard, former Minister of Environment in Prime Minister Mulroney's cabinet. He put his belief about Québec sovereignty succinctly: "It is not something to bargain for... It is taken by those who want it."[70] Under his tutelage the Bloc published a manifesto that clearly states their position on federalism:

> The Bloc Québécois' mission in Ottawa is solely to promote Québec's profound and legitimate interests and aspirations. On the federal scene, this formation is the single voice of those who, beyond partisan political allegiance, want to make Québec a sovereign, pluralistic state, open to the world.... After discharging its mission, the Bloc Québécois will have no more raison d'être.[71]

---

[68]   Parti Québécois, *La souveraineté* (Montréal: Service de communications du Parti Québécois, 1990).

[69]   Dominique Clift, *Le declin du nationalism au Québec* (Montréal: Editions Libre Expression, 1981).

[70]   *The Globe and Mail,* June 17, 1991.

[71]   Robert J. Jackson and Doreen Jackson, *Stand Up For Canada: Leadership and the Canadian Political Crisis* (Scarborough: Prentice-Hall, 1992), pp. 201–2.

In the October 25 General Election of 1993 the Bloc won 54 seats in the House of Commons, enough to become Her Majesty's Loyal Opposition. (See Chapter 11.) The Bloc's next stated goals are to help the Parti Québecois win the provincial election in 1994 and a referendum on sovereignty in 1995. The fact that they won only 49 percent of the vote in October 1993, a figure that included the votes of many disgruntled Liberals, suggests that they will have difficulty winning a referendum. The resignation of Premier Bourassa in the fall of 1993 has, however, weakened the provincial Liberal Party.

REGIONAL CHALLENGES

If the greatest modern challenge to Canadian federalism is the threat of Québec separatism, the next in significance is undoubtedly alienation in some of the regions. All the non-central provinces have some grievances against Ottawa, Ontario and Québec. The litany includes complaints about official bilingualism, monetary policy, tariff policy, spending decisions and the treatment of eastern fisheries and western resource industries. In the Atlantic provinces there has always been a fierce pride and independence but it is mitigated by the area's need for federal financial assistance. In the West, alienation has combined economic discontent and antipathy toward French and Québec in particular with a demand for greater western significance in the federation.

Largely because of the mix of a great many cultures and relatively few francophones in the West, political vision on the prairies is based more on economic development than cultural interests. Recent manifestations in the West grew out of economic prosperity in the period of the 1970s and early 1980s. The scarcity and high cost of non-renewable energy in the form of oil and gas spurred western economic development. Once among the weak partners of the federal union, the West began to acquire enormous economic power through its sale of natural resources. As this economic wealth was exploited, migration to the West increased and it finally found itself capable of challenging what it considered the insufferable domination of central Canada.

As we pointed out in Chapter 3, alienation is a major component of Western Canada's political culture.[72] Throughout the West's history there has been a strong belief that the resource-rich prairie provinces have been exploited by federal government policies representing central Canadian interests. Perennial issues of contention have centred on federal freight-rate and tariff policies, which were held responsible for making the West a captive market for higher-priced manufactured goods from central Canada. These policies concomitantly increased the cost of exporting products from the West. Thus, it is argued, such policies have allowed the East to remain the industrial heartland of Canada while the West has had to carry a disproportionate amount of the costs.[73]

Modern economic issues dividing western and central Canada continue to be interpreted within this context of alienation. Since the 1970s, regional criticism of the political and

---

[72] David Elton and Roger Gibbins, "Western Alienation and Political Culture," in Richard Schultz, et al., eds., *The Canadian Political Process*, 3rd ed. (Toronto: Holt, Rinehart and Winston, 1979), p. 85. On the concept of "western alienation" see Roger Gibbins, *Prairie Politics and Society* (Toronto: Butterworth, 1980); Robert R. Gilsdorf, "Western Alienation, Political Alienation and the Federal System," in Carlo Caldarola, ed., *Society and Politics in Alberta* (Toronto: Methuen, 1979), pp. 168–92; and Larry Pratt and Garth Stevenson, eds., *Western Separatism* (Edmonton: Hurtig, 1981).

[73] For an alternative view, see Kenneth H. Norrie, "Some Comments on Prairie Economic Alienation," *Canadian Public Policy*, vol. 2, no. 2 (Spring 1976), pp. 211–24. For a summary of centre-periphery issues see D.V. Smiley, *The Federal Condition in Canada* (Toronto: McGraw-Hill, 1987).

economic dominance of central Canada has been expressed in a desire for constitutional reform. The western provincial governments, for example, refused to compromise over patriation of the *Constitution* in 1982 unless the federal government would agree to reduce its power, especially on economic issues. In other words, the jurisdictional issue of whether the provinces or the federal government should control resource development flowed over into the constitutional arena.

Conflicts over western natural resources are essentially about public finance. Garth Stevenson describes the situation clearly:

> *Provincial efforts to collect larger "royalties" from their minerals in the early seventies were viewed by the federal government as surreptitious efforts to violate the arrangements for sharing tax revenue from corporations, while federal efforts to keep the price of oil below international levels are resented by Alberta and Saskatchewan as depriving them of revenue that would otherwise be available from their provincial treasuries.*[74]

The western provinces sought to secure not only a measure of financial independence from the federal government, but also to use the wealth generated from their natural resources to diversify their economies so that, when the non-renewable resources were depleted, economic prosperity would continue. The federal government, on the other hand, was concerned primarily about its own fiscal needs, as well as about ensuring an equitable sharing of western resource wealth throughout Canada. Many Westerners perceived the redistribution of this wealth as an attempt to keep the West in a position of permanent subordination.

The most significant public expression of western alienation was the formation in the early 1980s of various groups and political parties dedicated to the separation of the western provinces from Canada. The rise of western separatism was ignited by the re-election of the federal Liberal party in 1980, an event that resulted in the political disenfranchisement of western Canada, since the Liberals captured no seats west of Manitoba. Subsequently, the Liberal government initiated two aggressive federal policies: unilateral patriation of the *Constitution* despite provincial objections; and implementation of the National Energy Program, which many Westerners perceived as an attempt to rob them of their resource wealth.

The two leading separatist groups in that period were the Western Canadian Federation (West-Fed) and the Western Canada Concept (WCC). Frustrated by a lack of political power within the federal government, Westerners felt powerless against "centralist" policies, including bilingualism, metrication and immigration. One author summarized the separatist rationale as follows:

> *Without political power, this line of reasoning seems to go, there is nothing that can protect the [resource] wealth that exists. The national government can, if it so wishes, drain the West of its wealth and leave it both economically and politically impoverished within a few years.*[75]

Therefore, Western leaders argued, separation was the only solution.

Separatist meetings attracted hundreds of supporters (mostly in rural Alberta), climaxing with a November, 1980 Jubilee Auditorium rally where 2 700 gathered in Edmonton. Yet the popularity of western separatism dissipated as quickly as it had risen. As one observer

---

[74] Garth Stevenson, "Federalism and Intergovernmental Relations," in M.S. Whittington and G. Williams, eds., *Canadian Politics in the 1980s*, 2nd ed. (Toronto: Methuen, 1984), p. 381.

[75] Doug Owram, "Reluctant Hinterland," in Pratt and Stevenson, eds., *Western Separatism*, p. 61.

noted: "The spontaneity of the separatist movement was both the most important reason for its success and its greatest handicap in developing into a solid, permanent political movement."[76] While the movement provided an outlet for the expression of frustration, there was little agreement among the groups, let alone within them, concerning what strategy to follow. "Western separatism" provided an effective rallying cry, but masked the differing degrees of commitment to separatism within the movement. For example, the founder of West-Fed saw his organization as an interest group composed of members from all parties, while the leader of the WCC sought to build a unique separatist party. Infighting within the WCC as well as between West-Fed and WCC exposed long-term political and organizational differences, as well as the inability to mobilize western frustration.[77]

Nevertheless, the separatists did win a stunning victory in an Alberta provincial by-election when a WCC candidate was elected to represent the rural riding of Olds-Didsbury. Success, however, was short-lived; he was defeated nine months later in a provincial election. Although the WCC polled 10 percent of the total vote province-wide in this election, it received no seats. Their one sitting MLA had alienated separatists by his moderate stand on separatism, preferring to stress "free enterprise" and "good government." In a reflection of the fractious nature of separatist supporters, he was challenged by other separatist candidates. Similar internal dissension plagued the founder of the WCC in British Columbia. He was expelled from Alberta's WCC by the party's executive committee because of differences about the form of regime an independent West should adopt.

The acute western alienation the characterized the early 1980s declined after oil prices, which had underpinned provincialism, dropped and Brian Mulroney won the 1984 General Election.[78] With Mulroney's victory, the western separatists thought they would obtain strong and effective western representation in government. To some extent this expectation was valid; Mulroney's western accord dismantled the National Energy Program and the Trudeau marketing restrictions on the sale of oil and natural gas.

The feeling that the political system was stacked against the West still remained, however. In the 1988 General Election, a new movement called the Reform Party, headed by Preston Manning, son of the former Social Credit premier of Alberta, conducted a credible campaign for western interests. Its demands for free trade and Senate reform found a ready audience among small-c conservative voters. The party named 72 candidates and, while it did not win any seats, it did obtain 15 percent of the votes in Alberta and affected Conservative and NDP competitions throughout the West.

Despite its claim to be a national movement, by concentrating on the need to reduce federal deficits and debt the Reform Party continues to play on Western alienation. It calls for changes to the Senate in order to reduce the power of central Canada and for populist devices such as referendum, recall and initiative in order to reduce the power of the House of Commons. But the centrepiece of Reform policy is an implicit attack on bilingualism. As Manning's party puts it, attempts by the federal government to

> *politicize and institutionalize and constitutionalize English-French relations on a national basis and as a* raison d'être *for the nation itself — have led again, as they have in the past, not to unity but to crisis.*[79]

---

[76] Denise Harrington, "Who are the Separatists?" in Pratt and Stevenson, eds., *Western Separatism*, p. 24.

[77] Ibid., p. 31.

[78] See David Milne, *Tug of War: Ottawa and the Provinces under Trudeau and Mulroney* (Toronto: Lorimer, 1986).

[79] Jackson and Jackson, *Stand Up for Canada*, p. 198.

The party won 51 seats in 1993, mainly in Alberta and British Columbia. Given the collapse of the Conservative Party, Reform has the opportunity to develop a strong national party and take its place. However, the Reform Party would have to abandon some of the policies which attract protest votes in the West. The alternative is that it eventually whithers and dies, as the Progressive Party did in the 1920s.

The importance of such regional parties has often been disparaged. One commentator said of regional parties: "They're not going to amount to a hill of beans." We should remember, however, that they do have an effect on the programs of the major parties and they provide an outlet for the alienation that has been a tradition in western politics. And, in the case of the Reform Party, the West has brought a powerful voice into Ottawa.

To dismiss western separatism out of hand would be premature. Many Westerners feel that they put more into the federation than they receive in benefits. If Ottawa is not able to accommodate the ambitions of western Canadians, the potential for continued challenges remains — perhaps awaiting only the next very unpopular federal government decision.

OVERVIEW

This chapter has explored federalism and its challenges in Canada. Rather than being an esoteric topic, arguments about federalism shape many of the issues and controversies in contemporary politics. The chapter began with a general definition of federalism and examined some of the motives and justifications offered for the adoption of the federal form. As stressed, there is nothing intrinsically good or bad about this constitutional arrangement. At a minimum, federalism is simply a means of dividing political authority. In practice, however, federalism assumes a number of other meanings and implications that may lead some to believe that it is synonymous with "the nation."

A careful review of the history of federalism in Canada reveals pendulum swings of centralization and decentralization. The history of federal/provincial fiscal relations, for example, has been characterized by the waxing and waning of federal dominance. These shifts were due to individual interpretations of the *Constitution* as well as to the impact of particular individuals and historical events.

The best known Father of Confederation, Sir John A. Macdonald, thought of federalism as a means of subordinating provincial governments in the national system. His has been called a "quasi-federalist" position. Others have interpreted federalism as an agreement or "compact" between the English and French.

Sometimes, federalism has been described as a clear-cut or "classical" division of powers between the federal and provincial governments.[80] However, over time, the original financial and legislative powers have had to be changed on several occasions. Adjustments to economic reality and societal concerns forced the constitutional system to move from a strict separation of powers to a more "co-operative" system. In recent years, some authors have characterized the federal system as one of federal/provincial "diplomacy" rather than "cooperation" to indicate how the process has evolved and how much the provinces have been asserting their power in the state. The First Ministers' Conferences, which bring together

---

[80] See Edwin R. Black, *Divided Loyalties: Canadian Concepts of Federalism* (Montréal: McGill-Queen's University Press, 1975) and J.R. Mallory, *The Structure of Canadian Government* (Toronto: Macmillan of Canada, 1971), pp. 325–69.

the Prime Minister and the ten premiers, is the most public manifestation of this form of federalism. Also inseparable from modern concepts of federalism have been the proliferation of ministerial conferences, interprovincial coordinating meetings and the development of entire government departments devoted to federal/provincial relations.

At least five models of federalism have been advanced by Canadian scholars. These models, known by the names quasi-federalism, compact, classical, cooperative and diplomatic federalism, may be used to help explain various aspects of federal/provincial relations. While they are often put forward as if they refer to the evolution of federalism, they more adequately depict which relationships between the federal and provincial governments predominate at any one time. Moreover, there are many other ways to define federalism.

In order to understand Canadian federalism we must also bear in mind how it is buttressed by social and political forces. The federal dimension provides both advantages and disadvantages to Canada. It decentralizes some decision-making and allows a degree of cultural and linguistic autonomy. But it may give too much weight to either the federal or the provincial governments. In the former case there can easily be an erosion of provincial prerogatives, as when the federal government is required to aid the provinces in new, but essentially localized, matters. On the other hand, too much provincial control makes it difficult to handle nation-wide problems: unless the federal government makes inroads into provincial activities, it cannot disseminate national standards and values.

Despite a few difficult periods, federalism in Canada has proven remarkably resilient and adaptable. A degree of movement along the centralization/decentralization continuum is to be expected and is not in itself a matter for much concern. However, Québec and, to some extent the western provinces, continue for quite different reasons to seek changes in the present relationship. The possibility that provinces or regions of Canada may eventually break away from the federal union is not to be totally discounted. Neither should feelings of alienation in Western or Atlantic Canada be dismissed. The problem, as we have suggested, is not so much with federalism as it is with the deep cleavages and divisions in our society. There is nothing very new in regional pressures. Such challenges go back a long way in Canadian history.

In the search for a creative compromise, politicians will have to enunciate and examine Canada's fundamental problems. Any redefinition of federal arrangements must rest between national and provincial aspirations. Reconciliation must be built on a recognition that Canada has two linguistic groups and several cultures that are often in conflict, as well as heterogeneous socio-economic regions. The first fact demands constitutional and institutional guarantees; the second, a proper division of the public purse and power. While provincial distinctiveness is the fundamental reason for all federal systems, a sense of positive consensus among the different regional groups is also imperative if unity is to persist.

SELECTED BIBLIOGRAPHY

Aucoin, P., ed., *Regional Responsiveness and the National Administrative State*, vol. 37, Royal Commission on the Economic Union and Development Prospects for Canada (Toronto: University of Toronto Press, 1985).

Bakvis, Herman and William M. Chandler, eds., *Federalism and the Role of the State* (Toronto: University of Toronto Press, 1987).

Banting, Keith, *The Welfare State and Canadian Federalism*, 2nd ed. (Kingston, Ont.: McGill-Queen's University Press, 1987).

———— and Richard Simeon, eds., *And No One Cheered: Federalism, Democracy and the Constitution Act* (Toronto: Methuen, 1983).

Bickerton, James, *Nova Scotia, Ottawa and the Politics of Regional Development* (Toronto: University of Toronto Press, 1990).

Black, Edwin R., *Divided Loyalties: Canadian Concepts of Federalism* (Montréal: McGill-Queen's University Press, 1975).

Clift, Dominique, *Le Déclin du Nationalisme au Québec* (Montréal: Editions Libre Expression, 1981).

Coleman, William, *The Independence Movement in Quebec 1945–80* (Toronto: University of Toronto Press, 1984).

Courchene, Thomas J., David W. Conklin and Gail C.A. Cook, eds., *Ottawa and the Provinces: The Distribution of Money and Power*, 2 vols. (Toronto: Ontario Economic Council, 1985).

Dodge, William, ed., *Boundaries of Identity: A Quebec Reader* (Toronto: Lester Publishing, 1992).

Forsey, Eugene, *A Life on the Fringe: The Memoirs of Eugene Forsey* (Toronto: Oxford University Press, 1990).

Gagnon, Alain G., ed., *Quebec: State and Society* (Toronto: Methuen, 1984).

Gibbins, Roger, *Prairie Politics and Society* (Toronto: Butterworths, 1980).

Gillespie, W. Irwin, *Tax, Borrow and Spend: Financing Federal Spending in Canada* (Ottawa: Carleton University Press, 1991).

Hodgins, Bruce W. et al., *Federation in Canada and Australia* (Peterborough, Ont.: Frost Centre, 1989).

Hogg, Peter, *Constititonal Law of Canada*, 2nd ed. (Toronto: Carswell, 1985).

Krasnick, M., ed., *Fiscal Federalism*, vol. 65, Royal Commission on the Economic Union (Toronto: University of Toronto Press, 1985).

————, *Perspectives on the Canadian Economic Union*, vol. 60, Royal Commission on the Economic Union (Toronto: University of Toronto Press, 1985).

Latouche, Daniel, *Canada and Quebec, Past and Future: An Essay*, vol. 70, Royal Commission on the Economic Union (Toronto: University of Toronto Press, 1986).

Leslie, Peter M., *Canada: The State of the Federation 1985* (Kingston, Ont.: I.I.R., 1986).

————, *Federal State, National Economy* (Toronto: University of Toronto Press, 1987).

————, *Rebuilding the Relationship* (Kingston, Ont.: I.I.R., 1987).

Mahler, Gregory S., *New Dimensions of Canadian Federalism* (Cranbury, N.J.: Associated University Presses, 1987).

Mathews, Georges, *Quiet Resolution* (Toronto: Summerhill Press, 1990).

McRoberts, Kenneth, *Quebec: Social Change and Political Crisis*, 3rd ed. (Toronto: McClelland & Stewart, 1988).

Meekison, J. Peter, ed., *Canadian Federalism: Myth or Reality*, 3rd ed. (Toronto: Methuen, 1977).

Milne, David, *Tug of War: Ottawa and the Provinces Under Trudeau and Mulroney* (Toronto: Lorimer, 1986).

Milner, Henry, *Politics in the New Quebec* (Toronto: McClelland & Stewart, 1977).

Norrie, K., R. Simeon and M. Krasnick, *Federalism and Economic Union in Canada*, vol. 59, Royal Commission on the Economic Union (Toronto: University of Toronto Press, 1985).

Olling, R.D. and M.W. Westmacott, eds., *Perspectives on Canadian Federalism* (Scarborough, Ont.: Prentice-Hall Canada, 1988).

Pratt, Larry and Garth Stevenson, eds., *Western Separatism: The Myths, Realities and Dangers* (Edmonton: Hurtig, 1981).

Richards, John and Larry Pratt, *Prairie Capitalism: Power and Influence in the New West* (Toronto: McClelland & Stewart, 1979).

Riker, William H., *Federalism: Origin, Operation, Significance* (Boston: Little, Brown, 1964).

Russell, Peter et al., *Federalism and the Charter* (Ottawa: Carleton University Press, 1989).

Shugarman, David and Reg Whitaker, eds. *Federalism and Political Community* (Peterborough: Broadview Press, 1989).

Simeon, R. and I. Robinson, *The Political Economy of Canadian Federalism: 1940–1984*, vol. 71, Royal Commission on the Economic Union (Toronto: University of Toronto Press, 1985).

Smiley, Donald V., *Canada in Question; Federalism in the Eighties*, 3rd ed. (Toronto: McGraw-Hill Ryerson, 1980)

———, *The Federal Condition in Canada* (Toronto: McGraw-Hill, 1987).

——— and Ronald L. Watts, *Intrastate Federalism in Canada*, vol. 39, Royal Commission on the Economic Union (Toronto: University of Toronto Press, 1985).

Stevenson, Garth, *Unfulfilled Union: Canadian Federalism and National Unity*, 3rd ed. (Toronto: Gage, 1987).

———, *Federalism in Canada: Selected Readings* (Toronto: McClelland & Stewart, 1989).

Trudeau, Pierre, *Federalism and the French Canadians* (Toronto: Macmillan Canada, 1977).

Whittington, Michael S., ed., *The North*, vol. 72, Royal Commission on the Economic Union (Toronto: University of Toronto Press, 1985).

Young, Brian and John A. Dickinson, *A Short History of Quebec* (Mississauga, Ont.: Copp Clark Pitman, 1988)

CHAPTER 7

THE PRIME MINISTER, MINISTRY AND CABINET
POLICY-MAKING AT THE CENTRE

The intent of this chapter is to describe and explain the nature of executive power in Canada and to analyze how government policy is established. In many respects, executive power is comparable to a Shakespearean drama: there is a world of difference between appearance and reality.

The nature of political power and its exercise are exceedingly complex and fascinating phenomena. The analysis of leaders and their policies has always been a favourite pursuit of political scientists and pundits, regardless of country or type of political system. Perennial debates and studies consider who really exercises power, what the machinery of leadership is and whether power is shifting in some fashion. A factor complicating the analysis is that political power is an abstract commodity, changing in response to the dynamic political and social environment in which a variety of issues, problems and personalities come and go. It is difficult to isolate power analytically from social influence. Political power is, in a manner of speaking, like a complex mathematical equation in which there are a few constant values and many indeterminate ones.

In contemporary states the task of applying the rules of society is concentrated in an **executive**. This broad term is used to depict the institutions, personnel and behaviour of governmental power. Generally, there are two kinds of rules in a society — constitutional laws, or the basic rules of the game, and less fundamental laws, policies and resolutions. Both types of rules are implemented by the executive, which, in performing this function, plays a vital role in the political system.

Canada's constitutional heritage from Britain includes a formal executive, the Crown and the Governor General (discussed in Chapter 5). In this chapter, we emphasize the political executive and the realities of power in contemporary Canadian politics. We begin by examining the heritage of parliamentary government and its effects on executive power. Next, we outline the role of the Prime Minister and the structure of Cabinet decision-making, including the organization of the 1993 Chrétien government. Studies of conflict of interest and patronage fill out this section. These analyses are followed by an examination of the administrative agencies that support the executive by providing specialized research, advice and assistance in policy formation and implementation. We conclude by evaluating the ongoing debate about the expanding role of the Prime Minister and its implications for Canadian politics.

The reader should be conscious of how much easier it is to describe the machinery of government and what it can accomplish than it is to assess the nature of political power itself. One should also be aware that much important information about the modus operandi of the executive is shrouded in mystery. Important parliamentary traditions, as well as such legal devices as the *Official Secrets Act* have, for the most part, shielded the executive from penetrating scrutiny by the press or the public. Canada has never experienced anything quite like the Crossman Diaries affair, in which the inner workings of the British Cabinet in the late 1960s were laid bare through the posthumous publication of the daily journal of a high-ranking Cabinet minister. Nevertheless, despite certain obvious gaps in understanding, a significant amount is known about the executive in Canada.

WHAT IS THE CANADIAN EXECUTIVE?

Apart from the ceremonial functions of government discussed in Chapter 5, the main task of the executive is providing leadership. The determination of which bodies constitute the executive is complex, as there is no accepted view about how government should be organized.[1] As a result, executive leadership may refer to formal roles, to individuals, to types of activities or to the results of such activities. The executive leaders discussed here have been selected on the basis of their formal roles. They include the Prime Minister, ministry — including the Cabinet — and their immediate staff.

In modern times, executives have become the organizational centre of the political system.[2] The traditional areas of executive action, such as foreign policy and defence, have been augmented by the growing role of governments in managing the economy and social policy. These newer functions have added immensely to the complexity of the policy process, increased the size of bureaucracies and made it difficult to coordinate government activities.

The central feature of any survey of Canada's political heritage must be the pervasive impact of the British model of parliamentary government. Though other aspects of Canadian life have been strongly influenced by the United States, the parliamentary form of government is firmly entrenched and has proven remarkably resistant to change. As discussed in Chapters 5 and 6, the *Constitution* established a type of government based on the British example, with the exception that there was to be a federal division of legislative powers in recognition of the diversity of the country. Canada was to be governed by a parliamentary system with British historical traditions and procedures, and by a constitutional monarch represented by an appointed Governor General.

Although the *Constitution* makes it clear that the Governor General is the country's formal executive, his or her powers and prerogatives are in fact severely limited.[3] Only in

---

1   See Jean Blondel, *The Organization of Governments* (London: Sage, 1982).

2   Richard Rose and Ezra N. Suleiman, eds., *Presidents and Prime Ministers* (Washington: A.E.I., 1980).

3   For a thorough discussion of the role of the Crown in Canada see J.R. Mallory, *The Structure of Canadian Government* (Toronto: Macmillan, 1971), pp. 32–68.

extraordinary situations has a Governor General attempted to interfere directly in the political process. Executive power, though carried out in the name of the Governor General, resides elsewhere in the political structure.

The *Constitution* also established the Queen's **Privy Council** for Canada. This body was created to assist and advise the Governor General. The members of this largely ceremonial body are nominated by the Prime Minister and appointed for life. As it includes current and former Ministers of the Crown, as well as a few other politically prominent individuals, it cannot function as a decision-making body.[4] In reality, a committee of the Privy Council known as the **Cabinet**, comprising current Ministers of the Crown, constitutes the real executive power in Canada. The authority of the Prime Minister and the Ministers rests not on the written *Constitution* but on convention. As members of the Privy Council, the Ministers have the right to the titles 'honourable' and Privy Councillor for life, while the Prime Minister is designated as Right Honourable for life.

The term **governor-in-council** refers to the formal executive authority of the Governor General carried out upon the advice and consultation of this committee of the Privy Council, today known as the Cabinet. The decisions rendered by Cabinet on specific matters carrying legal force are referred to as **orders-in-council**. Technically speaking, a Cabinet directive is an agreement arrived at in Council with the Governor General absent. However, the Governor General is obliged by convention to grant formal approval to virtually any Cabinet decision or bill approved by Parliament. Thus, while Canada does have a monarchical form of government embodied in the Governor General and certain legal procedures, there is no doubt that real executive power belongs to the Cabinet. Its power, in turn, comes from maintaining at least a plurality of supporters in the House of Commons.

The foregoing passage described the largely ceremonial role of the formal executive in the parliamentary system. There are other, as significant, features of the monarchical form of government that impinge upon the operations and powers of the political executive in Canada. Perhaps most significant is the fact that, as in the British parliamentary system, the executive and legislative powers are combined. Today, Canadians vote for 295 Members of the House of Commons; the Prime Minister and almost all members of the Cabinet emerge from this body of representatives. Earlier in Canadian history, during the 1890s, Sir John Abbott and Sir Mackenzie Bowell were in the Senate at the time of their appointment as Prime Minister, but convention now demands that the Prime Minister be a member of the House of Commons either before or shortly after investiture.

The Prime Minister and his or her personally selected Cabinet constitute the government; they formulate policy and direct administrative operations as long as they are supported by the House of Commons. When they no longer receive such support they are replaced, or Parliament is dissolved and elections are called. The crucial point is that both the Prime Minister and the Cabinet Ministers are simultaneously members of the legislature and the executive. In contrast, the United States' presidential form of government provides a clear separation of executive and legislative powers. The American Constitution is based on the premise that a concentration of power is undesirable and that law-making and implementation should be separated by preventing the overlap of key personnel. The presidential/congressional system of checks and balances creates an atmosphere of public political bargaining not found in Canada. For example, in the United States the executive must

---

4   For example, all provincial premiers were made Privy Councillors in 1967 to celebrate Canada's Centennial.

rely on Congress to authorize funds to implement policy, and the Senate must confirm presidential appointments to Cabinet, the diplomatic service, federal courts and other boards and commissions.[5]

Also in contrast to the Canadian Constitution, the American chief executive is elected independently by voters, and tenure in office is in no way dependent on the fate of the legislative program. The executive can frustrate Congress because, for instance, Congress is dependent on the President to implement its policies, and the executive often controls the information needed to formulate effective policies in Congress. On the other hand, the American legislature can and often does reject executive proposals, an exceedingly rare event in Canada, where such rejection could cause the government to fall and a new election to take place.

Both houses of the American Congress share fully in legislative activity, and there is often rivalry between them. Unlike their Canadian counterparts, national parties in the United States have little power as organizations over the Congressmen or Senators they may help to elect. Once in office, American politicians have greater latitude on issues and are much more independent than Canadian MPs, who belong to disciplined, tightly controlled parties. Figure 7.1 illustrates the fusion of power in the Canadian system, where the Prime Minister is both the leader of the largest party in the legislature and the leader of the administration, and compares it to the American presidential system. Anyone familiar with the parliamen-

FIGURE 7.1   PARLIAMENTARY AND PRESIDENTIAL GOVERNMENT

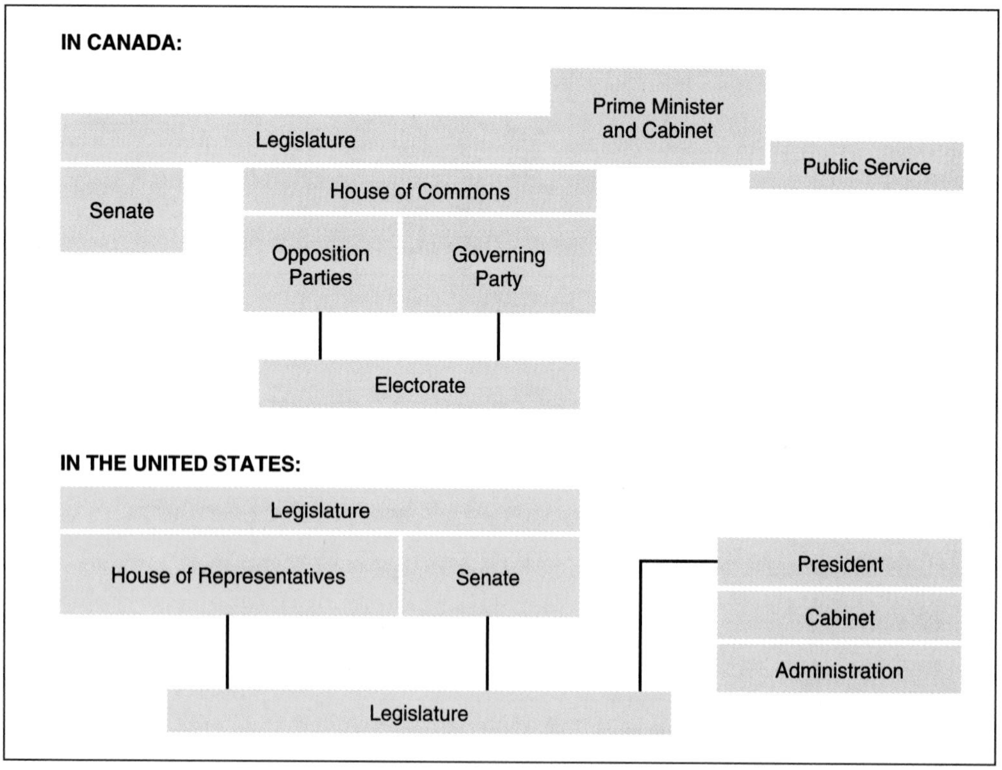

---

[5] Robert J. Jackson and Doreen Jackson, *Contemporary Government and Politics: Democracy and Authoritarianism* (Scarborough, Ont.: Prentice-Hall, 1993), chs 12 and 13.

tary system and the relatively smooth flow of operations resulting from the fusion of executive and legislative powers may wonder how the American system with its built-in conflict and rivalry can possibly work effectively.

Whereas in the United States it is forbidden for an individual to hold a post in Congress and an executive position at the same time, precisely the opposite is true in Canada. All members of Cabinet including the Prime Minister must be elected to the House of Commons or at least be appointed to the Senate. What is perhaps most important to remember in considering the implications of different types of governmental structures is that the principle of fusion of powers creates, at least theoretically, a form of government that is more coherent and responsive to the will of the people. The Canadian executive, assuming it is backed by a parliamentary majority, can be assured of legislative support on most of the bills and programs it wishes to enact. It will of course be held accountable by the people at the next election, but during the interim it is relatively free to pursue its goals.

THE POWERS OF THE PRIME MINISTER

The Prime Minister is unquestionably the central figure in Canadian politics. As we have suggested, the pre-eminence of the Prime Minister and the Cabinet has evolved more from tradition than from any specific part of the *Constitution* or statute. What is the basis of the power of the Prime Minister and Cabinet? How is this power exercised?

The basis of the Prime Minister's power and authority is leadership of the party that commands at least a plurality and normally a majority of the seats in the House of Commons. The Prime Minister is, above all else, an elected Member of Parliament, who has been chosen national leader of the party at a leadership convention. As leader of the party that has been victorious at the polls, the Prime Minister can claim that the "right" to govern is based on a popular mandate. The link with the people gives the Prime Minister enormous legitimacy and authorizes the pursuit of his or her programs and policies under the cloak of popular support until the next election. This legitimacy is not only important in dealings with the bureaucracy and the press, but it also helps in controlling the party. As leader of the party and the holder of this mandate, the Prime Minister can command obedience and support from Cabinet Ministers and backbenchers alike.

The Prime Minister and Cabinet together control the making and signing of treaties and the conduct of international relations, including the declaration of war and peace, as these are prerogative powers of the Crown. Another major source of the Prime Minister's power is control over appointments. The Prime Minister selects the members of the ministry (which includes all Ministers and Secretaries of State whether in Cabinet or not) from the membership of the parliamentary caucus. In 1993, Prime Minister Chrétien inaugurated a new ministry system based on that of Britain. Thirty members of the ministry were appointed, but only 22 were appointed to the Cabinet as Ministers, the other eight were made Secretaries of State to Assist without membership in the Cabinet and with a reduced ministerial salary.

Choice of Ministers may be the most difficult task of Prime Ministers. In fact, in signing a visitor's book, Sir John A. Macdonald entered his occupation as "Cabinet-Maker."[6] A number of factors may influence the Prime Minister's choice of Ministers. Most importantly, there

---

[6] Cited in R.M. Punnett, *The Prime Minister in Canadian Government and Politics* (Toronto: Macmillan, 1977), p. 56.

is an obvious advantage in appointing Ministers to reflect the regional and ethnic diversity of the country. In this regard, a persistent effort is made to have at least one Minister from every province and significant representative from the largest ethnic and religious groupings in the country. This practice is frustrated, of course, when the party does not hold any seats in a particular province or has not attracted any candidates from a specific ethnic or religious group.

Another factor in the selection process is that posts may be used as a reward for favours or services rendered to the Prime Minister or the party. Conversely, positions may be withheld as a punishment for some misdemeanour. On occasion, a talented but troublesome member or a rival for the party leadership may be included in the ministry (usually in a difficult but not too prestigious portfolio) in order to silence his or her opposition to the leader. The Prime Minister may also appoint a particular MP on the basis of his or her ability and popular appeal. It is evident that the Prime Minister must have a certain number of energetic and effective Ministers to run the key portfolios of the government, because there could be political repercussions if Ministers were perceived as bumbling and incompetent. On the other hand, the Prime Minister cannot afford to be constantly upstaged and overshadowed by clever Ministers. One Ottawa journalist likes to tell a story about Jack Pickersgill's view of Cabinet appointments during Prime Minister Lester B. Pearson's period in office. Pickersgill told him that there "must be some slow members in every Cabinet or nothing would ever get accomplished."

The Prime Minister, in consultation with other Ministers, is also responsible for appointing Parliamentary Secretaries. The first two were appointed by order-in-council in 1916, and thereafter their numbers slowly increased until proper legislative recognition was given them with the 1959 *Parliamentary Secretaries Act*. That *Act*, as amended in 1971, provides for the appointment of the same number of parliamentary secretaries as there are Ministers. **Parliamentary Secretaries** are appointed by the Prime Minister and aid Ministers in their duties, but have no statutory authority. As one Parliamentary Secretary put it: "There's no rule; it depends entirely on the Minister you are dealing with. Some are given considerable responsibility, others very little. It depends on the understanding between the two people concerned."[7] Usually, parliamentary secretaries have at least the agreement of their Minister before being appointed, but even this is not always the case. The Prime Minister may make an appointment without any consultation whatsoever.[8]

The Prime Minister, in addition to choosing the members of the executive, also makes a great many other crucial appointments: senators, judges and the senior staff of the public service. Through these selections the Prime Minister makes his or her influence felt throughout the governmental structure. Legally, the Prime Minister's appointments are mere recommendations of appointment, forwarded to the Governor General for formal approval. However, despite the Governor General's apparent power of discretion, a modern Prime Minister's appointees are never rejected. In fact, as we have seen, the Prime Minister chooses the Governor General.

Yet another significant basis of the Prime Minister's power is the right to advise the Crown to dissolve Parliament. The Prime Minister alone can determine the timing of an election within the five-year term of Parliament. This power can be used to impose discipline or

---

[7] Quoted in Claude Majeau, "The Job of a Parliamentary Secretary," Parliamentary Government, vol. 4, no. 3 (1983), p. 3.

[8] Judy LaMarsh, *Memoirs of a Bird in a Gilded Cage* (Toronto: McClelland & Stewart, 1969), p. 57.

solidarity on a fractious Cabinet or caucus. Fraught with uncertainty, election campaigns are expensive and risky for most MPs. If the government is clearly defeated on a major bill, due to breakdown of party discipline or loss of confidence of the House of Commons, the Prime Minister has little choice but to call an election to seek a new mandate. However, this is a rare occurrence. Except in minority situations such as the defeat of Joe Clark's Conservatives in December 1979, the Prime Minister determines the date of elections. Normally, Parliament is dissolved only when the Prime Minister believes that the party has a good chance of victory at the polls, though he or she may be constrained by the five-year limit or may misjudge the popular mood. Nonetheless, for the most part, the Prime Minister's power of dissolution is a potent weapon, helping to maintain the discipline and solidarity of the party and the stability of the Cabinet system.

A final major basis of the Prime Minister's pre-eminence is his or her power to control the organization of government. Nearly every Prime Minister has plans for a new organizational structure to streamline or modernize the government. Cabinet structure can be modified, portfolios limited or amalgamated, bureaucratic agencies abolished, Crown corporations created and Royal Commissions appointed — all on the initiative of the Prime Minister. However, while the power to make these changes certainly exists, the Prime Minister must be mindful that unwarranted or unnecessary modifications may generate significant opposition. The Prime Minister's power to initiate organizational changes extends across the entire government, but there is a tendency to focus on the various executive coordinating agencies that fall directly under his or her jurisdiction. Each Prime Minister can therefore be expected to make some changes in the Prime Minister's Office (PMO) and the Privy Council Office (PCO) to reflect his or her own interests or special needs.

The Prime Minister chairs the Cabinet and is the pivotal figure in the Cabinet committee system. No Prime Minister, however, can possibly deal with the multifarious matters needing attention. The Prime Minister must therefore delegate authority and responsibility to Cabinet members. Before turning to a consideration of the operations of the Cabinet and its methods of arriving at policy decisions, we shall briefly examine the history and approaches of Canada's Prime Ministers.

PRIME MINISTERS IN PRACTICE

Canada has had 20 Prime Ministers since 1867, eight Liberal and twelve Conservative. All but Kim Campbell, who was Prime Minister for a few months in 1993, were male. Joe Clark, at the age of 39, was the youngest Prime Minister in Canadian history. As of Jean Chrétien's election in 1993, the average age of a new Prime Minister was 56. The selections of Kim Campbell and Jean Chrétien continued the tradition of highly educated party leaders; every appointment since the First World War has gone to a university graduate. With regard to area of residence in adult life, there have been three Maritimers as Prime Ministers, six Québécois, six Ontarians and five Westerners (see Table 7.1). Three provinces — Prince Edward Island, Newfoundland and New Brunswick — have never had a Prime Minister elected in one of their federal constituencies. Kim Campbell was the second Prime Minister from British Columbia; as John Turner, the first, became a British Columbia Member of Parliament shortly before he was replaced as Prime Minister.

The regional pattern of electoral support for parties in Canada is illustrated by the fact that all eight Liberal Prime Ministers have come from Ontario or Québec (John Turner's western credentials notwithstanding), whereas the Conservatives have come from various parts of the country. On the other hand, the Liberals have balanced Canada's religious and ethnic diversity better than the Conservatives in their choice of Prime Ministers. Of the twenty Prime Ministers, seven have been Roman Catholic and thirteen Protestant; the Liberals have had five Roman Catholics and three Protestants. Moreover, since the 1880s, Liberal Party leaders have been drawn alternately from English Canada (Blake, 1880; King, 1919; Pearson, 1958; Turner, 1984) and French Canada (Laurier, 1887; St. Laurent, 1948; Trudeau, 1968; Chrétien, 1993).

Until recently, Conservative Prime Ministers have had much more parliamentary experience than their Liberal counterparts. Until Clark, Mulroney and Campbell, all Conservative PMs had 10 years' or more legislative experience at the federal or provincial level before their appointments. Experience in Cabinet before becoming PM, however, has been minimal for both parties; all but four had only two years' experience or less. Sir Charles Tupper had the most experience in federal and provincial Cabinets, but he lasted only two months as PM. Pierre Trudeau, by contrast, with no provincial experience and only one year of Cabinet experience, survived 11 years in his first period as Prime Minister and after an electoral defeat was re-elected to a further mandate. Brian Mulroney had no Cabinet experience when he became Prime Minister in 1984.

The durability of Canadian Prime Ministers varies enormously. Unlike American Presidents, who may serve only two terms, Canadian Prime Ministers retain power as long as the public and House of Commons support them. Prime Ministers in Canada have lasted longer than those in almost all Anglo-American and continental European countries.

The 20 Canadian Prime Ministers can be divided into three broad groups on the basis of their tenure in office. The shortest careers were those of Meighen, Thompson, Abbott, Bowell, Tupper, Clark, Turner and Campbell who all served for less than two years (the shortest periods were held by Sir Charles Tupper — 69 days; John Turner — 80 days; and Kim Campbell —133 days). Seven Prime Ministers stayed in office for five to eleven years: Borden, St. Laurent, Mackenzie, Bennett, Diefenbaker, Pearson and Mulroney. Four have towered above the rest: King, 22 years; Macdonald, 20 years; Trudeau, $15^1/_2$-years; and Laurier, 15 years. Laurier's fifteen consecutive years in office was the longest continuous term enjoyed by any PM; Trudeau's $15^1/_2$-year term was broken by an electoral loss. These four individuals held the office of Prime Minister for well over half of Canada's history since Confederation: 72 out of 126 years, as of 1993.

How are Prime Ministers' terms ended? Few of Canada's Prime Ministers have retired entirely of their own choice; their careers usually were ended by defeat in a general election. Abbott, Borden, King, Pearson, Trudeau and Mulroney retired. Twelve PMs lost their positions through defeat in a general election; one (Mackenzie Bowell) because of a Cabinet revolt, two (Macdonald and King) through defeats in Parliament. Only Macdonald, King, Meighen and Trudeau managed to stay on as leader and win another general election after their party was defeated in an election. Macdonald and Thompson died in office.

Getting rid of a Prime Minister, even via the electoral route, is extremely difficult. The statistics show that in about one-third of all elections Prime Ministers were defeated, whereas in about two-thirds they were returned to the House of Commons, albeit more than half the time with a reduced majority. Brian Mulroney chose to stand down in June 1993 rather than go into an election with high personal unpopularity. His replacement, Kim Campbell, lost the October 25, 1993, General Election but remained as party leader for a short time before being replaced by Jean Charest.

TABLE 7.1 THE PRIME MINISTERS OF CANADA

Prime Minister	Party	Tenure	Birthplace	Adult Residence	Age as PM	Occupation
Sir John A. Macdonald	Lib.-Con.	July 1, 1867– Nov. 5, 1873	Britain	Ontario	52–76	Law
Alexander Mackenzie	Lib.	Nov. 5, 1873– Oct. 9, 1878	Britain	Ontaio	51–56	Journalist/ Stonemason
Sir John A. Macdonald	Con.	Oct. 9, 1878– June 6, 1891				
Sir John Abbott	Con.	June 15, 1891– Nov. 24, 1892	Québec	Québec	70	Law/Lecturer
Sir John Thompson	Con.	Nov. 25, 1892– Dec. 13, 1894	Nova Scotia	Nova Scotia	48–50	Law/Lecturer
Sir Mackenzie Bowell	Con.	Dec. 13, 1894– Apr. 27, 1896	Britain	Ontario	70–72	Journalist
Sir Charles Tupper	Con.	Apr. 27, 1896– July 8, 1896	Nova Scotia	Nova Scotia	74	Doctor
Sir Wilfrid Laurier	Lib.	July 9, 1896– Oct. 6, 1911	Québec	Québec	54–69	Law
Sir Robert Borden	Con.	Oct. 7, 1911– July 10, 1920	Nova Scotia	Nova Scotia	57–65	Law
Arthur Meighen	Con.	July 10, 1920– Dec. 29, 1921	Ontario	Manitoba	46–52	Law/Business
W.L. Mackenzie King	Lib.	Dec. 29, 1921– June 28, 1926	Ontario	Ontario	47–73	Civil Service
Arthur Meighen	Con.	June 28, 1926-- Sept. 25, 1926				
W.L. Mackenzie King	Lib.	Sept. 25, 1926– Aug. 7, 1930				
R.B. Bennett	Con.	Aug. 7, 1930– Oct. 23, 1935	New Brunswick	Alberta	60–65	Law/Business
W.L. Mackenzie King	Lib.	Oct. 23, 1935– Nov. 15, 1948				
Louis St. Laurent	Lib.	Nov. 15, 1948– June 21, 1957	Québec	Québec	66–75	Law
John Diefenbaker	Con.	June 21, 1957– Apr. 22, 1963	Ontario	Saskatchewan	51–67	Law
Lester B. Pearson	Lib.	Apr. 22, 1963– Apr. 20, 1968	Ontario	Ontario	65–70	Civil Service
Pierre Elliott Trudeau	Lib.	Apr. 20, 1968– June 4, 1979	Québec	Québec	48–65	Law/Lecturer
Joseph Clark	Con.	June 4, 1979– Mar. 3, 1980	Alberta	Alberta	39–41	Journalist
Pierre Elliott Trudeau	Lib.	Mar. 3, 1980– June 30, 1984				
John Turner	Lib.	June 30, 1984– Sept. 17, 1984	Britain	Ontario	55	Law
Brian Mulroney	Con.	Sept. 17, 1984– June 25, 1993	Québec	Québec	54–54	Law/Business
Kim Campbell	Con.	June 25, 1993– Nov. 4, 1993	British Columbia	British Columbia	46	Law
Jean Chrétien	Lib.	Nov. 4, 1993–	Québec	Québec	59–	Law

Source: Government of Canada, *Guide to Canadian Ministries Since Confederation 1867–1957* (and supplement 1957–67)
(Ottawa: Public Archives of Canada, 1957 and 1967). J.K. Johnson, ed., *The Canadian Directory of Parliament 1867–1967*
(Ottawa: Public Archives of Canada, 1968).

THE MINISTRY AND CABINET

We have said that the Prime Minister determines which individuals serve as Ministers and Secretaries of State, and also the extent of their duties. In some parliamentary countries, such as Australia and New Zealand, particular caucuses select the Ministers and the PM merely assigns the portfolios. In Canada, however, the Prime Minister has a free hand, although traditionally most members of the ministry are selected from the House of Commons and, more rarely, the Senate.

In selecting future colleagues for the front bench, the Prime Minister takes into consideration a number of factors, one of them Cabinet size. Until 1993, all members of the ministry were in Cabinet — there were no Ministers outside of it — so with the appointment of each new Minister the size of Cabinet grew. Over time, the size of Cabinets gradually increased. By the end of the second Trudeau administration in 1984, the Cabinet included 37 Ministers. John Turner's appointments temporarily reduced this number, but the situation was immediately reversed when Brian Mulroney was appointed Prime Minister. He named the largest number in Canadian history to Cabinet — 40 Ministers.

After Brian Mulroney's resignation in 1993, Kim Campbell downsized the Cabinet and restructured the government considerably. She reduced the number of Cabinet Ministers to 24. When Jean Chrétien became head of government in November 1993 he left most of Campbell's departmental changes in place (see Chapter 9) but he adopted a new system for central government administration. Two types of Ministers were appointed — 22 politicians were appointed to full Cabinet and 8 were made Secretaries of State to Assist. Like full Ministers, the latter eight were sworn to the Privy Council and bound by the rules of collective responsibility. But they were only allowed to attend meetings of Cabinet on request and were given a reduced salary and staff compared to full Cabinet Ministers.

Needless to say, nearly all Cabinet Ministers are chosen from the Commons, although in some historical periods a number have been appointed from the Senate, particularly when the governing party lacked elected representatives from a particular region — as the Conservatives did from Québec in 1979 and the Liberals did from the West in 1980–84. In 1993, Senator Joyce Fairbairn from Alberta, for example, was appointed as Government Leader in the Upper House and was designated Minister responsible for literacy.

The composition of the ministry and Cabinet also depends on how many seats the government controls in the House of Commons. Most elections have produced **majority governments**, based on the support of only one party in the House of Commons. Only twice — in 1867 under Macdonald and in 1917 under Borden — have *coalition* Cabinets been formed from more than one party. On other occasions — six times since 1945 — the government had to persist with less than a majority of the Members of Parliament. It had to select its Cabinet members carefully to ensure a majority of Members would support it. Such **minority governments** have proved quite unstable and have tended to pass less legislation than governments based on single-party, majority control of the House.

Cabinet positions are all doled out to members of the Prime Minister's own party in Parliament or the Senate. There have been few exceptions. General McNaughton was Defence Minister in 1944–45 without holding a position in either House. After being defeated twice at the polls he gave up the post. On the other hand, Lester Pearson was appointed Secretary of State for External Affairs in 1948, then stood for election in a by-election and won. As noted earlier, the Prime Minister's choice of Ministers is limited essentially by certain considerations, foremost among them regional, ethnic and religious representation. Regional representation is the first of these, but not necessarily the most important. There is usually a Cabinet member from each province (with the frequent exception of Prince Edward Island) and from the largest cities, with the more important urban regions receiving extra members.

The correspondence between distribution of Cabinet Ministers and provincial population has been relatively constant since Confederation.[9] As a general rule, Ontario has had more members in Cabinet than any other province, with Québec second. However, in recent years this principle has varied somewhat. Trudeau usually had one more Cabinet member from Québec than from Ontario. And on his election in 1984, Mulroney awarded an unusually large number of Cabinet seats to the West. His Cabinet consisted of 13 Ministers from the four western provinces and the North, 11 from each of Ontario and Québec and 5 from the Atlantic provinces. Because of his landslide victory in Ontario and slim results from his own province, Jean Chrétien chose 12 Ministers from Ontario and only 6 from Québec for his 1993 ministry. (See Table 7.2.)

TABLE 7.2   THE 1993 LIBERAL MINISTRY BY REGION AND GENDER

A. Region	Ministry Membership
Québec	6
Ontario	12
West	7
East	5
North	1
B. Gender	
Male	24
Female	7

Ministry includes Prime Minister, Ministers and Secretaries of State.

Ethnicity is also significant. According to Malcolm Punnett, of the total number of Cabinet Ministers serving between 1867 and 1965, 28 percent were French Canadians, a figure that is remarkably close to the French Canadian percentage of the population.[10] Prime Ministers also attempt to appoint a chief lieutenant from the opposite official language group. The most successful alliance, for example, may have been between Macdonald and Cartier. Jean Chrétien, a francophone, appointed Sheila Copps from Ontario as his Deputy Prime Minister. Joe Clark found it necessary to appoint three French-speaking members of the Senate to his Cabinet to balance his weak support in Québec. Brian Mulroney, a Québecker, appointed his first chief lieutenant from Yukon. Other, smaller ethnic groups have usually been under-represented in Cabinet. Religion has also been balanced in Cabinet composition: "Between Confederation and 1965, there were almost equal numbers of Anglican, Presbyterian and United Church or Methodist Cabinet ministers while about 35% of Cabinet ministers were Catholics."[11]

---

9   Richard J. Van Loon and Michael S. Whittington, *The Canadian Political System* (McGraw-Hill Ryerson, 1981), p. 445.

10   Punnett, *The Prime Minister*, passim.

11   Van Loon and Whittington, *The Canadian Political System*, p. 458.

Certain posts are distributed according to traditional rules. The post of Minister of Agriculture usually goes to a Westerner, as it did in 1993 when Ralph Goodale from Saskatchewan received the post. When this is difficult, as in the Trudeau Cabinet, a Western Minister may receive control of the Wheat Board. A Maritime province usually gets the Ministry of Fisheries, as in the appointment of Newfoundlander Brian Tobin in 1993. The distribution of seats that the government has obtained throughout the country is also an important factor in determining many assignments. In the case of the Liberals, the department of Finance has usually been held by an Ontarian, but in the 1980 Trudeau government a French Canadian was appointed to that post to bolster Québec strength in Cabinet. Joe Clark was even more daring — in 1979 he went to Newfoundland for his Finance Minister. Brian Mulroney returned to tradition when he appointed Michael Wilson from Toronto to the position, but Jean Chrétien nominated a bilingual anglophone from Québec, Paul Martin, to this position.

Practically all of Canada's minority groups, as well as one majority group — women — consistently have been unrepresented or under-represented in Cabinet. No significant room has been made in Cabinet for Native Peoples, for workers and unskilled labourers or for the poor, all of whose interests have been consistently under-represented. Over-represented are those with higher education and high social status occupations. The most over-represented group has been lawyers, who have held approximately half the positions in Cabinet since Confederation; they are an elite, extremely well educated, financially successful group representing less than one percent of the population. Historically, about one-fifth of Cabinet members have been businesspeople; fewer than one-tenth, farmers; and fewer still have come from the public sector.

The composition of the 1993 Chrétien ministry follows these principles closely. As Table 7.2 indicates, in the 1993 Chrétien ministry every province had one or more Ministers. The ministry was reasonably representative of the provinces on a basis proportional to their population with the evident distortion of Québec. Prime Minister Chrétien said he wished he could have nominated more Ministers from Québec but that he had to work with a very small number of Liberal MPs from *la belle province*. In 1989, francophones constituted a higher proportion of the Cabinet membership than they did in the country's population as a whole, while in 1993 their proportion has been reduced far below their population share.

The new government members remained highly educated and professionally trained; they still did not form a social or economic cross-section of Canadians. Business and law continued to be the leading employment areas of Ministers. There were few farmers and, as usual, labourers and the poor were not represented at all. The number of women continues to grow — 7 Ministers and Secretaries of State out of a ministry of 30 appointed in the 1993 Liberal administration were female. (During Trudeau's period there were only three female Ministers in Cabinet.)

In theory, the Canadian system of government is premised on both *collective* and *individual ministerial responsibility*. Cabinet solidarity, or **collective ministerial responsibility**, allows Ministers to be frank in private but support the government in public. As a group, Ministers are supposed to be held accountable for their government's actions. In this sense, they may speak about policy only after it has been agreed to in private by their colleagues. The convention of collective responsibility is so pervasive that Ministers are expected to support each other even before the issue has been discussed in Cabinet. The Ministers act collectively in Cabinet to develop policy, approve draft legislation, manage the country's finances and adopt orders-in-council. Cabinet deliberations are held in secret, individual opinions are not publicly voiced, and Ministers are not supposed to speak or act except in the name of the entire Cabinet.

The personal responsibility of each Minister is referred to as **individual ministerial responsibility**. Ministers receive confidential advice from the public service, make important decisions and then are held accountable for these decisions in Parliament and the country. In other words, there is a trade-off: the public servants forego public praise in order to avoid public blame, while the Ministers accept both credit and criticism.

As we shall see in Chapters 13 and 14, public policy derives from a multitude of sources, but it is the individual Minister who puts the final stamp of approval on departmental initiatives. Politicians cannot hope to duplicate the expertise that derives from administration or the information that comes from permanent contact with interest groups. And yet only a Minister may carry forward departmental requests to the Cabinet. This iron-clad relationship between Minister and department places approval or disapproval upon the appropriate and responsible political official. While Ministers may delegate authority to their officials, they remain at the apex for appeals of administrative decisions and must be involved in the initiation and defence of new policies. The complexity of a Minister's task can be illustrated by the work of the Minister for Industry, Trade and Commerce in 1982. That year, the department took 4700 decisions — the Minister kept control of only 190 of them, but these constituted well over half the department's expenditures.[12]

In practice, however, it is nearly impossible to adhere at all times to these constitutional doctrines. Where is the line to be drawn between ministerial and departmental responsibility? Ministers do not even know most of the details of decisions that are carried out in their names. They cannot be held responsible for every activity, and, increasingly, Ministers have been voicing this problem openly. One even claimed he could not be held accountable for the "shabby research" in his department. The main check on ministerial responsibilities, therefore, is not the Minister's will nor his public servants' activities, but the free and open debate that takes place in Parliament and society about Ministers' actions. The Minister is judged in the department, in Cabinet, in Parliament, before the media and on the hustings.

The Prime Minister and Cabinet are assisted in their tasks by the central agencies discussed in the following section. Individual Ministers are supported by their departments and by their political appointees. The personnel budget for each Minister's office is used to employ an executive assistant, special assistants, a private secretary and other support personnel. At the end of the Mulroney period in 1993, there were hundreds of such political aides in Ottawa, not including those in the Prime Minister's Office. Ministers also second departmental employees to their offices and hire policy and communications advisors under contract. When the Tories came to office in 1984, they operated on the assumption that since all of the deputy ministers and other senior officials had been appointed by Liberal governments, they must be partisan. To counteract this, they tried to insulate Ministers from the bureaucracy by creating a new layer of political appointee, the Chiefs-of-Staff, through which all communications between Ministers and departments had to flow. Ministers' budgets for other political

---

[12] Ian Clark, "A 'Back to Basics' Look at the Government Decision-making Process," unpublished paper, Nov. 4, 1983, p. 13.

staff were also augmented. On his appointment, Prime Minister Jean Chrétien said he would take a fundamentally different approach. He declared his intent to rebuild the relationship between the Ministers and the bureaucracy. When he appointed his ministry in 1993, he halved the staff of Ministers, reduced their overall budgets and axed the highly paid position of Chief-of-Staff (except for his own Chief-of-Staff!).

Political aides are part of what Blair Williams has called the "para-political bureaucracy."[13] They are hired by Ministers on an individual basis in order to perform largely partisan tasks. They are not subject to the regulations of the public service (and hence are called "exempt staff") and, under provisions of the 1967 *Public Service Employment Act*, they are given high priority for permanent positions in the administration after a period of three years of consecutive political service.

The importance of these staffs is debatable. Depending on the Ministers' views and confidence, they are engaged in any number of personal concerns. Liaison work with the department, constituency, party and Parliament is perhaps the most important. Their partisan work for the Ministers is clearly significant. If competent, they strengthen both the Minister and the party in power. Their work on policy is underdeveloped, possibly because, with some exceptions, they usually do not have the necessary competence or experience. Their most important policy work is possibly in their "gatekeeping" functions: determining who gets an appointment with the Minister and what documents, papers and letters he or she reads. As Williams concluded, "there is little doubt…that ministerial exempt staffs play a fundamental and legitimate role at the executive level of the government process."[14] The Liberals, however, say that they will decrease the importance of the exempt staff. Marcel Massé, Minister in charge of reorganizing the bureaucracy, captured the philosophy behind their declared intent: "Good government required a close and congenial relationship between public servants of every level and politicians."[15]

CONFLICTS OF INTEREST

One issue that haunts members of the Cabinet as well as other politicians is conflict of interest. A **conflict of interest** is a situation in which a Prime Minister, Minister, Member of Parliament or public servant has knowledge of a private, personal economic interest sufficient to influence the exercise of public duties and responsibilities.[16] Even if the conflict is not illegal, it may create doubts or suspicions that the decisions or actions of such individuals are not impartial.

Public attitudes about which situations constitute conflict of interest for Ministers have changed considerably over the years; behaviour that was considered normal a few decades ago now engenders cynicism, suspicion and moral condemnation. Until the 1960s, MPs routinely carried on with their private businesses after they became Ministers, and conflict-of-interest queries were raised only when their ministerial decisions clearly produced private

---

[13] Blair Williams, "The Para-Political Bureaucracy in Ottawa," in Harold D. Clarke et al., eds., *Parliament, Policy and Representation* (Toronto: Methuen, 1980), p. 218; Brooke Jeffrey, *A Comparison of the Role of the Ministers' Office in France, Britain, Canada*, Research Branch, Library of Parliament, Ottawa, October, 1978.

[14] Williams, "The Para-Political Bureaucracy," p. 225

[15] *The Globe and Mail*, Oct. 29, 1993.

[16] This is essentially the definition used by Justice William Parker in his 1987 report on the conflicts of interest of former cabinet minister Sinclair Stevens. See p. 294.

advantage. In those years, politics was still a part-time, rather poorly paid, occupation, and Ministers and Prime Ministers openly and frequently engaged in potentially conflicting activities; they sat on boards of directors, carried on legal practices and accepted private trust funds.

After several mini-scandals in the Pearson government, public tolerance of such practices began to wane. In 1972, Prime Minister Trudeau issued formal guidelines for Cabinet Ministers.[17] Like Pearson, he chose to rely on guidelines rather than legislation to handle the problem:

> *An element of discretion, to be exercised by a minister on the basis of discussion with the Prime Minister of the day, seems the best solution.... A minister will be expected in the future, as is the policy today, to resign any directorships in commercial or other profit-making corporations that he may have held before becoming a minister.*[18]

A registry of Ministers' financial holdings was to be kept, and they could choose one of three options:

1. Divest themselves of their financial holdings; or
2. Place their financial holdings in a blind trust (which meant, in theory, that ministers should not know what their holdings are and therefore not be able to act on privileged information); or
3. Place them in a frozen trust (meaning that ministers could know what their assets were but not be able to change them).[19]

These guidelines provided rather undefined and ambiguous instructions for Ministers about how to arrange their personal affairs to avoid the possibility of conflict of interest. Possible disclosure of conflict situations was considered to be a sufficient deterrent, since it would cause political embarrassment and negative publicity to the extent that a Cabinet Minister might feel it necessary to resign in order to protect the government's integrity. However, the guidelines did not provide sufficient sanctions to deter potential conflicts, nor did they establish appropriate mechanisms to determine whether such violations were taking place.

Prime Minister Joe Clark made the guidelines more stringent by extending them to the immediate families of Ministers. Blind trusts became mandatory, and for two years after leaving Cabinet ex-Ministers could not serve on boards of directors of corporations with which they dealt as Ministers; they could not act on behalf of such people or corporations, or act as lobbyists. For one year they could not accept jobs with companies with which they had dealt, nor could they act as consultants for them. These guidelines were maintained from the Clark government through to the Mulroney government in 1984.

Prime Minister Mulroney abolished the code and introduced new conflict of interest guidelines for Cabinet Ministers (also guidelines for civil servants) in 1985. Like the earlier version, it stopped short of full, mandatory disclosure in order to strike a balance between protecting the public interest and protecting the private affairs of Ministers. The restric-

---

[17] In 1973, a Green Paper on conflict of interest for MPs was brought before Parliament for discussion, and while no legislation was passed, the government did issue conflict of interest guidelines for federal civil servants.

[18] Pierre Trudeau, Statement on Conflict of Interest, House of Commons, July 18, 1973.

[19] See Jackson and Atkinson, *Canadian Legislative System*, pp. 209–10.

tions on business dealings of immediate family members were dropped. It did, however, make it explicit that Ministers must not hire their own immediate relatives (or other Ministers' relatives) for government jobs.

Reproduced with permission, Dennis Pritchard

The ambiguity and lack of enforcement provisions in the new Code led to a major conflict of interest case when Cabinet Minister Sinclair Stevens was faced with a series of conflict allegations in 1986–87. A key charge against Stevens was that his wife obtained a $2.6 million loan from a consultant to a company that had obtained grants through Stevens' government department. Stevens had ostensibly placed his business holdings in a blind trust; however, the trust was considerably less than "blind" because of his connections with several involved individuals, including his wife (who remained an officer of the company) and his secretary, who could have provided Stevens with information about the affairs of his "blind" trust.

The Parker Commission was established to determine whether such transparency actually existed in handling the trust, and after an eight-month investigation Judge Parker declared that Stevens had violated the conflict Code 14 times. He recommended, among other things, that blind trusts be abolished or limited to assets that can be sold at arm's length, since it is difficult in practice to ensure that they are indeed "blind." He also recommended full disclosure and, if necessary, divestiture of assets, and said that the mere appearance of conflict, whether or not an advantage was actually obtained, sufficed to place a Minister in a conflict situation. Judge Parker was particularly concerned with "the need to rebuild public confidence in politicians and in the objectivity, integrity and impartiality of government."[20]

Concerned that Canadians were indeed losing confidence in the integrity of politicians and politics in general, and also that his government had an extremely poor image in this regard, Mulroney decided that guidelines were no longer sufficient and introduced conflict of interest legislation in early 1988. The legislation stopped short of mandatory, full disclosure for Cabinet Ministers; it required a mix of public and private disclosure of assets as well as limiting, but not foreclosing, the use of blind trusts. Spouses would have to comply with some of the provisions, and a gentler version of the new rules would cover all members of Parliament and Senators. The legislation, Bill C114, would have required the government to appoint an independent three-member ethics commission to act as a watchdog, implement the rules and impose penalties on members of Parliament who engaged in unethical activities. This commission was to alleviate the necessity, under the previous guidelines, for the Prime Minister to act as judge, jury and executioner in conflict of interest cases.

Recognizing the need for legislation, as opposed to simple guidelines, was a major step forward for the government. The bill that was put forward attempted to force enough disclosure to keep the government leaders honest, yet not infringe on their private lives so much that highly qualified individuals would be deterred from practising politics. However, Bill C114 died on the order paper when the 1988 General Election was called. Various other attempts to legislate about conflict of interest have also failed. In the dying days of the Mulroney government in 1993 another, more stringent, bill was introduced but it, too, died on the order paper when the 34th Parliament was dissolved.

The 1993 Liberal Prime Minister took a somewhat different approach to conflict of interest. Jean Chrétien hired former minister Mitchell Sharp as a special advisor on integrity of government for one dollar a year. Arguing that "integrity in government is not simply a matter of rules and regulations — it is also a matter of personal standards and conduct"[21] — the Prime Minister affirmed a commitment "to reform MP's pensions, end double-dipping, regulate the activities of lobbyists and examine contracting practices, appointments, conflict of interest and the whole area of advertising, polling and communications." The country awaits the concrete results of this somewhat optimistic philosophy.

PATRONAGE

A little-studied field closely linked to conflict of interest is the world of political patronage and its near-relative, pork-barrelling. **Patronage**, in the broad sense, concerns the awarding of contracts, employment and other material benefits to individuals or groups on the basis of partisan support rather than according to merit. It means granting jobs and contracts for political reasons. It can include illegal practices such as vote-buying, "treating" (paying for votes with liquor) and other forms of bribery. **Pork-barrelling**, on the other hand, extends favours to whole regions or communities as an inducement

---

20 *The Globe and Mail*, Feb. 25, 1988.

21 Office of the Prime Minister, *Press Release*, Nov. 4, 1993, p. 3.

for support. Patronage and pork-barrelling usually break no laws but often raise serious questions about ethical conduct.[22]

Some regard patronage and its less attractive cousin as essential parts of politics, providing the oil that makes the system run smoothly and the glue that keeps parties together and keeps the political system stable. For others patronage and pork-barrelling are corrupt, immoral activities that impede honest, efficient government services. All would agree that it is an enduring feature of the Canadian political system.

Journalist Jeffrey Simpson calls patronage "the pornography of politics, enticing to some, repulsive to others, justified as inevitable, condemned as immoral, a practice seldom fit for polite discussion."[23] It is in this shadowy world — where interest group behaviour, patronage and pork-barrelling meet, and where connections between influence and favours result from secret negotiations — that corruption is generally found adding its cynical, malodorous quality to Canadian politics.

Patronage has been an important part of the Canadian political culture since the pre-1867 colonial period of Canadian history.[24] The notion that only party supporters have the right to government positions and favours was imported from Britain, and has become a distinctive feature of Canadian politics that has been modified somewhat over time. Patronage provided an inducement for loyalty and for mobilizing participation. The early history of patronage in Canada reflects the struggle to shift control over the distribution of political favours from the Monarch and government in Britain to the Prime Minister and Cabinet in Canada; in effect, to "patriate" the power of patronage.

Four distinct stages have been noted in the development of patronage in Canada.[25] In the colonial years the British governors dispensed patronage, using it to maintain deference and loyalty from the colonists. With the advent of responsible government, these rights to dispense patronage shifted to the elected representative. In the second stage, after Confederation, patronage was used first by Sir John A. Macdonald and later by Sir Wilfrid Laurier to help build national parties that would unite a widely scattered population. The Prime Ministers used material benefits openly and freely to recruit and maintain an active party organization. The third stage of patronage development began about the time of the First World War when Mackenzie King began his long career as Prime Minister. Patronage and pork-barrelling remained an important part of party management, but during this period the civil service became separate from the party in power, dramatically changing the close relationship that had previously existed between the government and the public sector. The final stage of patronage development began in the 1960s as technological and cultural changes contributed to public intolerance of some of the traditional inducements for loyalty and participation.

Patronage still flourishes, but it has lost its aura of respectability. Its place in the political "natural order of things" is being questioned. The shift toward this new situation is reflected in two quotations from former prime minister Pierre Trudeau: "Patronage is

---

[22] This topic is well covered in the *Journal of Canadian Studies/Etudes Canadiennes*, vol. XXII, no. 2 (Summer, 1987) which is devoted to patronage.

[23] Jeffrey Simpson, *Spoils of Power* (Toronto: Collins, 1988), p. 6.

[24] Gordon T. Stewart, *The Origins of Canadian Parties* (Vancouver: University of British Columbia Press, 1986).

[25] Simpson, *Spoils of Power*, pp. 6–10.

incompatible with modern government"; and "Of course, I'm not against helping a friend of the Liberal Party when I get a chance."[26]

Modern Prime Ministers endeavour to find more acceptable inducements for loyalty and discipline, such as the strength of their personality and popular policies. They use the media — television in particular — to appeal directly to citizens. However strong these direct appeals have become, they have not yet supplanted patronage. It is no surprise that opposition parties seem to have more trouble than governing parties in maintaining internal party cohesion; the government holds all the patronage and pork-barrelling resources in its hands and is often able to secure loyalty from those who expect or receive favours.

There are several aspects of patronage that have contributed to its sullied reputation. It plays to human weaknesses, encouraging unethical behaviour by individuals, institutions, and groups in society. It also has an inflationary aspect; one reward creates a demand for more, and the demand always exceeds supply. The use of patronage to bind together religious, French/English and regional interests is no longer sufficiently broad; it must now extend to women, youth, natives and those of other ethnic groups. As well, as Simpson points out, the advent of deficit financing "widened the patron's opportunities for pork-barrelling," with the result that demands escalated and were met through public resources.[27]

Recent Prime Ministers have been plagued with the problem of dispensing patronage without compromising their public position.[28] Joe Clark incurred the wrath of party rank-and-file when he delayed too long in filling patronage positions. He lost his chance to dispense rewards when his minority government was defeated in 1979. John Turner lost the 1984 election when he declared he had "no option" but to honour the "orgy" of appointments demanded by departing Prime Minister Trudeau. Brian Mulroney also saw his own popularity, and that of his party, fall to record lows after patronage binges during his two governments.

Despite the fact that Mulroney had made a major issue out of patronage in his 1984 election campaign, calling the actions of Turner and Trudeau "scandalous," "vulgar" and "unacceptable," he proceeded to fill patronage positions and award government business to party and personal friends. In 1993 the new Chrétien government promised to increase integrity in government and decrease patronage appointments. The country waits for the concrete results of these assertions.

POLICY-MAKING IN CENTRAL GOVERNMENT

In recent years, the government has made major alterations to its internal organization. In the 1963 Pearson administration, full Cabinet was the major vehicle for Cabinet decision-making: it reviewed almost every decision taken in committee. After Trudeau came to

---

[26] Quoted in Simpson, *Spoils of Power*, p. 331. Simpson sees Trudeau as a transitional figure in terms of patronage: "accepting many of the traditional practices while groping towards new forms of political mobilization" (p. 332).

[27] Ibid., p. 15. Patronage is discussed further in Chapter 10, under the role of party leaders.

[28] John Sawatsky, *The Insiders: Government, Business and the Lobbyists* (Toronto: McClelland & Stewart, 1987), chs 17–19.

office in 1968, Cabinet and committee meetings were scheduled on a more regular basis and *committees* became much more powerful. The 1979 Clark and 1980 Trudeau Cabinets decentralized decision-making even further with the introduction of a Policy and Expenditure Management System. Under Mulroney, committees made many important decisions, but all major decisions were ratified by the full Cabinet or by the Committee on Priorities and Planning, both chaired by the Prime Minister.

The most precise change in Cabinet committee structure came in 1979 with Joe Clark's concept of an "inner" and "outer" Cabinet. It had generally been accepted until that time that a division of senior and junior Ministers in Canada would not be possible because of the need for regional and ethnic balance in the Cabinet. G. Bruce Doern had even predicted that "such a full-blown inner and outer cabinet system will never occur in Canada, given the strength and importance of regional and ethnic representation in the cabinet."[29] In fact, some Ministers had always been more important than others; Clark merely institutionalized this division of status.[30] He appointed 12 members to an "inner Cabinet" and 30 to full Cabinet. The Inner Cabinet's potential for usurping the power of Cabinet as a whole was quickly found to be exaggerated. In reality, it functioned in much the same way as the old Priorities and Planning Committee of Cabinet. When Trudeau returned to office in 1980, he abolished the name "Inner Cabinet" and replaced it with the former system. In 1984 and 1989 Mulroney also retained the old name.

In January 1989, Prime Minister Mulroney announced a major structural rearrangement of Cabinet and its committees as well as the process for Cabinet deliberation. A large Cabinet (39 members) was appointed by Mulroney that year with an eye to adequate representation of all the regions. The efficient operation of such a body, however, necessitated a smaller committee approach. Cabinet was divided into 15 committees, ranging from 8 members on some to 19 on the important Priorities and Planning Committee.

Priorities and Planning, chaired by the Prime Minister and consisting mainly of the chairpersons of Cabinet's other committees, continued to be responsible for setting the government's overall agenda and determining major policies; it prescribed what found its way onto the Cabinet agenda. This committee assumed responsibilities for such activities as preparing the broad policy goals concerning free trade, the Speech from the Throne, the legislative program, macro-economic policy, constitutional questions, and so on. An additional structure was added to ensure coordination: a new Operations committee, chaired by the Deputy Prime Minister, controlled the flow of policy issues into Priorities and Planning and dealt with political crises. This Operations committee began to operate informally as early as 1986, and later gained official status, meeting regularly before Priorities and Planning each Monday morning.[31]

In the 1989 system, seven committees were responsible for answers to substantive policy questions. The committees were Economic Policy, Trade Executive, Environment, Cultural Affairs and National Identity, Human Resources, Federal-Provincial Relations, and

---

[29] G. Bruce Doern, "The Development of Policy Organizations in the Executive Arena," in G. Bruce Doern and Peter Aucoin, eds., *Structures of Policy-Making in Canada* (Toronto: Macmillan, 1971), p. 74.

[30] See Jackson and Atkinson, *Canadian Legislative System*, ch. 4. On PEMS see Richard Van Loon, "The Policy and Expenditure Management System in the Federal Government," *CPA*, vol. 26, no. 2 (Summer 1983), pp. 255–85.

[31] Control over this committee gave rise to the popular notion that Don Mazankowski was "in charge of everything."

Foreign and Defence Policy. These "subject-matter" committees were each chaired by the Minister who held the Cabinet portfolio most directly associated with the subject-matter. They did not have a responsibility for expenditures, but had to go to Priorities and Planning to obtain permission to spend government funds.

Four committees were given broader co-ordination roles — Legislation and House Planning, Special Committee of Council, Communications, and Security and Intelligence. The Government House Leader (who in 1989 was also Minister of Justice), chaired Legislation and House Planning. This committee co-ordinated the flow of legislation, reviewed and drafts bills and supervised all matters pertaining to Parliament. The Special Committee of Council, chaired by the Deputy Prime Minister, met weekly. In 1989, this committee was given the responsibility of controlling regulatory activities and of reviewing proposals for the privatization of Crown corporations. Its main order of business, however, was to deal with regulations and routine orders requiring governor-in-council approval. That is, it passed uncontroversial orders-in-council made pursuant to statutory authority that requires the government, and not an individual Minister, to make a decision.

Orders-in-council are issued by Cabinet to carry out government rule-making and administration. In most cases, they are authorized by provisions contained in statutes. Some orders, however, fall under the Royal Prerogative. Upon passage, all orders-in-council are published in the Canada Gazette. Until recently, their numbers increased yearly. For example in 1982, 4379 were passed, ranging from the most trivial to the most urgent. By 1988, however, the number had dropped to 3223. This was not due to a reduction in Cabinet activities, but rather to a new process in which more than one appointment was made in the same order. Approximately a quarter of the orders consisted of regulations for administering the country; the next greatest number and the most visible, however, were those for appointments. By convention the Prime Minister recommends about a hundred deputy head positions on his own authority. The other 2000 full-time order-in-council positions involve the Prime Minister and/or other ministerial decisions.

Under Mulroney, the Communications committee of the Cabinet, chaired by the Conservative Leader in the Senate, was responsible for information, publicity and (some would say) the "propaganda" of the government. Security and Intelligence, chaired by the Prime Minister, met irregularly. It was responsible for protecting the internal security of Canada and its institutions.

The most important change in 1989, however, came in the form of a new Cabinet committee system to control expenditure. Control over policy initiation and expenditure was divided for the first time since 1979; Priorities and Planning retained the power of final decision over expenditure, the Treasury Board enhanced its authority and a new Expenditure Review committee was set up.

The Treasury Board is the only statutory committee of the Privy Council. Chaired by the President of the Treasury Board, it has legal responsibility for the authorization of expenditures and is the committee that allocates resources within the government. It is the only committee that does not position itself into a circle for policy deliberations, but sits like a jury, facing any petitioners and acting as a tribunal. Expenditure Review was mandated to see that government expenditures are related to government priorities, including deficit reduction. The committee was often referred to as the "search-and-destroy" committee.

The Mulroney committee system reduced the power of many Ministers, constructing a senior and junior ministerial system almost like the British one. Power was centralized in the hands of the Prime Minister, his Priorities and Planning Committee and the new Expenditure committee. Many Ministers were reduced almost to the status of eunuchs. Pressures from less powerful Ministers to reform this system increased over the life of the government.

As discussed above, in 1993 Jean Chrétien changed the basic nature of the government system. Full Cabinet membership was reduced to 23 members out of a ministry of 31. The new ministry was also given a new committee system. Priorities and Planning was dropped as a steering committee with Cabinet-as-a-whole resuming that function. Cabinet was divided into only four committees — economic development, social policy development, special committee of Council and Treasury Board (see Figure 7.2). Unlike recent Prime Ministers, Jean Chrétien reverted to the secretive practice of neither publicly naming the members of these committees nor specifying their functions. While Canada for two decades named all members of Cabinet committees (as Britain has done since 1992), the 1993 Liberal government has reduced transparency at the very core of democratic government.

Figure 7.2   The Ministry and Cabinet in the 1993 Liberal Government

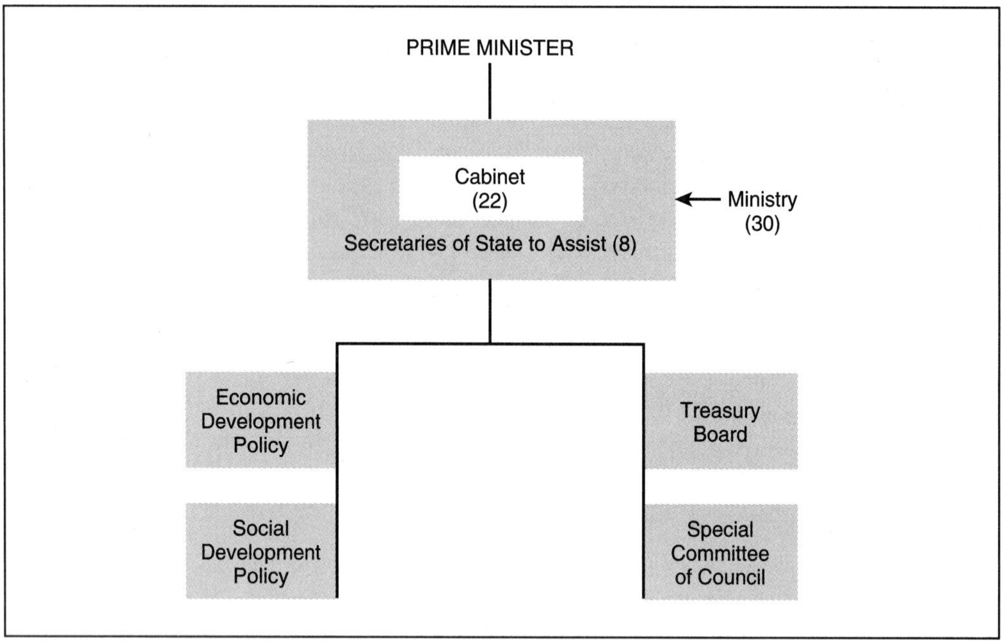

In principle, Cabinet and its committees are assembled at least once a week during parliamentary sessions. In 1956, under St. Laurent, Cabinet met 91 times. In 1969, under Trudeau, full Cabinet met 73 times, and there were 369 meetings of its committees. Under Clark's "Inner Cabinet" system, the number of full Cabinet meetings was further reduced to approximately twice a month, while the Inner Cabinet met weekly. By 1982 this number was reduced to 50 full Cabinet meetings and 232 meetings of committees. Under Mulroney's Cabinet process, the workload was altered. Since Priorities and Planning acted in the name of Cabinet for many decisions, meetings of full Cabinet were reduced by almost 50 percent. However, Priorities and Planning met almost weekly (in 1987 it met 44 times) and thus the combined final decision-making meetings were about the same number as in earlier years under the Liberals. The number of ordinary policy committee meetings, however, was sharply reduced to less than half (see Table 7.3). At the time of writing it is too early to assess the activities and workload of the 1993 Liberal ministry and Cabinet.

TABLE 7.3   CABINET WORKLOAD

	1982 (Liberal)	1987 (P.C.)
Cabinet meetings	50	26
Cabinet committee meetings	232	147
Memoranda to Cabinet and discussion papers	747	424
Draft Bills	68	63
Cabinet Decisions	716	738

Source: Derived from private communication from the Privy Council Office, December 1, 1983, and February 17, 1989.

Ministers are expected to bring substantial policies to their Cabinet colleagues for resolution. The formal process for Cabinet approval of a document is illustrated in Figure 7.3. The Minister's memorandum is forwarded to the Privy Council Office, which distributes it to the Cabinet members. The memorandum is then discussed by the appropriate Cabinet committee and forwarded to Cabinet for final determination. As Figure 7.3 indicates, the PCO briefs the Prime Minister, as does the PMO. This series of actions completes the process and Cabinet gives final approval or disapproval in a record of decision. Of course, private conversations about government policies, over the telephone and in person, add immeasurably to the complexity of Cabinet business.

FIGURE 7.3   THE FORMAL CABINET POLICY PROCESS, 1994

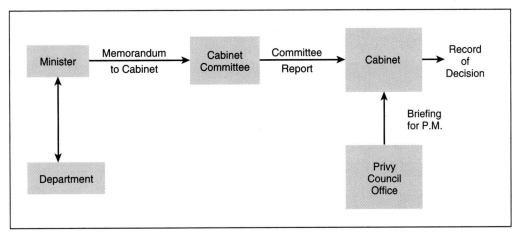

Cabinet documents proliferated rapidly after the Second World War. In 1982, there were 1533 documents: 747 memoranda, 68 draft bills and 716 Cabinet decisions. During the Mulroney government, the volume of work accomplished remained approximately the same with 63 draft bills and 738 Cabinet decisions. Every Cabinet document is numbered and awarded a security classification.

All Ministers are allowed to place some major policy areas and legislative proposals on Cabinet's list of priority problems. Cabinet cohesiveness is maintained by encouraging each

Minister to believe that he or she will succeed in persuading colleagues to accept some of these proposals. If serious Cabinet dissent emerges over a Minister's ideas, he or she will be asked to reconsider and resubmit them. Each Minister is made to feel part of a team that values his or her proposals. The participants are united for their own survival — and they know it!

How successful the Cabinet will be depends to a large extent on its management of several critical factors, including taxation, expenditures and the legislative program. By controlling these, as well as the machinery of government and senior personnel, the government is able to effect major decisions. Through strategic planning the government attempts to employ all these resources to accomplish its goals and to resolve policy issues. In theory the government places all the goals and issues into a hierarchy of interests, but in practice this rarely works. For one thing, long-term policy requirements often have to give way to short-term administrative matters. Second, the issues change over time, and the government must be prepared to adjust its targets. Finally, ultimate determination occurs within the ephemeral world of politics, where politicians come and go, change their opinions and are themselves divided over policies. A slight change in personnel may affect the distribution of power that first caused the priority. Nevertheless, the idea of strategic planning comes from the desire to achieve comprehensive, non-urgent policy-making to help counter the piecemeal policies emanating from individual departments. The government is aided in these various tasks by the central co-ordinating agencies.

THE CENTRAL COORDINATING AGENCIES

In response to the large scope of the government's role in Canadian society and to the corresponding need for innovative and effective policy formation and implementation, new executive agencies have been either created or expanded. Some of these central coordinating agencies have a special responsibility to support the Prime Minister, Cabinet and ministry. They are not part of the regular line departmental infrastructure. Some of these bodies have little legal authority, but are organized under the Prime Minister's prerogative for machinery of government. While their stated purpose is to streamline the governmental process, the executive agencies have recently received considerable public attention and have drawn accusations that Canada is being run by a cabal of "superbureaucrats" who have become powers unto themselves. The closed nature of these agencies makes them a target for criticism. To a considerable extent they also have become recruiting grounds for senior positions in the public service.

The centralization of power in the hands of the Prime Minister as well as in these co-ordinating agencies appears indisputable. It is also clear, however, that this development has probably been inevitable, given the range of demands for government action in Canada. We shall evaluate the nature of this controversy in the concluding section of this chapter, "Prime Ministerial Government?". For now, we discuss briefly the duties and responsibilities of the four most important executive agencies: the Prime Minister's Office; the Privy Council Office (now including the Federal-Provincial Relations Office); the Treasury Board; and the Department of Finance. The first two report directly to the Prime Minister; the other two have their own Ministers.

It is important to bear in mind that both the individuals within these agencies and the institutions themselves are important. One of Colin Campbell and George Szablowski's interviewees listed the basic ingredients for success at the top:

> Both senior officials and ministers are candidates for the inner circle. With respect to officials, there are three important elements. First, the person has to have an excellent knowledge of government procedure, the "rules of the game." Second, he has to be persuasive, the logical force of his arguments has to come across. Third, he has to be a team player, willing to help his colleagues.[32]

THE PRIME MINISTER'S OFFICE

Of the various executive support agencies, the Prime Minister's Office (PMO) is the most overtly political. The upper echelon of the PMO is composed of personal appointees of the Prime Minister and sometimes includes those referred to as "Ottawa's best and brightest." It is the largest and most important of the "exempt" staffs, and only very rarely are public servants employed in this central agency.

On the advice of Ministers and other advisors the PMO drafts the Speech from the Throne. Perhaps the most crucial task of the PMO, however, is to act as a monitoring agency tracing political developments and their implications for the Prime Minister and his career. (For an outline of the traditional structure of the PMO see Figure 7.4.)

An official explained the PMO's role as follows:

> We are just a valve at the junction of the bureaucratic and the political. We add a little of the political ingredient when it appears that it has been overlooked. For instance, if I know that an official in PCO is working on a briefing note to the PM on an issue which I am responsible for, I'll go to him and express the political point of view. — I guess we are sort of a Distant Early Warning System for things that are going to cause trouble politically.[33]

While the PMO lacks the statutory authority of the other executive agencies, it became important because of the style and personality of Pierre Elliott Trudeau. Consistent with Trudeau's quest for rationality and the scientific analysis of political problems, the PMO was enlarged and staffed with technocrats and so-called "whiz kids."

The Prime Minister's Office has grown immensely. Near the end of the Trudeau years (1983–84), the office had a budget of just over $4 million per annum, and in the first year of Mulroney's government it spent over $6 million.[34] The importance of the Office is determined solely by the Prime Minister's personality and needs. Yet, as Blair Williams points out,

> Today in its advisory, administrative, and political functions the PMO is the most significant element of the para-political bureaucracy in Ottawa. Indeed, as the events of August, 1978 [when Trudeau announced economic initiatives which have been alleged to have been wholly devised by his advisors] seemed to reflect, the PMO might, in many respects, be the most important element of the total governmental policy-making apparatus.[35]

---

[32] Cited in Colin Campbell and George J. Szablowski, *The Superbureaucrats: Structure and Behaviour in Central Agencies* (Toronto: Macmillan, 1979), p. 172.

[33] Ibid., p. 66.

[34] *Main Estimates*, 1983-84 (Ottawa: Supply and Services, 1983); and *Toronto Star*, Oct. 6, 1985.

[35] Williams, "The Para-Political Bureaucracy," p. 218. Material in square brackets added.

FIGURE 7.4   THE PRIME MINISTER'S OFFICE (BASIC FORM)

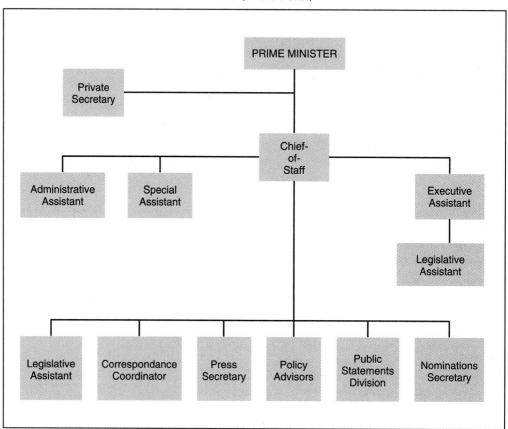

In concert with the Privy Council Office, the PMO provides the Prime Minister with a range of technical and political advice that may not be available from the more established bureaucratic structures. The emphasis of the PMO is on the development of practical policy suggestions relevant to the political fortunes of the Prime Minister and his party. In addition, the PMO does much public relations work. It gathers surveys on the popularity of the Prime Minister and specific policy initiatives, and helps in preparing press conferences and in dealing with the media generally. As a rule, officials in the PMO know and understand the marketing maxim that "It's the sizzle not the steak that sells." Other related responsibilities include answering the Prime Minister's mail, coordinating his daily appointment schedule and searching for candidates for nomination and awards.

The organization and structure of the PMO remain the prerogative of the Prime Minister. Throughout Canada's early history, the PMO was a small, relatively insignificant body. However, under Trudeau it achieved unprecedented importance. In 1968 Trudeau appointed Marc Lalonde, who had been with the Pearson administration, to the position of Principal Secretary. Lalonde, a confidant of Trudeau's, came to hold a very sensitive position at the apex of decision-making and was in control of information flowing to the Prime Minister. In 1984 Brian Mulroney went even further by putting many friends in the PMO. He appointed his law school friend, Bernard Roy, as his Chief of Staff. Later, Roy was replaced in turn by Derek Burney, a career public servant; Norman Spector, from FPRO; Stanley Hartt, an old friend; and the staunchest Tory of them all, Hugh Segal. The extent of the power and influence of this position depends in large measure on the ability of the individual and on the amount of authority the Prime Minister is willing to delegate. Burney's 1989 appointment as Canada's Ambassador to Washington illustrates his importance to Prime Minister Mulroney. In 1993 Prime Minister Chrétien appointed Jean Pelletier, former mayor of Québec and a defeated Liberal candidate, as his first Chief-of-Staff, and Eddie Goldenberg, a life-long friend, as Senior Policy Advisor.

Other changes have occurred in the Prime Minister's Office. The "regional desks" concept was introduced in 1968 but was abandoned after the Liberals' near defeat in 1972. The regional desks were designed to provide the Prime Minister with up-to-date information from the significant regions of the country. While the idea of a regional monitoring apparatus may have been sensible from the point of view of rational decision-making, it nonetheless revealed a certain insensitivity to the role and prerogatives of local MPs, as it was perceived to undermine their jealously guarded positions. Somewhat more successful than the regional desks idea was the creation of an office to monitor developments in foreign affairs. Through his personal rapport with the Prime Minister, Ivan Head came to take on a crucial role in external affairs analogous to that of Henry Kissinger in the first years of the Nixon administration. In delegating many important foreign policy matters to Head, Trudeau indicated a desire to control more directly the country's foreign affairs. In bypassing External Affairs, the traditional source of foreign policy advice and coordination, Trudeau indicated his distrust of older bureaucratic structures and his desire to create alternative sources of policy and information. Jean Chrétien has indicated that he intends to rely on public service advice rather than setting up a countervailing structure in the PMO.

The PMO has achieved considerable importance and is likely to continue to be extremely influential in policy-making at the political apex. With a budget of over $6 million and a staff of 68 person-years in 1993, the PMO is believed to be crucial to the government of the day.

THE PRIVY COUNCIL OFFICE

The Queen's Privy Council for Canada was established by the *BNA Act* to advise the Governor General. It is a ceremonial body comprised mostly of current and former Ministers of the Crown. The Cabinet, as we have seen earlier, is a committee of the Privy Council. The main organization supporting the Cabinet and Prime Minister is the Privy Council Office. The top position in the Office is held by the Clerk. This position, which has existed since 1867, is mentioned in the *Constitution*. It was combined with the function of Secretary to the Cabinet in 1940.

The PCO performs some of the same functions as the PMO but is staffed by career bureaucrats seconded from various government departments. It has responsibility for the development and coordination of overall government policy. Although the top echelon staff of the PCO is appointed by the Prime Minister on the advice of the Clerk, there is little emphasis on partisan politics — at least there had been little until Prime Minister Mulroney appointed his friend and political advisor, Dalton Camp, as the Senior Policy Adviser in the PCO. Under all recent Prime Ministers the PCO, like the PMO, has flourished in size and scope of responsibility, but it has rarely had political appointees on its staff.

The Privy Council Office possesses an impressive research capability and acts as the "eyes and ears" of the Cabinet in coordinating the numerous governmental departments and agencies. With a staff of over 300 officers and support personnel, the PCO is divided into three principal divisions: Plans, Operations and Senior Personnel. Each of these divisions has its own staff and is responsible for advising the Prime Minister, the plenary Cabinet and the various Cabinet committees on matters of national policy. To achieve this, the PCO employs a wide range of talent — from clerical staff and legal counsel to technical and scientific experts.

The **Clerk of the Privy Council** ranks at the top of Canada's civil service. The role and stature of the Clerk of the Privy Council, like those of the officers of the PMO, depend to a great extent on his rapport with the Prime Minister. Any Prime Minister would likely consider the Clerk to be one of his most crucial appointments. He is in charge of coordinating Cabinet activities. His staff set agendas, take the minutes of Cabinet meetings and convey Cabinet decisions to the bureaucracy.

The relationship between Cabinet Ministers and officers of the PCO is for the most part cordial and constructive. There is, of course, always the possibility of a rift or tension. Although the staff of the Privy Council may be expert on specific matters of policy, in the end it is the elected Ministers, whatever their knowledge or qualifications, who must make decisions. In principle, the PCO exists to advise and suggest alternatives in an objective and dispassionate manner, since the weight of public responsibility is not on its shoulders.

In an article describing developments in the PCO, a former Clerk, Gordon Robertson, suggested that it should be non-partisan, politically sensitive and governed by four principles.[36] The first principle is that the PCO should act as a source of policy ideas and should not construe its role as that of an administrative body. Responsibility for implementation and action lies with the various departments headed by the Ministers of the Crown. The PCO may play a coordinating role or provide specialized assistance, but should do nothing to undercut the authority of departments charged with specific responsibilities. The second principle is that the divisions within the PCO should work together and provide mutual assistance. In Robertson's opinion, unless there is coordination within the PCO itself, it will not be able to provide coherence to overall government policy. The third principle is that the PCO should be maintained as a non-career agency. As indicated earlier, the PCO is for the most part staffed by career bureaucrats on loan from various government departments. Robertson suggested that there be a continual turnover of staff in order to provide fresh talent and prevent anyone from becoming too settled or perhaps too deeply identified with a particular line of government policy. In his opinion, the task of liaison and coordination is far too sensitive to be left in the hands of a true believer. The fourth principle, Robertson argued, is that the PCO should be kept small in size. While it has grown dramatically since the Second World War, the present professional and clerical staff of approximately 300 is probably adequate for meeting its current needs and objectives. A further increase in staff would likely be counterproductive.

The PCO has a difficult task to perform within the Canadian government. It must be able to offer expert advice to the Prime Minister on a wide range of problems and policies.

---

[36] Gordon Robertson, "The Changing Role of the Privy Council Office," *CPA*, vol. 14, no. 4 (Winter 1971), pp. 487–508.

Given such expectations, it is not surprising that the PCO is considered one of the most prestigious agencies of the government.

Issues of concern to Ottawa and the provinces are periodically negotiated and adjusted through the mechanism of federal/provincial conferences. As we discussed in Chapter 6, this "executive" federalism has recently been characterized by a strong challenge to federal power, particularly from the richer western provinces and Québec. The holding of numerous federal/provincial meetings on a wide range of issues, especially constitutional revisions, necessitates intensive planning and preparation on the part of Ottawa. Within the Privy Council Office a new central agency — the Federal-Provincial Relations Office (FPRO) was established in 1974 and was designated a separate department under the Prime Minister in 1975. Until 1993 it functioned independently of PCO while reporting directly to the Prime Minister. As part of the 1993 restructuring it has been subsumed once again inside the PCO.

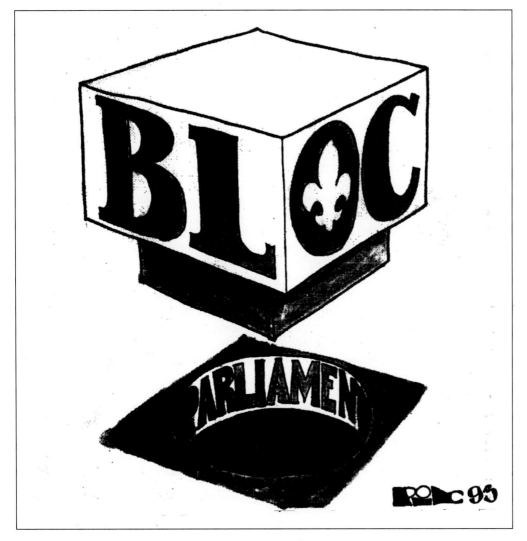

Reproduced with permission, PIC, *Ottawa Citizen*

PCO now carries out the traditional FPRO responsibilities for conducting research and analysis to help in coordinating Ottawa's interaction with the provinces and in anticipating provincial reactions. In particular, it has a special mandate to monitor events in Québec and prepare scenarios for action vis-à-vis its government and the issue of independence. It also has ongoing duties in the areas of aboriginal rights, the infrastructure program and constitutional planning. Given the continuous and increasing challenges to federalism, it is likely that the federal/provincial functions of the PCO will continue to increase.

THE TREASURY BOARD

The third central coordinating agency is the Treasury Board, which, as we have noted, is constitutionally a committee of the Privy Council, i.e., of Cabinet. In 1966, following recommendations of the Glassco Royal Commission on Government Organization, the staff of Treasury Board was removed from the jurisdiction of the Department of Finance and elevated to the legal status of a separate government department. Treasury Board and its Secretariat are headed by a Cabinet Minister, the President of the Treasury Board. The Treasury Board itself includes five other Cabinet Ministers, one of whom is usually the Minister of Finance. Aided by its Secretariat, the Treasury Board is charged with two broad areas of responsibility: review of government expenditures and personnel management.[37]

Responsibility for the review of expenditures means that the annual budgets of all government departments are screened and approved by this agency. The Treasury Board monitors all requests for money, evaluates them and provides an overall budget in keeping with the priorities and objectives expressed by the Prime Minister and Cabinet. There is continuous consultation and negotiation between the Treasury Board and the spokesmen for each department, usually senior level bureaucrats and the Minister. Each department attempts to maximize its share of the government's budget, and it is up to the Treasury Board to assess these requests and make its recommendations.

The task of the Treasury Board would be exceedingly difficult, if not chaotic, were it not for improvements in policy-making techniques during the past three decades. The first major reform came in the 1960s with the introduction of a Program, Planning and Budgetary System (PPBS). The second was the 1979 introduction of Public Expenditure Management Systems (PEMS) discussed in Chapter 9. Despite the government's decision to disband the overall PEMS system in 1989, the financial control procedures remain in place. In theory, these procedures force departments to frame their budgetary requirements in terms of government goals and objectives. Whether the Treasury Board has been fully able to meet its heavy responsibility in budgetary control is a matter of contention for various disgruntled department heads and, of course, for the loyal opposition. In fairness, it should be noted that the task it faces is complex. It is continually faced with pressure from both within and without Cabinet. Inevitably, no matter how worthwhile certain programs may be, there is only a finite amount of money to pay for them. It is the task of the Treasury Board and Cabinet to maximize the return.

The second major responsibility entrusted to the Treasury Board is management of civil service personnel. In 1967 the Treasury Board replaced the Public Service Commission

---

[37] See A.W. Johnson, "The Treasury Board of Canada and the Machinery of Government in the 1970s," *CJPS*, vol. 4, no. 3 (September 1971), pp. 346–66; and Michael Hicks, "The Treasury Board of Canada and its Clients: five years of change and administrative reform 1966–1971," *CPA*, vol. 16, no. 2 (Summer 1973), pp. 182–205.

as the official employer of government personnel; it is thus the responsible party in any collective bargaining negotiations. It exerts control over salaries and job classifications across the civil service, and its purpose is to expand the application of the merit principle. Motivating the Treasury Board above all else is a desire to encourage the effective utilization of human resources.

To assist the six Cabinet members of the Treasury Board there is a highly qualified staff — the Treasury Board Secretariat. Among the staff of the TBS are some of the brightest and most efficient members of the public service. Its economists, statisticians and efficiency experts conduct much of the preliminary analysis of departmental budgets. The TBS often makes various preliminary budgetary adjustments and other decisions that may be challenged by department heads or Ministers at the formal meetings of the Board itself. Needless to say, the specialized staff of the TBS can also play an important role in policy-making.

THE DEPARTMENT OF FINANCE

The fourth central coordinating agency of the executive is the Department of Finance. While it is a regular government department, by virtue of its subject matter it is one of the most politically sensitive. Created in 1967 out of the financial bodies that predated Confederation, its authority is assigned under the *Financial Administration Act*. The Department of Finance shares some of the general concerns of the Treasury Board, but its chief preoccupation is analyzing taxation policy and the impact of government activity on the economy. That is, the Department is concerned with monitoring Canada's economic prospects and predicting the probable level of tax revenues available to the government. It also engages in long-range economic forecasting and suggests ways to maximize the performance of the economy.

The Department of Finance provides most of the information that reaches the Cabinet on the performance of the economy. It is on the basis of these facts that Cabinet committees weigh and sift various programs and proposals to establish priorities. Its predictions and analyses greatly assist other policy-makers in achieving maximum use of available resources. Public servants employed by the Department of Finance concentrate on the analysis of four areas that comprise the Department's statutory authority: taxation policy, economic development and government finance, fiscal policy and economic analysis, and international trade and finance.

Taxation policy is handled by individual units within the Department. Specialists analyze existing tax measures from the perspective of the business community. A personal income tax unit examines proposals relating to personal taxation, deferred income plans such as retirement savings plans and trusts and partnerships. Other tax units attempt to determine the effects of taxation on the distribution of income, on the long-term growth of the economy and on the behaviour of individuals and corporations. Finally, the Department of Finance maintains an international tax policy unit that negotiates tax treaties with foreign countries and examines the effects of foreign taxation on the Canadian economy.

With respect to economic development, the Department seeks to devise policies and strategies encouraging the overall growth of the Canadian economy. For instance, policy analysts study plans to foster the development of Canada's natural resources and to promote industrial growth in such diverse fields as communications, transportation, nuclear energy and manufacturing. The Department of Finance is also involved in providing government loans to promote economic development and in negotiating financial guarantees to Crown corporations.

The third responsibility of the Department of Finance is fiscal policy and economic analysis. The Department monitors all indicators of the overall economic conditions of the country and prepares forecasts used in the development of the annual government budget. This involves establishing the annual fiscal framework and maintaining a close link with the Treasury Board Secretariat.

The fourth concern of the Department of Finance is international trade. It investigates and reports on proposals concerning the Canadian customs tariff and its relation to the General Agreement on Tariffs and Trade (GATT) and various bilateral trade agreements such as the Canada–United States Free Trade Agreement and the North American Free Trade Agreement. Recommendations on international trade policy, particularly imports, are formulated. The Department maintains a liaison with international financial organizations and, of course, seeks to promote export development. The international finance section is also concerned with the balance of payments and foreign exchange matters.

The Department of Finance maintains a relatively high profile among government departments. Its Minister is more than a spokesman for economic decisions made by the Cabinet. While he or she must carry out Cabinet's directives, other Ministers become involved so late in the budget planning process that, in effect, the Finance Minister has the dominant voice. It is the Minister who presents the government's budget to Parliament and is inevitably the object of criticism or praise by the press and the Opposition. Because taxation policy is usually the target of public scorn, however, the finance portfolio has traditionally been considered the graveyard of many a political career. The public servants in finance, however, remain to advise the next Minister.

A PROFILE OF SUPERBUREAUCRATS

The combined weight of the four organizations discussed above in bolstering the roles of the Prime Minister, ministry and Cabinet is beyond dispute. Their interactions with Ministers and each other are extensive. For example, Campbell and Szablowski found that 39 percent of their sample of "superbureaucrats" in these agencies had had contact with the PM, 60 percent with their own Minister, 73 percent with other Ministers and 62 percent with MPs. They also found that 72 percent of their respondents attended Cabinet committee meetings on a fairly regular basis.[38]

Who serves in these central agencies? Perhaps surprisingly, it has been found that superbureaucrats do not come from a socio-economic elite. Campbell and Szablowski's sample of central agents showed that their socio-economic backgrounds were more similar to those of the country's general populace than were the backgrounds of bureaucratic elites in other western democracies.[39] The study also revealed that central agents averaged 45 years of age. Québécois were the most under-represented proportionately, as they obtained only 15 percent of the positions. Ontario had 38 percent, Westerners 22 percent and the Maritimes only 4 percent. A full 21 percent came from outside Canada. It was found that 80 percent were of English or French origin; 20 percent came from other ethnic groups. Catholics and Protestants were equally represented with 38 percent each, while 9 percent were Jewish and 15 percent had no religious affiliation. The backgrounds of the parents of superbureaucrats were startling — many members of the bureaucratic elite were found to come from reasonably humble ori-

---

[38] Campbell and Szablowski, *The Superbureaucrats*, p. 167.

[39] Ibid., p. 105 and passim.

gins. "Only 37 percent of central agents' fathers attended university, while 29 percent never even attended high school. In addition, although, 30 percent of central agents' fathers had professional or technical occupations and 36 percent were businessmen or managers, a fairly large 34 percent had clerical or blue-collar jobs."[40]

What distinguishes central agents from the general populace, and indeed from the average bureaucrat, is their level of education. Like the majority of Ministers and Prime Ministers, members of the central agencies are highly educated. Nine out of ten graduated from university, seven out of ten received graduate degrees and many obtained foreign degrees. Many central agents began their careers outside the federal public service. The largest single group, 23 percent, came from the universities; 15 percent came from private corporations, 11 percent from Crown corporations, 9 percent from provincial government, 9 percent from media backgrounds, 8 percent from law firms and 4 percent from high school teaching. Educational achievement has clearly been a prime factor in rapid upward mobility. Such backgrounds, especially those in the social sciences and law, account for much of the pragmatism and professionalism found in the central agencies.

PRIME MINISTERIAL GOVERNMENT?

Considerable disquiet exists today among observers of the Canadian political scene. One basis for this uneasiness is the suggestion that the political executive has overstepped its proper authority; such encroachment is seen as portending grave consequences for responsible government and the parliamentary system. Changes in the rules of House of Commons procedure and the expanding jurisdiction of the central coordinating agencies have lessened the effectiveness of Parliament in its role of scrutiny and deliberation. The result is that the Prime Minister is beginning to exercise a scope of authority analogous to that of the American President.

In an early article discussing this issue, Denis Smith suggested that Parliament had surrendered its important roles of providing a forum for serious public debate and developing public policy.[41] He argued that the establishment of a presidential-style control of government had been evolving well before the election of Pierre Trudeau in 1968. Rather than establishing the trend, Trudeau merely refined and consolidated it. According to Smith, the source of the Prime Minister's predominance is that the system is devised in such a way that a great deal ultimately depends on him or her. The Prime Minister appoints Ministers and controls their tenure almost entirely. Although Cabinet may include some unusually powerful and prestigious figures such as C.D. Howe, John Turner and Joe Clark, in the end the decisions it reaches depend on the priorities and orientations of the Prime Minister. Cabinet policy becomes government policy, and backbenchers have little choice but to vote in obedience to the party and their Prime Minister. The recent reforms in House rules permit the government to guide legislation through with a minimum of delay or modification. The opposition parties, lacking adequate research and basic information, may resort to fiery oratory but are rarely able to conduct thorough scrutiny and effective criticism.

The office of Prime Minister in Canada today is very strong. Whether the current situation is beneficial for the country and its political process is a matter that will continue

---

[40] Ibid., p. 116.

[41] Denis Smith, "President and Parliament: The Transformation of Parliamentary Government in Canada," in Hockin, ed., *Apex of Power*, pp. 308–25.

to be debated for years to come. Without taking one side in the argument, we can consider what has given rise to this argument about executive leadership. While Canada's total population has been rising gradually, the demand for services of all kinds has risen exponentially. To meet these needs, the government developed large departments and bureaucracies. Their size and the variety of needs they must address made it increasingly difficult to control government spending. Faced with this cumbersome and ever-expanding government sector, Prime Ministers Trudeau, Clark and Turner introduced aspects of systematic planning to replace the somewhat haphazard, ad hoc policy-making of previous administrations. While pushing for the reform of House procedural rules to streamline the legislative process, the government simultaneously expanded the size and functions of the central coordinating agencies, especially the PMO and PCO. Prime Ministers Mulroney and Campbell inherited and used this system to their political advantage. Although a "brokerage" style of politics dominated Conservative decision-making, the role and significance of the Prime Minister continued to increase along with the role of central agencies.

> *When you're in government...the choices you make are not between...strawberries and cream or crème caramel for dessert. You have to sometimes choose between cod liver oil or cough syrup.*[42]

The take-over of exceptional policy-making authority by the Prime Minister and central executive agencies is resented by Ministers, middle and upper echelons of the civil service and Members of Parliament, and distrusted by the press and opposition. Journalistic reports abound of the existence of a coterie of insiders who, being outside the bounds of parliamentary control, are able to manipulate the levers of power in Canada. While the descriptions of flagrant abuse of power may be overstated,[43] the potential for its occurrence has been very real indeed. The power of the Prime Minister and the executive staff has become enormous and pervasive. Once elected, a Prime Minister can shape the direction and content of policy and, except in extraordinary situations, can count on dominating the political process until he or she decides to call an election.

While our discussion has justifiably focused on the powers and advantages of the Prime Minister's position, at the same time we must not overlook certain limits on it. It is our contention that, in fact, Canada does *not* have Prime Ministerial government. The political resources of the Prime Minister are undeniably potent and broad. But the power of the Prime Minister is not exercised in isolation. The Prime Minister and his or her colleagues must take care to guide the Cabinet and caucus toward policies that avoid hostile reactions from Parliament and the public. As well, the Prime Minister must secure the loyalty of followers or risk being voted out of office. As summarized in *The Canadian Legislative System*:

> *The Prime Minister's influence stems from an ability to command the maximum possible amount of information about the political environment and to use this resource in persuading political actors to follow his policy initiatives. Administrative secrecy and collective ministerial responsibility permit the executive to acquire requisite political knowledge without revealing conflicts or divisions which may occur within its ranks. However, the ability to conceal the process of decision making at this level in government has sustained the erroneous idea that the executive*

---

[42]   Ontario Premier Bob Rae in an interview as he launched his social contract to control the Ontario deficit.

[43]   Walter Stewart, *Shrug: Trudeau in Power* (Toronto: New Press, 1971).

works in isolation from parliamentary influence and has contributed significantly to the impression that the government acts independently of public opinion.[44]

At certain times, the Prime Minister can act independently; at others, the PM is forced to rely on party colleagues. Malcolm Punnett has provided the most succinct criticism of the thesis of Prime Ministerial government. After a detailed examination of the governing style of Canada's Prime Ministers, he concluded that the argument is not justified "because of the fundamental distinction that exists between the seeming concentration of power in the hands of the Prime Minister of the day and the realities of his position."[45] The Prime Minister is constrained in the choice of Ministers by the difficulties of holding a Cabinet together, of directing a complex government machine and of securing agreements to his proposals from the Cabinet, backbench and often other parties.

There are four basic models of executive government in the political science literature:

1. Prime Ministerial, in which decisions are taken by the Prime Minister acting alone.
2. Ministerial, in which decisions are taken by individual Ministers in their own spheres of interest.
3. Cabinet, in which Cabinet under the direction of the Prime Minister collectively takes decisions.
4. Inner-Group, in which decisions are taken by a sub-group of Cabinet along with the Prime Minister.[46]

In view of the constraints listed above, it is our view that the first model does not apply to Canada. No Canadian Prime Minister can really act alone and all of these models fail to take Ministers and bureaucrats into account. Of course, some Prime Ministers have tried to take more than their share of decision-making responsibility. R.B. Bennett simultaneously held the posts of Prime Minister, Minister of Finance and External Affairs, and is said to have acted independently of his Cabinet colleagues. A splendid joke was told about him in the 1930s:

Visitor to Ottawa — "*Who is that man coming toward us?*"

Ottawa Resident — "*Mr. R.B. Bennett, the new Prime Minister.*"

Visitor to Ottawa — "*Why is he talking to himself?*"

Ottawa Resident — "*He is holding a Cabinet meeting.*"[47]

However, even Bennett had to avoid coalitions of conflicting interests and often ran into difficulties.

Prime Ministers obtain much of their strength from holding their team together. This must be done with conciliation, tact and only rarely with force. Most Prime Ministers bring particular skills to bear on this responsibility. For example, Pearson was a master chairman-of-the-board type of leader; Mackenzie King was a master electioneer. Mulroney combined both talents. The skills required are so varied that no Prime Minister can be said to have had all of them. What all Prime Ministers must demonstrate is the ability to coordinate their colleagues and, hence, policy. The primary ingredient of this ability is anticipation

---

[44] Jackson and Atkinson, *Canadian Legislative System*, p. 56.

[45] Punnett, *The Prime Minister*, p. 157.

[46] Ibid., p. 86.

[47] Ernest Watkins, *R.B. Bennett: A Biography* (London: Secker and Warburg, 1963), p. 167.

of the actions of all the major actors in the political system. Recent Prime Ministers have accomplished this by relying on a small coterie of Ministers to help them come to compromises and conclusions. Prime Ministers Trudeau and Mulroney both employed a Priorities and Planning committee of Cabinet to obtain information and enhance consensus. Clark constructed an Inner Cabinet to accomplish the same end. On this evidence, the usual prime ministerial pattern could therefore be described as setting up an informal partial Cabinet to help run the government. This is a far cry from the arrangement suggested by those who contend that Canada now has Prime Ministerial government. Jean Chrétien eliminated these special committees and intends to govern with a small Cabinet of only 22 members. It remains to be seen whether this process will enhance or reduce Prime Ministerial power.

OVERVIEW

The centralization of power in the hands of the executive and its specialized agencies is a matter for serious attention. While some will find even the appearance of presidential-style government difficult to accept, it is likely inevitable. The centralization of power is a political reality, although critics should not overlook the obvious constraints and limitations within which the Prime Minister must operate. An extraordinary apparatus and structure of power has been built over the years; fortunately for Canada, its Prime Ministers have thus far been enlightened figures.

This chapter has sought to illuminate the nature of executive power in Canada. While the *Constitution Act* of 1867 established a formal executive in the person of the Governor General, there is no question that real political power is exercised by the Prime Minister and Cabinet, based on the possession of an electoral mandate. The fusion-of-powers principle, along with other aspects of the British parliamentary tradition such as party discipline and Cabinet solidarity, confers upon the political executive the opportunity to carry out its program knowing that it can count on consistent legislative support except during minority governments. The Prime Minister has extraordinary powers, such as the authority to make Cabinet appointments, reorganize the government structure and dissolve Parliament at his or her discretion. In order to run the government apparatus efficiently the Prime Minister must delegate some authority to the members of the ministry and Cabinet. In recent years the government has evolved an elaborate system of committees and subcommittees, all of which are ultimately responsible to the Prime Minister. In the last two decades the various executive coordinating agencies have grown greatly in size and authority. Unquestionably, power is becoming centralized as never before in the hands of the executive. Whether this is necessary or inevitable will be debated for years to come.

SELECTED BIBLIOGRAPHY

Bakvis, H. *Regional Ministers: Power and Influence in the Canadian Cabinet* (Toronto: University of Toronto Press, 1991).

Bercuson, David et al., *Sacred Trust: Brian Mulroney and the Conservative Party in Power* (Toronto: Doubleday, 1986).

Blondel, Jean, *The Organization of Governments* (Beverly Hills, Cal., and London: Sage, 1982).

———, World leaders (Beverly Hills, Cal. and London: Sage, 1980).

Cameron, Stevie, *Ottawa Inside Out: Power, Prestige and Scandal in the Nation's Capital* (Toronto: Key Porter, 1990).

Campbell, Colin, *Governments Under Stress: Bureaucrats and Political Leaders in Washington, London and Ottawa* (Toronto: University of Toronto Press, 1983).

——— and George Szablowski, *The Superbureaucrats: Structure and Behaviour in Central Agencies* (Toronto: Macmillan of Canada, 1979).

——— and M.J. Wyszomirski, eds., *Executive Leadership in Anglo-American Systems* (Pittsburgh: University of Pittsburgh Press, 1991).

Clarkson, Stephen and Christina McCall, *Trudeau and Our Times*, 2 vols (Toronto: McClelland & Stewart, 1990 and 1992).

Donaldson, Gordon, *Eighteen Men: The Prime Ministers of Canada* (Toronto: Doubleday, 1985).

Gossage, P., *Close to Charisma: Between the Press and the Prime Minister* (Toronto: McClelland & Stewart, 1986).

Gordon, Walter, *A Political Memoir* (Toronto: McClelland & Stewart, 1977).

Graham, Ron, *One-Eyed Kings: Promise and Illusion in Canadian Politics* (Toronto: Collins, 1986).

Hockin, Thomas A., ed., *The Apex of Power: The Prime Minister and Political Leadership in Canada*, 2nd ed. (Scarborough, Ont.: Prentice-Hall Canada, 1977).

LaMarsh, Judy, *Memoirs of a Bird in a Gilded Cage* (Toronto: McClelland & Stewart, 1969).

Martin, Lawrence, *Pledge of Allegiance: The Americanization of Canada in the Mulroney Years* (Toronto: McClelland & Stewart, 1993).

———, *The Presidents and the Prime Ministers* (Toronto: Doubleday, 1982).

Matheson, William A., *The Prime Minister and the Cabinet* (Toronto: Methuen, 1976).

McCall-Newman, Christina, *Grits* (Toronto: Macmillan, 1982).

Ondaatje, Christopher, *The Prime Ministers of Canada: Macdonald to Mulroney* (Toronto: Pagurian, 1985).

Pal, Leslie A. and David Taras, eds., *Prime Ministers and Premiers* (Scarborough, Ont.: Prentice-Hall Canada, 1988).

Punnett, R. Malcolm, *The Prime Minister in Canadian Government and Politics* (Toronto: Macmillan of Canada, 1977).

Rose, Richard and Ezra N. Suleiman, eds., *Presidents and Prime Ministers* (Washington: American Enterprise Institute for Public Policy Research, 1980).

Sawatsky, John, *Mulroney: The Politics of Ambition* (Toronto: Macfarlane Walter & Ross: 1991).

Weller, Patrick, *First Among Equals: Prime Ministers in Westminster Systems* (London: Allen and Unwin, 1985).

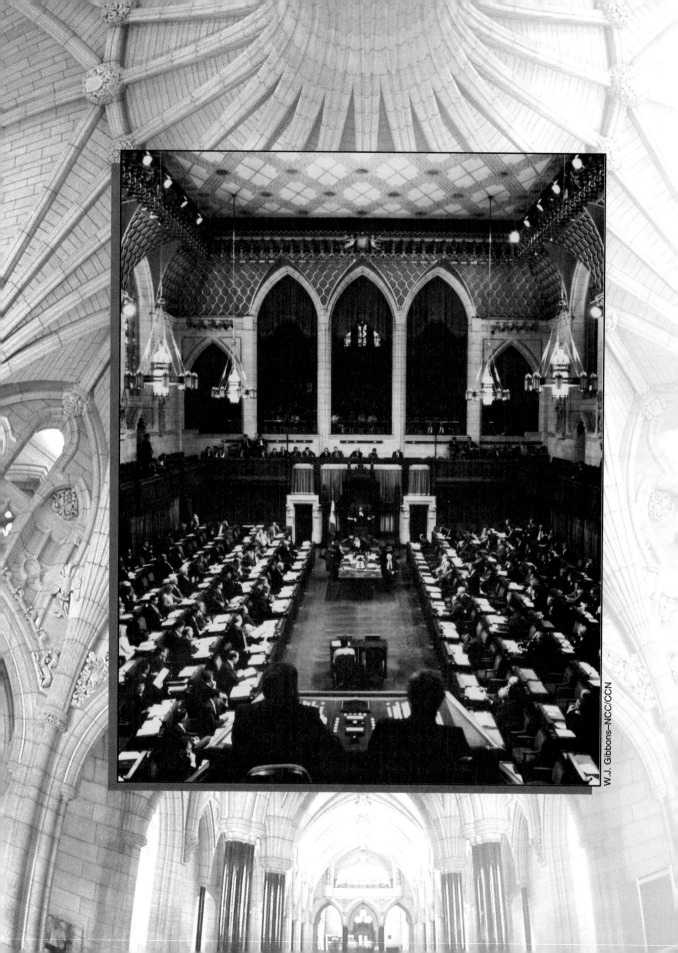

LEGISLATIVE POLITICS
SYMBOLISM OR POWER?

In a parliamentary democracy, the federal legislature, or Parliament, should be one of the most important institutions in the political life of the country. However, in Canada a certain degree of dissatisfaction exists among academic and media observers, sections of the general public and even parliamentarians themselves about the role of Parliament. There is perennial debate on the subject of parliamentary reform. At times, dissatisfaction with Parliament verges on outright cynicism. But the reality is that Canadian democracy could not function without this institution.

In a parliamentary democracy, in contrast to a presidential system, the political executive receives its power to govern from the legislature. The government needs the approval of Parliament to legitimate its policies and activities, particularly for the expenditure of public funds. In return, the Prime Minister and Cabinet must hold themselves accountable to Parliament, and may continue to govern only as long as they retain the "confidence" of Parliament or, more correctly in the case of Canada, at least the tacit support of a majority of the House of Commons. Thus, while Parliament gives the executive the authority to govern, it also serves as a check on the absolute or irresponsible use of government power.

Parliament, moreover, provides an arena for debate in which the major political issues of the day may be aired — and subsequently relayed to the public by the mass media. As such, it is a public forum for opposition parties to criticize the government of the day and to demonstrate why they, not the governing party, should be returned with a majority of seats at the next general election.

Last, but not least, Parliament serves important functions on behalf of Canadian citizens. In the theory of **parliamentary democracy**, Parliament is the "repository of popular sovereignty" — in making laws and ensuring the responsibility of government, Parliament exercises power on behalf of the general public, power vested in it through the electoral process. It is not possible in a country the size of Canada for all citizens to participate directly in the legislative process. Instead, Canada is a **representative democracy** in which, from time to time, we choose certain individuals (Members of Parliament) to represent our interests in the making of national policies. But, on a more practical level, a significant part of the role of parliamentarians is catering to the needs of their constituents. Members of Parliament and their staff spend much of their time taking up the problems of citizens with ministers, public servants or representatives of government agencies. Such personal problems may seem prosaic compared with issues such as inflation and military helicopters, but they are important to the people they affect. All Canadians, especially those with no well-organized business lobby or trade union to represent them, need Parliament.

Thus, Parliament is indeed an important institution in Canadian political life. The ongoing debates about parliamentary reform reflect its significance. But it is not always easy to determine whether the importance of Parliament is derived from its *power* to enact legislation, hold the government accountable and control the public purse-strings, or from its perceived *symbolic role* as the repository of popular sovereignty, an arena for political debate and the legitimizer of the actions of government and, perhaps, of the entire policy process.

Like other legislatures, the Parliament of Canada is a multifunctional institution. It plays several roles of importance to the political process and to the Canadian people. Accordingly, its members have a multitude of tasks to perform — as Senators and MPs, as members of Cabinet and opposition, as members of party caucuses and parliamentary committees and as individual representatives of their constituents. There is a constant tension, visible in many of the reform debates, among the various roles of Parliament and among the tasks that members are expected to carry out.

In this chapter, we examine how these tensions are reconciled through the process of *legislative politics*. We look at several aspects of this reconciliation: how the parliamentary timetable and procedures reflect the competing demands of a government wishing to govern and an opposition seeking to air public issues and criticize the government's method of handling them; how the working sub-groups of parliamentarians in committees and party caucuses contribute to the overall work of Parliament; how individual MPs attempt to manage the competing demands on their time; how the Senate continues to make a positive contribution and how adherence to the parliamentary "rules of the game" generally imposes a workable peace on an adversarial system of politics. We commence our examination by defining what a legislature is. Then, in the section that follows, we consider the role of legislatures in comparative perspective, with particular reference to the concepts of the *power* and *symbolism* of parliaments and to the various meanings that may be attached to the term *legislative politics*.

WHAT IS A LEGISLATURE?

Legislatures are among the most pervasive of political institutions. In 1994, almost all of the more than 185 independent states had some kind of parliamentary chamber; many of these also had legislative assemblies at the sub-national level such as the state legislatures of the United States, the provincial assemblies in Canada, and so on. The very ubiquity of the institution makes the definition of a "legislature" and the specification of its functions difficult. It was once common, if not entirely correct, to base such a definition on the characteristics of the American Congress or the British Parliament. However, easy conceptualization has been hindered by the development, particularly in the Third World, of many institutions that call themselves "legislatures" or "parliaments" but which possess methods of recruitment, powers and relations to other political structures widely divergent from those of the two traditional models.

Some authors avoid this matter of definition altogether — taking for granted that their readers already know what a legislature is — and plunge directly into their analyses.[1] An

---

[1] For example, Jean Blondel, *Comparative Legislatures* (Englewood Cliffs; N.J., Prentice-Hall, 1973).

alternative strategy to such avoidance *and* to offering a precise definition is the presentation of a checklist of characteristics that, taken together, are both necessary and sufficient to distinguish legislatures from other political institutions. Thus, Nelson Polsby argues that a

> ...*mélange of characteristics — officiality, a claim of legitimacy based on links with the people, multi-memberedness, formal equality, collective decision-making, deliberativeness — typifies and distinguishes legislatures in a wide variety of settings.*[2]

While Polsby's approach is primarily structural, an alternative is the functional perspective that defines legislatures in terms of their tasks or the purpose they serve in the political system. The latter approach shows legislatures performing a multitude of functions — in addition to the apparently tautological "legislative" or "law-making" role — that vary in salience from country to country and even over time within the same political system. The role of the Congress of People's Deputies in Russia, for example, was very different from that of the American Congress; and the functions of the British Parliament today have changed considerably since its so-called "Golden Age" over a century ago. Furthermore, the fact that many of the functions attributed to legislatures are also performed by other political institutions merely adds to the terminological confusion.

In a recent comparative study of legislatures, Michael Mezey offers a personal perception of the concept in which both structural and functional elements are combined:

> *I think of a legislature as a predominantly elected body of people that acts collegially and that has at least the formal but not necessarily the exclusive power to enact laws binding on all members of a specific geopolitical entity.*[3]

This constitutes a valid definition, but there is one major problem with Mezey's conceptualization in the Canadian context. In applying his definition individually to each chamber or "house" of bicameral parliaments, he specifically excludes the Canadian Senate from consideration as a legislature, since its members are appointed rather than "predominantly elected." On the other hand, he does not tell the reader just what a senate is, if it is not a legislature or at least a part of one. Of course, there would be no problem in the Canadian case if the definition were applied to the whole Parliament of Canada (i.e., the Senate and the House of Commons) since it is "predominantly elected"; but the usage could not then be extended to the British Parliament, wherein the membership of the House of Lords, recruited by appointment or by heredity, exceeds that of the popularly elected House of Commons. The application of Mezey's definition may therefore be broadened to cover bicameral parliaments if both chambers collectively are considered to constitute the legislature, as long as the lower house (or, in parliamentary systems, the house to which the government is officially responsible) is predominantly elected. With the addition of this proviso, the simplicity and clarity of Mezey's conceptualization make it a suitable working definition for this chapter.

THE ROLES OF LEGISLATURES

A frequent source of confusion in the study of parliamentary institutions is the notion that "legislatures must legislate." Given the similarity between the two words and the mythology

---

[2]   Nelson Polsby, "Legislatures," in F. Greenstein and N. Polsby, eds., *Handbook of Political Science*, vol. 5 (Reading, Mass.: Addison-Wesley, 1975), p. 260.

[3]   Michael L. Mezey, *Comparative Legislatures* (Durham, N.C.: Duke University Press, 1979), p. 6.

surrounding the role of legislatures, this assumption is not surprising. But neither should it be encouraged since it may lead to unfulfilled expectations of what legislatures ought to do and to overly simplistic criticisms of parliamentary institutions. For this reason, one author justifies his usage of "parliament" as a generic term for national legislative assemblies in preference to "legislature" in that the latter is "too restrictively an implied definition of what these bodies do."[4] On the other hand, most legislatures do spend a substantial portion of their time in consideration and passage of legislation. For instance, approximately one-third of all oral debates in the Canadian House of Commons are devoted to discussion of government legislation, and between one-quarter and one-half of all Commons committee meetings are on the same subject.[5] The essential point is that a distinction must be drawn between the legislative function — the task of initiating, formulating and enacting bills or statutes — and the legislature as an institution. The legislative function is a complex one that involves various other actors in the process of devising and drafting bills before the legislature gives them consideration and decides whether the proposals are to become part of the law of the land. As institutions, legislatures are multifunctional and the passage of legislation is but one of a number of roles they perform.

The delineation of the roles of legislatures has a long history in the study of political institutions, with the result that a bewildering array of functions now appears in the literature. More than a century has passed since the famous English constitutionalist Walter Bagehot described the major roles of the British House of Commons as *elective, expressive, teaching, informing* and *legislative*.[6] Given the reputation of the British legislature as "the mother of parliaments," it is perhaps not surprising that many subsequent classifications have been based more or less loosely upon Bagehot's classic formulation, although his categories have often been re-labelled with more current terminology or jargon. However, after the Second World War, as political scientists increasingly oriented their research to non-western societies, it became apparent that some legislatures had no real power to make laws, to constitute or remove governments or to articulate the grievances of the population. New functions had to be added to the list to describe the roles of what were little more than "rubber stamp" assemblies; as a result, attention was drawn to the more symbolic functions of parliaments, such as *legitimation* of the regime and *integration* of the political community.

So numerous have the proposed functions of legislatures become that some scholars have turned to a process of consolidation. To take one example, Mezey suggests that, "with only a modest amount of pushing and shoving," all the activities of legislatures and their members "can be grouped into three broad categories: policy-making activities, representational activities, and system-maintenance activities."[7] From this perspective, **policy-making activities** include not only the traditional legislative function (the initiation and passage of legislation), but also all attempts to influence the content of government policy, the

---

4   David M. Olson, *The Legislative Process: A Comparative Perspective* (New York: Harper & Row, 1980), p. 11.

5   See Thomas A. Hockin, "Adversary Politics and Some Functions of the Canadian House of Commons," in R. Schultz et al., eds., *The Canadian Political Process*, 3rd ed. (Toronto: Holt, Rinehart and Winston, 1979), p. 318; and Robert J. Jackson and Michael M. Atkinson, *The Canadian Legislative System*, 2nd rev. ed. (Toronto: Macmillan of Canada, 1980), p. 187.

6   Walter Bagehot, *The English Constitution*, 1st ed. 1867 (London: Fontana/Collins, 1963), pp. 150–54.

7   Mezey, *Comparative Legislatures*, p. 7 ff. For an application of these broad categories to the literature on the Canadian House of Commons, see Allan Kornberg and Colin Campbell, "Parliament in Canada: A Decade of Published Research," *Legislative Studies Quarterly*, vol. III, no. 4 (November 1978), pp. 555–80.

publication of political issues through parliamentary debate and the scrutiny or control of the activities of government and bureaucracy. The **representational activities** of parliamentarians consist largely of expressing the interests and opinions of their respective electorates and dealing with the problems of constituents, particularly with regard to mediating with the bureaucracy on their behalf. Finally **system-maintenance activities** are the often primarily symbolic functions that contribute to the viability and legitimacy of other parts of the political system or the regime itself. Hence, legislatures often participate in the recruitment and socialization of future members of the political elite; they aid in the regulation and management of conflict and may serve to integrate and build consensus among rival political elites; they frequently elect and thus help to legitimate governments and, through their participation in the decision-making process, they legitimate public policies.

The relative importance of the various activities of legislatures and their members varies from country to country and, over time, within individual systems. As a consequence of erroneous preconceptions of what legislatures *ought* to do, this change in the relative salience of different functions over time has led some commentators to lament the "decline of legislatures." Here, "decline" refers to a waning of the power vested in the more established parliaments of western Europe and the original members of the British Commonwealth. Particular attention is given to the dominance of cabinet and the bureaucracy in the legislative process. Much of the blame for this situation has been placed upon the growing volume and increasingly technical nature of legislation in the modern state and the lack of resources available to parliamentarians for coping with this complexity, or on the adverse effect of the emergence of cohesive, disciplined political parties upon the role of individual parliamentarians.

The bemoaning of a decline in the powers of parliaments is largely based on an inappropriate comparison of their present roles with an ideal-typical measure, the so-called "Golden Age of Parliament" in Britain. Admittedly, there was a time when much legislation was either initiated or introduced by private members; when the volume of parliamentary business was sufficiently small to allow members to spend long hours in debate and individual displays of grandiose rhetoric; when legislators were virtual independents and formed ad hoc majorities on an issue-to-issue basis and when governments were frequently removed and replaced by Parliament without resorting to general elections. But this situation existed only in a few countries and only for a short period during the mid-nineteenth century. It was an era in which the business of the state was minimal and parliaments were well-suited "to operate by competition between political parties responsible to a non-democratic electorate."[8] But, although a dominant executive has historically been the norm in Britain, it is in this brief and rather exceptional interlude that many of the myths currently surrounding legislatures originate. Not unnaturally, given the time at which the Parliament of Canada was established, on British principles, some idealistic views entered the mythology of Canadian parliamentary democracy.

Although, as we have said, the activities of legislatures have changed over time in response to alterations in the political and socio-economic environment, it must be pointed out that the decline of some functions has been matched by an enhancement of others.[9] To talk of the "strength" or "weakness" of a legislature is difficult in any case. The concept of power

---

8   C.B. Macpherson, *The Real World of Democracy* (Toronto: CBC Publications, 1965), p. 35.

9   Gerhard Loewenberg, "The Role of Parliaments in Modern Political Systems," in Loewenberg, ed., *Modern Parliaments: Change or Decline?* (Chicago: Aldine-Atherton, 1971), p. 15.

is extremely complex, particularly as it relates to the legislative process. If a given parliament accepts the vast majority of the legislation placed before it by the government, it is not possible to be sure whether this demonstrates the weakness of the legislature vis-à-vis the executive or its strength in forcing the government to introduce only those measures that have a high probability of success.

Similarly, *power* and *symbolism* are often posed as dichotomous concepts: a legislature is either powerful or its weakness makes its role primarily symbolic. While this may be partly true in the short term, it may also be argued that, in the long term, only a powerful or effective legislature will have sufficient efficacy to perform a symbolic role in maintaining the legitimacy of the policy process and its outputs. All too often, the power of a legislature is equated with the extent of its involvement in the legislative process, especially with the initiation of legislation or the frequency of rejection of government policies. But legislatures are multifunctional institutions, and many of their activities other than law-making are symptomatic of their importance in the political system and contribute to their public image and symbolic capabilities. Thus, "power" and "symbolism," rather than constituting polar opposites, are parallel concepts that may be applied to each of the many activities undertaken by legislatures.

LEGISLATIVE POLITICS

As the title of this chapter suggests, legislative behaviour in an assembly such as the Parliament of Canada is highly political.[10] But what is meant by the term **legislative politics**? Perhaps the closest analogy we can draw is to the concept of politics as it appears in the popular phrase "office politics" — that is, the interaction and competition among workers in the same organization for status, influence and power in the life of that institution. Whether in the form of opposition parties seeking to influence or change the policy of the government, the legislature as a whole seeking greater opportunities for effective participation in the decision-making process or members of the same party vying for advancement in the legislative or government hierarchy, there is constant politicking in the life of a legislature.

Nonetheless, all members of the legislature are bound together by their common participation in the institution and by codes of ethics and behaviour that are often incomprehensible to the outsider. Political foes on the floor of the House may be friends outside the chamber, while colleagues from the same party may be fiercely antagonistic. Similarly, members from polar extremes of the political spectrum may join forces in defence of the sovereignty of Parliament in the face of encroachment by the government or some other institution. Or, as occurred when Stanley Knowles was made an honorary officer of the Canadian House of Commons for life, all members of the legislature, partisan allies and foes alike, may put aside their differences to unite in paying tribute to one of their number for long and distinguished service. Meanwhile, through it all may rage a fierce war of rhetoric between rival parties and competing ideologies. Such is the stuff of legislative politics.

THE LEGISLATIVE PROCESS IN PARLIAMENT

The *Constitution Act, 1867* established the Parliament of Canada as a bicameral legislature consisting of an appointed upper house, the Senate, and a popularly elected lower house, the

---

[10] The electoral system and the composition of Parliament after the 1993 election is discussed in Chapter 11.

House of Commons. In addition, the Monarch plays a formal role in the legislative process through his or her representative, the Governor General, inasmuch as all bills must receive Royal Assent before becoming part of Canadian law.

In strictly legal terms, the two chambers of the Parliament of Canada have coequal legislative powers in that all bills must be passed in their entirety by both houses in order to receive Royal Assent, and neither chamber has the power to override the veto or the amendments of the other. In this regard, the Senate appears to be stronger than its British counterpart, the House of Lords, because the former can defeat legislation, whereas the latter can only exercise a suspensory veto.[11] However, the Senate rarely employs its amendment powers or vetoes bills; it usually backs down in the case of dissension between the two chambers. As a result, many commentators view the Senate as the junior partner in the parliamentary process and often virtually ignore the upper house in analyzing the Canadian legislature. The fact remains, however, that all bills must be passed by both chambers before becoming law. The free-trade gambit of 1988, when the Liberal-dominated Senate forced a general election over the issue by refusing to pass the required legislation, is undoubtedly the most important recent example of Senatorial power. The Liberal-dominated Senate, however, did not act entirely on its own. Liberal senators acted on the direction of opposition leader John Turner.

THE PARLIAMENTARY LIFE CYCLE

The Senate and the House of Commons may meet as legislative bodies only during a parliamentary session. Parliaments are labelled by consecutive numbers, changing after each general election. For example, the 295 MPs returned in the 1993 election collectively constitute the 35th Parliament. In each Parliament there may be one or a number of **sessions**, depending upon the wishes of the government of the day and its ability in managing its legislative program, and upon the length of the Parliament — that is, how much time elapses between general elections.

Each parliamentary session begins with the Governor General summoning the MPs and Senators to Parliament at the request of the Prime Minister. Members of both Houses come together in the Senate Chamber, amid great pomp and ceremony, to hear the Governor General deliver the speech from the throne, outlining the government's proposed legislative program for the forthcoming session. They then return to their respective chambers to commence business. In the Commons, the debate on the throne speech usually occupies the first few days of the session; afterward, the normal timetable of the House comes into effect. A break period taken by the House within a session is called an **adjournment**.

Another ceremonial occasion, known as the **prorogation of Parliament**, brings a session to a close. The Governor General again acts upon the advice of the Prime Minister to prorogue Parliament; therefore, the length of a session is often determined by the government's ability to tidy up the loose ends in its legislative program. Unless there is prior agreement, any legislation that has not successfully completed all the stages of the process automatically dies when Parliament is prorogued: if the government is still committed to it, the bill must go through the entire process again in the next session. This fact explains the phenomenon of so-called "trial-balloon bills" that governments sometimes introduce close

---

[11] In contrast to this view, see Thomas A. Hockin, *Government in Canada* (Toronto: McGraw-Hill Ryerson, 1976), p. 173.

to the end of a session to test parliamentary and public reactions before the bill is redrafted for introduction in the next session.

At one time, each session of Parliament lasted a year or less, but sessions have generally become longer in recent years. Thus, the first session of the 32nd Parliament lasted an unprecedented three years and eight months. Also in the past, MPs and Senators used to enjoy a break between sessions, in addition to their vacations from Ottawa when Parliament was adjourned or in recess. Today, prorogation of one session is often followed immediately by the summoning of the next. However, at least once every five years, there has always been and continues to be a proclamation by the Governor General announcing the dissolution of the House of Commons. **Dissolution**, which occurs at the request of a Prime Minister who seeks a new mandate or whose government has been defeated in the House,[12] brings in its wake a general election.

As we have noted, one of the reasons MPs and Senators are summoned to Ottawa is to participate in the legislative process through which bills must pass before being given Royal Assent. The parliamentary stages are only the final elements of a much longer process that begins with the initiation, formulation and drafting of bills by a number of institutions such as the Prime Minister, Cabinet, the Privy Council Office, the drafting office of the Department of Justice and other departments. What happens to bills once they enter the parliamentary deliberation stage of the legislative process? Before examining this question, we shall make a brief but necessary aside on the nature of bills.

TYPES OF BILLS

It is necessary to distinguish between the various types of legislation, since the nature of a bill helps determine its route through Parliament. Parliamentary procedure distinguishes among bills on constitutional and legal grounds on three major levels (see Figure 8.1). First, legislation can be divided into **private** and **public bills**. Private bills are those that confer special powers or rights upon specific individuals, groups or corporations, rather than upon society as a whole. They are sometimes utilized to incorporate companies or certain religious and charitable organizations and, until 1964, were required for granting divorces to residents of Québec and Newfoundland. These bills constitute an extremely small proportion of total legislative activity.

Second, public bills, which seek to change the law concerning the public as a whole, are themselves divided into two types: **government bills**, those introduced by the Cabinet as government policy; and **private members' bills**, those introduced by individual members of Parliament. In the nineteenth century, when the business of government was relatively limited, private members' bills were an important component of legislative activity. Today, with a restricted number of specific slots in the parliamentary timetable, few even come to a vote and it is quite unusual for Parliament to pass even one private member's bill during a session.

Finally, government bills are further divided into **financial** and **non-financial bills**. Under the *Constitution*, money bills, which authorize taxation and appropriations or expenditures, must be introduced first into the House of Commons, and then only by a Minister of the Crown.[13] These special provisions relate to the traditional right of Parliament to de-

---

12 In theory, the Governor General retains some discretionary power in the matter of dissolution; see Chapter 5.

13 The device is called a Royal Recommendation.

FIGURE 8.1   THE TYPES OF BILLS

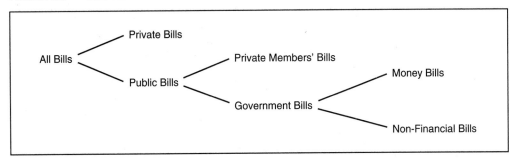

mand that the Crown hear grievances from the people before **granting supply** — that is, before approving the funds necessary to conduct the Crown's affairs. The consideration of financial measures is therefore intended to be a time when the Cabinet accounts for its management of the economy, listens to complaints brought forward by private members of Parliament and (usually but not always) survives an opposition motion to the effect that the government has failed in its responsibilities.

Before we leave the subject of the types of legislation, a comment should be made about **delegated** or **subordinate legislation**. This type of legislation refers to the power to make decisions, called "regulations" or "statutory instruments," having the force of law. Such legislative power is delegated by Parliament under various statutes to the governor-in-council (the Cabinet), to ministers of individual government departments and to a number of agencies and boards. For example, the *Fisheries Act* allows the passage of subordinate legislation on issues such as fishing seasons, numbers and types of fish that may be caught and the dates for opening and closing the fishing season. Such subordinate legislation takes the form of "regulations" and is, in principle, approved by Council (i.e., Cabinet) but is only scrutinized by Parliament *after* it is announced in the *Canada Gazette*.

Delegated legislation constitutes a large and ever-increasing proportion of all government legislative decisions. The Special Committee on Statutory Instruments reported in 1969 that, of 601 Acts of Parliament examined, 420 provided for delegated legislation. And, an average 530 regulations per annum had been published in the *Canada Gazette* over the previous 12 years.[14] An enormous volume of legislation (much of it technical) is therefore not subjected to the full parliamentary legislative process. However, one of the consequences of the Special Committee Report was the establishment, in 1973, of the Standing Joint Committee on Regulations and Other Statutory Instruments, the purpose of which is to review delegated legislation and report possible abuses to Parliament.[15] Today, the Joint Committee (composed of MPs and Senators) may examine a regulation according to specific criteria and even recommend that it be rescinded. Unless the government receives a vote of the House of Commons against the Joint Committee's recommendation, the regulation is automatically repealed.[16]

---

[14] House of Commons Special Committee on Statutory Instruments, *Third Report* (Ottawa: Queen's Printer, 1969).

[15] See James R. Mallory, "Parliamentary Scrutiny of Delegated Legislation in Canada: A Large Step Forward and a Small Step Back," *Public Law* (Spring 1972), pp. 30–42; Graham Eglington, "Scrutiny of Delegated Legislation in the Parliament of Canada," *The Parliamentarian*, vol. 59 (October 1978), pp. 271–75; and Gary Levy, "Delegated Legislation and Standing Joint Committee on Regulations and other Statutory Instruments," *CPA*, vol. 22, no. 3 (Fall 1979), pp. 349–65.

[16] See House of Commons, *Standing Orders* (Ottawa: Supply and Services, November, 1988).

THE STAGES OF LEGISLATION

The vast majority of bills passed by the Canadian Parliament are government bills. Although government legislation may be introduced first in the Senate (this is an increasingly rare occurrence) money bills are constitutionally prohibited from this route. Figure 8.2 illustrates the following brief overview of the major stages in the passage of a typical government bill originating in the lower house.

FIGURE 8.2   HOW A BILL BECOMES LAW

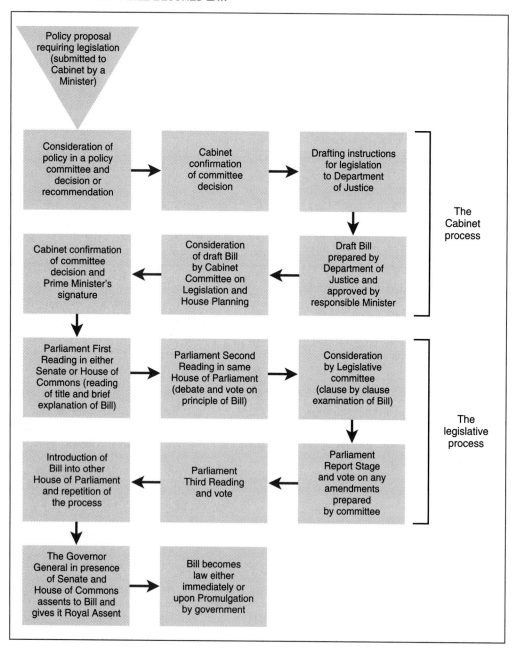

After the pre-parliamentary processes of policy formulation are over, the minister responsible for the legislation asks the House for leave to introduce the bill. This motion is not debatable. A short description of the aims of the bill may be given. Acceptance of the **First Reading** motion "that this bill be read a first time and be printed" is usually a matter of course. It allows the bill to be printed, numbered (with a 'C' prefix if it originates in the House of Commons, 'S' if in the Senate) and distributed to MPs. Numbers C2 to C200 are reserved for government bills, C201 to C1000 for private members' public bills, and C1001 on for private members' private bills. The bill is now on the **order paper**, the schedule of pending parliamentary business. The **Second Reading** motion, usually proposed by the sponsoring minister, permits debate on the principle of the bill; no amendments are accepted by the Speaker. The debate is monopolized by the government and opposition front benches. Normally, the opposition attempts to prove that the legislation is inadequate because it does not address the needs of some "sector" or "regions" while the government defends the overall content and principles of the proposed legislation.

After Second Reading, the Standing Orders stipulate that unless otherwise ordered a bill must be sent directly to a House of Commons Legislative Committee. This is the **Committee Stage**. (For money bills and certain other legislation upon which the House agrees, the Committee Stage is undertaken by the Committee of the Whole, the whole chamber sitting in committee chaired by the Deputy Speaker.) At this stage, the bill undergoes detailed clause-by-clause consideration. Amendments may be moved by both government and opposition members. The amended bill is then voted on as a whole.

Except in the case of bills examined by the Committee of the Whole, which go straight to **Third Reading**, the recommendations of the appropriate committee are presented to the House at the **Report Stage**. Debate is allowed on both the principle and the details of the bill, amendments proposed by the committee are voted on and further amendments may be introduced. Sometimes the opposition reintroduces amendments defeated in committee or the government seeks to reinstate original clauses altered by the committee. At the conclusion of the debate, a vote is taken on the whole bill, including amendments. Unless unanimously agreed otherwise by the House, after the Report Stage, Third Reading commences with the motion "that the bill be now read a third time and passed." Debate is not unknown at this point, but usually takes place only at the insistence of the opposition. A final vote is then taken on the bill.

When the bill has successfully negotiated the various debates, amendments, attempted hoists and divisions (formal votes) in the House of Commons, it has to begin the whole process again in the Senate. However, the upper house usually provides a smoother path for government legislation than the lower chamber. First and Second Readings are over quickly. It is at the Committee Stage that the major legislative work of the Senate is done. While the upper house rarely uses its powers to amend the substance of a bill, "it does do considerable work 'cleaning up' sloppily drafted bills."[17] The Senate is not allowed to increase taxation or spending. As in the House of Commons, the bill as amended in committee is reported back to the Senate for debate, possible further amendment and acceptance. After the final consideration of the bill by the Senate and the Third Reading vote, it is reported to the House of Commons whether the Senate has rejected, amended or passed the bill.[18]

---

[17] Hockin, "Adversary Politics," p. 174.

[18] See F.A. Kunz, *The Modern Senate of Canada 1925–1963: A Re-Appraisal* (Toronto: University of Toronto Press, 1965), pp. 338–39.

Richard Row Illustration, Toronto.

If the bill is defeated by the Senate (which is extremely unlikely), it is lost and must pass through the entire process again, from the start. A bill passed by the Commons but amended by the Senate returns to the lower house for consideration of the amendments. Since such changes are more often to the wording or to a minor detail of the bill (rather than its substance), they are often accepted by the responsible minister. Once this has happened, or if the bill is passed intact by the Senate, it is ready for Royal Assent. In this final stage of the process the Governor General, sitting in the Senate before the assembled members of both houses, puts the final seal of approval on the bill. The bill thereby becomes an Act of Parliament of Canada and, henceforth, is law unless a requirement for formal government proclamation is contained within it.

Money bills follow the same general process as other government legislation, but are unique for four reasons. First, as noted above, they must originate in the House of Commons. Second, revenue-raising bills are not considered in legislative committees in the Commons but by the Committee of the Whole. Third, there are political limitations upon the Senate's ability to amend such bills. Fourth, they tend to have a longer gestation period than other bills, because they are not themselves the only, or even the most important, basis for debate. In the case of tax bills, much debate centres on the budget speech delivered by the Minister of Finance, which outlines the government's economic policy and summarizes the changes that will subsequently appear in tax legislation. With appropriation bills — those that authorize the spending of public money by government departments and other agencies — the key debates occur during the consideration of departmental estimates by standing committees. Once the estimates are examined, appropriation bills are usually passed quickly to give legislative effect to the government's spending proposals.

The entire legislative process is thus complex and variable. The time taken by a bill to pass and its likelihood of success depend upon a number of factors: the importance or controversial nature of the given bill and of other legislation under consideration at the same time; the partisan composition of the two chambers and the presence or absence of a government majority; the willingness of the government to impose, and of Parliament to accept, procedural devices to shorten debate and speed passage of the bill; and last, but not least because Parliament is composed of human beings, the mood of the House at a particular moment.[19] Despite the apparent dominance of governments over the legislative process, to the minister introducing a piece of contentious legislation the whole procedure looks very much like an obstacle course.

Having briefly reviewed the legislative process, it is time for us to focus on the component parts of the legislature. The role of the Monarch, through his or her representative, the Governor General, has already been examined in Chapter 5. There remains the analysis of the legislative politics of the two chambers, the House of Commons and the Senate.

THE HOUSE OF COMMONS

It is probably not unreasonable to suggest that, when most Canadians talk about "Parliament," they really mean "The House of Commons." After all, when people vote for a Member of Parliament, they are electing a member of the House of Commons, not the Senate. And when they write to their MP about some personal or public matter, they expect their constituency representative in the Commons to take action on their behalf. Moreover, media attention is focused mainly on the House of Commons, because it is the chamber to which the

---

[19] On the last point, in particular, one study evaluating Canadian legislative activity suggests that "in each parliament the lowest performance levels appear during the final session… Parliaments, it seems, become cantankerous as they get older." Jackson and Atkinson, *Canadian Legislative System*, p. 181.

government is responsible and because the more newsworthy and dramatic confrontations in Canadian legislative politics usually occur there.

CONFLICT AND COMPROMISE

The tone of legislative politics in the House of Commons is profoundly affected by two key inheritances from the British political tradition: first, an adversarial system of party politics, with a clear dichotomy between government and opposition; second, a code of rules and procedures governing the behaviour of members that serves to counteract, to some extent, potential hostility arising from the partisan nature of the House.

The adversarial pattern of relations between government and opposition is clearly reflected in and, perhaps reinforced by, the physical layout of the House. In many legislative chambers, such as the U.S. House of Representatives or the German Bundestag, all elected members sit in a semicircle facing the Speaker of the House. However, the seating plan of the Canadian House of Commons follows the British model in forcing government and opposition to face one another across the floor of the House, the government to the Speaker's right and the opposition on the left. The leaders of the two major parties confront each other like old-time gunfighters, each surrounded by his or her immediate lieutenants and backed by the rest of the supporters. The smaller parties also take their place on the opposition side of the House. This face-to-face confrontation, separated only by the open floor of the House, serves to demarcate clearly the government from the opposition and to reinforce the sense of political identity and party cohesion on both sides of the Commons.

In the central area of the chamber, between the two main rivals, sit the officials of the House. Most conspicuous among them is the Speaker who, under the Constitution "shall preside at all meetings of the House of Commons." The Speaker is officially an impartial arbiter chosen by the whole House. He or she is not permitted to vote in the House (votes are cast when a "division" is called), except for casting the deciding vote in the event of a tie, when convention dictates that the Speaker support the government of the day.

Until recently, the Prime Minister nominated the Speaker; however, the position has become increasingly independent or non-partisan. After 1963, the Leader of the Opposition seconded the Prime Minister's nomination and, in 1979, Liberal James Jerome became the first Speaker to serve under two different parties when Prime Minister Joe Clark nominated him to continue the role he had fulfilled under the previous Liberal administration. Discussions about how to reform the process for selecting a Speaker were carried on for several years until both the Lefebvre and McGrath parliamentary reform committees recommended that the Speaker be elected by secret ballot. Eventually, the government agreed with this proposal and new Standing Orders to that effect were passed in February, 1986. On September 30, for the first time, the Speaker was elected by a secret ballot of all Members of the House.[20] It took the Members 12 hours and 11 ballots to elect John Fraser from among the 39 candidates. The process was repeated on December 12, 1988 but that time Mr. Fraser was elected after only one ballot. This new system provides Canada with a more impartial, less partisan Speaker in the House of Commons. As Fraser put it after his second

---

[20] Gary Levy, "A Night to Remember: The First Election of a Speaker by Secret Ballot," *Canadian Parliamentary Review*, vol. 9, no. 4 (Winter 1986–87), pp. 10–14. Also see Robert J. Jackson "Executive-Relations in Canada: The Search for a New Balance," in Robert J. Jackson, Doreen Jackson, Nicolas Baxter-Moore, eds., *Contemporary Canadian Politics: Readings and Notes* (Scarborough, Ont.: Prentice-Hall, 1987).

election, "this is going to change me, put constraints on me, change the political career that I've been having."[21] In January 1993, he became the second elected speaker.

The Speaker is in charge of the administration of the House of Commons. First, he or she oversees the staffing of the House with secretaries, clerks and so on. As well, the Speaker is jointly responsible, with the Board of Internal Economy (a body composed of the Speaker and House representatives from all parties), for the economic management of the House and prepares and steers through the House the annual estimates of the cost of running the House of Commons. In the political function of chairing the House, the Speaker is aided by a Deputy Speaker, also elected by fellow MPs at the beginning of each Parliament. The Speaker also is assisted by two chief permanent employees of the Commons, the Clerk of the House and an Administrator. The Clerk is responsible for ensuring that relevant documents are printed and circulated and advises the Speaker on the day's parliamentary business. In recent years, a senior bureaucrat, called the Administrator, has been added to the House staff to deal with financial and management issues.

In keeping with the Westminster model, the Speaker is simultaneously an ordinary member of the House of Commons and an impartial arbiter removed from the political struggle both by the conventions and traditions that surround the office and by the elevated position of the chair on a dais at one end of the chamber. In the midst of the potential chaos and conflict engendered by the partisan nature of the Commons, the Speaker is responsible for enforcing the rules designed to permit the orderly functioning of the House. The Speaker must therefore be a skilled parliamentarian, well-versed not only in the formal rules contained in the Standing Orders of the House but also in unwritten conventions established by past practice.

Certain rules of the House are explicitly designed to reduce the temperature of party politics in the legislature by limiting the direct personal interaction of the members. Verbal confrontations during debate are somewhat constrained by the requirements that no member may speak officially without recognition by the Speaker and that all statements must be addressed to the Chair. Thus, members do not speak to one another directly. Neither may they speak *of* one another directly, inasmuch as individuals are referred to not by name but through more impersonal titles, such as "The Prime Minister," "The Leader of the Opposition" or "The Honourable Member for Constituency X."

If all else fails and the debate becomes heated, as it does on occasion, the dignity of individual members and of the House as a whole is protected by the proscription of certain terms deemed to constitute "unparliamentary language."[22] It is not permitted, for example, to use expressions that cast doubt on the legitimacy of a member's birth nor to allege that a speech has been inspired by intoxicating substances. One of the most common infringements of the rule is the suggestion that another member is "lying" to the House. In March, 1993, New Democratic MP Dave Barrett was suspended from the Commons for a day after refusing to withdraw an accusation that the government was telling "lies."

The rules of unparliamentary language often have the effect of testing the verbal ingenuity of members in order to convey the sense of a particular epithet without the use of forbidden terms. There may also be other ways of getting one's point across without

---

[21] *The Globe and Mail*, Dec. 13, 1988.

[22] See the discussion of "Parliamentary Language" and "Parliamentary Behaviour" in R.M. Dawson, *The Government of Canada*, 5th ed., revised by Norman Ward (Toronto: University of Toronto Press, 1970) pp. 110–17.

breaching the rules. Former Conservative MP Gordon Aiken reports the clever and entirely legitimate device employed by one member exasperated by criticism from the other side of the House:

> *"Mr. Speaker," he asked, properly addressing the Chair, "would it be out of order if I called the honourable Member a son-of-a-bitch?" The Speaker nodded his head. "I thought so," said Clancy, resuming his seat.*[23]

Also among the conflict-regulating devices in the House of Commons are the Standing Orders, the procedures and regulations adopted by members for their internal self-government, and the rules of debate. Perhaps most important among the latter is the principle that, once recognized by the Speaker, every MP has the right to speak for a certain length of time without interruption, as long as the speech remains relevant to the motion before the House. The Speaker has to ensure that members from both sides of the House get a fair hearing, but it is not unknown for the opposition parties to complain that the Chair is favouring the government side. The rules also protect certain persons (especially the royal family, the Governor General and the Senate) from explicit attacks in the Commons.[24]

Once a member has the floor, the member's colleagues or opponents are not always capable of containing themselves; thus, some expressions of support and disagreement are, within certain bounds, sanctioned by the Speaker. Outbursts of laughter and cheering or antagonistic remarks are accepted as part of the debate; the euphemistic reporting in *Hansard* of "hear-hear!" or "oh-oh!" may disguise a multitude of sins.

All of these formal devices help in maintaining peace and reducing conflict emanating from the partisan composition of the House. Other effective mitigating factors are the sense of corporate identity shared by members of the Commons, and the extent to which MPs from both sides of the House interact in informal situations outside the chamber, often forging friendships across party lines. In the midst of the rhetoric, the struggle is, after all, "often carried on more in the spirit of a game than a war."[25]

THE BUSINESS OF THE HOUSE

Once the currents of conflict and compromise within the House of Commons are appreciated, the way in which the House works can perhaps best be understood with reference to the business of a typical day in the House.[26] The timetable of the House of Commons reflects a compromise between the competing demands of the various groups within it. The business of the House may be arranged, on the basis of practical usage rather than procedural formality, into five broad categories: routine business, urgent business, government business, private members' business and opposition business.

The **routine business** of the House usually begins after the daily Question Period and consumes 15 to 20 minutes. The Speaker reads through a list of routine proceedings, not all

---

[23] Gordon Aiken, *The Backbencher* (Toronto: McClelland & Stewart, 1974), p. 66.

[24] Through precedent established by past Speakers, this protection has been extended to the judiciary, lieutenant-governors and others of "high official station."

[25] Dawson, *The Government of Canada*, p. 356.

[26] House of Commons, *Standing Orders of the House of Commons* (Ottawa: Supply and Services, Nov., 1988). For a succinct summary of procedural rules see House of Commons, *Précis of Procedure*, 2nd ed. (Ottawa: Published under authority of the Clerk, 1987).

of which will arise on any particular day: announcements and the raising of questions of privilege; the presentation of reports from inter-parliamentary delegations and committees; the tabling of documents and government papers for the notice of members; statements by ministers regarding government policy; the introduction and First Reading of Commons bills and the First Reading of public bills originating in the Senate; government notices of motions to be introduced later in the Orders of the Day and other motions, particularly those requesting concurrence in committee reports and those pertaining to special arrangements for the sittings and proceedings of the House.

Next, the Speaker calls upon the Parliamentary Secretary to the Government House Leader to notify the House regarding government responses to **Questions on the Order Paper** (written questions which, after a minimum 48 hours' notice, are usually answered in print in the day's *Debates*) and, on occasion, to reply to requests from members for the tabling of government papers in the House.[27] The Commons is then ready to proceed with what the government regards as the main business, the Orders of the Day, unless there is first an interjection under the Standing Orders.

The Standing Orders, or rules of the House, permit any member to move "that this House do now adjourn" in order to discuss "a specific and important matter requiring urgent consideration." This motion could, at one time, exhaust considerable time in the House, even if not eventually granted. As a result, "it became the practice for members to discuss the matter proposed for discussion if leave were given under the guise of discussing the urgency of discussing it."[28] The Speaker rules immediately upon the validity of the request but, in order that the entire day may not be wasted, gives leave to the member to introduce the adjournment motion. The Standing Order concerned is primarily utilized by the opposition to introduce debate on an issue that is not on the government Order Paper or to criticize the government.

The other procedure classified as "urgent" business is the opportunity for MPs to make statements to the House under Standing Order 31, immediately preceding the Question Period. This provision has replaced the old SO 43 that permitted private members, usually from the opposition, to introduce without prior notice a motion relating to a matter of "urgent and pressing necessity." Since the unanimous consent of the House was required for debate to take place, the "necessity" was rarely established, and most members making use of SO 43 were, in fact, primarily concerned with focusing attention on themselves or on some particular issue in the presence of a packed House and a crowded press gallery gathered for the upcoming Question Period. The new SO 31 effectively recognizes this fact; it was introduced to prevent the widespread abuse of House time and patience that occurred formerly under SO 43. Thus, SO 31 permits members to make only a very brief statement to the House, allowing them to make a point or gain the desired media exposure without going through the pretense of formulating a motion or of attempting to establish "urgent and pressing necessity." It is an excellent example of sensible and pragmatic innovation in House rules to satisfy the needs of individual members without making a mockery of the formal proceedings of the Commons.

---

[27] For a detailed explanation of each of the "routine proceedings" before 1982, see John B. Stewart, *The Canadian House of Commons: Procedure and Reform* (Montréal: McGill-Queen's University Press, 1977), pp. 57–67.

[28] Ibid., p. 68.

The bulk of the time of plenary sessions of the Commons is consumed by the Orders of the Day, during which the House deals with the public business placed before it. The greater part of this period is devoted to **government business** in the form of the throne speech debate, motions dealing with the passage of bills and the referral of legislation, estimates and investigatory tasks to standing and special committees. **Orders** are the prime means through which the House of Commons formulates instructions in response to motions. They serve to guide the Speaker and other members and to direct the officers of the House to pursue particular courses of action. Some orders, for example **Standing Orders**, are general and more or less permanent, applying mainly to the procedures of the House. Others are more particular: for example, that a bill "now be read a second time" or that it be sent to committee. In the long run, of course, these latter cases result in a change in public policy through new laws. However, some motions result not in orders but in **resolutions**. Herein lies a source of confusion for many observers of Parliament. From time to time, the House makes a resolution on a particular issue on which the government subsequently takes no action. With the exception of *constitutional resolutions*, resolutions are *not binding* on anybody: they are simply expressions of the *opinion* of the Commons, as opposed to orders, which express the *will* of the House. While orders reflect the power of the Commons to impose its will on others, resolutions are the primarily symbolic outputs of "Parliament as rhetoric," although they may often be influential in legitimating policies for which the government wants a public expression of support from the House.

Not all of the business conducted during the working week is instigated by the government. **Private members' business** is listed under four categories: requests for the tabling of papers and documents; private members' bills; private members' motions; and private bills, although very few of the latter are now introduced in the Commons. Since 1986, private member's motions and bills have been handled under new procedures. Today, all of them are placed in a lottery or draw. The first 20 items chosen are placed in an "order of precedence" and a Standing Committee on Private Members' Business selects up to six items that will be voted on automatically. This means that the old system, in which almost every private member's motion or bill was debated and then "talked out," has been replaced by a compulsory vote on at least six items after as much as five hours debating time. Under the new rules, therefore, more private members' bills are assured a guaranteed vote, but much proposed legislation may be prevented from being considered at all.

On certain sitting days during the year, the Orders of the Day are not dominated by government motions. These are the days officially designated for **opposition business**, when the opposition has a chance to lead major debates on government policy. As of 1991, at the start of the session, the House is permitted eight days to debate the Address in Reply to the Speech from the Throne: since the Throne Speech contains only vaguely worded policy outlines, rules of relevancy are relaxed and debate takes a very general course. A further four days are allocated for the Budget Debate — officially, to discuss the Finance Minister's proposals but effectively, again, to articulate broad criticism of the government's record. As well, after the abolition of the old Committee of Supply in 1968, the opposition parties were compensated by the allocation of 20 **Supply** (or **Opposition**) **Days**, spread unevenly over the three supply periods of the session, on which opposition motions can be debated. Such debates rarely focus specifically on government expenditures, although that was the original intention. Instead, Opposition Days provide time for individual opposition parties to mount their own attacks on the government, to propose alternative policies and to introduce motions of non-confidence in the government. There are, however, both practical and political limitations on the ability of the opposition parties to effect radical criticism of government activities or produce startlingly different policy proposals. Hence, Opposition Days serve more as a symbolic recognition of the opposition's right to criticize the government than as a forum for policy initiation.

Far more effective as an instrument for the opposition — primarily because of the amount of media attention devoted to it and because no notice of content is required — is the **Oral Question Period**.[29] This is invariably the high point of the sitting day in the Commons. In theory, it provides an opportunity for any member who can catch the Speaker's eye to ask a question of the Prime Minister or a member of Cabinet — in fact, the Speaker calls almost all members according to lists supplied by the party whips. Although, technically, questions should be for the purpose of eliciting information and be "concise, factual and free of opinion and argument which might lead to debate,"[30] the Question Period in fact provides a forum for the Opposition parties to embarrass the government, criticize its policies and force discussion on issues of the day, frequently based "on news stories, on leaks by indiscreet or disaffected public servants, and on complaints from the public."[31]

As a mechanism for surveillance and accountability of the government, the Oral Question Period has many advantages. Still, it is not perfect. Although supplementary questions are permitted by the Speaker, no formal debate is allowed, and ministers can often manoeuvre to avoid the main substance of a question. The time limit of 45 minutes each day is often too short for the number of questions that members wish to raise, yet government backbenchers use up some of the period to ask questions of "minor" constituency interest or to feed "friendly" queries to their own front bench. Finally, the division of the opposition into two or more parties frequently results in a lack of structure or continuity to the proceedings.

To surmount this problem, each party caucus orchestrates its efforts at Question Period in order to provide a more effective attack on specific government ministers. To this end, the opposition parties have a "tactics" meeting each day during parliamentary sessions. At these meetings, they analyze press clippings, determine the order of the questions and practice their political stances. Despite problems, well-directed opposition tactics can make the daily Question Period into an important occasion for calling the executive to account for its actions, for effective participation by backbenchers and for the public to see responsible government at work. Considerable effort goes into ensuring that the right "clip" will appear on the television evening news.

Occasionally during the Question Period, a member who is dissatisfied with the response from a minister will shout "six o'clock" across the floor of the chamber. This refers to what is commonly known as "The Late Show," more formally the **Daily Adjournment Debate**, which takes place three days a week at 6:00 p.m. Unless the house has agreed to sit beyond the normal hour of adjournment for some special purpose, the Speaker proposes at 6:00 p.m. on these days "that this House do now adjourn," then recognizes in turn a maximum of three members who have made it known that they wish to speak. Members

---

[29] The first oral question was asked within three weeks of the first session of the first Parliament in 1867. For a complete history see W.F. Dawson, *Procedure in the Canadian House of Commons* (Toronto: University of Toronto Press, 1962); and Francis J. Schiller, "The Evolution of Oral Question Period" (unpublished BA thesis, Carleton University, September 1992).

[30] Ruling given by then-Speaker of the House, Roland Michener, cited in *House of Commons Debates*, February 26, 1959, p. 1393.

[31] Stewart, "The Canadian House of Commons," p. 56.

usually take up unresolved issues from the Oral Question Period; they are permitted to speak for up to seven minutes, addressing their point to a minister or parliamentary secretary, who is given three minutes in which to reply. At 6.30 p.m. the Speaker adjourns the House until the next sitting.

Under contemporary rules, the House has a five-day working week that may be increased by evening sittings for emergency debates or long series of divisions continuing after the normal hours of adjournment. The House is by no means full most of this time: in fact, it is usually crowded only for Question Period, for important divisions on major items of government legislation and for non-confidence motions. Since October 1977, the public has been able to see empty spaces in the chamber on televised House proceedings, despite occasional attempts by members to arrange themselves around and behind whoever is on camera.

But the average viewer may not be aware that attendance at plenary sessions of the House of Commons is only a part of the total workload of MPs. Apart from their role as members of the House, MPs serve on parliamentary committees, are members of parliamentary parties or caucuses and have large caseloads of constituency duties to perform. An analysis of procedure and legislative politics in the chamber of the House of Commons is therefore only a part of the story of how Parliament works: the next three sections provide a more complete picture by discussing the role of committees, party competition and individual MPs in the life of the House.

MPS IN GROUPS — THE COMMITTEE SYSTEM

Much of the significant work of Members of Parliament does not take place in plenary sessions but in committees. In 1986, the House of Commons adopted a new committee system that was slightly amended in 1991.[32] There are now four basic kinds of committees.

First is the **Committee of the Whole**, in which the entire complement of MPs sits in the chamber in one large committee under the chair of the Deputy Speaker or the Deputy Chair of Committees, and uses committee rules rather than House procedures to govern its activities. At one time, the majority of bills were considered by the Committee of the Whole rather than being sent to smaller, more specialized, standing committees, but enormous pressures on the timetable of the House and the workload of MPs have resulted in much more limited use of this procedure. Today, the use of Committee of the Whole is largely reserved for money bills or, on very rare occasions, to expedite the passage of other legislation.

The second type of committee consists of the relatively permanent House Standing Committees (see Table 8.1). **Standing Committees** are set up for the life of a Parliament.

---

[32] The 1991 rules grouped the committees into envelopes for administrative reasons — namely to allow the whips to better handle substitutions on committees. See House of Commons, *Standing Orders of the House of Commons* (Ottawa: Supply and Services, Nov. 1988), plus the amendments of April 5, 1989 and April 11, 1991. An assessment of these basic reforms is found in Robert J. Jackson, "Executive Legislative Relations in Canada," in Robert J. Jackson et al., eds., *Contemporary Canadian Politics* (Scarborough, Ont.: Prentice-Hall, 1984), pp. 111–24; and in Magnus Gunther and Conrad Winn, eds., *House of Commons Reform* (Ottawa, Parliamentary Internship Programme, 1991).

Their composition of 7 to 15 members is proportional to party standings in the House. In principle they elect their own chairmen, but the selection is controlled by the government and opposition House Leaders. These committees are empowered by the Standing Orders to study and report on all matters relating to the mandate, management and operations of the department or departments that are assigned to them. In particular, they are to report on program and policy objectives and effectiveness; immediate, medium and long-term expenditure plans; the relative success of the department(s) and all other matters of mandate, management, organization and operation. These responsibilities are usually carried out by studying the department's annual report and estimates as well as particular problems and future policy alternatives.

TABLE 8.1   STANDING COMMITTEES IN THE HOUSE OF COMMONS, APRIL 1993

A.   House Committees

Aboriginal Affairs
Agriculture
Citizenship and Multiculturalism
Communications and Culture
Consumer and Corporate Affairs and Government Operations
Elections, Privileges, Procedure and Private Members' Business
Energy, Mines and Resources
Environment
External Affairs and International Trade
Finance
Forestry and Fisheries
Health and Welfare, Social Affairs, Seniors and the Status of Women
Human Rights and the Status of Disabled Persons
Industry, Science and Technology, Regional and Northern Development
Justice and the Solicitor General
Labour, Employment and Immigration
Management and Members' Services
National Defence and Veterans Affairs
Public Accounts
Transport

B.   Joint Committees with the Senate

Official Languages
Regulations and Other Statutory Instruments

The Standing Committees are empowered to form subcommittees and to "send for persons, papers and records" to aid them in their deliberations. Moreover, all individuals appointed by order-in-council are scrutinized by the committees and may be called before their members after their appointments have been published in the *Canada Gazette*. This includes an examination of all deputy ministers, heads of Crown corporations, ambassadors and others appointed to high government positions (excluding judges).

The two **Joint Standing Committees** are composed of members of both the House of Commons and the Senate. The Official Languages Committee reviews and reports on official language policies and programs, including the annual report of the Commissioner of Official Languages. The role of the Standing Joint Committee on Regulations and other Statutory Instruments is much wider. It scrutinizes all delegated legislation by departments, agencies, boards or other authorities.

The third type, the **Legislative Committees**, receive all bills for examination, except those based on a Supply motion,[33] after Second Reading. The duty of each committee is limited to an examination of its bill and witnesses are called only on "purely technical" matters. The number of Legislative committees depends on the amount of legislation before the House: sometimes there are very few committees, at other times a large number. Thus, at times nearly all members will serve on at least one committee while at other times there will not be nearly enough work to go around. After the committee reports back to the House on its bill, the committee is dissolved. Members of legislative committees are appointed by the parties, and their numbers, up to 30, are proportionate to party standings in the House. The chairmen, however, are *not* appointed from within the committee membership. Instead, at the beginning of each session, the Speaker appoints at least 10 members as chairs of legislative committees. Together with the Chairmen of Committee of the Whole, they constitute the Panel of Chairmen. The Speaker then selects which chair will head each new Legislative Committee as bills are presented to the House.

COMMITTEE RECRUITMENT, COMPOSITION AND STAFFING

Membership in the Standing and Legislative committees is allocated by the Committee of Selection, more commonly known as the "Striking Committee," which is composed of seven MPs, including the Chief Whip of each party and one representative of the Cabinet. The partisan composition of each committee is roughly proportional to the Commons as a whole — although a majority government always claims more than 50 percent of the members and the official Opposition is usually over-represented compared with minor parties. Individual MPs are appointed to committees on the basis of their Chief Whip's recommendations, although these often reflect the personal preferences of the member and, in the case of the Conservative and Liberal parties, are usually in accordance with membership in party caucus committees. Recent procedural changes, in addition to reducing the number of MPs on each committee permit only pre-selected alternate members to substitute for absentees.

The chairman and vice-chairman of standing committees are elected at the start of each session by the committee members and, since 1968, have almost all been members of the governing party. By convention, however, the opposition always provides the chairmen of the Public Accounts Committee and the Management and Members' Services Committee, as well as the vice-chairman of the Standing Committee on Procedure and Organization, and the chairman of the Joint Committee on Regulations. Given the preponderance of government members filling these offices, committee chairs are frequently placed in an ambiguous position by conflicting expectations of their roles: while their responsibility for presiding over committee meetings requires them to be as impartial as the House Speaker, their selection by the government majority results in pressure to serve the interests of the government in pursuance of its policy goals.

---

[33]   A **Supply motion** is a motion of the House of Commons to supply funds for governments to spend. A **Ways and Means motion** is a motion of the House of Commons to raise taxes.

Committee deliberations are expedited by the work of several parliamentary organizations. The Committees and Private Legislation Branch of the Commons staff provides procedural and administrative support. Research assistance comes from the Research Branch of the Library and outside consultants. In recent years, standing committees have been allocated funds by the Board of Internal Economy. This money may be used by the leadership of the committee to retain the services of experts and professional, technical and clerical staff. The significance of this fund should not be exaggerated, however.

Some commentators have insisted that Canadian committees should have the high level of staffing and research resources enjoyed by Congressional committees in the United States, but such an increase would be unlikely, in itself, to enhance the influence of committees in the legislative process:

> *Until committees are given an independent capacity to influence public policy, it is unlikely that the addition of even the most competent of research assistants will do more than contribute to the frustrations of MPs and researchers alike.*[34]

As this quotation suggests, there have long been doubts among both politicians and academic observers as to whether the committee system in the House of Commons is effectively fulfilling its major functions.[35] Despite recent innovations many misgivings persist.

THE COMMITTEE SYSTEM AT WORK: AN EVALUATION

The Committee system has been completely restructured in recent years. Committees in the House of Commons now have three principal areas of operation: detailed consideration of legislation after a bill has passed Second Reading in the House; scrutiny of the financial aspects of government and bureaucracy; and investigation of reports, policy proposals and other items.

CONSIDERATION OF LEGISLATION

The Committee Stage of the legislative process is designed to provide an opportunity for the clause-by-clause examination of the details of each bill by a small group of relatively specialized MPs in legislative committees. Amendments to bills may be proposed in committees and, if accepted, subsequently will be recommended for adoption by the whole House at the Report Stage. Sometimes, the Opposition members of a committee will try to investigate the general policy behind a bill, especially since they have an opportunity, denied them during debates in the House, to question public servants and other witnesses. However, amendments of principle or major policy differences introduced by the Opposition have little hope of adoption in committee, especially if party divisions have been reinforced by heated debate at the Second Reading. Hence, such amendments are usually presented solely for propaganda purposes. Other amendments may be introduced to force the government to explain or defend a particular provision in the bill. Finally, many amendments constitute genuine attempts to improve the bill — either by

---

[34] Jackson and Atkinson, *The Canadian Legislative System.*

[35] For the views of politicians on the committee system, see the results of surveys of MPs reported by Paul Thomas, *The Role of Committees in the Canadian House of Commons* (unpublished Ph.D. Thesis, University of Toronto, 1975).

making substantive changes to its provisions or by altering technical details, wording or the administration of the legislation.

Amendments may be introduced by the government itself to correct problems that have become apparent in committee, or in response to interest group pressure or provincial government or departmental concerns. Thus, although some observers have suggested that the number of amendments accepted at this stage may indicate the influence of the committees, the sources of amendments are so many and varied that the measure is at best imprecise.

Once adopted by a committee, the fate of amendments in the House usually depends upon the minister's willingness to accept them at the Report Stage. The government is more likely to agree to amendments when they are supported by influential groups or by provincial governments, are technical rather than substantive in content and relate to bills of minor or relatively non-partisan nature.[36] Some notable amendments to government legislation have been achieved, but in general the committees do not permit a significant increase in the ability of the opposition parties to influence the executive's legislative program. Usually, the "majority government exerts tight control over what amendments will be accepted within the committees, and most of the successful amendments originate with the government."[37]

SCRUTINY OF PUBLIC EXPENDITURE

The second main function of the committee system is the scrutiny of public expenditure. It is performed through two mechanisms: first, detailed examination of the main estimates — proposals to spend money — of individual departments by the appropriate Standing committees each spring;[38] second, investigation of the government's spending practices by the Standing Committee on Public Accounts.

The **estimates** represent the government's projected spending patterns for the forthcoming financial year. They are approved by the Treasury Board and tabled in Parliament each February in the so-called "Blue Book." Before 1968, the main estimates were considered in Committee of Supply (i.e., the whole House), wherein the supply motion gave the opposition a chance to criticize the government's policies and management of the nation's finances. Since 1968, the supply procedure has been replaced by the introduction of Supply or Opposition Days and the referral of estimates to the newly established standing committees. Today, main estimates should be referred to committees on March 1st and must be reported back by May 31st. If a committee has not reported by that date, the Standing Orders provide that the estimates "shall be deemed to have been reported" anyway.

Theoretically, "the opportunity for parliamentary scrutiny of government policy is best afforded by consideration of departmental estimates."[39] Since the government cannot spend money for any purposes not specifically approved by Parliament and, since the estimates procedure allows MPs to investigate the aims of public expenditure,

---

[36] Paul Thomas, "The Influence of Standing Committees of Parliament on Government Legislation," *Legislative Studies Quarterly*, vol. 3, no. 4 (August 1978), p. 700.

[37] Ibid., p. 699.

[38] Supplementary estimates, which detail additional funds required to meet unforeseen circumstances or to compensate for inflation, are tabled later in the financial year.

[39] Jackson and Atkinson, *The Canadian Legislative System*, p. 99.

the process could permit the committees to scrutinize and influence the direction of government policy. However, this opportunity is by and large not realized to its full potential. Since only ministers of the Crown can propose public spending, no committee can recommend an increase in estimated funding for any program that it considers desirable — committees can only accept, reduce or reject outright the proposed amounts. Thus, in reality, members avoid cutting the estimates and only on the rarest of occasions ever do so. The opportunity to influence financial planning is further limited by infrequent ministerial attendance at committee sessions, and by the considerable information gap that exists between MPs and the departmental officials defending their proposed expenditures.

Then there is the attitude of MPs themselves. To many committee members, the estimates procedure is a boring, routine task, devoid of publicity and offering little political mileage. Hence, many meetings are conducted in the absence of a quorum, and it is "by no means unusual for committees to approve votes at the outset of the meeting — when a quorum is present — and then proceed to question witnesses on the millions of dollars that have just been approved."[40] Those who do participate are most likely to use the estimates process to relay constituents' complaints to departmental bureaucrats or to gain information that may be of use in their constituencies or in embarrassing the government at some future time. Even where there does exist "that rare bird, 'the economy hawk,' who swoops down on the plentiful bait of departmental spending…[he]…saves his attacks for the minor items, like trips and potted plants, that indicate waste and extravagance."[41]

In general, therefore, it is clear that MPs show little commitment to reducing public expenditure or to increasing the efficiency of government departments — however much lip-service they may pay to these aims. Such goals are hampered by the fact that each committee considers the estimates of only one government department at a time, with few opportunities for comparing spending patterns among departments or evaluating the total projected expenditure. One recent change in the publication of estimates has helped: the Blue Book in which they are published is now accompanied by an overall government fiscal plan. But there is still need for a separate committee to review the finances of Crown corporations[42] and for a general estimates committee to undertake a comparative analysis of all departments and provide a more comprehensive view of government expenditure.[43]

Despite its many weaknesses as a mechanism for parliamentary surveillance of government, the current estimates procedure does have some redeeming qualities. Its very existence leads government departments to take extra care in the preparation of estimates and to eliminate potential excesses before they are spotted by MPs. It also provides an opportunity for members to meet bureaucrats face-to-face and carry out representative functions on behalf of their constituents. As well, committee debate provides an additional forum for the opposition to criticize government policies and program priorities implic-

---

[40] Ibid., p. 101.

[41] Paul Thomas, "Parliament and the Purse Strings," in H.D. Clarke et al., eds., *Parliament, Policy and Representation* (Toronto: Methuen, 1980), pp. 166–67.

[42] Thomas d'Aquino, G. Bruce Doern and Cassandra Blair, *Parliamentary Democracy in Canada: Issues for Reform* (Toronto: Methuen, 1983), pp. 69–70.

[43] Thomas, "Parliament and the Purse Strings," pp. 175–76.

it in the projected spending patterns. But, overall, the standing committees, in their estimates function, are incapable of exercising adequate control over government finance or substantially influencing the content of government policy.

The second mechanism for overseeing public expenditure is the post-audit function of the Standing Committee on Public Accounts. This committee is somewhat unusual in that, since 1967, it has always been chaired by a member of the opposition. As well, it receives expert assistance from the Auditor-General, an independent officer of Parliament. The Committee's examination of the annual Public Accounts has often resulted in criticisms of government inefficiency and recommendations for improvements in spending practices.

INVESTIGATIONS

Part of the conventional wisdom concerning committees is that, as small groups, they permit MPs to interact in a manner rather different from their behaviour in the House.[44] In particular, the less formal environment and the relative absence of publicity surrounding committee deliberations permit the development of a less partisan atmosphere and enhance corporate identity. This facilitates the objective criticism of government policies and increases the opportunity for meaningful participation by members. It is in the performance of their investigative function that Canadian standing committees most often live up to conventional wisdom by displaying non-partisanship, group cohesion and autonomy from party and government control. Possibly the best example of such activities was found in the Standing Committee on Finance in 1987. Combining the new reforms with good leadership and expertise, the committee produced excellent investigations of the government's White Paper on tax reform, the near collapse of the Canadian Commercial Bank, the Green Paper on financial services, credit card rates, and the designation of Vancouver and Montréal as international banking centres.[45]

Investigations may take place at three stages in the policy process. A committee may hear evidence from interested parties and formulate recommendations to help the government establish priorities on an issue for which no policy has yet been formulated. Alternatively, a committee may be utilized to establish reactions to a particular set of policy proposals, usually contained in a government White or Green paper.[46] Or, a committee may evaluate the strengths and weaknesses of existing policies and their administration, especially in an extension of its estimates scrutiny role.

In most policy areas, investigatory tasks are referred to the appropriate standing committee, but certain complex or contentious issues require the establishment of an ad hoc special committee.[47]

---

[44] On the application of small group theory to legislative committees, see Malcolm Shaw, "Conclusion," in Lees and Shaw, eds., *Committees in Legislatures*, esp. pp. 412–18.

[45] See Robert J. O'Brien, "The Financial Committee Carves out a Role," *Parliamentary Government*, vol. 8, no. 1 (1988), pp. 3–10. Both White and Green papers are published government documents. A **White paper** is intended to state fairly firm government policy. A **Green paper** is a government document with suggested policy options. In Canada, this distinction is not held rigidly; on rare occasions the government has even published papers with other colours, thus distorting the distinction further.

[46] See Douglas C. Nord, "MPs and Senators as Middlemen: The Special Joint Committee on Immigration Policy," in Clarke et al., eds., *Parliament, Policy and Representation*, pp. 181–93.

[47] Robert J. Jackson, "The Unreformed Canadian House of Commons," *Les Cahiers de Droit*, vol. 26, no. 1 (March 1985), pp. 161–73.

COMMITTEES: PROBLEMS AND REFORMS

Certain of the problems experienced by the House of Commons committee system since its inception in the late 1960s have been resolved by the reforms introduced in the 1980s. First, a reduction in the number of members of each committee has permitted individual MPs to become more specialized. Second, it was hoped that smaller committees could operate more efficiently than their larger predecessors and reduce partisan conflict.

The reforms also introduced the practice of drawing up a list of alternate members for each committee. Now, when committee members are unable to attend a meeting, only designated alternates may substitute for them. Previously, any member of the House could substitute in committee hearings, usually to maintain the government's majority when votes were held. This resulted, according to one opposition MP, in

> ...*roving squads of Members whose chief ability is to sit on committees, read newspapers, sign letters and at the same time raise their right hands in approval of matters on which they have no previous experience. These members have not participated in the committee discussions and are merely present to fill a seat or fill out a quorum.*[48]

Today, alternate members are kept informed of the business before the committee, so they at least know which piece of legislation they are voting on!

An unresolved criticism of the committee system relates to the lack of autonomy of Commons committees. Committees cannot operate unless their activities are specified in the Standing Orders or unless they receive a reference from the House instructing them to pursue a particular topic. This referral process is effectively controlled by the government through its majority in the House. Thus, the government may limit the number of referrals to a given committee, or so overburden it with work that there is insufficient time for detailed consideration of any item. In the last resort, the government may create a hand-picked special committee to investigate particularly contentious legislation or issues, or to bypass a committee that is displaying too much independence. However, recent reforms give committees the power to generate their own references for investigations based on the annual reports of Crown corporations and government departments, without referral from the House.

Lack of autonomy is further complicated by the fact that committees do not enjoy an even workload throughout the year. At the beginning of a session, the workload is usually light. The major bills in the government's program usually reach the legislative committees in the spring, just when members of the standing committees are supposed to be carefully scrutinizing the spending proposals in the main estimates. The expenditure scrutiny function is therefore undermined as some of the most experienced members have little time for deliberation. Reports on the estimates are often brief and hastily written and some committees never do report to the House.[49]

Another traditional problem faced by committees has been the fate of their final reports. Prior to 1982, there was no guarantee that a report would ever get a hearing in the House or provoke any government reaction. The frustrations of a committee member were well expressed by a former New Democrat MP, Stanley Knowles:

---

[48] Marcel Lambert, *House of Commons Debates*, October 15, 1970, p. 156.

[49] In the 3rd session of the 28th Parliament, for example, the main estimates of 10 departments or agencies were "deemed to have been reported" in the absence of committee reports — see Thomas, "Parliament and the Purse Strings," p. 170.

> *What is the point of talking about the committee system and matters being referred to a*
> *committee for detailed study if, after all this is done and a thoroughly researched report is tabled,*
> *the government takes no action....Surely there comes a time when pleading which is consistent,*
> *unanimous and responsible ought to have some effect on the cabinet.*[50]

Under the new House rules, at the request of a committee the government must table a comprehensive response to its report within 150 days. However, it is still too easy for the government to ignore committee proposals and criticisms. The Communications and Culture Committee was simply told that its 1987 report was rejected — all 100 recommendations were to be reconsidered — and that the job of the committee was to recommend policy, not legislation. However, even if, under the new rules, it is not obliged to adopt recommendations put forward by committees, the government does have to explain its reaction to Parliament.

The procedural reforms of the 1990s, which originate in the Lefebvre and McGrath reports, have thus gone some way toward resolving the problems experienced by committees in the House of Commons and alleviating some MPs' deep-seated dissatisfaction with the committee system.[51] But problems do remain. First, in order to function effectively, committees require more professional research staff, expanded budgets for financial autonomy and more generalized references in the Standing Orders to reduce government control over referrals and committee workloads.

In addition, partisanship continues to dominate committee activities. The House has very few members who are so secure of re-election and independent of party finances that they can ignore the directives of their leader or the party whip. Thus, partisanship remains paramount at all times. Since only about a quarter of MPs are very active in committees, there are many operational difficulties — overlapping memberships, scheduling conflicts and other practical irritants such as lack of adequate staff and even meeting rooms.

But the area of committee work most in need of reform may well be the expenditure scrutiny function. A paper prepared for the Special Committee on Procedure by MPs Ron Huntington and Claude-André Lachance made specific proposals (not subsequently adopted) for increasing financial accountability, as did the Final Report of the Lambert Royal Commission in 1979.[52] We have already mentioned proposals for the establishment of a General Estimates Committee that would develop an overview of total government spending. Perhaps reform needs to go even further — and establish a National Finance Committee, similar to that proposed by the Lambert Commission, that would analyse both revenues and expenditures in order to bridge the gap between standing committees' consideration of individual departmental estimates, the debate in the whole House on the Finance Minister's economic review and taxation proposals in the budget.[53]

---

[50] *House of Commons Debates,* December 11, 1975, pp. 9930–33.

[51] See, for example, the comments by a selection of MPs interviewed in Parliamentary Centre, "Looking Toward Committee Reform."

[52] House of Commons Special Committee on Procedure, *Seventh Report* (Ottawa: Queen's Printers 1982); Royal Commission on Financial Management and Accountability ("Lambert Commission"), *Final Report* (Ottawa: Ministry of Supply and Services, 1979), especially ch. 22.

[53] "Lambert Commission," *Final Report,* ch. 21; and Jackson, "The Unreformed Canadian House of Commons," p. 11.

MPS IN PARTIES: GOVERNMENT AND OPPOSITION

In contrast to the nineteenth century, it is now rare to find independent members in the House of Commons. The only independent member of the 32nd Parliament, William Yurko, who resigned from the Conservative caucus in 1982 because "he could not abide his party's stand on the Constitution,"[54] failed to retain his seat in the 1984 General Election. The sole independent elected in September 1984 was Anthony Roman. No independents were elected in November 1988. After the 1988 election, however, more than a dozen MPs crossed the floor. Seven members resigned the Conservative whip and two Liberals resigned theirs to form the Bloc Québécois after the failure of the Meech Lake accord and Jean Chrétien's victory at the Liberal leadership convention. (One of the Tory dissenters subsequently rejoined his party.) Another Conservative party deserter, Pat Nowlan, left the Tory party because of differences over Meech Lake and the GST. Two Conservative MPs, David Kilgour and Alex Kindy were expelled from the Conservative party for voting against the GST. (Kilgour then sat with the Liberals while Kindy remained an independent.) Finally, one Tory became an independent before resigning from the House after being charged with a criminal offence.

The role of the independent or floor-crossing MP is tenuous indeed. From 1940 to 1992, 31 MPs ran for re-election in the next general election after the parliamentary sittings during which they crossed the floor. Only 12 were successful and three ran under their original party banner. These figures show that although an MP may think he or she is acting on his or her constituent's interests when breaking party ranks, the electorate does not reward such behaviour at the polls. This finding is in direct contrast to the idea that the people want MPs to be "free."[55]

Today, political parties are an inescapable fact of life in the Canadian Parliament and have a profound effect upon legislative politics in both chambers and their committees. The government relies on cohesion among its backbenchers to keep it in office and to secure the passage of its legislative proposals. Effective opposition likewise depends on the ability of minority party leaders to mobilize their MPs in specific directions. In both cases, individual members often have to compromise their own short-term interests and aims in order that party goals may be achieved.

INTRA-PARTY RELATIONS: REBELS AND WHIPS

Some observers argue that cohesion is imposed upon MPs through party discipline; that backbenchers, especially on the government side, are forced to adhere to the directives laid down by the party leadership. Others portray cohesion as the product of a commonality of views among members of the same party and as the result of consensus arrived at through regular meetings of the party caucus.

Former Conservative MP Gordon Aiken has asserted that party discipline is imposed equally on both sides of the House to turn opposition backbenchers as well as government

---

[54] "Independent's decision good news for Grits," *Globe and Mail*, Toronto, July 14, 1984.

[55] See Robert J. Jackson and Paul Conlin, "The Imperative of Party Discipline in the Canadian Political System," in Mark Charlton and Paul Basher, eds., *Contemporary Political Issues*, 2nd ed. (Scarborough: Nelson, 1994).

supporters into what he calls "trained seals."[56] Certainly, party leaders, especially of the governing party, have a number of sanctions at their disposal to ensure or at least encourage backbenchers to toe the party line. On the negative side, individual members who consistently oppose the party leadership or fail to vote with their colleagues on important issues may be coerced in a number of ways, culminating in the threat of expulsion from the party. Without the official backing of the party, a rebellious MP would have to contest the next election as an independent candidate with little probability of success. More sizable revolts within the governing party may be met by the threat of dissolution of Parliament. Given the high turnover of seats at every general election, this may serve to quell dissent, especially among those backbenchers who represent marginal constituencies. But the dissolution of Parliament on these grounds is a double-edged sword, since it constitutes a public admission of division within the government party and the possible defeat of the Prime Minister in a general election.

While these negative sanctions are the "sticks" in the enforcement of party discipline, party leaders also have a number of "carrots" available. The Prime Minister has a large patronage fund that may be used to reward loyal, well-behaved members: promotion to Cabinet minister, parliamentary secretary or committee chair; appointment to the Senate; and numerous positions in public corporations and Crown agencies. Some of these perks are also potentially available to the leadership of the major opposition party, but the government generally has considerably more of them at its disposal.

The discussion of party discipline tends to imply a *conflict approach* to the maintenance of party unity according to which inherent divisions between leaders and backbenchers exist that can be overcome only through coercion. On the other hand, it may be argued equally that party cohesion is based primarily on the existence of consensus (rather than conflict) among MPs in each parliamentary party.[57] According to the latter view, party unity may be based on a "value-consensus," a commonality of opinions on major issues shared by members of the same political movement and reinforced by regular meetings of the party caucus. However, while political parties in Canada do not have the organized political tendencies found in some other countries, it should not be forgotten that they are broad "brokerage" coalitions of a variety of regional and other interests. Another view is that unity may be based on the deference of backbenchers toward party leaders — a willingness to accept the decisions of those who derive their legitimacy from selection by national conventions and who, in this era of personality politics, may be perceived as largely responsible for the electoral success of the party. It may also be argued that peer-group pressure from fellow party members serves to reinforce party solidarity. But potentially the most effective instruments of cohesion in the House of Commons are the party organizations and regularity of party caucus meetings.[58]

---

[56] Aiken, *The Backbencher*, passim. For anecdotal description of the life of an MP, there are few studies to match this book. For parallels with Britain see Robert J. Jackson, *Rebels and Whips* (London: Macmillan, 1968).

[57] The consensus view of party cohesion is emphasized by Allan Kornberg, "Caucus and Cohesion in Canadian Parliamentary Politics." *APSR*, vol. 60, no. 1 (March 1966), pp. 83–92.

[58] On the origin of the caucus, see Mark MacGuigan, "Backbenchers, The New Committee System, and the Caucus," in Paul Fox, ed., *Politics: Canada*, 4th ed. (Toronto: McGraw-Hill Ryerson, 1977), pp. 431–38.

Each party leader appoints an MP to act as the party organizer in the House of Commons. This person, known as the House Leader, is assisted by other MPs — a **Chief Whip** and assistant whips — who help to maintain party cohesion and manage parliamentary activities. The number of whips depends on the size of caucus, but their role is invariable. They keep in close touch with the members, informing them of their duties in the House and in committees. While the whips can make use of some minor rewards and punishments, caucus cohesion is maintained more by party and leader loyalty than by the whips' ability to sanction members. The **party caucus** is a uniquely Canadian institution. Every Wednesday morning when Parliament is in session, all members of the House of Commons (together with any Senators who wish to attend) meet in their respective party groups. Caucus meetings are held in private, away from the press and public. Commentators feel that there are differences in the extent to which each party caucus permits backbenchers to influence the formulation of party positions. In the opposition parties, there is relatively little distinction in status between leaders and backbenchers: consequently, all MPs feel equally entitled to their point of view, and debate is often quite heated. However, even in opposition there are no formal votes and the party leader sums up the caucus consensus.

In the governing party, the overall situation is different. Since the prevailing attitude is that the primary task of government backbenchers is to support the executive and its legislative program, and since members are often consulted only after policies have already been decided by cabinet, the major function of the government caucus is to enforce party discipline and ensure cabinet control of the policy process. Thus, according to former Liberal MP Mark MacGuigan, there is "little doubt that the government caucus is of greater utility to the ministry than to the members, and that it is in effect the chief instrument of government control of the House of Commons."[59]

Elsewhere, however, while re-emphasizing his view of the caucus as an instrument of party discipline, MacGuigan admitted that "strong caucus opposition to any government proposal imposes an absolute veto on that proposal. The government has shown time and again that it does not act in the face of clear caucus opposition."[60] On numerous occasions the government caucus has challenged, and sometimes persuaded its leaders to amend or reject, policy proposals agreed upon by Cabinet.[61] Such cases, added to evidence drawn from surveys of MPs,[62] suggest that government backbenchers, like their opposition counterparts, view their caucus as a major opportunity to influence the content of party policy.

INTER-PARTY RELATIONS

Whatever its source, whether enforcement by sanctions or consensus based on common values and agreement in caucus, the existence of a strong degree of party cohesion in the House of Commons is an integral part of representative and responsible government. The emergence of responsible parliamentary government has produced, and is in turn reinforced by,

---

[59] MacGuigan, "Backbenchers, The New Committee System, and the Caucus," pp. 436–37. See also Aiken, *The Backbencher*, pp. 114–23.

[60] Mark MacGuigan, "Parliamentary Reform: Impediments to an Enlarged Role for the Backbencher," *Legislative Studies Quarterly*, vol. 3, no. 4 (November 1978), p. 676.

[61] For examples, see Jackson and Atkinson, *The Canadian Legislative System*, pp. 50, 80.

[62] Kornberg, Allan and William Mischler, *Influence in Parliament* (Durham N.C.: Duke University Press, 1976), pp. 177–87.

an adversarial relationship between government and opposition. The government requires unified support from its backbenchers to retain office and realize its policy goals. At the same time, the opposition has to mobilize all its resources to criticize the government and portray itself to the public as a viable, alternative administration.

Although the relationship between government and opposition is basically one of confrontation, both sides of the House have developed specific behavioural norms to restrain unbridled competition and make Parliament work. Opposition members recognize the government's responsibility to carry on the business of governing and sometimes lend their support to that end; simultaneously, they retain the right to criticize government policy. The government, in turn, recognizes the opposition's right to criticize, but denies it the right to obstruct. The debates on the budget and the throne speech, and the allocation of Supply Days on which the opposition parties may choose the topics for debate, constitute formal recognition of the right to criticize the government's record in general. The rules of debate, the committee system and the Question Period permit criticism of individual items of policy or administration. Less formally, although the governing party has final control over the timetable of the House, both government and opposition recognize the value of agreements between respective House Leaders or party whips concerning the disposal of parliamentary time in order to foster a spirit of cooperation.[63]

Occasionally, however, cooperation breaks down. This occurs usually when the government, confronted with what it views as obstruction by the opposition, attempts to push through a bill with what the opposition regards as unseemly haste. When this occurs, both sides of the House have various procedural weapons at their disposal. The government may seek to terminate debate by resorting to **closure** (Standing Order clause 57), an extremely unpopular measure whereby all outstanding discussion and divisions on a particular stage of a bill must be completed within the next sitting day instead of being adjourned from one day to the next, as unfinished business usually is. Closure is a device to which governments turn with the greatest reluctance because of its procedural complexity and political ramifications.[64] As one author has commented, notice of closure "resembles so much a death sentence and a public execution that ministers shrink from using it; and when they do, the opposition, regardless of their true sentiments, feels obliged to lament the end of a thousand years of freedom and democracy."[65] A less drastic alternative to closure as a means of limiting debate lies in a pre-arranged allocation of time to a particular bill or its various stages under Standing Order 78. Here, a balance of power is maintained between government and opposition by rules that become more complex procedurally as they require less inter-party cooperation.[66]

In the 32nd Parliament, for example, the opposition found dramatic weapons to confront an uncooperative government. In March and April 1981, the Progressive Conservatives tied up the business of the House of Commons with a collective "filibuster" — an apparently endless series of "points of order" and "questions of privilege" in order to prevent further discussion of the resolution on patriation of the Constitution until after it had been ruled

---

[63] See Paul G. Thomas, "The Role of House Leaders in the Canadian House of Commons," *CJPS* vol. 15, *Parliamentary Review*, vol. 6, no. 3 (Autumn 1983), pp. 14–19.

[64] On the origins, procedural details and use of "closure" see Dawson, *Procedure in the Canadian House of Commons*, pp. 121–30.

[65] Stewart, *The Canadian House of Commons*, p. 244.

[66] For a detailed explanation see ibid., pp. 250–58.

upon by the Supreme Court. For two weeks in March 1982, the division bells were left ringing on Parliament Hill as the opposition boycotted the House in protest against the Liberals'
omnibus bill on energy security. In both cases, the government was forced to compromise
its original proposals in order to get the House back to work. The McGrath reforms have ended
the future use of a "bell ringing filibuster." Now, by Standing Order, the bells can ring only
for 15 minutes, unless it is on a non-debatable motion, in which case 30 minutes is required.
The whips may request that a vote be delayed for a day, but during the deferral the bells may
not ring and the House continues its normal business.

In the 34th Parliament, the Conservative government's use of closure and time allocation
took on a new and harsh quality. From 1913, when closure was first used, until the 1984
election the device was employed only 19 times. During the 33rd Parliament it was used only
twice. But from 1988 until mid-April 1993 it was employed 15 times — in other words almost as many times as in the whole history of closure since 1913. To top it off, time allocation was used 25 times in the 34th Parliament (up to mid-April 1993) compared to many
fewer times in earlier Parliaments. The partisan nature of the use of closure and time allocation can be shown by indicating that these "gag" rules were nearly always imposed on fairly controversial legislation such as the free trade legislation, the Goods and Service Tax and
the *Drug Patent Act*.

In its adversarial relationship with the government, the opposition is disadvantaged
by the former's control over the parliamentary timetable and access to departmental information. But the opposition does have sanctions to prevent what it sees as abuse of the
parliamentary process. Even the complaint that opposition parties lack the research facilities
to compete with the government's monopoly on bureaucratic information has been partly blunted by the provision of public funding for partisan activity by caucus research
groups.

Indeed, many of the difficulties encountered by the opposition in formulating effective
criticism of government policy have less to do with House of Commons procedures or research facilities than with more fundamental problems that also afflict parliamentary oppositions in other western democracies.[67] One is that the official Opposition in Parliament
often has difficulty in making itself heard above the "hubbub" coming from other political
actors. Major interest groups and private research institutes frequently offer articulate and
well-publicized criticisms of government policy, and, in a federal context such as Canada,
"there is little doubt that the clashes between the provinces and the federal government...detract attention from the federal parliamentary opposition on some of the most
important issues in Canadian politics."[68]

Sometimes, too, it may be difficult for the opposition parties to offer clear-cut alternatives to government policy. Some issues do not lend themselves to a confrontational style
of politics, since they cut across party lines and strain party cohesion on both sides of the
House. This is especially true of moral issues such as abortion, AIDS, capital punishment or
euthanasia. On other social and economic policy issues, the development of an ideological
consensus supportive of the mixed-economy and the welfare state has tended to preclude
the presentation of radical policy alternatives by a "loyal" opposition.

---

[67] For an extended discussion see Andrew J. Milnor and Mark N. Franklin, "Patterns of Opposition
Behaviour in Modern Legislatures," in A. Kornberg, ed., *Legislatures in Comparative Perspective* (New York:
David McKay, 1973), p. 84; Jackson, "Models of Legislative Reform," p. 4.

[68] Jackson and Atkinson, *Canadian Legislative System*, p. 119.

Oppositions have increasingly had to be content with criticizing the specifics of government policy and its administration (rather than developing comprehensive alternatives) and with presenting themselves as an alternative source of leadership and government personnel. In this regard, the opposition parties have been greatly aided by the introduction of television cameras into the House of Commons. The broadcasting of Question Period and major debates not only provides a wider audience for their criticisms of the government, but also gives nation-wide exposure to the leaders of the opposition parties and their "teams." Direct communication with the electorate via television may in fact have greatly facilitated the major task of contemporary parliamentary oppositions — that of presenting themselves as viable alternatives.[69] Increasingly, the chief efforts of parliamentary oppositions are directed at explaining to the electorate why the government is making mistakes and why the opposition should be returned to power at the next election.

THE PRIVATE MEMBER: LEGISLATOR OR OMBUDSMAN?

In parliamentary systems, where cohesive parties are the main actors and the mass media focus upon leading personalities from the government and opposition front benches, it is easy to lose sight of the private member. Furthermore, the myths of "legislative decline" and "executive dominance" have tended to stress the political impotence of the individual backbencher. In contrast to the nineteenth century, private members' bills today constitute a tiny fraction of the total legislative output of the House of Commons, but to be accurate the narrow view of the member of a legislature as an initiator of legislation should be revised to take into account the many other demands on an MP's time.

Former Liberal MP and cabinet minister Mark MacGuigan has provided a guide to the workload of an average member of the House of Commons. As a freshman backbencher, MacGuigan found that "parliamentary demands on my time were considerable, and the burden of constituency cases staggering."[70] His catalogue of responsibilities and activities included:

> ...at least three half-days each week in the House to ensure that a quorum was always maintained; attendance at major debates and divisions; attendance at Question Period "for both excitement and information"; membership in two standing committees and, later, the Chairship of the Special Committee on Statutory Instruments; caucus meetings for three hours each Wednesday morning and caucus committee meetings in lunch and dinner breaks; twice-weekly French classes, "being determined to become bilingual"; a one thousand mile round trip each weekend to constituency and home in Windsor; approximately 200 public functions and 200 visits to the homes of constituents in each year; and a large volume of constituency business (some 5500 cases a year) which arrived by mail and by telephone.[71]

Even a list of this length excludes attendance at the routine proceedings of the House and attempts to develop expertise in one or more policy areas. Furthermore, new MPs are expected to become familiar with the rules and procedures governing behaviour in the House.

---

[69] On the role of the media in Parliament, especially television, see the entire issue of *Parliamentary Government*, vol. 3, no. 1 (1982).

[70] MacGuigan, "Parliamentary Reform," p. 673.

[71] Ibid., pp. 673–75.

Complaints concerning the inadequacy of staffing and research resources for legislators are neither new nor restricted only to Canada.[72] However, the lot of private members has improved considerably over the last three decades.[73] In earlier days, when parliamentary sessions were much shorter, permanent assistance for MPs was considered unnecessary. Today, MPs have a salary and expense allowance equal to about $100 000 of taxed income and an annual overall budget of at least $166 400 for staff. (See Table 8.2.) They usually hire four full-time assistants in their Ottawa offices, and at least one more to manage inquiries at their constituency office. Still, for most members, this increase has barely kept pace with the immense caseload of constituency business in the form of correspondence, telephone calls and personal contacts. Thus, a former clerk of the House of Commons has suggested that, while most MPs are adequately staffed for their role as constituency representative, they are not "over serviced" with respect to either their legislative functions or active participation in the committee system.[74]

We have said that the job of an MP is multifunctional. In theory at least, members of the Commons are constituency representatives, caucus members, orators, law-makers and watchdogs over the government and bureaucracy. Most of the time, however, members are bound by party discipline and can show little initiative. Canadian political parties are very "cohesive." That is, the caucus members act together on major policy issues and follow their whips when they vote in divisions. On occasion, there are "free" votes in which members are "free" to follow the dictates of their conscience, interest groups or their constituencies. Capital punishment was turned down in a free vote in 1987. In 1988 there were a series of House of Commons free votes on abortion (none of which were successful) and a free vote in the Senate (that killed a government proposal by ending in a tie).

Some recent reforms and innovations have enhanced the ability of individual MPs to perform their parliamentary tasks more effectively. The new standing committees enable MPs to have more input into policy formulation. Even government backbenchers in the 32nd Parliament took advantage of the new Standing Orders to voice independent opinions and mild criticism of Cabinet policy.[75] Reduction of the maximum length of speeches in the House allows more members to take part in debates, and the possibility of a ten-minute rebuttal/ debate after each speech has provided more interest and flexibility for MPs. But, by and large, effective participation in debate or in the scrutiny of government legislation and estimates is hampered by lack of information, resources and policy expertise. The development of a heightened role for the backbencher in the legislative process requires more than procedural reform of the House of Commons.

Of course, there are exceptions — MPs who carve out a particular area of specialization or who adopt some issue as their own. In the 34th Parliament, Liberal Charles Caccia was the dean of commentators on the environment while Conservative Patrick Boyer shone on subjects such as election and referendum law. But for every activist back-

---

[72] A comparative appreciation of the problem is offered by James A. Robinson, "Staffing the Legislature," in A. Kornberg and L. Musolf, eds., *Legislatures in Developmental Perspective* (Durham, N.C.: Duke University Press, 1970), pp. 366–90.

[73] On the development of legislative staffing for MPs, see Alistair Fraser, "Legislators and their Staffs," in Clark et al., eds., *Parliament, Policy and Representation*, pp. 230–40.

[74] Ibid., p. 240. For a description of the structure of an MP's office see Barbara Reynolds, "Organizing the MP's Office," *Parliamentary Government*, vol. 8, no. 2 (1988) pp. 9–10.

[75] See "Liberal seals are showing some bite," *Globe and Mail*, Toronto, February 15, 1983.

bencher in Parliament, there are many more who, however diligently they may serve their constituents, play a minimal part in the legislative process. Lack of opportunity is clearly one factor involved in this syndrome. But it may also be true that, as one study alleges, "private members do not seem to take full advantage of the opportunities available to them" to introduce legislation and initiate criticism of the government.[76]

TABLE 8.2   SALARIES AND BENEFITS FOR PARLIAMENT AND GOVERNMENT (APRIL 1993)

I Members of Parliament

Salary	$64 800.00
Expense Allowance (receipts required)	$21 400.00
Supplement (for large ridings, etc.)	$21 400.00 – $28 000.00
Pensions (they pay 10% of annual salary)	75% of average of best six years service (at the rate of 5% per year with minimum of 6 years service.
Staff (divided between office in constituency and House of Commons)	$166 400.00 – $172 200.00
Travel	64 return trips between Ottawa and constituency
Telephone, mail, equipment and supplies	paid and basically unlimited

II Senators

Salary	$64 000.00
Expense allowance	$10 100.00

III Officers of Government or Parliament (in addition to the above)

Prime Minister	$74 000.00
Leader of Official Opposition, Speaker and all Ministers	$49 400.00
Parliamentary Secretaries	$10 000.00
Other officials (leaders, deputy speakers, whips)	$7 500.00 – $25 800.00

IV Parliamentary Parties (at least 12 MPs)

Progressive Conservatives	$1 348 700.00
Liberal Party	$1 095 800.00
New Democratic Party	$765 300.00

The attitudes of MPs themselves, and their relations with their constituents, also encourage the concentration on representational activities. The electorate is becoming more demanding. With the ever-increasing volume of government legislation and the

---

[76] Kornberg and Mischler, *Influence in Parliament*, p. 311. See also John M. Reid, "The Backbencher and the Discharge of Legislative Responsibilities," and subsequent comments (especially those of Paul G. Thomas) in W.A.W. Nielson and J.C. MacPherson, eds., *The Legislative Process in Canada: The Need for Reform* (Montréal: IRPP 1978), ch. 5.

seemingly omnipresent role of the government, there is significant pressure from constituents for MPs to act as intermediaries on their behalf in disputes with departments and other central agencies. Such "ombudsman" work usually involves simple, concrete problems readily solved by a telephone call to a department or a brief negotiation with a minister. Policy-making, on the other hand, requires abstract, generalized conceptualization of an issue and a long-term commitment to pursue a particular solution. In terms of results for effort expended, the role of ombudsman is more rewarding than that of a law-maker for the majority of members. Furthermore, the bottom line is that the political future of many MPs depends upon them satisfying their constituents.

Reproduced with permission, Dennis Pritchard.

SYMBOLISM OR POWER? OBJECTIVES OF HOUSE OF COMMONS REFORM

The reform of parliamentary procedure should be an ongoing process. Parliament is in a constant state of evolution, and if its practices are to be effective, they must be adapted when necessary to meet the changing needs of Parliament and reflect the changing conditions of society and the nation.[77]

---

[77] House of Commons: Special Committee on Standing Orders and Procedures, *Third Report* (Ottawa: 1982), p. 5.

As this passage from a report by a recent Special Committee on Standing Orders and Procedures illustrates, members of the House of Commons appear to be perfectly aware of the necessity to reform the roles, procedures and customs of the chamber in order to maintain Parliament as a central institution in Canadian society. Yet it has also been observed that possibly the most enigmatic feature of parliamentary democracies is that ordinary members know that they possess limitless authority to change the structures of their legislatures but nevertheless persist in ignoring this power.[78]

Periodically, Canadian MPs undertake systematic reforms of the way in which they conduct their activities. After a wave of reforms in the late 1960s, notable among them the establishment of the modern system of committees, more than a decade elapsed until the next round of innovation and experimentation. In the early 1980s, the Lefebvre and McGrath reform committees ushered in major innovations in the election of the Speaker, private members' business, committee structure, scheduling and other items of importance.

Consequently, a voluminous body of literature exists on proposals for House of Commons reform.[79] This is not the place to add to it, although we have drawn attention in the preceding pages to areas in which reform may be desirable, and have made some specific proposals. It may even be justifiably argued that little new or innovative can be added to the catalogues of recommendations. What may be more useful is to provide some criteria for evaluating existing and future reform proposals.

First, it should be emphasized that one cannot turn back the clock to the "Golden Age of Parliament" of the mid-nineteenth century. Former Progressive Conservative leader Robert Stanfield, in a keynote address to a Conference on Legislative Reform a few years ago, asserted that

> ...we no longer have parliamentary responsible government in Ottawa. I assert that
> parliamentary government is not fitted for what it is being asked to do: that both the government
> and the Parliament are overloaded to the point that we have poor government and Parliament
> cannot cope with government.[80]

Stanfield prescribed a reduction of the "all-pervasive" influence of government through the decentralization of decision-making. Only by cutting the workload of the federal government and Parliament, he argued, could parliamentary control over the executive be restored while policy-making efficiency was maintained. However, though it is clear that the expansion of federal government activities has influenced the role of Parliament, there is little reason to believe that a reduced role for government in society is either necessary or sufficient for re-establishing parliamentary control.

Those who cling to the myth that Parliaments were once more important because governments were less so appear to forget that the growth of the public sector and state intervention are not all that has changed. Constituents today expect more of both their governments and their Members of Parliament, and there are more of them to bring problems to each MP. Traditional federal government responsibilities such as defence

---

[78] Jackson, "Models of Legislative Reform," p. 4.

[79] Among the many comprehensive "reform designs," the reader may wish to consult the discussion in Robert J. Jackson and Michael M. Atkinson, *The Canadian Legislative System*, 1st and 2nd eds. (Toronto: Macmillan, 1974 and 1980).

[80] Robert L. Stanfield, "The Present State of the Legislative Process in Canada: Myths and Realities," in Neilson and MacPherson, eds., *The Legislative Process in Canada*, p. 42.

policy have become increasingly technical in nature, placing additional burdens on parliamentarians. Television and other mass media have created direct channels of communication between government and the general public that have altered the representative, intermediary functions of MPs. Such trends cannot be reversed. Nor, in the absence of substantial realignment in the perceptions of Canadian citizens about the role of government in society, can the scope of federal government activities be significantly reduced. Realistic proposals for reform of the House of Commons must therefore be formulated within this context.

The objectives of parliamentary reform may be grouped under the two broad headings "power" and "symbolism" — the central themes of this chapter. Some reforms are oriented toward increasing the power of Parliament — to strengthening the House of Commons vis-à-vis other institutions and to increasing its ability to control, criticize and hold government accountable for its actions. Other proposals are primarily symbolic in nature inasmuch as they seek to enhance the image of the House of Commons as a key institution in the democratic process. As we noted earlier, these two categories are not necessarily mutually exclusive, since a Parliament that is perceived as weak and ineffective will not be able to sustain, in the long run, the degree of legitimacy necessary to fulfill its symbolic functions. However, the concepts "power" and "symbolism" do serve as useful organizing devices.

When it comes to a reform measure designed to increase the power of the House of Commons, the probability of success depends upon various implicit norms and constraints that result from the realities of legislative politics in the chamber. First, governments will not accept organizational or procedural changes unless they are assured that changes favourable to the government will also be adopted. Thus, reform packages must be designed in such a way that they maintain a balance between the competing needs of government and opposition. If, for example, the opposition is to gain increased opportunities for surveillance and criticism of the administration, the government must be guaranteed certain concessions with regard to limiting debate without fearing outbreaks of bell-ringing or other such measures. Political reality dictates that the government will simply deploy its majority in the House to defeat "unbalanced" reform proposals.

And we may be sure that governments will continue to deploy their forces in a cohesive fashion on matters affecting their interests. Proposals that seek to enhance the influence of backbenchers by advocating, for example, that "leaders of both government and opposition parties recognize and adopt in practice a less stringent approach to the question of party discipline and the rules governing confidence"[81] are politically naïve and based on misleading comparisons with the United States, where members of Congress are deemed to be more powerful because they work in a state of partisan anarchy.

As we have already pointed out, the principle of responsible party government in Canada is different from that in the United States, where the President is directly elected and not dependent upon a majority in Congress in order to stay in office. Therefore, pressures in favour of party cohesion are much stronger in Canada — and not only in the government party, since opposition party leaders also rely on support from their MPs to maintain pressure on the government and to present themselves to the electorate as a responsible alternative administration.

Finally, with respect to measures to enhance the power of the House of Commons, it must be emphasized that it is much easier to alter procedures and institutions than to

---

[81] d'Aquino et al., *Parliamentary Democracy in Canada*, p. 30.

change the attitudes and behaviour of politicians. Many reformers criticize the lack of opportunities for ordinary members to participate in the policy process or to effectively control government spending, without acknowledging that many MPs fail to take advantage of the opportunities that already exist — either because they choose not to, or because pressures of work and competing commitments prevent them from doing so. Thus, members do not take the scrutiny of government estimates very seriously, because much of it is boring, routine work. More committees or more powers for committees will not help; rather, there must be some perceived reward for effective participation, such as exposure to constituents through the televising of committee hearings. If MPs are too overworked to fulfill all expectations of them, giving them more powers will have little effect on their performance.

Reforms designed to increase the power of Parliament vis-à-vis other actors such as the government and the bureaucracy may well have a beneficial effect on the symbolic functions of the House of Commons in legitimating the government policies and many other aspects of the political system. But other reforms might also enhance the symbolic role of the House by raising the level of esteem in which it is held by the Canadian public. Thus, although the members of the 35th Parliament and the government they sustain are reasonably representative of Canadian voters across the country, electoral reform might assure the integrative capacity of the House as a representative institution.[82] Increased travel by committees and country-wide consultation would bring Parliament closer to the people. So too would more interesting televising of House proceedings — for example, letting cameras do more than merely focus on one talking head at a time; or, following the popular precedent set with the Special Committee on the constitution, allowing cameras more consistently into committee meetings, where so much work of the House is done.

As reformers seek to strengthen the House of Commons, all too often the other potential strengths of the House, as a representative institution, as a symbol of societal integration, as a link between government and citizens, are neglected. Both power and symbolic changes should be advocated.

THE SENATE

As of 1993, Canada is one of approximately 53 countries in the world with a bicameral legislature — that is, with a second chamber or upper house in addition to the (usually) popularly elected lower house.[83] Second chambers have been adopted or retained for a number of purposes, among them, the representation at the national level of the constituent parts of a federal system and the representation of a particular class (or estate) to act as a conservative restraint upon the potentially unbridled progressivism of the lower house. But the essential case for an upper house has always been that the formulation of legislation and policy issues ought to receive a second consideration, and possibly be rejected, or delayed, by a chamber different from the first in character and composition.[84]

---

[82]　See the discussion of the impact of the electoral system in Chapter 11.

[83]　I.P.U., *Electoral Systems: A World-Wide Comparative Study* (Geneva, 1993).

[84]　Michael Curtis, *Comparative Government and Politics: An Introductory Essay in Political Science,* 2nd ed. (New York: Harper & Row, 1978), p. 195.

While the notion of the second chamber as a provider of "sober second thought" concerning legislation from the lower house is almost universal, the other functions of upper houses can often be related to their mode of selection. In federal systems, all of which give their sub-national territorial units some representation in the national legislature, membership in the upper house is determined in different ways. Sometimes members are directly elected by the public, as in the United States and Australia. Sometimes they are delegates from the state governments or legislatures, as in Germany. Elsewhere, members are appointed as representatives of various economic, occupational or cultural associations, as in the Portuguese Corporative Chamber before 1975. In still other countries (notably Belgium, Italy and Japan), the upper house is popularly elected, but is designed to give rise to a chamber with a political complexion different from that of the lower house. Finally, the predominantly conservative and upper class mood of the British House of Lords has been modified by the appointment of Life Peers. Approximately three-quarters of the 1062 members of the Lords are hereditary peers and the remainder are appointed as Life Peers by successive governments.

RECRUITMENT AND FORMAL ROLES

The Senate of Canada appears, at first glance, to fit none of these models. It is the only legislative chamber in the western world where members are all appointed. They receive their positions from the Governor General at the behest of the government of the day. Thus, Canadian Senators cannot claim to represent directly, or to be delegates of, any electorate, any subordinate level of government or any specific interests within society.

Although Canada is unique in appointing its Senators, as in most other countries, there is a regional basis to the system. Since 1975, the membership of the Senate has been fixed at 104, with 24 each from four main regions — Ontario, Québec, the West (six from each of the four provinces west of Ontario) and the Maritimes (ten each from New Brunswick and Nova Scotia, four from Prince Edward Island) — together with six from Newfoundland and one each from Yukon and the Northwest Territories. There is also provision in the *Constitution* for the appointment of an additional four or eight Senators (drawn equally from the four main regions) to allow for breaking a deadlock within the Senate and the Commons. After the 1988 election, Conservative Prime Minister Brian Mulroney used this procedure to prevent the Liberal-dominated upper house from blocking the Goods and Service Tax legislation. For the first and only time in Canadian history eight additional Senators were appointed — temporarily increasing the number to 112.

A Senator nominally "represents" the province for which he or she was appointed and, unlike a member of the House of Commons, must reside and own property in that province. Thus there is a regional or provincial underpinning to the composition of the Senate, and the Fathers of Confederation did perceive the Second Chamber as a "federal" institution. According to Sir John A. Macdonald:

> In order to protect local interests and to prevent sectional jealousies, it was found requisite that the great divisions into which British North America is separated should be represented in the Upper House on the principle of equality.[85]

---

[85] *Parliamentary Debates on Confederation of the British North American Provinces.* Québec City, 1865 (Ottawa: Supply and Services, 1951), p. 29.

Most federal systems give their constituent states equal representation in the upper house or at least some modified form of representation by population.[86] Although the "great divisions" of Canada are equally represented in the Senate, there are obvious inequities in representation among Canadian provinces, particularly to the detriment of the West.

The unique appointment process means that Canadian Senators cannot be held accountable or responsible either to the provinces or to the regions they were originally intended to represent. Instead, the representation of provincial or regional interests in the federal policy-making process has become increasingly institutionalized in the form of Federal/Provincial Conferences and in the regional composition of the Cabinet.

If the Senate does not fill the role of guardian of regional or provincial interests in a federal system, neither does it necessarily seem oriented toward providing a more mature or conservative restraint upon the youthful enthusiasm of the House of Commons. Senators must be at least 30 years of age, but this is considerably younger than new MPs entering the lower house. And although the *Constitution* determined that Senators must own property exceeding $4000 in value — a sum that in the mid-nineteenth century limited potential membership to a fairly narrow and privileged minority — this figure has not been revised since 1867. Thus, the constitutional requirements for membership in the Senate are no longer of great relevance to its composition or perceived role within the legislative process.

Senators were originally appointed for life but, since 1965, they have retired at age 75. One observer noted, with a touch of black humour, that this formal change would have little practical relevance:

> Senators, on the average, die at the age of 74….Therefore, the introduction of a compulsory retiring age at 75 would by no means seriously affect the existing situation in the Senate; it would rather formalize a practice already present.[87]

One potential advantage of the process of appointment is that it can be used to give recognition to economic, ethnic and religious groups that are under-represented in the House of Commons. Thus, members of organized labour have been appointed, as have farmers — though not nearly as many as their numbers in the population would warrant. The Protestant minority in Québec and English-speaking Catholics elsewhere have also tended to be over-represented in the Senate to compensate for their relative lack of seats in the Commons.[88]

As of 1993, however, only very few women have been appointed to the Senate. The first woman Senator, Cairine Wilson, was appointed in 1930, after a long constitutional wrangle that was resolved by a decision from the Judicial Committee of the Privy Council that women were equally "persons" under the relevant sections of the *BNA Act*.[89] The fact that only 14 of 97 Senators in 1993 are women demonstrates that Senate appointments have not been systematically used as a means of redressing inequities of representation in the House of Commons.[90] Rather, appointments of women as well as leading figures from minority

---

[86] The United States and Switzerland, for example, permit each state and full canton respectively, two members in the federal chambers. The German *Länder* send three, four or five members, weighted according to population, to the federal *Bundesrat*.

[87] Kunz, *The Modern Senate of Canada*, p. 71.

[88] Robert A. Mackay, *The Unreformed Senate of Canada*, rev. ed. (Toronto: McClelland & Stewart, 1963), pp. 148–49.

[89] On the question of previous women in the Senate, and the development of minority group representation in the upper house, see Kunz, *The Modern Senate of Canada*, pp. 46-56.

[90] For details on earlier periods see Brodie and Vickers, *Canadian Women in Politics: An Overview* (Ottawa: Canadian Research Institute for the Advancement of Women, 1982), p. 42.

groups have been symbolic, "a token of recognition of their relative importance in the social and political system of the country."[91] Often, it has been motivated by purely partisan
interests in an attempt to win electoral support from certain groups.

This last point underlines the true nature of the system used in appointing Senators.
Although in formal terms "qualified persons" are "summoned" to the Senate by the
Governor General, in practice, as with other such appointments, the real power of selection
rests with the Prime Minister. The fact is, therefore, that the primary basis of appointment
to the Senate is unashamedly partisan. Senatorships have invariably been regarded as the
choicest plums in the patronage basket and they have been used continually as rewards for
faithful party service. There have been few more blatant examples of this in recent years than
the appointments of former Prime Minister Trudeau as he retired, and former Prime Minister
Mulroney's nominations of former ministers, MPs, fundraisers and former employees to the
Senate as part of veritable orgies of patronage appointments.

It must be acknowledged that the partisan nature of Senate appointments may have some
positive value for the political system. It does allow Cabinet ministers and other long-
serving party members to be "promoted" to secure, well-paid Senate seats rather than
being "relegated" to the backbenches. In this way, the Prime Minister can make room to manoeuvre, to reshuffle the Cabinet and introduce new blood without appearing to demote
colleagues. It also sometimes occurs that a party candidate regarded as potential ministerial material fails to win or retain a seat in the House of Commons. The Senate provides two
alternative strategies for a Prime Minister wishing to have such an individual available for
inclusion in the government. One is to elevate to the Senate a member of the caucus who
holds a safe seat into which the promising candidate can be "parachuted" at the ensuing election. Otherwise, the potential minister may be directly appointed to the Senate and allowed to hold a ministerial portfolio as a member of the upper house. Thus, when Robert
René de Cotret failed to win a seat in 1979, he was appointed to the Senate and the federal Cabinet by Prime Minister Clark.

Although this "renewal" function tends to give rise to a Senate composed mainly of semi-
retired party faithfuls, the upper house is far from being a geriatric retreat. The number of
appointments of relatively young Senators has increased in recent years, and some members have played important roles within their national party organizations. Senators are, for
example, in an ideal position to direct election campaigns, since they are close to the centres of power in Ottawa but do not have to seek personal re-election. Thus, Senators
Michael Kirby (Liberal) and Lowell Murray (PC) served as their respective parties' chief strategists in the 1988 election campaign.[92]

From the foregoing discussion, it is apparent that the Senate fulfills only imperfectly many
of the formal roles normally ascribed to second chambers. It is not manifestly a representative of provincial rights nor of minority groups; neither is it a straightforward champion
of a particular class, nor a sanctuary for aging politicians. Therefore, to ascertain the place
of the upper house within the Canadian legislative process, we need to consider the actual work done by the Senate and Senators' own perceptions of their task.

---

[91] Kunz, *The Modern Senate of Canada*, p. 46.

[92] See J. McMenemy et al., "Party Structures and Decision-Making," in C. Winn and J. McMenemy, eds.,
Political Parties in Canada, pp. 184–85.

LEGISLATIVE POLITICS IN THE SENATE

The status of the Senate as an independent and non-partisan counterweight to the Commons has been challenged by many observers. According to this view, Senators are partisan appointments; as such, they are vulnerable to external pressures and vested interests. According to one author:

> *The fact that they are still associating with their old colleagues and are only a few feet away from the thickest of the fight, makes party detachment and independence little more than a fanciful aspiration which has lost contact with the facts of life.*[93]

A contrary view is posited by F.A. Kunz. While admitting that "it would be rather naïve to expect a person who is summoned to the Senate at the (average) age of fifty-eight to forget his entire political background,"[94] he argues that strongly-held partisan convictions are counterbalanced by the process of socialization into the norms of the upper chamber that a new Senator undergoes.[95]

Certainly, the career backgrounds of Senators show them to be highly political.[96] However, there is also strong evidence that, once institutionalized into the norms and values of the upper house, Senators often forego overt displays of partisan attachment in favour of other roles. Many perceive themselves as independent elder statesmen placing their expertise and experience at the service of the country as a whole rather than serving particular party interests. The higher incidence of cross-voting (voting across party lines) in the upper house on important issues of government legislation would suggest that partisanship is lower in the Senate than in the House of Commons.[97] In 1993, five Senators had no declared loyalties to any of the political parties.

On the whole, the Senate does not reject government legislation.[98] Despite the fact that the Canadian upper house is one of the few second chambers to retain a full set of legislative teeth (including absolute veto over bills passed by the Commons), it has usually failed to make full use of them. On the few occasions when the upper house has thrown caution to the winds and blocked government initiatives, it has been threatened with dire consequences. Most Senators are fully aware of the erosion of powers, and in some cases even the abolition, of second chambers elsewhere. Moreover, the self-perceived role of elder statesman would appear to forbid the obstruction of legislation passed by a House of Commons mandated by popular will. Instead, one of the most important legislative functions performed by the Senate consists of the detailed scrutiny of bills with a view to removing ambiguities of interpretation in the original wording and amending technical items that fall within the particular expertise of individual members.

On occasion, however, the Senate has acted decisively to reject government legislation. As early as 1875 the Senate blocked the construction of an Esquimalt-Nanaimo railway. In 1913 it defeated the Borden Naval Bill and in 1926 it terminated MacKenzie King's old age

---

[93] Dawson, *The Government of Canada*, p. 285.

[94] Kunz, *The Modern Senate of Canada*, p. 113.

[95] Ibid., p. 115.

[96] Colin Campbell, *The Canadian Senate: A Lobby from Within* (Toronto: Macmillan, 1978), p. 53 and Appendix II.

[97] Several examples are offered by Kunz, *The Modern Senate of Canada*, Table XIX, p. 118, and ch. 4, passim.

[98] Ibid., Tables XV–XVIII, pp. 116–17.

pension legislation. During Prime Minister Mulroney's tenure from 1984 to 1993 there were constant clashes between the House and Senate. The Senate interfered or delayed a borrowing bill and the drug patent bill, copyright, immigration and income tax legislation. It tried to amend the Meech Lake accord, unemployment insurance payments and the Goods and Service Tax. It succeeded in rejecting an abortion bill when a free vote was called. While technically this was the first senatorial veto in three decades, it did not truly represent a rebellion against the government.

The most important incidence of the Senate blocking the elected house, however, was the decision of the Liberal Senators, at the request of John Turner, to prevent the passage of free trade legislation. When the trade bill reached second reading, Liberal Senators abstained and allowed it to go to the Foreign Affairs Committee. In a deliberate provocation of the Conservative government, the Liberal-dominated committee set up an extensive program of hearings. The government was forced to call an election for November 20, 1988: an election for which the Senate had helped to set the date and the agenda — a partisan act of the highest order.

Despite these occasions of grand obstruction, the Senators normally spend their time in leisurely debates or in committee deliberations. Committee work is their most significant contribution. For example, in 1991–92, Senate committees held 301 meetings to discuss legislation, estimates and special studies. In fact, most of the time (62.7 percent) was spent in special committees discussing key social issues and making recommendations for new policy initiatives. (See Figure 8.3.)

In the 1960s and early 1970s, Senate Special Committees on such diverse issues as poverty, the mass media, aging, and science helped to build social consensus around particular

Reproduced with permission, Dennis Pritchard.

problems and alternative responses. But, like recent House of Commons Task Forces, these special committees were frequently critical of existing government policy. In fact, they were probably too critical and non-partisan for their own good, because there has been a tendency in recent years for Government House Leaders in the Senate to allocate investigatory tasks to Standing committees, which can be more easily controlled. Reports in the 1980s and 1990s include those on unemployment insurance, the security service, national defence, youth and terrorism.

FIGURE 8.3   TIME SPENT IN SENATE COMMITTEES, 1991–92

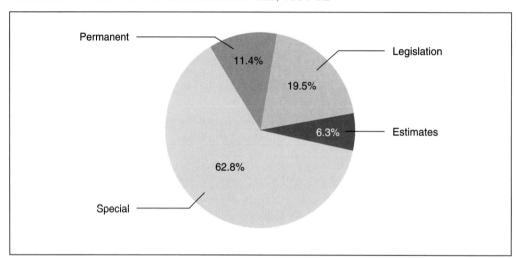

* Permanent refers to Internal Economy, Privileges, Selection and Scutiny of Regulations.

Source: Compiled from information in Committees and Private Legislation Branch, *Senate Committees* (Ottawa: Senate, 1992).

Prior to the 1984 General Election, it appeared that the Senate was developing a new role in the legislative process — that of a supplier of ministers. Ministers in the Senate ensured regional and linguistic balance in the Cabinet to parties denied House of Commons representation from major regions of the country. In 1979, Prime Minister Clark, with only two Conservative MPs elected in Québec, recruited three ministers from the Senate to bolster francophone representation in his Cabinet. Similarly, after the 1980 General Election, with no Liberal MPs from the three western provinces, Prime Minister Trudeau included three Senators in his government. Although the appointments were criticized by opposition MPs on the grounds that these ministers held no popular mandate, they did provide the Senate with an enhanced opportunity to oversee the work of government and to participate more fully in legislative/executive relations. In the 34th Parliament, with a majority of Conservative MPs elected from all parts of the country, Prime Minister Mulroney had little need of Senators to build his Cabinet. However, Senator Lowell Murray played an important role in the Conservative Cabinet, as does Senator Joyce Fairburn in the 1993 Liberal Cabinet.

SYMBOLISM OR POWER? OBJECTIVES OF SENATE REFORM

Like the House of Commons, the Senate is the subject of ongoing debate on parliamentary reform. As Henri Bourassa claimed half a century ago, such debate is something that "comes periodically like other forms of epidemics and current fevers."[99] However, in the last two decades, a qualitative shift in the motivation for reform has occurred. With reference again to the central concepts of this chapter, it might be said that the objectives have changed from altering somewhat the power and symbolism of the Senate to radically restructuring the Senate's role in the *Constitution*. The overall pattern of Senate reform proposals and constitutional change is discussed in Chapters 5 and 6.[100]

In the past, demands for restrictions on the power of the upper house came, not surprisingly, from governments confronted by a "hostile" Senate. Mackenzie King in 1927, Diefenbaker in 1962 and Mulroney in 1988 sought or threatened Senate reform after government legislation had been blocked by an opposition majority in the second chamber. It is also unsurprising that proposals designed to enhance the effective functioning of the upper house or to reassert its legislative significance have often come from within the Senate itself.

Some critics of the role of the Senate have not contented themselves with proposing minor reforms or even reduced powers. The Progressive Party of the 1920s, the CCF and its descendant the NDP have all advocated nothing less than abolition of the second chamber, arguing at times that an unelected body has no place in the legislative process of a democratic society. But total abolition of the upper house is not only constitutionally difficult, it is also politically impractical.

At one time, both demands for abolition and attempts at reform derived from dissatisfaction with the role and powers of the Senate as second chamber in the parliamentary system. More recent proposals, from the 1969 federal government White Paper that set out Prime Minister Trudeau's draft for a new Canadian *Constitution* through the various constitutional discussions of the late 1970s, the Alberta success in "electing" a Senator in 1989,[101] and the provisions in the Meech Lake and Charlottetown accords were predicated upon the assumption that the upper house could be reshaped into an institution designed to correct perceived deficiencies elsewhere in the political system. As federal/provincial and regional tensions became more acute, reform of the Senate was viewed as a panacea for all manner of perceived ills afflicting Canadian society.

The many reform designs produced a variety of schemes for a more equitable geographical distribution of seats in the upper house, usually to the potential benefit of Western Canada.[102] They ranged from allowing some provincial input into the existing appointment system,[103] through joint selection by the federal Parliament and the provincial legislatures in a proposed "House of the Federation," to having an upper house consisting of delegates chosen by and representing provincial governments in a so-called "House of the Provinces" modelled after the West German *Bundesrat*.[104]

---

[99] *House of Commons Debates*, 1926, p. 648.

[100] See also Robert J. Jackson and Doreen Jackson, *Stand Up for Canada; Leadership and the Canadian Political Crisis* (Scarborough, Ont.: Prentice-Hall, 1992).

[101] In 1989, the province of Alberta held a "senatorial election" when a vacancy opened during the period when Prime Minister Mulroney said he would appoint Senators from provincial "lists." A Reform party candidate won the election and Mulroney felt duty bound to appoint him. No other province has followed the precedent.

[102] See West Foundation, *Regional Representation: The Canadian Partnership* (Calgary: Canada West Foundation, 1981).

[103] The 1969 White Paper and the 1972 Special Committee Report proposed that the provinces would submit short-lists of nominees from which the Prime Minister would choose one-half of the future appointees.

[104] The *"Bundesrat* model," first discussed by academics in the 1960s, was subsequently endorsed by some provincial governments and other public bodies. See, among others: Canadian Bar Association, *Towards A New Canada* (Ottawa: Canadian Bar Association, 1978); Government of British Columbia, *Reform of the Senate: Paper 3: British Columbia's Constitutional Proposals* (Victoria: Government of British Columbia, 1978).

When the Constitution of Canada was patriated in 1982, the Senate's powers were left virtually intact with one important exception. Today, the Senate acting alone can block legislation on Senate reform for 180 days. After that time a constitutional amendment regarding the Senate can be made without its approval.

The January 1984 Report of the Special Joint Committee on Senate Reform recommended that Senators be directly elected by the citizens of Canada in order to give it legitimacy.[105] It also proposed amendments to the traditional powers of the Senate. In particular, it suggested that the present absolute veto be replaced by a suspensory veto of up to 120 days by which legislation passed by the House of Commons could be delayed but not rejected outright. Only on legislation of linguistic significance would the absolute veto power be retained. The Report argued that, while this may represent a diminution of the formal powers of the upper house, Senators might be more willing to exercise lesser powers in exchange for playing a more effective role in the legislative process. Other proposals — a suggestion that no more Cabinet ministers be recruited from the Senate, for example — might weaken the ability of the upper house to scrutinize the work of government. And the proposed direct election of Senators for a non-renewable term of nine years would do little to enhance the accountability of Senators: since they could not seek re-election, there would be no mechanism by which they could be held responsible by the electorate.

In the 1990s, a western initiative for a new "Triple E" Senate became prominent among the reform proposals. The desire for a Senate that would be *elected, effective* and *equal* for all provinces received the support of the smaller provinces. They favoured the idea of an equal number of Senators from each province, regardless of its size or population base. In the early deliberations, larger provinces tended to support the idea of a "Double E" Senate — one that would be *elected* and *effective* in its functioning but whose membership would be based on some principle of representation by population.

During the 1987 impasse over Senate reform, Prime Minister Mulroney gave a political commitment that until there was a comprehensive constitutional change concerning the Senate, he would nominate Senators only from lists supplied to him from provincial governments. This commitment was given in order to obtain a consensus over the Meech Lake accord. This practice had no constitutional authority, however, and quickly evaporated after Meech Lake died. Stan Waters from Alberta was the only *elected* Senator to be appointed under these rules.

Finally, in 1992, another constitutional package known as the Charlottetown accord was agreed upon by federal and provincial leaders and their assemblies. It proposed a modified "Triple E" Senate, with special guarantees for Québec representation in the House of Commons. Under Charlottetown there would have been 62 Senators — six from each province and one from each territory. Except in Québec, where they would have been appointed by the National Assembly, the Senators would have been elected directly by the people. The details of this proposal and the story of its defeat in the October 1992 referendum are discussed in Chapters 5 and 11. Suffice it to say here that the defeat of the Charlottetown accord left Canada with the same method of selecting Senators and with the same senatorial powers as described above in this chapter.

---

[105] Special Joint Committee of the Senate and of the House of Commons on Senate Reform, *Report* (Ottawa: Queen's Printer, 1984). For the author's more detailed views on Senate reform, see Robert J. Jackson, "Remarks to the Special Joint Committee of the Senate and of the House of Commons on Senate Reform," June 23, 1983.

And so the debate continues.[106] While the internal organization and procedures of the Senate have evolved over the last three decades, and one minor adjustment has been made to Senate tenure, the objectives of Senate reform have changed, perhaps rendering the task more difficult. The principle of producing an effective second chamber has largely been abandoned in favour of creating an institution valued more for its symbolic contribution to Canadian unity and maintenance of the federal system than for its role in the legislative process. However, as long as federal/provincial wrangling over the *Constitution* continues, and until an accepted means of amendment can be found, the Senate will maintain its role as a usually cooperative, sometimes cantankerous, but invariably dignified part of the legislative process. And as long as the Senate continues, so too will demands for its reform or abolition.

OVERVIEW

Throughout this chapter we have used the twin concepts of *power* and *symbolism* as reference points in describing the various roles performed by the two chambers of the Canadian Parliament and as an organizing device to evaluate certain proposals or directions for future reform. But we have also stressed that these two concepts are not mutually exclusive. In a relatively open society such as Canada, where the activities of Parliament and its members are subjected to fierce, often critical, scrutiny by the mass media, only a legislative body that is perceived to be powerful will be able to maintain sufficient legitimacy to fulfill its symbolic roles. Reform designs must therefore maintain the delicate balance between power and symbolism if Parliament is to continue to fulfill the many functions demanded of it as a key institution linking citizens with their federal government. Proposals that threaten to upset this balance are effectively doomed to failure.

Thus, for example, demands that Parliament be made more powerful like the American Congress or the West German *Bundestag*, must take into account the fact that the Canadian legislature performs different roles. In the United States, members of Congress are perceived to be more influential because they are relatively independent of party ties: but Congress does not have the same importance in sustaining the political executive in office and legitimizing its policies. Hence, any attempt to reduce the level of discipline in the Canadian House of Commons must be accompanied by a careful reconsideration of the concept of government responsibility, which is based currently on the assumption of cohesive party behaviour.

Similarly, the German *Bundestag* is perceived to be influential in part because much of its work is carried out by parliamentary committees working in relative isolation from media and public scrutiny: but debates in the legislative chamber itself are often quite stilted and boring affairs, since most issues have already been decided elsewhere. The Canadian House of Commons could grant increased powers and delegate much heavier workloads to committees, but only at the risk of reducing the current importance of plenary sessions to the House both as a forum for debate and as a place where the business of government and opposition is *seen* to be done.

---

[106] See Robert J. Jackson, "Reforming an Unreformed and Unreformable Senate," remarks to the Senate and staff, March 29, 1993 and published by the Senate.

The same delicate balance between power and symbolism must also appear in attempts to reform the upper house. Admittedly, the Senate as currently constituted has rather more formal power than legitimacy in the eyes of most Canadians. But many of the reform designs would tilt the balance too far the other way. The proposed "House of the Federation," for example, would almost certainly have a constantly shifting membership, which would undermine many of the traditional strengths of the upper house such as the expertise and parliamentary skills accumulated by experience in the legislature. Under this scheme, the upper house would become an empty shell, full of short-term symbolism, but lacking any real political clout. Some actual and proposed reforms do manage to maintain the balance of power and symbolism. The McGrath reforms increased the influence of backbench members and strengthened the investigative and policy-making roles of the House of Commons while enhancing the representative and symbolic functions of the legislature. It is not always so easy to kill two birds with one stone. However, more comprehensive reform packages can be designed to take into account both the need to strengthen Parliament and the requirement that it continue to serve as the representative and symbolic cornerstone of the governmental process. As society continually evolves in complexity, as the state plays an ever-expanding role in the lives of its citizens, as technological advances provide new links between government and the people, Parliament is struggling to keep up. If Parliament is to maintain its status as the most important institution in Canadian political life, it must evolve too, adjusting both its internal procedures and its external relations with other political actors.

SELECTED BIBLIOGRAPHY

Aiken, Gordon, *The Backbencher* (Toronto: McClelland & Stewart, 1974).

Aucoin, Peter, ed., *Institutional Reforms for Representative Government*, vol. 38, Royal Commission on the Economic Union and Development Prospects for Canada (Toronto: University of Toronto Press, 1985).

Beauchesne, A., *Rules and Forms of the House of Commons*, 5th ed. (Toronto: Carswell, 1978).

Bourinot, J.G., *Parliamentary Procedure and Practice in the Dominion of Canada*, 3rd ed. (Toronto: Canada Law Book Co., 1903).

Campbell, Colin, *The Canadian Senate: A Lobby from Within* (Toronto: Macmillan Canada, 1978).

Clarke, Harold D., Colin Campbell, F.Q. Quo and Arthur Goddard, eds., *Parliament, Policy and Representation* (Toronto: Methuen, 1980).

Courtney, J.C., ed., *The Canadian House of Commons: Essays in Honour of Norman Ward* (Calgary: University of Calgary Press, 1985).

d'Aquino, Thomas, G. Bruce Doern and Cassandra Blair, *Parliamentary Democracy in Canada: Issues for Reform* (Toronto: Methuen, 1983).

Dawson, William F., *Procedure in the Canadian House of Commons* (Toronto: University of Toronto Press, 1962).

Eagles, Munroe et al., *The Almanac of Canadian Politics* (Peterborough: Broadview, 1991).

Fife, Robert and John Warren, *A Capital Scandal* (Toronto: Key Porter, 1991).

Fleming, R.J., *Canadian Legislatures* (Ottawa: Ampersand, 1988).

Franks, C.E.S., *The Parliament of Canada* (Toronto: University of Toronto Press, 1987).

Gunther, J. and C. Winn, eds., *House of Commons Reform* (Ottawa; Parliamentary Internship Programme, 1991).

Head, Andrew, *Canadian Constitutional Conventions* (Toronto: Oxford University Press, 1991).

House of Commons, *Précis of Procedure*, 2nd ed. (Ottawa: Clerk of the House of Commons, 1987).

House of Commons, *Standing Orders* (Ottawa: Supply and Services, November 1988).

Jackson, Robert J. and Michael M. Atkinson, *The Canadian Legislative System*, 2nd rev. ed. (Toronto: Macmillan Canada, 1980).

Kornberg, Allan and William Mischler, *Influence in Parliament* (Durham N.C.: Duke University Press, 1976).

Kunz, F.A. *The Modern Senate of Canada* (Toronto: University of Toronto Press, 1965).

Lees, J.D. and M. Shaw, eds., *Committees in Legislatures* (Durham, N.C.: Duke, 1976).

Lijphart, A., ed., *Parliamentary versus Presidential Government* (Oxford: Oxford University Press, 1992).

Mackay, R.A., *The Unreformed Senate of Canada* (Toronto: McClelland & Stewart, 1967).

March, Roman, *The Myth of Parliament* (Scarborough, Ont.: Prentice-Hall, 1974).

Mezey, Michael M., *Comparative Legislatures* (Durham N.C.: Duke University Press, 1979).

Neilson, William A.W. and James C. MacPherson, eds., *The Legislative Process in Canada: The Need for Reform* (Montreal: IRPP, 1978).

Olson, David M., *The Legislative Process: A Comparative Perspective* (New York: Harper & Row, 1980).

Robertson, G. A., *House Divided: Meech Lake, Senate Reform and the Canadian Union* (Halifax: IRPP, 1989).

Stewart, J., *The Canadian House of Commons* (Montreal: McGill-Queen's University Press, 1977).

Taras, D., ed., *Parliament and Canadian Foreign Policy* (Toronto: CIIA, 1985).

Special Issue on "Legislatures in Canada," *Legislative Studies Quarterly*, vol. 3, no. 4 (November 1978).

Special Issue on "Responsible Government Reconsidered," *Journal of Canadian Studies*, vol. 14, no. 2 (Summer 1979).

See also the periodicals, *Canadian Parliamentary Review* and *Parliamentary Government*.

BUREAUCRACY AND DEMOCRACY

PUBLIC SERVANTS, BUDGETS AND CONTROLS

In Canada, as in most democratic societies, there is a distinction between transient politicians, who come and go, and permanent administrators who carry out the goals and purposes of their political masters. Constitutionally, the elected executive of the federal government is responsible for formulating policies. The administrative process of implementing those policies is entrusted to permanent state officials employed by the departments, agencies and Crown corporations that constitute the federal bureaucracy.

In the modern state, however, the traditional dichotomy between "politics" and "administration" is not as clear as it once appeared. First, the vastly expanded scope and complexity of contemporary public policy have rendered politicians increasingly dependent upon permanent administrators for information, advice and execution of government policy. Furthermore, as noted in Chapter 8, Parliament has delegated to the bureaucracy substantial decision-making autonomy in many areas of technical policy-making in the fields of regulation and administrative procedure. Fears have consequently been expressed about the increasingly "political" role of the bureaucracy and about a perceived lack of bureaucratic accountability in many areas of government policy-making.

At the same time, expansion of the responsibilities and activities of the Canadian government has effected a commensurate growth in the size and scope of public administration. The sheer size and complexity of the bureaucratic leviathan give cause for concern. As well, administrative secrecy, the apparent impenetrability of bureaucratic processes and lack of open accountability have been cited as threats to responsible, democratic government.

In this chapter, the primary focus is on the machinery and budgets of the Canadian government and on the major issues relating to the efficient implementation of government policy. However, since it is not easy to separate the administrative process of policy implementation from the political process of policy formulation, it is impossible to ignore the controversies surrounding the role of bureaucracy and the influence of public servants in Canadian politics.

WHAT IS BUREAUCRACY?

For centuries, political rulers have relied on permanent officials to carry out the routine tasks of administering government policies. From tax collectors and magistrates of old to modern government departments, public administration is as old and ubiquitous as government itself.

Bureaucracy, on the other hand, is a relatively new and more limited phenomenon. The term originated as a satirical combination of the French *bureau* (desk) and the Greek *kratein* (to rule), on the analogy of "democracy" and "aristocracy."[1] In popular parlance, it has come to signify depersonalization, inefficiency and inflexibility. But, while anyone who has encountered bureaucratic "red tape" may feel such characterizations are appropriate, these organizations are central to the effective management of modern life.

Similarly, bureaucrats, who comprise and carry out the functions of bureaucracies, are regularly condemned as overpaid, under-employed, inefficient and self-serving.[2] They are the objects of numerous anecdotes and popular jokes. Witness this quip by the Honourable Member from Kicking Horse Pass (alias Dave Broadfoot of the Royal Canadian Air Farce):

> Q: *"How many civil servants does it take to screw in a light-bulb?"*
> A: *"One, but he's been promoted three levels by the time it's all screwed up."*[3]

Yet Canadians turn to public servants to solve the toughest of problems on society's behalf. Politicians routinely run for office on promises of reducing bureaucracy, then discover that they cannot do without its officials.

THE CONCEPT OF BUREAUCRACY

The term **bureaucracy** may be applied to complex organizational forms in a variety of contexts — business corporations, churches, political structures such as party organizations, among others. But the term is most clearly and most often identified in people's minds with the administrative machinery of government. The size of contemporary states and the myriad of governmental responsibilities entailed in the management of modern societies necessitate complex structures that can routinize the administrative decision-making process.

The starting point for most studies of bureaucracy is the "ideal-typical" bureaucratic organization formalized by the German social scientist Max Weber. His ideal-typical bureaucracy was to be characterized by

1. the specialization of official duties;
2. the hierarchical organization of authority;
3. operations governed by a consistent application of abstract rules to particular cases;
4. impersonal detachment toward subordinates and clients;
5. employment based on merit and protection from arbitrary dismissal; and
6. maximization of technical and organizational efficiency.[4]

---

1   Florence Elliott, *A Dictionary of Politics*, 7th ed. (Hardmondsworth: Penguin Books, 1973), p. 71.

2   For an overview and examples of the widespread negative attitudes to bureaucracy, see Robert F. Adie and Paul G. Thomas, *Canadian Public Administration: Problematic Perspectives*, 2nd ed. (Scarborough, Ont.: Prentice-Hall, 1987).

3   From the Royal Canadian Air Farce recording, *Air Farce Live* (CBC Enterprises, 1983).

4   Summarized by Peter M. Blau, *Bureaucracy in Modern Society* (New York: Random House, 1956), pp. 28–31, passim. See also Max Weber, *The Theory of Social and Economic Organization*, ed. and trans. by A.M. Henderson and Talcott Parsons (Glencoe: Free Press, 1947), pp. 329–41.

In theory, organizations adopting the characteristics of Weber's model would maximize administrative efficiency and the rationalization of social activity. In reality, however, no bureaucracy conforms exactly to this ideal type: indeed, the concept of ideal-type implies a near-perfect standard against which examples in the observable world can be evaluated. Nonetheless, all these characteristics are found to some extent in Canadian federal administrative structures and, as Weber predicted, they have developed partly as a result of "the increasing complexity of civilization," which encourages bureaucratization.[5]

Many characteristics of bureaucracy developed as a consequence of the emergence of democratic forms of government. As the idea of alternation of power between competing parties became accepted under the doctrines of parliamentary democracy and representative government, it became necessary to separate the bureaucracy from the political executive. The bureaucracy has thus been able to maximize rational administration free from political concerns, and individual public servants are protected from arbitrary dismissal on political grounds (e.g., when government changes hands) as long as they maintain partisan neutrality.

The development of liberal democracy also saw demands for the substitution of *merit* for patronage as the primary method of recruitment to government service and promotion within it. Appointments to administrative office were once made on the basis of family and "old school tie" networks or as a reward for political services rendered. Democratization of the public service brought a merit system involving open competition.

Finally, certain characteristics of bureaucracy identified by Weber — the making of decisions through "the constant application of abstract rules to particular cases" and the display by bureaucrats of "impersonal detachment toward...clients" — enhance administrative efficiency by routinizing the decision-making process. They are also democratic inasmuch as they protect individuals from arbitrary decisions and ensure that all clients are treated equally. Where there may once have been one law for the rich and another for the poor, operations of the ideal-type bureaucracy apply the same rules to all citizens.

Thus, a neutral, professional public service based on the organizational principles of modern bureaucracy has emerged alongside, and partly as a consequence of, the development of liberal democracy. Yet a fundamental contradiction exists in the coexistence of bureaucracy and democracy in a society such as Canada.

BUREAUCRACY VERSUS DEMOCRACY

Bureaucratic and democratic structures are, in part, founded upon different organizing principles: bureaucracy is based primarily on a clearly defined hierarchy of authority established in the interests of efficiency; democracy is based on the principle of fundamental political equality that permits majority rule while respecting minority rights and freedom of dissent. But, as Peter Blau points out, democratic values also demand that social goals be implemented by the most effective means available so that the "will of the majority" may be seen to be done. Effective methods, suggests Blau, are more likely to be governed by the dictates of bureaucracy than by those of democracy.[6] Since bureaucratic efficiency is aided by the routinization of decision-making, the quest for effective implementation may result in

---

[5]   H.H. Gerth and C. Wright Mills, eds. and trans., *From Max Weber: Essays in Sociology* (New York: Oxford University Press, 1946), p. 212.

[6]   Blau, *Bureaucracy in Modern Society*, pp. 106–107.

uniform standards that reflect the will of the majority but neglect minority interest. In a country like Canada, where minority ethnic, linguistic and regional interests are particularly sensitive, the result may be the exacerbation of potential conflicts and a loss of legitimacy for both the bureaucracy and the entire policy-making process.

This problem has become particularly acute in the modern era, since many areas of government policy are now so complex that the means of implementing public policies are often as important to their outcomes as the choice of goals. Therefore, it is becoming increasingly difficult to maintain the distinction between administrative and political processes.

We have pointed out that in Canada, ultimate decision-making power in many fields resides constitutionally with the federal government; the bureaucracy is designated as the neutral, professional administrator of policy. But in practice it is difficult to separate the political and administrative dimensions of government action. While not political per se, the bureaucracy does influence the actual formation of public policy in a number of ways.

First, Cabinet ministers who are formally responsible for defining public policies rarely enjoy sufficient tenure to permit the acquisition of a high degree of expertise in the affairs of their respective ministries. Not only does government occasionally change hands at general elections, but there are also periodic Cabinet shuffles in which ministers are moved from department to department and hence from one policy area to another. Each time this occurs, it takes a while for a minister to come to grips with a new role. Since the average departmental tenure of Canadian Cabinet ministers has been very short, it is clear that the average federal minister spends considerable time learning the workings of the department.

In contrast, the permanence of public servants allows them to develop expertise and practical knowledge on which politicians can draw in formulating policies. Consequently, if, as Max Weber maintained, "knowledge is power,"[7] then the bureaucracy in a complex, technical society may have great political power. It may screen the data furnished to its political masters, and such filtered information may be fundamental to the direction of government policy.

The relative permanence and access to information enjoyed by bureaucrats may influence the policy process in a number of other ways as well. Bureaucratic tenure permits public servants to develop a more long-term view of policy formulation than is possible for politicians, who must be more responsive to short-term shifts in public opinion. Also, administrative personnel who have close links with "client" interest groups may be in a better position than politicians to identify certain public needs.

Furthermore, the bureaucracy (or its components) may constitute an "interest group" in its own right.[8] Policy proposals generated within the bureaucracy may influence the government's choice among competing alternatives. Most government departments contain a policy analysis unit that monitors and evaluates the impact of ongoing policies. Here again bureaucrats may be in a better position than politicians to recommend fine-tuning of, or wholesale changes in, existing policies. Finally, even after a political choice has been made by the government, a degree of discretion has to be left to public servants with regard to policy implementation.

The bureaucracy therefore has numerous opportunities to influence the policy-making process in Canada. But why should the bureaucracy, and especially its expanded role in the

---

[7]   Gerth and Wright Mills, *From Max Weber*, pp. 232–35.

[8]   See the discussion in Chapter 13 on public policy theory.

policy-making process, be viewed as a threat to democracy? Critics propose several arguments.

First, they allege that the bureaucracy is unrepresentative of the general public and therefore is not sensitive to the requirements of citizens. Minority groups and interests that are not adequately represented within the bureaucracy may be neglected.

A second, related argument is that the bureaucracy is steered by a narrow and cohesive elite that seeks to impose its own vision of society and the role of the state on the rest of the country. This argument is sometimes linked to "elite" or "class" theories of politics, which posit that the elitist family and educational backgrounds of bureaucrats render them sympathetic to the interest of friends, relatives and former business colleagues and the upper class.[9]

Third, the growth of the state, the rise in public expenditures, tax increases and escalating budgetary deficits incurred by most western governments are all blamed upon the expansionary tendencies of bureaucracy and the "empire-building" of individual bureaucrats.[10] Supporters of this argument aver that new government programs serve the interests of administrators rather than those of the general public. Furthermore, critics allege that bureaucratic inefficiency wastes economic resources and demand that measures be initiated to increase financial accountability and bureaucratic efficiency.

Fourth, arguments about the lack of financial accountability are often extended to more general criticisms of the lack of popular, parliamentary or governmental control over the bureaucracy. Politicians may be held accountable through the ballot box: if they have not adequately served the needs of the public then they may be removed at the next election. However, there are no such mechanisms by which permanent public servants may be held accountable. For this reason, too, critics regard bureaucracy as inimical to the democratic process.

In later sections of this chapter, we examine various aspects of the bureaucracy and the administrative process in Canada in relation to these arguments. But first it should be noted that most critics of bureaucracy tend to view it as an undifferentiated, monolithic monster. Nothing could be further from the truth. The Canadian administrative apparatus is a complex hierarchy of different types of government departments, Crown corporations, agencies and other bodies serving a wide range of functions. The next section provides a brief guide to the major structures of the administrative apparatus and their respective roles and responsibilities.

STRUCTURES OF THE FEDERAL BUREAUCRACY

The two formal structures of government with which Canadians most frequently come into contact are government departments and Crown corporations (or public enterprises). Few citizens escape encounters — some pleasant, some less so — with institutions such as the Department of National Revenue that collects taxes and customs duties. Its employees may embarrass us by searching our luggage for contraband at the airport; but it may also provide a welcome tax rebate. Most Canadians deal with Crown corporations every day, for example, by watching CBC television.

---

9   See, for example, Ralph Miliband, *The State in Capitalist Society* (London: Weidenfeld & Nicholson, 1969), ch. 5, esp. p. 111.

10   See, for example, Thomas E. Borcherding, ed., *Budgets and Bureaucrats: The Sources of Government Growth* (Durham, N.C.: Duke University Press, 1977).

But departmental officials and public enterprises that interact directly with the public are merely the most visible tip of the administrative iceberg. Three basic organizational forms are found in the Canadian federal bureaucracy: departments, Crown agencies and advisory bodies. Government **departments** are each headed by a Cabinet minister and are largely responsible for the administration of programs serving the public (e.g., Transport) or for the provision of services to the government itself (e.g., Supply and Services). **Crown agencies** include public enterprises (e.g., Canadian National North America) and regulatory commissions (e.g., the Atomic Energy Control Board). **Advisory bodies** consist of Royal Commissions, government and departmental task forces and a range of advisory councils that collectively provide alternative sources of research and advice for the political executive.

Because of their special role in the policy process and their often exaggerated elite status, it is possible to classify **central agencies** (introduced in Chapter 7) as a fourth type of bureaucratic organization. However, with the exception of the Prime Minister's Office (PMO), these agencies are staffed almost exclusively by career public servants appointed under the aegis of the Public Service Commission. They are all formally headed by a Cabinet minister and in all structural and legal respects closely resemble the departmental form of organization. For the purposes of this discussion, therefore, central agencies are viewed as a sub-category of government departments.

FEDERAL DEPARTMENTS

According to J.E. Hodgetts, a department is "an administrative unit comprising one or more organizational components over which a minister has direct management and control."[11] Each government department is created by a statute, which outlines generally the reason for the department's creation and its administrative duties. However, the *Transfer of Duties Act* of 1918 allows the government considerable latitude in altering internal structures and re-allocating departmental responsibilities.

The growing complexity of the institutional structures of government has been accompanied by an increase in the number of federal departments. In the years following Confederation, the work of the federal government was carried out by only 13 ministries. The titles and duties of these first departments reflected what were then perceived to be the dominant functions of the federal government: the maintenance of law, order and security (Justice, Militia and Defence); the coordination of government policy and service (Privy Council, Secretary of State, Secretary of State for Provinces, Finance, Receiver General, Customs, Inland Revenue); and the provision of communications networks and some limited encouragement to economic development (Public Works, Post Office, Agriculture, Marine and Fisheries). Most of these have survived to the present day, albeit with many alterations and additions to their duties and functions. But a few have disappeared, for example the Post Office Department, which was transformed into Canada Post, a Crown corporation, in 1981.

New responsibilities acquired by the federal government were often added to the duties of existing departments, until the latter became so unwieldy that reorganization was imperative. The major expansion in the number of departments occurred between 1966 and 1971, in part reflecting the continuing growth of state activities in the postwar period. But

---

[11]   J.E. Hodgetts, *The Canadian Public Service: A Physiology of Government 1867–70* (Toronto: University of Toronto Press, 1973), p. 89.

it was also a product of attempts by Prime Ministers Pearson and Trudeau to modernize the policy-making process. This five-year period witnessed the establishment of the Treasury Board (formally separated from the Department of Finance in 1966), Manpower and Immigration (1966), Consumer and Corporate Affairs (1967), Communications (1968) and Energy, Mines and Resources (1970). Lastly, 1971 saw the emergence of a new type of department, the **ministry of state**. The Ministries of State for Urban Affairs (MSUA) and for Science and Technology (MOSST) were created to provide research, information and policy planning and to encourage the coordination of policies and programs administered by other departments concerning these issue areas.[12]

The process of reorganizing existing departments, creating new ones and juggling their responsibilities continued. In 1978 the Urban Affairs ministry disappeared. As part of the new Policy Expenditure Management System (PEMS), a Ministry of State for Economic Development (MSED) and the Ministry of State for Social Development (MSSD) were established in December 1978 and June 1980 respectively. Like their predecessors, they were intended to be small departments aiding the coordination of other departments' efforts. But unlike the earlier versions, the two new ministries of state had genuine budgetary clout. In addition to their policy development roles, they also acted as "quasi-central agencies," providing advice and support to Cabinet committees. These new ministries were disbanded in 1984.

Meanwhile, other changes had occurred. We have already noted the transformation of Canada Post from a government department into a Crown corporation in 1981. In the same year, the government merged parts of the Department of Regional Economic Expansion (DREE) and of Industry, Trade and Commerce (IT&C) into a new Department of Regional and Industrial Expansion (DRIE); the "trade" component of IT&C was transferred to the Department of External Affairs. And so the process continues. Sometimes new departments are created or duties are shuffled among existing departments in the interest of policy-making effectiveness and administrative efficiency. But, on occasion, political and symbolic motivations prevail in that the reorganization of departments is designed to display the government's sensitivity to particular problems or to the concerns of special interest groups.[13]

At the end of Mulroney's tenure in 1993 there were 32 government departments and agencies as defined in the 1993–94 budgetary estimates. Table 9.1 presents a typology that divides these departments into three major categories — Vertical "Line" or "Constituency," Horizontal "Administrative Coordinative" and Horizontal "Policy Coordinative" — on the basis of their major functions and the clienteles whom they serve.[14]

---

[12] On the origins and rationales of the new ministries of state, see Peter Aucoin and Richard French, *Knowledge, Power and Public Policy* (Ottawa: Science Council of Canada, 1974).

[13] Sometimes, rather than creating a new department, Prime Ministers have appointed Ministers of State with special responsibilities within an existing department — for example, the Minister of State for Small Business and Tourism, the Minister of State for Multiculturalism and Citizenship, the Minister of State for Forestry, the Minister of State for Grains and Oil Seeds, the Minister of State for Privatization and Regulatory Affairs, the Minister of State for Seniors and the Minister of State for Housing.

[14] Our typology of government departments is an adaptation of an approach to classifying ministerial portfolios first suggested by G. Bruce Doern, "Horizontal and Vertical Portfolios in Government," in G. Bruce Doern and V. Wilson, eds., *Issues in Canadian Public Policy* (Toronto: Macmillan Canada, 1974), pp. 310–36.

TABLE 9.1   FEDERAL GOVERNMENT DEPARTMENTS AND AGENCIES, UNTIL 1993

Vertical "Line" or "Constituency Coordinative" Departments	Horizontal "Administrative Coordinative" Departments	Central Agencies	Horizontal "Policy" Departments
Agriculture	National Revenue	Finance	External Affairs
Atlantic Canada	Public Works	Privy Council Office	Justice
Opportunity Agency	Supply and Services	Treasury Board Secretariat	
Communications	Public Service Commission	*Federal-Provincial	
Consumer and		Relations Office	
Corporate Affairs		*Prime Minister's Office	
Employment and			
Immigration			
Energy, Mines			
and Resources			
Environment			
Fisheries and Oceans			
Forestry			
Indian Affairs and			
Northern Development			
Industry, Science &			
Technology			
Labour			
National Defence			
National Health			
and Welfare			
Secretary of State			
Solicitor General			
Transport			
Veterans' Affairs			
Western Economic			
Diversification			

*Agencies that serve as functional equivalents to departments but that are not recognized as government departments in standard, legal or financial terms.

Of the 32 departments and agencies, most may be classified as **Vertical "Constituency"** departments, those ministries whose primary function is the provision of services directly to the general public (e.g., National Health and Welfare, Transport) or to some particular constituency or clientele (e.g., Indian Affairs). These departments are described as "vertical" because they represent direct links between government and citizens, while the two "horizontal" categories primarily serve the government. Often, constituency departments are also referred to as "line" or "program-oriented" ministries since their administrative structures are chiefly geared toward a kind of assembly-line delivery of programs or services to Canadian citizens.

The second category, **Horizontal "Administrative Coordinative"** departments, are those ministries whose main function is providing services to other departments or to the entire governmental structure. Duties performed by these departments include the collection of taxes and other government revenues by Revenue Canada; management of the government's real estate and office buildings by Public Works; and the wide variety of financial, management, consulting, purchasing, printing and publishing services provided to government agencies by the twin administrative structures under the Minister of Supply and Services.

The chief roles of the third group, **Horizontal "Policy Coordinative"** departments, consist of developing a broader policy framework within which other governmental functions are carried out and of coordinating policies and programs across all departments, rather than administering services to the public or to the government itself. Thus, in addition to the Department of Finance and other central agencies such as the Privy Council Office (PCO) and Treasury Board Secretariat, policy coordinative departments include the Departments of External Affairs and Justice that provide respectively the foreign policy and legal frameworks for the program and policy activities of other departments.

In June 1993, the new Prime Minister, Kim Campbell, announced what she called "The most significant downsizing and restructuring of government ever undertaken in Canada."[15] The number of departments was reduced from 32 to 23. Eight new departments were created or fundamentally redesigned, three received new mandates and 15 were merged or broken up. One central agency, FPRO, was merged into PCO.

Some of these massive changes will require legislation but the government outlined what the public service would look like when completed (see Table 9.2). These changes were only partially implemented before the 1993 election during which the leader of the Liberal Party, Jean Chrétien, announced that most but not all of the innovations would go ahead if he won the election. In particular, he said the ministry of Public Security would revert to the ministry of the Solicitor General.

TABLE 9.2   CONSERVATIVE GOVERNMENT PROPOSED DEPARTMENTAL AND AGENCY
STRUCTURE OF THE PUBLIC SERVICE, 1993

	Departments	**Central Agencies**
Former, Remaining	Dept. of Agriculture & Agrifood Finance Fisheries & Oceans External Affairs and International Trade* Environment Justice Transport Indian Affairs & Northern Development National Defence Veterans' Affairs Atlantic Canada Opportunities Agency Western Economic Diversification Federal Office of Regional Development — Québec	Privy Council Office Treasury Board Secretariat
Additional	Human Resources & Labour Canadian Heritage Public Security* Industry and Science National Resources National Revenue Government Services Health	

*These changes were put in place by a dying Conservative government in 1993. However, the Liberals decided that Public Security would revert to the Ministry of the Solicitor General and that the immigration components would be sent back to the Department of Citizenship and Immigration. They also gave notice of introducing legislation to rename the Department of External Affairs the Department of Foreign Affairs and International Trade.

[15] Office of the Prime Minister, *Press Release*, June 25, 1993.

The primary function of a government department is a key determinant of its internal structure. Each department is headed by a Cabinet Minister. But while the minister is politically responsible for the activities of the department and for formulating general policy, the administrative and managerial head of each ministry is its senior public servant, the Deputy Minister or DM.[16] The Deputy Minister is at the apex of a pyramidal structure of authority and organizational agencies. Two or more Assistant Deputy Ministers (ADMs), heading branches or bureaus, report directly to the DM. Below the ADMs are directorates or branches, each headed by a Director General or Director. These directorates are in turn composed of divisions, headed by Directors or Divisional Chiefs; the divisions are further broken down into sections, offices and units. The exact titles of departmental subunits and their respective senior officials vary from department to department.

The number of senior officials, and the range of sub-units and employees for which they are responsible, differ according to the type of department. Vertical Constituency or Line departments generally consist of a large number of sub-units and employ more staff to deal with the general public. Agriculture Canada, for instance, employs several thousand people across the country. The Administrative Coordinative ministries also tend to be large, complex structures. However, the Policy coordinative departments, with the exception of External Affairs, are generally much smaller and have more simplified organizational forms, in part because they have few, if any, program- or service-delivery functions.

CROWN AGENCIES

The second basic organizational form in the federal bureaucracy is the Crown agency. This category includes a wide variety of non-departmental organizations including Crown corporations, regulatory agencies, administrative tribunals and, strictly speaking, some of the advisory bodies discussed separately below. The rationale for distinguishing the latter from Crown agencies is that they are primarily involved in the process of policy formulation, while Crown agencies are charged directly with attaining government policy objectives — through public ownership, regulation of the private sector and so on. Depending on the definition employed, there are approximately 400 federal Crown agencies.[17] A number of characteristics serve to distinguish Crown agencies from government departments. A.M. Willms identified four of the persisting differences:

1. Departments are answerable directly to a Cabinet minister and that minister takes responsibility for their actions. Agencies usually have a minister designated to them through whom they report to Parliament but the degree of supervision and accountability varies and is much smaller than that with departments....

2. Departments are all subject to the estimates system of budgeting, that is, revenues coming from the Crown must be spent exactly as directed by Parliament and Treasury Board. Agencies vary widely in their budget practices.

3. The personnel of departments are generally recruited by the Public Service Commission and their promotion and transfer is closely supervised by the

---

[16] Formerly, in departments where the minister's official designation was "Secretary of State for...," as in "Secretary of State for External Affairs," the senior public servant was known as the "Undersecretary of State..." rather than the "Deputy Minister."

[17] According to the Lambert Commission, "as of January 1979 the official count was 426." Royal Commission on Financial Management, *Final Report* (Ottawa: Supply and Services, 1979), p. 277.

Commission. Only a few of the agencies recruit through the Public Service Commission. Generally speaking they are responsible for their own personnel matters.

4. Departments have deputy ministers as the administrative heads while agencies vary widely in the nature of their management. Some have boards of directors, others have chairmen, commissioners, or directors.[18]

Many observers are concerned about the independence and perceived non-accountability of Crown agencies. J.E. Hodgetts labelled them "structural heretics" within the Canadian political system because of their non-departmental form, and argued that to varying degrees they do "violence to the constituted form of ministerial responsibility."[19] It is too easy for ministers to disclaim responsibility for the functioning of agencies nominally under their jurisdiction, by stating that "this is a matter involving an independent agency and one can only answer in so far as the agency sees fit to provide one with the information."[20]

Despite such concerns, a number of formal mechanisms do exist by which Parliament and Cabinet can seek to control these quasi-independent agencies. Many of their statutes require them to respond to ministerial or Cabinet policy directives. Cabinet may appoint and dismiss top management and board members and determine the number of years an appointee may serve. In addition, a degree of financial control is exercised: at least part of most agencies' proposed spending is subject to parliamentary scrutiny in the estimates process. Furthermore, agencies are subject to audit by the Auditor General who reports to Parliament and, usually, they must submit to Parliament an annual report that is automatically referred to the appropriate standing committee for investigation. Perhaps most important, all agencies ultimately receive their powers either from Orders-in-Council or from statutes, either of which may be amended or revoked by politicians if an agency abuses its independent status.

Thus, while much reform debate has revolved around the need to strengthen parliamentary and Cabinet control over the activities of Crown agencies, there have also been arguments in favour of reducing the extent of government intervention via the regulatory process and public ownership. Some of these ideas have received active political support. The Conservative government privatized a large number of Crown corporations between 1984 and 1993, including important bodies such as deHavilland, Canada Air, Teleglobe and Petro-Canada (see Chapter 13).

CROWN CORPORATIONS

According to John Langford, "a crown corporation is (or should be) a wholly owned, semi-autonomous agency of government organized under the corporate form to perform a task or group of related tasks in the national interest."[21] Despite the relative precision of this definition, the exact delineation of the universe of Crown corporations at the federal level is a difficult task. The usual starting place for defining and classifying these agencies is the *Financial Administration Act* (FAA), which sets out the financial relationship between different

---

[18] A.M. Willms, "Crown Agencies," in W.D.K. Kernaghan and A.M. Willms, eds., *Public Administration in Canada: Selected Readings*, 2nd ed. (Toronto: Methuen, 1971), p. 103.

[19] Hodgetts, *The Canadian Public Service*, p. 141 and ch. 7, passim.

[20] J.E. Hodgetts, "The Public Corporation in Canada," in J.E. Hodgetts and D.C. Corbett, eds., *Canadian Public Administration* (Toronto: Macmillan, 1960), p. 199.

[21] John Langford, "Crown Corporations as Instruments of Policy," in G.B. Doern and P. Aucoin, eds., *Public Policy in Canada; Organization, Process and Management* (Toronto; Macmillan, 1979), pp. 239–74.

Reproduced by permission, J. Beutel, New Brunswick.

types of Crown corporations and the federal government. The FAA classifies Crown corporations into three categories — "departmental," "agency" and "proprietory" — according to their main functions and degree of financial autonomy.

The variety of crown corporations is immense. The Bank of Canada regulates the money supply, the Royal Mint prints money and Canada Mortgage and Housing Corporation guarantees housing loans. Transportation Crown corporations include the Canadian National North America, Via Rail, Canada Ports Corporation and the St. Lawrence Seaway Authority. Economic development is fostered by the Canadian Saltfish Corporation, Canadian Wheat Board, Cape Breton Development Corporation, Export Development Corporation, Farm Credit Corporation and the Federal Development Bank. National integration is aided by the Canada Post Corporation, the Canadian Broadcasting Corporation and the National Film Board.

REGULATORY AGENCIES

Regulation is "the imposition of constraints, backed by government authority, that are intended to modify economic behaviour of individuals in the private sector significantly."[22] Regulation may be conducted through any of three mechanisms: **direct regulation**, in which constraints on behaviour are clearly specified in legislation, leaving little discretion to implementing authorities (usually government departments); **delegated self-regulation**, in which private actors such as the medical and legal professions or agricultural marketing boards are given substantial power to regulate their own activities, subject to certain conditions and **independent regulatory commissions**.[23] Our concern here is with the last of these, the independent regulatory agency or commission, another non-departmental structure or "structural heretic." A list of the important regulatory agencies would include the Atomic Energy Control Board, Canadian Labour Relations Board, Canadian Pension Commission, Canadian Radio-televison and Telecommunications Commission, Immigration and Refugee Board, Income Tax Appeal Board, National Energy Board, National Parole Board, National Transportation Authority and the Tariff Board.

---

22 Economic Council of Canada, *Interim Report: Responsible Regulation* (Ottawa: Minister of Supply and Services 1979), p. xi.

23 See Michael J. Trebilcock et al., *The Choice of Governing Instrument* (Ottawa: Minister of Supply and Services, 1982), pp. 88–92.

Among other functions, regulatory agencies may be required by government to influence private or corporate behaviour with respect to prices and tariffs, supply, market entry and conditions of service, product content and methods of production. In order to meet their objectives, agencies may be granted a variety of powers. Most agencies have quasi-judicial power, "that is, the power to judge specific cases involving the granting, denial or removal of licences, the approval of rates or fares and the censuring of failure to comply with terms of licences."[24] Furthermore, some agencies have developed quasi-legislative powers that permit them to formulate general rules applicable to all cases under consideration: an example is the "Canadian content" regulations applied by the Canadian Radio-television and Telecommunications Commission (CRTC). Most agencies also enjoy investigative powers allowing them to undertake research and pursue inquiries within their field of competence.

Independent regulatory agencies receive their major powers from enabling legislation that also sets out the agency objectives. Commission members are appointed by the governor-in-council, usually for fixed terms of from five to ten years. On the whole, the chair and members of the commission are patronage appointments. However, while most agencies are subject to ministerial directives, ministers usually are loathe to infringe upon the traditional arm's-length relationship. Regulatory bodies are required to submit their budgets to the Treasury Board (and usually, also, to the Auditor General) for review, and to present annual reports through the responsible minister to Parliament.

The autonomy enjoyed by many regulatory commissions — the consequence of broad mandates, tenure of office, lack of ministerial direction and often inadequate Parliamentary scrutiny — leads some observers to question whether these agencies always act in the public interest. The most prevalent such argument is the so-called "capture thesis" that suggests that regulatory bodies often end up serving the interests of the industries and firms they are supposed to regulate.

ADVISORY BODIES

Federal departments and Crown agencies are designed to deal primarily with the implementation and administration of government policies. There are other federal structures, however, whose activities are more closely related to the formulation of public policies. This third group, advisory bodies, comprises royal commissions, government and departmental task forces and advisory councils.[25]

Royal Commissions and task forces are widely employed as sources of public policy advice to the executive. They are generally asked to investigate an area of critical public concern and to issue a report recommending a suitable course of action. Typical issues in recent years have included the economy (the Macdonald Royal Commission on the Economic Union and Development Prospects for Canada), business and corporate policy (the Bryce Royal Commission on Corporate Concentration), cultural policy (the Applebaum-Hébert Federal Cultural Policy Review Committee), aboriginals (the Royal Commmission on Aboriginal Issues) and human reproduction (the Royal Commission on Reproductive Technologies).

Such bodies attempt to encourage wide public understanding of serious national problems and at the same time provide an informed basis for future policy-making by the

---

[24] Richard Schultz, "Regulatory Agencies," in M.S. Whittington and G. Williams, eds., *Canadian Politics in the 1980s*, 2nd ed. (Toronto: Methuen, 1984), p. 438.

[25] "Governmental" task forces should not be confused with the small Special Committees of the House of Commons, otherwise known as "Parliamentary Task Forces" described in Chapter 8.

government. Their investigations are carried out in part by soliciting outside views through public hearings and inviting individuals, groups and organizations to submit briefs. But they also initiate programs of directed and commissioned research.

ROYAL COMMISSIONS

Royal Commissions are established by the executive through an order-in-council under the *Public Inquiries Act*. There is no consistent policy governing the procedure of royal commissions, although a time limit is sometimes set for their report to the government. Royal commissions have some advantages over committees of Parliament, in that they are given their own budgets and may meet and travel when and where they wish. Governments are not legally bound to release commission reports, though it would generally be politically unwise not to do so. With few exceptions, the work of a commission is solely of an advisory nature and does not confer any power or responsibility regarding implementation of recommended policy. This characteristic is frequently cited as the greatest weakness of royal commissions. At the same time, it permits them the latitude to formulate progressive policy positions that are visionary yet could not possibly be legislated by the government under existing political conditions. Commission proposals are generally incorporated into government action as incremental policy change, the process having allowed the executive to sound out the limits of intended action.[26]

TASK FORCES

Some so-called "task forces," such as the Task Force on National Unity, are little more than a variation on the royal commission theme. They, too, are set up by order-in-council under the *Public Inquiries Act*. They usually do less extensive research than royal commissions, concentrating primarily on obtaining public input into the consultative process.[27] As ad hoc bodies, they suffer from the same problem as royal commissions in that, once their reports are published, no entity is empowered to force follow-up discussion in either Parliament or the mass media.

Other task forces are constituted on a less grandiose scale within the bureaucracy, consisting of representatives from a single department, from a number of ministries or from the public and private sectors. The rationales for employing these advisory bodies to tackle particular policy problems are that they require less staffing and funding than royal commissions and, most importantly, that they tend to produce results much more quickly.[28] Critics question the use of task forces rather than royal commissions because the former are more prone to interference from ministers and because there is no requirement for their reports to be made public. However, for quick responses in "trouble-shooting" situations, the flexibility of executive task forces gives them an advantage over the more formal, public and stately royal commissions.

ADVISORY COUNCILS

Frustration with the ad hoc, short-term work of royal commissions and task forces has caused the Canadian government to create a number of permanent advisory councils whose purpose is to study public policy questions, offer appropriate advice, monitor ongoing policies in their area of expertise and act as funding agencies. Thus, there are bodies such as the Canada Council and the National, Medical and Social Science and Humanities Research Councils. The Advisory Council for the Status of Women (ACSW) is charged with producing "recommendations to the

[26]   Vincent S. Wilson, "The Role of Royal Commissions and Task Forces," in G.B. Doern and P. Aucoin, eds., *The Structures of Policy-Making in Canada* (Toronto: Macmillan, 1971), pp. 119–20.

[27]   Doerr, *The Machinery of Government in Canada*, p. 151.

[28]   Wilson, "The Role of Royal Commissions and Task Forces," pp. 121–22.

Government on legislation on programs to improve the status of women; research on matters pertaining to the status of women in Canada; and publication of reports on areas of concern and an annual report on the progress being made in improving the status of women."[29] All advisory councils are given permanent research staffs to assist the full-time and part-time board members, who are appointed for fixed terms by the governor-in-council.

Most advisory groups representing specific constituencies or sub-groups of the population act as both government policy advisors and interest groups lobbying government departments on behalf of their respective clienteles. Consequently, they have to tread a fine line between being co-opted into the bureaucratic process and taking too independent a stance that might alienate them from access to government funding.

In 1992–93 the Tory government began to reduce the number of advisory councils. It cut, sold or merged 46 government agencies. It eliminated the Economic Council of Canada, the Canadian Institute for International Peace and Security, the Law Reform Commission, the Science Council and the Pay Research Bureau. In a rare rebellion, however, the Senate of Canada vetoed the government's effort to merge the Canada Council with the Social Sciences and Humanities Research Council.

ORGANIZING PRINCIPLES AND LINKAGES

An inventory of the main organizational forms within the Canadian federal bureaucracy illustrates the diversity of bureaucratic structures but does not provide a complete picture of the way the bureaucracy operates. One also requires an appreciation of the basic principles on which the bureaucracy is organized as well as of the various linkages that exist, first, among different structures within the bureaucracy and, second, between the bureaucracy and the more overtly political institutions of Cabinet and Parliament.

The chief organizing principle of the bureaucracy is the concept of **departmentalization**, whereby, at least in theory, every administrative function in the federal government is allocated to a single government department. Two reasons may be cited for a clear apportionment of duties among government departments or agencies: it avoids financial waste and administrative confusion; and it helps to clarify lines of accountability for administrative actions and thus strengthens another principle of bureaucratic organization in Canada — ministerial responsibility and accountability.

The allocation of duties to government departments may be based on one or more of the following criteria: common purpose, clientele, territory or place, expertise, process. Thus, for example, the Department of Veterans' Affairs caters to a specific clientele. So, too, in part does the Department of Indian Affairs and Northern Development, although that ministry's traditional responsibility for overseeing the administration of government in Yukon and the Northwest Territories has also been based on the criterion of "place." The Department of Supply and Services is organized around the use of common facilities — "process" — in acting as a printing and publishing house for almost the entire federal government.

In many cases, however, there is no perfect correspondence between these organizational criteria and the activities of individual departments. Consequently, different organizational criteria force some departments to pursue internally contradictory goals. In the case of the Department of Indian Affairs and Northern Development cited above, it has been argued that

---

[29] Government of Canada, *Estimates for the Fiscal Year Ending March 31, 1985* (Ottawa: Minister of Supply and Services, 1984), Sections 24–32.

the function of protecting and enhancing the interest and way of life of Native people in the North is irreconcilable with the objective of promoting northern resource development.[30]

The processes of policy-making and conflict resolution within and between government departments and agencies are often referred to as **bureaucratic politics**. This term is usually associated with the work of Graham Allison, who argued that the conventional model of foreign policy decision-making, the so-called "rational actor" model, did not adequately explain the actions of policy-makers in the 1962 Cuban Missile Crisis. The rational actor model suggests that government is effectively a unitary, monolithic actor, with a single set of goals or objectives, which selects from a range of alternatives the policy that best serves its perception of the national interest. Allison contended instead that the policy decisions in the Missile Crisis might better be explained by the "bureaucratic politics" model, which assumes that government consists of a variety of individuals, groups and agencies pursuing divergent interests and policy goals and competing to have their respective values and objectives supported in the final policy outcome.[31] (See Chapter 13.)

Clearly, the Canadian federal bureaucracy is far from being a homogeneous, monolithic entity. The diversity of structural forms found in departments and agencies; the different philosophies of policy-making and administration that develop in each agency; the periodic conflicts that arise between agencies with regard to policy objectives, jurisdictions and modes of implementation — all suggest that the Canadian bureaucracy is relatively pluralistic. On the other hand, Ottawa is not a state of anarchy. Inter-agency competition and bureaucratic infighting are not always destructive. Disputes between agencies or departments may be constrained by parameters established by Cabinet on the range of possible policy alternatives that may be considered on a particular issue.[32] It might even be argued that bureaucratic politics has its advantages. The greater the degree of competition between agencies, the more information and alternative choices Cabinet has at its disposal in making policy decisions, the greater the extent of political control over the policy-making process.

But what control does Cabinet have over the administrative process to ensure that policies, once made, are actually implemented? The second major principle of government organization in Canada — and the primary link between the bureaucracy and the overtly political realm of Cabinet, Parliament and the people — is the doctrine of **ministerial responsibility**. The Prime Minister appoints members of the Cabinet to assume responsibility for particular ministries or portfolios, and their associated departments, commissions, boards and corporations. Ministers are constitutionally responsible for all of the operations of their departments. Thus, legally, it is ministers who are assigned the powers and duties to be exercised by their departments. Departmental officials, on the other hand, are given scant attention in the law and are responsible exclusively to their ministers, not to Parliament. They are supposed to be non-partisan, objective and anonymous — shielded from the glare of public attention and from the partisan political arena of Parliament by their minister — in

---

[30] Simon McInnes, "The Policy Consequences of Northern Development," in M. Atkinson and M. Chandler, eds., *The Politics of Canadian Public Policy* (Toronto: University of Toronto Press, 1983), pp. 247–66.

[31] Graham T. Allison, *Essence of Decision: Explaining the Cuban Missile Crisis* (Boston; Little, Brown, 1971). See also J.C.H. Jones, "The Bureaucracy and Public Policy: Canadian Merger Policy and the Combines Branch, 1960–71." *CPA*, vol. 18, no. 2 (Summer 1975), esp. pp. 272–73; Richard D. French, *How Ottawa Decides*, 2nd ed. (Toronto: Lorimer, 1984); and Richard J. Schultz, *Federalism, Bureaucracy and Public Policy: The Politics of Highway Transport Regulation* (Montréal: McGill-Queen's University Press, 1980), esp. chs. 5 and 6.

[32] See, for example, Michael M. Atkinson and Kim Richard Nossal, "Bureaucratic Politics and the New Fighter Aircraft Decisions," *CPA*, vol. 24, no. 4 (Winter 1981), pp. 531–62.

order to safeguard their neutrality and ensure their ability to serve faithfully whichever government is in power. In the event of a serious error in the formulation or administration of policy within a department, convention dictates that the minister, rather than officials, be held responsible to Parliament; and if the minister cannot account for failures to the satisfaction of Parliament, then convention dictates that the minister should resign.

Experience has shown, however, that there are severe limitations to the actual realization of the doctrine of ministerial responsibility.[33] The individual responsibility of ministers for the operations of their departments is often sacrificed in favour of another principle or responsibility, the **collective responsibility** of the Cabinet to Parliament. Unless political expediency dictates otherwise, as long as a minister retains the confidence and support of the Prime Minister, that minister is extremely unlikely to be asked to resign. Another problem is the fact that ministers cannot be held personally responsible for administrative matters occurring before their current appointments. Thus, when questions were raised in the House of Commons in the late 1970s about RCMP wrongdoings, the then-Solicitor General took refuge behind this convention, saying that the events had taken place prior to his appointment; neither could three former Solicitor Generals sitting in the House be called to account for the activities of a department for which they were no longer the minister!

Perhaps it is reasonable that ministers should not be held responsible to the point of resignation for the administrative errors of public servants. The relative impermanence of Cabinet ministers and their multifunctional roles make it impossible for ministers to involve themselves extensively in the management of their departments. Ministers are expected to direct their attention to policy matters rather than to the details of departmental administration. For this reason, one observer argues, it is "unrealistic to expect a minister to accept personal responsibility for all the acts of his departmental officials. Why should a minister 'carry the can' when he has little or no knowledge of its contents?"[34]

If Cabinet ministers cannot, will not, or should not be held responsible to Parliament for the administrative functioning of their departments, then who can? The Lambert Commission proposed that "the minister's responsibility must be shared with the deputy [minister], who should be accountable to Parliament through the Public Accounts Committee as the chief administrative officer for the day-to-day operations which are, in practical terms, beyond the minister's control."[35] This recommendation is suspect in that it reflects adherence to the distinction between policy matters and administrative tasks, which is at best fuzzy and at worst likely to distort an understanding of the role of the bureaucracy. Moreover, the Commission may well have underestimated the extent to which some ministers seek to participate in the internal administration of their departments, while others seek to deflect criticism to the Deputy Minister and deny responsibility for policy failures.[36] Though sound

---

[33] See T.M. Denton, "Ministerial Responsibility: A Contemporary Perspective," in R. Schultz et al., eds., *The Canadian Political Process*, 3rd ed. (Toronto: Holt, Rinehart and Winston, 1979), pp. 344–63; and Sharon Sutherland "Responsible Government and Ministerial Responsibility," *CJPS*, vol. 24, no. 1 (March 1991), pp. 91–120 and "The Al-Mashat Affair: Administrative Responsibility in Parliamentary Institutions," *Canadian Public Administration* (Winter 1991), pp. 573–603.

[34] Kenneth Kernaghan, "Power, Parliament and Public Servants in Canada: Ministerial Responsibility Re-examined," in H.D. Clarke et al., eds., *Parliament, Policy and Representation* (Toronto: Methuen, 1980), p. 128.

[35] Royal Commission on Financial Management and Accountability, *Final Report* (Ottawa: Minister of Supply and Services, 1979), p. 57.

[36] See Paul Thomas, "The Lambert Report: Parliament and Accountability," *CPA*, vol. 22, no. 4 (Winter 1979), esp. pp. 561–62.

reasons exist for re-evaluating the doctrine of ministerial responsibility, there appears to be little point in adding to existing ambiguities surrounding the role of the Deputy Minister.

If the minister is the key link between the bureaucracy and Cabinet for the purposes of formal political accountability, the role of the **Deputy Minister** (DM) is equally crucial to effective administration and the coordination and direction of policy implementation. Certain financial and managerial responsibilities are laid down by the *Financial Administration Act* and the *Public Service Employment Act*, or are delegated to the DM by the Treasury Board and the Public Service Commission. Otherwise, the DM possesses only that power that the minister chooses to delegate. In fact, the *Interpretation Act* indicates that ministers may delegate any and all of their powers under the law to their Deputies, except for the power to make regulations and, of course, their parliamentary duties.[37] Exactly how much a minister chooses to delegate is a personal decision.[38]

The main function of the Deputy Minister, outside the administrative responsibilities of managing the department, is to act as the minister's chief source of non-partisan advice on public policy. The problem for the DM is how to initiate policy proposals and studies without appearing to undermine the ultimate policy-making responsibility of the minister.[39] In their policy-advisory roles, Deputies have to strike a delicate balance between political sensitivity and bureaucratic objectivity — especially when they are led by their experience and expertise to disagree with policies put forward by the minister. In such cases, the DM may stress the potential difficulties of implementing the policy — although perhaps not in the forthright fashion attributed to a senior British civil servant who reportedly told his minister that

> ...he could not stop his political master taking a damn silly decision but thought it justifiable to question whether he need carry it out in such a damn silly way.[40]

Deputy Ministers are appointed by the governor-in-council on the recommendation of the Prime Minister. Their office is held "during pleasure," which means that they can be dismissed or transferred at any time without assigned cause and that they are not protected by the provisions of the *Public Service Employment Act*. This insecurity of tenure naturally creates further ambiguity about the role of the Deputy Minister. Deputies who advise against "damn silly decisions" risk being viewed as obstacles to the government in pursuit of its partisan political objectives and being removed.

On the other hand, Deputies who are perceived as being successful in administering certain government policies may become identified with programs unpopular with the opposition and therefore risk losing their jobs when the reins of government change hands. The principle of "rotation in office," whereby Deputy Ministers and other senior public servants are replaced with each change of government, is not as widely accepted in Canada as in, for example, the United States. The political neutrality and relative permanence of Deputy

---

37 Denton, "Ministerial Responsibility."

38 The Conservative governments of 1984 and 1988 tried to insulate Ministers from the bureaucracy by creating a new level of political appointee, the Chiefs of Staff, through which all communication between departments and Ministers was routed. The Liberal government elected in 1993 began its term in office by eliminating the Chiefs of Staff and announcing that it intended to rebuild the relationship between Ministers and deputies. (*The Globe and Mail*, October 29, 1993).

39 See A.W. Johnson, "The Role of the Deputy Minister," in Kernaghan, ed., *Public Administration in Canada: Selected Readings*, 4th ed., pp. 262–63.

40 Cited in Herbert R. Balls, "Decision-making: the role of the deputy minister," *CPA*, vol. 19, no. 3 (Fall 1976), p. 419.

Ministers is viewed as both a safeguard against a return to political patronage and partisan bureaucracy and a source of continuity in administration amid political changes.[41]

While the primary tasks of Deputy Ministers concern their own departments — including managerial functions and advisory roles — they also help coordinate the activities and policies of government. Most important issues discussed by Cabinet or its committees involve more than one department. Consequently, Deputy Ministers can advise and prepare their Ministers effectively only if there has been prior interdepartmental consultation. This may take place in an informal way, or it may be routinized through regular meetings of interdepartmental committees. The Coordinating Committee of Deputy Ministers (CCDM), which is chaired by the Secretary to the Cabinet, serves as an important source of policy advice for the Prime Minister. Other committees of Deputy Ministers help coordinate and advise on administrative, rather than policy, concerns. The Committee of Senior Officials on Executive Personnel in the Public Service (COSO) advises the Prime Minister on the management, performance and recruitment of senior officials appointed by the Cabinet. Lastly, there is a host of interdepartmental committees and working parties at the level of Assistant Deputy Minister and below that help coordinate the work of government departments and solve common problems.

The Canadian federal bureaucracy is an extremely complex and diverse organization whose historical development reflects constant tension between the competing demands of democracy and efficiency. The fragmentation of the bureaucracy into many departments and Crown agencies in the interests of efficiency somewhat impedes policy coordination. At the same time, the principle of departmentalization underlies the doctrine of ministerial responsibility that, ideally, should enhance the democratic process by providing a line of accountability to Parliament and the people. And between the Cabinet and the great mass of the bureaucracy, the Deputy Ministers and other senior officials play key pivotal roles. They not only advise their respective ministers on how best to serve the interests of the people and attempt to ensure the efficient management and functioning of their own departments, but also play an important part in the coordination of policy advice and effective policy implementation throughout the bureaucracy as a whole.

THE PUBLIC SERVICE

While "bureaucracy" refers to the structures and principles of organization in the administrative arm of government, **public service** is the collective term in Canada for the personnel employed in those structures. Like other political institutions described in this book, the public service of Canada has undergone many profound changes since Confederation. It has evolved from a loosely organized, patronage-based service in which most people were recruited on the basis of political connections to a modern professionalized bureaucracy appointed on the principle of merit; from a predominantly anglophone and almost exclusively male preserve to an equal opportunity employer that consciously attempts to reflect Canada's ethnic and linguistic diversity and that has introduced affirmative action programs designed to promote the participation of women, indigenous peoples, visible minorities and disabled persons.

---

[41] On this and related issues of bureaucratic neutrality, see, for example: Mitchell Sharp, "Neutral Superservants," *Policy Options*, vol. 3, no. 6 (Nov./Dec. 1982), pp. 32–34; Gordon Robertson, "The Deputies' Anonymous Duty," *Policy Options*, vol. 4, no. 4 (July/Aug. 1983), pp. 11–13; Thomas D'Aquino, "Political Neutrality is Right," *Policy Options*, vol. 5, no. 1 (Jan./Feb. 1984), pp. 23–26.

DEVELOPMENT OF THE PUBLIC SERVICE

Since 1867 the federal public service has gone through many major transitions, partly in reflection of changes occurring in the society it serves.[42] At Confederation the civil service consisted of bureaucratic structures from Upper and Lower Canada, and did not include a central personnel agency. Appointment to the civil service was exclusively on the basis of political patronage. In the 1880s, a Board of Civil Service Examiners was created to help select candidates, but this had a negligible impact on the mode of recruitment.

The *Civil Service Act* of 1908 sought to replace patronage with the merit principle. The **merit principle** is actually based on two interrelated ideas: first, that all Canadian citizens "should have a reasonable opportunity to be considered for employment in the public service" and, second, that selection must be based "exclusively on merit, or fitness to do the job."[43] The *Act* formally divided the bureaucracy into two services: the Inside Service, which consisted of all persons employed at headquarters in Ottawa, and the Outside Service, comprised of federal employees outside the national capital. The *Act* also created a Civil Service Commission (CSC) to enforce the merit principle in the recruitment and promotion of government employees. However, at the time of its creation, the Commission controlled only the Inside Service; the Outside Service, which comprised about five-sixths of all federal civil servants, was still governed by patronage. Thus, thousands of Outside civil servants were dismissed when the Conservatives ousted the Liberal government in the 1911 election.[44]

In 1918, the *Civil Service Act* extended the method of appointment by competitive examination to the entire service and re-emphasized the role of the CSC in enforcing implementation of the merit principle. To aid its task, the Commission was required to reorganize the whole service on the basis of a classification of all positions within the bureaucracy. Over the next four decades the CSC had considerable success in enforcing the merit principle.

The *Civil Service Act* of 1961 came about largely as an effort to resolve a power struggle over common areas of responsibility that had built up between the CSC and the Treasury Board. By this Act, the Treasury Board was given sole responsibility for pay determination and administrative organization. The CSC kept its merit-related responsibilities with regard to staffing, appointments, promotions, conditions of employment and classification. Perhaps most important, this *Act* provided the context within which collective bargaining could develop, since final decisions on pay "now lay squarely between Treasury and the organized public servants," without any CSC activity as an independent arbiter.[45]

In 1967, two Acts were passed that further affected the role of the CSC and permitted it to become a more specialized staffing body. The *Public Service Staff Relations Act* (1967) created a collective bargaining regime in the public service with the power to enter into collective agreements in the name of the government. Responsibility for classification, pay determination and most conditions of employment rested with the Board. The *Public Service Employment Act* (1967) gave the renamed Public Service Commission (PSC) ultimate responsibility for all elements of the staffing process and staff training, especially language training. The PSC is for-

---

[42] For a comprehensive examination of the historical evolution of the federal public service see J.E. Hodgetts, William McCloskey, Reginald Whitaker and V. Seymour Wilson, *The Biography of an Institution: The Civil Service Commission of Canada 1908–1967* (Montréal: McGill-Queen's University Press, 1972).

[43] R.H. Dowdell, "Public Personnel Administration," in Kernaghan, ed., *Public Administration in Canada*, p. 196.

[44] Robert B. Best, "The Meaning of 'Merit' in Canadian Public Administration," in Adie and Thomas, *Canadian Public Administration*, p. 197.

[45] Hodgetts, et al., *The Biography of an Institution*, p. 274.

mally an agency reporting to Parliament, not to the executive — a status that permits it a degree of independence in investigating complaints and hearing appeals against the government. However, its independent status is somewhat compromised by the fact that the three PSC Commissioners are appointed for a set term by Cabinet.

In 1989, the government set up Public Service 2000 in an attempt to reorganize the public service to make it more service-oriented and reduce morale problems caused by fiscal restraint.[46] This new set of proposals to streamline public service practices was incorporated into the *Public Service Reform Act*, 1992 that constituted the first major amendments to staffing legislation in 25 years. Bill C-26 provided for more flexible staffing arangements — allowing managers to move employees to new positions more easily — and mandated the PSC to initiate employment equity programs while retaining the merit principle.

THE MERIT PRINCIPLE IN THE 1990S

There are two sides to the **merit principle**. One is that all appointments to, and promotions within, the public service are to be based on ability to do the job, in the interest of creating a qualified and efficient public service, The other, which also guards against patronage and helps safeguard the neutrality of the bureaucracy, is that public servants are expressly forbidden to engage in partisan political activities.

With respect to the first aspect, the role of the Public Service Commission in implementing government directives to promote participation by under-represented groups has threatened to compromise its application of the merit principle. This is not a new issue in public service staffing. Both the 1918 and the 1961 *Civil Service Acts* entrenched absolute preference in hiring for war veterans. Then, following the passage of the *Official Languages Act* of 1969, which required the provision of minority language services in areas where numbers warranted, the designation of many public service positions as bilingual brought accusations of "reverse discrimination" and "contravention of the merit principle" from unilingual employees and from public service unions.[47]

The *Public Service Employment Act* forbids discrimination in hiring or promotion on the basis of "race, national or ethnic origin, colour, religion, age, sex, marital status, disability, or conviction for an offence for which a pardon has been granted." However, certain groups have remained persistently under-represented in the public service, especially in senior positions. To address this, the PSC in 1983 introduced a service-wide affirmative action program. Affirmative action should not automatically be equated with quota systems or negative discrimination. Much of the affirmative action program is oriented toward education, training and career counselling through such agencies as the Office of Equal Opportunities for Women, rather than toward providing special treatment in hiring or promotion. The PSC insists that "the affirmative action program implemented in 1983 does not conflict with

---

[45] Canada, *Public Service 2000* (Ottawa: Supply and Services, 1990); David Zussman, "Managing the Federal Public Service as the Knot Tightens," in Katherine Graham, ed., *How Ottawa Spends, 1990-91* (Ottawa: Carleton University Press, 1991). A. Fly, A. Gray, and W. Jenkins, "Taking the Next Steps: The Changing Management of Government," *Parliamentary Affairs*, vol. 43, no. 2 (April 1990), pp. 159–78.

[46] See P.K. Kuruvilla, "Bilingualism in the Canadian Federal Public Service," in K. Kernaghan, ed., *Public Administration in Canada: Selected Readings*, 3rd ed. (Toronto: Methuen, 1977), pp. 81–90; and Kenneth Kernaghan, "Representative Bureaucracy — the Canadian Perspective," *CPA*, vol. 2, no. 4 (Winter 1978), pp. 489–512.

[47] Ibid., p. 16

merit, which requires that only qualified persons be appointed."[48] The fact that the Commission justifies its programs in such terms reveals its sensitivity to potential criticisms that affirmative action might "unwisely and unnecessarily undermine the merit system of recruitment and promotion and the efficiency of the public service."[49]

The enforcement of the other side of the merit principle (the limitations imposed on political activity to safeguard the neutrality of the public service) has become a sensitive issue. Traditionally, most public servants were permitted to contribute money to a political party and to attend their meetings, but neither to stand for public office nor indulge in overtly partisan activity. Such transgressions might result in suspension or, ultimately, dismissal. Until recently, most cases were fairly straightforward.

Take one case. According to the Public Service Staff Relations Board (PSSRB), Neil Fraser, a senior tax auditor with Revenue Canada, went well beyond the limits of proscribed political activity in 1982. After two suspensions and repeated warnings from senior officials, Fraser was dismissed from his job for criticizing the federal government's compulsory metric conversion program and the proposed *Charter of Rights*. When Fraser appealed to the PSSRB, the Board quashed one of his suspensions, upholding the right of public servants to speak out on political issues not directly connected with their own department or jobs. However, the other suspension and his dismissal were confirmed since, according to the Board, "…Mr. Fraser engaged in rhetoric that was vitriolic in the denunciation of his Government and its leaders" to the extent that he "had assumed the mantle of a 'politician' and as such was acting in a manner incompatible with his duties as a public servant."[50]

The Fraser case provoked a storm of protest. Calling his dismissal "unjustified," an editorial in *The Ottawa Citizen* complained, "It is obvious rights don't have the sanctity in practice they seem to have in speeches."[51] Of course, no government would relish the prospect of being criticized by its own employees. Even if the issue concerned is not directly related to the employee's job, a public servant's criticisms may well receive more press attention and be accorded more credibility that those of "ordinary" citizens.[52] The adoption of the *Charter of Rights and Freedoms* in 1982 has altered these traditions. In June 1991, the Supreme Court struck down the section of the *Public Service Employment Act* that forbids an employee of the government to "engage in work for or against a candidate…engage in work for or against a party or…be a candidate." The Court said that this restriction violated those sections of the *Charter of Rights* on freedom of expression. Top bureaucrats — those involved in policy-making — were still prohibited from political activity but the case has opened up the possibility that most public servants may now engage in political activity.[53]

1993 PROFILE OF THE PUBLIC SERVICE

The federal government is a major employer in Canada. In 1992, the federal government employed well over half a million people. These employees are spread throughout the

---

[49] One of the potential criticisms reported but dismissed by P.K. Kuruvilla in "Still Too Few Women," *Policy Options*, vol. 4, no. 3 (May/June 1983), p. 55.

[50] Extracts of the decision rendered by David Kates, Deputy Chairman of the PSSRB, reported in Public Service Staff Relations Board, *PSSRB Decisons* (1982) vol. 1, pp. 52–53.

[51] "The right to speak out," *The Citizen*, Ottawa, March 24, 1982.

[52] For a critical view of the difficulties with the merit principle, see Robert J. Jackson, "Politicization of the Public Service?" (unpublished paper, Royal Australian Institute of Public Administration, Sydney, Australia, Nov. 1985).

[53] *The Globe and Mail*, June 7, 1991.

FIGURE 9.1   FEDERAL GOVERNMENT EMPLOYMENT IN 1992

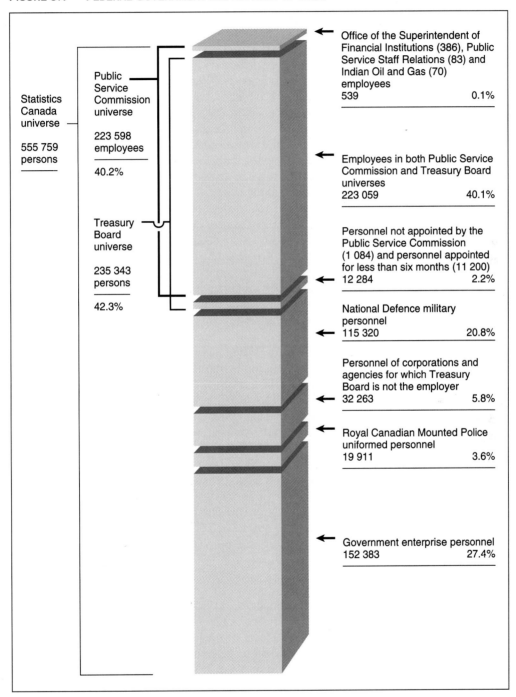

Source: Public Service Commision, *Annual Report, 1992* (Ottawa: Supply and Services, 1993), p. 8.
Reproduced by authority of the Minister responsible for Statistics Canada 1993.

country and work in the public service, military, corporations, agencies, enterprises and the Royal Canadian Mounted Police (see Figure 9.1).[54]

In the discussion of the characteristics of public servants that follows, we refer only to those employed under the auspices of the Public Service Commission. In 1992 these totalled 223 059 persons. The hierarchical system also fosters a definitive chain of responsibility within the bureaucracy. Within each department a descending order of command is evident, with each employee responsible to a superior. This chain of command, which begins with a government minister, protects against the arbitrary assumption of power by individuals within the bureaucracy. Bureaucratic red tape in the guise of triplicate copies, codes, memos and standard forms is a necessary part of the process of horizontal and vertical communication among employees and departments in the federal government. Given the immense number of people within the public service and the diversity of their duties, it is easy to appreciate why the bureaucracy's primary goal of efficiency is sometimes difficult to achieve.

Entrance into the public service is open and carries no restrictions as to age, race, sex, religion, colour, national or ethnic origin, marital status or disability. Recruitment is carried out across Canada on the basis of merit. Qualifications are determined through an entrance exam, the results of which determine the applicant's capabilities and job placement. Recruitment programs are sponsored by the Public Service Commission. Following the *Public Service Reform Act, 1992* the PSC is to continue basing its employment practices on merit, but may initiate employment equity plans to right historical imbalances for designated groups, which include women, aboriginal peoples, persons with disabilities and those from visible minorities.

Once within the public service, competition and appeal procedures ensure that virtually every employee can elevate his or her status. When a position is created or becomes vacant it is advertised. Depending upon the job, the competition will be "open" (available to candidates from both within and outside the public service) or "closed" (available only to those already in the public sector). Once a suitable candidate has been selected the appeal procedure allows complaints and criticisms against the appointment to be formally voiced; a board is convened to consider the appeal. In 1992, 3754 such appeals were lodged with the Public Service Commission. The PSC prides itself on this procedure, which in combination with the competition process provides an assurance of unbiased hiring and promotion practices.

To some extent, the bureaucracy is expected to be representative of the society it serves. Yet factors such as region, religion, ethnicity, social class, education, language and sex all render Canada a highly heterogeneous society. This situation might potentially hinder egalitarian representation. In what follows, we outline and assess the composition of the public service with reference to some of these factors in order to illuminate the patterns of employment found in the bureaucracy.

REGIONAL DISTRIBUTION

It is commonly assumed that most federal employees work in Ottawa or, more properly, in the National Capital Region (NCR). In 1992, however, only 32 percent were located in the NCR. Approximately 31 percent of all federal employees were located in Ontario and Québec outside the NCR. In total, Ontario and Québec had 63 percent — their approximate share of the total Canadian population. A further 17 percent of public servants were based in the Atlantic

---

Unless otherwise acknowledged, figures relating to Public Service employees are drawn from the Annual Reports of the Public Service Commission. For an excellent discussion of earlier changes in public service employment see S.L. Sutherland, "Federal Bureaucracy: The Pinch Test," in Michael J. Prince, ed., *How Ottawa Spends 1987–88* (Toronto: Methuen, 1987) pp. 38–128.

Provinces; about 24 percent worked in the western provinces, Yukon and Northwest Territories and outside Canada. In relation to regional populations, this means that the Atlantic area has rather more than its fair share of federal employees, while the West is slightly under-represented. By and large, these figures reflect the success of a deliberate attempt by the federal government to decentralize the bureaucracy away from Ontario in general and the NCR in particular.

LANGUAGE

The early failure to acknowledge the French fact in Canada has been seen by some commentators as the most damning indictment of the recruitment methods of the public service. Below, we present a brief history of francophone participation in the public service, in order to place in perspective today's francophone representation and to underline the importance of "bilingualization" in the public service.

Prior to 1918, at least adequate francophone representation was assured through patronage appointments made by French-speaking Cabinet ministers. But with the rationalization of the bureaucracy on the basis of merit, no procedure evolved to replace the patronage system's assurance of adequate representation based on language. The majority of the public service tended to define "merit" and "efficiency" in accordance with its own cultural and educational values; the result was that "with few francophones in the guiding councils of the public service, its explicit qualifications and implicit assumptions tended to become more unfavourable to francophones."[55]

Thus, while in 1918, 22 percent of government employees were French-speaking, by 1936 only 20 percent were,[55] and, by 1945, the figure was only 12 percent.[57] In 1965, only 5 percent of senior executives appointed by the Public Service Commission were French, while 16.5 percent of political appointees to the bureaucracy were francophone. It was only in the 1960s, after the Glassco Report and the bilingualism and biculturalism Report, that there was widespread recognition of the need to increase francophone representation in the federal government. In reaction, a tendency developed to "parachute" French-speakers into top-level political appointments in the bureaucracy.

Many factors combined during these years to reduce levels of francophone recruitment in the federal bureaucracy. The public service became less attractive for French Canadians because no provisions were made to ensure service to French Canadians. Nor were francophones' bilingual skills included in an assessment of their qualifications. Francophones were also hindered by the merit system's examinations and interviews, which reflected the patterns of thought and cultural style of English-speaking Canada.[58] The competitions also emphasized the technical and commercial skills taught in the English educational system, placing French-Canadians, with their classical education, at a disadvantage. It is sometimes argued that it is because of this "unsuitable" education that French Canada did not produce the type of administrator who could be used in the public service. However, as Nathan Keyfitz has pointed out, it is precisely such a classical curriculum that equipped many an "empire-builder" with the skills to become an effective "generalist" administrator.[59]

---

[55] From the Report of the Royal Commission on Bilingualism and Biculturalism as quoted in Vincent Seymour Wilson, *Staffing in the Canadian Federal Bureaucracy* (Unpublished Ph.D. dissertation, Kingston, Ont.: Queen's University, 1970), p. 244.

[56] Hodgetts, et al., *The Biography of an Institution*, p. 473.

[57] Wilson, *Staffing in the Canadian Federal Bureaucracy*, p. 236.

[58] Hodgetts, et al., *The Biography of an Institution*, p. 475.

[59] Nathan Keyfitz, "Canadians and Canadiens," *Queen's Quarterly*, vol. 70, no. 2 (Summer 1963), p. 173.

In finally assuming responsibility for language training in the late 1960s, the Public Service Commission found itself at the centre of one of the most significant transformations ever attempted in the bureaucracy. The Commission was directed to aid the government in achieving full and equal participation of anglophones and francophones in the public service while preserving the merit principle in recruitment and promotion.

Progress is slowly being made towards this goal. The percentage of francophone employees in the public service has increased, so that now participation is more comparable to their distribution in the national population: by 1992, their numbers had increased to 29 percent of all public servants (see Table 9.3).

However, closer examination of the distribution of anglophones and francophones within the public service shows that French-speaking Canadians are still relatively disadvantaged. In 1992, francophones were somewhat under-represented in the executive group category of employment (23 percent), and somewhat over-represented in the administrative support group (34 percent). There may, however, be grounds for optimism regarding a public service more representative in terms of language. In 1992, approximately 32 percent of all public servants under the age of 40 were francophones, and of the external appointments made in 1992, 24 percent were francophones and 76 percent were anglophones, proportionally very close to the Canadian labour force. Language training continues as well. In 1992, 5553 public servants were studying French and 405 English.

TABLE 9.3   LANGUAGE AND AGE GROUP OF PUBLIC SERVANTS, 1991

Age	Anglophones	Francophones
under 20	65.1	34.9
20–24	68.3	31.7
25–29	69.8	30.2
30–34	67.5	32.5
35–39	68.3	31.7
40–44	70.7	29.3
45–59	72.7	27.3
50–54	75.9	24.1
55–59	80.8	19.2
60–64	83.3	16.7
65 & over	87.0	13.0
Total	71.4	28.6

Source: Adapted from Public Service Commission, *Annual Report, 1992* (Ottawa: Supply and Services, 1993), p. 9.

Through these measures, successive federal governments have tried to reduce the under-representation of French Canadians in the federal bureaucracy. While there is still room for improvement, especially at higher salary levels and ranks, the federal public service is gradually becoming more representative of the official language composition of the Canadian population.

WOMEN AND EQUITY DESIGNATED GROUPS

If the federal government is to be congratulated for creating a public service more representative of Canada's two main language communities, it has little reason for complacency with regard to its representation of the gender division in Canadian society. Although the federal government is Canada's largest single employer of women, with 102 632 female employees in 1992, women have long faced both institutional and attitudinal barriers to advancement in the bureaucracy that are only slowly being broken down by more sensitive recruitment, training and affirmative action programs.[60]

Discrimination against women in the bureaucracy was officially endorsed in varying degrees until 1967. In direct contradiction of the merit principle, anti-female prejudice was built into the very fabric of civil service legislation and personnel practice.[61] As early as 1908, the CSC admitted that "there are women who have as good executive ability as men, and who might, on the *mere* ground of personal qualifications, fill the higher positions in the service.[62]

In order to "protect the merit principle from itself," deputy heads were instructed to segregate occupational categories into male and female groups, with women being limited to the lowest clerical levels. Since inequality of opportunity thus became a foregone conclusion, and women were not given access to middle-level positions, the issue of equal pay for equal work could not arise. As Kathleen Archibald points out, this occupational sex-typing of jobs was later used as "evidence" to show why women were not capable of filling higher executive positions.[63] In the 1918 *Civil Service Act*, gender was mentioned as a "limiting" factor on an individual's qualifications, and in 1921 formal restrictions were placed on employing married women.

Over the next five decades, the concentration of women in the lower white-collar ranks provided the CSC with a cheap labour supply. During the Second World War, however, it became the patriotic duty of women to fill "male" jobs, so that while in 1938 only 17 percent of public service appointees were female, by 1943 this figure had risen to 65 percent. With the enforcement of the "veterans' preference" in 1946 the proportion of female appointees was halved, and restrictions were once again placed on employing married women.

In 1955, when one-third of all Canadian working women were married, the CSC finally lifted restrictions on their appointment. The 1950s also witnessed the appointment of the first female Civil Service Commissioner, Ruth Addison. But it was only with the promulgation of the 1967 *Public Service Employment Act* that "sex" was added to "race, national origin, colour and creed" as grounds upon which an individual could not be discriminated against.

Legally, the federal administration's position on sex discrimination has altered; but the actual situation of women in the bureaucracy is little improved. While women have constituted an increasingly larger percentage of public servants over time, from 27 percent in 1943 to 46 percent in 1992, they are still very slightly under-represented in proportion to the total population. Much more importantly, effective segregation by occupational category is still occurring. In 1992, 83 percent of the Administrative Support category were women who tended to be concentrated in traditional job ghettos within Administrative Support, serving as clerks, secretaries, stenographers and typists. In the executive group category, on the other hand, while their numbers have certainly increased, women are still seriously under-represented in proportion to their total employment in the public service. In 1992, female employees formed only 17 percent of senior management. Women constitute less than 20 percent of public servants who earn more than $50 000.

---

[60] On institutional and attitudinal barriers to female employees, see the critical review by Kuruvilla, "Still Too Few Women," pp. 54–55.

[61] Hodgetts, et al., *The Biography of an Institution*, p. 483.

[62] Ibid., p. 485 (emphasis in original).

[63] Kathleen Archibald, *Sex and the Public Service: A Report to the Public Service Commission of Canada* (Ottawa: Queen's Printer, 1970), pp. 18–23.

Reproduced with permission, Dennis Pritchard.

There are signs of improvement in the position of women in the public service. Women constituted 51 percent of all public servants under 40 years of age in 1992. But it is also clear that current lines of occupational segregation must be broken down if women are to achieve genuine equality of opportunity in the bureaucracy. While the just application of the merit principle might permit women to increase their representation gradually in the long term, in the short term there is manifestly a need in the public service for serious commitment to continued and expanded affirmative action programs.

The question of fairness for other historically deprived groups in Canada is a hot topic. Following the *Public Service Reform Act, 1992*, the PSC has inaugurated several new programs to improve the recruitment of aboriginal peoples, persons with disabilities and members of minority groups. There has been some improvement because of these new procedures. In the executive group — i.e., senior management — the numbers are still small: 1.1 percent aboriginal peoples; 1.8 percent persons with disabilities and 2.4 percent members of visible minorities. At lower levels there has been more rapid progress. Table 9.4 shows the relation between labour market availability in general and the rate at which these designated groups have been recruited into the public service during 1992. It also indicates the rate of female recruitment by comparison with their availability.

In summary, the Canadian public service has, over the last 40 years, become more representative of the society it serves. There has been an increased sensitivity to the under-representation of francophones, women and other historically disadvantaged groups in the bureaucracy. At the same time, more readily available university education helped to enhance opportunities for the appointment and advancement of individuals from middle- and lower-class backgrounds.

TABLE 9.4 LABOUR MARKET AVAILABILITY AND PUBLIC SERVICE RECRUITMENT FOR EQUITY DESIGNATED GROUPS, 1992

Non-Executive Categories	Labour Market Availability (%)	Public Service Recruitment Share (%)
Aboriginal peoples	1.8	3.4
Persons with Disabilities	4.5	2.5
Members of Visible Minority Groups	5.9	5.5
Women (by category)		
Scientific & Professional	35.9	42.6
Administrative & Foreign Service	32.3	41.9
Technical	20.1	28.8
Administrative Support	79.8	81.0
Operational	21.7	19.9

Source: Adapted from Public Service Commission, *Annual Report, 1992* (Ottawa: Supply and Services, 1993). Reproduced by authority of the Minister responsible for Statistics Canada 1993.

BUREAUCRATS AND BUDGETS

If the general public has a single dominant image of the federal bureaucracy it is perhaps that of a rather large drain down which their hard-earned tax dollars are poured. In one sense, this view is not entirely inaccurate. No government can govern without spending money. But, since most of the money expended by government finds its way back into the Canadian economy, boosting the demand for goods and services, the drain might be as accurately described as a well that in many periods of Canadian history has helped to irrigate the economy, providing a stimulus to economic growth.

This having been said, the government is also responsible to Parliament and to the Canadian taxpayer for ensuring that there is not too much seepage from the well. Consequently, a major focus of political and administrative reform over the past quarter-century has been the search for increased efficiency in government spending and greater control over it. During this period, the federal government has gone through several different expenditure/budgetary systems to arrive at the current restraint process. In the sections that follow, we briefly examine the budgetary process, and discuss the efficacy of some of the techniques introduced to monitor public spending.

POLICY AND BUDGET

The days are long gone when Ministers of Finance could present their budget from a few notes written on the back of an old envelope. Total federal expenditure in 1993–94 was $161 billion. Of this total, public debt interest payments consumed 25 percent, payments to other governments 18 percent and transfers to individuals 26 percent. The remainder of the funds went to support Crown corporations and defence, and such policy fields as justice and legal affairs and industrial, regional, scientific and technological fields. See Figures 9.2 and 9.3.

The Canadian budget shares with others in parliamentary systems of British origin the peculiar characteristic of containing no detailed proposals for spending: the spending estimates are tabled separately. In most political systems and private businesses, budgets contain detailed targets for both spending and revenues.

The budget has a lengthy preparation process. Preliminary discussions are held in the Department of Finance to fix an approximate level of expenditures for the fiscal year. These

FIGURE 9.2   FEDERAL GOVERNMENT EXPENDITURES BY TYPE OF PAYMENT, 1993–94
($161 BILLION)

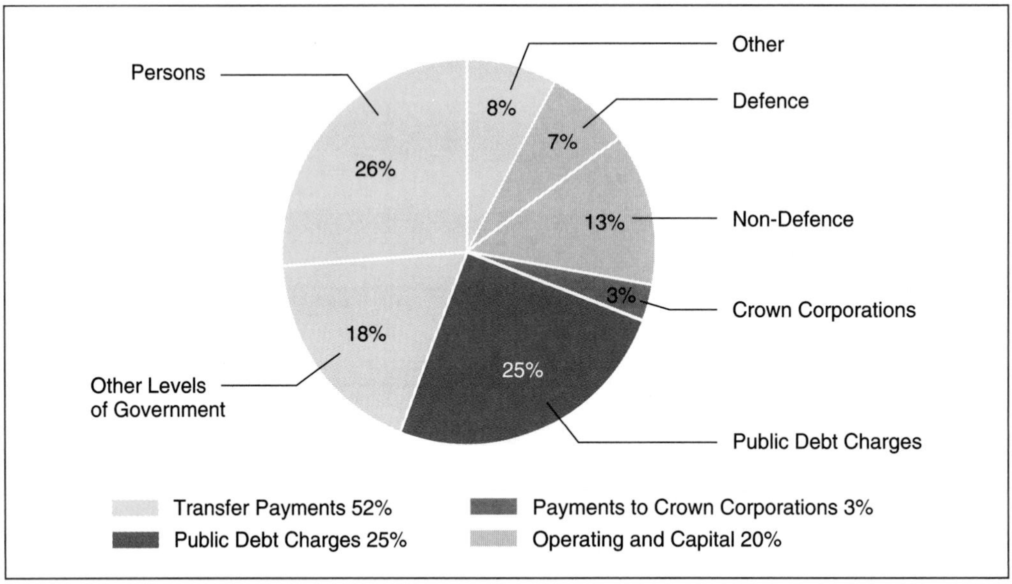

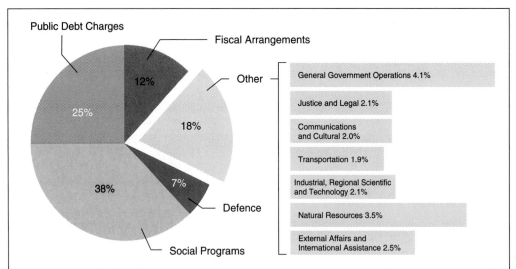

Source: *Estimates*, 1993–94.

FIGURE 9.3   FEDERAL GOVERNMENT EXPENDITURES BY SECTORS, 1993–94 ($161 BILLION)

Source: *Estimates*, 1993–94.

talks also establish estimates of revenues expected to be realized from existing tax rates. From these two estimates, expenditure and revenue, emerges a surplus or a deficit. In recent years the government has usually had to borrow money by issuing securities in order to finance its deficits. The accounts predicted that in 1993–94 the government would spend at least $33 billion to service the public debt. (This figure was later shown to be too low.)

To help determine the appropriate fiscal stance, the Minister of Finance receives an analysis of the economic situation and outlook from departmental officials. These deliberations are also aided by information from the Governor of the Bank of Canada on general economic conditions, conditions in the money markets, monetary policy and the market's capacity to absorb government bonds. This provides the foundation for judgements about the amount of taxes to be collected. When matched with proposed expenditures, the result is an indication of the appropriate budget surplus or deficit and, in the latter event, how the deficit can be financed. From this emerges the proper overall strategy to employ.

In matters of taxation, departmental officials advise the Minister of tax loopholes that can be closed, public reactions concerning taxes, tax reform proposals from external sources and proposals for changes in the customs tariff. From these discussions a general pattern of taxation policy emerges. Costs of tax reduction and revenues from tax raises are totalled and compared with the estimates and the desired fiscal stance. The road is then clear to begin drafting the budget speech. As well, the Minister can begin consulting Cabinet colleagues to obtain their agreement to the budget proposals. Sometimes Finance Ministers spring the budget on the Cabinet at the last possible moment before budget day. Recently, however, there has been a strong tendency to undertake more lengthy consultation.[64]

The actual address and the debate are regulated by the Standing Orders of the House as discussed in Chapter 8. The budget speech is often delivered in the evening after the markets have closed. The speech reviews the fiscal plan, the state of the national economy and the financial operations of the government over the past fiscal year, and provides a forecast of spending requirements for the year ahead, taking into account the estimates. Mitchell Sharp commented about these speeches that in his career as a Minister of Finance he

> *...found all of those speeches excessively long and incredibly dull. On one occasion I was so overwhelmed, I read so fast that a member of the opposition called out "whoa"! I wanted to get it over with and did not think anyone was any more interested than I was in the presentation, except for the final paragraphs.*[65]

Four days of debate follow in the House of Commons during which the opposition discusses almost everything, sometimes even the details of the Fiscal Plan.

THE BUDGETARY PROCESS

As we noted in the preceding paragraphs, the finances of the federal government are managed through two separate but interrelated processes, involving two different sets of actors. The first, the **expenditure process**, is centred on the consolidation of the estimated spending requirements of all government departments and agencies for the next fiscal year, under the watchful eye of the Treasury Board (a Cabinet committee). These estimates are subsequently submitted to Parliament and its committees for scrutiny and approval via appropriations bills that grant the government the requisite permission to spend public funds. The second, the **revenue process**, concerns the means by which those funds are to be raised — taxation and other measures — and is largely the responsibility of the departments of Finance and Revenue. Its Parliamentary focal point is, of course, the Budget Speech delivered by the Minister of Finance, in which the government's economic policy outlook, fiscal plan and revenue-raising proposals are announced to the House of Commons amid great media attention.

---

[64] See remarks by Mitchell Sharp at a Seminar on *The Budgetary Process* (Ottawa: Queen's Printer, 1977). See also Douglas G. Hartle, *The Expenditure Budget Process in The Government of Canada* (Toronto: Canadian Tax Foundation, 1978).

[65] Sharp, ibid., p. 1:8.

Before the mid-1960s and the quest for more "rational" policy-making under Prime Ministers Pearson and Trudeau, the expenditure budget process could best be described as a department-centred, "bottom-up" process. Individual departments determined their own spending requirements, usually based on an "incremental" increase over the previous year's budget for ongoing programs plus additional resources for new commitments, then sent their respective ministers to bat for them in Cabinet. The departmental estimates presented to the government and the House of Commons were aggregated into "standard objects" of expenditure (i.e., administrative inputs such as salaries and supplies) for the whole department, rather than being broken down into the costs of individual programs, functions and objectives. Consequently, parliamentary and auditing control emphasized strict legal accounting for the correct expenditure of funds according to the standard objects, rather than the elimination of potential waste caused by the duplication of programs or functions among departments. Any centralized control exercised by Cabinet was largely over the total level of spending across all government departments, reflecting a concern arising out of Keynesian economic principles for the assumed impact of aggregate public expenditure on the economy.

The "control" aspect of this traditional budget process was strongly criticized in the report of the Glassco Commission. It urged that public service managers be allowed increased autonomy to manage their departments and programs within guidelines established by the Treasury Board. It was also recommended that the latter should be separated from the Department of Finance. Furthermore, the Glassco Report proposed that the preparation of departmental estimates be made on the basis of programs and their objectives.[66]

An approach that would more effectively link expenditure to the outputs of government was found in the Planning Programming Budgeting System (**PPBS**), first popularized in the United States by Secretary of Defense Robert McNamara. Starting with an experimental period in four departments in 1963, PPBS was gradually adopted by the government until the whole federal bureaucracy was committed to this model by 1968. As its name implies, PPBS marked a deliberate step toward a more "planned" approach to government, with estimates for various departmental programs being evaluated by the Treasury Board and the new Cabinet committee on Priorities and Planning. Thus, in place of the "bottom-up" approach of the traditional expenditure budget, PPBS was supposed to be a "top-down" system, providing for a more controlled allocation of resources according to the priorities determined by Cabinet.[67]

As it happened, PPBS was little more effective than its predecessor in either restraining the overall growth in government expenditures or ensuring that funds were allocated according to Cabinet priorities. In part, this was due to political failures. At no time was the Cabinet able to produce a sufficiently detailed and comprehensive list of government objectives by which departmental programs could be evaluated. The PPBS experiment also suffered from the fact that departments and program managers learned quickly "how to work the system." In preparing annual expenditure plans, departments were initially required to divide their estimates into three categories. The "A" budget specified the cost of maintaining programs at their current levels, with allowances made for inflation, population growth, etc.; the estimated cost of expanding existing programs or introducing new ones was to comprise the "B" budget; and the "X" budget was to provide a forecast of savings that would accrue from curtailing or eliminating those programs that had lowest priority in the department. But so few de-

---

[66] Royal Commission on Government Organization, *Report, Volume I: Management of the Public Service* (Ottawa: Queen's Printer, 1962).

[67] For a description of the key elements of the PPB system, see A.W. Johnson, "Planning, Programming, and Budgeting in Canada," *Public Administration Review*, vol. 33, no. 1 (Jan./Feb. 1973), pp. 23–31.

partments were willing to identify "X" budget items (largely because there was no guarantee that the savings would be reallocated to other programs in the same department) that this part of the system soon became unworkable.

Amid growing criticism of the federal government's financial management, PPBS gradually faded into history. In the last months of the 1974–79 Liberal government, work was already underway on a new expenditure budget process. First announced publicly in a paper accompanying the ill-fated Conservative government budget in December 1979, the **Policy and Expenditure Management System** (PEMS) came into full operation during the fiscal year 1981–82.[68] Its general purpose was to integrate the processes of policy-making and fiscal and expenditure planning within the Cabinet committee system.

The PEMS was designed to ensure that the government's decisions on priorities and policies were integrated closely with the allocation of resources. Before 1980, a considerable problem existed in this regard: the ideas for policies and their projected costs were worked out by separate Cabinet committees and at different times. The result was an increased probability that ministers would accept new programs without considering the overall costs to the government. With the introduction of the PEMS, policy decisions were to be made and expenditure limits set simultaneously by the same Cabinet committee. In addition, the new system was to ensure that priorities and expenditure limits were set before expenditure plans were developed.

The PEMS involved the addition of two new features to the Cabinet system. First, a five-year fiscal plan was to be developed to outline the overall financial constraints within which policy choices must be made. This plan was to be revised each year. Second, specific expenditure limits, called "resource envelopes," were to be set. Responsibility for managing these within the expenditure limits was assigned to Cabinet policy committees and Priorities and Planning. The ministers on a policy committee allocated the money in the envelope among themselves. In this way, they were forced to choose the policies to support and to make trade-offs. If a department wished to spend more money on either an old or a new program, it had to delete programs or convince the ministers on the appropriate Cabinet policy committee to reduce allocations elsewhere in that policy sector.

The Treasury Board remained responsible for the preparation of the **Main Estimates** (spending proposals for the upcoming fiscal year), which were based on decisions of the policy commitees. Departmental plans were reviewed in the late fall and in February. The Main Estimates were then tabled in Parliament for the next fiscal year (April 1–March 31). At the departmental level, strategic overviews, multi-year operational plans and budget-year operational plans were made and circulated to the policy committees and central agencies as a basis for decision on departmental requests for policies, programs and funds.

It was the Prime Minister's committee, Priorities and Planning, that determined overall government priorities, established the multi-year fiscal plan and set the size of the resource envelopes. In recent years the funding decisions have been taken at ministerial deliberations at so-called "Lakes and Lodges" meetings. These annual Cabinet retreats are used to develop the highlights of the government's expenditures, the budget and the speech from the throne. The development of these items was based on advice from the central agencies (the Prime Minister's Office, the Privy Council Office, Finance and Treasury Board) and the chairpersons of the Cabinet policy committees.

---

[68] On the origins of the envelope system, see Sandford F. Borins, "Ottawa Expenditure 'Envelopes': Workable Rationality at Last?" in G.B. Doern, ed., *How Ottawa Spends Your Tax Dollars:...1982* (Toronto: Lorimer, 1982), esp. pp. 64–66; The Government of Canada, Privy Council Office, *The Policy and Expenditure Management System* (Ottawa: Minister of Supply and Services, 1981), pp. 3–5.

The PEMS system could therefore be interpreted as an attempt to strengthen collective government control over aggregate government expenditure. This was accomplished in part through the centralization of overall limit setting and envelope allocation in the Priorities and Planning (P&P) Committee, chaired by the Prime Minister. At the same time, the decentralization of expenditure decision-making to the sectoral policy committees was designed to enhance individual ministerial responsibility for departmental expenditure management and planning.

The PEMS approach was not perfect. Among the problems peculiar to PEMS was the fact that it was not a single integrated system at all. According to Richard Van Loon, there were actually *four* systems for policy and expenditure management in the federal government, played out among different sets of actors in different arenas:

1. the budgetary and macro-economic management system, including the revenue budget process, dominated by the Minister of Finance;
2. the A-base management system for ongoing programs, under the control of the Treasury Board;
3. the macro-policy or major governmental priorities system, in which the Cabinet Committee on Priorities and Planning was the major actor; and
4. the system for managing new policies and expenditures, involving the sectoral policy committees of Cabinet and their constituent departments.[69]

The existence of these four systems or sub-systems within PEMS resulted in competition among the various central agencies involved and gave rise to immense problems of coordination which resulted in an apparent lack of overall direction of government policy.

As well, the early years of PEMS implementation were bedevilled by inaccurate economic forecasting. While this problem is common to all budgetary systems, PEMS was particularly dependent upon long-range economic forecasting because of the central importance of the Multi-Year Fiscal Plan as a basis for all planning. Even short-term forecasting was risky and "forecasts further ahead than one year could have been as accurately divined from reading the entrails of small birds as from reading the printouts of anyone's computers."[70] Inaccurate economic forecasting made nonsense of estimates for statutory programs whose expenditure levels were determined by Canadian citizens' demand for programs rather than by the government's willingness to supply them. Thus, as government revenues failed to meet expectations in the early 1980s, and the recession brought growing demand for unemployment and other social welfare expenditures, the long-range planning process was undermined and the federal deficit escalated to alarming proportions.

Like most other budgetary systems, PEMS was not immune to "end-runs" — techniques used by departments and politicians alike to circumvent the process or the spirit of the approach.[71] A number of financial instruments did not appear in, or were poorly integrated with, the PEMS process — for example, non-governmental borrowing by Crown corporations; tax expenditures; loan guarantees and the practice of "netting," whereby depart-

---

[69]   Richard Van Loon, "Ottawa's Expenditure Process: Four Systems In Search of Coordination," in G.B. Doern, ed., *How Ottawa Spends...1983* (Toronto: Lorimer, 1983), pp. 100–101.

[70]   Ibid., p. 106.

[71]   On the phenomenon of "end-runs" in general, see Aaron Wildavsky, *How to Limit Government Spending* (Los Angeles/Berkeley: University of California Press, 1980), ch. 6; and Wildavsky, "From chaos comes opportunity: the movement toward spending limits in American and Canadian budgeting," *CPA*, vol. 26, no. 2 (Summer 1983), pp. 163–81.

ments discount revenues received from programs in calculating their costs.[72] Departments learned a number of new techniques, including the inflation of A-base estimates to provide reserves for later in the year; these could be reallocated without the need to compete with rivals in the sectoral policy committees. They also realized that their chances of getting new expenditures were increased if they flooded the system with demands, one or two of which might be satisfied, rather than putting up a single proposal.[73]

Moreover, Cabinet ministers demonstrated an understandable reluctance to assume responsibility for cutbacks in their departments and programs; consequently, it was difficult to achieve redistribution of funds within policy sectors or to reallocate funds to policy reserves for the financing of new programs. Instead, most major new projects were announced as "special allocations" by the P&P Committee, with little reference to envelope ceilings or to the appropriate sectoral policy committee.

In summary, then, given the trying economic circumstances under which it was introduced, the Policy and Expenditure Management System could be labelled a qualified success. By and large it did increase both collective and individual ministerial responsibility for public spending. However, it was not successful in restraining the escalation of public spending and government deficits. For this reason the 1988 Conservative government decided to put an end to this process and return to the more "politicized" model of earlier years. The basic system remained in place — only without the "envelopes" and the nomenclature. (see Tables 9.5 and 9.6.)

In 1989, Prime Minister Mulroney disbanded PEMS at the Cabinet level. The envelope system was dropped; control over the relation between policy and expenditure was taken away from sectoral policy committees and given over to a triumvirate of committees — Priorities and Planning, Treasury Board and Expenditure Review. These committees were to review the costs of existing programs as well as new ideas coming up from the policy committees of Cabinet. The envelope system had been set up with the assumption of rational policy-making (relating policies to expenditures) and a rising supply of funds. With the 1989 Mulroney government set on a deficit-cutting strategy, the Prime Minister believed there would be no purpose to the envelopes. The overall expenditure control within the public service as a whole, however, did not differ greatly from that of the PEMS system (see Chapter 6 for the 1993 Liberal cabinet structures and expenditure control mechanisms).

DEMOCRATIC CONTROL OF THE BUREAUCRACY

The Weberian concept of bureaucracy, outlined at the beginning of this chapter, posited an organizational form ideally suited to providing the most efficient means of achieving a given end. In a parliamentary democracy such as Canada, the selection of "ends" or policy objectives should be the task of the political executive, responsible through Parliament to the people. The bureaucracy's role, in theory, should be primarily that of implementing the goals chosen by politicians through the most efficient and effective means possible.

---

[72] On loan guarantees as "end-runs," see Allan M. Maslove, "Loans and Loan Guarantees: Business as Usual Versus the Politics of Risk," in Doern, ed., *How Ottawa Spends...1983*, pp. 121–132; and on "netting," see Rod Dobell, "Pressing the Envelope: The Significance of the New, Top-Down System of Expenditure Management in Ottawa," *Policy Options*, vol. 2, no. 6 (Nov./Dec. 1981), pp. 13–18.

[73] Richard Van Loon, "The Policy and Expenditure Management System in the Federal Government," *Canadian Public Administration*, vol. 26, no. 2 (1983), pp. 269–72.

TABLE 9.5   SUPPLY PROCESS FOR MAIN AND SUPPLEMENTARY ESTIMATES

	MAR.	APR.	MAY	JUNE	SEPT.	OCT.	NOV.	DEC.	JAN.	FEB.
PARLIAMENT (House of Commons and the Senate)	Standing Cttees Review S.E. Considers S.E. and Interim Supply Bills	Standing Cttees Review S.E. and Report by May 31		Supply debate on M.E. by June 30 Consider M.E. Supply Bill		Receives Public Accounts for Previous Fiscal Year — Referred to Public Accounts Cttee	Receives First Regular S.E. Cttee review of S.E.	Considers Supply Bill for First Regular S.E. December 10		Receives Budget speech and M.E.
GOVERNOR GENERAL	Grants Royal Assent to Supply Bills; Signs Warrant to Release Monies			Grants Royal Assent to Supply Bill; Signs Warrant to Release Monies				Grants Royal Assent to Supply Bill; Signs Warrant to Release Monies		
TREASURY BOARD	President Tables S.E. and refers them to Cttees; Introduces S.E. and Interim Supply Bills			President Introduces M.E. Supply Bill			President Tables First Regular S.E. and refers them to Cttees	President Introduces S.E. Supply Bill		President Tables M.E. and refers them to Cttees
TB SECRETARIAT	Informs Departments that Supply has been approved		Prepares Supply Bill for M.E.	Informs Departments that Supply has been approved			Preparation of First Regular S.E. and Supply Bill	Informs Departments that Supply has been approved	Prepares M.E.	Prepares S.E. and Supply Bills

Legend: Main Estimates (M.E.)
　　　 Supplementary Estimates (S.E.)
　　　 Committees (Cttees)

Source: Adapted from the Government of Canada, *Fiscal Plan, 1991–92* (Ottawa: Supply and Services, 1992). Reproduced by the authority of the Minister responsible for Statistics Canada 1993.

TABLE 9.6 BUDGET PLANNING CYCLE

	JUNE	JULY	AUG.	SEPT.	OCT.	NOV.	DEC.	JAN.	FEB.	MAR.
PRIORITIES AND PLANNING CABINET COMMITTEE		Review of Government Priorities and Status of Fiscal Plan				Confirmation of Budget Strategy		Finalization of Budget Details		
TREASURY BOARD (President of TB)		Development of Resourcing Strategy for Review of Multi-year Operational Plans				Approval of Departmental Allocation of Resources and items to be included in M.E.			Approve items for Final S.E.; Tabling of M.E.	Tabling of S.E.; Introduction of S.E. and Interim Supply Bills
TB SECRETARIAT		Review of Spending Pressures	Technical Instructions for Multi-year Operational Plans (MYOPs)			Review of MYOPs		Preparation of Estimates Parts I and II		Preparation of S.E. and Interim Supply Bills
DEPARTMENT OF FINANCE (Minister of Finance)		Budget Consultation Process Begins			Preparation of Economic and Revenue Forecast and Fiscal Strategies			Budget Preparation	Presentation of Budget Documents and Budget Speech	
SPENDING DEPARTMENTS		Review of Strategic and Operational Plans		Preparation of MYOPs	Submission of MYOPs to TB			Preparation of Estimates Part III		Finalize New Year Operational Plans Based on M.E.

Legend: Main Estimates (M.E.)
Supplementary Estimates (S.E.)

Source: Adapted from the Government of Canada, *Fiscal Plan, 1991–92* (Ottawa: Supply and Services, 1992). Reproduced by the authority of the Minister responsible for Statistics Canada 1993.

However, as we noted earlier in this chapter, in a complex modern society governed by a highly interventionist state, the distinction between means and ends or administration and politics is at best unclear and at worst untenable. The relative permanence and immense organizational resources of the bureaucracy confer upon public servants considerable influence in the policy-making process. Moreover, discretionary power has been given to the bureaucracy in many areas of policy implementation, especially where Parliament has delegated regulatory or administrative decision-making authority to government departments, agencies and tribunals. Given these trends, peaceful coexistence between bureaucracy and democracy cannot be maintained by seeking restoration of the distinction between politics and administration. The policy-making or policy-influencing activities of the bureaucracy have to be controlled by representative political institutions such as Parliament in such a way that the bureaucracy can be held accountable for its operations.

PARLIAMENTARY CONTROLS

Parliamentary reforms enacted over the last two decades have been oriented in part toward government's dependence on the bureaucracy as a source of information and policy advice. The effectiveness of parliamentary committees is increasing, and their reports necessarily present a view of government policy that differs from that of the public service. Opposition parties receive research funds to assist them in achieving more effective policy input or, at least, in developing more informed criticism of existing policy-making and implementation. Increased staff support for individual MPs, while still not sufficient, does provide some research potential that enables MPs to question bureaucratic decisions more effectively.

Perhaps the most important asset of Parliament's scrutiny of the work of the bureaucracy arises in the expenditure budget process. Here, too, parliamentary and administrative reforms have enhanced the potential for democratic control. The presentation of estimates in program format (rather than by standard objects of expenditure) facilitates the comparison of spending with policy outputs and government priorities. The development of multi-year fiscal plans provides a broader and more long-range context for the evaluation of both overall spending plans and individual estimates. The role of the Auditor General permits a critical appraisal of the effectiveness of both public spending and accounting practices by the Public Accounts Committee. The Auditor is directly responsible to Parliament — not the executive — and his reports trigger major debates in the House of Commons about government policy-making.

There remain some problems, however. One is the perceived lack of accountability of Crown corporations to Parliament identified by the Lambert Commission. Although the reports of public enterprises and regulatory agencies are now automatically referred to the appropriate standing committees, inadequate auditing provisions and difficulties in imposing ministerial responsibility for these semi-autonomous agencies hinder effective parliamentary control. A number of measures have been proposed for strengthening the accountability of Crown agencies,[74] but legislation has always failed to secure passage before its proponents forced an election.

With this exception, the mechanisms for parliamentary control of the bureaucracy are largely in place. The key question thus remains, as we suggested in Chapter 8, whether MPs have the inclination or the time to devote themselves to ensuring bureaucratic accountability.

---

[74] See Government of Canada, Privy Council Office, *Crown Corporations: Direction, Control and Accountability* (Ottawa: Queen's Printer, 1977); and Royal Commission on Financial Management and Accountability, *Final Report*.

The Lambert Commission called on parliamentarians to "treat their surveillance role with the same seriousness they accord their political responsibilities"[75] but, in the absence of structural and/or widespread attitudinal change in the House of Commons, it seems likely that MPs will continue to have little inclination to fully utilize the opportunities available to them.

ALTERNATIVE MECHANISMS FOR CONTROL

Other non-parliamentary means of controlling the bureaucracy's role in policy-making have also been proposed over the years. The judicial process, for example, might be called on to play a greater role in protecting citizens against arbitrary bureaucratic decisions. But, although there has been an increase in court challenges to bureaucratic decisions since the *Charter of Rights* has been implemented, we have to agree with the conclusion drawn by one opponent of judicial review of the bureaucracy:

> *It would be wrong to abandon democratic processes working through Parliament to check bureaucratic power in favour of a more elitist approach based upon courts, lawyers and tribunals as the primary mechanisms for safeguarding the rights of individuals.*[76]

As an alternative means of protecting individual citizens against arbitrary decision-making, there has been some debate concerning the establishment of a federal "ombudsman," an independent officer who would be responsible to Parliament for the investigation of citizens' complaints against the bureaucracy.[77] The establishment of an ombudsman at the federal level (most provinces already have provincial ombudsmen) was recommended by an investigatory committee in 1977,[78] but legislation introduced the following year failed to pass beyond Second Reading.[79] However, although an ombudsman might provide an additional mechanism of overall surveillance of the bureaucracy, it should be noted that Canada already has a number of more specialized ombudsman-like officers, including the Commissioner of Official Languages, a Privacy Commissioner and a Correctional Investigator for Penitentiary Services, who all act as watchdogs over certain aspects of bureaucratic activity.

The federal government took one step to provide for more open government. In 1983, the *Access to Information Act* was finally promulgated after over twenty years of debate within and outside Parliament.[80] With a number of controversial exceptions, Canadian citizens and permanent residents now have the right to obtain or examine records that were previously kept secret by federal government institutions. At stake in many cases is the individual's right to

---

[75]   Royal Commission on Financial Management and Accountability, *Final Report*, p. 388.

[76]   Paul Thomas, "Courts Can't be Saviours," *Policy Options*, vol. 5, no. 3 (May/June 1984), p. 27

[77]   See D.C. Rowat, "An Ombudsman Scheme for Canada," *CJEPS*, vol. 28, no. 4 (November 1962), pp. 543–56; his comparative survey in D.C. Rowat, ed., *The Ombudsman*, 2nd ed. (Toronto: University of Toronto Press, 1968); and "Reflections on the Ombudsman Concept," Nova Scotia Ombudsman's *Annual Report*, Dec. 31, 1990, pp. 26–34.

[78]   Government of Canada, Committee on the Concept of the Ombudsman, *Report* (Ottawa: Queen's Printer, 1977).

[79]   For a critique of the proposed Ombudsman Act, see K.A. Friedmann and A.G. Milne, "The Federal Ombudsman Legislation: A Critique of Bill C-43," *Canadian Public Policy*, vol. 6, no. 1 (Winter 1980), pp. 63–77.

[80]   On the history of the "Freedom of Information" debate, see Adie and Thomas, *Canadian Public Administration*, and the overview in Donald C. Rowat, "The Right of Public Access to Official Documents," in O.P. Dwivedi, ed., *The Administrative State in Canada: Essay for J.E. Hodgetts* (Toronto: University of Toronto Press, 1982), p. 177–92.

know why certain government decisions were taken, or to determine whether they were fairly arrived at or whether mistakes were made. The *Act* is intended to make government more accountable and to reverse whatever public image exists of public servants scheming to hide blunders or alleged corruption from innocent victims.

Nonetheless, some observers are skeptical of the value of the *Act* in its present form. Donald Rowat has argued that some of the exceptions to access "go against the whole spirit of a freedom of information act by absolutely prohibiting certain types of records from being released, thus turning these exemptions into an extension of the *Official Secrets Act*."[81] Also disturbing is the long list of subjects on which discretionary exemptions can be made by bureaucrats, which may well "limit the accountability of the government to Parliament."[82] Moreover, if the government refuses to disclose information on request, appeal can be made first to an Information Commissioner. Ultimate recourse, however, is via the Federal Court — an expensive procedure that raises the undesirable prospect of having the judicial process replace Parliament as the primary mechanism for ensuring bureaucratic accountability. In 1991–92 use of the *Act* to obtain information was slightly declining, progress was slow and only 69 percent of requests were fully met.[83]

In the final analysis, public confidence will depend on how well the mechanics of releasing information work and on whether information which should be released is actually made public. This, in turn, will depend upon the extent to which the Cabinet and the bureaucracy are willing to comply with the spirit as well as the letter of the new law. The issue of freedom of information will undoubtedly remain on the agenda of public debate in the late 1990s as the *Act* continues to be evaluated.

OVERVIEW

Many Canadians are extremely suspicious, if not downright cynical, about the federal bureaucracy. In part, as we have argued, this suspicion stems from fear of the unknown, or, at least, the inadequately understood. The bureaucracy is not a single monolithic entity whose size and organizational structure automatically present a threat to democratic government. Rather it is a complex of competing departments, corporations and agencies established to meet the perceived economic, social and political goals of the public. Neither is the bureaucracy an elite group, dominated by a single class or ethnic/linguistic group and thereby unrepresentative of and unresponsive to the Canadian population. Concerted efforts have been made over the last few decades to make the bureaucracy more representative, although there is still substantial room for improvement, especially with regard to increasing opportunities for women and Native people. Nor is there an absence of mechanisms through which control or accountability might be imposed on the bureaucracy by elected institutions. Rather, if there is a problem it may well be described as a lack of political will to make use of these control mechanisms.

Elected politicians in both Cabinet and Parliament feel bound to respond to the immediate demands of constituents and voters in order to secure their re-election. And, since voters and interest groups tend to rush to the defence of threatened programs from which they benefit, reduction of the size of public spending levels is relatively low in the political

---

[81] Rowat, "The Right of Public Access," pp. 185–86.

[82] Ibid., p. 187.

[83] *The Ottawa Citizen*, April 5, 1993.

priorities of Canadians. As long as the bureaucracy continues to serve the needs of most segments of Canadian society, there will not be sufficient impetus for a serious assault on the public service and its programs. Ultimately, as with governments, it may be argued that societies get the bureaucracies they deserve.

SELECTED BIBLIOGRAPHY

Adie, Robert F. and Paul G. Thomas, *Canadian Public Administration*, 2nd ed. (Scarborough, Ont.: Prentice-Hall Canada, 1987).

Albo, Gregory, David Langille and Leo Panitch, eds., *A Different Kind of State? Popular Power and Democratic Administration* (Toronto: Oxford University Press, 1993).

Bernier, I. and A. Lajoie, eds., *Regulations, Crown Corporations and Administrative Tribunals*, vol. 48, Royal Commission on the Economic Union and Development Prospects for Canada (Toronto: University of Toronto Press, 1985).

Blau, Peter M., *Bureaucracy in Modern Society* (New York: Random House, 1956).

Bourgault, J. and Dion, S., *The Changing Profile of Federal Deputy Ministers, 1867–1988* (Ottawa: Centre for Management Development, 1990).

Brooks, Stephen, *Who's in Charge? The Mixed Ownership Corporation in Canada* (Halifax: IRPP, 1987).

Clark, Jon D., *Getting the Incentives Right; Toward a Productivity-oriented Management Framework for the Public Service* (Ottawa: Treasury Board, 1993).

Doern, G. Bruce, Allan Maslove and Michael Prince, *Public Budgeting in Canada; Politics, Economics and Management* (Ottawa: Carleton University Press, 1988).

Butler, Stuart M., *Privatizing Federal Spending: A Strategy to Eliminate the Deficit* (New York: Universe Books, 1985).

Doerr, Audrey D., *The Machinery of Government in Canada* (Toronto: Methuen, 1981).

Dwivedi, O.P., ed., *The Administrative State in Canada: Essays for J.E. Hodgetts* (Toronto: University of Toronto Press, 1982).

Granatstein, J.L., *The Ottawa Men: The Civil Service Mandarins 1935–57* (Toronto: Oxford University Press, 1982).

Hardin, Hershel, *The Privatization Putsch* (Halifax: IRPP, 1989).

Hodgetts, J.E., *The Canadian Public Service 1867-1970: A Physiology of Government* (Toronto: University of Toronto Press, 1973).

——————, *Public Management: Emblem of Reform of the Canadian Public Service* (Ottawa; Canadian Centre for Management Development, 1991).

Hood, C., *The Tools of Government* (London: Chatham House, 1986).

Kernaghan, Kenneth, *Canadian Public Administration: Discipline and Profession* (Toronto: Butterworths/Institute of Public Administration of Canada, 1983).

——————, ed., *Public Administration in Canada; Selected Readings*, 5th ed. (Toronto: Methuen, 1985).

—————— and John Langford, *The Responsible Public Servant* (Halifax: IRPP, 1990).

—————— and David Siegal, *Public Administration in Canada*, 2nd ed. (Scarborough: Nelson, 1991).

Lane, J.E., ed., *Bureaucracy and Public Choice* (London: Sage, 1989).

Laux, Jeanne and Maureen Molot, *State Capitalism: Public Enterprise in Canada* (Ithica: Cornell Unversity Press, 1988).

Morgan, Nicole, *Implosion* (Ottawa: IRPP, 1986).

————, *Nowhere to Go* (Montréal: IRPP, 1981).

Osbaldeston, Gordon F., *Keeping Deputy Ministers Accountable* (Toronto: McGraw-Hill Ryerson, 1989).

————, *Organizing to Govern*, vols I and II (Toronto: McGraw-Hill Ryerson, 1992).

Plumptre, Timothy, *Beyond the Bottom Line: Management in Government* (Halifax: IRPP, 1988).

Pritchard, J.R.S., ed., *Crown Corporations in Canada* (Toronto: Butterworths, 1983).

Self, Peter, *Administrative Theories and Politics*, 2nd ed. (Toronto: University of Toronto Press, 1977).

Simeon, R., ed., *Division of Powers and Public Policy*, vol. 61, Royal Commission on the Economic Union (Toronto: University of Toronto Press, 1985).

Stanbury, W.T. and Thomas E. Kierans, eds., *Papers on Privatization* (Montréal: IRPP, 1985).

Sutherland, Sharon L. and Y. Baltaciogla, *Parliamentary Reform and the Federal Public Service* (London, Ont.: School of Business Administration, University of Western Ontario, 1988).

Sutherland, Sharon L. and G. Bruce Doern, *Bureaucracy in Canada: Control and Reform*, vol. 43, Royal Commission on the Economic Union (Toronto: University of Toronto Press, 1985).

Swimmer, G. and M. Thompson, eds., *Public Sector Industrial Relations in Canada* (Montréal: IRPP, 1983).

Treasury Board of Canada, *Modernizing the Federal Government* (Ottawa, 1993).

Tupper, Allan and Bruce Doern, eds., *Public Corporations and Public Policy in Canada* (Montréal: IRPP, 1981).

Wilson, V. Seymour, *Canadian Public Policy and Administration: Theory and Environment* (Toronto: McGraw-Hill Ryerson, 1981).

See also the periodical *Canadian Public Administration*.

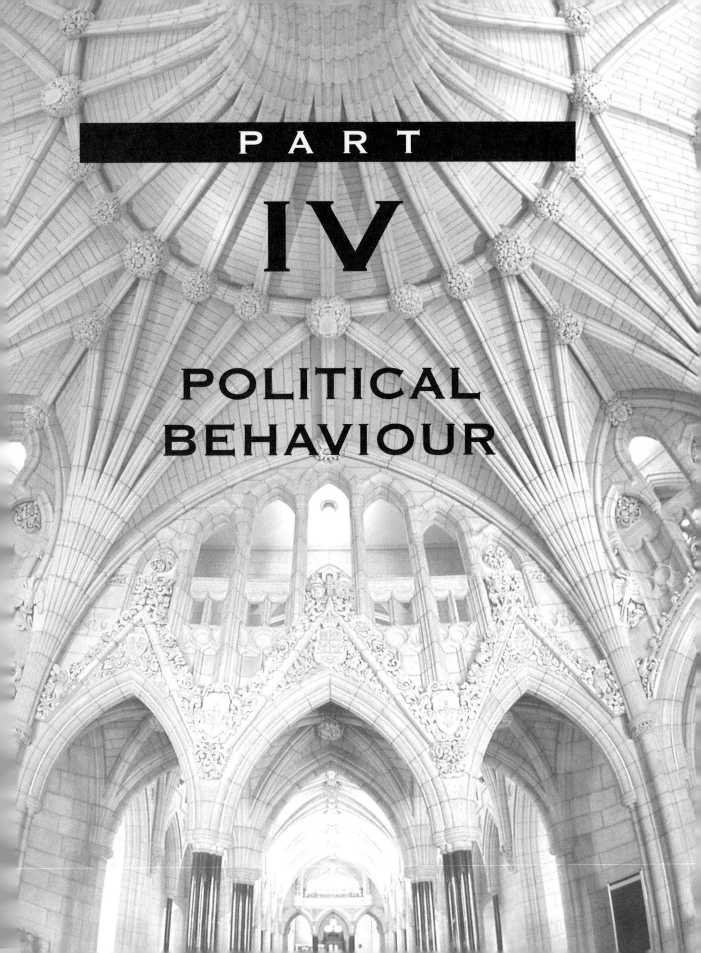

PART

IV

POLITICAL BEHAVIOUR

On se donne le Vrai POUVOIR

POLITICAL PARTIES
PERSISTENCE AND CHANGE

Political parties are a vital part of the Canadian political system. They are agents of representative democracy. With few exceptions, local party organizations select candidates who stand for election as Members of Parliament. The Prime Minister, although formally named by the Governor General, almost invariably is leader of the party that holds the greatest number of elected representatives and is therefore most likely to form a viable government. In short, the party system provides essential organizing and stabilizing functions for government in a large, bureaucratic state.

In spite of their important role, organized political parties are a relatively recent historical phenomena. As vehicles of mass participation in politics, they became increasingly significant and formalized as the franchise was extended, providing voters with progressively clearer alternatives. In Canada, the Liberal and Conservative parties have assumed an important place in the political culture for over a century, while the New Democratic Party's historical roots go back almost half that length of time. In the 1993 General Election, however, two new, regionally based parties, the Reform Party and the Bloc Québécois, burst dramatically onto the federal scene, cutting into the traditional bases of support of all three established parties and threatening two of them with extinction.

The federal parties provide a common political focus for Canadians, including a real-life national soap opera complete with heroes, rogues and villains. Party leaders are the object of rapt media attention: their political views, personal foibles and even their families provide fodder for discussion and personal gossip from coast to coast. Today, more than ever, they focus public attention on the national stage of Canadian politics.

Yet, for many decades, federal political parties have had a divisive influence on the country. Their leaders often have proven powerless to prevent the regionalization of their bases of support; indeed, at times they appeared to encourage it. The failure to achieve strong *national* representation remains a serious challenge for modern Canadian political parties. When the main parties are unable to represent the country from sea to sea, the party system fragments and new parties arise to promote specifically regional causes, balkanizing the country and providing few voices at the centre to stand up for Canada.

In this chapter, we examine the origins and development of Canadian parties and their organization and structure outside of Parliament. What are their basic functions and how well do they perform them? How representative of the Canadian public are they?

How democratic are they in formulating party policy? We also examine the role of the party leader and consider the selection process that thrusts individuals into that prestigious and potentially powerful position. First, however, we examine the definition and role of parties, and survey the wide range of party types and party systems that exist as possible alternatives.

WHAT ARE POLITICAL PARTIES?

Political parties have been defined in a number of ways. Karl Marx, for example, considered them to be a manifestation of class conflict and struggle. Benjamin Disraeli saw them as organized opinion. However, perhaps the most useful definition for our purposes is simply that **political parties** are organizations designed to secure the power of the state for their leaders. The goal of political parties is to gain control of the levers of government and therefore realize their policies or programs. In democratic systems this is achieved through open competition in the electoral process.[1] The voluminous literature on political parties provides general (though not unanimous) agreement that parties constitute a crucial link between society and government.[2]

PARTY FUNCTIONS

Political parties have certain tasks or functions to perform in society; these vary according to the political system in which they operate.[3] It has already been mentioned that political parties add an important element of stability to the political system by legitimizing the individuals and institutions that control political power. In addition, they help to organize the electorate by recruiting candidates, organizing campaigns, encouraging partisan attachments, helping individual voters get their names on polling lists and generally stimulating voter participation. As well, they help to organize the government by providing a degree of policy direction and supplying party leaders as potential Prime Ministers and Cabinet Ministers. The winning party serves to fuse the executive and legislative branches of government in Canada, providing the foundation of Cabinet government.

Within the broad task of organizing the electorate and the government, there are several specific party functions that deserve elaboration.

---

[1] At a practical level, of course, countries have different rules defining what constitutes an officially recognized political party. In Canada, to be recognized on a ballot at election time, and receive other privileges such as tax credits and advertising broadcast time, a party must field a minimum of 50 candidates. To be officially recognized in the House of Commons, a party must have 12 MPs — though the House may allow exceptions.

[2] Parties are relatively modern phenomena, playing a major role in Britain for the first time in the eighteenth century. There has been considerable controversy over their desirability, epitomized in the classic works of M.I. Ostrogorski, *Democracy and the Organization of Political Parties*, 2 vols., trans. by Frederick Clarke (New York: Macmillan, 1902) and Robert Michels, *Political Parties: A Sociological Study of Oligarchical Tendencies of Modern Democracy*, trans. by Eden and Cedar Paul, with introduction by S.M. Lipset (New York: The Free Press, 1966). Modern classics include Leon D. Epstein, *Political Parties in Western Democracies* (New York: Praeger, 1967).

[3] See a classic article by Anthony King, "Political Parties in Western Democracies," *Polity*, vol. II, no. 2 (Winter 1969), pp. 111–141.

RECRUITMENT, NOMINATION AND ELECTION OF POLITICAL OFFICEHOLDERS

It is the task of every political party to enlist suitable candidates for the positions of MPs, government ministers and Prime Minister, and then get them elected to form a government. To achieve this, each party must select and present candidates and mobilize voters by waging a campaign. The winning party forms the government and largely decides who will occupy the major policy-making posts, the most powerful tool a party can control. It gains control of numerous patronage appointments throughout the government structure, and is able to reward its own supporters while extending its power and influence. Party leaders therefore recruit public appointees such as Senators and members of Crown agencies, as well as helping to elect representatives to the House of Commons.

INTEREST ARTICULATION AND AGGREGATION

A vast number of interests are present in modern, complex societies. Parties articulate or express those interests in many ways; they educate public opinion by debating important issues; and they provide a legitimate outlet for dissent and pressure for change. The latter is particularly important for accommodating regional or sectional interests. In fact, parties are often referred to as "gatekeepers" in the political system because they allow certain demands to pass directly to decision-makers, while they eliminate or combine others. Political parties also perform the valuable function of bringing together, then reducing and simplifying the morass of interests to manageable sets of policy alternatives. By appealing to the many classes, regions, interests and ethnic groups that make up the country, political parties modify conflict and facilitate decisions. This process, known as **aggregation** of interests, is performed by a variety of structures in society, but political parties may be the most important. Parties constantly monitor the electorate for ideas and conduct opinion polls to help them transform public concerns into vote-winning policies. Effective interest aggregation is important for electoral success in Canada.

FORMULATION OF PUBLIC POLICY

By winning elections, parties form the government and acquire the ability to formulate and present public policy. The Cabinet, along with senior civil servants who have an important role in drafting policies, leads the policy-making function in the legislative process. Parties provide platforms for election campaigns, but these are rarely very restrictive in terms of subsequent policy decisions.

POLITICAL SOCIALIZATION

In stable democracies, political parties normally play a fairly conservative role, reinforcing the established system in order to keep the political process running smoothly. A revolutionary situation would, of course, bring on different types of parties. In a parliamentary democracy such as Canada, which lacks a strong, homogeneous political culture, there is a special need for political parties to play a unifying role as "agencies for the creation of national symbols, experiences, memories, heroes, and villains."[4] The failure of Canadian parties to bind regional cleavages by building strong national bases of representation limits their effectiveness.[5]

---

[4]   John Meisel, "Recent Changes in Canadian Parties," in Hugh G. Thorburn, ed., *Party Politics in Canada*, 2nd ed (Scarborough, Ont.: Prentice-Hall Canada, 1967), p. 34.

[5]   Alan Cairns was one of the first to argue that the party system "conditioned by the electoral system, exacerbates the very cleavages it is credited with healing." Alan C. Cairns, "The Electoral System and the Party System in Canada, 1921–1965," *CJPS*, vol. 1, no. 1 (March 1968), p. 62.

They do, however, inform and educate the public, enlisting a high percentage of Canadians to participate in the electoral process through volunteer work as well as through voting.

OTHER FUNCTIONS

Parties sometimes participate in community activities outside the political arena in an attempt to influence constituents indirectly. They also provide a training ground for future political leaders. For those who do not aspire to leadership positions they give social, psychological and sometimes economic benefits and the opportunity to participate in party decisions.

PARTY TYPES AND PARTY SYSTEMS

Political parties can be classified in a great number of ways. Maurice Duverger formulated a widely used, simple scheme that divides political parties into three categories — mass, cadre or devotee — according to their type of organization.[6] **Mass parties** recruit across class lines to achieve the largest possible membership and then allow that membership a significant role by functioning democratically. Members have significant power over their executive and the parliamentary wing — including the leader, whom they elect — and a meaningful say in policy formulation. The party is financed by membership fees. The theoretical rationale behind mass parties is that a large membership across social class lines helps to counter the power of establishment parties, whose leaders come mainly from the economic, political and social elite of society.

Cadre parties, on the other hand, are highly centralized and recruit only from the politically active elite. They are much less democratic than mass parties in that the elite runs the party and allows the rest of the party to fall dormant until election time. The parliamentary wing of the party selects the leader, who has no formal accountability. Financing is from a relatively narrow base, usually corporations. Today, they are often associated with developing nations but are found throughout the developed world as well.

Duverger's third category, **devotee parties**, are those built around a charismatic leader; an example would be the Nazi party under Adolf Hitler. As we examine Canadian parties we will see that the Liberals and Conservatives began as cadre parties, but over time they have taken on some features of the mass party model. The NDP began, and remains, close to the mass party model, as does Reform. The Bloc Québécois has many features of a cadre party.

The series of relationships among parties in a political system constitutes the **party system**. Party systems, too, can be classified to assist in making gross comparisons among states. One way to categorize them is by the number of active parties. Around the world there are one-party, dominant party, two-party and multi-party systems.[7]

In the **one-party state**, a single party — which is the only legal party — controls every level of government. Communist and authoritarian regimes such as the former Soviet Union, Cuba, the People's Republic of China and some Marxist-inspired African states are examples.

A **dominant party** system exists when a single party regularly wins almost every election, though opposition parties are allowed to function freely. An example is in Mexico

---

[6]   The classic discussion of party organization is found in Maurice Duverger, *Political Parties: Their Organization and Activity in the Modern State* (London: Methuen, 1954).

[7]   Of course, there are more complex definitions and typologies of party systems. See, for example, Giovanni Sartori, *Parties and Party Systems: A Framework for Analysis* (London: Cambridge University Press, 1976).

where the Institutional Revolutionary Party (PRI) invariably defeats all minor parties in congressional and presidential elections.

The **two-party system** is characteristic of much of the English-speaking world. In this system, two major parties dominate; others have only minor political strength. The United States has a classic two-party system. Great Britain, Australia, New Zealand and Canada all have a tradition of two dominant parties that vie for power as well as one or more weaker third parties. This model offers the electorate a choice of policies and leaders, and at the same time promotes governmental stability by making it possible for one party to win a majority or near-majority in the legislature.

In the **multi-party system**, popular support is divided among several parties, so that the party in power must generally form coalitions to retain its position. This system, of which present-day Italy, the Third and Fourth French Republics and Weimar Germany are major examples, is often criticized as being unstable. However, there are many examples of multi-party systems with stable governments — notably Switzerland, the Netherlands and Austria. Advocates of this type of system argue that it allows a wide expression of the many interests of a complex society.

More sophisticated classification systems for parties have been devised to distinguish with greater precision among party systems on a world-wide basis. Joseph LaPalombara and Myron Weiner, for example, introduced a *competitive/non-competitive* classification of party systems that has since been expanded by others (see Table 10.1).[8]

TABLE 10-1   PARTY SYSTEMS BASED ON PARTY COMPETITION

Non-Competitive Systems	1. Communist (China)
	2. Authoritarian (Franco's Spain)
Mixed and Low-Competitive Systems	1. Low Competition (Mexico)
Competitive Systems	1. Dominant One-Party (Japan until 1993)
	2. Two-Party (United States)
	3. Multi-Party Dominant (three or more parties; one regularly receives about 40% of the vote) (Canada)
	4. Multi-Party Loose (three or more parties; none regularly receives 40% of the vote) (Italy)

Source: Adapted from Joseph LaPalombara and Myron Weiner, eds., *Political Parties and Political Development* (New Jersey: Princeton University Press, 1966) and Joseph LaPalombara, *Politics Within Nations* (Englewood Cliffs, N.J.: Prentice-Hall, 1974), ch. 13.

Competitive systems are classified by the number of parties that compete for and have access to legislative power. In the **dominant one-party** system a single party regularly wins almost every election, even though opposition parties function freely. In the **two-party** system, two major parties dominate; others have only minor political strength. In the **multiparty** system, popular support is divided among several parties so that the largest party must generally form a coalition with one or more other parties to form a government. As indicated in Table 10.1, multi-party systems can be divided further into multi-party dominant or

---

8   Joseph LaPalombara and Myron Weiner, eds., *Political Parties and Political Development* (Princeton, N.J.: Princeton University Press, 1966), pp. 33–41.

multi-party loose. **Non-competitive systems**, in which one party dominates, are classified by other variables, such as how repressive their governments are. A few have been called **mixed and low competitive** because they include elements of the other two types. In Mexico, for example, opposition parties are allowed, but one party dominates to such an extent that the system is almost non-competitive.[9]

Classification systems are intended for gross comparisons between states. Not all countries fit neatly into any one category, and a country's classification may change over time. Canada is a prime example. It has a competitive party system, but, partly because this system has changed over time, Canada does not clearly belong in any of the above categories. Until the rise of third parties in 1921, when the Progressives suddenly won 23 percent of the federal vote, the Canadian party system was developing along the lines of a classic two-party system. Since then, and particularly since the advent of the NDP in 1961, third parties have fairly consistently captured about a quarter of the federal vote. They never come very close to winning power in Ottawa, but nine times (six since the Second World War) they have prevented one of the major parties from winning a clear majority in a general election. Until 1993, the Canadian system, therefore, fell somewhere between the two-party and multi-party systems in the classification scheme set out above. Because of this, the arrangement in Canada has often been called a "two-and-a-half party" system. With the election of five parties in 1993, there are indications that the party system could be shifting further toward the multi-party end of the spectrum.

There are both pros and cons to the two-and-a-half system as it appeared in Canada in recent years. In general it worked quite smoothly. The two major parties were lodged so firmly in the centre of the political spectrum that they were often portrayed as Tweedledum and Tweedledee. They appealed to the same middle-of-the-road electoral supporters, constantly shifting their principles in search of electoral success. This type of flexible, non-ideological party system is known as a **brokerage** party system because the two main parties act as brokers of ideas, selecting those that have the widest appeal and the best likelihood of attracting electoral support.

George Perlin called the Liberal and Conservative parties "modified brokerage parties" because there were "some basic differences between them, partly explained by a different internal balance in ideological perspectives and partly by their long-term competitive relationship."[10] The Liberals have been considered centre-left and the Progressive Conservatives centre-right, because of a few alleged historical differences such as the Conservative support of free enterprise and the Liberal leadership in social legislation and public ownership. However, they have both displayed remarkable flexibility within this broad range. For example, free trade with the United States historically was a Liberal policy until the Conservatives took it up in 1985.

---

[9] For a classification of the world's states see Robert J. Jackson and Doreen Jackson, Contemporary Government and Politics: Democracy and Authoritarianism (Scarborough, Ont.: Prentice-Hall, 1993), pp. 68–83 and 398–481.

[10] George Perlin, ed., *Party Democracy in Canada* (Scarborough, Ont.: Prentice-Hall Canada, 1988). See especially articles in this volume by Donald Blake, "Division and Cohesion: The Major Parties," pp. 32–53 and Richard Johnston, "The Ideological Structure of Opinion on Policy," pp. 54–70. Christian and Campbell challenge the brokerage theory with an ideological interpretation in William Christian and Colin Campbell, *Political Parties and Ideologies in Canada* (Toronto: McGraw-Hill Ryerson, 1983), and in an article of the same title in Alain G. Gagnon and A. Brian Tanguay, *Canadian Parties in Transition* (Scarborough: Nelson, 1989), pp. 45–63.

Advocates of brokerage theory argue that the many cleavages in the country — ethnic, geographic, economic and demographic — have forced parties in Canada to occupy the middle of the road in their attempts to win majorities. Brokerage parties do not appeal to specific socio-economic groupings, and they are flexible and opportunistic in order to keep the country united. By usurping the middle ground the Liberals and Conservatives largely restricted radical parties to the sidelines.

History and traditional loyalties, rather than logic or ideology behind party platforms, have been the distinguishing features of Canadian political parties.[11] Divisions such as ethnicity and region have always taken precedence over class.[12] With the Conservatives reduced to only two seats in 1993, and a separatist party in official Opposition, the basic nature of the party system has changed, at least temporarily.

THE ORIGIN, DEVELOPMENT AND MODERNIZATION OF CANADIAN PARTIES

It is difficult to pinpoint the date of origin of political parties in Canada. Until shortly after Confederation, Canadian politics was characterized by factionalism. Party structures as we know them today had not had time to form, and the problems of the day did not require a comprehensive set of policies. Often, candidates did not even commit themselves to a party until they had determined who would win.

Early parties were loosely organized and even less encumbered by ideology than they are today. In their early years, Upper and Lower Canada, Nova Scotia and Prince Edward Island were all governed by oligarchies. The Family Compact, the Château Clique, the Halifax Compact and the landed proprietors in Prince Edward Island controlled the economic and political power in their particular areas. Any opposition that existed was fragmented and factional. The prime requisite for the emergence of parties was, in each case, increased competition for power within the legislature. Nowhere did the factions and interest groups mature into parties until the advent of responsible government. In fact, the formation of parties occurred even after that in the case of PEI, where religious rights and land settlement problems cut across party lines. Only when the executive became responsible to the legislature was there a genuine need for political parties to develop. As legislative responsibilities were extended, the franchise expanded, and other electoral reforms such as the secret ballot were introduced, the pressure for party cohesion increased and recognizable political parties emerged.[13]

---

[11] Paul W. Fox, "Political Parties in Canada," in Paul W. Fox, ed., *Politics: Canada*, 4th ed. (Toronto: McGraw-Hill Ryerson), pp. 253–357.

[12] See Jon Pammett, "Class Voting and Class Consciousness in Canada," *Canadian Review of Sociology and Anthropology*, vol. 24, no. 2 (1987) pp. 269–90; Keith Archer, "The Failure of the New Democratic Party: Unions, Unionists and Politics in Canada," *CJPS* (June, 1985) pp. 353–66; and Richard Johnston et al., *Letting the People Decide* (Montréal: McGill-Queen's University Press, 1992).

[13] See J.M. Beck, "Nova Scotia, the Party System in Nova Scotia: Tradition and Conservatism," in Martin Robin, ed., *Canadian Provincial Politics* (Scarborough, Ont.: Prentice-Hall Canada, 1972). Also Beck, *The Government of Nova Scotia* (Toronto: University of Toronto Press, 1957); and Frank Mackinnon, *The Government of Prince Edward Island* (Toronto: University of Toronto Press, 1951).

The origin and development of parties were directly influenced by the system of government. Canadian parties developed within the framework of a democratic parliamentary system and, after 1867, a federal constitutional arrangement. They were further influenced by internal factors such as national and industrial development, and external stimuli, such as historical precedents and ideological influences from Britain and the United States.

Until the 1920s, two major parties, the precursors of today's Liberals and Progressive Conservatives, were able to aggregate the various interests, which were not very complex. The economy prospered; regional and rural/urban cleavages were minimal. After this date the first minor parties appeared on the political scene.

Canada's party system has had to adapt over time to social, demographic and institutional changes. Ken Carty identifies three successive, distinctive Canadian party systems since Confederation. He called the first system, from 1867 to 1917, a "patronage" system. At that time, the parliamentary caucus was, in effect, the party, and parties focused on parochial constituency issues. This system ended when civil service reform deprived the parties of their state-building role. The second party system spanned the years 1921–57 when "brokerage politics" dominated and the focus of party politics shifted from constituency to region. It ended when federal/provincial diplomacy usurped the nation-building role of parties. The brokerage nature of Canadian parties continued, but Carty suggests that, in 1963, a third pattern emerged that continues today. He calls it an "electronic" party system, characterized by politics with a technical, modern, national focus. The electronic mobilization of information — most notably by television and opinion-polling — revolutionized the patterns of communication between party and voter.

We could also say that, since 1921, the party system has generally had the characteristics of a one-party dominant system where one party receives at least 40 percent of the vote.[14] For the first seven decades of this century the Liberals dominated. Until 1984, they had fallen below 40 percent of the vote in a federal election only three times: in 1958, 1962 and 1972. In only one of those cases — the Diefenbaker sweep of the country — did the Conservative Party receive a significantly higher percentage of the vote than the Liberals. In terms of seats, the Liberals won 18 of the 25 General Elections from 1896 to 1984. Until 1984, therefore, the Liberals, as the government party, monopolized bureaucratic and senatorial appointments and all the other advantages of holding power, including the psychological advantages of being perceived as the government party. During this period, the Conservatives were the main opposition party. Being much less successful, they were prone to factionalism that further decreased their chances of electoral success. From 1984 to 1993 the situation was temporarily reversed and the Conservatives dominated the party system for nine years until their disasterous defeat in 1993. Given the fact that as of 1993 the Liberals are the only nationally based party, the one-party dominant character of the party system has strengthened. (See Figure 10-1.)

Since 1921, there has always been at least one minor party represented in Parliament. From 1961 to 1993, the only significant "third" party was the NDP. On the moderate left of the political spectrum, it has often acted as a social conscience, initiating innovative ideas for social programs that were too extreme for the major parties but that, over time, were taken into the Liberal or Conservative party platforms and eventually implemented in watered-

---

[14] See Hugh G. Thorburn, "Interpretations of the Canadian Party System," in Thorburn, ed., *Party Politics in Canada*, 6th ed; or Reginald Whitaker, *The Government Party: Organizing and Financing the Liberal Party of Canada, 1930–50* (Toronto: University of Toronto Press, 1977).

FIGURE 10.1   PARTIES IN PARLIAMENT: PERCENT OF SEATS WON BY PARTY IN
GENERAL ELECTIONS, 1945–93

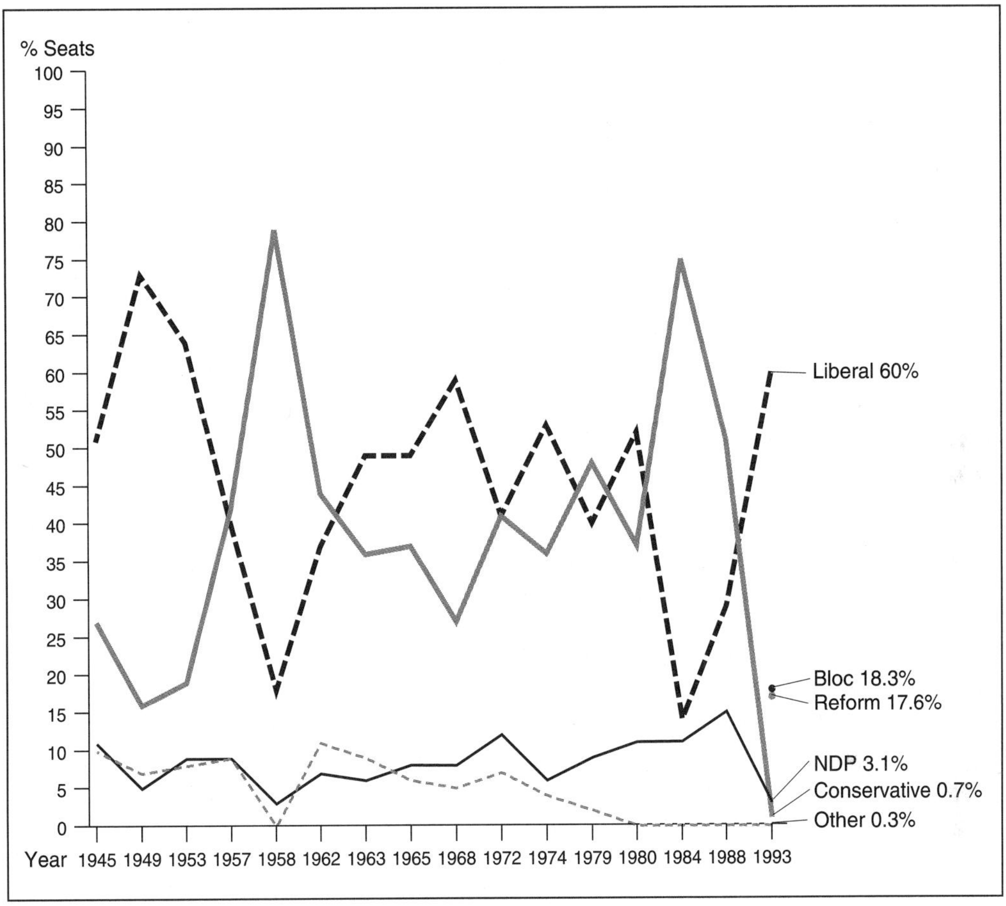

Source: Adapted from Pierre F. Normadin, ed., *Canadian Parliamentary Guide* (Ottawa, 1989).

down form. A case in point was the implementation of provincial health care plans. From more radical left-wing origins, the NDP gradually adopted a moderate-left reform position that, at times, overlaps with centre-left Liberal positions. The middle-of-the-road tendency of all the parties is evident, but the historical relationship between the parties is sufficient to warrant their relative positions on the left-right continuum.[15]

Until 1993, the two major parties together consistently won about 75–80 percent of the vote; the NDP, about 15–20 percent. By helping to broaden the spectrum of political views represented in Parliament, minor or third parties provide a legitimate outlet for political dissent, giving a voice to minority opinion that might otherwise be forced to work outside the system. In this respect, they are particularly effective at the provincial level where they often form provincial governments. For example, the CCF-NDP has governed in

---

[15]   On problems encountered in placing Canadian parties on an ideological left-right spectrum, see David Elkins, "The Perceived Structure of the Canadian Party System," *CJPS*, vol. 7, no. 3 (September 1974), pp. 502–24. See also Thorburn, "Interpretations of the Canadian Party System," in Thorburn, *Party Politics in Canada*, 5th ed., pp. 20–40.

Saskatchewan, Manitoba, British Columbia and Ontario; Social Credit in Alberta and British Columbia; the Union Nationale and the Parti Québécois in Québec.

In the late 1980s, Canada's modified two-party system began to show signs that it was shifting toward a multi-party system. The Mulroney Conservative government was highly unpopular, the Liberals were not regarded as a satisfactory alternative in Québec and parts of western Canada and the New Democratic Party remained unable to create a bridge between French- and English-speaking populations. Two new parties, the Reform Party and the Bloc Québécois, filled the breach, sapping the support of the established parties in Québec and the West, particularly that of the Conservatives and the NDP. Blessed with militants, money and simple messages the Bloc and Reform attracted 33 percent of the popular vote in the 1993 General Election.

There are several factors involved in the rise of minor parties including ethnicity, regionalism, poor economic conditions, charismatic leadership and ideology. Maurice Pinard theorizes that minor parties arise from a period of one-party dominance when voters are dissatisfied with the traditional party and do not like the weak existing alternative party.[16] They prefer instead a new minor party. At best, minor parties provide flexibility in Canadian politics; at worst they fragment the country, pitting region against region and creating political instability.

The Canadian party system is plagued by other problems as well. Party image, like that of politics and politicians generally, has deteriorated; ties to parties have withered and supporters drifted away. John Meisel maintains that political parties are in decline, as their traditional functions have been taken over by other institutions.[17]

Canadians have become cynical and distrustful of politics, politicians and political parties. In the late 1980s, this was fuelled by the belief that the Meech Lake accord was formed by a few men behind closed doors, and the Charlottetown accord was "sold" by an elite to an unwilling public. Following the 1988 General Election campaign, charges were made that groups such as the Business Council on National Issues had spent huge sums of money and interfered in the electoral process by running a parallel campaign to support free trade. Discussions of how to reform parties and make them more democratic and responsive to public needs culminated in a Royal Commission on Electoral Reform and Party Financing (RCERPF) headed by Pierre Lortie. Their report, *Reforming Electoral Democracy*, was produced in February, 1992. In concluding its study, it stated that

> *Canadians appear to distrust their political leaders, the political process and political institutions.... Canadian political parties are held in low public esteem, and...their standing has declined steadily over the past decade. They are under attack from citizens for failing to achieve a variety of goals deemed important by significant groups within society.*[18]

---

[16] On third parties see Maurice Pinard, "One Party Dominance and the Rise of Third Parties," *CJPS*, vol. 33, no. 3 (August 1967), pp. 358–73. See also Pinard, *The Rise of a Third Party: A Study in Crisis Politics* (Englewood Cliffs, N.J.: Prentice-Hall, 1971); and "Third Parties in Canada Revisited: A Rejoinder and Elaboration of the Theory of One-Party Dominance," *CJPS*, vol. 6, no. 3 (September 1973), pp. 439–60; Graham White, "One Party Dominance and Third Parties: The Pinard Theory Reconsidered," *CJPS*, vol. 6, no. 3 (September 1973), pp. 399–421; and A. Blais, "Third Parties in Canadian Provincial Politics," *CJPS*, vol. 6, no. 3 (September 1973), pp. 422–38.

[17] John Meisel, "Decline of Party in Canada" in Thorburn, ed., *Party Politics in Canada*, 5th ed.; John Meisel, "The Dysfunction of Canadian Parties: An Exploratory Mapping," in ibid., 6th ed.; and Ian Ward, "'Media Intrusion' and the Changing Nature of the established Parties in Australia and Canada," *CJPS*, vol. XXVI, no. 3 (Sept. 1993), pp. 477–506.

[18] The Royal Commission on Electoral Reform and Party Financing (RCERPF), *Reforming Electoral Democracy*, vol. 1 (Ottawa: Supply and Services, 1992), p. 221.

The Report challenged the parties to reform themselves and become more democratic, and suggested many ways that they might do so, including having meaningful political debates to elevate political discourse, giving their members a larger role to play and fighting fair elections with limited expenditures. As we shall see in the next chapter, virtually all of the recommendations have been ignored.

In the Report, criticism of parties centred on features that are endemic to brokerage politics.[19] Accommodation of interests tends to become the prerogative of "back-room boys" and party elites who discourage interference of non-elites. Elements of society may be excluded or under-represented. In Canada, as we have seen, regions are not consistently well represented in each party, nor are women, aboriginals, visible minorities or the poor. When groups are traditionally under-represented, they seek alternative routes to representation. Protest parties, social movements and interest groups organize and offer themselves as alternatives to the three main parties, weakening them, and sometimes threatening their very existence, as in the 1993 General Election.

Since brokerage parties are non-ideological, they rarely offer alternative, comprehensive manifestos from which the public can choose. This, too, weakens the party system. The RCERPF recommended measures to enhance fairness and electoral competition, increasing the spectrum of ideas and widening the range of choices for electors. Most such recommendations were financial — such as extending the existing reimbursment of allowable election expenses (up to 50 percent) to candidates who received as little as one percent of the vote in their constituency. Currently, individuals must win 15 percent of the vote to get the refund.

The recommendations of this Royal Commission were dramatic, but somewhat naïve. The proposals would weaken the parties that put them in place. It was not surprising, therefore, that the ideas were not acted on before the 1993 election. (In retrospect, the Conservatives might wish they had done so!)

FEDERALISM, REGIONALISM AND THE PARTY SYSTEM

In addition to being competitive the Canadian party system is both federal and highly regional. While they parallel the federal organization of government, the *provincial* party systems are not necessarily identical to their federal counterparts. Provincially, as federally, the classic two-party system is found consistently only in the Atlantic provinces, where third parties rarely win more than 5 percent of the vote. Federal and provincial parties of the same name generally have separate elites, organizations, financial support and, often, separate platforms.[20] Only in the Atlantic provinces are federal/provincial party ties fairly integrated. For this reason, a federal party cannot assume ideological congruence or policy support from its provincial counterparts. The federal Liberal Party and the Québec Liberal Party, for example, share neither organization nor ideas. The Bloc and the Parti Québécois, on the other hand, share

---

19 Brokerage politics in Canada has been criticized for many years. See, for example, F.H. Underhill "The Canadian Party System in Transition," *Canadian Journal of Economics and Political Science*, vol. IX, 1943, pp. 300–13; and Gad Horowitz, "Toward the Democratic Class Struggle," in Trevor Lloyd and Jack McLeod, *Agenda 1970: Proposals for a Creative Politics* (Toronto: University of Toronto Press, 1968).

20 Donald V. Smiley, *Canada in Question: Federalism in the Eighties*, 3rd ed. (Toronto: McGraw-Hill Ryerson, 1980), pp. 83–113. Also see Rand Dyck, "Relations Between Federal and Provincial Parties," in Gagnon and Tanguay, *Canadian Parties in Transition*, pp. 186–219.

both. Provincial governments generally win support by pugnacious behaviour in taking strong stands for provincial concerns against the federal government. As Garth Stevenson speculates, this

peculiar separation of the party system into federal and provincial layers is perhaps in part a consequence of the intensity of federal-provincial conflict, which makes it difficult for a party affiliated with the federal government to appear as a credible defender of provincial interests.[21]

For whatever reason, voters do not necessarily support the same parties federally and provincially.

Although the Liberal Party dominated the federal government for most of this century, after the Second World War it gradually lost support at the provincial level. By the late 1970s, it was reduced to the role of major opposition party provincially or even the third party, as in Alberta and British Columbia. In fact, when it was defeated federally in 1979 and again in 1984, not a single Liberal provincial government existed anywhere in Canada. During the next nine years of federal Conservative rule, however, Liberal fortunes revived in most provinces and provincial Conservative governments lost. In the same vein, provincial success does not necessarily carry over into the federal sphere.

The federal structure also encourages the establishment of new parties at the provincial level. Some remain unique to one or to a few provinces and never move into the federal system, while others do enter the federal contest but never come close to power. The Parti Québécois, for example, is an important provincial one-province party. In the 1993 General Election it threw its weight behind the new Bloc Québécois as the standard bearer of Québec separatism in the federal Parliament. The English equivalent of the Parti Québécois in Québec, the Equality Party, is a minor, provincial-level party also unique to that province. The Social Credit Party, on the other hand, has existed at both levels. It established roots at the provincial in three provinces. It also flourished briefly federally, but won no federal seats after 1979.

Perhaps the most interesting, but also the most worrisome, feature of the Canadian party system is its strong regional character. In recent years, with the exceptions of 1984 and 1988, general elections increasingly have produced governments with great regional distortions because the parties were unable to build strong national bases. In the 1980 election, for example, the Liberals won 99 percent of the seats in Québec, 55 percent of those in Ontario, 59 percent in the Atlantic region, but just under 3 percent in the West (see Table 10.2 for an overview of elections from 1867 to 1993). Translated into parliamentary seats, 74 of the Liberal government's 147 seats came from Québec, 52 from Ontario, 19 from the Atlantic provinces and only two from the West (both from Manitoba). This meant that the four Western provinces were virtually excluded from the government caucus: they only had about one percent of the membership. They were severely under-represented in virtually all Liberal government caucuses from 1963 to 1993. In fact, from 1921 until 1984, the West was mildly or severely under-represented in almost *all* government caucuses.[22] Conversely, Québec was highly over-represented in all Liberal government caucuses during the same period.

---

[21] Garth Stevenson, *Unfulfilled Union: Canadian Federalism and National Unity*, rev. ed. (Toronto: Gage, 1982), p. 182.

[22] The only exceptions were during three Progressive Conservative governments, which lasted in total only about six years.

TABLE 10.2   PERCENTAGE OF SEATS IN EACH REGION WON BY GOVERNING PARTY IN
CANADIAN GENERAL ELECTIONS, 1867-1993

		% Seats Won by Governing Party in Each Region				
Election	Governing Party	Canada	West	Ontario	Québec	Atlantic
1867	CONSERVATIVE	55.8	–	56.1	69.2	29.4
1872	CONSERVATIVE	51.5	90.0	43.2	58.5	48.6
1874	LIBERAL	64.6	20.0	72.7	50.8	79.1
1878	CONSERVATIVE	66.5	90.0	67.0	69.2	55.8
1882	CONSERVATIVE	66.2	72.7	59.3	73.8	67.4
1887	CONSERVATIVE	57.2	93.3	56.5	50.8	55.8
1891	CONSERVATIVE	57.2	93.3	52.2	46.2	72.1
1896	LIBERAL	54.9	47.1	46.7	75.4	43.6
1900	LIBERAL	62.0	70.6	39.1	87.7	69.2
1904	LIBERAL	65.0	75.0	44.2	83.1	74.3
1908	LIBERAL	60.2	51.4	41.9	81.5	74.3
1911	CONSERVATIVE	60.2	51.4	83.7	41.5	45.7
1917	UNIONIST (CONSERVATIVE)	65.1	96.5	90.2	4.6	67.7
1921	Liberal	49.4	8.8	25.6	100.0	80.6
1925	Liberal	40.4	33.3	13.4	90.8	20.7
1926	Liberal	47.3	34.8	28.0	92.3	31.0
1930	CONSERVATIVE	55.9	44.9	72.0	36.9	79.3
1935	LIBERAL	69.8	48.6	68.3	84.6	96.2
1940	LIBERAL	72.7	59.7	67.1	93.8	73.1
1945	LIBERAL	51.0	26.4	41.5	83.1	69.2
1949	LIBERAL	72.5	59.7	67.5	90.4	73.5
1953	LIBERAL	64.2	37.5	58.8	88.0	81.8
1957	Progressive Conservative	42.3	29.2	71.8	12.0	63.6
1958	PROGRESSIVE CONSERVATIVE	78.5	91.7	78.8	66.7	75.8
1962	Progressive Conservative	43.8	68.1	41.1	18.7	54.5
1963	Liberal	48.7	13.9	61.2	62.7	60.6
1965	Liberal	49.4	12.5	60.0	74.7	45.5
1968	LIBERAL	58.7	40.0	72.7	75.7	21.9
1972	Liberal	41.3	10.0	40.9	75.7	31.2
1974	LIBERAL	53.4	18.6	62.5	81.1	40.6
1979	Progressive Conservative	48.2	73.8	60.0	2.7	56.3
1980	LIBERAL	52.1	2.5	54.7	98.7	59.4
1984	PROGRESSIVE CONSERVATIVE	74.8	76.3	70.5	77.3	78.1
1988	PROGRESSIVE CONSERVATIVE	57.3	53.9	46.5	84.0	37.5
1993	LIBERAL	60.9	32.6	99.0	25.3	96.9

LIBERAL/PROGRESSIVE CONSERVATIVE — Majority Government
Liberal/Progressive Conservative — Minority Government
(NOTE: "West" includes NWT and Yukon)

TABLE 10.3   REGIONAL COMPOSITION OF GOVERNMENT CAUCUS AND HOUSE OF COMMONS, CANADIAN GENERAL ELECTIONS, 1867–1993

Election	Governing Party	% Regional Composition of Government Caucus				% Regional Composition of House of Commons			
		West	Ont.	Qué.	Atl.	West	Ont.	Qué.	Atl.
1867	CONSERVATIVE	—	45.5	44.6	9.9	—	45.3	35.9	18.8
1872	CONSERVATIVE	8.7	36.9	36.9	17.5	5.0	44.0	32.5	18.5
1874	LIBERAL	1.5	48.1	24.8	25.6	4.9	42.7	31.6	20.9
1878	CONSERVATIVE	6.6	43.1	32.8	17.5	4.9	42.7	31.6	20.9
1882	CONSERVATIVE	5.8	38.8	34.5	20.9	5.2	43.3	31.0	20.5
1887	CONSERVATIVE	11.4	42.3	26.8	19.5	7.0	42.8	30.2	20.0
1891	CONSERVATIVE	11.4	39.0	24.4	25.2	7.0	42.8	30.2	20.0
1896	LIBERAL	6.8	36.8	41.9	14.5	8.0	43.2	30.5	18.3
1900	LIBERAL	9.1	27.3	43.2	20.5	8.0	43.2	30.5	18.3
1904	LIBERAL	15.1	27.3	38.8	18.7	13.1	40.2	30.4	16.4
1908	LIBERAL	13.5	27.1	39.8	19.5	15.8	38.9	29.4	15.8
1911	CONSERVATIVE	13.5	54.1	20.3	12.0	15.8	38.9	29.4	15.8
1917	UNIONIST (CONSERVATIVE)	35.9	48.4	2.0	13.7	24.3	34.9	27.7	13.2
1921	Liberal	4.3	18.1	56.0	21.6	24.3	34.9	27.7	13.2
1925	Liberal	23.2	11.1	59.6	6.1	28.2	33.5	26.5	11.8
1926	Liberal	20.7	19.8	51.7	7.8	28.2	33.5	26.5	11.8
1930	CONSERVATIVE	22.6	43.1	17.5	16.8	28.2	33.5	26.5	11.8
1935	LIBERAL	20.5	32.7	32.2	14.6	29.4	33.5	26.5	10.6
1940	LIBERAL	24.2	30.9	34.2	10.7	29.4	33.5	26.5	10.6
1945	LIBERAL	15.2	27.2	43.2	14.4	29.4	33.5	26.5	10.6
1949	LIBERAL	22.6	29.5	34.7	13.1	27.5	31.7	27.9	13.0
1953	LIBERAL	15.9	29.4	38.8	15.9	27.2	32.1	28.3	12.5
1957	Progressive Conservative	18.8	54.4	8.0	18.8	27.2	32.1	28.3	12.5
1958	PROGRESSIVE CONSERVATIVE	31.7	32.2	24.0	12.0	27.2	32.1	28.3	12.5
1962	Progressive Conservative	42.2	30.2	12.1	15.5	27.2	32.1	28.3	12.5
1963	Liberal	7.8	40.3	36.4	15.5	27.2	32.1	28.3	12.5
1965	Liberal	6.9	38.9	42.7	11.5	27.2	32.1	28.3	12.5
1968	LIBERAL	18.1	41.3	36.1	4.5	26.5	33.3	28.0	12.1
1972	Liberal	6.4	33.0	51.4	9.2	26.5	33.3	28.0	12.1
1974	LIBERAL	9.2	39.0	42.6	9.2	26.5	33.3	28.0	12.1
1979	Progressive Conservative	43.4	41.9	1.5	13.2	28.4	33.7	26.6	11.3
1980	LIBERAL	1.4	35.4	50.3	12.9	28.4	33.7	26.6	11.3
1984	PROGRESSIVE CONSERVATIVE	28.9	31.8	27.5	11.8	28.9	33.7	26.6	11.3
1988	PROGRESSIVE CONSERVATIVE	28.4	27.2	37.3	7.1	30.2	33.6	25.4	10.8
1993	LIBERAL	37.7	55.4	10.7	17.5	30.2	33.6	25.4	10.8

LIBERAL/PROGRESSIVE CONSERVATIVE — Majority Government
Liberal/Progressive Conservative — Minority Government
(N.B.: Rows may not add up to 100.0% because of rounding)
Note: "West" includes NWT and Yukon.

Over the century the Liberal Party increasingly became the party of central Canada, winning 85 percent of its seats there in the 1980 election. Prime Minister Trudeau had summarized the dismal condition of the Liberal Party in a speech at a Liberal Conference in 1976:

> West of the Manitoba border we exist as a third party and not a strong one at that. We have in a sense almost local representation amongst the French-speaking part of New Brunswick but very little, just one member, in the English-speaking part of the province. Just one member out of four in PEI, two members in Nova Scotia. So, you know, I think we have to worry as Liberals about our future as a national party... Indeed, the governments of Canada for a large part of the period of Liberal holding of office have been the governments of a majority of French-speaking Canada, plus a minority of English-speaking Canada.[23]

In 1984 the Liberals lost their hold on central Canada and did poorly in every other province. In 1988, they increased their support in Ontario, the Maritimes and Manitoba, but did poorly again in Québec.

The Progressive Conservatives, for their part, had won 50 percent of their seats in 1980 in the Western provinces, and only one seat in Québec. In 1984, however, they won 29 percent in the West and 28 percent in Québec. But their 1984 electoral breakthrough in Québec finally gave Canada a government with a strong national mandate. As Table 10.3 shows, in 1984 and 1988, for the first time since 1958, the percentage regional composition of the PC caucus was extremely close to the percentage regional composition of the House of Commons.

On return to power in 1993, for the first time in many years the Liberal caucus reflected the regional balance of the country. Ironically, its main opposition was from new regionally based parties, the separatist Bloc Québécois and the western-based Reform Party.

These severe regional imbalances in the party system make it difficult for the parties to perform many of their important functions. For decades, selection for political patronage positions was distorted by Liberal Party domination of the government, as was recruitment to Cabinet. Interest aggregation and articulation by the parties is also distorted when regions are severely over- or under-represented in governments on a regular basis over several decades. When it happens on a regular basis, as it has in Canada in recent years, it can be expected that regional parties will flourish as a protest against exclusion. Even the socialization function is distorted when there are regional imbalances, because regional cleavages are exacerbated instead of smoothed over. The different political traditions and social and economic cleavages in the regions tend to encourage viewpoints that are parochial and narrow rather than national, and make Canada difficult to govern.

ESTABLISHED PARTIES: HISTORY AND IDEAS

THE PROGRESSIVE CONSERVATIVE PARTY

The oldest party in a country is often the party of established interests, and this is certainly the case in Canada. The privileged elements of Canadian society banded together as early as 1854, when John A. Macdonald gathered a working coalition of various interests under the label Liberal-Conservative. It was an alliance that included eastern commercial interests, conservative French Canadians and Ontario Tories. Their objectives were to bring about Confederation and then work toward a National Policy — basically through encouraging national unity and developing the country by promoting a national railway, industry and

---

[23] *The Globe and Mail*, Toronto, Oct. 4, 1976.

commerce. Maintenance of the British connection was fundamental to the early Conservatives, as was the establishment of relatively high tariffs.

The Conservative Party was traditionally disliked by farmers in the West because of its empathy for big business, and French Canadians were wary of it because of its strong British interest. These latter attitudes were consolidated by both the execution of Riel and the Conscription Crisis of 1917. Conservative support in French Québec disintegrated, and the Conservative party structure became centralized in Ontario. In the West as well during the pre-war period, there was no strong, single party tradition, and voters withheld support from the Conservatives. After the first World War, Westerners formed the Progressive Party, which allied itself uneasily with the Liberals.

Another misfortune for the Conservatives was that they were in power during the Depression, a situation that assured further unpopularity and erosion of support. Their adversities were compounded by a serious leadership vacuum: neither Arthur Meighen nor R.B. Bennett could make inroads in Québec. Then, in the 1940s, the party wooed Progressive support in the West and chose John Bracken, the Liberal-Progressive Premier of Manitoba, as its leader, renaming the party the Progressive Conservatives (PC). George Drew became leader in 1948, but still the party remained in the political wilderness.[24] Not until John Diefenbaker, another Westerner, emerged as leader did Tory fortunes improve. The Conservatives formed a minority government in 1957, followed by a landslide, majority victory the next year.

In 1958, John Diefenbaker's charismatic personality and his appeal to diverse Canadian ethnic, economic, religious and regional groups brought his native Prairies into the fold, along with 50 seats from Québec. The Progressive Conservative Party appeared to take over the Liberal stand of moderate reform. However, Diefenbaker's capricious leadership in difficult times ultimately alienated French Canada, the large urban centres, business and industry and the intellectual community. Only the West, his gift to the party, remained loyal. Diefenbaker's electoral defeat in 1963 left the Conservatives floundering and unable to re-enlist the Québec votes they had briefly recaptured; the charismatic leader who had reunited and led the party to victory had lost his magic.

When Diefenbaker failed to resign, Dalton Camp, the party president, engineered his removal at the party convention of 1967. The conflict over "the Chief's" leadership and forced retirement created deep factions within the party that plagued the Stanfield era which followed.[25] Enough local members abandoned active politics to seriously weaken party organization at the local level. The six years of power under Diefenbaker's leadership preceded the Conservatives' second longest continuous period as the major opposition party. Diefenbaker's successor, Robert Stanfield, with his honest but plodding image, lost his third and final campaign in 1974 by advocating wage and price controls. He was replaced by thirty-six-year-old Joe Clark, Member of Parliament for Rocky Mountain, Alberta, who assumed the leadership after a photo-finish win against Québec's Claude Wagner in the 1976 leadership convention. This move consolidated western support, but by then the PC's other bases of strength had dwindled to the Atlantic provinces and rural and small-town Ontario.

The 1979 election gave the Progressive Conservatives their first hold on power in 16 years, but the prize was snatched from their hands just eight months later when their minority government was defeated on a vote on the budget. Joe Clark accepted the results of the vote

---

24 See W.L. Morton, *The Progressive Party in Canada* (Toronto: University of Toronto Press, 1950).

25 See, for example, Peter Newman, *The Distemper of Our Times: Canadian Politics in Transition, 1963–1968* (Toronto: McClelland & Stewart, 1968).

as a want of confidence in the government and advised the Governor General to dissolve Parliament. The consequence of that combination of events was a severe Conservative defeat in the 1980 election and Clark's own ultimate rejection and defeat as party leader. At the ensuing party policy convention in Winnipeg, Clark submitted to a routine vote of confidence. Although he won 67 percent of the delegate vote, which was technically more than adequate, he asked the executive to call a leadership convention and declared his candidacy. His defeat by Brian Mulroney at that spring convention was a personal humiliation. Mulroney, who had run unsuccessfully against him in the 1976 convention, had had no experience in public office. He was, however, an extremely astute politician who had diligently paved the way to this leadership position over many years.[26] As a bilingual native of Québec of Irish-French descent, with family connections to the Yugoslavian community, his qualifications were tailor-made to win support from the two major constituencies the Conservatives desperately needed: French Canadians in Québec and ethnic groups, particularly in key Toronto ridings. Mulroney's challenge was to build a significant and durable electoral base in French Canada. In the 1984 General Election and to a lesser extent in 1988, he won relatively evenly across the entire country. In the spring of 1993, however, in the wake of constitutional reform failures, scandals and unpopular policies the Prime Minister resigned. In June 1993, Kim Campbell became leader of the party and Prime Minister. She led the party into a fall campaign that left the party in ruins. She lost her own seat and ended up with only two MPs, well below the requirement for official party recognition in the House. Two months later, she resigned and Jean Charest became interim leader. The party retained its majority in the Senate and it fell to the 58 Conservative Senators to keep the party alive and functioning on Parliament Hill.

The Tory party in Canada is not doctrinaire and has never sought ideological purity. The early Conservative Party under Macdonald was dominated by the themes of Canadian nationalism and support for British imperialism with its "innate assumption of moral and racial superiority."[27] Years in the political wilderness and the pressures resulting from expanding American influence in Canada as well as the growing anachronism of British imperialism undermined these Tory traditions. As they entered the 1980s, Conservatives themselves agreed that their party was "hampered by its public image of being pro-big business and anti-labour, anti-ethnic, anti-women and anti-youth, as well as reactionary on most social issues."[28]

This harsh assessment was a formidable burden, and efforts to soften the image, particularly in accommodating women and youth, culminated in the election, in 1993, of the party's first female leader and Canada's first female Prime Minister. In broad general terms, the modern Progressive Conservative Party represents a "conservative-radical mix which is based on a sense of community and order, a feeling for the land, a respect for human diversity and human rights, a concern for social justice, and a non-ideological approach to the problems of political and economic organization."[29] The party is committed to upholding the private enterprise system, but on occasion has been willing to let the government intervene in the

---

[26] Patrick Martin, Allan Gregg and George Perlin, *Contenders: The Tory Quest for Power* (Scarborough, Ont.: Prentice-Hall Canada, 1983). Also see John Sawatsky, *Mulroney: The Politics of Ambition* (Toronto: Macfarlane Walter & Ross, 1991).

[27] Charles Taylor, *Radical Tories: The Conservative Tradition in Canada* (Toronto: Anansi, 1982), p. 211.

[28] Ibid., p. 211.

[29] Ibid., p. 213.

[30] See Robert Stanfield, "Conservative Principles and Philosophy," in Fox, ed., *Politics: Canada*, pp. 260–64.

economy to protect broad collective interests.[30] The party was traditionally less sensitive to francophone interests than were the Liberals, but that changed after 1984 with a leader from Québec. Historically, the party was wary of American influence; it was also pro-British and supportive of agricultural interests. But, again, this changed dramatically under Mulroney, who led the party to a staunch pro–United States position and brought forth both the *Canada-United States Free Trade Agreement* and the *North American Free Trade Agreement*. Mulroney's electoral success relied heavily on the West and Québec. It was an unlikely union that held together partly because of the desire of both regions for free trade with the United States. In 1993, when those regions deserted the Conservatives, the party was crushed. The great party of Sir John A. Macdonald has been forced to reassess its policies and even its very existence.

THE LIBERAL PARTY

The Liberal Party was slower than the Conservative to develop as a national force. Its predecessors were the early reformers who generally advocated a radical transformation of society and wanted to solve major inequities through governmental reform. The opposition to Sir John A. Macdonald's first government consisted of Clear Grits from Ontario, the Parti rouge from Québec, and anti-Confederation Nova Scotia MPs. It was generally considered a more egalitarian grouping than the Conservatives. However, there was no real unity among the groups until Wilfrid Laurier became leader in 1887 and transformed them into the national Liberal Party. As Canada's first French Canadian Prime Minister, Laurier firmly entrenched the Liberal Party in Québec, with assistance from people like Honoré Mercier and Israel Tarte. Laurier still holds the record for the longest continuous term in office as Prime Minister — from 1896 to 1911.

After Laurier, the Liberal Party endured a decade of discontent that climaxed in bitter division over the Conscription Crisis in Québec. In 1919, the party elected William Lyon Mackenzie King as party leader. The Liberals won the 1921 election, and King rebuilt the party into a strong organization that dominated Canadian government for most of the next six decades. Mackenzie King set a record for total years in power; he was Prime Minister for 21 years and 5 months. During his early years in office he astutely tried to accommodate the agrarian protest from the West by forming an alliance with the Progressives, but that initiative collapsed. Louis St. Laurent, who succeeded King (and who was defeated by John Diefenbaker in 1957), his successor Lester Pearson (party leader from 1958 to 1968, Prime Minister from 1963 to 1968) and Pierre Trudeau (Prime Minister 1968–79 and 1980–84) who followed Pearson, all more or less successfully accommodated Québec discontent but gradually lost the West.

Trudeau's ascent to the leadership in April 1968 was dramatic — a victory by an attractive political neophyte over well-known, experienced Liberal leaders. It spurred a wave of "Trudeaumania" that swept the country and gave his party a large majority in the ensuing election. Throughout the 1960s the Liberal popular vote had increased in the West and, although the 1968 sweep was not as extensive there as in Ontario and Québec, it represented a Liberal high point. Following that election, the party endured an unrelenting decline in support west of Ontario.

As the initial wave of Trudeaumania wore thin, Liberal support began to fluctuate. In the wake of accusations of arrogance and insensitivity, the Liberals suffered near-defeat in the 1972 election. However, they won another strong mandate in 1974. Five years later they received another rebuff at the polls. It was not a crushing defeat, just severe enough to allow the Conservatives a tenuous minority hold on power. The Liberals' serious problem in 1979 was the fact that half of their MPs were elected from one province — Québec. That November, Trudeau publicly stated his intention to resign as leader, but within weeks the Conservative government was toppled and a new election called. Endowed with a new mandate in 1980, Trudeau's stated intent to resign dissolved.[31]

In the spring of 1984, having led his party for over 16 years, with all but nine months as Prime Minister, Pierre Trudeau resigned. John Turner won the ensuing party leadership convention and called an election within days. The Liberal Party won only 28 percent of the popular vote in the 1984 election, the worst result ever for the Liberals in a federal election. Turner stayed on as leader, but his new party caucus was dispirited, fractious and poorly prepared for the realities of opposition status. Issues such as the Meech Lake accord and the Free Trade Agreement with the United States were particularly divisive, and the party went into the 1988 election in debt and divided over both issues and leadership. It lost again but improved its share of the popular vote to 32 percent. Within months Turner resigned and Jean Chrétien was elected party leader to become Canada's 20th Prime Minister in November, 1993.

The philosophical base of the Liberal Party derived originally from British liberalism, but Canadian Liberal leaders have tended to adopt a distinctively pragmatic approach to issues as they arise. Traditional liberal themes such as reform, individual rights, state intervention to enhance the lives the underprivileged, national and international conciliation have recurred in various concrete forms in Liberal Party platforms and policies. However, as we have noted, practical politics in Canada tend to be ideologically fuzzy and opportunistic.[32] As one observer put it, "certainly there have been sporadic tremors of small 'l' liberalism. But whether unemployment insurance or the National Energy Program, the tremors have usually been in isolation, a reflection of an individual minister rather than concerted Government policies."[33]

After the Second World War, successive Liberal governments gradually expanded their influence in the social and economic spheres. They introduced important social welfare legislation and assumed more responsibility for directing the Canadian economy, particularly by enforcing wage and price controls in 1975. In the late nineteenth century, when the Liberal Party was generally in opposition in Ottawa and in government in the provinces, it was a staunch defender of provincial rights. When the Liberals held power in Ottawa, however, they gradually moved into the position of the major opposition party or worse in the provinces, and correspondingly espoused strong centralizing policies. In foreign affairs, Liberal policies have been judged to be selectively internationalist.[34] Internally, bilingualism and a broad commitment to individual and minority rights, both linguistic and legal, were perhaps the most coherently pursued liberal policies under Trudeau, Turner and Chrétien.

Having been the dominant party for most of the period from the 1920s to 1984, the Liberals benefited from their monopoly on patronage appointments and built strong ties with the mushrooming mandarinate of the public service. Somewhat ironically, massive patronage appointments made on behalf of Trudeau as he left office raised the ire of the

---

[31] Pierre Elliot Trudeau, *Memoirs* (Toronto: McClelland & Stewart, 1993).

[32] William Christian and Colin Campbell, *Political Parties and Ideologies in Canada* (Toronto: McGraw-Hill Ryerson, 1974), p. 41.

[33] John Gray, "Who will be the Liberals' New Skipper?" *The Globe and Mail*, Toronto, Jan. 6, 1982.

[34] See Chapter 14 on Canadian foreign policy.

electorate against John Turner and the Liberal Party, and became a major campaign issue in 1984. There was also a negative side to the Liberal Party's strong ties to the federal bureaucracy: Liberal Party members and observers alike deplored the extent of government dependence on the bureaucracy and the diminishing relevance of the political party in policy-making.[35] Given the fact that as of 1993 it is the only national party in Canada, its prospects for forming the government for some time are high.

THE CCF/NDP

The roots of the NDP are in the Co-operative Commonwealth Federation (CCF), which held its founding convention in 1933. The original CCF was an assortment of Fabian socialists, Marxists, farmers and labourers under the leadership of J.S. Woodsworth.[36] The party had a predominantly western rural backing, and in the ensuing 28 years never attracted more than 14 to 16 percent of the popular vote. In 1958, the Canadian Labour Congress (CLC) made formal overtures to the party, proposing the need for a broadly based people's movement that would embrace the CCF, the labour movement, farm organizations and professionals. The CCF set up a joint committee with the CLC to create a new party.

In 1961, the CCF was dissolved and the New Democratic Party, with its social democratic platform, was born. The new party retained many CCF leaders, but the participation of organized labour caused difficulties, and tensions between farmers and workers often ran high. The extent to which the party should be influenced by trade unions is still a divisive issue.[37]

Vigorous leadership by Tommy Douglas in the early years, and then by David Lewis and Ed Broadbent, was never enough to overcome the lack of funds and the ideological divisions that kept the New Democratic Party as a third party at the federal level. It has never been able to expand its territorial base to Québec and the Maritimes.[38] In 1988, it achieved its best results ever: 43 seats in the House of Commons and 20.2 percent of the popular vote. Despite this good showing, Broadbent resigned and was replaced as leader by Audrey McLaughlin. In 1993, the party was reduced to nine seats and forced to re-think its purpose and direction.

There are several reasons why the NDP failed to become a national winner. As a left-wing party, it has had no strong position or impact on the country's major French/English cleavage. In the early years, it attracted the votes of discontented Westerners. From the 1960s to 1988 the Conservatives encroached on that base, but in the 1988 election the NDP captured 33 of their 43 seats in the West, mostly in British Columbia and Saskatchewan and it appeared that the party might flourish. However, its traditional protest role was usurped by the Reform Party and it was left defending the status quo. In 1993 Reform and the Liberals cut NDP seats in its western stronghold to five in Saskatchewan, one in Manitoba and two in B.C.

---

[35] Joseph Wearing, *The L-Shaped Party: The Liberal Party of Canada 1958–1980* (Toronto: McGraw-Hill Ryerson, 1981), p. 241. Also see John Meisel, "The Decline of Party in Canada," in Thorburn, ed., *Party Politics in Canada*, 5th ed., pp. 98–114.

[36] W.D. Young, *The Anatomy of a Party: The National CCF 1932-61* (Toronto: University of Toronto Press.)

[37] See, for example, Norman Penner, *The Canadian Left* (Scarborough: Prentice-Hall Canada, 1977).

[38] The NDP has never won a seat in Québec in a General Election. They did win a by-election seat there in 1990, but afterward were consistently embarrassed by their new Québec MP's independence and nationalist views.

Reproduced with permission, Gable, *The Globe and Mail.*

The NDP is considerably stronger at the provincial level than it is federally. In 1993 it held the reigns of government in three provinces — British Columbia, Saskatchewan and Ontario. The party has used the issues of provincial health insurance and foreign domination of the economy to its advantage in these provinces. Federally as well, the NDP has played a larger role in Canadian politics than its success at the polls would indicate. During the 1972 minority government, for example, tacit support from the NDP was vital to the Liberals.

In general, the NDP platform is based on democratic socialist goals. The NDP is a fairly ideologically based left-wing party. It advocates policies such as government regulation of the economy, including more government control of private enterprise, higher taxes for big business and industry, increased social welfare, and protection from American influence.[39] NDP Premier Bob Rae's tough measures to reduce the Ontario deficit in 1993 offended many of the NDP's traditional supporters and caused a rift in the national party. In the 1993 General Election the NDP lost all of its seats in Ontario. The ruling NDP in British Columbia also cost the federal party support by its pragmatic environmental policies.

---

[39] For further reading on the NDP, see N.H. Chi and George Perlin, "The New Democratic Party: A Party in Transition," in Thorburn, 4th ed., *Party Politics in Canada,* pp. 177–87; Desmond Morton, *The Dream of Power* (Toronto: Hakkert, 1974); Janine Brodie and Jane Jensen, *Crisis, Challenge and Change: Party and Class in Canada* (Toronto: Methuen, 1980); Alan Whitehorn "The New Democratic Party in Convention," in Perlin, ed., *Party Democracy in Canada: The Politics of National Party Conventions* (Scarborough, Ont.: Prentice-Hall, 1988), pp. 272–300; and Janine Brody, "From Waffles to Grits: A Decade in the Life of the New Democratic Party," in Thorburn, ed., *Party Politics in Canada,* 5th ed.

NEW PARTIES

THE REFORM PARTY

The Reform Party, led by Preston Manning, was founded in late 1987. Like other western protest parties, Reform tapped into feelings of economic and political alienation in southern Alberta in particular, and the West in general. Its rallying cry was "the West wants in." (See Chapter 6.) It fielded candidates in the 1988 General Election and won no seats but captured 15 percent of the popular vote in Alberta. A few months later it won a by-election in Alberta, electing Deborah Grey as its first MP. By April 1991, when opinion polls indicated that it led all parties in the Prairies and some polls even put it ahead of the unpopular ruling Conservatives nationwide, it decided to send organizers east of Manitoba.[40] In the 1993 General Election it ran candidates in all provinces except Québec.

Reform benefited from widespread cynicism toward politicians in general, and a feeling that the traditional parties had atrophied. It appealed particularly to farmers and others who felt outraged and abandoned by the established political parties. The cornerstone of the right-wing Reform policy platform in the 1993 General Election was slashing the deficit, which it promised to accomplish in three years. To do this it vowed to cut programs such as maternity leave and reduce transfer payments for welfare. Job creation was seen primarily as the responsibility of the private sector. It espoused the virtues of thrift and self-reliance, cheaper and less intrusive government. As a populist party it appealed to "plain folks" with "plain talk." Aspects of its platform harked back to the defunct Progressive Party and Social Credit. For example, it included support for more democratic input into policies, based on initiative, referendum, recall of MPs, free voting in the Commons and a Triple-E Senate. Economic difficulties and social problems were blamed on scapegoats such as immigrants, bilingualism, multiculturalism, the GST and feminists. The party therefore attracted elements of society that resented immigrants and special status for French-speaking Canadians.

By the latter part of the 1993 election campaign Reform was running first in the polls in British Columbia and Alberta. In the end it won 52 seats with 19 percent of the popular vote. It remains to be seen whether Reform will retain its appeal and grow into a nationally based party, or whether it will wither and die like other western, populist movements such as the Progressive Party in the 1920s. Preston Manning positioned himself early on as a voice of English-speaking Canada against Québec. His restricted mandate and the election of a nationally based majority Liberal government undermined that claim.

THE BLOC QUÉBÉCOIS

The Bloc Québécois was the first separatist party to sit in Parliament. Party leader Lucien Bouchard founded the party from dissidents within Parliament. His own background showed lack of consistent direction. He supported sovereignty-association in 1982, but when the opportunity arose he changed his tune to federalism and accepted Tory patronage to become Canada's Ambassador to France. He came to Ottawa in 1988 as a federal Minister and friend of Prime Minister Brian Mulroney. In May, 1990, apparently slighted by Mulroney's handling of constitutional negotiations, Bouchard quit Cabinet and the Conservative Party. In resigning he cast himself as spokesman for a monolithic, humiliated Québec. He said Canada was not even worth attempting to save.

---

[40] *The Globe and Mail*, editorial, October 7, 1991.

We must stop trying to fit Québec into the mould of a province like the others. Beyond the legal arguments, there is one argument that is unanswerable. Quebeckers do not accept this mould. Their very reality shatters it.[41]

When the Meech Lake accord died in June 1990, Bouchard set up a legislative group in the House of Commons to work for the dismantling of Canada — following essentially the same path as the provincial Parti Québécois under Jacques Parizeau. A handful of MPs followed him to create the Bloc Québécois. Most MPs had defected from the Conservative Party, but two were Liberal. They were soon joined by Gilles Duceppe who was elected in a by-election under the Bloc Québécois banner.

As we noted in Chapter 6, the Bloc Québécois stated its purpose in a draft manifesto as "solely to promote Québec's profound and legitimate interests and aspirations."[42] In the 1993 General Election it did not present a comprehensive platform because it did not have, or want to have, any coherent ideas about how to run Canada. Its limited platform placed the Bloc left of centre on the political spectrum, defending progressive social policies but also fiscal conservatism, and reconciling the demands of business and labour under the sovereignty banner. Bouchard advocated free trade to create resources with which to implement social policies. Many of his economic policies mirrored the demands made by Québec businesspeople at the Bélanger-Campeau commission, which had examined Québec's political options after the failure of the Meech Lake accord. Although polls showed that only a fraction of Québec voters supported the separatist option for Québec, the Bloc appealed for voters to "shake up" the old-line parties. To this end he talked about cutting government waste, job creation and social programs. The party's raison d'être, however, was sovereignty. It appealed to uninformed passion — anger, fear and ethnic pride. The Bloc went into the 1993 General Election with 8 seats and came out with 54. It won 14 percent of the popular vote in Canada, but 49 percent in Québec where it ran all of its candidates. It was an impressive win, enough to make it the Official Opposition party, but was not the landslide it had hoped for. Many of its votes came from disgruntled federalists, indicating that the Bloc would need increased support to win a referendum on sovereignty.

MINOR AND HISTORICAL FRINGE PARTIES

There have been and continue to be several minor parties on the fringes of the party system in Canada that never win enough support to gain any influence or credibility. Some are serious, others less so. None has had any lasting significance. In the 1993 election, 14 political parties officially recorded their names with the Chief Electoral Officer and fielded the 50 candidates required to be officially recognized as a political party.[43] No candidates from fringe parties won seats in the 1993 election, but some of them showed pockets of strength. Some, such as the National Party, the Christian Heritage Party and the Libertarian Party had

---

[41] Quoted in Robert J. Jackson and Doreen Jackson, *Stand Up for Canada: Leadership and the Canadian Political Crisis*, (Scarborough: Prentice-Hall, 1992), p. 201.

[42] Ibid., pp. 201–2.

[43] The 14 parties and the number of candidates they fielded were: Liberal (295), Conservative (295), NDP (294), Natural Law (231), Reform (207), National (171), Abolitionist (80), Green (79), Bloc Québécois (75), Christian Heritage (59), Commonwealth of Canada (59), Canada (56), Libertarian (52) and Marxist-Leninist (51). Fifty-two candidates appeared on the ballot as independents; 99 appeared with no affiliation. The Social Credit, communist and Rhinoceros parties were among those that failed to field the required number of candidates to receive official recognition.

sufficient organization and appeal to become "spoilers" in some ridings, preventing the party that might otherwise have won from doing so. The proliferation of new parties is a recent development in Canada. It was countered somewhat by the more stringent official requirements in 1993 that deprived parties such as the Rhinoceros and the Communists of official party standing in the election.

One reason fringe parties proliferated in the 1980s was the rise of powerful single-interest lobbies. Some groups that support issues such as English-first, ecology, or "family" issues are choosing not to work through the traditional parties but are trying to form new parties instead. Generally, fringe parties do not attempt to develop policies on a cross-section of issues, but field candidates on a limited platform or single issue only. Two fringe parties of historical significance federally are Social Credit and the Progressives.

SOCIAL CREDIT

The Social Credit Party originated in the West. It was always a regional party, never more than a third party federally and never a serious threat to the party in power. During the Depression and the agricultural failures of the 1930s, a charismatic preacher, William Aberhart, captured the political imagination of Albertans with the unorthodox financial theories of Major C.H. Douglas (which were often labelled "funny money"). Under Aberhart's leadership the Social Credit Party advocated the principle of monetary re-form, or more explicitly, the right of the provinces to issue money and credit. In 1935, the party flooded the Alberta legislature with members and sent fifteen MPs to Ottawa as well. The party's attempts to institute their radical financial reforms in Alberta were declared unconstitutional by the Supreme Court, but Social Credit persisted as a populist conser-vative party.

At about the time that the Social Credit Party appeared in Alberta, Social Credit ideas also took root in Québec. The Québec wing was a failure until the fiery orator Réal Caouette revived it as the Ralliement des Créditistes. In 1961, the Créditistes joined the national Social Credit Party, but the two groups were never fully integrated. No Social Credit mem-ber has been elected to the federal Parliament from Western Canada since 1965, but the Ralliement maintained a small representation for about another decade.[44] It has not won any seats since 1979.

THE PROGRESSIVE PARTY

Also of historical interest is the Progressive Party, which appeared briefly on the national scene in the 1920s. It consisted of a loose coalition of provincial United Farmers, and was based largely in Manitoba, Saskatchewan and Alberta, with some support in Ontario. The party opposed the National Policy tariff that kept the price of central Canada's manufactured goods relatively high and drove up the costs of farming. It also opposed discriminatory freight rates that made it cheaper to ship manufactured goods from central Canada to the West than to ship grain eastward.

---

[44] The best discussion of the Ralliement in Québec is in Michael Stein, *The Dynamics of Right-Wing Protest: A Political Analysis of the Social Credit in Quebec* (Toronto: University of Toronto Press, 1973). See accounts of the Social Credit Movement in Alberta in C.B. Macpherson, *Democracy in Alberta: The Theory and Practise of a Quasi-Party System* (Toronto: University of Toronto Press, 1953); J.R. Mallory, *Social Credit and the Federal Power in Canada* (Toronto: University of Toronto Press, 1954); and J.A. Irving, *The Social Credit Movement in Alberta* (Toronto: University of Toronto Press, 1959).

The Progressive Party made a startling appearance in the 1921 election, sending 65 MPs to Ottawa, 15 more than the Conservatives. However, they refused to form the official Opposition and, with no organization, the party quickly disintegrated as a national movement. Four elections later it disappeared on the federal scene; its adherents drifted into other parties. In the early 1940s, John Bracken, former Progressive Party leader from Manitoba, became the national leader of the Conservatives and, to take advantage of the potency of the Progressive label in the West, the Conservatives adopted "Progressive" as part of their party's name.

PARTY STRUCTURE AND ORGANIZATION

We have noted that one outstanding feature of the system within which Canadian parties operate is its federal nature. Parties at the federal and provincial levels may bear the same name but act quite independently. They may not even exist at both federal and provincial levels in any given province. Or, at the other extreme, like the Bloc Québécois, they may be closely allied to a provincial party.

The three traditional parties — Liberal, Conservative and NDP — have relatively similar organizations that are outlined in their constitutions. These documents reveal little about power and influence; they simply set out the general structure of the party and describe the basic functions of each part of it. As well, the constitutions authorize the appointment of bureaucracies and the establishment of standing committees with appointed memberships, and guarantee regional and bicultural party representation at the executive level.[45] They also indicate the basic philosophical leanings of the parties.

The traditional parties consist of two wings: the parliamentary wing, comprised of the party leader and caucus; and a very large, three-tier extra-parliamentary wing. Both wings are dominated by the party leader, whose role and selection are discussed later in this chapter.

The basic pyramidal structure of the extra-parliamentary party, which is linked at the upper levels to the parliamentary wing, is similar for both federal and provincial parties. As Figure 10.2 shows, an executive body and a small permanent office stand at the apex of the federal parties; a very wide but fluid base of party voters is at the foundation. Between elections, virtually all of the structure below the apex dissolves, and communication with the party is through the national organization or the parliamentary wing. This is not true of Britain and other western parliamentary democracies, where the extra-parliamentary party continues to function, mobilizing citizens and participating in the dialogue between citizen and state. As well, none of the Canadian parties has a permanent office or professional staff that can compare in size or sophistication with those of British parties. The major parties in Canada have had permanent offices only since the mid-1940s. Until their establishment, the entire extra-parliamentary wing of each party was dormant until an election was called, and then it would arise spontaneously to coordinate the campaign. The extra-parliamentary wing was at one time, therefore, even more cut off from dialogue with the parliamentary wing than it is today.

---

[45] John McMenemy, John Redekop and Conrad Winn, "Party Structures and Decision-making," in C. Winn and J. McMenemy, eds., *Political Parties in Canada* (Toronto: McGraw-Hill Ryerson, 1976), pp. 167–90.

FIGURE 10.2   CANADIAN POLITICAL PARTIES: GENERAL STRUCTURE

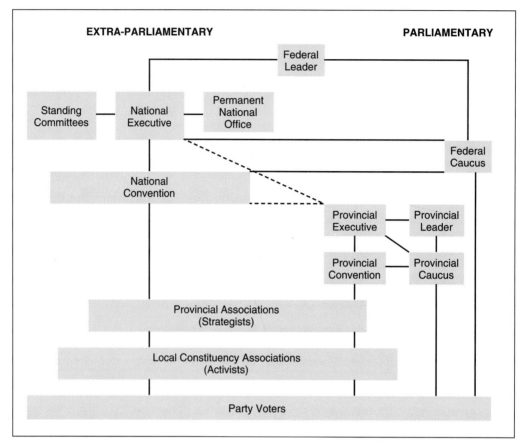

CONSTITUENCY AND PROVINCIAL LEVELS

The constituency is the locus of the grassroots organization of each federal party. Constituency executives represent the party in the ridings, recruit local volunteers and raise campaign funds. The constituency level of the party also elects convention delegates and plays a major role in choosing federal candidates. The dedication of members to this basic unit is vital to party fortunes, but it is a relatively weak body within the power structure of the party.

The national office normally sets procedures governing party membership and the selection of delegates to conventions, but formal decisions fall under the jurisdiction of the provincial party organizations.[46] Therefore, rules vary from province to province and even within a province. Neither the Liberals nor the Conservatives have standardized membership qualifications or dues, although many associations do charge a small fee. Constituency

---

[46] Recruitment drives are often innovative. In 1982 the Liberal party headquarters prepared a controversial guide for local associations on how to recruit new members. The manual urged party associations to sponsor Canadian citizenship classes, preparing flyers in different languages and inviting immigrants to speak with a citizenship judge. This procedure would, it noted, encourage Canadian citizenship and bring "potential members of the Liberal Party into contact with established associations." *The Globe and Mail*, Toronto, Dec. 15, 1982.

organizations in these two parties issue membership cards easily — indeed, on rare occasions, they have been known to sign up children and derelicts when the need for votes for certain delegates or candidates was pressing! Before the 1993 election, the Liberals implemented residency requirements for those who vote for candidates, requiring them to sign up in advance of the vote.

The NDP organization is slightly different, as one would expect of a social democratic organization. It has dues; it also prohibits members from belonging to another party and requires them to pledge support to the constitution and principles of the NDP. An individual who joins the provincial wing of the NDP automatically becomes a member of both the federal and provincial constituency organizations. Fees are shared by the constituency, provincial and federal levels of the party. One must be a member at least 30 days and live in the constituency in order to vote at nomination meetings.

In spite of large membership bases there are few active members in any of the parties at this level, and the constituency associations meet infrequently — usually only when it is necessary to elect the executive, choose delegates for conventions or prepare for an imminent general election. One reason for the usual lassitude between elections is that parties do not normally contest municipal elections in Canada, and, therefore cannot draw on the forum of local government for support. As well, there is little congruence between provincial and federal party constituency boundaries. Another factor that hampers party activity at a local level is that constituency units are often very large and their members widely scattered. If the party is weak electorally in a particular constituency, funds are inevitably scarce, and it becomes difficult to hold activities and attract new members. The Reform Party has pledged to increase the relative importance of the constituency level organizations in the party structure.

The provincial organization of each of the traditional federal parties forms the intermediate level of the extra-parliamentary party pyramid. Individuals at this level coordinate and plan strategy and activities for implementation at the constituency level. The provincial executive has the ultimate responsibility for all federal constituencies in the province. In some provinces there are regional organizations within the provincial structures. Provincial level organization may be shared with provincial party counterparts, although the relationship varies from party to party and province to province. As we have seen, provincial parties in Canada are very independent, and generally like to keep their distance from their federal partners, particularly when those partners are in power in Ottawa.

NATIONAL LEVEL

At the upper level of the extra-parliamentary party pyramid is the national organization of each party that unites the provincial associations.

EXECUTIVES AND NATIONAL OFFICES

The national executive appears in a different form in each party, but it consists essentially of a small elite that conducts party business on behalf of the mass party. In each case, it includes a president, vice president and other officers and several executive committees.

As we have noted, each party maintains a small permanent office or headquarters at the national level. This body contains a handful of bureaucrats and staff who are responsible to the executives from the extra-parliamentary organization and also to the party leader. The national offices of the traditional parties function as links between the provincial organizations and the elected Members of Parliament and act as clearing houses for intra-party communications.

Despite its permanent position at the top of the extra-parliamentary party, this body is engaged mainly in service and coordinating functions: it organizes conventions, by-elections and general elections. As Joseph Wearing commented about the Liberal National Office, the duties of a National Office are chiefly those of keeping the party alive between elections.[47] After their 1993 defeat, the Conservatives had a debt of well over $7 million and were forced to cut their national and regional offices to mere skeletal services.[48]

The organization of the Reform Party reflects its grassroots, populist philosophy. Constituency associations meet regularly, and have vital organizational, policy-development and election-readiness functions. Elected convention delegates vote into office members of the Executive Council, the governing body of the party.

The organization of the Bloc Québécois reflects its separatist philosophy. It is very closely tied to the provincial Parti Québécois. PQ leader Jacques Parizeau campaigned for the Bloc, and long-standing PQ members were elected and assigned key positions in the Bloc shadow cabinet and as House Leader. Close ties were established between the House leaders and the whips of the two parties so that common positions could be co-ordinated. All Bloc critics were asked to work closely with their provincial counterparts.

WOMEN AND YOUTH

Women were relative latecomers to Canadian politics. They did not have the right to vote federally until 1918 (much later in some provincial elections — Québec was the last to grant the franchise to women, in 1940) nor did they have a representative of their own gender in the federal Parliament until 1921, the first federal election held after the franchise was extended. This first woman MP was Agnes MacPhail, who originally sat as a member of the Progressive party and later joined the CCF.[49]

Until the 1950s political parties, too, were male preserves despite the individual contributions of such women as MacPhail. Women and also youth were gradually acknowledged and accepted, but certainly not as full partners. In the Liberal Party, for example, young people were hived off into affiliated organizations: the Young Liberal Federation and the Canadian University Liberal Federation.[50] Women, who did much of the background work in the ridings licking stamps and providing tea, were diverted to the Women's Liberal Federation (WLF). Both groups were effectively barred from any significant part in the National Federation.

As the novelty of such low-grade participation gradually wore off, the demand grew for women and youth to be integrated into the main organizations. By the 1960s, the old organizations were faltering for lack of participants; fewer than one-third of the ridings had youth organizations left. Finally, in 1973, the affiliated organizations were replaced by two new ones, the Liberal Commission (for women) and the National Youth Commission, that now elect their own executives and "are responsible to caucuses

---

[47] Wearing, *The L-Shaped Party*, p. 214.

[48] *The Globe and Mail*, Nov. 18, 1993.

[49] MacPhail served as an MP until she was defeated in 1940 and then moved to provincial politics in her native Ontario. She died in 1954 just before her appointment to the Senate was to be announced.

[50] Reginald Whitaker, *The Government Party: Organizing and Financing the Liberal Party of Canada 1930-1958* (Toronto: University of Toronto Press, 1977), pp. 78–9 and 194–95.

of women or youth delegates respectively at national meetings."[51] They are intended to represent and promote the interests of students, youth and women in the party and encourage their participation and party activities.

In time, special organizations designed to encourage women to participate in the parties may be abandoned because women's participation can be taken for granted. In the meantime, however, to ensure female participation, both the PC and Liberal constitutions guarantee officials of the women's groups positions on the party executive committees and specify that a certain number of voting delegates at the conventions must be women. Partly because of these guaranteed positions, women have achieved higher visibility within party organizations in recent years. In 1983, for example, for the first time in Canadian history a woman, Iona Campagnolo, was elected Liberal Party President.

The NDP constitution contains few guarantees with respect to female participation, on the general understanding that there is no need for such measures. By 1981, however, the party had an internal affirmative action program, and two years later approved a requirement for equal representation of men and women on its executive and council. In December of 1989 the NDP elected Audrey McLaughlin as its national party leader, making her the first woman ever to lead a national party in Canada.

This trend to more active female participation and leadership in parties reflects prevalent changes in the role of women in society.[52] The 1992 report of the Royal Commission on Electoral Reform and Party Financing identified women as the most under-represented of the social categories it considered, saying that their "virtual exclusion" from the corridors of power is "no longer acceptable."[53] It made recommendations aimed at reducing financial barriers to seeking party nominations and contesting elections, as well as a scheme to include child-care expenses as an allowable tax deduction. The recommendations were ignored by the Conservative government, but it was a sign that women's groups are becoming increasingly forceful in ensuring that these concerns appear on the political agenda.

Women continue to be poorly represented in the parliamentary wings of all parties. However, as we see in the next chapter, since about 1979 parties have taken significant steps to accept, and even search for and assist, women as candidates, and women's representation continues to increase.[54]

Youth, too, have won a fairly prominent role in all three traditional parties. However, some have argued that youth are guaranteed more voting delegates at conventions than would seem reasonable based on their membership numbers, or that they are allowed to vote in leadership conventions even though they may be too young to vote in federal elections. None of the party constitutions establishes a minimum age for young members, though the Liberals have 25 as a maximum, and the PCs, 29.

---

[51] Wearing, *The L-Shaped Party*, p. 218. For detailed studies of gender and age factors at recent conventions see Janine Brodie, "The Gender Factor and National Leadership Conventions in Canada," and George Perlin, Allen Sutherland, and Marc Desjardins, "The Impact of Age Cleavage on Convention Politics," in Perlin, *Party Democracy in Canada*, pp. 172–87 and 188–201.

[52] Heather Conway, "Edging Towards Equality," *Policy Options*, vol. 9, no. 1 (May 1988), pp. 20–22.

[53] *Reforming Electoral Democracy*, vol. l, pp. 7–8.

[54] Political participation by women in recent years is documented by Sylvia Bashevkin, *Toeing the Lines; Women in Party Politics in English Canada* (Ottawa: Carleton University Press, 1985).

PARTY FINANCE

Political parties require funds for three basic purposes. The first and most widely recognized is that they must support expensive election campaigns. Second, they must maintain a small permanent staff between elections. Third, they need money to support research and advisory services for the party leader and elected representatives.

Where do these funds come from and who obtains them? In Chapter 8 we discussed the formula by which party caucuses receive money for research and for leaders' salaries from the House of Commons. To get such funds parties must have a minimum of 12 elected members in Parliament. It is difficult for parties to operate effectively or even stay alive without this funding. The Social Credit Party, for example, lost this funding when it dropped to 11 seats in 1974, and it never recovered. The Conservatives and NDP face a similar prospect after 1993.

Besides this internal funding however, parties are actively engaged in seeking funds outside of Parliament. In the early years of two-party politics in Canada, both major parties were financed largely from the same corporate contributors. Provincial and federal parties received allotments from central party funds; this highly centralized organization of party finance had an integrative effect that helped counter the centrifugal forces of the federal system. Party leaders played a key role in collecting and distributing campaign funds because there was no special fund-raising structure or permanent party organization.

With the advent of minor parties on the federal scene and the increased economic and political strength of the provinces vis-à-vis the federal government, the centralized nature of party financing began to change. After the Second World War the concentration on resource and extractive industries, which are under provincial jurisdiction, increased provincial wealth. Large corporations began to seek direct access to provincial governments and to make party contributions directly at the provincial as well as the federal level. Provincial parties in western and central Canada, in particular, were adept at gathering funds. As the provincial governments and provincial parties increased their wealth and power, they were able to compete more and more successfully with their federal counterparts. Gradually, party financing became decentralized; today, it retains little of its earlier integrative role.

The *Election Expenses Act*, which was passed in 1974, had a profound influence on the fund-raising patterns of all Canada's parties.[55] The new law was intended to bring party financing into the open and at the same time cap election spending. Until that time, parties were reluctant to admit the extent of their financial dependence on specific sources. There was always a suspicion that those who contributed might have undue influence on the selection of leaders or the determination of party policies. The motivation of donors was suspect even though their reason for contributing might have been as innocent as a desire to do their civic duty.

There were two early political scandals in Canada resulting from parties accepting money from "unsavoury" sources: the Pacific Scandal of the 1870s in the Conservative Party, and the Beauharnois affair of the 1930s in the Liberal Party. The 1960s brought more scandals, particularly the Rivard affair, in which a narcotics smuggler, Lucien Rivard,

---

[55] See F. Leslie Seidle and Khayyam Zev Paltiel, "Party Finance, the Election Expenses Act, and Campaign Spending in 1979 and 1980," in John Penniman, *Canada at the Polls* (Washington: AEI, 1981) pp. 226–79; and W.T. Stanbury, "Financing Federal Political Parties in Canada, 1974–1986," in Gagnon and Tanguay, *Canadian Parties in Transition*, pp. 354–83.

was linked to the Liberal "old guard" in Québec. These events increased the pressure for full disclosure of sources and amounts of party funds so that parties would be free of the danger of hidden manipulation by contributors. It was hoped that the *Election Expenses Act* would prevent further financial scandals. The resultant changes in campaign spending practices and reimbursements to the parties from public funds are discussed in the following chapter; here we are concerned primarily with party fundraising.

Since the passage of the *Election Expenses Act*, contributors are named publicly if they donate more than $100 to a party, and those making contributions up to $500 may claim a tax credit. Each national party must file a detailed expenditure and revenue report within six months of the end of its fiscal year. It also must submit an annual report of contributions received and income tax receipts issued to the Department of National Revenue. Before 1974, businesses often donated 60 percent of their total political contribution to the party in office and the balance to the official Opposition, a decision that favoured the Liberal Party because of its dominant position. The belief behind the 1974 legislation was that it would encourage corporations to contribute relatively equal amounts to the major parties, both of which relied heavily on corporate contributions. Since disclosure has been mandatory, equal contributions have been the general rule. Many large corporations have donated about $50 000 a year to both parties; only a few private companies have not felt obliged to provide equal treatment.[56]

The Liberal and Conservative parties traditionally were financed by businesspeople, trade associations and, most importantly, by the corporate financial structures of Toronto and Montréal. Only a few donors and collectors, or "bagmen" as they are known, were involved.[57] Two years after the new regulations were introduced, Prime Minister Trudeau expressed concern that the large sources of funds were "drying up." The party's fund-raising base was broadened considerably, so that individual donors in the $100 to $1 000 range now contribute about half of the party's funds. The Liberals did not, however, do nearly as well in this respect as the Conservatives who, from 1974 to 1993, made extraordinary progress in direct-mail funding. In the decade after 1983, the Conservatives collected significantly more money than either of their competitors in this manner. However, after their 1993 defeat, this pattern is not likely to continue. While in opposition, the Liberal Party accumulated a large debt that caused considerable internal dissension in the three years preceeding the 1988 election. They went into that election several million dollars in debt, and were still in debt by the 1993 election. Now in government, their financial situation can be expected to improve.

The NDP has always relied to a considerable extent on small donations from many sources. It continues to collect substantial amounts from membership fees and individual donations as well as affiliation fees from some trade unions. The new parties in Parliament, Reform and the Bloc Québécois, have to date relied almost entirely on membership fees, individual donations and fundraising events to finance their parties. Reform has proved particularly adept in this regard and emerged from the 1993 campaign with more money than it started with.[58]

Taxpayers pick up the tab for most party spending during election campaigns — over $7 million in 1993. (See Chapter 11 for details of election financing.)

---

[56] Wearing, *The L-Shaped Party*, p. 232.

[57] Khayyam Zev Paltiel, *Political Party Financing in Canada* (Toronto: McGraw-Hill, 1970), p. 14.

[58] *The Ottawa Citizen*, Nov. 7, 1993.

PARTY CONVENTIONS

About every two years, the national association of each party holds a convention in order to elect party officials and debate policy resolutions. These resolutions have no formal authority and are not binding on the Liberal or Conservative party leadership. However, the debates do give delegates the opportunity to air their views and communicate their policy concerns to the political wing; further, they allow the party to benefit from free publicity. Party leadership conventions are particularly important in marshalling enthusiasm to help heal divided parties, particularly following difficult periods in opposition. Conventions also have an important centralizing influence on the Canadian political system.

Party conventions in the three traditional parties are large, widely representative gatherings of several thousand delegates, most of whom have already invested considerable time and energy as executive officers for the party or as members of women or youth associations. The Liberal and Conservative parties send an equal number of delegates from each constituency to their conventions, joining Senators, MPs and defeated candidates. A number of delegates-at-large from the provinces also attend, including people who are prominent in party affairs but are not eligible to become delegates in one of the other categories. Both the Liberals and Conservatives allow appointed delegates-at-large and committee members to attend their National Conventions, often in the face of vociferous objections that such appointments are elitist and undemocratic.

As a social democratic party, the NDP emphasizes the importance of the individual member; not surprisingly, it has the longest history of regular meetings. The NDP's National Conventions include broad representation from Parliament, constituencies, youth groups and affiliated organizations such as trade unions and farm groups. Unlike the other two parties, the number of delegates from any particular constituency is based on how many members it has. This rewards active associations but does not help the party make inroads into areas where it is weak. Compared to the Liberal and Conservative parties, there are fewer delegates who attend purely by virtue of their official position. The Reform Party, too, emphasizes grassroots participation. It holds conventions approximately every two years to review policy and affirm the party leader.

Party conventions clearly are not designed to be representative of Canadian society as a whole, but of that party in society. They normally are more inclusive of the various age, sex, occupational and religious groups than are the party caucuses, but there are glaring deficiencies in comparison to the total population.[59] Delegates are much better educated and economically better off than the general population. Conventions cannot, therefore, be defended as truly representative in any strict sense. Terms such as "democratic" and "representative" are merely part of the rhetoric used by parties and commentators to generate respect and approval for their party conventions.[60]

---

[59] John Courtney, *The Selection of National Party Leaders in Canada* (Toronto: Macmillan, 1973), p. 106. Also see J. Lele, G.C. Perlin and H.G. Thorburn, "The National Party Convention," in Thorburn, 5th ed., *Party Politics in Canada*, pp. 89–97. For more detail on the attendance at party conventions, see John Courtney, "Leadership Conventions and the Development of the National Political Community in Canada," in R. Kenneth Carty and W. Peter Ward, eds., *National Politics and Community in Canada* (Vancouver, B.C.: University of British Columbia Press, 1986).

[60] The most recent comprehensive study of party conventions can be found in Perlin ed., *Party Democracy in Canada*.

PARTY PROGRAM FORMULATION

At the national level, the extra-governmental party takes part in drafting policy resolutions at national conventions that currently are held at least every two years by all three traditional parties. The trend in recent years has been to keep leadership and policy conventions separate because of their complexity. Before a policy convention assembles, party associations are invited to send in suggestions to a resolutions committee that sorts and prepares them for consideration by the convention. In theory, the resolutions presented to the delegates are debated and passed item by item. However, in fact, the resolutions committee often determines the success of resolutions.

We have pointed out that parties must aggregate, rank and articulate claims of interest in the competition for votes and decide which to present to the electorate as their party platform. Party platforms have contributions from both intra- and extra-parliamentary branches of the parties; they are generally what R.M. Dawson called "conspicuously unsatisfactory documents."[61] Of necessity, items must be vague enough to carry wide appeal — examples are "social reform" or "improved education" — and so end up reading rather like a list of New Year's resolutions. They must also appeal to regional interests such as maritime rights or economic sectors such as wheat exporters. Party platforms are therefore deliberately vague, broadly based documents of compromise that can be used to unite the party nationally. As the three traditional parties have vied for the middle ground, their policy resolutions have often overlapped.

Even after the platform is drawn up and approved by the national convention, it is little more than a guide, or, as Mackenzie King was fond of stating, a "chart and compass" for the party leader to interpret and follow as deemed opportune when steering the ship of state. The party constitutions give no official status to policy resolutions emanating from the National Associations; this situation has been reinforced by successive party leaders.

The issue of extra-parliamentary involvement with policy decisions has been contentious for several decades. Until the late 1950s, party memberships were generally content to provide services at election time. However, by the 1960s both the Liberal and Conservative party federations were demanding to be involved in party affairs on a continuing basis. We have already noted several concrete steps that were taken to make the parties more democratic. Full-time national directors were hired, and national offices were established to operate between elections. Conventions gradually became more regular, and measures were taken to bring women and youth into the main body of the parties. The philosophical justification for conventions in these parties continues to be that their decisions are representative of the party, and consequently are more democratic than those reached by the parliamentary caucus.

One innovation intended to allow wider policy input into the Liberal and Conservative parties was the "Thinkers Conference." These meetings were attended by MPs, MLAs, academics and other invitees who wished to contribute to policy initiatives. The Liberals held their first one in 1933, but the most notable were held in 1960 by the Liberals at Kingston and in 1967 by the Conservatives at Montmorency Falls. Both these conferences made recognized contributions to party policy and were followed by others. A Liberal meeting at the elegant mountain resort of Harrison Hot Springs in British Columbia in 1969 was to be the first phase in a more ambitious operation intended to stimulate floods of public

---

[61] R.M. Dawson, *The Government of Canada*, 5th ed. (Toronto: University of Toronto Press, 1970), p. 504.

participation, but the public showed little interest in the follow-up meetings. When the steam went out of that particular participatory experiment, the Thinkers Conference became unfashionable and was not revived on the same scale until 1987, when the opposition Liberal Party instigated a series of "Canada Conferences" to encourage wide, grassroots discussion and input into policy formulation. The conferences made a significant contribution to the "40 point" progressive platform that the Liberal Party unveiled just before the 1988 election.[62]

The Reform Party, more than any of the traditional parties, emphasizes grassroots input into policy-making. Convention delegates meet with constituency members to discuss policies that will be voted on in convention. Once accepted, policies are recorded in a "Statement of Principles and Policies" and are considered binding on the leadership.

Party conventions may also be used to ensure leadership accountability. In 1966 the Liberal Party added a clause to its constitution requiring the leader to report to future policy conventions on "the consideration given, the decisions made and the reasoning therefore regarding resolutions passed at the previous Convention." This has become known as an "accountability session" at which, theoretically at least, the leader is peppered with difficult questions about the conduct and policies of the parliamentary wing for which the leader is responsible. In fact, the sessions usually produce little serious dialogue and more accolades than criticisms.

Despite such attempts to keep the parliamentary party in touch with the grassroots of the party and allow wider participation in policy discussions, the locus of party power remains with the leader and a small group of chosen associates. Liberal activists expressed the same frustration in 1984 as their predecessors had two decades earlier when, fearful of the consequences of a long period of miserable showings in opinion polls, they complained that the Liberal Party had become a closed, elitist organization that was out of touch with ordinary Canadians.

The extra-parliamentary wings of the traditional parties have slowly strengthened their hand, but the leader and parliamentary caucus remain by far the dominant partners. The extra-parliamentary wing still largely evaporates between elections; only an elite executive group (which has a symbolic share in party decisions) remains, and it is dominated by the party leader. All party appointments are made by the leader or on his or her approval.

Another factor that increases the dominance of the parliamentary party is that, particularly when in government, it has a large support staff that it prefers to consult rather than the national office. As described in earlier chapters, the Prime Minister's Office, the Privy Council Office, the Ministers' "exempt" staffs and the party research offices all have specialized personnel at the disposal of the parliamentary party and Cabinet.

In many ways, the NDP has been the most democratic of the established parties, as would be expected of a social democratic party. It has the longest history of regular conventions and, unlike the two other parties, does not allow delegates to be appointed by the party elite. NDP policy conventions have also been the most serious and binding on the leadership, a situation that might well have changed if the party had come to power in Ottawa. The Reform Party promises to outdo the NDP in terms of grassroots democracy, but it remains to be seen if it will actually do so once in Ottawa.

A grave shortcoming of the pragmatic policy formulation procedures followed by modern Canadian parties as they vie for electoral success is that parochial concerns often dominate at the expense of a national vision. As Gordon Stewart comments:

---

[62] A more modest convention at the beginning of the Chrétien leadership resulted in a volume of essays. See Cleo Mowers, ed., *Towards a New Liberalism: Re-creating Canada and the Liberal Party* (Victoria: Orca, 1991).

From the time that modern party formulation began in the 1840's Canada's political culture encouraged only the party leader/prime minister and perhaps one or two lieutenants to take long-term national interests into account.[63]

This has tended to discourage creative thinking about long-term policy solutions to problems such as French-English relations in Canada. Stewart goes so far as to call the parties "political dinosaurs" — with great weight and presence but small brains.

NATIONAL PARTY LEADERSHIP SELECTION

Until 1919, leadership selection in Canada followed the British model. Members of the parliamentary caucus and the retiring leader selected the new leader, occasionally with the advice of the Governor General, and then presented him to the party. The Liberal Party was the first national political party in Canada to select a leader with the active participation of its extra-parliamentary wing. It happened almost accidentally. The 1919 convention was not intended to be a leadership convention; it was instigated by the Prime Minister as a policy convention to help reunite his badly divided party. However, Laurier's sudden death, "combined with the peculiar internal conditions of the parliamentary Liberal Party, made the convention appear to be a natural way of selecting the next leader of the Liberal party."[64] Mackenzie King became the first party leader selected by a national convention.

The Conservatives chose one more leader — Arthur Meighen — by the caucus method in 1920, but when the party was defeated, and Meighen subsequently resigned in 1926, the party felt compelled to follow the democratic precedent set by the Liberals. In 1927, they elected R.B. Bennett at a national convention. The British leadership selection model whereby party leaders "emerged" after consultations generated by the retiring leader and the party caucus with the parliamentary party was thus abandoned. Open, more American-style conventions were established, gradually becoming more lavish. Liberals have subsequently held leadership conventions in 1948, 1958, 1968, 1984 and 1990; the Conservatives in 1938, 1942, 1948, 1956, 1967, 1976, 1983 and 1993; and the NDP in 1971, 1975 and 1989. (See Table 10.4 for a list of major-party leaders.)

The appeal of the convention method is that it gives the impression, justified or not, that the party is "open," "democratic" and "representative" in making its decisions. A drawback is that it was not designed for parliamentary government, but rather for a system with separate legislative and executive offices. It has been adapted to Canada's unique federal, parliamentary needs, but not without leaving inevitable contradictions in the Canadian system. For example, leadership candidates must support their party in Parliament at the same time that they appeal for delegate support — something very difficult to do when Cabinet solidarity is at stake. There is often a legacy of bitter feelings that makes it difficult for the new leader to command the full support of the caucus.

As long ago as 1968, Don Smiley pointed out that the nature of the convention was changing, that a new "openness" was being established. He cited five examples. There were many more serious candidates than in early conventions, the major candidates conducted elaborate competitive campaigns across Canada, mass media coverage was extensive, the rank and file of the parties was more involved and influential and token candidates were treated generously.[65]

---

[63] Gordon T. Stewart, *The Origins of Canadian Politics* (Vancouver: University of British Columbia Press, 1986), p. 100.

[64] Courtney, *The Selection of National Party Leaders*, p. 78.

[65] D.V. Smiley, "The National Party Leadership Convention in Canada: A Preliminary Analysis," *CJPS*, vol. 1, no. 4 (December 1968), pp. 373–97.

These changes have all been confirmed; to them must be added the beneficial effect of the secret ballot on leadership selection. It would be unthinkable today for outgoing leaders to designate their successors and have the convention duly annoint them, which happened as recently as 1942 for the Conservatives and 1948 for the Liberals. At the same time, however, as we have noted, conventions are far from representative of Canadian society, and the "establishment" within each party tend to appoint a large number of delegates.

TABLE 10.4 PARTY LEADERS: CONSERVATIVE, LIBERAL, NDP, BLOC QUÉBÉCOIS AND REFORM

Progressive Conservative Party	Liberal Party	New Democratic Party	Bloc Québécois	Reform Party
Sir John A. Macdonald (1854–81)	Alexander Mackenzie (1873–80)	Tommy Douglas (1961–71)	Lucien Bouchard (1991–)	Preston Manning (1987–)
Sir J.J.C. Abbott (1891–92)	Edward Blake (1880–87)	David Lewis (1971–75)		
Sir John Thompson (1892–94)	Sir Wilfrid Laurier (1887–1919)	Ed Broadbent (1975–89)		
Sir Mackenzie Bowell (1894–96)	Daniel D. McKenzie* (1919–19)	Audrey McLaughlin (1989 -)		
Sir Charles Tupper (1896–1901)	W.L. Mackenzie King (1919–48)			
Sir Robert Borden (1901–20)	Louis St. Laurent (1948–58)			
Arthur Meighen (1920–26)	Lester B. Pearson (1958–68)			
Hugh Gutherie* (1926–27)	Pierre E. Trudeau (1968–84)			
R.B. Bennett (1927–38)	John Turner (1984–90)			
R.J. Manion (1938–40)	Jean Chrétien (1990–)			
R.B. Hanson* (1940–41)				
Arthur Meighen (1941–42)				
John Bracken (1942–48)				
George Drew (1948–56)				
John Diefenbaker (1956–67)				
Robert L. Stanfield (1967–76)				
Joe Clark (1976–83)				
Erik Nielsen* (1983)				
Brian Mulroney (1983–93)				
Kim Campbell (1993)				
Jean Charest* (1993-)				

* Interim leader

Leadership conventions are similar to policy conventions in terms of basic organization and participation, and their general rules are common to all three parties, although specific details vary. Leadership conventions are called when a leader resigns or dies, and sometimes even if he or she does not score sufficiently high on a leadership review vote. Rules about when a leadership review will be held differ from party to party. Currently, the Liberal constitution states that a leadership review will be held only during the first national convention after a General Election. In practice, Liberal convention delegates have always voted against calling a leadership convention, but the procedure remains a significant reminder that the leader is responsible to the party. In 1992 the Liberals approved giving all party members a direct say in reviewing the leader's performance after each election, thereby ending the practice of choosing delegates to vote on the leader's performance at a national convention. This will take place for the first time to judge the performance of Jean Chrétien after the 1993 election.

In the Conservative Party, leadership reviews were first initiated to assess John Diefenbaker's performance in 1967. They later became a regular feature of party conventions.[66] Technically, a Tory leader needs to win only 50 percent of the leadership review vote to continue in office. In 1983, however, Joe Clark resigned as Conservative leader after he failed to secure more than 67 percent of the voting delegate's support. He then submitted himself as a leadership candidate in a final effort to consolidate his party support. The caucus chose a temporary leader from its own membership, and at a subsequent leadership convention the party elected a new leader, Brian Mulroney. The Conservative Party amended its review procedure at the 1983 convention to reduce the opportunities for a leadership review vote. Reviews are now held only at the first convention within a year of a federal general election in which the party does not form the government.

The NDP has no leadership review procedure as such, but requires its leader to seek re-election automatically at biennial national conventions. It opens nominations for the position of leader, but if there is no challenger, no vote is needed. In practice, an incumbent has never been defeated. In line with its general philosophy of accountability, the Reform Party also asks delegates at every convention whether they want a leadership review. To date that option has always been turned down.

Leadership conventions take several months to organize once a leader announces the decision to step down. Delegates must be chosen, and the manner in which this is done has important consequences for the leadership candidates. Most delegate positions are fixed. The Conservative convention in 1993 allowed each of the 295 ridings to send four senior and two youth delegates, and university campus clubs were also allotted delegates. All Conservative MPs or candidates, Tory members of provincial legislatures, executive officers and a fixed number of delegates-at-large were included, for a total of about 3 800. To discourage "nuisance" candidates, contestants had to file nomination papers with a minimum number of signatures and make a financial deposit. Five candidates competed. The rules were fairly standard: voting was by secret ballot; any candidate with fewer than 50 votes was automatically dropped off the next ballot; if all candidates had 50 votes or more, the candidate in last place was dropped automatically; a tie for last place meant all candidates would remain on the ballot; eventually the winning candidate had to receive a majority of the votes cast.

---

[66] Diefenbaker's leadership was in dispute following his defeat in the 1963 General Election, and party President Dalton Camp seized the opportunity to argue for the need to "democratize" the party by assessing the leadership. After a bitter struggle, the Camp faction won and a leadership convention was called in 1967.

Recent leadership conventions have adopted the festive atmosphere of American conventions, with flamboyant speeches, entertainment and full national television coverage. There are some important differences, however. Balloting at U.S. conventions is by states rather than individuals, and the votes are announced openly, making the event quite ritualistic and predictable. The American primary system and open delegate selection process tend to produce a winner long before the convention. In Canada, the secret ballot (and the not-so-genteel tendency of some delegates to vote differently than they have promised candidates) lends a degree of suspense that is missing in the American process. Nuisance candidates, though kept to a minimum, are not totally discouraged in either system because of the colour and democratic element they add. In Canada, having several ballots also allows the serious candidates to learn the absolute voting figures and gain time to bargain between ballots while the token candidates are being eliminated. Delegates normally give little public indication of who they will support if their first choice candidate is eliminated.

At the end of each session of balloting, the votes are counted and results announced as a total — there is no potentially divisive breakdown. Victory on the first ballot does not necessarily indicate who will win; Clark won the first ballot in 1983, well ahead of Mulroney, but that lead narrowed in the next two ballots and was finally reversed on the fourth and final vote. With the withdrawal or elimination of a candidate, coalitions shift and delegates disperse. When Jean Chrétien was elected leader in Calgary in June 1990, he won on the first ballot over four other candidates. Audrey McLaughlin won on the fourth ballot. (See Tables 10.5 and 10.6.) Preston Manning was elected leader of the Reform Party at a 1987 convention after Stan Roberts withdrew his candidacy. Bloc Québécois leader Lucien Bouchard was acclaimed at a party congress in June 1991.

Leadership campaign costs have escalated dramatically in recent years. In order to keep costs low, and also to discourage candidates from relying on large sums of money from one or two donors who hope for future considerations, the Liberal Party constitution provides for the appointment of a Leadership Expenses Committee whenever a leadership convention is called. The committee is empowered to set a maximum limit for candidates' spending prior to and at the convention, to enforce compliance with that limit and to ensure complete disclosure of all contributions to leadership campaigns. The Conservative Party had no such provisions at its 1983 convention, claiming that they were unenforceable. Candidates were left with large debts, and the Tory party received negative publicity from accusations that "offshore" financing had been used to defeat the incumbent leader. Partly because of this bad press, the Conservative executive placed a $900 000 spending limit per candidate, plus unlimited travel for the 1993 convention. In 1993, funds collected by leadership candidates were to be processed through the PC Canada Fund and tax receipts issued for contributions (meaning that anyone contributing up to $1 100 could deduct the contribution from their taxes). There were, however, few penalties for breaking the rules. Kim Campbell was reported to have spent at least four times the allowed limit.[67]

The 1993 Conservative contest may be the last of the mega-conventions that began with the 1967 Tory convention in Toronto's Maple Leaf Gardens. The Liberal Party decided in 1992 to use a combined direct-vote/convention model when the time comes to replace Jean Chrétien. Under the new process, federal leaders will be elected by a system similar to that used by the Ontario Liberals for the first time in 1992, combining the concept of party members' suffrage with the old system of electing delegates to attend leadership conventions.

---

67 *The Globe and Mail*, Oct. 30, 1993.

The hope is to avoid the kind of embarrassing spectacles suffered by the party in 1984 and 1990 when candidates wooed members of specific ethnic groups and used anti-abortion activists to stack meetings and elect slates of delegates. For the next Liberal leadership selection, all party members in each riding will vote for their preferred candidate and each riding will then send delegates, proportional to the support garnered by each candidate, to a national convention.[68]

TABLE 10.5   1990 LIBERAL LEADERSHIP CONVENTION BALLOTING RESULTS

Candidate	First Ballot
Jean Chrétien	2 662
Paul Martin	1 176
Sheila Copps	499
Tom Wappel	267
John Nunziata	64

TABLE 10.6   1989 NDP LEADERSHIP CONVENTION BALLOTING RESULTS

Candidate	First Ballot	Second Ballot	Third Ballot	Fourth Ballot
Audrey McLaughlin	646	829	1072	1 316
Dave Barrett	566	780	947	1 072
Steven Langdon	351	519	393	—
Simon de Jong	315	289	—	—
Howard McCurdy	256	—	—	—
Ian Waddell	213	—	—	—
Roger Lagasse	53	—	—	—

The general criticism that the convention process is too expensive and allows those with the money to walk away with the prize persists. It is highly unlikely, however, that the parties will forfeit the prolonged media exposure the convention method provides, or risk returning to the earlier model of parliamentary selections that were swift and inexpensive but smacked of elitism and anti-democracy.

THE 1993 CONSERVATIVE LEADERSHIP CONVENTION

Leadership conventions give parties precious media coverage. The Conservative convention of June 1993 was a typical entertainment extravaganza. In the initial phase, amid great speculation about who would run, the candidates slowly entered the contest. It did not begin as a race at all, but as a coronation. Kim Campbell was first to enter the contest, and the media

---

[68] Reported in *The Ottawa Citizen*, February 22, 1992.

helped make her an "overnight sensation," setting exaggerated expectations. Four other candidates, none of them senior Conservatives, declared, but with considerably less fanfare: Jean Charest, Jim Edwards, Patrick Boyer and Garth Turner.

Campbell campaign organizers took advantage of the media hype that preceded her entry into the race by signing up thousands of new Tories, sending them to the delegate selection meetings and having them vote for Campbell delegates. In spite of the fact that she had been in federal politics for only five years, and for two years before that in provincial politics, she began the leadership campaign so strongly that other senior Conservative Ministers withheld their names and threw their support behind her. During delegate selection meetings

DELEGATE WOOING

Reprinted with permission, Gable, *The Globe and Mail.*

in May, her two main rivals, Jean Charest and Jim Edwards, were still struggling to organize national campaigns while she was consolidating delegate support. Campbell's opponents hoped that her delegate support was based on media hype and would collapse over the three-month campaign. To a degree this happened; as Charest's popularity increased the coronation was turned into a race. Modern technology enabled candidates to keep daily delegate counts, monitoring trends, shifts, second choice preferences, and so on.

In the second phase of the contest, policy rallies were held across the country to introduce the candidates and gain more media attention. Leadership debates were fully covered by the media, giving the entire country a look at the candidates and the issues. Meanwhile, pollsters and candidates showered delegates with attention by mail, telephone and personal contact. At the same time, candidates were concerned about firming up the support of fellow MPs and raising funds for the three-month campaign. Polls indicated that Jean Charest's campaign was gaining momentum and, by the time of the convention, that he could possibly win.

On convention weekend, the Landsdowne Park site in Ottawa was crammed with about 3 800 registered voters, alternatives, and several thousand observers and media representatives. Delegates were pestered and pampered: the wooing included free drinks, a huge B.C. salmon barbecue, youth delegate parties, hospitality suites with free beer and a plethora of souvenirs. Competing television networks sought to capture as much of the convention drama and gossip as possible as they fought for a larger share of the viewing audience. The convention gave the party hours of prime-time coverage and commentary. Amid the hoopla, the candidates each made major speeches, poll results were "leaked" and politicking was intense. At convention events, Campbell youth delegates and volunteers arrived well before Charest's team. They got the best locations on the arena floor and created the appearance of dominance. Campbell supporters were outfitted with shocking pink hats and a sea of "KIM" placards.

Kim Campbell went into the convention well ahead in the polls, followed by Jean Charest as the only realistic contender. Campbell had the support of most Tory establishment figures. Her platform was based on deficit reduction and making the democratic process more open to more people — "the politics of inclusion." She went into the convention with enough support to win a majority and retained most of that support. Although it was widely agreed that Charest outperformed her in the debates, he was handicapped by the fact that he was young (34 years old) and from Québec, and because Campbell's campaign organization had been prepared well in advance of her announced candidacy.

There were only two ballots. The first placed Kim Campbell within 71 votes of victory. Charest was second, but not close enough to have a realistic chance of closing the gap. Alberta MP Jim Edwards, who was a distant third with 307 votes, quickly moved to Campbell with the comment "I think this is probably the best way to unify the party and I hope we'll be able to all come together for the next election."[69] Toronto MP Patrick Boyer, who placed fifth, tried to take his 53 votes to Charest, while Toronto-area MP Garth Turner, who had 76 first-ballot votes, released his delegates. Campbell won easily on the second ballot. (See Table 10.7.)

TABLE 10.7 1993 CONSERVATIVE LEADERSHIP CONVENTION BALLOTING RESULTS

Candidate	First Ballot	Second Ballot
Kim Campbell	1 664	1 817
Jean Charest	1 369	1 630
Jim Edwards	307	
Garth Turner	76	
Patrick Boyer	53	

Although Charest lost the leadership, he came out of the convention with increased recognition and respect. Jim Edwards was expected to be the king- or queen-maker at the convention, but Ms. Campbell was very close to winning without him, and his 9 percent finish left him with less support than he had expected. Not many of his delegates moved with him to Campbell.

---

[69] Quoted in *The Ottawa Citizen*, June 14, 1993.

PARTY LEADERS

Candidates who win leadership conventions are likely to exhibit similar characteristics though these vary somewhat depending on the party to which he or she belongs. Almost all who enter the fray are university-educated professionals. The leader of the NDP has always been from Ontario, the West or the North, a tradition that reflects the party's inability to make political inroads in Québec and the Maritimes. Audrey McLaughlin was the first woman and the first person from the North to lead a national political party.

In the past, the typical Conservative leader was a lawyer, a Protestant and from one of the Prairie Provinces, Ontario or the Maritimes. Today, it is expected that he or she will be bilingual. Brian Mulroney was the party's first elected leader from Québec. Kim Campbell was the Conservative's first leader from British Columbia, and the first woman to lead the party. The typical Liberal leader has been a lawyer — though this is less likely than for the Conservatives — a Roman Catholic and bilingual. Except for John Turner (who lived in Ontario but ran for office in British Columbia), the Liberals have always chosen their leaders from Ontario or Québec; normally they have alternated between French and English leaders, a tendency that has become a matter of principle for many Liberals. This was also a factor in the 1993 Conservative convention. To counter the criticism that he could be the second Québec leader in a row, Charest argued: "As far as the rule of alternation [between a Québécois and non-Québécois leader] is concerned, having had only one leader from Québec in 125 years, we haven't exactly abused the rule."[70]

Prior to the introduction of leadership conventions, leaders of both Liberal and Conservative parties were likely to have been experienced career parliamentarians. Since then, previous parliamentary experience has become less significant for party leaders. Brian Mulroney was the first leader of either party to win the position with no legislative experience whatsoever. Not until he won a seat in a by-election several months after the convention was Mulroney sworn in as Member of Parliament and therefore able to be Leader of the Official Opposition as well as Leader of the Progressive Conservative Party. Mackenzie King, Pierre Trudeau and Audrey McLaughlin had all been in Parliament less than three years when they were elected leader. In Kim Campbell's case it was four years. At recent conventions Stanfield, Clark, Mulroney, Trudeau and McLaughlin were all relatively unknown even by party activists until shortly before the conventions at which they were chosen. John Turner had been out of politics and disassociated from the Liberal government for years, but still remained the darling of the media while he waited in the wings. Reform leader Preston Manning had never been in Parliament when he became leader of the party he had started. Lucien Bouchard was first elected to Parliament, as a Conservative, in 1988. It would appear that a fresh image counts more at a leadership convention than does the experience of a party veteran, although Jean Chrétien was able to counter the epithet "yesterday's man" and turn his many years of parliamentary experience into an asset.

THE ROLE OF THE LEADER IN THE PARTY

The party leader has a pre-eminent role as decision-maker, figurehead and spokesperson of both the parliamentary and extra-parliamentary branches of a party. The image a leader projects is extremely important because it provides a simple, differentiating feature between the

---

[70] *The Globe and Mail*, March 17, 1993, p. 1.

parties, which otherwise often appear very similar to the electorate. A leader with a poor image can ruin the electoral chances of even the most vital party; this fact encourages enormous preoccupation with image building and the appearance and personality of the leader, to the detriment of policy issues. The leadership position is a prestigious one carrying considerable powers in the parliamentary system. National party leaders ideally are symbols of unity, figures above sectional interests. The more regionalized the party system becomes, the less this ideal can be met.

The Prime Minister's position at the apex of government, public service and political party was discussed in Chapter 7. Here it is sufficient to note that the office includes a large support staff and many other perquisites of which political patronage is foremost. As Gordon Stewart points out, patronage has, since colonial days, been relatively openly entrenched as a legitimate activity. Prime Ministers have used patronage to help build and maintain broad bases necessary for national parties.

The Prime Minister's political patronage powers are second to none. As the top member of the government hierarchy he or she has Cabinet, government bureaucracy and Senate positions to fill, as well as party appointments. Opposition leaders, whose capacity for largesse is extremely limited, have a much more difficult time keeping a united party.

Much of the prestige of the official Leader of the Opposition lies in the fact that he or she is a potential Prime Minister, and could inherit the superior status and authority of that coveted position. But because the job is to lead the offensive against the party in power, opposition leaders are often accused of carping and sometimes even unpatriotic behaviour for attacking the government.

We have already noted the extensive authority the leader has over the extra-parliamentary wing of his or her party, including the power to approve or disapprove the budget for the activities of the party organization. Another power arises from the right to make key appointments on the national executive and to create ad hoc committees whose authority may supersede that of the officers elected by the national association. For example, the leader makes appointments to the election campaign committee. Within the parliamentary party the Opposition leader appoints a "shadow cabinet," and in many ways enjoys more flexibility than the Prime Minister does in choosing a Cabinet.

The Leader of the Official Opposition has special status at official functions and in parliamentary ceremonies and even an international standing with foreign governments, but this position is nevertheless very inferior compared to that of the Prime Minister.[71] Though his or her functions are not governed by statute, the role is officially recognized in the procedures of the House of Commons. Canada first officially recognized the existence of the Leader of the Opposition in 1905 by granting the occupant of that position a salary equal to that of a Cabinet minister. Surprisingly, Canada was well ahead of Britain in doing so, for it was not until 1937 that the British officially recognized their Opposition leader along with their Prime Minister.[72]

While the Prime Minister enjoys the many perquisites of government and the official residences at 24 Sussex Drive and Harrington Lake, the Opposition leader receives, in addition to a salary and expense allowance as a Member of Parliament, other perks such as a

[71] R.M. Punnett, *Front-Bench Opposition* (London: Heinemann, 1973), p. 99.

[72] Ghita Ionescu and Isabel de Madariaga, *Opposition: Past and Present of a Political Institution* (London: C.A. Watts and Co., Ltd., 1968), p. 69.

car allowance and an official residence — Stornoway in Rockcliffe Park. As for facilities on Parliament Hill, the Opposition leader is provided with a large staff and offices in the House of Commons similar to that allocated to the Prime Minister. In addition, as a Member of Parliament, he or she is entitled to a suite of offices and to a constituency office with a full-time staff in Ottawa and in his or her riding.[73] In Parliament, the Opposition leader has the right to ask the lead question in Question Period and benefit from the attendant publicity that entails.

The party leader is accountable to the caucus. Without the support of the caucus and the national association the leader cannot hope for sufficient party unity to achieve electoral victory. The leader's relationship with these two important sectors of the party is complicated because the caucus basically represents federal interests, while the national association tends to be more representative of provincial interests. As leaders from both the Liberal and Conservative parties can testify, the task of placating the two is especially difficult for an opposition leader who has general responsibility for the conduct of the members of his caucus but few rewards to offer them. Internecine battles over the leadership during Joe Clark's tenure contributed to and reinforced the Conservative image of a fragmented party in electoral decline.[74] Similar problems beset John Turner in the Liberal Party before the 1988 election.

Nonetheless, the power of the parliamentary caucus is limited vis-à-vis the leader because regular meetings are held only a half-day each week and even then no votes are taken. The leader simply interprets the general mood in what he or she determines is the party's best interests. This means, as George Perlin notes, that there is no recognized independent body within the caucus that can challenge the leader.[75] Getting rid of an unpopular leader who is determined to stay on is a difficult matter that requires a vote of non-confidence at a leadership review, as discussed earlier.

The superior status of the party leader in the Canadian system is deeply rooted in parliamentary tradition. The leader is the only party member who can claim broadly based legitimacy. Leaders like Preston Manning and Lucien Bouchard who found new parties are quick to legitimate their position by a vote. Chosen by the national convention but also the voice of the parliamentary caucus, the party leader is the most powerful individual in the creation of party policy. The position is, at least theoretically, a symbol of coherence and cohesion for the party.

OVERVIEW

The Canadian party system strongly reflects the decentralized nature of the federal system of government within which it operates. Federal and provincial parties operate independently. And the relationships among the constituency, provincial and federal structures of federal parties are relatively weakly articulated.

At the beginning of the chapter we outlined the essential functions of all political parties. An examination of the recent history and organization of Canadian parties reveals

---

[73] Alastair Fraser, "Legislators and their Staffs," in Harold Clarke et al., eds., *Parliament, Policy and Representation* (Toronto: Methuen, 1980), p. 232.

[74] George Perlin, *The Tory Syndrome* (Montréal: McGill-Queen's University Press, 1980), p. 103.

[75] Ibid., p. 26.

that the traditional parties have not performed many of those functions well, thereby facilitating the growth of new, regionally based parties at the federal level.

Important party functions include the effective aggregation of demands from society. The Liberal and Conservative parties, which have always supplied the managers and decision-makers of Canadian federal politics, have maintained their dominant roles by bringing together coalitions of ethnic and regional interests, thereby allowing a means of expression to those interests and providing an integrative force in Canadian society. Often, however, major distortions in regional representation in the two parties have weakened their ability to be truly national parties. Other parties have arisen to fill the vacuum, but they have been even less successful in aggregating interests across the country. Most have attempted to capture votes by presenting a program based on a single ideology or principle.

Canadian political parties are also limited in their ability to articulate interests. They are effective "gatekeepers," allowing certain demands, and not others, to reach decision-makers. But party programs, expressed as coordinated and consistent politics aimed at achieving specific goals with which the parties are associated, are rare in the Canadian system. Because they have attempted to mediate diverse interests the Liberal and Conservative parties in past could not afford the rigidity of firm policy commitments. Issues are discussed and developed for election campaigns, but, as we shall see in the next chapter, elections are a very poor source of policy communication, with policies often being advanced in a random fashion as ad hoc responses to specific problems. Even after winning an election, parties can rarely claim clear policy directives from the electorate, or even that the electorate supports one or all of their policies.

Party organizations are designed to achieve electoral victory for their party, and their members are concerned with policy-making mainly as a means to achieve that goal. Between elections they hold policy conventions to agree on policies that are generally designed to win electoral support where they are weak. However, Canadian political parties are not organized very well for policy formulation, and the impact of policy decisions made at conventions on the party leadership is uncertain. Convention policy statements are not binding on the leadership and, although steps are taken to avoid embarrassing contradictions or inconsistencies in party and government policies, such gaffes still happen. The mass party does not have much influence over policy formation; senior party bureaucrats and members of the parliamentary party have more. This is especially true in the government party, because the government caucus, or private meeting of the parliamentary party, has the opportunity to discuss most policy matters before they reach the House of Commons.

By their very nature, political parties are flawed, as Lord Macaulay pointed out in this irreverent analogy:

> *Every political sect...has its altars and its deified heroes, its relics and its pilgrimages, its canonized martyrs and confessors, and its legendary miracles.*[76]

Political parties in this electronic age still use all the devices of superstition to win converts and maintain their loyalty: conventions are but pilgrimages; heroes and martyrs provide the spiritual glue of the party; relics are the venerated policies and records that provide the proof of vision and ideas of substance. Along with the manipulation, patronage and distortions, however, parties in Canada allow for the orderly election of representatives and leaders to government and are the means by which thousands of Canadians can

---

[76] Quoted by Neil A. McDonald in *The Study of Political Parties* (New York: Random House, 1955), p. 20.

actively participate and express themselves in the process. In short, parties are a colourful and important part of the democratic process in Canada, and even with their shortcomings it is difficult to conceive of political representation in this country without them. The next chapter examines the electoral system within which the parties vie for power.

SELECTED BIBLIOGRAPHY

GENERAL

Aucoin, Peter, ed., *Party Government and Regional Representation in Canada*, vol. 36, Royal Commission on the Economic Union and Development Prospects for Canada (Toronto: University of Toronto Press, 1985).

Bashevkin, Sylvia B., *Toeing the Lines: Women in Party Politics in English Canada* (Ottawa: Carleton University Press, 1985).

Blake, Donald E., *Two Political Worlds: Parties and Voting in British Columbia* (Vancouver: University of British Columbia Press, 1985).

Brodie, M. Janine and Jane Jensen, *Crisis, Challenge and Change: Party and Class in Canada* (Toronto: Methuen, 1980).

Brooks, Stephen, ed. *Political Thought in Canada* (Toronto: Irwin, 1984).

Carty, K.R., ed., *Canadian Political Party Systems* (Toronto: Broadview, 1992).

————, and W.P. Ward, eds., *Canada and the National Political Community* (Vancouver: University of British Columbia Press, 1986).

Christian, W., and C. Campbell, *Political Parties and Ideologies in Canada* (Toronto: McGraw-Hill Ryerson, 1983).

Duverger, Maurice, *Political Parties: Their Organisation and Activity in the Modern State* (London: Methuen, 1954).

Gagnon, Alain G. and A. Brian Tanguay, eds., *Canadian Parties in Transition: Discourse, Organization and Representation* (Toronto: Nelson, 1989).

Jackson, Robert J. and Doreen Jackson, *Stand Up For Canada: Leadership and the Canadian Political Crisis* (Scarborough, Ont.: Prentice-Hall, 1992).

Kerr, Donald C., *Western Canadian Politics: The Radical Tradition* (Edmonton: West Institute for Western Canadian Studies, 1981).

Megyery, Kathy, ed., *Women in Canadian Politics: Toward Equity in Representation*, Research Studies of the Royal Commission on Electoral Reform and Party Financing, vol. 6 (Toronto: Dundurn Press, 1991).

Meisel, John, *Cleavages, Parties and Values in Canada* (Beverly Hills, Cal. and London: Sage Publications, 1974).

Perlin, George, ed., *Party Democracy in Canada: The Role of National Party Conventions* (Scarborough, Ont.: Prentice-Hall Canada, 1988).

Polsby, N.W., *Consequences of Party Reform* (New York: Oxford University Press, 1983).

Sartori, Giovanni, *Parties and Party Systems: A Framework for Analysis* (London: Cambridge University Press, 1976).

————, *Spoils of Power: The Politics of Patronage* (Toronto: Collins, 1988).

Thorburn, Hugh G., ed., *Party Politics in Canada*, 6th ed. (Scarborough, Ont.: Prentice-Hall Canada, 1991).

Wearing, Joseph, *Strained Relations: Canadian Parties and Voters* (Toronto: McClelland and Stewart, 1988).

Winn, Conrad, and John McMenemy, eds., *Political Parties in Canada* (Toronto: McGraw-Hill Ryerson, 1976).

CONSERVATIVE PARTY

Dobbin, Murray, *The Politics of Kim Campbell* (Toronto: James Lorimer, 1993).

Granatstein, J.L., *The Politics of Survival: The Conservative Party of Canada 1939–1945* (Toronto: University of Toronto Press, 1967).

Martin, P., A. Gregg and G. Perlin, *Contenders: The Tory Quest for Power* (Scarborough, Ont.: Prentice-Hall Canada, 1983).

Perlin, George, *The Tory Syndrome: Leadership Politics in the Progressive Conservative Party* (McGill-Queen's University Press, 1980).

Simpson, Jeffrey, *Discipline of Power: The Conservative Interlude and the Liberal Restoration* (Toronto: Personal Library, 1981),

Taylor, Charles, *Radical Tories* (Toronto; House of Anansi, 1982).

LIBERAL PARTY

Clarkson, Stephen and Christina McCall, *Trudeau and Our Times: The Magnificent Obsession* (Toronto: McClelland and Stewart, 1990).

Chrétien, Jean, *Straight from the Heart* (Toronto: Key Porter, 1985).

Goldfarb, Martin and Thomas Axworthy, *Marching to a Different Drummer* (Toronto: Stoddart, 1988).

McCall Newman, Christina, *Grits: An Intimate Portrait of the Liberal Party* (Toronto: Macmillan, 1982).

Roberts, John, *Agenda for Canada: Towards a New Liberalism* (Toronto: Lester and Orpen Dennys, 1985).

Smith, David E., *The Regional Decline of a National Party: Liberals on the Prairies* (Toronto: University of Toronto Press, 1981).

Trudeau, Pierre Elliot, *Memoirs* (Toronto: McClelland & Stewart, 1993).

Wearing, Joseph, *The L-Shaped Party: The Liberal Party of Canada 1958–1980* (Toronto: McGraw-Hill Ryerson, 1981).

Whitaker, Reginald, *The Government Party: Organizing and Financing the Liberal Party of Canada 1930-1958* (Toronto: University of Toronto Press, 1977).

Wilson, Barry, *Politics of Defeat: The Decline of the Liberal Party in Saskatachewan* (Saskatoon: Western Producer Books, 1980).

CCF/NDP

Bradley, Michael, *Crisis of Clarity: The New Democratic Party and the Quest for the Holy Grail* (Toronto: Summerhill Press, 1985).

Brennan, J.W., ed., *Building the Co-operative Commonwealth: Essays on the Democratic Socialist Tradition in Canada* (Regina: Canadian Plains Research Center, 1985).

Horn, M., *The League for Social Reconstruction: Intellectual Origins of the Democratic Left in Canada 1930–1942* (Toronto: University of Toronto Press, 1980).

McDonald, Lynn, *The Party that Changed Canada: The New Democratic Party, Then and Now* (Toronto: McClelland & Stewart, 1987).

Morton, Desmond, *The New Democrats 1961–1986* (Toronto: Copp Clark Pitman Ltd., 1986).

Whitehorn, Alan, *Canadian Socialism: Essays on the CCF and the NDP* (Toronto: Oxford University Press, 1992).

Wilson, Donna, ed., *Democratic Socialism: The Challenge of the Eighties and Beyond* (Vancouver: New Star Books, 1985).

Wiseman, Nelson, *Social Democracy in Manitoba: A History of the CCF/NDP* (Winnipeg: University of Manitoba Press, 1984).

OTHER PARTIES

Bouchard, Lucien, *Un nouveau parti pour l'étape décisive* (St. Laurent, PQ:, Fides, 1993).

Dobbin, Murray, *Preston Manning and the Reform Party* (Toronto: Lorimer, 1991).

Hurtig, Mel, *A New and Better Canada: Principles and Policies of a New Canadian Political Party* (Toronto: Stoddart, 1992).

Manning, Preston, *The New Canada* (Toronto: Macmillan, 1992).

Morton, W.L., *The Progressive Party in Canada* (Toronto: University of Toronto Press, 1950).

Stein, Michael B., *The Dynamics of Right-wing Protest: A Political Analysis of the Social Credit in Quebec* (Toronto: University of Toronto Press, 1973).

Sydney Sharpe and Don Braid, *Storming Babylon: Preston Manning and the Rise of the Reform Party* (Toronto: Key Porter, 1992).

Elections Canada

CHAPTER 11

ELECTIONS AND ELECTORAL BEHAVIOUR
LETTING THE PEOPLE DECIDE

Elections, like parliamentary assemblies, are almost universal. In the past decade, only a handful of UN member states have failed to hold a national election to choose either an assembly or a head of state. These include traditional societies (such as Oman and the United Arab Emirates) in which heredity or family ties determine political office, long-term military dictatorships (such as Upper Volta) and communist or socialist states (such as Angola, Ethiopia and Laos). The vast majority of countries have held elections at least once during this period, including all liberal democracies. Some countries have fallen by the wayside as far as elections are concerned, especially those where the military have intervened, but other states have restored elections after long periods with no opportunity for citizens to vote.

Although elections are held in a wide variety of political systems, they assume special significance in liberal democracies. In the latter, they afford citizens the opportunity to choose political representatives from competing candidates and, in principle at least, give citizens a voice in the governance of their society. The electoral process aggregates various demands in society into a limited number of choices and assures the representation of diverse opinions in the policy-making arena. As a result, the process accords political leaders legitimacy on which to base their rule and their policies. Elections also have a more direct strategical importance: they decide which parties and leaders achieve political power within the political system.

Electoral outcomes are shaped by many factors. Electoral law defines who has the right to participate in the electoral process — parties, candidates and voters. It may also limit the absolute sum and means of spending the financial resources used by candidates. The type of electoral system is also significant. The method by which voter preferences are translated into representation in political institutions affects the outcome and has a long-term impact on the nature of the party system.

Since the electoral process involves an aggregation of the choices made by each voter — first, whether or not to vote; then, which party and/or candidate to vote for — patterns of individual electoral behaviour clearly determine electoral outcomes. The activities of the mass media and the conduct of election campaigns also influence voter choices.

Elections in Canada, as elsewhere, are thus affected by a number of forces. In this chapter, we examine the mechanics of the Canadian electoral process, including the franchise (the means by which candidates are selected) and the legal constraints on election spending; the factors that shape individual electoral behaviour; the role of the media; a brief review of the 1988 election campaign; and a case study of the unique 1993 election that returned the Liberal Party to power after nine years in opposition, and made the separatist Bloc Québécois Her Majesty's Official Opposition. First, however, we shall consider the topic of elections in comparative terms, examining their role in the overall political process and the various ways by which other countries elect their political representatives.

REPRESENTATION AND ELECTIONS

In large states such as Canada, it is not possible for everyone to be directly involved in the day-to-day policy-making process. In earlier times, when societies consisted mainly of small, more-or-less autonomous communities, direct democracy was possible: all citizens in a community could participate personally in collective deliberation and decision-making about how they would be governed. To some, this represented the ideal form of democracy. Eighteenth century philosopher Jean-Jacques Rousseau believed that true political freedom could exist only in societies small enough for all citizens to meet together to govern themselves.[1]

Today, town meetings in some small New England communities and the *Landesgemeinde* in certain Swiss communes are legacies of a time when collective self-government was a simpler process. These are exceptions. As societies grew larger and more complex, direct democracy was replaced by **representative democracy**, wherein certain individuals are selected to represent the interests of their fellow citizens in the policy-making process. In most societies, the means by which such representatives are chosen is the electoral process. For the most part, democratic government now means government by representatives of the people, chosen by their peers in elections. However, there are occasions on which citizens can participate more directly in policy-making.

REFERENDUMS

The major exception to the general rule of indirect representation in modern democracies is the "referendum." A **referendum**, sometimes known as a **plebiscite** (there is no clear universally accepted distinction between the two, although in Canada a plebiscite is taken to mean a non-binding referendum), is a means by which a policy question can be submitted directly to the electorate for decision rather than being decided exclusively by elected representatives. A referendum may consist of a single direct question or statement requiring a simple *yes* or *no* vote of the public, or a selection of one alternative from several policy options.

Referendums may be used in various ways. Some are merely *consultative*, providing a kind of official public opinion poll on an issue in order to guide politicians. Others are *binding* in

---

[1]   A.H. Birch, *Representation* (London: Pall Mall, 1971), p. 35.

that they force the government to follow the majority decision in the referendum. Still others are essentially *instruments of ratification*, the final seal of approval on a course of action adopted by a law-making institution; this is the case, for example, where proposed constitutional amendments must be ratified by the electorate.

Not all referendums are designed to permit the electorate a voice in how their country is governed. Especially in non-democratic systems, referendums may be used primarily as symbolic devices, giving the illusion of popular participation without any meaningful choice. Such referendums may be useful in lending an air of legitimacy to decisions on which the ruling elite is already agreed. Not surprisingly, their results often provide almost unanimous support for the government's policies — for example, all nine referendums held in Egypt between 1956 and 1976 yielded a *yes* vote of at least 99.8 percent.[2]

Where referendums do allow a meaningful choice, however, they can be said to enhance the democratic process. Proponents of referendums argue that they represent a form of direct democracy — an example of popular participation in government policy-making. Voters are given an opportunity to have a much more immediate influence on public decisions than is possible through the election of representatives. Advocates also point out that widespread consultation increases the legitimacy of political decisions. This legitimizing function of referendums is particularly important when it comes to fundamental changes in the political system such as, for example, the ratification of significant constitutional amendments.

Notwithstanding these apparent advantages, referendums are not widely used in most liberal democracies, though there are exceptions such as Switzerland and Australia. Critics argue that it detracts from the sovereignty of Parliament; bypassing Parliament by appealing directly to the voters downgrades the importance of the sovereign law-making body. Others argue that it is unreasonable to ask relatively uninformed citizens to make decisions, especially on technical or legal matters, since they have neither the time nor the expertise to evaluate complex issues. Furthermore, it is not feasible to consult citizens on every issue that might be regarded as fundamental.

Another basic criticism of referendums concerns their inflexibility — they usually require a straight *yes/no* decision that may oversimplify complex political problems and make subsequent compromise difficult. As well, there is always the danger that unscrupulous politicians could use the referendum, as Hitler did, to appeal to populist sentiments and gain support for extremist and non-democratic measures. Finally, it is argued that referendums, especially if used frequently, pose a threat to minorities. In a country as diverse as Canada, the final and uncompromising nature of a referendum is potentially divisive. Majority rule, while a central component of democracy, must be tempered by the protection of minorities, lest it turn into a the "tyranny of the majority."

Therefore, most countries tend to use referendums with extreme caution and only in specific circumstances. The most frequent use, perhaps, is associated with the process of constitutional amendment to ratify changes. Referendums are also widely employed to decide questions of national importance such as sovereignty, secession or autonomy. Another common use of referendums is in allowing citizens to decide what might be called "moral" issues over which political parties are internally divided. Thus, a number of countries have held national or local referendums on such matters as prohibition, licensing laws and drinking hours, divorce, abortion and nuclear energy. On such sensitive issues politicians often

---

[2] David Butler and Austin Ranney, eds., *Referendums: A Comparative Study of Practice and Theory* (Washington, D.C.: American Enterprise Institute for Public Policy Research, 1978), p. 9 (fn. 9) and Appendix A, p. 232.

appear happy to allow parliamentary sovereignty to be bypassed and let the citizens decide for themselves!

REFERENDUMS IN CANADA

Federal politicians in Canada have tended to share the mistrust of referendums and concern for parliamentary sovereignty displayed by their counterparts elsewhere. There have been only three referendums at the national level in Canada, and all were consultative.[3]

The first was held in 1898, when the federal government was contemplating prohibition of alcohol. Although a small majority voted in favour of prohibition (51 percent), there was a very low turn-out (44 percent) and Prime Minister Wilfrid Laurier did not believe that support was strong enough to go ahead. It should be noted that the proposal was massively rejected in Laurier's home province of Québec, a fact that undoubtedly influenced his decision not to proceed.

The second national referendum was during the Conscription Crisis of 1942. Prime Minister Mackenzie King only proceeded with conscription after a referendum that asked whether the federal government could overturn its previous pledge not to institute a draft. The referendum received the support of 65 percent of the voters. Québec, however, voted heavily against conscription (71 percent), thus exacerbating relations between English and French Canadians. Mackenzie King was able to delay the implementation of conscription so long that the conscripts were never used in battle.

The third national referendum was on the Charlottetown constitutional accord in 1992. The result was a 54.4 percent popular vote against the accord and 44.6 percent for it. Because of the significance of this event for contemporary politics the 1992 referendum is discussed in detail below.

Referendums have also been used by other levels of government in Canada. At the provincial level, Newfoundland held a referendum on the question of joining Confederation — in fact, it held two.[4] In the first, in June 1948, Newfoundlanders were given three choices as to their future status. Responsible self-government was supported by 45 percent of the voters; joining Canada by 41 percent; and remaining under the control of a board of commissioners appointed by the British government by 14 percent. Six weeks later, the choice having been narrowed to self-government or Confederation, 52 percent voted in favour of joining Canada.

The only other province to hold a referendum relating to the question of sovereignty was Québec. In May 1980 the Parti Québécois government held a referendum asking the voters of the province for "a mandate to negotiate sovereignty-association" with the rest of Canada. Sixty percent of the voters voted *non*, and the status quo was maintained. The threat of a future referendum on this question continues to plague Canadian and Québec politics.

Referendums have been used for other questions. Practically every province has had at least one vote on alcohol regulations, and many municipalities have asked their residents

---

[3] Patrick Boyer, *The People's Mandate: Referendums and a More Democratic Canada* (Toronto: Dundern, 1992); and Richard Theoret, "The Uses of the Referendum in Canada," in D.C. Rowat, ed., *The Referendum and Separation Elsewhere: Implications for Québec* (Ottawa: Carleton University, 1978), pp. 23–26.

[4] See Henry B. Mayo, "Newfoundland's Entry into the Dominion," *CJPS*, vol. 15, no. 4 (November 1949), pp. 505–22.

to choose between "wet" and "dry" — in other words to decide whether or not they wanted liquor outlets in their area. In addition, some municipalities have held votes on other issues, sometimes even on matters outside their jurisdictions, such as votes to be "nuclear-free" zones. Finally, during the discussions on constitutional patriation in 1982, Prime Minister Trudeau suggested that a referendum might be used as a means of ratifying amendments on which the federal and provincial governments were unable to agree, although no such provision was included in the amending formula in the new *Constitution*.

THE 1992 REFERENDUM

In Chapter 5, we outlined the constitutional issues surrounding the Charlottetown accord. In their effort to achieve a political consensus Prime Minister Brian Mulroney and the 10 premiers met in Charlottetown. They gave final agreement to the accord and unanimously decided to hold a national referendum to legitimate the proposal. In the House of Commons the three party leaders, Brian Mulroney, Audrey McLaughlin and Jean Chrétien all agreed to defend the accord. They were joined by provincial, territorial and aboriginal leaders as well as business, labour and other elites and organizations such as *The Globe and Mail.*

For a time it appeared that the accord would obtain an absolute majority in every province. However, eventually three major opposition groups developed. In Québec, the Bloc Québécois and the provincial Parti Québécois argued that Charlottetown was weaker than Meech Lake and did not give enough powers to Québec. In the West, the Reform Party, led by Preston Manning, campaigned against the accord on the basis that it gave too much to Québec and did not assure sufficient protection for the interests of the less populous provinces. Across the country "no" committees sprang up at the grassroots level. The most important of these, "Canada for all Canadians," argued that the document was incomplete, incoherent and took away rights already accorded to Canadians under the *Charter of Rights and Freedoms*. Their message was buttressed by former Prime Minister Pierre Trudeau in a well-publicized speech that galvanized Canadians who had been unaware of the significance of the proposed constitutional change. In the final analysis, aboriginal people, too, were divided on the provisions for self-government.

The "yes" forces, massively funded by corporations and governments, launched a highly professional campaign based on the election machinery of all three parties and their experts. They campaigned essentially on the basis that a "yes" vote was a vote for Canada and national unity, obscuring the fact that there was no legal text to the agreement, and that it would entail massive reorganization of Canadian government. Their appeal was directed essentially to the emotions of Canadians.

Rag-tag groupings of "no" forces battered the details of the deal, maintaining that approximately one-third of the Canadian *Constitution* was being amended in one vote. There was little organization to their attacks, but their lack of cohesion allowed different groupings to focus on specific sectors of the country and particular issues in the agreement.

The proponents of Charlottetown had a difficult task to perform. In order for the referendum to be passed, it had to receive a majority vote in each and every province as well as in the country as a whole. This requirement was due to the fact that the amendments proposed in Charlottetown required the unanimous approval of the legislatures of every province. Morally, no provincial legislative assembly could approve the Charlottetown resolution if their electorate voted "no." This led the "no" forces to attempt to stop the referendum in at least one province.

In the final analysis, the emotional rhetoric and massive advertising of the "yes" forces worked to their disadvantage. Opinion polls showed that many voters used the vote to vent their anger and frustration against the Prime Minister, premiers, politicians and governments in general. Only in the Maritimes was there a solid "yes" vote for the accord. Québec and all of the western provinces voted strongly "no." As Table 11.1 shows, in Ontario the "yes" forces won — but only by a whisker.

TABLE 11.1   1992 REFERENDUM RESULTS BY PROVINCE

Province	% Yes	% No
Newfoundland	62.9	36.5
P.E.I	73.6	25.9
Nova Scotia	48.5	51.1
New Brunswick	61.3	38.0
Québec	42.4	55.4
Ontario	49.8	49.6
Manitoba	37.8	61.6
Saskatchewan	44.5	55.2
Alberta	39.7	60.1
British Columbia	31.7	68.0
N.W.T.	60.6	38.7
Yukon	43.4	56.1

The result was a national humiliation for Prime Minister Mulroney, the 10 premiers and politicians generally. When the numbers were announced, Canada's leading politicians reversed their dire predictions and said that Canada was not in danger. In fact, they shelved the constitutional issue in favour of pressing economic issues.

However, the defeat of Charlottetown did not end the need to accommodate a wide range of interests from Québec nationalism to aboriginal self-government. What it did do was end the career of Prime Minister Brian Mulroney and set the stage for the massive defeat of the Progressive Conservative Party in the 1993 General Election.

FUNCTIONS OF ELECTIONS

At the most basic level, the primary function of elections is to provide a mechanism for selecting the individuals who will occupy seats in representative institutions. Hence, in Canada, the federal electoral process is the means by which voters in various constituencies throughout the country choose which men and women will represent their interests in the House of Commons.

But in liberal democratic societies such as Canada elections fulfill an even more important function: they provide for the orderly succession of government, by the peaceful transfer of authority to new rulers. Elections held at regular intervals provide citizens with opportunities to review the record of the government, to assess its mandate, and to replace it with an alternative administration. In certain countries, such as the United States, the political executive (the President) is elected, reconfirmed or replaced by the people directly through the electoral process. In Canada and other parliamentary democracies, however, the election of constituency representatives to the House of Commons assumes additional significance in that the government arises out of the majority within the legislature and is subsequently responsible to the legislature for the exercise of executive power until the next election.

Once a government has been elected, directly or indirectly, it may claim a mandate from the voters to rule on their behalf. Thus, the electoral process helps to legitimate the government of the day and also the policies that it has been elected to carry out. Furthermore, elections also legitimate the entire system of government. To the extent that Canadians, for example, turn out in relatively large numbers at the polls (on average, around 74 percent of the electorate have voted in federal general elections in this century), they are expressing confidence in the system by their very participation.

It is this function of legitimation of the political system that makes elections so common around the world, not just in liberal democracies, but also in communist regimes and other forms of government where no real element of choice is put before the voters. Elections in all countries provide an opportunity for citizens to participate in the political process and to express their support for the system. But they serve an additional role in many countries, since in non-competitive state-controlled systems, *international* acceptance counts for at least as much as national legitimation. "Elections are signs of good conduct to the outside world."[5]

Election campaigns also serve as agents of political socialization and political integration. For a few weeks at least, the whole society is joined together in one common enterprise — the election of a new government or the reaffirmation of an existing one. Extensive media coverage is given to election campaigns in most countries, airing national political issues that transcend local or regional concerns and providing widespread dissemination of information about current politics.

In **competitive elections** — those involving more than one party with a chance of forming a government — political parties are forced to aggregate interests in their search for a political majority. Through campaign literature, speeches and personal contacts, candidates attempt to "educate" voters and to persuade them to vote the "right" way. But even where there may be only a single slate of candidates for the voters to ratify, as in elections in the former Soviet Union, the campaigns provide "an immediate and solemn occasion for the transmission of orders, explanations and cues from the government to the population."[6]

Finally, in competitive systems at least, elections provide a forum for airing views not heard in everyday political debate. Widespread media coverage, all-candidates meetings and the distribution of political literature all allow minor parties, interest groups, independent politicians and the occasional "odd-ball" an opportunity to air their ideas and opinions. Thus, while in the normal course of events political debate at the federal level in Canada is dominated by a very few parties, an election campaign exposes Canadians to the views of many others. To the extent that some people vote for minor parties and independent candidates, elections may be viewed as a kind of safety valve that allows voters to express dissatisfaction with the major parties and support ideas not generally represented in the federal political arena.[7]

---

[5]   Guy Hermet, "State Controlled Elections: A Framework," in G. Hermet, et al., eds., *Elections Without Choice* (London: Macmillan, 1978), p. 15.

[6]   Ibid., pp. 13–14.

[7]   Andrew J. Milnor, *Elections and Political Stability* (Boston: Little, Brown, 1969).

TYPES OF ELECTORAL SYSTEMS

There is a tendency to believe that one's own electoral system is the best way of choosing a government. But history reminds us that there are many perceptions of what is best; different electoral systems may be viewed as institutional expressions of these competing values.

According to one observer of electoral practices around the world, there are four primary objectives of elections, which may be regarded as the principles upon which different electoral systems are based:

1. A legislature reflecting the main trends of opinion within the electorate.
2. A government according to the wishes of the majority of the electorate.
3. The election of representatives whose personal qualities best fit them for the function of government.
4. Strong and stable government.[8]

Some electoral systems place a high premium on the concept of "representation," inasmuch as they are designed to ensure that all significant shades of public opinion are represented in Parliament. Others appear to be concerned more with providing majority governments that are commonly assumed to be stronger and more stable than minority or coalition governments.

To illustrate these points, we outline next the major types of electoral systems and their effects on party competition and government outcomes. In essence, two factors are determined by electoral systems: how many candidates are elected in each geographical district (usually known as "constituencies" or "ridings"); and how votes are translated into parliamentary seats. Using these criteria, we can identify four basic varieties of electoral systems: single-member plurality, single-member majoritarian, multi-member proportional representation and mixed systems.

SINGLE-MEMBER PLURALITY

The single-member **plurality** system is used primarily in the "Anglo-American" democracies of the United Kingdom, the United States, New Zealand and Canada. Under this system, one member or representative is elected from each constituency. Each elector has one vote, which is cast by indicating (usually with an "X") one's favourite candidate. The translation of votes into seats is based on the achievement of a plurality — that is, the candidate with the most votes wins. It is important to note that the victorious candidate is not required to gain an absolute majority of votes, but merely to receive more votes than anyone else. For this reason the system is sometimes known by other labels, such as the "simple majority" or "relative majority" (as opposed to "absolute majority") system.

In Canada, all members of the House of Commons are now elected by plurality voting in single-member constituencies. But it is also theoretically possible to conduct elections under the plurality formula in districts returning more than one member. In such systems, the rules are essentially the same, except that the voter has as many votes as there are seats to be filled in the geographical territory. Thus, in a two-member constituency, each voter marks two

---

8   Enid Lakeman, *How Democracies Vote: A Study of Electoral Systems*, 4th rev. ed. (London: Faber and Faber, 1974), p. 28.

names, and the two candidates with the most votes are the winners. As recently as the 1965 General Election there were federal constituencies in Canada returning two members to the House of Commons.[9] Even today, the 32 members of the provincial legislature of Prince Edward Island are elected in 16 two-member ridings, and many municipal councils and school boards are still elected "at large" or in multi-member districts using the plurality formula. However, most contemporary national elections that use the plurality formula, including those in Canada, employ single-member constituencies.

SINGLE-MEMBER MAJORITARIAN

In plurality systems, the candidate receiving the most votes is the winner whether or not he or she has an absolute majority of all votes cast. Other electoral systems based on single-member constituencies are designed to increase the likelihood of the winning candidate's receiving an absolute majority of votes cast in the constituency. These "majoritarian" formulas are essentially of two types: the alternative vote (AV) and the second ballot.

Under the **alternative vote** system, used, for example, in elections to the federal House of Representatives in Australia, for example, voters rank candidates in order of preference. They place "1" beside their favourite candidate, "2" beside their second choice and so on. When the votes are counted, each ballot is assigned to the candidate it ranks first. If a candidate has an absolute majority of votes, that candidate is declared elected. Otherwise, the candidate with the least votes is excluded and his or her supporters' ballots are transferred to the remaining candidates according to their second preferences. This process of excluding candidates and transferring votes continues until one candidate has an absolute majority over all other remaining contenders.

Another variation on the single-member constituency format is the **second ballot** system, used on occasion in France. There, electors initially opt for a single candidate, but if no one obtains an absolute majority on this first vote, a run-off election is held, usually a week or two later. On this second ballot, candidates who failed to get a specified proportion of the votes the first time around are excluded; usually, only the two leading candidates reappear and, therefore, the elected representative normally can claim the support of a majority of voters in the constituency.

The second-ballot system has never been used in Canada, but the alternative vote has, though not at the federal level. In the provincial elections of 1952 and 1953, the entire legislature of British Columbia was elected by the AV system, although plurality voting was subsequently reintroduced. In Alberta from 1926 to 1959, rural MLAs were returned from single-member ridings using AV, while those from Calgary and Edmonton were elected by the multi-member proportional representation (PR) system described below. Similarly, rural MLAs in Manitoba were elected by AV from 1927 to 1936, while members from Winnipeg were again elected under a PR formula.

MULTI-MEMBER PROPORTIONAL REPRESENTATION

Multi-member proportional representation (PR) systems provide an opportunity to elect two or more members from each constituency. They are designed to ensure that parties, or groups of voters, are represented more fairly than is often the case under single-member

---

[9] See T.H. Qualter, *The Election Process in Canada* (Toronto: McGraw-Hill, 1970), pp. 118–23, for a discussion of a single-member and multi-member constituencies in Canadian elections.

plurality or majoritarian formulas. In other words, PR formulas attempt to ensure that parties receive representation in parliament in proportion to their respective shares of the popular vote. PR systems are essentially of two types: party list systems and the single transferable vote (STV) formula.

Party list systems of PR are used extensively in western Europe. In its simplest form, the **party list** system allows electors in a multi-member constituency to vote for a party or a slate of candidates, rather than for one or more individuals. Seats are allocated to each party roughly in proportion to its share of the popular vote. Assume, for example, that a constituency sends 10 members to the parliament and that 100 000 people turn out to vote. Theoretically, if Party A receives 50 000 votes, Party B 30 000 and Party C 20 000, the resulting seat distribution will be 5, 3 and 2 respectively — i.e., each party will receive exactly the same percentage of seats as votes. In real life, the percentages of voters are rarely distributed so conveniently, and a number of different procedures exists to allocate seats. But the general effect is that parties receive representation approximately proportional to their popular support.

In party list systems, seats are usually awarded to individual candidates on the basis of their position on the party's slate. Before the election, each party publishes a list of candidates in order of rank and, under normal circumstances, if Party A receives five seats in our hypothetical constituency, the top five names on the party list will be declared elected. In some countries, however, the electoral rules permit voters to express preferences for one or more individuals within the party list and, therefore, to effect a change in the rank ordering of candidates. The basic principle of all party list systems is that seats are awarded in the first instance to political parties according to their relative shares of the popular vote; the actual representatives who will occupy those seats are essentially a secondary concern. This is in direct contrast to single-member constituency systems, where the election of individual members is the immediate objective, and the relative strengths of the parties in Parliament is the product of the individual constituency races.

The second variety of proportional representation places greater emphasis on individual candidates than does the party list system. The **single transferable vote** formula is used in the Republic of Ireland and also in Australia for electing the Senate. Again, representatives are elected from multi-member constituencies, but electors vote for individual candidates rather than for a party list.

In the STV, as in the alternative vote system, voters rank candidates in order of preference, and ballot papers are initially assigned to the first-choice candidate. To be elected, a candidate must obtain a specified number of votes or "quota." Candidates receiving first preference votes in excess of the quota are declared elected and their "surplus" votes (those in excess of the quota) are transferred to the remaining candidates according to subsequent preferences. If no candidate receives a quota on the first count, or if seats remain to be filled after all surpluses have been distributed, the least popular candidate is excluded and his or her votes are transferred. This process continues until all seats have been allocated. Although the STV system need not be used with proportional representation of political parties in mind, its effect in countries such as the Irish Republic is very similar to electoral outcomes under other PR formulas.

Unlike the party list form of PR, the STV system has been used in Canada, though again not at the federal level. Members of the Alberta legislature from Calgary and Edmonton were elected by this system from 1926 to 1959, as were Winnipeg's representatives in the Manitoba provincial assembly from 1920 to 1953. STV was also used for municipal elections in Winnipeg until 1972.

MIXED SYSTEMS

Mixed systems or **additional member** systems (AMS) represent a combination of plurality and PR formulas. A certain percentage of the seats is filled by plurality voting in single-member constituencies, while the remainder are awarded to parties according to their popular support in order to achieve an approximately proportional representation in the legislature.

Such a system is used in Germany for electing both the federal *Bundestag* (analogous to Canada's House of Commons) and the *Land* (provincial) legislatures. Under the German system, each elector has two votes, one for a constituency candidate and one for a party list. The "first" votes, those for candidates in single-member constituencies, determine half the seats in the *Bundestag*. The "second" votes, cast for a party list, determine the share of total seats each party will obtain. Parties are awarded additional seats if the number of representatives directly elected in the constituencies is less than their overall proportional entitlement based on their shares of the "second" votes.

While the German system represents an equal mix of the plurality and PR party list systems, the AMS places greater emphasis on the plurality formula. Here, the majority of seats in the legislature are still elected in single-member constituencies, but a small reserve of seats is allocated to parties according to their share of the popular vote in order to alleviate some of the disproportional effects of the plurality system. Variations on the AMS have been proposed by several contributors to the debate on electoral reform in Canada.

THE EFFECTS OF ELECTORAL SYSTEMS

There is a large body of literature on the effects that different electoral systems have on the politics of their respective countries.[10] Many of these works are highly polemical since they are contributions to debates on electoral reform, either defending the existing system or propounding the adoption of an alternative method. In the following discussion, therefore, we outline what might be called the "conventional wisdom" on the effects of different electoral systems, keeping in view three main criteria: their impact on representation at the constituency level; the representation of political parties and effects on the party system; and the type of governmental outcome that each system typically produces. These effects are summarized in Table 11.2.

One of the advantages claimed for single-member formulas (plurality or majoritarian) is that they maintain the traditional link between the individual MP and the constituents. There is no ambiguity about who is designated to represent the voters and, since the representatives owe their election to the voters rather than to their positions on a party list, it is in their personal interest to represent their constituents if they wish to be re-elected. Furthermore, the representatives' task is made easier because, even in relatively large and populous countries, division into a large number of single-member districts limits the size

---

[10] Among many others, see Maurice Duverger, *Political Parties*, translated by B. and R. North (London: Methuen, 1954), Book II, ch. 1; Douglas Rae, *The Political Consequences of Electoral Laws* (New Haven: Yale University Press, 1967). On Canada, see also Alan C. Cairns, "The Electoral System and the Party System in Canada, 1921–1965," *CJPS*, vol. I, no. 1 (March 1968), pp. 55–80; William P. Irvine, *Does Canada Need a New Electoral System?* (Kingston, Ont.: Queen's University, Institute of Intergovernmental Relations, 1979), especially ch. 3; J.A.A. Lovink, "On Analyzing the Impact of the Electoral System on the Party System in Canada," *CJPS*, vol. 3, no. 4 (December 1970), pp. 497–516.

of both the area and the electorate of each constituency. These generalizations apply equally to representatives elected in single-member constituencies under a mixed or AMS formula.

TABLE 11.2   TYPES OF ELECTORAL SYSTEMS AND THEIR EFFECTS

Electoral System (Examples)	Constituency Representation	Representation of Parties	Governmental Outcome
Single-Member Plurality (U.K., U.S., New Zealand, Canada)	– Maintains traditional link between MP and constituents. – MPs often elected on a minority of total votes. – Discourages multiplication of parties — tendency towards two-party system.	– Distortion of votes/ seats ratio. – Minor parties disadvantaged unless support is regionally of government between two dominant parties.	– Tends to "over represent" largest party. – Usually single-party majority government. – Some alternation
Single-Member Majoritarian (a) Alternative Vote (AV) (Australia, House of Reps.) (b) Second Ballot (France)	– Both maintain traditional link between MP and constituents. – Representatives usually elected by a majority. – Tendency towards multi-party system.	– Distortion of votes/ seats ratio. – "Wasted vote" thesis does not apply — therefore, small parties survive even if unsuccessful.	– Tends to "over-represent"largest party (parties). – Usually single-party majority government or stable coalition.
Proportional Representation (PR) (a) Party List (Italy, Netherlands, Switzerland) (b) Single Transferable vote (STV) (Rep. of Ireland, Australia, Senate)	(a) Individual representatives usually owe election more to party than to voters (b) Representatives forced to compete for "first preference" votes.	– Approximate congruence between vote shares and seat allocations. – Minor parties usually gain "fair" represen-tation — easy entry for new parties. – Tendency towards multi-party systems.	– Coalition governments — may be stable (Sweden) or unstable (Italy). – Alternation of government rare.
Mixed Plurality/PR (Germany)	– Maintains traditional link between MP and constituents. – Minor parties usually gain "fair" represen-tation, unless measures are adopted (as in Germany) to prevent representation of "splinter" groups.	– Approximate congruence between vote shares and seat allocations.	– Reasonably stable coalition government.

In party list systems of PR, on the other hand, MPs owe their election (especially their position on the party list) more to their party than to their constituents. Furthermore, constituencies may be too large for individual representatives to maintain contact with all constituents, making it difficult to establish representative responsibility. Thus, members may focus on maintaining their popularity within the party, and hence their standing on the party list, rather than on representing the interests of their constituents. This is less true with the STV system of PR, especially as it operates in Ireland. There, since each candidate attempts to gain as many first preference votes as possible, members do have to pay considerable attention to constituency interests.

What effect do electoral systems have on political representation and party competition within a society? Proportional representation systems are by definition designed to achieve a more-or-less proportional allocation of seats to parties according to their respective shares of the popular vote. However, the degree of congruence between the percentage of votes and the number of seats won by each party tends to vary from country to country. A key factor here is the number of members returned by each constituency. The Netherlands, which elects its legislative chamber, the *Tweede Kamer*, by treating the whole country as if it were a single constituency, achieves an almost perfect correspondence between votes and seats for each party. However, where constituencies are smaller, returning, say, three or four members each, it is more difficult to achieve congruence when allocating seats according to popular votes: there is the likelihood that some parties will be persistently over- or under-represented in each constituency, and thus overall in the legislature.

If we take the argument concerning constituency size to its logical conclusion, it follows that the proportional allocation of seats according to shares of the popular vote is least likely to occur in systems where electoral districts return only one member each — i.e., in single-member plurality and majoritarian systems. This can easily be illustrated with reference to the 1979, 1980 and 1984 General Elections in Canada (see Table 11.3), all of which were conducted under single-member plurality voting rules. In 1979, the Progressive Conservatives gained more seats than the Liberals and thus formed the government, although they received a smaller share of the popular vote, 36 percent to the Liberals' 40 percent. This outcome was rather exceptional, and the normal pattern reasserted itself in 1980, with the Liberals getting the most votes and the most seats. In 1984 the Conservatives returned with a massive majority of both votes and seats.

Table 11.3 demonstrates some of the negative characteristics typically associated with the plurality system: a tendency to favour the two largest parties, with an additional "bonus" of seats for the largest party; and, conversely, a tendency to under-represent third or minor parties, especially those whose support is spread fairly evenly but thinly across the country.

TABLE 11.3   CANADIAN GENERAL ELECTION RESULTS 1979, 1980, 1984: SHARES OF VOTES AND SEATS BY PARTY

	1979			1980			1984		
	% Votes	% Seats	No. of Seats	% Votes	% Seats	No. of Seats	% Votes	% Seats	No. of Seats
LIB	40	40	(114)	44	52	(147)	28	14	(40)
PC	36	48	(136)	33	37	(103)	50	75	(211)
NDP	18	9	(26)	20	11	(32)	19	11	(30)
SC	5	2	(6)	2	0	(0)	0	0	(0)
Other	2	0	(0)	1	0	(0)	3	0	(1)

Note: Percentages may not add up to 100% because of rounding.

In 1988, the Conservatives won 169 seats with 43 percent of the vote. In 1993 the Liberals won 177 seats with only 41 percent. And, the Conservatives were reduced to two seats even though they had won 16 percent of the vote — more than the BQ, which won only 14 percent of the vote but got 54 seats. (See Table 11.4.) Because its votes were concentrated in Québec, the Bloc also gained more seats than Reform, which got 52 seats for 19 percent of the vote. In this electoral system it does not matter how well you do in second place — the system loves only winners. Note that in 1993 it took about 31 320 votes to elect a Liberal, but more than one million to elect a Conservative!

TABLE 11.4   FIRST PAST THE POST: HOW VOTES TRANSLATED INTO SEATS, 1988 AND 1993

	PC 1988	PC 1993	Lib. '88	Lib. '93	NDP '88	NDP '93	Reform '88	Reform '93	BQ '88	BQ '93
No. of seats	169	2	83	177	43	9	0	52	–	54
% of total seats*	57	0.7	28	60	15	3.1	0	17.6	–	18.3
% of votes*	43	16	32	41	20	7	2	19	–	14

*Total seats and % of votes exclude 1 independent elected in 1992.

Source: Based on provisional data from the office of Elections Canada.

According to Maurice Duverger, there are two reasons why a single-member plurality system tends to reward the party that comes first with more seats than it deserves, and the second and following parties with fewer seats. First, an arithmetical consequence rewards the party that gets the largest share of the vote with more seats. The exception to this general rule occurs when a minor party has its support strongly concentrated in a particular region as happened in 1993 with the Bloc Québécois in Québec and to a slightly lesser extent with the Reform Party in the West, or in some earlier elections with the Social Credit and Créditiste parties in Alberta and Québec. Second, voters who might otherwise support a minor party tend to refrain from voting for it for fear of "wasting" their votes — casting votes that have no effect on the election of individual representatives or on the formation of a government. Thus, Duverger suggested that the association between the plurality electoral formula and the two-party system is close to being a "true sociological law."[11] (For seats won by region by each party see Table 11.5.)

As a consequence of the tendency to under-represent minor parties, the plurality system is often said to favour the development or maintenance of a two-party system of electoral competition.

Like the plurality system, the alternative vote and second ballot formulas both tend to result in severely disproportional allocations of seats, often in favour of the largest parties.[12] But they do not tend to "squeeze out" minor parties to the same extent as the plurality formula. Voters do not have to worry about wasting their votes, as the majoritarian formulas effectively give them a "second bite at the cherry." Electors can give their first

[11] Duverger, *Political Parties*, p. 217. For a test of Duverger's hypothesis regarding the plurality formula and bipartism, see Rae, *The Political Consequences of Electoral Laws*, pp. 93ff.

[12] In particular, both the alternative vote and the second ballot tend to "over-represent" parties that can reach agreements or alliances with other parties regarding the destination of second preferences or second ballots. Thus centrist or moderate parties are often "over-represented" compared with extremist parties of either the right or left, since the latter often cannot persuade supporters of other parties to transfer allegiance to them in the latter stages of voting.

preferences (under the AV) or their "first ballots" (under the second ballot system) secure in the knowledge that, if their favourite candidate is unsuccessful, subsequent preferences or the "second ballot" will be used to choose between the major protagonists in the constituency.

TABLE 11.5   SEATS WON IN GENERAL ELECTIONS BY REGION 1945-1993

	1945	1949	1953	1956	1958	1962	1963	1965	1968	1972	1974	1979	1980	1984	1988	1993
Atlantic																
LIB	19	25	27	12	8	14	20	15	7	10	13	12	19	7	20	31
PC	6	7	5	21	25	18	13	18	25	22	17	18	13	25	12	1
SC	–	–	–	–	–	–	–	–	–	–	–	–	–	–	–	–
CCF-NDP	–	1	1	–	–	1	–	–	–	–	1	2	–	–	–	–
Reform	–	–	–	–	–	–	–	–	–	–	–	–	–	–	–	–
BQ	–	–	–	–	–	–	–	–	–	–	–	–	–	–	–	–
Other	1	1	–	–	–	–	–	–	–	–	1	–	–	–	–	–
Total	27	34	33	33	33	33	33	33	32	32	32	32	32	32	32	32
Québec																
LIB	54	66	66	63	25	35	47	56	56	56	60	67	74	17	12	19
PC	1	2	4	9	50	14	8	8	4	2	3	2	1	58	63	1
SC	–	–	–	–	–	26	20	–	–	15	11	6	–	–	–	–
CRED	–	–	–	–	–	–	–	9	14	–	–	–	–	–	–	–
CCF-NDP	–	–	–	–	–	–	–	–	–	–	–	–	–	–	–	
Reform	–	–	–	–	–	–	–	–	–	–	–	–	–	–	–	–
BQ	–	–	–	–	–	–	–	–	–	–	–	–	–	–	–	54
Other	9	5	5	3	–	–	–	2	–	1	–	–	–	–	–	1
Total	64	73	75	75	75	75	75	75	74	74	74	75	75	75	75	75
Ontario																
LIB	34	56	50	20	14	43	52	51	64	36	55	32	52	14	43	98
PC	48	25	33	61	67	35	27	25	17	40	25	57	38	67	46	–
SC	–	–	–	–	–	–	–	–	–	–	–	–	–	–	–	–
CCF-NDP	–	1	1	3	3	6	6	9	6	11	8`	6	5	13	10	–
Reform	–	–	–	–	–	–	–	–	–	–	–	–	–	–	–	1
BQ	–	–	–	–	–	–	–	–	–	–	–	–	–	–	–	–
Other	–	1	1	1	1	1	–	–	1	1	–	–	–	1	–	–
Total	82	83	85	85	85	85	85	85	88	88	88	95	95	95	99	99
West*																
LIB	19	43	27	10	1	7	10	9	2	7	13	3	2	2	8	29
PC	11	7	9	21	66	49	47	46	26	43	50	59	51	61	48**	–
SC	13	10	15	19	–	4	4	5	–	–	–	–	–	–	–	–
CCF-NDP	27	10	21	22	5	12	11	12	16	20	7	18	27	17	33	9
Reform	–	–	–	–	–	–	–	–	–	–	–	–	–	–	–	51
BQ	–	–	–	–	–	–	–	–	–	–	–	–	–	–	–	–
Other	–	–	–	–	–	–	–	–	–	–	–	–	–	–	–	–
Total	71	71	72	72	72	72	72	72	70	70	70	80	80	80	89	89

*including the Northwest Territories and Yukon

**48 Conservatives were elected, but one died before being sworn in, leaving the official party standing as 47 from the West, with one vacant.

Source: Adapted from the *Canadian Parliamentary Guide.*

Under PR formulas where all parties, including minor ones, receive seats more-or-less in proportion to their shares of the popular vote, there is also a tendency toward multiple political parties. Some countries attempt to counteract this tendency by imposing a threshold — a certain proportion of votes that small parties must exceed before they are allotted any seats. Germany, for example, modifies the proportional element of its mixed system to make things more difficult for new or splinter parties by requiring that they must gain at least 5 percent of the popular vote or win seats in three single-member constituencies.

Lastly, the electoral system has an impact on the formation of governments. Because the plurality formula favours the development of a two-party system (or at least of two dominant parties) and because the largest single party in any election receives a "bonus" of seats, elections conducted by single-member plurality voting are more likely to result in the creation of relatively stable single-party governments. Frequently these governments enjoy majority support in Parliament, although minority governments may sometimes occur.

A further characteristic of the plurality system is that relatively small swings in votes between parties often result in large numbers of seats changing hands. Perhaps the most outstanding example in Canada occurred in the 1935 General Election, when the Liberals swept back into power. Although their share of the popular vote increased by less than one percent, their number of seats nearly doubled, from 91 to 173. Such amplification of small voting shifts across the country into large-scale changes in seat allocation causes the plurality system to tend to encourage alternation in government between the two dominant parties.

Most of the typical characteristics ascribed here to the plurality system are also true of the majoritarian AV and second ballot formulas. The major exception is that coalition governments are more frequent than under the plurality system. Australia was ruled by a coalition of the Liberal and Country Parties from 1975 to 1983, and French governments have often had to rely on support from more than one party in the National Assembly during the Fifth Republic.

Since PR systems do not give significant bonuses of seats to any party, and since they are usually associated with multi-party systems, it often happens that no single party is in a position to form a majority government. In such cases, coalition or minority governments often result. Sometimes such governments can be highly unstable, as in Italy, which has had more than one new government annually since the Second World War. Elsewhere, however, PR formulas may be associated with stable coalitions, as in Austria, Holland or Switzerland.

Because PR formulas do not exaggerate vote swings to the extent that single-member systems do, alternation of government between major parties or blocs of parties is less frequent in the former. Changes of administration usually result from changes in the alliance strategies of parties in and around the governing coalition, rather than from mass changes in voter allegiance at elections.

Electoral systems do not completely determine the nature of party systems, nor the type of government, majority or minority, single-party or coalition, in any country. Governmental outcomes are largely a function of the balance of party forces: the party system, in turn, is largely shaped by a country's political culture and social structure and by the electoral behaviour of its citizens. However, the electoral system — which translates votes into seats — is a powerful intermediary force, modifying the competition among parties, distorting or faithfully reproducing the electoral preferences of the voters. Since elections provide the chief mechanism of political participation for most people, the means of translating individual votes into political representation is naturally an important factor in a country's political system.

Having provided a general, comparative introduction to elections and electoral systems, we can now examine in detail the mechanics of the electoral process in Canada.

ELECTIONS IN CANADA

THE FRANCHISE AND THE RIDINGS

At Confederation the electoral rules were unjust. The federal **franchise** — the right to vote — was based on provincial laws and was restricted to male property owners. There was flagrant discrimination in favour of the upper classes and the ruling Conservative Party.

The property qualification was doubly discriminatory because of plural voting; that is, citizens were allowed to vote in each area in which property was owned. Instead of having a single election day, voting was staggered, so the government could control the timing of elections in each region. Elections were held first in those areas where the government was most popular, moving to areas of lesser support only later. The government benefited from this arrangement, since areas in which government support was not as prevalent were encouraged to fall into line, supporting the likely "winner" in order to gain favours from the future government.

In 1885, balloting was brought under federal jurisdiction. Former restrictions remained, however, and a new one, the disenfranchisement of Asians, was added. The two World Wars also affected the development of the franchise. In 1917, Canadians of Central European descent lost their vote. On the other hand, women, if they were relatives of soldiers, were given the right to vote for the first time, along with Native Indians serving in the Armed Forces, in the expectation that they would support the Union government's call for conscription. The following year all women were granted equal voting rights. Canadians of Asian descent were not granted normal voting privileges until 1948 and the Inuit, who were disenfranchised in 1934, did not have that right restored until 1950. Religious conscientious objectors, mainly Mennonites, who had been disenfranchised as early as 1920, did not receive voting rights until 1955. Reservation Indians received voter status as late as 1960.

In the light of the *Charter of Rights*, which states that every citizen of Canada has the right to vote, the Chief Electoral Officer recommended in 1983 that Parliament reconsider the status of the approximately 80 000 Canadians who continued to be denied that right. Resulting amendments to the *Canada Elections Act* in 1993 removed disqualifications for several groups including judges, persons who are "restrained of their liberty of movement or deprived of the management of their property by reason of mental disease" and inmates serving sentences of less than two years in a correctional institution.

New mechanisms were also established to allow Canadian citizens to vote if they are absent from Canada for less than five consecutive years and intend to return to reside in Canada, or if they are temporarily outside of the country or outside of their electoral district. Very few persons are still specifically prohibited from voting. They include the Chief Electoral Officer, the Assistant Electoral Officer, returning officers in each riding, inmates of penal institutions serving a sentence of more than two years and individuals disqualified by law for corrupt or illegal practices.

CONSTITUENCY BOUNDARIES

Under federal election law, independent, three-member commissions in each province re-draw constituency boundaries once every 10 years in order to ensure that each riding has roughly the same number of voters. The rules for carrying out this readjustment of electoral district boundaries are laid out in the *Electoral Boundaries Readjustment Act* (EBRA). Since the

1940s, there have been three fundamental changes to the representation formula and one major change in the boundary readjustment process.[13] In 1985, the *Representation Act* simplified the formula for calculating representation. (See Figure 11.1.)

FIGURE 11.1 FORMULA FOR CALCULATING REPRESENTATION IN THE HOUSE OF COMMONS

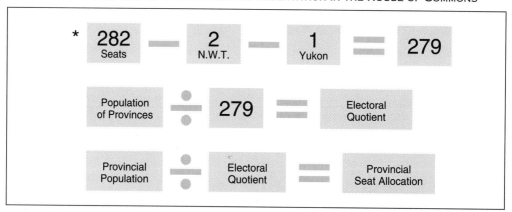

*The calculation starts with the 282 seats that the House of Commons had in 1985. There are now 295 seats.

The formula for calculating representation in the House of Commons also includes a "Senatorial clause" guarantee (from the *Constitution*) that no province has fewer members in the House of Commons than it has in the Senate; and a "Grandfather clause" guarantee (based on the 33rd Parliament) that no province shall have fewer seats than it had in 1976, during the 33rd Parliament.

Source: *Representation in the Federal Parliament* (Ottawa: Chief Electoral Officer of Canada, 1993), p. 5.

The average number of constituents in the new ridings is about 85 800, but because of demographic differences the numbers still vary widely. Ontario, with 8.9 million people and 99 seats is proportionally under-represented; Prince Edward Island, which is guaranteed four MPs under the Constitution, is over-represented with an average of 31 661 constituents per riding.

Readjustments following the 1991 census were delayed because of constitutional deliberations and were not in place for the 1993 General Election. If a new redistribution goes ahead according to plan for the next election, the 1991 census figures will increase the size of the House of Commons to 301 and increase the number of seats for Ontario and British Columbia.

ELECTORAL PROCEDURE

According to the Constitution, the Prime Minister must ask the Governor General to dissolve Parliament and call an election at least once every five years. The opposition parties may, as they did, for example, in 1974 and 1979, defeat the government and force the Prime Minister to call an election at an earlier date. Technically, however, they have no part to play in the choice of election date. The Prime Minister's decision is usually taken some time in the fourth year, at the most favourable opportunity for the governing party.[14] The election

---

[13] R. Kenneth Carty, "The Electoral Boundary Revolution in Canada," *The American Review of Canadian Studies*, vol. 15, no. 3 (1985), pp. 273–87; John C. Courtney, "Parliament and Representation: The Unfinished Agenda of Election Redistributions," *CJPS*, vol XXI, no. 4 (1988), pp. 657–90; Andrew Sancton, "Eroding Representation-by-Population in the Canadian House of Commons: The Representation Act, 1985," *CJPS*, vol. XXIII, no. 3 (1990), pp. 441–57.

[14] Four of the 11 elections since 1958 were held in the government's fifth year. The 1962 and 1972 elections resulted in the party in power being reduced to a minority, and the 1979, 1984 and 1993 elections brought government defeats.

is always held on a Monday, except if the Monday in question is a statutory holiday, in which case it is held on the next day, a Tuesday. The Cabinet (officially the governor-in-council) formally instructs the Chief Electoral Officer, an independent official responsible to the House of Commons, to set the election machinery in motion. The Chief Electoral Officer issues the writs of election to the Returning Officers in all constituencies or ridings, who in turn supervise the collation of voters' lists, appoint Deputy Returning Officers for each polling subdivision and receive nominations of candidates.

The government assumes responsibility for enrolling the voters. In the seventh week before an election, an army of canvassers, in couples representing the two leading parties in each constituency (except in rural areas, where one enumerator suffices), visits every residence to register the names of eligible voters.[15] There follows a period where voters missed or wrongly included in the blitz may apply to the courts of revision. Finally, 17 days before election day, the voting lists are closed. From the issuing of the writ to the closing of the polls the 1993 election campaign lasted 48 days. In 1993 no enumeration was conducted outside of Québec because it had been carried out for the Charlottetown referendum and the lists were re-used.

The enumeration process is slow and expensive. Jean-Marc Hamel, former Chief Election Officer, commented:

> *"It's like pushing a big locomotive... The idea is to get the thing started. We have to open the equivalent of 295 branch offices within 48 hours [of an election call]...We need office space, telephones, furniture, supplies. We have to recruit enumerators to knock on every door in the country."*[16]

The length of this pre-election period could be reduced, but at the expense of accuracy. Leaving the lists open until 17 days before the election ensures that extremely few eligible voters are left off the lists. Other types of systems present different problems. Britain, for example, has a "permanent voters' list" that allows shorter campaigns — about three weeks. Citizens are required by law to register once a year, and the voters' list is revised only at this time. Thus, it can be quite out-of-date when an election is called, eliminating voters who have moved, married or divorced.

Voting procedure is carefully controlled. Each Returning Officer designates the locations of the polling stations in his or her constituency, such as church halls or schools. On election day, the balloting is overseen at each polling station by Deputy Returning Officers and their polling clerks, and two scrutineers are allowed for each candidate. The voter identifies himself or herself to the polling clerk, who has a list of eligible voters for that polling station and gives the voter an official, bilingual ballot listing in alphabetical order the official candidates and their party affiliations. Candidates not representing a registered party are listed as independents, unless they request the Returning Officer to show no designation.

Voters mark their ballot in a private booth, and (in 1993 for the first time) may place their own ballots in the ballot box.[17] When the polling booth closes, the Deputy Returning Officer, with the polling clerk and scrutineers, counts the ballots, seals them in the box and delivers them to the Returning Officer. An unofficial result is made public shortly after

---

[15] As of 1993, enumeration by mail or fax is possible.

[16] Quoted in the *Toronto Star*, Mon. Oct. 10, 1988.

[17] Previously this was done by the Deputy Returning Officer who first verified that it was a valid ballot. Also, for the first time as of the 1993 General Election, the sale of alcohol was no longer prohibited on polling day.

balloting is closed. The official count by the Returning Officer is not made until later, in some cases not for several days when the vote from overseas is in. A recount is automatically requested by the returning officer if the difference between the first and second candidates is less than one one-thousandth of the ballots cast. In the very rare event of a tie vote, the Returning Officer casts the deciding ballot.

When a seat is vacated by any party for any reason during a Parliament, it is up to the Prime Minister to call a by-election to elect a new representative. If it is an opposition seat, the Prime Minister can hold it vacant for many months. Or, if a vacancy represents an opportunity to place a colleague in the House of Commons, a by-election can be called very quickly by the Prime Minister. Obviously, governments often use by-elections as barometers to measure popularity, and, as with general elections, they attempt to time them to their best advantage.

If the leader of a winning party is defeated in his or her own constituency, an apparently safe seat is quickly found. When Brian Mulroney became PC leader in 1983 he had not yet been elected to the House, and the Member from Central Nova in Nova Scotia resigned to let him contest and win that seat in a by-election.

ELECTORAL IRREGULARITIES

We have noted that Canadians did not benefit from a universal franchise until relatively recently. **Gerrymandering** — deliberate manipulation of boundaries by a governing party for their own benefit — and maldistribution were not brought under control until 1964 with the *Electoral Boundaries Commission Act*. While different patterns of boundaries clearly produce different electoral outcomes, mischievously redrawn boundaries are not necessarily illegal acts. In 1986, for example, when the electoral commission began drawing the new electoral boundaries, the Conservative Party was accused of coordinating efforts to influence the redistribution in the party's favour.[18] Tories were coached on how to make cases at public hearings for certain boundaries based on "community of interest or community of identity" such as school districts and transportation routes. They did not, of course, reveal that most of their proposals were also strategically advantageous for themselves. The Liberal and NDP parties had little influence in the boundary changes at that time, largely because they were preoccupied with internal party matters. When the boundaries were settled and Elections Canada transposed the 1984 votes into the new ridings, it showed the Tories would have won 17 extra seats using the new boundaries. This was not "gerrymandering" as such, but a legal use of influence. However, there are other ways in which elections in this country have been and, in some cases, remain, less than just.

In the past, fraudulent election irregularities have included multiple voting (ballot stuffing), impersonating, bribing, intimidating and either excluding real names from (false enumeration) or adding fictitious names to (padding) voters' lists. None of these actions is an accepted part of the national political culture today and, if discovered, would damage the popularity and credibility of the candidate involved. Two examples of false enumeration occurred in Toronto in 1957 and 1962, when blocks of names were left off the voters' lists. "Padding" also occurred in Toronto in the 1988 municipal election. Among eligible voters listed were "residents" of gas stations as well as deceased persons. In all of these instances court cases led to prosecutions. Most irregularities that occur now are at the municipal or provincial rather than the federal level. Gifts of money or liquor to voters, for example, have

---

[18] *Maclean's*, Oct. 10, 1988, p. 18.

been an accepted part of the Maritime political culture, though the practice is much less common than even a generation ago. In any case, the secret ballot renders such favours almost meaningless today.

One of the most unusual situations in Canadian electoral history occurred in the riding of York North, Ontario in the 1988 federal election. The Conservative candidate was declared the winner on election night. Three days later, a recount awarded the seat to the Liberals. A judicial recount gave the seat back to the Conservatives before yet another recount returned it to the Liberals, who kept the seat. The exchange was accompanied by charges of double voting, illegal voting and the exclusion of thousands of eligible votes.[19]

THE CANDIDATES

Virtually any elector can become a candidate.[20] All that is necessary is to file nomination papers with the signatures of 100 other electors and deposit $1000 with a Returning Officer.[21] The deposit is intended to discourage nuisance candidates, but still allow participation by interested citizens. Local party organizations usually pay the deposit fee for their candidates. It is refundable as follows: 50 percent if the candidate submits the required election expenses return and unused official receipts within the prescribed time limit, and 50 percent if the candidate obtains 15 percent of the ballots cast in the electoral district. Candidates may withdraw until 3 hours after the close of nominations (the 28th day before polling day). A prospective candidate need not have the backing of a political party or even reside in the constituency he or she would like to represent. However, it is extremely difficult for a candidate without party endorsement to be elected in Canada.[22]

As we saw in the preceding chapter, near the time of Parliamentary dissolution party organizations spring to life and rush to legitimate their candidates through the nomination process. The procedure varies from one constituency to the next. Local party organizations generally take the initiative in candidate recruitment, and, although automatic renomination of candidates sometimes occurs, locally controlled delegate conventions are usually held. Local organizations use this opportunity to recruit new members and raise money. The openness of the procedure has some problems. In 1984 and 1988, for example, many Tories complained that certain ridings had been "captured" by anti-abortionists, and in 1988 some Liberal constituencies were "seized by the mobilization of one ethnic group" who are asked to make almost no commitment to the party.[23]

In only exceptional cases does the national party headquarters or the party leader interfere with local nominations, although since 1970, by virtue of the *Canada Elections Act*, all party leaders have had a veto over the choice of party candidates. A statement signed by the party leader or a designated representative confirming the party's endorsement must be filed with a candidate's nomination papers. Although local party associations for the most part

---

[19] *The Globe and Mail*, Jan. 12, 1989.

[20] Persons convicted of certain crimes, mental patients and those holding certain public offices or appointments are excluded.

[21] The number of signatures and the deposit were revised upwards to these amounts in the 1993 Amendments to the *Canada Elections Act*.

[22] Robert J. Williams, "Candidate Selection," in Howard R. Penniman, ed., *Canada at the Polls, 1979 and 1980* (Washington D.C.: AEI, 1981), pp. 86–120. In 1993, one candidate (a former Conservative in Québec) was elected as an Independent.

[23] *The Globe and Mail*, editorial, November 23, 1992.

continue to have the main responsibility for candidate recruitment, this requirement for endorsement allows the party leader to reject candidates nominated by the local riding association, furthering the protection of "national" party interests. Brian Mulroney took advantage of this rule in the nomination of Conservative candidates in 1984 and 1988, as did Kim Campbell in 1993 during her short period as Prime Minister. The National Council of the Reform Party recommended that leader Preston Manning not sign some nomination papers, and also stripped several Ontarians of membership because of their extreme views, thereby preventing them from seeking nominations as Reform candidates in 1993.[24]

In February 1992, a Liberal convention gave party leader Jean Chrétien a unique power: the leader can now appoint candidates directly without having to go through the local riding associations. Chrétien used the power in a handful of ridings to "parachute" in "star" candidates in 1993. In York Centre, for example, Mr. Chrétien cancelled the nomination meeting and announced that Art Eggleton would be the riding's Liberal candidate.

THE CAMPAIGNS

With the announcement of an election, the national headquarters of the largest parties become nerve centres of nation-wide campaigns. Their functions include coordinating the meetings and tours of party leaders, issuing literature, arranging broadcasts, employing public relations firms, issuing news releases and collecting public opinion data. All major parties have two foci during an election campaign: the national campaign, the aim of which is electing the party; and 295 separate constituency campaigns, which aim to elect individual candidates.

In all parties, the leader's role in the campaign is paramount. The personal charisma and flamboyant campaign style exhibited by Diefenbaker in 1958, Trudeau in 1968 and Mulroney in 1984 are credited with the large majorities won by their parties. When leaders are popular, they and their families are paraded before party gatherings from coast to coast and photographed shaking hands with as many people as possible in an effort to have some of their charisma rub off onto the local candidates.

The candidates, meanwhile, are busy making themselves as visible as possible in their constituencies. Speeches, door-to-door canvassing, coffee parties and media appearances fill each day. A campaign manager makes efficient use of the candidate's time and organizes financing and other details. Party advisors include a large percentage of media people: communications strategists, advertising personnel, public relations experts and public opinion pollsters. It is their job to plan strategy, obtain maximum media coverage for their candidate, communicate the party's promises and build images. The basic duties of phoning constituents, distributing literature and organizing babysitting and rides to and from the polling booths on election day all fall to volunteers.

A candidate plans campaign strategy with two goals in mind: retaining traditional party supporters and attracting as many undecided and opponent votes as possible. To achieve these aims, analysis and targeting of the various voting groups in the constituency is essential. Their importance to the candidate depends on their size, turnout on election day and party commitment. What percentage of time should a particular candidate spend wooing the farm or trade-union vote? What issues should be emphasized or avoided? Voting behaviour studies obviously have important practical applications here.

---

[24] *The Globe and Mail*, August 4, 1993.

At the party level, the same knowledge is essential to plan a competent overall campaign strategy. Here, too, the growing complexity of campaigns necessitates professional help. In what geographical areas does a party have a great chance of winning? Where is there little chance? What issues should be stressed? How should financial and other resources be allocated? Party campaign strategists must answer many such questions.

PUBLIC OPINION SURVEYS

The first psephologist, R.B. McCallum, remarked after completing his study of the 1945 General Election in Britain that election studies should cease, or they would take all the mystery out of voting.[25] His advice, of course, went unheeded, and survey research now plays a large role in both pre- and post-election analyses in most western countries.

A great fund of election data is available in Canada. Major opinion surveys have been conducted by academics in most elections since 1965.[26] Recent elections have also witnessed a proliferation of pre-election polls, which are commonly used to predict election outcomes and probe specific issues. Perhaps the most widely known survey organizations are Canadian Gallup, Reid, Environics and Compass, which publish their results in various newspapers. The media compete by offering their own polls. Both major television networks, the CBC and CTV, conduct national surveys. Local television and broadcasting stations often do their own polls at the town or city level. Besides these sources, there exist many other private surveys, done for various groups by either Canadian or American firms. Large numbers of polls are also commissioned for the private use of political parties. Decima Research, for example, advised the Conservatives from 1979 to 1993, conducting increasingly elaborate polls.

Canada's immense size and uneven population distribution causes pollsters two major problems. First, it is expensive to sample an adequate number of Canadians to represent the whole population. Second, regions often differ dramatically in their opinions, and often are at variance with the national pattern. Whereas in a geographically smaller country like Britain it is usually possible to measure the swing of votes for or against the government as a uniform movement across the country, it is sometimes impossible in Canada. This situation is caused by strong regional differences, but it is compounded by the fact that some parties that are important in certain regions are often non-existent in others. These and other factors make Canadian election forecasters extremely reluctant to predict the distribution of seats in Parliament from the national opinion trend.

In 1993, for the first time, polling was banned from midnight the Friday before polling day until the close of all polling stations. In general elections before 1993, polling was often controversial; pollsters were accused of leading public opinion rather than reporting it. Although there is no conclusive evidence that polls influence voting behaviour, critics argue that they can cause a "bandwagon" effect whereby undecided or weakly committed voters decide to vote for a winner — or conversely they see that a particular candidate is going to win and decide not to vote at all. Negative polls can also be extremely dispiriting to party workers, causing them to give up.

---

[25] R.B. McCallum and A. Readman, *The British General Election of 1974* (Oxford: Macmillan, 1974).

[26] The most extensive study to date was of the 1988 General Election: Richard Johnston, André Blais, Henry E. Brady and Jean Crête, *Letting the People Decide: Dynamics of a Canadian Election* (Montréal: McGill-Queen's University Press, 1992).

The essential problem is that polls are often presented as factual data that require no explanation. In fact, they are a mere collection of attitudinal information on a given day from a random sample of the population used to assess attitudes of the population as a whole. There is always a margin of error and they require proper interpretation. Attention to the following six items could serve as a check on the quality of a poll:

1. Examine the wording of the question to be sure it is clear. Also check the question ordering to see if it could affect responses. For example, leading questions are sometimes asked just before a question on voting intentions.

2. Check the polling time. When was it taken? Over what length of time? A poll represents a snapshot of attitudes at a given time period, not on the day it is published. The specific day, or even the time of day it was taken can affect results.

3. Note the percentage of "undecideds"; high numbers can render the results meaningless.

4. Note the size of the sample and the sample error factor; the sample error depends on the sample size. In extrapolating from a few thousand to many million there will always be a statistical error. In reputable election polls the margin is usually between plus or minus three. In Canada, a representative sample of 1500 people, for example, is generally considered to be an accurate reflection of the national opinion within plus or minus 2.5 percentage points, 95 percent of the time.

5. Watch for the percentage of "soft" voters who are only weakly decided and could easily change.

6. Consider the name and reputation of the polling firm and who paid for the survey.

Despite having been curtailed in the final two days of the election campaign, polls are here to stay. Proponents of polls argue that they provide valuable aid for parties and governments in reading public opinion. Journalists and political scientists defend the public's right to have the same information that the politicians have. Moreover, the results of polls have proven remarkably accurate. In 1993, for example, the last Gallup Poll indicated the Liberals would win a majority government with 44 percent of the popular vote. They actually won 41 percent and majority status.

MEDIA AND VOTERS

The relationship between the campaign and media coverage is reciprocal: each wants something of the other and affects the other's conduct. Party strategists structure their daily campaign itineraries around the demands of television and, to a lesser extent, radio. For example, the timing and presentations of policy pronouncements can ensure inclusion on network evening newscasts. Policy statements delivered early in the day allow reporters enough time to meet their deadlines. Television crews are provided the best vantage points at campaign rallies and other "media events." Appropriate photogenic backgrounds are arranged to highlight the theme of policy pronouncements. And, "advance crews" are sent ahead to campaign stops to ensure a proper expression of support for their candidate.

The importance that parties attach to the role of the media is indicated in the amounts they spend on broadcast and print advertising. For example, the 1988 PC advertising campaign was reported to cost $4.7 million; the Liberals' $3.8 million; and the NDPs' $3.1 million. Even more instructive is the percentage that advertising comprised of the parties' total campaign expenditures: 59 percent, 56 percent and 44 percent, respectively.[27]

The mass media therefore play a crucial role in helping voters choose among parties at election time. There is, however, a growing concern about how well they are performing this role. Many observers resent the excessive concentration placed on style rather than on substance and complain that Canadian election coverage is analogous to a horserace or a game. Emphasis tends to be placed on polls, campaign strategies and party prospects in individual ridings, in an attempt to determine which party is "winning." Serious analysis of party pronouncements or investigation into areas of voter concern are for the most part ignored. Thus the voter is provided little information on which to base a decision. Fred Fletcher traces the origins of this "horserace" coverage of Canadian elections back to the 1974 election. It is his contention that the media have been reacting to what they perceived as manipulation by the Liberals during that campaign. To prevent recurrence of such events, journalists were instructed not only to convey what the parties said, but also to report on the tactics and purposes underlying media events. The result of this brand of "judgemental journalism" has not been without disadvantages. Penetrating the motives of the party campaigns, and thereby focusing on the campaign style of each party, is done at the expense of analyzing campaign issues.[28]

Emphasis on style also results in a "leader fixation," since campaigns are based around leaders' tours. Polls conducted throughout the campaign also focus on leadership in an attempt to predict the outcome of the election and to explain it in terms of leader appeal. The polls are presented as measures to gauge how the leaders' campaigns are faring. In this sense media coverage misrepresents the political system, narrows the focus of public debate, and denigrates political leaders and institutions.[29] A study of the 1984 election showed that there was "less reporting of the leaders' statements and more assessments of their performances." Almost 60 percent of news reports on The National (CBC) and in *The Globe and Mail* concerning the party leaders made an explicit assessment of the leader or his performance.[30] In 1993 the media spotlight was almost entirely on the party leaders, rather than on the "team" seeking election.

We noted earlier that the media are highly political instruments. Television is the most powerful medium of all because of the vast number of voters who can be reached. One recent poll indicated that about 52 percent of the respondents obtained most of their campaign information from television, 30 percent from newspapers and 11 percent from radio.[31] A 1988 post-election poll found that 51 percent of respondents found the media helpful in deciding how to vote, with television debates ranked as the most helpful.[32]

Until 1993, television and radio coverage tended to be partisan toward established parties. The bias against minor parties was evident in newspapers as well, where editors propagandized through editorials and influenced the contents of the headlines and news

---

[27] *Report of the Chief Electoral Officer Respecting Election Expenses, 1988* (Ottawa: Supply and Services, 1988), p. 2-1.

[28] Frederick Fletcher, "Playing the Game,: The Mass Media and the 1979 Campaign," in H.R. Penniman, ed., *Canada at the Polls 1979 and 1980*, p. 295.

[29] Ibid.

[30] Fletcher, "The Media and the 1984 Landslide," p. 169.

[31] Fletcher, "Playing the Game," p. 285.

[32] The 1988 poll was by *Maclean's*/Decima, reported in *Maclean's*, Dec. 5, 1988, p. 19.

pages.[33] Minor parties were thus at a severe disadvantage, especially if no alternative sources of information were available. As we noted in Chapter 4, many newspapers across the country are under the same ownership — and that ownership sometimes extends to the local radio and television stations. In 1993, the Bloc Québécois and Reform parties, because of their strong regional support, captured considerable media attention. A contributing factor was that they already had membership in Parliament, and therefore were eligible to be represented in the nationally televised leadership debates.

Media time for parties during election campaigns is strictly governed by law. According to the *Election Expenses Act*, all broadcasters are required to sell up to a maximum of six-and-one-half hours of prime-time spots to registered political parties at a most-favoured advertising rate. The number of hours is divided among the parties according to a formula revised in August 1993 to allow smaller parties more advertising than in the 1988 campaign. The formula is based on the number of Commons seats held, the number of candidates each party ran in the previous election and the percentage of the popular vote each party won. In 1993, the Conservatives were allowed to buy 116 minutes, the Liberals 78, the NDP 55, Reform 17, and the BQ 5 minutes. Often, only a fraction of the time is actually used because it is so expensive.

Free time is allocated on the same basis as paid advertising; naturally, all of it is used. These media time regulations were designed to provide registered political parties with a reasonable opportunity to present themselves directly to the public and help equalize access to the airwaves. However, it is important to note that, while this law establishes some equity for the largest federal parties represented in Parliament, it also reinforces the bias against minor and new parties and independent candidates. Political advertising is also regulated. None is allowed during the first four weeks of the campaign, nor on the last two days before the election nor on polling day itself. The object is to prevent a last-minute "ad blitz."[34] In time for the 1993 election, an amendment to the *Canada Election Act* was passed placing a $1000 limit on advertising expenses incurred by non-party organizations for the purpose of promoting or opposing a particular registered party or candidate. The restrictions, supported by the three major parties, were intended to prevent individuals or groups from dominating political discourse during the election campaign. However, an Alberta trial judge ruled in the spring of 1993 that the changes in the *Elections Act* that limited spending in election campaigns violated freedom of expression under the Charter. The federal government launched an appeal, but Jean-Pierre Kingsley, Canada's Chief Electoral Officer, lifted restrictions on the right of citizens and lobby groups to buy political advertising during the 1993 campaign.[35]

Elections have become big business, with the establishment of public relations firms whose primary purpose is to build the leaders' images and direct political campaigns. Typically, public relations experts determine the voters' key prejudices by means of public opinion polls, then tailor the campaign to avoid unpopular subjects that might alienate large voting blocs. They devise catchy slogans like "The Just Society," or "The Politics of Inclusion" that fix a name and personality in the voters' minds in connection with a positive proposal.

---

[33] T.H. Qualter and K.A. MacKirdy, "The Press of Ontario and the Election," in John Meisel, ed., *Papers on the 1962 Election* (Toronto: University of Toronto Press, 1964), pp. 151–54.

[34] See the introduction to the 1993 election case study. See page 499.

[35] *The Globe and Mail*, August 20, 1993. In 1988 individuals and advocacy groups such as the National Citizen's Coalition had the right to spend any amount of money to publicize their viewpoints, and no time limits — although party and candidate spending were restricted. This ruling set the stage for a war of wealth in the 1988 election in which an unprecedented number of advocacy groups spent millions of dollars on advertising, direct mail, phone banks, canvassing, information booths and the like to influence voters.

According to K.Z. Paltiel, the Liberal and Conservative Parties first used advertising agencies to plan their campaigns in the 1940s. In 1948 the Walsh Advertising Agency, in *A Formula for Liberal Victory*, wrote "we stripped away all the mysticism of political campaigns and 'sold' Liberalism as we would sell any other product or service...by modern merchandising methods."[36] Of course, the opposite effect can occur if the slogan is badly chosen. The 1972 Liberal slogan "The Land is Strong" drew this widely repeated comment in rural areas: "What makes my land strong is horse shit."

Parties make extensive preparations before the election is called — money spent then is not deducted from the party's spending limits — later, in the midst of a campaign, more commercials may be produced quickly as pollsters target issues of most concern to voters. While there may be something degrading about politicians being packaged and sold like soapflakes, advertising does have positive aspects. Despite evident media distortions, the simplification of issues and the personalization of the political campaigns arouse wide interest, and therefore probably increase awareness and participation in the political process.

ELECTION FINANCING

The rising costs of financing general election campaigns raise questions about the degree and fairness of political competitiveness. Does the expense hinder or exclude individuals, groups and parties from active involvement in the election process? The 1974 enactment of the *Election Expenses Act*, discussed in the previous chapter, represented an important attempt to address such questions. Many ideas in the *Act* originated with the Task Force on Election Expenses and received its main thrust from Privy Council Office President Allan MacEachen and his aides from 1970 to 1974. According to its provisions, which were embodied in a series of amendments to the *Canada Elections Act*, the *Broadcasting Act* and the *Income Tax Act*, federal candidates, for the first time, were required to give a detailed accounting of money received and spent. They were also compelled to observe spending limits, and candidates who received 15 percent of the votes were eligible for subsidies from the national treasury.

F. Leslie Seidle and K.Z. Paltiel ascribe the motivating forces behind the adoption of the *Election Expenses Act* partly to financial difficulties encountered by political parties: between 1957 and 1965 Canada experienced a rapid succession of five elections, which taxed the fund-raising capabilities of the major parties.[37] Compounding this problem was the increasing cost of elections, arising mainly from the accelerated use of television advertising. Another motivation was the party financing scandals that aroused the ire of the public. Seidle and Paltiel note that:

> *Party leaders since Confederation have attempted to overcome through financing the problems created by the absence of cohesive parliamentary factions and extra-parliamentary organizations. They were faced with the task of raising and allocating funds to finance campaigns as well as to weld together a loyal and disciplined legislative following. As a result, they were inevitably vulnerable to the temptation of fund-raising abuses and to their subsequent exposure.[38]*

Continued concerns about party fund-raising activities and the influence of the Watergate scandal in the United States encouraged politicians to take steps to prevent further mistrust on the part of the public.

---

[36] R. Whitaker, "The Liberal Party Enters the Age of the Ad Man: Advertising Agencies and the National Liberal Party 1943–58," unpublished paper.

[37] F. Leslie Seidle and K.Z. Paltiel, "Party Finance, the Election Expenses Act and Campaign Spending in 1979 and 1980," in H.R. Penniman, ed., *Canada at the Polls, 1979 and 1980*, pp. 229–30.

[38] Ibid., p. 227.

Perhaps the most important aspect of the *Election Expenses Act* is that it recognizes parties as legal entities, thereby rendering them publicly accountable. They can therefore benefit but also be prosecuted for infractions of the *Act*.[39] The *Act* controls election spending by limiting the campaign costs of both parties and candidates to a base formula linked to the consumer price index and adjusted before every election. (For 1993 party limits see Table 11.6.) It also encourages the parties to develop broader financial bases by granting generous tax credits, primarily for small donations, as a balance against reliance on corporate funds.[40] A further provision to reduce the reliance of political parties and their candidates on large contributors is the refunding of deposits and partial reimbursement of election expenses for candidates: as we have noted, a candidate who obtains 15 percent of the valid votes cast in his or her electoral district is refunded the $1000 deposit and partially reimbursed by the Receiver General of Canada for election expenses. Provided that they comply with the requirements concerning the filing of a return of election expenses,[41] registered parties are reimbursed for one-half the costs incurred in the purchase of permitted radio and television advertising time. More importantly, recognized national parties can also get taxpayers to subsidize 22.5 percent of their campaign costs if they spend just 10 percent of the expense limit set by Elections Canada. (See Table 11.6.) The total projected spending by Liberal, Conservative, NDP, Bloc and Reform parties on national campaigns in 1993 was $32 million, which would make them eligible for $7.2 million in public subsidies.[42]

TABLE 11.6   ALLOWABLE SPENDING BY PARTIES ON THEIR 1993 NATIONAL CAMPAIGNS

Party	No. of candidates	Spending ceiling ($)
Conservatives	295	10.5 million
Liberals	295	10.5 million
New Democrats	294	10.5 million
Natural Law	231	8.6 million
Reform	207	7.5 million
National	171	6.4 million
Abolitionist	80	3.0 million
Green	79	3.0 million
Bloc Québécois	75	2.7 million
Christian Heritage	59	2.2 million
Commonwealth	56	2.3 million
Canada Party	56	1.9 million
Libertarian	52	2.1 million
Marxist-Leninist	51	1.9 million

Note: Parties that spend at least 10 percent of their ceiling are eligible for a 22.5% taxpayer subsidy.
Source: Elections Canada.

---

[39] A "registered" political party is defined as a political party that was either (a) represented in the House of Commons on the day before the dissolution of Parliament, immediately preceding the General Election, or (b) 30 days before polling day at the General Election, had officially nominated candidates in at least 50 electoral districts in Canada. The Chief Electoral Officer maintains a register of political parties.

[40] Seidle and Paltiel, "Party Finance," pp. 227–28.

[41] Only "registered" political parties can take advantage of these income tax credits. However, a contribution during a federal election made directly to a candidate allows the contributor to claim a tax credit whether or not the candidate represents a registered political party.

[42] Ron Eade, *The Ottawa Citizen*, Oct. 23, 1993. In addition to campaign reimbursements for national and riding campaigns, the cost of the election includes staff salaries, compiling the voter list, computerization, mail-in ballots, printing ballots and running polling stations — for a grand total of about $160 million in 1993.

We stated in the previous chapter that the *Election Expenses Act* requires parties to provide audited financial statements in order to expose fund-raising practices and election expenses to public scrutiny. All expenses and the amount and sources of contributions must be disclosed. Six months after the end of the party's fiscal year, an audited return containing a detailed statement of the party's contributions and operating expenses must be sent to the Chief Electoral Officer. Contributors of $100 or more during the fiscal year must be named. Candidates are also required to file detailed, audited returns after each general or by-election. These are public documents and are thus available for scrutiny. In order to prevent outside interference in elections, a 1993 amendment to the *Canada Elections Act* prohibited contributions to a candidate from sources outside the country.[43] Apart from this, there are no limits placed on the amount that individuals or organizations may donate to a political party.

BY-ELECTIONS

By-elections are held to fill vacancies of legislative seats that occur between general elections. The timing of federal by-elections is at the discretion of the Prime Minister, who, within six months of the date the Speaker issues the notification warrant acknowledging the vacancy, may name any date. By-elections may be held soon after a vacancy appears, a year or more later or not at all if the writs for a general election are issued before the by-election takes place.

While much fanfare and attention accompanies most by-elections, their significance is limited as a predictor of party fortunes in general elections. By-elections tend to be idiosyncratic because of a variety of factors, including the small number of seats contested at any given time (and therefore the lack of regional representativeness), their inability to alter the government's status, changing political conditions between the time of by-elections and the general election and the absence of national campaigns by the political parties.[44] The lack of congruence between by-election and general election results is demonstrated by the Conservative failure to win a majority government in 1979, although the federal Liberal government had lost 13 of 15 by-elections the previous year.

Nevertheless, by-elections are an important part of the democratic process, providing an outlet for voters to air their frustrations and send the government a message. They also are important in maintaining representation. It is in the performance of this latter function that Canada's election laws are lacking. Outrageous delays have sometimes occurred between the time seats became vacant and the calling of subsequent by-elections. In 1975, for example, Trudeau left St. John's West with no representative for 13 months and 10 days.[45] The Prime Minister and his advisors are not anxious to call a by-election if they believe the result will be perceived as unfavourable. This hesitancy is reinforced by the tendency of governments to lose by-elections. However, most reformers agree that political considerations should not obstruct the basic right of citizens to representation in Parliament for very long.

---

[43] Specifically, contributions are prohibited from 1. an individual who is not a Canadian citizen or permanent resident in Canada, 2. an association that does not carry on activities in Canada, 3. a union that is not entitled to bargain collectively in Canada and 4. a foreign state or political party.

[44] See Barry J. Kay, "By-Elections as Indicators of Canadian Voting," *CJPS*, vol. XIV, no. 1 (March 1981), pp. 37–52.

[45] This has been the longest vacancy to date.

ELECTORAL BEHAVIOUR

Studies of electoral behaviour attempt to describe how and explain why people vote as they do and what impact political events, personalities, issues and other factors have on their decisions.

As we have noted, virtually every Canadian 18 years of age and over has the right to vote. However, certain citizens are more apt to exercise their franchise than others. Comparative studies in the United States and Canada show that there are several standard factors involved in whether a person votes or not.[46] First, some individuals are more socially at ease and gregarious and find interaction with others rewarding. Such people are more likely to have a psychological predisposition to participate actively in the electoral process. As well, the poor and the uneducated are much less apt to vote than are individuals in the higher income levels with a college education.[47] The wealthy are more apt to vote because they feel they have more at stake in an election outcome, and more highly educated people are more interested and better informed than others. The abstention rate also reflects feelings of efficacy that increase from the lower to upper middle classes. In general, lower class workers have a low feeling of efficacy; that is, they don't feel their vote matters, while corporation presidents, at the other extreme, tend to believe that they can further their interests by electing the right candidate. Voter turnout in Canada is highest in the middle-aged range; the youngest and the oldest tend to abstain more. Men cast their vote more often than women.[48] Incidental factors such as issues and campaigns may also affect non-voting and so, too, may the level of civic responsibility instilled in some voters through socialization.

Although meaningful generalizations about political participation are difficult to make with precision, it would appear that while socioeconomic factors are significant in motivating participation there is little substantial variation based on ethnicity or regionalism. Interestingly, no significant difference between ethnic groups in terms of their overall index of electoral activity has been found at the federal level. Moreover, levels of participation in the various regions have also been discovered to be roughly similar across the country. A stereotypical Canadian voter, then, is a middle-aged, white-collar worker with at least some post-secondary education. The counterpart, the typical non-voter, would be a young person with little formal education and a blue-collar job. These are of course crude generalizations, but they are supported by studies that show that political participation is basically a middle-class affair.

Many factors influence how and why Canadians vote. These can be grouped loosely, as indicated in Figure 11.2, into long-term and short-term factors. Long-term factors contribute to an individual's basic identification with a political party. They include socioeconomic indicators such as class, religion, gender and ethnicity, urban/rural distinctions and so on. Short-term factors arise from the specifics of an election campaign, including issues, leaders, candidates, debates, polls and media coverage. It is possible to visualize voting behaviour as a funnel, that has flowing into it long-term factors that endure over time and then short-term factors that have an impact just before the vote emerges at the tip of the funnel.

---

[46] W. Mishler, *Political Participation in Canada* (Toronto: Macmillan of Canada, 1979), pp. 88–97.

[47] See Anthony Downs, "The Causes and Effects of Rational Abstention," in his *Economic Theory of Democracy* (New York: Harper & Row, 1957), pp. 260–75.

[48] See B.J. Kay, R.D. Lambert, S.D. Brown and J.E. Curtis, "Gender and Political Activity in Canada," *CJPS*, vol. 20, no. 4 (1987), pp. 851–63.

FIGURE 11.2 FUNNEL OF INFLUENCE IN VOTING BEHAVIOUR

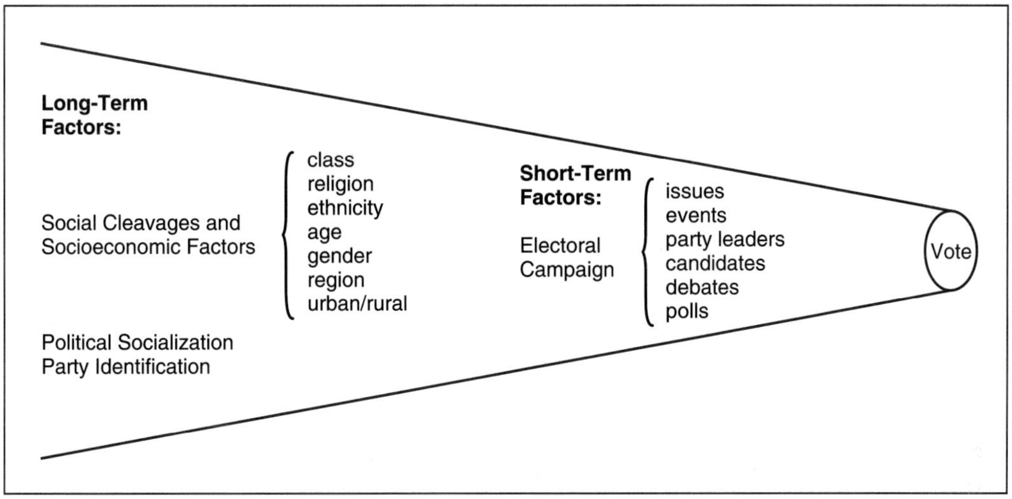

Long-term factors begin early in an individual's life, as attitudes toward politics and political parties are acquired through socialization and social group factors. These factors have a bearing on one's political ideas (see Chapter 4), party identification and voting intentions to varying degrees. Long before an election campaign starts, an individual may have acquired a degree of party identification. The *configuration* and *intensity* of social divisions are important factors in whether or not those divisions affect electoral behaviour.

> Where cleavages such as class and religion run deep and reinforce each other, so as to give sharply-etched sub-cultures, voting choice merely reflects communal loyalties. But where divisions are cross-cutting or simply less intense, voting becomes a genuinely political act, shaped but not dominated by an elector's social identity.[49]

During the campaign, short-term factors have an impact on the voter confirming or changing the effect of long-term factors. Two short-term factors in particular are significant: leadership and issues. Short-term factors can cause significant fluctuation in public opinion. Changing technology, campaign strategies and media, especially television, have increased the impact of short-term factors on voting in recent years at the expense of long-term factors including regionalism, religion, urban/rural environment, ethnicity, gender and age.[50]

LONG-TERM FACTORS AND ELECTORAL OUTCOMES
REGIONALISM
In order that voting behaviour may be explained by regionalism, there must exist both a regional identity and a party politization of that identity. Regions in Canada have often been associated with particular political parties, but the pattern has changed considerably over time.

---

[49] Martin Harrop and William L. Miller, *Elections and Voters: A Comparative Introduction* (London: Macmillan, 1987), p. 211.

[50] For a more extensive review of the debates about the role of class, region and religion in Canadian voting, and of the concept of party identification, see Elisabeth Gidengil, "Canada Votes: A Quarter Century of Canadian National Election Studies", *CJPS.*, vol. XXV, no. 2 (June, 1992), pp. 219–48.

As a long-term factor, region has shown wide variations.[51] We have noted, for example, that the Liberals dominated Québec for decades, but were severely defeated there by the Conservatives under Diefenbaker in 1958 and then by Mulroney 1984 and 1988. In 1993, however, the Conservatives won only one Québec seat, and the Liberals ran a weak second to the separatist Bloc Québécois. In the West in 1993, where the Conservatives, along with the NDP, had dominated in the previous decade, the upstart Reform Party captured the bulk of the vote, with the Liberals running second.

CLASS

Class has not proven to be a significant determinant of Canadian voting behaviour.[52] Only a proportion of working class voters support the NDP; the Liberal Party attracts support from all classes. Although it may be argued that the results of some opinion polls have shown a degree of class awareness in Canada, there is no evidence to indicate that it has had a significant impact on electoral choice. Alan Cairns has suggested that Canada's electoral system itself and its homogenizing effect works against the emergence of class-based politics.[53] As class orientations are spread relatively evenly across the country, their political impact is effectively nullified by the single-member plurality electoral system.

On the other hand, the question of the ideological content of Canadian electoral behaviour remains unresolved. In his study of identification with federal political parties 1977–81, Michael Stevenson found "a slight bias toward more upper-class identification with the Progressive Conservative Party and more lower-class identification with the Liberal Party."[54] Analysis of the 1988 election results confirmed this voting pattern because of the free trade issue. The Conservative Party was strongly supported by higher income business groups while the Liberals and New Democrats tended to receive their support from lower income groups.[55]

RELIGION

Religion has had a fairly strong impact on voting behaviour in Canada. For decades Roman Catholics have shown a strong tendency to vote Liberal regardless of their ethnicity, region or class.[56] This held true in 1988, when Protestants tended to be Conservatives, Catholics Liberals, and the NDP had no religiously differentiated base. Canadians of "other" or "no" religion were the least partisan politically.[57] Ontario, in particular, has stood out as a province

---

[51]   See Roger Gibbins, *Regionalism: Territorial Politics in Canada and the United States* (Toronto: Butterworths, 1982) and, by the same author *Prairie Politics and Society: Regionalism in Decline* (Scarborough: Butterworths, 1980).

[52]   John Pammett, "Class Voting and Class Consciousness in Canada," *Canadian Review of Sociology and Anthropology*, vol. 24, no. 2 (1987), pp. 269–90; Elisabeth Gidengil, "Class and Region in Canadian Voting: A Dependency Interpretation," *CJPS* (Sept. 1989), pp. 563–87; Ronald D. Lambert et al., "Social Class and Voting," in James Curtis et al., eds., *Social Inequality in Canada* (Scarborough, Ont: Prentice-Hall, 1988); and Keith Archer, *Political Choice and Electoral Consequences* (Montréal: McGill-Queen's University Press, 1990).

[53]   Cairns, "The General Election and the Party System."

[54]   H. Michael Stevenson, "Ideology and Unstable Party Identification in Canada: Limited Rationality in a Brokerage Party System," *CJPS*, vol. 20, no. 4 (Dec. 1987), pp. 813–50.

[55]   Johnston et al., *Letting the People Decide*, ch. 3.

[56]   Mildred A. Schwartz, "Canadian Voting Behaviour," in Richard Rose, ed., *Electoral Behaviour: A Comparative Handbook* (New York: Free Press, 1974), pp. 571–74. Also see Laurence LeDuc, "The Flexible Canadian Electorate," in H. Penniman, *Canada at the Polls, 1984* (Durham, N.C.: Duke University Press, 1988), pp. 37–54; Richard Johnston, "The Reproduction of the Religious Cleavage in Canadian Elections," *CJPS*, vol. 25, no. 1 (March 1985), pp. 99–113, and the rejoinder by William P. Irving in the same volume, pp. 115–17.

[57]   Johnston et al., *Letting the People Decide*, p. 86.

characterized by strong religious divisions. Ontario Catholics have tended to vote very strongly Liberal, while Protestants have lined up consistently behind Conservative or NDP candidates.

No simple logic is adequate to explain the impact of religious affiliation on voting preference. The answer is perhaps intertwined with the historical evolution of Canada and its party system. An anti-Catholic sentiment on the part of some Tories during the nineteenth century may have alienated English Canadian Catholics. As well, French Canadians are overwhelmingly Catholic and, until 1984 tended to vote strongly Liberal. However, religion is often confounded with linguistic and regional patterns. Results of the 1984, 1988 and 1993 elections show that the Liberal hold on their French, Catholic base has been greatly weakened in Québec.

URBAN/RURAL ENVIRONMENT

Despite its relatively small population and its enormous land mass, Canada has a remarkably large urban population. Although to some people "urban" may connote a particular viewpoint rather than a place of dwelling, for our purposes the term is defined as habitation in a town or city of at least 5000 people. As we noted in Chapter 1, the Canadian population is overwhelmingly concentrated in urban regions in the provinces of Ontario, Québec and British Columbia. The Conservatives have traditionally received a significant degree of rural support, while the Liberals tend to attract a disproportionate number of urban voters.[58] Support for the New Democratic Party also tends to be urban. Reform has a strong rural appeal. In most twentieth-century federal elections, the Liberal Party, while receiving considerable urban support, has appeared to be best able to attract a variety of voters by cutting across urban/rural lines.

The impact of community size on voting is likely to be associated with several other cleavages and voting influences. In order to prove its independent effect, a researcher would have to control for the various historical influences and factors in the political demography of the constituencies being examined.

ETHNICITY

As we indicated in Chapters 3 and 4, a number of political culture and socialization studies have documented the degree to which French Canadians and English Canadians hold different attitudes and values. What complicates the analysis of voting behaviour in this regard is that ethnicity, language and religion are interrelated.

Traditionally, the Liberal Party received a consistently high level of support from French Canadians while simultaneously attracting a significant proportion of English Canadian and post-Second-World-War immigrant voters, especially from France and Southern Europe. The Progressive Conservatives, on the other hand, have attracted "disproportionate support" from Canadians of British descent, those from the Protestant monarchies of Northern Europe and those of Eastern European origin.[59] Ethnic voting support for the NDP has been confined primarily to non-French Canadians. The ability of the Liberal Party to bridge the two founding ethnic groups and at the same time to appeal to immigrant voters was the principal reason for its dominance in Canadian politics during most of the twentieth century.

---

[58] Harold D. Clarke, Jane Jenson, Lawrence LeDuc and Jon Pammett, *Political Choice in Canada* (Toronto: McGraw-Hill Ryerson, 1979), ch. 4.

[59] Richard Johnston et al., *Letting the People Decide*, p. 86

GENDER AND AGE

Gender and age are not significant factors in voting behaviour in Canada. However, some elections have indicated that women and first-time voters have tended to vote Liberal, while elderly Canadians have tended to vote Conservative.[60]

PARTY IDENTIFICATION

One of the most controversial topics in the field of electoral studies is the role of **party identification** — the degree to which citizens identify with a particular party. It is thought by some that parental party identification is transmitted to children through the socialization process and that the resulting attachment has a long-term effect on voting behaviour, filtering the effects of short-term factors such as party leaders or campaign issues. While in the preceding analysis we have discussed essentially "group" phenomena such as region, class, religion and ethnic identity, the question of party identification directs us to the level of the individual voter. How important is this factor in influencing voting behaviour?

Studies of electoral behaviour indicate that party identification is widespread in Canada but is relatively low in intensity.[61] In 1988, only 35 percent of the electorate did not identify themselves with a party. This was similar to percentages of non-identifiers in the previous four elections.[62] Non-partisans are particularly susceptible to issues, leaders and other short-term factors in the election campaign. Transient and newly eligible voters generally seem to favour the incumbent government.[63] The impact of specific issues and the image of the leader are credited with many recent defections from party loyalty. While there continues to be a small, stable core of loyalists, a significant proportion shifts from one party affiliation to another. Party identification volatility is tending to increase over time, and this suggests the increasing possibility of large pendulum swings of political support. Michael Stevenson has found that unstable partisanship is at least partially related to ideology. His research indicates that in the 1977–88 period "the largest bloc of unstable partisans was closest ideologically to the more left-wing stable New Democratic Party partisans, and shifted only between the New Democratic and Liberal Parties." He also found that the smaller bloc of unstable partisans, which moved to the Conservative Party, "was ideologically closest to its more right-wing stable partisans."[64]

SHORT-TERM FACTORS AND ELECTION OUTCOME

Issues, along with other factors in electoral campaigns such as party leadership, candidates, leadership debates and specific events may play an important part in influencing the individual voter's decision. Voters in Canada shift their attention to new problems in each election. Although free trade, for example, played a major role in determining voter choice in the 1988 election, it was relatively insignificant in 1993 (much to the chagrin of the NDP).[65]

---

[60] Peter Wearing and Joseph Wearing, "Does Gender Make a Difference in Voting Behaviour?" in Joseph Wearing, *The Ballot and its Message: Voting in Canada* (Toronto: Copp Clark Pitman, 1991).

[61] See Lawrence LeDuc, "The Flexible Canadian Electorate," in Penniman, *Canada at the Polls, 1984*, pp. 40–41.

[62] This is close to the non-partisan rates in the United States. Party identification percentages for the main parties in 1988 were Conservative 29; Liberal 24; NDP 11. Johnston et al., *Letting the People Decide*, pp. 82–84.

[63] Alan Frizzell et al., *The Canadian General Election of 1988* (Ottawa: Carleton University Press, 1989).

[64] H. Michael Stevenson, "Ideology and Unstable Party Identification in Canada," p. 815.

[65] Johnston et al., *Letting the People Decide*, chapter 5.

For an issue to have an impact on the outcome of an election it must meet three conditions.[66] First, it must be salient to voters; that is, voters must have an opinion on it and they must consider it relatively important. Second, the issue must be linked with partisan controversy. It will have little impact on election outcomes if all the parties are perceived to have the same position on it. Third, opinion must be strongly skewed in a single direction and not simply reflect the usual degree of attachment to the various political parties.

The perception that issues are an important factor in a voter's choice leads strategists to rely heavily on public opinion surveys. Party planners identify those groups that contain possible supporters and strive to mobilize their support through appeals and policies tailored to a winning electoral coalition. The measure of success, of course, is the election result.

Political leaders in Canada tend to embody the party image. This is largely due to television coverage. Leaders put a personal stamp on their parties. John Turner, Pierre Trudeau and Jean Chrétien had very different personal images that adhered to the Liberal Party. Although Canada has a parliamentary system, the leader plays a central role in determining voter choices. Leadership was an important issue early in the 1988 campaign, and again in the final week. Inevitably, complex political issues are personalized; personality is often easier for the electorate and the media to evaluate. John Turner's leadership ability was undermined by his poor performance in 1984, and he never fully recovered from that negative perception. His strong performance in the 1988 debate helped him considerably, but negative Conservative ads in the last week of the campaign reinforced the previous image of him as an indecisive, weak leader. In the 1993 campaign, Jean Chrétien trailed PC leader Kim Campbell in popularity by a wide margin at the start of the campaign, but passed her by the last week. Campbell's stumbles and indiscretions had caused public rifts in the party.

It is evident that a number of factors influence voting. The contradictory perceptions and influences weighing on voters' minds as they enter the polling booths are indeed difficult to disentangle. We have identified a number of the leading factors in an attempt to understand electoral choice. There is undoubtedly a degree of interaction and reinforcement among the factors that makes the precise independent effect of each difficult to determine. A useful guide to voting behaviour in any single election is to think of the factors that influence voters as a triangle with leaders, issues and party identification each constituting one of its angles. The degree of party identification indicates the percentage of votes that are likely to change hands, while leaders and issues influence voters in the short-term. Each campaign is unique in the extent to which leaders and issues are influential.

GENERAL ELECTION RESULTS, 1867–1993

Since Confederation, Canada has held 35 General Elections. Either the Liberals or Conservatives have won each time. As we saw in Figure 10.1, the Conservative Party dominated federal politics from 1867 until nearly the turn of the century (1896), with the exception of the Liberal victory of 1874. The Liberal Party was ascendant until 1984, holding power for most of the present century. (See Table 11.7.) The most important element in the Liberals' success during these years was the capture and maintenance of Québec.

---

[66] Ibid., p. 20.

Table 11.7   General Election Results, 1878 – 1993

Election Year	Gov't Formed	Total Seats	Con Seats	Con % votes	Lib Seats	Lib % votes	CCF/ NDP Seats	CCF/ NDP % votes	Ref Seats	Ref % votes	Bloc Seats	Bloc % votes	Oth Seats	Oth % votes
1878	Con	206	140	53	65	45	–	–	–	–	–	–	1	2
1882	Con	211	138	53	73	47	–	–	–	–	–	–	–	–
1887	Con	215	128	51	87	49	–	–	–	–	–	–	–	–
1891	Con	215	122	52	91	46	–	–	–	–	–	–	2	2
1896	Lib	213	88	46	118	45	–	–	–	–	–	–	7	9
1900	Lib	213	81	47	132	52	–	–	–	–	–	–	–	1
1904	Lib	214	75	47	139	52	–	–	–	–	–	–	–	1
1908	Lib	221	85	47	135	51	–	–	–	–	–	–	1	2
1911	Con	221	134	51	87	48	–	–	–	–	–	–	–	1
1917	Con[1]	235	153	57	82	40	–	–	–	–	–	–	–	3
1921	Lib	235	50	30	116	41	–	–	–	–	–	–	69[2]	29
1925	Lib	245	116	46	99	40	–	–	–	–	–	–	30[3]	14
1926	Lib	245	91	45	128	46	–	–	–	–	–	–	26[4]	9
1930	Con	245	137	49	91	45	–	–	–	–	–	–	17[5]	6
1935	Lib	245	40	30	173	45	7	9	–	–	–	–	25	16
1940	Lib	245	40	31	181	51	8	8	–	–	–	–	16	10
1945	Lib	245	67	27	125	41	28	16	–	–	–	–	24	16
1949	Lib	262	41	30	190	49	13	13	–	–	–	–	18	8
1953	Lib	265	51	31	170	49	23	11	–	–	–	–	21	9
1957	Con	265	112	39	105	41	25	11	–	–	–	–	23	9
1958	Con	265	208	54	48	34	8	9	–	–	–	–	1	3
1962	Con	265	116	37	99	37	19	14	–	–	–	–	31	12
1963	Lib	265	95	33	129	42	17	13	–	–	–	–	24	12
1965	Lib	265	97	32	131	40	21	18	–	–	–	–	16	10
1968	Lib	264	72	31	155	45	22	17	–	–	–	–	15	7
1972	Lib	264	107	35	109	38	31	18	–	–	–	–	16	9
1974	Lib	264	95	35	141	43	16	15	–	–	–	–	12	6
1979	Con	282	136	36	114	20	26	18	6	6	–	–	–	–
1980	Lib	282	103	33	147	44	32	20	–	–	–	–	0	3
1984	Con	282	211	50	40	28	30	19	–	–	–	–	1	3
1988	Con	295	169[6]	43	83	32	43	20	–	–	–	–	–	5
1993	Lib	295	2	16	177	41	9	7	52	19	54	14	1	4

[1] Wartime coalition

[2] Includes 65 Progressives

[3] Includes 24 Progressives

[4] Includes 20 Progressives

[5] Includes 12 Progressives

[6] 169 Conservatives were elected on Nov. 21, 1988, but one died before being official sworn in, leaving the seat technically vacant.

CASE STUDY OF THE 1993 GENERAL ELECTION

BACKGROUND: THE 1984 AND 1988 ELECTIONS

The 1993 General Election campaign and results can be understood best in light of the two preceding elections. The 1984 General Election produced a landslide victory for the Conservatives. Brian Mulroney became Prime Minister and John Turner was leader of the Liberal Official Opposition. The Conservative success in Québec was due to a coalition of Nationalists, Créditistes and disaffected Liberals. It was the first win for the Conservatives in that province since Diefenbaker's sweep there in 1958. However, the new government was plagued by a series of ministerial scandals. Within months the Conservatives were overtaken in the popularity polls by the Liberals. They remained in second or a record third position until shortly before the November 1988 election. The NDP, meanwhile, enjoyed unprecedented support, reaching a record peak of 41 percent in the polls in July 1987, ahead of both major parties.

As for the Liberals, after forming the government for so many years the party had severe problems adjusting to its new role in opposition, and, soon after the election defeat, many of the internecine battles that had characterized the Tories during their years in opposition surfaced in Liberal ranks. John Turner's leadership rival Jean Chrétien eventually resigned his Commons seat, but his supporters did not give up his cause. By the time the Meech Lake accord was signed with the provincial premiers on April 30, 1988, the Liberal Party was publicly warring over Turner's decision that the party would support the agreement. Mr. Turner survived well-publicized caucus revolts and unsubstantiated rumours about his character and ability to lead, but these damaged his personal credibility and also that of the party.

In January 1988, United States President Ronald Reagan and Prime Minister Mulroney signed a preliminary agreement concerning free trade. The Liberals faced renewed publicity about internal dissension over the party stand opposing the Free Trade Agreement. Their anti-free trade position put them in direct confrontation with big business so they were unable to rely on much financial support from that quarter.

In a determined effort to capture the initiative in the forthcoming election, on July 20, 1988, Turner asked Liberal Senate Leader Allan MacEachen to have the Liberal majority block the free trade legislation in the Senate and force Prime Minister Mulroney to call an election on the issue of free trade. The Liberal Senators agreed, despite some misgivings about the possibility of making Senate reform an issue by thwarting the will of the government.

The Conservatives, knowing they would need a majority in the next government to pass the free trade legislation, followed their own pre-election agenda. Throughout the late summer, Prime Minister Mulroney and his ministers had announced more than 70 government initiatives costing more than $8 billion. Since Parliament was not sitting, the Liberals and NDP could not compete for media attention and the Conservatives gradually moved from second place into first place in the polls.

The Liberals, in an attempt to arrest their slide in public opinion, took the unprecedented step of unveiling their 40-point policy program for the 1988 campaign even before the election was called. It was a wide-ranging document built around the theme of social and economic justice, and party strategists hoped it would clarify the Liberal vision for the decades ahead and give them some momentum going into the campaign.

The New Democratic Party, meanwhile, was interpreting private polls conducted over the summer that indicated that free trade was not a positive issue for them. Respondents viewed it as an economic and international issue, and did not believe the NDP was best qualified to manage either the economy or international affairs. The party's election strategy was built on their interpretation of these polls. The November 21, 1988, election was remarkable in many respects; extreme voter volatility, near dominance of a single issue and involvement of outside community leaders and advocacy groups.

The Conservatives went into the 1988 election with by far the richest and fittest organization; they had more candidates nominated, more advertising ready, faster communications with all ridings, more sophisticated polling, and more money; they even had a bigger airplane.

They were returned to power with a comfortable majority on November 21, 1988. At age 49, Brian Mulroney became the most successful Conservative prime minister since Sir Robert Borden and the first leader of any party to win back-to-back majorities since Louis St. Laurent had done it for the Liberals in 1949 and 1953. The Conservatives' share of the popular vote fell from 50 percent in 1984 to 43 percent, but they maintained strong representation in every region of the country and captured 169 seats.

The Liberals increased their standing to 83 seats from 38, and won 32 percent of the popular vote, up from 28 percent. The election was a personal victory for John Turner whose strong performance countered the personally negative images that had persisted from his 1984 loss. The only region where the party won a majority of the seats, however, was in the Maritimes where they won 20 of 32. In Québec they did even worse than in 1984, winning only 12 seats. In Ontario they climbed from 14 to 43, and in Manitoba they increased from 1 to 5. However, representation in the rest of the West was still bleak; only the party leader himself was elected in British Columbia, 2 seats were captured in the Northwest Territories, but none at all from Saskatchewan, Alberta or Yukon.

The New Democrats climbed from 30 seats to 43, but still won only 20 percent of the popular vote — hardly changed from their 19 percent share in 1984. Expectations had been higher and Ed Broadbent and his strategists were severely criticized after the election for their failure to take advantage of Liberal weaknesses early in the campaign. In an attempt to win, the party had moved too far from its ideological, social democratic roots. It won a record 19 seats in B.C., 10 in Saskatchewan, 1 in Alberta and 1 in Yukon. However, it dropped to 2 in Manitoba. It won only 10 in Ontario and none in Québec or the Maritimes.

Probably the most significant election result was in Québec, where the Conservatives consolidated and even improved upon their 1984 victory. Prime Minister Mulroney, a native son, filled the vacuum left by the federal Liberals when they had patriated the Constitution without Québec's approval in 1982. By engineering the Meech Lake accord and winning the support of Liberal Premier Robert Bourassa for free trade, Mulroney established the Conservatives as the party that had done the most for Québec. Combined with his stress on cooperation and conciliation, an appeal to Québec nationalism and widespread support among opinion leaders in Québec, he left little opening for the Liberals. His party even took 14 of the 23 ridings in the former Liberal bastion of Montréal; 63 of 75 of the province's total seats.

In Ontario, Tory organizers had anticipated severe losses in Toronto, but still did relatively well, winning 8 of the 23 Toronto seats (compared to 14 in 1984). Just a one percent increase in the Liberal popular vote in Ontario would have given them about 25 more seats there.[67]

---

[67] Based on Goldfarb's calculations, *Maclean's*, Dec. 5, 1988, p. 25.

In the West in 1984, the Conservatives had won a strong majority of seats in all four western provinces. In 1988, they maintained their western majority only in Alberta, and even there the NDP made a one-seat breakthrough. Fringe parties did exceptionally well. The western-based Reform Party, led by Preston Manning, ran 72 candidates. None won, but they attracted support with a platform backing free trade and calling for increased western participation in federal affairs.[68] Their candidates placed second in 10 Alberta ridings and third in 6. Many experts thought they would have done even better if free trade had not been the dominant issue.

In British Columbia the protest vote went largely to the New Democrats who attributed their gains there to what they described as a widespread feeling that Ottawa had ignored the province's interests. Fringe parties may also have undermined some Conservative candidates; in some ridings fringe candidates won as much as 14 percent of the vote.

THE 1993 CAMPAIGN

When Prime Minister Mulroney stepped down as Prime Minister in the spring of 1993, the coalition he had built to give the Conservatives their 1984 and 1988 victories was in tatters. He had taken Québec separatists into his party and government and they were deserting to the Bloc; Reformers were eating into his support in the West. There were several overlapping crises in the country: a leadership vacuum, widespread cynicism and distrust of politicians and government, a growing philosophy of difference that pitted groups of Canadians against each other, shattered aspirations for constitutional change and a record economic debt and high unemployment. Alienation and regionalism were rampant. The combination of problems called for a new kind of politics. The new Conservative leader, Kim Campbell, took advantage of the opportunity to appeal for a new "politics of inclusiveness." The circumstances also gave ideal conditions for protest parties like the Reform Party and the Bloc Québécois to flourish.

The Conservative government was in the last year of its mandate when Mr. Mulroney resigned his party leadership. In many ways the election campaign began when Kim Campbell was sworn in as party leader on June 25, 1993. The new leader spent the summer on the barbeque circuit building her image.

Mulroney left ample funds ($5.9 million) for the campaign and an election strategy including a throne speech and an electoral platform.[69] Campbell discarded both. Caught in the dilemma of having to disassociate herself from the unpopular former government of which she had been a prominent member, she replaced experienced strategists and fundraisers associated with her predecessor and cut ties with many senior ministers.

When she called the election on September 8, the new Prime Minister was still riding a wave of personal popularity, and the party was running close to the Liberals in terms of percentage of support. The polls began to plummet almost immediately. The Conservatives ran one of the most disastrous political campaigns in modern Canadian history. Much as John Turner had done in 1984, Campbell lost public respect through a series of blunders. Her problems began with an announcement that she would cut a few of the proposed EH-101 helicopters in order to save some money. She was immediately tagged as indecisive.

---

[68]   In March, 1989, Reform party candidate Deborah Grey won a federal by-election in Beaver River, Alberta.

[69]   *The Globe and Mail*, October 27, 1993.

Reprinted with permission, Allan King, *The Ottawa Citizen*.

As a leader, Campbell was seen to be outspoken, inexperienced, naïve and overconfident. She began the campaign by saying that unemployment would continue to be high to the end of the century; she could not explain her deficit projections; she blamed her problems on "bad government bookkeeping"; and she said that the election was the "worst possible time" to debate social programs, indicating that she had a secret agenda. She was advised by Allen Gregg, pollster for the Conservatives to concentrate on personality over policies.[70] Unfortunately, Campbell's personality could not live up to the billing. When it became obvious that she needed policies, a "Blue Book" outlining them was hastily prepared, but it did not stand up to scrutiny.

Campbell compared badly with Mulroney on the hustings. Her team was disorganized — it was still hiring key players during the campaign, and communications were poor — and workers complained they weren't sure who was in charge. In Québec the Campbell and Jean Charest forces did not mesh and by the end of the campaign squabbled openly. Donors fled, and the Conservative campaign that had begun with so much promise ended over $7 million in debt.

The Liberals under Jean Chrétien's leadership, by contrast, ran a flawless campaign. They were tagged by their opponents as a "tax-and-spend," patronage-hungry, Québec-focused party led by "yesterday's man." In reply they picked a simple message — the theme of "Jobs" — and stuck to it. They played to their leader's strength, which was his expe-

---

[70] *The Globe and Mail*, October 30, 1993

rience and which contrasted favourably with his inexperienced opponents. John Rae, who directed the campaign, made the decision to bring out the party's "Red Book" of policies early in the campaign.[71] The heart of the policy book was a two-year program of spending on infrastructure to create thousands of new jobs annually, replace the GST, cancel the $5.8 billion helicopter program and make other defence cuts, and reduce the deficit to 3 percent of Gross Domestic Product by the end of the term.

"MEDIA-OCRACY" IN THE CAMPAIGN

The 1993 election demonstrated once again the key role of the media and opinion polls in the process of modern Canadian elections. On the basis that campaign events have little impact unless they are noticed by the media, campaign strategists tried to harness the media and employ it for their own purposes. Since paid ads and free time broadcasts are strictly regulated, party strategists focused on the "earned media" of news broadcasts. The introduction of CBC's all-news network *Newsworld*, which runs regular television news reports, compressed the news cycle of the election. This required some timing adjustments for the campaign managers. PC advisor John Tory commented, "before, you'd wait to react until 3 in the afternoon on something that happened at 10, because you knew if you were looking at TV it wasn't going to get on until 6 anyway."[72] The CBC network also allowed greater coverage of regional and minor parties than was possible in any previous election.

As usual, the media focused public attention on the leaders throughout the campaign. Did they act as a conduit or as a filter? Did they convey reality or did they distort? Observers generally agreed that Campbell was more closely criticized than Chrétien. The state of the Progressive Conservative campaign and whether Ms. Campbell would be able to hang on to her job as Prime Minister dominated the coverage.

The media had been part of the "elite" rejected by the Charlottetown referendum. Despite earnest pre-election vows to concentrate less on opinion polls and more on issues this time, the news agencies, particularly television, fell back on their traditional patterns of concentrating on the "horse race" and party strategy and personalities rather than on ideas. There was also a visible attempt to give "power to the people," with different election features from town halls to CBC's bizarre "down-home" coverage that plotted, graphed and analyzed statistically meaningless reactions of a handful of people to the political rhetoric of the week.

There were two leadership debates, one in each official language. It normally takes a few days for a consensus to form about who won, so following the debate teams of party "spin-doctors" cast their leaders' performances in the best possible light. In the 1988 debates, the immediate surge in John Turner's competence ratings occurred first among those who actually had watched the debates. Within a week, people who had not seen the debate were showered with media reports and opinion polls until they shared the same views. The scenario was repeated in 1993.[73]

As usual, the media tended to focus on who won or lost and whether there was a "defining moment" rather than on the issues debated. Campbell was judged to have functioned

---

[71] *Creating Opportunity: The Liberal Plan for Canada* (Ottawa: the Liberal Party of Canada, 1993).

[72] *The Globe and Mail*, Sept. 10, 1993.

[73] *The Globe and Mail*, October 5, 1993

reasonably well in the French debate, but not adequately enough to challenge Lucien Bouchard, leader of the Bloc Québécois. While the Conservative and Bloc leaders engaged in acrimonious exchanges, Jean Chrétien stood above the fray and looked Prime Ministerial. Preston Manning, being unilingual, was unable to take part except for brief, prepared statements.

The English debate had no clear winner, but Campbell aroused some concern in Québec by saying that "Only Quebeckers will get sucked in" by Bouchard. Bouchard again scored points by forcing her to look evasive when he asked about the real size of the federal government's deficit.

Clearly the biggest winners for both debates were Lucien Bouchard and Reform leader Preston Manning who had access to national audiences merely by being in the debate. They were part of the proceedings by virtue of the fact that they had representation in Parliament when the election was called. Another television debate was held later for the leaders of the parties that were not qualified to enter the main events.

The impact of party advertising was relatively insignificant in this election except for a negative ad that the Tories used in the last week of the campaign. In 1988 negative adds had worked to halt what appeared to be a surge by John Turner in the polls. This time they backfired. Ads concentrating on Chrétien's physical disfigurement inspired public outrage and Campbell was forced to pull them off the air and apologize.

There were only half as many editorial polls disseminated as in 1988, but they provided a clear expression of public opinion until they were banned at midnight the Friday before the election. There was every indication that they encouraged **strategic voting** — votes for second choices designed to defeat one's last choice. An Angus Reid Poll published on October 19 showed that Liberal support outside Québec would rise by 5 percent if the Bloc seemed on the verge of sweeping the Québec seats.[74] Another Reid poll indicated that 1 in 5 voters would vote strategically.[75] Some wanted to help elect a minority or majority Liberal government. Many NDP supporters moved to the Liberals — not because they lost faith in the NDP, but because they were afraid the Reform Party would "end up dictating the agenda" if the Liberals won only a minority.[76] By the end of the campaign the Tories were apparently mortally wounded, and some protest voters were able to turn back to the Liberals as the only viable national alternative.

ISSUES IN THE CAMPAIGN

No single issue in the 1993 campaign had the compelling importance that free trade policy had in 1988. In 1993, free trade and the NAFTA were barely mentioned; the general economy was by far the biggest issue, even in Québec. With the country coming out of a recession and with unemployment levels stubbornly high, the Liberals managed to capture the initiative on the need to create jobs. (See Figure 11.3.) Chrétien committed the Liberals to policies generating 300 000 jobs a year in each year of a Liberal mandate. Much of the money was to come from canceling the contract for EH-101 helicopters. Polls showed 60 percent of the public opposed buying the helicopters at a time of high unemployment.[77]

---

74 *The Globe and Mail,* October 19, 1993

75 *The Ottawa Citizen,* October 22, 1993.

76 Angus Reid Poll, *The Globe and Mail,* October 19, 1993

77 *The Globe and Mail,* September 3, 1993.

The other major issue was the deficit. (See Figure 11.4.) The Conservatives and Liberals both made projections for cutting the deficit of $35.5 billion in 1992–93 (after the election the deficit was found to be over $40 billion). The Conservatives promised to cut it to $8 billion in four years; the Liberals said they would reduce it over the next five years to 3 percent of Gross Domestic Product. The deficit was the most important issue for the Reform Party, which promised to eliminate it completely in three years by combining $19 billion in spending cuts with $16.5 billion in increased tax revenue from improved economic activity.

FIGURE 11.3   AVERAGE UNEMPLOYMENT IN CANADA, 1966–93

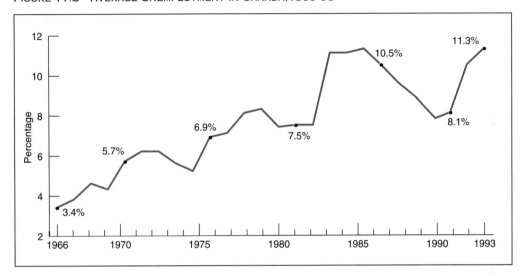

Source: Statistics Canada. Reproduced by authority of the Minister responsible for Statistics Canada 1993.

As in 1988, the NDP had difficulty finding and settling upon a winning issue. In the early stages of the campaign it flogged two dead issues — the GST and free trade. It ignored the deficit and produced a comprehensive job plan that made economists cringe. In the latter stages of the campaign, they switched the emphasis to the more viable policy of maintaining medicare.

Reform and the Bloc brought some new issues to the campaign, concerns that had been dismissed by the other parties. Preston Manning positioned himself as the spokesman for English-speaking Canada in its relations with Québec. He also raised the issue of immigration, saying that the number of immigrants Canada accepts should be tied to how many the economy can absorb.

As usual, many important issues were ignored, including foreign policy, internal trade barriers and national educational standards.

THE OUTCOME

The Liberals, who had already held power for 65 of the last 100 years, swept to a majority government, making Jean Chrétien the 20th Prime Minister. The turnout was lower than average, only 71 percent nationally. However, the results created a massive turnover of seats: of the 295 MPs elected, over 200 were newcomers to the House. There was a record

FIGURE 11.4   GROWING DEFICIT 1987–94

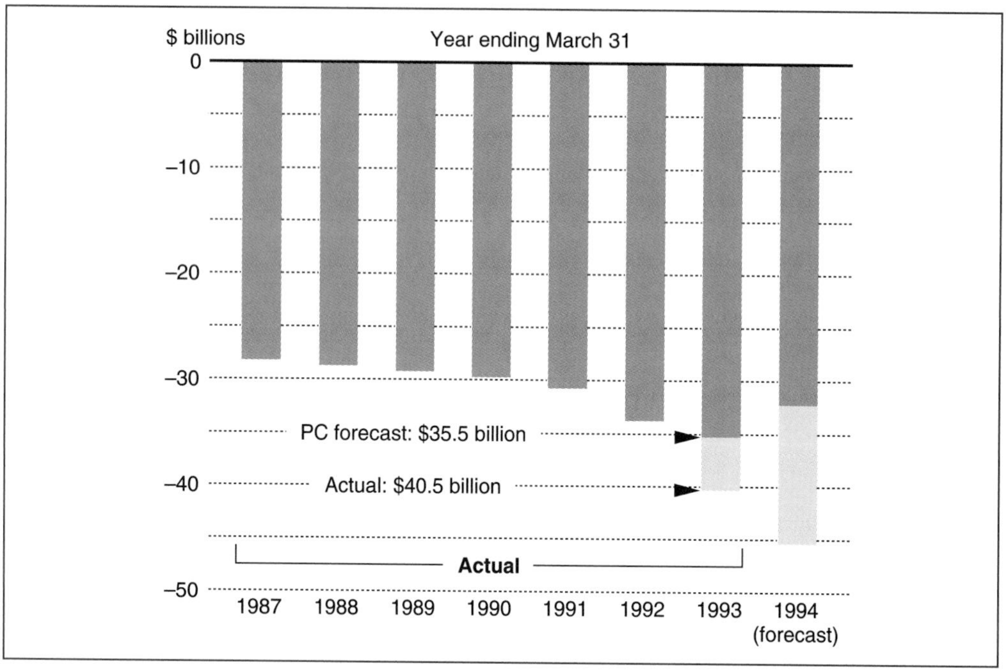

Source: Department of Finance, Canadian Press. Reported in *The Globe and Mail* (November 30, 1993.)

number of women elected, 53 compared to 39 in 1988. Proportionally, women still represent only 18 percent of the House, but the trend continues the considerable and steady gains made since 1980. (See Figure 11.5.)

The Liberal share of the popular vote was 41 percent with representation from all provinces and Northwest Territories contributing to their 177 seats. They won 31 of 32 Atlantic seats and 98 of 99 in Ontario. And, they had their best results in the West for many elections: no federal Liberal had been elected in Alberta since 1968 — now they had 4. They had an embarrassment of riches in terms of talent and background, a mix of experienced MPs and former ministers and new talent, a wide range of ethnic representation and an ability to field ministers from every region. (See Tables 11.8, 11.9, and 11.10.)

The Conservative Party was dealt a stunning defeat, winning only two seats in Parliament with 16 percent of the popular vote. It was a dramatic repudiation of the party and its record. Leader Kim Campbell lost her seat after only four months as Canada's first female Prime Minister. With just four years of experience as a party member, with no party roots or debts to call in she became an unpaid, interim caretaker leader. Within two months she retired and was replaced as interim leader by Jean Charest. The election put the party in financial ruin, and with no official status in the House it will be extremely difficult for it to recover.

The NDP faced its worst electoral defeat in history. Its predecessor, the CCF, had been reduced to 8 seats in 1958, but shortly afterward it dissolved and a new party took its place.

The Reform Party went into its second national election with only one seat, which it had won in a by-election. It emerged from the campaign with greatly increased credibility and almost enough seats to be the Official Opposition. It won 52 seats altogether. In its western base it won 51 seats: 22 in Alberta, 24 in British Columbia, 4 in Saskatchewan and one in

FIGURE 11.5 WOMEN IN THE HOUSE OF COMMONS, 1921–1993

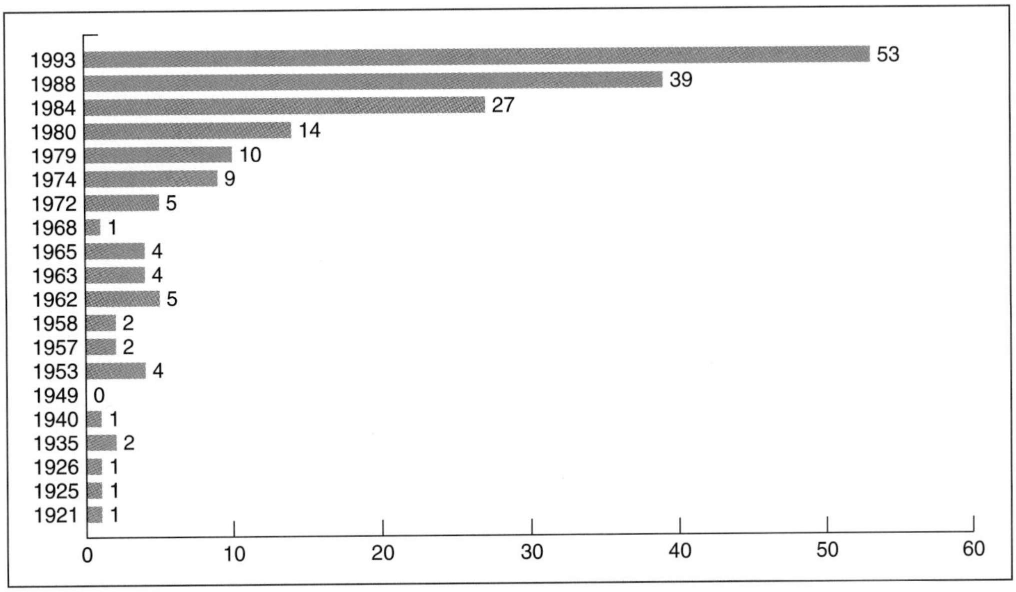

Source: Robert Cross, *The Ottawa Citizen*.

Manitoba. Outside of western Canada it won only one seat in Ontario, although it finished in second place in 56 Ontario ridings.

The Bloc Québécois went into its first election with 8 MPs. It came out as the party with the second highest number of seats in the House of Commons and a healthy majority in Québec. It won 54 seats and 14 percent of the popular vote in Canada, 49 percent in Québec where it ran all of its candidates.

TABLE 11.8 1993 GENERAL ELECTION SEATS BY PROVINCE

Party	Total	Nfld	PEI	NS	NB	Que	Ont	Man	Sask	Alta	BC	Y	NWT
Lib	177	7	4	11	9	19	98	12	5	4	6	–	2
Bloc	54	–	–	–	–	54	–	–	–	–	–	–	–
Reform	52	–	–	–	–	–	1	1	4	22	24	–	–
NDP	9	–	–	–	–	–	–	1	5	–	2	1	–
PC	2	–	–	–	1	1	–	–	–	–	–	–	–
Ind	1	–	–	–	–	1	–	–	–	–	–	–	–
Total	295	7	4	11	10	75	99	14	14	26	32	1	2

Source: Elections Canada.

TABLE 11.9 1993 GENERAL ELECTION PERCENTAGE POPULAR VOTE BY PROVINCE

Party	Canada	Nfld	PEI	NS	NB	Que	Ont	Man	Sask	Alta	BC	Y	NWT
Lib	41.2	67.5	60.2	52.0	56.0	33.0	52.8	45.0	32.1	25.0	28.1	23.2	65.4
Bloc	13.5	–	–	–	–	49.2	–	–	–	–	–	–	–
Ref	18.7	1.0	1.0	13.3	8.5	2.7	20.1	22.4	27.3	52.1	36.3	13.1	8.4
NDP	6.9	3.6	5.2	6.8	4.9	1.6	6.0	16.6	26.6	4.1	15.6	43.4	7.7
PC	16.0	26.5	31.9	23.5	28.0	13.6	17.7	11.9	11.3	14.6	13.4	17.8	16.3
Other	3.6	1.5	1.7	4.5	2.7	2.7	3.4	4.2	2.7	4.3	6.6	2.5	2.3

Note: Provisional percentages from Elections Canada.

TABLE 11.10   1993 GENERAL ELECTION RESULTS IN CANADA'S MAJOR CITIES

	Total Seats	Vote
Toronto	23	23 Liberal
Montreal	23	13 Liberal, 10 Bloc
Vancouver	15	1 NDP, 5 Liberal, 9 Reform

ANALYSIS

The 1993 federal election was a watershed for the country — what one expert called "the domestic equivalent of the 1989 fall of the Berlin Wall in Europe."[78] Canada has entered a transitional stage of party development. The election created a fundamental realignment of parties from which the Liberals profited. Capturing 41 percent of the vote, the Liberals obtained 177 seats in the House of Commons, regained power and formed a majority government. It is the only party that can claim national status. The opposition in Parliament is fragmented and regionalized. Canada appears to be undergoing a fundamental change from a two or two-and-a-half party system toward one that is one-party dominant or multi-party.

The Conservative Party was reduced to a historic low of two seats. Early in the campaign it was clear that the coalition Mulroney had built in Québec and also in the West had collapsed. By capturing the traditional Conservative vote in western Canada, the Reform Party has an opportunity to become a new national right-wing party. In 1993, Québec, too, abandoned the Conservative Party that it had massively supported since 1984 under Brian Mulroney. However, rather than moving back to the Liberal Party, francophones in Québec gave the Liberals only token support and opted heavily for the separatist Bloc Québécois. All Liberal seats but one in Québec were captured in ridings with a high proportion of anglophones or allophones. It is not clear whether Liberal roots in the province will be strong enough to win back their former bastion of support in future elections.

The New Democratic Party, reduced from 43 seats to 9, has lost its role as third party in Parliament and will have great difficulty achieving that status again. The Conservative Party, with two seats, is now the fifth party in the House. Both the Conservatives and the NDP fell well below the numbers needed to be recognized as an official party in Parliament.[79] As we have seen, the law and parliamentary convention confer financial advantages on officially recognized parties. Extra allowances are given to the leaders, House leaders and whips of parties with 12 MPs or more. And parliamentary convention since 1969 has dictated the provision of research funds for parties with 12 or more Members in the House. As well, House procedures give prominence in debates and committees to parties with 12 MPs or more. Without official recognition, therefore, both the NDP and the Tories will have a difficult time regaining their former stature.

The Reform Party won support from disaffected Tories and Social Credit supporters. The fact that it is concentrated in British Columbia and Alberta reinforces the regional cleavage

---

[78]   Patrick J. Monahan, Osgoode Hall Law School, *The Globe and Mail*, October 11, 1993.

[79]   Funding decisions are made by the Board of Internal Economy, which oversees the operation of the House. The party rule has been bent twice before — in 1963 for the Social Credit's 11 MPs and in 1974 for 11 Créditistes.

in Canadian voting patterns. Populism and alienation are common in the West. A Depression-era mayor of Vancouver captured the mood that still pervades the province: "It's 3000 miles from Vancouver to Ottawa, but 3 million miles from Ottawa to Vancouver."[80] British Columbia has not elected a Liberal or Conservative provincial government for 40 years, and it was the first province to pass an initiative demanding the recall of MLAs. BC was, thus, fertile ground for the Reform Party — it gave Westerners a vehicle to protest against the political establishment.

True to tradition, Québec voted as a group. The Bloc's win in Québec was impressive, but was not the tidal wave its leaders had sought in order to claim they could win a provincial referendum on sovereignty. As Her Majesty's Official Opposition, the Bloc's strong voice in Ottawa gives it prestige, resources and assured media coverage. Leader Lucien Bouchard made it clear that this electoral victory was just the first of three steps the party intended to take; the second was to help the Parti Québécois win the Québec provincial election in 1994 and the third was to win a referendum on sovereignty in 1995.

In many ways the 1993 campaign was less significant than that of 1988 in determining the electoral results. In 1988 the Liberals began behind the incumbent Conservatives but came within reach of winning due in large part to John Turner's performance in the leadership debates and his forceful stand on the free trade issue. The Liberals lost ground during the final week of the campaign due to negative advertising. In 1993, however, the Conservatives were at an almost record low in the polls when Brian Mulroney resigned. When Kim Campbell was elected leader, her fresh, new image appealed to Canadians and revived the party's hopes. Exposure during the campaign convinced voters that her new face only masked the same old Conservative policies and ideas, and Conservative support on election day was close to what the polls had shown they had been when Mulroney stepped down. (See Figure 11.6.)

The Conservatives ran a poor campaign. They had no vision or deep-seated policy change to offer the country. They underestimated Manning's appeal in the West and in Ontario, and they thought Bouchard could be dealt with by Jean Charest. In 1988 there had been just one target for them to attack — John Turner. In 1993 there were several targets, and their response was scattered and ineffectual.

The NDP lost votes to Liberals and also to Reform. It collapsed even before the campaign began. Many of its good ideas had already been taken up by other governments. The Reform Party challenged existing social programs and forced the NDP to become an agent of the status quo, thus usurping its traditional role as an agent of change. The NDP was also hurt by the unpopular economic policies of the NDP government in Ontario, which had produced splits in the party ranks, and by the controversial environmental policies of the NDP government in British Columbia.

In Québec, the vote for the Bloc Québécois was remarkably similar to the vote a year earlier on the Charlottetown referendum. Of the 51 (of 75) Québec ridings that voted *non* in the referendum, all but three elected Bloc MPs in 1993 — two of the exceptions were the ridings of Jean Chrétien and Jean Charest. All but eight ridings where francophones made up more than two-thirds of the population voted Bloc, and all but 10 of these ridings voted *non* in the referendum.

This was not the first Canadian federal election in which five prominent parties contended for office: it also happened in 1935 when William Lyon Mackenzie King, the "yesterday's

---

[80] Quotation from former mayor Gerry McGeer quoted in *The Globe and Mail*, October 11, 1993.

FIGURE 11.6   CHRONOLOGY OF A CAMPAIGN: ANGUS-REID POLLS OF PARTY SUPPORT, 1993

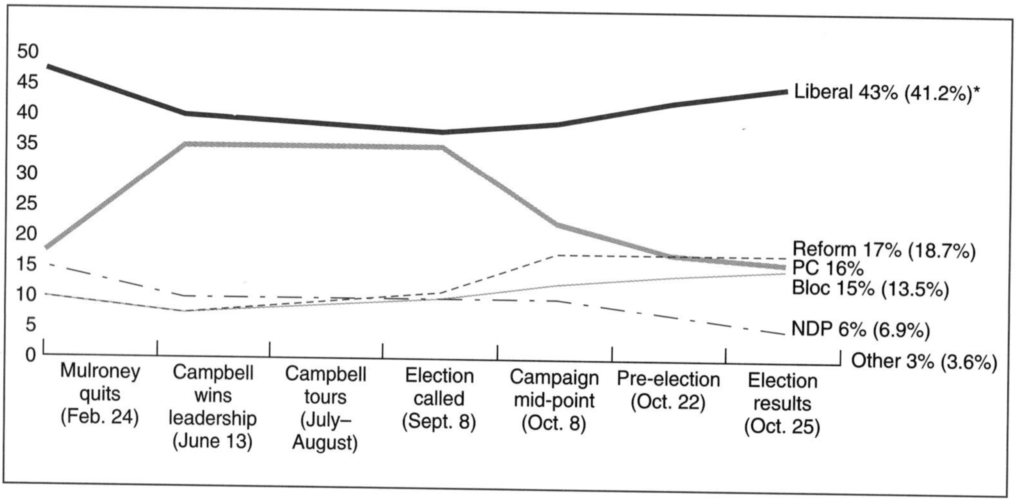

*The bracketed numbers alongside the Angus-Reid poll results show the actual results of the October 25 election.

Source: Adapted from Angus Reid polls. Reported in the Ottawa Citizen (October 26, 1993.)

man" who had been prime minister for most of the 1920s, severely defeated R.B. Bennett of the Conservatives. At that time there were two new right-wing parties, the Reconstruction Party and Social Credit, and on the left, the Co-operative Commonwealth Federation, which also ran federally for the first time. The big difference in 1993 was that the Conservatives were cut to only 2 seats, not 40, and both of the new parties did very well — almost tying for second place.

In the end, Canadians seem to have wanted a change of government more than anything else. This sentiment defeated the Conservatives and also allowed the Reform Party to fill the gap in the West and the Bloc to do the same in Québec. Clearly, the Bloc vote was not a vote for separatism. However, as Québec professor Stephan Dion remarked when asked if the vote meant Québec would separate — "No, but you never know."[81] Neither was the vote for Reform a vote to make that party the voice of "English Canada" to balance the voice of "Quebec." There is no mechanism for such a voice to exist. As the only national party, the Liberals alone can claim to speak for all of Canada.

OVERVIEW

Elections have an important role in Canadian politics. By providing a stable means of transferring government office between contesting political parties as well as an opportunity for voters to express their acceptance of or displeasure with the decisions of the government, elections legitimate the exercise of political power. Furthermore, the mobilization of voters' interest in electoral contests confers legitimacy on the political regime itself, as well as on the individual office-holders.

Through the party organizations based upon them, elections are vital in reconciling diverse interests within society. They provide a national forum for discussion and allow issues

---

[81]   At a conference on the 1993 Election in Mexico City, November 13, 1993.

Reproduced with permission, Allan King, *The Ottawa Citizen.*

to be raised and compromises to be arrived at, leading thereby to a measure of consensus. However, there are grounds to question the performance of this role in Canada. The results of Canadian general elections often appear to be more divisive than consensual, pitting region against region and eroding the legitimacy of the "national" government. This concern has motivated calls for electoral reform. Yet elections continue to generate support for Canada's political system. It may even be that the viability of elections themselves in the long run may be more significant than the actual partisan results.

Elections also have an impact on government decision-making. By determining which party will form the government, elections influence the choices made by policy-makers. Elections also help to establish the broad policy parameters of political parties and the government. Issues perceived as important during the campaign must usually be addressed by the government; otherwise, it risks defeat in the next general election. Defeated parties may also adjust their behaviour and policy positions both to prevent repetition of their mistakes and to broaden their support. To this extent, therefore, elections help provide politicians with a reference for guiding their actions.

In summary, the main importance of elections in Canada stems from the legitimacy they confer on government and its actions. Because of the democratic and consistent nature of elections, most voters perceive that the government is representative of their interests. Although few would express unqualified support of government, most Canadians are committed to Canada's basic electoral structures and their results.

The 1993 General Election created a dramatic realignment of Canada's party system. For the first time, a separatist party moved into the heart of the federal Parliament as Official Opposition. It is not yet clear whether the regional fragmentation that brought five parties to the House of Commons in this election will become a permanent feature of politics in Canada.

SELECTED BIBLIOGRAPHY

Archer, Keith, *Political Choices and Electoral Consequences* (Montréal: McGill Queen's University Press, 1990).

Bashevkin, Sylvia, ed. *Canadian Political Behaviour* (Toronto: Methuen).

Blake, Donald E., *Two Political Worlds: Parties and Voting in British Columbia* (Vancouver, B.C.: University of British Columbia Press, 1985).

Bognador, Vernon and David Butler, eds., *Democracy and Elections: Electoral Systems and their Political Consequences* (Cambridge, Eng.: Cambridge University Press, 1983).

Boyer, J. Patrick, *Political Rights and the Legal Framework of Elections in Canada* (Toronto: Butterworths, 1982).

————, *The People's Mandate: Referendums and a More Democratic Canada* (Toronto: Dundurn, 1992).

Brook, Tom,*Getting Elected in Canada* (Stratford: Mercury Press, 1991).

Butler, David, Howard R. Penniman and Austin Ranney, eds., *Democracy at the Polls: A Comparative Study of Competitive National Elections* (Washington: American Enterprise Institute for Public Policy Research, 1981).

Butler, David and Austin Ranney, eds., *Referendums: A Comparative Study of Practice and Theory* (Washington: American Enterprise Institute for Public Policy Research, 1978).

Caplan, Gerald, Michael Kirby and Hugh Segal, *Election: The Issues, the Strategies, the Aftermath* (Scarborough, Ont.: Prentice-Hall, 1989).

Clarke, Harold D., Jane Jensen, Lawrence LeDuc and Jon H. Pammett, *Absent Mandate: The Politics of Discontent in Canada* (Toronto: Gage, 1984).

————, *Political Choice in Canada* (Toronto: McGraw-Hill Ryerson, 1979).

Dalton, Russell J., Scott C. Flanagan and Paul Allen Beck, eds., *Electoral Change in Advanced Industrial Democracies: Realignment or Dealignment?* (Princeton, N.J.: Princeton University Press, 1984).

Elections Canada, *Annual Reports of the Chief Electoral Officer* (various years).

Elton, David and Roger Gibbins, *Electoral Reform: The Time is Pressing, The Need is Now* (Calgary: Canada West Foundation, 1980).

Fraser, Graham, *Playing for Keeps: The Making of the Prime Minister, 1988* (Toronto: McClelland and Stewart, 1989).

Frizzel, Alan and Anthony Westell, *The Canadian General Election of 1984: Politicians, Parties, Press and Polls* (Ottawa: Carleton University Press, 1985).

Frizzel, Alan, Jon H. Pammett and Anthony Westell, *The Canadian General Election of 1988* (Ottawa: Carleton University Press, 1988).

Goldfarb, Martin and Thomas Axworthy, *Marching to a Different Drummer* (Don Mills, Ont.: Stoddart, 1988).

Gollner, Andrew B. and Daniel Salee, eds., *Canada Under Mulroney* (Montréal: Véhicule Press, 1988).

Irvine, William P., *Does Canada Need a New Electoral System?* (Kingston, Ont.: Queen's University Institute of Intergovernmental Relations, 1979).

Johnston, J. Paul and Harvey Pasis, *Representation and Electoral Systems* (Scarborough, Ont.: Prentice-Hall, 1990).

Johnston, Richard, André Blais, Henry E. Brady and Jean Crête, *Letting the People Decide* (Montréal: McGill-Queen's University Press, 1992).

Lakeman, Enid, *How Democracies Vote: A Study of Electoral Systems*, 4th rev. ed. (London: Faber and Faber, 1974).

Meisel, John, *Working Papers on Canadian Politics*, 2nd enlarged ed. (Montréal: McGill-Queen's University Press, 1975).

Penniman, Howard R., ed., *Canada at the Polls 1979 and 1980: A Study of the General Elections* (Washington: American Enterprise Institute for Public Policy Research, 1981).

————, ed., *Canada at the Polls, 1984* (Durham, N.C.: Duke University Press, 1988).

Qualter, T.H. *The Election Process in Canada* (Toronto: McGraw-Hill Ryerson, 1970).

Rae, Douglas W., *The Political Consequences of Electoral Laws* (New Haven, Conn.: Yale University Press, 1967).

Royal Commision on Electoral Reform and Party Financing, *Final Report*, vol. 1 *Reforming Electoral Democracy* (Ottawa; Supply and Services, 1992).

Soderlund, Walter C., Walter I. Romanow, E. Donald Briggs and Ronald H. Wagenburg, *Media and Elections in Canada* (Toronto: Holt, Rinehart and Winston of Canada, 1984).

Wearing, Joseph, ed., *The Ballot and Its Message* (Toronto: Copp Clark Pitman, 1991).

INTEREST GROUPS AND POLITICAL MOVEMENTS

INFLUENCING PUBLIC POLICY

Canadians are organized in numerous and novel ways. There are organizations to represent business, labour, loyalists, separatists, nature lovers and economic developers. Practically everyone belongs to some organization or other. Large or small, these groups are active in pressing their needs, principles and demands on other Canadians. When such groups act in the political arena without becoming full-fledged political parties they are usually called interest groups or, more pejoratively, pressure groups.

Sometimes broad collective identities form that are neither organized interest groups nor political parties. They too seek social change, but they are based on ideas and altruism rather than organizational form. These are movements. Movements may subsume interest groups, and both interest groups and movements may transform themselves into political parties. Movements are tied to ideologies that seek broad social change — such as nationalism, the women's movement, the environmental movement and gay or other minority rights movements. As their goals are universal in spirit, movements may flow across state boundaries. Interest groups are more particularistic and tend to reside inside of specific countries.

Groups are an important element in the political life of all modern societies, but their form and importance varies from one country to the next. In Japan, for example, the *chingodan*, a group of rural petitioners, often bearing gifts of fruit, traditionally visits Tokyo when the national budget is being prepared in order to present their arguments to government officials and politicians. In some communist countries, on the other hand, where citizens have few legal rights to organize associations, unauthorized interest groups attempt to influence the government by means of dramatic events such as strikes intended to attract international publicity, such as happened at China's Tiananmen Square. These cases illustrate that the structure and behaviour of interest groups and movements are closely related to the political system in which they operate.

In Canada, interest groups organize legally to petition and cajole the government. They operate in and help to mould the federal political system. They are ubiquitous, representing interests as varied as business (Canadian Manufacturers Association), labour (Canadian Labour Congress), agriculture (Canadian Federation of Agriculture), professionals (Canadian Medical Association), consumers (Consumers' Association of Canada), women (National Action Committee on the Status of Women), religious groups (Canadian Council of Churches), ethnic groups (Canadian Jewish Congress) and even public interests such as a clean environment (Greenpeace or Energy Probe) and foreign affairs and development issues (Canadian Action for Nicaragua or Tools for Peace). Canadians are very familiar with organizations such as the Brewer's Association of Canada, which attempts to prevent the import of inexpensive foreign beer, and the Canadian Federation of Students, which demands lower fees for university students.

Thousands of individuals work in Ottawa representing these multifarious interests. Some organizations are powerful; others are practically insignificant. Some interest groups employ experts such as professional lobbyists, public relations firms or highly paid lawyers to promote their interests. Others occasionally send their local officials or chief executive officers to argue their cases. Still others attempt to attract public attention through the media. What they all have in common is the desire to influence government policy, legislation, regulation or expenditures.

Much of the public is dismayed by the power of these interest groups and their shadowy connections with patronage and pork-barrel activities by the government. Citizens' groups complain about big business; businesspeople admonish the special pleading of narrowly formed organizations. Some skeptics complain that interest groups are associated with unethical means such as bribery or blackmail. Many even harbour the suspicion that they are "evil because they conflict with the fundamental attributes of democracy."[1] Political scientists, on the other hand, usually counter that such groups are inevitable and important for the political process.

This chapter is concerned initially with descriptions and explanations of interest groups and their activities (especially lobbying) and then turns to discuss political movements and in particular the women's movement as a case study of movements in action.

WHAT ARE INTEREST GROUPS?

There are many sociological meanings to the word "group." But, in this volume, "interest groups" are distinguished from others by their orientation to the political system.[2] We are not interested in groups with no relation to the political system or with no organizational element. Thus, an **interest group** is here defined as an "organized association which engages in activity relative to governmental decisions."[3]

This is a very wide definition that includes many types of groups, from those that are relatively transient and issue-oriented to others that are institutionalized, with many general as well as specific interests. The common denominator is, as the definition states, that they are non-publicly accountable organizations that attempt to further their common interest by affecting public policy.

---

[1]   Harmon Zeigler, *Interest Groups in American Society* (Englewood Cliffs, N.J., Prentice-Hall, 1964), p. 33.

[2]   Mildred A. Schwartz, "The Group Basis of Politics," in John A. Redekop, ed., *Approaches to Canadian Politics*, 2nd ed. (Scarborough, Ont.: Prentice-Hall Canada, 1983), p. 316.

[3]   Robert H. Salisbury, "Interest Groups," in Fred I. Greenstein and Nelson W. Polsby, eds., *Handbook of Political Science*, vol. 4 (Reading, Mass.: Addison-Wesley, 1975), p. 175.

Paul Pross identifies four prime characteristics of interest groups.[4] First, they have a formal structure of organization that gives them continuity. Organization is essential to allow them to determine their objectives and strategies for action. Second, interest groups are able to articulate and aggregate interests. Third, they attempt to act within the political system to influence policy outputs. Fourth, they try to influence power rather than exercise the responsibility of government themselves.

Mobs are not interest groups because they lack organizational structure. Political parties too are excluded, although the first three of these criteria apply equally to them. However, parties have different goals than interest groups; they seek political power by having their candidates elected to government office, whereas interest groups try to influence political parties and government officials toward certain policies rather than enacting these policies themselves. Interest groups can, and often do, try to win the support of all parties. The similarities between parties and groups have led to different opinions about how the two are related. Some analysts, for example, believe that a rise in interest group power has been at least partially responsible for the decline in the role of political parties. In countries like Canada, where traditionally there have been two dominant political parties, the distinction between parties and interest groups is fairly evident. However, in countries where many small parties compete, minority parties often represent the very narrow interests of one group, and then the distinction becomes less clear. The Bloc Québécois is a political party, but it represents only the interest of one group — Québec nationalists.

ANALYZING INTEREST GROUPS

The study of interest groups by political scientists grew out of a sociological revolt against the narrow confines of formal institutional analysis. Politics came to be viewed as something associated with, but much larger than, "government."

Of seminal importance to the theory of politics that centred around the interaction of social groups was the work of A.F. Bentley. His *Process of Government*, published in 1908, cited the "group" as the basic unit of all political life.[5] Rejecting the concept of the state as "no factor in our investigation" and the idea of sovereignty as a "piteous, threadbare joke,"[6] Bentley put the case for identifying the group as the fundamental point of departure for the study of politics:

> *All phenomena of government are phenomena of groups pressing one another, forming one another, and pushing out new groups and group representatives (the organs or agencies of government) to mediate the adjustments. It is only as we isolate these group activities, determine their representative values, and get the whole process stated in terms of them, that we approach a satisfactory knowledge of government.*[7]

While Bentley displayed a disinclination to indulge in precise definitional rigour, even a cursory review of monographic group studies from the 1930s onward serves to illustrate

---

4 A. Paul Pross, "Pressure Groups: Adaptive Instruments of Political Communication," in A. Paul Pross, ed., *Pressure Group Behaviour in Canadian Politics* (Toronto: McGraw-Hill Ryerson, 1975).

5 Arthur F. Bentley, *The Process of Government, A Study of Social Pressures,* edited by Peter H. Odegard (Cambridge: Harvard University Press, 1967).

6 Ibid., pp. 263–64.

7 Ibid., p. 269.

the power of his influence. These works were in fundamental agreement with Ambrose Bierce's definition of politics as "a strife of interest masquerading as a contest of principles."[8] Earl Latham's research on the evolution of American anti-trust legislation, for example, began with the assertion that organized groups, as "structures of power," are the vehicles through which social values cherished by individuals are realized, and concluded that one of the ways in which politics can be properly understood is as "the struggle of groups to write in their favor the rules by which the community is governed."[9]

It is indicative of Bentley's influence on American political science that works such as Latham's, published in the early 1950s, actually represent comparatively late research on interest group activity. As early as the late 1920s, books such as Peter Odegard's on the prohibition movement and Pendelton Herring's on interest group representation in Congress laid the foundation of a rich body of interest group literature very much within the Bentley tradition.[10] The work of greatest theoretical importance to the contemporary study of interest groups, however, is unquestionably David Truman's monumental work on interests and public opinion, *The Governmental Process.*[11] For Truman, the fundamental justification for emphasizing groups as basic social units lay in "the uniformities of behaviour produced through them."[12] Uniformity of behaviour, he pointed out, does not deny the existence of individual will; on the contrary, the nature and frequency of interaction between individuals determine the existence or nonexistence of a group:

> If a motorist stops along a highway to ask directions of a farmer, the two are interacting, but they can hardly be said to constitute a group except in the most casual sense. If, however, the motorist belongs to an automobile club the staff of which he and the other members more or less regularly resort to for route information, then staff and members can be designated as a group.[13]

Truman's primary concern was the functioning of groups in the political process. He arrived at an unusually broad definition of interest group as "any group that, on the basis of one or more shared attitudes, makes certain claims upon other groups in society for the establishment, maintenance, or enhancement of forms of behaviour that are implied by the shared attitudes."[14] At the same time, he inveighed against the popular inclination to credit interest groups with inherently sinister intentions — an inclination typified by the use of terms such as "vested interest," "special interest" and "pressure group."

Indeed, the concept of interest group as found in Bentley, Truman and their theoretical disciples can be said to be an indispensable component of later pluralist theories.[15] To pluralist scholars interest groups represent highly functional cogs in the variegated machinery

---

8   Ambrose Bierce, *The Devil's Dictionary* (New York: Dover, 1958), p. 101.

9   Earl Latham, *The Group Basis of Politics: A Study in Basing-Point Legislation* (Ithaca: Cornell University Press, 1952), p. 1, p. 12, p. 209.

10 Peter H. Odegard, *Pressure Politics: The Story of the Anti-Saloon League* (New York: Columbia University Press, 1928); E. Pendelton Herring, *Group Representation Before Congress* (Washington: Brookings Institute, 1929).

11 David B. Truman, *The Governmental Process: Political Interests and Public Opinion* (New York: Alfred A. Knopf, 1951).

12 Ibid., p. 23.

13 Ibid., p. 24.

14 Ibid., p. 33.

15 See Robert A. Dahl, *Who Governs? Democracy and Power in an American City* (New Haven: Yale University Press, 1961) and *Polyarchy: Participation and Opposition* (New Haven: Yale University Press, 1971).

of the participatory democratic process. As aggregators and articulators of the needs of their constituent membership, interest groups serve to place issues on the political agenda of society, pre-digest the disparate views of individual members and formulate coherent demands for insertion into the legislative process.[16] (See Chapter 13.)

Yet no matter how political scientists have come to evaluate the role of interest groups in contemporary politics, most have found it necessary to begin with a definition of "interest group" that is more discriminating than the one offered by Truman. We have defined interest group as an "organized association which engages in activity relative to government decisions."[17] **Lobbying** is activity aimed at securing favourable policy decisions or the appointment of specific government personnel. It is the narrow political activity of an interest group thus defined.

Political science has identified several contributions of interest groups to liberal democratic politics. Interest groups are a major source of mediation between the government and the individual, articulating aggregated opinions and protecting the individual from undue control by the state. They provide a mechanism for political representation that supplements the electoral process, assisting the political system by marshalling support for issues and providing ideas for public policy. Interest groups allow the political process to be more responsive than the electoral process to social and economic differences in society.[18] Such groups also feed the government valuable information, both facts and opinion, that can be used to help formulate policies and test policy proposals. This circular process of communication provides a valuable link between citizens and public policy by helping to keep the government in touch with shifts of opinion in society.

Groups also supplement government agencies: bureaucrats delegate administrative responsibilities to certain groups. For example, the Canadian Medical Association actually regulates its own professional activity. This largely unpaid service can be an enormous assistance to the government bureaucracy. As well, professional groups indirectly help the civil service to disseminate information by publishing explanations of government policy in their journals.

Finally, interest groups have valuable internal functions. Membership in a group offers benefits won through communication with government such as tax incentives or other legislation. Of course, not only the membership at large benefits from the organization; there are also career rewards for those who hold leadership positions within subgroups. For example, David Kwavnick has shown that the Québec-based Confederation of National Trade Unions' "leadership risked and ultimately sacrificed the most vital interests of the Lapalme drivers in a dispute which ultimately concerned only those leaders' ambitions for organizational aggrandizement."[19]

---

[16] See David Easton, *The Political System: An Inquiry into the State of Political Science* (New York: Alfred A. Knopf, 1953); David Easton, "An Approach to the Analysis of Political Systems," *World Politics*, vol. 9, no. 3 (April 1957), pp. 383–400; Gabriel A. Almond and G. Bingham Powell Jr., *Comparative Politics: A Developmental Approach* (Boston: Little, Brown, 1966).

[17] This is the definition offered by Robert H. Salisbury in Greenstein and Polsby, *Handbook of Political Science*.

[18] Adapted from a list by Amitai Etzioni, "Making Interest Groups Work for the Public," *Public Opinion*, vol. 5, no. 4 (Aug./Sept. 1982), pp. 53–5.

[19] David Kwavnick, "Pressure Group Demands and Organizational Objectives: The CNTU, the Lapalme Affair and National Bargaining Units," *CJPS*, vol. VI, no. 4 (December 1973), p. 583. For a perceptive analysis of the broader question raised here, see David Kwavnick, *Organized Labour and Pressure Group Politics; The Canadian Labour Congress: 1956–1968* (Montréal: McGill-Queen's University Press, 1972).

THE UNIVERSE OF CANADIAN INTEREST GROUPS

Interest groups in Canada reflect a wide range of issues and concerns. The number and variety of groups is immense and has not been fully catalogued. The *Associations Canada* directory lists several thousand organizations. In Ottawa alone there are well over 300 trade and professional organizations. It has been estimated that these groups, representing only the tip of a giant iceberg, employ several thousand staff to improve "public relations" with the government.

Few individual corporations can afford to have full-time employees in Ottawa. Instead, their interests are "protected" by their public relations departments and chief executive officers. According to one survey, 27 percent of chief executive officers had been before a parliamentary committee at least once; 33 percent had direct regular contact with the government; 29 percent were on a government board or in an advisory group; and 42 percent had made a personal representation to the government.[20]

If all these types of activities were summed one would obtain a complete list of the interest group universe. Doing this would be so difficult and the results so transitory, however, that political scientists have attempted to avoid the problem of tabulation by classifying the types of interest groups instead.

CLASSIFICATION OF INTEREST GROUPS

Two typologies of interest groups have had lasting acceptance in Canadian political science. Engelmann and Schwartz divide interest groups into economic and non-economic categories, then subdivide the first into agriculture, labour and business groups. The non-economic category is further subdivided into nine subtypes.[21] Such distinctions, based on the primary basis of affiliation for their members, help to explain the basic differences in origin, activities and goals of the groups. This typology was used by others, for example, by W. Blair Dimock and later by Elizabeth Riddell-Dixon to discuss the impact of groups on Canadian foreign policy.[22]

The economic/non-economic distinction, however, does not convey any information about the activities or relative importance of the various groups. There is a wide disparity in their powers. They range from relatively transient issue-oriented groups to others that are well-established and assert a strong influence on political and economic life. They differ in terms of structure, resources, tactics and goals. These differences seem to affect the success or failure of groups in reaching their goals.

Paul Pross has addressed this omission in the most satisfactory categorization of Canadian interest groups to date.[23] His typology is designed to relate the groups to one another and

---

[20] James Gillies, *Why Business Fails* (Montréal: IRPP, 1981). On business and politics, see Robert J. Jackson, "Politics and Business: Partners and Antagonists," in Rinus Van Schendelen and Robert J. Jackson, eds., *The Politicization of Business in Western Europe* (London: Croom Helm, 1986).

[21] F.C. Engelmann and M.A. Schwartz, *Political Parties and the Canadian Social Structure*, 2nd ed. (Scarborough, Ont.: Prentice-Hall Canada, 1975).

[22] W. Blair Dimock, "The Involvement and Influence of Domestic Interest Groups in Canadian Foreign Policy Making" (M.A. Dissertation, Carleton University, 1980); and Elizabeth Riddell-Dixon, *The Domestic Mosaic: Domestic Groups and Canadian Foreign Policy* (Toronto: CIIA, 1985).

[23] Pross, "Pressure Groups," pp. 9–18. See also, by the same author, *Group Policy and Public Policy* (Toronto: Oxford University Press, 1986).

to the policy system at large. Groups are classified as institutionalized, issue-oriented, fledgling, or mature; each is then categorized according to its objectives, organizational features and levels of communication with government. Of course, the distinction between the categories is not clear-cut, and any one group may not conform exactly to this pattern.

Institutionalized groups are relatively well-structured and enduring. In Pross's definition they have five main characteristics: organizational continuity and cohesion; exclusive knowledge of the appropriate sectors of government and their clients; stable membership; operational objectives that are clear and concrete; and organizational imperatives on which the credibility of the organization is based that generally are more important than any particular objective. At the opposite extreme of institutionalized interest groups are **issue-oriented** groups. Their organizational continuity and cohesion are weak, their knowledge of government poor and their membership fluid. They also have trouble formulating and adhering to long-range objectives, and maintain a low regard for their own organizational mechanisms. What issue-oriented groups lack in size and organization they make up for in flexibility; they can be excellent vehicles for generating immediate public action on specific issues. They are little constrained by fear of disturbing their relationship with government officials. Good examples were some of the early environmental groups and peace organizations in Canada that were short-lived but very active publicly. The **fledgling** and **mature** groups fall, in that order of organization, between these two extremes.

CANADIAN GROUPS: A CATALOGUE

In order that readers become aware of the main groups and lobbyists who participate in the political area, we summarize here the activities of some of the largest and most active. It is not an exhaustive list but does indicate the multiplicity of groups in Canada. Because of the federal political structure of the country, most of the major interest groups have federated organizations. Interests in the economic sphere, for example, are regulated by both federal and provincial governments; as a result, groups representing the various agriculture, labour and business interests may require federated organizations with bureaucracies in Ottawa and the provincial capitals. It should also be noted that while the majority of interest groups are privately funded, a number of them are financed by government.

BUSINESS

Business groups are especially active in political persuasion. The economic viability of the businesses they represent is often directly dependent on government policies and contracts. Large organizations like the Canadian Manufacturers Association and the Canadian Trucking Association retain offices in the national capital, while others send public relations officers on regular or irregular visits to Ottawa.

The largest business association in Canada is the Canadian Chamber of Commerce representing some 500 local chambers and boards of trade. While its headquarters is in Montréal, its president is constantly in Ottawa representing the business community that funds it. Another large organization that aims at influencing government policy in such fields as corporate regulation and taxation is the Canadian Manufacturers Association. It represents about 80 percent of Canadian manufacturing and is funded by this corporate membership. Yet another organization, the Business Council on National Issues (BCNI), represents the executives of 150 of the largest firms in the country.

Business interests in domestic affairs are also defended and promoted by associations representing particular sectors. These include the Canadian Industries Association, which represents manufacturing companies, and the Canadian Nuclear Association, representing companies and organizations interested in the development of nuclear energy. The interests of manufacturing groups can often be recognized by their names: examples are the Automobile Industries Association, the Canadian Chemical Producers Association, the Mining Association of Canada, the Canadian Pulp and Paper Association, and even the Confectionery Manufacturers' Association and the Shoe Manufacturers' Association.

The petroleum industry is represented by the huge Canadian Petroleum Association, which has member companies involved in the exploration and production of oil and gas, as well as by the far smaller Independent Petroleum Association.

The various financial interests are also well organized. The Canadian Life and Health Insurance Association represents all companies in the insurance business. The Canadian Bankers' Association represents all banks. Small business is centralized as an interest group by the Canadian Federation of Independent Business, which consists of private enterprises.

Business groups also try to influence government foreign policies. Probably the most significant of these groups is the Canadian Business and Industry International Advisory Committee. The CBIIAC is an umbrella organization that includes the Canadian Chamber of Commerce, the Canadian Manufacturers Association, the Canadian Export Association, the Canadian Import Association and other organizations concerned with trade policy. Of course, this means there can be incongruities in the CBIIAC. The CIA wants reduction of tariffs and non-tariff barriers, while the CEA, representing 500 corporations, wants to increase access to foreign markets and obtain government assistance and tax concessions.

AGRICULTURE AND FISHERIES

The Fisheries Council of Canada is the largest organization representing fishing interests. It is comprised of provincial associations of companies in fishing and fish processing.

Agriculture has two major organizations. The largest, the Canadian Federation of Agriculture, enrolls about two-thirds of the country's farmers. It is composed of provincial federations of agriculture and many commodity organizations such as the Canadian Pork Council. The CFA makes representations to the federal government, but is somewhat less willing to engage in direct confrontation with the government than is the smaller National Farmers' Union.[24]

LABOUR

Labour can be a powerful force in Canadian politics. Approximately one out of every three paid workers outside agriculture is a member of a labour union. The major umbrella organization is the Canadian Labour Congress. It consists of affiliated trade unions. The CLC is a federation with 12 regional offices and 120 local councils. Representation is geographically dispersed: the Ottawa office deals with issues at the national or international levels, and the regional and local branches focus on issues under provincial jurisdiction. Unlike most interest groups, the Canadian Labour Congress supports one political party — the NDP.

A second major worker association, the Canadian Federation of Labour, comprises 10 building-trade unions. It differs from the CLC in emphasizing cooperation with the government and in being non-partisan; it does not uniquely support the NDP. Québec has its own major

---

24 See Riddell-Dixon, *The Domestic Mosaic*, p. 25. Also see Helen Jones Dawson, "The Consumers' Association of Canada," *CPA*, vol. 4, no. 1 (March 1963), pp. 92–118; W.T. Stanbury, *Business Interests and the Reform of Canadian Competition Policy* (Toronto: Carswell, 1977); and Jonah Goldstein, "Public Interest Groups and Public Policy," *CJPS*, vol. 12, no. 1 (March 1979), pp. 137–56.

labour organization, the Confederation of National Trade Unions, which represents members in a number of Québec labour unions.

Workers are also affiliated with their particular sector of the economy or trade; examples are the Québec Woodworkers Federation and the United Automobile Workers of America. Government employees are represented by organizations such as the Canadian Union of Public Employees (CUPE) and the Canadian Union of Postal Workers (CUPW).

OTHER ECONOMIC GROUPS

Another prominent category of economic interest groups comprises those representing consumers. The Consumers' Association of Canada represents the interests of consumers to government. This function often brings it in conflict with both business and labour.

In a separate category are professional workers. The Canadian Bar Association, the Canadian Association of Broadcasters and the Canadian Council of Professional Engineers, among others, attempt to secure government policies conducive to their professional interest. Perhaps the best-known group in this category is the powerful Canadian Medical Association; other prominent organizations in the health field are the Canadian Dental Association and the Canadian Nurses Association.

Reproduced with permission, Dennis Pritchard.

NON-ECONOMIC GROUPS

This category is possibly the largest; it is certainly the most diffuse. As indicated earlier, such groups may be transitory or permanent. Religious interests are fostered by the Canadian Council of Churches, the Canadian Conference of Catholic Bishops and the Christian Movement for Peace. Ethnic representation is made by groups such as the Canadian Jewish Congress, the Arab Palestine Association, the Ukrainian National Association, and the

Canadian Polish Congress. Women are represented by the National Action Committee on the Status of Women, which represents some 600 women's organizations, REAL Women and the YWCA.

Weaker and more transitory than the above-named are public interest groups. Issue-oriented groups can develop anywhere and at any time a corrosive issue arises. Motivated by a mixture of principle and ideology, these groups usually see themselves as representing the unrepresented or under-represented. Usually they are dependent on favourable media coverage. Of course, all groups believe they represent the "public interest," but these particular groups specialize in this approach rather than in one based on occupation, nationality, religion, sex or ethnicity. They include such vocal advocates of environmental causes as Friends of the Earth, Greenpeace, Energy Probe, and such peace organizations as Amnesty International and Operation Dismantle. Also well recognized as interest groups of this type are the Non-Smokers' Rights Association and the National Poverty Organization.

INGREDIENTS FOR INTEREST GROUP SUCCESS

Perhaps the most fundamental ingredient for the political success of an interest group is that its values, goals and tactics are compatible with the country's political culture and therefore are perceived as legitimate. Without public support a group has very little chance of receiving government recognition.[25] Groups that use the tactic of violent demonstration rather than negotiation meet rigid resistance in the Canadian system, as do those that approve goals foreign to the Canadian political culture such as, say, state control of family planning.

Another ingredient for success is an appealing issue — one that will gather very broad public sympathy and increase the size of the group, or at least increase its support. Good leadership is also important; a strong, vocal and prestigious leader brings valuable publicity and direction. A high-status general membership further increases the chance of success, since distinguished, influential people bring contacts and other resources, and have easier personal access to bureaucrats and politicians. Similarly, large budgets naturally assist in achieving and maintaining access to policy-makers. Prosperity does not guarantee success, but it certainly increases its possibility.[26]

A permanent organizational structure is important because it helps the group act cohesively. Internal divisions weaken the group. Sections of society that have common interests but are unorganized, such as homemakers or pensioners, usually have little long-term impact on public policy.

Flexibility is another important factor in achieving success, since it is often necessary to compromise one part of a demand to achieve another. As one lobbyist said: "We are often forced to ask ourselves should we shoot for the moon or try to give suggestions politicians might accept. It is an important calculation in our work." Successful groups often join at least temporarily with other groups to bolster each others' claims. Interest groups must also be flexible enough to make use of all the areas of access available to them. They there-

---

25 Kwavnick, *Organized Labour and Pressure Group Politics*, passim.

26 An interesting case against this argument is made by Francis Piven and Richard Cloward in *Poor People's Movements* (New York: Pantheon Books, 1977). In a study of four large mass movements of the poor lower class in the U.S., they conclude that one of the main reasons the poor are unsuccessful in winning concessions is that their leaders are overconcerned with organization and so lose the anger, spontaneity and solidarity that could force government response. Concessions to the poor are not made through established political channels, but to placate mass defiance.

fore need to know where to plug into the policy-making system. An important condition of success consists of knowing where and at what state access to policy-makers can be achieved.

Attempts to measure the success of lobbying activities statistically have had only limited utility. Observations of the frequency and nature of the contact between interest groups, legislators and bureaucrats have often led to disappointing assessments that border on truisms. One such study of Canadian interest group activity concluded that

> *Legitimate, wealthy, coherent interests having multiple sources of access to the legislative process would tend to be much more influential than less legitimate, poor, diffuse interests having few sources of access to the legislative process.*[27]

It is true but regrettable that interest group politicking is a well-practised but little understood art.[28] Part of the problem is definitional. David Truman's definition of "interest group," for example, does not specify a political content to "interest,"[29] while, at the other extreme, the state of Texas has designated as a political lobbyist anyone who comes in contact, however casual, with a legislative representative. Political lobbying is a poorly studied phenomenon generally, and has been the victim of misunderstanding on a number of levels.

LOBBYING IN CANADA

The term "lobby" comes from the corridor in the British House of Commons where constituents may meet their MPs to cajole or pressure them about policy or legislation. One of the more useful texts on the subject of political lobbying in Canada begins with the observation that interest groups "live in the half-light of politics."[30] For all too many Canadians the "half-light" is in fact a shroud of suspicion. While nothing is more proper in a democratic process than for individuals to attempt to influence their government, social taboos construe such activity as embarrassing and imprudent.

Yet, for all the prudery, Ottawa and the provincial capitals *are* full of lobbyists. It is worth noting that while businessmen, for example, display contempt for the dirty world of politics, they exhibit remarkable ability to hold their noses and socialize when something is to be gained. These relationships are both accommodating and antagonistic. Government regulates business yet also subsidizes and protects it.

Lobbyists are paid to influence the government. Their organizations break down roughly into two groups: those focused primarily on general government policy, such as the Business Council on National Issues, and those with a more specific focus, typified by the Pharmaceutical Manufacturers Association or the Mining Association of Canada. Trade and umbrella groups send scores of lawyers before regulatory tribunals to secure the modification of regulations, while voluntary groups press their causes with MPs, Cabinet ministers and bureaucrats. One organization, the Canadian Federation of Independent Business, actually created the Ministry of State for Small Business. Yet the entire scene remains

---

27 Fred Thompson and W.T. Stanbury, *The Political Economy of Interest Groups in the Legislative Process in Canada* (Reprinted by permission of the IRPP, May 1979), p. 48 (emphasis in original).

28 See Robert J. Jackson, "An Underdeveloped Art: Analysing Interest Groups and Lobbying in Canada," paper prepared for Conference on Foreign Lobbies, Johns Hopkins University, 15–16 June 1983.

29 See Truman, *The Governmental Process*, p. 33.

30 Pross, "Pressure Groups," p. 1.

obscure and a substantial portion of Ottawa's lobbyists describe their occupation simply as "public relations."

Given the complexity of government, lobbying is essential. As previously noted, lobbyists provide valuable assistance to government and Parliament in that they assemble and provide facts that are necessary for informed decisions. Governments use lobbyists, too, periodically calling them together for advice or research. And they hire lobbyists of their own, as the Canadian government did to represent Canadian interests in the acid rain issue in the United States. Lobbyists are useful to governments because their information enables bureaucrats and politicians to develop policies that will gain votes. As one former senior government official put it, "being able to develop a policy that will gain votes is worth more than a contribution to the party...Whatever the contribution, you could blow it away if you lose votes."[31]

Since it is so widely practised, and performs a valuable function, why then does lobbying have such an unsalubrious reputation? Obviously, the concern is not about the provision of facts but its close relation to influence peddling in which money is exchanged for favours. Influence peddling comes under the Criminal Code and carries a five-year prison term.

While many interest groups lobby on their own behalf, others hire professionals to carry out this function. Since the enactment of the *Lobbyists Registration Act*, the members and organizations of this profession have become well known through publications such as the *Lobby Digest* and *Lobby Monitor*. A list of the leading lobby firms would include Executive Consultants, Government Consultants International, Public Affairs International, William H. Neville and Associates, the Capitol Hill Group, S.A. Murray Consulting, Government Policy Consultants and Fred Doucet Consulting International. But these are not the only professional hired guns in the Lobbying business. Most law firms in Canada's capitals also lobby — although they prefer to be called consultants or lawyers. Many single individuals, too, such as former MPs, Senators and bagmen of parties are paid by organizations to work on their behalf.

LEGISLATION TO CONTROL LOBBYING

To make lobbying more open and fair, Parliament has frequently considered establishing rules to regulate it. In 1978 and 1985, for example, private members' bills to control lobbyists failed to secure passage through the House of Commons. However, in 1985 when the Mulroney Conservative government finished its first year in office plagued with scandals and shrouded in perceptions of patronage and favouritism, the incentive for regulations gained impetus. To improve his government's tarnished image Mr. Mulroney promised a new code of conduct. Hearings of the Commons Standing Committee on Elections, Privileges and Procedure ensued. Not surprisingly, the lobbying profession generally was against any form of registration. In its submission to the committee, for example, Canada's largest consulting firm, Public Affairs International, argued that it "plays a positive catalytic role in the interface between government and Parliament and the private sector."[32] It does not lobby, it said, but simply ensures "that our clients are enlightened and constructive partners in the development of public policy." On the other hand, two other lobbyists who worked for the

---

[31]   Quoted in Margot Gibb-Clark, "Lobbying: No respect but it gets things done," *The Globe and Mail*, Dec. 14, 1987.

[32]   Hugh Winsor, "Lobbyists liken role to lawyers," *The Globe and Mail*, May 28, 1986.

non-profit Canadian Coalition on Acid Rain argued that comprehensive registration and dis-closure should be required of all paid lobbyists. Citing their experience in Washington, where they were required by law to register as lobbyists and foreign agents, they maintained that public disclosure provided "a level playing field" in that it helped balance the advantages of powerful and well-financed business lobby groups over smaller non-profit organizations in influencing Government officials.[33] They also argued that the reporting requirements nec-essary for them to lobby in the United States were not unduly onerous even for a group with limited resources; and the rules were helpful in allowing them to monitor the activities of their opponents, the well-funded U.S. coal interests and the electrical utilities.

By January 1987, the parliamentary committee released a unanimous report recom-mending that registration should be required of paid lobbyists, listing the name of the lob-byist, the client and the issue. Five months later, Consumer and Corporate Affairs Minister Harvie André tabled Bill C-82, *The Lobbyists Registration Act*. It was a rather weak bill that did not include many of the more stringent recommendations of the Standing Committee. It did not attempt to regulate lobbyists, but simply required registration. Lobby groups were rel-atively satisfied with such weak measures and, in September 1988, the bill was finally given Royal Assent, to be proclaimed in June 1989, when the infrastructure for implementing the bill was in place.

The long-awaited new bill was a watered-down compromise that did little more than keep a current list of some of the lobbyists operating in and around Ottawa. The *Financial Times* said it had "a hole big enough to drive a tank through."[34]

The *Act* divides lobbyists into two tiers — "professional lobbyists" and "paid lobbyists" — and sets out different requirements for each.

Tier I includes "an individual who, for pay, provides certain types of lobbying services on behalf of a client." These *professional* lobbyists must 1) file a new registration for every lobbyist-client relationship, 2) include in every registration their own name; the name and address of their firm; name of client; name of corporate owners or subsidiaries of the client; general area of concern of the lobbying effort; and the class of undertaking that the lobby-ing was intended to influence.

Tier II includes those "whose job involves a 'significant' amount of government lobbying for his or her employer" — lobbyists employed by corporations, umbrella associations and public interest groups. These lobbyists are required to register within two months of initi-ating the lobbying activity and once a year thereafter. They need only give their name and the name and address of the corporation that employs them. Neither group has to provide any financial information. The penalties for non-compliance are a maximum fee of $100 000 and/or a two-year prison sentence.

Incorporated into the new act was a provision to review the legislation three years after it came into effect. The review took place in 1993 and it was evident that reformers want-ed major changes while others, particularly lobbyists, desired to leave the law intact. On the positive side, the new *Act* confirmed the legitimacy of lobbying the government in Canada and set up a registry of lobbyists. However, as it stands there are several serious faults in the legislation. They can be summarized as follows:

---

[33] Ibid. When the Acid Rain Coalition went to Washington to press Congress for legislation limiting emis-sions it had to register under the *Foreign Agents Registration Act* and the *Federal Regulation of Lobbying Act*. All bills above $10 and every meeting with officials and every brief distributed had to be recorded.

[34] *Financial Times*, October 9, 1989.

1. Only paid lobbyists have to register — others have *no obligation* to file or disclose information. This provides a gigantic loophole through use of contingency fees. Essentially, lobbyists who do not receive payment until *after* contacting the office holder or bureaucrat, can avoid disclosing information, because he or she has not been paid.

2. The *definition* of Tier II lobbyists is particularly weak. It only includes someone who devotes a "significant" part of his or her duties to lobbying. A lobbyist who does not want to register can simply maintain that lobbying is not a "significant" part of his or her duties.

3. Not enough information is required, especially of Tier II lobbyists. Spending *disclosure* might relieve the negative image of lobbyists. As well, the subject categories given are too vague and can be used to mislead rivals or critics.

4. Interest groups do not have to file any *information* about their objectives.

5. *Enforcement* is inadequate. The Registrar has no power to verify the information submitted by the lobbyists. The RCMP, which enforces the *Act*, will only launch an investigation when a complaint is raised against an individual. The Criminal Code's statute of limitations on summary offences limits the ability of the RCMP to obtain prosecutions under the *Act* to a period of six months. By the time a complaint is made it may prove too late to punish the perpetrator.

6. *Non-compliance* is a problem. Many lobbyists are reportedly refusing to register at all and are getting away with it. A bureaucrat or individual being lobbied is not required to ensure that the lobbyist is registered.

7. There is a strong argument that *all* lobbyists should have the same requirements. The two-tier system creates a hierarchy of lobbyists, inferring that some individuals have the potential to be more subversive to the policy process than others.

Furthermore, one of the main factors behind public cynicism about interest groups is that governments spend more money because of lobbying. Governments make direct payments to some groups, they allow corporations to treat lobbying as a business expense, and certain types of interest groups are allowed to register as charities and receive tax credits for charitable donations.[35] It can be argued that a more open system would eliminate the source of public discontent. Reformers argue, therefore, that it is in the public interest that the lobbying registration procedure provide *access* and *transparency*. Access to the public should be equitable, not selective or priviledged. And the public should have the opportunity to know who is attempting to influence the government. Instead, the current legislation provides what one expert calls "little more than a registry of the more professionally minded lobbyists."[36] The public is given the impression that lobbying in Ottawa is controlled, when it is not.

Still other reformers argue that the problem is more fundamental. Interest groups, they say, are a bad thing and would ideally be abolished because they harm the role of the legislature in Canadian democracy:

> ... the practices engaged in by those who insert themselves between the people and those in government and extract a fee for doing so...[are] fundamentally undermining representative democracy and eclipsing Parliament.[37]

---

[35] See, for example, W.T. Stanbury, *Business-Government Relations in Canada* (Toronto: Nelson, 1992) pp. 137–40.

[36] A. Paul Pross and Iain Steward, "Lobbying, the Voluntary Sector and the Public Purse," in Susan D. Phillips, ed., *How Ottawa Spends 1993–94* (Ottawa: Carleton University Press, 1993) p. 121.

[37] Patrick Boyer, House of Commons *Debates*, Nov. 20, 1992, p. 14292.

The debate continues. One can expect that in the near future minor amendments will be made to the *Lobbyists Registration Act*, but there will be no fundamental change in the system.

COMMON TACTICS AND STRATEGIES

The lobbying strategy chosen by an interest group depends largely on the type of group it is, its resources and the type of issues involved. Some groups concentrate on the pre-parliamentary stages of government, while others prefer buttonholing MPs. In all cases, the strategies used must include more than an attempt to influence legislators and bureaucrats. Public opinion must be aroused too. No amount of persuasion of the government will be effective unless public opinion is in agreement with a lobby, or at least not hostile to its demands.

Many lobbyists establish friendly relationships with legislators, bureaucrats and media or other group contacts, in order to present their cases in informal, friendly ways. Robert Presthus' research showed that about 75 percent of MPs of all parties had frequent or occasional contact with interest groups. This contact generally concerned interests that the MPs already supported, and was aimed at convincing them to influence their colleagues.[38] Lobbyists also disseminate literature, present briefs, provide research results, promote letter writing campaigns, support groups at committee hearings and entertain. At the same time, they must keep close track of what is happening in Parliament, so that they and the group they represent will know when and where to take appropriate action.

In his study of the Canadian Medical Association (CMA) Bernard Blishen shows the multiple ways in which a pressure group promotes its interests. Positive relations with the press and personal contacts are considered important to the CMA. Both formal and informal contacts between the profession and government are pursued. This is facilitated by the fact that many senior officials of the federal and provincial government health departments, as well as Ministers of Health, have been physicians. In addition to these contacts, "institutional patterns" between the CMA and the government are well established. For example, close contacts are fostered between the profession and the public service by the "medical care prepayment" plans in the area of health insurance. A final significant tactic used by this group is referred to as the "tie-in-endorsement," which refers to the effort to "tie members in" with related groups such as other health professionals, hospital associations, insurance industries, and other health programs in an effort to protect similar interests and policies. In all its activities, group members make every effort to act in unison, in the knowledge that their influence depends to a large degree on the cohesion of the Association.[39]

Lobbying MPs is probably *least effective* when the policy concerned is already before Parliament in the form of proposed legislation. Policies are made before they reach Parliament, and by the time they are set in a bill it is difficult for any group to have an effect on them. At this stage, legislation is more apt to be blocked or delayed than changed. The *most effective* form of lobbying is probably to target key bureaucrats and ministers while policy is in the gestation stage.

Occasionally, interest groups use the judicial process to pursue their goals. It is possible for group leaders to initiate suits directly on behalf of their group. Or they may

---

[38] Robert Presthus, "Interest Groups and Parliament Activities, Interaction, Legitimacy and Influence," *CJPS* vol. 4, no. 4 (December 1971), p. 460.

[39] Bernard R. Blishen, *Doctors and Doctrines: The Ideology of Medical Care in Canada* (Toronto: University of Toronto Press, 1969), p. 101.

support in the courts an individual who seeks to achieve the same goals as their own. For example, a stay-at-home-mother might obtain the support of a women's organization before the courts because the interest group considers that her case provides the best opportunity to have the law interpreted in favour of the women's movement. Or parents who take court action against a provincial government because their child is not allowed to attend the school of their choice might be supported by a group whose own cause is thereby represented.

We have pointed out that public relations campaigns are expensive, and, as a result, groups with large memberships, extensive financial resources and influential connections often have major advantages. Direct advertising or program sponsorship are often too expensive for many groups. However, because it is the function of the media in a democratic system to inform the public, poorer interest groups often create newsworthy events so that information about their group and their activities will be publicized without charge.

Some groups employ other tactics to obtain *free* media coverage. For example, they may stage employee strikes against management in order to force the government to listen to their demands through the media. Picketers affect not only management but also public opinion. Or an angry consumer group may gain publicity by picketing a business to protest high prices or poor services.

Non-violent demonstrations are yet another means of seeking publicity. The tactic has become increasingly popular since the non-violent U.S. civil rights movement in the 1950s and 1960s. It is especially popular with minority and low income groups. But neither non-violent nor violent protest fits within the norms of mutual accommodation between interest groups and policy-makers in Canada. Such a tactic presents an ultimatum that precludes negotiation of individual group claims; on the whole, groups that use this strategy are likely to be ignored, discredited or placated with purely symbolic action. Lobbyists sometimes get pushed by their clients to act harshly, but when they do so they are often ostracized from government circles.

One of the most sophisticated lobbying campaigns in modern Canadian history was waged in 1987–88 over the Government's bill (C-51) to ban tobacco advertising and promotion. The two sides on the issue used unique lobbying and public relations techniques. On one side, the tobacco manufacturers engaged an influential, well-connected lobbyist, William Neville, to stop Bill C-51. On the other side, health groups banded together to support the bill and counter every tactic Neville and his clients mounted. In the summer of 1987, the tobacco manufacturers took out full-page advertisements in newspapers, and Neville conducted a sophisticated direct-mail campaign to mobilize all those who profit from tobacco, and enlist the support of those who benefit from tobacco company sponsorship. The anti-tobacco campaign retaliated by publishing full-page ads in 24 newspapers attacking the direct-mail campaign. And the Canadian Medical Association asked "two physicians in every riding to get in touch with their MP directly and asked all 59 000 physicians in the country to write their MPs in support of the bill."[40]

The tobacco industry organized a press conference; the health groups held one too. The industry contacted tobacco retailers and provided them with an information kit, which included a computer-generated letter of protest to the store owner's MP, then made three follow-up phone calls to encourage the merchants to sign and mail the letters. The Canadian

---

[40] Graham Fraser, "Lobby fight on tobacco legislation smolders on," *The Globe and Mail,* Dec. 16, 1987.

Cancer Society responded with 35 000 black-edged postcards to MPs (one for each tobacco-related death forecast for the MP's riding).

MP Ronald Stewart spoke out against Bill C-51, and the coalition of health groups promptly sent out letters to every household in Mr. Stewart's riding, pointing out that he was involved in the wholesale tobacco distribution business. One of the coalition's members commented: "We're trying to be sophisticated enough to use our relatively modest resources to blow the industry's multi-million-dollar campaign out of the water." Mr. Neville, on the other hand, claimed that he was merely trying to inform those who would be affected by the legislation.[41]

Besides the sophisticated lobbying techniques employed by the two sides in this affair, this contest was unusual in that the tobacco industry did not try to lobby individual MPs to kill the bill, but only to reduce its priority on the legislative agenda. They knew that delay can kill a bill as effectively as a defeat. The bill had broad public support, confirmed health benefits, and the support of a minister and a majority of MPs, but effective lobbying delayed its passage for a considerable time. Bill C-51 did not receive Royal Assent until June 1988, and only took effect in January 1989, with rules for advertising and labelling to be phased in over a five-year period.

ACCESS POINTS

One lobbyist has commented that "our political system is great if the government is doing what you like — otherwise there are never enough access points."[42] To be successful, groups must be flexible enough to approach and adapt to all of the available access points. "We throw out our line everywhere," is the usual approach.

We have seen that access is available to the policy process through individual MPs via the committee system or caucus and, of course, the Cabinet. But interest groups operate even more outside Parliament. Since the bureaucracy is concerned with policy in its earliest formation it is often the most important focus of lobbying. Such activity has been known to provoke complaints that interest groups bypass Parliament and the elected representatives.

In both arenas, the interaction between pressure group leaders and politicians or bureaucrats is characterized by a spirit of cooperation that has been termed an "ethos of mutual accommodation."[43] All parties must receive some benefits and value the interaction. This ethos is evident in the following remark by an interest group leader: "We are concerned to always give full and accurate information to bureaucrats because if we don't create a confidence and they depend on advice which is biased towards us — they have a long memory and will hold it against us later."[44]

It is important for interest groups to use the access points provided within the political system and establish a framework for mutual consultation. Once a pattern is established, it indicates that the group has obtained recognition as the representative for its particular interests. The interaction is a symbol of the compatibility of its goals and tactics with both Canadian political culture and the goals of the government.

---

[41] Ibid.

[42] Based on personal interviews.

[43] Robert J. Jackson and Michael M. Atkinson, *The Canadian Legislative System,* 2nd rev. ed. (Toronto: Gage, 1980), p. 36.

[44] Based on personal interviews.

Successful access to the policy-making process necessitates knowledge of the institutional and procedural structures of government and the legislative system, such as, for instance, how a bill originates and what affects its passage. The early stages of a bill are particularly important for interest groups because, as we noted in an earlier chapter, Parliament passes laws but rarely originates them. Legislation and expenditures are generally approved by the executive as a package. By the time a particular package reaches Parliament, the government has publicly committed itself to the policies therein, and little can be done to change the details of single bills or estimates without destroying the delicate compromises on which the "deal" has been constructed.

If we trace the course of a bill through the pre-parliamentary to the parliamentary stages, the relative importance of the various access points becomes clearer. The interaction process can be very complex, and most of it takes place on an informal and secret basis. The bureaucracy and Cabinet are significant access points in the pre-parliamentary stages of a bill. Many political analysts believe that the bureaucracy is the most widely used arena for successful pressure group activity.

There is a close relationship between civil servants and pressure groups for many reasons. The most obvious is that civil servants are required by their ministers to research and evaluate policy proposals for Cabinet, to give advice on the public acceptability of these policies and even to help educate and inform the public about them. Another opportunity for pressure exists again during the drafting and amendment of a bill, but this is a difficult stage at which to have much influence. One lobbyist stated his preferences this way: "After a bill is printed it is almost impossible to have a great effect. We prefer the white paper process so that the minister is not married to his bill." Professional lobbyists are particularly critical about the lack of influence in the closed atmosphere around taxation legislation: "Too few people get involved in the final projects....We prefer the American system where there is a greater airing of views on each bill."[45]

Since responsibility for initiation and control of legislation is in the hands of the government, the Cabinet is a natural target for interest group activity. In the pre-parliamentary stages of a bill the minister preparing a new policy is responsible for gathering information from interest groups. At the same time, government secrecy requires that the groups not be informed about the government's intentions regarding decisions or policy details. This relationship can be exceedingly complex or simple. Sometimes the relationships between ministers and interest groups are extremely close: for example, when Mitchell Sharp and C.M. Drury entered the Cabinet they were both members of the Canadian Manufacturers Association.

An interest group leader's approach to a Cabinet minister may be illustrated by an incident in 1977. A Toronto lobbyist asked an acquaintance who was a friend of Cabinet Minister A.C. Abbott to tell the Minister over lunch that he wanted to be sure that an insurance company would have the opportunity to present a brief at the committee stage of a certain bill (*The Borrowers and Depositors Protection Act*, 1977). Abbott assured him that they would be heard, and they were.[46] Some interest group relations with Cabinet are more formalized. Every year specific national groups are invited to present annual briefs to the whole

---

[45] Personal interview.

[46] Grace Skogstad examines the activities of interest groups in parliamentary committees in "Interest Groups, Representation and Conflict Management in the Standing Committees of the House of Commons." *CJPS*, vol. XVIII, no. 4 (Dec. 1985), pp. 739–72.

Cabinet. This recognition, which has been achieved by only a few organizations, such as the CLC, is greatly valued. Apart from publicity and prestige, it gives these groups an opportunity to air their views directly to ministers.

Paul Pross has argued convincingly that interest groups have contributed to the enhancement of Parliament's role in the policy process. Approaches by interest groups to MPs have increased because they have "found it useful to exploit the legitimacy and publicizing capacities of parliament."[47] Interest groups seek access to individual MPs more for their long-term political influence than because the groups need immediate assistance. Because legislation is approved and passed, rather than initiated, in the House of Commons, unless an MP has special information or interest (or is strategically located in a minority government situation) he or she can be of little direct help. Also, interest group leaders complain that "it is almost impossible to get backbenchers involved in the technical details of bills" and that "there has to be public appeal in order to get backbenchers involved." On the other hand, it is always possible that a friendly member may bring an issue to the attention of a Cabinet minister, become a Cabinet minister or, together with fellow backbenchers, force desired change in Cabinet decisions. In addition, since opposition MPs may, after the next election, gain key positions in the government they cannot be ignored. As a rule, however, opposition MPs receive most interest group attention during minority governments, when their vote is more significant.

An MP may take up the cause of an interest group for various reasons. It could be politically expedient to do so. Or the group might provide information for a well-informed question or speech in the House, which would earn the MP credit and recognition within party caucus.

Caucus gives individual MPs an opportunity to express their views. On the government side, the outline of bills that are about to be introduced in the House are presented first to the caucus. Caucus committee meetings follow in which the MPs have an opportunity to express the interest of groups that have approached them. Caucus continues to debate bills even after they have been introduced in the House, and, on occasion, can even prevent the moving of Second Reading. If Cabinet and interest groups' opinions diverge, it is usual for interest groups to attempt to form a coalition of anti-government forces. Jackson and Atkinson note that

> *Generally cabinet opinion prevails when the caucus, the provinces, or the relevant interest groups can be attracted to cabinet's side. Cabinet has the least chance of imposing its views where all three of these elements resist its direction.*[48]

The committee system is yet another attractive access point for interest groups because the very purpose of committees is to gather information. In fact, Presthus found that committees were the most frequent site of interest group impact on legislators. It is not uncommon for interest groups, both in Ottawa and the provincial capitals, to have their own representatives on legislative committees. The Royal Canadian Legion, for example, is usually well represented on the committee for Veterans' Affairs.

Some interest groups prefer Senate committees over House committees as a lobbying forum. Senate committees tend to handle testimony from corporations less politically than

---

[47] A. Paul Pross, "Parliamentary Influence and the Diffusion of Power," *CJPS*, vol. XVII, no. 2 (June, 1985), p. 263.

[48] Jackson and Atkinson, *The Canadian Legislative System*, p. 40.

do House of Commons committees. Business people, for example, find dealing with committees of the House of Commons unsatisfactory because the deliberations are unsystematic and partisan.

When legislation is before a House committee, all interests are invited to present briefs. As we have already noted, even after bills are before the House a great many devices exist for slowing down their progress. Passage of legislation is at best a very lengthy process, often taking several years, thereby giving interest groups extensive opportunities to lobby and conduct public relations campaigns. And, in many circumstances, delaying a bill may be just as effective as killing it.

Although organized groups normally prefer to transmit their demands directly through the bureaucracy or legislative system, political parties constitute a further possibility for access to decision-making. Interest groups attempt to influence party policy resolutions because political parties supply the government leaders; party decisions therefore may become government policy decisions. However, fearing that such an attachment will close their routes of access to other parties, many groups declare non-partisanship. The Canadian Manufacturers Association is a classic example of a group that has achieved success by avoiding identification with a single party. On the other hand, some interests, particularly labour associations, not only openly identify themselves with specific political parties, but also affiliate with them, providing both financial and political support. For example, the Canadian Labour Congress first openly identified with, then directly associated with, the CCF/NDP. In 1943 it endorsed the CCF as the political arm of labour in Canada, and in 1961 the joint CLC-CCF Committee founded the NDP.

PRIMARY INTEREST GROUP TARGETS

As a whole, Cabinet is closely involved in the policy-making process and is the target for intense lobbying. It is not, however, a monolithic block of power, but rather the sum of its ministerial parts. While the whole Cabinet is involved in major issues because of the principle of collective responsibility, its committee system forms the nexus of many significant decisions. In fact, the majority of significant Cabinet decisions are made in committee; they are merely ratified by Cabinet. Moreover, for the lobbyist, access to the committee system involves contact with the relevant minister, often via the ministerial bureaucracy or exempt staff.

Reinforcing the myth of Cabinet monopoly is the handy commonplace that, while the members of the House of Commons pass legislation, very few of them initiate it. At face value the statement is true; however, on close examination of the workings of the House, it is revealed as an unscholarly distortion. To be sure, lobbyists do spend less time approaching MPs than their American counterparts do Congressmen. Nevertheless, Members of Parliament are now more significant in terms of briefings, committee hearings and new task forces than ever before. Proof of this assertion can be found in a survey that showed that some 75 percent of the chief executive officers of Canadian business corporations or their representatives have frequent contact with Members of Parliament.[49]

Since Members of Parliament have a small staff, lobby groups become a major source of information. In a period of a week, a total of two hundred briefs, magazine articles and letters was forwarded to one MP from groups eager to inform him of their points of view and perhaps win support. Thus, backbenchers often become a barometer of the political climate:

---

[49] Robert J. Jackson, "Lobbying and the Political Process," paper prepared for the Social Science Federation of Canada, October 22, 1982, p. 12.

> *...special interest groups can give an MP a reading of the political pros and cons of a particular proposal. This is very important to the MPs who are often more concerned about public attitudes on legislation than are members of the bureaucracy or the Cabinet. Moreover, MPs usually have more time to see lobbyists than do Cabinet ministers or senior bureaucrats.*[50]

Consequently, interest groups or their representative public relations firms often distribute responsibility for all the legislators among members of their organizations in order to provide a consistent and geographically based influence. For organizations that can afford such a broad and sustained effort, this strategy represents a calculated investment in the future. As we said earlier, Cabinet ministers are, to a large degree, recruited from the ranks of the government backbench, and neither they nor opposition backbenchers can be allowed to feel isolated or ignored.

Yet even in the short term the skillful lobbying of backbenchers can have considerable impact on the legislative output of the government. The primary forum for backbench influence is caucus. When a substantial coalition of backbenchers with the support of one or more concerned interest groups opposes the Cabinet's position, the likelihood that the government's proposals will be reviewed increases. Further leverage is often available via a three-way alliance between lobbyists, backbenchers and disgruntled provincial governments.

Thus, backbench MPs provide a substantial link to the executive. Unfortunately, many scholars underestimate this feature of the Canadian legislative process because of the inclination to oversimplify the structural features of Canadian government and its points of contrast with the American system. In just one example, Robert Presthus asked nearly 1 000 directors of interest groups in Canada and the United States which arm of government received the most attention in their lobbying efforts.[51] The results are presented in Table 12.1. From these data Presthus drew the unjustified conclusion that Canadian interest groups direct the greater part of their lobbying efforts at the Cabinet and federal bureaucracy. The error emanates from making a distinction between "Cabinet" and "legislators." While this division is certainly valid for the American figures, Canadian Cabinet ministers are also legislators, in spite of their special status. According to Presthus' statistics, therefore, Canadian lobbyists target legislators, defined in general terms, 51 percent of the time. This results in a difference of only 8 percent in interest group contact with legislators between the U.S. and Canada — a figure of little statistical significance. Presthus' table represents an effort to explain differences in lobbying activity in two countries through quantification without sufficient regard for the subtle relationships between the executive and legislature in Canada.

TABLE 12.1   INTEREST GROUP ACTIVITY

Target of Interest Group	Canada	U.S.
Bureaucracy	40%	21%
Cabinet and Executive Assistants	24%	75%
Legislators and Legislative Committees	27%	59%
Judiciary	3%	3%
Other	6%	9%
	100%	100%
	N = 393	N = 604

Source: Robert Presthus, *Elite Accommodation in Canadian Politics* (Toronto: Macmillan, 1973), p. 255.

---

[50]   J. Gillies and J. Pigott, "Participation in the Legislative Process," *CPA*, vol. 25, no. 2 (Summer 1982), p. 256.

[51]   Robert Presthus, *Elite Accommodation in Canadian Politics* (Toronto: Macmillan, 1973), p. 256.

Presthus' findings indicate that Canadian interest groups seem more inclined to petition the federal bureaucracy than are their American counterparts. Certainly business groups exhibit a tendency to approach lower- and middle-level bureaucrats "on the premise that policy becomes more set and less easy to change the higher up it moves and that the lower level bureaucrats rely on business for information."[52] Hence there exists a reciprocity of dependency. Effective lobbying of the public service presupposes, of course, a fairly sophisticated understanding of the bureaucratic process and sufficient knowledge about the best timing and point of contact. In the perception of one former lobbyist, the campaign to influence legislative outputs cannot begin too early "because you don't even see the tip of the iceberg until there's a hell of a lot of ice down there."[53]

The effectiveness of focusing on public servants at the pre-parliamentary stage of the process is augmented at later stages. Legislation is often returned to departments for further consideration; thus, the entire process is reopened to groups that seek to block or stall disadvantageous proposals. The complexities of the legislative system and the rough landscape of Canadian politics give some indication of why it is often "considered easier to block or slow down proposals than to initiate them."[54]

The increased salience of bureaucracy is general to all advanced industrial societies. There is, however, a tendency to overstress the political significance of the bureaucratic process. This is especially true of journalists, for whom the use of the word "mandarin" in reference to senior civil servants carries an aura of omnipotence. Observations to the effect that "Any lobbyist who is worth either the handsome retainer or the comfortable salary that goes with the title will tell you that the real levers of power in Ottawa lie within the bureaucracy" abound.[55] Those wasting their time with MPs and Cabinet ministers, so the reasoning goes, are simply not in the know.

The habit of using language such as "the real levers of power" stems from the mechanization of the concept of political "power." The competition for access to government decision-makers is seen as a zero-sum game. Power is viewed as a kind of football in the lobbyists' free-for-all; if one group has it, other groups do not.

The fact is that while certain interests single out specific components of the legislative system for special attention, no successful group fosters illusions about "power" having a single address. Flexibility and concern to touch all the bases are the hallmarks of the most seasoned practitioners of the art of lobbying. When business groups suspect, for example, that their efforts at the mid-level of bureaucracy are too late or simply insufficient, chief executive officers will engage jointly in discussions with members of Cabinet — an activity that is frequently coordinated by a large umbrella organization. All groups appreciate the importance of monitoring developments in Ottawa very closely and making regular contact with government officials.

Despite this common characteristic, no two groups are identical in goals or resources, organization or methods. The National Farmers' Union (NFU) does not hesitate to employ

---

[52] Riddell-Dixon, *The Domestic Mosaic*, p. 7.

[53] Quoted in John Gray, "Insiders go to Mandarins Before Minister," *The Globe and Mail*, Toronto, October 25, 1980.

[54] Jackson and Atkinson, *The Canadian Legislative System*, p. 39.

[55] Gray, "Insiders go to Mandarins Before Minister."

confrontational tactics when they are deemed necessary. The larger Canadian Federation of Agriculture (CFA) makes representations to the federal government on matters of macro- and micro-agricultural policy, paying special attention to the development of export markets. While the NFU has placed greater emphasis on the economic viability of the family farm and the dignity of the Canadian farmer, it does have a community of interest with the CFA in promoting trade policies that will increase exports and protect domestic producers generally.[56]

The Canadian Business and Industry International Advisory Committee (CBIIAC) represents a major umbrella organization responsible for the interests of the Canadian business community in matters of foreign policy. Its members include some of the most respected business groups in the country, including the Canadian Chamber of Commerce and the Canadian Manufacturers Association. The CBIIAC traditionally worked closely with the Department of Industry, Trade and Commerce, but departmental reorganization now requires it to give greater attention to the Department of External Affairs. While this group's broad membership dictates concern with a very wide range of issues, other groups feature more exclusive membership and a concomitantly narrower focus, stressing a specific geographic area or a particular sector of the economy.[57]

Depending on their styles and resources, certain groups consistently stress one link of the legislative process over others. According to Robert Presthus, religious, educational and business groups focus most frequently on Cabinet, welfare groups on the bureaucracy and labour organizations on the legislature.[58] While the financial capacity of certain lobbies may enable them to wage a long-term campaign at every level, one should be careful of the assumption that wealthy lobbies are necessarily the most influential. An aide to the Minister of Energy, Mines and Resources described the tactics of oil interests as "unbelievably bad." Their attempts at dramatizing first Canada's oil wealth, and later her relative poverty, contributed to a substantial erosion of their credibility in government circles.[59] Moreover, even enormous financial resources may not be enough to offset salient political factors.

While the industry in general lacks credibility, there are exceptions. Dome Petroleum Ltd. and Nova, both large Calgary-based companies, and many of the medium and smaller companies are heard and listened to in Ottawa. The primary reason for this is that they can drape themselves in the maple leaf flag.[60]

Regionalism has a considerable impact, especially when federalism affords interest groups differing areas of opportunity. David Kwavnick has noted how competition between the Canadian Labour Congress and the Québec-based Confederation of National Trade Unions demonstrates that "rival groups representing the same interest, but having access to different levels of government in a federal system, will attempt to shift power to the level of government to which they enjoy access."[61]

---

[56] Riddell-Dixon, *The Domestic Mosaic*, p 24.

[57] Ibid., pp. 6–7.

[58] Presthus, *Elite Accommodation*, ch. 6.

[59] James Rusk, "Powers in the Oil Lobby Cull Clout from the Flag," *The Globe and Mail*, Toronto, October 27, 1980.

[60] Ibid.

[61] David Kwavnick, "Interest Group Demands and the Federal Political System: Two Canadian Case Studies," in Pross, *Pressure Group Behaviour*, p. 77. For a broader perspective see Stephen McBride, "Public Policy as a Determinant of Interest Group Behaviour," *CJPS*, vol. XVI, no. 3 (September 1983), pp.

All these groups recognize the multi-faceted nature of the legislative process and exert a long-term, systematic yet flexible effort at as many points of access as possible. Lobbyists are aware that political power is not some finite substance that necessarily ebbs in the legislature as it flows in the bureaucracy. They know that government structures are not held together by nuts and bolts; a search for the "real lever of power" is for bare-handed amateurs. Government, like a growing onion, continues to change size; the political process features so many different but similar layers that it is impossible to distinguish which of them really counts. Successful lobbyists have learned that they *all* count — in fact, each layer has meaning only because of its relation to the others.

The relative utility of any one facet of the legislative system to lobbyists can and does change over time. This is true in regard to backbench MPs, who are now considered more suitable targets for lobbying than in the past. Here again, zero-sum assumptions about the exercise of influence and political authority have tended to cloud an understanding of the subtle relations between administrative and legislative branches of government. Rare indeed is the contemporary political science text that does not make much ado about the increasing importance of specialized, bureaucratized expertise to government in the contemporary welfare state. Students of politics seem to regard knowledge held by the bureaucrat to be knowledge lost to the politician; elected representatives are held to be overshadowed by civil service technocrats. Whatever political analysts may have accused politicians of having been in the past two decades, few elected representatives would claim to have been the artless victims of manipulative bureaucrats or lobbyists.

This does not mean that MPs cannot be manipulated unwittingly. Consider, for example, the story of an official attached to a certain foreign embassy in Ottawa who thought that an issue concerning some aspect of his country's relation with Canada should have an airing in the House of Commons. This official contacted an opposition member and armed him with a particularly contentious question with which to confront the government. When the Secretary of State for External Affairs asked his staff to brief him on the substance of the matter, they of course required information from a foreign embassy — information they received from the very man who had originally formulated the question and inserted it into the system.[62] The diplomat had, in fact, both set the question and determined the answer. Yet politicians are neither unaware of such manoeuvring nor unappreciative of the perceptions and ideas that filter through this way. To paraphrase Senator Duff Roblin, former Conservative Premier of Manitoba, "I've never had an original idea in my life, but I know one when I see it!"

When substantive legislation is the target of interest group activity, a sustained campaign is important. It is perhaps in endurance that well-financed lobbies have great advantages. The controversial Drug Bill was tabled in the House of Commons in 1962, yet by the time all concerned interests had aired their views and conducted their public relations blitzes two governments had been in power, and the bill did not become law until 1968.[63] The legislation, which was designed to reduce the retail cost of pharmaceuticals by encouraging druggists to substitute generic alternatives for more expensive brand-name products, never sat well with foreign-based multinationals. The law provided that Canadian pharmaceutical manufacturers be granted licences to produce the drugs of foreign companies domesti-

---

[62] Anecdote based on personal interviews.

[63] Donald Coxe, "A License to Loot: How Ottawa Promotes Drug Piracy and Drives Away R & D," *Canadian Business*, March 1982, p. 142.

cally after just four years of patent protection. One hysterical voice went so far as to claim that the principle of private property in Canada was being subverted by "Godless Consumerism." After years of counteroffensive the law was changed again in 1987 and 1993, this time in favour of the multinationals.[64]

Reproduced with permission, Dennis Pritchard.

LOBBYING IN CANADA: CASTING THE NET WIDE

It should by now be apparent that the relatively unregulated practice of lobbying in Canada is an art of enormous complexity. Far from operating in a "restricted" environment, interest groups have the advantage of multiple access points to the legislative process. It is also obvious that scenarios that speak of the "virtual monopoly" of Cabinet clash with those that view federal bureaucrats as unseen power brokers in Ottawa. Both are misrepresentations of a complicated reality.

The relationship of lobbyists, bureaucrats and politicians in Canada is not one of zero-sum games or of sinister cabals in the corridors of power. The interaction of interest groups with the political system is at all points permeated by an ethos of mutual accommodation. Each party involved in the process recognizes that all other parties have an investment in

---

[64] "Critics Say Ottawa Drug Changes Will Add Millions to Consumer Cost," *The Globe and Mail,* Toronto, May 28, 1983. This case is discussed in John Sawatsky, *The Insiders: Government, Business and the Lobbyists* (Toronto: McClelland & Stewart, 1987), pp. 315–17. In February, 1993, Bill C-91 became law. It eliminates compulsory licencing, extending full patent protection of 20 years to all new, innovative drugs. *The Globe and Mail,* Feb. 5, 1993.

the outcome of the legislative process and hence a legitimate share in the formulation of public policy. The spirit of accommodation thrives where no party is seen to dominate all of the time and when each party receives sufficient satisfaction to justify further participation.

In Canada this process of *elite accommodation* tends to include interest groups, particularly business, the Cabinet and the bureaucracy. To some extent labour is left out of the process. In many industrialized democracies a social partnership or consensus known as **corporatism** exists instead of Canadian-style accommodation. In the corporatist model, a formal or institutionalized process of consultation between the state, business and labour shapes economic policy for society as a whole. Normally, such a process cannot take place in Canada because no single business or labour association can claim to represent all the significant interests in their respective communities and even the largest associations are accorded no functional representation in government policy-making.

In Canada, a successful and fruitful relationship with government actors begins with a group's recognition of the complexity of the contemporary democratic state and the opportunities that such complexity offers. A concern to leave no point of contact or influence untried, to cast one's net in as wide an arc as possible, is the cardinal rule of serious interest group politics. This means that while certain components such as Cabinet and the bureaucracy may be more significant than others, no facet of the process can be dismissed as unimportant.

The Canadian Senate, for example, is popularly considered to be the inconsequential artifact of a British political heritage. We have remarked that this contention is incorrect from the point of view of the lobbyist. Indeed, one author has called the Senate "a lobby from within," by which he meant that most Senators already represented lobbying interests before they were appointed to the upper house.[65] Formally, the Senate is responsible for detailed amendments to legislation from the House of Commons, a task for which it possesses a committee system capable of analyzing the impact details of legislation have on the business community.

Often the key to lobbying success is a sense of timing. Clause-by-clause consideration of bills, for example, almost always takes place in one of the several committees of the House of Commons after the Second Reading. MPs representing all parties are members of these committees. And, while the government side of each committee is "whipped" to ensure the bill's passage, lobbyists have a good chance to secure amendments at this time either by serving as witnesses or prompting backbench initiatives.

Finally, it should be stressed that interest group activities do not occur in a social vacuum. Casting a wide net can also involve the careful nurturing of broad public support or opposition to certain policies by interest groups. The size of the social constituency sought will of course depend on the nature and substance of the issue. The past record and perceived social "legitimacy" of an interest group affects its ability to harness social support. John Bullock, representative of the interests of Canadian small business and a very successful lobbyist himself, estimates that 90 percent of lobbyists are ineffectual because they lack either the necessary knowledge to articulate their case or sufficient public support to legitimate it.[66]

In recent years another political phenomenon that aims to influence governments and change social policy has become influential within many countries and also inter-

---

[65] Colin Campbell, *The Canadian Senate: A Lobby From Within* (Toronto: Macmillan, 1978).

[66] Quoted in *The Globe and Mail*, Toronto, October 25, 1980.

nationally. We turn next to a brief study of such movements, and an examination of the women's movement in particular.

WHAT ARE POLITICAL MOVEMENTS?

Return for a moment to the four prime characteristics of interest groups. They 1) have an organization, 2) articulate and aggregate interests, 3) act within the political system to influence policy and 4) seek to influence rather than exercise responsibility of government themselves.

Movements are another political phenomenon that share some of these interest group characteristics. **Movements** are rather fluid expressions of interests or collective identities with a broad, utopian appeal that often flows across state boundaries. They generally have no well developed formal organization. Rather, they loosely subsume a variety of interest groups that may have different aspirations and agendas, although they share the same broad philosophy. Peace movements, labour movements, nationalist movements and those supporting gay, disabled and animal rights are examples of broad, unstructured movements that offer a particular vision of how people should live. They may include coalitions of many associations and interest groups that support the same general cause. Such movements bring new issues and problems to public attention outside of the channels of political parties. Most are broadly based and inclusive, emphasizing citizen participation. They emphasize that citizens should be equal to enjoy the goods and services of society and to participate in the political decision-making process. Susan Phillips says social movements

> ...have accentuated a decline in the public's acquiescence and deference to elites and experts, and accelerated an increase in the public's interest in creating opportunities for direct participation and improving mechanisms for holding public officials accountable for policy decisions.[67]

Movements may remain in a loose form as innovators or they may harden into organized cohesive pressure groups or even become new political parties.[68]

Some movements have a long history. Nationalist movements, for example, have roots extending back to the seventeenth century. Nationalist and ethnic movements espouse the belief that a group of people represents a "natural" community and should be united under one political system. They stress local identities and loyalties based on ethnicity, language, culture, and so on, which may or may not correspond to state boundaries. Sometimes nationalist movements create a political party, or parties, as in Québec with the Parti Québécois and Bloc Québécois. We saw the same kind of transformation in a loose farmers' movement in Alberta at the beginning of the century. In the early 1900s, farmers organized pressure groups to fight for their interests in Ottawa. Discouraged with their results in the early 1920s they entered the political forum as the Progressive Party. However, in spite of considerable electoral success, they soon withdrew their party status and returned to pressure group activity. What began as a farmers' movement hardened into a pressure group, then a political party and finally reverted back to pressure group activity.

---

[67] Susan D. Phillips, "A More Democratic Canada...?" in Susan D. Phillips, *How Canada Spends* (Ottawa: Carleton University Press, 1993).

[68] See Claude Galipeau, "Political Parties, Interest Groups and New Social Movements: Toward New Representation?" in Alain Gagnon and Brian Tanguay, eds., *Political Parties in Transition* (Scarborough: Nelson, 1989).

As well as movements with deep historical roots, there are a multitude of modern movements related to what is sometimes called "the new politics." These concern issues, such as environmentalism, feminism and various other group rights, that began to emerge in western democracies in the 1960s and 1970s.

The environmental movement appeared in western societies as people became concerned with the deteriorating quality of the environment and the depletion of world resources. Broadly speaking, environmentalists regard economic growth as less important than the protection of "quality of life." They support pollution controls even though they may mean greater expense, hamper industrial development and limit or decrease material affluence. A great many interest groups come under the umbrella of the environmentalist movement, such as those seeking government regulations on acid rain, reforestation, preservation of threatened animal species, and so on. In some countries the environmental movement has established political parties. In many European countries these parties regularly receive up to five percent of the vote at general elections and, where voting systems allow, they have minor representation in legislative chambers. In Canada, the environmental movement includes the Canadian Environmental Network, which contains about 200 groups as well as small Green Parties in several provinces and at the federal level. The federal Green Party is extremely weak, undoubtedly because established parties also have taken up ecological issues.

Ron Inglehart has offered a theory to explain the proliferation of these new movements. He suggests that western democracies have undergone social, economic and cultural changes that have contributed to a growing politicization of their citizens. At the same time, political behaviour is moving beyond the constraints of traditional organizations like parties. He says that elite-directed participation is giving way to ad hoc groups concerned with specific issues and policy changes. There are growing numbers of people with high political skills but without close party ties.[69] Because of this he predicts more movements and parties will appear. The established parties, he says, came into being in an era dominated by social class conflict and economic issues, and tend to remain polarized on this basis. But in recent years, a new axis of polarization has arisen based on cultural and quality of life issues. He goes on to say that parties today:

> ...do not adequately reflect the most burning contemporary issues, and those who have grown up in the postwar era have relatively little motivation to identify with one of the established parties.[70]

Whether or not Inglehart's explanation for the rise of new movements is valid, there has been a proliferation of new parties around issues such as the environment.

The word "movement" has been used to capture these new interests because it implies broad, mass appeal and the notion that there is inevitability for the success of these causes. Recognizing the emotional appeal of movements, parties everywhere have adjusted their platforms to accommodate their demands. In Canada today, the Bloc Québécois espouses nationalist rhetoric and all three traditional federal parties all have adopted policy positions that give credence to the philosophies of environmentalism, feminism,

---

[69] Ron Inglehart, *Culture Shift in Advanced Industrial Society* (Princeton, N.J.; Princeton University Press, 1990), pp. 363–68. For a commentary on Inglehart's ideas see Thomas M. Trump, "Value Formation and Postmaterialism: Inglehart's Theory of Value Change Reconsidered," *Comparative Political Studies*, vol. 24, no 3 (Oct. 1991), pp. 365–90.

[70] Ibid., p. 363.

and so on. To explore these relations among movements, interest groups and parties and the general appeal of political movements, we assess the women's movement in Canada.

THE WOMEN'S MOVEMENT: A CASE STUDY

The women's movement is one of the most active and widespread movements reaching across state borders today. It has manifested itself on and off since the nineteenth century seeking rights for women to vote and to hold political positions and appointments for paid employment. The women involved share no doctrine per se and, in fact, are often in bitter disagreement about how to achieve their goals. Since the 1960s, the movement generally has focused on women's liberation, denouncing traditions of male supremacy in the family, and in other political and social structures that assign women an inferior position in society. In short, it seeks women's equal social and political rights with men and shares a theoretical assumption that historically men have exploited women based on gender differences that established a division of labour, limiting women's role in society to child rearing and domestic chores.

To achieve their ends, women's movements have built solid organizational and leadership structures within many countries and also at the international level.[71] At this broad level the women's movement has no unified ideology, but a neo-Marxist framework has provided much of its ideological basis. Capitalism and its social and political superstructures are often identified as the forces behind the oppression of women. It is argued that since men control the means of production, they have used their position to institutionalize norms and values that keep women in an inferior position.[72] To this end they identify and expose perceived cultural stereotyping, socialization and distortions of history that have been and continue to be used to ensure male dominance.

To date, the women's movement has generally sought to influence the policies of existing political parties rather than institute their own, although there are women's political parties in Columbia and Iceland. Since the rise of the modern women's movement, female politicians have become increasingly prominent. Sirimavo Bandarana-Ike of Sri Lanka was the first woman prime minister (1960–65, 1970–77). She was followed, for example, by Indira Gandhi in India (1966–77; 1980–84), Golda Meir in Israel (1969–70), Benazir Bhutto in Pakistan (1988–90) and Kim Campbell in Canada (1993). Although female politicians are particularly evident in Scandinavia, in most national legislatures their numbers are disproportionately low compared to their share of the population.

In Canada today, several groups advance women's causes.[73] The 1970 Royal Commission on the Status of Women provided the impetus to make gender an important factor in Canadian social and political life. The National Action Committee on the Status of Women (NAC) was established in 1972 to pressure for implementation of the recommendations of

---

[71] See Mary Fainsod Katzenstein and Carol McClurg Mueller, eds., *The Women's Movement of the United States and Western Europe* (Philadelphia: Temple University, 1987), pp. 64–88.

[72] See Robert J. Jackson and Doreen Jackson, *Contemporary Government and Politics: Democracy and Authoritarianism* (Scarborough, Ont.: Prentice-Hall, 1993), pp. 296–97.

[73] For the history of the women's movement see M. Janine Brodie and Jill McCalla Vickers, *Canadian Women in Politics: An Overview* (Ottawa: Canadian Research Institute for the Advancement of Women, 1982); and Sylvia B. Bashevkin, *Toeing the Lines: Women and Party Politics in English Canada* (Toronto: University of Toronto Press, 1985).

the Royal Commission. It has become an umbrella lobbying group for about 580 local and national member groups representing about three million women. The Canadian Advisory Council on the Status of Women (CACSW), set up by the government in 1973, is composed of government appointees who give advice to the responsible minister. Susan Phillips' study of 33 national Canadian women's organizations shows that the diverse groups "form an expansive, but loosely coupled, network, that is bound by a collective identity of 'liberalized' feminism."[74] Canadian women do not, however, speak with one voice. REAL Women (Realistic, Equal, Active for Life), formed in 1974, opposes feminist demands, and various anti-abortion groups also attack feminist viewpoints.

The women's movement in Canada has raised the awareness of women's position in society, changed attitudes and introduced many issues into the policy agendas of political parties. It has not tried to create a party itself, but has stayed outside of traditional political and interest group organization. Lynn McDonald, former President of NAC commented: "We have decided that at no time will we support one party.... Our members come from all political parties and we have to work with whomever is in government."[75]

The women's movement can be credited with concrete improvements in legislation concerning women as well as with attitudinal changes concerning participation.[76] Details of women's achievements in Canadian society have been discussed in the preceeding chapters on political culture, the *Constitution*, Parliament, political parties and the public service.

OVERVIEW

Lobbying in Canada is a well-practised but poorly studied art. Simplistic interpretations of the relationship between government and interest groups stem from a lack of appreciation of the complexity and evolution of the Canadian legislative process. It is quite likely that if a government were to establish more rigorous rules for lobbying and draw back the veil of obscurity and suspicion, social scientists would be able to bring greater sophistication to their study of the phenomenon. Above all, tired clichés, conspiracy scenarios and zero-sum characterizations of power and influence should be abandoned. The multi-faceted and changing relationship between public and private actors must be acknowledged in future studies of interest groups in Canada. Sensitive description must precede analysis. Accurate diagnosis must precede prescription.

How well do interest groups serve the average Canadian? We have seen that interest groups are a widely accepted part of the political culture. The interaction between groups and the political system is characterized by an ethos of accommodation or cooperation in which the interaction is deemed mutually worthwhile. The fact that interest groups are accepted within the political culture means that there is a legitimate channel for complaints and frustrations, an opportunity for citizens to articulate viewpoints and defend them, so that citizens do not have to resort to extra-legal behaviour to be heard. Once they are part of such a legitimized group, the members are committed to acting within the system. Interest groups in this sense act as a safety valve for individual frustrations by allowing the

---

[74] Susan D. Phillips, "Meaning and Structure in Social Movements: Mapping the Network of National Canadian Women's Organizations," *CJPS*, vol. 24, no. 4 (December 1991), p. 757.

[75] *Ottawa Citizen*, May 16, 1979.

[76] See Anne Phillips, *Engendering Democracy* (London: Polity Press, 1991).

possibility of joining with others to influence legislation. They thus provide a crucial and culturally acceptable link between citizen and public policy.

Interest groups widen the range of interests that are taken into account in the legislative process. On the premise that more information can help achieve fairer laws, this is good — but what assurance is there that the most worthy groups are heard? Deserving groups might be ignored because of lack of funds or prestige, or competition from more powerful groups. And where is the fine line between information and propaganda in the expert advice offered to lawmakers? Groups can be expected, even within the realm of mutual accommodation, to give selective information, making their own cases as strong as possible and not making the cases for their competitors. We know too that interest groups are elite dominated. People with higher status participate more, and groups tend to be dominated by the most active and vocal members. And what of unorganized interests? Who is to press the urgent claims of pensioners, children or stay-at-home mothers? To be fair the system must be responsive to those who do not have the resources to sustain mass organization.

Representation in the Canadian political system is sought through the electoral process. It is clear that interest groups, as we have described them, constitute another legitimate form of political representation. Yet these representatives seek influence on their own initiative and are responsible only to themselves. Some seek the good of the whole, but never to the detriment of their own interests. Interest group supporters say that extra representation through interest groups is good because the constituency form of representation cannot meet all the demands of groups in the political system, and that the modern welfare state makes interest group representation a necessary adjunct to government activity.

However, should interest groups play such an important role in making public policy? Could the representation allowed to interest groups erode political responsibility in a representative democracy? This problem within the system is aggravated when one political party dominates the government for a long period of time and relationships become well-ingrained. Then we find more highly placed and experienced bureaucrats leaving the public service to sell their knowledge and contacts to interest groups through private consulting services. If interest groups are to exist as representative bodies complementary to the elected representatives, steps should be taken to eliminate some of these injustices. The 1988 legislation to register lobbyists in Ottawa is just a beginning.

In recent years another influence on policy-making in Western societies has become widespread. Movements have become a powerful force in changing societal attitudes and influencing governments. They are amorphous currents of interest that flow easily across borders because of their broad and inclusive philosophies. They often subsume existing interest groups and stimulate new ones; sometimes they stay as movements and sometimes they solidify as political parties. When political parties fragment and represent narrow, regional interests or groups, movements often help to unify people by embracing national and even international issues or points of view.

SELECTED BIBLIOGRAPHY

Banting, Keith, ed., *The State and Economic Interests* (Toronto: University of Toronto Press, 1986).

———, and R. Simeon, *And No One Cheered* (Toronto: Methuen, 1983).

Black, Hawley, *How to Sell to the Government: The 30 Billion Dollar Market* (Toronto: Macmillan, 1989).

Bliss, Michael, *Northern Enterprise: Five Centuries of Canadian Business* (Toronto: McClelland & Stewart, 1987).

Campbell, Colin, *The Canadian Senate: A Lobby From Within* (Toronto: Macmillan, 1978).

Clark, S.D., J.P. Grayson and Linda Grayson, eds., *Prophecy and Protest: Social Movements in Twentieth-Century Canada* (Toronto: Gage, 1975).

Coleman, William, *Business and Politics* (Montréal: McGill-Queen's University Press, 1988)

————, and Grace Skogstad, *Policy Communities and Public Policy in Canada* (Mississauga: Copp Clark Pitman, 1990).

Eckstein, Harry, *Pressure Group Politics* (London: Allen and Unwin, 1960).

Economic Council of Canada, *Institutional and Influence Groups in the Canadian Food System Policy Process* (Ottawa: Minister of Supply and Services, January 1982).

Eggerton, Bill, "Belling the Cat: The Lobbyists Registration Act" (M.J. Thesis, Carleton University, 1992).

Gibbons, Kenneth and Donald Rowat, eds., *Political Corruption in Canada* (Toronto: Macmillan, 1976).

Gilles, James, *Where Business Fails: Business-Government Relations at the Federal Level in Canada* (Montréal: IRPP, 1981).

Greenwald, C.S., *Group Power: Lobbying and Public Policy* (New York: Praeger, 1977).

Horowitz, Gad, *Canadian Labour in Politics* (Toronto: University of Toronto Press, 1980).

Kwavnick, David, *Organized Labour and Pressure Politics: The Canadian Labour Congress 1956–1968* (Montréal: McGill-Queen's University Press, 1972).

Laxer, Robert, *Canada's Unions* (Toronto: Lorimer, 1976).

Malvern, Paul, *Persuaders: Influence Peddling, Lobbying and Political Corruption in Canada* (Toronto: Methuen, 1985).

March, James G., *Decisions and Organizations* (Oxford: Blackwell, 1988).

Panitch, Leo, ed., *The Canadian State: Political Economy and Political Power* (Toronto: University of Toronto Press, 1977).

Presthus, Robert, *Elite Accommodation in Canadian Politics* (Toronto: Macmillan, 1975).

Pross, A. Paul, ed., *Pressure Group Behaviour in Canadian Politics* (Toronto: McGraw-Hill Ryerson, 1975).

————, *Group Politics and Public Policy* (Toronto: Oxford University Press, 1986).

Sarpkaya, S., *Lobbying in Canada — Ways and Means* (Toronto: CCH Canadian Ltd., 1988).

Sawatsky, John, *The Insiders: Government, Business and the Lobbyists* (Toronto: McClelland & Stewart, 1987).

Schultz, Richard J., *Federalism, Bureaucracy and Public Policy: The Politics of Highway Transport Regulation* (Montréal: McGill-Queen's University Press, 1980).

Seidle, F. Leslie, ed., *Interest Groups and Elections in Canada*, vol. 2 of the Research Studies of the Royal Commission on Election Financing and Party Reform (Toronto: Dundurn Press, 1991).

Simpson, Jeffrey, *Spoils of Power: The Politics of Patronage* (Toronto: Collins, 1988).

Skogstad, Grace, *The Politics of Agricultural Policy-Making in Canada* (Toronto: University of Toronto Press, 1987).

Stanbury, William T., ed., *Business Interests and the Reform of Canadian Competition Policy* (Toronto: Carswell/Methuen, 1977).

————, *Business Government Relations in Canada: Grappling with Leviathan* (Toronto: Methuen, 1986).

Thompson, Fred and William T. Stanbury, *The Political Economy of Interest Groups in the Legislative Process in Canada* (Toronto: Butterworths, 1979).

Thorburn, Hugh G., *Interest Groups in the Canadian Federal System*, vol. 69, Royal Commission on the Economic Union and Development Prospects for Canada (Toronto: University of Toronto Press, 1985).

Van Schendelen, R. and Robert J. Jackson, eds., *The Politicization of Business in Western Europe* (London: Croom Helm, 1986).

Vickers, Jill, Christine Appelle and Pauline Rankin, *Politics as if Women Mattered* (Toronto: University of Toronto Press, 1993).

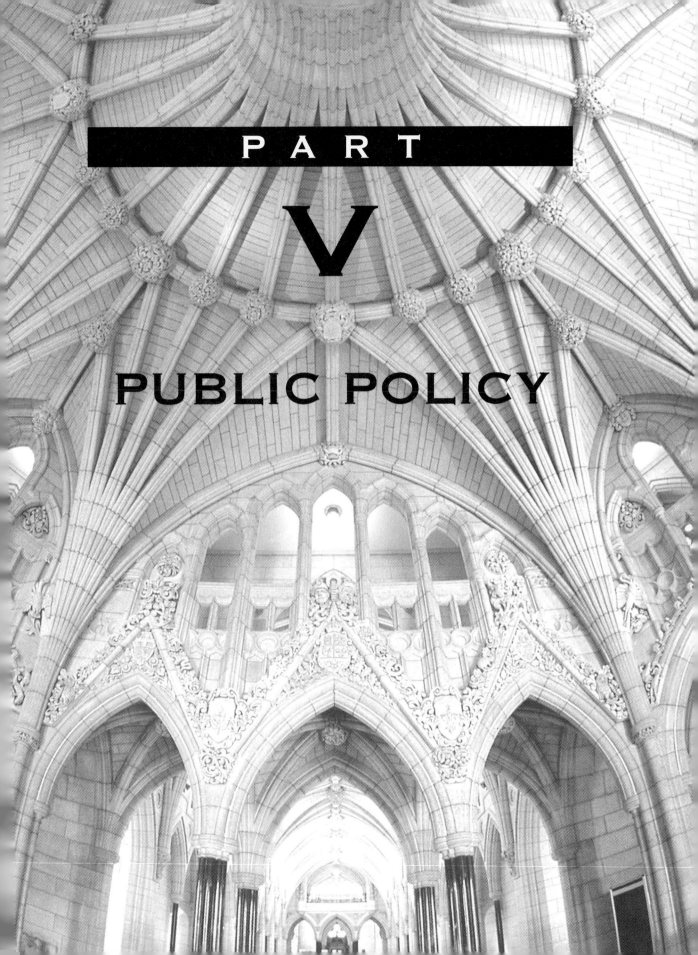

PART

V

PUBLIC POLICY

CHAPTER 13

PUBLIC POLICY AND PUBLIC EXPENDITURES
CHOICE AND CONSTRAINT

No study of politics is complete without an examination of what governments actually do. Thus, one of the burgeoning fields within the discipline of political science is the study of public policy. In fact, research and writing about public policy has become a major growth industry.

In the world of social science, as one author puts it, "concepts, like clothes, are trendy."[1] Consequently, as a particular concept, theme or area of study becomes fashionable, there is a tendency to dress up rather dowdy subjects in more colourful and popular attire. Like other "chic" topics, the concept of public policy has occasionally endured such a fate — an unfortunate occurrence, because much insightful research has been done under the rubric of public policy analysis, and it has greatly augmented our understanding of politics in Canada and elsewhere.

In earlier chapters we examined the expansion of the role of government in Canada, and noted the increase in intervention by governments at all levels in most western industrialized states in recent years. State action is more complex than formerly and therefore more difficult to understand. The current popularity of the study of public policy stems from the realization that governments have come to play an ever more important role in the social and economic life of the country.

Thus, when governments decide to increase or decrease public spending, or raise taxes or abolish a Crown corporation, we want to know why they have chosen a particular course of action and what has influenced and shaped their decisions.

Sometimes governments fail to act on a particular issue. This, too, is of interest to students of public policy. The study of non-decisions, or situations in which the government fails to act on public demands, helps one understand some of the constraints within which policy-makers operate. The options open to policy-makers may be limited by the availability of resources in the physical and economic environments and, also, by the cultural, institutional and behavioural patterns examined in earlier chapters.

---

[1]   The "fashion" metaphor is employed by Leo Panitch, "Corporatism in Canada," *Studies in Political Economy*, no. 1 (Spring 1979), p. 43ff.

In the policy process, these other elements — culture, institutions and behaviour — all come together. The *culture* of a society shapes the demands placed before policy-makers and imposes constraints on the range of possible responses. Some forms of government activity may be legitimized by prevailing ideas and cultural norms, others precluded.

The *institutional structure* of Canadian politics also has a crucial influence on the policy-making process. Room for policy-makers to manoeuvre is limited by the federal nature of the political system, by aspects of the Canadian *Constitution*, by the dictates of governmental responsibility and accountability to Parliament, as well as by non-institutional factors such as relations with the United States and the available levels of finances.

Political *behaviour*, manifested through parties, interest group activity and the electoral arena, is one important means whereby the demands of citizens are articulated and channelled to policy-makers. Moreover, in a liberal democracy such as Canada, the electoral process is significant in determining who will occupy some of the formal policy-making positions. The electoral process requires that governments display a measure of responsiveness to public opinion and may also influence the timing of key policy initiatives.

In this chapter, we attempt to demonstrate the nature and extent of linkages between culture, institutions, behaviour and public policy. We then consider questions about the relations between public policy and public expenditure. Our first task, however, is to define what we mean by the term "public policy."

WHAT IS PUBLIC POLICY?

One of the most common problems in any field of study is securing agreement on the definition and scope of its subject matter. This has certainly been the case in public policy analysis. The word "public" here merely points out that the policy in question is initiated and carried out by "public authorities" — those involving the state or government, or the "public" sector — as opposed to policies of "private" institutions such as chartered banks, private sector corporations or other social organizations. The primary distinguishing feature of "public" policy, therefore, is that it is ultimately backed by the force of law and the coercive sanctions of the state.

The second half of the concept, the word "policy," has proven more difficult to delineate. As one author complained, "no term in social science has suffered more ambiguity and abuse."[2] This ambiguity stems largely from the many contexts in which the term is employed. "Policy" is applied to phenomena ranging from narrow individual decisions, such as building an airport in a particular location, to broad philosophical precepts such as a vague commitment to a "just society." However, the concept "policy" may more usefully be employed as involving a series of more-or-less related activities, rather than a single decision, since grandiose objectives like "balancing the budget" or a "just society" involve changes in a wide range of public policies.[3]

Between these two extremes, "policy" is used somewhat indiscriminately in at least three contexts: "to refer to the *intentions* of politicians...to the *actions* of government...or to the

---

[2] Eliot J. Feldman, "Review Article: Comparative Public Policy: Field or Method?" *Comparative Politics,* vol. 10, no. 2 (January 1979), p. 288.

[3] Richard Rose, "Introduction," in Richard Rose, ed., *Policy-Making in Britain: A Reader in Government* (London: Macmillan, 1969), p. x.

impact of government."[4] These three usages reflect different dimensions of public policy. A policy, whether public or private, is first and foremost a program or course of action pursued in response to a particular problem or issue.[5] But it is also, in most cases, linked to particular goals or objectives (the "intentions" of politicians). Further, the study of public policy is concerned with the effects of policies on society ("the impact of government"), whether such results are the intended or unintended consequences of pursuing a certain course of action.

There is one further dimension of policy that is not revealed by any of the above interpretations of the term. On occasion, a government or some other actor may decide *not* to take action on a given problem. In this case, "policy" takes the form of inaction or non-intervention rather than a positive series of activities. This aspect of policy is well illustrated by Thomas Dye's much-quoted definition of public policy as "whatever governments choose to do or not to do."[6] We are now in a position to propose a definition: **public policy** is the broad framework within which decisions are taken and action (or inaction) is pursued by governments in relation to some issue or problem. The study of public policy is "the study of *how*, *why* and to *what effect* different governments pursue particular *courses of action and inaction*."[7] Thus, when we examine Canadian foreign policy in the next chapter, we outline the broad framework of goals, objectives, decisions and activities of the federal government with regard to Canada's place in the world and its relations with other states and international actors.

This definition raises a further dimension of public policy analysis. How can we divide the total activities of government into more manageable chunks for the purpose of analyzing public policy? A number of classifications of types of public policy may be proposed.

The most obvious division is the traditional separation of foreign policy from domestic public policy. **Foreign policy** shapes Canada's place in the international political system and determines Canada's relations with other states and international organizations such as the United Nations and NATO. **Domestic public policy**, on the other hand, is directed toward the internal economic, social and political environment.

As the world becomes more interdependent, a sharp distinction between domestic and foreign policy is increasingly difficult to maintain. This is especially the case for a country like Canada whose economy is closely integrated with that of a much larger and more powerful neighbour. But, despite the grey areas created by growing interdependencies, there remains a sufficiently clear distinction between domestic and foreign policy, and the respective policy-making processes, to justify the division of these two types of government activity. Therefore, we shall conform to conventional usage by restricting our discussion of public policy to the domestic activities of government, and examine foreign policy separately in Chapter 14.

As the umbrella term "foreign policy" covers a number of government activities — ranging from functional areas such as defence, foreign aid and trade policy to policies toward

---

4 Richard Rose, "Models of Change," in Richard Rose, ed., The Dynamics of Public Policy: A Comparative Analysis (Beverly Hills, Ca.: Sage Publications, 1976), p. 9 (emphasis added).

5 See the definition of "policy" as "A cluster of related activity organized around some general purpose," in Marsha A. Chandler and William M. Chandler, *Public Policy and Provincial Politics* (Toronto: McGraw-Hill Ryerson, 1979), p. 2.

6 Thomas R. Dye, *Understanding Public Policy*, 3rd ed. (Englewood Cliffs, N.J.: Prentice-Hall, 1978), p. 3.

7 Arnold J. Heidenheimer, et al., *Comparative Public Policy*, 2nd ed. (New York: St. Martin's Press, 1983), p. 4 (emphasis in original).

specific regions or countries — so, too, may the domestic activities of government be divided into different policy areas. Again, we find that a much-used dichotomy — social policy and economic policy — serves as a basic organizing device, but may also be less meaningful when applied to specific activities and programs of government.

"Social policy" is perhaps the more easily defined. In general terms, **social policy** encompasses those activities oriented toward the education, health and welfare of the population. The term "economic policy," on the other hand, may be applied to two different levels of government activity. From a macro perspective, **economic policy** refers to the overall management and stabilization of the country's economic environment; that is, to government attempts to control the money supply and interest rates, manage government spending and taxation and foster balanced economic growth — without incurring the "twin evils" of rampant inflation and mass unemployment. Social policy cannot be divorced from economic policy in this broad sense, because public spending on social programs is manipulated to increase or deflate aggregate demand in the economy. Social expenditure is therefore one of the tools available to governments in implementing macroeconomic policy.

On another level, **economic policy** is also a generic term for a number of sectoral policy frameworks to develop or conserve national resources, promote industrial growth, reduce regional disparities or provide communications and transportation systems. In this sense, "economic policy" and "social policy" are more easily distinguished. Even so, some overlaps persist. The objectives of regional development or transportation policy may be as much social as economic, insofar as they attempt to ensure access to services in all parts of the country. Some authors include certain aspects of social policy in their considerations of Canadian economic policies. Education, for instance, is closely linked to the provision of adequately trained personnel for the labour market.[8]

However, in addition to social policy and the two levels of economic policy there are a number of policy areas or frameworks in which governments have become active. These include subsidizing performing arts (ballet, opera, theatre, and so on), regulating the mass media (especially broadcasting), preserving the physical environment and enhancing the multicultural fabric of society. To the extent that these policies are not directly linked to economic development, they appear to be more closely related to "social" concerns. But they are clearly of a different nature from the traditional concerns of social policy and the priorities of the welfare state. Rather than pertaining to standards of living (in quantitative or material terms), they are oriented toward preserving or enhancing the quality of life of Canadian citizens.

We classify the multiplicity of domestic activities in Figure 13.1. "Macroeconomic Policy" comprises those activities that pertain to the federal government's role as the central manager of the overall domestic economy, including control of the currency and money supply, manipulation of interest rates via the Bank of Canada, managing public expenditures and taxation, and so on. Since priorities under this general heading influence the resources available for, or the constraints upon, the attainment of other public objectives, "Macroeconomic Policy" is placed at the centre of the figure; dotted lines indicate its relation to other policy fields. While macroeconomics deals with broad categories of the economy such as employment, investment, inflation, growth and trade, microeconomics draws attention to components of the economy such as markets, industries, firms and consumers.

---

[8]   See, for example, Ingrid Bryan, *Economic Policies in Canada* (Toronto: Butterworths, 1982).

FIGURE 13.1 A TYPOLOGY OF SELECTED DOMESTIC POLICY AREAS

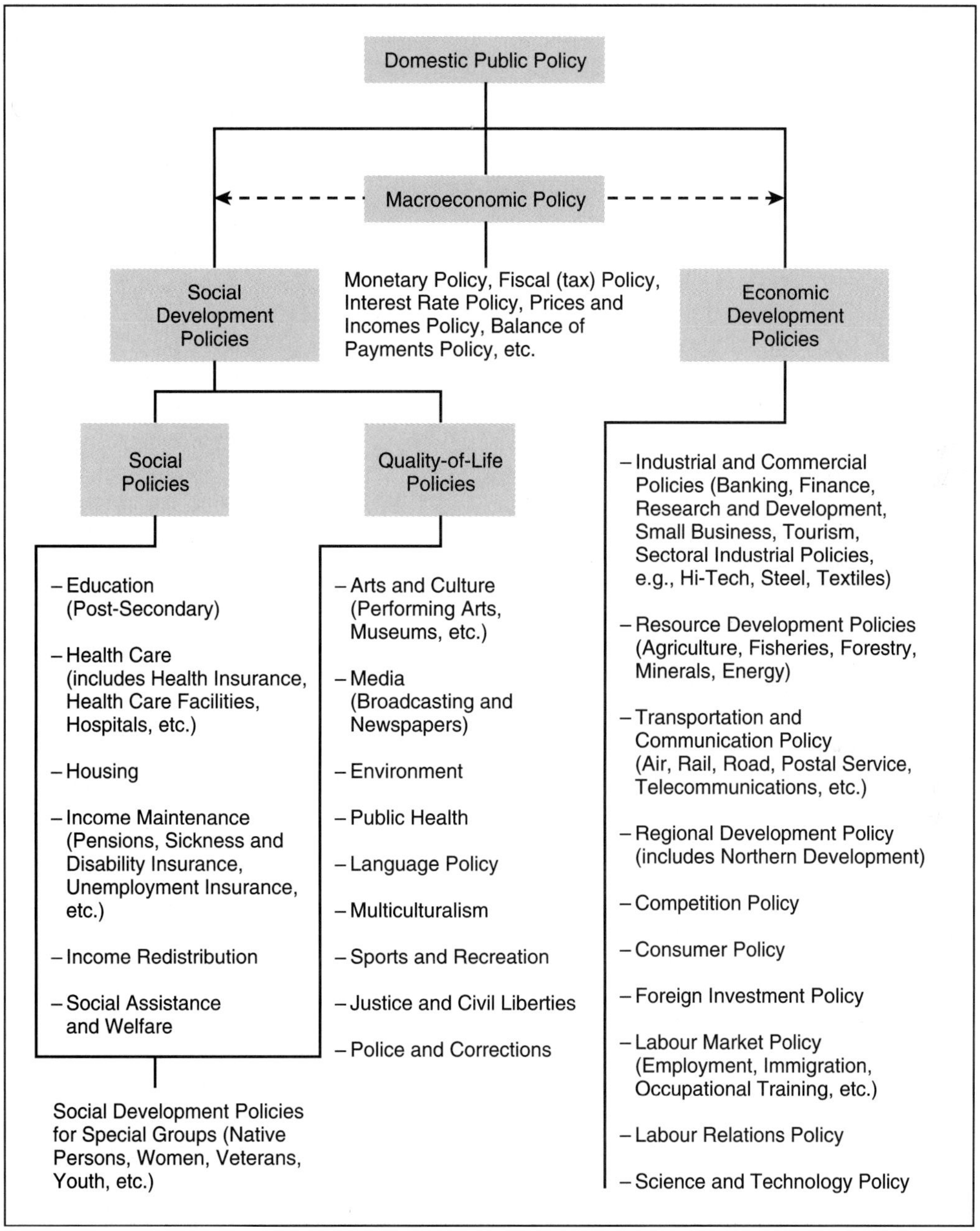

```
                          ┌──────────────────────────┐
                          │  Domestic Public Policy  │
                          └──────────────────────────┘
                                      │
          ┌───────────────────────────┼───────────────────────────┐
          │       ┌──────────────────────────────────┐            │
     <────┼──────>│      Macroeconomic Policy         │<───────────┤─────>
          │       └──────────────────────────────────┘            │
   ┌────────────┐   Monetary Policy, Fiscal (tax) Policy,   ┌────────────┐
   │   Social   │   Interest Rate Policy, Prices and         │  Economic  │
   │Development │   Incomes Policy, Balance of               │Development │
   │  Policies  │   Payments Policy, etc.                    │  Policies  │
   └────────────┘                                            └────────────┘
```

Social Development Policies → Social Policies / Quality-of-Life Policies

Social Policies

– Education (Post-Secondary)

– Health Care (includes Health Insurance, Health Care Facilities, Hospitals, etc.)

– Housing

– Income Maintenance (Pensions, Sickness and Disability Insurance, Unemployment Insurance, etc.)

– Income Redistribution

– Social Assistance and Welfare

Social Development Policies for Special Groups (Native Persons, Women, Veterans, Youth, etc.)

Quality-of-Life Policies

– Arts and Culture (Performing Arts, Museums, etc.)

– Media (Broadcasting and Newspapers)

– Environment

– Public Health

– Language Policy

– Multiculturalism

– Sports and Recreation

– Justice and Civil Liberties

– Police and Corrections

Economic Development Policies

– Industrial and Commercial Policies (Banking, Finance, Research and Development, Small Business, Tourism, Sectoral Industrial Policies, e.g., Hi-Tech, Steel, Textiles)

– Resource Development Policies (Agriculture, Fisheries, Forestry, Minerals, Energy)

– Transportation and Communication Policy (Air, Rail, Road, Postal Service, Telecommunications, etc.)

– Regional Development Policy (includes Northern Development)

– Competition Policy

– Consumer Policy

– Foreign Investment Policy

– Labour Market Policy (Employment, Immigration, Occupational Training, etc.)

– Labour Relations Policy

– Science and Technology Policy

The other general categories, "Social Development Policies" and "Economic Development Policies," reflect other divisions of responsibilities in the federal government.[9] The latter category includes a wide range of sectoral and regional frameworks designed to deal with

---

[9] For a similar division of public policies at the provincial level in Canada, see Chandler and Chandler, *Public Policy and Provincial Politics.*

different aspects of the Canadian economy. In keeping with our earlier discussion, we have divided "Social Development Policies" into two sub-categories. "Social Policies" reflect the traditional concerns of the welfare state with providing adequate minimum standards of education, health care, housing and income security for all citizens. "Quality-of-Life-Policies," on the other hand, are oriented toward preserving and enhancing the country's artistic, cultural and environmental heritage and with civil liberties, human rights and opportunities for individuals and groups.

Even with this comprehensive classification of the activities of government, many omissions remain. The government's interventions on behalf of certain designated groups, such as youth, Native peoples, handicapped persons and women, do not fit easily into any classification since they entail both social and economic activities. For example, in tackling the position of women in Canadian society, public policy has to be directed toward reforming traditional social policies (such as the provision of adequate pensions for elderly single women), providing new social programs (such as day care), taking into account quality-of-life issues (such as the elimination of sexist bias in advertising, media reporting and publishing) and promoting equal employment and training opportunities for women as part of labour market policy.

These caveats aside, the typology of government activities or policy areas in Figure 13.1 provides a guide to the many major policy concerns of governments in Canada while grouping them into manageable bundles to facilitate analysis.

PUBLIC POLICY AND THEORIES OF POLICY-MAKING

As the literature on public policy has grown, analysts have embraced a number of alternative theoretical models and approaches to explain how policy decisions were made and how public policy frameworks developed, why various governments have adopted different courses of action and inaction in response to apparently similar problems and issues, and to what effect governments have intervened or refrained from acting to resolve the problems that confront them. The theories are "as indispensable to political analysis as a map or compass is to a traveller crossing unknown terrain."[10]

These models and approaches may be distinguished from one another by their portrayal of the major actors in the policy process, their assumptions regarding the nature of society and politics and the role of government/state and their evaluation of the interests served by public policy outputs. Each model or approach directs the student's attention to different features of public policy — they are like different lenses through which policy may be observed. There is no universally accepted theory. Consequently, we shall outline some of the more frequently used approaches and note some of their respective strengths and weaknesses. To organize our discussion, we have divided the contending theories into two categories: micro-level models, which focus mainly on the making of individual policy, decisions, and macro-level approaches, which are more concerned with accounting for broader patterns of public policy as part of the relationship between the state and society.[11]

---

[10]   Stephen Brooks, *Public Policy in Canada* (Toronto: McClelland & Stewart, 1989), p. 41.

[11]   For other categorizations see Bruce Doern and Richard W. Phidd, *Canadian Public Policy* (Toronto: Methuen, 1983), ch. 1; and Michael Atkinson and Marsha Chandler, eds., *The Politics of Canadian Public Policy* (Toronto: University of Toronto Press, 1983), pp. 3–5.

MICRO-LEVEL APPROACHES TO PUBLIC POLICY ANALYSIS

Micro-level models or theories of decision-making are intended to explain how individual decisions are taken within a broad framework of public policy. It must be made clear that, in our terms, policy-making and decision-making are not the same thing. Rarely will a policy consist of a single decision. If **decision-making** is defined as the process whereby one course of action (or inaction) or one objective is chosen from a number of competing alternatives, then each public policy will involve at least the following:

1. A decision whether or not government should intervene in a particular issue area;
2. A decision on the goals or objectives of governmental involvement;
3. A decision on the best available means of achieving the goals and instruments to be used; and
4. A decision to maintain, alter or discontinue the chosen course of action once some evaluation of its effectiveness can be undertaken.

Decision-making therefore is clearly a *part* of the policy-making process, but not the whole process. Decision-making models, by and large, concentrate on the third stage outlined above — the selection of the best available means of achieving the goals of governmental intervention. They assume that governmental priorities and objectives have already been established via the political process, and tend to focus instead on the choice of means to attain those goals via the administrative process.

Over the years, the relative merits of different theories of decision-making have been debated.[12] The most widely known debate has centred on the confrontation between advocates of the *rationalist* and *incrementalist* approaches to decision-making.[13]

THE RATIONAL-COMPREHENSIVE MODEL

The usual point of departure for this debate over theory is the *rational-comprehensive* model of decision-making. This model can best be described by the following elements or stages of the process:

1. The rational decision-maker is presented with a problem that can be distinguished from other problems, or at least compared meaningfully with them.
2. The values, goals and objectives that guide the decision-maker are reviewed and ranked in order of priority.
3. A list of alternative means of achieving these goals is compiled.
4. The consequences (costs and benefits) that would ensue from each alternative are estimated.
5. Each alternative, and its likely consequences, is then compared with all other alternatives.

---

[12] See Chapter 9 and Graham T. Allison, *Essence of Decision: Explaining the Cuban Missile Crisis* (Boston: Little, Brown, 1971).

[13] See, especially, Charles E. Lindblom, "The Science of 'Muddling Through,'" *PAR*, vol. 19, no. 2 (Spring 1959), pp. 79–88; the critique by Yehezkel Dror, "Muddling Through — 'Science' or Inertia?"; and Lindblom's response, "Contexts for Change and Strategy: A Reply," both in *PAR*, vol. 24, no. 3 (September 1964), pp. 153–57 and l57–58.

6. Finally, the rational decision-maker will select the course of action, and its consequences, that offers maximum attainment of the values, goals or objectives identified in Step 2.[14]

According to the advocates of this model, the end product of the process will be a "rational" decision — that is, one that selects the most effective and efficient means of achieving a given end.

Ideally, the rational-comprehensive process may be the way that some decisions *ought* to be made; but does it describe accurately the way in which all, or even most, decisions are made? Critics maintain that the rationalist model is wrong on both counts — it neither describes reality nor represents an ideal to be emulated.[15] First, it is argued that, in a complex industrial society, very few of the issues confronting governments can be singled out easily for this kind of comprehensive analysis. Second, such a process makes totally unreasonable demands on decision-makers with regard to information needed and the time and resources necessary to evaluate the costs and benefits of all possible alternative courses of action. Thus, the model is claimed to be impractical and, perhaps, not entirely "rational." The costs of undertaking a search for the most efficient means of implementation may well be greater than the savings realized by deploying it.

Third, it is argued that the rational-comprehensive approach is a normative or prescriptive model: it does not describe how decisions are actually made; rather, it *prescribes* how some people think policies and decisions *ought* to be made. Thus, there is a danger that means become confused with ends, that the ultimate objectives of government become less important than the quest for the most efficient or rational means of achieving those goals. When technocratic models of decision-making or policy-making come to value rationality and efficiency as ends in themselves, the outcome may be as Theodore Lowi trenchantly expressed with reference to a convicted war criminal: "There is neither politics nor political science left when we can look at Eichmann and ask only whether his policy-making system was as good as it could have been."[16]

THE INCREMENTALIST MODEL

Charles Lindblom has advocated an alternative to the rational-comprehensive model that, he argues, is more descriptive of the way decision-makers actually proceed. This alternative approach has been variously labelled "disjointed incrementalism," "policy-making by successive limited comparisons," "the science of muddling through" or, in its simplest form, "incrementalism."[17]

---

[14] Adapted from Anderson, *Public Policy-Making*, pp. 9–10.

[15] See among others, Lindblom, "The Science of 'Muddling Through"; reviews by Anderson, *Public Policy-Making*, pp. 10–1; G. Smith and D. May "The Artificial Debate between Rationalist and Incrementalist Models of Decision-making," in A.G. McGrew and M.J. Wilson, eds., *Decision-Making Approaches and Analysis* (Manchester: Manchester University Press, 1982), pp. 116–24; and Ronald Manzer, "Public Policy-Making as Practical Reasoning," *CJPS*, vol. 17, no. 3 (Sept. 1984), pp. 577–94.

[16] Theodore Lowi, "Decision Making vs. Policy Making: Toward an Antidote for Technocracy," *PAR*, vol. 30, no. 3 (May 1970), p. 319.

[17] Lindblom, "The Science of 'Muddling Through'"; David Braybrooke and Charles Lindblom, *A Strategy of Decision* (New York: Free Press, 1963), especially ch. 5; and Lindblom, "Still Muddling, Not Yet Through," *PAR*, vol. 39, no. 6 (Nov./Dec. 1979), pp. 517–26.

The **incrementalist** model assumes that the majority of problems facing decision-makers are complex and interrelated, and that decision-makers operate in a climate of uncertainty and limited resources. In contrast to the rationalist approach, the point of departure for incremental decision-making is not some ideal goal to be attained in the most efficient manner, but the policies and programs already in place in a given issue area. From that basis, only a limited number of policy alternatives are considered, and only a few foreseeable consequences are evaluated for each alternative. Incrementalism therefore results in alterations at the margins of existing policies.

The incrementalist model claims to resolve the problem of inadequate information and uncertainty, since marginal adjustments to policies and programs can easily be reversed or altered. Thus, incrementalism may be the more "rational" way to proceed, because it avoids making serious, lasting errors. Moreover, successive limited comparisons consume less time and other resources than the exhaustive search process of the rational-comprehensive model. Finally, since there is rarely agreement on the values and objectives of government intervention, an incremental approach to decision-making offers endless opportunities for a redefinition of goals and the adjustment of both the means (programs, activities) and ends (values, priorities) of public policy-making.

The incrementalist approach, too, has been criticized on a number of grounds. Many criticisms are essentially subjective in nature, arguing that, whether or not the model is empirically valid, it is just not the way that decisions should be made. Given the preoccupation of advocates of rationalism with "improving" the decision-making process in the interests of technical efficiency, it is perhaps not surprising that they are appalled by the prospect of decision-makers "muddling through" on most issues. Yehezkel Dror, for example, has labelled Lindblom's model an inherently "conservative" recipe for maintaining the status quo since it provides an "ideological reinforcement of the pro-inertia and anti-innovation forces prevalent in all human organizations, administrative and policy-making."[18]

A much more important problem, in our view, is the fact that although the incrementalist model is supposed to provide a general description of how policy decisions are made by making marginal adjustments to the policies and programs already in place, it quite clearly cannot account for occasional radical departures from existing patterns of activity or inactivity. Thus, it cannot explain the entry of governments into new areas of policy intervention, nor can it account for drastic alterations to, or innovations in, existing policy.

RESOLVING THE RATIONALIST VERSUS INCREMENTALIST DEBATE

In an attempt to overcome both the descriptive shortcomings of incrementalism and the impracticality of the rational-comprehensive model, Amitai Etzioni has proposed a third theory of decision-making known as **mixed-scanning**.[19] Etzioni differentiates two kinds of decisions. "Contextual" or "fundamental" decisions establish the broad framework of goals and long-term action in a given policy area and are made through a modified, more realistic, form of the rationalistic process. "Incremental" decisions are based on marginal adjustments and fill in the short-term details of policy implementation within the contexts set by fundamental decisions.

---

[18] Dror, "Muddling Through — 'Science' or Inertia?", p. 155.

[19] Amitai Etzioni, "Mixed-Scanning: A Third Approach to Decision Making," *PAR*, vol. 27, no. 5 (December 1967), pp. 385–92.

The central problem in the rationalist/incrementalist debate is that the two sides have different conceptions of the term "model" and its functions. In political science, as in every-day language, "model" is sometimes used to refer to a normative ideal that all should seek to emulate, as in "she is a model citizen." But "model" is more rigorously used in the sense of a simplified version of reality designed to show how various components fit together and work, as in a "working model" of a car or steam engine. The rational-comprehensive model is of the former type, since it assumes that general agreement can be reached on long-term values and goals and prescribes how decisions ought to be made in the interests of techni-cal efficiency. It is, therefore, a prescriptive model to which decision-makers and policy an-alysts may aspire, but is strictly impractical for routine decision-making. Incrementalism, on the other hand, is a simplified "working model" that purports to explain and describe how decision-makers actually proceed, given the constraints within which they operate. To a great extent, therefore, the two sides are advocating totally different things, and the debate between incrementalists and rationalists is based on differing conceptions of the roles and purposes of decision making models.[20]

As a theoretical approach to aid our understanding of how decisions are made within the broader framework of public policy, the rational-comprehensive model is faulty in many respects. Incrementalism, on the other hand, is a more descriptive model that may accurately portray the tendency of governmental decision-makers to "muddle through" from day to day on many issues. But it also has limitations, inasmuch as it cannot account for key decisions such as government involvement in a new issue area, where no clear policy programs existed previously. Neither of these contending models, nor any attempt to develop a middle ground between them, has yet provided a comprehensive and generally accepted theory of decision-making. However, decision-making is only a part of the over-all process of public policy activity. Therefore, to the extent that any model can tell us *how* policy decisions are made, it still could not provide guidance as to *why* governments pursue particular directions in public policy, nor *to what effect*. That requires a broader perspective on the role of the state and its relationship with society than decision-making theories can provide.

MACRO-LEVEL APPROACHES TO PUBLIC POLICY ANALYSIS

Macro-level approaches are those that focus on the wider relationship between state and society, and therefore on the broad patterns of public policy, rather than on the details of how individual policy decisions are made within the government. These theories tend to differ from one another with respect to both the relative emphasis they place on economic, social and political factors and their views of the interests served by the government in its policy activities. In the pages that follow, we briefly outline five of these approaches: "environmental determinism," "pluralism," "public choice theory," "neo-Marxism" and "state centred," together with some of their respective strengths and weaknesses, as frameworks for analyzing Canadian public policy.

ENVIRONMENTAL DETERMINISM

The **environmental determinist** approach to the study of public policy is the least "political" of the five macro-level frameworks considered here. Its methodology is based

---

[20]   Smith and May, "The Artificial Debate," pp. 121–23.

upon "the systematic comparative analysis of public policies the objective of which is to discover the relationship between various environmental factors and public policy."[21] The approach calls for the study of a number of political systems or sub-national political units (e.g., Canadian provinces) in order to obtain sufficient data for statistical analysis of the relationships between public policy outputs (usually measured in terms of public expenditure) and socio-economic variables (such as economic or technological developments, affluence or the demographic structure of populations). At the same time, it tends to ignore or downplay the importance of explicitly political actors such as parties or interest groups, as well as other major political variables such as ideology and the distribution of power in society.

The theoretical origins of this approach lie in the political science frameworks that were popular during the so-called behavioural revolution in the late 1950s and the 1960s. These models viewed the political system as a sub-system of society as a whole, as the complex set of roles and structures concerned with the "authoritative allocation of values" for a society.[22] From this perspective, public policies are "authoritative allocations" designed to maintain or restore an equilibrium between the political system and its environment. Policies, therefore, are largely determined by changes in the economic, physical, social and technological environments, both domestic and external, as well as in the international political system.

A number of studies in political science supported this thesis by showing that public policy outputs were more strongly related statistically with socio-economic environmental variables than with political factors such as the nature of party competition or the extent of electoral participation, both in cross-national analyses[23] and in intra-societal comparisons among the American states.[24] Attempts to reproduce these findings in the Canadian context met with mixed results. While, for example, Falcone and Whittington found that political variables were less relevant than socio-economic factors in predicting federal policy outputs over time,[25] studies of provincial policy innovation by Poel and Chandler re-emphasized the importance of political characteristics such as the partisan complexion of government, the size of the public service, constituency representation and the nature of party competition.[26]

However, even where statistical analyses do suggest a strong relationship between socio-economic and other environmental factors on the one hand, and public policy outputs on the other, their explanatory power is limited. As one critic observes, "the fact that socio-

---

[21] Peter Aucoin, "Public Policy Theory and Analysis," in G.B. Doern and P. Aucoin, eds., *Public Policy in Canada: Organization, Process and Management* (Toronto: Macmillan, 1979), p. 11.

[22] Hence, the environmental determinist model is sometimes labelled the "sociological" approach to politics and public policy.

[23] For example, Phillips Cutright, "Political Structure, Economic Development and National Programs," *American Journal of Sociology*, vol. 70, no. 5 (March 1965), pp. 537–50.

[24] For example, Thomas R. Dye, *Politics, Economics and the Public: Policy Outcomes in the American States* (Chicago: Rand McNally, 1966).

[25] David Falcone and M.S. Whittington, "Output Change in Canada: A Preliminary Attempt to Open the 'Black Box,'" unpublished paper delivered to the Canadian Political Science Association, Annual Meeting, Montréal, June 1972.

[26] Dale H. Poel, "The Diffusion of Legislation among the Canadian Provinces: A Statistical Analysis," *CJPS*, vol. 9, no. 4 (December 1976), pp. 605–28; William M. Chandler, "Canadian Socialism and Policy Impact: Contagion from the Left," *CJPS*, vol. 10, no. 4 (December 1977), pp. 755–80.

economic variables are closely associated with political or policy variables does not in it-self show that one 'causes,' 'shapes,' 'determines,' or 'accounts for' the other."[27] This is not to say that environmental factors are unimportant to the study of public policy. It may reasonably be expected that broad social and economic changes such as the changing age structure of the population, urbanization, industrialization or a recession may generate new demands for government intervention. But we need to know how those demands be-come mobilized and why public policy-makers respond to them in a particular fashion. We need to know which social groups are affected by environmental changes and whether they have the political resources to channel demands to policy-makers, as well as why gov-ernments appear willing to respond to some interests and not to others.[28]

In our view, the vast majority of economic, geographical, social and technological factors in the environment of the policy-making process should be regarded not as causal determinants of public policy but as strictly environmental variables — that is, as part of the broader context of resources and constraints within which policy-makers op-erate and make political choices. The next model, pluralism, attempts to fill some of the gaps. To be sure, economic growth may lead to an expansion of the government's tax base, thereby providing greater revenues to finance public expenditure, but it will not in itself cause governments to spend more, nor determine which programs, if any, will benefit from increased resources. In a recession, the revenue base may shrink, placing constraints on the government's freedom of action but not necessarily determining that the government will reduce spending in general or on any particular program.

PLURALISM

The **pluralist** approach to the study of public policy emphasizes political actors and organized interests in the policy process, especially on the role of parties and pressure groups. Pluralists treat economic factors, cultural and ideological differences as sources of political conflict. They do not posit, as Marxists do, that society is comprised of antagonistic classes. Pluralists see shifting groups all seeking to have their members' preferences translated into public policy. These groups may be based on ethnicity, language, religion, gender, region, province, ideology or class. For pluralists, politics is the process whereby individuals and groups seek to promote their interests through organization, political mobilization and alliance-building in order to influence the policy outputs of government. Political parties are seen as broad coalitions of interests, seeking legislative majorities in the electoral arena. Government is viewed as a neutral arbiter that referees the group struggle, adju-dicates among competing group demands and implements and enforces public policies in the national interest or, at least, according to the wishes of the majority on each issue.

Thus, pluralists regard public policies as the outcomes of competition between groups and parties. The essence of the pluralist approach is the assumption that power is widely dispersed in society. Since, in its *extreme* forms, pluralism does not admit to the existence of structural inequalities within society, all individuals and groups are seen as having approx-imately equal access to the policy-making process. Therefore, they all have potentially equal influence on public policy outputs as long as they organize themselves and play by the

---

[27] Joyce M. Munns, "The Environment, Politics and Policy Literature: A Critique and Reformulation," *Western Political Quarterly*, vol. 28, no. 4 (December 1975), p. 658.

[28] Richard Simeon, "Studying Public Policy," *CJPS*, vol. 9, no. 4 (December 1976), pp. 567–68.

"rules of the game" — that is, as long as they abide by the underlying consensus on political values and procedures. The tendency for coalitions and alliances of groups to change composition from one issue to another means that there are no permanent winners and losers in the group struggle. Power, defined in simple terms as "the ability to get things done," therefore shifts from coalition to coalition according to the issue at stake and is never the exclusive preserve of any one group or elite.[29]

The more advanced schools of pluralism assert the importance of the competition between elites within an overall consensus from the mass public. In his famous volume *Capitalism, Socialism and Democracy*, Joseph Schumpeter showed how elitist decision-making could be reconciled with democracy. He compared the competition between elites for democratic votes with the operation of an economic market.[30] Later Robert Dahl invented the term *polyarchy* to depict how minority rule could take place within a consensus on democratic values.[31]

Critics argue that some groups never get a fair hearing for their interests because obstacles prevent them from placing certain issues on the agenda of political debate. For example, it may be argued that the federalist organization of Canadian political life is more conducive to the expression of linguistic and regional issues than to the mobilization of redistributional issues based on social class. Since many class-based issues such as labour legislation and welfare policies fall under provincial jurisdiction, it is more difficult to mobilize these interests across provincial boundaries. Thus, they are partially "organized out" of federal politics, while cultural and regional issues are "organized in."[32]

In any case, it is harder for the poor and the working class to become politically organized than for the rich or for business interests. The latter groups have more political and economic resources and their relatively small numbers facilitate mobilization.[33] Consequently, "the flaw in the pluralist heaven is that the heavenly chorus sings with a strong upper-class accent. Probably about 90 percent of the people cannot get into the pressure (group) system."[34]

The idea that some issues are "organized out" of politics by the "mobilization of bias" inherent in all political systems is taken a step further in the concept of *non-decision-making*. Peter Bachrach and Morton Baratz condemned the pluralists for emphasizing one aspect of power, "the ability to get things done," to the exclusion of "the ability to stop things getting done," which is the power of non-decision.[35] They argued that elite groups within or outside government take advantage of the "mobilization of bias," a set of predominant values, beliefs, rituals and institutional procedures that operate systematically and consistently to the

---

[29] The classic pluralist statement of the diffusion of political power is found in Robert A. Dahl, *Who Governs?* (New Haven: Yale University Press, 1961).

[30] Joseph A. Schumpeter, *Capitalism, Socialism and Democracy* (New York: Harper, 1943).

[31] Robert Dahl, *A Preface to Democratic Theory* (Chicago: University of Chicago Press, 1956).

[32] For a comprehensive critique of this position, see Charles Lindblom, *Politics and Markets* (New York: Basic Books, 1977) and Stephen Brooks, *Public Policy in Canada*, ch. 2.

[33] Schattschneider's arguments about the effects of group size on political mobilization are supported by Mancur Olson, Jr., *The Logic of Collective Action* (Cambridge: Harvard University Press, 1965).

[34] E.E. Schattschneider, *The Semisovereign People: A Realist's View of Democracy in America* (Hinsdale: Dryden Press, 1975), pp. 34–35.

[35] Peter Bachrach and Morton S. Baratz, "The Two Faces of Power," *APSR*, vol. 56, no 4 (December 1962), pp. 947–52.

benefit of certain persons and groups at the expense of others in order to prevent some issues from ever reaching the agenda of political debate.[36]

Obviously, non-decisions present serious methodological problems since by their very nature they cannot readily be identified, especially where issues have been successfully suppressed or excluded from the political agenda.[37] However, this critical approach does serve to sensitize one to the facts that some interests and issues are more easily organized than others and that various groups do not have equal political resources or enjoy equal access to the policy-making process.

To be sure, interest groups do organize in attempts to influence policy-makers, and it is necessary to examine their effects when studying public policy, especially in a liberal democracy such as Canada where governments must maintain a degree of responsiveness to pressures from society. But, for a variety of reasons, some groups have greater influence on policy-making than others. The next three macro-level approaches attempt to explain why this is the case.

PUBLIC CHOICE THEORY

Public choice can be defined as "the economic study of non-market decision-making or simply the application of economics to political science."[38] The basic premise of this theory, borrowed directly from classical liberal economics, is that each individual is essentially a self-interested, rational, utility-maximizing actor. Individual wants are constrained by a world characterized by scarcity and populated by other individuals who want the same things. Thus, when people engage in collective non-market decision-making in the political arena (making "public" choices), they behave in exactly the same way that many economists believe they do when making market-oriented choices in the economic sphere — that is, they act in a rational and calculating fashion to maximize their own interests. Voters, for example, will give electoral support to the party that offers a package of programs most likely to maximize their individual well-being.[39] Interest groups will lobby for their particular concerns. And, when politicians and bureaucrats formulate policies, they do so not according to some vague notion of "the public interest" or even "the will of the majority" but largely to satisfy their own narrow individual interests.

Individuals do not have equal opportunities to realize their respective interests in the public choice model, however. The average voter, for example, is fairly peripheral to the public choice view of the policy process. Voters are important only when they have the periodic opportunity to choose, through elections, which politicians will have most influence in government. Otherwise, except when they participate in an effective special-interest group, ordinary citizens are little more than consumers of public policies.

According to public choice theorists, the central actors in the policy-making process are special interest groups, bureaucrats and politicians (especially the leaders of the governing

---

[36] Peter Bachrach and Morton S. Baratz, *Power and Poverty: Theory and Practice* (New York: Oxford University Press, 1970), p. 43ff.

[37] See Geraint Parry and Peter Morriss, "When is a Decision not a Decision?" in McGrew and Wilson, eds., *Decision-Making: Approaches and Analysis*, pp. 19–35.

[38] Dennis C. Mueller, *Public Choice* (Cambridge: Cambridge University Press, 1979), p. 1.

[39] Anthony Downs, *An Economic Theory of Democracy* (New York: Harper and Row, 1957), esp. ch. 3.

party).[40] But this is not just pluralism in disguise. First, in the public choice approach, the primary unit of political action is the individual, not the group. Although individuals may join forces in pursuit of their interests, they do so only when collective action promises greater rewards than acting alone and when the benefits of collective action outweigh the costs of group participation. When the benefits of group action are uncertain, or when they might possibly be derived without paying the costs of group membership, it is often more rational for the individual not to participate in collective action.

Some groups have much more difficulty organizing and mobilizing support than do others. Small, relatively homogeneous groups with much to win or lose from public policy changes, such as specific business interests, are more easily mobilized and enjoy proportionately greater resources than larger, disparate groups like consumers or environmentalists.[41] Thus, in contrast to the extreme pluralists, who consider that all groups have equal access to and potentially equal influence on the policy-making process, public choice analysts argue that "there is no reason to believe that the pressure exerted on decision-makers by special interest groups…is in any sense balanced or fair or offsetting."[42]

The third major departure from pluralism is that public choice views government not as a neutral arbiter refereeing the group struggle in the public interest, but rather as a complex process of interaction and bargaining among bureaucrats and politicians seeking to maximize their own individual self-interests. Thus, for example, it is assumed that politicians will support policies that benefit marginal voters in order to maximize the likelihood of their election or re-election to office. Bureaucrats, on the other hand, will use the information at their disposal to push for policies that will expand their departmental budgets, increase the number of programs or staff under their responsibility or enhance opportunities for promotion and influence in the policy process.[43]

Although it draws upon the long-established tradition of classical economic theory, public choice as an approach to politics and public policy analysis is still a young and relatively underdeveloped art. Its application has produced some interesting insights into the policy-making process — especially in its recognition that politicians and bureaucrats are not mere servants of external pressures, but rather have their own interests and objectives.[44] However, its focus remains rather restrictive. Despite its ambitions toward formulating a more general theory of the political process, public choice theory is, at best, only a partial aid for understanding how and why public policies are developed.

NEO-MARXIST ANALYSIS

An alternative political economy approach to public policy is **neo-Marxist analysis**. Neo-Marxism is a generic label for various contemporary theories and propositions that seek to

---

[40] Some public choice writers also include the media as a fourth influential actor in the policy process, because the media helps to structure the agenda of political debate. See, for example, Michael J. Trebilcock et al., *The Choice of Governing Instrument: A Study Prepared for the Economic Council of Canada* (Ottawa: Supply and Services, 1982), ch. 2.

[41] Olson, *The Logic of Collective Action*, pp. 53–7 and ch. 7.

[42] Trebilcock, et al., *The Choice of Governing Instrument*, p. 10.

[43] See Mark Sproule-Jones, "Institutions, Constitutions and Public Policies," in Atkinson and Chandler, *The Politics of Canadian Public Policy*, p. 127.

[44] See, for example, Allan M. Maslove and G. Swimmer, *Wage Controls in Canada 1975–78: A Study of Public Decision-Making* (Montreal: IRPP, 1980).

develop a systematic conceptualization of politics and the role of the state in capitalist society based upon assumptions originally formulated by Karl Marx concerning the relationships among economic, social and political structures. There are, at present, a number of strands of neo-Marxist theory; the following brief overview attempts to simplify some fairly complex concepts and arguments.

The essence of Marxist theory is that, at all stages of historical development, social and political relations are determined largely by the economic basis of society. The relations between classes necessarily are antagonistic and are based on the mode of production that exists at any given time. In the present era (the capitalist mode of production), two main social classes are differentiated by their respective economic roles: the capitalist class, or bourgeoisie, that owns and controls the means of production (factories, financial capital, and so on) and the working class, or proletariat, that sells its labour to the capitalists. According to Marx's economic theory, the dynamics of capitalism require that capitalists extract "surplus value" from labour — that they effectively exploit the working class — because this is the chief mechanism whereby capitalists make profits for further investment and the accumulation of capital. This exploitative economic relationship between capital and labour forms the basis for unequal, conflictual class relations in social and political life.

According to Marxists, the primary function of the state in capitalist society is to serve the interests of capitalism by creating and maintaining conditions favourable to profitable capital accumulation. However, in order to reduce conflict between classes and forestall the possibility of revolution by the exploited working class, the state also has to create and maintain conditions of social harmony by providing policies that legitimize the capitalist society.[45] Marxists believe that one of the factors in state survival is the dominant ideology of capitalist countries. This includes beliefs about private property, the possibility of upward socio-economic mobility and the economic market, all of which buttress the role of the state and make it difficult for the vast majority of individuals to understand that they are being exploited.

Most public policies, in the neo-Marxist view, may be categorized roughly according to their intentions or effects as serving either the *accumulation* or *legitimation* functions of the capitalist state. Examples of accumulation-oriented policies in the Canadian context include the provision of industrial infrastructure (e.g., transportation networks, public utilities such as hydro), subsidies or tax expenditures for private sector businesses and fiscal and monetary policies aimed at creating a healthy climate for investment. Legitimation policies would include most social welfare programs, occupational health and safety regulations, environmental pollution controls and language and cultural policies. Some programs or policies, however, may serve both accumulation and legitimation roles; hence these two functions are not necessarily mutually exclusive. For example, the introduction of free, mass education in response to working class demands may enhance the legitimacy of the state in the short term but, by providing a better-trained, more skilled labour force, it may also aid capital accumulation.[46]

The key question in neo-Marxist analysis, of course, is why the state pursues particular public policies and courses of action. The **instrumentalist** view of the state suggests that

---

[45] See James O'Connor, *The Fiscal Crisis of the State* (New York: St. Martin's Press, 1973), p. 6.

[46] For further discussion of the functions of the Canadian state, see Leo Panitch, "The Role and Nature of the Canadian State," in Panitch, ed., *The Canadian State: Political Economy and Political Power* (Toronto: University of Toronto Press, 1977), pp. 3–27.

it serves the interests of the capitalist class because of the strong links (common class backgrounds, family ties and old school networks) that exist between political and bureaucratic elites and the business community.[47] The **structuralist** view argues that the capitalist class is itself internally divided into a number of competing elements or *factions* (finance capital, manufacturing capital, resource capital, etc.). Hence, the state must be *relatively autonomous* or independent so that it can serve the long-term interests of capitalism rather than the short-term profit-maximizing interests of individual capitalists.[48] Therefore, the state often pursues policies such as social welfare programs that respond to working class demands even if these policies are opposed by much of the capitalist class. According to structuralist neo-Marxists, the capitalist state operates in this apparently contradictory way because it is the political expression of the conflictual, but unequal, relationship between social classes.

If one can accept the premises on which their arguments are based, neo-Marxist analyses can be seen to account for broad patterns in public policy in different societies and for the expanding economic and social activities of the state over time. For example, since Marxist economics predicts that the rate of return on capital investment will tend to fall as capitalism progresses, it becomes increasingly necessary for governments to underwrite some of the costs of production (e.g., by subsidizing research and development expenditures). Neo-Marxist analysis is also explicitly oriented toward matters of inequality and distribution of power in Canadian society. In addition, more than any other approach considered here, it addresses issues of external constraints on Canadian policy-making, especially in an era of extensive foreign ownership, multinational corporations and the interdependence of capitalist economies. But, despite numerous attempts to get inside the policy process and to develop a neo-Marxist approach to public policy analysis,[49] neo-Marxism remains unclear on exactly how the state makes specific policy choices or decisions at particular moments in time.

STATE-CENTRED ANALYSIS

A state-centred approach has blossomed in the study of comparative politics and, to a lesser degree, in the examination of Canadian public policy in the 1980s and 1990s.[50] Its advocates object to the notion that social forces determine what state authorities do. Instead they view the state as able to act independently of the demands of society. The state is visualized as "autonomous," independent of the public's interests, as expressed in the environmentalist, pluralist and public choice models; and certainly not derivative of class interests, as found in neo-marxist thought.

---

[47] See, for example, Ralph Miliband, *The State in Capitalist Society* (London: Weidenfeld and Nicolson, 1969).

[48] The state is only "relatively" autonomous because its activities are constrained by the underlying social and economic (class) relations in society. See Nicos Poulantzas, *Political Power and Social Classes* (London: New Left Books, 1973).

[49] See especially Rianne Mahon, "Canadian Public Policy: The Unequal Structure of Representation," in Panitch, ed., *The Canadian State*, pp. 165–98; and Mahon, *The Politics of Industrial Restructuring: Canadian Textiles* (Toronto: University of Toronto Press, 1984).

[50] The burgeoning literature includes James G. March and Johan P. Olsen, "The New Institutionalism: Organizational Factors in Political Life," *APSR*, vol. 78, no. 3 (September 1984), pp. 734–49; and Peter B. Evans, Dietrich Rueschemeyer and Theda Skocpol, eds., *Bringing the State Back In* (Cambridge: Cambridge University Press, 1985). For a critique, see Gabriel A. Almond, *A Discipline Divided: Schools and Sects in Political Science* (Newbury Park: Sage, 1990).

According to the rawest form of this type of explanation of public policy, politicians and bureaucrats can act in any way they determine is best for the country — irrespective of demands from society. In other words, the argument is state-centred and not society-centred. Although some attention is paid to the role of elected politicians, much of the research based on this approach focuses on bureaucratic politics: how unelected officials (public servants, judges, police and military) initiate and implement public policy.

This state-centred approach is based on the assumption that those individuals with the greatest knowledge will determine to a great extent the policy outputs of a society. Apparently, the modern world requires legislation and policy that is based on expertise not possessed by the mass public, interest groups or transient politicians. Since the bureaucracy is the only permanent repository of the knowledge required to carry out modern government, it is able to use this information to manipulate societal forces. Bureaucrats derive their power from the institutions that empower them, and the perceptions and actions of these officials are in turn shaped by the very institutions that they serve.

This approach has been attacked as being based on untenable assumptions. There certainly are grounds for this criticism in Canada. First, the knowledge required to govern the country is not "scientific." Those who determine the direction of public policy are those who possess and convince others to accept a guiding philosophy for the direction of governmental action. After the politicians determine the priorities — which is more a question of philosophy or personal choice than knowledge — the public servants are left with the administration of this choice, which is much less significant than the choice of policy orientation. Second, many members of the senior bureaucracy are as transient as some leading politicians. Deputy ministers may be dismissed, and often are, while some cabinet members remain in the government longer than a decade. Third, despite the state-centred assumption that political parties do not present policy alternatives — which is often the case in Canada — it is not always true. The 1988 election provided a clear-cut choice between those parties that favoured a free trade deal with the United States and those that did not. Moreover, referendums, such as that on the Charlottetown accord, allow the public direct decision-making power. In that particular vote, the people chose a course of action diametrically opposed to that put forward by almost every political leader and bureaucrat in the country.

Fourth, the bureaucracy cannot act in isolation. Even if the politician's role is discounted, the bureaucrats need the help of interest groups in order to get their own way. Specific sectors of the public service ally themselves with societal interests — pressure groups — to forge "policy communities."[51] This effort to save the hypothesis of the state-centred contention that the state drives public policy by adding pluralist assumptions to the model merely highlights the weaknesses in the argument.

The extent to which the state-centred approach provides a new paradigm for analysis is hotly contested. Some theorists have even called it a pernicious fad that caricatures pluralism, neo-marxism and environmental determinism without itself being able to sustain its argument without adding ideas from earlier approaches.[52]

---

[51] William Coleman and Grace Skogstad, eds., *Policy Communities and Public Policy in Canada* (Mississauga: Copp Clark Pitman, 1991).

[52] See Gabriel A. Almond, "The Return to the State," *APSR*, vol. 82, no. 3 (September 1988), pp. 853–74, and David Easton, "The Political System Besieged by the State," *Political Theory*, vol. 9, no. 3 (1981), pp. 303–25.

THE APPROACHES COMPARED

Richard Simeon has argued that a comprehensive approach to the study of public policy must involve at least three levels of analysis.[53] According to Simeon, although the policy process itself has "some independent effect on policy outcomes," it also reflects and is shaped by a broader framework that imposes constraints on the alternative policies considered by policy-makers and on their freedom of action. This broader framework consists of two sets of factors. Furthest removed from the policy process are the resources and constraints flowing from the social and economic environments. But the effects of these influences are profoundly shaped by a number of important intervening factors, including the system of power relations, the dominant values and ideas of society and the structure of political institutions. The combination of these three levels of analysis "suggests a sort of funnel of causality."[54] In this model of policy analysis, all three groups of factors are considered relevant, but the relative importance of factors in determining actual policy outputs increases as the "funnel" narrows from left to right (see the graphic portrayal in Figure 13.2).

FIGURE 13.2 POLICY "FUNNEL OF CAUSALITY"

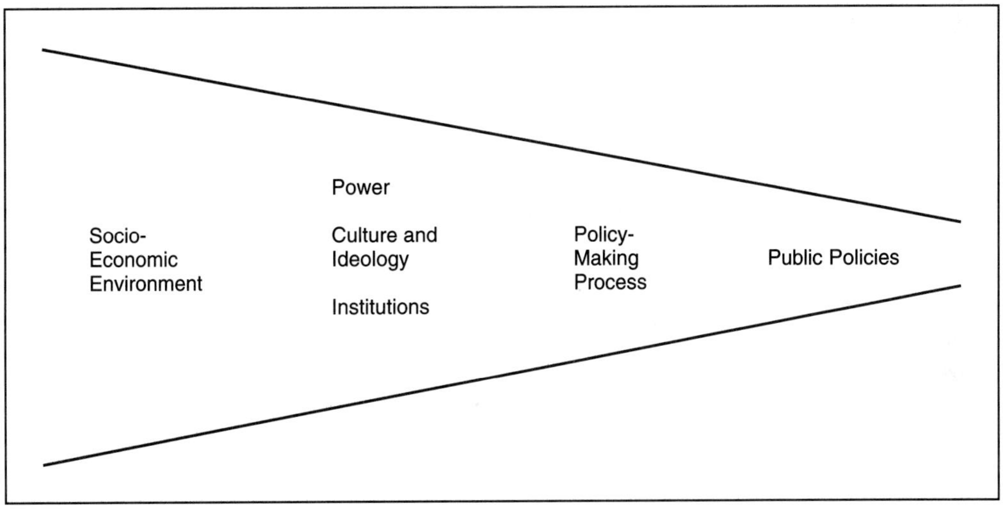

Source: Graphic adaptation of ideas discussed in Richard Simeon, "Studying Public Policy," *Canadian Journal of Political Science*, vol. 9, no. 4 (December 1976), esp. p. 556.

We have noted that no single approach to policy analysis has gained overall acceptance. One reason is that the various approaches tend to focus on particular aspects of the policy process — on different parts of the "funnel." For example, micro-level models such as incrementalism and rationalism and, to a lesser extent, the public choice approach, are more concerned with the process of policy-making *inside* government than with the wider relationship *between* government and its socio-economic environment or broader questions of the distribution of power, ideas and institutions. At the other extreme, the environmental determinist approach also ignores both these distributional questions and the decision process. It seeks to link public policy outputs directly to aggregate economic and social variables.

---

[53] See Simeon, "Studying Public Policy," esp. pp. 555–6 and pp. 566–78.

[54] Ibid., p. 556.

The neo-Marxist and pluralist approaches bring together more elements from the "funnel." Neo-Marxists explicitly address the influence of the economic and social environments, linking the role of the state to changes in the social structure and the economy. In addition, inequalities in power, income and resources between social classes, and the role of ideology and values are central themes in neo-Marxist analysis. However, as we have already noted, this approach has not yet come to terms with the independent influence of actors within the policy-making process in determining public policy outcomes such as are found in the state-centred approaches.

The pluralist approach implicitly takes into account the socio-economic environment, since the growing complexity of industrial society gives rise to more and more issues and interests around which groups may be mobilized. Pluralists emphasize the interaction of interest groups with the policy-making process; they also stress the mediating effects of institutions such as the electoral process. However, the traditional pluralist view has often been criticized for its failure to recognize inequalities of power and influence and for its emphasis on government as a reactive agent — as a neutral arbiter that responds only to the balance of group pressures. The admission by Dahl and Lindblom that business enjoys a privileged position in the interest group struggle still does not go far enough for some critics who argue that pluralists are unwilling to acknowledge that inequalities in power and resources are structurally based.[55] Today, many authors in the pluralist tradition allow that the modern state possesses its own dynamic in the policy process.[56] But, while the granting of "autonomy" to the state or government frees it from being a mere cipher of group demands, the argument fails to develop a comprehensive analysis of how, why and to what effect the state takes advantage of its newly discovered freedom.

A further problem that has served to inhibit the emergence of a generally accepted approach to public policy analysis lies in the ideological and political rhetoric associated with some of the theories sketched out above. Too often, theoretical models of public policy are used for support rather than illumination. This problem is particularly acute in the case of the two so-called political economy approaches — public choice and neo-Marxism.

The public choice argument that politicians and bureaucrats pursue their own interests in formulating public policies rather than some vague notion of the public interest is attractive to those who think that government has grown too large and that public expenditures have risen out of control. By providing a theoretical rationale for allegations of bureaucratic empire-building and for the supposed self-serving actions of politicians, public choice lends additional weight to the arguments of neo-conservatives who wish to lower tax rates, reduce the size of the bureaucracy and social programs and generally 'get government off the backs of the private sector.'

While public choice theory may reinforce the prejudices and negative views that many people hold toward bureaucrats and politicians, the assumptions of neo-Marxism tend to challenge the way most North American citizens think about politics. Indeed, it provides a critical, alternative way of looking at the role of the state in Canada and makes one question

---

[55] See Robert A. Dahl and Charles E. Lindblom, *Politics, Economics and Welfare* (Chicago: University of Chicago press, 1976); Charles Lindblom, *Politics and Markets* (New York: Basic Books, 1977); and the critique by John F. Manley, "Neo-Pluralism: A Class Analysis of Pluralism I and Pluralism II," *APSR*, vol. 77, no. 2 (June 1983), pp. 368–83.

[56] Eric A. Nordlinger, *On the Autonomy of the Democratic State* (Cambridge: Harvard University Press, 1981). Michael Laslovich has applied this idea to Canadian transportation policy. See his "Changing the Crow Rate: State-Societal Interaction" (unpublished Ph.D thesis, Carleton University, 1987).

assumptions about the way government operates. However, neo-Marxist analysis often is also difficult to disentangle from ideological rhetoric. Many critics believe that it is impossible to use neo-Marxist concepts as an approach to analysis without also adhering to the ideology of Marxism, with its prescription for the revolutionary overthrow of capitalist society. Others simply refuse to accept the premises of class division and conflict on which neo-Marxist theories of the state are based. In either case, strong opposition is further reinforced by the determinist and hyper-theoretical nature of much neo-Marxist writing.

Rather than promoting research that will enhance understanding of the policy process and the role of the state or government in formulating and implementing public policies, both public choice and neo-Marxist analysis may be reduced to facile sloganeering. By attributing every perceived evil of the modern state to the self-interest of bureaucrats or to the inequities of capitalism, political economy is reduced to *polemical* economy.

For a variety of reasons, therefore, it is extremely unlikely that any of the approaches outlined in this section will emerge as a universally accepted theory of public policy-making. But these models do represent the dominant frameworks of analysis found in the current literature on public policy. Each approach has its strengths and weaknesses in explaining how, why and to what effect governments choose to act on certain issues. Students of Canadian politics should be conversant with these models and be able to apply them to policy decisions and policy frameworks.

POLICY INSTRUMENTS AND PROCESSES

Public policy-making and decision-making are not restricted to setting governmental objectives and priorities; they also entail selecting means by which these ends are to be achieved. **Policy instruments** relate to the methods used by governments to attain their policy goals. This section illustrates the range of instruments that governments have at their disposal when attempting to put policy proposals into effect.

The instruments of policy implementation are often portrayed as part of a continuum on which they are arranged according to the degree of legitimate coercion each one implies. Thus, exhortation is viewed as the least coercive instrument, since it entails requests for voluntary compliance with government policies in the absence of any explicit sanctions. Expenditures attempt to secure compliance through the provision of financial inducements — with, perhaps, the implied threat that funding will be withdrawn if government objectives are not met. Although taxation may be viewed as a separate policy instrument, in some formulations it is grouped with regulation, in that both impose rules of behaviour on citizens "backed up directly by the sanctions (penalties) of the state."[57] Finally, public ownership is considered the most coercive form of policy instrument (see Figure 13.3). We shall return to the idea of the continuum and its utility for analyzing public policies at the end of this section.

EXHORTATION AND SYMBOLIC OUTPUTS

Exhortation (or, as it is sometimes called, "suasion") consists of a variety of attempts by policy-makers to induce individuals and groups to comply voluntarily with government objectives. Whatever the examples cited — from television chats by the Prime Minister

---

[57] Doern and Phidd, *Canadian Public Policy*, p. 112.

FIGURE 13.3 INSTRUMENTS OF GOVERNING

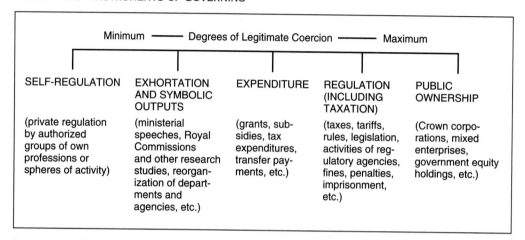

Source: Adapted from G. Bruce Doern and Richard W. Phidd, *Canadian Public Policy: Ideas, Structure, Process* (Toronto: Methuen, 1983), Figure 5.1, p.111 and Figure 5.3, p. 134.

urging economic restraint, through government-sponsored advertising extolling the benefits of the Charlottetown accord — exhortation is widely used by governments trying to change patterns of private behaviour.[58]

Exhortation is often used in pursuit of specific objectives when the government is unable to resort to other policy instruments such as taxation or regulation. **Symbolic policy outputs**, on the other hand, are mainly ways of demonstrating government concern over an issue; they are often used when no clear policy response has yet been formulated, but the government must be seen to be "doing something" about the perceived problem. Examples of symbolic policies include ministerial speeches and resolutions on pressing issues, or the establishment of special committees or royal commissions on matters of public concern. Sometimes these symbolic acts are accompanied or quickly followed by more substantive policy responses, such as the allocation of new public funds to deal with a problem area. But they may also be used as a form of "non-decision-making," to defuse or deflect public opinion and to delay action on an issue of perceived importance. Too much smoke and mirrors, however, may eventually alienate rather than placate the electorate.

EXPENDITURE INSTRUMENTS

To a certain extent, all government actions involve public expenditure — for example, advocacy advertising must be paid for, as must the administrative costs of regulatory agencies. As a distinct category of policy instruments, however, **expenditures** refer to those funds that are explicitly directed toward achieving government objectives. The most obvious is the provision of direct transfers to individuals — old-age pensions, child allowances, unemployment insurance — in order to redistribute income. As well, the federal government also makes fiscal transfers to provinces, to ease regional disparities and contribute to the funding of social programs such as health care and post-secondary education. These transfer

---

[58] For further discussion of these and other examples of suasion or exhortation see William T. Stanbury and Jane Fulton, "Suasion as a Government Instrument," in A.M. Maslove, ed., *How Ottawa Spends 1984: The New Agenda* (Toronto: Methuen, 1984), pp. 282–324.

POLITICAL PLOY # 3726

GST

BEER

DO IT DURING THE PLAYOFFS!...

Reproduced with permission, Dennis Pritchard.

expenditures (directly to individuals or via transfers to provinces) account for more than half of federal government spending.

But expenditure instruments may also be used in other policy areas. In recent years, the federal government has employed a broad array of subsidies, grants, loans and loan guarantees to aid new enterprises, to bail out troubled firms, to promote small business and so on. Further, the government's own capital expenditures not only attain immediate objectives such as the modernization of port and rail facilities, but may also serve indirectly to approach other goals, for instance, through the awarding of contracts to firms from economically depressed areas.

Also of interest to policy analysts is a less visible sub-category of expenditure instruments, the phenomenon known as "tax expenditures." **Tax expenditures** are the revenues foregone by the government through the provision of tax deductions or tax credits to individuals and corporations. Some deductions for individual tax-payers are intended to encourage personal spending on "socially desirable" purposes such as charitable donations and Registered Retirement Savings Plans (RRSPs) while others, including medical expense deductions and child tax credits for low-income families, are part of the social safety net of the welfare state.[59] In the corporate tax sector, too, there are two major categories of tax expenditures: those that give preferential treatment to certain kinds of income (e.g., small business tax credits) and those that reward certain objectives of corporate spending. Examples of the latter are investment tax credits and allowances for research and development expenditures.

Since tax expenditures are revenues foregone by the government rather than funds collected and subsequently disbursed, they are less easily quantified than ordinary expenditures, which must be accounted for in the expenditure-budgetary process. However, studies estimate that the volume of tax expenditures has grown rapidly in recent years.[60] At the same time, there has been concern that tax expenditures tend to favour upper-income earners and profitable corporations, thereby counteracting redistributive effects elsewhere in the expenditure and tax processes.

---

[59] See Allan M. Maslove, "Tax Expenditures, Tax Credits and Equity," in G.B. Doern, ed., *How Ottawa Spends Your Tax Dollars: Federal Priorities 1981* (Toronto: Lorimer, 1981) pp. 232–54.

[60] See Kenneth Woodside, "The Political Economy of Policy Instruments: Tax Expenditures and Subsidies in Canada," in Atkinson and Chandler, eds., *The Politics of Canadian Public Policy*, esp. pp. 176–8.

REGULATION

A regulation "can be viewed *politically* as a rule of behaviour backed up more directly by the legitimate sanctions of the state."[61] From this rather broad perspective, the concept of **regulation** comprises all rules of conduct imposed by government on individual and corporate citizens. It encompasses statutory legislation (including, for example, the *Criminal Code*), since such laws establish general rules of behaviour; the tax system, which imposes special rules concerning the payment of money to government; as well as the activities of semi-autonomous regulatory agencies that lay down more restricted codes of conduct within their respective spheres of operation. In this broad sense, in addition to regulatory agencies, the actors in the regulatory process include Parliament and Cabinet, which formulate regulations, and bureaucratic departments, the police and the court system, which administer and enforce them. However, much of the emphasis in the public policy literature on regulation is on the more limited area of regulation of private economic activity. From this narrower perspective, regulation is sometimes seen as a policy instrument that is aimed at forcing private economic actors to adopt behaviour that they would not normally choose in the absence of regulation, that is, in a completely laissez-faire, free-market economy. The study of economic regulation therefore focuses on "public intervention by way of non-market controls in a mixed but primarily market-oriented economy."[62]

In what circumstances, and to what end, do governments intervene to impose non-market controls on private economic behaviour? In the area of direct economic regulation, governments may act to control prices and rates of return (e.g., telephone rates), entry to the market (e.g., broadcasting licences for television and radio stations), market exit (e.g., ensuring that railways or public utilities serve remote communities) and output (e.g., supply management by agricultural marketing boards). In addition, governments may also regulate economic behaviour in pursuit of social objectives such as "health, safety and fairness."[63]

In summary, then, governments use regulation as a policy instrument for one of three purposes: to remedy market failures, to serve as an instrument of redistribution and to meet social and cultural objectives.[64] However, to the extent that some of these objectives might be met by other policy instruments there may be, in addition to economic, social and cultural objectives, a political rationale for the choice of regulation to achieve policy goals. Regulation may be managed directly by government departments, as in the case of most forms of social regulation; it may be delegated to semi-autonomous agencies such as the Canadian Radio-television and Telecommunications Commission, the Canadian Transport Commission and the National Energy Board; or powers of self-regulation may be granted to professional associations like medical and bar associations.

In any event, regulatory regimes are comparatively inexpensive. According to the Economic Council of Canada, in 1979 "the total budgetary cost of all federal regulatory programs amount[ed] to less than 2 percent of the total federal budget."[65] In an era of widespread criticism of growing federal spending and budgetary deficits, regulation is therefore an attractive option for governments seeking an instrument to realize policy goals. The major cost of regulation, it is argued, is that of compliance, borne not by government,

---

[61]   G. Bruce Doern, "Regulatory Processes and Regulatory Agencies," in Doern and Aucoin, eds., *Public Policy in Canada*, p. 150 (emphasis in original).

[62]   Richard J. Schultz, *Federalism and the Regulatory Process* (Montreal: IRPP, 1977), p. 8.

[63]   Economic Council of Canada, *Responsible Regulation*, pp. 43–5.

[64]   Ibid., pp. 45–52; Schultz, *Federalism and the Regulatory Process*, pp. 9–12.

[65]   Economic Council of Canada, *Responsible Regulation*, pp. 43–4.

but by businesses, shareholders and consumers in the private sector. Consequently, there has been growing support in Canada for "deregulation," for a lessening of constraints on private behaviour in certain sectors of the economy — recently evidenced, for example, by the abandonment of regulated oil and gas pricing. At the same time, however, it is apparent that powerful vested interests support the continuation of regulatory regimes.

PUBLIC OWNERSHIP

Public ownership or **public enterprise** — the direct provision of goods and services by corporations owned partly or wholly by the government — has a long history in Canada at both the federal and provincial levels. Indeed, some observers have labelled Canada a "public enterprise culture."[66] Among major federal enterprises, the oldest is the Canadian National Railways, established soon after the First World War, but it was predated by provincially owned enterprises such as Ontario Hydro and publicly owned telephone systems in the Prairies. From these early beginnings, public ownership has expanded to other transportation, energy and communications facilities, as well as resource development, manufacturing, finance and a number of other sectors of the economy. Today, several federal public corporations can be found among Canada's largest business enterprises (see Table 13.1).[67]

TABLE 13.1   MAJOR FEDERAL PUBLIC ENTERPRISES IN CANADA, 1992*

Corporation	Federal Ownership	Operating Revenue ($,000)	Employees	Rank**
CNR	100%	4 051 459	35 281	25
Canada Post Corp.	100%	3 804 000	56 000	29
Canadian Wheat Board	100%	3 503 910	491	31
Via Rail	100%	487 089	4 494	201
Royal Mint	100%	377 002	763	258
CBC	100%	376 732	9 337	259
Atomic Energy of Canada	100%	267 000	4 500	311
Cape Breton Development Corp.	100%	254 625	2 554	322
Marine Atlantic Inc.	100%	201 262	2 797	367
The St. Lawrence Seaway Authority	100%	67 786	862	590

* Major industrial enterprises only — excludes financial institutions and subsidiaries included under parent corporation.

** "Rank" shows corporation's ranking among all private and public corporations by operating revenue.

Source: Adapted from *The Financial Post 500* (Toronto: Maclean Hunter Ltd., 1993).

The realm of public ownership partly overlaps that of Crown corporations (discussed in detail in Chapter 9) but the two are not identical. Federal agencies classified as Crown corporations may be mechanisms for policy implementation or advisory bodies that contribute to the formation of public policy. On the other side of the coin, public ownership need not entail 100 percent government ownership and control. Apart from wholly owned Crown

---

[66] Herschel Hardin, *A Nation Unaware: The Canadian Economic Culture* (Vancouver: J.J. Douglas Ltd., 1974).

[67] For more extended discussion of the origins and growth of public enterprise in Canada, see Allan Tupper and G. Bruce Doern, eds., *Public Corporations and Public Policy in Canada* (Montreal: IRPP, 1981) and Marsha Gordon, *Government in Business* (Montreal: C.D. Howe Institute, 1981).

corporations and their subsidiaries, governments may turn to mixed (public-private) enterprises or to equity- (share-) holding in a private company in their attempts to realize certain policy goals.

As these examples illustrate, the objectives of public ownership as a policy instrument are many and varied. Some early public enterprises, such as state-owned railways and Trans-Canada Airlines (later Air Canada), were established to develop essential economic infrastructure in situations where "the private sector was unwilling or unable to take the initiative."[68] These transportation facilities also played a part in national integration; a similar motive lay behind the creation of the Canadian Radio Broadcasting Commission (now the CBC) in 1932. Other public enterprises have been founded to provide financial infrastructure for the Canadian economy. Thus, the Canadian Business Development Bank and the Export Development Corporation were designed to "fill gaps in the financial system and to assist interests whose financial needs were only partially met by established (private) leaders."[69] As well, public ownership has been used to develop pioneer enterprises involving high cost or commercial risks that were deemed to be in the long-term public interest. For example, federal government involvement in Atomic Energy of Canada is intended to foster the development of new technologies and processes and to encourage diversification of the Canadian economy.[70]

In many of these cases, public enterprises complemented, rather than competed with, the interests of the private sector. In recent years, however, more controversial examples of government ownership have brought the public sector into conflict with private enterprise over market shares and investment resources. Opposition to public ownership has crystallized around two major issues: first, the growing concern about a perceived lack of accountability of Crown corporations; second, the losses suffered in recent years by some corporations. These issues have lent extra ammunition to arguments that resources devoted to public enterprise might be more profitably and efficiently allocated in the private sector. Critics of public ownership have adopted as a solution to both problems the concept of "privatization" of a number of Crown corporations.[71]

Between 1984 and 1993, the federal Conservative government privatized many Crown corporations, in particular those that functioned as private enterprises. Arguing that the private sector operates more efficiently than the public sector, and that the government had to reduce the deficit, the Tories sold off such illustrious Crown corporations as Air Canada, CN hotels, CN Route, Canadair, de Havilland Aircraft, Eldorado Nuclear, Fisheries Products International, Northern Transportation Commission, Petro-Canada and Teleglobe Canada. As well, Canada Post Corporation was changed from a government department to a Crown corporation so that it could function like a private enterprise. Despite these efforts to reduce the "public enterprise spirit" at the federal level, the federal government kept some enterprises intact (see Table 13.1) and the provinces retained their public enterprises such as Ontario Hydro and Hydro-Québec. Federal and provincial public enterprise together continued to dominate the fields of electric power, communications and transportation.

Public ownership continues to be under fire from neo-Conservatives, who view any government intervention as an infringement upon the supremacy of the free market economy.

---

68   John W. Langford, "Crown Corporations as Instruments of Policy." in Doern and Aucoin, eds., *Public Policy in Canada*, p. 248.

69   Allan Tupper and G. Bruce Doern, "Understanding Public Corporations in Canada," *Canadian Business Review*, vol. 9, no. 3 (Autumn 1982), p. 34.

70   Gordon, *Government in Business*, ch. 6.

71   T.M. Ohashi and T.P. Roth, *Privatization: Theory and Practice* (Vancouver; Fraser Institute, 1980). See also Tom Kierans, "Commercial Crowns," *Policy Options*, vol. 5, no. 6 (Nov./Dec. 1984), pp. 23–9.

Thus, while it is improbable that privatization will be carried as far as it has been in some countries, it seems certain that public ownership will be less prominent within the federal government's arsenal of new public policy instruments during the next decade.

POLICY INSTRUMENTS AND THE POLICY PROCESS

There are several academic approaches to explain how and why particular policy instruments are chosen by governments. One is based on the continuum of governing instruments mentioned earlier in this section. Doern and Wilson hypothesize that "politicians have a strong tendency to respond to policy issues by moving successively from the *least coercive* governing instrument to the *most coercive*."[72] Applied to the continuum (as shown in Figure 13.3), this hypothesis suggests that governments will tend to respond first with symbolic outputs such as the establishment of a royal commission and with attempts to secure voluntary compliance through exhortation. Later, however, they may shift to expenditure instruments and, if these incentives are insufficient to ensure compliance with policy objectives, they may subsequently deploy more coercive measures such as regulation or even public ownership. Thus, Tupper and Doern suggest that in the majority of cases they studied "the direct ownership instrument was selected *after* extensive use of other instruments including regulation, spending and taxation."[73]

However, when adopting new instruments as they move along the continuum, policy-makers rarely discontinue the use of less coercive means. Instruments, differentiated from each other by the degrees of coercion attributed to them, are therefore additive or complementary in nature, rather than constituting alternatives. Thus, when public enterprises are established, rather than replacing other measures, "public ownership is more frequently *added* to an array of existing instruments that have been tried and found wanting, or at least are *believed* to be found wanting."[74]

At first glance, this hypothesis of instrument choice also appears plausible, although both it and the continuum from which it is derived are based on a number of assumptions that might not be acceptable to all public policy analysts. It does have the advantage that it can be tested empirically. However, applications of the hypothesis to different fields of Canadian public yield mixed results. While the study of some policy areas such as energy policy lends support to the contention that governments progress along the continuum in developing policy responses, leaving regulation and especially public ownership as a last resort, examination of other sectors such as broadcasting indicates that public ownership was among the first instruments deployed by the federal government.

A full explanation of the selection of policy instruments by governments has to take into account a multiplicity of economic, legal, political and external constraints on governmental freedom of choice. For example, within a federal system such as Canada, governments may be precluded from using the full range of instruments in some policy areas by the constitutional division of powers among jurisdictions. Thus, the federal government is effectively limited to exhortation and spending in many fields of Canadian social policy. Economic constraints in a period of growing criticism of the expansion of public expenditures and budgetary deficits make both regulation and relatively hidden tax incentives more attractive than large, visible spending programs. International agreements such as the General Agreement on Tariffs and Trade (GATT) militate against raising tariffs (a form of

---

[72] Doern and Wilson, eds., *Issues in Canadian Public Policy*, p. 339 (emphasis in original).

[73] Tupper and Doern, "Public Corporations and Public Policy in Canada," p. 19 (emphasis in original).

[74] Ibid.

taxation or regulation) and force governments to resort to alternative methods (non-tariff barriers) to control the volume of imports flowing into the country. Even the nature of the policy-making process itself may have an effect. While routine, day-to-day or year-to-year policy-making may tend toward the kind of incrementalist instrument selection hypothesized above, a study by Robert J. Jackson of policy-making in crisis management situations shows that, after initial symbolic responses, governments are most likely to resort to highly coercive instruments, including emergency regulations and the deployment of armed forces. Only after the crisis is over will they return to legislation and public spending in order to pre-empt the occurrence of further crises.[75]

Clearly, we need to learn more about the dynamics of public policy-making in order to reach a more complete explanation of the choice of policy instruments by governments. But while the concept of a continuum of governing instruments has weaknesses, it has proven to be a useful heuristic device in promoting research and in sensitizing policy analysts to the multiplicity of means of policy implementation that governments have at their disposal.

THE GROWTH AND SIZE OF THE CANADIAN STATE

The proportion of total national income spent by the various levels of government has increased greatly over the years. However, the rate has by no means been constant; there have been distinct periods of growth and decline. Moreover, the overall growth disguises substantial shifts in the relative importance of different levels of government. Seventy years ago, local and municipal governments were the biggest spenders, since they were primarily responsible for

FIGURE 13.4 BUDGETARY REVENUES AND EXPENDITURES, 1971–92

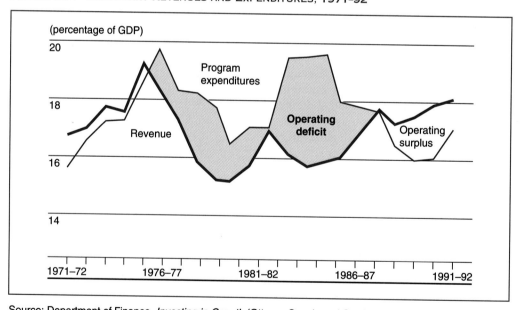

Source: Department of Finance, *Investing in Growth* (Ottawa: Supply and Services, 1992).

---

[75] Robert J. Jackson, "Crisis Management and Policy-Making," in Richard Rose, ed., *The Dynamics of Public Policy*, p. 214.

FIGURE 13.5 G-7 IN THE HOLE

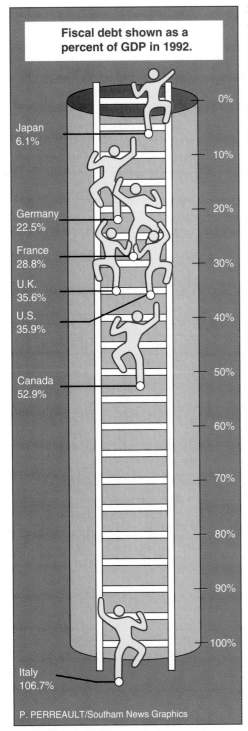

Fiscal debt shown as a percent of GDP in 1992.

Japan 6.1%

Germany 22.5%

France 28.8%

U.K. 35.6%

U.S. 35.9%

Canada 52.9%

Italy 106.7%

0%
10%
20%
30%
40%
50%
60%
70%
80%
90%
100%

P. PERREAULT/Southam News Graphics

Source: *The Ottawa Citizen* (June 6, 1993).

financing education and limited social welfare functions. During the Depression, local and provincial governments were unable to cope with demands on their budgets, so the federal government began to spend more; it continued to do so to meet the costs of the war effort. Since the mid-1960s the largest increase in expenditure has occurred at the provincial level. However, it is also true that in recent years federal spending in dollar terms has risen substantially.

In 1993–94, the federal government spent about 161 billion dollars, compared with only 13 billion in 1971. Of course, government expenditure has to be paid for out of revenues. Like expenditures, the revenues of all levels of government have had to increase over the last half century. In 1993–94, the federal government raised about 127 billion dollars, leaving a federal deficit of approximately 34 billion (more than twice the entire federal budget of two decades earlier). That deficit was later found to be more than $40 billion, greatly increasing the national debt which, by the end of 1993, was projected to be about $500 billion. (See Figure 13.4.) Of course, it is important to relate the size of the Canadian deficit/debt to the size and strength of the economy. For a comparison of Canada with other G-7 countries, see Figure 13.5. The financial problems are not limited to the federal government; provincial deficits, too, have escalated in the 1990s. (See Figure 13.6.) As well, Canada's *international* debt is expected to be about 45 percent of the GNP by the end of 1993, dramatically higher than comparable United States' statistics.[76] This chronic shortfall between government revenue and its expenditures has become a major issue in Canadian politics. (Figure 13.7 shows how much is spent paying merely the interest on the debt.)

Not all state activity is measurable in terms of public expenditure. While many public policies do require the outlay of money, others need very little — particularly those that seek to regulate or control the behaviour of either individual or

---

[76] See Bruce Wilkinson, "Canada's Balance of Payments and International Indebtedness," in *How Ottawa Spends 1993–94*, pp. 291–332.

corporate members of society. Thus, as the state has become more involved in its citizens' lives, the volume of legislation, statutes and regulations has increased. This aspect of the growth of the Canadian state was aptly summarized by former Conservative Justice Minister Senator Jacques Flynn in a speech to the Canadian Bar Association.

We recently published a consolidation of federal regulations — 15,563 pages of them. Add to that 10,000 pages of Revised Statutes (Canada's Statutes were last revised and consolidated in 1970) and 8,000 to 10,000 pages of Statutes since the revision, plus hundreds of thousands of pages of provincial laws and regulations to say nothing of municipal by-laws, orders and regulations. Now you begin to realize that we've come a long way from 10 clauses on a slab of stone.[77]

FIGURE 13.6 GOVERNMENT NET DEBT — PUBLIC ACCOUNTS BASIS

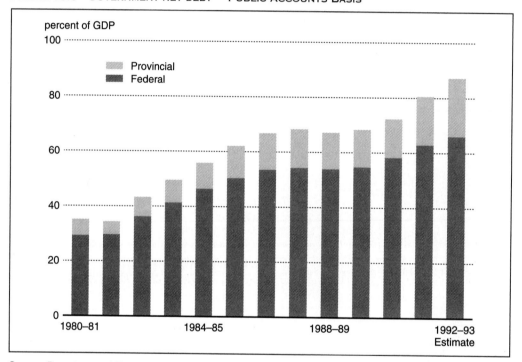

Source: Department of Finance, *The Budget Story in Charts* (Ottawa: Supply and Services, 1993). Reproduced by authority of the Minister responsible for Statistics Canada 1993.

Finally, as the state has increasingly intervened in social and economic life, so the actual machinery of government has become more complex. The number of federal government departments and branches quadrupled between 1870 and 1990. There are approximately 400 federal government Crown corporations and agencies, of which almost half were created after 1970. Similarly, the number of people employed by the state has also grown to about half a million. As in the case of public expenditure, however, the "real" growth in terms of the percentage of total employment in the public sector has been relatively much smaller.[78]

---

[77] Quoted by Donald John Purich, "Too Many Laws? There may not be enough!" *The Chronicle-Herald*, Halifax, February 2, 1980.

[78] Richard M. Bird et al., *The Growth of Public Employment in Canada* (Scarborough, Ont.: Butterworths, for the IRPP, 1979), p. 43.

FIGURE 13.7 THE INTEREST BITE

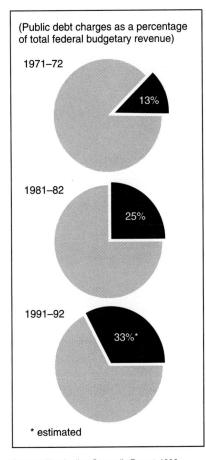

(Public debt charges as a percentage
of total federal budgetary revenue)

1971–72

13%

1981–82

25%

1991–92

33%*

* estimated

Source: *The Auditor General's Report,* 1992

In 1960, for example, federal government employment constituted 5.2 percent of the total labour force; in 1982 the public sector employed 18.6 percent of the total labour force, higher than in the United States but lower than in Britain, France, Germany, Italy and Sweden.[79]

Whichever indicators we choose, it is unarguable that in Canada the state has grown over the last century — or even the last twenty years — although when measured in real terms this expansion is by no means as large as some critics of government intervention would suggest. Still, the question remains: How do we account for the growth of the state?

EXPLANATIONS FOR THE GROWTH AND SIZE OF THE STATE

Why has the government, or the public sector, grown in Canada? So many authors have attempted to explain the growth of the state in Canada that, according to Richard Bird,

> ...the problem is not that there are no explanations of the growth of government in Canada since the war: it is rather that there are too many explanations, each one of which probably contains both some truth and some misleading elements.[80]

In the following discussion, we focus on the more pertinent among this plethora of explanations.[81] We begin with historical and theoretical arguments.

Most of the major federal programs that comprise the modern Canadian welfare state were initiated or consolidated in the quarter-century after the Second World War, including hospital and medical insurance, the Canada and Québec pension plans, the Canada Assistance Plan and federal participation in other shared-cost programs such as post-secondary education. These were added to such war-time initiatives as unemployment insurance and family allowances to create a comprehensive package of social and welfare programs.

---

[79] See Tables 2-1 and 2-3 in S.L. Sutherland, "Federal Bureaucracy: The Pinch Test," in *How Ottawa Spends 1987–88,* edited by Michael J. Prince (Toronto: Methuen, 1987).

[80] Richard M. Bird, *Financing Canadian Government: A Quantitative Overview* (Toronto: Canada Tax Foundation, 1979), p. 82 (emphasis in original).

[81] For a more comprehensive discussion, see Richard M. Bird, *The Growth of Government Spending in Canada* (Toronto: Canada Tax Foundation, 1970), Part II, ch. 4–7. For briefer overviews see Bird, *Financing Canadian Government,* ch. 7; Bird et al., *The Growth of Public Employment in Canada,* ch. 8; Butler and Macnaughton, "Public Sector Growth in Canada," pp. 97–102; James Gillies, *Where Business Fails: Business-Government Relations at the Federal Level in Canada* (Montreal: IRPP, 1981), pp. 5–7. For the most recent data see the many studies prepared for the Royal Commission on the Economic Union and Development Prospects for Canada, included in the select bibliographies at the end of the chapter.

Reprinted with permission, Gable, *The Globe and Mail.*

The expansion of state activities can be attributed to a number of factors. First, the period was marked by the emergence of Keynesian economics as the dominant paradigm of macro-economic management in Western industrial societies. The Keynesian model legitimized large-scale government intervention as a means of manipulating the level of aggregate demand to control the kind of extreme cyclical fluctuations in the economy that had given rise to the Great Depression of the 1930s. It should be noted, however, that Keynesian economics was never fully implemented in Canada since, although successive federal governments intervened to boost aggregate demand as an incentive to economic growth, they rarely followed Keynes' prescriptions of expenditure cutbacks and tax hikes to deflate the economy in times of expansion and inflation.

Second, the period from 1945 to 1970 was, by and large, an era of rapid and sustained economic growth fuelled by post-war reconstruction, the injection of foreign investment and the spread of mass affluence. This economic growth led to an expansion of government revenues through increasing tax returns and enhanced the fiscal capacity of the state to intervene. It also enabled the government to involve itself in major redistributive programs, since there were sufficient resources to distribute to the less privileged without depriving more affluent and politically influential groups of a share of the ever-expanding national pie.

From a pluralist perspective, therefore, the government as neutral arbiter was able to satisfy the demands of more societal groups, including an increasingly influential labour movement that had organized behind the trade unions and the growing electoral force of the CCF. In the public choice and state-centred views, however, the growth of the state could be attributed to the competitive bidding practices of party politicians anxious to gain governmental power and to the expansionist tendencies of bureaucrats seeking to enlarge their spheres of influence in the policy process.

The neo-Marxist approach would interpret the growth of the state in different terms again. The need to promote private capital accumulation after the war required the state to intervene on behalf of capital through incentives to investment, by boosting aggregate demand (e.g., universal child allowances) and by helping to underwrite the costs of reproducing the labour force (e.g., health and education policies). At the same time, the growing power of organized labour led the state to introduce programs that helped to legitimate its capital accumulation role and disguise the exploitative nature of capitalism. As capitalism becomes increasingly monopolistic and as the rate of profit falls (a central tenet of Marxian economics), the state will intervene more and more to maintain both capital accumulation and legitimation until it reaches what James O'Connor has called "fiscal crisis," a situation in which government revenues can no longer satisfy the simultaneous demands of the dual role of the state.[82] Thus, for some analysts, the current language of restraint and the social policy cutbacks undertaken by neo-conservative governments in Britain, the United States and Canada are natural consequences of fiscal crisis and the fundamental contradiction between the state's accumulation and legitimation functions.

There are many other less theoretical approaches to the growth of the state. Some are essentially apolitical in that they view the expansion of the role of government as a product of exogenous (externally determined) forces. For example, the growth and changing age structure of the population may call for increased state activity. More expenditure and more government personnel are needed to provide even a fixed level of services to a larger number of people, and the fact that more people are living longer necessitates more services to provide pensions and health care for the aged. Alternatively, the vast technological development undergone by Canadian society in the last century may be said to have increased the scope for government intervention. The coming of the motor vehicle alone has given rise to a great variety of government activity: road building and maintenance, traffic laws, seatbelt legislation, driver and vehicle licensing, exhaust emission controls, vehicle safety regulations, and much more.

But the growth of the state is not the *direct* consequence of demographic change or technological innovation; these are background factors that create increased potential for state intervention. The current extent of state activity *is* the result of an extensive series of political decisions — to increase public expenditure on a particular item, to move into a new functional area, to create another regulatory agency — each one taken by politicians acting in the context of the political process. Therefore, although the number of people over 65 already exceeded 5 percent of the population in 1901 (compared with around 11 percent in 1986) it was another quarter-century before government pensions were introduced for some people over the age of 70, and 50 years before pensions were granted to those over 65.

Since the state is first and foremost a political phenomenon, many attempts to explain its growth focus on the bureaucratic forces that underlie its activities. It is sometimes argued that bureaucrats judge their personal success by the growth rate of the budgets, number of employees and volume of programs administered by their departments. Although the proposition smacks of individual "empire-building," such may not be the case. A more benevolent view might ascribe it to genuine concern for the target population or to a response to political pressures. The dominant modes and structures of policy-making in state bureaucracies may also play a part, especially with respect to the growth of public spending. Incremental decision-making has predominated in the budgetary process over much of

---

[82] James O'Connor, *The Fiscal Crisis of the State* (New York: St. Martin's Press, 1973), passim.

the past century. While attempts have been made to reform the budgetary process in recent years it has proven difficult to counterbalance the tendency toward continued expansion of public expenditure. The budgetary process was covered in Chapters 7 and 9.

The role of political ideas or ideologies is sometimes overlooked in explorations of the decisions underlying the growth of the state. However, it may be argued that an interventionist role for the state has traditionally been considered legitimate in the Canadian political culture. Canadians do not share the anti-statist liberalism and the free enterprise ethic to the same extent as the general public in the United States. Thus, according to one author, Canada "is a public enterprise country, always has been, and probably always will be."[83] In the nineteenth century, the Canadian versions of "Toryism" and nationalism motivated state intervention in the interests of private enterprise and national economic development through the National Policy. Since the Second World War, the acceptance of Keynesian economics and the embracing of a "welfare state ideology" have served to legitimate an even more interventionist role for the state.

At the more overtly political level of elections, political parties vie with one another to provide the best package of state services for voters, and generally offer the electorate more services rather than fewer taxes. Why do political parties compete to expand government services and public expenditure rather than to reduce state intervention and cut tax-rates? One answer lies in the public expectations of the role of the state in Canada, although, as Richard Bird points out, "the popular postwar ideology that government can — and should — solve most problems is now, however, increasingly being questioned in the face of the strong evidence that it cannot."[84] An alternative suggestion is that support for tax cuts is much more diffuse than opposition to reductions in services — that reductions are more deeply felt and are more likely to be translated into votes against the party proposing such measures. This may especially be the case in Canada where approximately 40 percent of the electorate is employed in some way by government and is therefore in favour of public sector expansion and opposed to any reduction of the role of the state.[85]

Last among the political factors is the proposition that the very structure of key political institutions in Canada, expressly the Cabinet system of government and federalism, may militate in favour of the growth of the state. Just as in the bureaucracy "success" may be measured in terms of departmental expansion, so in Cabinet the "success" or influence of individual ministers may be evaluated by the extent to which they have defended or enhanced the budgets and programs of their departments. Consequently, even if a Cabinet were collectively to commit itself to reducing public expenditure or cutting government services, it would be difficult to find any particular minister who would say "let us start with my department." Moreover, the federal nature of the Canadian political system may be a contributory factor in accelerating the growth of government as a whole. The competitive relationship between federal and provincial governments means that, as new areas of potential public sector growth have opened up, governments have rushed in, motivated as much by desire to upstage the other level of government as by their concern for the public welfare.

With so many alternatives to choose from, it is perhaps not surprising that no universally accepted explanation of the growth of the Canadian state has emerged. One point upon

---

[83] Herschel Hardin, *A Nation Unaware: The Canadian Economic Culture* (Vancouver: J.J. Douglas, 1974), p. 140.

[84] Bird, *Financing Canadian Government*, p. 85.

[85] Don McGillivray, "40% of Canadian Voters are on Government Payroll," *Financial Times of Canada*, Toronto, June 27, 1977.

which most authors agree is that, while demographic, technological and economic factors provide the contextual background to the growth of the state the key to a comprehensive and satisfactory explanation lies more in the political field than in other processes.

POLICY-MAKING IN AN AGE OF RESTRAINT

In the late 1970s, and particularly after the Conservative victory of 1984, "restraint" became a watchword of federal policy-making, as successive governments attempted to cope with inflation, recession, declining tax revenues, growing deficits and the task of reviving a faltering Canadian economy. One major consequence of the slowdown in economic growth has been the advent of what American economist Lester Thurow has labelled "the zero-sum society."[86] In earlier times, governments could redistribute resources to the underprivileged without eroding at least the money income, if not the relative position, of more affluent groups. The growing national pie permitted "positive-sum" politics. However, once the pie stopped growing, redistribution to some groups could be undertaken only at the expense of others. In the zero-sum society, then, distributional conflicts become more polarized, since somebody must "lose" for someone else to "win." Thus, new or expanded social programs must be financed either from savings or from increased revenues. But, as the recession lengthened unemployment lines and squeezed corporate profit margins, government revenues have fallen below expected levels — just when demand has been increasing for social expenditures such as unemployment insurance benefits and welfare, and pressure has mounted for the government to bail out failing businesses.

In the short term, of course, governments can try to escape from this dilemma by deficit financing — that is, by borrowing money to meet the shortfall between revenues and expenditures. But in recent years, the annual federal deficit has come to exceed 33 billion dollars; interest on the net public debt of over 459 billion dollars now consumes over one-quarter of annual spending by Ottawa. Many politicians and external observers alike have argued that the limits of deficit financing, and perhaps even of the public sector, have been exceeded, causing an unacceptable drain on private capital investment and on the economy in general.

It is under these conditions that restraint has become a recurring theme in federal political discourse. It was already evident in the late 1970s, both in the Liberals' sweeping expenditure cuts of 1978–79 and in John Crosbie's "short-term pain for long-term gain" Conservative Budget of December 1979. It resurfaced in the Liberals' "six and five" program of June 1982, which imposed limits on annual increases in public sector salaries and many social programs and, indirectly, attempted to reduce public expectations of government. But the concept of restraint really came to the fore with the 1984 and 1988 elections of Conservative governments committed to trimming the federal deficit and privatizing a good proportion of the federal Crown corporations. In the 1993 General Election, Prime Minister Kim Campbell promised to eliminate the national debt completely within five years. She did not have the opportunity to fulfill her promise before losing the General Election. The new Prime Minister, Jean Chrétien, promised to reduce the deficit to 3% of the GDP in five years.

The Conservatives' bark may have been worse than their bite. During their years in office, they demonstrated that their economic policies could be incrementalist and responsive to political pressure from voters. By attempting, for example, to bail out the Canadian

---

[86] Lester C. Thurow, *The Zero-Sum Society: Distribution and the Possibilities for Economic Change* (New York: Basic Books, 1980).

Commercial Bank, providing loan guarantees to the Domtar paper mill in Windsor, Quebec, and committing federal funds for large energy projects such as Hibernia, they added to federal spending commitments despite their efforts at deficit cutting and gaining greater control over government expenditures. Despite their fiery rhetoric the national debt tripled and the Tories never managed to reduce the annual deficit, as they had promised. The politics of restraint by Conservatives, Liberals, or New Democrats, must be understood along with the higher political goal of ensuring re-election in a competitive party democracy, with the entrenched interests of bureaucrats and client interest groups, with the pressures of provincial governments in a federal system — in short, with the realities of politics in Canada.

OVERVIEW

It is not possible to explore all the facets of federal policy-making in a chapter of this length. The primary objectives here have been to introduce some of the central concepts in policy-making and the most commonly used approaches to public policy analysis, as well as to illustrate some of the constraints within which federal policy-makers have to operate. Whichever perspective one takes on the role of the state in Canadian society, it is clear that certain fundamental realities of Canadian political life have a major influence on federal policy-making, and that their net effect is to militate against comprehensive decision-making in favour of a general tendency toward incremental policy-making or the fine art of "muddling through."

First, Canada is a liberal democracy in which political parties must compete for electoral support and governments must remain responsive to the promptings of key interest groups, both as lobbyists and as potential organizers of public opinion and votes. The need to win, and especially to maintain, electoral support from societal groups usually requires that governments refrain from making major policy changes that might alienate significant portions of the electorate.

Second, Canada has a federal system of government in which the constitutional division of powers imposes both legal and political constraints upon federal policy-makers. The legal constraints limit the instruments available to the federal government in pursuit of its objectives in many policy areas, while the values and goals of provincial governments and the policies these governments implement often contradict and reduce the effectiveness of federal policy outputs. The need to secure federal/provincial cooperation in many policy areas again dictates that policy-making must move in small, incrementalist steps rather than in giant strides.

Third, Canada is not a political system in isolation. Changes in the world economic and political environments create a climate of uncertainty for policy-makers of all states. But the political and economic influence of the United States and of U.S.-based multinational corporations impose extra demands and constraints on policy-makers in Canada; federal policy-makers constantly have to adjust their priorities and instruments of policy implementation in response to events south of the 49th Parallel.

None of this is intended to argue against policy-makers attempting to make better policy decisions. All Canadians would like to think that their federal government makes the most rational policy choices available to it, subject to the constraints under which it is working. However, the requirements of a democratic political process, a federal institutional structure and the constraints imposed by the domestic and international economies usually combine with short-term political expediency to ensure that policy-makers follow the path of least resistance by "muddling through." Canadians should, perhaps, demand of their governments that, if they are going to "muddle through," they at least do so in a more "rational" way.

SELECTED BIBLIOGRAPHY

Abele, Frances, ed., *How Ottawa Spends: The Politics of Competitiveness 1992–93* (Ottawa: Carleton University Press, 1993).

Atkinson, Michael M. and Marsha A. Chandler, eds., *The Politics of Canadian Public Policy* (Toronto: University of Toronto Press, 1983).

———— and William Coleman, *The State, Business and Industrial Change in Canada* (Toronto: University of Toronto Press, 1989).

Banting, K. ed., *The State and Economic Interests*, vol. 32, Royal Commission on the Economic Union and Development Prospects for Canada (Toronto: University of Tornoto Press, 1985).

Blais, A., ed., *Industrial Policy* (Toronto: University of Toronto Press, 1985).

————, *The Political Sociology of Industrial Policy* (Toronto: University of Toronto Press, 1985).

Brandes, James A., *Government Policy Toward Business* (Toronto: Butterworths, 1988).

Brooks, Stephen and Andrew Stritch, *Business and Government in Canada* (Scarborough, Ont.: Prentice-Hall, 1991).

Chandler, Marsha A. and William M. Chandler, *Public Policy and Provincial Politics* (Toronto: McGraw-Hill Ryerson, 1979).

Coleman, William, *Business and Politics* (Montréal: McGill-Queen's University Press, 1988).

———— and Grace Skogstad, eds., *Policy Communities and Public Policy in Canada* (Mississauga: Copp Clark Pitman, 1991).

Doern, G. Bruce, ed., *The Politics of Economic Policy*, vol. 40, Royal Commission on the Economic Union (Toronto: University of Toronto Press, 1985).

———— and P. Aucoin, *Public Policy in Canada: Organization, Process and Management* (Toronto: Macmillan, 1979).

———— and Richard Phidd, *Canadian Public Policy: Ideas, Structure, Process*, 2nd ed. (Toronto: Nelson, 1992).

Fleck, J.D. and I.A. Litvak, eds., *Business Can Succeed: Understanding the Political Environment* (Toronto: Gage, 1984).

Hartle, D.G., *Public Policy, Decision-Making and Regulation* (Toronto: Butterworths, 1979).

Jackson, Robert, et al., eds., *Contemporary Canadian Politics* (Scarborough, Ont.: Prentice-Hall, 1987).

Johnston, Richard, *Public Opinion and Public Policy in Canada* (Toronto: University of Toronto Press, 1986).

Laidler, D., ed., *Responses to Economic Change*, vol. 27, Royal Commission on the Economic Union (Toronto: University of Toronto Press, 1985).

March, J.G., *Rediscovering Institutions* (New York: Free Press, 1989).

McGrew, Anthony G. and M.J. Wilson, eds., *Decision-Making: Approaches and Analysis* (Manchester: Manchester University Press, 1982).

Nordlinger, Eric, *On the Autonomy of the Democratic State* (Cambridge Mass.: Harvard University Press, 1981).

Osborne, David and Ted Gaebler, *Reinventing Government* (New York: Addison Wesley, 1992).

Ostrom, E., *Governing the Commons* (Cambridge: Cambridge University Press, 1990).

Pal, Leslie A., *Public Policy Analysis* (Toronto: Methuen, 1987).

————, *State, Class and Bureaucracy* (Montréal: McGill-Queen's University Press, 1988).

Philips, Susan D. ed., *How Ottawa Spends 1993–94* (Ottawa: Carleton University Press, 1993).

Poggi, G., *The State: Its Nature, Development and Prospects* (Cambridge: Polity Press, 1990).

Rea, K.J. and N. Wiseman, eds., *Government Enterprise in Canada* (Toronto: Methuen, 1985).

Reich, Robert, *The Work of Nations* (New York: Simon and Schuster, 1991).

Riddell, C., ed., *Labour-Management Cooperation in Canada*, vol. 15, Royal Commission on the Economic Union (Toronto: University of Toronto Press, 1985).

Stanbury, W.T., *Business-Government Relations in Canada* (Toronto: Methuen, 1986).

————, ed., *Government Regulation: Scope, Growth and Process* (Montréal: IRPP, 1980).

Sutherland, S.L. and G.B. Doern, *Bureaucracy in Canada: Control and Reform*, vol. 43, Royal Commission on the Economic Union (Toronto: University of Toronto Press, 1985).

Treibilcock, Michael, Douglas G. Hartle, J. Rober, S. Prichard and Donald N. Dewees, *The Choice of Governing Instrument*, a study prepared for the Economic Council of Canada (Ottawa: Supply and Services, 1982).

Tuohy, Carolyn J. *Policy and Politics in Canada: Institutionalized Ambivalence* (Philadelphia: Temple University Press, 1992).

Tupper, Allan and G. Bruce Doern, eds., *Public Corporations and Public Policy in Canada* (Montréal: IRPP, 1981).

Vaillancourt, F., ed., *Income Distribution and Economic Security in Canada*, vol. 1, Royal Commission on the Economic Union (Toronto: University of Toronto Press, 1985).

Weaver, R.K. and B.A. Rockman, eds., *Do Institutions Matter?* (Washington: The Brookings Institution, 1992).

CANADA IN THE WORLD

FOREIGN TRADE AND DEFENCE POLICY

S ince the last world war, the world has entered an era of rapid technological change and increasing economic interdependence. Canada is far from self-sufficient with regard to either economic prosperity or national security. Increasingly, the well-being and security of Canadian citizens depend on how they collectively respond to the constraints, opportunities and dangers that flow from the international environment.

What is Canada's place in the international order; how does it rank in terms of power, influence and prosperity? Measuring Canada's precise position in the world is difficult, if not impossible. Intuitive measures may be distorted by personal observations or national biases. Empirical measures based on indexes such as primary resources may fluctuate wildly because of changes in world supply and demand, and give an equally distorted view. However, some approximations of Canada's relative position are both necessary and instructive.

Remaining cognizant of the problems involved in acquiring equivalent data from various countries, *The New Book of World Rankings* placed Canada tenth in the world in terms of "Total Power."[1] It based its Power index on a combination of several factors, including population, territory, economy and military capability, as well as such factors as national will. According to its author, Canada ranks not only below the superpowers (United States and the former U.S.S.R.) and the standard great powers of Germany, France, Britain, Japan and China but also below Brazil and Australia.

Determining Canada's relative economic performance in terms of GDP is of course much easier than measuring power and influence. By this economic measure, too, Canada hovers in the elite top ten. In the global perspective, Canadians are economically very well off. They have a high standard of living that furnishes them with many items, from

---

[1] George Thomas Kurian, *The New Book of World Rankings*, 3rd ed. (New York: Facts on File, Inc., 1991) p. 47ff. See also George P. Miller, *Comparative World Data* (Baltimore: Johns Hopkins, 1988).

automobiles to television sets, that citizens of other countries consider extreme luxuries. As John Holmes put it, Canada is regarded as "filthy rich."[2]

Official relationships outside our borders are conducted in two ways. One involves maintaining active multilateral relations, particularly through international institutions. The other is through selective bilateral relations; Canada has 105 missions abroad. Canada's foreign policy generally aims to build strong relationships with countries that are most important to Canada's economic development and offer long-term markets for Canadian exports. The parameters of these relationships are determined to a large degree by defence arrangements with Western Europe and the United States.

In this chapter, we shall first examine the concept of foreign policy. Then, we turn to an examination of the sources of foreign policy in Canada. The balance of the chapter discusses the four main components of Canadian foreign policy: trade policy, activity in international organizations, bilateral relations and defence policy. The last among these focuses on the international strategic environment, our role in major defence organizations, peacekeeping, arms control and disarmament.

WHAT IS FOREIGN POLICY?

The domain of **foreign policy** includes all state behaviour that has external ramifications. It includes government actions and objectives and excludes those of private actors in civil society.[3] As Kal Holsti put it, students of foreign policy analyze "the actions of a state toward external environment and the conditions — usually domestic — under which those actions are formulated."[4] Therefore, the study of foreign policy can be distinguished from that of general international relations: while the former consists of an examination of government behaviour, the latter refers to the broader relations between states and includes other non-governmental activity of citizens and corporations.

Foreign policy is not one-dimensional. It has many components including national security and economic and political interests. A Canadian government trade policy document defined foreign policy as "the end product of an integration and balancing of the range of Canadian interests after the international environment in which these interests are pursued has been taken into account."[5] One of the most important aspects of that environment is, of course, the network of defence commitments. But, in recent years, the economic component of foreign policy has become increasingly important because of the growing interdependence of states and the competitive search for economic growth.

---

[2]   John Holmes, cited in Peyton V. Lyon and Brian Tomlin, *Canada as an International Actor* (Toronto: Macmillan, 1979), p. 70. For other ideas about Canada's international status see David B. Dewitt and John J. Kirton, *Canada as a Principal Power* (Toronto: Wiley, 1983); and John W. Holmes, *Canada: A Middle-Aged Power* (Toronto: McClelland & Stewart, 1976).

[3]   For comprehensive discussions of the definitional problem involved see the following general texts on international affairs: Karl W. Deutsch, *The Analysis of International Relations*, 3rd ed. (Englewood Cliffs, N.J.: Prentice-Hall, 1988); K.J. Holsti, *International Politics*, 4th ed. (Englewood Cliffs, N.J.: Prentice-Hall, 1983); Daniel S. Papp, *Contemporary International Relations*, 2nd ed. (N.Y.: Macmillan, 1988); James Lee Ray, *Global Politics* (Boston: Houghton Mifflin, 1987); Bruce Russett and Harvey Starr, *World Politics* (San Francisco: Freeman, 1985); and Robert L. Wendzel, *International Politics* (New York: Wiley, 1981).

[4]   Holsti, *International Politics*, p. 19.

[5]   *Canadian Trade Policy for the 1980s, A Discussion Paper* (Ottawa: Minister of Supply and Services, 1983), p. 40.

The process of making foreign policy is considerably different from that of making domestic policy, and coordination is not always easy or even possible. The state is able to achieve domestic objectives because it has sovereign authority over its internal environment. A government has no legal authority outside its borders; as a result, foreign policy decisions must be set within the context of the opportunities and constraints of the international system. In concrete terms, foreign policy-making in Canada differs from domestic policy-making because the former sometimes amounts to little more than striking an image. Only rarely is legislation necessary; often Parliament and even the bureaucratic elite have little more than spectator status as the Prime Minister, the Secretary of State for External Affairs and the Departments of External Affairs and National Defence determine initiatives.

SOURCES OF CANADIAN FOREIGN POLICY

The traditional view of the relationship between politicians and civil servants depicts elected politicians as responsible for the determination of policy that bureaucrats administer. Politicians make decisions; bureaucrats merely implement them. However, as we have shown in Chapter 13, the government bureaucracy has always been involved in policy-making. This development is especially evident in the formulation of foreign policy, an area where Canada's political leadership depends heavily on the bureaucracy's expertise and advice concerning the conduct of its international affairs. Nonetheless, the Prime Minister and the Ministers of Foreign Affairs and National Defence remain at the apex of decision-making.

PRIME MINISTER AND CABINET

At the level of political leadership, responsibility for foreign policy falls primarily on the Prime Minister and the Minister of Foreign Affairs. In fact, until 1946 the PM personally retained the External Affairs portfolio. It is only recently that foreign affairs have begun to involve the participation of other Cabinet members, as a result of efforts to strengthen the collective involvement of Cabinet in decision-making.[6] Today, greater use of committees and the insistence that the bureaucracy and ministers provide Cabinet with alternatives rather than allowing single-option recommendations and attempts to establish national priorities at the Cabinet level have helped to open the foreign-policy process to other departments and ministers. Still, the PM remains the central political actor, able to

Reprinted with permission, Gable, *The Globe and Mail*

---

[6] Kim Richard Nossal, *The Politics of Canadian Foreign Policy*, 2nd ed. (Scarborough, Ont.: Prentice-Hall Canada, 1989).

provide leadership and place his or her concerns high on the government's political agenda. Prime Minister Trudeau's promotion of a North/South dialogue and proposals for talks among the world's nuclear powers are examples from the early 1980s. In 1984, Brian Mulroney temporarily "institutionalized" the Prime Minister's authority in international affairs by disbanding the Cabinet committee on External Affairs and National Defence and assigning its responsibilities to Priorities and Planning, the committee that he chaired. Prime Minister Mulroney's implementation of a free trade arrangement with the United States in 1988 and the signing of the *North American Free Trade Agreement* with Mexico and the United States in 1992 are dramatic examples of the strong role the Prime Minister plays in external affairs.

The role of the Minister of Foreign Affairs (renamed from Secretary of State for External Affairs by the Liberals in 1993) is also extremely important. This Minister is not only the chief spokesman on international affairs and the top administrator for the Department of External Affairs, but often also the second most powerful person in the Cabinet. Louis St. Laurent and Lester Pearson both became Prime Ministers after being Secretary of State; Allan MacEachen held the dual position of Secretary of State and Deputy Prime Minister for several years. Joe Clark became Secretary of State after being ejected as leader of the Conservative Party and Prime Minister of Canada and André Ouellet took on the office after being the Liberal Party co-campaign manager during the 1993 election.

DEPARTMENT OF EXTERNAL (FOREIGN) AFFAIRS

The Department of External Affairs (DEA) is at the centre of the bureaucratic complex responsible for Canada's foreign relations. (See Figure 14.1.) The term "External" was originally used rather than "Foreign" affairs because many of the relationships Canada had with other countries used to involve other members of the British Empire and therefore were not regarded as "foreign" in the strict sense. Currently, the Liberal government intends to revert to the term "Foreign" in 1994. The 1909 Act of Parliament that established the Department

FIGURE 14.1   EXTERNAL (FOREIGN) AFFAIRS PERSONNEL BY REGION, 1990–91

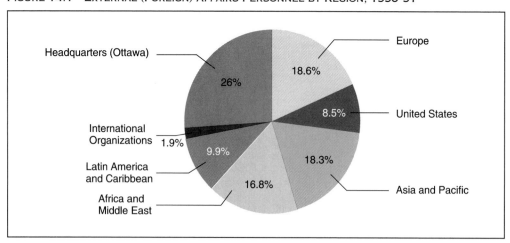

Source: Adapted from The Department of External Affairs, *Annual Report*, 1990–91 (Ottawa: Supply and Services, 1991).

---

[7]   As cited in the *Royal Commission on Conditions of Foreign Service* (Ottawa: Minister of Supply and Services, 1981), p. 64.

and charged it with "the conduct of all official communications between the Government of Canada and the government of any other country in connection with the external affairs of Canada."[7] These responsibilities have grown substantially over time. Today, the Department performs three interrelated functions: the provision and integration of policy advice, the coordination and integration of Canada's foreign relations and the implementation of foreign operations. The Liberal government intends to initiate legislation to change the institution into the Department of Foreign Affairs and International Trade.

As the repository of policy advice the Department conducts research and analysis, contributes to domestic-policy formulation and provides leadership in establishing policies in the international sphere. The coordination and integration of foreign policy involves providing a framework for the full range of governmental activities overseas, monitoring and influencing other departments and other Canadian governments' international activities and bringing coherence to a patchwork of priorities and programs. Foreign operations include representation of Canada's interests to other countries, analysis of information regarding developments abroad, negotiation and management and supervision of programs overseas. Figures 14.1 to 14.3 indicate the Department's activities at home and abroad.

FIGURE 14.2   EXTERNAL (FOREIGN) AFFAIRS PROGRAM DELIVERY PERSONNEL BY FUNCTION, 1990-91

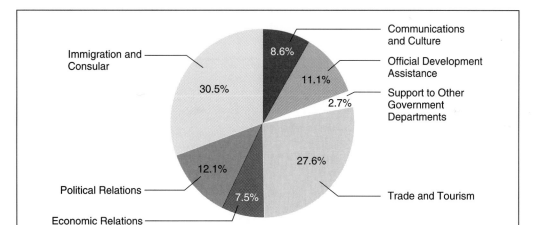

Source: Adapted from the Department of External Affairs *Annual Report*, 1991 (Ottawa: Supply and Services, 1991), p. 8. In 1992, responsibility for immigration was transferred to the Department of Employment and Immigration.

While the DEA retains primary responsibility for the conduct of Canada's foreign policy, other governmental and non-governmental bodies have become increasingly salient in the foreign policy-making process. What were once considered purely domestic matters have increasingly taken on an international dimension. The foreign policy process has become more diffuse within government and also more open in that non-governmental groups increasingly are involved. Domestically, interest groups, private citizens, business people, as well as regional interests and their provincial government representatives seek to influence foreign policy decisions. Internationally, a new layer of non-governmental organizations is active, including multinational firms pursuing commercial relations and private groups

---

[7]   As cited in the *Royal Commision on Conditions of Foreign Service* (Ottawa: Minister of Supply and Services, 1981), p.64.

FIGURE 14.3   ORGANIZATION OF THE DEPARTMENT OF EXTERNAL (FOREIGN) AFFAIRS*

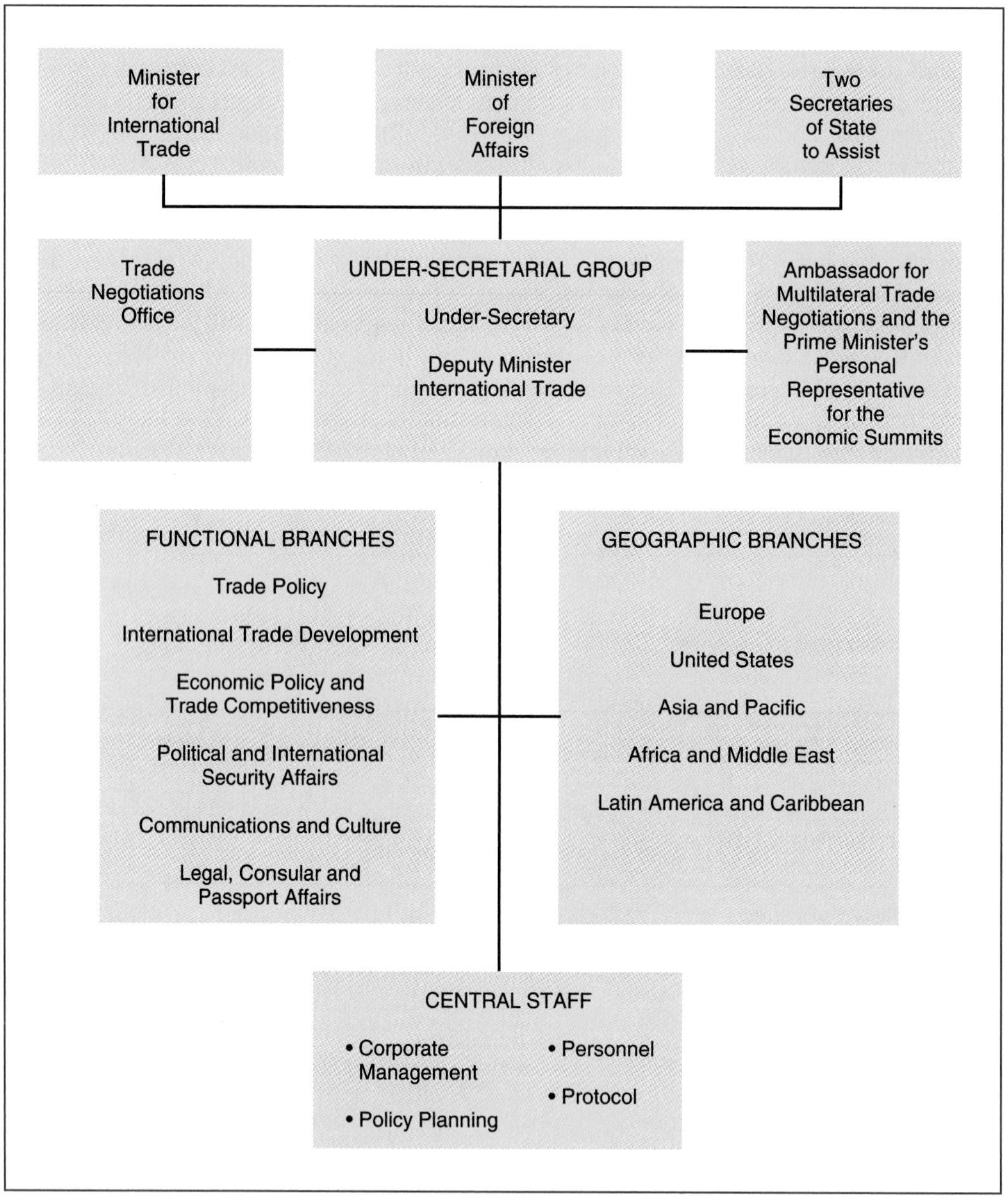

```
┌─────────────────┐   ┌─────────────────┐   ┌─────────────────┐
│     Minister    │   │     Minister    │   │       Two       │
│       for       │   │       of        │   │   Secretaries   │
│  International   │   │     Foreign     │   │    of State     │
│      Trade      │   │     Affairs     │   │    to Assist    │
└─────────────────┘   └─────────────────┘   └─────────────────┘

┌─────────────────┐   ┌─────────────────────────┐   ┌─────────────────┐
│      Trade      │   │  UNDER-SECRETARIAL GROUP│   │   Ambassador for│
│   Negotiations  │   │                         │   │ Multilateral Trade│
│      Office     │   │     Under-Secretary     │   │   Negotiations and the│
│                 │   │                         │   │  Prime Minister's│
│                 │   │     Deputy Minister     │   │     Personal    │
│                 │   │   International Trade    │   │   Representative│
│                 │   │                         │   │      for the    │
│                 │   │                         │   │ Economic Summits│
└─────────────────┘   └─────────────────────────┘   └─────────────────┘

┌─────────────────────────┐       ┌─────────────────────────┐
│   FUNCTIONAL BRANCHES    │       │   GEOGRAPHIC BRANCHES    │
│                         │       │                         │
│      Trade Policy       │       │         Europe          │
│                         │       │                         │
│ International Trade     │       │      United States      │
│      Development        │       │                         │
│                         │       │     Asia and Pacific    │
│   Economic Policy and   │       │                         │
│  Trade Competitiveness  │       │  Africa and Middle East │
│                         │       │                         │
│ Political and International│     │ Latin America and Caribbean│
│    Security Affairs     │       │                         │
│                         │       │                         │
│ Communications and Culture│     │                         │
│                         │       │                         │
│   Legal, Consular and   │       │                         │
│     Passport Affairs    │       │                         │
└─────────────────────────┘       └─────────────────────────┘

              ┌─────────────────────────┐
              │      CENTRAL STAFF      │
              │                         │
              │ • Corporate   • Personnel│
              │   Management            │
              │               • Protocol│
              │ • Policy Planning       │
              └─────────────────────────┘
```

* In November 1993, the new Liberal government took tentative steps to reorganize the department. Henceforth, it would be called the Department of Foreign Affairs and International Trade. Two Ministers — the Minister of Foreign Affairs and the Minister of International Trade — and two Secretaries of State to Assist — one for Latin America and Africa and another for Asia-Pacific — were appointed. Legal changes will require legislation to be passed by Parliament

Source: Adapted from The Department of External Affairs, *Estimates*, Part III, 1993–94 (Ottawa: Supply and Services, 1993), pp. 2–18. Reproduced by authority of the Minister responsible for Statistics Canada 1993.

advocating protection of human rights. Consequently, traditional foreign-policy-makers have had to accept increasing levels of participation by other actors in international affairs.

Changes in federal intra-governmental structures have also eroded the DEA's dominance in conducting Canada's foreign relations. The introduction of a formal Cabinet committee system subjected the Department's activities and policy proposals to scrutiny from other departments. Further, the Prime Minister's support agencies — the Prime Minister's Office and the Privy Council Office — have become more influential in foreign policy decisions. New or revamped departments have also eroded the former predominance of the DEA, to the point of duplicating some of the Department's functions. Many contemporary issues require expertise that External Affairs does not possess: the law of the sea, acid rain, energy policy and nuclear and grain exports, to name a few. The participation of such diverse departments and government bodies as Environment Canada; Energy, Mines and Resources; the National Energy Board; Atomic Energy of Canada; the Department of Agriculture and the Canadian Wheat Board is therefore essential.

Provincial governments and their agencies and Crown corporations, too, have become important actors in the foreign policy process. While Québec's international activities tend to receive most publicity, nearly all the provinces are active on the international scene. Western provinces concern themselves with such matters as resource exports and tariffs, while Atlantic Canada has interests in fisheries, the law of the sea and offshore resources — all issues with important foreign policy implications. In addition, the provinces are all concerned with federal government policies that affect international trade.

As a response to the diffusion of the contemporary foreign policy-making process, attempts have been made to coordinate the various departments, groups and policies involved. In 1962 the Glassco Commission, in its review of the DEA, recommended structural changes and suggested periodic reviews and reforms of the department's internal structure. Further studies resulted in a 1970 federal White Paper, Foreign Policy for Canadians, that led to the establishment of the Interdepartmental Committee on External Relations. In March 1980, the federal government announced further consolidation of responsibilities. Foreign service officers from the Department of Industry, Trade and Commerce and the Canadian Employment and Immigration Commission were integrated into the DEA, along with foreign service officers from Employment and Immigration at the operational level and the field staff from the Canadian International Development Agency (CIDA). The stated purposes of the consolidation were to improve the economy and efficiency of foreign operations without affecting the policy and program development roles of the departments involved; to create a more cohesive and coherent foreign service; to strengthen the role of heads of post and to improve the career prospects and experiences of foreign service personnel.[8]

The Department of External Affairs was restructured further in January 1982. Its aims were to enhance Canada's ability to pursue international markets and give greater priority to economic matters in the development of foreign policy or, in the words of then-Undersecretary of External Affairs, "to give greater weight to economic factors in the design of foreign policy,

---

[8]   Gordon Osbaldeston, "Reorganizing Canada's External Affairs," *International Journal*, vol. XXXVII, no. 3 (Summer 1982), p. 461. See also W.M. Dobell, "Is External Affairs a Central Agency?" *International Perspectives* (May/July, 1979), pp. 8–11; Daniel Madar and Denis Stairs, "Alone on Killers' Row: The Policy Analysis Group and the Department of External Affairs," *International Journal*, vol. XXXII, no. 4 (August 1977), pp. 727–55; Kim Richard Nossal, "Allison through the (Ottawa) Looking Glass: Bureaucratic Politics and Foreign Policy in a Parliamentary System," *CPA*, vol. 22, no. 4 (Winter, 1979), pp. 610–26; and G.A.H. Pearson, "Order Out of Chaos? Some Reflections on Foreign Policy Planning in Canada," *International Journal*, vol. XXXII, no. 4 (August 1977), pp. 756–68.

to ensure the conduct of foreign relations serves Canadian trade objectives, to improve the service offered exporters in an increasingly competitive international marketplace and to ensure policy and program coherence in the conduct of Canada's range of relations with the outside world."[9] Trade policy and trade promotion functions of the Department of Industry, Trade and Commerce were therefore transferred to External Affairs, completing the consolidation on economic matters. Then, in 1992 another shuffle took place and the primary responsibility for immigration was returned to the Department of Employment and Immigration.

As late as 1993, the prominence of economic objectives is reflected in a two-minister team at External Affairs (see Figure 14.3). The Secretary of State for External Affairs (Minister of Foreign Affairs) is responsible for the management of the department, integrating its various parts as well as relating the department to the rest of the government. He or she is supported by the Minister of State for International Trade. They, in turn, are backed up by two Secretaries of State to Assist — one for Asia and one for Africa and Latin America. These Ministers are charged with providing a link between the concerns of government outside and within Canada. Concern for coordination is also evident at the senior bureaucratic level of the department (refer again to Figure 14.3). At the head of the department is the Undersecretary, who is supported by a Deputy Minister of International Trade.

The Department of External (Foreign) Affairs is now expected to be responsible for the delivery of almost all government programs abroad, through a single, unified foreign service. All positions are filled by career civil servants who are normally admitted into the service as junior officers on the basis of open competitive examination. There are exceptions. For example, the Canadian Ambassadors in Paris and Washington and High Commissioner in London are often political appointees. Normally, officials change their postings every two or three years, with occasional intervals in Ottawa to broaden their experience. The most senior officials, for example, sometimes alternate high-level positions in domestic government agencies with ambassadorships abroad.

PARLIAMENT AND POLITICAL PARTIES

In western liberal democracies, legislatures and political parties provide an important link between citizens and their government. In Canada, Parliament provides a forum for public debate, while parties mobilize public opinion, coordinate political activity and function as intermediate instruments of political activity for those not elected to office. Therefore, in the realm of foreign policy formulation, Parliament and political parties provide channels through which diverse pressures from the domestic community are brought to bear on the policy process.[10]

For example, Question Period in the House of Commons provides MPs the opportunity to raise foreign policy issues. The House of Commons Standing Committee on External Affairs, the Standing Committee on National Defence and the Senate Committee on Foreign Affairs have conducted major reviews of various aspects of Canadian foreign and defence policy in addition to performing their routine function of examining the budgetary estimates of the foreign policy establishment. Special parliamentary task forces and subcommittees have been formed to report on important issues such as Canadian/American relations, North/South relations, peacekeeping, and others.

---

9   Marcel Massé, "Department of External Affairs: Changes to Organizational Structure," memo no. USS-241, (Department of External Affairs, July 8, 1983), p. 1.

10   The following discussion is derived from Denis Stairs, "The Foreign Policy of Canada," in James N. Rosenau, Kenneth W. Thompson and Gavin Boyd, eds., *World Politics: An Introduction* (New York: The Free Press, 1976), pp. 187–89.

However, the role of Parliament and political parties in making foreign policy is constrained by the powers of the government. While Cabinet takes into consideration the anticipated reaction of Parliament in its policy deliberations, only a few cases exist in which formal parliamentary debate can be said to have had a decisive impact on government behaviour in the foreign policy field.[11] Because of the nature of diplomacy, governments have almost exclusive control over information in this area. Requirements of discretion over matters involving national security and relations with foreign countries therefore limit the impact of outside groups and individuals on the foreign policy process: the government's ability to assume policy and make treaties with foreign countries without ratification by Parliament constrains the impact of opposition parties and societal groups.

NON-GOVERNMENTAL ACTORS: INTEREST GROUPS, THE MEDIA AND PUBLIC OPINION

Other means of expression of international policy interests include representations from private interest groups, the media and popular opinion as measured by polling. How much influence each has varies from issue to issue, yet politicians cannot remain long in office without taking these views into consideration.

Interest groups attempt to reach those who have influence in the foreign policy-making process, primarily members of the government and appropriate members of the public service.[12] Some groups possess sufficient expertise or political clout to be asked by government to participate in the process. For example, representatives of domestic interest groups are included among the advisors to Canadian delegations attending international conferences.[13] Most groups, however, must gain access to politicians and bureaucrats through meetings, presentation of position briefs, the media and/or mobilization of their constituents.

The number of interest groups concerned with foreign policy has grown substantially in recent years. New issues such as nuclear radiation and waste, acid rain, survival of whales and seals and the disruption of Arctic communities by resource development have joined traditional foreign policy issues, including global security and nuclear proliferation.

The media's impact on the foreign-policy process is indirect. According to a prominent observer, the press "has little effect upon the substance of foreign policy per se, but...it exerts a very significant impact upon the day-to-day activities of the men who make it."[14]

---

[11] Important exceptions include the Suez Crisis of October 1956, in which the Liberal government supported American-sponsored efforts to force British, French and Israeli forces to withdraw from captured Egyptian territory; the issue of equipping Canadian fighter planes and missile system with nuclear warheads during Diefenbaker's prime ministership and the TransCanada Pipeline debate. See D.B. Dewitt and J.J. Kirton, *Canada as a Principal Power*, pp. 171–77; Lawrence Martin, *The Presidents and the Prime Ministers* (Toronto: Doubleday, 1982), ch. 12; and William Kilbourn, *Pipeline: TransCanada and the Great Debate — A History of Business and Politics* (Toronto: Clarke, Irwin, 1970).

[12] On the impact of interest groups and the media on foreign policy see Special Issue "Domestic Causes of Canada's Foreign Policy," *International Journal*, vol XXXIX, no. 1 (Winter 1983–84); Elizabeth Riddell-Dixon, *The Domestic Mosaic: Domestic Groups and Canadian Foreign Policy* (Toronto: CIIA, 1985); Donald Barry, "Interest Groups and the Foreign Policy Process," in A. Paul Pross, ed., *Pressure Group Behaviour in Canadian Politics* (Toronto: McGraw-Hill Ryerson, 1975), pp. 115–47.

[13] Jack Davis, *Conference on the Human Environment: A Report of Canada's Preparation for and the Participation in the United Nations Conference on Human Environment*, Stockholm, Sweden, June 1972 (Ottawa, 1972), cited in Denis Stairs, "Public Opinion and External Affairs: Reflections on the Domestication of Canadian Foreign Policy," *International Journal*, vol. XXXIII, no. 1 (Winter 1977–78), pp. 128–49.

[14] Denis Stairs, "The Press and Foreign Policy in Canada," *International Journal*, vol. XXXI, no. 2 (Spring 1976), p. 238.

By providing coverage of external events, reports on specific issues and editorial positions, the media disseminates information and opinion and, at times, prescribes solutions, thereby articulating public and elite foreign policy concerns.

Professional diplomats' feelings toward the proper role of public opinion in foreign policy-making are critical or ambivalent; many believe that it is not an appropriate guide for the conduct of foreign policy.[15] Because of the constraints diplomats face in the international arena, as well as the complexity of the issues, the impact of public opinion may at times be detrimental. According to Denis Stairs,

> From the professional's traditional perspective the international working environment is…a world of nuance and subtlety and craft, and certainly no place for the amateur. But nuance, subtlety, and craft are not the most obvious characteristics of the constituent public, or of their opinions. Public reactions to foreign policy issues, especially but not solely in political-security contexts, are often one sided, ill informed, transient, fickle, and given, at their worst, to emotional excess.[16]

While public opinion may not have an immediate impact on the determination of policy, it has the capacity to set limits on what policy-makers can do "politically." Policy-makers must take account of latent opinions and anticipate the public's reactions to various policy alternatives. Thus, decision-makers consult public opinion polls not as a source of policy ideas but rather as an indicator of the public's potential response to various policy options. It is in this negative sense of ruling policy options out (that is, determining not so much what the public wants as what it does not want) that public opinion has its most significant influence.[17]

PROVINCES AND FOREIGN POLICY

Provincial governments have a keen interest in the conduct of Canadian foreign policy and have attempted to increase their international visibility by opening foreign offices.[18] Such offices are important to provinces that depend heavily on external trade. Provincial governments sponsor trade and cultural missions, receive visiting foreign dignitaries, participate in ongoing multilateral conferences and become involved in joint federal/provincial programs.

Fields over which provinces have concurrent or exclusive jurisdiction have become increasingly important in the international arena, and this necessitates the inclusion of provincial concerns in the formation of Canada's foreign policy. Within the context of growing provincial power in Canadian federalism, provincial interests are important to the extent that, according to one author, "the range and frequency of provincial international activity is now sufficient to complicate the design and conduct of Canadian foreign policy, indeed, to frustrate central control over foreign policy in some areas."[19]

Increased international activity on the part of provincial governments has not been without periods of confrontation and conflict. This is not surprising, given that matters of national interest in a country as large and disparate as Canada are in question. The federal government, presiding over a varied populace, is sometimes faced with incompatible demands.

---

[16] Ibid., p. 142.

[17] Ibid., pp. 133–34.

[18] For further discussion see Ronald G. Atkey, "The Role of Provinces in International Affairs," *International Journal*, vol. XXVI, no. 1 (Winter 1970–71), pp. 249–73; P.R. Johannson, "Provincial International Activities," *International Journal*, vol. XXXIII, no. 2 (Spring 1978), pp. 357–78; and David B. Dewitt and John J. Kirton, *Canada as a Principal Power*, pp. 186–92.

[19] Johannson, "Provincial International Activities," p. 357.

Federal/provincial conflict in this field is exacerbated by the absence of a clear delineation of constitutional authority regarding treaties and international relations. Section 132 of the *Constitution Act*, for example, refers only to the implementation of treaties affecting the British Empire. Moreover, the range of powers vested in the provinces necessitates at least some measure of involvement in foreign policy. Consequently, there has been, and to some extent continues to be, both legal and political debate over the proper role of the provinces in foreign affairs.[20]

Those who argue for independent provincial international competence believe that the *Constitution*'s silence on foreign relations implies that the provinces have a legal right to negotiate and sign treaties *on provincial subjects*. Support for this position is based on a number of factors.[21] First, the provinces were judicially conceded the exclusive right to implement treaties in the 1936 *Labour Conventions* case. Since treaty-making and treaty implementation are virtually inseparable, it is argued that if provincial governments can legally implement provisions of treaties, they should also be able to negotiate them.

Second, international law, specifically the 1966 *International Law Commission* of the United Nations, adds support to the concept of provincial competence. According to Article 3(2): "State members of a federal union may possess a capacity to conclude treaties if such capacity is admitted by the federal constitution and within the limits laid down."[22] The silence of the *Constitution* is again assumed to be supportive of the provincial case.

Third, the experiences of other federal states where component units have been allowed to make treaties are noted as precedents. For example, treaty-making powers exist in the subunits in Switzerland and the Federal Republic of Germany.

Fourth, efforts of various Québec governments to obtain recognition of their special linguistic and cultural status are claimed to have provided precedents strengthening the position of the provinces. For example, in 1964 Québec concluded an educational exchange agreement with France without the participation of or prior consultation with Ottawa. In November 1965, Canada and France signed a cultural agreement and arranged an exchange of letters recognizing possible *ententes* providing for educational and cultural exchanges between France and the provinces of Canada. However, that same month, Québec and France concluded an *entente* on cultural cooperation without reference to the Ottawa/France agreement. Although the federal government gave its consent to both the 1964 and 1965 exchanges, the agreements were initiated by Québec alone and implemented by Québec officials. Such actions are said to be creating a de facto provincial competence in international affairs.

Advocates of exclusive federal competence in all international matters view the situation differently.[23] The prerogative of treaty-making power for Canada, it is argued, was vested exclusively in the Queen in 1867, as stated in section 9 of the *BNA Act*. Through a process of evolution from 1871 to 1939, direct foreign affairs power devolved to Canada to be exercised by the government in the name of the Governor General. At no time during this period did

---

[20] For an excellent discussion see R. McGregor Dawson, *The Government of Canada*, 5th ed., rev. by N. Ward (Toronto: University of Toronto Press, 1970), passim.

[21] The various arguments are taken from Atkey, "The Role of Provinces."

[22] Ibid., p. 262.

[23] For a discussion of the exclusive federal competence view, see the federal government's White Paper, Canada, Department of External Affairs, *Federalism and International Relations* (Ottawa: Queen's Printer, February, 1968) and its supplement, *Federalism and International Conferences on Education* (Ottawa: Queen's Printer, 1968). As well, see Ontario Advisory Committee on Confederation, *Confederation Challenged: Background Papers and Reports*, vols. I and II (Toronto: 1967, 1970).

the provinces acquire treaty-making power. Rather, as evidenced by the new letters patent issued to the Governor General by the Crown in 1947 and the *Seals Act* of 1939, the federal government was given all powers previously exercised by the British Crown.

Several Supreme Court judgements also support the federalist position. For example, before the 1936 *Labour Conventions* case was appealed to the Judicial Committee of the Privy Council, it drew comments from several Supreme Court justices, including Chief Justice Duff, that the authority to enter into international agreements resided exclusively in the federal government even on matters of provincial legislative competence. However, since the case concerned the power to implement and not negotiate treaties, the JCPC did not consider this issue relevant.

Finally, support for the exclusivity of federal treaty-making power is derived from the international law of recognition. Advocates of this position argue that, during Canada's evolution to independence, only the federal government, not the provincial governments, was recognized as having responsibility for foreign affairs.

Thus, both sides have recourse to legal precedents that make it difficult if not impossible to arrive at a legal solution by unilateral action. The dispute has necessitated a more functional approach that recognizes the concerns of both levels of government; it is this approach that has been adopted by the federal government. Reacting to the demands of Québec, the federal government issued what it perceived to be the proper international role for the provinces:

1. The provinces have no treaty-making powers, but they do have the right to enter into private commercial contracts with foreign governments, as well as to make bureaucratic agreements of a non-binding nature with foreign governments.
2. The provinces may open offices in foreign countries in pursuit of their legitimate needs and interests in that country, so long as the office only engages in arrangements of a non-binding nature.
3. The provinces claim the right to be involved in the formulation stages of treaty-making activities when the subject matter of the treaty falls within provincial legislative competence.
4. The provinces may be included in Canadian delegations attending international gatherings and play a role in formulating and enunciating the Canadian position, when the subject matter falls within provincial legislative competence.[24]

While the federal government's purpose was to prevent provincial government initiatives when possible, jurisdictional realities necessitated a framework that would accommodate provincial interests to some extent. Ottawa's policy of primacy in external affairs has therefore been tempered by accommodation, allowing provinces to participate within Canadian international delegations.

It is evident, then, that foreign-policy-making in Canada is becoming ever more diffuse. While the Department of External (Foreign) Affairs remains the most important bureaucratic component, other departments have become more prominent. The increased activity of non-governmental actors continued the trend. The response of the federal government has been to initiate bureaucratic reorganization and to continue to seek accommodation of regional interests as expressed by provincial governments, in an attempt to provide a coherent and effective foreign policy.

---

[24] Johannson, "Provincial International Activities," pp. 361–62.

CANADIAN TRADE POLICY

Foreign trade is vital to Canadian interests. Canada possesses a low ratio of population to land and resources and is by necessity, therefore, one of the largest trading nations in the world. The domestic market of 27 million is too small to sustain flourishing industries, so about one-third of GDP depends on exports.[25] Most of these exports come from primary industries based on natural resources, of which Canada has an abundance.

Canada has three main kinds of natural resources. The first is agricultural land, which climatic and soil conditions make amenable to cultivating crops and raising livestock. It is limited to the southernmost part of the country and, particularly in central Canada, is steadily being encroached upon by industrial development and urban sprawl. The second category is non-renewable resources, such as mineral deposits. Canada is a leading exporter of minerals — crude petroleum, natural gas, iron ore, nickel and copper, in that order. The third type of natural resource consists of renewable resources, of which wood, fish and fur are, or have been, particularly important to Canada's economic growth.

This present-day pattern of the Canadian economy essentially was laid out in the colonial period. Basically, Canada exports primary goods and imports secondary or manufactured goods. Most Canadians live and work in urban, industrialized areas, but it is agricultural products, lumber and mineral resources that continue to provide the bulk of our exports and pay for imported manufactured goods. Yet only about 7 percent of the population is employed in primary industries.

During the 1970s, while defence issues were largely dormant in Canadian politics, successive Trudeau governments concentrated on elevating other issues in foreign policy. The first step was the 1970 foreign policy White Paper. In the ensuing years, the so-called Third Option was pursued, and the Department of External Affairs was restructured to provide better coordination and a higher profile for foreign trade policy. Then, in August 1983, for the first time, the Department issued two related documents dealing with Canadian trade policy. One, *Canadian Trade Policy in the 1980s*, was a discussion paper; the other, *A Review of Canadian Trade Policy*, was a background paper.[26] Both attempted to link trade policy to other government concerns such as monetary, taxation, subsidies, transport and labour policies. Unlike the Third Option, which had called for building markets in countries other than the United States, these documents argued that Canada should promote both multilateral and regional or bilateral initiatives, stressing particularly the need to develop bilateral relations with the U.S. We examine the results of these policies, in particular the *Canada–United States Free Trade Agreement* and the *North American Free Trade Agreement* below.

Canadian trade is conducted on a bilateral basis, and requires careful day-to-day management of issues that arise between Canada and her main trading partners. However, the fact that the contractual framework for most of Canada's bilateral trade is provided by the *General Agreement on Tariffs and Trade* (GATT) illustrates the important multilateral dimension of international economic relations.

---

[25]   Questions about Canadian trade policy assumed a new importance in the 1980s and 1990s. For discussion of the topic see Rodney de C. Grey, *Trade Policy in the 1980s* (Montréal: C.D. Howe Institute, 1981); and Special Issue on "Trade Policy," *International Perspectives*, March/April 1984. The Canadian Government also assessed the trade environment in *A Review of Canadian Trade Policy: A Background Document to Canadian Trade Policy for the 1980s* (Ottawa: Minister of Supply and Services, 1983), p. 3.

[26]   *Canadian Trade Policy for the 1980s, A Discussion Paper* (Ottawa: Department of External Affairs, 1983); *A Review of Canadian Trade Policy*, ibid.

THE GATT

After the Second World War, the U.S., Britain and Canada were the principal proponents of a new trading order that resulted in 1947 in the *General Agreement on Tariffs and Trade* (GATT), an agreement that seeks to establish a trading order based on reciprocity, non-discrimination and multilateralism.[27] It covers over 80 percent of world trade and includes most major industrialized countries. The **GATT** is both a treaty and an institution. As a treaty, it sets out a code of rules for the conduct of trade; as an institution, it oversees the application of the trade rules and provides a forum in which countries can discuss trade problems and negotiate reductions in trade barriers.

The main benefit for Canada of the GATT is that it provides a contractual basis for Canada/U.S. trade relations while facilitating the expansion of trade relations with other countries. As a signatory of the GATT, Canada can negotiate basic resource needs with its powerful southern neighbour more easily. At the time of writing, the members of GATT have just completed the Uruguay Round of multilateral trade negotiations.

Some Facts About GATT

- The GATT was extablished in 1947. It was intended as a temporary measure that would lead to a World Trade Organization.

- There have been eight trade liberalization negotiations. The latest, started in Uruguay in 1986, terminated successfully in 1993. The four key sectors under discussion involved textiles, intellectual property, agriculture and services. Difficulties were primarily over agricultural subsidies.

- The 108 countries participating in the Uruguay Round of the GATT have agreed to abide by the trade rules set down in the deal.

World trade grew steadily after the GATT was founded and then slowed in the 1970s, with the Organization of Petroleum Exporting Countries (OPEC) showing most rapid growth during that decade. In 1981, for the first time since the GATT was established, there was no real growth in world trade. Since then, the world economy has demonstrated three significant characteristics: slow international market growth, financial instability and increased international competitiveness. Financial markets have been volatile, with developing countries building enormous debt loads that threaten to disrupt the international economic system.

The changing structure of the world economy has seriously affected the Canadian economy. There has been a pronounced shift in industrial power toward Japan, Europe and the so-called Newly Industrialized Countries (NICs). Major oil exporting countries have retained their vastly increased purchasing power. New technologies are developing rapidly and forcing industries in developed countries to adapt to increasingly competitive conditions or be left behind as standard technologies are taken over by developing countries with low labour costs.

---

[27] For discussion on Canada and the world economy see A.F.W. Plumptre, *Three Decades of Decision: Canada and the World Monetary System, 1944–75* (Toronto: McClelland & Stewart, 1980); Robert Bothwell, Ian Drummond and John English, *Canada Since 1945: Power, Politics and Provincialism* (Toronto: University of Toronto Press, 1981); and Donald J. Daly, *Canada in an Uncertain World Economic Environment* (Montréal: IRPP, 1982). On general international economic organizations see Joan Edelman Spero, *The Politics of International Economic Relations* (New York: St Martin's Press, 1977); and C. Fred Bergsten and Lawrence B. Krause, eds., *World Politics and International Economics* (Washington: Brookings Institution, 1975).

There are some disturbing signs about the capability of Canada to adapt to this new world situation. While the volume of Canadian trade has continued to grow, its share of total world trade has steadily declined in the postwar years.[28] During the 1970s especially, Canada was unable to hold its own in world markets as an exporter of capital goods. During the same period the European Community became the world's largest trading bloc, its external trade equalling the combined shares of the United States and Japan.[29] While Germany and Japan in particular made spectacular gains in their share of world exports, other countries, including Canada, the U.S. and the U.K., saw their shares of world trade decline considerably. In relative terms, Canada's share of world trade underwent the largest decline among industrialized countries. For details of Canadian trade in 1990 see Table 14.1.

TABLE 14.1   CANADA'S PRINCIPAL TRADING REGIONS: MERCHANDISE EXPORTS, IMPORTS AND TRADE BALANCES, 1990

Merchandise Trade With	Exports 1990	Imports 1990	Trade Balance 1990
World	148 665	136 224	12 440
United States	111 381	87 895	23 486
Europe	15 780	20 227	(4 446)
Western Europe	14 459	19 627	(5 167)
of which EC (12)	12 191	15 616	(3 425)
Eastern Europe & Former USSR	1 321	600	721
Asia–Pacific	16 237	19 535	(3 299)
Asia	15 143	18 540	(3 397)
of which Japan	8 230	9 523	(1 293)
of which China	1 655	1 394	262
Pacific	1 094	995	99
Latin America	2 703	4 582	(1 879)
South America	1 378	2 198	(821)
Central America & Caribbean	1 325	2 383	(1 058)
Africa–Middle East	2 521	2 283	238
Middle East	1 434	1 157	277
Africa	1 087	1 126	(39)

Source: Adapted from the Department of External Affairs, *Annual Report 1990–91* (Ottawa: Supply and Services, 1991).

INTERNATIONAL AND MULTILATERAL ORGANIZATION

For historical and political reasons, Canadian foreign policy has always been directed predominantly toward Europe (especially Britain) and the United States. Political relations, defence and economic policies therefore have all developed certain basic continuities. Longstanding defence ties, which are considered in detail later in the chapter, are with the United States and western Europe through NATO and NORAD. Multilateral relations are primarily conducted through the United Nations and its related agencies. Bilateral political and economic relations are strongest with the U.S., the Commonwealth, western Europe and the French-language community. But Asia, especially Japan, recently has become even more important to Canada than Europe in purely economic relations.

---

[28] *Canadian Trade Policy for the 1980s*, p. 4

[29] *A Review of Canadian Trade Policy*, p. 19.

CANADA AND THE UNITED NATIONS

Canada played a central role in creating the United Nations and in directing its evolution as an international organization. Sponsorship of the United Nations by the Canadian government demonstrated the radical change from the prewar policy of isolationism to postwar internationalism as a means of avoiding war. Both Louis St. Laurent, who became Secretary of State for External Affairs in 1946, and Lester Pearson, who followed in that position, were avowed internationalists. Pearson wrote in his memoirs, "everything I learned during the war confirmed and strengthened my view as a Canadian that our foreign policy must not be timid or fearful of commitments but activist in accepting international responsibility."[30] The United Nations seemed the natural medium for bringing states together to promote peace.

Initially, the UN had 57 charter members and, in the 1950s, Canada was a major participant. But the club was too restrictive. In 1955 Paul Martin, Chairman of the Canadian UN delegation, persuaded the UN Security Council to agree to a package deal for accepting new member states. New members flooded in, and today Canada is no longer a principal player, but merely one of 181 countries in an institution that is no longer dominated by western democratic powers. As president of the UN General Assembly, Lester Pearson was responsible for introducing one of the UN's most important innovations: the peacekeeping force. The UN Charter provided for a standing army, but one was never created.

In recent years, the UN has been severely criticized, particularly by the United States, because the large membership with equal voting rights among very unequal states restricts what the Assembly can accomplish. The General Assembly too often is used as a platform for public denunciations of states by their enemies rather than as a forum for rational debate of the issues. One of Canada's former ambassadors to the UN, William Barton, described the situation as follows: "What we have is a UN where…weak powers pay two percent of the budget and a small percentage of the nations have the muscle, pay the bills and call the shots because they have the real power. So a dispute between small nations and big ones becomes a struggle against people with real power."[31]

However, no other organization has arisen to replace the UN as a forum for the discussion of world problems. Canada has been involved at the UN in several significant issue areas during recent years, including the Law of the Sea, the North/South dialogue between rich and poor nations, human rights and chemical warfare. Canada is also a strong supporter of the UN's many specialized multilateral agencies — the World Health Organization, the International Labor Organization, International Postal Union and the International Monetary Fund, among others — that have earned considerable respect throughout the world. Another agency, the International Civil Aviation Organization, has its headquarters in Montréal. These agencies are all working to improve the quality of life, particularly in the large number of new states represented at the UN, which look to it as a source of security and development assistance.

The rather tarnished contemporary image of the UN may be a result of exaggerated expectations of what it can accomplish. John Holmes, one of Canada's leading authorities on the UN, summarized the situation in this way: "When people worry whether the UN has lived up to the ideals of the Charter, in some ways it's the wrong question. Rather than see whether it has been able to carry out a mandate carved in stone it may be better to ask whether

---

[30] Lester B. Pearson, *Mike: The Memoirs of Lester Pearson, Vol. I: 1897–1948* (Toronto: University of Toronto Press, 1972), p. 283.

[31] *The Toronto Star*, November 20, 1982.

it has been able to grow and fit in with changing circumstances... To a great extent it has."[32] Holmes was correct. In 1993, for example, the United Nations had almost 85 000 troops acting as peacekeepers around the world, including in Cambodia, Somalia and the former Yugoslavia.

THE COMMONWEALTH

At Confederation Canada was part of the British Empire, exercising autonomy in domestic policy but dependent on Britain in foreign affairs. The First World War was the catalyst in the attainment of complete autonomy for Canada and in the transformation of the Empire into the Commonwealth. The transition was achieved at a succession of Imperial Conferences in the 1920s that culminated with the Balfour declaration in 1926. The dominions within the British Empire were equal, autonomous communities "united by a common allegiance to the Crown, and freely associated as members of the British Commonwealth of Nations."[33] This sentiment was enshrined in the 1931 *Statute of Westminster* that formally laid the old Empire to rest. The Commonwealth at that time consisted of Britain, Australia, Canada, Newfoundland, the Irish Free State, the Union of South Africa and New Zealand. Now, just over six decades later, it numbers 50 member states and embraces more than a billion people and about a quarter of the earth's surface. Louis St. Laurent and Lester Pearson played an important role in the evolution of this radically new Commonwealth. Pearson particularly was a key figure in negotiating an acceptable formula for admission of new republics — a development that changed the essentially anglocentric focus of the Commonwealth association.[34] Canada has consistently encouraged the advancement and strengthening of the association as a vehicle for practical cooperation among member states.

At the practical level, Commonwealth heads of government meet regularly every two years and sponsor various fields of technical cooperation, scholarships and the Commonwealth games. There are no binding rules of membership, and decisions at these meetings are by consensus rather than vote. Perhaps the most valuable feature of Commonwealth meetings, however, is simply the opportunity for heads of state to meet relatively informally and discuss a variety of vital common issues such as human rights and intra-Commonwealth aid. For instance, at the meeting in Lusaka in 1979, in an atmosphere of civil war, the issue was how to end Rhodesia's illegal white supremacist regime. The Commonwealth meeting provided a forum for negotiations, and its result was an independent Zimbabwe. As Prime Minister Joe Clark put it at the time, the informality limited posturing and encouraged frankness; whereas the "economic summits allow leaders to appear to be addressing problems, to make statements...the Commonwealth meetings, I believe, allow leaders to try to resolve important issues."[35] Concrete progress is not always evident, however. The 1991 meeting in Harare, Zimbabwe was used by Canada mainly to highlight issues of human rights, democratic development and equality for women, but there was little instrumental effect from all the talk.

---

[32] John Holmes, quoted in *The Toronto Star*, November 20, 1982.

[33] Glazebrook, *A History of Canadian External Relations*, pp. 90–1.

[34] See John Holmes, *Shaping of Peace*, vol. 2 (Toronto: University of Toronto Press, 1982), ch. 8.

[35] *The Globe and Mail*, Toronto, September 30, 1981.

LA FRANCOPHONIE

In recent years, the French-language community has built its own organization similar to the British Commonwealth. Under Lester Pearson's leadership and especially under Pierre Trudeau, the Canadian federal government encouraged strengthening Canada's ties with francophone countries, mainly in the form of increasing representation and development aid in these nations through multilateral programs and organizations such as the Agency for Cultural and Technical Cooperation. The Agency programs centre on three main areas: development, education and scientific and technical cooperation. The issue of Québec's participation as distinct from Canada's has occasionally caused overt hostility between the respective governments when the federal government interpreted Québec's actions as a challenge to its primacy in foreign policy. However, since 1971 Québec has had "participating government" status in the Agency, a privilege that also was extended to New Brunswick in 1977. Finally, in Paris in 1986 *la Francophonie*, with a membership of 41 countries, was born. Canadian representation was fleshed out with members from Québec and New Brunswick using a controversial formula that implied an enhanced role for the provinces in foreign affairs. In 1991, Canada attended the fourth francophone conference at which it advocated more human rights and democracy in the world.

ECONOMIC SUMMITS

Canada belongs to many multilateral organizations concerned with the global economy and development. The best known and most prestigious of them are the economic summits, annual gatherings of the seven largest industrialized democracies and the Commission of the European Community. The summits, which began in 1975 at Rambouillet in France, have taken on a semi-permanent character, although there is no permanent secretariat. They have become huge media events, but despite the potential for grandstanding, they provide the opportunity for leaders to discuss trade issues and international economic topics.

The meetings are particularly important to Canada for several reasons. First of all, the economic summits provide recognition of status; political leaders want to be part of this elite group. Canada joined the group largely through United States and Japanese sponsorship. But more importantly, Canada has a major stake in the economic relationships among the "Big Seven." Of the seven, Canada is the most affected by the economic policies of the United States.

Still, many observers believe that the summits are meaningless exercises. A balanced view is that they are significant, but their importance is easy to exaggerate. As Prime Minister Margaret Thatcher remarked in a pre-summit briefing, "Blessed is he that expecteth nothing and he shall not be disappointed."[36]

CANADA AND FOREIGN AID: CIDA AND THE IDRC

Canada's official development assistance is channelled through the Canadian International Development Agency (CIDA). It operates two types of assistance programs, multilateral and bilateral, but Canada's major contribution is in the form of bilateral aid. Multilateral assistance programs are directed mainly toward the UN, its affiliated agencies and the World Bank.

---

[36] Quoted in *The Globe and Mail*, Toronto, June 8, 1984. The global economy is described in David H. Blake and Robert S. Walters, *The Politics of Global Economic Relations*, 2nd ed. (Englewood Cliffs, N.J.: Prentice-Hall, 1976). For a general description of international doctrines and decisions as they apply to Canada see Dewitt and Kirton, *Canada as a Principal Power*.

In 1993, the Canadian government proposed to spend over three billion dollars on foreign aid. Africa was by far the largest recipient, followed by Asia, Latin America and the Caribbean. In 1981, the UN had recommended that, in order to prevent large-scale global starvation and privation, the rich nations should pledge 0.7 percent of their GNP to foreign aid by 1985. By 1991, Canada had only reached 0.45 percent of GNP. In 1993, the government was still far under the figure of 0.7 percent but maintained a commitment to the goal — offering to complete it eventually.[37]

The bilateral programs are controversial and often have drawn criticism because of their self-serving nature. The point of contention is that Canada's bilateral aid requirements are designed to tie aid to helping Canadian industries. There are various ways of doing so, but in this circumstance the consequences of "tied" aid are that recipients of the aid are required to buy goods and services from Canada even if they are more expensive than those available from other countries. Former CIDA President Marcel Massé defended this type of bilateral aid, arguing that Canadian goods and services may be expensive but are of high quality. Moreover, procurement in Canada creates jobs and assists Canadian industry, thereby increasing support for foreign aid. "Development is just not charity any more," he asserted.[38]

The sad truth about foreign aid is that most programs are undertaken for reasons that are not solely humanitarian; as a result, assistance often does not go to the countries that need it most. Generally, aid is designed to help the donor achieve certain political objectives: for example, to create political stability in the recipient country for strategic motives, to obtain or support allies or to influence the recipient's domestic or foreign policies.[39] However, by international standards, a very high percentage of Canadian aid money reaches low-income countries.

While CIDA administers development assistance, another small agency sponsors research. When it became evident in the 1960s that developing countries lacked the research capacities and facilities to identify and define their own problems and find solutions, an International Development Research Centre (IDRC) was set up in Canada to meet that need. Devoted to research, it is separate from CIDA, and more isolated from political pressures. Although it is financed by the Canadian government, an effort has been made to give the IDRC an international character. Half of the board of governors and one-third of its staff are non-Canadians. The IDRC does no research itself, but provides aid and scientific advice to help countries solve their own problems. Most of the IDRC's work is in rural areas, with an emphasis on such basic matters as agriculture, health, nutrition and hygiene.

CANADA AND THE OAS

One international organization that Canada was late to join is the Organization of American States (OAS), the main institution that unites the states of the western hemisphere. It was formed in 1948 from the Pan-American Union at a time when Canada was primarily concerned with seeking security through NATO and the UN and hence did not seriously consider joining the organization. The issue of Canadian membership first became significant in the early 1960s. Proponents argued that Canada should accept responsibility for being a member of the hemisphere and thereby establish prestige in the region and increase trade

---

[37] CIDA, *Estimates*, part III, 1993–94, p. 5.

[38] *The Ottawa Citizen*, May 14, 1982.

[39] See Holsti, *International Politics*, pp. 231–39, for a discussion of this problem.

opportunities. Antagonists warned that if Canada did join the OAS the country soon would become embroiled in disputes between the United States and Latin America. The latter view was accepted by the government and the issue was not seriously raised again as a foreign policy option until the 1980s.[40] During this period Canada maintained "permanent observer" status at the OAS, a position that provided a limited, but practical, forum for communication and cooperation with OAS members.

Over time, arguments for joining the OAS became stronger. Advocates believed that membership would give Canada a stronger voice in planning development strategies for Latin America, as well as allow Canada to make a contribution in the field of human rights.[41] As countries like Mexico and Venezuela have become stronger, the strength of the argument that Canada would be caught in disputes between the United States and Latin America has diminished. Canada finally ratified full membership of the OAS in January 1990. One of the most important results has been increased cooperation between Canada and other OAS members to establish democracy throughout South America.

CANADIAN RELATIONS WITH THE UNITED STATES

President John F. Kennedy said, on a visit to Ottawa, that geography made us neighbours, history made us friends and economics made us partners. The simple fact is that there is no more important external relationship for Canada than that with the United States. Approximately 200 billion dollars in merchandise trade crossed the border in 1991 — by a large margin the world's leading trade relationship. The U.S. accounted for 75 percent of Canadian exports and 65 percent of all imports, making it our most important trading partner. On the other hand, Canada took only a small percent of total American exports and provided even less of its imports. Even at these significantly lower percentages of total trade, Canada is the United States' most important trading partner.[42] Leading Canadian exports to the U.S. include passenger autos and chassis, communications and electronic equipment, aerospace components, natural gas, forest products, crude petroleum and petrochemicals. In turn, Canada imports motor vehicle parts, passenger autos and chassis, electronic computers, crude petroleum and aircraft. In spite of efforts to diversify Canadian trade, both import and export trade with the U.S. has grown dramatically in recent years. (See the next section on free trade.)

Relations with the United States clearly are critical to Canada's economic well-being. The high degree of dependence is not, however, mutual. Though both geography and history provided the backdrop for an early special relationship between Canada and the United States,

---

[40] Robert J. Jackson, "Canadian Foreign Policy in the Western Hemisphere," in Viron P. Vaky, ed., *Governance in the Western Hemisphere* (New York: Praeger, 1984), pp. 119–34.

[41] Minutes of Proceedings of the Standing Committee on External Affairs and National Defence on *Canada's Relations with Latin America and the Caribbean*, Issue no. 48, December 8, 1981, p. 8. Hereafter cited as *Interim Report*.

[42] Literature on the Canadian/U.S. relationships is voluminous. Some of the multiple perspectives are provided in the Special Issue on "The Canada-United States Relationship," *International Journal*, vol. XXXVI, no. 1 (Winter 1980–81). For a standard Canadian view see John W. Holmes, *Life with Uncle* (Toronto: University of Toronto Press, 1981). For an American view of Canada see Willis C. Armstrong and Francis O. Wilcox, eds., *Canada and the United States* (Cambridge, Mass.: Ballinger, 1982); and Charles F. Doran, "The United States and Canada: Invulnerability and Interdependence," *International Journal*, vol. XXXVIII, no. 1 (Winter 1982–83), pp. 128–46.

inevitably it has often been one-sided. This fact was perhaps best illustrated in symbolic terms by the relative urgency assigned to initial political visitations at the highest level. The first Canadian Prime Ministerial visit to Washington was in 1871, only four years after Confederation; the first Presidential visit to Ottawa did not occur until over eight decades later, in 1943. The relationship between these unequal neighbours over the years has been friendly, but, on the part of Canadians, necessarily guarded, as the attitudes of American leaders were perceived to fluctuate from the extremes of annexation to complete indifference. Ulysses S. Grant, for example, aspired to absorb Canada in time for his 1872 election bid — in fact, he wanted the British to cede Canada in exchange for damage caused by a British ship![43]

With regard to defence, the long history of cooperation through NATO and NORAD belies the fact that much of Canada's history, including Confederation itself, was inspired by deliberate efforts to be independent of the United States and protected from American domination.

Because the Canadian economy is so closely entwined with that of the United States, a priority in foreign policy must be the solution of bilateral irritants. History has made Canada and the U.S. friends but, in spite of obvious similarities in origins and aspirations, there are also significant differences that affect every aspect of the relationship. Our governments are different in structure and functions, and these subtle differences are not always understood or appreciated. In the early 1980s, for example, a bilateral fishing agreement was scuppered after long negotiations when the United States Senate refused to give its assent. This ratification procedure, which is foreign to the Canadian political system, brought howls of outrage. In Canada, ratification is part of the powers of the executive. There is no constitutional need for the government to seek parliamentary approval. This incident was particularly well-publicized, but not unusual. In fact, according to specialist Christian Wiktor there have been more than 200 treaties negotiated by American administrators with various countries over the past 200 years that were never ratified by the Senate, 18 of them concerning Canada directly.[44]

There are other important differences. The two governments have disparate approaches to the roles of government in the economy. In Canada, both federal and provincial governments take an active role in the marketplace to a degree unknown and unacceptable in the United States.

Perhaps the most obvious difference, however, is that Canada's population is only one-tenth that of the U.S. We discussed in Chapters 2 and 4 some of the inevitable repercussions of such a disparity; basically, it makes Canada vulnerable to pressures from the United States in the fields of culture, economy and defence. A few facts will serve to indicate the economic issue: in 1991 Canada's net international investment position was negative. The amount Canadians owed non-residents over what they owed residents was 269.9 billion dollars; 30 percent of the leading 65 000 corporations were foreign-controlled; and, of the largest 500 companies in Canada, 38 percent were foreign-controlled and 28 percent fully foreign-owned.[45]

Underlying economic and cultural differences between the two countries surface periodically as policy conflicts between Ottawa and Washington. This was particularly evident in the late 1970s, a decade of growing tension between the two countries, both of which were caught in a deep economic recession.[46] The poor economic climate exacerbated cleavages when each country acted to protect and strengthen its home industries. Management of

[43] Martin, *The Presidents and the Prime Ministers*, p. 12.

[44] *The Globe and Mail*, May 7, 1981.

[45] Statistics Canada, *Canada's Investment Position 1988–91* (Ottawa: Supply and Services, 1992), pp. 42–3. See charts and details in Mel Hurtig, *The Betrayal of Canada*, 2nd ed. (Toronto: Stoddart, 1992), ch. 11. And see Rowland C. Frazee in "Canada-U.S. Relations," paper delivered to the Economic Club of Detroit, Michigan, February 22, 1982.

bilateral irritants, which is an important part of the relationship between Canada and the United States, assumed major proportions. Disputes arose in such areas as fisheries, trucking regulations and advertising rights.

Most conflict, however, centred around the Liberal government's Foreign Investment Review Agency, set up to monitor and restrict foreign investment, and the National Energy Program, designed to increase Canadian ownership of natural resources. Both impinged on foreign interests, especially those of the United States. The conflict continued until the 1984 Conservative government got rid of the NEP and undermined FIRA, turning it into Investment Canada.

Measures such as the NEP and FIRA were adopted by the Canadian government to regulate escalating foreign ownership, which was seen as depriving Canadians of the ability to control and benefit from the country's industries, particularly resource industries. Canada's prosperity is linked to the rest of the world through not only trade, but also the importation of foreign capital. We have seen that the level of foreign investment is particularly high. As one expert put it, "Canada cannot be compared with capital-rich economies such as the American and British. The combination of a small population and huge natural resources necessitate, even in the best of economic times, reliance on external financing to satisfy our economic expansions."[47] Individual Canadians save at double the rate of Americans, but the country does not come close to satisfying its own capital requirements. In recent years, much foreign investment has not been "new" American capital but has come from within Canada itself. Foreign subsidiaries simply retain earnings and depreciation reserves and put them back into the economy as investments.

Most foreign capital comes in the form of direct investment, not interest or portfolio investment. This means that rather than involving bank loans or bonds, which can be paid off, investment in the Canadian economy brings a high degree of control and ownership by foreigners, especially in the manufacturing and resource sectors. Such branch plants allow the importation of American technology and market access as well as American values. They are subject not only to market forces and Canadian government regulation but also to American interests. John H. Redekop provides a classic instance: the incorporation of the Ford Motor Company of Canada gave "the Canadian firm market rights in all British Commonwealth countries (excluding the best, the U.K.), while the rest of the world is reserved for the U.S. parent firm or its other subsidiaries."[48]

There can be no doubt that foreign investment improves Canada's standard of living and has helped to transform Canada into an industrialized country. However, there is equally no doubt that it has greatly increased the dependence of the economy on that of the United States.

FREE TRADE

One of the most controversial trade issues concerns free trade, a recurring theme in Canada's relationship with the United States. The issue originated, and caused heated debate, as far back as the 1800s. In the early years of statehood, Sir John A. Macdonald won the hearts

---

[46] For an interesting view of Canada/U.S. tensions see Stephen Clarkson, *Canada and the Reagan Challenge* (Toronto: James Lorimer & Co., 1982). Also see Rowland C. Frazee in "Canada-U.S. Relations," paper delivered to the Economic Club of Detroit, Michigan, February 22, 1982.

[47] James R. Niniger, President, The Conference Board of Canada, quoted in *The Ottawa Citizen*, May 14, 1984.

[48] John H. Redekop, "Continentalism: The Key to Canadian Politics," in Redekop, ed., *Approaches to Canadian Politics*, 2nd ed. (Scarborough, Ont.: Prentice-Hall Canada, 1983) p. 45.

of Canadians with his National Policy of high tariffs to protect fledgling Canadian industries. Much later, in 1911, Sir Wilfrid Laurier failed to win re-election partly because he wanted to eliminate tariffs on less than one-quarter of cross-border trade. He could not compete with the opposition slogan of "No truck or trade with the Yankees." More recently, many tariff cuts were made following the GATT agreement. Some Canadian tariffs remained high — for example, those on petrochemicals and textiles. Other selected markets were protected by indirect means such as quotas, government "standards and specifications," health and safety regulations and even drawn-out customs inspections (such as those that delayed the 1983 delivery of Japanese cars by holding them in the port of Vancouver).

In the early 1980s, the controversy was over whether to move toward full free trade across the border or, as the Liberal government recommended in 1983, to build "sectoral free trade" in selected items, among them steel, agricultural equipment, urban mass transit equipment and "informatics" such as computer communications services. Free trade with the United States, even in specific sectors, would have been a major political undertaking. Advocates argued that it would raise productivity, lower inflation and create jobs, unlike protectionism, which hinders global trade. The sectoral free trade policy was dropped after the Conservatives came to office in 1984. Their position was buttressed by the 1985 report of the Royal Commission on the Economic Union and Development Prospects for Canada (the Donald Macdonald Commission), which argued strongly in favour of general free trade.[49] Opponents argued that free trade would destroy many Canadian companies (especially in textiles and footwear) and inevitably lead to the formation of common institutions that would be dominated by the U.S. and would therefore erode Canada's political sovereignty.

In the course of his first mandate, Prime Minister Mulroney reversed his earlier position against free trade and entered into negotiations for a comprehensive trade agreement with the United States. The reasons for this shift are not completely known, but he received strong support from Québec and the Western provinces for doing so. At the time, however, many Canadian businesspeople were worried about a growing demand for protectionism in Washington due to the United States' massive trade deficit; obviously the Prime Minister thought free trade might reduce recurrent trade problems between the two countries. In fact, two major trade disputes did come to the fore while Canada–U.S. trade negotiations were taking place. In 1986, the United States introduced a countervailing duty against softwood lumber imported from Canada; a source of trade worth about four billion dollars annually to Canadian companies. Canada successfully negotiated to apply its own 15 percent export tax instead of submitting to the proposed countervailing duty. Later the same year the United States also imposed a five-year tariff on Canadian red cedar shakes and shingles and Canada was forced to retaliate.[50] These examples were considered dangerous signs of a growing American trend toward trade protectionism.

On September 26, 1985, Canada formally requested that the United States enter negotiations for a comprehensive free trade agreement. Two years later, the deal was concluded; the legal text was released and signed by President Reagan and Prime Minister Mulroney on January 2, 1988; the agreement came into force on January 1, 1989.

---

[49] *Report of the Royal Commission on the Economic Union and Development Prospects for Canada*, vol. 1 (Ottawa: Minister of Supply and Services, 1985).

[50] For a summary of these disputes see Leyton-Brown, "Canada-U.S. Trade Disputes and the Free Trade Deal," in Maureen Molot and Brian W. Tomlin, eds., *Canada Among Nations 1987: A World of Conflict* (Toronto: Lorimer, 1988).

Reproduced with permission, Raeside, *Victoria Times.*

In the meantime, Federal Liberal leader John Turner called on the Liberal-controlled Senate to block the agreement. The 1988 election ensued with the free trade deal as the primary election issue. It was debated in detail by the politicians. The 1988 election is discussed in Chapter 10, but it is important to bear in mind here how questions about Canada's domestic and international affairs interacted in this policy debate.

The *Canada-United States Free Trade Agreement* is intended to enhance market access and reduce trade conflicts between the two countries. The agreement provides a set of dispute resolution mechanisms and the goal of gradual elimination of all tariffs between the two countries. Special and technical agreements have been made in services, investment, financial services, energy, agriculture, automobiles, cultural industries and even alcoholic beverages.

However, free trade was never completed. Each country reserved the right to continue to impose trade retaliation, such as countervailing duties, anti-dumping and other trade remedies. Each country also reserved the right to change its trade legislation even after the agreement came into force on January 2, 1989; new laws will only apply to the partner country if it is so specified in the legislation.

Canadian opposition to this deal was widespread and centred on three issues. First, it was argued that the deal did not obtain secure access to the American market for Canadian products since American trade remedies continued to apply. Second, the agreement was attacked as giving away too much (especially in investment, financial services, agriculture, energy and the service sectors) and getting too little in return. An important issue also centres around the definition of what constitutes a trade "subsidy"; opponents of the deal argue that Canadian social programs — such as UI and provincial health insurance — could fall into such a category. And, lastly, the deal was attacked by some provincial leaders for eroding provincial powers and by some federal politicians for reducing the ability of Canadian governments to act freely in the economy and hence reducing Canadian sovereignty.

FIGURE 14.4 THE NAFTA EQUATION, 1992

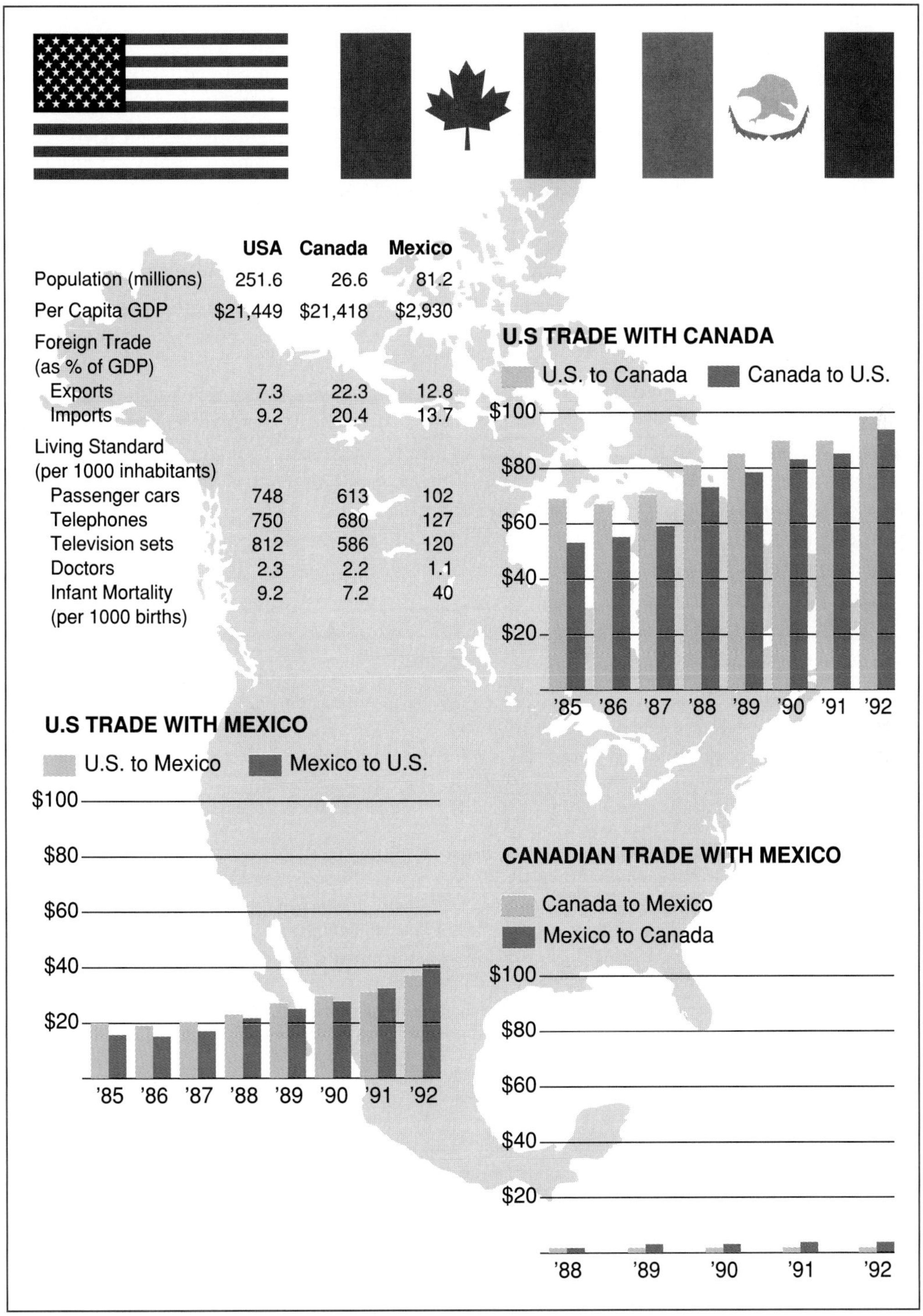

	USA	Canada	Mexico
Population (millions)	251.6	26.6	81.2
Per Capita GDP	$21,449	$21,418	$2,930
Foreign Trade (as % of GDP)			
Exports	7.3	22.3	12.8
Imports	9.2	20.4	13.7
Living Standard (per 1000 inhabitants)			
Passenger cars	748	613	102
Telephones	750	680	127
Television sets	812	586	120
Doctors	2.3	2.2	1.1
Infant Mortality (per 1000 births)	9.2	7.2	40

U.S TRADE WITH CANADA

U.S. to Canada ■ Canada to U.S.

U.S TRADE WITH MEXICO

U.S. to Mexico ■ Mexico to U.S.

CANADIAN TRADE WITH MEXICO

Canada to Mexico
Mexico to Canada

Sources: Statistics Canada; U.S. Commerce Dept.; OECD Survey of Mexico, current price numbers.

Although the 1988 election settled the basic question about the free trade deal,[51] questions about the impact of the trade agreement on Canadian interests and indeed on Canadian sovereignty remain.[52] In the 1993 General Election, the Liberals under Jean Chrétien promised to re-open some of the most controversial parts of the agreement for renegotiation. Almost before the ink was dry on the free trade agreement, the Canadian government began negotiations with Mexico and the United States for a *North American Free Trade Agreement* (NAFTA).[53] This document calls for a three-country deal that incorporates the *Canada-United States Free Trade Agreement* and expands it to include clauses on intellectual property, all medical services and more explicit rules about national treatment. In May 1993, Parliament approved the legislation, allowing the government the right to implement the agreement if side deals on labour and the environment were worked out among Canada, Mexico and the United States. On January 1, 1994, the agreement was made law despite the fact that the Liberal government had not achieved its goals, especially on energy protection. (See Figure 14.4 for basic information on NAFTA.)

NAFTA was discussed in the 1993 General Election (see chapter 11) but did not prove nearly as significant an issue as free trade in the 1988 election because the Liberals did not directly oppose the deal. All five major parties seemed to agree that as captive neighbours on this continent, the only reasonable policy for the three states to adopt is to foster a mutually satisfactory relationship. In the coming years, the advent of free trade with Mexico and the United States may well transform the nature of politics in Canada. See Table 14.3 for NAFTA highlights.

TABLE 14.3   NAFTA FRAMEWORK

Facts about the North American Free Trade Agreement for 360 million people

Tariffs:	Eliminated over a 15-year period. Levies on half of the more than 9 000 products to be phased out immediately, 65 percent of them within five years.
Agriculture:	Some tariffs on all farm products will be phased out but producers will be given 15 years to adjust to a duty-free status on sensitive products.
Automobiles:	To qualify for duty-free treatment, the North American content of cars, now 50 percent, will have to reach 62.5 percent after 8 years.
Financial Services:	Mexico will allow U.S. and Canadian banks, brokerage firms and insurance companies free access after a six-year transition period during which bans on foreign ownership will be phased out.
Textiles:	Mexico will be able to escape high duties on shipments to the U.S. and Canada as long as the clothing is made from yarns and fabrics from North America.
Trucking:	Mexico will allow foreigners to invest in its trucking firms, and U.S., Mexican and Canadian trucking companies will be allowed to do business on cross-border routes that are now prohibited.
Side Agreements:	Will establish trinational commissions to oversee environmental and labour laws with the possibility of sanctions, either punitive trade tariffs in the case of the U.S. and Mexico or fines in the case of Canada, for failure of a country to enforce its own laws.

Implementation date: January 1, 1994.

---

[51] It should be noted, however, that more Canadians voted *against* the Conservatives who espoused free trade than voted for them. See election figures in Chapter 10.

[52] The arguments in favour of the free trade deal have been carefully summarized in John Crispo, ed., *Free Trade: The Real Story* (Toronto: Gage, 1988). A delightful summary of the opposition arguments is found in Marjorie M. Bowker, *On Guard for Thee* (Hull: Voyageur, 1988). For a longer view see Robert Bothwell, *Canada and the United States* (Toronto: University of Toronto Press, 1992).

[53] Much more opposition comes from outsiders than from political parties — see Maude Barlow and Bruce Campbell, *Take Back the Nation* (Toronto: Key Porter, 1991); and Mel Hurtig, *Betrayal of Canada,* 2nd ed. (Toronto: Stoddart, 1992).

CANADIAN RELATIONS WITH OTHER AREAS

CANADA AND WESTERN EUROPE

Canada's historical and cultural ties with Western Europe have always been close, and Canadian governments have counted on this region of the world to counterbalance American influence. In the 1970s in particular, fears were rife that Canada was too dependent on American markets. It was at this time that Trudeau initiated his Third Option to increase trade with Western Europe and Japan. As an extension of that philosophy, Trudeau achieved a weak contractual link with the European Community. However, little but platitudes came from this agreement, and trade with the United States continued to increase.

The Canadian-British link, the strongest tie Canada had in Western Europe, became weaker after Britain entered the European Common Market in 1973. The Canadian share of the British market decreased, and the trade balance eventually tilted in the U.K.'s favour, largely because of North Sea oil exports to Canada. In the 1990s, Britain remains Canada's third-largest trading partner, its second-largest investor, and educational and travel links remain very strong.

The twelve countries that make up the European Community constitute the world's largest trading entity. The EC is one of Canada's largest markets for agricultural products and several resource-based products, including forest products and fish. In 1990, the EC imported less than 10 percent of Canada's total merchandise exports. Since this figure represented an even smaller percent of total EC imports, however, the relationship is much more important to Canada than it is to the EC.

Community members generally desire access to Canada's pulp, oil, uranium and other mineral resources, and in return would like to offer Canadians manufactured goods. The Canadian government is justifiably reluctant to accept these nineteenth-century conditions of trade. On the other hand, access to European Community markets is also difficult for Canadians to achieve, and despite traditional political ties the trade relationship is unlikely to improve much. As of 1994 the Community is officially called the European Union (EU).

CANADA AND THE PACIFIC RIM

While Canadian trade with western Europe stagnated in recent years, it increased rapidly in the Pacific Rim. In 1983, for the first time, Canada traded more with Asia than with Western Europe. By 1990, exports to Asia totalled 16.2 billion dollars, compared to 14.5 billion dollars with Western Europe.[54] It is increasingly evident that trans-Pacific trade is another opportunity for a counterbalance in the American-dominated Canadian economy: it may eventually be Canada's new Third Option.[55]

Countries of the Pacific Rim — Japan, Korea, Taiwan and Singapore — in particular are challenging world markets with outstanding management, technological and production techniques. Their economies are growing more rapidly than those of Europe or any other major region. Since 1973, Japan has been Canada's second-largest national trading partner. In 1990, two-way trade reached over 18 billion dollars. Japan is Canada's fastest growing export market among our major trading partners. Canadian-Japanese trade relations are those of a resource-rich supplier and a resource-poor industrial nation: almost all of Japan's exports to Canada are fully manufactured, while most of Canada's exports are either raw

---

[54] Department of External Affairs, *Annual Report* (Ottawa: Supply and Services, 1991), pp. 39 and 48.

[55] See H.E. English, "National Policy and Canadian Trade," *International Perspectives* (March/April, 1984), pp. 3–6.

materials or semi-processed products. China too is looming as an important trade partner for Canada.

CANADA, DEVELOPING COUNTRIES AND THE REST OF THE WORLD

Under the GATT, the developing countries of the world enjoy various types of differential and preferential treatment in the effort to nurture their nascent agricultural and manufacturing industries. Canadian trade with developing areas is relatively modest, although it has grown slightly in recent years. Most developing countries have economic situations similar to that of Canada and therefore compete in many of the same areas. They generally export tropical foodstuffs and raw materials. The more industrialized among them, including Brazil, Venezuela, Mexico, China, Korea and Saudi Arabia, also produce labour-intensive standard technology goods and were considered by the Canadian government to be the best targets for expanded exports in the 1980s.[56] On the whole, developing countries continue to be more important trade partners for Japan, the U.S. and the EC than for Canada, because Canada competes with these developing countries to sell raw materials. Another serious problem inhibiting trade with developing countries is their enormous debt burden — estimated at US\$1280 billion in 1993.[57]

Since Canada has no coherent foreign policy that embraces the entire hemisphere, Canadian relations with countries in South and Central America and the Caribbean consist mainly of bilateral trade, political, economic and humanitarian interests.[58] In 1990, Canadian trade with these countries amounted to about seven billion dollars. A high percent of these exports were processed or manufactured goods. Canadian imports from the area were about twice the volume of the exports. They consisted primarily of petroleum products, particularly from Venezuela and Mexico, and tropical food products, as well as some manufactured products from Brazil and Mexico. Although trade is paramount, Canada is also an active investor in the region. Canadian banks have been active in Latin America and the Caribbean since the nineteenth century.

Economic and commercial matters are the most concrete evidence of Canadian relations south of the United States, but political and humanitarian issues, too, concern Canadians. Despite protest from the United States, Canada maintained political relations with Cuba after the 1959 revolution. As well, Canada continued trade relations even in the face of a U.S. embargo. The Canadian government has disagreed with the ideological commitment and some of the policies and activities of the Cuban government, but, unlike some American administrations, it does not condemn Cuba and communism as the only sources of conflict in Central America and the Caribbean.[59]

---

[56] *A Review of Canadian Trade Policy*, p. 224.

[57] CIDA, *Estimates*, Part III (1993–94), p. 27.

[58] These are considered in detail in Robert J. Jackson, "Canadian Foreign Policy and the Western Hemisphere." For a historical summary, see D.R. Murray, "The Bilateral Road: Canada and Latin America in the 1980s," *International Journal*, vol. XXXVII, no. 1 (Winter 1981–82), pp. 108–31.

[59] For more information on Canadian-Cuban relations see Baudouin St-Cyr, *Canadian Policy Towards Cuba: A Case Study in U.S. Influence and External Constraints on Canadian Foreign Policy* (Unpublished M.A. thesis: McMaster University, 1987); and Kenneth McNaught, "Canada, Cuba and the U.S." *Monthly Review*, vol. XII (April 1961), pp. 616–24.

Considerable media coverage has been devoted to Central America in the past decade. The region has had a troubled history of coups, assassinations, rigged elections, human rights violations, and foreign-financed military intervention. None of the six countries in the region — Nicaragua, El Salvador, Panama, Honduras, Costa Rica, and Guatemala — has remained untouched by these troubles. In recent years, however, these countries have tried to move away from American influence in order to solve their own problems.[60] Despite criticism, the Canadian government's position has been that a political solution, not a military one, is required to resolve the continued crises in the region.

Canada's best relations in the area are with Mexico, Brazil and Venezuela. All three have been given priority ratings by the Canadian government. Their large markets and relatively stable political systems, a contrast to those of many nations in the region, provide the foundation for increased, successful ties.

Canada naturally has links with other countries and areas, which, though important in other ways, are not very significant in an economic sense. Relations with Australia and New Zealand are long-standing and close because of the early Commonwealth connection. These countries are a small but important part of Canada's global trade relationship. Mention must also be made of Russia, the republics of the former U.S.S.R. and other eastern European countries. These states account for only a tiny percentage of Canada's total trade, but Russia is a major grain importer and therefore economically important to Canada.

CANADIAN DEFENCE AND SECURITY POLICY

The objectives of defence and security policy are intertwined with foreign policy objectives and, more specifically, with deterring war. Over time, Canadian objectives in this field have varied according to changes in the international strategic environment and the political configuration of the country. But at all times there have been commitments to preserving the independence of Canada, its borders, institutions and values; to pursuing the peaceful settlement of disputes and to preventing hostilities and warfare.

Such aspirations are accepted by almost all Canadians. However, the policies and programs required to fulfill these goals are constantly in dispute. Should Canada continue to be a part of a collective security arrangement such as NATO or, like Sweden, be more independent? Should Canada be part of the nuclear bomb club or keep nuclear devices off native soil? Even if there were agreement on such general policies, an analyst would still need to know what programs would be required to execute them. For example, should more government funds be spent on arms than butter? Should Canadians be deployed overseas in potential combat zones? Should Canadians participate in international peacekeeping missions?

These are deep and difficult questions that touch on the basic values of the country. Given that Canadians are essentially a non-militaristic people, what visible security policies have been developed? Furthermore, what set of policies could be designed to protect Canadian citizens and to defend the second-largest land mass and the longest coastline in the world?

---

[60] For more information see the conference report *Canada, The United States and Latin America: Independence and Accommodation* (Washington D.C.: The Woodrow Wilson International Center for Scholars/Latin American Program, April 1984); Steven Baranyi, "Peace in Central America?" *Background Paper*, Canadian Institute for Peace and Security, #8 (October 1986), pp. 1–8.

The ingredients of Canada's policy have remained essentially the same since the end of the Second World War. Canada has sought security in collective agreements — it has not been neutral. Canada's security policy has rested on three complementary foundations:

- prevention of war and deterrence of aggression through collective defence arrangements of NATO and NORAD;
- pursuit of verifiable arms control and disarmament agreements;
- commitment to the peaceful settlement of disputes and collective efforts to resolve the underlying causes of international tensions.[61]

CANADIAN SECURITY POLICY

The basic pattern of the international environment today is one of sharply decreased East/West differences and an increase in local and regional conflicts throughout the world, particularly in the developing Third World but also in middle and eastern Europe. Explanations for the continuation of hostile acts throughout the globe are beyond the scope of this book, but they include economic, cultural, religious and ideological frustrations and aggression.[62]

In 1993, there were more than 40 wars going on around the world. In the face of such intractable conflicts it could be said that Canada's defence forces are insignificant. However, given the size of Canada's population and the few direct conflicts in which Canada is engaged, the military commitment is reasonable. In 1993–94, just over 8 percent of the federal government's budget — $11 970 million — was in the defence envelope.

ORGANIZATION OF NATIONAL DEFENCE

The Department of National Defence (DND) was created by the *National Defence Act* in 1922. Led by the Minister of National Defence, the DND is involved in both the formulation and implementation of Canadian defence policy. Foreign affairs and defence policies are inextricably interrelated, and therefore they concern both the Minister of Foreign Affairs and the Minister of National Defence. The Defence Minister specifically, and the Cabinet generally, are accountable to Parliament for national defence matters.

The responsibilities of the Minister of National Defence include the control and management of the Department itself, the Canadian Armed Forces and all matters relating to works and establishments concerned with Canada's defence. The Minister is also responsible for Defence Construction Canada, a Crown corporation that functions as a contracting and construction supervisory agency for major construction and maintenance projects of the DND. It ensures that adequate standards of supervision and inspection are maintained throughout the life of construction contracts.

The Deputy Minister of the DND is the senior civilian advisor to the Minister.[63] The DM ensures that governmental policy direction is reflected in the administration of the DND and in military plans and operations. The senior military advisor to the Minister is the Chief of

---

61 Minister's Statement, *Defence Estimates 1984–85*, p.13. Hereafter cited as *Defence Estimates 1984–85*.

62 See Robert J. Jackson and Doreen Jackson, *Contemporary Government and Politics: Democracy and Authoritarianism* (Scarborough, Ont.: Prentice-Hall, 1993) ch. 21.

63 C.J. Marshal, "Canada's Defence Structure Review," *International Perspectives* (Jan./Feb. 1976), pp. 26–9. Little has been written on the domestic sources of Canadian military policy. One exception is Kim Richard Nossal, "On the Periphery: Interest Groups and Canadian Defence Policy in 1970s," unpublished paper, June 1982.

the Defence Staff (CDS), who is responsible for the conduct of military operations and for the preparedness of the Canadian Forces to meet commitments assigned by the government.

THE CANADIAN FORCES

The Canadian Forces are the military element of the Canadian Government and are part of the Department of National Defence.[64] In 1993, the total personnel in the Canadian Forces was 70 799 — 5 632 of whom were serving outside the country.[65] Since 1968, the Canadian Forces have had a unified structure to carry out their tasks. They perform a number of roles, including surveillance of Canadian territory and coastlines to protect Canadian sovereignty; defence of North America in cooperation with American forces; fulfillment of NATO commitments and performance of international peacekeeping roles. The military also provides assistance to other federal government departments, civil authorities and civilian organizations; for example, air and ground transportation for royal visits, meetings of foreign government officials and sporting events; emergency and disaster relief and a search and rescue program. Finally, the Forces provide training for allied military personnel in Canada and aid in the form of military training to developing countries.[66]

Defence expenditures are not, however, without their critics. The charges of opponents are often based on the belief that there is a so-called military-industrial complex that controls the government, especially in the United States. The basic argument is that there is collusion between powerful industrialists and military planners to keep international tension high in order to sell expensive weapons to the government. This assertion is usually coupled with a belief that such expenditures would be better used in other fields such as health, education and social welfare. Its exponents believe that the costs of Canadian defence could be reduced by a radical shift towards neutralism in international affairs. This argument will be further discussed below; the issue is raised here to point to the fundamental debate over whether government funds should be spent on guns or butter.

What does Canada do with these expenditures on defence? Figure 14.5 shows the 1993–94 forecast for defence spending. Approximately two-thirds of the funds are for the combined Maritime, Land and Air Forces in Canada, while Canadian combat forces in Europe consume less than 7 percent of defence expenditures. This figure has been decreasing in recent years due to the government's decision to remove Canadian bases from Europe. This is lower than our NATO allies would prefer. Canada still remains the second-lowest among NATO partners with regard to concrete support for defence measures.[67]

Canadian military expenditures basically cover protection of Canada's territory, a special partnership with the U.S. in the North American Aerospace Defence Command and membership in the North Atlantic Treaty Organization. Although Canada is involved in strategic nuclear planning, the country's chief role in NATO has involved stationing Canadian land and air forces in Europe as part of the forward defence strategy. The total peace-time

---

[64] Formally the Governor General of Canada, as the Sovereign's representative, is Commander-in-Chief of the Canadian Forces.

[65] The government plans to reduce the regular force again by 1995–96. See *Canadian Defence Policy*, April 1992, p. 14.

[66] Training teams have been sent to Ghana, Cameroon, Jamaica, Kenya, Tanzania, Malaysia, Nigeria, Zambia and other countries. Allied countries that have used training facilities in Canada include Great Britain, Germany, Denmark, Norway, the Netherlands and the United States.

[67] For a discussion of this issue see Robert J. Jackson, ed., *Europe in Transition* (New York: Praeger, 1992).

FIGURE 14.5   DEFENCE EXPENDITURE FORECAST 1993–94 (IN MILLIONS)

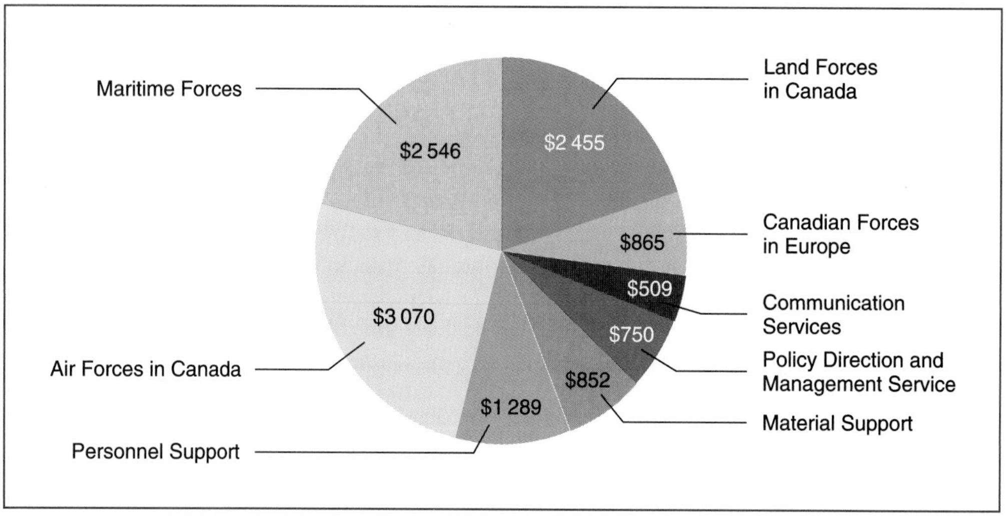

Maritime Forces — $2 546
Land Forces in Canada — $2 455
Canadian Forces in Europe — $865
Communication Services — $509
Policy Direction and Management Service — $750
Material Support — $852
Air Forces in Canada — $3 070
Personnel Support — $1 289

Source: Adapted from DND, *Estimates*, Part III (1993–94), p. 10.

strength of Canadian forces in Europe reached approximately 7 700, most of them stationed in Lahr and Baden-Soellingen in the Federal Republic of Germany. In case of war, the two European-based formations, four Canadian Mechanized Brigade Groups and one Canadian Air Group, would have been assigned to NATO's Supreme Commander. Canada is closing these bases and will bring all troops home from Europe by 1994. The Liberal Party has suggested that Lahr become a peace-keeping base.

PEACEKEEPING

In keeping with the fundamentally non-military nature of Canadian security policy, the government's most visible activity has been in the field of international peacekeeping. In early 1993 the largest overseas forces were with the United Nations troops in Yugoslavia (UNPROFOR I and II), Somalia (UNSOM) and Cyprus (UNFICYP). In the former Yugoslavia and in Somalia, Canadians were involved in supplying humanitarian aid and relief. In Cyprus, they have been responsible for patrolling the Nicosia area as part of a multilateral contingent to prevent hostilities between Greek and Turkish Cypriots. At the time of writing, Canadian peacekeeping troops are still serving in the former Yugoslavia but those in Somalia and Cyprus will soon be removed. Canada has troops serving in Cambodia (UNTAC), the Golan Heights (UNDOF), Jerusalem (UNTSO), Kuwait (UNIKOM), Angola (UNAVEM), West Sahara (UNIMRWS), El Salvador (UNUSAL), Egypt/Israel (MFO), the former Yugoslavia (ECMM), and various smaller miscellaneous operations. Canada, of course, also makes financial contributions without troops as, for example, in India and Pakistan (UNMOGIP) and Afghanistan/Pakistan (OSGAP). (See Figure 14.6.)

In total there were 4754 personnel serving in these missions with a cost of $559 million in the fiscal year 1992–93. Canada supplies about 10 percent of all UN peacekeepers, which is certainly much larger than its share. On the whole, however, Canadian participation in peacekeeping represents an important contribution to global and Canadian security and enhances Canada's international reputation.

FIGURE 14.6 PEACEKEEPING: A CANADIAN CONTRIBUTION TO THE WORLD

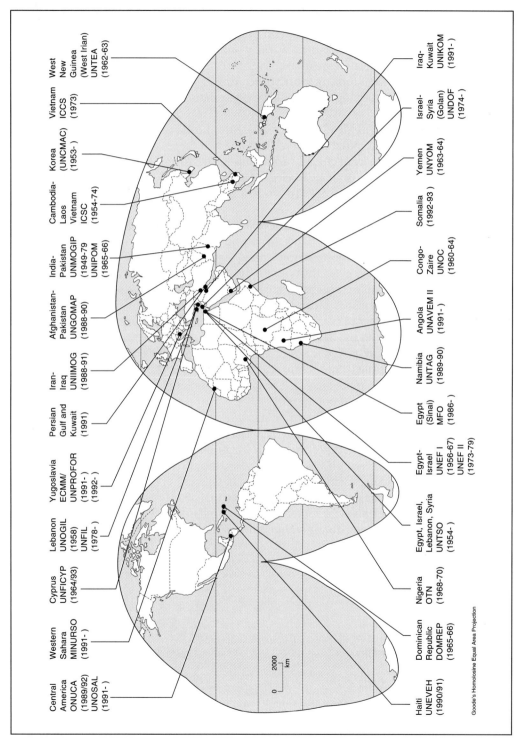

Source: *Peacekeeping: A Canadian Contribution to the World* (Ottawa: Department of National Defense, 1991–92).

DETERRENCE, ARMS CONTROL AND DISARMAMENT

Despite the end of the Cold War, the complexities of the issues surrounding the arms race are daunting.[68] Today, well over 50 billion warheads are held in the world's arsenals. Though peace and security have been dreamed about for centuries, the world continues producing ever-more sophisticated weapons. Over three decades ago U.S. President John F. Kennedy observed that the topic of world peace was so vital that he intended to devote a portion of every day to studying what could be done about it. The problems continue to be pressing today.

The options facing world leaders today range from total disarmament to constant development of newer, more powerful weapons. Between these two extremes lies the rationale that has delivered us from global war for almost half a century — the policy of deterrence. Deterrence rests on a strategic nuclear equilibrium between the U.S. and Russia and other former republics of the U.S.S.R. To work, it must provide security for both sides. But the paradox is that in order to attain this security, both powers must remain insecure about their own defences. Neither side may achieve a perfect defence system, because the danger of war increases as soon as one side gains the advantage. Stable mutual deterrence exists between the superpowers because the United States and Russia both have the capability of obliterating each other, even after sustaining a nuclear strike. In military parlance, this policy is explained in terms of "second-strike capability": deterrence is measured by the usable strength of the survivable second-strike force. Both sides must retain a sufficient amount of retaliatory power to withstand a first strike and remain capable of making an unacceptable second strike on the aggressor.

This type of deterrence policy is required because despite the end of a basic conflict in ideology between the United States and Russia neither one can realistically expect that the other side will ever eliminate its nuclear arsenal completely. Deterrence is a two-sided affair; nothing can be achieved unilaterally.

Proponents of general disarmament hold a different view. They warn that armaments themselves are a fundamental cause of international hostility. Members of the peace movement expound the risks of deterrence, including the possibility of human error, the expansion of the number of countries with nuclear weapons, the threat of biological and chemical weapons, as well as the increasing sophistication of delivery systems and the possible stationing of nuclear weapons on satellites. They believe that all countries should disarm to prevent world destruction. However, such a proposal is regarded sceptically by the leaders of all major states. But, if general disarmament is discounted by governments, arms control or limited disarmament is not. Arms control offers "the prospect of reducing threats, constraining the competition for military advantage, increasing stability and providing a predictable international environment."[69]

---

[68] The literature on weapons is voluminous. On Canadian concerns in the nuclear field see Special Issue, "Arms Control," *International Journal*, vol. XXXVI, no. 3 (Summer, 1981). For an introduction to the general topic see Spurgeon M. Keeny Jr. and Wolfgang K.H. Panofsky, "Nuclear Weapons in the 1980s," *Foreign Affairs*, vol. 60, no. 2 (Winter 1981–82), pp. 287–346 and the Harvard Study Group, *Living with Nuclear Weapons* (Cambridge, Mass.: Harvard University Press, 1983). On Canada, see Ernie Regehr and Simon Rosenblum, eds., *The Road to Peace* (Toronto: Lorimer, 1988), especially John Barrett's piece on Mulroney's defence policy, pp. 76–103.

[69] Government of Canada, *Challenge and Commitment: A Defence Policy for Canada* (Ottawa: Minister of Supply and Services, 1987), p. 7.

Several arms control agreements have been reached in recent years. In 1968, the nuclear powers signed a Nonproliferation Treaty pledging not to disseminate nuclear devices to non-nuclear countries. At least six countries are known to be technically capable of detonating a nuclear bomb: the U.S., Russia, Britain, France, China and India. There are also countries, such as Israel, Brazil, Pakistan, and South Africa, which have some nuclear capability but do not admit it. The total number of countries capable of detonating a nuclear bomb could grow to include South Korea, Iraq, Libya and many others. It is difficult to predict whether any of these countries could develop an adequate delivery system or whether they would use the nuclear power for aggressive purposes, but the risks are clear. A strengthening of the nuclear non-proliferation regime is still required despite the end of the Cold War.

In 1972, the United States and the U.S.S.R. signed two agreements based on the Strategic Arms Limitation Talks (SALT I). These agreements included limiting the number and deployment of anti-ballistic missiles (ABMs). These modest achievements were improved in the SALT II Treaty, but it was never ratified by the U.S. Senate. In 1991, Strategic Arms Reduction Talks (START), which will reduce the number of strategic nuclear weapons that Americans and Russians can aim at each other's territory, was signed between the United States and Russia.

At the strategic level, there is to be a rough nuclear parity between the United States and Russia. Each side is to reduce strategic offensive arms by 30 percent in seven years and to possess no more than 1 600 strategic nuclear delivery vehicles and 6 000 strategic nuclear warheads. Both sides will continue to possess adequate retaliatory power to prevent aggression and the SALT and START agreements provide some measure of protection. The results in Intermediate-Range Nuclear Forces (INF) talks have been more definitive. In December 1987, the U.S. and U.S.S.R. made a historic agreement that eliminated all land-based INF in the super powers' arsenals. The treaty concluded with an asymmetrical compromise by the Soviet Union and a verification regime that includes on-site inspection of the destruction of all these missiles. By May 1991 the destruction of all these weapons in Europe had been completed.

There has been considerable progress in conventional arms control in recent years. In November 1990, a Conventional Force Europe Agreement (CFE) was signed that reduced conventional forces in Europe. The destruction and verification of the CFE were to be conducted under the auspices of the 51-member Conference on Security and Cooperation in Europe (CSCE).

Various other options for changing the nuclear death-game are proffered from time to time by concerned citizens and experts. They include declaring a freeze on the building of new nuclear weapons; setting up geographical zones where nuclear weapons will not be kept during peace-time (one of them is Canada); preventing the stationing of nuclear weapons in space and declaring that the West will not employ nuclear weapons unless they are used first by an aggressor.

In our view, arms control measures to reduce weaponry, without going as far as total disarmament, constitute the only possible solution for the time being. Unless and until states learn to live with the values and philosophies that separate them, a sound defence policy accompanied by arms control agreements is the best that can be expected.

In the near future, Canadian arms control goals should include even further reductions in nuclear weapons, a strengthened nuclear non-proliferation treaty, a global chemical weapons ban, a comprehensive test ban treaty, prevention of an arms race in outer space and a comprehensive treaty for the Arctic. The agreements should be balanced and verifiable. Unfortunately, this subject is much plagued by extreme rhetoric. As one astute observer put it, "The howls of the macho school for crude assertions of virility are matched by the wails of the utopians, paralyzed by the challenge of an international system devised by man rather than by God."[70]

OVERVIEW

Canada's role in world affairs continues to develop. Among states Canada is one of the most powerful both economically and politically. This relative position makes it mandatory that Canada participate fully in international organizations such as the United Nations and its specialized agencies. Canada's international importance has also increased because of economic and security requirements.

The importance of international relations to Canada is also illustrated by its defence policies. While Canada contributes to the security of the West by membership in NATO and NORAD, its overall military budget is small compared to that of most countries. Because of an essentially non-militaristic position Canada is acceptable to many countries as an intermediary in troubled areas. The most concrete example is the Canadian contribution to peacekeeping.

The international strategic environment, however, is changing. Most conflicts take place outside the Western European theatre and Canada has had little role to play in the ethnic superpower and religious conflicts of the Middle East and the Balkans. In the remainder of the world, essentially south of the Tropic of Cancer, Canada plays a modest, usually rhetorical, role. Efforts to make NATO into a world policeofficer have largely failed. The United States and the states of the former Soviet Union have been left to conduct these tasks on their own. Canadian efforts to help end apartheid in South Africa, and to bring a political solution to other troubled areas have sometimes landed on fertile ground. In sum then, the Canadian contribution to world politics outside North America, Europe and a few countries with old Commonwealth ties is marginal and largely symbolic, except at the important humanitarian and peacekeeping levels.

Decision-making in domestic and international policy spheres has been quite dissimilar. However, the foreign policy process has been changing due to widespread concern for international peace and disarmament issues and a growing awareness of the importance of trade to the Canadian economy. Many new actors are now involved in foreign policy-making. The historically important roles of the Prime Minister and the Ministers of External Affairs and National Defence remain but the relative significance of other departments and agencies has grown, as have interest group activities.

As Canada evolved into a full-fledged state it gradually adopted an internationalist posture and dropped its older style of isolationism. Issues of peace, world trade and humanitarian concerns actively interest many Canadians, and political leaders have forced the government towards a foreign policy that is in tune with Canada's domestic concerns and issues. Today the realization that no country can be totally self-sufficient is an accepted maxim of international and Canadian politics.

---

[70] John W. Holmes, "The Way of the World," *International Journal*, vol. XXXV, no. 2 (Spring 1980), p. 211

SELECTED BIBLIOGRAPHY

Barlow, Maude and Bruce Campbell, *Take Back the Nation* (Toronto: Key Porter, 1991).

Bothwell, Robert, *Canada and the United States* (Toronto: University of Toronto Press, 1992).

Brzezinski, Zbigniew, *Out of Control: Global Turmoil on the Eve of the 21st Century* (NY: Scribners, 1993).

Bowker, Marjorie M., *On Guard for Thee* (Hull, Qué.: Voyageur, 1988).

Cameron, Duncan, ed., *The Free Trade Deal* (Toronto: Lorimer, 1988).

Clarkson, Stephen, *Canada and the Reagan Challenge: Crisis and Adjustment 1981–1985*, 2nd ed. (Toronto: Lorimer, 1985).

Cox, David and Mary Taylor, eds., *A Guide to Canadian Policies on Arms Control, Disarmament, Defence and Conflict Resolution, 1986–87* (Ottawa: CIIPS, 1987).

Crispo, John, ed., *Free Trade: The Real Story* (Toronto: Gage, 1988).

Daly, Donald J., *Canada in an Uncertain World Environment* (Montréal: IRPP, 1982).

Dewitt, David B. and John J. Kirton, *Canada as a Principal Power* (Toronto: John Wiley, 1983).

Doern, G. Bruce and Brian W. Tomlin, *Faith and Fear* (Toronto: Stoddart, 1991).

Doran, Charles F. and John H. Sigler, eds., *Canada and the United States* (Englewood Cliffs, N.J.: Prentice-Hall, 1985).

Granatstein, J.L., ed., *Canadian Foreign Policy: Historical Readings* (Toronto: Copp Clark Pitman, 1986).

———— and Robert Bothwell, *Pirouette: Pierre Trudeau and Canadian Foreign Policy* (Toronto: University of Toronto Press, 1990).

Hampson, Fen Osler and Christopher J. Maule, *Canada Among Nations 1993: Global Jeopardy* (Ottawa: Carleton University Press, 1993).

Head, Ivan L., *On a Hinge of History: The Mutual Vulnerability of South and North* (Toronto: University of Toronto Press, 1991).

Holsti, Kal J., *International Politics; A Framework for Analysis*, 4th ed. (Englewood Cliffs, N.J.: Prentice-Hall, 1983).

Holmes, John W., *Life with Uncle* (Toronto: University of Toronto Press, 1981).

———— and John Kirton, eds., *Canada and the New Internationalism* (Toronto: Centre for International Studies, 1988).

Hurtig, Mel, *The Betrayal of Canada*, 2nd ed. (Toronto: Stoddart, 1993).

Jackson, Robert J., ed., *Continuity of Discord: Crises and Responses in the Atlantic Community* (New York: Praeger, 1985).

————, ed., *Europe in Transition* (New York: Praeger, 1993).

Jockel, Joseph T., *No Boundaries Upstairs: Canada, The United States and the Origins of North American Air Defence* (Vancouver: University of British Columbia Press, 1987).

————, and Joel J. Sokolsky, *Canada and Collective Security* (New York: Praeger, 1986).

Kennedy, Paul, *Preparing for the Twenty-First Century* (New York: Harper Collins, 1993).

————, *The Rise and Fall of Great Powers* (New York: Random House, 1988).

Lipsey, R.G. and W. Dobson, eds., *Shaping Comparative Advantage* (Toronto: C.D. Howe Institute, 1987).

Middlemiss, D.W. and J.J. Sokolsky, *Canadian Defence: Decisions and Determinants* (New York: Harcourt Brace Jovanovich, 1989).

————, and Murray G. Smith, *Taking the Initiative: Canada's Trade Options* (Montréal: C.D. Howe Institute, 1985).

Lyon, Peyton V. and Brian Tomlin, eds., *Canada as an International Actor* (Toronto: Macmillan of Canada, 1979).

Mathews, Robert O. and Cranford Pratt, eds., *Human Rights in Canadian Foreign Policy* (Montréal: McGill-Queen's University Press, 1988).

Miall, Hugh, *The Peacemakers* (London: Macmillan, 1992).

Moynihan, Daniel Patrick, *Ethnicity in International Politics* (New York: Oxford University Press, 1992).

Nossal, Kim Richard, *The Politics of Canadian Foreign Policy*, 2nd ed. (Scarborough, Ont.: Prentice-Hall Canada, 1989).

Pammett, J. and B. Tomlin, eds., *The Integration Question* (Toronto: Addison-Wesley, 1984).

Regehr, Ernie and Simon Rosenblum, eds., *The Road to Peace* (Toronto: Lorimer, 1988).

Riddell-Dixon, Elizabeth, *The Domestic Mosaic* (Toronto: CIIA, 1985).

Rosenau, James N., *Turbulence in World Politics* (New York; Harvester Wheatsheaf, 1990).

Stairs, D. and G.R. Winham, eds., *Canada and the International Political/Economic Environment*, vol. 28, Royal Commission on the Economic Union and Development Prospects for Canada (Toronto: University of Toronto Press, 1985).

————, eds., *The Politics of Canada's Economic Relationship with the United States*, vol. 29, Royal Commission on the Economic Union (Toronto: University of Toronto Press, 1985).

Stone, Frank, *Canada, The GATT and the International Trade System* (Montréal: IRPP, 1984).

Tomlin, Brian W., ed., *Canada's Foreign Policy: Analysis and Trends* (Toronto: Methuen, 1988).

Tucker, Michael, *Canadian Foreign Policy* (Toronto: McGraw-Hill Ryerson, 1980).

Whalley, J., et al., *Canadian Trade Policies and the World Economy*, vol. 9, Royal Commission on the Economic Union (Toronto: University of Toronto Press, 1985).

————, ed., *Canada-United States Free Trade*, vol. 11, Royal Commission on the Economic Union (Toronto: University of Toronto Press, 1985).

————, ed., *Canada's Resource Industries and Water Export Policy*, vol. 14, Royal Commission on the Economic Union (Toronto: University of Toronto Press, 1985).

Williams, Glen, *Not for Export* (Toronto: McClelland & Stewart, 1983).

See also the periodicals *International Journal* and *Peacekeeping and International Relations*.

A P P E N D I X

A
CONSOLIDATION
OF THE
CONSTITUTION
ACTS
1867 TO 1982

CONSTITUTION ACT, 1867

(THE BRITISH NORTH AMERICA ACT, 1867)

[Note: The present short title was substituted for the original short title (in italics) by the *Constitution Act, 1982* (No. 44 *infra*).]

30 & 31 Victoria, c. 3 (U.K.)

An Act for the Union of Canada, Nova Scotia, and New Brunswick, and the Government thereof; and for Purposes connected therewith

[29th March 1867]

Whereas the Provinces of Canada, Nova Scotia, and New Brunswick have expressed their Desire to be federally united into One Dominion under the Crown of the United Kingdom of Great Britain and Ireland, with a Constitution similar in Principle to that of the United Kingdom:

And whereas such a Union would conduce to the Welfare of the Provinces and promote the Interests of the British Empire:

And whereas on the Establishment of the Union by Authority of Parliament it is expedient, not only that the Constitution of the Legislative Authority in the Dominion be provided for, but also that the Nature of the Executive Government therein be declared:

And whereas it is expedient that Provision be made for the eventual Admission into the Union of other Parts of British North America:

Be it therefore enacted and declared by the Queen's most Excellent Majesty, by and with the Advice and Consent of the Lords Spiritual and Temporal, and Commons, in this present Parliament assembled, and by the Authority of the same, as follows:

[Note: The enacting clause was repealed by the *Statute Law Revision Act, 1893* (No. 17 *infra*).]

I. PRELIMINARY

Short Title

1. *This Act may be cited as The British North America Act, 1867.*

Short title

1. This Act may be cited as the *Constitution Act, 1867*.

[Note: Section 1 (in italics) was repealed and the new section substituted by the *Constitution Act, 1982* (No. 44 *infra*).]

Application of Provisions referring to the Queen

2. *The Provisions of this Act referring to Her Majesty the Queen extend also to the Heirs and Successors of Her Majesty, Kings and Queens of the United Kingdom of Great Britain and Ireland.*

[Note: Repealed by the *Statute Law Revision Act, 1893* (No. 17 *infra*).]

II. UNION

DECLARATION OF UNION

Declaration of Union

3. It shall be lawful for the Queen, by and with the Advice of Her Majesty's Most Honourable Privy Council, to declare by Proclamation that, on and after a Day therein appointed, not being more than Six Months after the passing of this Act, the Provinces of Canada, Nova Scotia, and New Brunswick shall form and be One Dominion under the Name of Canada; and on and after that Day those Three Provinces shall form and be One Dominion under that Name accordingly.

[Note: The first day of July, 1867 was fixed by proclamation dated May 22, 1867.]

4. *The subsequent Provisions of this Act shall, unless it is otherwise expressed or implied, commence and have effect on and after the Union, that is to say, on and after the Day appointed for the Union taking effect in the Queen's Proclamation; and in the same Provisions*, unless it is otherwise expressed or implied, the Name Canada shall be taken to mean Canada as constituted under this Act.

Construction of subsequent Provisions of Act

[Note: The words in italics were repealed by the *Statute Law Revision Act, 1893* (No. 17 *infra*).]

5. Canada shall be divided into Four Provinces, named Ontario, Quebec, Nova Scotia, and New Brunswick.

Four Provinces

[Note: Canada now consists of ten provinces (Ontario, Quebec, Nova Scotia, New Brunswick, Manitoba, British Columbia, Prince Edward Island, Alberta, Saskatchewan and Newfoundland) and two territories (the Yukon Territory and the Northwest Territories). See the note to section 146.]

6. The Parts of the Province of Canada (as it exists at the passing of this Act) which formerly constituted respectively the Provinces of Upper Canada and Lower Canada shall be deemed to be severed, and shall form Two separate Provinces. The Part which formerly constituted the Province of Upper Canada shall constitute the Province of Ontario; and the Part which formerly constituted the Province of Lower Canada shall constitute the Province of Quebec.

Provinces of Ontario and Quebec

7. The Provinces of Nova Scotia and New Brunswick shall have the same Limits as at the passing of this Act.

Provinces of Nova Scotia and New Brunswick

8. In the general Census of the Population of Canada which is hereby required to be taken in the Year One thousand eight hundred and seventy-one, and in every Tenth Year thereafter, the respective Populations of the Four Provinces shall be distinguished.

Decennial Census

III. Executive Power

9. The Executive Government and Authority of and over Canada is hereby declared to continue and be vested in the Queen.

Declaration of Executive Power in the Queen

10. The Provisions of this Act referring to the Governor General extend and apply to the Governor General for the Time being of Canada, or other the Chief Executive Officer or Administrator for the Time being carrying on the Government of Canada on behalf and in the Name of the Queen, by whatever Title he is designated.

Application of Provisions referring to Governor General

11. There shall be a Council to aid and advise in the Government of Canada, to be styled the Queen's Privy Council for Canada; and the Persons who are to be Members of that Council shall be from Time to Time chosen and summoned by the Governor General and sworn in as Privy Councillors, and Members thereof may be from Time to Time removed by the Governor General.

Constitution of Privy Council for Canada

12. All Powers, Authorities, and Functions which under any Act of the Parliament of Great Britain, or of the Parliament of the United Kingdom of Great Britain and Ireland, or of the Legislature of Upper Canada, Lower Canada, Canada, Nova Scotia, or New Brunswick, are at the

All Powers under Acts to be exercised by Governor General with Advice of Privy Council, or alone

Union vested in or exerciseable by the respective Governors or Lieutenant Governors of those Provinces, with the Advice, or with the Advice of Consent, of the respective Executive Councils thereof, or in conjunction with those Councils, or with any Number of Members thereof, or by those Governors or Lieutenant Governors individually, shall, as far as the same continue in existence and capable of being exercised after the Union in relation to the Government of Canada, be vested in and exerciseable by the Governor General, with the Advice or with the Advice and Consent of or in conjunction with the Queen's Privy Council for Canada, or any Members thereof, or by the Governor General individually, as the Case requires, subject nevertheless (except with respect to such as Exist under Acts of the Parliament of Great Britain or of the Parliament of the United Kingdom of Great Britain and Ireland) to be abolished or altered by the Parliament of Canada.

[Note: See the note to section 129.]

Application of Provisions referring to Governor General in Council

13. The Provisions of this Act referring to the Governor General in Council shall be construed as referring to the Governor General acting by and with the Advice of the Queen's Privy Council for Canada.

Power to Her Majesty to authorize Governor General to appoint Deputies

14. It shall be lawful for the Queen, if Her Majesty thinks fit, to authorize the Governor General from Time to Time to appoint any Person or any Persons jointly or severally to be his Deputy or Deputies within any Part or Parts of Canada, and in that Capacity to exercise during the Pleasure of the Governor General such of the Powers, Authorities, and Functions of the Governor General as the Governor General deems it necessary or expedient to assign to him or them, subject to any Limitations or Directions expressed or given by the Queen; but the Appointment of such a Deputy or Deputies shall not affect the Exercise by the Governor General himself of any Power, Authority, or Function.

Command of Armed Forces to continue to be vested in the Queen

15. The Command-in-Chief of the Land and Naval Militia, and of all Naval and Military Forces, of and in Canada, is hereby declared to continue and be vested in the Queen.

Seat of Government of Canada

16. Until the Queen otherwise directs, the Seat of Government of Canada shall be Ottawa.

IV. LEGISLATIVE POWER

Constitution of Parliament of Canada

17. There shall be One Parliament for Canada, consisting of the Queen, an Upper House styled the Senate, and the House of Commons.

Privileges, etc., of Houses

18. *The Privileges, Immunities, and Powers to be held, enjoyed, and exercised by the Senate and by the House of Commons and by the Members thereof respectively shall be such as are from Time to Time defined by Act of the Parliament of Canada, but so that the same shall never exceed those at the passing of this Act held, enjoyed, and exercised by the Commons House of Parliament of the United Kingdom of Great Britain and Ireland and by the Members thereof.*

18. The privileges, immunities and powers to be held, enjoyed, and exercised by the Senate and by the House of Commons, and by the members thereof respectively, shall be such as are from time to time defined by Act of the Parliament of Canada, but so that any Act of the Parliament of Canada defining such privileges, immunities, and power shall not confer any privileges, immunities, or powers exceeding those at the passing of such Act held, enjoyed, and exercised by the Commons House of Parliament of the United Kingdom of Great Britain and Ireland, and by the members thereof.

[Note: Section 18 (in italics) was repealed and the new section substituted by the *Parliament of Canada Act, 1875* (No. 13 *infra*).]

19. The Parliament of Canada shall be called together not later than Six Months after the Union.

First Session of the Parliament of Canada

[Note: The first session of the first Parliament began on November 6, 1867.]

20. *There shall be a Session of the Parliament of Canada once at least in every Year, so that Twelve Months shall not intervene between the last Sitting of the Parliament in one Session and its first sitting in the next Session.*

Yearly Session of the Parliament of Canada

[Note: Repealed by the *Constitution Act, 1982* (No. 44 *infra*). See also section 5 of that Act, which provides that there shall be a sitting of the Parliament at least once every twelve months.]

The Senate

21. The Senate shall, subject to the Provisions of this Act, consist of *Seventy-two* Members, who shall be styled Senators.

Number of Senators

[Note: The Senate now consists of 104 Members, as amended by the *Constitution Act, 1915* (No. 23 *infra*) and modified by the *Newfoundland Act* (No. 32 *infra*) and as again amended by the *Constitution Act (No. 2), 1975,* (No. 42 *infra*).]

22. In relation to the Constitution of the Senate Canada shall be deemed to consist of *Three* Divisions:

Representation of Provinces in Senate

1. Ontario;
2. Quebec;
3. *The Maritime Provinces, Nova Scotia and New Brunswick*;

which *Three* Divisions shall (subject to the Provisions of this Act) be equally represented in the Senate as follows: Ontario by Twenty-four Senators; Quebec by Twenty-four Senators; and the Maritime Provinces by Twenty-four Senators, *Twelve* thereof representing Nova Scotia, and *Twelve* thereof representing New Brunswick.

In the case of Quebec each of the Twenty-four Senators representing that Province shall be appointed for One of the Twenty-four Electoral Divisions of Lower Canada specified in Schedule A. to Chapter One of the Consolidated Statutes of Canada.

[Note: Prince Edward Island, on admission into the Union in 1873, became part of the third division with a representation in the Senate of four members, the representation of Nova Scotia and New Brunswick being reduced from twelve to ten members each. See section 147.

A fourth division represented in the Senate by twenty-four senators and comprising the Western Provinces of Manitoba, British Columbia, Alberta and Saskatchewan, each represented by six senators, was added by the *Constitution Act, 1915* (No. 23 *infra*).

Newfoundland is represented in the Senate by six members. See the *Constitution Act, 1915* (No. 23 *infra*) and the *Newfoundland Act* No. 32 *infra*).

The Yukon Territory and the Northwest Territories are represented in the Senate by one member each. See the *Constitution Act (No. 2), 1975* (No. 42 *infra*).]

Qualifications of
Senator

23. The Qualifications of a Senator shall be as follows:

1. He shall be of the full age of Thirty Years:

2. He shall be either a natural-born Subject of the Queen, or a Subject of the Queen naturalized by an Act of the Parliament of Great Britain, or of the Parliament of the United Kingdom of Great Britain and Ireland, or of the Legislature of One of the Provinces of Upper Canada, Lower Canada, Canada, Nova Scotia, or New Brunswick, before the Union, or of the Parliament of Canada after the Union:

3. He shall be legally or equitably seised as of Freehold for his own Use and Benefit of Lands or Tenements held in Free and Common Socage, or seised or possessed for his own Use and Benefit of Lands or Tenements held in Franc-alleu or in Roture, within the Province for which he is appointed, of the Value of Four thousand Dollars, over and above all Rents, Dues, Debts, Charges, Mortgages, and Incumbrances due or payable out of or charged on or affecting the same:

4. His Real and Personal Property shall be together worth Four thousand Dollars over and above his Debts and Liabilities:

5. He shall be resident in the Province for which he is appointed:

6. In the Case of Quebec he shall have his Real Property Qualification in the Electoral Division for which he is appointed, or shall be resident in that Division.

[Note: For the purposes of the *Constitution Act (No. 2), 1975* (No. 42 *infra*), the term "Province" in section 23 has the same meaning as is assigned to the "province" by section 35 of the *Interpretation Act* (Canada).]

Summons of
Senator

24. The Governor General shall from Time to Time, in the Queen's Name, by Instrument under the Great Seal of Canada, summon qualified Persons to the Senate; and, subject to the Provisions of this Act, every Person so summoned shall become and be a Member of the Senate and a Senator.

*Summons of First
Body of Senators*

25. *Such Persons shall be first summoned to the Senate as the Queen by Warrant under Her Majesty's Royal Sign Manual thinks fit to approve, and their Names shall be inserted in the Queen's Proclamation of Union.*

[Note: Repealed by the *Statute Law Revision Act, 1893* (No. 17 *infra*).]

Addition of
Senators in certain
Cases

26. If at any Time on the Recommendation of the Governor General the Queen thinks fit to direct that *Three or Six* Members be added to the Senate, the Governor General may by Summons to *Three or Six* qualified Persons (as the Case may be), representing equally the *Three* Divisions of Canada, add to the Senate accordingly.

[Note: The number of members who may be added to the Senate was increased from three or six to four or eight, representing equally the four divisions of Canada. See the *Constitution Act, 1915* (No. 23 *infra*).]

Reduction of
Senate to normal
number

27. In case of such Addition being at any Time made, the Governor General shall not summon any Person to the Senate, except on a further like Direction by the Queen on the like Recommendation, until each of the *Three* Divisions of Canada is represented by Twenty-four Senators and no more.

[Note: Superseded by the *Constitution Act, 1915*, paragraph 1(1)(iv), No. 23 *infra*). This paragraph reads as follows:

"In case of such addition being at any time made the Governor General of Canada shall not summon any person to the Senate except upon a further like direction by His Majesty the King on the like recommendation to represent one of the four Divisions until such Division is represented by twenty-four senators and no more:"]

28. The Number of Senators shall not at any Time exceed *Seventy-eight*.

[Note: The maximum number of senators is now 112, as amended by the *Constitution Act, 1915 (No. 23 infra)* and the *Constitution Act (No. 2), 1975 (No. 42 infra).*]

Maximum Number of Senator

29. *A Senator shall, subject to the Provisions of this Act, hold his Place in the Senate for Life.*

Tenure of Place in Senate

29. (1) Subject to subsection (2), a Senator shall, subject to the provisions of this Act, hold his place in the Senate for life.

Tenure of place in Senate

(2) A senator who is summoned to the Senate after the coming into force of this subsection shall, subject to this act, hold his place in the Senate until he attains the age of seventy-five years.

Retirement upon attaining age of seventy-five years

[Note: Section 29 (in italics) was repealed and the new section substituted by the *Constitution Act, 1965 (No. 39 infra).*]

30. A Senator may by Writing under his Hand addressed to the Governor General resign his Place in the Senate, and thereupon the same shall be vacant.

Resignation of Place in Senate

31. The Place of a Senator shall become vacant in any of the following Cases:

1. If for Two consecutive Sessions of the Parliament he fails to give his Attendance in the Senate:

2. If he takes an Oath or makes a Declaration or Acknowledgement of Allegiance, Obedience, or Adherence to a Foreign Power, or does an Act whereby he becomes a Subject or Citizen, or entitled to the Rights or Privileges of a Subject or Citizen, of a Foreign Power:

3. If he is adjudged Bankrupt or Insolvent, or applies for the Benefit of any Law relating to Insolvent Debtors, or becomes a public Defaulter:

4. If he is attainted of Treason or convicted of Felony or of any infamous Crime:

5. If he ceases to be qualified in respect of Property or of Residence; provided, that a Senator shall not be deemed to have ceased to be qualified in respect of Residence by reason only of his residing at the Seat of the Government of Canada while holding an Office under that Government requiring his Presence there.

Disqualification of Senators

32. When a Vacancy happens in the Senate by Resignation, Death, or otherwise, the Governor General shall by Summons to a fit and qualified Person fill the Vacancy.

Summons on Vacancy in Senate

33. If any Question arises respecting the Qualification of a Senator or a Vacancy in the Senate the same shall be heard and determined by the Senate.

Questions as to Qualifications and Vacancies in Senate

34. The Governor General may from Time to Time, by Instrument under the Great Seal of Canada, appoint a Senator to be Speaker of the Senate, and may remove him and appoint another in his Stead.

Appointment of Speaker of Senate

[Note: See also the *Canadian Speaker (Appointment of Deputy) Act, 1895* (No. 18 *infra*) and the provisions concerning the Speaker of the Senate in the *Parliament of Canada Act* (Canada).]

Quorum of Senate

35. Until the Parliament of Canada otherwise provides, the Presence of at least Fifteen Senators, including the Speaker, shall be necessary to constitute a Meeting of the Senate for the Exercise of its Powers.

Voting in Senate

36. Questions arising in the Senate shall be decided by a Majority of Voices, and the Speaker shall in all Cases have a Vote, and when the Voices are equal the Decision shall be deemed to be in the Negative.

The House of Commons

Constitution of House of Commons in Canada

37. The House of Commons shall, subject to the Provisions of this Act, consist of *One hundred and eighty-one* Members, of whom *Eighty-two* shall be elected for Ontario, *Sixty-five* for Quebec, *Nineteen* for Nova Scotia, and *Fifteen* for New Brunswick.

[Note: On October 31, 1987, the House of Commons consisted of 282 members: 95 for Ontario, 75 for Quebec, 11 for Nova Scotia, 10 for New Brunswick, 14 for Manitoba, 28 for British Columbia, 4 for Prince Edward Island, 21 for Alberta, 14 for Saskatchewan, 7 for Newfoundland, 1 for the Yukon Territory and 2 for the Northwest Territories.

These figures result from the application of section 51 as re-enacted by the *Constitution Act, 1974* (No. 40 *infra*) and amended by the *Constitution Act (No. 1), 1975* (No. 41 *infra*), and of the *Electoral Boundaries Readjustment Act* (Canada).]

Summoning of House of Commons

38. The Governor General shall from Time to Time, in the Queen's Name, by Instrument under the Great Seal of Canada, summon and call together the House of Commons.

Senators not to sit in House of Commons

39. A Senator shall not be capable of being elected or of sitting or voting as a Member of the House of Commons.

Electoral Districts of the Four Provinces

40. Until the Parliament of Canada otherwise provides, Ontario, Quebec, Nova Scotia, and New Brunswick shall, for the Purposes of the Election of Members to serve in the House of Commons, be divided into Electoral Districts as follows:

1. ONTARIO

Ontario shall be divided into the Counties, Ridings of Counties, Cities, Parts of Cities, and Towns enumerated in the First Schedule to this Act, each whereof shall be an Electoral District, each such District as numbered in that Schedule being entitled to return One Member.

2. QUEBEC

Quebec shall be divided into Sixty-five Electoral Districts, composed of the Sixty-five Electoral Divisions into which Lower Canada is at the passing of this Act divided under Chapter Two of the Consolidated Statutes of Canada, Chapter Seventy-five of the Consolidated Statutes for Lower Canada, and the Act of the Province of Canada of the Twenty-third Year of the Queen, Chapter One, or any other Act amending the same in force at the Union, so that each such Electoral Division shall be for the Purposes of this Act an Electoral District entitled to return One Member.

3. Nova Scotia

Each of the Eighteen Counties of Nova Scotia shall be an Electoral District. The County of Halifax shall be entitled to return Two Members, and each of the other Counties One Member.

4. New Brunswick

Each of the Fourteen Counties into which New Brunswick is divided, including the City and County of St. John, shall be an Electoral District. The City of St. John shall also be a separate Electoral District. Each of those Fifteen Electoral Districts shall be entitled to return One Member.

[Note: The federal electoral districts of the 10 provinces and the Northwest Territories are now set out in the schedule to Proclamations issued from time to time pursuant to the *Electoral Boundaries Readjustment Act* (Canada), as amended for particular districts by other Acts of Parliament.

The electoral district of the Yukon Territory is set out in section 30 of the *Electoral Boundaries Readjustment Act* (Canada).]

41. Until the Parliament of Canada otherwise provides, all Laws in force in the several Provinces at the Union relative to the following Matters or any of them, namely,—the Qualifications and Disqualifications of Persons to be elected or to sit or vote as Members of the House of Assembly or Legislative Assembly in the several Provinces, the Voters at Elections of such Members, the Oaths to be taken by Voters, the Returning Officers, their Powers and Duties, the Proceedings at Elections, the Periods during which Elections may be continued, the Trial of controverted Elections, and Proceedings incident thereto, the vacating of Seats of Members, and the Execution of new Writs in case of Seats vacated otherwise than by Dissolution,—shall respectively apply to Elections of Members to serve in the House of Commons for the same several Provinces.

Continuance of existing Election Laws until Parliament of Canada otherwise provides

Provided that, until the Parliament of Canada otherwise provides, at any Election for a Member of the House of Commons for the District of Algoma, in addition to Persons qualified by the Law of the Province of Canada to vote, every Male British Subject, aged Twenty-one Years or upwards, being a Householder, shall have a Vote.

[Note: The principal provisions concerning elections are now found in the *Parliament of Canada Act, Canada Elections Act* and *Dominion Controverted Elections Act* (all three enacted by Canada). The right to vote and hold office is provided for in section 3 of the *Constitution Act, 1982* (No. 44 *infra*).]

42. *For the First Election of Members to serve in the House of Commons the Governor General shall cause Writs to be issued by such Person, in such Form, and addressed to such Returning Officers as he thinks fit.*

Writs for first Election

The Person issuing Writs under this Section shall have the like Powers as are possessed at the Union by the Officers charged with the issuing of Writs for the Election of Members to serve in the respective House of Assembly or Legislative Assembly of the Province of Canada, Nova Scotia, or New Brunswick; and the Returning Officers to whom Writs are directed under this Section shall have the like Powers as are possessed at the Union by the Officers charged with the returning of Writs for the Election of Members to serve in the same respective House of Assembly or Legislative Assembly.

[Note: Repealed by the *Statute Law Revision Act, 1893* (No. 17 *infra*).]

As to Casual Vacancies

43. *In case a Vacancy in the Representation in the House of Commons of any Electoral District happens before the Meeting of the Parliament, or after the Meeting of the Parliament before Provision is made by the Parliament in this Behalf, the Provisions of the last foregoing Section of this Act shall extend and apply to the issuing and returning of a Writ in respect of such Vacant District.*

[Note: Repealed by the *Statute Law Revision Act, 1893* (No. 17 *infra*).]

As to Election of Speaker of House of Commons

44. The House of Commons on its first assembling after a General Election shall proceed with all practicable Speed to elect One of its Members to be Speaker.

As to filling up Vacancy in Office of Speaker

45. In case of a Vacancy happening in the Office of Speaker by Death, Resignation, or otherwise, the House of Commons shall with all practicable Speed proceed to elect another of its Members to be Speaker.

Speaker to preside

46. The Speaker shall preside at all Meetings of the House of Commons.

Provision in case of Absence of Speaker

47. Until the Parliament of Canada otherwise provides, in case of the Absence for any Reason of the Speaker from the Chair of the House of Commons for a Period of Forty-eight consecutive Hours, the House may elect another of its Members to act as Speaker, and the Member so elected shall during the Continuance of such Absence of the Speaker have and execute all the Powers, Privileges, and Duties of Speaker.

[Note: See also the provisions concerning the Speaker of the House of Commons in the *Parliament of Canada Act* (Canada).]

Quorum of House of Commons

48. The Presence of at least Twenty Members of the House of Commons shall be necessary to constitute a Meeting of the House for the Exercise of its Powers, and for that Purpose the Speaker shall be reckoned as a Member.

Voting in House of Commons

49. Questions arising in the House of Commons shall be decided by a Majority of Voices other than that of the Speaker, and when the Voices are equal, but not otherwise, the Speaker shall have a Vote.

Duration of House of Commons

50. Every House of Commons shall continue for Five Years from the Day of the Return of the Writs for choosing the House (subject to be sooner dissolved by the Governor General), and no longer.

[Note: See for an extension of this term the *British North America Act, 1916* (No. 24 *infra*). See also section 4 of the *Constitution Act, 1982* (No. 44 *infra*).]

Decennial Readjustment of Representation

51. *On the Completion of the Census in the Year One thousand eight hundred and seventy-one, and of each subsequent decennial Census, the Representation of the Four Provinces shall be readjusted by such Authority, in such Manner, and from such Time, as the Parliament of Canada from Time to Time provides, subject and according to the following Rules:*

1. Quebec shall have the fixed Number of Sixty-five Members:

2. There shall be assigned to each of the other Provinces such a Number of Members as will bear the same Proportion to the Number of its Population (ascertained at such Census) as the Number Sixty-five bears to the Number of the Population of Quebec (so ascertained):

3. In the Computation of the Number of Members for a Province a fractional Part not exceeding One Half of the whole Number requisite for entitling the Province to a Member shall be disregarded; but a fractional

Part exceeding One Half of that Number shall be equivalent to the whole Number:

4. On any such Re-adjustment the Number of Members for a Province shall not be reduced unless the Proportion which the Number of the Population of the Province bore to the Number of the aggregate Population of Canada at the then last preceding Re-adjustment of the Number of Members for the Province is ascertained at the then latest Census to be diminished by One Twentieth Part or upwards:

5. Such Re-adjustment shall not take effect until the Termination of the then existing Parliament.

51. (1) The number of members of the House of Commons and the representation of the provinces therein shall, on the coming into force of this subsection and thereafter on the completion of each decennial census, be readjusted by such authority, in such manner, and from such time as the Parliament of Canada from time to time provides, subject and according to the following rules: | Readjustment of representation in Commons

    1. There shall be assigned to each of the provinces a number of members equal to the number obtained by dividing the total population of the provinces by two hundred and seventy-nine and by dividing the population of each province by the quotient so obtained, counting any remainder in excess of 0.50 as one after the said process of division. | Rules

    2. If the total number of members that would be assigned to a province by the application of rule 1 is less than the total number assigned to that province on the date of coming into force of this subsection, there shall be added to the number of members so assigned such number of members as will result in the province having the same number of members as were assigned on that date.

    (2) The Yukon Territory as bounded and described in the schedule to chapter Y-2 of the Revised Statutes of Canada, 1970, shall be entitled to one member, and the Northwest Territories as bounded and described in section 2 of chapter N-22 of the Revised Statutes of Canada, 1970, shall be entitled to two members. | Yukon Territory and Northwest Territories

[Note: The original section 51 (in italics) was repealed and a new section 51 substituted by the *British North America Act, 1946* (No. 30 *infra*).

The section enacted in 1946 was repealed and a new section 51 substituted by the *British North America Act, 1952* (No. 36 *infra*).

Subsection (1) of the section 51 enacted in 1952 was repealed and a new subsection 51(1) substituted by the *Constitution Act, 1974* (No. 40 *infra*). The subsection 51(1) enacted in 1974 was repealed and the present subsection 51(1) substituted by the *Constitution Act, 1985 (Representation)* (No. 47 *infra*).

Subsection (2) of the section 51 enacted in 1952 was repealed and the present subsection 51(2) substituted by the *Constitution Act (No. 1), 1975* (No. 41 *infra*).

The words from "of the census" to "seventy-one and" and the word "subsequent" of the original section had previously been repealed by the *Statute Law Revision Act, 1893* (No. 17 *infra*).]

51A. Notwithstanding anything in this Act a province shall always be entitled to a number of members in the House of Commons not less than the number of senators representing such province. | Constitution of House of Commons

[Note: Added by the *Constitution Act, 1915* (No. 23 *infra*).]

52. The Number of Members of the House of Commons may be from Time to Time increased by the Parliament of Canada, provided the pro- | Increase of Number of House of Commons portionate Representation of the Provinces prescribed by this Act is not thereby disturbed.

Money Votes; Royal Assent

Appropriation and Tax Bills

53. Bills for appropriating any Part of the Public Revenue, or for imposing any Tax or Impost, shall originate in the House of Commons.

Recommendation of Money Votes

54. It shall not be lawful for the House of Commons to adopt or pass any Vote, Resolution, Address, or Bill for the Appropriation of any Part of the Public Revenue, or of any Tax or Impost, to any Purpose that has not been first recommended to that House by Message of the Governor General in the Session in which such Vote, Resolution, Address, or Bill is proposed.

Royal Assent to Bills, etc.

55. Where a Bill passed by the Houses of the Parliament is presented to the Governor General for the Queen's Assent, he shall declare, according to his Discretion, but subject to the Provisions of this Act and to Her Majesty's Instructions, either that he assents thereto in the Queen's Name, or that he withholds the Queen's Assent, or that he reserves the Bill for the Signification of the Queen's Pleasure.

Disallowance by Order in Council of Act assented to by Governor General

56. Where the Governor General assents to a Bill in the Queen's Name, he shall by the first convenient Opportunity send an authentic Copy of the Act to One of Her Majesty's Principal Secretaries of State, and if the Queen in Council within Two Years after Receipt thereof by the Secretary of State thinks fit to disallow the Act, such Disallowance (with a Certificate of the Secretary of State of the Day on which the Act was received by him) being signified by the Governor General, by Speech or Message to each of the Houses of the Parliament or by Proclamation, shall annul the Act from and after the Day of such Signification.

Signification of Queen's Pleasure on Bill reserved

57. A Bill reserved for the Signification of the Queen's Pleasure shall not have any Force unless and until, within Two Years from the Day on which it was presented to the Governor General for the Queen's Assent, the Governor General signifies, by Speech or Message to each of the Houses of the Parliament or by Proclamation, that it has received the Assent of the Queen in Council.

An Entry of every such Speech, Message, or Proclamation shall be made in the Journal of each House, and a Duplicate thereof duly attested shall be delivered to the proper Officer to be kept among the Records of Canada.

V. PROVINCIAL CONSTITUTIONS

Executive Power

Appointment of Lieutenant Governors of Provinces

58. For each Province there shall be an Officer, styled the Lieutenant Governor, appointed by the Governor General in Council by Instrument under the Great Seal of Canada.

Tenure of office of Lieutenant Governor

59. A Lieutenant Governor shall hold Office during the Pleasure of the Governor General; but any Lieutenant Governor appointed after the Commencement of the First Session of the Parliament of Canada shall not be removeable within Five Years from his Appointment, except for

Cause assigned, which shall be communicated to him in Writing within One Month after the Order for his Removal is made, and shall be communicated by Message to the Senate and to the House of Commons within One Week thereafter if the Parliament is then sitting, and if not then within One Week after the Commencement of the next Session of the Parliament.

60. The Salaries of the Lieutenant Governors shall be fixed and provided by the Parliament of Canada.
[Note: See the *Salaries Act* (Canada).]

Salaries of Lieutenant Governors

61. Every Lieutenant Governor shall, before assuming the Duties of his Office, make and subscribe before the Governor General or some Person authorized by him Oaths of Allegiance and Office similar to those taken by the Governor General.

Oaths, etc., of Lieutenant Governor

62. The Provisions of this Act referring to the Lieutenant Governor extend and apply to the Lieutenant Governor for the Time being of each Province, or other the Chief Executive Officer or Administrator for the Time being carrying on the Government of the Province, by whatever Title he is designated.

Application of Provisions referring to Lieutenant Governor

63. The Executive Council of Ontario and of Quebec shall be composed of such Persons as the Lieutenant Governor from Time to Time thinks fit, and in the first instance of the following Officers, namely,—the Attorney General, the Secretary and Registrar of the Province, the Treasurer of the Province, the Commissioner of Crown Lands, and the Commissioner of Agriculture and Public Works, within Quebec the Speaker of the Legislative Council and the Solicitor General.
[Note: See the *Executive Council Act* (Ontario) and the *Executive Power Act* (Quebec).]

Appointment of Executive Officers for Ontario and Quebec

64. The Constitution of the Executive Authority in each of the Provinces of Nova Scotia and New Brunswick shall, subject to the Provisions of this Act, continue as it exists at the Union until altered under the Authority of this Act.
[Note: The instruments admitting British Columbia, Prince Edward Island and Newfoundland contain similar provisions and the *Manitoba Act, 1897, Alberta Act* and *Saskatchewan Act* establish the executive authorities in the three provinces concerned. See the note to section 146.]

Executive Government of Nova Scotia and New Brunswick

65. All Powers, Authorities, and Functions which under any Act of the Parliament of Great Britain, or of the Parliament of the United Kingdom of Great Britain and Ireland, or of the Legislature of Upper Canada, Lower Canada, or Canada, were or are before or at the Union vested in or exerciseable by the respective Governors or Lieutenant Governors of those Provinces, with the Advice or with the Advice and Consent of the respective Executive Councils thereof, or in conjunction with those Councils, or with any Number of Members thereof, or by those Governors or Lieutenant Governors individually, shall, as far as the same are capable of being exercised after the Union in relation to the Government of Ontario and Quebec respectively, be vested in and shall or may be exercised by the Lieutenant Governor of Ontario and Quebec respectively, with the Advice or with the Advice and Consent of or in conjunction with the respective Executive Councils, or any Members thereof, or by the

Powers to be exercised by Lieutenant Governor of Ontario or Quebec with Advice, or alone

Lieutenant Governor individually, as the Case requires, subject nevertheless (except with respect to such as exist under Acts of the Parliament of Great Britain, or of the Parliament of the United Kingdom of Great Britain and Ireland,) to be abolished or altered by the respective Legislatures of Ontario and Quebec.

[Note: See the note to section 129.]

Application of provisions referring to Lieutenant Governor in Council

66. The Provisions of this Act referring to the Lieutenant Governor in Council shall be construed as referring to the Lieutenant Governor of the Province acting by and with the Advice of the Executive Council thereof.

Administration in Absence, etc., of Lieutenant Governor

67. The Governor General in Council may from Time to Time appoint an Administrator to execute the Office and Functions of Lieutenant Governor during his Absence, Illness, or other Inability.

Seats of Provincial Governments

68. Unless and until the Executive Government of any Province otherwise directs with respect to that Province, the Seats of Government of the Provinces shall be as follows, namely,—of Ontario, the City of Toronto; of Quebec, the City of Quebec; of Nova Scotia, the City of Halifax; and of New Brunswick, the City of Fredericton.

Legislative Power

1. ONTARIO

Legislature for Ontario

69. There shall be a Legislature for Ontario consisting of the Lieutenant Governor and of One House, styled the Legislative Assembly of Ontario.

Electoral districts

70. The Legislative Assembly of Ontario shall be composed of Eighty-two Members, to be elected to represent the Eighty-two Electoral Districts set forth in the First Schedule to this Act.

[Note: See the *Representation Act* (Ontario).]

2. QUEBEC

Legislature for Quebec

71. There shall be a Legislature for Quebec consisting of the Lieutenant Governor and of Two Houses, styled the Legislative Council of Quebec and the Legislative Assembly of Quebec.

[Note: The Legislative Council was abolished by the *Act respecting the Legislative Council of Quebec*, Statutes of Quebec, 1968, c. 9. Sections 72 to 79 following are therefore spent.]

Constitution of Legislative Council

72. The Legislative Council of Quebec shall be composed of Twenty-four Members, to be appointed by the Lieutenant Governor, in the Queen's Name, by Instrument under the Great Seal of Quebec, one being appointed to represent each of the Twenty-four Electoral Divisions of Lower Canada in this Act referred to, and each holding Office for the Term of his Life, unless the Legislature of Quebec otherwise provides under the Provisions of this Act.

Qualification of Legislative Councillors

73. The Qualifications of the Legislative Councillors of Quebec shall be the same as those of the Senators for Quebec.

74. The Place of a Legislative Councillor of Quebec shall become vacant in the Cases, *mutatis mutandis*, in which the Place of Senator becomes vacant.

Resignation, Disqualification, etc.

75. When a Vacancy happens in the Legislative Council of Quebec by Resignation, Death, or otherwise, the Lieutenant Governor, in the Queen's Name, by Instrument under the Great Seal of Quebec, shall appoint a fit and qualified Person to fill the Vacancy.

Vacancies

76. If any Question arises respecting the Qualification of a Legislative Councillor of Quebec, or a Vacancy in the Legislative Council of Quebec, the same shall be heard and determined by the Legislative Council.

Questions as to Vacancies, etc.

77. The Lieutenant Governor may from Time to Time, by Instrument under the Great Seal of Quebec, appoint a Member of the Legislative Council of Quebec to be Speaker thereof, and may remove him and appoint another in his Stead.

Speaker of Legislative Council

78. Until the Legislature of Quebec otherwise provides, the Presence of at least Ten Members of the Legislative Council, including the Speaker, shall be necessary to constitute a Meeting for the Exercise of its Powers.

Quorum of Legislative Council

79. Questions arising in the Legislative Council of Quebec shall be decided by a Majority of Voices, and the Speaker shall in all Cases have a Vote, and when the Voices are equal the Decision shall be deemed to be in the Negative.

Voting in Legislative Council

80. The Legislative Assembly of Quebec shall be composed of Sixty-five Members, to be elected to represent the Sixty-five Electoral Divisions or Districts of Lower Canada in this Act referred to, subject to Alteration thereof by the Legislature of Quebec: Provided that it shall not be lawful to present to the Lieutenant Governor of Quebec for Assent any Bill for altering the Limits of any of the Electoral Divisions or Districts mentioned in the Second Schedule to this Act, unless the Second and Third Readings of such Bill have been passed in the Legislative Assembly with the Concurrence of the Majority of the Members representing all those Electoral Divisions or Districts, and the Assent shall not be given to such Bill unless an Address has been presented by the Legislative Assembly to the Lieutenant Governor stating that it has been so passed.
[Note: Declared to be of no effect by the *Act respecting electoral districts*, Statutes of Quebec, 1970, c. 7.]

Constitution of Legislative Assembly of Quebec

3. ONTARIO AND QUEBEC

81. *The Legislatures of Ontario and Quebec respectively shall be called together not later than Six Months after the Union.*
[Note: Repealed by the *Statute Law Revision Act, 1893* (No. 17 *infra*).]

First Session of Legislatures

82. The Lieutenant Governor of Ontario and of Quebec shall from Time to Time, in the Queen's Name, by Instrument under the Great Seal of the Province, summon and call together the Legislative Assembly of the Province.

Summoning of Legislative Assemblies

83. Until the Legislature of Ontario or of Quebec otherwise provides, a Person accepting or holding in Ontario or in Quebec any Office, Commission, or Employment, permanent or temporary, at the Nomination of the Lieutenant Governor, to which an annual Salary, or any Fee,

Restriction on election of Holders of offices

Allowance, Emolument, or Profit of any Kind or Amount whatever from the Province is attached, shall not be eligible as a Member of the Legislative Assembly of the respective Province, nor shall he sit or vote as such; but nothing in this Section shall make ineligible any Person being a Member of the Executive Council of the respective Province, or holding any of the following Offices, that is to say, the Offices of Attorney General, Secretary and Registrar of the Province, Treasurer of the Province, Commissioner of Crown Lands, and Commissioner of Agriculture and Public Works, and in Quebec Solicitor General, or shall disqualify him to sit or vote in the House for which he is elected, provided he is elected while holding such Office.

[Note: See also the *Legislative Assembly Act* (Ontario) and the *National Assembly Act* (Quebec).]

Continuance of existing Election Laws

84. Until the Legislatures of Ontario and Quebec respectively otherwise provide, all Laws which at the Union are in force in those Provinces respectively, relative to the following Matters, or any of them, namely,— the Qualifications and Disqualifications of Persons to be elected or to sit or vote as Members of the Assembly of Canada, the Qualifications or Disqualifications of Voters, the Oaths to be taken by Voters, the Returning Officers, their Powers and Duties, the Proceedings at Elections, the Periods during which such Elections may be continued, and the Trial of controverted Elections and the Proceedings incident thereto, the vacating of the Seats of Members and the issuing and execution of new Writs in case of Seats vacated otherwise than by Dissolution,—shall respectively apply to Elections of Members to serve in the respective Legislative Assemblies of Ontario and Quebec.

Provided that, until the Legislature of Ontario otherwise provides, at any Election for a Member of the Legislative Assembly of Ontario for the District of Algoma, in addition to Persons qualified by the Law of the Province of Canada to vote, every Male British Subject, aged Twenty-one Years or upwards, being a Householder, shall have a Vote.

[Note: See also the *Election Act* and *Legislative Assembly Act* (Ontario) and the *Elections Act* and *National Assembly Act* (Quebec).]

Duration of Legislative Assemblies

85. Every Legislative Assembly of Ontario and every Legislative Assembly of Quebec shall continue for Four Years from the Day of the Return of the Writs for choosing the same (subject nevertheless to either the Legislative Assembly of Ontario or the Legislative Assembly of Quebec being sooner dissolved by the Lieutenant Governor of the Province), and no longer.

[Note: Now five years in both provinces: see the *Legislative Assembly Act* (Ontario) and the *National Assembly Act* (Quebec). See also section 4 of the *Constitution Act, 1982* (No. 44 *infra*).]

Yearly Session of Legislature

86. There shall be a Session of the Legislature of Ontario and of that of Quebec once at least in every Year, so that Twelve Months shall not intervene between the last sitting of the Legislature in each Province in one Session and its first Sitting in the next Session.

[Note: See section 5 of the *Constitution Act, 1982* (No. 44 *infra*).]

Speaker, Quorum, etc.

87. The following Provisions of this Act respecting the House of Commons of Canada shall extend and apply to the Legislative Assemblies of Ontario and Quebec, that is to say,—the Provisions relating to the

Election of a Speaker originally and on Vacancies, the Duties of the Speaker, the Absence of the Speaker, the Quorum, and the Mode of voting, as if those Provisions were here re-enacted and made applicable in Terms to each such Legislative Assembly.

4. NOVA SCOTIA AND NEW BRUNSWICK

88. The Constitution of the Legislature of each of the Provinces of Nova Scotia and New Brunswick shall, subject to the Provisions of this Act, continue as it exists at the Union until altered under the Authority of this Act; *and the House of Assembly of New Brunswick existing at the passing of this Act shall, unless sooner dissolved, continue for the Period for which it was elected.*

[Note: The words in italics were repealed by the *Statute Law Revision Act, 1893* (No. 17 *infra*). The note to section 64 also applies to the Legislatures of the provinces mentioned therein. See also sections 3 to 5 of the *Constitution Act, 1982* (No. 44 *infra*) and sub-item 2(2) of the Schedule to that Act.]

Constitutions of Legislatures of Nova Scotia and New Brunswick

5. ONTARIO, QUEBEC, AND NOVA SCOTIA

89. *Each of the Lieutenant Governors of Ontario, Quebec and Nova Scotia shall cause Writs to be issued for the First Election of Members of the Legislative Assembly thereof in such Form and by such Person as he thinks fit, and at such Time and addressed to such Returning Officer as the Governor General directs, and so that the First Election of Member of Assembly for any Electoral District or any Subdivision thereof shall be held at the same Time and at the same Places as the Election for a Member to serve in the House of Commons of Canada for that Electoral District.*

[Note: Repealed by the *Statute Law Revision Act, 1893* (No. 17 *infra*).]

First Elections

6. THE FOUR PROVINCES

90. The following Provisions of this Act respecting the Parliament of Canada, namely,—the Provisions relating to Appropriation and Tax Bills, the Recommendation of Money Votes, the Assent to Bills, the Disallowance of Acts, and the Signification of Pleasure on Bills reserved,—shall extend and apply to the Legislatures of the several Provinces as if those Provisions were here re-enacted and made applicable in Terms to the respective Provinces and the Legislatures thereof, with the Substitution of the Lieutenant Governor of the Province for the Governor General, of the Governor General for the Queen and for a Secretary of State, of One Year for Two Years, and of the Province for Canada.

Application to Legislatures of Provisions respecting Money Votes, etc.

VI. DISTRIBUTION OF LEGISLATIVE POWERS

Powers of the Parliament

91. It shall be lawful for the Queen, by and with the Advice and Consent of the Senate and House of Commons, to make Laws for the Peace, Order, and good Government of Canada, in relation to all Matters not coming within the Classes of Subjects by this Act assigned exclusively to the Legislatures of the Provinces; and for greater Certainty, but not so as to restrict the Generality of the foregoing Terms of this Section, it

Legislative Authority of Parliament of Canada

is hereby declared that (notwithstanding anything in this Act) the exclusive Legislative Authority of the Parliament of Canada extends to all Matters coming within the Classes of Subjects next hereinafter enumerated; that is to say,—

Amendment as to legislative authority of Parliament of Canada

1. *The amendment from time to time of the Constitution of Canada, except as regards matters coming within the classes of subjects by this Act assigned exclusively to the Legislatures of the provinces, or as regards rights or privileges by this or any other Constitutional Act granted or secured to the Legislature or the Government of a province, or to any class of persons with respect to schools or as regards the use of the English or the French language or as regards the requirements that there shall be a session of the Parliament of Canada at least once each year, and that no House of Commons shall continue for more than five years from the day of the return of the Writs for choosing the House: Provided, however, that a House of Commons may in time of real or apprehended war, invasion or insurrection be continued by the Parliament of Canada if such continuation is not opposed by the votes of more than one-third of the members of such House.*

[Note: Class 1 was added by the *British North America Act (No. 2), 1949* (No. 33 *infra*) and repealed by the *Constitution Act, 1982* (No. 44 *infra*).]

1A.   The Public Debt and Property.

[Note: Re-numbered 1A by the *British North America Act (No. 2), 1949* No. 33 *infra*).]

2. The Regulation of Trade and Commerce.

2A.   Unemployment insurance.

[Note: Added by the *Constitution Act, 1940* (No. 28 *infra*).]

3. The raising of Money by any Mode or System of Taxation.

4. The borrowing of Money on the Public Credit.

5. Postal Service.

6. The Census and Statistics.

7. Militia, Military and Naval Service, and Defence.

8. The fixing of and providing for the Salaries and Allowances of Civil and other Officers of the Government of Canada.

9. Beacons, Buoys, Lighthouses, and Sable Island.

10. Navigation and Shipping.

11. Quarantine and the Establishment and Maintenance of Marine Hospitals.

12. Sea Coast and Inland Fisheries.

13. Ferries between a Province and any British or Foreign Country or between Two Provinces.

14. Currency and Coinage.

15. Banking, Incorporation of Banks, and the Issue of Paper Money.

16. Savings Banks.

17. Weights and Measures.

18. Bills of Exchange and Promissory Notes.

19. Interest.

20. Legal Tender.

21. Bankruptcy and Insolvency.

22. Patents of Invention and Discovery.

23. Copyrights.

24. Indians, and Lands reserved for the Indians.

25. Naturalization and Aliens.

26. Marriage and Divorce.

27. The Criminal Law, except the Constitution of Courts of Criminal Jurisdiction, but including the Procedure in Criminal Matters.

28. The Establishment, Maintenance, and Management of Penitentiaries.

29. Such Classes of Subjects as are expressly excepted in the Enumeration of the Classes of Subjects by this Act assigned exclusively to the Legislatures of the Provinces.

And any Matter coming within any of the Classes of Subjects enumerated in this Section shall not be deemed to come within the Class of Matters of a local or private Nature comprised in the Enumeration of the Classes of Subjects by this Act assigned exclusively to the Legislatures of the Provinces.

[Note: Legislative authority has also been conferred by the *Rupert's Land Act, 1868* (No. 6 *infra*), *Constitution Act, 1871* (No. 11 *infra*), *Constitution Act, 1886* (No. 15 *infra*), *Statute of Westminster, 1931* (No. 27 *infra*) and section 44 of the *Constitution Act, 1982* (No. 44 *infra*), and see also sections 38 and 41 to 43 of the latter Act.]

Exclusive Powers of Provincial Legislatures

92. In each Province the Legislature may exclusively make Laws in relation to Matters coming within the Classes of Subjects next hereinafter enumerated; that is to say,—

Subjects of exclusive Provincial Legislation

1. *The Amendment from Time to Time, notwithstanding anything in this Act, of the Constitution of the Province, except as regards the Office of Lieutenant Governor.*

[Note: Class 1 was repealed by the *Constitution Act, 1982* (No. 44 *infra*). The subject is now provided for in section 45 of that Act, and see also sections 38 and 41 to 43 of the same Act.]

2. Direct Taxation with-in the Province in order to the raising of a Revenue for Provincial Purposes.

3. The borrowing of Money on the sole Credit of the Province.

4. The Establishment and Tenure of Provincial Offices and the Appointment and Payment of Provincial Officers.

5. The Management and Sale of the Public Lands belonging to the Province and of the Timber and Wood thereon.

6. The Establishment, Maintenance, and Management of Public and Reformatory Prisons in and for the Province.

7. The Establishment, Maintenance, and Management of Hospitals, Asylums, Charities, and Eleemosynary Institutions in and for the Province, other than Marine Hospitals.

8. Municipal Institutions in the Province.

9. Shop, Saloon, Tavern, Auctioneer, and other Licences in order to the raising of a Revenue for Provincial, Local, or Municipal Purposes.

10. Local Works and Undertakings other than such as are of the following Classes:—

a. Lines of Steam or other Ships, Railways, Canals, Telegraphs, and other Works and Undertakings connecting the Province with any other or others of the Provinces, or extending beyond the Limits of the Province:

b. Lines of Steam Ships between the Province and any British or Foreign Country:

c. Such Works as, although wholly situate within the Province, are before or after their Execution declared by the Parliament of Canada to be for the general Advantage of Canada or for the Advantage of Two or more of the Provinces.

11. The Incorporation of Companies with Provincial Objects.

12. The Solemnization of Marriage in the Province.

13. Property and Civil Rights in the Province.

14. The Administration of Justice in the Province, including the Constitution, Maintenance, and Organization of Provincial Courts, both of Civil and of Criminal Jurisdiction, and including Procedure in Civil Matters in those Courts.

15. The Imposition of Punishment by Fine, Penalty, or Imprisonment for enforcing any Law of the Province made in relation to any Matter coming within any of the Classes of Subjects enumerated in this Section.

16. Generally all Matters of a merely local or private Nature in the Province.

Non-Renewable Natural Resources, Forestry Resources and Electrical Energy

Laws respecting non-renewable natural resources, forestry resources and electrical energy

92A. (1) In each pro-vince, the legislature may exclusively make laws in relation to

(a) exploration for non-renewable natural resources in the province;

(b) development, conservation and management of non-renewable natural resources and forestry resources in the province, including laws in relation to the rate of primary production therefrom; and

(c) development, conservation and management of sites and facilities in the province for the generation and production of electrical energy.

Export from provinces of resources

(2) In each province, the legislature may make laws in relation to the export from the province to another part of Canada of the primary production from non-renewable natural resources and forestry resources in the province and the production from facilities in the province for the generation of electrical energy, but such laws may not authorize or provide for discrimination in prices or in supplies exported to another part of Canada.

Authority of Parliament

(3) Nothing in subsection (2) derogates from the authority of Parliament to enact laws in relation to the matters referred to in that subsection and, where such a law of Parliament and a law of a province conflict, the law of Parliament prevails to the extent of the conflict.

Taxation of resources

(4) In each province, the legislature may make laws in relation to the raising of money by any mode or system of taxation in respect of

(a) Non-renewable natural resources and forestry resources in the province and the primary production therefrom, and

(b) sites and facilities in the province for the generation of electrical energy and the production therefrom,

whether or not such production is exported in whole or in part from the province, but such laws may not authorize or provide for taxation that differentiates between production exported to another part of Canada and production not exported from the province.

(5) The expression "primary production" has the meaning assigned by the Sixth Schedule.

"Primary production"

(6) Nothing in subsections (1) to (5) derogates from any powers or rights that a legislature or government of a province had immediately before the coming into force of this section.

Existing powers or rights

[Note: Added by section 50 of the *Constitution Act, 1982* (No. 44 *infra*).]

Education

93. In and for each Province the Legislature may exclusively make Laws in relation to Education, subject and according to the following Provisions:—

Legislation respecting Education

(1) Nothing in any such Law shall prejudicially affect any Right or Privilege with respect to Denominational Schools which any Class of Persons have by Law in the Province at the Union:

(2) All the Powers, Privileges, and Duties at the Union by Law conferred and imposed in Upper Canada on the Separate Schools and School Trustees of the Queen's Roman Catholic Subjects shall be and the same are hereby extended to the Dissentient Schools of the Queen's Protestant and Roman Catholic Subjects in Quebec:

(3) Where in any Province a System of Separate or Dissentient Schools exists by Law at the Union or is thereafter established by the Legislature of the Province, an Appeal shall lie to the Governor General in Council from any Act or Decision of any Provincial Authority affecting any Right or Privilege of the Protestant or Roman Catholic Minority of the Queen's Subjects in relation to Education:

(4) In case any such Provincial Law as from Time to Time seems to the Governor General in Council requisite for the due Execution of the Provisions of this Section is not made, or in case any Decision of the Governor General in Council on any Appeal under this Section is not duly executed by the proper Provincial Authority in that Behalf, then and in every such Case, and as far only as the Circumstances of each Case require, the Parliament of Canada may make remedial Laws for the due Execution of the Provisions of this Section and of any Decision of the Governor General in Council under this Section.

[Note: Altered for Manitoba by section 22 of the *Manitoba Act, 1870* (No. 8 *infra*) confirmed by the *Constitution Act, 1871* No. 11 *infra*); for Alberta, by section 17 of the *Alberta Act* (No. 20 *infra*); for Saskatchewan, by section 17 of the *Saskatchewan Act* (No. 21 *infra*); and for Newfoundland, by Term 17 of the Terms of Union of Newfoundland with Canada, confirmed by the *Newfoundland Act* (No. 32 *infra*). See also sections 23, 29 and 59 of the *Constitution Act, 1982* (No. 44 *infra*).]

Uniformity of Laws in Ontario, Nova Scotia, and New Brunswick

94. Notwithstanding anything in this Act, the Parliament of Canada may make Provision for the Uniformity of all or any of the Laws relative

Legislation for Uniformity of Laws in Three Provinces

to Property and Civil Rights in Ontario, Nova Scotia, and New Brunswick, and of the Procedure of all or any of the Courts in those Three Provinces, and from and after the passing of any Act in that Behalf the Power of the Parliament of Canada to make Laws in relation to any Matter comprised in any such Act shall, notwithstanding anything in this Act, be unrestricted; but any Act of the Parliament of Canada making Provision for such Uniformity shall not have effect in any Province unless and until it is adopted and enacted as Law by the Legislature thereof.

94A. The Parliament of Canada may make laws in relation to old age pensions and supplementary benefits, including survivors' and disability benefits irrespective of age, but no such law shall affect the operation of any law present or future of a provincial legislature in relation to any such matter.

Legislation respecting old age pensions and supplementary benefits

[Note: Substituted by the *Constitution Act, 1964* (No. 38 *infra*) for the section 94A that was originally added by the *British North America Act, 1951* (No. 35 *infra*).]

Agriculture and Immigration

95. In each Province the Legislature may make Laws in relation to Agriculture in the Province, and to Immigration into the Province; and it is hereby declared that the Parliament of Canada may from Time to Time make Laws in relation to Agriculture in all or any of the Provinces, and to Immigration into all or any of the Provinces; and any Law of the Legislature of a Province relative to Agriculture or to Immigration shall have effect in and for the Province as long and as far only as it is not repugnant to any Act of the Parliament of Canada.

Concurrent Powers of Legislation respecting Agriculture, etc.

VII. JUDICATURE

96. The Governor General shall appoint the Judges of the Superior, District, and County Courts in each Province, except those of the Courts of Probate in Nova Scotia and New Brunswick.

Appointment of Judges

97. Until the Laws relative to Property and Civil Rights in Ontario, Nova Scotia, and New Brunswick, and the Procedure of the Courts in those Provinces, are made uniform, the Judges of the Courts of those Provinces appointed by the Governor General shall be selected from the respective Bars of those Provinces.

Selections of Judges in Ontario, etc.

98. The Judges of the Courts of Quebec shall be selected from the Bar of that Province.

Selection of Judges in Quebec

99. *The Judges of the Superior Courts shall hold Office during good Behaviour, but shall be removable by the Governor General on Address of the Senate and House of Commons.*

Tenure of Office of Judges of Superior Courts

99. (1) Subject to subsection (2) of this section, the judges of the superior courts shall hold office during good behaviour, but shall be removable by the Governor General on address of the Senate and House of Commons.

Tenure of office of judges

(2) A judge of a superior court, whether appointed before or after the coming into force of this section, shall cease to hold office upon attaining the age of seventy-five years, or upon the coming into force of this section if at that time he has already attained that age.

[Note: Section 99 (in italics) was repealed and the new section substituted by the *Constitution Act, 1960* (No. 37 *infra*).]

100. The Salaries, Allowances, and Pensions of the Judges of the Superior, District, and County Courts (except the Courts of Probate in Nova Scotia and New Brunswick), and of the Admiralty Courts in Cases where the Judges thereof are for the Time being paid by Salary, shall be fixed and provided by the Parliament of Canada.
[Note: See the *Judges Act* (Canada).]

Salaries, etc., of Judges

101. The Parliament of Canada may, notwithstanding anything in this Act, from Time to Time provide for the Constitution, Maintenance, and Organization of a General Court of Appeal for Canada, and for the Establishment of any additional Courts for the better Administration of the Laws of Canada.
[Note: See the *Supreme Court Act, Federal Court Act* and *Tax Court of Canada Act* (Canada).]

General Court of Appeal, etc.

VIII. Revenues; Debts; Assets; Taxation

102. All Duties and Revenues over which the respective Legislatures of Canada, Nova Scotia, and New Brunswick before and at the Union had and have Power of Appropriation, except such Portions thereof as are by this Act reserved to the respective Legislatures of the Provinces, or are raised by them in accordance with the special Powers conferred on them by this Act, shall form One Consolidated Revenue Fund, to be appropriated for the Public Service of Canada in the Manner and subject to the Charges in this Act provided.

Creation of Consolidated Revenue Fund

103. The Consolidated Revenue Fund of Canada shall be permanently charged with the Costs, Charges, and Expenses incident to the Collection, Management, and Receipt thereof, and the same shall form the First Charge thereon, subject to be reviewed and audited in such Manner as shall be ordered by the Governor General in Council until the Parliament otherwise provides.

Expenses of Collection, etc.

104. The annual Interest of the Public Debts of the several Provinces of Canada, Nova Scotia, and New Brunswick at the Union shall form the Second Charge on the Consolidated Revenue Fund of Canada.

Interest of Provincial Public Debts

105. Unless altered by the Parliament of Canada, the Salary of the Governor General shall be Ten thousand Pounds Sterling Money of the United Kingdom of Great Britain and Ireland, payable out of the Consolidated Revenue Fund of Canada, and the same shall form the Third Charge thereon.
[Note: See the *Governor General's Act* (Canada).]

Salary of Governor General

106. Subject to the several Payments by this Act charged on the Consolidated Revenue Fund of Canada, the same shall be appropriated by the Parliament of Canada for the Public Service.

Appropriation from Time to Time

107. All Stocks, Cash, Banker's Balances, and Securities for Money belonging to each Province at the Time of the Union, except as in this Act mentioned, shall be the Property of Canada, and shall be taken in Reduction of the Amount of the respective Debts of the Provinces at the Union.

Transfer of Stocks, etc.

Transfer of Property in Schedule

108. The Public Works and Property of each Province, enumerated in the Third Schedule to this Act, shall be the Property of Canada.

Property in Lands, Mines, etc.

109. All Lands, Mines, Minerals, and Royalties belonging to the several Provinces of Canada, Nova Scotia, and New Brunswick at the Union, and all Sums then due or payable for such Lands, Mines, Minerals, or Royalties, shall belong to the several Provinces of Ontario, Quebec, Nova Scotia, and New Brunswick in which the same are situate or arise, subject to any Trusts existing in respect thereof, and to any Interest other than that of the Province in the same.

[Note: The Provinces of Manitoba, British Columbia, Alberta and Saskatchewan were placed in the same position as the original provinces by the *Constitution Act, 1930* (No. 26 *infra*).

Newfoundland was also placed in the same position by the *Newfoundland Act* (No. 32 *infra*).

With respect to Prince Edward Island, see the Schedule to the *Prince Edward Island Terms of Union* (No. 12 *infra*).]

Assets connected with Provincial Debts

110. All Assets connected with such Portions of the Public Debt of each Province as are assumed by that Province shall belong to that Province.

Canada to be liable for Provincial Debts

111. Canada shall be liable for the Debts and Liabilities of each province existing at the Union.

Debts of Ontario and Quebec

112. Ontario and Quebec conjointly shall be liable to Canada for the Amount (if any) by which the Debt of the Province of Canada exceeds at the Union Sixty-two million five hundred thousand Dollars, and shall be charged with Interest at the Rate of Five per Centum per Annum thereon.

Assets of Ontario and Quebec

113. The Assets enumerated in the Fourth Schedule to this Act belonging at the Union to the Province of Canada shall be the Property of Ontario and Quebec conjointly.

Debt of Nova Scotia

114. Nova Scotia shall be liable to Canada for the Amount (if any) by which its Public Debt exceeds at the Union Eight million Dollars, and shall be charged with Interest at the Rate of Five per Centum per Annum thereon.

[Note: As to sections 114, 115 and 116, see the *Provincial Subsidies Act* (Canada).]

Debt of New Brunswick

115. New Brunswick shall be liable to Canada for the Amount (if any) by which its Public Debt exceeds at the Union Seven million Dollars, and shall be charged with Interest at the Rate of Five per Centum per Annum thereon.

Payment of interest to Nova Scotia and New Brunswick

116. In case the Public Debts of Nova Scotia and New Brunswick do not at the Union amount to Eight million and Seven million Dollars respectively, they shall respectively receive by half-yearly Payments in advance from the Government of Canada Interest at Five per Centum per Annum on the Difference between the actual Amounts of their respective Debts and such stipulated Amounts.

Provincial Public Property

117. The several Provinces shall retain all their respective Public Property not otherwise disposed of in this Act, subject to the Right of Canada to assume any Lands or Public Property required for Fortifications or for the Defence of the Country.

118. *The following Sums shall be paid yearly by Canada to the several Provinces for the Support of their Governments and Legislatures:*

Grants to Provinces

	Dollars
Ontario	*Eighty thousand.*
Quebec	*Seventy thousand.*
Nova Scotia	*Sixty thousand.*
New Brunswick	*Fifty thousand*

Two hundred and sixty thousand;

and an annual Grant in aid of each Province shall be made, equal to Eighty Cents per Head of the Population as ascertained by the Census of One thousand eight hundred and sixty-one, and in the Case of Nova Scotia and New Brunswick, by each subsequent Decennial Census until the Population of each of those two Provinces amounts to Four hundred thousand Souls, at which Rate such Grant shall thereafter remain. Such Grants shall be in full Settlement of all future Demands on Canada, and shall be paid half-yearly in advance to each Province; but the Government of Canada shall deduct from such Grants, as against any Province, all Sums chargeable as Interest on the Public Debt of that Province in excess of the several Amounts stipulated in this Act.

[Note: Repealed by the *Statute Law Revision Act, 1950* (No. 34 *infra*). The section had been previously superseded by the *Constitution Act, 1907* (No. 22 *infra*). See the *Provincial Subsidies Act* and the *Federal-Provincial Fiscal Arrangements and Federal Post-Secondary Education and Health Contributions Act* (Canada).]

119. New Brunswick shall receive by half-yearly Payments in advance from Canada for the Period of Ten Years from the Union an additional Allowance of Sixty-three thousand Dollars per Annum; but as long as the Public Debt of that Province remains under Seven million Dollars, a Deduction equal to the Interest at Five per Centum per Annum on such Deficiency shall be made from that Allowance of Sixty-three thousand Dollars.

Further Grant to New Brunswick

120. All Payments to be made under this Act, or in discharge of Liabilities created under any Act of the Provinces of Canada, Nova Scotia, and New Brunswick respectively, and assumed by Canada, shall, until the Parliament of Canada otherwise directs, be made in such Form and Manner as may from Time to Time be ordered by the Governor General in Council.

Form of Payments

121. All Articles of the Growth, Produce, or Manufacture of any one of the Provinces shall, from and after the Union, be admitted free into each of the other Provinces.

Canadian manufactures, etc.

122. The Customs and Excise Laws of each Province shall, subject to the Provisions of this Act, continue in force until altered by the Parliament of Canada.

[Note: See the current federal customs and excise legislation.]

Continuance of Customs and Excise Laws

123. Where Customs Duties are, at the Union, leviable on any Goods, Wares, or Merchandises in any Two Provinces, those Goods, Wares, and Merchandises may, from and after the Union, be imported from one of those Provinces into the other of them on Proof of Payment of the Customs Duty leviable thereon in the Province of Exportation, and on Payment of

Exportation and Importation as between Two Provinces

such further Amount (if any) of Customs Duty as is leviable thereon in the Province of Importation.

Lumber Dues in New Brunswick

124. Nothing in this Act shall affect the Right of New Brunswick to levy the Lumber Dues provided in Chapter Fifteen of Title Three of the Revised Statutes of New Brunswick, or in any Act amending that Act before or after the Union, and not increasing the Amount of such Dues; but the Lumber of any of the Provinces other than New Brunswick shall not be subject to such Dues.

Exemption of Public Lands, etc.

125. No Lands or Property belonging to Canada or any Province shall be liable to Taxation.

Provincial Consolidated Revenue Fund

126. Such Portions of the Duties and Revenues over which the respective Legislatures of Canada, Nova Scotia, and New Brunswick had before the Union Power of Appropriation as are by this Act reserved to the respective Governments or Legislatures of the Provinces, and all Duties and Revenues raised by them in accordance with the special Powers conferred upon them by this Act, shall in each Province form One Consolidated Revenue Fund to be appropriated for the Public Service of the Province.

IX. MISCELLANEOUS PROVISIONS

General

As to Legislative Councillors of Provinces becoming senators

127. *If any Person being at the passing of this Act a Member of the Legislative Council of Canada, Nova Scotia, or New Brunswick, to whom a Place in the Senate is offered, does not within Thirty Days thereafter, by Writing under his Hand addressed to the Governor General of the Province of Canada or to the Lieutenant Governor of Nova Scotia or New Brunswick (as the Case may be), accept the same, he shall be deemed to have declined the same; and any Person who, being at the passing of this Act a Member of the Legislative Council of Nova Scotia or New Brunswick, accepts a Place in the Senate, shall thereby vacate his Seat in such Legislative Council.*

[Note: Repealed by the *Statute Law Revision Act, 1893* (No. 17 *infra*).]

Oath of Allegiance, etc.

128. Every Member of the Senate or House of Commons of Canada shall before taking his Seat therein take and subscribe before the Governor General or some Person authorized by him, and every Member of a Legislative Council or Legislative Assembly of any Province shall before taking his Seat therein take and subscribe before the Lieutenant Governor of the Province or some Person authorized by him, the Oath of Allegiance contained in the Fifth Schedule to this Act; and every Member of the Senate of Canada and every Member of the Legislative Council of Quebec shall also, before taking his Seat therein, take and subscribe before the Governor General, or some Person authorized by him, the Declaration of Qualification contained in the same Schedule.

Continuance of existing Laws, Courts, Officers, etc.

129. Except as otherwise provided by this Act, all Laws in force in Canada, Nova Scotia, or New Brunswick at the Union, and all Courts of Civil and Criminal Jurisdiction, and all legal Commissions, Powers, and Authorities, and all Officers, Judicial, Administrative, and Ministerial, existing therein at the Union, shall continue in Ontario, Quebec, Nova

Scotia, and New Brunswick respectively, as if the Union had not been made; subject nevertheless (except with respect to such as are enacted by or exist under Acts of the Parliament of Great Britain or of the Parliament of the United Kingdom of Great Britain and Ireland,) to be repealed, abolished, or altered by the Parliament of Canada, or by the Legislature of the respective Province, according to the Authority of the Parliament or of that Legislature under this Act.

[Note: The restriction against altering or repealing laws enacted by or existing under statutes of the United Kingdom was removed by the *Statute of Westminster, 1931* (No. 27 *infra*), except in respect of certain constitutional documents. See also Part V of the *Constitution Act, 1982* (No. 44 *infra*).]

130. Until the Parliament of Canada otherwise provides, all Officers of the several Provinces having Duties to discharge in relation to Matters other than those coming within the Classes of Subjects by this Act assigned exclusively to the Legislatures of the Provinces shall be Officers of Canada, and shall continue to discharge the Duties of their respective Offices under the same Liabilities, Responsibilities, and Penalties as if the Union had not been made.

Transfer of Officers to Canada

131. Until the Parliament of Canada otherwise provides, the Governor General in Council may from Time to Time appoint such Officers as the Governor General in Council deems necessary or proper for the effectual Execution of this Act.

Appointment of new Officers

132. The Parliament and Government of Canada shall have all Powers necessary or proper for performing the Obligations of Canada or of any Province thereof, as Part of the British Empire, towards Foreign Countries, arising under Treaties between the Empire and such Foreign Countries.

Treaty Obligations

133. Either the English or the French Language may be used by any Person in the Debates of the Houses of the Parliament of Canada and of the Houses of the Legislature of Quebec; and both those Languages shall be used in the respective Records and Journals of those Houses; and either of those Languages may be used by any Person or in any Pleading or Process in or issuing from any Court of Canada established under this Act, and in or from all or any of the Courts of Quebec.

Use of English and French Languages

The Acts of the Parliament of Canada and of the Legislature of Quebec shall be printed and published in both those Languages.

[Note: See also section 23 of the *Manitoba Act, 1870* (No. 8 *infra*) and sections 17 to 23 of the *Constitution Act, 1982* (No. 44 *infra*).]

Ontario and Quebec

134. Until the Legislature of Ontario or of Quebec otherwise provides, the Lieutenant Governors of Ontario and Quebec may each appoint under the Great Seal of the Province the following Officers, to hold Office during Pleasure, that is to say,—the Attorney General, the Secretary and Registrar of the Province, the Treasurer of the Province, the Commissioner of Crown Lands, and the Commissioner of Agriculture and Public Works, and in the Case of Quebec the Solicitor General, and may, by Order of the Lieutenant Governor in Council, from Time to Time prescribe the Duties of those Officers, and of the several Departments over which they shall preside or to which they shall belong, and of the Officers and Clerks

Appointment of Executive Officers for Ontario and Quebec

thereof, and may also appoint other and additional Officers to hold Office during Pleasure, and may from Time to Time prescribe the Duties of those Officers, and of the several Departments over which they shall preside or to which they shall belong, and of the Officers and Clerks thereof.

[Note: See the *Executive Council Act* (Ontario) and the *Executive Power Act* (Quebec).]

Powers, Duties, etc. of Executive Officers

135. Until the Legislature of Ontario or Quebec otherwise provides, all Rights, Powers, Duties, Functions, Responsibilities, or authorities at the passing of this Act vested in or imposed on the Attorney General, Solicitor General, Secretary and Registrar of the Province of Canada, Minister of Finance, Commissioner of Crown Lands, Commissioner of Public Works, and Minister of Agriculture and Receiver General, by any Law, Statute, or Ordinance of Upper Canada, Lower Canada, or Canada, and not repugnant to this Act, shall be vested in or imposed on any Officer to be appointed by the Lieutenant Governor for the Discharge of the same or any of them; and the Commissioner of Agriculture and Public Works shall perform the Duties and Functions of the Office of Minister of Agriculture at the passing of this Act imposed by the Law of the Province of Canada, as well as those of the Commissioner of Public Works.

Great Seals

136. Until altered by the Lieutenant Governor in Council, the Great Seals of Ontario and Quebec respectively shall be the same, or of the same Design, as those used in the Provinces of Upper Canada and Lower Canada respectively before their Union as the Province of Canada.

Construction of temporary Acts

137. The Words "and from thence to the End of the then next ensuing Session of the Legislature," or Words to the same Effect, used in any temporary Act of the Province of Canada not expired before the Union, shall be construed to extend and apply to the next Session of the Parliament of Canada if the Subject Matter of the Act is within the Powers of the same as defined by this Act, or to the next Sessions of the Legislatures of Ontario and Quebec respectively if the Subject Matter of the Act is within the Powers of the same as defined by this Act.

As to Errors in Names

138. From and after the Union the Use of the Words "Upper Canada" instead of "Ontario," or "Lower Canada" instead of "Quebec," in any Deed, Writ, Process, Pleading, Document, Matter, or Thing, shall not invalidate the same.

As to Issue of Proclamations after Union

139. Any Proclamation under the Great Seal of the Province of Canada issued before the Union to take effect at a Time which is subsequent to the Union, whether relating to that Province, or to Upper Canada, or to Lower Canada, and the several Matters and Things therein proclaimed, shall be and continue of like Force and Effect as if the Union had not been made.

As to issue of Proclamations before Union, to commence after Union

140. Any Proclamation which is authorized by any Act of the Legislature of the Province of Canada to be issued under the Great Seal of the Province of Canada, whether relating to that Province, or to Upper Canada, or to Lower Canada, and which is not issued before the Union, may be issued by the Lieutenant Governor of Ontario or of Quebec, as its Subject Matter requires, under the Great Seal thereof; and from and after the Issue of such Proclamation the same and the several Matters and Things therein proclaimed shall be and continue of the like force and Effect in Ontario or Quebec as if the Union had not been made.

141. The Penitentiary of the Province of Canada shall, until the Parliament of Canada otherwise provides, be and continue the Penitentiary of Ontario and of Quebec.

[Note: See the *Penitentiary Act* (Canada).]

Penitentiary

142. The Division and Adjustment of the Debts, Credits, Liabilities, Properties, and Assets of Upper Canada and Lower Canada shall be referred to the Arbitrament of Three Arbitrators, One chosen by the government of Ontario, One by the Government of Quebec, and One by the Government of Canada; and the Selection of the Arbitrators shall not be made until the Parliament of Canada and the Legislatures of Ontario and Quebec have met; and the Arbitrator chosen by the Government of Canada shall not be a Resident either in Ontario or in Quebec.

Arbitration respecting Debts, etc.

143. The Governor General in Council may from Time to Time order that such and so many of the Records, Books, and Documents of the Province of Canada as he thinks fit shall be appropriated and delivered either to Ontario or to Quebec, and the same shall thenceforth be the Property of that Province; and any Copy thereof or Extract therefrom, duly certified by the Officer having charge of the Original thereof, shall be admitted as Evidence.

Division of Records

144. The Lieutenant Governor of Quebec may from Time to Time, by Proclamation under the Great Seal of the Province, to take effect from a Day to be appointed therein, constitute Townships in those Parts of the Province of Quebec in which Townships are not then already constituted, and fix the Metes and Bounds thereof.

Constitution of Townships in Quebec

X. Intercolonial Railway

145. *Inasmuch as the Provinces of Canada, Nova Scotia, and New Brunswick have joined in a Declaration that the Construction of the Intercolonial Railway is essential to the Consolidation of the Union of British North America, and to the Assent thereto of Nova Scotia and New Brunswick, and have consequently agreed that Provision should be made for its immediate Construction by the Government of Canada: Therefore, in order to give effect to that Agreement, it shall be the Duty of the Government and Parliament of Canada to provide for the Commencement, within Six Months after the Union, of a Railway connecting the River St. Lawrence with the City of Halifax in Nova Scotia, and for the Construction thereof without Intermission, and the Completion thereof with all practicable speed.*

[Note: Repealed by the *Statute Law Revision Act, 1893* (No. 17 *infra*).]

Duty of Government and Parliament of Canada to make Railway herein described

XI. Admission of Other Colonies

146. It shall be lawful for the Queen, by and with the Advice of Her Majesty's Most Honourable Privy Council, on Addresses from the Houses of the Parliament of Canada, and from the Houses of the respective Legislatures of the Colonies or Provinces of Newfoundland, Prince Edward Island, and British Columbia, to admit those Colonies or Provinces, or any of them, into the Union, and on Address from the

Power to admit Newfoundland, etc., into the Union

Houses of the Parliament of Canada to admit Rupert's Land and the North-western Territory, or either of them, into the Union, on such Terms and Conditions in each Case as are in the Addresses expressed and as the Queen thinks fit to approve, subject to the Provisions of this Act; and the Provisions of any Order in Council in that Behalf shall have effect as if they had been enacted by the Parliament of the United Kingdom of Great Britain and Ireland.

[Note: Rupert's Land and the North-Western Territory (subsequently designated the Northwest Territories) became part of Canada, pursuant to this section and the *Rupert's Land Act, 1868* (No. 6 *infra*), by the *Rupert's Land and North-Western Territory Order* (June 23, 1870) (No. 9 *infra*).

The Province of Manitoba was established by the *Manitoba Act, 1870* (No. 8 *infra*). This Act was confirmed by the *Constitution Act, 1871* (No. 11 *infra*).

British Columbia was admitted into the Union pursuant to this section by the *British Columbia Terms of Union* (May 16, 1871) (No. 10 *infra*).

Prince Edward Island was admitted into the Union pursuant to this section by the *Prince Edward Island Terms of Union* (June 26, 1873 (No. 12 *infra*).

The Provinces of Alberta and Saskatchewan were established, pursuant to the *Constitution Act, 1871* (No. 11 *infra*), by the *Alberta Act* (July 20, 1905) (No. 20 *infra*) and the *Saskatchewan Act* (July 20, 1905) (No. 21 *infra*) respectively.

Newfoundland was admitted as a province by the *Newfoundland Act* (March 23, 1949) (No. 32 *infra*), which confirmed the Agreement containing the Terms of Union between Canada and Newfoundland.

The Yukon Territory was created out of the Northwest Territories in 1898 by *The Yukon Territory Act* (No. 19 *infra*).

As to Representation of Newfoundland and Prince Edward Island in Senate

147. In case of the Admission of Newfoundland and Prince Edward Island, or either of them, each shall be entitled to a Representation in the Senate of Canada of Four Members, and (notwithstanding anything in this Act) in case of the Admission of Newfoundland the normal Number of Senators shall be Seventy-six and their maximum Number shall be Eighty-two; but Prince Edward Island when admitted shall be deemed to be comprised in the third of the Three Divisions into which Canada is, in relation to the Constitution of the Senate, divided by this Act, and accordingly, after the Admission of Prince Edward Island, whether Newfoundland is admitted or not, the Representation of Nova Scotia and New Brunswick in the Senate shall, as Vacancies occur, be reduced from Twelve and Ten Members respectively, and the Representation of each of those Provinces shall not be increased at any Time beyond Ten, except under the Provisions of this Act for the Appointment of Three or Six additional Senators under the Direction of the Queen.

[Note: See the notes to sections 21, 22, 26, 27 and 28.]

CANADA ACT, 1982

including the

CONSTITUTION ACT, 1982

1982, c. 11 (U.K.)
[29th March 1982]

[Note: The English version of the *Canada Act 1982* is contained in the body of the Act; its French version is found in Schedule A. Schedule B contains the English and French versions of the *Constitution Act, 1982.*]

An Act to give effect to a request by the Senate and House of Commons of Canada

Whereas Canada has requested and consented to the enactment of an Act of the Parliament of the United Kingdom to give effect to the provisions hereinafter set forth and the Senate and the House of Commons of Canada in Parliament assembled have submitted an address to Her Majesty requesting that Her Majesty may graciously be pleased to cause a Bill to be laid before the Parliament of the United Kingdom for that purpose.

Be it therefore enacted by the Queen's Most Excellent Majesty, by and with the advice and consent of the Lords Spiritual and Temporal, and Commons, in this present Parliament assembled, and by the authority of the same, as follows:

1. The *Constitution Act, 1982* set out in Schedule B to this Act is hereby enacted for and shall have the force of law in Canada and shall come into force as provided in that Act.

Constitution Act, 1982 enacted

2. No Act of the Parliament of the United Kingdom passed after the *Constitution Act, 1982* comes into force shall extend to Canada as part of its law.

Termination of power to legislate for Canada

3. So far as it is not contained in Schedule B, the French version of this Act is set out in Schedule A to this Act and has the same authority in Canada as the English version thereof.

French version

4. This Act may be cited as the *Canada Act, 1982.*

Short title

SCHEDULE B

CONSTITUTION ACT, 1982

PART I

CANADIAN CHARTER OF RIGHTS AND FREEDOMS

Whereas Canada is founded upon principles that recognize the supremacy of God and the rule of law:

Guarantee of Rights and Freedoms

Rights and freedoms in Canada

1. The *Canadian Charter of Rights and Freedoms* guarantees the rights and freedoms set out in it subject only to such reasonable limits prescribed by law as can be demonstrably justified in a free and democratic society.

Fundamental Freedoms

Fundamental freedoms

2. Everyone has the following fundamental freedoms:

(a) freedom of conscience and religion;
(b) freedom of thought, belief, opinion and expression, including freedom of the press and other media of communication;
(c) freedom of peaceful assembly; and
(d) freedom of association.

Democratic Rights

Democratic rights of citizens

3. Every citizen of Canada has the right to vote in an election of members of the House of Commons or of a legislative assembly and to be qualified for membership therein.

Maximum duration of legislative bodies

4. (1) No House of Commons and no legislative assembly shall continue for longer than five years from the date fixed for the return of the writs at a general election of its members.

Continuation in special circumstances

(2) In time of real or apprehended war, invasion or insurrection, a House of Commons may be continued by Parliament and a legislative assembly may be continued by the legislature beyond five years if such continuation is not opposed by the votes of more than one-third of the members of the House of Commons or the legislative assembly, as the case may be.

Annual sitting of legislative bodies

5. There shall be a sitting of Parliament and of each legislature at least once every twelve months.

Mobility Rights

Mobility of citizens

6. (1) Every citizen of Canada has the right to enter, remain in and leave Canada.

Rights to move and gain livelihood

(2) Every citizen of Canada and every person who has the status of a permanent resident of Canada has the right
(a) to move to and take up residence in any province; and
(b) to pursue the gaining of a livelihood in any province.

Limitation

(3) The rights specified in subsection (2) are subject to

(a) any laws or practices of general application in force in a province other than those that discriminate among persons primarily on the basis of province of present or previous residence; and

(b) any laws providing for reasonable residency requirements as a qualification for the receipt of publicly provided social services.

(4) Subsections (2) and (3) do not preclude any law, program or activity that has as its object the amelioration in a province of conditions of individuals in that province who are socially or economically disadvantaged if the rate of employment in that provide is below the rate of employment in Canada.

Affirmative action programs

Legal Rights

7. Everyone has the right to life, liberty and security of the person and the right not to be deprived thereof except in accordance with the principles of fundamental justice.

Life, liberty and security of person

8. Everyone has the right to be secure against unreasonable search or seizure.

Search or seizure

9. Everyone has the right not to be arbitrarily detained or imprisoned.

Detention or imprisonment

10. Everyone has the right on arrest or detention

Arrest or detention

(a) to be informed promptly of the reasons therefor;

(b) to retain and instruct counsel without delay and to be informed of that right; and

(c) to have the validity of the detention determined by way of *habeas corpus* and to be released if the detention is not lawful.

11. Any person charged with an offence has the right

Proceedings in criminal and penal matters

(a) to be informed without unreasonable delay of the specific offence;

(b) to be tried within a reasonable time;

(c) not to be compelled to be a witness in proceedings against that person in respect of the offence;

(d) to be presumed innocent until proven guilty according to law in a fair and public hearing by an independent and impartial tribunal;

(e) not to be denied reasonable bail without just cause;

(f) except in the case of an offence under military law tried before a military tribunal, to the benefit of trial by jury where the maximum punishment for the offence is imprisonment for five years or a more severe punishment;

(g) not to be found guilty on account of any act or omission unless, at the time of the act or omission, it constituted an offence under Canadian or international law or was criminal according to the general principles of law recognized by the community of nations;

(h) if finally acquitted of the offence, not to be tried for it again and, if finally found guilty and punished for the offence, not to be tried or punished for it again; and

(i) if found guilty of the offence and if the punishment for the offence has been varied between the time of commission and the time of sentencing, to the benefit of the lesser punishment.

12. Everyone has the right not to be subjected to any cruel and unusual treatment or punishment.

Treatment or punishment

Self-crimination

13. A witness who testifies in any proceedings has the right not to have any incriminating evidence so given used to incriminate that witness in any other proceedings, except in a prosecution for perjury or for the giving of contradictory evidence.

Interpreter

14. A party or witness in any proceedings who does not understand or speak the language in which the proceedings are conducted or who is deaf has the right to the assistance of an interpreter.

Equality Rights

Equality before and under law and equal protection and benefit of law

15. (1) Every individual is equal before and under the law and has the right to the equal protection and equal benefit of the law without discrimination and, in particular, without discrimination based on race, national or ethnic origin, colour, religion, sex, age or mental or physical disability.

Affirmative action programs

(2) Subsection (1) does not preclude any law, program or activity that has as its object the amelioration of conditions of disadvantaged individuals or groups including those that are disadvantaged because of race, national or ethnic origin, colour, religion, sex, age or mental or physical disability.

[Note: This section became effective on April 17, 1985. See subsection 32(2) and the note thereto.]

Official Languages of Canada

Official languages of Canada

16. (1) English and French are the official languages of Canada and have equality of status and equal rights and privileges as to their use in all institutions of the Parliament and government of Canada.

Official languages of New Brunswick

(2) English and French are the official languages of New Brunswick and have equality of status and equal rights and privileges as to their use in all institutions of the legislature and government of New Brunswick.

Advancement of status and use

(3) Nothing in this Charter limits the authority of Parliament or a legislature to advance the equality of status or use of English and French.

Proceedings of Parliament

17. (1) Everyone has the right to use English or French in any debates and other proceedings of Parliament.

Proceedings of New Brunswick legislature

(2) Everyone has the right to use English or French in any debates and other proceedings of the legislature of New Brunswick.

Parliamentary statutes and records

18. (1) The statutes, records and journals of Parliament shall be printed and published in English and French and both language versions are equally authoritative.

New Brunswick statutes and records

(2) The statutes, records and journals of the legislature of New Brunswick shall be printed and published in English and French and both language versions are equally authoritative.

Proceedings in courts established by Parliament

19. (1) Either English or French may be used by any person in, or in any pleading in or process issuing from, any court established by Parliament.

Proceedings in New Brunswick courts

(2) Either English or French may be used by any person in, or in any pleading in or process issuing from, any court of New Brunswick.

20. (1) Any member of the public in Canada has the right to communicate with, and to receive available services from, any head or central office of an institution of the Parliament or government of Canada in English or French, and has the same right with respect to any other office of any such institution where

    (a) there is a significant demand for communications with and services from that office in such language; or

    (b) due to the nature of the office, it is reasonable that communications with and services from that office be available in both English and French.

Communications by public with federal institutions

(2) Any member of the public in New Brunswick has the right to communicate with, and to receive available services from, any office of an institution of the legislature or government of New Brunswick in English or French.

Communications by public with New Brunswick institutions

21. Nothing in sections 16 to 20 abrogates or derogates from any right, privilege or obligation with respect to the English and French languages, or either of them, that exists or is continued by virtue of any other provision of the Constitution of Canada.

Continuation of existing constitutional provisions

22. Nothing in sections 16 to 20 abrogates or derogates from any legal or customary right or privilege acquired or enjoyed either before or after the coming into force of this Charter with respect to any language that is not English or French.

Rights and privileges preserved

Minority Language Educational Rights

23. (1) Citizens of Canada

    (a) whose first language learned and still understood is that of the English or French linguistic minority population of the province in which they reside, or

    (b) who have received their primary school instruction in Canada in English or French and reside in a province where the language in which they received that instruction is the language of the English or French linguistic minority population of the province,

have the right to have their children receive primary and secondary school instruction in that language in that province.

[Note: See also section 59 and the note thereto.]

Language of instruction

(2) Citizens of Canada of whom any child has received or is receiving primary or secondary school instruction in English or French in Canada, have the right to have all their children receive primary and secondary school instruction in the same language.

Continuity of language instruction

(3) The right of citizens of Canada under subsections (1) and (2) to have their children receive primary and secondary school instruction in the language of the English or French linguistic minority population of a province.

    (a) applies wherever in the province the number of children of citizens who have such a right is sufficient to warrant the provision to them out of public funds of minority language instruction; and

    (b) includes, where the number of those children so warrants, the right to have them receive that instruction in minority language educational facilities provided out of public funds.

Application where numbers warrant

Enforcement

Enforcement of guaranteed rights and freedoms

24. (1) Anyone whose rights or freedoms, as guaranteed by this Charter, have been infringed or denied may apply to a court of competent jurisdiction to obtain such remedy as the court considers appropriate and just in the circumstances.

Exclusion of evidence bringing administration of justice into disrepute

(2) Where, in proceedings under subsection (1), a court concludes that evidence was obtained in a manner that infringed or denied any rights or freedoms guaranteed by this Charter, the evidence shall be excluded if it is established that, having regard to all the circumstances, the admission of it in the proceedings would bring the administration of justice into disrepute.

General

Aboriginal rights and freedoms not affected by Charter

25. The guarantee in this Charter of certain rights and freedoms shall not be construed so as to abrogate or derogate from any aboriginal, treaty or other rights or freedoms that pertain to the aboriginal peoples of Canada including

(a) any rights or freedoms that have been recognized by the Royal Proclamation of October 7, 1763; and

(b) any rights or freedoms that may be acquired by the aboriginal peoples of Canada by way of land claims settlement.

(b) any rights or freedoms that now exist by way of land claims agreements or may be so acquired.

[Note: Paragraph 25*(b)* (in italics) was repealed and the new paragraph substituted by the *Constitution Amendment Proclamation, 1983* (No. 46 *infra*).]

Other rights and freedoms not affected by Charter

26. The guarantee in this Charter of certain rights and freedoms shall not be construed as denying the existence of any other rights or freedoms that exist in Canada.

Multicultural heritage

27. This Charter shall be interpreted in a manner consistent with the preservation and enhancement of the multicultural heritage of Canadians.

Rights guaranteed equally to both sexes

28. Notwithstanding anything in this Charter, the rights and freedoms referred to in it are guaranteed equally to male and female persons.

Rights respecting certain schools preserved

29. Nothing in this Charter abrogates or derogates from any rights or privileges guaranteed by or under the Constitution of Canada in respect of denominational, separate or dissentient schools.

Application to territories and territorial authorities

30. A reference in this Charter to a province or to the legislative assembly or legislature of a province shall be deemed to include a reference to the Yukon Territory and the Northwest Territories, or to the appropriate legislative authority thereof, as the case may be.

Legislative powers not extended

31. Nothing in this Charter extends the legislative powers of any body or authority.

Application of Charter

Application of Charter

32. (1) This Charter applies

(a) to the Parliament and government of Canada in respect of all matters within the authority of Parliament including all matters relating to the Yukon Territory and Northwest Territories; and *(b)* to the legislature and government of each province in respect of all matters within the authority of the legislature of each province. Exception

(2) Notwithstanding subsection (1), section 15 shall not have effect until three years after this section comes into force.

[Note: This section came into force on April 17, 1982. See the proclamation of that date (No. 45 *infra*).]

33. (1) Parliament or the legislature of a province may expressly declare in an Act of Parliament or of the legislature, as the case may be, that the Act or a provision thereof shall operate notwithstanding a provision included in section 2 or sections 7 to 15 of this Charter. Exception where express declaration

(2) An Act or a provision of an Act in respect of which a declaration made under this section is in effect shall have such operation as it would have but for the provision of this Charter referred to in the declaration. Operation of exception

(3) A declaration made under subsection (1) shall cease to have effect five years after it comes into force or on such earlier date as may be specified in the declaration. Five year limitation

(4) Parliament or the legislature of a province may re-enact a declaration made under subsection (1). Re-enactment

(5) Subsection (3) applies in respect of a re-enactment made under subsection (4). Five year limitation

Citation

34. This Part may be cited as the *Canadian Charter of Rights and Freedoms*. Citation

Part II

Rights of the Aboriginal Peoples of Canada

35. (1) The existing aboriginal and treaty rights of the aboriginal peoples of Canada are hereby recognized and affirmed. Recognition of existing aboriginal and treaty rights

(2) In this Act, "aboriginal peoples of Canada" includes the Indian, Inuit and Métis peoples of Canada. Definition of "aboriginal peoples of Canada"

(3) For greater certainty, in subsection (1) "treaty rights" includes rights that now exist by way of land claims agreement or may be so acquired. Land claims agreements

(4) Notwithstanding any other provision of this Act, the aboriginal and treaty rights referred to in subsection (1) are guaranteed equally to male and female persons. Aboriginal and treaty rights are guaranteed equally to both sexes

[Note: Subsections 35(3) and (4) were added by the *Constitution Amendment Proclamation, 1983* (No. 46 *infra*).]

35.1 The government of Canada and the provincial governments are committed to the principle that, before any amendment is made to Class 24 of section 91 of the "*Constitution Act, 1867*", to section 25 of this Act or to this Part, Commitment to participation in constitutional conference

    (a) a constitutional conference that includes in its agenda an item relating to the proposed amendment, composed of the Prime Minister

of Canada and the first ministers of the provinces, will be convened by the Prime Minister of Canada; and

(b) the Prime Minister of Canada will invite representative of the aboriginal peoples of Canada to participate in the discussions on that item.

[Note: Added by the *Constitution Amendment Proclamation, 1983* (No. 46 *infra*).]

PART III

EQUALIZATION AND REGIONAL DISPARITIES

Commitment to promote equal opportunities

36. (1) Without altering the legislative authority of Parliament or of the provincial legislatures, or the rights of any of them with respect to the exercise of their legislative authority, Parliament and the legislatures, together with the government of Canada and the provincial governments, are committed to

(a) promoting equal opportunities for the well-being of Canadians;

(b) furthering economic development to reduce disparity in opportunities; and

(c) providing essential public services of reasonable quality to all Canadians.

Commitment respecting public services

(2) Parliament and the government of Canada are committed to the principle of making equalization payments to ensure that provincial governments have sufficient revenues to provide reasonably comparable levels of public services at reasonably comparable levels of taxation.

PART IV

CONSTITUTIONAL CONFERENCE

Constitutional conference

37. *(1) A constitutional conference composed of the Prime Minister of Canada and the first ministers of the provinces shall be convened by the Prime Minister of Canada within one year after this Part comes into force.*

Participation of aboriginal peoples

(2) The conference convened under subsection (1) shall have included in its agenda an item respecting constitutional matters that directly affect the aboriginal peoples of Canada, including the identification and definition of the rights of those peoples to be included in the Constitution of Canada, and the Prime Minister of Canada shall invite representatives of those peoples to participate in the discussions on that item.

Participation of territories

(3) The Prime Minister of Canada shall invite elected representatives of the governments of the Yukon Territory and the Northwest Territories to participate in the discussions on any item on the agenda of the conference convened under subsection (1) that, in the opinion of the Prime Minister, directly affects the Yukon Territory and the Northwest Territories.

[Note: Part IV was repealed effective April 17, 1983 by section 54 of this Act.]

PART IV.1

CONSTITUTIONAL CONFERENCES

Constitutional conferences

37.1 *(1) In addition to the conference convened in March 1983, at least two constitutional conferences composed of the Prime Minister of*

Canada and the first ministers of the provinces shall be convened by the Prime Minister of Canada, the first within three years after April 17, 1982 and the second within five years after that date.

(2) Each conference convened under subsection (1) shall have included in its agenda constitutional matters that directly affect the aboriginal peoples of Canada, and the Prime Minister of Canada shall invite representatives of those peoples to participate in the discussion on those matters.

Participation of aboriginal peoples

(3) The Prime Minister of Canada shall invite elected representatives of the governments of the Yukon Territory and the Northwest Territories to participate in the discussions on any item on the agenda of a conference convened under subsection (1) that, in the opinion of the Prime Minister, directly affects the Yukon Territory and the Northwest Territories.

Participation of territories

(4) Nothing in this section shall be construed so as to derogate from subsection 35(1).

Subsection 35(1) not affected

[Note: Part IV.1 was added by the *Constitution Amendment Proclamation, 1983* (No. 46 *infra*). By the same proclamation, it was repealed effective April 18, 1987. See section 54.1 of this Act.]

PART V

PROCEDURE FOR AMENDING CONSTITUTION OF CANADA

38. (1) An amendment to the Constitution of Canada may be made by proclamation issued by the Governor General under the Great Seal of Canada where so authorized by

General procedure for amending Constitution of Canada

(a) resolutions of the Senate and House of Commons; and
(b) resolutions of the legislative assemblies of at least two-thirds of the provinces that have, in the aggregate, according to the then latest general census, at least fifty per cent of the population of all the provinces.

(2) An amendment made under subsection (1) that derogates from the legislative power, the proprietary rights or any other rights or privileges of the legislature or government of a province shall require a resolution supported by a majority of the members of each of the Senate, the House of Commons and the legislative assemblies required under subsection (1).

Majority of members

(3) An amendment referred to in subsection (2) shall not have effect in a province the legislative assembly of which has expressed its dissent thereto by resolution supported by a majority of its members prior to the issue of the proclamation to which the amendment relates unless that legislative assembly, subsequently, by resolution supported by a majority of its members, revokes its dissent and authorizes the amendment.

Expression of dissent

(4) A resolution of dissent made for the purposes of subsection (3) may be revoked at any time before or after the issue of the proclamation to which it relates.

Revocation of dissent

39. (1) A proclamation shall not be issued under subsection 38(1) before the expiration of one year from the adoption of the resolution initiating the amendment procedure thereunder, unless the legislative assembly of each province has previously adopted a resolution of assent or dissent.

Restriction on proclamation

Idem

(2) A proclamation shall not be issued under subsection 38(1) after the expiration of three years from the adoption of the resolution initiating the amendment procedure thereunder.

Compensation

40. Where an amendment is made under subsection 38(1) that transfers provincial legislative powers relating to education or other cultural matters from provincial legislatures to Parliament, Canada shall provide reasonable compensation to any province to which the amendment does not apply.

Amendment by unanimous consent

41. An amendment to the Constitution of Canada in relation to the following matters may be made by proclamation issued by the Governor General under the Great Seal of Canada only where authorized by resolutions of the Senate and House of Commons and of the legislative assembly of each province:

(a) the office of the Queen, the Governor General and the Lieutenant Governor of a province;

(b) the right of a province to a number of members in the House of Commons not less than the number of Senators by which the province is entitled to be represented at the time this Part comes into force;

(c) subject to section 43, the use of the English or the French language;

(d) the composition of the Supreme Court of Canada; and

(e) an amendment to this Part.

Amendment by general procedure

42. (1) An amendment to the Constitution of Canada in relation to the following matters may be made only in accordance with subsection 38(1):

(a) the principle of proportionate representation of the provinces in the House of Commons prescribed by the Constitution of Canada;

(b) the powers of the Senate and the method of selecting Senators;

(c) the number of members by which a province is entitled to be represented in the Senate and the residence qualifications of Senators;

(d) subject to paragraph 41(d), the Supreme Court of Canada;

(e) the extension of existing provinces into the territories; and

(f) notwithstanding any other law or practice, the establishment of new provinces.

Exception

(2) Subsections 38(2) to (4) do not apply in respect of amendments in relation to matters referred to in subsection (1).

Amendment of provisions relating to some but not all provinces

43. An amendment to the Constitution of Canada in relation to any provision that applies to one or more, but not all, provinces, including

(a) any alteration to boundaries between provinces, and

(b) any amendment to any provision that relates to the use of the English or the French language within a province,

may be made by proclamation issued by the Governor General under the Great Seal of Canada only where so authorized by resolutions of the Senate and House of Commons and of the legislative assembly of each province to which the amendment applies.

Amendments by Parliament

44. Subject to sections 41 and 42, Parliament may exclusively make laws amending the Constitution of Canada in relation to the executive government of Canada or the Senate and House of Commons.

Amendments by provincial legislatures

45. Subject to section 41, the legislature of each province may exclusively make laws amending the constitution of the province.

46. (1) The procedures for amendment under sections 38, 41, 42 and 43 may be initiated either by the Senate or the House of Commons or by the legislative assembly of a province.

Initiation of amendment procedures

(2) A resolution of assent made for the purposes of this Part may be revoked at any time before the issue of a proclamation authorized by it.

Revocation of authorization

47. (1) An amendment to the Constitution of Canada made by proclamation under section 38, 41, 42 or 43 may be made without a resolution of the Senate authorizing the issue of the proclamation if, within one hundred and eighty days after the adoption by the House of Commons of a resolution authorizing its issue, the Senate has not adopted such a resolution and if, at any time after the expiration of that period, the House of Commons again adopts the resolution.

Amendments without Senate resolution

(2) Any period when Parliament is prorogued or dissolved shall not be counted in computing the one hundred and eighty day period referred to in subsection (1).

Computation of period

48. The Queen's Privy Council for Canada shall advise the Governor General to issue a proclamation under this Part forthwith on the adoption of the resolutions required for an amendment made by proclamation under this Part.

Advice to issue proclamation

49. A constitutional conference composed of the Prime Minister of Canada and the first ministers of the provinces shall be convened by the Prime Minister of Canada within fifteen years after this Part comes into force to review the provisions of this Part.

Constitutional conference

PART VI

AMENDMENT TO THE CONSTITUTION ACT, 1867

50. The *Constitution Act, 1867* (formerly named the *British North America Act, 1867*) is amended by adding thereto, immediately after section 92 thereof, the following heading and section:

Amendment to Constitution Act, 1867

"Non-Renewable Natural Resources, Forestry Resources and Electrical Energy

92A. (1) In each province, the legislature may exclusively make laws in relation to
  (a) exploration for non-renewable natural resources in the province;
  (b) development, conservation and management of non-renewable natural resources and forestry resources in the province, including laws in relation to the rate of primary production therefrom; and
  (c) development, conservation and management of sites and facilities in the province for the generation and production of electrical energy.

Laws respecting non-renewable natural resources, forestry resources and electrical energy

(2) In each province, the legislature may make laws in relation to the export from the province to another part of Canada of the primary production from non-renewable natural resources and forestry resources in the province and the production from facilities in the province for the generation of electrical energy, but such laws may not authorize or provide for discrimination in prices or in supplies exported to another part of Canada.

Export from provinces of resources

Authority of
Parliament

(3) Nothing in subsection (2) derogates from the authority of Parliament to enact laws in relation to the matters referred to in that subsection and, where such a law of Parliament and a law of a province conflict, the law of Parliament prevails to the extent of the conflict.

Taxation of resources

(4) In each province, the legislature may make laws in relation to the raising of money by any mode or system of taxation in respect of
(a) non-renewable natural resources and forestry resources in the province and the primary production therefrom, and
(b) sites and facilities in the province for the generation of electrical energy and the production therefrom,
whether or not such production is exported in whole or in part from the province, but such laws may not authorize or provide for taxation that differentiates between production exported to another part of Canada and production not exported from the province.

"Primary production"

(5) The expression "primary production" has the meaning assigned by the Sixth Schedule.

Existing powers or rights

(6) Nothing in subsections (1) to (5) derogates from any powers or rights that a legislature or government of a province had immediately before the coming into force of this section."

Idem

51. The said Act is further amended by adding thereto the following Schedule:

"THE SIXTH SCHEDULE

Primary Production from Non-Renewable Natural Resources and Forestry Resources

1. For the purposes of Section 92A of this Act,
(a) production from a non-renewable natural resource is primary production therefrom if
(i) it is in the form in which it exists upon its recovery or severance from its natural state, or
(ii) it is a product resulting from processing or refining the resource, and is not a manufactured product or a product resulting from refining crude oil, refining upgraded heavy crude oil, refining gases or liquids derived from coal or refining a synthetic equivalent of crude oil; and
(b) production from a forestry resource is primary production therefrom if it consists of sawlogs, poles, lumber, wood chips, sawdust or any other primary wood product, or wood pulp, and is not a product manufactured from wood."

PART VII

GENERAL

Primacy of
Constitution of
Canada

52. (1) The Constitution of Canada is the supreme law of Canada, and any law that is inconsistent with the provisions of the Constitution is, to the extent of the inconsistency, of no force or effect.

Constitution of
Canada

(2) The Constitution of Canada includes
(a) the *Canada Act 1982*, including this Act;

(b) the Acts and orders referred to in the schedule; and

(c) any amendment to any Act or order referred to in paragraph *(a)* or *(b)*.

(3) Amendments to the Constitution of Canada shall be made only in accordance with the authority contained in the Constitution of Canada.

Amendments to Constitution of Canada

53. (1) The enactments referred to in Column I of the schedule are hereby repealed or amended to the extent indicated in Column II thereof and, unless repealed, shall continue as law in Canada under the names set out in Column III thereof.

Repeals and new names

(2) Every enactment, except the *Canada Act 1982*, that refers to an enactment referred to in the schedule by the name in Column I thereof is hereby amended by substituting for that name the corresponding name in Column III thereof, and any British North America Act not referred to in the schedule may be cited as the *Constitution Act* followed by the year and number, if any, of its enactment.

Consequential amendments

54. Part IV is repealed on the day that is one year after this Part comes into force and this section may be repealed and this Act renumbered, consequentially upon the repeal of Part IV and this section, by proclamation issued by the Governor General under the Great Seal of Canada.

[Note: On October 31, 1987, no proclamation had been issued under this section.]

Repeal and consequential amendments

54.1 *Part iv.1 and this section are repealed on April 18, 1987.*

[Note: Added by the *Constitution Amendment Proclamation, 1983* (No. 46 *infra*).]

Repeal of Part iv.1 and this section

55. A French version of the portions of the Constitution of Canada referred to in the schedule shall be prepared by the Minister of Justice of Canada as expeditiously as possible and, when any portion thereof sufficient to warrant action being taken has been so prepared, it shall be put forward for enactment by proclamation issued by the Governor General under the Great Seal of Canada pursuant to the procedure then applicable to an amendment of the same provisions of the Constitution of Canada.

[Note: On October 31, 1987, no proclamation had been issued under this section.]

French version of Constitution of Canada

56. Where any portion of the Constitution of Canada has been or is enacted in English and French or where a French version of any portion of the Constitution is enacted pursuant to section 55, the English and French versions of that portion of the Constitution are equally authoritative.

English and French versions of certain constitutional texts

57. The English and French versions of this Act are equally authoritative.

English and French versions of this Act

58. Subject to section 59, this Act shall come into force on a day to be fixed by proclamation issued by the Queen or the Governor General under the Great Seal of Canada.

[Note: The *Constitution Act, 1982* was, subject to section 59 thereof, proclaimed in force on April 17, 1982 (No. 45 *infra*).]

Commencement

59. (1) Paragraph 23(1) (a) shall come into force in respect of Quebec on a day to be fixed by proclamation issued by the Queen or the Governor General under the Great Seal of Canada.

Commencement of paragraph 23(1)(a) in respect of Quebec

Authorization of Quebec

(2) A proclamation under subsection (1) shall be issued only where authorized by the legislative assembly or government of Quebec.

Repeal of this section

(3) This section may be repealed on the day paragraph 23(1)(a) comes into force in respect of Quebec and this Act amended and renumbered, consequentially upon the repeal of this section, by proclamation issued by the Queen or the Governor General under the Great Seal of Canada.

[Note: On October 31, 1987, no proclamation had been issued under this section.]

Short title and citations

60. This Act may be cited as the *Constitution Act, 1982*, and the Constitution Acts 1867 to 1975 (No. 2) and this Act may be cited together as the *Constitution Acts, 1867 to 1982*.

References

61. A reference to the *"Constitution Acts, 1867 to 1982"* shall be deemed to include a reference to the *"Constitution Amendment Proclamation, 1983."*

[Note: Added by the *Constitution Amendment Proclamation, 1983* (No. 46 *infra*). See also section 3 of the *Constitution Act, 1985 (Representation)* (No. 47 *infra*).]

INDEX

Q

R